Andreas Lammer

The Elements of Avicenna's Physics

Scientia Graeco-Arabica

Herausgegeben von
Marwan Rashed

Band 20

Andreas Lammer

The Elements of Avicenna's Physics

Greek Sources and Arabic Innovations

DE GRUYTER

In summer 2016, this study was accepted as a doctoral dissertation at the Faculty of Philosophy, Philosophy of Science and the Study of Religion at LMU Munich.

The BRAIS-De Gruyter Prize for 2017 has been awarded to Andreas Lammer for this monograph.

ISBN 978-3-11-071019-9
e-ISBN (PDF) 978-3-11-054679-8
e-ISBN (EPUB) 978-3-11-054608-8
ISSN 1868-7172

Library of Congress Cataloging-in-Publication Data
A CIP catalog record for this book has been applied for at the Library of Congress.

Bibliographic information published by the Deutsche Nationalbibliothek
The Deutsche Nationalbibliothek lists this publication in the Deutsche Nationalbibliografie; detailed bibliographic data are available on the Internet at http://dnb.dnb.de.

This volume is text- and page-identical with the hardback published in 2018.
Typesetting: Andreas Lammer
Arabic font: Amiri, © Khaled Hosny, http://www.amirifont.org/
Printing and binding: CPI books GmbH, Leck

♾ Printed on acid-free paper
Printed in Germany

www.degruyter.com

To my parents, Ingrid and Herbert Lammer,
with gratitude.

So eine Arbeit wird eigentlich nie fertig;
man muß sie für fertig erklären,
wenn man nach Zeit und Umständen
das Möglichste gethan hat.

Johann Wolfgang von Goethe
in Caserta am 16. März 1787

Contents

List of Abbreviations — XI

List of Figures and Tables — XII

Preface — XIII

Acknowledgements — XIX

Introduction — 1

1 **The Arabic Fate of Aristotle's *Physics* — 9**
1.1 Transmission and Translation — **10**
1.2 The Commentators on the Aristotelian Text — **20**
1.3 On Avicenna's Copy of the *Physics* — **37**

2 **The Methodology of Teaching and Learning — 43**
2.1 The Method of Physics — **43**
2.2 Method and Principles between Physics and Metaphysics — **81**

3 **The Subject-Matter of Physics — 111**
3.1 Body, Substance, and Corporeality — **114**
3.2 Matter and Form as Common Principles — **154**
3.3 Change and an Additional Principle — **201**

4 **Nature and Power — 213**
4.1 Nature, and Soul, in the Greek Philosophical Tradition — **213**
4.2 Avicenna's Commentary on *Physics* II.1, 192b20–23 — **225**
4.3 Avicenna, and Philoponus, on Inclination — **240**
4.4 Bad Readings of Aristotle — **252**
4.5 Avicenna's Account of Nature and its Relation to Soul — **280**

5 **Putting Surface Back into Place — 307**
5.1 A Troubled Account of Place — **311**
5.2 Clarifying Aristotle's Troubled Account of Place — **326**
5.3 Eliminating Void and Space — **367**

6 **Time and Temporality in the Physical World — 429**
6.1 A New Approach to an Old Definition — **431**
6.2 The Before and After — **462**

List of Abbreviations

Plato

Alc. I	Alcibiades I
Leg.	Laws
Parm.	Parmenides
Phd.	Phaedo
Phdr.	Phaedrus
Plt.	Politicus
Rep.	Republic
Tim.	Timaeus

Aristotle

Cat.	Categories
De int.	De interpretatione
An. pr.	Prior Analytics
An. post.	Posterior Analytics
Top.	Topics
De soph. el.	De sophisticis elenchis
Rhet.	Rhetoric
Poet.	Poetics
Phys.	Physics
Cael.	De caelo
De gen. et corr.	De generatione et corruptione
Meteor.	Meteorologica
De an.	De anima
De mem.	De memoria et reminiscentia
Hist. anim.	Historia animalium
De part. anim.	De partibus animalium
De motu anim.	De motu animalium
De gen. anim.	De generatione animalium
Met.	Metaphysics
Eth. Nic.	Nicomachean Ethics
Eth. Eud.	Eudemian Ethics

Plotinus

Enn.	Enneads

https://doi.org/10.1515/9783110546798-201

List of Figures and Tables

Table 1.1	Arabic Translations of Aristotle's *Physics* with and without commentaries — 16
Table 4.1	Avicenna's fourfold classification of natural powers — 289
Figure 6.1	A complete schema of Avicenna's analysis of motion at different speeds — 434
Figure 6.2	A vertical relation of things to time — 474
Figure 6.3	A vertical relation of a thing's states to time — 482
Figure 6.4	A horizontal relation between a thing's states in time — 483

https://doi.org/10.1515/9783110546798-202

Preface

This study is an examination of texts of historic value, in particular those that were composed by the philosopher and physician Avicenna (d. 428/1037). For this reason, it relies heavily on quoting, reading, translating, and understanding passages from primary texts. The following rules have been adopted in presenting and working with these passages.

Passages in quotation are presented in their original language together with an English translation. In the case of Aristotle, texts are quoted in Greek and English together with a historical Arabic translation, if extant and available.[1] Given that some of Aristotle's works were more than once translated into Arabic, in addition to the lack of reliable, or in any way precise, information about which translations Avicenna used and knew, it must be noted that the Arabic versions of passages from Aristotle that are quoted in this study may not necessarily be those which Avicenna was most familiar with or primarily worked from. This is especially true in the case of the *Physics*.[2] At the same time, it should be clear that simply *any* Arabic translation from the second/eighth to the fourth/tenth century provides a modern interpreter with valuable information about a certain terminology and understanding that was used to render the Greek text into Arabic at around Avicenna's own times.

In this regard it is to be noted, too, that the historical Arabic translations may naturally deviate from our established Greek texts in various respects. Such differences are only occasionally mentioned, as it is not the subject of this study to assess the quality and accuracy of the Arabic translations or of the Greek manuscripts and Syriac intermediaries from which they were produced. Moreover, such remarks are clearly only of limited value in a study on Avicenna's philosophy as long as we continue to lack reliable information about which translations he primarily relied on in his philosophical education and formation.

All Greek texts are quoted following the available, often critical, editions listed in the bibliography. Arabic texts are quoted on the basis of the available, rarely critical, editions listed in the bibliography but have silently been adapted so as to conform to a consistent orthography and punctuation.

The transliteration of Arabic terms follows, for the most part, the rules laid down by the Deutsche Morgenländische Gesellschaft. Exceptions include the handling of sun letters (e.g., *al-ṭabīʿa* instead of *aṭ-ṭabīʿa*) and of diphthongs (*aw* and *ay* instead of

1 If a quoted passage is provided in three languages, then the English translation at the *bottom* always translates the version on *top*, and not that of the version between these. So, if the order of the versions of a given passage is Greek-Arabic-English, then the English translation at the bottom renders the Greek text on top, whereas if the order is Arabic-Greek-English, then the English translation at the bottom renders the Arabic text on top.

2 q.v. below, 37ff.

https://doi.org/10.1515/9783110546798-203

au and *ai*). In the transliteration of Persian terms, I decided against classicising the spelling, taking my cue from contemporary pronunciation (e.g., *ketāb* instead of *kitāb*).

Furthermore, I took the liberty of adding Greek and Arabic terms in brackets at any time and to any quotation, be that from primary texts or from the secondary literature. Likewise, I have allowed myself the removal of any such earlier addition by the original editor, translator, or author from a quoted passage, if I deemed it inadequate or distracting.[3]

It often happens that I quote from an earlier published translation and indicate that this translation has been "modified." This can mean either that the text of the earlier translation has been *slightly* modified (such as changing the tense of a verb or replacing a noun) or that it has been *heavily* modified (such as changing the structure of the sentence). As it is, most quoted translations have been modified, not only in order to provide what I consider to be a better or more correct translation but also to obtain a clear and straightforward terminology throughout this study. Terms such as ἀρχή and *mabdaʾ*, for example, have been translated usually and consistently as "principle," even though other translators, in various contexts, chose different expressions, such as "beginning," "source," and "origin."

In my own translations, I often strive to follow the Arabic original closely, even in its syntax and word order.[4] On occasion, the resulting translations may appear to be less fluent, or pleasant, in English but, so I hope, no less adequate for a thorough examination of text, thought, and terminology.

As a rule, references to primary texts always indicate the title of the work, the part, the chapter, and the subsection, if applicable, to which a certain passage refers or from which a given translation has been taken *in addition* to page numbers with line numbers. It is my sincere belief that modern scholarship would benefit from a strict observance of this rule.

Aristotle's works are referenced with their established English or Latin titles: for example, *Posterior Analytics*, *Physics*, *De generatione et corruptione*, and *De anima*. Corresponding titles of Avicenna's works are always given in their transliterated Arabic form: for example, *al-Burhān*, *al-Samāʿ al-ṭabīʿī*, *al-Kawn wa-l-fasād*, and *al-Nafs*. If the title of an Arabic work of another author is identical with, or too similar to, the title of one of Avicenna's works, then the former is given in English translation, instead of the transliterated Arabic, in an attempt to avoid confusion: for example, Abū Naṣr al-Fārābī's *Kitāb al-Burhān* is referred to as *Book of Demonstration*.

3 In like manner do I quote from Gutas' *Avicenna and the Aristotelian Tradition* without keeping the capitalisation of technical terms, which is pointless to retain anywhere outside the original work.
4 cf. also the advice given by Gutas in "The Study of Avicenna," 55.

With regard to Aristotle's works, I quote from the following Arabic translations:

- *Posterior Analytics*: Abū Bišr Mattā ibn Yūnus on the basis of a Syriac translation by Isḥāq ibn Ḥunayn; published by Badawī and by Ǧabr.
- *Rhetoric*: an unknown translator; published by Badawī and by Lyons.
- *Physics*: Isḥāq ibn Ḥunayn presumably on the basis of a Syriac translation either by himself or by his father Ḥunayn ibn Isḥāq; published by Badawī.[5]
- *De caelo*: Yaḥyā ibn al-Biṭrīq (somewhat revised) on the basis of an unknown Syriac translation; published by Badawī.[6]
- *De generatione et corruptione*: Isḥāq ibn Ḥunayn on the basis of a Syriac version by his father Ḥunayn ibn Isḥāq; extant in a Hebrew and a Latin translation, the latter of which was produced by Gerard of Cremona and still remains unpublished.[7]
- *De anima*: an unknown translator, erroneously attributed to Isḥāq ibn Ḥunayn; published by Badawī.[8]
- *De partibus animalium*: Usṭāṯ, erroneously attributed to Yaḥyā ibn al-Biṭrīq, on the basis of an unknown Syriac translation; published by Kruk.[9]
- *De generatione animalium*: Usṭāṯ, erroneously attributed to Yaḥyā ibn al-Biṭrīq, on the basis of an unknown Syriac translation; published by Brugman and Drossaart Lulofs.[10]
- *Metaphysics*: primarily Usṭāṯ, preserved in the lemmata of Averroes' *Tafsīr Mā baʿd al-ṭabīʿa*; published by Bouyges.[11]
- *Nicomachean Ethics*: Isḥāq ibn Ḥunayn (for books I–IV) probably on the basis of a Syriac version by his father Ḥunayn ibn Isḥāq as well as Usṭāṯ (for books V–X); published by Badawī and by Akasoy and Fidora.[12]

5 For more information on the transmission of Aristotle's *Physics*, q.v. below, 9ff.

6 cf. Endreß, "Averroes' *De Caelo*," 47f.

7 cf. Eichner's remarks in the introduction of her edition of Averroes, *Mittlerer Kommentar zu Aristoteles'* De generatione et corruptione, 1–6. I am grateful to Marwan Rashed, who kindly provided me with his personal transcript of Gerard of Cremona's Latin translation, which I shall quote in lieu of Isḥāq ibn Ḥunayn's not extant Arabic version.

8 For a discussion of the attribution to Isḥāq ibn Ḥunayn, cf. Frank, "Some Fragments of Isḥāq's Translation of the *De anima*"; Gätje, *Studien zur Überlieferung der aristotelischen Psychologie im Islam*, 20–44

9 For a discussion of the attribution to Yaḥyā ibn al-Biṭrīq, cf. the remarks by Brugman and Drossaart Lulofs as well as Kruk in their respective editions of the Arabic translations of Aristotle's *De generatione animalium*, 1–10; *De partibus animalium*, 18–23. For the attribution to Usṭāṯ, cf. the extensive discussion in Ullmann, *Die Nikomachische Ethik des Aristoteles in arabischer Überlieferung*, vol. 2, 15–56.

10 q.v. the preceding footnote.

11 For a discussion of the various translations of Aristotle's *Metaphysics* and of those preserved and attested through Averroes' commentary, cf. Bertolacci, *The Reception of Aristotle's* Metaphysics *in Avicenna's* Kitāb al-Šifāʾ, ch. 1, being a moderately reworked version of his earlier article "On the Arabic Translations of Aristotle's *Metaphysics*."

12 For the textual transmission of the *Nicomachean Ethics*, cf. the extensive discussion in Ullmann, *Die Nikomachische Ethik des Aristoteles in arabischer Überlieferung*, vol. 2, 15–56.

With regard to Avicenna's works, I use the following editions and cite according to the following pattern:

- *al-Ḥikma al-ʿArūḍiyya*: Title, part, chapter, page, line; following Ṣāliḥ's edition.[13]
- *ʿUyūn al-ḥikma*: Title, part, chapter, page, line; following Badawī's first edition from 1954.
- *Kitāb al-Ḥudūd*: Title, paragraph, page, line; following Goichon's edition.
- *al-Mabdaʾ wa-l-maʿād*: Title, part, chapter, page, line; following Nūrānī's edition.
- *al-Hidāya*: Title, part, chapter, page, line; following ʿAbduh's edition.
- Works from *al-Šifāʾ* are quoted by title, book, chapter, page, line; following the "Cairo edition" of *al-Šifāʾ*; with the exception of:
  - *al-Samāʿ al-ṭabīʿī*: Title, book, chapter, paragraph (of McGinnis' edition and translation) with both page and line (of the Cairo edition by Zāyid).
  - *al-Ilāhiyyāt*: Title, book, chapter, paragraph (of Marmura's edition and translation) with both page and line (of the Cairo edition by Qanawātī, Zāyid, Mūsā, and Dunyā).
- *al-Naǧāt*: Title, part, section chapter, page, line; following Dānešpažūh's edition.[14]
- *Dānešnāme-ye ʿAlāʾī*: Title, part, chapter, page, line; following the editions by Moʿīn and Meškāt.
- *al-Ḥikma al-mašriqiyya*: Title, part, chapter, page, line; following the editions by al-Ḫaṭīb and al-Qatlān (for logic), and by Özcan (for physics).[15]
- *al-Išārāt wa-l-tanbīhāt*: Title, part, chapter, section, page, line; following Forget's edition.[16]

---

13 The chapters on physics in *al-Naǧāt* are largely identical with those in *al-Ḥikma al-ʿArūḍiyya*. I shall refer to *al-Naǧāt* in the main body and supply the corresponding passages of *al-Ḥikma al-ʿArūḍiyya* in the footnote.

14 Dānešpažūh's division of the work into eleven *aǧzāʾ* (sg. *ǧuzʾ*) should be disregarded, as that division has no correspondence whatsoever with the content of the work and presumably reflects some arbitrary division – into quires (*aǧzāʾ*)? – in the manuscript which Dānešpažūh used as the basis for his edition (manuscript *dāl*); cf. his remarks in the introduction to his edition (xcix). Other than that, Dānešpažūh did not edit the part on mathematics, which in his edition is provided only in the form of a facsimile from manuscript *dāl*, perhaps because this part was not written by Avicenna himself but was compiled by his closest disciple Abū ʿUbayd al-Ǧūzǧānī; cf. Gutas, *Avicenna and the Aristotelian Tradition*, 422–424.

15 I would like to express my gratitude to Jules Janssens for providing me with a copy of Özcan's doctoral dissertation containing the edition.

16 Avicenna's *al-Išārāt wa-l-tanbīhāt* is commonly referenced as if it were a work consisting of four parts, viz., logic, physics, metaphysics, and mysticism. This fourfold division seems to have been introduced through Dunyā's four-volume edition of the text and gained prominence through the widespread use of that edition. This, however, is a habit which is entirely misled and must be avoided. Avicenna's *al-Išārāt wa-l-tanbīhāt* does not consist of four but of two parts, viz., logic and all the rest, and should be quoted accordingly.

Occasionally, I have compared the editions of Avicenna's works, in particular of his *al-Šifāʾ*, with manuscripts at my disposal.[17] My comparison, however, did not follow a systematic rule nor did I consistently compare every passage that I quote. I drew upon the manuscripts only when the text established by the editions appeared to be especially dissatisfying. In a number of cases, I preferred readings found in these manuscripts to those found in the editions. These cases are always noted in the footnotes.

Two final remarks: first, in my footnotes, I use the Latin abbreviation "cf.," in order to refer to further evidence in another work or study. In doing so, I do not observe and emulate the distinction between "see" and "cf." and, for this reason, only use the latter. Second, the fact that I do not make use of feminine pronouns when, for example, referring to a generic person ("a student of nature ... *he* may acquire knowledge ...") should not be interpreted as displaying a sexist or anti-feminist stance. With my native German background, I find it more convenient and less confusing to use masculine pronouns, hoping that the reader is not offended by this idiosyncrasy or – failing that – accepts my apologies.

---

17 Especially the manuscripts Leiden or. 4 and or. 84 proved to be helpful in assessing the text of the Cairo edition of *al-Šifāʾ*. Neither of them has been taken into consideration by previous editors of the work. On these manuscripts, cf. Witkam, "Avicenna's Copyists at Work." Due to the close textual relation between the works contained in Avicenna's *al-Šifāʾ*, on the one hand, and Avicenna's later composition *al-Ḥikma al-mašriqiyya*, on the other, it is evident that any future critical edition of one of the works contained in *al-Šifāʾ* needs to investigate the text of the manuscripts that preserve *al-Ḥikma al-mašriqiyya* and examine the *variae lectiones* they provide. In this study, however, I abstained from comparing the text of the section on physics of *al-Ḥikma al-mašriqiyya*, as established in Özcan's edition, with the texts contained in the editions of *al-Samāʿ al-ṭabīʿī* and the two mentioned Leiden manuscripts of *al-Šifāʾ*, because Özcan's edition, despite all its merits, is full of mistakes and typographical errors and, thus, greatly unreliable.

Acknowledgements

I always like to read the acknowledgements of academic books, because they show so vividly that we never walk alone, that the human desire for knowledge and more complexity in understanding is a group effort, and that we should not be ashamed to admire the truth and to acquire it from wherever it comes, even if it should come from distant nations and foreign peoples.

Besides, I think they are a fantastic place for expressing one's sincere gratitude to those people without whom the present book would have been much worse and the process of writing it much more painful. It is in this sense, then, that I thank most sincerely two excellent mentors and supervisors: Peter Adamson and Dag Nikolaus Hasse. I am immensely grateful that it was them who guided my readings, corrected my mistakes, and also – years ago – instilled and, then, promoted my interest in Avicenna and the history of Arabic philosophy and science.

Secondly, I would like to express my gratitude to a number of friends who kindly provided me with their help during the last years of working on Avicenna's natural philosophy and to whom I am immensely indebted in various ways. These are: Jon McGinnis, Fedor Benevich, Hanif Amin Beidokhti, and Nora and Alexander Kalbarczyk.

Furthermore, I have received help from a number of people who devoted their time to reading earlier drafts of this book. Their remarks were gratefully received and I did my best to implement them into the text. My thanks go, above all, to Bethany Somma and Jens Ole Schmitt as well as to Nadja Germann and Benjamin Morison. I am also grateful to Marwan Rashed, who was so kind to include my book in his excellent series *Scientia Graeco-Arabica*, to read the manuscript, and to send me a number of insightful comments from which I could profit very much in the final stages of completing the book.

I wrote this book as a doctoral fellow at the *Munich School of Ancient Philosophy* (MUSAΦ) at the LMU Munich. Consequently, I would like to express my gratitude for the generous institutional support and even more for the valuable comments and remarks I have received on numerous occasions from my friends and colleagues there. In particular, I would like to mention Christof Rapp, Oliver Primavesi, Rotraud Hansberger, Matteo Di Giovanni, Laura Castelli, Christian Pfeiffer, Davlat Dadikhuda, Máté Herner, Jonathan Greig, Mirjam Engert Kotwick, Mareike Jas, and Christopher Noble.

I am also grateful to my friends from the philosophy department at the Julius-Maximilians-Universität Würzburg (above all, Anna-Katharina Strohschneider, Katrin Fischer, Jon Bornholdt, Jörn Müller, Stefan Georges, and Raphael Kretz) and at the Thomas-Institut at the University of Cologne (above all, Andreas Speer, David Wirmer, Guy Guldentops, and Roland Hissette) for years of support and friendship.

Moreover, during the last years of attending conferences and other academic events, I have had the pleasure to meet many colleagues and friends who both encouraged me to continue my work and provided helpful comments in numerous conversations.

https://doi.org/10.1515/9783110546798-204

Among these are Jon Hoover, Ayman Shihadeh, Jules Janssens, Matthias Perkams, Elvira Wakelnig, Frank Griffel, Richard Taylor, Dimitri Gutas, Jari Kaukua, David Bennett, Janis Esots, Eric van Lit, and Laura Hassan. I also wish to thank the team of De Gruyter, especially Katrin Hofmann, Olena Gainulina, and Sophie Wagenhofer, for their professional support in finishing and publishing this book.

Finally I am grateful to my family, Katja, Henri, and Jarne, especially for their patience; to my older brother, Martin, for challenging all this history of philosophy caboodle and for eventually letting me convince him that it is, after all, fairly interesting and worthwhile; and to my parents, Ingrid and Herbert Lammer, for their guidance, education, encouragement, and constant support.

Far from comparing *The Elements of Avicenna's Physics* with the masterful *Iphigenie auf Tauris*, I am deeply sympathetic to the sentiment Goethe expressed about his own work in the lines I chose as the epigraph of this book, and duly acknowledge all remaining shortcomings as being due to the limitations of time and circumstances as well as of my own possibilities.

Thank you very much.

Andreas Lammer
Munich, December 2017

Introduction

It is the aim of this study to analyse the core concepts of Avicenna's physics. Particular attention is devoted to a work called *al-Samāʿ al-ṭabīʿī*, which is the first section (*fann*) of the second part (*ǧumla*) of Avicenna's comprehensive collection *al-Šifāʾ* and, by all appearance, was the first section to be written and completed around the year 412/1022. In his *al-Samāʿ al-ṭabīʿī*, Avicenna formulated his most extensive account of physics in general, and of the concepts of matter and form, nature, motion, place, and time in particular. It is for this reason that this work is at the heart of this study.

Avicenna also authored a number of less exhaustive, even if not necessarily less complete, philosophical compendia, viz., *al-Ḥikma al-ʿArūḍiyya*, *ʿUyūn al-ḥikma*, *al-Hidāya*, *al-Naǧāt*, *Dānešnāme-ye ʿAlāʾī*, *al-Ḥikma al-mašriqiyya* and *al-Išārāt wa-l-tanbīhāt*. Some of these works have been neglected by modern scholarship almost in their entirety.[1] In this study, it is my firm intention to consider all these eight works, and to compare, contextualise, and assess their respective contents in an attempt to provide a full and coherent picture of the key concepts of Avicenna's natural philosophy. In addition to that, other sections of *al-Šifāʾ*, in particular *al-Ilāhiyyāt*, *al-Samāʾ wa-l-ʿālam*, *al-Kawn wa-l-fasād*, *al-Burhān*, and *al-Maqūlāt*, are often consulted, as they provide important information without which many details cannot adequately be evaluated or even understood.[2]

---

1 Of these, only *al-Naǧāt* and, especially, *al-Išārāt wa-l-tanbīhāt* now have spurred the interest of scholars, while only *al-Išārāt wa-l-tanbīhāt* and the *Dānešnāme-ye ʿAlāʾī* have been published in their entirety in modern translation. Avicenna's *al-Ḥikma al-mašriqiyya* is a special case in its almost universal neglect, as it still seems to be the established opinion that it is "lost except for its inlogic [sic!]" (Endreß, "The Cycle of Knowledge," 119), despite that it appears to be largely extant except for its metaphysics. In fact, the sections on physics from *al-Ḥikma al-mašriqiyya* have been edited by Özcan as part of his 1993 Turkish doctoral dissertation almost twenty-five years ago, and also Hasse showed in his 2000 monograph *Avicenna's* De Anima *in the Latin West* how the transmitted text of the psychological sections of *al-Ḥikma al-mašriqiyya* can be put to great use in an examination of Avicenna's philosophy in general, and of the arguments in *al-Šifāʾ* in particular. In terms of its physics, it is plainly clear that *al-Ḥikma al-mašriqiyya* is overall very similar to – not to say largely identical with – what Avicenna set forth in his other works, and primarily consists of a series of shorter and longer quotations from different chapters of *al-Samāʿ al-ṭabīʿī*, joined by a number of explanatory or connecting phrases. A detailed comparison shows that in composing his *al-Ḥikma al-mašriqiyya*, Avicenna's reliance on the text of his own *al-Šifāʾ* is greater than even Gutas suggested (cf. "Avicenna's Eastern ('Oriental') Philosophy," esp. 178–180). Here in this study, I decided not to mark all the many identical passages that can be found in these two works and, instead, to refer to *al-Ḥikma al-mašriqiyya* in just the same manner as I refer to Avicenna's other works as providing further evidence. However, I am currently working on an article – tentatively titled "Avicenna's Oriental Physics Unmasked: The Truth about *al-Ḥikma al-mašriqiyya*" – in which I shall examine the content of *al-Ḥikma al-mašriqiyya*, also in comparison to *al-Samāʿ al-ṭabīʿī*, in more detail.

2 It is a perplexing datum of reality that, even despite the commonly acknowledged importance of *al-Šifāʾ* as such, most of its volumes have so far not been published in modern translation and are often

https://doi.org/10.1515/9783110546798-001

Avicenna's *al-Samāʿ al-ṭabīʿī* is neither a commentary on Aristotle's *Physics* nor is it an interpretation of that work. It is more adequately described as Avicenna's own version of that science whose subjects have traditionally been transmitted and discussed under the title of Aristotle's Greek work *Φυσικὴ ἀκρόασις*, in Arabic *Samʿ al-kiyān* or *al-Samāʿ al-ṭabīʿī* and in English *Lecture on Physics* or simply *Physics*. According to Avicenna's understanding, the subjects discussed in Aristotle's work belong to, and make up, the science of "physics," which he conceives as the most common science or discipline within the area of natural philosophy. With regard to Avicenna's *al-Šifāʾ*, then, the contents of *al-Samāʿ al-ṭabīʿī* lay the foundation for the more specific investigations carried out in the particular disciplines presented in *al-Samāʾ wa-l-ʿālam*, *al-Kawn wa-l-fasād*, *al-Afʿāl wa-l-infiʿālāt*, *al-Maʿādin wa-l-āṯār al-ʿulwiyya*, *al-Nafs*, *al-Nabāt*, and *al-Ḥayawān*.[3] Together, these eight disciplines complete the scientific area of *al-Ṭabīʿiyyāt*: the philosophy concerned with "natural [things]" – i.e., natural philosophy.

Since Avicenna's various works on physics provide us with insights into his personal reading of Aristotle's *Physics*, and into his own appropriation of Aristotelian physics and natural philosophy, any engagement with Avicenna's texts recommends a preceding engagement with Aristotle's writings on these subjects as well as with a range of further works from the philosophical tradition they initiated. It is for this reason that I shall make constant use of Aristotle's *Physics* alongside a number of Greek and Arabic sources which, in one way or another, comment on or expound Aristotle's work in a way that helps us understand and contextualise the various views and positions which Avicenna presented and discussed in his major works, especially in his *al-Samāʿ al-ṭabīʿī*. That said, I shall *never* intend to engage in an attempt to understand or to interpret Aristotle's *Physics* in light of Avicenna's works. To put it simply: Aristotle's *Physics* is a valuable resource for understanding Avicenna's *al-Samāʿ al-ṭabīʿī* – but not vice versa. Consequently, I consider Avicenna as a Peripatetic and a genuine follower of Aristotle, even though his positions may often not be genuinely Aristotelian.[4] Indeed, in his own systematic works, Avicenna is no commentator on Aristotle and in many ways even exceeds Aristotle by providing novel ways of how Aristotelian materials can be interpreted and integrated, rearranged and refined in innovative ways, often

---

only marginally treated – if at all – by western scholars. Notable exceptions include *al-Ilāhiyyāt* (with several translations) and *al-Samāʿ al-ṭabīʿī* (translated by McGinnis in 2009).

3 Most of these works correspond thematically to a work from the canon of Aristotle's writings. For example, Avicenna's *al-Samāʾ wa-l-ʿālam* corresponds to Aristotle's *De caelo*, *al-Kawn wa-l-fasād* to *De generatione et corruptione*, *al-Nafs* to *De anima*. The cases of *al-Afʿāl wa-l-infiʿālāt*, *al-Maʿādin wa-l-āṯār al-ʿulwiyya*, *al-Nabāt*, and *al-Ḥayawān* are more complicated; cf. also Gutas, *Avicenna and the Aristotelian Tradition*, 103–105.

4 Here I adopt and follow Hasse's distinction between the adjectives "Aristotelian" and "Peripatetic" as a means to describe Aristotle's "Aristotelian" doctrines as opposed to the "Peripatetic" interpretations of his followers and commentators; cf. Hasse, *Avicenna's* De Anima *in the Latin West*, x. An analogous distinction is applied to Plato's "Platonic" doctrines as opposed to later "Platonist" or "Neoplatonic" appropriations.

in light of later developments. The result of this appropriation, viz., Avicenna's own philosophy, as expressed in his various works, must not be taken as a way to comment on Aristotle but as a way to transform and to develop Aristotle.[5]

This understanding of the place of Avicenna's works within the history of Peripatetic philosophy, and of the relation between the Aristotelian corpus and the Avicennian oeuvre, leads to a simple but crucial question: is Avicenna's natural philosophy as rich and innovative as his logic and his metaphysics already proved to be? As it happens, this is a question which has not yet received an adequate answer, even though, given the fruitful research on other areas of his philosophy, it clearly deserves a thorough investigation.[6] In fact, it appears that in the field of natural philosophy in general, and of physics in particular, Avicenna's contributions are not widely acknowledged. It seems to be commonly believed that Avicenna simply was a follower of Aristotle and that, for this very reason, his physical theory is just Peripatetic. While it is certainly correct that Avicenna is – and, more importantly, that he considered himself to be – a follower of Aristotle, and while it is also true that his physical theory is Peripatetic, it is not *just* Peripatetic or *simply* so. In fact, it is *prima facie* unreasonable to assume that someone of Avicenna's stature should have been so absolutely ingenious in certain fields of philosophy and science but utterly dull and uninteresting in another.

However, this does not mean that *no* study of Avicenna's natural philosophy has so far been undertaken that would highlight his originality in this field. During the last couple of years, a number of insightful and accurate studies on various aspects have been published in the West, in particular by two scholars: Jon McGinnis and Ahmad Hasnawi.[7] Their contributions provide valuable information on certain concrete aspects of, and novel insights in, Avicenna's physics, ranging from the structure of his *al-Samāʿ al-ṭabīʿī* as a whole to specific concepts and their history in Greek, Arabic, and Latin philosophy (as, for example, the concepts of motion or time), and to

5 It is interesting to note nonetheless that contemporary Aristotelian interpretations sometimes arrive at conclusions which, incidentally, resemble those found in Avicenna. Two striking examples are Morison's solution to the question about the place and motion of the outermost sphere, set out in his *On Location*, and Roark's interpretation of Aristotle's definition of motion and its relation to time, elaborated in his *Aristotle on Time*.

6 Apart from Marmura's articles collected in *Probing in Islamic Philosophy*, the pioneering studies on Avicenna's metaphysics, in particular as developed in *al-Ilāhiyyāt*, and on the ways in which Avicenna conceived of the text of Aristotle's *Metaphysics*, restructured its contents, interpreted its concepts in light of other sources in the preceding Greek and Arabic traditions, and formed his own understanding of the ontology of the world are Wisnovsky, *Avicenna's Metaphysics in Context*, and Bertolacci, *The Reception of Aristotle's* Metaphysics *in Avicenna's* Kitāb al-Šifāʾ. Regarding Avicenna's logic, perhaps the best overview is given in Street, "Arabic Logic." The importance of Avicenna as a logician has already been acknowledged fifty years ago by Rescher; cf. *The Development of Arabic Logic*, esp. 50.

7 cf. esp. Hasnawi, "La dynamique d'Ibn Sīnā"; "La définition du mouvement dans la *Physique* du *Shifāʾ* d'Avicenne"; "La *Physique* du *Šifāʾ*"; "Le statut catégorial du mouvement chez Avicenne"; "La théorie avicennienne de l'*impetus*"; McGinnis, "Ibn Sīnā on the Now"; "Positioning Heaven"; "A Penetrating Question"; "Avoiding the Void"; "Avicennan Infinity"; "Avicenna's Natural Philosophy."

particular arguments within Avicenna's discussions (as, for example, the proof against circular motion in a void). Nonetheless, what has so far been missing is a study of the foundations of Avicenna's natural philosophy (i) as a whole, (ii) in all his major works, and (iii) in light of the preceding Greek and Arabic traditions. Providing such a study has become the aim of this monograph.

Avicenna's *al-Samāʿ al-ṭabīʿī* consists of four books (*maqālāt*, sg. *maqāla*). All the basic concepts of natural philosophy are discussed within the first two books.[8] It is an investigation into these concepts which forms the core of the present study. More precisely, it examines Avicenna's accounts of corporeality, matter, form, and privation (in chapter three); nature and inclination (in chapter four); place, space, and void (in chapter five); and time (in chapter six). In addition to that, Avicenna's way of presenting his thoughts in *al-Samāʿ al-ṭabīʿī*, in particular those on matter and form, together with the fact that the first chapter in both Aristotle's *Physics* and Avicenna's *al-Samāʿ al-ṭabīʿī* is devoted to methodological concerns of inquiry, argumentation, and presentation within the area of natural philosophy, made it necessary to investigate the overall method adopted in *al-Samāʿ al-ṭabīʿī* as a whole (in chapter two).

There are two concepts which I decided not to investigate in detail, viz., the concepts of motion and causation. The primary reason for leaving Avicenna's account of motion aside is that there are already two studies which have considerably furthered our understanding of this subject, viz., Hasnawi's article "La définition du mouvement dans la *Physique* du *Shifāʾ* d'Avicenne" and Robert Wisnovsky's monograph *Avicenna's Metaphysics in Context*.[9] In the former, Hasnawi not only offered an accurate treatment of Avicenna's notion as expressed in his *al-Samāʿ al-ṭabīʿī* but also provided valuable material about the history of the definition of motion from Aristotle through the commentators up to Avicenna and, among other things, highlighted the influence of Themistius, John Philoponus, and Abū Naṣr al-Fārābī on Avicenna's views on motion. Wisnovsky, on the other hand, meticulously analysed Avicenna's understanding of "perfection," "actuality," or "entelechy" (ἐντελέχεια, *kamāl*) which, since Aristotle, had been the central notion within the definition of motion. While Avicenna's account of motion is not investigated in this study *as such*, it will, nonetheless, figure prominently and frequently be mentioned, outlined, or discussed in various contexts, so

8 These first two books correspond to the first four books of Aristotle's *Physics*; cf. also Hasnawi, "La *Physique* du *Šifāʾ*." The third book of *al-Samāʿ al-ṭabīʿī* is concerned with questions that arise from the notion of continuity with regard to natural things and, thus, thematically relates in various ways to matters discussed in *Physics* V–VI. It contains, for example, a refutation of atomism (chs. 2–5) and a discussion of the infinite (chs. 8–9) along with a number of important issues that relate to the notion of quantity in natural things, such as the finitude of power (ch. 10) and the finitude of natural motion (ch. 14). The fourth book, then, is more miscellaneous in content and provides a number of various, even though important, studies, most of which are concerned with some aspect of motion, such as the numerical unity of motion (ch. 3), contrary motions (ch. 6), accidental (ch. 13) and forced motions (ch. 14), thus relating, more or less, to Aristotle's examination of motion in *Physics* VII–VIII.

9 cf. now also Ahmed, "The Reception of Avicenna's Theory of Motion in the Twelfth Century."

that the core idea of Avicenna's account of motion will eventually have been treated *en passant*. On the other hand, Avicenna's discussion of causation in *al-Samāʿ al-ṭabīʿī*, have only peripherally been taken into consideration, primarily because Avicenna's main exposition of causation and the categorisation of causes is carried out in book six of his *al-Ilāhiyyāt*.[10] Although Avicenna frequently refers to different kinds of cause throughout his writings, and although he offers a distinct treatment of causes in the first book of *al-Samāʿ al-ṭabīʿī*, questions about causation are not as such investigated in *al-Samāʿ al-ṭabīʿī*. Having said this, the notion of cause – in particular in its application to matter and form, to nature, and to God, for example – is at appropriate places integrated and discussed.[11]

In addition, this study does not contain an examination of Avicenna's treatment of the infinite.[12] Although the infinite was an integral part of the first half of Aristotle's *Physics*, having been treated exhaustively in the third book, Avicenna moved it to what he considered to be a more appropriate place, viz., the discussion of continuity in relation to the natural bodies insofar as they have quantity, inspired by Aristotle's treatment in *Physics* V–VI and carried out in the third book of *al-Samāʿ al-ṭabīʿī*. That is to say, the infinite is itself not a fundamental concept of natural things alongside, for example, motion, time, and place, or even a principle alongside matter and form. Instead, it is a subordinate feature, i.e., a feature that follows from concepts that truly are fundamental and which, in one way or another, relate to the category of quantity, especially motion and magnitude.

Apart from the noted exceptions, this present study investigates all the most important and fundamental concepts that are central to Avicenna's natural philosophy with an eye both to significant developments in the preceding Greek and Arabic traditions, and to parallel or supplementary materials from his other major works, in order to examine thoroughly and accurately Avicenna's position within the history of natural philosophy by providing a comprehensive understanding of the key concepts, i.e., elements, of Avicenna's physics.

---

10 Some of these aspects have been treated in publications or monograph-length studies by Bertolacci, Richardson, and especially Wisnovsky; cf. Wisnovsky, *Avicenna on Final Causality*; "Final and Efficient Causality in Avicenna's Cosmology and Theology"; "Towards a History of Avicenna's Distinction between Immanent and Transcendent Causes"; Bertolacci, "The Doctrine of Material and Formal Causality"; Richardson, "Avicenna's Conception of the Efficient Cause."

11 This study also does not discuss Avicenna's account of chance and luck in *al-Samāʿ al-ṭabīʿī* I.13–14. For Avicenna, chance and luck are merely accidental causes. This means that, in the final analysis, they have no bearing on the natural world, because a more proper investigation of why a certain effect has come about will eventually reveal its essential causes – and it is these essential causes which are relevant for the science of nature. Moreover, Belo has already provided an investigation of Avicenna's views on chance and luck in her book *Chance and Determinism in Avicenna and Averroes*.

12 cf. McGinnis, "Avicennan Infinity."

I regret that I could include an investigation of Avicenna's engagement with Muʿtazilī and early Ašʿarī theology only occasionally.[13] Likewise, close to no mention is made of later Andalusian figures such as Abū Bakr Muḥammad ibn Bāǧǧa, Abū Bakr Muḥammad ibn Ṭufayl, and Averroes, whose works may contain further material on the development of natural philosophy from Antiquity to Avicenna.[14] Perhaps most regrettably, the materials contained in Averroes' commentaries on Aristotle's *Physics* could also not be taken into consideration. Moreover, I could not take into account the Latin tradition of reading both Avicenna's *al-Samāʿ al-ṭabīʿī* and Aristotle's *Physics* or of Averroes' commentary on the latter.[15] Finally, the later Islamic tradition of philosophy and kalām in reaction to Avicenna's philosophical system has almost entirely been neglected in this study; yet, the rich materials of the post-Avicennian tradition have already riveted my attention within the research project "The Heirs of Avicenna: Philosophy in the Islamic East from the Twelfth to the Thirteenth Century."[16]

Structure and Prospect

The first chapter of this study is concerned with providing an account of the transmission of Aristotle's text of the *Physics* and its Greek commentaries into Arabic, and additionally also surveys a number of other sources which were significant in the history of natural philosophy up to Avicenna. Most of the texts mentioned in this first chapter will reappear, often prominently, in the remainder of this study and illuminate either how Avicenna himself conceived of certain concepts or how certain figures in the preceding history did to whose conception, then, Avicenna reacted. While Avicenna's *al-Samāʿ al-ṭabīʿī* is at the heart of this study, this first chapter seeks to describe the wide range of texts which form its basis.

The second chapter is concerned with Avicenna's methodology in his writings on natural philosophy. It expounds how Avicenna conceives of his own philosophy in most of his major works and especially in his *al-Šifāʾ*. The general picture drawn out in this chapter is not entirely new and has, in other publications, either implicitly assumed or explicitly addressed.[17] Yet, it has not been canvassed from the specific viewpoint of natural philosophy for which it is, in fact, of utmost importance, not least because in his major works, Avicenna usually comments on his methodology precisely at the beginning of the sections on natural philosophy.

---

13 A full investigation of this interesting facet is yet to be carried out.

14 cf. Lettinck, *Aristotle's* Physics *and its Reception in the Arabic World*; Belo, *Chance and Determinism in Avicenna and Averroes*; Glasner, *Averroes' Physics*; Cerami, *Génération et substance*.

15 cf. esp. Trifogli, *Oxford Physics in the Thirteenth Century*.

16 This project started in the Spring of 2016; it is directed by Peter Adamson and funded by the *German Research Foundation* (DFG).

17 cf. esp. Bertolacci, *The Reception of Aristotle's* Metaphysics *in Avicenna's* Kitāb al-Šifāʾ, ch. 6.

The exposition of Avicenna's views on the principles of natural things, which is carried out in the third chapter, may be the most "metaphysical" topic of this study. Incidentally, this is the reason why in this chapter, more than in the others, I shall engage with the interpretations and views expressed by various authors in the secondary literature, for there simply exist more scholarly contributions on Avicenna's views on matter, form, and corporeality than on other aspects that are immediately relevant for his natural philosophy. However, this does not also entail that the scientific community has already formed a correct understanding of Avicenna's account. To the contrary, it will be shown that the interpretations that have been presented so far in the secondary literature are, more often than not, inaccurate, as they misrepresent Avicenna's intentions and testify to a misunderstanding of his words.

Avicenna's account of nature as a principle of motion within natural things is an apparent case for Avicenna's engagement with earlier opinions or, more precisely, with one particularly influential earlier opinion. That this earlier opinion has its roots in late-ancient developments in reading Aristotle's *Physics* was to be expected; that it must also be understood in light of the writings of Avicenna's immediate contemporaries, and that Avicenna is effectively reacting to an entire, and hitherto unnoticed, tradition of, as he would say, misunderstanding the power of nature, is the central theme of the fourth chapter.[18]

Regarding the philosophical understanding of place, Avicenna finds himself in a difficult situation. Rigorously accepting Aristotle's definition with all its consequences, he has to face the opposition of virtually the entire preceding Greek philosophical tradition which, as is well-known, had turned against Aristotle. As is shown in the fifth chapter, Avicenna was probably the first in the history of philosophy systematically to defend, and successfully to restore, what for centuries had been ridiculed as an implausible, even crazy, understanding of the reality of place. In addition to the materials drawn from the Greek tradition, Avicenna is also reacting to certain trends and tendencies of his own time, most notably the views about space and void expressed by the members of the Baṣrian strand of Muʿtazilism.

Time is arguably the most complex notion discussed in Avicenna's *al-Samāʿ al-ṭabīʿī* – more complex than the others and also more complex than previous studies have so far noticed. According to the commonly accepted interpretation, Avicenna was influenced by ancient and late ancient readings of Aristotle which described time in terms of a flowing now which generates time much like the tip of a ballpoint pen could be seen as producing a line through its motion on a sheet of paper. It will be shown in chapter six that this understanding of Avicenna's account of time is inadequate. For one thing, Avicenna rejected the idea of a flowing now as the cause of time's existence. More importantly, however, the now is also not relevant for his understanding of time's

18 I have recently published some materials from this fourth chapter in an article with the title "Defining Nature."

essence. The complexity of Avicenna's account of time as the magnitude of motion and the universal source of beforeness and afterness within the world can only be unravelled if his account is read against the background of a common Peripatetic confusion about the relation between motion and time, on the one hand, and a well-known attack that charges the Aristotelian definition with circularity, on the other. It is the traces of this confusion in Avicenna, together with his defence against this charge, which is ultimately responsible for the increasing complexity of his account, as he struggled to – unwittingly – combine seemingly incompatible Neoplatonic and Peripatetic elements within a single coherent and more robust theory.

Taking it all together, this study shows that Avicenna's analysis of the central concepts and the core issues of natural philosophy is innovative and resourceful in the highest degree. His discussions are rich, his material is vast, his positions are intriguing, and his stance is both rigorously Peripatetic and characteristically Avicennian. Although on a large scale, the structure of his *al-Samāʿ al-ṭabīʿī*, and in particular of its first two books, may appear to follow closely the order of exposition in Aristotle's *Physics*, a more detailed analysis reveals that Avicenna's independence in execution, his resolution in argument, and his innovative power in discussion are tremendous and unmistakable – just as one, given the fruitful research on his logic and metaphysics, should have expected.

1 The Arabic Fate of Aristotle's *Physics*

In this chapter, I survey the transmission of Aristotle's *Physics* into Arabic, in order to set the basis for my subsequent investigation of the central concepts of Avicenna's physics. Since Avicenna formed his philosophy by engaging with the materials from the preceding Greek and Arabic traditions, it is important to bring to mind which texts were available to him and what he might have known, used, and reacted to. Accordingly, the contents of this chapter not only indicate the wide range of texts that need to be taken into consideration if the assessment of Avicenna's natural philosophy is to be adequate, they also provide information on translators and translations that will be presupposed and referred to in the remainder of this study.

Much information here derives from the famous *Kitāb al-Fihrist*, an annotated bio-bibliographical catalogue composed by the Baġdādī book merchant Abū l-Farağ Muḥammad ibn Isḥāq al-Nadīm (d. ~ 385/995). This catalogue contains primarily two passages which report on translations of Aristotle's *Physics* that either were available to Ibn al-Nadīm, had been in his possession, or were simply known by him.[1] Many sections of the *Kitāb al-Fihrist*, including one on Aristotle's *Physics*, have been copied verbatim by the historian ʿAlī ibn Yūsuf ibn al-Qifṭī (d. 646/1248) into his own *Taʾrīḫ al-ḥukamāʾ*, often furnished with additional information.[2]

Ibn al-Nadīm's catalogue has received a large share of attention among scholars. With regard to its information on the Arabic transmission of the *Physics*, particular mention is to be made of Moritz Steinschneider's well-known study *Die arabischen Übersetzungen aus dem Griechischen* and Francis Peters' partial translation and study *Aristoteles Arabus*.[3] Elias Giannakis' unpublished doctoral dissertation on *Philoponus in the Arabic Tradition of Aristotle's* Physics as well as a number of subsequently published articles provide valuable information on the context of reading Aristotle's *Physics* in fourth/tenth-century Baġdād.[4] Moreover, important information concerning the Graeco-Arabic translation movement, in particular regarding its influence on Avicenna's philosophy, can be gathered from Amos Bertolacci's assessment of the sources for Avicenna's *al-Ilāhiyyāt* as well as from Dimitri Gutas' analysis of the philosophical curriculum outlined in the *Kitāb fī aṣnāf al-ʿulūm al-ḥikmiyya* of Abū Sahl al-Masīḥī (d. 401/1010).[5]

1 Ibn al-Nadīm, *Kitāb al-Fihrist*, vol. 1, 244.5f., 250.7–27 (ed. Flügel)/vol. 2, 145.5f., 166.1–167.12 (ed. Sayyid).

2 cf. Ibn al-Qifṭī, *Taʾrīḫ al-ḥukamāʾ*, 38.9–39.21; cf. also Ḥāğğī Ḫalīfa, *Kašf al-ẓunūn*, §§7258, 10190, 10193.

3 cf. esp. Steinschneider, *Die arabischen Übersetzungen aus dem Griechischen*, 50–55; Peters, *Aristoteles Arabus*, 30–34.

4 cf. esp. Giannakis, "The Structure of Abū l-Ḥusayn al-Baṣrī's Copy of Aristotle's *Physics*"; "Fragments from Alexander's Lost Commentary on Aristotle's *Physics*."

5 cf. Bertolacci, *The Reception of Aristotle's* Metaphysics *in Avicenna's* Kitāb al-Šifāʾ, ch. 11; Gutas, *Avicenna and the Aristotelian Tradition*, 169–179.

https://doi.org/10.1515/9783110546798-002

1.1 Transmission and Translation

The transmission of Aristotle's *Physics* into Arabic is intimately related to the transmission of the Greek commentaries on the *Physics*, especially those written by Alexander of Aphrodisias (fl. ~ 200) and John Philoponus (d. 574).[6] As it turns out, this circumstance is to the detriment of anyone hoping to acquire an *exact* understanding of the scope and nature of the Arabic translations of the *Physics*, as the information we can gather from our bibliographical sources concerns more the commentaries than the text commented upon. Of course, the Greek commentaries as we know them are, for the most part, lemmatised expositions, i.e., commentaries which, first, quote some lines from the Aristotelian text and, then, engage in a more or less free analysis of the quoted passage before turning to the next few lines from the text. Lemmatised commentaries, thus, provide in and of themselves a relatively complete version of the Aristotelian text.[7] Yet, it is also clear that any information on the Graeco-Arabic translations of *commentaries* does not as such tell us anything exact about whether, and to what extent, an Arabic version of Aristotle's *text* itself existed, circulated, and was used at a certain time in an intellectual milieu, or whether an interested reader had to turn to an Arabic version of (some parts of) a commentary and from there come to know (some parts of) the Aristotelian text. This is particularly problematic, when – as in the case of Aristotle's *Physics* – the bibliographical sources allow for different interpretations.

Translations Mostly "with" the Commentaries of Alexander and Philoponus

The earliest attested translation of Aristotle's *Physics* is that by Sallām al-Abraš (fl. mid second/late eighth century), who worked under the reign of Hārūn al-Rašīd (d. 193/809; r. 169/786–193/809), the fifth ʿAbbāsid caliph at Baġdād.[8] According to Peters, Ibn al-Nadīm did not specify the language into which Sallām al-Abraš translated the *Physics*, suspecting that the translation "may have provided the Syriac *Vorlage* for Ibn Naʿimah's

6 For the Greco-Arabic translation movement, cf. esp. Endreß, "Die wissenschaftliche Literatur"; Gutas, *Greek Thought, Arabic Culture*; "Greek Philosophical Works Translated into Arabic."

7 It is worth noting that the lemmata of a commentary follow a different line of transmission than both the running text of the commentary itself and the passages quoted or paraphrased within the running text of the commentary; cf. Primavesi's remarks in Aristotle, *Metaphysics A*, 407f. as well as Barnes, "An Introduction to Aspasius," 37. For a more positive evaluation, in particular regarding the lemmata in Alexander's commentary on the *Metaphysics*, cf. Kotwick, *Alexander of Aphrodisias and the Text of Aristotle's* Metaphysics, esp. 38–50.

8 cf. Endreß, "Die wissenschaftliche Literatur," 422; Gutas, *Greek Thought, Arabic Culture*, 72f.; D'Ancona, "Greek Sources in Arabic and Islamic Philosophy," ch. 2. In Sayyid's recent edition of Ibn al-Nadīm's *Kitāb al-Fihrist*, vol. 2, 145.5, "Salām [sic] and al-Abrša [sic]" appear to be two translators. The textual variant *Sallām wa-l-Abraš*, however, is also noted by Endreß, "Die wissenschaftliche Literatur," fn. 38, 422.

Arabic" version, subsequently produced in the early third/early ninth century.[9] Apparently, Peters overlooked that in the heading of the section that mentions Sallām al-Abraš as a translator of the *Physics*, Ibn al-Nadīm informs us of his intention to list the names of translators who translated "into the Arabic language" (*ilā l-lisān al-ʿarabī*).[10] We should, therefore, assume that the target language of Sallām al-Abraš's efforts was Arabic. Perhaps we may even surmise, despite the lack of any further information, that his translation covered the whole of Aristotle's *Physics*.[11]

Later, Ibn al-Nadīm reports that a translation of Aristotle's *Physics* "with the commentary" (*bi-tafsīr*) of Porphyry (d. ~ 305) on books I–IV was extant. As the translator, he names a certain Basīl (fl. early third/early ninth century), whose son Iṣṭifān ibn Basīl was a translator of medical texts in the circle of Ḥunayn ibn Isḥāq (d. 260/873) and arguably the brother of Taḏārī ibn Basīl, the translator of the extant Arabic version of Aristotle's *Prior Analytics*.[12] Not much is known of Basīl's translation or even of Porphyry's commentary.[13] Ibn al-Nadīm mentions Basīl's translation of Porphyry's commentary in a general section which lists "the *Physics* with various commentaries of numerous philosophers" (*bi-tafāsir ǧamāʿat falāsifa mutafarriqīn*). The expression *bi-tafsīr* (pl. *bi-tafāsir*) is sufficiently ambiguous to conceal whether Basīl translated Aristotle's *Physics* in full (and then continued with a translation of books I–IV of Porphyry's commentary) or whether he translated only the first four books of Porphyry's commentary (which contained at least parts of the Aristotelian text of the first four books in the form of lemmata). We also have no information about whether his translation was made on the basis of the Greek text or an earlier Syriac version.

In the same section on "the *Physics* with various commentaries of numerous philosophers," Ibn al-Nadīm also mentions Ibrāhīm ibn al-Ṣalt (fl. third/ninth century) as the translator of book one of "this book" (*hāḏā l-kitāb*).[14] Just as before in that section, the expression "this book" may seem to refer to Aristotle's *Physics*, mentioned in the section heading. Yet, the question arises why his translation is mentioned in a section

---

9 Peters, *Aristoteles Arabus*, 32.

10 Ibn al-Nadīm, *Kitāb al-Fihrist*, vol. 1, 244.1 (ed. Flügel)/vol. 2, 144.2 (ed. Sayyid).

11 Gutas mentions that Sallām al-Abraš's translation may have been used by the second/eighth century theologian Hišām ibn al-Ḥakam in his attack on the concept of God developed in the eighth and last book of the *Physics* (*Greek Thought, Arabic Culture*, 73).

12 cf. Lameer, *al-Fārābī and Aristotelian Syllogistics*, 3f. Steinschneider refers to some variant readings in the apparatus of Flügel's edition of the *Kitāb al-Fihrist* and considers the possibility that not Basīl but one of his sons translated Porphyry's commentary; cf. *Die arabischen Übersetzungen aus dem Griechischen*, 51f., referring to Ibn al-Nadīm, *Kitāb al-Fihrist*, vol. 2, 115.

13 Apart from the fragments collected by Romano (*Porfirio e la fisica aristotelica*) and by Smith (Porphyry, *Fragmenta*), the Greek original of Porphyry's commentary is not known to be extant. A potential fragment of the Arabic translation is found in Abū Bakr al-Rāzī, *Maqāla fī-mā baʿd al-ṭabīʿa*, 120.19–121.19, and has been included as frgm. 463F in Smith's collection; cf. also Adamson, "*Porphyrius Arabus* on Nature and Art," discussing the fragment and its context.

14 Ibn al-Nadīm, *Kitāb al-Fihrist*, vol. 1, 250.25 (ed. Flügel)/vol. 2, 167.10 (ed. Sayyid).

that reports on "the *Physics* with various commentaries," even though it is precisely a translation of the *Physics without* a commentary. Alternatively, then, "this book" could refer to whatever book was mentioned immediately before the information on Ibn al-Ṣalt's efforts, and this was a commentary on parts of the first book of the *Physics* composed by Ṯābit ibn Qurra (d. 288/901). Now, the mother tongue of Ṯābit ibn Qurra was Syriac, so it is possible that he composed a Syriac commentary on parts of the first book of Aristotle's *Physics*, which was, then, translated into Arabic by Ibn al-Ṣalt. Here, however, it is problematic that Ṯābit ibn Qurra could just as well also have written his commentary in Arabic (in fact, we might even expect that he did); that Ibn al-Nadīm used the expression "this book" before, albeit in order to refer to the *Physics*; and that Ṯābit ibn Qurra's commentary covered only *part of* the first book of Aristotle's *Physics*, whereas Ibn al-Ṣalt's translation was of "the first book," i.e., *the whole* of the first book.

The next translation that is known is the one produced by ʿAbd al-Masīḥ ibn Nāʿima al-Ḥimṣī (fl. ~ 215/830), who was already mentioned above in a quote from Peters' study. He was active in the circle of Abū Yaʿqūb ibn Isḥāq al-Kindī (d. ~ 256/870) and is known for his involvement in the production of the Arabic *Theology of Aristotle* and the Arabic (or rather Syriac?) translation of *De sophisticis elenchis*.[15] Regarding the *Physics*, Ibn al-Nadīm attributes to Ibn Nāʿima a translation of Aristotle's work "with the commentary of John Philoponus" (*bi-tafsīr Yaḥyā al-Naḥwī*) on books V–VIII. Again, the expression *bi-tafsīr* does not make clear whether Ibn Nāʿima produced a translation of Aristotle's entire *Physics* (to which he, then, added a translation of books V–VIII of Philoponus' commentary) or whether he simply translated the last four books of Philoponus' commentary (together with whatever these four books contained of the Aristotelian text in the form of lemmata). We likewise do not know whether Ibn Nāʿima translated from the Greek text or, as may seem more likely, from an earlier Syriac version, as Peters also suggested.

What we do know, however, is that before the Arabic tradition came to refer to Aristotle's *Physics* with the title *al-Samāʿ al-ṭabīʿī*, it was known as *Kitāb al-Kiyān* or *Samʿ al-kiyān*, even though it is uncertain whether this title ought to be associated primarily with Sallām al-Abraš's translation of Aristotle, or with Basīl's or Ibn Nāʿima's partial translation of one of the two commentaries, or even with whatever it was Ibn al-Ṣalt translated. The title *Samʿ al-kiyān* stems from the Syriac expression *Šemʿā kyānāyā*, which is a perfectly literal rendering of the Greek title traditionally given to Aristotle's *Physics*, viz., *Φυσικὴ ἀκρόασις*.[16] If neither Basīl's nor Ibn Nāʿima's translation provided the full text of Aristotle's *Physics*, covering it only partially, i.e., to the extent it was contained in the lemmata of those parts of Porphyry's and Philoponus' commentaries

15 cf. Zimmermann, "The Origins of the So-Called *Theology of Aristotle*"; Adamson, *The Arabic Plotinus*. As I have been informed by Pieter Sjoerd Hasper and Gerhard Endreß, the involvement of Ibn Nāʿima in the translation of *De sophisticis elenchis* is uncertain.

16 cf. esp. Arzhanov and Arnzen, "Die Glossen in Ms. *Leyden or. 583*," 425–429; cf. also Kraus, "Zu Ibn al-Muqaffaʿ," fn. 2, 7f.; Hein, *Definition und Einteilung der Philosophie*, 288, 407f.

which they translated, and if Ibn al-Ṣalt's translation was incomplete at any rate, then we may perhaps hesitate to assume that the title *Samʿ al-kiyān* was meant to refer to any of these incomplete versions and, instead, surmise that the older and complete translation of Sallām al-Abraš already circulated under this title.[17] However, the alternative assumption that there may have existed a full translation of Aristotle's *Physics* by Ibn Nāʿima, i.e., one which additionally included the second half of Philoponus' commentary, might find some support in the information which Ibn al-Nadīm provides about al-Kindī, who reportedly composed a treatise *Fī samʿ al-kiyān*.[18] Since Ibn Nāʿima was an active member of al-Kindī's circle, it may well have been his translation of Aristotle which al-Kindī read before he composed his own treatise. This, in turn, would indicate that al-Kindī either had no access to Sallām al-Abraš's earlier translation or that he considered it to be of such poor quality, that he requested from Ibn Nāʿima a new full translation of the *Physics* (including the second half of Philoponus' commentary).[19] It may, however, also simply mean that al-Kindī, having access the Sallām

---

17 Two minor caveats should be mentioned here. In his *Kitāb al-Fihrist*, Ibn al-Nadīm provides three pieces of information about Sallām al-Abraš: that he was one of the "old translators" (*min al-naqala al-qudamāʾ*), that he was active "during the days of the Barmakids" (*min ayyām al-barāmika*), and that "the *Physics* exists in his translation" (*wa-yūǧadu bi-naqlihī al-Samāʿ al-ṭabīʿī*; vol. 1, 244.5f. (ed. Flügel)/vol. 2, 145.5f. (ed. Sayyid)). The first of these minor caveats, then, is that the last piece of information here could be taken to mean that Sallām al-Abraš's translation was precisely not called *Samʿ al-kiyān* but already carried the title *al-Samāʿ al-ṭabīʿī*, the same title by which Aristotle's work will later commonly be known. It should be clear, though, that far from stating that Sallām al-Abraš's translation was called *al-Samāʿ al-ṭabīʿī*, Ibn al-Nadīm merely mentions that Sallām al-Abraš translated *inter alia* that work which *he*, i.e., Ibn al-Nadīm in Baġdād in the fourth/tenth century, calls *al-Samāʿ al-ṭabīʿī* – and we do know from other sections in his *Kitāb al-Fihrist* that this is, indeed, how Ibn al-Nadīm refers to Aristotle's *Physics*. The second caveat is that according to Kraemer, Sallām al-Abraš translated the *Physics* "from Persian into Arabic" (*Humanism in the Renaissance of Islam*, 134). If true, this could undermine the present suggestion that it may have been Sallām al-Abraš's translation that was referred to as *Samʿ al-kiyān* – a title indicating a Syriac (and not a Persian) intermediary in the line of transmission. Neither of the two references which Kraemer provides, however, mentions a Persian intermediary for Sallām al-Abraš's translation. It may perhaps be that Kraemer silently identified Sallām al-Abraš with another person by the name of Salm, whom Ibn al-Nadīm elsewhere reports to have translated "from Persian into Arabic" (*min al-fārisī ilā l-ʿarabī*; *Kitāb al-Fihrist*, vol. 1, 120.16f. (ed. Flügel)/vol. 1, 374.9–11 (ed. Sayyid)). However, as Endreß already noted, Salm and Sallām al-Abraš were probably two different translators; cf. "Die wissenschaftliche Literatur," 422; cf. also Peters, *Aristoteles Arabus*, 11. Moreover, Ibn al-Nadīm's description of Sallām al-Abraš specifically as having been active "during the days of the Barmakids" seems to serve the exclusive purpose of a temporal designation, stressing the point that Sallām al-Abraš really was one of the "old translators," so that he was active during the reign of caliph Hārūn al-Rašīd, but not that he translated from Persian; cf. also Gutas, *Greek Thought, Arabic Culture*, 72.

18 *Kitāb al-Fihrist*, vol. 1, 256.16 (ed. Flügel)/vol. 2, 185.8 (ed. Sayyid). Surprisingly, Ibn al-Nadīm lists this treatise as one of al-Kindī's "logical works" (*kutubuhū l-manṭiqiyya*).

19 According to Kraus, it was, indeed, Ibn Nāʿima's translation that was known as *Samʿ al-kiyān*; cf. Kraus, "Zu Ibn al-Muqaffaʿ," fn. 2, 7f. His argument, however, does not rule out that the title was already in use before and merely confirms that Ibn Nāʿima's translation was made from a Syriac intermediary.

al-Abraš's translation, requested a translation only of the important second half of Philoponus' commentary. Additionally, it may also well be that Ibn Nāʿima's translation of Philoponus' commentary on books V–VIII was meant to complement Basīl's translation of Porphyry's commentary on books I–IV. Although this remains a purely speculative hypothesis, it could at least explain the otherwise puzzling fact that Ibn Nāʿima apparently began his translation efforts with the fifth book, i.e., in the middle of the work.[20]

What seems to be the most convincing interpretation of the evidence so far is to assume that Sallām al-Abraš translated the *Physics* in full, that his translation was known as Aristotle's *Samʿ al-kiyān*, and that Basīl's and Ibn Nāʿima's new translations of the first and the second half of the *Physics* together "with the [partial] commentaries" of Porphyry and Philoponus, may have circulated under the same already known title, before it became customary to refer to Aristotle's *Physics* as *al-Samāʿ al-ṭabīʿī* instead.[21]

20 That Basīl apparently stopped his translation efforts likewise in the middle of the work after the fourth book is less puzzling and, in fact, corresponds to Romano's claim that Porphyry properly commented only on books I–IV, to which he added a mere compendium on book V, altogether neglecting the remaining books VI–VIII; cf. Romano, *Porfirio e la fisica aristotelica*, esp. 54–56. Romano's assertion is accepted by Urmson in fn. 3, 124, to his translation of Simplicius' commentary on the fifth book of the *Physics*; cf. also Moraux, "Porphyre, commentateur de la *Physique* d'Aristote"; Adamson, "*Porphyrius Arabus* on Nature and Art"; A. Smith, "The Significance of 'Physics' in Porphyry."

21 The title *al-ḫabar al-ṭabīʿī* is also attested in the third/ninth century as referring to Aristotle's *Physics*, for example, by al-Kindī in his *Risāla fī kammiyyat kutub Arisṭūṭālīs wa-mā yuḥtāğu ilayhi fī taḥṣīl al-falsafa*, vol. 1, 382.14f.; cf. also Arzhanov and Arnzen, "Die Glossen in Ms. *Leyden or. 583*," 426. Philosophers who used the title *Samʿ al-kiyān* in their Arabic works include, apart from al-Kindī, the Ps.-Aristotle who composed the *Kitāb al-Ḥaraka*, Abū Bakr Muḥammad ibn Zakariyāʾ al-Rāzī, the Iḫwān al-Ṣafāʾ, Abū Naṣr al-Fārābī, and Avicenna. In the *Kitāb al-Ḥaraka*, the title is mentioned three times (cf. the searchable online version of the *Kitāb al-Ḥaraka* and the excerpt (containing only two occurrences) in Wakelnig, *A Philosophy Reader from the Circle of Miskawayh*, appx. 2, 486.4, 12); Abū Bakr al-Rāzī uses it in his *Maqāla fī-mā baʿd al-ṭabīʿa*, 121.6, and his *Kitāb al-Sīra al-falsafiyya*, 109.1f.; the Iḫwān al-Ṣafāʾ refer with it to their epistle on physics in *Rasāʾil Iḫwān al-Ṣafāʾ* XVI.1, 67.9; al-Fārābī uses it in his *Risāla fī-mā yanbaġī an yuqaddama qabla taʿallum al-falsafa*, 51.2; the expression *ṣināʿat al-kiyān* occurs in al-Fārābī (?), *Kitāb al-Ğamʿ bayna raʾyay al-ḥakīmayn Aflāṭun al-ilāhī wa-Arisṭāṭālīs*, 45.12; Avicenna uses *Kitāb al-Kiyān* in his *Risāla fī aqsām al-ʿulūm al-ʿaqliyya*, 108.17, and *Samʿ al-kiyān* in his correspondence with Abū Rayḥān al-Bīrūnī, known as *al-Asʾila wa-l-ağwiba*, 18.7, 23.13; finally, Avicenna's disciple Abū Saʿīd Aḥmad ibn ʿAlī al-Maʿṣūmī also uses *Samʿ al-kiyān* in his reply – on behalf of Avicenna – to al-Bīrūnī's response (68.10). Moreover, Gutas notes that at least in some (early?) recensions of Avicenna's *Risāla fī l-ağrām al-ʿulwiyya*, the term *kiyān* is found to designate the concept of nature; cf. Gutas, "The Study of Avicenna," 61. Even after Avicenna, the term was in use, as is evinced by the brief preface to the final four chapters from the area of natural philosophy in Abū Ḥāmid al-Ġazālī's *Tahāfut al-falāsifa*, 268.9. Whether or not this indicates that al-Ġazālī, in composing this preface, relied upon Avicenna's *Risāla fī aqsām al-ʿulūm al-ʿaqliyya* remains to be seen. At any rate, Avicenna's and al-Ġazālī's enumerations of the natural sciences share many conspicuous similarities. On Avicenna's treatise, cf. also Michot's annotated translation published as Avicenna, *Les sciences physiques et métaphysiques selon la Risālah fī Aqsām al-ʿulūm d'Avicenne*.

Ibn al-Nadīm attributes, in the same ambiguous way, a translation of Aristotle's work "with the commentary" (*bi-tafsīr*) of Philoponus' on books I–IV to the translator Qusṭā ibn Lūqā al-Baʿlabakkī (d. 300/912). The natural assumption would be that Qusṭā's translation of the first and Ibn Nāʿima's translation of the second half of Philoponus' commentary were meant to complement each other. In addition to that, Qusṭā is also said to have translated Aristotle's work "with the commentary" (*bi-tafsīr*) of Alexander on books IV, V, and VII. Once more, we do not know whether we should understand Ibn al-Nadīm's expression *bi-tafsīr* in such a way that Qusṭā produced a complete Arabic version of Aristotle's *Physics* together with one half of Philoponus' and (at least) one third of Alexander's commentary or whether Qusṭā only translated parts of these two commentaries together with the Aristotelian text inasmuch as it was contained in their lemmata. Since it is unlikely that Qusṭā translated the complete text of Aristotle's *Physics* twice, i.e., once together with parts of Philoponus' commentary and once together with parts of Alexander's commentary, we might have to understand *bi-tafsīr* generally as indicating that Aristotle's text was translated only insofar is it was contained in the lemmata of the commentaries. This would further mean that Basīl's and Ibn Nāʿima's translations were just as incomplete as Qusṭā's, and suggest that the title *Samʿ al-kiyān* originally, indeed, referred to the translation by Sallām al-Abraš, which is the only complete – and incidentally also the oldest – translation so far mentioned. Moreover, in light of its title, Sallām al-Abraš may have produced his translation on the basis of an earlier Syriac version. Additionally, it is also possible that Qusṭā's translation was also complete in the sense that he translated the first half of the *Physics* "with the commentary" of Philoponus and the second half "with the commentary" of Alexander, which, then, would indicate that Qusṭā is also the translator of books VI and VIII of Aristotle "with" Alexander, i.e., those books that are mentioned by Ibn al-Nadīm without being linked to the name of a translator.

What is more, Ibn al-Nadīm also credits Abū ʿUṯmān al-Dimašqī (fl. late third/early tenth century) with an extant version of Alexander's commentary on *Physics* IV. While this could mean that al-Dimašqī was yet another translator who produced an Arabic version of Aristotle's *Physics* together with parts of Alexander's commentary, it is more plausible to assume, again, that the expression *bi-tafsīr* indicates merely that parts of Alexander's commentary were translated together with the Aristotelian text contained therein or, as a third alternative in this case, that al-Dimašqī's contribution was overall limited to revising some of the work of his older contemporary Qusṭā, so that it was *his* revision that was reportedly more widely distributed (*al-ẓāhir al-mawǧūd*) at the time of Ibn al-Nadīm.[22]

22 In any case, Giannakis notes that al-Dimašqī "is known to have taken a special interest in Alexander" (*Philoponus in the Arabic Tradition of Aristotle's* Physics, 90; "Fragments from Alexander's Lost Commentary on Aristotle's *Physics*," 157); cf. also Arzhanov and Arnzen, "Die Glossen in Ms. *Leyden or. 583*," 462. It should further be noted that al-Dimašqī is explicitly mentioned as the translator of

Concerning Alexander's commentary, there is also Yaḥyā ibn ʿAdī (d. 363/974), who is credited with having revised an Arabic translation by Abū Rawḥ al-Ṣābiʾ (fl. late third/early tenth century) of book I of Aristotle's *Physics* "with the commentary" (*bi-tafsīr*) of Alexander and said to have translated book II, again "with the commentary" (*bi-tafsīr*) of Alexander, on the basis of an earlier Syriac version by Ḥunayn ibn Isḥāq.[23] The third book of Aristotle's *Physics* "with the commentary" (*bi-tafsīr*) of Alexander was, according to Ibn al-Nadīm, not extant.

Tab. 1.1: Arabic Translations of Aristotle's *Physics* with and without commentaries.

					Physics				
		I	II	III	IV	V	VI	VII	VIII
Sallām al-Abraš:	Aristotle	×	×	×	×	×	×	×	×
Ibrāhīm ibn al-Ṣalt:	Aristotle?	×							
Basīl:	Porphyry	×	×	×	×				
Ibn Nāʿima:	Philoponus					×	×	×	×
Qusṭā ibn Lūqā:	Philoponus	×	×	×	×				
Qusṭā ibn Lūqā:	Alexander				×	×	?	×	?
al-Dimašqī:	Alexander				×				
Abū Rawḥ al-Ṣābiʾ:	Alexander	×							
Yaḥyā ibn ʿAdī:	Alexander	×	×						
Isḥāq ibn Ḥunayn:	Aristotle	×	×	×	×	×	×	×	×

At best, this information attests to four complete translations of Aristotle ("with" different parts of various commentaries), viz., those by Sallām al-Abraš, Basīl, Ibn Nāʿima, and Qusṭā (or five, should we consider Qusṭā to have translated it twice, once with Alexander's and once with Philoponus' commentary; or even eight, if we wanted to include the efforts of Ibn al-Ṣalt, al-Dimašqī, and Ibn ʿAdī with the help of al-Ṣābiʾ as well). At worst, we have to be content with only one complete translation – that by Sallām al-Abraš – together with several parts from Alexander's, Porphyry's, and Philoponus' commentaries, sometimes in multiple translation, which may or may not

the *Risālat al-Iskandar al-Afrūdīsī fī anna kull mā yataḥarraku fa-innamā yataḥarraku ʿan muḥarrik*, which is jointly preserved through Ms. Carullah 1279 at Süleymaniye Kütüphanesi in Istanbul and Ms. arab. 794 at Real Biblioteca del Monasterio de San Lorenzo in El Escorial. Now, according to a suggestion by Pines, this work may not be one of Alexander's independent treatises against Galen but an "extract from Alexander's lost *Commentary* on Aristotle's *Physics*" ("Omne quod movetur necesse est ab aliquo moveri," 22). Pines' suggestion was critically discussed, and ultimately rejected, by Rescher and Marmura in their edition of the treatise (esp. 60–62). Following Rescher's and Marmura's criticism, I do not consider the Arabic version of Alexander's treatise as evidence indicating that al-Dimašqī translated (or revised) not only the fourth but also (parts of) the seventh book of Aristotle's *Physics* "with the commentary" (*bi-tafsīr*) of Alexander into Arabic.

23 According to Ḥāğğī Ḫalīfa, it was the third book, and not the second; cf. *Kašf al-ẓunūn*, vol. 3, 619.7.

have contained lemmatised quotations of the Aristotelian text.[24] In that case, however, we might cherish the prospect that Basīl's and Ibn Nāʿima's combined activities as well as Qusṭā's double effort, if accumulated, may have amounted to a second and even a third full translation of the *Physics*.

All this remains speculation, because none of these translations has survived in any substantial form.

Ms. Leiden or. 583

Finally, there is the Arabic translation by Isḥāq ibn Ḥunayn (d. 298/910–11), which, as far as I can see, is not mentioned in either Ibn al-Nadīm's *Kitāb al-Fihrist* or Ibn al-Qifṭī's *Taʾrīḫ al-ḥukamāʾ*. It is the only Arabic translation of Aristotle's *Physics* that is known to be extant today. Isḥāq ibn Ḥunayn produced it presumably on the basis of an earlier Syriac version of his own or his father Ḥunayn ibn Isḥāq.[25] His Arabic translation survives in the manuscript or. 583 from the collection which Levinus Warner (d. 1665) bequeathed to the University of Leiden.[26] The manuscript contains 233 folia and was transcribed in 524/1129–30 by the physician and poet Abū l-Ḥakam al-Maġribī (d. 549/1155) from a copy of an earlier annotated exemplar of Isḥāq ibn Ḥunayn's translation.[27] This earlier exemplar was prepared by the Muʿtazilī theologian Abū l-Ḥusayn al-Baṣrī (d. 436/1044) around the year 395/1004 and copied by an anonymous scribe in 470/1077, this latter being the copy from which Abū l-Ḥakam al-Maġribī transcribed the manuscript which we today know as Ms. Leiden or. 583.[28]

The original exemplar of Abū l-Ḥusayn was the result of his own studies in philosophy within the school of the so-called Baġdād Peripatetics under Abū ʿAlī ibn al-Samḥ (d. 418/1027) and Abū l-Faraǧ ʿAbd Allāh ibn al-Ṭayyib (d. 435/1043).[29] Ibn al-Samḥ was a pupil of Ibn ʿAdī, whereas Ibn al-Ṭayyib was taught by Ibn ʿAdī's students, among

24 In this regard, one should mention Endreß' general warning that it is not certain whether the translator of a commentary would also have translated the text that was commented upon; cf. "Die griechisch-arabischen Übersetzungen und die Sprache der arabischen Wissenschaften," 108.

25 cf. Peters, *Aristoteles Arabus*, 32; Arzhanov and Arnzen, "Die Glossen in Ms. *Leyden or. 583*," 439–442.

26 For information on the manuscript, cf. Peters, *Aristoteles Arabus*, 31f.; Witkam, *Seven specimens of Arabic Manuscripts*, 14f.; Kraemer, *Humanism in the Renaissance of Islam*, 109; Giannakis, *Philoponus in the Arabic Tradition of Aristotle's* Physics, 19–30; "The Structure of Abū l-Ḥusayn al-Baṣrī's Copy of Aristotle's *Physics*"; Lettinck, *Aristotle's* Physics *and its Reception in the Arabic World*, 1–6; Arzhanov and Arnzen, "Die Glossen in Ms. *Leyden or. 583*," 431–434.

27 For the identification of the scribe Abū l-Ḥakam with the poet Abū l-Ḥakam al-Maġribī, cf. Stern, "Ibn al-Samḥ," 34–36.

28 For the identification of Abū l-Ḥusayn with the Muʿtazilī theologian, cf. Stern, "Ibn al-Samḥ," 36–38; cf. also Kraemer, *Humanism in the Renaissance of Islam*, 131; Madelung, "Abū 'l-Ḥusayn al-Baṣrī."

29 On the Baġdād Peripatetics, cf. Kraemer, *Humanism in the Renaissance of Islam*, 104–139.

whom was Ibn al-Samḥ's fellow al-Ḥasan ibn Suwār ibn al-Ḫammār (d. after 407/1017). Ibn ʿAdī himself studied under Abū Bišr Mattā ibn Yūnus (d. 328/940).[30]

What we today find in Ms. Leiden or. 583, then, is a faithfully transcribed text of Isḥāq ibn Ḥunayn's translation supplemented with comments, notes, objections, and philological remarks by Abū l-Ḥusayn, Ibn al-Samḥ, Ibn al-Ṭayyib, Ibn ʿAdī, Abū Bišr, and an otherwise little known Abū ʿAmr (or Abū ʿUmar) al-Ṭabarī, who probably was a student of Abū Bišr and Ibn ʿAdī.[31] All these thinkers drew upon Arabic translations of Alexander's commentary on the *Physics* as well as the paraphrase by Themistius (d. ~ 385) and, most of all, the commentary of Philoponus.[32] It is no exaggeration to say that they used Philoponus as their guide and model for reading Aristotle's *Physics*. Moreover, the Leiden manuscript also attests to the translation efforts of Qusṭā and al-Dimašqī – at times discussing variant readings to Isḥāq ibn Ḥunayn's translation, and even to Syriac sources of Aristotle's work and Alexander's commentary.[33]

Giannakis' analysis of the manuscript and its contents suggests that Abū l-Ḥusayn's compilation, which combined the Arabic text of Aristotle's *Physics* together with comments and remarks from his teachers, was only one of a number of such compilations. In fact, it is reasonable to assume that students, if they themselves possessed a copy of a text, may have taken notes from the lessons they had with their teachers. Likewise, it is no less plausible that teachers preserved their own readings together with the results of their own examination of a text in the form of a personal copy enriched with glosses and annotations of their own as well as quotations from the available secondary literature. In particular, Giannakis hints towards the possible existence of similar compilations by Ibn al-Samḥ and Ibn al-Ṭayyib (recording material from their lessons with Ibn ʿAdī), by Ibn ʿAdī himself, and by Abū ʿAmr al-Ṭabarī (recording material from his lessons with Abū Bišr) as potential models for Abū l-Ḥusayn's own compilation.[34] It could be that Ibn al-Samḥ's compilation is identical with the "commentary" or "compendium" (*šarḥ ka-l-ǧawāmiʿ*) which Ibn al-Qifṭī attributes to him in the *Taʾrīḫ al-ḥukamāʾ*.[35]

To what extent these compilations were circulating and, in turn, to what extent Avicenna knew these collections as commentaries on the Aristotelian text is unknown.

---

30 The list of Ibn ʿAdī's students also included eminent members of the philosophical circle around Abū Sulaymān al-Siǧistānī, among them ʿAlī Abū Ḥayyān al-Tawḥīdī and Abū ʿAlī Aḥmad Miskawayh; cf. Kraemer, *Philosophy in the Renaissance of Islam*, 30f.; *Humanism in the Renaissance of Islam*, 115.

31 On Abū ʿAmr al-Ṭabarī, cf. Hasnawi, "Un élève d'Abu Bišr Mattā b. Yūnus"; cf. also Giannakis, *Philoponus in the Arabic Tradition of Aristotle's* Physics, 34–37.

32 Badawī published the contents of the manuscript, i.e., both the Aristotelian text in the translation of Isḥāq ibn Ḥunayn and the various glosses and commentaries, under the title *al-Ṭabīʿa*; cf. also the brief information in Badawī, *La transmission de la philosophie grecque au monde arabe*, 79.

33 On these Syriac sources, cf. esp. Arzhanov and Arnzen, "Die Glossen in Ms. *Leyden or. 583*."

34 A puzzling feature of Abū l-Ḥusayn's compilation is that up to *Physics* VI.5 he seems to be drawing on Ibn al-Samḥ's work but then turns to Ibn al-Ṭayyib's for the rest of the *Physics*; cf. also Giannakis, "The Structure of Abū l-Ḥusayn al-Baṣrī's Copy of Aristotle's *Physics*."

35 Ibn al-Qifṭī, *Taʾrīḫ al-ḥukamāʾ*, 39.19f.

The mere fact that Abū l-Ḥakam al-Maġribī transcribed a copy of Abū l-Ḥusayn's own compilation, however, indicates that a certain circulation took place and that there was at least some interest in copying and reading such materials. In addition, we can be certain that Avicenna knew most of these figures, and in some of his writings he even responded directly to some of them.[36] Consequently, there is good reason to think that Avicenna was in one way or another aware of the fact that some of his contemporaries in Baġdād read and commented upon Aristotle's *Physics*, and that he may have known some of the interpretations they were putting forth.[37] Yet, Avicenna's relation to contemporary Baġdādī intellectuals clearly deserves more attention than my present study can provide.[38] What, nonetheless, emerges from this study is that Avicenna reacts critically to Philoponus and his way of reading and interpreting Aristotle's *Physics*. Thus, it is at least indirectly that Avicenna also reacts critically to his colleagues from Baġdād, because he criticises the very way in which they read Aristotle's *Physics*, viz., through Philoponus.[39]

So much, then, for the evidence about the transmission of the text of Aristotle's *Physics* into Arabic as such. I shall now turn to a more general survey of information about those thinkers from within the Aristotelian tradition whose works on natural philosophy were translated into Arabic, in order to introduce the texts that need to be taken into account – and that this study has taken into account – in elucidating and contextualising the various discussions and arguments we find in Avicenna works on physics. Without laying claim to completeness in any respect, this survey seeks to provide relevant information about those thinkers who, in one way or another, wrote on physics, commented on Aristotle, were translated into Arabic, were influential in their Arabic translation, or may otherwise have had an impact on the formation of Avicenna's thought on natural philosophy, and which, for this reason, will reappear, often prominently, in the remainder of this book.

---

36 cf. Pines, "La 'philosophie orientale' d'Avicenne et sa polémique contre les bagdadiens"; Brown, "Avicenna and the Christian Philosophers in Baghdad"; M. Rashed, "Ibn ʿAdī et Avicenne"; Ferrari's remarks in Ibn al-Ṭayyib, *Tafsīr Kitāb al-Maqūlāt*, 23–25; Menn, "Avicenna's Metaphysics," 153–159; Gutas, *Avicenna and the Aristotelian Tradition*, 53–67; Benevich, "Fire and Heat." Daiber notes that Ibn Suwār even met Avicenna, and al-Bīrūnī, at the court of the penultimate Maʾmūnid Ḫwārizmšāh Abū l-ʿAbbās Maʾmūn ibn Maʾmūn (r. 390–407/1000–1017); cf. "The *Meteorology* of Theophrastus," 220; cf. also Kraemer, *Humanism in the Renaissance of Islam*, 124–126.

37 What is revealing in this context is Avicenna's explicit reference to both the *Physics* and the inadequacy of the understanding both of the Baġdād Peripatetics and of Philoponus in his *Letter to Kiyā* contained in *al-Mubāḥaṯāt*, 373.7–11. For the identification of *fulān wa-fulān* in Avicenna's letter with the "Christians from Baġdād," cf. Gutas, *Avicenna and the Aristotelian Tradition*, 57.

38 For a valuable exploration of Avicenna's relation to his contemporaries, and in particular those appearing in his *al-Mubāḥaṯāt*, cf. Reisman, *The Making of the Avicennan Tradition*, ch. 3.

39 This is particularly evident in Avicenna's discussion of nature; q.v. below, 256ff.

1.2 The Commentators on the Aristotelian Text

Theophrastus

There is only scarce information about the Arabic transmission of the writings on physics and natural philosophy by Theophrastus of Eresus (d. ~ 287 BC). The evidence has conveniently been listed by Gutas.[40] Most important, perhaps, is the Arabic version of his *Metaphysics* produced by Isḥāq ibn Ḥunayn and recently edited by Gutas as well as his Arabic *Meteorology* translated by Ibn Suwār on the basis of an earlier Syriac version, both published by Daiber.[41] Moreover, Theophrastus was an influential figure in the development of the philosophical concept of place, as a handful of important fragments of his lost work on physics, preserved by Simplicius (d. ~ 560), evince. While it is not clear whether material from this work on physics circulated in Arabic translation and whether it reached Avicenna, his fragments inspired others to object to Aristotle's account and to shape the critical situation to which Avicenna will later react.[42]

Galen

One respect in which Galen (d. ~ 216) was of importance for Arabic philosophy, is as a transmitter of Plato. Generally, there was not much of Plato's works to be read for Muslim intellectuals.[43] That is to say, we find in Arabic works an abundance of sayings attributed to Plato and there certainly was a general and honest interest in – or as Franz Rosenthal put it: "an enthusiastic reception and a vivid echo" of – various aspects of his philosophy, which stands in stark contrast to the fact that not a single one of Plato's dialogues is known to have come down to us in Arabic.[44] Whether this was primarily due to the involved style of his dialogues or to another reason (or a complex of reasons) is still unknown. As a result, Plato was by all means a prominent figure and a famous philosopher, even though on the whole, his philosophy was overshadowed by the success of Aristotelianism, and ultimately and entirely "eclipsed by the triumph of Avicenna's Peripateticism," as Gutas put it.[45] With regard to natural philosophy,

40 cf. Gutas, "The Life, Works, and Sayings of Theophrastus in the Arabic Tradition," 80–82; cf. also Theophrastus, *Sources for his Life, Writings, Thought and Influence*, 276–435.

41 Theophrastus, *On First Principles* (known as his *Metaphysics*); *Meteorology*.

42 cf. also Steinmetz, *Die Physik des Theophrastos von Eresos* and the remarks by Daiber in "The *Meteorology* of Theophrastus," 167. Steinmetz suggests an influence of Theophrastus on Avicenna in matters of mineralogy (*Die Physik des Theophrastos von Eresos*, 322).

43 cf. Arnzen, "Plato's *Timaeus* in the Arabic Tradition," esp. 181–198; cf. also Hasse, "Plato arabico-latinus"; Gutas, "Platon."

44 Rosenthal, "On the Knowledge of Plato's Philosophy in the Islamic World," 393.

45 Gutas, "Platon," 849.

however, there was at least, thanks to Galen, a paraphrase of the *Timaeus*, which was translated into Syriac by Ḥunayn ibn Isḥāq and subsequently from Syriac into Arabic by his colleague ʿĪsā ibn Yaḥyā ibn Ibrāhīm. The Arabic version has been published by Paul Kraus and Richard Walzer in 1951 together with their own Latin translation.[46]

In addition to that, philosophers in the Arabic tradition were also informed about the opinions Galen himself held about some of the subjects usually treated in physics. In part, his views reached them through the writings of other or later authors and commentators. In particular, Alexander's critical engagement with Galen on time, place, and motion provided an, albeit biased, picture of Galen's sceptical attitude towards certain aspects of Aristotelian natural philosophy. An intriguing testimony in this regard is a letter written by Ibn Abī Saʿīd al-Mawṣilī (fl. fourth/tenth century) in Mosul and addressed to Ibn ʿAdī in Baġdād, containing philosophical questions on a number of subjects. One of the questions concerns the nature of time and asks whether Aristotle's or rather Galen's position is correct. It is in this context also explicitly stated that Ibn Abī Saʿīd derived his information from a treatise by Alexander that contradicts (*nāqaḍahū*) Galen's views on time and place.[47] One should, however, take notice also of the more reserved interpretation of Alexander's purported polemics against Galen advanced by Fritz Zimmermann and Silvia Fazzo.[48]

Apart from the indirect transmission of Galen's thoughts, there was also a direct transmission of his works into Arabic. This includes, of course, his medical corpus among which, for example, his *De elementis ex Hippocratis sententia* proved to be a particularly rich source for the discussion of corporeality as well as atomistic and non-atomistic elemental theories. The history of its transmission is complex. In addition to an Arabic translation the work itself, there exist epitomes of it in both Greek and Arabic as well as further abridgements and commentaries, attesting to its favourable reception and widespread dissemination.[49] One of the Greek epitomes was translated into both Syriac and Arabic by Ḥunayn ibn Isḥāq, and recently published in edition and translation by John Walbridge as *Ǧawāmiʿ Kitāb Ǧālīnūs fī l-ʿanāṣir ʿalā raʾy Ibuqrāṭ*.[50] Another important example is Galen's no longer extant work *On Demonstration*, which was at least partially available in a Syriac and Arabic versions produced, again, in the

---

46 Galen, *Compendium Timaei Platonis*.

47 Ibn ʿAdī, *Kitāb Aǧwiba Bišr al-Yahūdī ʿan masāʾilihī*, esp. 318.6–319.3; cf. also Furlani, "Le 'Questioni filosofiche' di Abū Zakarīyā Yaḥyà b. ʿAdī"; Pines, "A Tenth Century Philosophical Correspondence," 111f.; Sharples' remarks in Alexander of Aphrodisias, *On Time*, 72f.; Adamson, "Galen and al-Rāzī on Time."

48 Zimmermann, "al-Farabi und die philosophische Kritik an Galen"; Fazzo, "Alexandre d'Aphrodise contre Galien."

49 cf. De Lacy's remarks in Galen, *De elementis ex Hippocratis sententia*, 20–25; cf. also Langermann, "Islamic Atomism and the Galenic Tradition"; Bos and Langermann, "An Epitome of Galen's *On The Elements* Ascribed to Ḥunayn Ibn Isḥāq."

50 Walbridge, *The Alexandrian Epitomes of Galen*, 131–186.

circle of Ḥunayn ibn Isḥāq.[51] It is known that this voluminous work was not exclusively devoted to logic and covered several topics of cosmology and natural philosophy.[52] We shall come across it prominently when investigating Avicenna's views on time.

Alexander of Aphrodisias

Alexander's commentary on Aristotle's *Physics* is almost entirely lost in both Greek and Arabic. In fact, Ibn al-Nadīm's *Kitāb al-Fihrist* contains an anecdote which may suggest that copies of Alexander's commentary may already have been rare in the fourth/tenth century.[53] It is through the commentaries of later authors, in particular Simplicius, that we have the chance of retrieving fragments of his comments. Simplicius' writings are generally a rich source for statements of earlier authors, as he often provides or discusses selected passages from a variety of sources, including Alexander, whom he often quotes and sometimes mentions by name. Recently the situation concerning Alexander's commentary improved dramatically when Marwan Rashed published

51 cf. Ḥunayn ibn Isḥāq, *Risāla fī ḏikr mā turǧima min kutub Ǧālīnūs*, 47.10–48.8 (ed. Bergsträßer)/117.7–119.5 (ed. Lamoreaux); cf. also von Müller, *Ueber Galens Werk vom wissenschaftlichen Beweis*; Rescher, "New Light from Arabic Sources on Galen," 29f.

52 cf. Chiaradonna, "Le traité de Galien *Sur la démonstration*"; Adamson, "Galen and al-Rāzī on Time"; "Galen on Void," 197; Koetschet, "Galien, al-Rāzī, et l'éternité du monde."

53 Ibn al-Nadīm relates that the apparent bibliophile Ibn ʿAdī was offered copies of Alexander's commentaries on the *Physics* and the *Posterior Analytics* for one hundred and twenty dinars. While Ibn ʿAdī was trying to get the money together, the books were sold in a package with others to another customer for three thousand dinars, leaving Ibn ʿAdī probably somewhat disgruntled about the missed opportunity; cf. *Kitāb al-Fihrist*, vol. 1, 252.27–253.2 (ed. Flügel)/vol. 2, 174.5–9 (ed. Sayyid); cf. also Kraemer, *Humanism in the Renaissance of Islam*, 105. Unfortunately, it is not stated whether the offered codices were in Arabic, Syriac, or Greek, nor is it clear whether this anecdote took place before or after Ibn ʿAdī revised al-Ṣābiʾ's translation of Alexander's commentary on book I of the *Physics* and before he himself rendered book II into Arabic on the basis of Ḥunayn ibn Isḥāq's Syriac version. A second anecdote, however, specifically speaks of Isḥāq ibn Ḥunayn's *translations* of the *De sophisticis elenchis*, the *Rhetoric*, and the *Poetics* which Ibn ʿAdī tried to acquire all together for fifty dinars; cf. *Kitāb al-Fihrist*, vol. 1, 253.2–4 (ed. Flügel)/vol. 2, 174.9–11 (ed. Sayyid). Of these three works, Ibn al-Nadīm tells us elsewhere that Isḥāq ibn Ḥunayn, indeed, translated the *Rhetoric* into Arabic; cf. *Kitāb al-Fihrist*, vol. 1, 250.1 (ed. Flügel)/vol. 2, 164.15 (ed. Sayyid). If, then, the first anecdote is also concerned with (Arabic) translations, then this may suggest that there was a (complete?) Arabic translation of Alexander's commentary extant at the time of Ibn ʿAdī, which was probably a version not translated by himself, as otherwise he certainly would have kept a copy. However, it is not clear in light of the evidence discussed above who the translator of this complete version of Alexander's commentary would have been (Qusṭā?), so that the first anecdote, which does not explicitly mention translations, may rather have been about a Greek original. At any rate, the anecdote suggests that Alexander's commentary already may have been difficult to acquire in either language, especially as otherwise the anecdote would not be worth telling in the first place. What is more, Alexander's commentary on Aristotle's *Posterior Analytics* was apparently not extant either, as Ibn al-Nadīm states elsewhere, cf. *Kitāb al-Fihrist*, vol. 1, 249.13 (ed. Flügel)/vol. 2, 163.4f. (ed. Sayyid)

a volume containing 826 fragments from Alexander's commentary that have been preserved in the margins of two manuscripts stored in the Bibliothèque nationale de France in Paris (Ms. Supplément grec 643 and Ms. grec 1859).[54] Moreover, M. Rashed systematically compared these fragments with the testimony provided by Simplicius.

There are also a number of fragments preserved in Arabic in the marginal notes contained in Ms. Leiden or. 583, the manuscript of Isḥāq ibn Ḥunayn's translation of Aristotle's *Physics*. These have been extracted and published by Giannakis.[55] Most of them can be traced to quotations provided by Philoponus in his commentary on the *Physics*.[56] It is, therefore, not entirely clear from which translation they derive: a translation of Philoponus' commentary containing these passages, in which case we must consider Ibn Nāʿima and Qusṭā as the responsible translators, or a translation of Alexander's own commentary, in which case there are Ibn ʿAdī (book II), Qusṭā (at least books IV, V, VII), al-Dimašqī (book IV), and the translator of books VI and VIII, whose name is not known.[57]

In addition to this, a number of treatises attributed to Alexander are extant in Arabic. Among them is his already mentioned refutation of Galen's views on motion, which has been edited and translated by Nicholas Rescher and Michael E. Marmura.[58] It has been suggested by Shlomo Pines and Jules Janssens that this treatise influenced Avicenna's views on motion and natural motion.[59] There is, second, the well-known *Maqālat al-Iskandar al-Afrūdīsī fī l-zamān*. This treatise on time is extant in an Arabic version by Ḥunayn ibn Isḥāq, which was edited by ʿAbd al-Raḥmān Badawī, and a Latin translation from the Arabic by Gerard of Cremona (d. 1187), which was edited by Gabriel Théry.[60] It has been suggested by Théry, and accepted by Rescher and Marmura, that this treatise, too, is an excerpt from Alexander's commentary on the *Physics*.[61] However, it seems more likely that Alexander's extant treatise on time constitutes one

---

54 Alexander of Aphrodisias, *Commentaire perdu à la* Physique *d'Aristote*.

55 Giannakis, "Fragments from Alexander's Lost Commentary on Aristotle's *Physics*."

56 Giannakis, *Philoponus in the Arabic Tradition of Aristotle's* Physics, 75–80; "Fragments from Alexander's Lost Commentary on Aristotle's *Physics*," 158f. Peters notes about Alexander's commentary on Aristotle's *Posterior Analytics* that it may also have been known exclusively through quotations in other commentaries, especially in that of Philoponus; cf. *Aristoteles Arabus*, 18.

57 As mentioned above, the unknown translator may have been Qusṭā. Of book I, translated by al-Ṣābiʾ and revised by Ibn ʿAdī, no fragment of Alexander survives in the margins Ms. Leiden or. 583.

58 Alexander of Aphrodisias, *Risālat al-Iskandar al-Afrūdīsī fī anna kull mā yataḥarraku fa-innamā yataḥarraku ʿan muḥarrik*.

59 cf. Pines, "Omne quod movetur necesse est ab aliquo moveri," 49–54; Janssens, "L'Avicenne latin," 93–97; "Ibn Sīnā," 84; q.v. below, 242ff.

60 Badawī, *Šurūḥ ʿalā Arisṭū mafqūda fī l-yūnāniyya wa-rasāʾil uḫrā*, 19–24; Théry, *Autour du décret de 1210*, vol. 2, 92–97.

61 Théry, *Autour du décret de 1210*, 97; Alexander of Aphrodisias, *Risālat al-Iskandar al-Afrūdīsī fī anna kull mā yataḥarraku fa-innamā yataḥarraku ʿan muḥarrik*, fn. 8, 12.

half of his otherwise lost *Kitāb Radd ʿalayhi [sc. Ǧālīnūs] fī l-zamān wa-l-makān*, which is attested in Ibn al-Nadīm's *Kitāb al-Fihrist*.[62]

There is, furthermore, the influential *Maqāla fī l-qawl fī mabādiʾ al-kull*.[63] That its attribution to Alexander has been contested by Pines and Gutas (but defended by Charles Genequand) should not distract from the fact that Avicenna knew it as a treatise by Alexander and that he appreciated it as a philosophical work just as much as he valued its author as a philosophical writer and commentator.[64] The treatise is extant in two different Arabic translations, of which one is incomplete. The complete version was edited and translated first by Badawī and a second time, together with the incomplete version, by Genequand.[65] An abridged Syriac adaption from the hands of Sergius of Rēš ʿAynā (d. 536) has been edited by Emiliano Fiori.[66]

Finally, several extant fragments also attest to an Arabic translation of Alexander's *Quaestiones*. This work is an interesting collection of issues that seem to have arisen within the context of teaching Aristotelian philosophy together with proposed solutions. These questions may be read independently as an elaboration on specific problems of Aristotelian exegesis. However, due to the wide range of topics covered, they can also be used for the purpose of forming an idea about what Alexander may have argued for in his longer, but no longer extant, commentaries, not only the one on the *Physics* but also those on the *Categories*, *Posterior Analytics*, *De anima*, and *De caelo*, for example.[67] In the introduction to the first volume of his translation of the *Quaestiones*, Robert W. Sharples issues the note of caution that not all answers may have been written by Alexander himself, as he observed certain differences between some of the answers and what Alexander wrote elsewhere in his surviving works.[68] Again, questions about authenticity need not concern the historian interested in the formation of Avicenna's philosophy, because if there was a translation of the *Quaestiones* circulating under the

62 Ibn al-Nadīm, *Kitāb al-Fihrist*, vol. 1, 253.5f. (ed. Flügel)/vol. 2, 173.13 (ed. Sayyid); cf. also Zimmermann, "al-Farabi und die philosophische Kritik an Galen," fn. 49, 410; Sharples' remarks in Alexander of Aphrodisias, *On Time*, 67f., 72–78; Adamson, "Galen and al-Rāzī on Time," 6.

63 The treatise has been discussed in Pines, "Omne quod movetur necesse est ab aliquo moveri," esp. fn. 85, 42f. and more recently in Endreß, "Alexander Arabus on the First Cause"; D. King, "Alexander of Aphrodisias' *On the Principles of the Universe* in a Syriac Adaptation"; Fazzo and Zonta, "Towards a Textual History and Reconstruction of Alexander of Aphrodisias's Treatise *On the Principles of the Universe*."

64 cf. *al-Ilāhiyyāt* IX.2.25, 392.17–393.1 = *al-Naǧāt* IV.2.30, 635.6f. ≈ *al-Mabdaʾ wa-l-maʿād* I.45, 62.5; cf. also Bertolacci, *The Reception of Aristotle's* Metaphysics *in Avicenna's* Kitāb al-Šifāʾ, 443–447, esp. fn. 22, 444f. For Pines' and Gutas' arguments against the authenticity of the text, cf. Pines, "The Spiritual Force Permeating the Cosmos"; Gutas, *Avicenna and the Aristotelian Tradition*, 245–248, esp. fn. 46, 247; for Genequand's defence, cf. his notes in Alexander of Aphrodisias, *On the Cosmos*, 1–3.

65 Badawī, *Arisṭū ʿinda l-ʿarab*, 253–277; Alexander of Aphrodisias, *On the Cosmos*; cf. also Badawī's French translation in his *La transmission de la philosophie grecque au monde arabe*, 121–139.

66 Fiori, "L'épitomé syriaque du *Traité sur les causes du tout* d'Alexandre d'Aphrodise."

67 On Alexander's lost works, cf. D. Frede, "Alexander of Aphrodisias," ch. 1.2.

68 cf. Sharples' remarks in Alexander of Aphrodisias, *Quaestiones 1.1–2.15*, 3f.

name of Alexander, Avicenna would have duly appreciated its contents. In brief, we may say that whatever existed in Arabic translation in the name of Alexander must be considered as a potentially influential source for Avicenna's philosophy, irrespective of the correctness of that attribution.

Plotinus

There is no doubt about the importance of Plotinus (d. 270) for the study of Arabic philosophy. As is well known, parts of his *Enneads* were available in an Arabic version. This version has been produced in the circle of al-Kindī, primarily by Ibn Nāʿima, and was even redacted by al-Kindī himself. Later, part of it circulated under the titles *Kitāb Arisṭāṭālīs al-faylasūf al-musammā bi-l-yūnāniyya Uṯūlūǧiyā* and *Risāla fī l-ʿilm al-ilāhī*, and as a collection of sayings attributed to "the Greek Sage" (*al-šayḫ al-yūnānī*).[69] Most of the materials contained in them stem from Plotinus' *Enneads* IV–VI. It has convincingly been argued that these three separate collections go back to an earlier, and presumably more complete, compilation or translation of the *Enneads*.[70] Thus, there may have been more material from the whole of the *Enneads* that was in circulation – in one form or another – at the time of Avicenna, even though it is not known to be extant today.

What is more, in some parts of his *Enneads*, Plotinus carefully scrutinises various concepts which Aristotle had developed in his writings. One striking example in this regard is Plotinus' critical review of Aristotle's account of time in *Enneads* III.7.[71] It is, then, not only Plotinus' own Platonist philosophy as a whole but also the detailed criticism of Aristotle which was greatly influential on subsequent philosophers and commentators on Aristotle, shaping their way of reading and interpreting both Plato and Aristotle. It is, thus, again the whole of Plotinus' *Enneads*, and not only their famous second half, that is to be considered when investigating the influence Plotinus had on the Arabic philosophical tradition.

Porphyry

As already mentioned, it is known that Porphyry wrote a work on Aristotle's *Physics*. This work probably contained a commentary on books I–IV and a synopsis of book V. According to Ibn al-Nadīm, the commentary section on books I–IV was extant at his

---

69 They are edited by Badawī in *Aflūṭīn ʿinda l-ʿarab*, 1–164, 165–183, 184–194, respectively.
70 Kraus, "Plotin chez les Arabes," cf. Rosenthal, "aš-Šayḫ al-Yūnānī and the Arabic Plotinus Source"; Zimmermann, "The Origins of the So-Called *Theology of Aristotle*"; Adamson, *The Arabic Plotinus*; D'Ancona, "La Teologia neoplatonica di 'Aristotele.'"
71 cf. esp. *Enn.* III.7.9.

time in an Arabic translation by Basīl. Although it can be assumed that Basīl's translation may have been known in the circle of Ibn ʿAdī, it is not mentioned in any of the comments preserved in Ms. Leiden or. 583. Moreover, it cannot be determined whether Avicenna had access to Basīl's translation and made use of Porphyry's comments. Apart from fragments, the commentary is not known to be extant in any substantive form in Greek and even less so in Arabic.

Themistius

More obviously relevant is Themistius' explanatory, and at times quite elaborate, paraphrase of Aristotle's *Physics*. Its transmission, however, is complex and far from clear. There is, first, the information provided by Ibn al-Nadīm, which seems to attribute to Abū Bišr a Syriac translation of the commentary of Themistius on the *Physics* (*tafsīr tafsīr Ṯāmisṭiyūs li-hāḏā l-kitāb bi-l-suryāniyya*).[72] Yury Arzhanov and Rüdiger Arnzen convincingly argue that the term *tafsīr* in the first occurrence here means "interpretation" in the sense of "translation" rather than in the sense of "commentary."[73] This is supported by the fact that Ibn al-Qifṭī, and subsequently Ḥāǧǧī Ḫalīfa (d. 1657), replaced *tafsīr* in the first occurrence by *naql* ("translation").[74]

Arzhanov and Arnzen further maintain that it is this first occurrence of *tafsīr* that is specified by the subsequent expression *bi-l-suryāniyya*, so that the statement testifies to a *Syriac translation* of the commentary which Themistius wrote "on this book" (*li-hāḏā l-kitāb*), viz., the *Physics* of Aristotle. This, however, is puzzling, because we know Abū Bišr as a translator not from Greek into Syriac but from Syriac into Arabic.[75] Moreover, in the famous debate between Abū Bišr and the grammarian Abū Saʿīd al-Ḥasan al-Sīrāfī (d. 368/979), which was recorded by ʿAlī Abū Ḥayyān al-Tawḥīdī (d. 414/1023) in his *Kitāb al-Imtāʿ wa-l-muʾānasa*, al-Sīrāfī accuses Abū Bišr precisely of being ignorant of the language of the Greeks, stating that he translates only on the basis of earlier Syriac translations.[76] While it is, of course, possible that the information contained in al-Tawḥīdī's record of that debate is inaccurate regarding Abū Bišr's knowledge of the Greek language, this does not seem to be likely, as it would jeopardise one of the central points within the whole debate. It is, then, more plausible to read the information provided by Ibn al-Nadīm in such a way that Abū Bišr translated

72 Ibn al-Nadīm, *Kitāb al-Fihrist*, vol. 1, 250.22f. (ed. Flügel)/vol. 2, 167.6f. (ed. Sayyid); cf. Steinschneider, *Die arabischen Übersetzungen aus dem Griechischen*, 54; Arzhanov and Arnzen, "Die Glossen in Ms. *Leyden or. 583*," 430f.; Janos, "Active Nature and Other Striking Features," 137.

73 Arzhanov and Arnzen, "Die Glossen in Ms. *Leyden or. 583*," fn. 79, 430, referring to Gutas, "Aspects of Literary Form and Genre in Arabic Logical Works," 32f.

74 Ibn al-Qifṭī, *Taʾrīḫ al-ḥukamāʾ*, 39.7; Ḥāǧǧī Ḫalīfa, *Kašf al-ẓunūn*, §7258, 619.11.

75 cf. Endreß, "Mattā b. Yūnus," 844b.

76 al-Tawḥīdī, *Kitāb al-Imtāʿ wa-l-muʾānasa*, vol. 1, 111.11–14.

Themistius' commentary on the *Physics* on the basis of an earlier Syriac translation into Arabic. Moreover, the actual wording of Ibn al-Nadīm's text bears this out, as the specification *bi-l-suryāniyya* is modifying not the first but the second occurrence of *tafsīr*, just as the preceding qualification *li-hāḏā l-kitāb* does: what Abū Bišr translated, then, was the "commentary of Themistius " (*tafsīr Ṯāmisṭiyūs*) which is "on this book" (*li-hāḏā l-kitāb*), viz., the *Physics*, and which was "in the Syriac language" (*bi-l-suryāniyya*), translating it, of course, from Syriac into Arabic.[77] This interpretation has the further advantage that it actually explains the existence of an Arabic version of Themistius' commentary which, indeed, is attested through the following information.

In Ibn al-Qifṭī's *Taʾrīḫ al-ḥukamāʾ*, we read that the physician Abū l-Faraǧ Ǧūrǧīs ibn Ibrāhīm al-Yabrūdī (d. ~ 442/1050), who was a student of Ibn al-Ṭayyib, furnished the margins of an Arabic copy of Philoponus' massive, ten-volume long commentary with excerpts from – or perhaps even the whole of – Themistius' paraphrase.[78] Earlier this same codex had been in the possession of ʿĪsā ibn ʿAlī (d. 391/1001), the son of vizier ʿAlī ibn ʿĪsā ibn al-Ǧarrāḥ (d. 334/946) whose secretary, the above-mentioned al-Ṣābiʾ had translated the first book of Aristotle's work "with the commentary" of Alexander into Arabic. Subsequently, al-Ṣābiʾ's translation was revised by Ibn ʿAdī, who, Ibn al-Qifṭī continues, read together with the vizier's son Philoponus' commentary on Aristotle's *Physics* from the very copy into whose margins al-Yabrūdī later added Themistius' paraphrase (of course, after ʿĪsā ibn ʿAlī had added his own remarks on the basis of Ibn ʿAdī's teachings). Regardless of whether or not we believe every detail of this story, it certainly indicates that not long after the turn of the fifth/eleventh century, i.e., during Avicenna's most active phase, Themistius' paraphrase had gained a prominent place in philosophical study circles alongside Philoponus' famous commentary.

Taking it all together, then, knowledge about Themistius' interpretations of the topics discussed in Aristotle's *Physics* could be gathered from three distinct sources: first,

---

77 Ibn al-Nadīm, *Kitāb al-Fihrist*, vol. 1, 250.22f. (ed. Flügel)/vol. 2, 167.6f. (ed. Sayyid). Furthermore, Ibn al-Nadīm states that of Themistius' commentary only "part of the first book was extant in Syriac" (*mawǧūd suryānī bi-baʿḍ min al-maqāla al-ūlā*). This is to be taken as a statement about the defective condition of the Syriac text which Abū Bišr was translating into Arabic. Yet, whether the Syriac text was already incomplete before Abū Bišr's efforts, so that his translation would likewise only have covered parts of the first book, or whether it became defective afterwards, so that Abū Bišr's translation may have been complete after all, is not clear. At any rate, Ibn al-Qifṭī's version of the same report provides a textual variant to the testimony transmitted through Ibn al-Nadīm's *Kitāb al-Fihrist*. According to Ibn al-Qifṭī, it was only part of the first book which was *lacking* (*yanquṣu šayʾ min al-maqāla al-ūlā*), instead of only this part being *extant* (*Taʾrīḫ al-ḥukamāʾ*, 39.8, following the suggestion by Arzhanov and Arnzen to read *yanquṣu* for *bi-naqṣ*). In either case, however, it is clear that there was an Arabic translation of Themistius' commentary, that Abū Bišr produced it on the basis of an earlier Syriac version, and that it may have been incomplete. As we shall see now, it is most probable that Abū Bišr's translation was, in fact, complete or almost complete.

78 Ibn al-Qifṭī, *Taʾrīḫ al-ḥukamāʾ*, 39.14–19; cf. also Arzhanov and Arnzen, "Die Glossen in Ms. *Leyden or. 583*," 433, 443.

there was Abū Bišr's Arabic translation; second, there were more or less complete excerpts from that translation added to the margins of other works; and finally, there was the indirect transmission through occasional quotations in Philoponus' commentary.

Themistius certainly knew some of Galen's works on the subjects treated within natural philosophy, as he occasionally discusses his tenets critically, as we shall see. He was also acquainted with Alexander's commentary of the *Physics* as well as with some other treatises by Alexander, among which we may assume not only the polemics against Galen but also some of Alexander's more independent treatises, such as the *De mixtione*, to which Themistius explicitly refers in the discussion of place.[79] Furthermore, as has been shown by Ahmad Hasnawi, Themistius contributed significantly to Avicenna's understanding of motion.[80] It is also interesting to note that Avicenna explicitly refers to Themistius' paraphrases of the *Physics* and the *De anima* in his correspondence with Abū Rayḥān al-Bīrūnī (d. 440/1048), and that he illustrates in his *al-Samāʿ al-ṭabīʿī* two forms of accidental motion by means of examples which we find only in Themistius, as we shall see.[81] Finally, Janssens also detected traces of Themistius' paraphrase in Avicenna's discussion of luck and chance in *al-Samāʿ al-ṭabīʿī* I.13–14.[82]

Proclus

The *Institutio physica* of Proclus (d. 485) is not a commentary on Aristotle's *Physics*; it is, as Jan Opsomer called it, "a fairly intelligent summary" of Aristotelian materials drawn primarily from *Physics* VI and VIII as well as *De caelo* I.[83] As such, it constitutes a self-standing treatise on motion, culminating in the proposition that the first mover, which is responsible for circular motion, is incorporeal.[84] It has been translated into Arabic and was known to Ibn al-Nadīm under the title *Kitāb Ḥudūd awāʾil al-ṭabīʿiyyāt*.[85]

---

79 cf. Themistius, *In Phys.*, 104.20f. Alexander's treatise is translated and discussed by Todd in *Alexander of Aphrodisias on Stoic Physics*.

80 cf. Hasnawi, "La définition du mouvement dans la *Physique* du *Shifāʾ* d'Avicenne," §5; Wisnovsky, *Avicenna's Metaphysics in Context*, 52f.; cf. also Janssens, "Ibn Sīnā," 85; McGinnis, "A Medieval Arabic Analysis of Motion at an Instant."

81 For the reference to Themistius' writings, cf. Avicenna and al-Bīrūnī, *al-Asʾila wa-l-ağwiba*, 25.9–11, 28.13–29.1.

82 Janssens, "Ibn Sīnā," 84.

83 Opsomer, "The Integration of Aristotelian Physics in a Neoplatonic Context," 193.

84 The treatise certainly deserves more scholarly attention than it has received so far. A highly accurate outline is given by Opsomer, "The Integration of Aristotelian Physics in a Neoplatonic Context," 193–203; cf. also O'Meara, *Pythagoras Revived*, 177–179; Nikulin, "Physica more geometrico demonstrata"; Kutash, "Commentary on Nikulin"; Martijn, *Proclus on Nature*, 216–218.

85 Ibn al-Nadīm, *Kitāb al-Fihrist*, vol. 1, 252.13 (ed. Flügel)/vol. 2, 173.5 (ed. Sayyid); cf. also Endreß' remarks in Proclus, *Zwanzig Abschnitte aus der* Institutio theologica *in arabischer Übersetzung*, 27; cf.

Additionally, there are also traces of a partial Arabic translation of Proclus' seminal commentary on Plato's *Timaeus*.[86]

More prominently known was Proclus as the antagonist of Philoponus on the question over the eternity of the world in the latter's *De aeternitate mundi contra Proclum*. Proclus' own work, whose Greek text survives only to the extent it is quoted in Philoponus' refutation, was apparently (partially) translated into Arabic at least twice.[87] Its refutation by Philoponus likewise existed in an Arabic translation, of which so far only few substantial fragments have come to light, some of which transmitted under the name of Alexander.[88] This controversy between Proclus and Philoponus was certainly known at the time of Avicenna and was explicitly mentioned by al-Bīrūnī in his correspondence with the young Avicenna.[89] Together with the Arabic version of the *Institutio physica*, it was arguably possible to construct a picture – however exhaustive or accurate – of Proclus' basic views on physics and cosmology.

Proclus' greatest influence on the Arabic philosophical tradition, however, was rather oblique and circuitous. His *Institutio theologica* happened to be the main source for a compilation which was known in Arabic as the *Kalām fī maḥḍ al-ḫayr* or the *Kitāb al-Īḍāḥ fī l-ḫayr al-maḥḍ li-Arisṭūṭālīs*. It was attributed to Aristotle and even to Alexander but never to Proclus.[90] The *Kalām fī maḥḍ al-ḫayr* itself circulated in different versions, which were redacted in the circle of al-Kindī, maybe in part even by himself.[91] It has been argued that Avicenna was aware of the *Kalām fī maḥḍ al-ḫayr*

also Pines, "Hitherto Unknown Arabic Extracts from Proclus' *Stoicheiôsis Theologikê* and *Stoicheiôsis Physikê*"; R. Rashed, "Al-Sijzī and Maimonides," 161, and fn. 9, 171.

86 cf. Endreß' remarks in Proclus, *Zwanzig Abschnitte aus der* Institutio theologica *in arabischer Übersetzung*, 24–26; cf. also Arnzen, "Proclus on Plato's *Timaeus* 89e3–90c7."

87 cf. Endreß' remarks in Proclus, *Zwanzig Abschnitte aus der* Institutio theologica *in arabischer Übersetzung*, 15–18; cf. also Wakelnig, "The Other Arabic Version of Proclus' *De Aeternitate mundi*." There is now an independent publication of Proclus' work under the title *On the Eternity of the World* on the basis of the text provided in Philoponus' *De aeternitate mundi contra Proclum*; cf. the earlier translation in Baltes, *Die Weltentstehung des platonischen Timaios*, vol. 2, 134–164; cf. also Maróth, "Der erste Beweis des Proklos für die Ewigkeit der Welt."

88 cf. Hasnawi, "Alexandre d'Aphrodise *vs* Jean Philopon"; Fazzo, "L'Alexandre arabe et la génération à partir du néant"; M. Rashed, "Nouveaux fragments antiprocliens de Philopon en version arabe"; cf. also the minor fragments in al-Bīrūnī's *Kitāb fī taḥqīq mā li-l-Hind min maqūla maqbūla fī l-ʿaql aw marḏūla*, mentioned and discussed in Giannakis, "The Quotations from John Philoponus' *De aeternitate mundi contra Proclum* in al-Bīrūnī's *India*."

89 cf. Avicenna and al-Bīrūnī, *al-Asʾila wa-l-aǧwiba*, 52.1f.; cf. also Rowson's comments in al-ʿĀmirī, *A Muslim Philosopher on the Soul and its Fate*, 252, as well as Giannakis, "Proclus' Arguments on the Eternity of the World in al-Shahrastānī's Works"; Chase, "al-Šahrastānī on Proclus."

90 cf. Endreß' remarks and references in Proclus, *Zwanzig Abschnitte aus der* Institutio theologica *in arabischer Übersetzung*, 7f., 18–23; cf. also Pines, "Hitherto Unknown Arabic Extracts from Proclus' *Stoicheiôsis Theologikê* and *Stoicheiôsis Physikê*"; Zimmermann, "Proclus Arabus Rides Again"; Wakelnig, "Proclus in Aristotelian Disguise."

91 cf. D'Ancona, "Al-Kindī et l'auteur du *Liber de causis*"; Wakelnig, "Proclus in Aristotelian Disguise."

and implemented some of its features into his own metaphysics.[92] The influence of Proclus through the *Kalām fī maḥḍ al-ḫayr* on Avicenna, however, was surely more modest than that of Plotinus through the *Theology of Aristotle*, even though it had a severe impact on some of his contemporaries and predecessors.

It remains to be seen in the future to what extent Avicenna was acquainted with Proclus' works on natural philosophy. In the present study, Proclus does not emerge as a primary and direct source for Avicenna's thoughts on the natural world.

John Philoponus

It is no exaggeration to state that for an investigation of the central concepts of Avicenna's natural philosophy, Philoponus' works are the second most important source right after Aristotle's own work.[93] In addition to having been acquainted with Philoponus' commentaries on Aristotle, including the one on the *Physics*, Avicenna also must

---

92 cf. D'Ancona, "Avicenna and the *Liber de causis*"; Bertolacci, *The Reception of Aristotle's* Metaphysics *in Avicenna's* Kitāb al-Šifāʾ, 143f., 458–460.

93 Regarding Philoponus' commentary on the *Physics* as such, there has been quite some dispute during the last three decades, especially concerning its content and dating. In 1985, Verrycken argued that the commentary on the *Physics* bears clears signs of a much later revision, reflecting different stages in the philosophical development of Philoponus, which Verrycken labelled as "Philoponus 1" and "Philoponus 2." It was argued that a later revision would explain, for example, why we find the fierce and brilliant criticism which "Philoponus 2" expressed in his corollary on place alongside the otherwise rather uncritical and straightforward exposition of Aristotle's chapters on place by the hands of "Philoponus 1." According to Verrycken, the critical corollary on place was added to the commentary after the year 529 and represents the more mature position of "Philoponus 2"; cf. Verrycken, *God en wereld in de wijsbegeerte van Ioannes Philoponus*; "The Development of Philoponus' Thought and its Chronology." Verrycken's thesis was meet with criticism by a number of scholars and has been defended recently by Verrycken himself; cf. M. Rashed, "Alexandre d'Aphrodise et la 'magna quaestio,'" fn. 56, 100; de Haas, *John Philoponus' New Definition of Prime Matter*, 292f.; Golitsis, *Les commentaires de Simplicius et de Jean Philopon à la* Physique *d'Aristote*, esp. 27–37; Sorabji, *Philoponus and the Rejection of Aristotelian Science*, 14–18; for the recent defence, cf. Verrycken, "John Philoponus." A second suggestion in contrast to Verrycken's hypothesis was made by Golitsis on the basis of descriptions in the titles of Philoponus' commentaries. He argues that instead of having changed his mind and revising earlier written works at a later time, we should consider Philoponus to have separated between different activities as a commentator and amanuensis of Ammonius, resulting in different positions being expounded in one and the same work; cf. Golitsis, *Les commentaires de Simplicius et de Jean Philopon à la* Physique *d'Aristote*, esp. 22–27. A third, even though so far widely neglected, conciliatory interpretation of the available evidence has been advanced by Perkams, who investigates the student-teacher relation between Ammonius and Philoponus, and, after reviewing the evidence for Philoponus' commonly assumed year of birth, suggests the year 500 for Philoponus' birth; cf. Perkams, "Zwei chronologische Anmerkungen zu Ammonios Hermeiou und Johannes Philoponos"; cf. also Sorabji's remarks in his introduction to Broadie's translation of book IV.10–14 of Philoponus' commentary; cf. also Sorabji, "New Findings on Philoponus," 16–18, as well as, generally, Sorabji, "John Philoponus," 3–5, 37–40; "Dating of Philoponus' Commentaries on Aristotle."

have been aware of Philoponus' dispute with Proclus on the eternity of the world, as already mentioned, and there is no good reason that he should not also have known Philoponus' *De aeternitate mundi contra Aristotelem*.[94] Avicenna's views on the natural inclination of bodies, for example, clearly resemble those of Philoponus (and also those of Alexander). Likewise, Avicenna's understanding of the corporeality of natural bodies is coloured by a certain conception within the Peripatetic commentary tradition which found its expression also in the earlier works of Philoponus, in particular in his commentary on the *Physics*.

More often than not, however, Avicenna's stance towards Philoponus is critical rather than commending. Despite the similarities between Avicenna's account of corporeality and that in Philoponus' *early* works, Avicenna's argument for the existence of matter can be seen as a direct riposte to the argumentation expressed by Philoponus in his *late* works or, at least, to a reasoning very similar to the one we find in the *De aeternitate mundi contra Proclum*, in which Philoponus decided to abandon his early position and to introduce a new account of matter.[95] Other than that, Avicenna develops his understanding of nature as a principle of motion in explicit opposition to Philoponus' attempted improvement upon the original Aristotelian doctrine and elaborates his defence of Aristotle's notion of place in what appears to be a direct engagement with the criticism he found in Philoponus' commentary. He also seems to be less impressed by Philoponus' (and Alexander's) appeal to the flowing now as the ultimate cause for the existence of time than contemporary scholarship has so far realised. Moreover, Avicenna's general understanding of the nature of hypotheses and postulates is at variance with that of Philoponus (and Themistius), as will be shown. All this calls to mind how Avicenna, in his *Letter to Kiyā*, speaks disparagingly of Philoponus' wasted efforts in the science of physics.[96]

---

94 On Philoponus' refutation of Aristotle in the Arabic, cf. Kraemer, "A Lost Passage from Philoponus' *Contra Aristotelem* in Arabic Translation," esp. fn. 27, 323f.; Mahdi, "Alfarabi against Philoponus"; MacCoull and Siorvanes, "*PSI XIV* 1400"; M. Rashed, "The Problem of the Composition of the Heavens"; cf. also Hasnawi, "Alexandre d'Aphrodise *vs* Jean Philopon"; Giannakis, "The Quotations from John Philoponus' *De aeternitate mundi contra Proclum* in al-Bīrūnī's *India*." In addition to Philoponus' polemics against Proclus and Aristotle, and also to his *De opificio mundi*, which was not translated into Arabic, there must have been at least one further work in which Philoponus, non-polemically as it seems, set out his position regarding the creation of the world. This work, often referred to as *De contingentia mundi*, was apparently likewise available in Arabic, perhaps in an abridged version and may have been the same work as the one to which Simplicius reacted towards the very end of his commentary on the *Physics*; cf. Pines, "An Arabic Summary of a Lost Work of John Philoponus"; Troupeau, "Un épitomé arabe du 'De contingentia mundi' de Jean Philopon"; cf. also the Wildberg's introduction to his translation of that discussion by Simplicius, which was published as *Against Philoponus on the Eternity of the World*.

95 Sorabji, *Matter, Space, and Motion*, ch. 2; de Haas, *John Philoponus' New Definition of Prime Matter*.

96 q.v. fn. 37 above, 19.

In many ways, then, it appears that Avicenna formed his understanding of the core concepts of natural philosophy through a thorough and critical examination of the views expressed in Philoponus' works, and so it is only natural that a considerable amount of the following investigation is devoted to Philoponus' thought. This focus commends itself also because even before Avicenna, Philoponus has come to occupy a central position in the Arabic tradition of reading the *Physics*. In fact, his commentary is the most important commentary that was translated into Arabic and which is still extant today: Simplicius' commentary on the *Physics* might not have been translated at all; Themistius' paraphrase, though interesting and relevant, is naturally not as straightforward and rich as Philoponus' thorough and critical exposition; and the commentaries of Alexander and Porphyry, although translated into Arabic, are, apart from the indirect transmission and the newly discovered fragments, not extant in either Greek or Arabic.

So, it is *for us* and our analysis of Avicenna's *al-Samāʿ al-ṭabīʿī* that Philoponus' commentary emerges as the second most important source for physics right after Aristotle. *For Avicenna*, though, the situation may have been somewhat different. It is precisely because Alexander's commentary is not extant in any substantial form in *any* language, that we are frankly unable to assess both the scope of its direct influence on Avicenna's natural philosophy and the extent of its potential indirect influence on Avicenna through Philoponus. Since Avicenna rarely, if ever, cites his sources by name, it may well have been that *for him*, it was Alexander's – and not Philoponus' – commentary that was the second most important source after Aristotle's *Physics*, even though *for us* this simply cannot be determined. Unfortunately, all this is equally true with regard to Porphyry's commentary. What is more, among those works composed in Arabic, there is a potentially analogous case to the loss of Alexander's and Porphyry's Greek commentaries on Aristotle's *Physics*, as the major works on physics that were written by Abū Naṣr al-Fārābī (d. 339/950-51) have not survived either, even though it is virtually certain that Avicenna must have been acquainted with them.[97] This means that we are deprived of no less than two sources (or three when also counting Porphyry) which are potentially indispensable for a *truly* adequate understanding of the developments in interpreting the *Physics* of Aristotle that lead up to Avicenna's composition of *al-Samāʿ al-ṭabīʿī*.

On the other hand, the centrality and the dominance of comments ascribed to Yaḥyā al-Naḥwī (i.e., to John Philoponus, "the Grammarian") in the margins of Ms. Leiden or. 583 indicate that it was, nonetheless, Philoponus' commentary which, besides the riches of translated materials available between the second/eighth and fourth/tenth century, was the major source for reading and interpreting Aristotle's *Physics* – even

97 In fact, it is *in principle* even possible that Avicenna exclusively relied on al-Fārābī's commentary, so that all he knew of Alexander's and Philoponus' interpretations and theories on physics would have been derived from al-Fārābī. This is a possibility which cannot be ruled out as long as we lack the text of al-Fārābī's commentary or at least sufficient information about it.

more than Alexander's and certainly more than Porphyry's. As Giannakis has shown, most – even if not all – of the comments preserved in the margins of Ms. Leiden or. 583 that are ascribed to Alexander or Themistius can also be found in Philoponus.[98] Other than that, the name of Philoponus also occurs in Avicenna's correspondence with al-Bīrūnī on matters pertaining to natural philosophy (but so do Alexander and Themistius, admittedly).[99]

Finally, it ought to be noted that it is not entirely clear in what form Avicenna knew Philoponus' commentary on the *Physics*. As has been mentioned above, the second half of Philoponus' commentary was translated by Ibn Nāʿima and its first half by Qusṭā. Now, it has been argued by Giannakis that it is not certain whether Qusṭā produced a full translation of Philoponus' full commentary on books I–IV, or a full translation of an abridged commentary covering books I–IV, or an abridged translation of a full commentary on books I–IV, or whether his full translation of the commentary on books I–IV was later epitomised. As has also been noted, Qusṭā's translation may have been revised (partially) at one point by al-Dimašqī.[100] All this, however, does not change the fact that Avicenna made heavy use of Philoponus' commentary in whatever form he had access to it and that Philoponus' commentary is nothing other than an indispensable source for understanding the philosophical background to Avicenna's views on natural philosophy, in particular as they are expressed in his *al-Samāʿ al-ṭabīʿī*. This is all the more true in light of the additional information which Ibn al-Qifṭī provided in his *Taʾrīḫ al-ḥukamāʾ*. As already mentioned above, Ibn al-Qifṭī explains that Philoponus' commentary on the *Physics* existed in an Arabic translation as a single complete behemoth of ten volumes.[101] Specifically, he writes that Philoponus' work "was translated from Greek into Arabic, and it was a great book of ten volumes and once in my possession" (*malaktuhū dufʿatan*).[102] This can mean nothing other than that Philoponus' commentary was available as a complete translation in the seventh/thirteenth century and did not merely circulate in the form of summaries and excerpts.[103] We have already seen that Ibn al-Qifṭī, furthermore, reports that Avicenna's contemporary al-Yabrūdī, a student of Ibn al-Ṭayyib in Baġdād, added Themistius' "discussion" (*kalām*) to the margins of this very copy, so that it is clear that the whole of Philoponus' commentary was also accessible during Avicenna's own lifetime.

---

98 cf. Giannakis, *Philoponus in the Arabic Tradition of Aristotle's* Physics, 75–82; "Fragments from Alexander's Lost Commentary on Aristotle's *Physics*," 158; cf. also Lettinck, *Aristotle's* Physics *and its Reception in the Arabic World*, 339.

99 cf. Avicenna and al-Bīrūnī, *al-Asʾila wa-l-aǧwiba*, 13.7–9, 25.9–11, 28.13–29.1, 51.13f.

100 cf. Giannakis, *Philoponus in the Arabic Tradition of Aristotle's* Physics, 84–91; cf. also Arzhanov and Arnzen, "Die Glossen in Ms. *Leyden or. 583*," fn. 93, 433.

101 q.v. above, 27.

102 Ibn al-Qifṭī, *Taʾrīḫ al-ḥukamāʾ*, 39.14f.

103 Nothing, however, precludes the possibility that *additionally* it may have been available in the form of excerpts and summaries also.

Simplicius

Simplicius was a contemporary of Philoponus and responded to him critically. In the Arabic tradition, Simplicius' influence may have been restricted to his comments on Aristotle's *Categories* and the *De anima* as well as to some introductory remarks on the *Elements* of Euclid (fl. ~ 300 BC).[104] It is not clear whether his commentary on the *Physics* was translated into Arabic or not. It has long been accepted that it was not. Only recently have scholars started to question this traditional consensus.[105]

Having said this, Simplicius' commentary on the *Physics* still is an important text for the present study due to the following reasons. First, a comparison of Simplicius' comments with those of his contemporary Philoponus enables us to understand more properly the philosophical developments that took place in Neoplatonic circles in and before the sixth century, i.e., not all too long before the Graeco-Arabic translation movement set in and shaped the philosophical understanding in Arabic intellectual circles before Avicenna. Second, it is an invaluable source for opinions and positions expressed by earlier figures within the history of philosophy, such as Theophrastus, Eudemus of Rhodes (d. ~ 300 BC), and Porphyry, to name only a few. In many instances, Simplicius preserves material which is otherwise lost, so that it is only through the testimonies provided in his commentary that one can gather insights into earlier philosophical debates which ultimately may also have shaped Philoponus' understanding of physics and, thus, through Philoponus also Avicenna. Third, Simplicius is also the most important source for fragments of Alexander's commentary on the *Physics* in addition to the above-mentioned 826 fragments which were recently discovered and published by M. Rashed.

Arabic Commentaries

Of Arabic commentaries on the *Physics* up to the time of Avicenna, close to nothing is extant. Ibn al-Nadīm mentions a handful of commentaries on Aristotle's *Physics*, referring to Ṯābit ibn Qurra, Abū Aḥmād ibn Yazīḍ al-Kātib known as Ibn Karnīb (fl. late third/early tenth century), and Abū l-Faraǧ Qudāma ibn Ǧaʿfar al-Kātib al-Baġdādī (d. ~ 337/949).[106] Their commentaries or expositions – Ibn al-Nadīm uses the verb *fassara* – did not survive.[107] As already noted, Ibn al-Qifṭī additionally reports on the

104 cf. Gätje, "Simplikios in der arabischen Überlieferung"; Hadot, "The Life and Work of Simplicius in Greek and Arabic Sources"; Gutas, "Greek Philosophical Works Translated into Arabic."

105 In particular, Jens Ole Schmitt informed me of fragments and ideas from Simplicius' commentary that are preserved in the section on physics of Barhebraeus' Syriac compendium known as *Butyrum sapientiae*. Schmitt is currently preparing an edition with translation and commentary of that work.

106 On Ṯābit ibn Qurra's commentary, q.v. above, 12.

107 cf. Ibn al-Nadīm, *Kitāb al-Fihrist*, vol. 1, 250.23–27 (ed. Flügel)/vol. 2, 167.8–12 (ed. Sayyid); cf. also M. Rashed, "Thābit ibn Qurra, la *Physique* d'Aristote et le meilleur des mondes."

glosses which ʿĪsā ibn ʿAlī, the son of vizier ʿAlī ibn ʿĪsā ibn al-Ǧarrāḥ, added to his copy of Philoponus' commentary on the basis of his readings of the text with Ibn ʿAdī. This copy is not known to be extant. Ibn al-Qifṭī further mentions a commentary by Ibn al-Samḥ, yet this may merely be a reference to his glosses surviving in the margins of Ms. Leiden or. 583 alongside those of Abū l-Ḥusayn, Ibn al-Samḥ, Ibn al-Ṭayyib, Ibn ʿAdī, Abū Bišr, and al-Ṭabarī.[108]

It has also been mentioned already that according to Ibn al-Nadīm, al-Kindī composed a work on physics. We also know that Abū Bakr Muḥammad ibn Zakariyāʾ al-Rāzī (d. 313/925) wrote a work which he himself described as "our book on the introduction into natural philosophy called the *Physics* " (*kitābunā fī l-madḫal ilā l-ʿilm al-ṭabīʿī l-mawsūm bi-Samʿ al-kiyān*).[109] Neither is known to be extant.

Next, Ibn Abī Uṣaybiʿa (d. 668/1270) tells us that the philosopher Abū ʿAlī Muḥammad ibn al-Hayṯam (fl. fifth/eleventh century) wrote expositions or summaries (sg. *talḫīṣ*) of the *Physics*, of the *Meteorologica*, and of the "animal books" of Aristotle as well as a treatise on time and place in which he followed Aristotle's opinion (*yalzamu raʾy Arisṭūṭālīs*).[110] As Roshdi Rashed argued, repeatedly and convincingly, Muḥammad ibn al-Hayṯam should not be confused with the famous optician al-Ḥasan ibn al-Ḥasan ibn al-Hayṯam (d. after 430/1040) who, then, did *not* write a commentary on the *Physics*, as is usually assumed, but who, nonetheless, composed a treatise on the Aristotelian notion of place.[111]

Moreover, al-Bīrūnī had a great interest in physical matters, which is attested through his many scientific writings, but he did not write a commentary proper on Aristotle's *Physics*.[112] Nonetheless, some of his thoughts pertaining to natural philosophy are recorded in his correspondence with Avicenna.

In addition to that, there are, of course, the later commentaries by Abū Bakr Muḥammad ibn Bāǧǧa (d. 533/1139) and Averroes (d. 595/1198), which could not adequately been taken into account in this study, even though they surely contain valuable information about physical concepts and theories in the Greek and the Arabic philosophical traditions before Avicenna.[113]

---

108 Ibn al-Qifṭī, *Taʾrīḫ al-ḥukamāʾ*, 39.13–21.

109 Abū Bakr al-Rāzī, *Kitāb al-Sīra al-falsafiyya*, 198.1f.

110 Ibn Abī Uṣaybiʿa, *ʿUyūn al-anbāʾ fī ṭabaqāt al-aṭibbāʾ*, vol. 2, 97.3f., 17f.

111 cf. R. Rashed, *Les mathématiques infinitésimales*, vol. 2, 8–19; vol. 3, 937–941; vol. 4, 957–959.; cf. also Steinschneider, *Die arabischen Übersetzungen aus dem Griechischen*, 54, who lists "Ibn Heitham" as an author of a "paraphrase" of the *Physics* without, however, mentioning the rest of the name.

112 cf. the list of works al-Bīrūnī himself appended to his list of Abū Bakr al-Rāzī's writings, edited by Kraus as al-Bīrūnī, *Risāla li-l-Bīrūnī fī fihrist kutub Muḥammad ibn Zakariyāʾ al-Rāzī*, esp. 30–43 and translated by Boilot, "L'œuvre d'al-Beruni," esp. 176–215.

113 For information, the reader may be deferred to Lettinck, *Aristotle's* Physics *and its Reception in the Arabic World*; Belo, *Chance and Determinism in Avicenna and Averroes*; Glasner, *Averroes' Physics*; Wirmer, *Vom Denken der Natur zur Natur des Denkens*; Cerami, *Génération et substance*.

al-Fārābī

Particular mention should be made of al-Fārābī. It is known that he wrote several works on natural philosophy and that his works were prominent among Muslim and Jewish authors in Andalusia, such as Ibn Bāǧǧa, Averroes, and Maimonides (d. 1204).[114] The bio-bibliographical sources also tell us that al-Fārābī wrote at least one commentary on Aristotle's *Physics* – the *Kitāb Šarḥ al-Samāʿ*, as Ibn al-Qifṭī has it, or *Šarḥ Kitāb al-Samāʿ al-ṭabīʿī li-Arisṭūṭālīs ʿalā ǧiha al-taʿlīq*, according to Ibn Abī Uṣaybiʿa – and a further work called *Kitāb al-mawǧūdāt al-mutaġayyira al-mawsūm bi-l-kalām al-ṭabīʿī*.[115] As Steinschneider already noted, the latter is a distinct exposition, by and large concerned with Aristotle's argument for the eternity of motion and time from *Physics* VIII.1.[116]

The nature of the former work, i.e., of al-Fārābī's commentary proper, is more difficult to determine. More than eighty years ago, Alexander Birkenmajer discovered and edited a Latin translation produced by Gerard of Cremona (d. 1187) of a brief outline of Aristotle's *Physics* that is attributed to al-Fārābī under the title *Distinctio super Librum Aristotelis de naturali auditu*.[117] This outline cannot by itself be the entire commentary of al-Fārābī, as it is evidently too brief and does not correspond to the arguments and interpretations that are reported in al-Fārābī's name by Ibn Bāǧǧa and Maimonides, for example. Accordingly, and provided the attribution to al-Fārābī is correct, it either was or belonged to a separate treatise, composed in addition to his commentary, or was part of that same commentary.[118] If, in turn, Avicenna had access to these works, and in particular to al-Fārābī's commentary on the *Physics*, it is clear that the interpretations they contained must have had tremendous effect on Avicenna – and there is no reason that he should not have had access to them, even though we have no way to determine the precise ways in which they influenced Avicenna.

Indeed, al-Fārābī's influence on Avicenna can be verified at least on one point, viz., regarding the void. A short treatise in which al-Fārābī argues against the existence of the void is extant under the title *Maqāla fī l-ḫalāʾ*, and its influence on Avicenna is

---

114 cf. M. Rashed, "al-Fārābī's Lost Treatise *On Changing Beings*," 30; Janos, *Method, Structure, and Development in al-Fārābī's Cosmology*, 38.

115 Ibn al-Qifṭī, *Taʾrīḫ al-ḥukamāʾ*, 279.20f.; Ibn Abī Uṣaybiʿa, *ʿUyūn al-anbāʾ fī ṭabaqāt al-aṭibbāʾ*, vol. 2, 138.26, 139.10 (reading with Steinschneider *al-mawsūm* for *al-mawǧūd*), 140.6; cf. also Maimonides, *Dalālat al-ḥāʾirīn* II.19, 320.22: *ḥawāšīhi ʿalā al-Samāʿ*; cf. further Lettinck, *Aristotle's* Physics *and its Reception in the Arabic World*, 260, 265. Lettinck, however, seems to identify al-Fārābī's commentary with his *Kitāb al-mawǧūdāt al-mutaġayyira*; cf. also Janos, *Method, Structure, and Development in al-Fārābī's Cosmology*, fn. 60, 38.

116 Steinschneider, *al-Farabi (Alpharabius)*, 20; cf. M. Rashed, "al-Fārābī's Lost Treatise *On Changing Beings*"; Janos, *Method, Structure, and Development in al-Fārābī's Cosmology*, 38.

117 Birkenmajer, "Eine wiedergefundene Übersetzung Gerhards von Cremona."

118 It has been suggested by Birkenmajer that the outline may be the second half of a physical pendant to al-Fārābī's *Maqāla fī aġrāḍ al-ḥakīm fī Kitāb Mā baʿd al-ṭabīʿa*, thus indicating the goals and intentions of Aristotle's discourse in the *Physics*; cf. Birkenmajer, "Eine wiedergefundene Übersetzung Gerhards von Cremona," 474.

unmistakable, as we shall see. In addition, al-Fārābī also composed other works, such as the *Mabādi' ārā' ahl al-madīna al-fāḍila* and the *Kitāb al-Siyāsa al-madaniyya* (also known as *Mabādi' al-mawǧūdāt*). Each of these provides a comprehensive overview of emanation as well as the structure of the material world, yet they treat the topics relevant to the present investigation merely in a wholesale fashion, providing no detailed investigation of such concepts as corporeality and time, for example.

Finally, one further work should be mentioned here, viz., the *'Uyūn al-masā'il* by Ps.-al-Fārābī. This highly interesting treatise is strongly reminiscent of so many aspects of Avicennian philosophy that it is more likely to have been composed by someone close, or posterior, to Avicenna rather than by someone close to al-Fārābī, by al-Fārābī himself, or in fact by anyone before Avicenna.[119]

1.3 On Avicenna's Copy of the *Physics*

In the final section of this chapter, I would like to offer some thoughts regarding Avicenna's access to the works that have been mentioned, in particular insofar as his knowledge of the various Arabic translations of both the text of and the commentaries on Aristotle's *Physics* is concerned. It should be borne in mind that none of these translations – with the exception of that produced by Isḥāq ibn Ḥunayn – is extant, so that we simply lack a (sufficiently reliable) textual basis for any comparison of, say, the terminology used in Avicenna's works and in the attested Graeco-Arabic translations. Consequently, any attempt at identifying which translation of Aristotle's *Physics* Avicenna used and knew, or maybe even which translation he was primarily working from when he was composing his *al-Samāʿ al-ṭabīʿī*, is almost necessarily unavailing, so long as no more textual evidence comes to light. Yet, even despite this bleak prospect, some thoughts may indicate a partial answer, at least.

What Did Avicenna Know and What Did He Use?

There is no document informing us about which texts Avicenna used and knew in general, or which translation of Aristotle's *Physics* he was acquainted with in particular. Yet, there is one text informing us that, at the age of seventeen, Avicenna spent six months in the royal library of Nūḥ ibn Manṣūr (d. 387/997) in Buḫārā and that it was in this library that he "saw books whose very names are unknown to many and which I

119 cf. Rahman, *Prophecy in Islam*, fn. 2, 21f.; Black, *Logic and Aristotle's* Rhetoric *and* Poetics *in Medieval Arabic Philosophy*, fn. 53, 71; Janssens, "The Notions of *wāhib al-ṣuwar* and *wāhib al-ʿaql* in Ibn Sīnā," 559; Gutas, "The Study of Avicenna," 50f.; Janos, *Method, Structure, and Development in al-Fārābī's Cosmology*, fn. 91, 239 and appx. 1; Kaya, "Şukûk alâ 'Uyûn"; for a defence of the attribution to al-Fārābī; cf. Lameer, *al-Fārābī and Aristotelian Syllogistics*, 24f.

had never seen before nor have I seen since."[120] This, at least, is what his autobiography tells us. We cannot but take this account seriously, with the result that we are arguably bound to assume that Avicenna, at least at one (early) point in his career, had access to virtually all translations into Arabic that had been produced up to this time, i.e., all those translations of which we know (and maybe more), and this means more or less all translations which have been mentioned in this chapter.[121] Indeed, in light of this testimony from Avicenna's autobiography, the onus of proof seems to be on anyone who intends to argue that Avicenna did *not* know or could *not* have known (and, thus, was not influenced in any way by) a particular book or a particular translation. So, it appears that regarding Aristotle's *Physics*, we are forced to assume that Avicenna may have had access to all Arabic translations that were produced, at least for some limited time at some certain point before he turned eighteen.

This does not necessarily entail that Avicenna also read all texts to which he may have had access within these six months (or even later in other libraries), nor whether he could make copies of some of the works and translations he has read (or was not able to read within these six months), nor which works he had access to only in this library and which he had "ever since" not seen again in any other library, nor how well he, when composing his *al-Samāʿ al-ṭabīʿī*, for example, could remember what he has read more than twenty years earlier. Thus, in a way this tells us all and nothing.[122]

There is, however, more definite evidence regarding the *Physics*. In his correspondence with al-Bīrūnī and his *Risāla fī aqsām al-ʿulūm al-ʿaqliyya*, Avicenna refers to Aristotle's *Physics* as *Samʿ al-kiyān* and *Kitāb al-Kiyān*, respectively.[123] Both of these

120 Avicenna and al-Ǧūzǧānī, *Sīrat al-šayḫ al-raʾīs*, 36.5f., tr. by Gutas in *Avicenna and the Aristotelian Tradition*, 18; cf. Gutas, *Avicenna and the Aristotelian Tradition*, 169–179. Kraemer describes the same library as "extraordinary" and "wonderful" (*Humanism in the Renaissance of Islam*, 92f.).

121 Taking something seriously is clearly different from taking something for granted or accepting it unconditionally and without qualification.

122 This is especially true with regard to Avicenna's *al-Samāʿ al-ṭabīʿī*. In the preface to *al-Madḫal*, which serves as the universal introduction to the whole of *al-Šifāʾ* and was written by Avicenna's disciple Abū ʿUbayd al-Ǧūzǧānī, we are told that Avicenna composed the metaphysical and most of the physical parts of his *magnum opus* "without having available any book to consult ... relying solely upon his natural talents" (*al-Madḫal*, preface, 3.1f., tr. by Gutas in *Avicenna and the Aristotelian Tradition*, 32). Yet, al-Ǧūzǧānī also reports that Avicenna began to write his *al-Šifāʾ* around 411/1020 while being employed by Šams al-Dawla at the latter's court in Hamadān and that he, having begun to work on *al-Samāʿ al-ṭabīʿī*, was able to compose only the first "approximately twenty folia" before he was disturbed by administrative matters, had to go into hiding, and finally even left the area (*al-Madḫal*, preface, 2.14–18). Now, neither is it clear how much was covered by these "twenty folia" that Avicenna was apparently able to write in a promoting environment with sufficient access to books and libraries nor can we be sure about his access to books and libraries afterwards nor even do we know to what extent al-Ǧūzǧānī's testimony generally is to be trusted; cf. Gutas, *Avicenna and the Aristotelian Tradition*, 109–115, esp. 111.

123 Avicenna and al-Bīrūnī, *al-Asʾila wa-l-aǧwiba*, 18.7; 23.13; Avicenna, *Risāla fī aqsām al-ʿulūm al-ʿaqliyya*, 108.17.

works were composed relatively early in Avicenna's career. In his other – that is to say: later – works he no longer employs this title. One may brave the suggestion that Avicenna's use of this title is a relict of an early acquaintance with a translation that itself bore that title. Consequently, one may think of Sallām al-Abraš's translation of the *Physics* and perhaps also of Ibn Nāʿima's translation of Philoponus' commentary on books V–VIII. Thus, Avicenna may have come to know Aristotle's *Physics* first through one of these two early translations. In light of the fact that Ibn Nāʿima's translation was most probably incomplete, we may prefer to assume that it was the translation by Sallām al-Abraš which introduced Avicenna to Aristotle's *Physics*.

In addition, it is clear that Avicenna was acquainted with materials from Qusṭā's translation, given that he has good knowledge of Philoponus' commentary on the first half of the *Physics*. Whether al-Dimašqī was exclusively interested in Alexander or also in other commentators, and so whether he also revised some of Qusṭā's translation of Philoponus, as he seems to have done with his translation of Alexander's commentary, and, in effect, whether Avicenna, then, used al-Dimašqī's revision or Qusṭā's original, cannot be ascertained. Moreover, Avicenna's general interest in Philoponus' commentary certainly warrants the suggestion that he may have tried to obtain – and, thus, may have known – Ibn Nāʿima's translation of (at least) the second half of Aristotle's *Physics* with the second half of Philoponus' commentary. Regarding Isḥāq ibn Ḥunayn's translation, moreover, there is actually no reason that Avicenna should not have had access to it, as it was widely used in philosophical circles of Baġdād and it would not have been difficult for him to acquire a copy of that translation, given that we have textual evidence testifying to the fact that Avicenna did, indeed, send his associates to Baġdād to acquire books for him.[124]

However, there are many passages in *al-Samāʿ al-ṭabīʿī*, in which Avicenna's diction differs from that of Isḥāq ibn Ḥunayn (or also of Qusṭā, as far as it is attested or can be reconstructed). Let me just mention four examples. First, at the very beginning of his *Physics*, Aristotle expresses his intention to investigate the "principles or causes or elements" (ἀρχαὶ ἢ αἴτια ἢ στοιχεῖα) of natural things. This expression was faithfully translated by Isḥāq ibn Ḥunayn as *mabādiʾ aw asbāb aw usṭuqussāt* ("principles or causes or elements") but appears in Avicenna as *mabādiʾ wa-asbāb wa-ʿilal* ("principles and causes and causes"). It is puzzling to read here two different words for "cause" which are often said to be synonymous. There is no reason – at least no *apparent* one – for why Avicenna would have done so.[125] This passage led Paul Lettinck to assume that Avicenna must have used a translation different from the one produced by Isḥāq ibn Ḥunayn.[126]

124 cf. Gutas, *Avicenna and the Aristotelian Tradition*, 59f.

125 There certainly was a doctrinal reason, as will be explained below, 162ff.

126 Lettinck, *Aristotle's* Physics *and its Reception in the Arabic World*, 97.

Second, in Avicenna's discussion of the definition of nature, he explicitly claims the definition he provided was "taken from" Aristotle (*ma'ḫūḏ ʿan al-imām al-awwal*). Yet, the wording of his definition does not correspond to either Isḥāq ibn Ḥunayn or Qusṭā.

Third, Aristotle frequently emphasises in his *Physics* that time "follows" motion and that motion "follows" distance. The term he used in these contexts for "to follow" is a form of the Greek verb ἀκολουθεῖν. Isḥāq ibn Ḥunayn translated it with the Arabic verb *tabaʿa* ("to follow"). A gloss in Ms. Leiden or. 583 attributed to "Yaḥyā," which could be both by Ibn ʿAdī or Philoponus but probably refers to the latter, perhaps in the translation of Qusṭā, likewise gives *tabaʿa*. Avicenna, however, consistently uses forms of the verb *ṭābaqa* ("to conform to") whenever he expresses the same idea.

As a final example, Aristotle states that one of the important conditions of place is that it must be "unmoving" (ἀκίνητον). In fact, he eventually even defines place as an unmoving limit. The expression we find in Isḥāq ibn Ḥunayn's translation here is *ġayr mutaḥarrik*. A gloss in the margins of Ms. Leiden or. 583 which is attributed to "Yaḥyā" uses the expression *ġayr muntaqil*. Avicenna, who discusses this condition critically and, ultimately, rejects it, as we shall see, uses neither the expression we find in Isḥāq ibn Ḥunayn nor the one we find in "Yaḥyā's" gloss (and which may derive from Qusṭā's translation), writing *ġayr mustabdil*, instead.

Of course there are also numerous passages in Avicenna's *al-Samāʿ al-ṭabīʿī* which are in line with Isḥāq ibn Ḥunayn's terminology or may stem from Qusṭā's translation of Philoponus.[127] This is hardly surprising, because all the above evidence suggests that there is good reason to believe that Avicenna "possessed" the translations of materials directly relating to the text of Aristotle's *Physics* by Sallām al-Abraš, Qusṭā (and al-Dimašqī), Isḥāq ibn Ḥunayn, and perhaps Ibn Nāʿima.[128] One must also take into consideration that the translators may have rendered certain passages in a similar or even identical way. Yet, on the whole, it seems to be an altogether wrong question to ask, as I have deliberately phrased it above, which translation Avicenna was primarily working from when he was composing his *al-Samāʿ al-ṭabīʿī*, for most of the time he does not seem to *rely* upon any translation while writing; instead, he puts forth his own philosophy from his own point of view and in the terminology he himself deems most proper. Surely, it is an interesting detail that he has "taken" the definition of nature from Aristotle and that his definition, then, does not correspond to either Isḥāq ibn Ḥunayn or Qusṭā, so that, indeed, we may assume that he memorised – or quoted – the definition on the basis of a different translation, i.e., a translation with which he

---

127 Occasionally, I shall refer to some of these passages in my investigation.

128 By "possessed" here, I mean that there is no reason that one should deny that Avicenna either once had access to these materials or once has read them or at some point really was in the possession of them. In other words, Avicenna may, throughout his life, well have had *all* major translations at his disposal in one way or another and, thus, could have been influenced by various renderings of the Aristotelian text and different interpretations from the commentaries.

became familiar earlier in his career. So, he may have hit upon the definition of nature in his first read of Aristotle's *Physics* and was impressed by it so much that its particular wording stuck with him. Similarly, the fact that he uses *ṭābaqa* instead of *tabaʿa* or that he writes *ġayr mustabdil* instead of *ġayr mutaḥarrik* or *ġayr muntaqil* may, likewise, go back to the terminology with which he was primarily familiar through his studies of texts and may, again, testify to a different (i.e., earlier) translation he once was reading. The reason that he wrote *mabādiʾ wa-asbāb wa-ʿilal*, however, instead of something closer to the Greek text as, for example, Isḥāq ibn Ḥunayn's *mabādiʾ aw asbāb aw usṭuqussāt*, is certainly due to doctrinal reasons – and that is: doctrinal reasons of *his own philosophy*. Thus, in formulating his physical theories, Avicenna did not simply and primarily rely on *one text* or *one translation* which he had on his desk while he was composing his works on nature, constantly looking at it and copying from it. Avicenna was precisely no commentator; he was a philosopher who, in forming his ideas about the world, was certainly influenced by the texts he read but who, in formulating his ideas, was considerably independent.[129]

Clearly, a more comprehensive and systematic investigation and comparison of Avicenna's terminology would be required, in order to determine which translations he used or primarily worked from. Yet, I am sceptical whether any such study would yield a definitive result – in particular, because it would seem to underestimate the independence of Avicenna's reasoning, misunderstand the originality of his thought, and ultimately mistake the essence of Avicenna's philosophical activity.

With this remark, I would now like to turn precisely to Avicenna's natural *philosophy* as it reveals itself in the elements of his physics.

---

129 q.v. also fn. 122 above, 38, as well as below, 73ff.

2 The Methodology of Teaching and Learning

2.1 The Method of Physics

After a brief preface, Avicenna begins his *al-Samāʿ al-ṭabīʿī* with a chapter on method. This first chapter has the following heading:

في تعريف الطريق الذي نتوصّل منه إلى العلم بالطبيعيات من مبادئها.

> On making known the method by which we arrive at the knowledge of natural things from their principles. (*al-Samāʿ al-ṭabīʿī* I.1, 7.3f.)[1]

It is immediately conspicuous that this heading promises a method by which we are supposed to arrive *at* a certain kind of knowledge *from* the principles of a certain kind of things. In fact, some might have expected from a chapter on method to receive, more than anything else, some instruction on how to arrive at the *principles* through proper scientific inquiry, i.e., to be offered general advice on how to acquire or derive principles. Since principles are starting-points, we need to acquaint ourselves with universal principles, before we can understand particular objects. Here, however, we seem to be promised an inverse procedure at the end of which we shall arrive at, or obtain access to, knowledge, in this case, that of natural things.[2]

The first chapter of Aristotle's *Physics* is about method, too. It contains a particularly puzzling bit of methodological advice:

> πέφυκε δὲ ἐκ τῶν γνωριμωτέρων ἡμῖν ἡ ὁδὸς καὶ σαφεστέρων ἐπὶ τὰ σαφέστερα τῇ φύσει καὶ γνωριμώτερα ... διὸ ἐκ τῶν καθόλου ἐπὶ τὰ καθ' ἕκαστα δεῖ προϊέναι.
>
> ومن شأن الطريق أن يكون من الأمور التي هي أعرف وأبين عندنا إلى الأمور التي هي أبين وأعرف عند الطبيعة ... ولذلك قد ينبغي أن نتطرّق من الأمور المجملة إلى الجزئيات.
>
> The natural way is to start from the things which are more knowable and clear to us, and proceed towards those which are clearer and more knowable by nature ... Thus, we must advance from the universals to the particulars (ἐκ τῶν καθόλου ἐπὶ τὰ καθ' ἕκαστα, *min al-umūr al-muǧmala ilā l-ǧuzʾiyyāt*). (*Phys.* I.1, 184a16–24, tr. by Hardie/Gaye, modified)

1 It is known that medieval, and even ancient, authors often either penned the headings of their works themselves or drew up a table of contents, leaving space in the running text for their disciples or amanuenses to fill in the headings in their proper places. Regarding Muslim scholars, Rosenthal remarked that it "soon became the custom among scholars to prefix a short table of contents to their works" (*The Technique and Approach of Muslim Scholarship*, 40); cf. Gacek, *Arabic Manuscripts*, 57f. Bertolacci, too, considered extensively the content of chapter headings in Avicenna's *al-Ilāhiyyāt* in a recent article ("How Many Recensions of Avicenna's *Kitāb al-Šifāʾ*?").

2 Due to the double meaning of the Arabic noun *ʿilm*, it is implied that once we have acquired "knowledge" of a certain class of things, we also have mastered the "science" of these things; cf. *al-Qiyās* I.1, 3.8–10. In the case of natural things (*ṭabīʿiyyāt*), the corresponding science is natural philosophy (*ʿilm al-ṭabīʿiyyāt*).

https://doi.org/10.1515/9783110546798-003

According to Aristotle in *Physics* I.1, it is the universals which are more knowable and clear to us, so that it is also the universals from which we should start and venture towards the particulars. This advice, however, is bewildering, as it seems to contradict, and to reverse, his usual scientific tenet as expressed in the *Posterior Analytics*:

> λέγω δὲ πρὸς ἡμᾶς μὲν πρότερα καὶ γνωριμώτερα τὰ ἐγγύτερον τῆς αἰσθήσεως, ἁπλῶς δὲ πρότερα καὶ γνωριμώτερα τὰ πορρώτερον. ἔστι δὲ πορρωτάτω μὲν τὰ καθόλου μάλιστα, ἐγγυτάτω δὲ τὰ καθ' ἕκαστα.
>
> وأعني بالتي هي أقدم وأعرف عندنا أقدم وأعرف الأشياء التي هي أقرب إلى الحسّ وأمّا التي هي أقدم وأعرف على الإطلاق فهي الأشياء التي هي أكثر بعداً منه. والأشياء التي هي أبعد ما تكون منه هي الأمور الكلّية خاصّةً والتي هي أقرب ما يكون منه هي الأشياء الجزئية والوحيدة.
>
> I call prior and more familiar to us items which are nearer to perception, prior and more familiar *simpliciter* items which are further away. What is most universal (τὰ καθόλου μάλιστα, *al-umūr al-kulliyya ḫāṣṣatan*) is furthest away, and the particulars (τὰ καθ' ἕκαστα, *al-ašyāʾ al-ǧuzʾiyya wa-l-waḥīda*) are nearest. (*An. post.* I.2, 72a1–5, tr. by Barnes)[3]

The apparent tension between *Physics* I.1 and *Posterior Analytics* I.2 did not pass unnoticed within the commentary tradition.[4] John Philoponus (d. 574), for example, complained in his commentary on Aristotle's *Physics* that it has been "a matter of debate ... why Aristotle says [here in the *Physics*] that universals are posterior in nature and less clear, but to us prior and more clear, given that elsewhere he suggests the opposite."[5] That this debate has not yet come to an end is borne out by the ever increasing number of articles and monographs which have been devoted to the content and method of *Physics* I.1 since the late nineteenth century.[6] According to William David Ross, Aristotle's argument "is, superficially at least, opposed to what we find in *An. Post.*," while William Charlton calls the passage in the *Physics* "obscure" and Hans Wagner asserts that it caused "lots of trouble ever since."[7] Yet, despite its difficulties –

3 Prominent versions of this assertion include *Top.* VIII.1, 156a3ff; *De an.* I.2, 413a11–13; *Met.* A.2, 982a23–25; Z.3, 1029a33–b12; Z.4, 1029b13; *Eth. Nic.* VII.3, 1147a25f.

4 cf. Cerami, "Thomas d'Aquin lecteur critique du Grand Commentaire d'Averroès à *Phys.* I, 1," 191.

5 Philoponus, *In Phys.*, 10.23–25, tr. by Osborne.

6 cf. Tannery, "Sur un point de la méthode d'Aristote"; Owen, "Τιθέναι τὰ φαινόμενα"; Pines, "A New Fragment of Xenocrates"; Owens, "The Universality of the Sensible in the Aristotelian Noetic"; Wieland, "Aristotle's Physics and the Problem of Inquiry into Principles"; *Die aristotelische Physik*; Konstan, "A Note on Aristotle *Physics* 1.1"; Turnbull, "'Physics' I"; Fritsche, *Methode und Beweisziel*; Berti, "Les méthodes d'argumentation et de démonstration dans la 'Physique'"; Lettinck, *Aristotle's* Physics *and its Reception in the Arabic World*; "Problems in Aristotle's Physics I, 1"; Morrison, "Philoponus and Simplicius on Tekmeriodic Proof"; Kessler, "Method in the Aristotelian Tradition"; Horstschäfer, *"Über Prinzipien"*; Angioni, "Explanation and Definition in Physics I 1"; de Haas, "Modifications of the Method of Inquiry in Aristotle's *Physics* I.1"; Cerami, "Thomas d'Aquin lecteur critique du Grand Commentaire d'Averroès à *Phys.* I, 1"; Lesher, "Aristotle's Considered View of the Path to Knowledge."

7 Ross' comments in *Physics*, 456f.; Charlton's comments in *Physics*, 52; Wagner's comments in *Physikvorlesung*, 395: "Dieser Satz hat den Erklärern von jeher viel Mühe gemacht."

to some of which I shall return shortly – it is now universally agreed that in *Physics* I.1, Aristotle is proposing a *method of inquiry* similar to what he has developed in his *Posterior Analytics*, especially in chapters I.2 and II.19. Whereas *Posterior Analytics* I.2 emphasises the need of being acquainted with first principles as the starting points for scientific deductions, the final chapter II.19 appeals to an inductive inquiry (ἐπαγωγή) as the very method leading to such an acquaintance.[8]

The intention of the present chapter, now, is to ascertain the method which Avicenna sets out in the first chapter of *al-Samāʿ al-ṭabīʿī*. We shall see how this method differs from those which the late ancient commentators attributed to Aristotle's *Physics*; how Avicenna interpreted the actual wording of Aristotle's advice that we should progress ἐκ τῶν καθόλου ἐπὶ τὰ καθ' ἕκαστα; and, finally, how this Aristotelian *dictum* correlates with Avicenna's own general views about the structure of the scientific enterprise. To that end, I shall, first, outline briefly Avicenna's account of scientific inquiry with its emphasis on the concept of *taǧriba*, often translated into English as "experience" or "methodic experience." On the basis of an analysis of late ancient readings of *Physics* I.1, I shall suggest that, contrary to the commentators' understanding of Aristotle, Avicenna precisely does not adopt a method of inquiry in his *al-Samāʿ al-ṭabīʿī* and, thus, cannot be said to follow what is often considered to be Aristotle's stance in *Physics* I.1. Yet, it will be shown that Avicenna nonetheless follows Aristotle's advice that we should progress ἐκ τῶν καθόλου ἐπὶ τὰ καθ' ἕκαστα literally by adopting a *mode of instruction*, according to which he structures and develops his *al-Samāʿ al-ṭabīʿī* (and arguably his entire *al-Šifāʾ*) as a didactic work for his students and disciples to read and gather knowledge from. Finally, I shall expound how his method in *al-Samāʿ al-ṭabīʿī* correlates with his general views about the structure of the scientific enterprise as an, in the strict sense, interdisciplinary endeavour.

Avicenna on the Method of Science

A principle is something "first" or "primary." In this spirit, the Greek ἀρχαί are πρῶτα, the Latin *principia* are *prima*, and the Arabic *mabādiʾ* are *awāʾil*. This simple fact, however, is the source for the intricate question of how it could be possible for a human being to acquire knowledge of truths that are first in themselves. The answer given by Aristotle culminates in, whereas the one offered by Avicenna originates from,

8 For recent studies of these chapters and especially of *Posterior Analytics* II.19, cf. Bolton, "Definition and Scientific Method in Aristotle's *Posterior Analytics* and *Generation of Animals*"; "Aristotle's Method in Natural Science"; Pietsch, *Prinzipienfindung bei Aristoteles*; Bayer, "Coming to Know Principles in *Posterior Analytics* II 19"; Butler, "*Empeiria* in Aristotle"; LaBarge, "Aristotle on *empeiria*"; Anagnostopoulos, "Aristotle's Methods"; Tuominen, "Back to *Posterior Analytics* II 19"; Adamson, "*Posterior Analytics* II.19"; Herzberg, *Wahrnehmung und Wissen bei Aristoteles*; Mouzala, "Aristotle's Method of Understanding the First Principles of Natural Things in the *Physics* I.1"; Bronstein, "The Origin and Aim of *Posterior Analytics* II.19"; Hasper and Yurdin, "Between Perception and Scientific Knowledge."

Posterior Analytics II.19. Naturally, there are strong similarities between their solutions, above all, a heavy reliance upon sense perception and observation. Nonetheless, both philosophers take strikingly different views about the efficiency of induction (ἐπαγωγή, *istiqrāʾ*). Aristotle, for his part, chose to begin and to end his *Posterior Analytics* with remarks on the notion of ἐπαγωγή.[9] Eventually, he declares the following:

> δῆλον δὴ ὅτι ἡμῖν τὰ πρῶτα ἐπαγωγῇ γνωρίζειν ἀναγκαῖον·
>
> فمن بيّن إذن أنّه قد يلزم أن نعلم الأوائل بالاستقراء.
>
> Thus it is plain that we must get to know the primitives (τὰ πρῶτα, *al-awāʾil*) by induction (ἐπαγωγῇ, *bi-l-istiqrāʾ*). (*An. post.* II.19, 100b3f., tr. by Barnes)

Contrary to Aristotle's explicit approval of induction, Avicenna has been described as being rather "skeptical of the merit of induction as an adequate tool of science," disqualifying the notion as being "merely a pointer that draws one's attention to the pertinent facts surrounding some state of affairs ... and does not make clear what the cause of that state of affairs is or even that there must be a cause."[10] The main reason for Avicenna's reserved attitude towards induction, most thoroughly explained in *al-Qiyās* IX.22, is that induction fails to provide the necessity and certainty required for true knowledge and, at best, produces syllogisms that merely yield uninformative, i.e., scientifically nugatory, conclusions.[11]

In order to bridge the gap between induction and knowledge, Avicenna systematically develops the concept of *taǧriba* ("methodic experience") in *al-Burhān* I.9 in contrast to the notion of *istiqrāʾ* ("induction").[12] For Avicenna, methodic experience

---

9 In his critical remarks about induction, Avicenna focuses on Aristotle's use of ἐπαγωγή as it is outlined in *Prior Analytics* II.23 and on its particular application to the context of those issues to which *Posterior Analytics* II.19 seems to be the solution. For other uses of that concept, cf. von Fritz, *Die* ἐπαγωγή *bei Aristoteles*; Hamlyn, "Aristotelian Epagoge"; Engberg-Pedersen, "More on Aristotelian Epagoge"; Hintikka, "Aristotelian Induction;" cf. also Tuominen, *Apprehension and Argument*; Helmig, *Forms and Concepts*, chs. 3–4.

10 McGinnis, "Avicenna's Naturalized Epistemology," 144f., referring to *al-Burhān* III.5, 223.12–15.

11 The best summary of Avicenna's criticism is given in McGinnis, "Avicenna's Naturalized Epistemology," 145f.; cf. also Janssens, "'Experience' (*tajriba*) in Classical Arabic Philosophy," 60f. In the discussion of *taǧriba* in *al-Burhān* I.9, Avicenna seems to refer to his more complete (and at times rather technical) criticism of induction in *al-Qiyās* IX.22; cf. also *al-Naǧāt* I.111, 122.8f.; *Dānešnāme-ye ʿAlāʾī* I.23, 92.4–93.6; *al-Hidāya* I.4, 111.9–113.2; *al-Išārāt wa-l-tanbīhāt* I.7.1, 64.10–15.

12 That Avicenna draws a distinction between induction and methodic experience is clear from *al-Burhān* I.9, 95.1: "As for methodic experience, it is other than induction" (*wa-amma l-taǧriba fa-innahā ġayr al-istiqrāʾ*); cf. *al-Burhān* I.9, 95.17f. Towards the end of the chapter, however, Avicenna remarks that although induction is merely capable of producing a probable belief, it may still "lead to" (*yaʾūla*) methodic experience (98.5f.). Later in *al-Burhān* III.5, he states that methodic experience "is like something mixed from syllogism and induction" (*fa-ka-annahū maḫlūṭ min qiyās wa-stiqrāʾ*; 223.16). Other than that, the term *taǧriba* was employed to translate ἐμπειρία in *Prior Analytics* I.30 and *Posterior Analytics* II.19 and generally the Greek πεῖρα; cf. Janssens, "'Experience' (*tajriba*) in Classical Arabic

emerges from the rigorous recording of frequently repeated observations of particular events or facts over a long period of time, where these events or facts always or for the most part bring about the same result.[13] He describes it as a judgement of the mind (*ḥukm al-ḏihn*) formed on the basis of the repeated sensation (*al-ḥiss*) of individual particularities (*al-ǧuzʾiyyāt al-šaḫṣiyya*) such as an administration of scammony purging bile or a magnet attracting iron. More specifically, Avicenna maintains that we are able to construe a scientific syllogism on the basis of methodic experience. This syllogism links an observed major term (e.g., attracting iron) through a middle term (e.g., having the power to attract iron) to a minor term (e.g., a magnet). Within a syllogism, it is the middle term which is the explanation of the observed event and the cause for the major term's predication of the minor. In other words, whenever we determine the middle term of a syllogism, we detect a causal connection between the two extreme terms.

Moreover, if the syllogism is composed on the basis of multiple events that form a series of tests whereby each event proved to yield the same result, we no longer need to speak of a simple cause but are allowed to refer to a "power" (*quwwa*) or a "nature" (*ṭabʿ*) responsible for the observed result. It is this nature which, by belonging to the minor term, explains the occurrence of the major term "always or for the most part" (*dāʾimatan aw fī l-akṯar al-amr*). It is of the nature of scammony to purge bile when administered and it is of the nature of a magnet to attract iron in the immediate vicinity.

When Avicenna speaks of a regularity that holds "always or for the most part," he virtually means "always," for whenever some event that occurs "always or for the most part" does not occur, then there must have been some other reason that, unbeknownst to us, prevented its occurrence.[14] If, for example, fire usually burns wood but this morning did not, then it is highly probable, if not straightforwardly certain, that this morning there had been a further condition, which has so far not been taken into consideration. After further inspection, we may find out, for example, that this morning the wood was not dry enough to burn. However, if we record all the circumstances in which the observed events occurred and all conditions under which

Philosophy," 45. According to Gutas, the term was widely used in Arabic medical works, having been "at the heart of the medical epistemological process" ("Medical Theory and Scientific Method in the Age of Avicenna," 151.). Gutas also refers to Avicenna's use of the word in his autobiography; cf. "Certainty, Doubt, Error," 279f.; "Medical Theory and Scientific Method in the Age of Avicenna," 151f., 160.

13 The following outline primarily draws upon Avicenna's accounts in *al-Burhān* I.9 and III.5, esp. 223.16–224.5; *al-Naǧāt* I.148, 169.10–171.8; *al-Išārāt wa-l-tanbīhāt* I.6.1, 56.17–57.7. The greater part of *al-Naǧāt* I.148 is missing in the editions of al-Kurdī, Fakhry, and ʿUmayra but is contained in Dānešpažūh's edition and Ahmed's translation. For more detailed studies of Avicenna's account of methodic experience, cf. McGinnis, "Scientific Methodologies in Medieval Islam"; "Avicenna's Naturalized Epistemology"; Janssens, "'Experience' (*tajriba*) in Classical Arabic Philosophy"; cf. also Gutas, "The Empiricism of Avicenna" as well as Langermann's critical remarks on Gutas in "From My Notebooks," esp. 173–176.

14 cf. *al-Samāʿ al-ṭabīʿī* I.13, §6, 62.5–17; cf. also McGinnis, "Scientific Methodologies in Medieval Islam," 319; Belo, *Chance and Determinism in Avicenna and Averroes*, 24–26; cf. further Richardson, "Avicenna and the Principle of Sufficient Reason."

our series of tests was performed, then we are able to claim that we have acquired necessary and certain knowledge through methodic experience. As Avicenna explains, such knowledge, though universal, is only *conditionally* universal (*kulliyyan bi-hāḏā l-šarṭ lā kulliyyan muṭlaqan*), as it depends on precisely these conditions.[15]

Certain elements of this description of methodic experience already surface in the works of Abū Naṣr al-Fārābī (d. 339/950-51).[16] In both his *Book of Demonstration* and the *Kitāb al-Mūsīqā l-kabīr*, he shares – and, thus, anticipates – Avicenna's critical stance towards induction and presents methodic experience (*tağriba*) as a superior alternative.[17] In the *Book of Demonstration*, al-Fārābī writes:

وهي شبهة بالاستقراء غير أنّ الفرق بينها وبين الاستقراء أنّ الاستقراء هو ما لم يُحصَّل عنه اليقين الضروري بالحكم الكلّي والتجربة هي ما حُصِّل عنها اليقين بالحكم الكلّي.

> It [sc. methodic experience] is similar to induction (*šibha bi-l-istiqrā'*), except that the difference between it and induction is that induction is something from which the necessary certainty through a universal judgement (*al-yaqīn al-ḍarūrī bi-l-ḥukm al-kullī*) is not obtained, whereas methodic experience is something from which the certainty through a universal judgement is obtained. (al-Fārābī, *Book of Demonstration* 2, 24.21–25.3)[18]

At the heart of al-Fārābī's account of methodic experience, in contrast to induction, is the notion of a "universal judgement" which brings about "certainty." In his *Kitāb al-Mūsīqā l-kabīr*, al-Fārābī described this universal judgement as a "special act of the intellect" (*fi'l ḫāṣṣ li-l-'aql*).[19] It is this very notion of a universal judgement, being a special act of the rational intellectual capacities, which also marks what is perhaps the most striking difference between al-Fārābī and Avicenna regarding methodic experience, for according to al-Fārābī, this special act of the intellect consists in a "general judgement (*ḥukm 'āmm*) comprising both what has and what has not been examined."[20] The notion of universality in al-Fārābī's account is, thus, an unconditional or unres-

---

15 *al-Burhān* I.9, 96.4–7.

16 cf. Janssens, "'Experience' (*tajriba*) in Classical Arabic Philosophy," 47–52; Black, "Knowledge (*'ilm*) and Certitude (*yaqīn*) in al-Fārābī's Epistemology," 40–43; Janos, *Method, Structure, and Development in al-Fārābī's Cosmology*, 58–63.

17 The first two volumes of D'Erlanger, *La musique arabe* contain a French translation of al-Fārābī's *Kitāb al-Mūsīqā l-kabīr*. It needs to be noted regarding al-Fārābī's *Book of Demonstration* that it is only a relatively brief exposition of Aristotle's *Posterior Analytics*. The (presumably) much longer commentary on the *Posterior Analytics* is not known to be extant.

18 cf. al-Fārābī, *Kitāb al-Mūsīqā l-kabīr*, 96.1–7.

19 al-Fārābī, *Kitāb al-Mūsīqā l-kabīr*, 96.2. As Janos notes, al-Fārābī's criticism of induction may be inspired by Aristotle's claim in the *Posterior Analytics* that one "cannot understand anything through perception" and that "it is impossible to perceive what is universal and holds in every case" (*An. post.* I.31, 87b28, 30f., tr. by Barnes); cf. Janos, *Method, Structure, and Development in al-Fārābī's Cosmology*, fn. 118, 59. By bringing in an element of the intellect, al-Fārābī may have tried to overcome the limitations of pure sensory observation and perception.

20 al-Fārābī, *Book of Demonstration* 2, 25.5f.

tricted notion, as it extends beyond what has been observed empirically. It seems that for him, methodic experience leads to necessary certainty precisely because of the *unconditionally* universal judgement of the intellect that covers *all* cases, both observed and unobserved. Indeed, this is precisely why that act of the intellect is so "special." For Avicenna, by contrast, there are clear limitations to the knowledge derived through methodic experience, especially insofar as it is only *conditionally* universal and depends on – i.e., is valid only with regard to – the recorded circumstances.

Thus, it seems that, due to these limitations and the restriction to only the observed conditions and circumstances, Avicenna's concept of methodic experience does not bring us any closer to answering our initial question about how human beings could be able to acquire real knowledge of principles, because knowledge of principles cannot merely be restrictedly universal but must be absolutely so. In other words, if conditionally universal knowledge is the highest form of knowledge the human mind can obtain empirically through research on the basis of sensation, we end up still lacking any grasp of universal, explanatory, and absolute truths and principles.

However, in the concluding remarks on methodic experience in *al-Burhān* I.9, Avicenna points to a possible solution for this dilemma:

وبالجملة فإنّ التجربة معتبرة في الأمور التي تحدث على الشرط الذي شرطناه وفي اعتبار عللها فقط. فإن كان ضرب من التجربة يتبعه يقين كلّي حُتِمَ على غير الشرط الذي شرطناه لا شكّ فيه فيشبّه أن يكون وقوع ذلك اليقين ليس عن التجربة بما هي تجربة على أنّه أمر يلزم عنها بل عن السبب المباين الذي يفيد أوائل اليقين وخبره في علوم غير المنطق. فيشبّه حينئذ أن تكون التجربة كالمُعِدّ وليس بذلك المُعِدّ المُلزِم الذي هو القياس بل معدّ فقط.

On the whole, methodic experience considers things which occur on the basis of the condition which we have laid down and only with regard to their causes. So, if universal certainty follows from [some] sort of methodic experience without having been determined by the condition which we have unassailably laid down for it, then it seems that the occurrence of this certainty is not due to methodic experience insofar as it is methodic experience in the sense that it [sc. this certainty] is something following from it [sc. methodic experience] but, instead, from the separate cause which provides the primitives of certainty (*bal ʿan al-sabab al-mubāyin allaḏī yufīdu awāʾil al-yaqīn*). However, the investigation of it [sc. this separate cause] belongs to sciences other than logic. In this case, then, it seems that methodic experience is like something which prepares (*ka-l-muʿidd*); yet, not that which prepares by necessitating – which would be the syllogism (*al-qiyās*) – but only something which prepares. (*al-Burhān* I.9, 97.21–98.3)

There are three important points Avicenna distinctly states in this passage. First of all, universal certainty (*yaqīn kullī*) does not come about through methodic experience or more precisely through methodic experience alone. So, we cannot gather knowledge of principles through methodic experience, because methodic experience is always limited to the conditions mentioned.

Second, Avicenna does not deny the possibility of universal knowledge. Rather, what he says is that such knowledge follows "from the distinct cause" (*ʿan al-sabab al-mubāyin*). The active participle *mubāyin* does not only mean "separate" but also has the connotation of "extrinsic." It is clear, then, that Avicenna hints towards the

Active Intellect as "the separate cause which provides the primitives of certainty" and the ultimate source for true universal knowledge. Accordingly, universal knowledge is possible, yet the conditions and causes of it ought not to be examined in logic – instead, they belong to a different science, later in *al-Burhān* III.5 identified as the science of the soul (*ʿilm al-nafs*).[21] Thus, what Avicenna has in mind here are the concepts of abstraction (*taǧrīd*) and intuition (*ḥads*), through which, he claims, knowledge of first principles can be obtained with the help of the Active Intellect.[22]

Finally, Avicenna claims that methodic experience is not entirely without value for acquiring universal knowledge, as it seems to be "like something which prepares" (*ka-l-muʿidd*) for any such acquisition.[23] While it remains open whether that which prepares is a sufficient, a necessary, or only an auxiliary condition for universal knowledge, Avicenna clearly depicts methodic experience as beneficial for preparing our selves, and our souls, for further psychological processes which possibly end in the acquisition of universals and principles, provided that we diligently and carefully employed methodic experience in our quest for knowledge. The cognitive processes which constitute the intellectual aspect of methodic experience, i.e., the noting down of conditions, deliberation, assessing the evidence, trying to form syllogisms, and so on, are precisely what Avicenna in *al-Nafs* V.5 calls "thoughts and considerations" (*al-afkār wa-l-taʾammulāt*).[24] They, too, are further described in the same line as "movements that prepare (*ḥarakāt muʿidda*) the soul for the reception of the emanation." With "emanation," Avicenna does nothing other than to point towards the involvement of the Active Intellect in human knowledge acquisition through abstraction. The harmony of this passage from the psychology of *al-Šifāʾ* with the above passage in *al-Burhān* III.5 is perfect, when Avicenna continues in *al-Nafs* with a reference to the equally preparatory (*muʿidda*) function of middle terms for the obtainment of the conclusion within a scientific syllogism.[25] It is, then, not only the terminology of syllogisms, preparing factors, separate causes, and universal intelligibles that correspond to the above passage from Avicenna's *al-Burhān* – it is the entire psychological, epistemological, and cosmological framework that is invoked in both works to explain what appears to be the same phenomenon: the human grasp of universal, necessary, certain truths through methodic experience preparing for, and leading to, abstraction.

21 *al-Burhān* III.5, 222.12–13; cf. McGinnis, "Avicenna's Naturalized Epistemology," 131, 141. On the role of the Active Intellect, cf. esp. *al-Naǧāt* II.6.16, 394.9–396.7.

22 For Avicenna's theories of *taǧrīd* and *ḥads*, cf. Hasse, *Avicenna's* De Anima *in the Latin West*; "Avicenna on Abstraction"; "Avicenna's Epistemological Optimism"; Gutas, "Intuition and Thinking"; *Avicenna and the Aristotelian Tradition*; McGinnis, "Making Abstraction Less Abstract"; for competing accounts, cf. Davidson, *Alfarabi, Avicenna, and Averroes, on Intellect*, 94; Black, "Psychology," esp. 319f.; "How Do we Acquire Concepts?"; R. C. Taylor, "al-Fārābī and Avicenna," esp. 182.

23 cf. also McGinnis, "Logic and Science," 172.

24 *al-Nafs* V.5, 208.14.

25 *al-Nafs* V.5, 208.14f.; cf. esp. Hasse, *Avicenna's* De Anima *in the Latin West*, 184–188; "Avicenna on Abstraction," 53–58; Germann, "Avicenna and Afterwards," 86–88

On the whole, then, Avicenna's conception of methodic experience describes a method of inquiry which enables human beings to acquire knowledge of things that have not been known before. It is through intelligent and scientific cogitative acts of engaging with the phenomena of the natural world that we prepare our intellects for the acquisition of primary and universal principles. Methodic experience surely is an inductive method of inquiry, but it is a method more advanced and scientifically more rigorous than simple induction.[26]

Consequently, when we claim that both the first chapter of Aristotle's *Physics* and that of Avicenna's *al-Samāʿ al-ṭabīʿī* are chapters on method, is it, then, a method of inquiry which Aristotle and Avicenna set forth and intend to pursue in the course of their respective works? The ancient commentators argue that this, at any rate, should be answered in the affirmative with regard to Aristotle.

The Commentators on the Method of Science in the *Physics*

In their attempts to resolve the above-mentioned tension between *Physics* I.1 and *Posterior Analytics* I.2, the ancient commentators recommended that in the science of physics one employ a certain method of inquiry, viz., induction through tekmeriodic or "evidential" proof on the basis of the compounded and jumbled-up universals that are prior to us.[27]

While not explicitly mentioning tekmeriodic proof as such, we find already Themistius (d. ~ 385) referring to a demonstration of principles on the basis of what is prior to us. In his paraphrase of Aristotle's *Physics*, he states:

> ὅταν μὲν οὖν περὶ τῶν συγκειμένων ποιώμεθα λόγον, ἐκ τῶν φύσει προτέρων αὐτὸ ἀποδείξομεν· ὅταν δὲ περὶ τῶν ἀρχῶν, ἐκ τῶν πρὸς ἡμᾶς προτέρων. καὶ ἔστιν ἐκείνη μὲν ἡ κυρίως ἀπόδειξις, αὕτη δὲ εἰ καὶ μὴ κυρίως, ἀλλὰ ἡμῖν ἱκανῶς.
>
> Now, when we produce an account of compounds (συγκειμένων), we will demonstrate from things that are prior by nature, but when we produce an account of principles (ἀρχῶν), it is from things that are prior to us. And while the former is demonstration in its primary sense (κυρίως ἀπόδειξις), the latter, even if not so in a primary sense, still suffices for us (μὴ κυρίως, ἀλλὰ ἡμῖν ἱκανῶς). (Themistius, *In Phys.*, 1.20–2.3, tr. by Todd, modified)

---

26 That is not to say that Aristotle's answer to the question of how to acquire knowledge of universal principles was nothing but simple induction; cf. esp. *An. post.* II.19, 100a3–9, describing the four-stages of perception, memory, experience (ἐμπειρία, *tağriba*), and knowledge; cf. also *Met.* I.1, 980a27–981a3; cf. further Hasper and Yurdin, "Between Perception and Scientific Knowledge," 147f., describing Aristotelian experience as "knowledge of general facts, consisting in recognitional and practical abilities to detect and act on particulars of the relevant sorts" and as "the epistemic state in which one knows logically universal facts in such a way that one may go on to acquire scientific knowledge."

27 On tekmeriodic proof, cf. Morrison, "Philoponus and Simplicius on Tekmeriodic Proof"; Sorabji, *The Philosophy of the Commentators*, vol. III, ch. 9d.

Commenting on the same passage, Simplicius (d. ~ 560) claims the following:

> δῆλον ὅτι τεκμηριώδης ἐστὶν ἡ γνῶσις ἡ περὶ τῶν ἀρχῶν ἀλλ' οὐκ ἀποδεικτική.
>
> It is clear that the knowledge of the principles (τῶν ἀρχῶν) is evidential (τεκμηριώδης) but not demonstrative (ἀποδεικτική). (Simplicius, *In Phys.*, 18.28f.)

Finally, Philoponus appears to combine both assertions without, however, retaining Simplicius' somewhat reserved stance towards tekmeriodic argumentation:

> ἰστέον οὖν ὅτι αὐτὸς εἶπεν ἐν τῇ Ἀποδεικτικῇ, ὅτι δύο τρόποι εἰσὶ τῆς ἐπιστημονικῆς γνώσεως, πρῶτος μὲν ὁ ἀποδεικτικός, δεύτερος δὲ ὁ διδασκαλικός, οὗτοι δὲ ἀντιπεπονθότως ἔχουσι πρὸς ἀλλήλους. ὁ μὲν γὰρ ἀποδεικτικὸς ἐκ τῶν πρώτων τῇ φύσει καὶ ἀρχικωτέρων ἀποδείκνυσι τὰ δεύτερα, ὁ δὲ διδασκαλικός, ἀποδεικτικός τις ὢν καὶ αὐτός, κατὰ δεύτερα μέτρα ἀποδείξεως ἐκ τῶν ὑστέρων τῇ φύσει τὰ πρότερα ἀποδείκνυσιν, ὃν καὶ τεκμηριώδη καλεῖ. οἷον εἴ τις ἰδὼν καπνὸν εἴποι πῦρ εἶναι ἐνταῦθα· ἐκ γὰρ τοῦ τῇ φύσει ὑστέρου τὸ πρότερον κατεσκεύασε.
>
> We need to be aware that Aristotle himself said in the *Posterior Analytics* that there are two ways of acquiring scientific knowledge (ἐπιστημονικῆς γνώσεως): first, the demonstrative (ἀποδεικτικός) and, second, the didactic (διδασκαλικός) method, and that these are in opposition to each other, for the demonstrative method demonstrates secondary things from things that are first and more fundamental in nature, while the didactic method, although it is also somewhat demonstrative (ἀποδεικτικός τις), demonstrates things that are prior from things that are posterior in nature, using a second rate type of demonstration.[28] This [latter] approach he also calls "evidential" (τεκμηριώδη). An example [would be] if someone, upon seeing smoke, said that there was a fire there, because he has argued for what is prior from what is in nature posterior. (Philoponus, *In Phys.*, 9.11–19, tr. by Osborne, modified)[29]

With these words, the Greek commentators advertise a purportedly "irrefutable" proof (τῆς δείξεως τεκμηριῶδες καὶ ἄλυτον), as Philoponus puts it elsewhere.[30] This proof represents an inverted reasoning from a clear evidence (τεκμήριον) which is more readily accessible for us to what is further removed from us. The notion of τεκμήριον was introduced by Aristotle in his discussion of rhetorical syllogisms and enthymemes in *Rhetoric* I.2. There, Aristotle stated that of all signs (sg. σημεῖον, *rasm*), some are necessary and some are not. Necessary signs (sg. τεκμήριον, *dalāla*) are such that one can compose a valid syllogism on their basis. An example for a valid syllogism on the basis of necessary signs is that someone is sick, because he is running a fever. This syllogism is superior to a syllogism on the basis of a mere sign, whose conclusion can be called into question. If we were to say, for example, that someone has a fever, because he is breathing heavily, then someone might well challenge our conclusion merely by mentioning other reasons for why someone might be breathing heavily. By contrast, a necessary sign is clear evidence inevitably pointing to the conclusion:

---

28 Following the alternative translation offered by Osborne in fn. 40, 109, to her translation.

29 cf. Philoponus, *In Phys.*, 49.17–20; cf. also Simplicius, *In Phys.*, 15.12–29.

30 Philoponus, *In An. post.*, 31.8–17.

there is no fever without sickness and there is no smoke without fire.[31] A tekmeriodic proof, then, is a necessary and irrefutable argument, establishing a conclusion which is further removed from us on the basis of a sign which is near and clear to us. It is an inductive kind of reasoning, which some – but not all – commentators grant the status of being demonstrative, though maybe not in "its primary sense" (κυρίως), as Themistius carefully remarks and as Philoponus similarly seems to imply.[32] Demonstrative or not, the commentators are agreed that induction, or more precisely tekmeriodic induction, is the very method *Physics* I.1 advises us to choose:

> ἐπεὶ οὖν καὶ νῦν πρόκειται τὰς ἀρχὰς τῶν φυσικῶν πραγμάτων γνῶναι, ἀνάγκη θατέρῳ τούτων τῶν τρόπων γνῶναι. τῷ μὲν οὖν προτέρῳ ἀδύνατον·
>
> Since the present task is to get to know the principles of physical things, it is necessarily by the second of these methods [sc. by didactic and tekmeriodic induction] that we must get to know them; it is after all impossible to do so by the first method [sc. by demonstration]. (Philoponus, *In Phys.*, 10.8–11, tr. by Osborne)[33]

Consequently, the Greek commentators regard "the universal" (τῶν καθόλου) from the first chapter of Aristotle's *Physics* as the starting points for the tekmeriodic method. That is to say that τῶν καθόλου actually refers to the universal features that are exhibited by the compounded or confused things (τὰ συγκεχυμένα) of which Aristotle spoke only one line earlier. On this view, καθόλου means "universal" insofar as that which is said to be universal is a whole that encompasses several parts, viz., its principles, causes, and elements.[34] Since by sensation, the whole is better known than its parts, we cannot

---

31 *Rhet.* I.2, 1357b1–25; I.25, 1402b13–20, 1403a10–15; cf. also *An. pr.* II.27, 70a2–10. It should be noted that, strictly speaking, Aristotle does not define a tekmeriodic reasoning in causal terms as an inference from an effect to its cause, as his ancient and late-ancient commentators do.

32 cf. Alexander of Aphrodisias, *In Met.*, 13.27–31; Simplicius, *In Phys.*, 15.24f., 18.24–29. On the whole, it seems that Themistius, Simplicius, and Philoponus derived their theory from Alexander's commentary on *Physics* I.1; cf. M. Rashed, *Essentialisme*, 191–199; Cerami, "Thomas d'Aquin lecteur critique du Grand Commentaire d'Averroès à *Phys.* I, 1," 193–195. Morrison argues that tekmerioidc proof is both an un-Aristotelian theory and an implausible interpretation of *Physics* I.1; cf. Morrison, "Philoponus and Simplicius on Tekmeriodic Proof," 9–12; cf. generally Sorabji, *The Philosophy of the Commentators*, vol. III, ch. 9d; cf. also Ross' comments in *Physics*, 457; Osborne's fn. 41, 109, to her translation of the first part of Philoponus' commentary on the *Physics*.

33 cf. Simplicius, *In Phys.*, 15.11–25.

34 One might also like to take τῶν καθόλου as a reference to the first and primitive universal (πρῶτον μὲν ἐν τῇ ψυχῇ καθόλου) which "made a stand" in our mind (*An. post.* II.19, 100a15f.). This approach seems to be in line with how Simplicius reads the passage; cf. Simplicius, *In Phys.*, 17.38–18.23; cf. also Cerami, "Thomas d'Aquin lecteur critique du Grand Commentaire d'Averroès à *Phys.* I, 1," 191f.; Menn, "Simplicius on the *Theaetetus*"; cf. further Bolton, "Aristotle's Method in Natural Science," 7; de Haas, "Modifications of the Method of Inquiry in Aristotle's *Physics* I.1," 46. On both interpretations, it is the particular that is the starting point of the investigation. Other than that, it is important to note that the Neoplatonic understanding of what is common or universal became increasingly complicated. Proclus, Simplicius, and the author of the commentary on the second book of *Posterior Analytics* that is

get hold of these parts unless we start to examine the compounded whole that is prior to us. In the course of time, we will not only acquire knowledge of the things that are posterior to us and constitute the whole – its principles, causes, and elements – but also of the whole itself.

Philoponus, in particular, is famous for developing this strategy. In his commentary on Aristotle's *Physics*, he developed the concept of the "indiscriminate particular" (τὸ μερικόν συγκεχυμένον) as the actual meaning of Aristotle's καθόλου from which we should proceed. This interpretation proved to be highly influential and is still the more or less commonly accepted reading.[35]

Philoponus claims that Aristotle distinguished in *De interpretatione* the individual (τὸ καθ' ἕκαστον) from the particular (τὸ μερικόν) in calling the latter "'universal' because of its capacity to apply to many things, while the individual applies to only one; and 'indiscriminate' because it applies in an indeterminate and inarticulate manner to the things it does apply to."[36] Thus, although we see individuals, we, at first, perceive them as particulars in that we are not yet able to discern their individual characteristics – much like Aristotle's example of the child who calls "all men fathers."[37] In this case, what we perceive is a particular animal, a particular human, or a particular father, but we do not perceive them as individuals. Perceiving a particular means to have an indiscriminate idea of what is in front of our eyes, i.e., something of which we have a primary grasp, for which we have a more or less appropriate name, and from which we may now begin our inquiry into the world.[38] Philoponus voices his strong opposition

commonly ascribed to Philoponus, for example, distinguish between three different kinds of universals (*ante rem*, *in re*, and *post rem*), or, to be precise, of κοινά in Simplicius' case and καθόλου in Proclus' and Philoponus' (?) case; cf. Proclus, *In Eucl.* 50.18–51.13; Philoponus (?), *In An. post.*, 435.28–30; Simplicius, *In Cat.*, 82.35–83.10; cf. also Philoponus, *In Phys.*, 11.24–12.1; Simplicius, *In Phys.*, 17.38–18.23; cf. further Menn, "Simplicius on the *Theaetetus*," esp. fn. 4, 258; Helmig, *Forms and Concepts*, esp. 209–211. Richard Sorabji remarks that "[i]n a sufficiently broad sense, we can recognise not three, but seven, kinds that were recognised by Neoplatonist commentators," among them Platonic transcendent Forms, Aristotelian enmattered forms, universal concepts in the mind of God, universal concepts in the human mind, and so on (Sorabji, *The Philosophy of the Commentators*, vol. III, ch. 5c, 133ff.).

35 For various adaptations of this interpretation, cf. the commentaries by Ross and Wagner on *Physics* I.1 as well as Wieland, "Aristotle's Physics and the Problem of Inquiry into Principles"; Konstan, "A Note on Aristotle *Physics* 1.1"; Bolton, "Aristotle's Method in Natural Science"; Horstschäfer, *"Über Prinzipien"*; de Haas, "Modifications of the Method of Inquiry in Aristotle's *Physics* I.1"; Mouzala, "Aristotle's Method of Understanding the First Principles of Natural Things in the *Physics* I.1."

36 Philoponus, *In Phys.*, 11.1–3, tr. by Osborne; cf. Cerami, "Thomas d'Aquin lecteur critique du Grand Commentaire d'Averroès à *Phys.* I, 1," 196–198.

37 *Phys.* I.1, 184b12–14; this is the first of the two examples employed by Aristotle to illustrate his theory in chapter I.1. For the second example, q.v. below, 58f.

38 A common example for illustrating an inquiry on the basis of an indiscriminate perception is the case of seeing somebody from afar; cf. *De soph. el.*, 179a26–179b6; Themistius, *In Phys.*, 2.5–9; Philoponus, *In Phys.*, 11.11–18; Simplicius, *In Phys.*, 16.17–20; *al-Samāʿ al-ṭabīʿī* I.1, §§7–10, 9.17–11.9; cf. also Menn, "Simplicius on the *Theaetetus*," 257f.; Lagerlund, "Singular Terms and Vague Concepts."

to the view of some people that "Aristotle meant by 'universal' what is in the many things," i.e., the universal *in re*.[39] He emphasises that what we perceive is by no means *the* animal, *the* human, or *the* father, i.e., *the* universal as existing in the particulars, and draws the following conclusion:

> ὁ γὰρ παῖς εἰ καὶ πάντα ἄνθρωπον ὡς πατέρα γινώσκει, ἀλλ' οὖν τοῦ καθόλου ἔννοιαν οὐκ ἔχει, ἀλλὰ τοῦ μερικοῦ, τοῦ ἀορίστου ... "καθόλου" οὖν ἀκούσομεν ... τὸ μερικόν, ὅπερ τῷ ἀόριστον εἶναι καὶ συγκεχυμένον ἐστὶ καὶ καθόλου.
>
> Even if the child recognises every human being as father, yet he does not have an idea of the universal but of the particular; the indeterminate [particular] ... We shall, therefore, understand "universal" ... as the particular which, in virtue of being indeterminate, is indiscriminate and universal. (Philoponus, *In Phys.*, 12.29–13.6, tr. by Osborne, modified)

Starting from indiscriminate particulars, we can derive our knowledge of the universal through a comparative collation of several instances of particulars and the subsequent differentiation of the gathered data which leads up to a grasp of what is common to them, viz., their genus.[40] Thus, the comprehension of the universal genus is the result of a noetic process and is not achieved directly from perception. Just as the particular's individual features are posterior and less clear to us in terms of sensation, the universal genus is posterior and less clear to us in terms of intellection. For this reason, the perceived individual *qua* particular ought not to be identified with the genus "animal." It is only an instance of "animal" precisely in the universal and indiscriminate manner in which it is more clear and prior for us, viz., as an indiscriminate particular.

Seen in this light, Aristotle's *dictum* appears to be correct: we begin with what is prior to us, viz., the universal as the indiscriminate particular (ἐκ τῶν καθόλου), and proceed to what is posterior to us, viz., the principles, causes, and elements that constitute the whole (ἐπὶ τὰ καθ' ἕκαστα).[41] In fact, this reading amounts to grafting essential aspects of the account of *Posterior Analytics* I.2 onto the methodological advice of *Physics* I.1 by means of interpreting τῶν καθόλου in light of τὰ συγκεχυμένα as the starting point for an inductive and tekmeriodic reasoning. Actually, it even seems that Philoponus' commentary, and perhaps also those of most of the ancient commentators,

---

39 Philoponus, *In Phys.*, 11.24–13.4, tr. by Osborne.

40 cf. Philoponus, *In Phys.*, 12.25.

41 It should be noted that there is also no agreement on how to understand τὰ καθ' ἕκαστα; cf. Ross' comments in *Physics*, 457f.; *Methode und Beweisziel*, 171–187. In addition, interpreters have criticised Aristotle for offering two rather dissimilar, or even inappropriate, examples to clarify his account, viz., the child calling all men fathers and the circle whose definition is differentiated into its parts. It is difficult to see, for example, how Aristotle can claim that the universals are prior to us, when the parts of the definition of "circle" are both more universal and posterior to us; cf. Menn, "Simplicius on the *Theaetetus*," 257f.; q.v. also below, 58f. Moreover, it is obscure how the child's cognitive process from the καθόλου to the καθ' ἕκαστα, i.e., from the indiscriminate particular to the identification of its father and mother by recognising their individual features, illustrates a method for acquiring universal first principles, instead of scientifically irrelevant individual data.

would not have reached a very different conclusion in their interpretation of *Physics* I.1, if Aristotle's text would read διὸ ἐκ τῶν καθ' ἕκαστα ἐπὶ τὰ καθόλου instead of the reverse – certainly, however, they would have written less.

A distinctively different strategy from the one just expounded on the basis of the remarks in Philoponus' commentary, is to take τῶν καθόλου as meaning τὰ κοινά ("what is common"), as the beginning of chapter I.7 of Aristotle's *Physics* may suggest:

> Ὧδ' οὖν ἡμεῖς λέγωμεν πρῶτον περὶ πάσης γενέσεως ἐπελθόντες· ἔστι γὰρ κατὰ φύσιν τὰ κοινὰ πρῶτον εἰπόντας οὕτω τὰ περὶ ἕκαστον ἴδια θεωρεῖν.
>
> أمّا نحن فنبدأ بالبحث في الكون عامّةً إذ يتّفق مع الطبيعة أن نتحدّث أوّلاً عن الأمور المشتركة ثمّ بعد ذلك عن كلّ ما هو خاصّ بشيء شيء.
>
> We shall now give our own account, approaching the question first with reference to coming-to-be in general (πάσης, *'āmmatan*), for it is the natural order first to speak of what is common (τὰ κοινά, *al-umūr al-muštaraka*) and, then, to investigate what is particular in each case (τὰ περὶ ἕκαστον ἴδια, *mā huwa ḫāṣṣ bi-šay' šay'*). (*Phys.* I.7, 189b30–32, tr. by Hardie/Gaye, modified)

On this view, καθόλου means "universal" insofar as what is universal applies to many different objects or, as τὰ κοινά in this passage do, even to all natural things, apparently. If we inquire into and seek to understand nature, we may be well advised to examine, first, what applies to all or, at least, to many or most natural things, i.e., their more common features such as motion and corporeality. In the course of time, we would have acquired knowledge of the general aspects that universally apply to natural things, i.e., we would have grasped the fundamental universals and would be properly prepared to inquire into more particular aspects, such as the motion of the heavens, the transformation of the elements, or the soul.[42]

It is less widely known that Philoponus is also one of the proponents of this reading.[43] Both before and after his discussion of the "indiscriminate particular," Philoponus asserts that the *Physics* is an introductory work on general concepts and, thus, preparatory for the study of nature as undertaken in the more specialised sciences

---

42 Provided that the soul belongs to the subjects of natural philosophy at all; cf. the discussion in Falcon, *Aristotle and the Science of Nature*, 16–22, referring to earlier contributions in Wedin, *Mind and Imagination in Aristotle*, 3–9; Burnyeat, *A Map of* Metaphysics *Z*, fn. 15, 134; "*De anima* II 5," 36; "Aristotle on the Foundations of Sublunary Physics," 13. As Falcon remarks, the question of whether the study of the soul belongs to natural philosophy was implicitly raised by Aristotle himself and has been discussed since antiquity; cf. *Meteor.* I.1, 338a20–339a9; *De part. anim.* I.1, 641a32–b10; *Met.* E.1, 1025b25–1026a6; Simplicius (?), *In An.*, 1.23–3.28. Indeed, this is a question which exercised, and even troubled, Avicenna, too, as Gutas has shown; cf. *Avicenna and the Aristotelian Tradition*, 288–296.

43 Simplicius attributes such a reading to Alexander of Aphrodisias and criticises it; cf. *In Phys.*, 19.1–18. Themistius had a similar understanding; cf. *In Phys.*, 2.3–5, with the back-references at 23.20f., 67.16–18; cf. also Tannery, "Sur un point de la méthode d'Aristote," who was criticised by Konstan, "A Note on Aristotle *Physics* 1.1," 244f.; cf. further Ross' comments in *Physics*, *ad* 184a16–b14, attributing the idea to Pacius; Fritsche, *Methode und Beweisziel*, 15; Charlton's comments in *Physics*, *ad* 184a23–b14; de Haas, "Modifications of the Method of Inquiry in Aristotle's *Physics* I.1," 49–51; Corcilius, "Physik," 75.

that follow the *Physics*. It is the universal features of the compounded things (τὰ συγκεχυμένα) that we, at first, i.e., in the *Physics*, should be interested in. Later, we may start a new investigation of the very same compounded things, now concerned with their more particular features. Thereby, we work our way from the universals to the particulars, while progressing from the *Physics* to the more specialised disciplines of natural philosophy.[44]

Each of Aristotle's works on natural philosophy, Philoponus explains, covers only a part of nature: "eternal things ... in *De caelo*, ... generation and corruption in the *De generatione et corruptione*, ... in the *Meteorologica* and *On Minerals* ... matters that appertain to lifeless things [and] atmospherical phenomena in particular," and so on.[45] The sole exception being "[t]he book we have before us [which is] about the adjuncts that accompany *all* natural things in common" (περί τῶν κοινῇ πᾶσι τοῖς φυσικοῖς πράγμασι παρακολουθούντων), viz., matter, form, place, time, and motion.[46] He illustrates his view by making a distinction between the investigation of matter *qua* bodies, which is a task for the *Physics*, and that of matter *qua* meteorological, as carried out in the *Meteorologica*.[47] What is more, Philoponus even mentions that, strictly speaking, privation is sort of an alien element in the *Physics*, because although it is an adjunct of natural things, it is limited only to those things that are subject to generation and corruption.[48] Later, then, Philoponus provides an overall perspective of "the aim of the project and the direction of the discussion as a whole." The following is a selective summary of this outlook:

> Ἀλλὰ γὰρ ἄνωθεν τὸν σκοπὸν τῶν προκειμένων εἴπωμεν καὶ τοῦ ὅλου λόγου τὴν ἀγωγήν. πρόκειται, φησίν, ἡμῖν τὰ φυσικὰ πράγματα γνῶναι ... ἄρχεται γοῦν ἐντεῦθεν κοινῶς περὶ τῶν ἀρχῶν ζητεῖν πότερον μία ἢ πλείους, αὕτη δὲ ἡ διδασκαλία τῶν κοινοτέρων ἐστὶ καὶ συγκεχυμένων ... ὥστε κἂν περὶ τῆς ὕλης διδάσκῃ ἡμᾶς ἐν τούτοις, ἀλλὰ περὶ τῆς κοινότερον καλουμένης ὕλης, ἥτις ἐπὶ πάσης ὕλης κατηγορεῖσθαι δύναται.
>
> But let us explain what is the aim of the project and the direction of the discussion as a whole (τὸν σκοπὸν τῶν προκειμένων ... καὶ τοῦ ὅλου λόγου τὴν ἀγωγήν), starting from the beginning. Our project, Aristotle says, is to get to know physical objects ... Hence, he begins by enquiring about the principles generally (κοινῶς), whether they are one or many, and this is the study of things that are more general and indiscriminate (κοινοτέρων ἐστὶ καὶ συγκεχυμένων) ... So, even if he

44 Philoponus apparently combined his reading of τῶν καθόλου as τὰ συγκεχυμένα with his views on the relation of the *Physics* to the other disciplines of natural philosophy, arguably following Alexander; cf. his comments on the opening lines of *Physics* I.7 (*In Phys.*, 151.8–23).

45 Philoponus, *In Phys.*, 1.22–2.13, tr. by Osborne, modified.

46 Philoponus, *In Phys.*, 2.13–16, tr. by Osborne, emphasis added. In a similar manner, Proclus writes that in the *Physics*, Aristotle meant to treat the "common factors in all things that have come to exits by nature" (τὰ μὲν κοινὰ πάντων τῶν φύσει συνεστώτων), adding the "original source of motion" (τὸ ὅθεν ἡ ἀρχὴ τῆς κινήσεως) as a sixth item to Philoponus' just quoted list of five (*In Tim.* I, 6.24–26, tr. by Tarrant).

47 Philoponus, *In Phys.*, 8.18–25.

48 Philoponus, *In Phys.*, 2.35–37.

> teaches us about matter in these books, nevertheless it is about matter under its more general (κοινότερον) description, matter that can be predicated of every sort of matter (ἐπὶ πάσης ὕλης κατηγορεῖσθαι). (Philoponus, *In Phys.*, 14.21–16.1, tr. by Osborne, modified)

Since Aristotle began his treatment of nature with the most fundamental principles of natural things, the definition of nature, and the four causes, then progressed to motion as such and to the discussion of certain aspects and concomitants of motion, it seems that, indeed, it was Aristotle's plan to proceed from the general and the universally applicable to the particular, and, for example, to examine motion in general *before* accounting for specific sorts of motion, such as alteration, growth, and circular motion.[49] As a matter of fact, Aristotle even said so himself in *Meteorologica* I.1, where he laid out the general structure of his works on nature and how they should be ordered.[50]

This plan is, moreover, quite plausible. Standing at the beginning of our investigation as we are, it is only reasonable first to come to know basic truths, such that the term "circle" is a whole, indiscriminately describing something with a round shape. It is only thereafter that we come to distinguish particular cases of circularity from each other, like the oval and the sphere, through definition, i.e., by joining *differentiae* to the common *genus*.[51]

Support for this reading of *Physics* I.1 can be gathered from other chapters of the book. There is, for example, the conclusion of chapter I.9, where Aristotle states that the present discussion of the principles of natural change is sufficient only for now

---

49 Commenting on the opening lines of *Physics* I.7, Philoponus explains Aristotle's progression from the universals to the particulars as follows: "For the knowledge of the universals always precedes the knowledge of the particulars. Thus when he [sc. Aristotle] wants to explain the differences between syllogisms, he first explains what a syllogism is as a whole; for someone who does not know what a syllogism is, will never come to know what a demonstrative syllogism is" (Philoponus, *In Phys.*, 151.12–15 tr. by Osborne).

50 *Meteor.* I.1, 338a20–339a9; cf. Capelle, "Das Proömium der Meteorologie"; Burnyeat, "Aristotle on the Foundations of Sublunary Physics"; Falcon, *Aristotle and the Science of Nature*, ch. 1.

51 This is Aristotle's example of the circle and its definition. Alongside the child calling all men fathers, it is the second example used to illustrate the method proposed in *Physics* I.1. For the first example see above, 54ff. There are other possible interpretations of the example of the circle than the one here advanced. One may consider the "particulars" into which the definition of a circle divides the whole to be particular definitory statements such as "being at all points equidistant from the centre." Alternatively, one may think that the "particulars" in question are rather the genus and the difference of "circle," which is Aristotle's usual account of definition and the interpretation offered by Bostock and also by Menn; cf. Bostock's remarks in Waterfields translation of the *Physics*, 232; Menn, "Simplicius on the *Theaetetus*," 257; cf. also Simplicius, *In Phys.*, 16.20–25. Ross, however, writes that "dividing the whole into its καθ' ἕκαστα ... if taken strictly must mean the analysis of a genus into its species" (Ross' comments in *Physics*, 457); this is also the reading of *Physics* I.1, 184b11f. presently suggested here: "For [a word] signifies some whole, e.g., a circle, in an undifferentiated way, whereas the definition separates [that whole, i.e., the circle], into particular instances [of that whole, e.g., oval or sphere]" (ὅλον γάρ τι καὶ ἀδιορίστως σημαίνει, οἷον ὁ κύκλος, ὁ δὲ ὁρισμὸς αὐτοῦ διαιρεῖ εἰς τὰ καθ' ἕκαστα).

and that we should better postpone (ἀποκείσθω, *nurǧiʾahū*) specific questions about these principles until we have reached the *Metaphysics*.[52] There is also the opening of book III, where Aristotle claims that "the investigation of what is particular (τῶν ἰδίων, *amr al-ḫawāṣṣ*) comes after that of what is common [and universal]" (τῶν κοινῶν [καὶ καθόλου], *al-umūr al-ʿāmmiyya al-muštaraka*).[53]

The strongest support from among Aristotle's own writings, however, stems from *De generatione et corruptione* II.9.[54] There, having concluded his treatment of the elements, Aristotle finally commences his discussion of causes other than the material:

> λεκτέον περὶ πάσης γενέσεως ὁμοίως πόσαι τε καὶ τίνες αὐτῆς αἱ ἀρχαί· ῥᾷον γὰρ οὕτω τὰ καθ' ἕκαστα θεωρήσομεν, ὅταν περὶ τῶν καθόλου λάβωμεν πρῶτον.
>
> Tunc oportet ut ponamus sermonem nostrum ad omnem generationem, et ostendamus secundum similitudinem unam quot sint principia eius et que sint. Nam nos quando incesserimus hac via, erit statio nostra super particularia facilior, propterea quod determinabimus in primis res universales.
>
> We must say, concerning all generation alike, how many principles there are of it and what they are. We shall in this way be able more easily to study the particulars (τὰ καθ' ἕκαστα, *particularia*), namely when we have first obtained a grasp of the universals (τῶν καθόλου, *res universales*). (*De gen. et corr.* II.9, 335a25–28, tr. by Williams, modified)[55]

As it appears, understanding τὰ καθ' ἕκαστα and τῶν καθόλου in this passage turned out to be not particularly troublesome. Neither did Philoponus in his commentary on that work mention any difficulty in the text or a debate among fellow commentators, as we saw him doing in the case of Aristotle's *dictum* in *Physics* I.1, nor do modern translators diverge in their respective renderings of this sentence, for they all used either the pair specific-universal (Joachim) or particular-universal (Forster, Williams, Kupreeva, M. Rashed, Buchheim). To the contrary, there seems to be an unanimous agreement that at least in this work, Aristotle proposes to treat the universals *before* proceeding to the particulars.

Taking it all together, we are offered two interpretations for τῶν καθόλου in *Physics* I.1. On the first, Aristotle tells us his method for how to acquire knowledge of principles from compounded particular wholes through comparison and analysis. This describes a *method of inquiry* not unlike the one expounded in the *Posterior Analytics*. Through this method of inquiry, a student of nature, who does not yet have the knowledge he is hoping to acquire, is led to gather scientific knowledge through an inductive examination of the compounded things encountered in the natural world.

---

52 *Phys.* I.9, 192a34–b1.

53 *Phys.* III.1, 200b20–25, tr. by Hardie/Gaye, modified; cf. M. Rashed's remarks in Alexander of Aphrodisias, *Commentaire perdu à la* Physique *d'Aristote*, 33.

54 A passage most significantly at variance is *De motu animalium* 1, 698a1–7.

55 Marwan Rashed kindly provided me with his personal transcript of Gerard of Cremona's Latin translation. It is quoted here in lieu of the Arabic version by Isḥāq ibn Ḥunayn which is not known to be extant.

On the second, Aristotle is not giving advice on how to acquire knowledge of principles, as this has already been explained at length in the *Posterior Analytics*. Instead, he presents an outline of his plan and informs the reader about how he wants to proceed, which subjects he intends to treat when and where, and, finally, insinuates that in the present book – the *Physics* – he will confine himself to the basic and universal concepts of natural philosophy. This illustrates his *way of procedure*.[56] On this second interpretation, chapter I.1 no longer represents the introductory remarks only to the first book of the *Physics* or to the whole of the *Physics* but rather constitutes Aristotle's universal introduction to natural philosophy as such. It is a chapter on the broad method he intends to pursue throughout his works on natural philosophy. In this introduction, he states that he will begin with the fundamental concepts that pertain to all natural things alike, and that the scope of his investigation and his questions will continuously become more narrow, for example, from motion in general to locomotion to circular motion, and from soul in general to ensouled mobile beings (animals) to ensouled immobile beings (plants). This *way of procedure* displays the direction of his investigations in natural philosophy. Moreover, on this second interpretation, the *Physics* is naturally the first work in the venture into the study of nature, because its topics bear greatly on all other physical writings, such as *De generatione et corruptione*, *De caelo*, and *De anima*, which in dealing with more particular cases cannot do without the preliminary and general – at times rather metaphysical – remarks of *Physics* I–VIII.[57]

---

56 As the case of Philoponus shows, the *method of inquiry* and the *way of procedure* are not mutually exclusive. The former is a general method for acquiring knowledge of particular objects, whereas the latter is only a general plan of which objects ought to be treated first, in order to structure, and thereby to facilitate, the scientific enterprise. In other words, the *method of inquiry* would be Aristotle's answer to the question: "how to acquire knowledge of *x*?," with *x* representing the motion of the heavenly bodies, the growth of plants, or the coming-to-be of a human being, and so on. His answer is that we acquire knowledge of *x* by looking at particular instances of *x* and, thereby, try to grasp the universal of *x* through comparing and examining these particular instances. On the other hand, the *way of procedure* would be Aristotle's answer to another question: "should we apply the *method of inquiry* first to an investigation of the motion of the heavenly bodies, the growth of plants, or the coming-to-be of a human being?" Here, his advice is that we should, first, try to look at all kinds of particular processes or motions alike and figure out what motion is as such, before we devote our attention to the particular kinds of instances of motion.

57 It was perhaps in a similar vein that Bostock described Aristotle's discussion of the principles, especially as pursued in *Physics* I.7, as a "meta-investigation," claiming that "Aristotle is not after all engaging in physical enquiry himself … but rather trying to lay down in advance the general form which any physical enquiry must have" ("Aristotle on the Principles of Change in *Physics* I," 4). Fritsche similarly wrote: "Auf dem Hintergrund der Platonischen Philosophie kann man die *Physikvorlesung* als einen meta-naturwissenschaftlichen Text charakterisieren. In ihm werden … die Bedingungen der Möglichkeit einer Naturwissenschaft untersucht" (*Methode und Beweisziel*, 15). More recently, Corcilius described the *Physics* as divided into two parts, a general first part (books I–VI) which is supplemented by a particular application (books VII–VIII): "Die *Physik* … lässt sich grob in zwei Teile gliedern: Einerseits enthält sie eine Metaphysik naturphilosophischer Grundbegriffe … andererseits

That Aristotle's *Physics* provides its readers with basic and fundamental concepts that apply to all or most natural things is beyond doubt. It is equally clear that those works on natural philosophy that traditionally follow the *Physics* have a narrower scope and investigate particular applications of these fundamental concepts within the natural world.[58] A systematic and hierarchical understanding of the Aristotelian corpus has become a commonplace for philosophers in the ancient and late ancient tradition. This understanding of (Aristotelian) science, and of the place of physics within that schema, also shaped the thought of the early philosophers in the Islamic world. Both Abū Yaʿqūb ibn Isḥāq al-Kindī (d. ~ 256/870) and al-Fārābī composed treatises about the division of the sciences and the division of the Aristotelian works as well as the systematic relation between the various sciences and works. In al-Fārābī's *Risāla fī-mā yanbaġī an yuqaddama qabla taʿallum al-falsafa*, for example, we read the following:

فالكتب التي يتعلّم منها الأمور الطبيعية فمنها ما يتعلّم منها الأمور العامّة لجميع الطبائع ومنها ما يتعلّم منها الأمور التي تخصّ كلّ واحد من الطبائع. والكتاب الذي يتعلّم منه الأمور العامّة لجميع الطبائع هو كتابه المسمّى سمع الكيان.

> So, among the books from which one learns about the natural things, are those from which one learns the things that are common to all natural things (*al-umūr al-ʿāmma li-ǧamīʿ al-ṭabāʾiʿ*) as well as those from which one learns the things which are specific to each one of the natural things (*al-umūr allatī taḫuṣṣu kull wāḥid min al-ṭabāʾiʿ*). The book from which one learns the things that are common to all natural things is the book of his (*kitābuhū*) which is called the *Physics* (*Samʿ al-kiyān*). (al-Fārābī, *Risāla fī-mā yanbaġī an yuqaddama qabla taʿallum al-falsafa*, 50.22–51.2)[59]

This account of how science proceeds within the area of natural philosophy presents us with an explicit move from what is more universal to what is more particular. The first part of this enterprise is attained through "the book of his [i.e., Aristotle] which is called the *Physics* " and which is concerned with the fundamentals of natural philosophy. This agrees with Philoponus' above-mentioned perspective of "the aim ... and the direction" (τὸν σκοπὸν ... καὶ ... τὴν ἀγωγήν) of Aristotle's works on natural philosophy and also with the advice given in *Physics* I.1. Taking Aristotle's *dictum* in this light will become crucial, now that we will return to Avicenna.

---

aber auch Argumentationen für eine Reihe naturphilosophischer Thesen" ("Physik," 75). Charlton, less straightforwardly but still in similar fashion, attested Aristotle to write in the first two books "as a philosopher, not as a scientist," adding that "[n]evertheless, *Phys.* II, at least, seems to be addressed to the scientific student of nature ... the *phusikos*" (his introduction in *Physics*, ix).

58 Whether we would like to find this fact epitomised in the Aristotelian *dictum* of chapter I.1 is a different and more challenging question which, although raised by the preceding discussion, is not among the primary concerns of this study.

59 cf. al-Fārābī, *De scientiis*, 100.6–104.20. In the *Risāla fī kammiyyat kutub Arisṭūṭālīs wa-mā yuḥtāǧu ilayhi fī taḥṣīl al-falsafa*, al-Kindī uses a similar expression when he characterises the *Physics* as an exposition of "the things that are common to all natural things" (*al-ašyāʾ al-ʿāmma li-ǧamīʿ al-ašyāʾ al-ṭabīʿiyya*; vol. 1, 382.14–16); cf. also Avicenna, *Risāla fī aqsām al-ʿulūm al-ʿaqliyya*, 108.12–110.6, which will be mentioned below, 67; cf. further Hein, *Definition und Einteilung der Philosophie*, esp. 276–303.

Avicenna on the Mode of Instruction

On the basis of the concept of the "indiscriminate particular," Philoponus offered a sophisticated version of an approach to natural science which we saw him and others call ἐπαγωγή ("induction") or describe as τεκμηριώδης ("evidential"). Aristotle and the Peripatetics regarded induction – in particular: tekmeriodic induction – as one of two valuable and, for some thinkers in the tradition, even demonstrative (ἀποδεικτικός) ways for acquiring knowledge of things that have not been known before. Regardless of whether we prefer to read Aristotle's advice that we ought to proceed "from the universals to the particulars" as representing a *method of inquiry* or a *way of procedure* (or a combination of both), it seems that in the science of physics we ought to follow this lead and advance along the lines of induction or, in Avicenna's case, along the lines of methodic experience.

Yet, Avicenna does not mention methodic experience in *al-Samāʿ al-ṭabīʿī* I.1 nor anywhere else in that work.[60] This is surprising, because Avicenna himself stated in the preface:

> فجري بنا أن نفتتح الكلام في تعليم العلم الطبيعي على النحو الذي تقرّر عليه رأينا وانتهى إليه نظرنا وأن نجعل الترتيب في ذلك مقارناً للترتيب الذي تجري عليه فلسفة المشائين.
>
> The procedure of ours is that we commence the discussion on the teaching of natural philosophy in the manner on which our opinion has settled and which our inquiry has determined, and that we make the order (*al-tartīb*) in this correspond (*muqāranan*) to the order according to which the philosophy of the Peripatetics proceeds. (*al-Samāʿ al-ṭabīʿī*, preface, §1, 3.4–6)[61]

Of course, this statement does not entail that Avicenna always has to adopt the method, and to follow the structure, of Aristotle's *Physics* point by point. In his general introduction to *al-Šifāʾ* as a whole, being the first chapter of *al-Madḫal*, he announces his intention to include all that can be found in the books of the Ancients, while at the same time allowing himself to rearrange the systematic order of the subjects discussed whenever it appears to him to be "more appropriate" (*alyaq*).[62] Nonetheless, especially

---

60 Once, in *al-Samāʿ al-ṭabīʿī* III.4, §13, 195.3, Avicenna uses the passive voice of *ǧarraba*, which is the verb from which the verbal noun *taǧriba* is derived. Likewise, there is only one single mention of *istiqrāʾ*, in *al-Samāʿ al-ṭabīʿī* I.2, §15, 18.2. Both cases are negligible. Moreover, Avicenna begins his account of nature in *al-Samāʿ al-ṭabīʿī* I.5, §1, 29.4–11, with a survey of motions that can be observed by different kinds of natural things "in front of us" (*qablanā*). This is similar to the beginning of *al-Nafs* I.1, 5.3-8, in which Avicenna even employs forms of the verb *šāhada* ("to observe, to experience"). Avicenna uses these remarks in both cases, in order to appeal to our own everyday experience. This "experience" is distinctively not "methodic" and is not an instance of *taǧriba*. Avicenna uses it as a first pointer that indicates something to be demonstrated more rigorously in the remainder of the work; cf. also the remarks on *šāhada* and *ǧarraba* in Gutas, "The Empiricism of Avicenna," 428–430.

61 cf. *al-Madḫal* I.1, 11.1–4.

62 *al-Madḫal* I.1, 9.17–10.4; cf. *al-Madḫal*, preface, 2.11–13; both passages are translated in Gutas, *Avicenna and the Aristotelian Tradition*, 42–46, 29–34; cf. also Hasnawi, "La *Physique* du *Šifāʾ*," 67.

the first book of *al-Samāʿ al-ṭabīʿī* appears to be strikingly similar, both in order and in content, to books I and II of Aristotle's *Physics*: Avicenna enumerates and discusses the principles of natural things, rejects the views of the Presocratics on that subject, proceeds to defining nature and the four causes as well as chance and luck, and ends with a chapter on the scientific merit of these causes – this is exactly the agenda Aristotle set.[63] It is, thus, by no means surprising that the first chapter of his *al-Samāʿ al-ṭabīʿī* is – just as in Aristotle's *Physics* – a chapter on method. However, it is all the more surprising, in particular in light of the late ancient interpretations of *Physics* I.1, that Avicenna does not mention methodic experience, induction, or any other method of scientific inquiry. This already gives us some reason for doubting Paul Lettinck's claim that "Ibn Sina's interpretation of the statement that we should proceed from the general to the particular is about the same as Philoponus' interpretation," because Philoponus *did* elaborate upon methods of scientific inquiry.[64] As shall become clear shortly, this assertion is a misjudgement.

63 For a comparison of content between the *Physics* of Aristotle and *al-Samāʿ al-ṭabīʿī* of Avicenna, cf. Hasnawi, "La *Physique* du *Šifāʾ*," esp. 67–69.

64 Lettinck, *Aristotle's* Physics *and its Reception in the Arabic World*, 97; "Problems in Aristotle's Physics I, 1," 97. Lettinck founded his interpretation on the observation that Avicenna mentions the concept of a "vague individual" (*al-šaḫs al-muntašir*) in *al-Samāʿ al-ṭabīʿī* I.1, §§9–10, 10.12–11.9. This expression is reminiscent of Philoponus' "indiscriminate particular" (τὸ μερικόν συγκεχυμένον) which, as we have seen, served as the basis for interpreting *Physics* I.1 as recommending a method of inquiry. This reminiscence notwithstanding, Avicenna discusses the concept merely in passing, while digressing from his actual concerns. In fact, the notion of Philoponus' vague individual, the Aristotelian example of the child calling all men fathers, and the common case of seeing somebody from afar may *prima facie* seem to counter the claim Avicenna was just advancing that although common things are better known to our intellects, it is the individuals that are better known to our sensation. Consequently, Avicenna is required, in *al-Samāʿ al-ṭabīʿī* I.1, §§7–10, 9.17–11.9, to explain how these examples can be brought into conformity with his theory, which he, thereupon, continues to set forth. Avicenna's exposition of the "vague individual" remains a clear case of a digression and is not incorporated into the line of thought in *al-Samāʿ al-ṭabīʿī* I.1 nor is it employed or elaborated upon in the remainder of the chapter nor is it ever mentioned again anywhere in *al-Samāʿ al-ṭabīʿī*. Black suggested a connection between the "vague individual" in *al-Samāʿ al-ṭabīʿī* I.1 and the "vague human" (*insān muntašir*) in *al-Burhān* IV.10: "The specific occasion for introducing the vague individual [as known from *al-Samāʿ al-ṭabīʿī*] into the discussion [of *al-Burhān*] is to provide an interpretation of Aristotle's metaphor likening the process of grasping a universal to the re-formation of a battle line after a rout." On her interpretation, the vague individual serves an inductive or, more precisely, abstractive purpose that is supposed to elucidate "how the intellect derives the principles of demonstration from the senses" ("Avicenna's 'Vague Individual' and its Impact on Medieval Latin Philosophy," 266). While there is much to be learned from Black's paper, it is doubtful whether the "vague individual" and the "vague human" are meant to signify the same concept, just because both expressions are described by the participle *muntašir*. To the contrary, it seems that the "vague human" is rather a "vague universal" (instead of a "vague individual"), similar to the "primitive universal" (πρῶτον μὲν ἐν τῇ ψυχῇ καθόλου) which "made a stand" in our mind and which Aristotle discussed in *Posterior Analytics* II.19 – this inference, also drawn by Black, is all the more plausible, as the whole chapter in which the expression "vague human" appears – *al-Burhān* IV.10 – is precisely Avicenna's own version of *Posterior Analytics* II.19.

Avicenna begins the first chapter of *al-Samāʿ al-ṭabīʿī* with the distinction between universal and particular sciences known from *al-Burhān*.[65] Following this, he maintains that the subject-matter of physics is "the sensible body insofar as it is subject to change" (*al-ğism al-maḥsūs min ğihat mā huwa wāqiʿ fī taġayyur*); that natural bodies are called "natural" (*ṭabīʿī*) due to a "power called nature" (*al-quwwa allatī tusammā ṭabīʿa*), which Avicenna shall discuss and define later; and that natural things ought to be investigated with regard to their "principles, [external] causes, and [internal] causes" (*mabādiʾ wa-asbāb wa-ʿilal*), for one can acquire knowledge (*maʿrifa*) of things that have principles only by getting to know those principles.[66] With this last remark, Avicenna straightforwardly approaches the intricate issue of how to acquire knowledge of principles. This issue, however, will not be solved here in *al-Samāʿ al-ṭabīʿī* by referring to methods of inquiry. Instead, Avicenna writes the following:

In other words, the "vague human" illustrates an abstractive method of grasping a universal concept through the collection of individual instances, as Black rightly states. The "vague individual" from *al-Samāʿ al-ṭabīʿī*, however, serves as an example for how intellection naturally proceeds (and how it can be observed in infants whose cognitive apparatus is still pure and natural). It, thus, clarifies the opposite of an inductive approach, as it concerns the identification of a concrete individual through a reasoning from its general and universal descriptions to its particular and individual characteristics. In the end, Avicenna purposefully integrates the notion of the "vague individual" in his exposition here in *al-Samāʿ al-ṭabīʿī*, because it – just as much as the example of the child calling all men fathers and the case of seeing somebody from afar – nicely illustrates that common things are better known to the intellect and that, for this reason, any scientific instruction should begin with what is common and proceed to what is particular. It is not, however, about the acquisition of first knowledge through abstraction, which is precisely the concern of the passage about the "vague human" in *al-Burhān*.

65 cf. esp. *al-Burhān* II.6–7, II.9. This distinction is frequently encountered in the works of Avicenna. It is expounded in logic but often explicitly invoked in his philosophical compendia at the beginning of the first science after logic, which usually is physics; cf. *al-Nağāt* II.1, 189.13–190.8 ≈ *al-Ḥikma al-ʿArūḍiyya* II.1, 113.9–16; *ʿUyūn al-ḥikma* II.2, 17.12–15; *al-Ḥikma al-mašriqiyya* III, 2.3–7. A similar distinction is found at the beginning of the metaphysics of the *Dānešnāme-ye ʿAlāʾī* – instead of at the beginning of the section on natural philosophy – because in this work, Avicenna reversed his usual order of exposition and treats metaphysics before natural philosophy; cf. Avicenna's own remarks at *Dānešnāme-ye ʿAlāʾī* II.2, 8.7–10. It may seem surprising that in *al-Ḥikma al-mašriqiyya*, in which metaphysics likewise follows immediately upon logic, thus preceding natural philosophy, we find such a remark at the beginning of natural philosophy. Yet, this is surely explained by the close textual relationship between the texts of the sections on natural philosophy in *al-Ḥikma al-mašriqiyya* and *al-Šifāʾ*. Indeed, Avicenna's treatment of natural philosophy in *al-Ḥikma al-mašriqiyya* heavily relies on – and often reproduces verbatim – corresponding passages from *al-Šifāʾ*; cf. also Gutas, "Avicenna's Eastern ('Oriental') Philosophy," 177–180. Whether or not the section on metaphysics in *al-Ḥikma al-mašriqiyya* also mentioned the distinction between particular and universal sciences at the outset can no longer be determined due to the loss of that section. The distinction between universal and particular sciences, and its methodological implications, will be discussed in detail below, 81ff.

66 *al-Samāʿ al-ṭabīʿī* I.1, §1, 7.5–13. Although Avicenna's phrase *mabādiʾ wa-asbāb wa-ʿilal* clearly emulates Aristotle's ἀρχαὶ ἢ αἴτια ἢ στοιχεῖα, it has replaced the term for "elements" (στοιχεῖα) by just another seemingly redundant synonym for "cause." For an attempt to account for Avicenna's puzzling, even though arguably deliberate, divergence, q.v. below, 162ff.

فإن كان للأمور الطبيعية مبادئ وأسباب وعلل لم يتحقّق العلم الطبيعي إلّا منها فقد شُرِح في تعليم البرهان أنّه لا سبيل إلى تحقّق معرفة الأمور ذوات المبادئ إلّا بعد الوقوف على مبادئها والوقوف من مبادئها عليها فإنّ هذا النحو من التعليم والتعلّم هو الذي نتوصّل منه إلى تحقّق المعرفة بالأمور ذوات المبادئ.

If, then, natural things have principles, [external] causes, and [internal] causes, natural knowledge cannot be ascertained other than through them. So, it has been explained in the teaching about demonstration [i.e., in Aristotle's *Posterior Analytics*] that there is no way of ascertaining the knowledge (*taḥaqquq maʿrifa*) of those things which have principles except after understanding their principles and understanding them from their principles, for this way from teaching and learning (*al-taʿlīm wa-l-taʿallum*)[67] is the one through which we arrive at the ascertainment of knowledge of things which have principles. (*al-Samāʿ al-ṭabīʿī* I.1, §1, 7.13–15)

Avicenna's mention of *taʿlīm* ("teaching") and *taʿallum* ("learning") is reminiscent of the famous first sentence of Aristotle's *Posterior Analytics*: "All teaching (διδασκαλία, *taʿlīm*) and all intellectual learning (μάθησις, *taʿallum*) comes-to-be from pre-existent knowledge."[68] It is, moreover, also reminiscent of Philoponus' calling the inductive method of the *Posterior Analytics* (and of *Physics* I.1) "didactic" (διδασκαλικός).[69] A few lines later, Avicenna claims:

فإنّ وجه التعلّم والتعليم العقلي فيها أن يُبتدَأ ممّا هو أعمّ ويُسلَك إلى ما هو أخصّ.

So, indeed, the direction of intellectual learning and teaching (*al-taʿallum wa-l-taʿlīm al-ʿaqlī*) about them [sc. natural things] is to start[70] from what is more common (*aʿamm*) and to proceed[71] to what is more specific (*aḫaṣṣ*). (*al-Samāʿ al-ṭabīʿī* I.1, §3, 8.8)

The first half of this assertion is reminiscent, again, of *Posterior Analytics* I.1 and Philoponus' "didactic" method, while the second half resembles Aristotle's much-debated advice in *Physics* I.1. For several reasons, it is justified to regard this clause as Avicenna's version of the Aristotelian *dictum* of *Physics* I.1 and to assert that Avicenna understood Aristotle's rather enigmatic τῶν καθόλου, i.e., whatever he might have read in the Arabic translations at his disposal, as that which is common (*ʿāmm*) or more common (*aʿamm*), in Greek: κοινός or κοινότερος/κοινότατος.[72]

67 Reading *al-taʿlīm wa-l-taʿallum* with Mss. Leiden or. 4 and or. 84 for *al-taʿlīm aw al-taʿallum* in Zāyid, McGinnis, and Āl Yāsīn.

68 cf. *Posterior Analytics* I.1, 71a1f. In the Greek-Arabic translation movement, *taʿlīm* was often employed to render διδασκαλία and related expressions (e.g., δίδαξις), while *taʿallum* translated μάθησις and related expressions. Some ambiguity is introduced through the fact that *taʿlīm* is also the common translation for μάθημα, and so also came to signify the science of mathematics in particular.

69 cf. Philoponus, *In Phys.*, 9.11–19, tr. by Osborne.

70 Reading *yubtadaʾa* with Mss. Leiden or. 4 and or. 84 as well as Zāyid for *yubtadiʾa* in McGinnis and Āl Yāsīn.

71 Reading *yuslaka* with Mss. Leiden or. 4 and or. 84 for *nasluka* in Zāyid and *tasluka* in McGinnis and Āl Yāsīn.

72 cf. also Pines, "A New Fragment of Xenocrates," 32.

First of all, Avicenna presents a contraposition of what is specific and what is common, just as Aristotle contrasted what is particular with what is universal. It should further be noted that Aristotle himself does not strictly distinguish between common (κοινός) and universal (καθόλου), describing them at times in similar terms.[73]

Second, the ancient commentators as early as Alexander of Aphrodisias (fl. ~ 200) often took these two terms as conveying an equivalent meaning.[74] In any case, Alexander's account of universals had great influence on the Arabic and Latin Middle Ages.[75] Moreover, Neoplatonic theories of universals became increasingly complex. As already mentioned above, some thinkers distinguished three meanings of καθόλου, among them Proclus (d. 485), Simplicius, and the author of the commentary on the second book of *Posterior Analytics*, ascribed to Philoponus.[76] The exposition of these different meanings of "universal" in many cases employs, and indeed essentially relies upon, the term κοινός. What is more, the Neoplatonic differentiation of three kinds of universals has been absorbed by prominent figures in the Arabic philosophical tradition, as can be seen in the writings of, for example, Yaḥyā ibn ʿAdī (d. 363/974).[77]

Third, in his commentary on the *Physics*, Philoponus frequently describes the universal principles of book I as τὰς κοινοτάτας ἀρχάς and τὰς καθολικωτάτας πάντων τῶν ὄντων ἀρχάς, with the latter phrase bringing in yet another related term, albeit one that is not attested in Aristotle's works.[78] It seems that καθολικός is a term of Stoic provenance which we find more and more frequently used in the works of the later commentators.[79]

Fourth, it should not be forgotten that Aristotle, having declared that we ought to begin from the universals (ἐκ τῶν καθόλου) in *Physics* I.1, commences his own investigation of the principles of natural things in *Physics* I.7 with his explicit intention "first to speak of what is common" (τὰ κοινά, *al-umūr al-muštaraka*).[80] As already

---

73 For a description of καθόλου as that which is naturally such as to be predicated (κατηγορεῖσθαι) of many, cf. *De int.* 7, 17a39f.; for a description of κοινός as that which applies (ὑπάρχει) to many, cf. *Rhet.* II.22, 1396b12–20; cf. also *Met.* Z.13, 1038b9–12; *Phys.* III.1, 200b20–25.

74 cf. Sirkel, "Alexander of Aphrodisias's Account of Universals," esp. 301–304, discussing Alexander's *Quaestiones*, q. I.11, calling it "probably the most important and influential text on universals by Alexander." Earlier, Pines stated that, "*to koinon* is often regarded as including (and sometimes perhaps as a near-equivalent of) *to katholou*. However ... sometimes at least a certain difference is indicated between *to koinon* and *to katholou*" insofar as the former "may exist in one thing only," whereas the latter "must be predicated of more than one thing" ("A New Fragment of Xenocrates," 29).

75 Sorabji, *The Philosophy of the Commentators*, vol. III, ch. 5a, e.

76 q.v. fn. 34 above, 53.

77 cf. M. Rashed, "Ibn ʿAdī et Avicenne," translating and examining Ibn ʿAdī's *Maqāla fī tabyīn wuǧūd al-umūr al-ʿāmmiyya*.

78 cf. Philoponus, *In Phys.*, 122.18, 122.20; other instances include 122.1, 125.13, 126.24, 127.22 for κοινός and 7.21, 7.32, 14.17, 91.19 for καθολικός.

79 cf. Bett's comment in Sextus Empiricus, *Adversus ethicos*, 54f.

80 *Phys.* I.7, 189b30–32, tr. by Hardie/Gaye, modified; q.v. above, 56.

noted, this intention is reflected in Philoponus' statement that Aristotle's *Physics* is about what "all natural things [have] in common" (περὶ τῶν κοινῇ πᾶσι τοῖς φυσικοῖς πράγμασι παρακολουθούντων) and is, moreover, also present in al-Kindī's and al-Fārābī's descriptions of the *Physics* as a work concerned with "the things that are common to all natural things" (*al-umūr al-ʿāmma li-ǧamīʿ al-ṭabāʾiʿ*).[81] The same view is likewise found in Avicenna, who, in his own *Risāla fī aqsām al-ʿulūm al-ʿaqliyya*, uses the same formulation as al-Kindī and al-Fārābī when characterising the first part of natural philosophy:

> قسم به تُعرَف الأمور العامّة لجميع الطبيعيات مثل المادّة والصورة والحركة والطبيعة والإنسان بالنهاية وغير النهاية وتعلّق الحركات بالمحرّكات واثباتها الى محرّك أوّل واحد غير متحرّك وغير متناهى القوة لا جسم ولا فى جسم ويشتمل عليه كتاب الكيان.
>
> [The] part through which the things that are common to all natural things (*al-umūr al-ʿāmma li-ǧamīʿ al-ṭabīʿīyāt*) are known – such as matter, form, motion, nature, the acquaintance with the infinite and the finite, the dependence of motions upon movers and their bearing witness to a single first mover which is unmoved, of infinite power, and neither a body nor in a body – is what the *Physics* (*Kitāb al-Kiyān*) contains. (*Risāla fī aqsām al-ʿulūm al-ʿaqliyya*, 108.13–110.6)

Fifth, despite our lack of information about which Arabic translations of the *Physics* Avicenna used and knew and that, accordingly, almost nothing can be said for certain, it is by no means unlikely, given the terminology employed in late antiquity and in the writings of early Arabic philosophers such as Ibn ʿAdī, that here Avicenna relies on a translation which rendered καθόλου not with what was to become the standard term (*al-kullī*), but with another viable expression such as *al-ʿāmm* ("common" in the sense of "general") or *al-muštarak* ("common" in the sense of "shared").[82] This assumption is particularly justified in light of the apparent difficulties with which any interpreter of *Physics* I.1 is immediately confronted. The Arabic translation of Isḥāq ibn Ḥunayn (d. 298/910–11) is an obvious example, for he, too, refrained from using cognates of *al-kullī* in his version and rendered τῶν καθόλου as *al-umūr al-muǧmala* ("the compounded things"), instead. As already mentioned before, there are good reasons for believing that Avicenna knew several translations of the *Physics*.[83]

Finally, Avicenna's own words indicate that he took the common (*al-ʿāmm*) to be equivalent to the universal (*al-kullī*). In his *al-Ilāhiyyāt*, Avicenna employs *al-umūr al-ʿāmma* ("the common things") as an expression for "universals."[84] Beyond that, he writes in *al-Burhān* I.11:

---

81 q.v. above, 61f.

82 On these two terms, q.v. below, 154ff.; cf. also Pines, "A New Fragment of Xenocrates," 29.

83 q.v. above, 37ff.

84 cf. the discussion in, and the chapter heading of, *al-Ilāhiyyāt* V.1; cf. also Eichner, "al-Amidi and Fakhr al-Din al-Rāzi," fn. 26, 20; cf. generally, Eichner's remarks about the concept of *al-umūr al-ʿāmma* in *The Post-Avicennian Philosophical Tradition and Islamic Orthodoxy*.

وأمّا إذا رُتّبت الكلّيات النوعية بأزاء الكلّيات الجنسية كانت الكلّيات الجنسية أقدم بالطبع وليست أعرف عند الطبيعة وكانت الكلّيات الجنسية أيضاً أقدم وأعرف عند عقولنا.

When the specific universals (*al-kulliyyāt al-naw'iyya*) are ordered relatively to generic universals (*al-kulliyyāt al-ǧinsiyya*), the generic universals will be naturally prior (*aqdam bi-l-ṭab'*) but not better known by nature (*a'raf 'inda l-ṭabī'a*), but they will be both prior and better known to our intellects. (*aqdam wa-a'raf 'inda 'uqūlinā*). (*al-Burhān* I.11, 107.1f.)[85]

This description of "generic universals" (*al-kulliyyāt al-ǧinsiyya*) resembles Avicenna's description of "the common things" (*al-umūr al-'āmma*) in *al-Samā' al-ṭabī'ī* I.1:

فيجب أن نبتدئ في التعليم من المبادئ التي للأمور العامّة إذ الأمور العامّة أعرف عند عقولنا وإن لم تكن أعرف عند الطبيعة.

It is, thus, necessary that we begin in the teaching from the principles which belong to common things, since common things (*al-umūr al-'āmma*) are better known to our intellects (*a'raf 'inda 'uqūlinā*), even if they are not better known by nature (*a'raf 'inda l-ṭabī'a*). (*al-Samā' al-ṭabī'ī* I.1, §4, 8.13f., tr. by McGinnis, modified)

What these passages suggest is that the Arabic terms which have been used to render the meanings of such Greek expressions as καθόλου, καθολικός, and κοινός have come to converge just as much as the original Greek terminology had done in the writings of the late ancient commentary tradition, such that for Avicenna himself, the terms *'āmm* and *kullī* have likewise become, to a certain extent, equivalent to each other.

What is more, one might speculate that Avicenna's statement that "common things are better known to our intellects" stems directly from one of the Arabic translations of Aristotle's *Physics* Avicenna had at his disposal. In *Physics* I.5 we read:

τὸ μὲν γὰρ καθόλου κατὰ τὸν λόγον γνώριμον, τὸ δὲ καθ' ἕκαστον κατὰ τὴν αἴσθησιν· ὁ μὲν γὰρ λόγος τοῦ καθόλου, ἡ δ' αἴσθησις τοῦ κατὰ μέρος.

فإنّ الكلّي أعرف عند الفهم والجزئي أعرف عند الحسّ وذلك أنّ الفهم هو للكلّي فأمّا الحسّ فهو للجزئي.

For the universal is known according to λόγος, while the particular [is known] according to sensation, because λόγος is of the universal and sensation is of the particular. (*Phys.* I.5, 189a5-8)[86]

85 cf. *al-Samā' al-ṭabī'ī* I.1, §6, 9.7–14; I.1, §16, 12.15f.; cf. also *Met.* A.2, 982a19–982b10, esp. 982a23–25, 982b2; q.v. also the following footnote.

86 cf. *Met.* Δ.11, 1018b32–34. Aristotle often differentiates between two senses of γνώριμον and πρότερον, and contrasts "to us" (πρὸς ἡμᾶς) or "to sensation" (κατὰ τὴν αἴσθησιν) with "in nature" (τῇ φύσει), "as such" (ἁπλῶς), or "in account" (κατὰ τὸν λόγον). Avicenna, however, differentiates *three* aspects in *al-Burhān* I.11 and in *al-Samā' al-ṭabī'ī* I.1. He complements the twofold Aristotelian distinction of what is better known "to sensation" or "to us" (*'indanā*) and "to nature" (*'inda l-ṭabī'a*) with the further aspect of what is better known "to our intellects" (*'inda 'uqūlinā*): "common things (*al-umūr al-'āmma*) are better known to the intellect (*'inda l-'aql*) ... specific things (*al-umūr al-naw'iyya*) are better known by nature (*'inda l-ṭabī'a*) ... if we include the internal sensitive faculty, only then in that case the individuals (*al-šaḫsiyyāt*) are better known to us (*'indanā*) than universals (*al-kulliyyāt*)" (*al-Samā' al-ṭabī'ī* I.1, §6, 9.8–12, tr. by McGinnis, modified). Avicenna's addition may not be entirely

The relevance of this passage relies on our understanding of κατὰ τὸν λόγον and λόγος. As can be seen in the Arabic quotation, Isḥāq ibn Ḥunayn translated both through the term *fahm*, which means "understanding" or "scientific understanding," so that his Arabic translation reads in English:

> For the universal is better known to the understanding and the particular is better known to sensation, because understanding is of the universal and as to sensation, it is of the particular.

It is attested that Qusṭā ibn Lūqā al-Baʿlabakkī (d. 300/912), for example, sometimes translated λόγος by *ʿaql*, the Arabic word for "intellect."[87] If Qusṭā also translated καθόλου as *ʿāmm* or *muštarak*, as he did translate καθολικός, and if Avicenna used his *Physics* translation, we directly get from Aristotle the statement that "what is common is better known by the intellect" – the statement we read in *al-Samāʿ al-ṭabīʿī* I.1, §4, 8.13.[88] Regardless of whether or not Avicenna is here relying on Qusṭā's translation of the *Physics*, it is by no means an odd choice to translate λόγος by *ʿaql* nor to render καθόλου by *ʿāmm* – at least no less odd than Isḥāq ibn Ḥunayn's *fahm* for the former and *al-umūr al-muǧmala* for the latter. In fact, *ʿāmm* has been used in that sense for καθόλου in the translation of the *De caelo*, by Yaḥyā ibn al-Biṭrīq (d. ~ 215/830), as well as in the translation of the *Meteorologica* and the *De generatione animalium*, erroneously attributed to Yaḥyā ibn al-Biṭrīq. At any rate, in Greek we could read λόγος, like *ʿaql* in Arabic, along the lines of "understanding," "reason," or "intellect," and καθόλου, like *ʿāmm*, in terms of "common" or "general." Incidentally, this is exactly the reading Simplicius offered in his commentary on the *Physics*.[89]

In light of all this evidence, it emerges that Avicenna took Aristotle's τῶν καθόλου, i.e., whatever word or phrase he may have read in the Arabic translations of the *Physics*, more in terms of its usual meaning as "universals" which are better known to our intellects and most commonly applicable to natural things. Conversely, the individuals are better known to sensation and the specific things are better known to nature, as is asserted in *al-Samāʿ al-ṭabīʿī* I.1, §6, 9.7–14. Since Avicenna understands the Aristotelian *dictum* more literally as a recommendation to proceed "from the universals to the particulars," his position is much closer to the second of the two above-outlined

---

unprecedented. In *Metaphysics* A.2, Aristotle describes that what is most universal as most difficult to grasp, because it is furthest away from sensation, but adds a few lines later that the principles and causes (which presumably are most universal) are to the highest degree knowable (μάλιστα δ' ἐπιστητὰ τὰ πρῶτα καὶ τὰ αἴτια; *Met.* A.2, 982a23–25 and 982b2). The same idea seems to be expressed in *Topics* VI.4, 141b28–34, and also in *Posterior Analytics* I.2, 72a25–32. Thus, we find in Aristotle something very close to the Avicennian distinction between what is better known by our sensation and what is better known to our intellect. In this regard, cf. also the influential passage of *Metaphysics* α.1, 993b9–11.

87 cf. Daiber's glossary in Aetius Arabus, *Die Vorsokratiker in arabischer Überlieferung*, esp. #2223, 611.

88 cf. Qusṭā's translation of καθολικός as *ʿāmm* and *muštarak* in Ps.-Plutarchus, *Placita Philosophorum*, 428a.12, Arabic translation in Aetius Arabus, *Die Vorsokratiker in arabischer Überlieferung*, 71.14.

89 cf. Simplicius, *In Phys.*, 188.17–21, 190.9–12.

interpretations that Philoponus offered in his commentary, because the "universals" signify common matters, rather than jumbled-up compounds. Thus, for Avicenna, too, the *Physics* is a work about what is common to all natural things and, therefore, should naturally precede all other works on natural philosophy, as these have more particular concerns. However, there is also a crucial difference to that second interpretation, as my present analysis of Avicenna's method in *al-Samāʿ al-ṭabīʿī* also bears on the observation that Avicenna neither uses nor mentions methodic experience or any other method of scientific inquiry in his *al-Samāʿ al-ṭabīʿī*. In fact, once we have realised that Avicenna takes Aristotle's *dictum* literally, it becomes clear why Avicenna does not *need* to mention such methods of inquiry, for in his *al-Samāʿ al-ṭabīʿī* he is not engaged in research and inquiry at all, instead being concerned with another form of knowledge acquisition: that which is achieved through teaching and learning. Consequently, Avicenna does not present a *method of inquiry* – not even one that follows the *way of procedure* – as Aristotle and his Greek commentators, especially Philoponus, had done. Instead, Avicenna adopts a *mode of instruction*.

It is instruction and teaching which proceeds from the common and generic universals to the particulars, because what is common is better known to our intellects.[90] That is to say that in physics, *intellectual* comprehension begins with the universals and proceeds to the particulars. The validity of this claim extends even beyond the physical, for Avicenna asserts in *al-Ilāhiyyāt* I.5:

وأولى الأشياء بأن تكون متصوّرة لأنفسها الأشياء العامّة للأمور كلّها كالموجود والشيء والواحد وغيره. ولهذا ليس يمكن أن يبيَّن شيء منها ببيان لا دور فيه البتّة أو ببيان شيء أعرف منها.

> The things which deserve it most to be conceptualised through themselves are the things common to all things (*al-ašyāʾ al-ʿāmma li-l-umūr kullihā*), such as "existent," "thing," "one,"[91] and others. Because of this, it is not possible that any of these be proven by a proof without any circular [reasoning] in it at all or by a proof of something that is better known (*aʿraf*) than them. (*al-Ilāhiyyāt* I.5, §5, 30.3–5)

Accordingly, Avicenna also begins his metaphysical discourse in *al-Ilāhiyyāt* by stating the most common and universal principles and intends to develop the science on their basis in a demonstrative and deductive, i.e., in an apodictic, manner.[92] With regard to the subject-matter of metaphysics, viz., "the existent insofar as it is an existent" (*al-mawǧūd bi-mā huwa mawǧūd*), the most common concepts are, as Avicenna states in the

90 Avicenna further notes that "all men are as good as alike in knowing the common and generic natures (*al-ṭabāʾiʿ al-ʿāmma wa-l-ǧinsiyya*), and are distinguished only insofar as some know and reach the specific things and apply themselves to making differentiations, while others stop at the generic things" (*al-Samāʿ al-ṭabīʿī* I.1, §5, 9.3–5, tr. by McGinnis, modified).

91 Following Bertolacci's suggestion to correct *wa-l-šayʾ al-wāḥid* to *wa-l-šayʾ wa-l-wāḥid* (*The Reception of Aristotle's* Metaphysics *in Avicenna's* Kitāb al-Šifāʾ, 492).

92 cf. Bertolacci, *The Reception of Aristotle's* Metaphysics *in Avicenna's* Kitāb al-Šifāʾ, ch. 6; Gutas, *Avicenna and the Aristotelian Tradition*, 351–358.

above quote, "'existence,' 'thing,' 'one,' and others." Notions such as these, variously enumerated by Avicenna throughout his *al-Ilāhiyyāt*, are the proper starting points for the science of metaphysics precisely because they are both basic, fundamental or even transcendental, and more accessible and better known to the human intellect.[93] In physics, now, we are likewise urged to begin with the common principles, albeit, of course, not with those pertaining to "the existent insofar as it is an existent," which is the subject-matter of metaphysics, but with those that apply to "the sensible body insofar as it is subject to change," i.e., to the subject-matter of physics.[94]

Moreover, within each science, we pursue knowledge about essences by composing definitions from a common and generic universal that is joined by a specific difference. A definition, being the answer to the question "What is that thing?," ideally provides us with an understanding of that thing's essence. So, when we acquire knowledge through definitions, we naturally proceed from the more common to the more specific. Avicenna follows this schema – and this schema requires that we begin with whatever is most common and universal:

> فإنّ وجه التعلّم والتعليم العقلي فيها أن يُبتدَأ ممّا هو أعمّ ويُسلَك إلى ما هو أخصّ لأنك تعلم أنّ الجنس جزء حدّ النوع فتعرّف الجنس يجب أن يكون أقدم من تعرّف النوع لأنّ المعرفة بجزء الحدّ قبل المعرفة بالحدّ وتصوّره قبل الوقوف على المحدود ... فإذا كان كذلك فالمبادئ التي للأمور العامّة يجب أن تعرف أولاً حتّى تعرف الأمور العامّة والأمور العامّة يجب أن تعرف أولاّ حتّى تعرف الأمور الخاصّة.
>
> So, indeed, the direction of intellectual learning and teaching (*al-taʿallum wa-l-taʿlīm al-ʿaqlī*) about them [sc. natural things] is to start[95] from what is more common (*aʿamm*) and to proceed[96] to what is more specific (*aḫaṣṣ*), because you know that the genus is a part of the definition of the species (*ḥadd al-nawʿ*), and so the grasp (*taʿarruf*) of the genus is necessarily prior (*yağibu an yakuna aqdam*) to the grasp of the species, because the knowledge of a part of the definition precedes the knowledge of the definition and its conceptualisation precedes the understanding of what is defined ... If it is like this, then it is necessary that you come to know, first, the principles which belong to the common things, so that you come to know the common things, and it is necessary that you come to know the common things, first, so that you come to know the specific things. (*al-Samāʿ al-ṭabīʿī* I.1, §3, 8.8–12, tr. by McGinnis, modified)[97]

Thus, the key terms for understanding Avicenna's method and the first chapter of *al-Samāʿ al-ṭabīʿī* are *taʿlīm* ("teaching") and *taʿallum* ("learning") – and not methodic

93 For common notions and transcendentals in Avicenna, cf. Koutzarova, *Das Transzendentale bei Ibn Sīnā*; cf. also Eichner, "Dissolving the Unity of Metaphysics," 159f.

94 *al-Samāʿ al-ṭabīʿī* I.1, §1, 7.7f., tr. by McGinnis.

95 As in the first quotation of this passage above, 65, I prefer reading *yubtadaʾa* with Mss. Leiden or. 4 and or. 84 as well as Zāyid for *yubtadiʾa* in McGinnis and Āl Yāsīn.

96 Likewise, I prefer reading *yuslaka* with Mss. Leiden or. 4 and or. 84 for *nasluka* in Zāyid and *tasluka* in McGinnis and Āl Yāsīn.

97 cf. *al-Burhān* II.2, 125.9–12; *al-Ḥikma al-mašriqiyya* III, 3.3–8; cf. also *Top.* VI.4, 141b28–34; *An. post.* I.2, 72a25–32; *Met.* A.2, 982a23–25, 982b2; q.v. further fn. 86 above, 68f.

experience (*taǧriba*) or induction (*istiqrā'*). This is nowhere as apparent and explicit as in the final paragraph of the first chapter, in which Avicenna confirms once more that what is common and simple is better known to the intellect and states that, likewise, "learning begins from what is common and simple, and from there brings forth knowledge of the specific and composed things."[98]

That is to say, Avicenna's *al-Samā' al-ṭabī'ī* is no book of research and inquiry but a book of teaching and learning; it is a book which Avicenna designed and composed for the education and learning of his disciples and followers, and a book in which Avicenna followed the structure of intellectual understanding and, thus, naturally decided to begin with the common and universal generalities before getting into the intricate and complex issues with which the advanced student will be able to occupy himself only after having managed the basics.[99]

The Teaching and Learning of Avicenna's Philosophy

The preface of Avicenna's *al-Madḫal* serves as the general introduction of the whole *al-Šifā'*. This preface has been written by Avicenna's closest disciple, Abū 'Ubayd al-Ǧūzǧānī (d. ~ 462/1070).[100] In it, al-Ǧūzǧānī reports on the circumstances in which *al-Šifā'* has been composed:

> وإذا دعوته إلى التصانيف الكبار وإلى الشروح أحال على ما عمله من الشروح وصنفه من الكتب في بلاده وقد كان بلغني تفرّقها وتشتّتها وضنّ من يملك نسخة منها بها ... وكان قد وهن الرجاء أيضاً في تحصيل تصانيفه الفائتة فالتمسنا منه إعادتها فقال: أمّا الاشتغال بالألفاظ وشرحها فأمر لا يسعه وقتي ولا تنشط له نفسي فإن قنعتم بما يتيسّر لي من عندي عملت لكم تصنيفاً جامعاً على الترتيب الذي يتّفق لي. فبذلنا له منا الرضا به وحرصنا على أن يقع منه الابتداء بالطبيعيات.
>
> When I [sc. al-Ǧūzǧānī] appealed to him [sc. Avicenna] to compose long works and commentaries, he referred to the commentaries he had written and books he had composed in his native country. I had heard, however, that these were widely dispersed and that people who owned a copy of them

98 *al-Samā' al-ṭabī'ī* I.1, §16, 12.17.

99 Clearly, by "basics," I do not mean simple preliminary notions that are easy to comprehend even for beginners or those equipped with only mediocre intellectual capacities. Avicenna would not have had any interest in teaching such students. By "basics" I mean the fundamentals or cornerstones and elements, i.e., the *mabādi'* ("principles") and *uṣūl* ("roots"). However, it is not necessary that these principles are fully demonstrated and established before an understanding of what follows from them is possible. Avicenna repeatedly remarks – and, in fact, already did so at the very beginning of chapter I.1 – that in *al-Samā' al-ṭabī'ī*, the principles are merely postulated and, thus, have to be accepted by the natural philosopher. They will, however, be proven in metaphysics, i.e., in the course of his *al-Ilāhiyyāt*. On all this, cf. *al-Burhān* I.12, 114.4–11; II.6, 155.5–7; II.7, 165.11–13; *al-Naǧāt* I.128, 138.5–13; II.1, 189.13–190.8; *'Uyūn al-ḥikma* II.2, 17.12–15; *Dānešnāme-ye 'Alā'ī* II.2, 8.7; III.1, 2.10; *al-Ḥikma al-mašriqiyya* III, 2.4f., 2.21–3.8; *al-Išārāt wa-l-tanbīhāt* I.9.3, 83.2–9. This feature of Avicenna's understanding of science as a universal and interdisciplinary endeavour is investigated in detail below, 81ff.

100 On al-Ǧūzǧānī, cf. Wisnovsky, "Jowzjāni (Juzjāni), Abu 'Obayd 'Abd-al-Wāḥed b. Moḥammad."

withheld them [from others] ... In the meantime, the hope of ever obtaining his lost works having dimmed, we asked him to rewrite them and he said: "I have neither the time nor the inclination to occupy myself with close textual analysis and commentary. But if you would be content with whatever I have readily in mind [which I have thought] on my own (*bi-mā yatayassaru lī min ʿindī*), then I could write for you a comprehensive work arranged in the order which will occur to me." We readily offered our consent to this and urged that he start with the [works on] natural philosophy. (*al-Madḫal*, preface, 2.2–14, tr. by Gutas, modified)[101]

In the biography, which al-Ǧūzǧānī wrote shortly after Avicenna had died, the same story is retold only slightly differently:

ثمّ سألته أنا شرح كتب أرسطو فذكر أنّه لا فراغ له إلى ذلك في ذلك الوقت. ولكن إن رضيت منّي بتصنيف كتاب أورد فيه ما صحّ عندي من هذه العلوم بلا مناظرة مع المخالفين ولا اشتغال بالردّ عليهم فعلت ذلك. فرضيت به فابتدأ بالطبيعيات من كتاب سمّاه كتاب الشفاء.

Then I [sc. al-Ǧūzǧānī] asked him [sc. Avicenna] myself to comment on the books of Aristotle, but he brought up that he had no leisure for this at that time. "But if you would like me to compose a book in which I will set forth what, in my opinion, is sound of these [philosophical] sciences, without debating with those who disagree or occupying myself with their refutation, then I will do that." I was pleased with this, and so he began with the [works on] natural philosophy of a book which he called *al-Šifāʾ*. (Avicenna and al-Ǧūzǧānī, *Sīrat al-šayḫ al-raʾīs*, 54.1–5, tr. by Gutas, modified)[102]

It emerges from these testimonies, provided that they are reliable, that Avicenna wrote *al-Šifāʾ* upon request of his disciples and that he did so, because they wanted, as al-Ǧūzǧānī phrased it elsewhere, "to acquire true knowledge" (*iqtibās al-maʿārif al-ḥaqīqiyya*), i.e., they wanted to learn from their master and, thus, asked for commentaries, since commentaries had been the central medium of academic learning and teaching for centuries.[103] However, Avicenna is reported to have had no interest at all in writing works in the style his disciples requested, as he already had written some commentaries, which got lost, so that he now eschewed rewriting them.[104] This claim finds support in the second introduction to *al-Šifāʾ*, this time written by Avicenna:

فإنّ غرضنا في هذا الكتاب ... أن نودعه لباب ما تحقّقناه من الأصول في العلوم الفلسفية المنسوبة إلى الأقدمين المبنية على النظر المرتّب المحقّق والأصول المستنبطة بالأفهام المتعاونة على إدراك الحق المجتهد فيه زماناً طويلاً ...

101 Gutas, *Avicenna and the Aristotelian Tradition*, 31f.; cf. 103f.

102 Gutas, *Avicenna and the Aristotelian Tradition*, 103f.

103 *al-Madḫal*, preface, 1.8f., tr. by Gutas, *Avicenna and the Aristotelian Tradition*, 29; cf. also Endreß, "Reading Avicenna in the Madrasa."

104 Additionally, Gutas argues that Avicenna altogether "wished to abandon the commentary format as it was employed, for the works of Aristotle at least, from the time of Alexander to his own times. Instead he proposed to write a running exposition of the philosophical sciences as reconstructed according to his own opinion" (*Avicenna and the Aristotelian Tradition*, 104); cf. *Avicenna and the Aristotelian Tradition*, 252–255; cf. also Avicenna's remarks in *al-Samāʿ al-ṭabīʿī*, preface, §3, 4.3–9.

> وهذا الكتاب وإن كان صغير الحجم فهو كثير العلم ويكاد لايفوت متأمّله ومتدبّره أكثر الصناعة إلى زيادات لم تجرّ العادة بسماعها من كتب أخرى.
>
> Our purpose in this book [sc. *al-Šifāʾ*] ... is that we set down in it the gist of what we have ascertained in terms of the principles contained in the philosophical sciences attributed to the ancients based on methodical and verified theoretical analysis as well as the principles discovered by [a series of] acts of comprehension cooperating in the attainment of truth which was diligently pursued for a long time ... This book, though small in volume, contains much of knowledge. The person who studies it attentively and reflects on it will hardly fail to acquire most of the [philosophical] discipline, including the additions which were customarily omitted from other books. (*al-Madḫal* I.1, 9.7–10, 11.14–16, tr. by Gutas, modified)[105]

We are justified in assuming that *al-Samāʿ al-ṭabīʿī* was the first of the books Avicenna wrote and completed for his *al-Šifāʾ*, which he intended to be a collection of works from the attentive study of which his disciples, on whose request he composed it, could "acquire most of the philosophical discipline" and fulfil their desire for knowledge through intellectual learning and teaching.[106] In addition, he thought it both suitable and reasonable to follow the Aristotelian *dictum* of *Physics* I.1 and to proceed "from the

---

105 Gutas, *Avicenna and the Aristotelian Tradition*, 42, 46.

106 cf. Gutas' remarks on chronology in *Avicenna and the Aristotelian Tradition*, 106–109. It should not be forgotten in this regard that the title of Avicenna's *al-Šifāʾ* translates into English as *The Book of the Cure* – the "cure" in question is nothing other than the soul's cure from ignorance. On this basis, Koutzarova described *al-Šifāʾ* as "following the aspiration to provide an indispensable and complete educational programme for everyone" ("Wissenschaft als 'Genesung,'" 194: "Das 'Buch der Genesung' erhebt somit den Anspruch, unentbehrliches und vollständiges Bildungsprogramm für alle zu sein"); cf. also the recent reassessment of the traditional translations of the title of Avicenna's work by Saliba, arguing that *šifāʾ* should finally come to be understood in its metaphorical sense as "'finding one's fulfillment' or 'quenching one's thirst' in the matter of philosophy" ("Avicenna's *Shifāʾ (Sufficientia)*," 430). Other than that, Reisman emphasised that both Avicenna's autobiography and the biography written by his disciple al-Ǧūzǧānī "must be approached as tendentious literary documents" ("The Life and Times of Avicenna," 7). It would, thus, be inadvisable to accept their contents without reserve. Nonetheless, Reisman examined and verified certain aspects of these testimonies; cf. also Gutas' remarks on the composition of *al-Šifāʾ* in *Avicenna and the Aristotelian Tradition*, 106–109. What is more, Reisman distinguished several styles of writing within Avicenna's works. These styles were either determined by the events of his life and his general personal situation or consciously chosen by Avicenna for certain purposes and adjusted to certain audiences. Apart from the styles conditioned, for example, by his "final years of stability," his "evolving views of Aristotelianism," and the "rivalry and refutation" he had to face, Reisman stressed that Avicenna often wrote "for pupils, with an explicitly pedagogical purpose." While Avicenna frequently engaged in debates about the content of his *al-Šifāʾ*, it seems that this work as a whole – and most clearly during the initial stages of composition, i.e., in such parts written as early as *al-Samāʿ al-ṭabīʿī* – was intended to serve a pedagogical purpose and to initiate those discussions precisely by virtue of its pedagogical character. In turn, these discussions, partly preserved in his *al-Mubāḥaṯāt*, led to frequent revisions of *al-Šifāʾ*. Reisman also claimed that Avicenna's *al-Išārāt wa-l-tanbīhāt* must be regarded as a pedagogical work, as "Avicenna imposed the constraint that it could be studied only with him" ("The Life and Times of Avicenna," 7, 10–14); cf. Gutas, *Avicenna and the Aristotelian Tradition*, 169–225.

universals to the particulars." Thus, Avicenna, first, explains what the universals are and states that they are shared by all or most natural things. Thereupon, he begins to unpack the philosophical discipline of physics by delving deeper into concomitants and particular aspects of the very same natural objects to which the principles apply. His work thereby exhibits a *mode of instruction* and not a *method of inquiry*. Avicenna's approach to physics in *al-Samāʿ al-ṭabīʿī* is, therefore, profoundly different from Philoponus' and, in fact, from all Peripatetic interpretations of *Physics* I.1.

So, in *al-Samāʿ al-ṭabīʿī*, Avicenna presents himself more as teacher than as a student of nature or a scientist who seeks knowledge through posing ἀπορίαι and discussing ἔνδοξα. He rather seems to have set everything, or at least most things, "readily in his mind," so that he can now develop and explain – by way of instruction and teaching – the Aristotelian philosophical tradition as he himself deemed most proper.[107] Indeed, Avicenna does not have to acquire knowledge or to *inquire* into nature or into the true reading of Aristotle and his commentators anymore nor does he have to put forth his plan of *procedure*, which he then would mean to follow during his research. Rather, having accomplished and mastered the philosophical sciences already, he is now in a position to confine himself to preparing a proper presentation and delivering an adequate teaching of the knowledge that he has acquired beforehand.[108] This presentation proceeds along the lines of the literal meaning of Aristotle's remarks in *Physics* I.1 from the universals to the particulars.

However, there is still more to it. In the *Posterior Analytics*, Aristotle formulated the rigorous standards any truly demonstrative exposition of the truths of a science must conform to as follows:

> εἰ τοίνυν ἐστὶ τὸ ἐπίστασθαι οἷον ἔθεμεν, ἀνάγκη καὶ τὴν ἀποδεικτικὴν ἐπιστήμην ἐξ ἀληθῶν τ' εἶναι καὶ πρώτων καὶ ἀμέσων καὶ γνωριμωτέρων ἀληθῶν τ' εἶναι καὶ πρώτων καὶ ἀμέσων καὶ γνωριμωτέρων καὶ προτέρων καὶ αἰτίων τοῦ συμπεράσματος· οὕτω γὰρ ἔσονται καὶ αἱ ἀρχαὶ οἰκεῖαι τοῦ δεικνυμένου. συλλογισμὸς μὲν γὰρ ἔσται καὶ ἄνευ τούτων, ἀπόδειξις δ' οὐκ ἔσται· οὐ γὰρ ποιήσει ἐπιστήμην.
>
> وإن كان معنى أن يعلم هو على ما وضعناه فقد يلزم ضرورةً أن يكون العلم البرهاني من قضايا صادقة وأوائل غير ذات وسط وأن يكون أعرف من النتيجة وأن يكون أكثر تقدّماً منها وأن يكون عللها. وذلك أنّه بهذا النحو تكون مبادئ مناسبة أيضاً للأمر الذي يتبيّن. فإنّ القياس قد يكون من غير هذه أيضاً. وأمّا البرهان فلا يكون إذ لا يحدث علماً.

107 *al-Madḫal*, preface, 2.12, tr. by Gutas, *Avicenna and the Aristotelian Tradition*, 32; cf. also 103; cf. further *Metaphysics* A.2, 982a12–14, where Aristotle states that the one "who is more exact and more capable of teaching the causes (διδασκαλικώτερον τῶν αἰτιῶν) is wiser (σοφώτερον) in every branch of knowledge" (tr. by Ross). We lack an Arabic translation of the first half of *Metaphysics* A. Yet, as Bertolacci has shown, Avicenna certainly knew it; cf. Bertolacci, *The Reception of Aristotle's* Metaphysics *in Avicenna's* Kitāb al-Šifāʾ, fn. 49, 18, and generally 335–338.

108 For Avicenna having "mastered" (*ẓafirtu*) all the philosophical sciences, cf. Avicenna and al-Ǧūzǧānī, *Sīrat al-šayḫ al-raʾīs*, 36.6–8.

> If to understand something (τὸ ἐπίστασθαι, *ma'nan an ya'lamu*) is as what we have posited it to be, then demonstrative understanding in particular must proceed from items which are true (ἀληθῶν, *ṣādiqa*) and primitive (πρώτων, *awā'il*) and immediate (ἀμέσων, *ġayr ḏāt wasaṭ*) and more familiar than (γνωριμωτέρων, *a'raf*) and prior to (προτέρων, *akṯar taqadduman*) and explanatory of (αἰτίων, *'ilalahā*) the conclusions. (In this way the principles (αἱ αρχαί, *al-mabādi'*) will also be appropriate to what is being proved.) There can be a deduction (συλλογισμός, *al-qiyās*) even if these conditions are not met, but there cannot be a demonstration (ἀπόδειξις, *al-burhān*) – for it will not bring about understanding (ἐπιστήμην, *'ilman*). (*An. post.* I.2, 71b19–24, tr. by Barnes)

Avicenna clearly agrees with these conditions.[109] In addition, Aristotle described the principles of a demonstrative science, i.e., "the so-called common axioms," as "the primitives (πρώτων, *al-awā'il*) from which its demonstrations proceed."[110] Irrespective of whether or not this description, and its context, is representative of Aristotle's general view on principles, it very adequately captures how Avicenna conceived of principles.[111] This is clear from the following passage of Avicenna's *al-Burhān*:

والمبادئ هي المقدّمات التي منها تبرهن تلك الصناعة.

> Principles are the premisses from which that discipline is demonstrated.[112] (*al-Burhān* II.6, 155.5)

---

109 cf. Adamson, "On Knowledge of Particulars," 281; McGinnis, "Avicenna's Naturalized Epistemology," 131f.; cf. also *al-Naǧāt* I.120, 130.9–131.2.

110 *An. post.* I.10, 76b14f., tr. by Barnes; cf. *An. post.* I.7, 75a39–b2; I.11, 77a26–28; *Eth. Nic.* VI.3, 1139b26–31; for Aristotle's general description of principles, cf. *Met.* Δ.1.

111 *Posterior Analytics* I.10, in which Aristotle clarifies the notion of ἀρχαί and their relation to the sciences and especially to demonstrative sciences (ἀποδεικτικαὶ ἐπιστῆμαι), is exceptionally important and obscure. Let me just briefly highlight one aspect in Aristotle and mention its reverberation in Avicenna. In this chapter, Aristotle, *first*, distinguished between principles which are common (κοινά) to all sciences and principles which are proper (ἴδια) to individual sciences and, *then*, explained that demonstrative sciences employ common axioms, i.e., principles, in their demonstrations. It is not entirely clear how these two statements relate to each other, whether they are indeed related, and precisely which type of principles can be employed in the demonstrations of a (particular) science. (On all these issues, cf. Barnes' and Detel's commentaries on *Posterior Analytics* I.10.) Generally, however, Aristotle subscribes to the claim that demonstrations proceed from principles (ἐξ ὧν, *minhā*). What is important, now, is that we find this basic claim taking a more elevated position in Avicenna, as he reverses Aristotle's order of exposition from *Posterior Analytics* I.10 in his *al-Burhān* II.6. That is to say, Avicenna, *first*, states that generally "principles are the premisses from which that discipline is demonstrated" and only, *then*, divides these principles into principles which belong to all sciences and principles that belong to particular sciences. With this rearrangement, Avicenna emphasises the general applicability of what has now become the first claim, instead of burying it in the midst of an already complex and unclear context, as in the passage from Aristotle's *Posterior Analytics* I.10. While in the case of Aristotle, the claim that demonstrations proceed from "the so-called common axioms, i.e. the primitives" in isolation from its context provides only an abridged and incomplete – or at worst: distorted – picture of *Aristotle's* intentions, it, nonetheless, faithfully represents how *Avicenna* conceived of principles and how he understood *Posterior Analytics* I.10.

112 Reading *tabarhana* for *tubarhanu* with 'Afīfī and *tubarhinu* in Badawī. 'Afīfī's reading, followed by Eichner, results in the same translation, whereas Bertolacci, following Badawī, translates that

Thus, when Avicenna voices his intention to proceed from the universals to the particulars, what he means by this is that he wants to proceed in a demonstrative manner, beginning with the universal principles of a given discipline from which the whole of "that discipline is demonstrated." In a particular science such as physics, it is the common principles proper to that science that ought to be chosen as the starting points for the demonstrations that lead towards knowledge. For Avicenna, there are two ways in which knowledge can be ascertained and verified.[113] The first of these ways is "through intuition" (*bi-l-ḥads*), i.e., through research and inquiry. Here, the above-mentioned concept of methodic experience (*taǧriba*) is central, as it is through an investigative engagement with the natural world that a student of nature prepares his intellectual capacities for the reception of intelligibles. This reception may require more or less inquiry, depending on the natural cleverness and acumen of the scientist, i.e., on his natural aptitude for "intuition," but ultimately – even though not necessarily – leads to the acquisition of middle terms which complete demonstrative syllogisms and indicate the cause of the phenomenon that was to be explained, thus bringing about knowledge and completing the premisses that can, henceforth, be employed as ascertained principles in other demonstrations.[114]

The second of these two ways is "through teaching" (*bi-l-taʿlīm*). Two points are crucial, now. On the one hand, it is important to realise that Avicenna immediately states that the principle of teaching is, again, intuition. In other words, any present instance of teaching depends on an earlier instance of intuition. So, in order for there to be anything to teach, there already has to have been research which led to the successful acquisition of universal knowledge through methodic experience and intuition, i.e., to the discovery of causally explanatory middle terms. Now, according to Avicenna, there have been two people in particular within the history of philosophy who were responsible for establishing and verifying through intuition the corpus of knowledge that can now be taught to others: these are Aristotle and Avicenna himself. The first founded and developed Aristotelian philosophy, which Avicenna describes as the "most worthy" school of philosophy; the second completed and perfected it.[115]

On the other hand, it is crucial to recognise that Avicenna's *al-Samāʿ al-ṭabīʿī* is no book of scientific inquiry. Accordingly, a reader of this work is not advised to carry out

---

"principles are the premises from which that discipline demonstrates" (*The Reception of Aristotle's* Metaphysics *in Avicenna's* Kitāb al-Šifāʾ, 134); cf. Eichner, "al-Fārābī and Ibn Sīnā on 'Universal Science' and the System of Sciences," 92.

113 cf. *al-Nafs* V.6, 219.20–24 ≈ *al-Naǧāt* II.6.5, 340.5–8. It should be noted that the section in which this passage can be found begins with an explicit reference to "learning" (*taʿallum*; *al-Nafs* V.6, 219.8 = *al-Naǧāt* II.6.5, 339.2).

114 For the notion of intuition and *ḥads*, q.v. above, 49f.; q.v. also the literature in fn. 22 above, 50.

115 This description of "Aristotelian philosophy" is found in the preface to the logic of Avicenna's *al-Ḥikma al-mašriqiyya*, published as *Manṭiq al-Mašriqiyyīn wa-l-Qaṣīda al-muzdawiǧa fī l-manṭiq*, 3.13; for Avicenna's conception of the history of philosophy and of his own position in it as well as his relation to Aristotle's philosophy, cf. Gutas, *Avicenna and the Aristotelian Tradition*, chs. 4, 7.

experiments or to investigate nature or to engage with the phenomena, regardless of whether these phenomena are the theories and ἔνδοξα of the Presocratics and other predecessors or the concrete occurrences in the natural world.[116] Still, this is precisely what Avicenna himself has done already. He has conducted his research, both by reading the books of the ancients, especially (even if not exclusively) Aristotle and his commentators, and through independent investigation of his own, so that, through his extraordinary intellectual capacities and his intuition, he was able to acquire genuine knowledge of the truth.

What comes next, now, is the communication of this knowledge, i.e., Avicenna's teaching of this knowledge to his disciples. His immediate students – and generally the readers of his *al-Samāʿ al-ṭabīʿī* – are lacking knowledge of the natural world which they, nonetheless, are hoping to acquire. This acquisition of knowledge will be accomplished through instruction and teaching by Avicenna, being someone who already is in possession of that knowledge which they are hoping to acquire. If Avicenna, now, begins his teaching with what is universal, he begins with those things that are common to all instances of the subject-matter of the science under discussion (in this case: physics), and these are the principles of that science. Besides fulfilling many of the above-quoted conditions stipulated in *Posterior Analytics* I.2, these principles provide the aforementioned further advantage of being better known to the intellect and, as a consequence, should be particularly intelligible and plausible to a student's mind. On this epistemic basis, Avicenna can, then, develop his lessons in the form of a demonstrative deduction. Even if, in reality, he abstains from unleashing a cascade of demonstrative syllogisms – say, for didactic reasons – his explanations may still unfurl demonstratively in a deductive direction. What I mean by "deductive direction," here, accords with Dimitri Gutas' description of Avicenna's method as a "demonstrative method [that] involves exposition by demonstrative proofs (*burhān*) and arguments; it follows, in its strictest form, detailed syllogistic reasoning, and in its loosest, clear and sequential presentation of thoughts and arguments."[117] That is to say, the mode of instruction, which Avicenna adopts in his *al-Šifāʾ*, and specifically in his *al-Samāʿ al-ṭabīʿī*, and which we find epitomised in the literal understanding of the Aristotelian *dictum* to proceed from the universals to the particulars, entails the demonstrative exposition of philosophy, and specifically of natural philosophy. This method, moreover, is the realisation of the ideal state of a fully developed, i.e., a perfected, philosophy within any nation, as it was described by al-Fārābī in the *Kitāb al-Ḥurūf*:

ثمّ يُتداوَل ذلك إلى أن يستقرّ الأمر على ما استقرّ عليه أيام أرسطوطاليس. فيتناهى النظر العلمي وتُميَّز الطرق كلّها
وتكمل الفلسفة النظرية والعامّية الكلّية ولا يبقى فيها موضع لفحص. فتصير صناعة تُتعلَّم وتُعلَّم فقط ويكون تعليمها

116 For the meaning of the "phenomena" in Aristotle's philosophy, cf. the famous paper by Owen, "Τιθέναι τὰ φαινόμενα."
117 Gutas, *Avicenna and the Aristotelian Tradition*, 351.

تعليماً خاصّاً وتعليماً مشتركاً للجميع فالتعليم الخاصّ هو بالطرق البرهانية فقط والعامّ فهو بالطرق الجدلية أو بالخطبية أو بالشعرية.

Then, that [sc. the philosophy that has emerged within a nation] is discussed until the matter is settled the way it was settled in the days of Aristotle, and so the scientific inquiry comes to an end with all the distinctions being discerned, the theoretical, universal, and common philosophy being perfected, and without there being any place left for [further] investigation. So, it [sc. philosophy] becomes a discipline that is learned and taught only (*tuta'allamu wa-tu'allamu faqaṭ*). Its teaching comprises both a specific teaching and a common teaching for all. So, the specific teaching is in demonstrative ways only (*bi-l-ṭuruq al-burhāniyya faqaṭ*), whereas the common [teaching][118] is in dialectical, rhetorical, or poetical ways. (al-Fārābī, *Kitāb al-Ḥurūf*, 151.17–152.4)

Implicit in Avicenna's methodology, and certainly mediated through al-Fārābī's influence on Avicenna in these matters, is a certain interpretation of the contents of Aristotle's *Posterior Analytics*. Indeed, Avicenna would have agreed with Jonathan Barnes' claim that "the theory of demonstrative science [as developed in Aristotle's *Posterior Analytics*] was never meant to guide or formalise scientific research: it is concerned exclusively with the teaching of facts already won; it does not describe how scientists do, or ought to, acquire knowledge: it offers a formal model of how teachers should impart knowledge."[119] A similar view is shared by Wolfgang Wieland, who characterises the method of Aristotle's *Posterior Analytics* as "didactic."[120] However, Wieland sees a stark contrast between that method and the approach of the *Physics*, for the latter is concerned with discovering the principles, not with teaching them. Wieland, thus, maintains that Aristotle does not apply the method of the *Posterior Analytics* in his *Physics*. It is on this point, now, that Avicenna differs, for he is keen on putting this method of teaching and learning into practice in all disciplines covered by his works, and particularly in those contained in his *al-Šifā'*.

Amos Bertolacci has already convincingly shown that Avicenna intended his *al-Ilāhiyyāt* as improving upon Aristotle's *Metaphysics*. One of the most vital aspects of this improvement is that Avicenna develops metaphysics demonstratively along the lines of the conditions stipulated in the *Posterior Analytics*.[121] Accordingly, Avicenna's metaphysics begins with the principles of "the existent insofar as it is an existent," so that he can develop the science from there and on that basis. The same is true also of the science of physics, as Avicenna likewise begins with the common principles which pertain to *its* subject-matter. Thus, when Avicenna in the first chapter of his *al-Samā'*

118 I am not following Mahdi's addition here, assuming that al-Fārābī uses *'āmm* and *muštarak* interchangeably.

119 Barnes, "Aristotle's Theory of Demonstration," 138; cf. also "Proof and the Syllogism." Barnes' reading was subsequently criticised; cf. his own notes in Aristotle, *Posterior Analytics*, xviii–xx; it was recently defended by Bronstein, *Aristotle on Knowledge and Learning*, esp. 177–185.

120 Wieland, *Die aristotelische Physik*, e.g., 20, 43, 53.

121 cf. Bertolacci, *The Reception of Aristotle's* Metaphysics *in Avicenna's* Kitāb al-Šifā', ch. 6; cf. also Gutas, *Avicenna and the Aristotelian Tradition*, 351–358.

al-ṭabīʿī refers several times to the method of "teaching" (*taʿlīm*) and "learning" (*taʿallum*), he does not use these terms as a mere set phrase. To the contrary, he deliberately refers to διδασκαλία and μάθησις from the first line of Aristotle's *Posterior Analytics* to signal his readiness to be guided in his teaching of physics by the demonstrative method of teaching and learning offered in the *Posterior Analytics*.[122] Bertolacci's claim that Avicenna regards "metaphysics as an apodictic science," and his *al-Ilāhiyyāt* as an apodictic work, is, thus, equally applicable to Avicenna's *al-Samāʿ al-ṭabīʿī*.[123]

Above, my investigation of Avicenna's *al-Samāʿ al-ṭabīʿī* departed from a brief reflection on the heading of chapter I.1:

في تعريف الطريق الذي نتوصّل منه إلى العلم بالطبيعيات من مبادئها.

> On making known the method by which we arrive at the knowledge of natural things from their principles. (*al-Samāʿ al-ṭabīʿī* I.1, 7.3f.)

Whereas, initially, I remarked that it was a rather puzzling feature that this heading announces a method by which we are supposed to arrive *at* a certain kind of knowledge and the science of a certain class of things *from* the principles of these things, it can now be seen (i) how very fitting this heading delineates Avicenna's intention in the first chapter; (ii) how it relates to Avicenna's methodological approach as developed in *al-Burhān*; (iii) how Avicenna incorporates certain elements from Aristotle's discussion in both the *Physics*, the *Posterior Analytics*, as well as the late ancient commentaries on *Physics* I.1; and (iv) how we are supposed to regard Avicenna's *al-Samāʿ al-ṭabīʿī*, viz., as a work in which Avicenna teaches us the "truth" (*al-ḥaqq*) about physics.[124] He does so by guiding us from the principles of natural things along a demonstrative path until, eventually, we will have arrived at, and will have fully obtained, the theoretical science concerned with these things. In fact, Avicenna's intentions could not have been more aptly expressed nor could he have been more explicit than at the very beginning of *al-Samāʿ al-ṭabīʿī* I.1:

---

122 Again, this attitude was probably taken over by Avicenna from al-Fārābī. For al-Fārābī's emphasis on teaching and learning, and the related concepts of *taṣawwur* and *taṣdīq*, cf. Germann, "How Can I Know?"; cf. also Galston, "al-Fārābī on Aristotle's Theory of Demonstration"; Joep Lameer's study in al-Šīrāzī, *Conception and Belief in Ṣadr al-Dīn al-Shirāzī*, ch. 2; Black, "Al-Fārābī on Meno's Paradox"; cf. further Avicenna's own introductory remarks in *al-Madḫal* I.3, esp. 17.7–17; *al-Naǧāt* I.1, 7.3–8.6.

123 Bertolacci, *The Reception of Aristotle's* Metaphysics *in Avicenna's* Kitāb al-Šifāʾ, 215, 262, 473; cf. also Bertolacci's remarks on the stylistic feature of *tarfīʿ*, i.e., the deriving of corollaries, which he attributes to Avicenna's *al-Šifāʾ* as a whole arguing that "[t]he presence of *furūʿ* and the performing of *tafrīʿ*, therefore, can be regarded as an indicator of what will emerge as the main trend of Avicenna's method in the *Šifāʾ*, i.e. the adoption of syllogistic and demonstrative procedures" (*The Reception of Aristotle's* Metaphysics *in Avicenna's* Kitāb al-Šifāʾ, appx. E, esp. 611); cf. also Hasnawi, "Commentaire et démonstration," 512: "Le but ultime d'Avicenne, à travers ces remaniements, est de se conformer au modèle d'exposition de la science qui est celui des *Seconds Analytiques*."

124 *al-Madḫal* I.1, 9.10; q.v. above, 74.

فإن كان للأمور الطبيعية مبادئ وأسباب وعلل لم يتحقّق العلم الطبيعي إلّا منها فقد شُرِح في تعليم البرهان أنّه لا سبيل إلى تحقّق معرفة الأمور ذوات المبادئ إلّا بعد الوقوف على مبادئها والوقوف من مبادئها عليها فإنّ هذا النحو من التعليم والتعلّم هو الذي نتوصّل منه إلى تحقّق المعرفة بالأمور ذوات المبادئ.

If, then, natural things have principles, [external] causes, and [internal] causes, natural knowledge cannot be ascertained other than through them. So, it has been explained in the teaching about demonstration [i.e., in Aristotle's *Posterior Analytics*] that there is no way of ascertaining the knowledge (*taḥaqquq maʿrifa*) of those things which have principles except after understanding their principles and understanding them from their principles, for this way from teaching and learning (*al-taʿlīm wa-l-taʿallum*)[125] is the one through which we arrive at the ascertainment of knowledge of things which have principles. (*al-Samāʿ al-ṭabīʿī* I.1, §1, 7.13–15)

2.2 Method and Principles between Physics and Metaphysics

In the preceding section, it has been remarked frequently that although Avicenna's mode of instruction requires him to begin his course on nature with the universal principles common to all natural things, he neither establishes them inductively nor demonstrates them in any other way at the beginning of *al-Samāʿ al-ṭabīʿī*. Instead, he explicitly requires the students to accept their existence as a posit and conceptualise their essence as if it were already verified (*qubūl wuǧūdihā waḍʿan wa-taṣawwur māhiyyatihā taḥqīqan*).[126] This demand stands in stark contrast to the *Physics*, in which Aristotle sought to identify and establish matter, form, and privation as the principles of natural things (ἀρχαὶ τῶν φύσει ὄντων).[127] In fact, Avicenna openly acknowledges that some of what he is about to discuss in the first chapters of *al-Samāʿ al-ṭabīʿī* has "nothing to do with natural philosophy" at all (*lā yuḫāliṭu l-ṭabīʿiyyāt*) and that "we must ... content ourselves" (*yaǧibu an ... naqnaʿuhū*) with what is merely "posited for the natural philosopher" (*mawḍūʿ li-l-ṭabīʿī* or *yūḍaʿu li-l-ṭabīʿī*).[128] This all calls to mind the way in which the heading of *al-Samāʿ al-ṭabīʿī* I.2 describes what Avicenna is up to in that chapter:

في تعديد المبادئ للطبيعيات على سبيل المصادرة والوضع.

On the enumeration of the principles of natural things by way of postulation (*al-muṣādara*) and positing (*al-waḍʿ*). (*al-Samāʿ al-ṭabīʿī* I.2, 13.3)

---

125 As in the first quotation of this passage above, 64, I prefer reading *al-taʿlīm wa-l-taʿallum* with Mss. Leiden or. 4 and or. 84 for *al-taʿlīm aw al-taʿallum* in Zāyid, McGinnis, and Āl Yāsīn.

126 *al-Samāʿ al-ṭabīʿī* I.1, §2, 8.3f.

127 *Phys.* I.7, 190b17f.

128 These quotations are taken from *al-Samāʿ al-ṭabīʿī* I.2, §10, 16.8; §15, 18.1f.; §5, 14.1; §11, 16.17, tr. by McGinnis, modified. The translation of *mawḍūʿ* as "posit" or "posited," instead of the more common "subject" or "subject-matter," is demanded by the context and is by no means unusual in both *al-Samāʿ al-ṭabīʿī* and *al-Burhān*.

Even though we cannot explore in detail Avicenna's conception of scientific method within this present study, an analysis of the origin and meaning of the two notions "postulation" (*muṣādara*) and "positing" (*waḍʿ*) will already clarify some important aspects of how Avicenna conceived of science as a universal endeavour. We shall, thereby, also understand more fully the philosophical foundation of the principles of natural things as Avicenna developed them.

The Arabic term *waḍʿ* and the cognate passive participle *mawḍūʿ* have frequently been employed by the Graeco-Arabic translators to render a variety of terms, in particular to convey the meaning of θέσις and τιθέναι as well as ὑπόθεσις and ὑποτιθέναι. This is especially true of the Arabic versions of Aristotle's *Physics* and *Posterior Analytics*. Additionally, *mawḍūʿ* has been the standard term to render ὑποκεῖσθαι and ὑποκείμενον, in the logical sense of something's being a subject for a predicate, the ontological sense of something's being a substrate for an attribute, and the physical sense of something's being the underlying thing of change.

The Arabic root *w-ḍ-ʿ* signifies in its basic verbal form "to put (down), to lay (down), to set." It corresponds by and large to the meanings Liddell and Scott note for τιθέναι, and Lewis and Short for *iacere*. In effect, something which has been laid down or set up, i.e., an Arabic *mawḍūʿ*, can subsequently serve as the basis for further descriptions or further actions and, thus, is a proper ὑποκείμενον and *subiectum* for a predicate, an attribute, or a change. Moreover, the act of "putting down, laying down, and setting up" or of "making something into something" and "positing something as something," i.e., the precise meaning of the Arabic noun *waḍʿ*, aptly meets the Greek θέσις.

By contrast, we have only scant evidence of the term *muṣādara* in the Graeco-Arabic translations of philosophical texts.[129] Considering the Arabic, the term is a verbal noun of the third stem to the root *ṣ-d-r* which connotes the basic verbal meaning of "to go out, to proceed, to arise, to appear." The third stem conveys the sense of having the basic meaning as its aim and so, by signifying "to have the appearance of something as its aim," the third stem verbal noun stands for a "request" or a "demand." Consequently, *muṣādara* emerges as a perfect match for translating the Greek αἴτημα in its common meaning. Since, from all we have seen so far, *muṣādara* is used in a similar way as *waḍʿ*, it also conveys the technical sense of αἴτημα of a "postulate" or an "assumption" which was frequently used in mathematics and logic.[130] Scarce though the occurrence

129 The term, however, was widely employed in mathematical works and, above all, in the Arabic translations of Euclid's *Elements*.

130 cf. D. E. Smith, *The Teaching of Geometry*, 117, 125: "The distinction between axiom and postulate was not clearly made by ancient writers. Probably what was in Euclid's mind was the Aristotelian distinction that an axiom was a principle common to all sciences, self-evident but incapable of proof, while the postulates were the assumptions necessary for building up the particular science under consideration ... αἰτήματα (*aitemata*) were requests made by the teacher to his pupil that certain things be conceded"; cf. also Mendell's supplement "Aristotle and First Principles in Greek Mathematics" to his "Aristotle and Mathematics."

of *muṣādara* may be in texts of philosophy, it appears prominently as a translation of αἴτημα in *Posterior Analytics* I.10, together with derivatives from the root *w-ḍ-ʿ* for cognates of ὑπόθεσις. In this chapter, Aristotle defines both terms as follows:

> Οὐκ ἔστι δ' ὑπόθεσις οὐδ' αἴτημα, ὃ ἀνάγκη εἶναι δι' αὐτὸ καὶ δοκεῖν ἀνάγκη ... ὅσα μὲν οὖν δεικτὰ ὄντα λαμβάνει αὐτὸς μὴ δείξας, ταῦτ', ἐὰν μὲν δοκοῦντα λαμβάνῃ τῷ μανθάνοντι, ὑποτίθεται, καὶ ἔστιν οὐχ ἁπλῶς ὑπόθεσις ἀλλὰ πρὸς ἐκεῖνον μόνον, ἂν δὲ ἢ μηδεμιᾶς ἐνούσης δόξης ἢ καὶ ἐναντίας ἐνούσης λαμβάνῃ τὸ αὐτό, αἰτεῖται. καὶ τούτῳ διαφέρει ὑπόθεσις καὶ αἴτημα· ἔστι γὰρ αἴτημα τὸ ὑπεναντίον τοῦ μανθάνοντος τῇ δόξῃ, ἢ ὃ ἄν τις ἀποδεικτὸν ὂν λαμβάνῃ καὶ χρῆται μὴ δείξας.
>
> ولا شيء من الأصل الموضوع ولا من المصادرة أيضاً ما هو ضروري من أجل ذاته ويظنّ أنّه ضروري ... فجميع التي يأخذها وهي مقبولة من حيث لم يبيّنها إن كان أخذه لها هو مظنون عند المتعلّم فإنّما يضعها وضعاً وهي أصل موضوع أعني الوضع لا على الإطلاق لكنّها عند ذلك فقط. فأمّا إنّ هو أخذه من حيث ليس له فيه بعينه ولا ظنّ واحد أو من حيث ظنّه على ضدّ فإنّما يصادر عليه مصادرةً. وهذا هو الفرق بين المصادرة وبين الأصل الموضوع وذلك أنّ المصادرة هي ما كان مقابلاً لظنّ المتعلّم وهذا هو الذي يأخذه الإنسان وهو متبرهن ويستعمله من حيث لم يبيّنه.
>
> What must be the case and must be thought to be the case because of itself is not a hypothesis (ὑπόθεσις, *al-aṣl al-mawḍūʿ*) or a postulate (αἴτημα, *al-muṣādara*) ... If you take something which is provable without proving it yourself, then if it is something which the student (τῷ μανθάνοντι, *al-mutaʿallim*) thinks to be the case, you are positing it (ὑποτίθεται, *yaḍaʿu waḍʿan*) and it is a hypothesis (ὑπόθεσις, *al-aṣl al-mawḍūʿ*) not absolutely (οὐχ ἁπλῶς, *lā ʿalā l-iṭlāq*) but only in relation to the student (πρὸς ἐκεῖνον μόνον, *ʿinda ḏālika faqaṭ*). If, however, you take the same [proposition] (τὸ αὐτό, *bi-ʿaynihī*) when the student has no opinion or actually a contrary opinion on the matter, then you are postulating it (αἰτεῖται, *yuṣādiru ʿalayhi muṣādaratan*). It is in this that hypotheses and postulates differ: a postulate is something not in accordance with the opinion of the student which, though demonstrable, you assume and use without proving it. (*An. post.* I.10, 76b23–34, tr. by Barnes, modified)[131]

According to Aristotle, one and the same proposition (τὸ αὐτό, *bi-ʿaynihī*) could be either a hypothesis or a postulate. This is so, because they do not differ *per se* but are differentiated with respect to the student (τῷ μανθάνοντι, *al-mutaʿallim*). Thus, a proposition may be a hypothesis if (a) the student is ready to accept the proposition unquestioningly (i.e., if he thinks it is true) or a postulate if (b) the student is, for whatever reason, reluctant to do so (i.e., if he thinks it may not be true). Thus, the two criteria (a) and (b) discriminate between hypotheses and postulates. Since this discrimination is accomplished by means of a reference to the student, Aristotle calls these hypotheses and postulates relative and not absolute; they are "relative hypotheses" and "relative postulates." Whether Aristotle would also allow for the category of "absolute hypotheses" and "absolute postulates," and what these would mean, is not entirely clear.

131 The Arabic text here is a combination of the editions by Badawī and Ǧabr, the Paris Ms. ar. 2346, and Avicenna's quotation of it at *al-Burhān* I.12, 113.5–10.

What is clear, however, is that in the first line of this passage, Aristotle also draws another distinction, viz., between what "must be the case and must be thought to be the case because of itself," one the one hand, and hypotheses and postulates, on the other. Accordingly, Aristotle intends to distinguish axioms, which are necessarily and self-evidently true because of themselves, from hypotheses and postulates, which are not self-evidently true but, instead, require proof.[132] In fact, axioms are not even provable or demonstrable, i.e., they cannot be demonstrated on the basis of something even more self-evident. So, in addition to the first criterion distinguishing between (a) hypotheses and (b) postulates, there is a second criterion which discriminates between propositions that (1) are provable (viz., genuine hypotheses and postulates) and those that are (2) indemonstrable (viz., axioms). Clearly, then, Aristotle wanted to elucidate (a1) "relative hypotheses" and (b1) "relative postulates."

We also see that the translator of the Arabic *Posterior Analytics*, Abū Bišr Mattā ibn Yūnus (d. 328/940), who worked on the basis of the Syriac version produced by Isḥāq ibn Ḥunayn, rendered ὑπόθεσις as *al-aṣl al-mawḍūʿ*. Since he has already used *waḍʿ* for translating θέσις in the previous chapters, and since Aristotle explicitly distinguishes between θέσις and ὑπόθεσις, Abū Bišr may have felt the need to find a translation for ὑπόθεσις which both emphasised its semantic difference from θέσις as well as their common etymological origin. Thus, he coined the expression *al-aṣl al-mawḍūʿ* for ὑπόθεσις, in which the noun *aṣl* ("root," "source," "fundament") accounts for the meaning of the prepositional prefix ὑπό- ("under," "below," "beneath"), while the passive participle *mawḍūʿ* is responsible for conveying the meaning of θέσις.[133]

Avicenna is clearly influenced by these remarks in Aristotle's *Posterior Analytics* when he defines *waḍʿ* and *muṣādara* in the logic of his *al-Naǧāt* as follows:

فما كان من الأوضاع يتسلّمه المتعلّم من غير أن يكون في نفسه له عناد سُمِّيَ أصلاً موضوعاً على الإطلاق وما كان يتسلّمه مسامحاً وفي نفسه له عناد يُسمّى مصادرة.

So, whichever of the posits (*al-awḍāʿ*, sg. *waḍʿ*) the student (*al-mutaʿallim*) accepts without there being resistance to it in his soul (*fī nafsihī*) is called an absolute hypothesis (*aṣlan mawḍūʿan ʿalā l-iṭlāq*) and whichever he accepts as tolerated with resistance to it in his soul is called a postulate (*muṣādaratan*). (*al-Naǧāt* I.128, 138.11–13)[134]

Several aspects about this definition are noteworthy. First of all, Avicenna seems to express an idea that is approximately the same as Aristotle's, for he, too, regards hypotheses and postulates not as different from each other *per se* but distinguishes

---

132 cf. Barnes' comments in *Posterior Analytics, ad loc.*

133 Abū Bišr may have found a similarly composite expression already in Isḥāq ibn Ḥunayn's Syriac version from which he produced the Arabic translation. For the general method of turning Greek prefixes into the first, "governing" part ("*regens*") of an Arabic genitive construction, cf. Endreß, "Die griechisch-arabischen Übersetzungen und die Sprache der arabischen Wissenschaften," 115.

134 cf. *Dānešnāme-ye ʿAlāʾī* I.32, 144.8–146.5.

them on the grounds of their relation to the "student" (*al-muta ʿallim*), particularly to the student's readiness to accept them. Thus, a proposition is a hypothesis, if it is accepted by the student (a) without there being opposition in the student's soul (i.e., if he thinks it is true), whereas a postulate is accepted (b) with opposition (i.e., if he thinks it may not be true).

Second, Avicenna also picks up on Aristotle's remark that a ὑπόθεσις is such not absolutely (ἁπλῶς) but only "in relation to the student." Yet, Avicenna apparently states the reverse, as he claims that a posit of the former category "is called an absolute hypothesis" (*aṣlan mawḍūʿan ʿalā l-iṭlāq*). This is surprising, because, as has just been noted, Aristotle spoke of *relative* hypotheses and postulates, not of absolute ones. Indeed, it is not even clear whether an absolute category of posits exists at all in the Aristotelian schema of *Posterior Analytics* I.10 (with "posits" being the genus term that encompasses both hypotheses and postulates). Why, then, does Avicenna mention it and what does it really mean?

Finally, in all this Avicenna faithfully follows the terminology of Abū Bišr's Arabic translation of Aristotle's *Posterior Analytics*.[135] Thus, it seems to be unquestionable that the above passage from Avicenna's *al-Naǧāt* is either a loose quote or a close paraphrase of Aristotle's *Posterior Analytics* I.10, 76b23–34.

Looking for further evidence for Avicenna's understanding of hypotheses and postulates, we may turn to his *al-Burhān*, a work more elaborate than the brief, and comparatively early, logical section of *al-Naǧāt*.[136] There, we find chapter I.12 to be "on the principle of demonstration" (*fī mabdaʾ al-burhān*), in which Avicenna provides not a mere paraphrase of *Posterior Analytics* I.10 but a direct quotation from Abū Bišr's translation of 76b27–34.[137] Upon these words, Avicenna adds the following:

ظنّوا أنّ الأصل الموضوع هو الذي يتبيّن بأدنى تأمّل وأنّ المصادرة ما لا يتبيّن بأدنى تأمل بل كأنّ الأصل الموضوع
هو الذي يحضر المتعلّمَ حقيقته إذا فكر أدنى فكر وأن المصادرة هو ما لا سبيل له إلى ذلك وليس الأمر كذلك.

They believe (*ẓannū*) that a hypothesis (*al-aṣl al-mawḍūʿ*) is that which is proven (*yatabayyanu*) by the slightest reflection (*bi-adnā taʾammul*) and that a postulate (*al-muṣādara*) is what is not proven by the slightest reflection, indeed, as if (*bal ka-anna*) a hypothesis were that whose reality (*ḥaqīqatuhū*) is present in [the mind of] the student (*al-mutaʿallim*) if he thinks [about it] even slightly and a postulate were whatever is in no way like this – yet, this is not the case. (*al-Burhān* I.12, 113.10–13)

---

135 In other cases, however, Avicenna's terminology clearly deviates from Abū Bišr's translation, as Eichner has pointed out; cf. "al-Fārābī and Ibn Sīnā on 'Universal Science' and the System of Sciences," esp. 85–89. The exact reasons for this still need to be determined.

136 When Avicenna composed his *al-Naǧāt*, he incorporated his earlier treatise *al-Muḫtaṣar al-aṣġar fī l-manṭiq*, probably written between 403/1013 and 404/1014 in Ǧurǧān, as its section on logic; cf. Kalbarczyk, "The *Kitāb al-Maqūlāt* of the *Muḫtaṣar al-awsaṭ fī l-manṭiq*," 306–312; Gutas, *Avicenna and the Aristotelian Tradition*, 434.

137 *al-Burhān* I.12, 113.5–10

Besides the question of why Avicenna speaks of absolute hypotheses in the logic of his *al-Naǧāt*, there are two further questions about this passage from *al-Burhān* that ought to be addressed: first, why is what they believe "not the case" and, second, who are "they," i.e., who is the subject of the verb *ẓannū* ("they believe")?

Considering the latter, there seem to be the following possibilities. The plural may refer to the same people who uphold the theory expounded in the preceding lines, i.e., the passage quoted from the *Posterior Analytics*. Thus, *ẓannū* could ultimately include, or directly refer to, Aristotle and indicate that Avicenna interprets the Aristotelian text as claiming that the difference between hypotheses and postulates is in the fact that the former, but not the latter, can be grasped even "by the slightest reflection" (*bi-adnā ta'ammul*). If that were Avicenna's interpretation of *Posterior Analytics* I.10, it would be inadequate, as it simply does not follow from the Aristotelian text. Moreover, any such reading on Avicenna's part would appear to be quite unfair, because it would seem that Avicenna interpreted Aristotle that peculiar way only to be able to conclude that "this is not the case." It may, therefore, be more fruitful to consider another possibility, viz., that Avicenna puts forth an interpretation offered by a further group, the Greek or Arabic commentators, for example, and to have a brief glance at post-Aristotelian commentaries.

The famous Ms. ar. 2346 of the Bibliothèque nationale de France in Paris is, apart from al-Fārābī's logical works, our primary source for early Arabic interpretations of Aristotle's *Organon*. The editor of the manuscript, al-Ḥasan ibn Suwār ibn al-Ḫammār (d. after 407/1017), drew extensively on the commentaries by, or the teaching of, Ibn ʿAdī and Abū Bišr, in order to supply his edition with marginal notes.[138] The few preserved notes to *Posterior Analytics* I.2 and I.10, however, do not provide anything similar to the interpretation reported by Avicenna in *al-Burhān* I.12.[139]

Turning to al-Fārābī's brief *Book of Demonstration*, we find a section on "the principles of instruction" (*mabādi' al-taʿlīm*), which covers many of the aspects relevant to our present concern and, in particular, explicitly provides definitions of *al-uṣūl al-mawḍūʿa* and *al-muṣādarāt*.[140] This section contains the following passage:

والأصول الموضوعة هي التي إذا ذكّر بها المعلّم المتعلّم لم يكن عند المتعلّم اليقين بها ولا ما يزيّفها به وذلك أنّ لا يكون ذلك لا رأيه ولا مضادّاً لرأيه فيطالب المتعلّم بتسليمها. وأمّا المصادرات فهي التي يرى المتعلّم فيها خلاف ما

138 On the manuscript and its contents, cf. Peters, *Aristoteles Arabus*; Hugonnard-Roche, "Une ancienne 'édition' arabe de l'*Organon* d'Aristote"; "Remarques sur la tradition arabe de l'*Organon* d'après le manuscrit Paris, Bibliothèque nationale, ar. 2346"; Kraemer, *Humanism in the Renaissance of Islam*, 108; Lameer, "The *Organon* of Aristotle in the Medieval Oriental and Occidental Traditions"; Badawī's remarks in the introduction to his edition *Manṭiq Arisṭū*.

139 cf. also the account given by ʿĪsā ibn Zurʿa, a colleague of Ibn Suwār, who by and large followed Aristotle's *Posterior Analytics* in his *Kitāb al-Burhān li-Arisṭāṭālīs al-ḥakīm*, published in *Manṭiq Ibn Zurʿa* I.14, 242.1–4.

140 cf. al-Fārābī, *Book of Demonstration* 5, 87.15–90.16.

يراه المعلّم غير أنّ المتعلّم يطالَب بتسليمها فتستعمل. وهذه الأوضاع إنّما تكون أكثر ذلك أحد شيئين إمّا مقدّمات شأنها أن تتبرهن في صناعة أخرى لم يزاولها المتعلّم أو تكون ممّا يمكن أن تتبيّن في تلك الصناعة بأشياء متأخّرة تطول أو تعسر على المتعلّم فيترك بيانها إلى وقت آخر. وقد يمكن أن تستعمل ما شأنها أن تكون يقينية أوضاعاً متى لم يكن المتعلّم يعترف بها لأحد تلك الأسباب التي ذكرناها وأمثال هذه ليست هي أوضاعاً على الإطلاق لكنّ هي أوضاع بالقياس إلى ذلك المتعلّم فقط.

> Hypotheses (*al-uṣūl al-mawḍūʿa*) are those which, if the teacher (*al-muʿallim*) brings them to the student's (*al-mutaʿallim*) attention, the student has neither certainty about them nor does he have anything by virtue of which he could declare them to be false, because that it is false is neither his belief nor is it contrary to his belief, and so he [sc. the teacher] demands from the student to accept them. As for postulates (*al-muṣādarāt*), they are those about which the student believes something different from what the teacher believes, yet the student claims to concede them, and so they are employed. For the most part, these posits are only one of two things: either they are propositions that are such as to be demonstrated in another discipline not [currently] pursued by the student or they are among those [propositions] that can be proven in this [current] discipline by posterior things that [now would] take too long [to explain] or are [yet too] difficult for the student, and so their proof is put on hold for later. It may be possible that those that are such as to be axioms (*yaqīniyya*) are employed as posits, whenever the student does not recognise them [as such] due to one of the reasons we have [just] mentioned. Examples of these are not posits absolutely (*ʿalā l-iṭlāq*) but are posits in relation to this student only (*bi-l-qiyās ilā ḏālika l-mutaʿallim faqaṭ*). (al-Fārābī, *Book of Demonstration* 5, 90.4–13)

In this passage, al-Fārābī, too, draws two distinctions. The first is between hypotheses and postulates, the second between absolute posits and relative posits. About the first, al-Fārābī explains that a proposition is a hypothesis if (a) the student accepts them, because he has no opinion whatsoever about its being either true or false. In other words, he is in no position either to agree or disagree. Though slightly different, this corresponds structurally with the proposition "which the student thinks to be the case" from Aristotle's *Posterior Analytics*. By contrast, a proposition is a postulate if (b) he disagrees but is kind enough to concede it nonetheless or, as Aristotle had it, "the student has no opinion or actually a contrary opinion on the matter." Clearly, then, we find al-Fārābī employing roughly the same criteria as Aristotle to distinguish between hypotheses and postulates.

The second distinction, here, divides posits on the whole into two categories. There are those which (1) can be proven either in another discipline or later in the same discipline. It is important to recognise that these posits can be proven, i.e., they are "provable," to speak in Aristotle's terms. Moreover, al-Fārābī insinuates that the posits of this category, i.e., those that are provable, are absolute hypotheses and postulates, because he contrasts them with the second category of posits which (2) are actually unprovable axioms, even though they are currently not recognised by the student as such. Thus, these are not genuine posits – because, actually, they are axioms – and are employed as posits only due to the confusion of the student, who does not recognise their self-evident, axiomatic nature.

On the basis of these distinctions, al-Fārābī mentions four different kinds of posits: (a1) absolute hypotheses and (b1) absolute postulates as well as (a2) relative hypotheses and (b2) relative postulates. It is to be noted that what al-Fārābī calls (a1) absolute hypotheses and (b1) absolute postulates originally had been (a1) relative hypotheses and (b1) relative postulates in Aristotle's *Posterior Analytics*. In other words, al-Fārābī uses the same criteria to distinguish them but employs different terminology to name them, calling those "absolute" which Aristotle called "relative." Accordingly, al-Fārābī's terminology – and the influence of al-Fārābī on Avicenna – easily explains why Avicenna, too, speaks of "absolute hypotheses" in his *al-Naǧāt* if all he means is just what Aristotle described as non-absolute "relative hypotheses" in *Posterior Analytics* I.10.

Yet, in addition to this, al-Fārābī explicitly affirms the category of (a2) relative hypotheses and (b2) relative postulates – which in Aristotle's terminology would be (a2) absolute hypotheses and (b2) absolute postulates – which we were unsure Aristotle would recognise at all. Since for al-Fārābī, these are actually axioms, and are only employed as posits because of the students confusion about them, it seems that al-Fārābī simply combined the distinction which Aristotle made in the first line of the above passage between axioms and posits, on the one hand, and the subsequent differentiation of posits into hypotheses and postulates, on the other, thus fully establishing, on this basis, a further category of posits, i.e., one that was not explicit in Aristotle.

However, comparing al-Fārābī's passage to that in Avicenna's *al-Burhān*, it is obvious that it does not contain anything that would amount to the view that hypotheses are understood "by the slightest reflection" (and also does not contain this expression). It may well be that al-Fārābī's more comprehensive full commentary on Aristotle's *Posterior Analytics* contained some discussion either of the concepts of postulation and hypothesis or of the idea that some posits are understood already "by the slightest reflection." Since this work is not known to be extant, we are in no position to tell.

What is certain, though, is that in his full commentary, al-Fārābī would have discussed Greek sources mentioning these ideas and concepts. Of the Greek commentaries, the one written by Alexander is not known to be extant in any language, and the surviving fragments, collected by Paul Moraux, do not offer anything on this topic.[141] The commentaries by Themistius and Philoponus, on the other hand, are extant in Greek and even were translated into Arabic, arguably by the same figure who is responsible for the Arabic version of the *Posterior Analytics* itself, viz., Abū Bišr. It is in these works that we can find the materials Avicenna is reacting to.

In his paraphrase of Aristotle's *Posterior Analytics* I.2, Themistius makes the following distinction between hypotheses and postulates:

> κοινὸν μὲν οὖν ἁπάσης ὑποθέσεως τὸ μὴ ἐκ τῆς φυσικῆς ἐννοίας ἠρτῆσθαι ἀλλὰ τίθεσθαι παρὰ τοῦ τεχνίτου καὶ πρότασιν εἶναι ... ἀλλ' ὅσαι μὲν γνώριμοι τούτων εἰσὶ καὶ ὅσας ἅμα τῷ πυθέσθαι προσίεται ὁ μανθάνων, ὑποθέσεις αὗται καλοῦνται· ὅσαι δ' οὐ σαφεῖς καὶ οὐ γνώριμοι, αὗται

141 Alexander of Aphrodisias, *Le Commentaire aux "Seconds Analytiques" d'Aristote*.

αἰτήματα λέγονται ... ἁπλῶς μὲν οὖν αἱ τοιαῦται ὑποθέσεις τε καὶ αἰτήματα. ἤδη δὲ λέγονταί τινες ὑποθέσεις καί τινα αἰτήματα οὔτε ἄμεσα οὔτε ἀναπόδεικτα, ἀλλὰ δεόμενα <μὲν> ἀποδείξεως λαμβανόμενα δὲ χωρὶς ἀποδείξεως ἐν τοῖς λόγοις. καὶ εἰσὶν οὐχ ἁπλῶς ὑποθέσεις ταῦτα οὔτε αἰτήματα, ἀλλὰ πρὸς ἐκεῖνον μόνον τὸν διδόντα καὶ συγχωροῦντα·

Et communicat omnis radix posita quia non pendet per scientiam naturalem ex scientiis cognitionis; verum non ponit eam nisi positione auctor syllogismi et facit eamn propositionem ... Verumtamen quae ex istis propositionibus est manifesta ita ut recipiat eam discipulus cum quaestione quam facit ei magister de ea, appropriatur nomine radicis positae. Et quae ex eis non est manifesta neque cognita appropriatur nomine petitionum ... Et ad ultimum similes istis ex radicibus positis manifestis non sunt manifestae absque medio, neque sunt excusatae a demonstratione, sed indigent demonstratione; verumtamen sumuntur in sermone absque demonstratione. Et non sunt absolute radices positae neque ex petitionibus iterum. Verum ipsae non sunt ita nisi apud illum qui concedit eas et convenit super eas tantum.

Now, it is common to all hypotheses that they do not depend on natural knowledge but are posited by the expert and are a proposition ... Those of them, however, that are known (γνώριμοι, *manifesta*) and are such that the learner understands them as soon as they are heard, these are called hypotheses (ὑποθέσεις, *radicis positae*), whereas those that are not clear and not known (οὐ σαφεῖς καὶ οὐ γνώριμοι, *non est manifesta neque cognita*), those are called postulates (αἰτήματα, *petitionum*) ... Such hypotheses and postulates, then, are absolute. Now, however, some that are called hypotheses and postulates are neither immediate nor indemonstrable but require proof, even though they are assumed in the discourse without proof – and these are not hypotheses or postulates absolutely (ἁπλῶς, *absolute*) but only with respect to the one who concedes them and assents to them. (Themistius, *In An. post.*, 7.20–32)[142]

Here, in this passage, which is concerned with the second chapter of the first book of Aristotle's *Posterior Analytics*, Themistius likewise draws two distinctions. First, he employs the criteria that propositions may be (a) known and such as to be understood as soon as they are stated or (b) not known and not clear. Since these criteria distinguish between hypotheses and postulates, they are the same as those that can be found in Aristotle, even though Themistius' terminology differs greatly.[143] Second, he distinguishes between (1) absolute propositions and (2) relative propositions with respect to the interlocutor. The latter are explicitly said to be "not immediate" and "not indemonstrable," and such as to "require proof." This clearly corresponds to Aristotle's criteria that distinguish between (1) provable hypotheses and postulates, and

142 cf. also Maróth, *Die Araber und die antike Wissenschaftstheorie*, 141f. The Latin translation of Gerard of Cremona is taken from O'Donnell's edition of the text (Themistius, *Commentum super Librum posteriorum*). It is used here in lieu of Abū Bišr's Arabic translation, which is not known to be extant. Although it is at times difficult to map the Latin with the Greek, especially at the beginning of the latter half of the quote (ἁπλῶς μὲν οὖν ..., *Et ad ultimum* ...), the Latin text provides valuable information about the Arabic translation that was probably available to Avicenna and his contemporaries. The expression *radix posita*, for example, clearly derives from *aṣl mawḍūʿ* – Abū Bišr's choice for translating ὑπόθεσις.

143 Aristotle formulated (a) as the student's readiness to accept the proposition unquestioningly (i.e., thinking that it is true) and (b) as the student's reluctance to accept it (i.e., thinking that it may not be true).

(2) indemonstrable axioms. Thus, in Themistius, just as later in al-Fārābī, we get a full set of four different kinds of posits: (a1) absolute hypotheses, (a2) relative hypotheses, (b1) absolute postulates, and (b2) relative postulates.

Yet, there are two differences between Themistius and al-Fārābī. First, Themistius calls those propositions that are are provable (i.e., not axiomatic) "relative," whereas al-Fārābī will call them "absolute." Thus, Themistius' terminology is analogous to that in Aristotle. Unlike Aristotle, however, Themistius explicitly mentions the absolute cases of propositions. Again, these were, if at all, only implicit in Aristotle. These (a1) absolute hypotheses and (a2) absolute postulates, just as in al-Fārābī (even though with converse terminology), actually seem to be axioms, because they are said to be immediate and indemonstrable.

Besides this, Themistius' criterion that hypotheses are "known" and "such that the learner understands them as soon as they are heard" is similar to Avicenna's report that "they believe" that this criterion distinguishes between hypotheses and postulates. That is to say, Themistius' account has striking similarities to that about which Avicenna says that it is "not the case." Yet, again, the exposition in Themistius does not contain anything that really fits Avicenna's expression *bi-adnā taʾāmmul.* However, we may find something more suitable in Philoponus' commentary on the *Posterior Analytics*, which contains passages that are strikingly similar to what we have already read. Indeed, Themistius' explanation was apparently so appealing that two centuries later, Philoponus did not hesitate to reproduce it – to some extent verbatim – in his own comments on *Posterior Analytics* I.2.[144] Later, in his discussion of chapter I.10, Philoponus once more returns to the distinction he drew from Themistius and writes the following:

> καὶ τῶν ὑποθέσεων ὅσαι μὲν μετὰ τοῦ δοκεῖν τῷ προσδιαλεγομένῳ καὶ ἀληθεῖς εἶναι οὐ πολλῆς δέονται ἐπιστάσεως εἰς τὸ τὴν ἐν αὐτοῖς θεωρηθῆναι ἀλήθειαν, καλοῦνται κυρίως ὑποθέσεις ... καὶ ἐπὶ τῶν παραπλησίων ὡσαύτως ὀλίγης δεῖται ἐπιστασίας. ὅσαι δὲ δοκοῦσαι τῷ προσδιαλεγομένῳ ἀληθεῖς μέν εἰσι, ἀποδείξεως δὲ δεόμεναι καὶ ἐπεξεργασίας πλείονος, αὗται πρὸς τὸν μανθάνοντά εἰσι μὲν ὑποθέσεις, οὐ μὴν κυρίως.
>
> All hypotheses (τῶν ὑποθέσεων) that [are taken] in circumstances where they both appear true to the interlocutor and are true, and do not require much reflection (οὐ πολλῆς δέονται ἐπιστάσεως) for their truth to be observed, are called hypotheses absolutely (κυρίως ὑποθέσεις) ... [Philoponus provides some examples] ... And in similar cases it likewise requires little reflection (ὀλίγης δεῖται ἐπιστασίας). All those, however, that appear true to the interlocutor and are true but require demonstration and further elaboration are hypotheses (ὑποθέσεις) relative to the student (πρὸς τὸν μανθάνοντά) but not absolutely. (Philoponus, *In An. post.*, 127.31–128.15, tr. by McKirahan, modified)

---

144 cf. Themistius, *In An. post.*, 6.28–7.34, esp. 7.20–31; Philoponus, *In An. post.*, 34.9–36.4, esp. 35.21–36.3; cf. also Maróth, *Die Araber und die antike Wissenschaftstheorie*, 138–141.

Focusing on (a) hypotheses, Philoponus distinguishes an absolute meaning from a relative meaning. In doing so, his criterion is the amount of reflection required for the truth of a proposition to be realised. A hypothesis which (2) does "not require much reflection" is (a2) an absolute hypothesis, whereas one whose truth (1) requires "demonstration and further elaboration" is (a1) a relative hypothesis.

Apart from a striking similarity between Philoponus' explanation and the analysis in the paraphrase of his predecessor Themistius, one immediately recognises two things. First, Philoponus' expressions οὐ πολλῆς δέονται ἐπιστάσεως and, especially, ὀλίγης δεῖται ἐπιστασίας very aptly conform to Avicenna's *bi-adnā ta'āmmul*. Second, such propositions that "do not require much reflection" in Philoponus also appear to be similar to what Themistius called propositions which "the learner understands them as soon as they are heard." Yet, the appearance is deceitful, because in Themistius this criterion was meant to distinguish between (a) hypotheses and (b) postulates, whereas here in Philoponus it differentiates between (1) relative cases and (2) absolute ones.

Having identified the meaning of ὑπόθεσις, Philoponus continues with an analogous definition of αἴτημα:

> ὅσαι δὲ μὴ δοκοῦσι τῷ προσδιαλεγομένῳ, ἀληθεῖς δέ εἰσι καὶ ὀλίγης δεόμεναι παραμυθίας, καλοῦνται κυρίως αἰτήματα ... εἰ δὲ μὴ δοκοῦσαι, εἰ μὲν ψευδεῖς εἶεν ἐναντίαι δὲ τῇ τοῦ προσδιαλεγομένου δόξῃ, ἢ καὶ ἀληθεῖς μὲν πλείονος δὲ ἀποδείξεως δεόμεναι, καλοῦνται πρὸς τὸν μανθάνοντα αἰτήματα.
>
> But all that [are taken] though they do not appear true to the interlocutor, but are true and require but little explanation (ὀλίγης δεόμεναι παραμυθίας), are called postulates absolutely (κυρίως αἰτήματα) ... But if they [are taken] without appearing true, if they are false and contrary to the opinion of the interlocutor, or even if they are true and require more demonstration, they are called postulates relative to the student (πρὸς τὸν μανθάνοντα αἰτήματα). (Philoponus, *In An. post.*, 129.5–11, tr. by McKirahan, modified)

Now focusing on (b) postulates, Philoponus employs the same criteria again to distinguish (b2) absolute postulates from (b1) relative ones. Once more, the overall framework is identical to that in Themistius, yet, again, the characterisation of propositions that "require but little explanation" is meant to discriminate between (1) relative hypotheses and postulates from (2) absolute ones, which "require more demonstration." Thus, in Philoponus, too, we get the full list of four different kinds of posits: (a1) absolute hypotheses, (a2) relative hypotheses, (b1) absolute postulates, and (b2) relative postulates. Moreover, Philoponus follows Themistius' (and Aristotle's) terminology, thus differing from al-Fārābī who, as we have seen, reverses the application of "absolute" and "relative."

On the whole, we can say that Themistius and Philoponus adopted the meaning of hypotheses and postulates as it had been explained by Aristotle in *Posterior Analytics* I.10. A hypothesis is something which is accepted by the student unquestioningly, whereas a postulate is only conceded reluctantly. Probably inspired by Aristotle's own terminology, they added – or made explicit – a further distinction between relative and absolute cases. Relative cases are those which, despite being employed by the teacher and accepted by the student without proof, are themselves such as to require proof or demonstration. These are propositions which need to be proven somewhere in one of the sciences, even though they are currently accepted without proof for didactic reasons. Both Themistius and Philoponus state that these are such as to "require proof" or demonstration. Absolute cases, in turn, are the opposite: they are "immediate" and "indemonstrable" for Themistius and such as to require "little explanation" or "not much reflection" for Philoponus. It seems to be clear that both are talking about axioms here, even though al-Fārābī is the only one who really makes this explicit. Thus, all three allow for propositions that are hypotheses and postulates despite their being actually indemonstrable and immediate axioms – in short, they are propositions which the teacher posits for the student to accept, even though they should actually be clear by the slightest reflection.

Other than that, the similarities between Themistius and Philoponus – not only in content but even in terminology and actual wording – could indicate that both may have drawn on a common source. If so, then their common source may well have been Alexander's no longer extant commentary on the *Posterior Analytics*. This would mean that, with regard to our question about the target of Avicenna's criticism of what "they believe" (*ẓannū*), all three Greek commentators may be possible candidates (in addition to Arabic logicians such as al-Fārābī who were following them on this point). Nonetheless, it is equally clear that Philoponus' commentary stands out in that it alone seems to contain expressions that correspond closely to Avicenna's repeated phrase *bi-adnā ta'ammul*. Therefore, Philoponus together with Themistius and, possibly, Alexander as well as al-Fārābī emerge as likely candidates for being the target of Avicenna's critique that what "they believe ... is not the case."

If that is so and if Philoponus, even more than Themistius and al-Fārābī, is Avicenna's primary target, we have to admit that Avicenna misrepresents Philoponus' interpretation, for we saw Avicenna claiming that some people "believe that a hypothesis is what is proven by the slightest reflection and that a postulate is what is not proven by the slightest reflection." In other words, Avicenna presents the criterion of being accessible even by the slightest reflection as the distinctive feature that divides between (a) hypotheses and (b) postulates – much like the criterion of being known or clear and immediately understood does in Themistius – whereas Philoponus actually argued that both hypotheses and postulates are differentiated by this feature into (1) a relative and (2) an absolute sense. This discrepancy notwithstanding, the vocabulary expressed by the phrase *bi-adnā ta'ammul* is, indeed, very close to that of Philoponus.[145] Therefore, we have to ask why Avicenna misrepresents the conception

145 For further evidence that Avicenna had knowledge of, and in fact worked with, Philoponus' commentary on the *Posterior Analytics*, cf. Strobino, "Avicenna's Use of the Arabic Translations of the *Posterior Analytics* and the Ancient Commentary Tradition." That in the present passage Avicenna is

of hypotheses and postulates that Philoponus had expressed in his commentary (and which he took from Themistius or, perhaps, from Alexander).

To my mind, there are two possible answers to this question. First, Avicenna may not really have misrepresented Philoponus' distinction at all but may just have paraphrased from another part of his predecessors' commentary. In his comments on *Posterior Analytics* I.2, 72a14–16, Philoponus offers two examples of hypotheses and contrasts these with another kind of posits which he claims to be in need of demonstrative reasoning (δεόμεναι μὲν κατασκευῆς ἀναποδείκτως). This other kind he calls postulates.[146] The text of Philoponus' own commentary, thus, insinuates that hypotheses, as opposed to postulates, are not in need of proof and are grasped by the slightest reflection alone. This is certainly due to the fact that Philoponus' remarks on *Posterior Analytics* I.2 follow closely, and in part even literally derive from, Themistius' paraphrase, which draws the distinction between hypotheses and postulates precisely in this way, as we have seen. Moreover, since Philoponus refers the reader of his commentary to his discussion "further down" (παρακατιών), apparently pointing at his comments on *Posterior Analytics* I.10, he himself invited Avicenna to connect his simpler remarks on chapter I.2 with his more complex exposition of chapter I.10 and its central idea that some posits are grasped even by the slightest reflection. Avicenna, then, merely had to import the notion of *bi-adnā ta'ammul* from the commentary on I.10 into the passage from I.2 and to paraphrase it this way in his *al-Burhān* I.12.

For everyone thinking that this reconstruction is quite a stretch, the second answer will perhaps be more convincing, even though it intends to explain why it is actually irrelevant whether Avicenna presents Philoponus' conception correctly (and also why it is somewhat irrelevant whether Avicenna's primary target is, now, Themistius, Philoponus, or al-Fārābī). At the same time, this second answer will also explain why what "they believe ... is not the case," as Avicenna claims.

So, as we have seen, much of Philoponus' interpretation of hypotheses and postulates is about the amount of reflection required for ascertaining the truth of hypotheses and postulates. Indeed, the distinction between an absolute and a relative sense of hypotheses and postulates seems to have been Themistius' original contribution to *Posterior Analytics* I.2, on the one hand, and the backbone of Philoponus' commentary on *Posterior Analytics* I.10, on the other.[147] For Avicenna, though, the matter is entirely different, because the distinction of what is and is not immediately intelligible is not what *Posterior Analytics* I.10 is about. In effect, it does not matter whether Philoponus' original exposition is accurately portrayed in Avicenna's discussion, precisely because Avicenna thinks that the idea misses the point entirely: there is nothing about either

referring to Philoponus is apparent not only from the general idea and the terminology but is further borne out by the fact that he explicitly employs geometrical examples just as Philoponus did; cf. *al-Burhān* I.12, 114.16f. and *In An. post.*, 128.28f., for example.

146 Philoponus, *In An. post.*, 35.19–36.5.

147 Again, it may be possible that this distinction goes back to Alexander.

hypotheses or postulates that is grasped by the slightest reflection. They are, as we shall see, premisses that are "unknown in themselves" (*al-muqaddimāt al-mağhūla fī anfusihā*).[148] Consequently, Avicenna contends that both kinds of posits have to be rigorously demonstrated somewhere in one of the sciences – posits are precisely not indemonstrable, just as Aristotle said, too, when he distinguished them from axioms. Presently, they are only advanced by the teacher for the sake of the imminent argumentation and, in turn, taken or accepted by the student, because the teacher, in fact, is able to give a demonstration and, thus, to substantiate his current argument, even though he prefers to kindly ask the student to be content with accepting theses premisses for the time being as merely posited.

The difference, however, between Avicenna and his Greek and Arabic predecessors is not only that they allow for axioms to serve as hypotheses and postulates, but also that they – especially Themistius and Philoponus – accept more propositions as self-evidently, or almost self-evidently, true than Avicenna is willing to accept. This, again, comes to light in Philoponus' comments on *Posterior Analytics* I.2, 72a14–16. There, Philoponus provides the very same examples of hypotheses which Themistius had offered, viz., that "motion occurs in things" and that "nothing comes to be from what in no way or manner is."[149] Philoponus insinuates that these hypotheses could be grasped by the slightest reflection and Themistius stated that they are clear and known. Avicenna, however, vehemently disagrees with this, just as he disagrees with Aristotle's claim that the existence of nature does not require any proof – indeed, that it would be ridiculous to even attempt a proof – because nature "obviously" (φανερόν, *min al-umūr al-ẓāhira*) exists.[150] Whereas Philoponus in his commentary on the *Physics* professed his full agreement with Aristotle's claim that the existence of nature is self-evident, Avicenna is aghast, stating that this is something he is "not willing to listen to and support" (*lā uṣġiyu ilayhi wa-lā aqūlu bihī*).[151]

For Avicenna, there may be self-evident first principles or concepts, but there are no self-evident hypotheses and postulates, nor are there any sort-of-self-evident hypotheses or postulates which the student should be able to grasp immediately after having devoted only the lowest amount of reflection to it (although he sometimes may

148 *al-Burhān* I.12, 114.4.

149 Philoponus, *In An. post.*, 35.22f., tr. by McKirahan; cf. Themistius, *In An. post.*, 7.23.

150 *Phys.* II.1, 193a3f.

151 *al-Samāʿ al-ṭabīʿī* I.5, §4, 31.2f. Avicenna could refer to Aristotle's remark from *Physics* VIII.3 that "it is a hypothesis that nature is a principle of motion" (ὑπόθεσις γὰρ ὅτι ἡ φύσις ἀρχὴ τῆς κινήσεως, *wa-ḏālika anna l-aṣl al-mawḍūʿ lahū anna l-ṭabīʿa mabdaʾ li-l-ḥaraka*; 253b4f.). Since it is a hypothesis, Avicenna would say, it requires a proof. The proof is provided in *al-Ilāhiyyāt* IV.2, §§20–23, 179.4–181.10, and reappears, in an abbreviated form, in *al-Samāʿ al-ṭabīʿī* I.5, §§1–3, 29.4–30.7, where Avicenna even mentions that this is a principle to be posited in physics and proven in metaphysics. Versions of this proof are also found in *ʿUyūn al-ḥikma* III.3, 49.17–50.12; *al-Nağāt* IV.1.13, 526.1–529.2; *al-Ḥikma al-mašriqiyya* III.4, 9.20–10.12. For Philoponus' endorsement of Aristotle's earlier claim that it would be ridiculous to prove the existence of nature, cf. *In Phys.*, 205.25–207.14; cf. also *In Phys.*, 271.25–273.4.

fail to manage even that).[152] That is to say that for Avicenna, it may be that *principles* are absolute – but *posits* most definitely are not, as is explained at the very beginning of *al-Burhān* I.12:

> ومبدأ البرهان يقال على وخهين فيقال مبدأ البرهان بحسب العلم مطلقاً ويقال مبدأ البرهان بحسب علم ما. ومبدأ البرهان بحسب العلم مطلقاً هو مقدّمة غير ذات وسط على الإطلاق أيّ ليس من شأنها أن يتعلّق بيان نسبة محمولها إلى موضوعها كانت إخاباً أو سلباً بحدّ أوسط فتكون مقدّمة أخرى أقدم منها وقبلها. ومبدأ البرهان بحسب علم ما يجوز أن يكون ذا وسط في نفسه لكنّه يُوضَع في ذلك العلم وضعاً ولا يكون له في مرتبته في ذلك العلم وسط بل إمّا أن يكون وسطه في علم قبله أو معه أو يكون وسطه في ذلك العلم بعد تلك المرتبة كما ستعرّف الحال فيه.
>
> The principle of demonstration is said in two ways, and so the principle of demonstration is said with regard to science absolutely (*bi-ḥasab al-ʿilm muṭlaqan*) or it is said with regard to a certain science (*bi-ḥasab ʿilm mā*). The principle of demonstration with regard to science absolutely is a premiss that has no middle [term] absolutely, i.e., it is not such that the proof of the relation of its predicate to its subject – be that a affirmation or negation – depends on a middle term, so that another premiss would be prior to it and and before it. By contrast, the principle of demonstration with regard to a certain science may have a middle [term] in itself, yet it is laid down in that science as a posit (*yūḍaʿu fī ḏālika l-ʿilm waḍʿan*) and does not have a middle [term] at this stage in that science. Rather its middle [term] belongs to a science before it or on a par with it, or its middle [term] belongs to that [same] science after that stage, just as that whose state will be made known [later]. (*al-Burhān* I.12, 110.3–9)

As can be seen, Avicenna differentiates between two kinds of principles, absolute and non-absolute principles. The former are not such as to be proven, because there is nothing that could explain and demonstrate the relation between their subject and their predicate. They are genuinely self-evident, i.e., known in themselves, and are, thus, valid without qualification. Such absolute propositions are axioms, and they are sharply contrasted with another kind of principles, those that are commonly employed in the particular sciences. These are principles that are not valid without qualification and as such need to be posited conditionally, as the proof of their validity belongs to another science or to the same science later on. These principles are posits, i.e.,

---

152 There is one thing in *al-Samāʿ al-ṭabīʿī* which Avicenna claims to "be clear to us by the slightest reflection" (*yattaḍiḥu lanā bi-adnā taʾammul*) and that is the fact that in change, there is a third factor involved in addition to the underlying body and the form acquired through the change – a third factor commonly called "privation" (*ʿadam*; *al-Samāʿ al-ṭabīʿī* I.2, §14, 17.18f.). However, Avicenna does not consider privation to be a principle or posit. He merely remarks that it is clear, presumably from experience, that every changeable object is, prior to the change, in some way in a privative state and that this state is eliminated through the acquisition of a form during the change. If a person is already healthy, he cannot undergo a change so as to become healthy. The person needs to be deprived of health, i.e., needs to be sick in one way or another, in order to be able to undergo a change towards health. This situation is what Avicenna describes as fundamentally clear "by the slightest reflection." This also already indicates that privation, being a concept of natural philosophy, is only of subordinate relevance for his understanding of change and for the discussion of principles in *al-Samāʿ al-ṭabīʿī*, as I shall discuss below, 201ff.

hypotheses and postulates. It is clear, then, that *principles* can be self-evident and absolute – but only when they are axioms. Hypotheses and postulates, in turn, cannot be self-evident, simply because they are not axioms, nor can axioms be hypotheses and postulates, because they are self-evident.

For Avicenna, hypotheses and postulates are kinds of posits, precisely because their truth is not attained immediately, i.e., because their truth has to be demonstrated somewhere in one of the sciences – and this understanding of hypotheses or postulates is in broad disagreement with how Avicenna thinks Philoponus (as well as Themistius and al-Fārābī) presented hypotheses and postulates. It is on that note that Avicenna states his opposition to the interpretation introduced by *ẓannū* ("they believe") and eventually offers his own definition of hypotheses and postulates a few lines later in *al-Burhān* I.12:

> بل الأصول الموضوعة هي المقدّمات المجهولة في أنفسها التي من حقّها أن تُبَيَّن في صناعة أخرى إذ كان المتعلّم قد قبلها وظنّها بحسن ظنّه بالمعلّم وثقته بأنّ ما يراه من ذلك صدق. والمصادرة ما كان كذلك لكنّ المتعلّم لا يظنّ ما يراه المعلّم ظنّ مقابله أو لم يظنّ شيئاً. والمؤكد بالجملة فيه أن يكون عند المتعلّم ظنّ يقابله بل الأشبه أن تكون المصادرة هي ما تكلّف المتعلّم تسليمه وإن لم يظنّه، كان من المبادئ أو كان من المسائل في ذلك العلم بعينه لمسائل التي تتبيّن بعد فيستسمح بتسليمها في درجة متقدّمة. فيكون المبدأ الواحد الذي ليس بيّناً بنفسه أصلاً موضوعاً باعتبار ومصادرةً باعتبار.

> Rather, hypotheses (*al-uṣūl al-mawḍūʿa*) are premisses unknown in themselves (*al-muqaddimāt al-maǧhūla fī anfusihā*) which, with respect to their truth, are proven (*tubayyana*) in another discipline, since the student (*al-mutaʿallim*) has already accepted them and believes them on account of the high esteem in which he holds the teacher (*bi-ḥusn ẓannihī bi-l-muʿallim*) and his trust in him (*wa-ṯiqatihī*) in that what he thinks about this is true. A postulate (*al-muṣādara*) is something similar, but the student does not believe what the teacher thinks [and instead] believes the opposite[153] or does not believe anything. On the whole, what is certain about it is that the student has a belief which is contrary to [what the teacher believes] – indeed, what is most fitting is that the postulate is what the student accepts reluctantly (*takallafa ... taslīmahū*), even though he does not believe it, be it among the principles (*al-mabādiʾ*) or the questions (*al-masāʾil*) in this current science, because questions are what are proven later on, and so asking for accepting them as premisses is permitted. Thus, one [and the same] principle which is in itself not evident[154] at all may be a hypothesis (*aṣlan mawḍūʿan*) from one point of view and a postulate (*muṣādaratan*) from another. (*al-Burhān* I.12, 114.4–11)[155]

The theme of the teacher (*al-muʿallim*) and the student (*al-mutaʿallim*), which occurred frequently in many of the texts discussed so far, is nowhere as present and central as in this passage here.[156] This reminds us once more that the key terms of Avicenna's

153 Suggesting to read *muqābilahū* for *muqābila* in ʿAfīfī and Badawī.

154 Reading *bayyinan* with Mss. Leiden or. 4 and or. 84, and Badawī for *ʾa-b-y-n-ā* in ʿAfīfī.

155 cf. *al-Išārāt wa-l-tanbīhāt* I.9.3, 82.16–18, 83.2–6; cf. also Maróth, *Die Araber und die antike Wissenschaftstheorie*, 145.

156 cf. Philoponus, *In An. post.*, 34.22, 35.22, 36.1, 127.28, 129.31, 130.4f.

method in *al-Samāʿ al-ṭabīʿī* are teaching (*taʿlīm*) and learning (*taʿallum*). Thus, when Avicenna devotes the second chapter of *al-Samāʿ al-ṭabīʿī* to "the enumeration of the principles of natural things by way of postulation and positing" (*ʿalā sabīl al-muṣādara wa-l-waḍʿ*), he is providing a clear link, via his methodological account in *al-Burhān*, between the subsequent discussion of principles and his remarks on method in the preceding chapter, because both the latter and the former are tied to teaching and learning – but this is just the tip of the methodological iceberg.

The principles we are concerned with in the first chapters of *al-Samāʿ al-ṭabīʿī* are the principles of natural things, such as matter, form, and nature. Here in *al-Burhān*, however, the principles are said to be "premisses" (*muqaddimāt*) employed in demonstrative syllogisms.[157] Avicenna is surely not conflating an epistemological account of principles (on which principles are propositions one can assent to and employ as premisses in syllogisms) with an ontological account of principles (on which principles are real aspects and constituents of concrete objects) – at least no more than Aristotle did when he said the principles of demonstrations are causally explanatory (αἰτίων, *ʿilalahā*) of their conclusions.[158] For Avicenna, the syllogistic structure of true demonstrative argumentation only reflects the structure inherent in the reality of the world.[159] Thus, principles are, generally, what can be employed as premisses of scientific demonstrations and, in this function, are not only explanatory of the conclusion but also causally explanatory of the factual phenomenon which is expressed by the conclusion and which initially was to be explained.

Above, we were told that the principles of the first chapters of *al-Samāʿ al-ṭabīʿī* are not self-evident. In fact, they are characterised as being "unknown in themselves" (*al-maǧhūla fī anfusihā*). Thus, they belong to a subclass of principles that the sciences individually employ in their demonstrations. The technical term for principles is *mabādiʾ* and this is also what Avicenna usually calls them. Although he sometimes prefers to call them *uṣūl* (lit. "roots"), he always means the same collection of ἀρχαί:

الأصول التي تُعلَم أوّلاً قبل البراهين ثلاثة: حدود وأوضاع ويقينيات.

> The fundamentals (*al-uṣūl*) that are [to be] known first before any demonstration are three: definitions (*ḥudūd*), posits (*awḍāʿ*), and axioms (*yaqīniyyāt*). (*al-Naǧāt* I.128, 137.13f.)

---

157 Avicenna explicitly calls certain propositions which he has established in metaphysics "principles" for other sciences, such as physics and psychology. Chapter IV.1.7 of Avicenna's *al-Naǧāt* can serve as an example. There, Avicenna first explains that quantity (*al-kamm*) is not due to matter but to a form inhering in matter. This proposition is, then, explicitly called a principle which belongs to natural things (*wa-hāḏā ayḍan mabdaʾ li-l-ṭabīʿiyyāt*; 508.9); cf. the corresponding passage *al-Ilāhiyyāt* II.3, §15, 78.14. A little later, Avicenna establishes the impossibility of form's existence without matter and of matter's existence without form. These, again, are called principles in the same sense (*wa-ǧumla hāḏihī mabād li-l-ṭabīʿiyyāt*; 512.5); cf. also *al-Ilāhiyyāt* III.7, §13, 139.13; VI.5, §32, 294.4f.

158 *An. post.* I.2, 71b19–24.

159 cf. McGinnis, "Avicenna's Naturalized Epistemology."

We find a virtually identical statement in al-Fārābī:

ومبادئ التعليم في الصناعات أربعة: يقينية وحدود وأصول موضوعة ومصادرات.

> The principles of teaching (*mabādiʾ al-taʿlīm*) in the disciplines are four: axioms (*yaqīniyya*), definitions (*ḥudūd*), hypotheses (*uṣūl mawḍūʿa*), and postulates (*muṣādarāt*). (al-Fārābī, *Book of Demonstration* 5, 87.15f.)[160]

Both assertions ultimately derive from Aristotle's definition of θέσις, ὁρισμός, ὑπόθεσις, and αἴτημα in *Posterior Analytics* I.2 and I.10. The reason that the principles encompass four kinds according to al-Fārābī but three according to Avicenna is that Aristotle presents ὁρισμός and ὑπόθεσις as species of θέσις, and ὑπόθεσις and αἴτημα as species of the homonymously called genus ὑπόθεσις. So, al-Fārābī mentions four kinds of principles, because he subdivides the notion of posits into hypotheses and postulates, whereas Avicenna, in his *al-Naǧāt*, does not.[161] This step of dividing the posits into two subclasses is not explicitly taken by Aristotle but by his commentator Philoponus, who proposes the following hierarchical structure of "deductive principles" in his commentary in *Posterior Analytics* I.2:

> ἧς δὲ θέσεως εἴδη ταῦτα· ἡ μὲν γὰρ ὑπόθεσις ἡ δὲ ὁρισμός ... ἡ δὲ ὑπόθεσις πάλιν διαιρεῖται εἰς δύο εἴδη, ὧν τὸ μὲν ἕτερον ὁμωνύμως τῷ γένει καλεῖται ὑπόθεσις, τὸ δὲ αἴτημα.
>
> The species of posits are these: hypothesis (ὑπόθεσις) and definition (ὁρισμός) ... Hypothesis in turn is divided into two species, of which one is called a hypothesis homonymously with the genus (ὁμωνύμως τῷ γένει καλεῖται ὑπόθεσις), and the other [is called] a postulate (αἴτημα). (Philoponus, *In An. post.*, 35.1–20, tr. by McKirahan, modified)[162]

For Avicenna, then, there are principles such as the principle of non-contradiction or the principle that two things equal to a third are equal to each other. There are also primary notions and concepts such as "existent," "thing," and "necessary" which are famously "impressed in the soul in a primary way."[163] Avicenna, like al-Fārābī, calls all these propositions "axioms" (*yaqīniyyāt*).[164] In addition, however, there are also posits or theses (*awḍāʿ*, sg. *waḍʿ*) which are in need of demonstration. In his *al-Naǧāt*, Avicenna declares:

وأمّا الأوضاع فهي المقدّمات التي ليست بيّنة في نفسها ولكنّ المتعلّم يراود على تسليمها وبيانها إمّا في علم آخر وإمّا بعد حين في ذلك العلم بعينه.

160 Regarding the notions of hypotheses and postulates, cf. esp. also al-Fārābī, *Book of Demonstration* 5, 90.4–13, translated above, 86.

161 Elsewhere, for example in his *Dānešnāme-ye ʿAlāʾī*, for example, Avicenna likewise explicitly presents four kinds of principles; cf. *Dānešnāme-ye ʿAlāʾī* I.32, 143.8–146.5.

162 cf. Themistius, *In An. post.*, 6.28–7.34.

163 *al-Ilāhiyyāt* I.5, §1, 29.5f.; cf. also Aertsen, "Avicenna's Doctrine of Primary Notions."

164 cf. *al-Naǧāt* I.129, 138.15–139.5.

> Posits (*al-awḍāʿ*) are premisses which are not evident in themselves (*laysat bayyina fī nafsihā*), but the student (*al-mutaʿallim*) is tempted to accept them, while their proof (*bayān*) [occurs] either in another science or after a while in that same science. (*al-Naǧāt* I.128, 138.5–7)

This is also the gist of *al-Burhān* II.6, the *locus classicus* for Avicenna's understanding of principles, where he states the following:

> والمبادئ هي المقدّمات التي منها تبرهن تلك الصناعة ولا تُبرهَن هي في تلك الصناعة إمّا لوضوحها وإمّا لجلالة شأنها عن أن تُبرهَن فيها وإنّما تُبرهَن في علم فوقها وإمّا لدنو شأنها عن أن تُبرهَن في ذلك العلم بل في علم دونه وهذا قليل.
>
> Principles are the premisses from which that discipline is demonstrated (*minhā tabarhana tilka l-ṣināʿa*),[165] but they are not demonstrated in that discipline, either because they are evident or because they are of too high a rank to be demonstrated in it and are demonstrated only in a superior science or because they are of too low a rank to be demonstrated in that science but rather [are demonstrated] in an inferior science, even though this is rare. (*al-Burhān* II.6, 155.5–7, tr. by Bertolacci, modified)[166]

In *al-Burhān* II.6, Avicenna distinguishes and extensively discusses in general terms the principles (*mabādi'*), subject-matters (*mawḍūʿāt*), and questions (*masāʾil*) which each science is individually said to have. In the subsequent chapter II.7, he considers the relations between, and correlations among, the various sciences. In this chapter "on the differences of the sciences and their similarities," we read the following:

> ولأنّا قد وضعنا أنّ من مبادئ العلوم ما ليس بيّناً بنفسه فيجب أن يُبيَّن في علم آخر إمّا جزئي مثله أو أعم منه فنتهي لا محالة إلى أعم العلوم. فيجب أن تكون مبادئ سائر العلوم تصحّ في هذا العلم. فلذلك يكون كأن جميع العلوم تُبرهَن على قضايا شرطية متّصلة.
>
> Since we have laid down (*waḍaʿnā*) that among the principles of the sciences (*mabādiʾ al-ʿulūm*) [some] are not evident through themselves (*laysa bayyinan bi-nafsihī*), it is necessary that they are proven in another science, either in a particular [science] like it or in [a science] more common than it, so that we inevitably arrive at the most common of the sciences (*aʿamm al-ʿulūm*). It is, thus, necessary that the principles of the other sciences turn out to be true (*taṣiḥḥu*) in this [most

---

165 Reading *tabarhana* with Badawī (?) for *tubarhanu* in ʿAfīfī, whose reading results in the same translation.

166 Bertolacci, *The Reception of Aristotle's* Metaphysics *in Avicenna's* Kitāb al-Šifāʾ, 134. It is surprising that Avicenna does not mention here the option that these premisses may also be demonstrated after a while in the same science as he did in *al-Naǧāt* (and as al-Fārābī did in his *Book of Demonstration* 5, 90.8–11, translated above, 86). An example of this method is the investigation of the various powers of the soul in *al-Nafs*. There Avicenna states at the beginning that he shall, first, enumerate the various powers of the soul "by way of positing" (*ʿalā sabīl al-waḍʿ*) and, "then," engage in providing a proof for each of them (*al-Nafs* I.5, 32.3f.). Additionally, it is not clear what would be an adequate example for a principle that is demonstrated in a lower science. There is a nice example, however, already in *Posterior Analytics* I.13 that illustrates how different and remote two sciences can be, while still working together in the truly interdisciplinary endeavour of explaining reality. There, Aristotle mentions the case of the slower healing process of round-shaped wounds, which is relevant and well-known in medicine but explained only in geometry (79a13–16); cf. Philoponus, *In An. post.*, 182.9–183.3.

common] science. So, because of this, it is as though all sciences are demonstrated on the basis of combined conditional propositions (*ʿalā qaḍāyā šarṭiyya muttaṣila*). (*al-Burhān* II.7, 165.11–13)[167]

Previous research has already shown that for Avicenna, the Aristotelian division of the scientific enterprise as a whole into different disciplines follows a hierarchical structure.[168] This structure becomes particularly manifest in the relation of the principles, subject-matters, and questions of each science. The science of physics, for example, does not establish the existence of its subject-matter, the sensible body insofar as it is subject to change. It does not establish its principles, such as matter and form, agent and end, the four causes, or the existence of nature or of motion. All these principles were questions in the most common, i.e., the universal, science of metaphysics and were subsequently handed down as established premisses to the particular science of physics being the next lower science. In turn, the science of physics has questions of its own the answers to which may, again, become the principles and subject-matters of the next lower science, where they reappear as propositions in the demonstrations of that science. They are "conditional propositions" (*qaḍāyā šarṭiyya*) – i.e., hypotheses and postulates – insofar as they are employed but not proven in that science. Nonetheless, their truth is safeguarded by the higher sciences and ultimately by the highest of all, viz., metaphysics or "first philosophy."[169] This highest science of all is further characterised in *al-Burhān* II.7 along the following lines:

167 cf. *al-Ilāhiyyāt* I.1, §9, 5.7f.; I.3, §5, 18.12f.; *al-Naǧāt* I.131, 141.16–142.2; IV.1, 493.2–13; *ʿUyūn al-ḥikma* I.7, 11.15; *Dānešnāme-ye ʿAlāʾī* I.32, 144.8–145.1; *al-Hidāya* I.5.2, 123.1f.; *al-Ḥikma al-mašriqiyya* III, 3.2f.; *al-Išārāt wa-l-tanbīhāt* I.9.3, 83.8f.; cf. also Avicenna's Avicenna, *Risāla fī l-aǧrām al-ʿulwiyya* 2, 41.1–5, 42.3–8.

168 cf. Bertolacci, *The Reception of Aristotle's* Metaphysics *in Avicenna's* Kitāb al-Šifāʾ, chs. 6–7; cf. also Gutas, *Avicenna and the Aristotelian Tradition*; Maróth, "Das System der Wissenschaften bei Ibn Sina"; *Die Araber und die antike Wissenschaftstheorie*; Koutzarova, *Das Transzendentale bei Ibn Sīnā*; "Wissenschaft als 'Genesung'"; Eichner, "al-Fārābī and Ibn Sīnā on 'Universal Science' and the System of Sciences."

169 cf. Bertolacci, "The Doctrine of Material and Formal Causality," 141: "Avicenna conceives metaphysics as a discipline encharged with the epistemological foundation of all the other sciences. This is implicit, according to Avicenna, in one of the names that metaphysics bears in the *Ilāhiyyāt*, namely 'first philosophy' (*falsafa ūlā*): first philosophy is presented by Avicenna as the discipline that provides the verification of what he calls, broadly speaking, the 'principles' (*mabādiʾ*) of the other sciences. In the course of *Ilāhiyyāt* I, 2 the identity of these principles is clarified: on the one hand, they are the subject-matters of the particular sciences (like 'body' for natural philosophy, 'measurable quantity' for mathematics and so on), in so far as these are subdivisions of the species of 'existent'; on the other hand, they are certain notions that are common to, but not investigated by, the other sciences (like 'one *qua* one,' 'many *qua* many,' 'coincident,' 'different,' 'contrary' and so on), in so far as these are properties of 'existent.' Furthermore, metaphysics, in Avicenna's conception, also verifies the validity of the principles of the other sciences in the strict sense, i.e. of the axioms of non-contradiction and of the excluded middle (I, 8)."

وأمّا الذي عمومه عموم الموجود والواحد فلا يجوز أن يكون العلم بالأشياء التي تحته جزءاً من علمه ... بل يجب أن تكون العلوم الجزئية ليست أجزاء منه. ولأنّ الموجود والواحد عامّان لجميع الموضوعات فيجب أن تكون سائر العلوم تحت العلم الناظر فيهما ولأنّه لا موضوع أعمّ منهما فلا يجوز أن يكون العلم الناظر فيهما تحت علم آخر.

As for that [science] whose generality (*ʿumūmuhū*) is the generality of the existent and the one (*ʿumūm al-mawǧūd wa-l-wāḥid*), it is not possible that a science about things below [the generality of the existent and the one] could be a part (*ǧuz'an*) of the science of [this generality] ... Rather, it is necessary that the particular sciences are not part of [this general science]. Since the existent and the one are both common to all subject-matters (*ʿāmmān li-ǧamīʿ al-mawḍūʿāt*), it is necessary that the other sciences are below this science investigating these two [sc. the existent and the one]; and since there is no subject-matter more common than these two, it is not possible that the science investigating these two is below another science. (*al-Burhān* II.7, 165.3–7)[170]

First philosophy or metaphysics is the highest of all sciences, because its subject-matter is most general and common, viz., the existent and the one (*al-mawǧūd wa-l-wāḥid*).[171] Since everything that exists is one and existent, these are the most common principles of existing things, so that the science investigating these two is, by the same token, the most common science of all. Other sciences, investigating less common subject-matters, are also less common than this science whose generality and commonality surpasses all other sciences. This leads to a hierarchical structure of the sciences in accordance with the hierarchical structure of subject-matters due to each subject-matter's rank in commonality.

Put simply, one may, as an example, point to the motions of the celestial bodies and the transformations of the elements. It is the task for the metaphysician to establish the existence of the principles of natural bodies and their principles of motion. These results become principles for the physicist's inquiry into how natural powers, being principles of motion, enter into the investigation of natural bodies. The questions discussed in *al-Samāʿ al-ṭabīʿī* include "what" nature and "what" motion are, and generally *how* principles of motion ought to be classified. On the basis of these questions, whose answers become the principles for the sciences below, Avicenna discusses in *al-Samā' wa-l-ʿālam*, how the simple bodies, and especially the celestial bodies, perform their respective motions, while he examines in *al-Kawn wa-l-fasād*, how many simple bodies there are and how they perform other kinds of motion, like alteration and substantial change.[172] It is through considerations like these that Avicenna erects his system of philosophy.

---

170 cf. *al-Naǧāt* I.130, 140.9–14; IV.1, 493.10f.; IV.1.1, 493.16–494.2; *al-Išārāt wa-l-tanbīhāt* I.9.4, 84.1–7; cf. also *al-Ilāhiyyāt* I.3, §12, 21.9–11. For the subject-matter of metaphysics, cf. *al-Ilāhiyyāt* I.2.

171 On the existent and the one as the focus of Avicenna's *al-Ilāhiyyāt* and on their relation to other primary concepts such as "thing," "necessary," and so on, cf. Bertolacci, *The Reception of Aristotle's* Metaphysics *in Avicenna's* Kitāb al-Šifā', chs. 4–5.

172 Regarding the heavenly motion as a subject of scientific inquiry, cf. the particularly illuminating meta-reflection in *al-Burhān* II.9, 178.15–179.3.

It should be noted that Avicenna's understanding of the hierarchy of principles and subject-matters, and the conception of the scientific enterprise as a whole, reflects in an expanded and systematised way certain ideas and opinions that have been expressed, in one way or another, by various figures in the philosophical and scientific tradition before Avicenna, and even by Aristotle himself.[173] Aristotle, for example, mentions in his *Posterior Analytics* I.13 that different sciences my collaborate with one another insofar as they investigate different questions, so that some establish "the fact that" a certain phenomenon exists, whereas others determine "the reason why" this phenomenon occurs.[174] A little later, in *Posterior Analytics* I.27, Aristotle explicitly states that some sciences may be "more exact" (ἀκριβεστέρα, *akṯar istiqṣāʾan wa-yaqīnan*) and, thus, "prior" (προτέρα, *aqdam*) to others.[175] In *Metaphysics* E.1, Aristotle even describes the differences among various sciences in terms of their different subject-matters, in order to emphasise the exceptional position of the science of metaphysics against all other sciences.[176] There are also some passages in the *Physics* that suggest a hierarchical structure, or at least a division of labour, among the sciences.[177]

In the tradition following Aristotle, there was, first and foremost, Alexander, who is mentioned by Averroes in the course of the latter's discussion of *Metaphysics* Λ in the *Tafsīr Mā baʿd al-ṭabīʿa* and subsequently criticised for having held the opinion that "the practitioner of natural philosophy obtains its principles from the practitioner of metaphysics and that the practitioner of metaphysics is responsible for proving (*bayān*) the existence of these principles."[178] Moreover, we find Simplicius who, at the beginning of his commentary on the *Physics*, quotes a passage from Porphyry (d. ~ 305), stating the view that "it is not up to the physicist to investigate whether there are principles of natural things but to the one who ascends [to more sublime inquiries], for the physicist [merely] employs them as given" (ὡς δεδομέναις χρῆται).[179] Furthermore, Ahmad Hasnawi refers to Proclus' commentary on the *Elements* of Euclid (fl. ~ 300 BC) for a similar position, while Bertolacci mentions that Asclepius of Tralles (d. ~ 570)

173 A more detailed investigation of the historical background of Avicenna's conception lies outside the scope of this study.

174 cf. *An. post.* I.13, 78b34–79a16.

175 cf. *An. post.* I.27, 87a31.

176 cf. *Met.* E.1, 1025b3–1026a32; cf. also *Met.* K.4, 1061b17–33.

177 cf. *Phys.* I.9, 192a34–192b1; II.2, 194b14f.; cf. also Menn, "Avicenna's Metaphysics," fn. 10, 147. For the opposite view that "[t]here is no evidence that Aristotle has ever thought of the science of nature as a subordinated science, either in the Metaphysics or elsewhere," cf. Falcon, *Aristotle and the Science of Nature*, 28.

178 Averroes, *Tafsīr Mā baʿd al-ṭabīʿa*, 1429.6–9; this remark is classified as fragment 6F by Freudenthal in Alexander of Aphrodisias, *Die durch Averroes erhaltenen Fragmente Alexanders zur Metaphysik des Aristoteles*; cf. also the very similar statement in fragment 4aF (1420.6–13). A few lines after fragment 4aF, Averroes turns to Avicenna and reproaches him for having held the same view (1432.18–1424.4).

179 Porphyry *apud* Simplicium, *In Phys.*, 9.10–12 (= part of frgm. 119F Smith in Porphyry, *Fragmenta*); cf. Simplicius, *In Phys.*, 15.29–16.2.

ascribed this view in his commentary on the *Metaphysics* to his teacher Ammonius (d. ~ 520).[180] The references to Proclus and Euclid are particularly appropriate, because Avicenna's exposition of hypotheses and postulates in the *Dānešnāme-ye ʿAlāʾī* relies heavily on Euclid and, indeed, explicitly mentions Euclid as its model.[181]

That Avicenna points towards Euclid and the geometrical method makes it further reasonable to see his agenda of grounding physics in metaphysics as an extension of the Neoplatonic view that the physical and corporeal existence, as well as the science thereof, is entirely dependent upon the metaphysical and intelligible reality, as well as the science *thereof*. This is why, according to the Neoplatonists, Aristotle's physics, together with much of his entire philosophy, is only a part of the larger explanatory whole set out in Plato's writings: "So long as an Aristotelian realizes that physical science cannot be explanatorily exhaustive, its ambit is secure," as Lloyd Gerson writes.[182] This, furthermore, explains also why there can be a harmony between Aristotle and Plato in the first place, for what Aristotle wrote, though often correct, remains insufficient, because it lacks precisely its grounding in the metaphysical truth of the Forms and the One as it was delineated by Plato who – and this brings out the relation to geometry and Euclid – was regarded as a Pythagorean. Thus, for science as an enterprise, geometry is the model, and Euclid, Pythagoras, and Plato are its masters.[183]

In the Arabic tradition, then, Abū ʿAlī ibn al-Samḥ (d. 418/1027) interprets Aristotle's intentions in the *Physics* precisely along these lines. Commenting on the first words of chapter I.1, and its declared goal to investigate the "principles, causes, and elements" (ἀρχαὶ ἢ αἴτια ἢ στοιχεῖα, *mabādiʾ aw asbāb aw usṭuqussāt*) of natural things, he writes:

وليس يتكلّم في هذه الثلاثة الأشياء ليبيّن وجودها لأنّ الصنائع الجزئية لا تبيّن أسباب الأمور وإنّما تبيّنها صناعة الفلسفة الأولى.

180 cf. Hasnawi, "La *Physique* du *Šifāʾ*," 76; Bertolacci, *The Reception of Aristotle's* Metaphysics *in Avicenna's* Kitāb al-Šifāʾ, 81f.; "Avicenna and Averroes on the Proof of God's Existence and the Subject-Matter of Metaphysics," 71f.; cf. also Maróth, *Die Araber und die antike Wissenschaftstheorie*, 135–138.

181 cf. *Dānešnāme-ye ʿAlāʾī* I.32, 143.8–146.5; cf. also the reference to Euclid and his *Elements* in *al-Samāʾ wa-l-ʿālam* 5, 39.17–40.1.

182 Gerson, *Aristotle and Other Platonists*, 111.

183 Much of this was worked out in Proclus' commentaries on Euclid's *Elements* and on Plato's *Timaeus*, often in reaction to Iamblichus' "arithmetical version of Aristotelian physics," as it was called and discussed by O'Meara (*Pythagoras Revived*, chs. 8–9, here 178); cf. Martijn, *Proclus on Nature*, ch. 3; "Proclus' Geometrical Method"; cf. also Steel, "Why Should We Prefer Plato's Timaeus to Aristotle's Physics?," esp. 183–187; Nikulin, "Physica more geometrico demonstrata"; Kutash, "Commentary on Nikulin"; Opsomer, "The Natural World." It would be interesting to follow up on the connection between Avicenna and Euclid, and to see to what extent Avicenna is really committed to the Neoplatonic cause in this respect. Such an investigation, however, would carry us far beyond the limits of the present study.

He [sc. Aristotle] does not discuss these three things [sc. matter, form, and privation], in order to prove (*li-yubayyina*) their existence, because particular disciplines do not prove the causes of the things [which they investigate]; only the discipline of first philosophy proves them (*wa-innamā tubayyinuhā ṣināʿat al-falsafa al-ūlā*). (Ibn al-Samḥ's comment in Aristotle, *al-Ṭabīʿa* I.1, 2.4–6)[184]

A few decades before Ibn al-Samḥ, there is the theory we find explicated in al-Fārābī's *Book of Demonstration*, which, as Heidrun Eichner has shown, is to a similar degree comprehensive.[185] That al-Fārābī is, without doubt, the primary influence on Avicenna is particularly apparent from the facts that al-Fārābī's *Maqāla fī aġrāḍ al-ḥakīm fī Kitāb Mā baʿd al-ṭabīʿa* played a seminal role in the formation of Avicenna's understanding of Aristotelian philosophy – a treatise in which we find the following remarks:

وأمّا العلم الكلّي فهو الذي ينظر في الشيء العامّ لجميع الموجودات مثل الوجود والوحدة ... ولأنّ هذه المعاني ليست خاصّة بالطبيعيات بل أعلى من الطبيعيات عموماً فهذا العلم أعلى من علم الطبيعة وبعد علم الطبيعة فلهذا واجب أن يُسمّى علم ما بعد الطبيعة ... والموضوع الأوّل لهذا العلم هو الوجود المطلق وما يساويه في العموم وهو الواحد ... تتبيّن فيه مبادئ العلوم الجزئية وحدود موضوعاتها.

The universal science is the one which investigates the thing that is common to all existents (*al-šayʾ al-ʿāmm li-ǧamīʿ al-mawǧūdāt*), such as existence and oneness (*al-wuǧūḍ wa-l-waḥda*) ... Since[186] these meanings are not proper to natural things but are more exalted than natural things in terms of generality (*ʿumūman*), so this science is more exalted than the science of nature and [comes] after the science of nature (*baʿd ʿilm al-ṭabīʿa*). Thus, because of this, it is necessary that it is called "the science of what is after nature" (*ʿilm mā baʿd al-ṭabīʿa*) [i.e., metaphysics] ... The primary subject of this science is absolute existence and what is equal to it in commonality (*fī l-ʿumūm*), and this is the one ... In it [sc. the science of metaphysics], the principles of the particular sciences as well as the definitions of their subject-matters are proven. (al-Fārābī, *Maqāla fī aġrāḍ al-ḥakīm fī Kitāb Mā baʿd al-ṭabīʿa*, 35.8–36.19)[187]

This passage corresponds closely to what we have seen Avicenna expounding above in the passage from *al-Burhān* II.7. Like Avicenna will do later, al-Fārābī characterises metaphysics as the science concerned with the investigation of existence and oneness (*al-wuǧūḍ wa-l-waḥda*). These notions are highest in terms of generality (*fī l-ʿumūm*) and their common applicability to existing things, because all things that exist are one and existent. Thus, the science investigating these is even after, i.e., more exalted than, the science of nature, and so metaphysics is the highest science of all, providing the particular sciences with their principles and subject-matter.

184 cf. Abū Bišr' similar remarks in Aristotle, *al-Ṭabīʿa* II.7, 138.12–16; cf. also Janos, "Active Nature and Other Striking Features," 141f.

185 cf. Eichner, "al-Fārābī and Ibn Sīnā on 'Universal Science' and the System of Sciences."

186 Reading *wa-li-anna* with Druart, Gutas, and Bertolacci for *li-anna* in Dieterici; cf. Druart, "Le Traité d'al-Fārābī sur les Buts de la Métaphysique d'Aristote," fn. 26, 41; Gutas, *Avicenna and the Aristotelian Tradition*, 273; Bertolacci, *The Reception of Aristotle's* Metaphysics *in Avicenna's* Kitāb al-Šifāʾ, 68.

187 cf. al-Fārābī, *Iḥṣāʾ al-ulūm*, 120.10–121.1.

Regarding physics and its relation to metaphysics, there is one remark in Aristotle which is particularly interesting and relevant for understanding the hierarchy of the scientific enterprise as we have seen it outlined by all these thinkers and, above all, by Avicenna. In this passage from *Metaphysics* Γ.3, we read the following:

> ἐπεὶ δ' ἔστιν ἔτι τοῦ φυσικοῦ τις ἀνωτέρω (ἓν γάρ τι γένος τοῦ ὄντος ἡ φύσις), τοῦ καθόλου καὶ τοῦ περὶ τὴν πρώτην οὐσίαν θεωρητικοῦ καὶ ἡ περὶ τούτων ἂν εἴη σκέψις· ἔστι δὲ σοφία τις καὶ ἡ φυσική, ἀλλ' οὐ πρώτη.
>
> ولاكن إذا كان علم من العلوم أرفع من علم الطبيعيين لأنّ الطباع جنس واحد من أجناس الهوية لذلك ينبغي أن يكون النظر في هذه الأشياء للذين يفحصون عن معرفة الكلّ وعن الجوهر الأوّل فإنّ العلم الطبيعي واحد من أصناف العلوم إلّا أنّه ليس بالعلم المتقدّم الأوّل.
>
> However, since there is one kind of thinker who is even above the natural philosopher (for nature is only one particular genus of being), the discussion of these [things] also will belong to him whose inquiry is universal and deals with primary substance (τοῦ καθόλου καὶ τοῦ περὶ τὴν πρώτην οὐσίαν θεωρητικοῦ, *yafḥaṣūna ʿan maʿrifat al-kull wa-ʿan al-ǧawhar al-awwal*). Natural science also is a kind of wisdom (σοφία τις, *wāḥid min aṣnāf al-ʿulūm*), but it is not the first kind (ἀλλ' οὐ πρώτη, *illā anna laysa bi-l-ʿilm al-mutaqaddim al-awwal*). (*Met.* Γ.3, 1005a33–b2, tr. by Ross, modified)

Although physics is a "kind of wisdom," it is neither the first kind nor is it a universal science. For Avicenna, too, physics is a particular science dependent upon metaphysics for its ultimate foundation and validity.[188] The science of physics may be the most common science within natural philosophy, but it is not universal. This is the reason for why, at the outset of physics, we have to be informed about the principles of that science "by way of postulation and positing" (*ʿalā sabīl al-muṣādara wa-l-waḍʿ*).[189] This, in turn, entails that those chapters of Avicenna's *al-Samāʿ al-ṭabīʿī* which provide an account of the principles of natural things, i.e., most of the entire first book, strictly speaking, have "nothing to do with natural philosophy" at all (*lā yuḫāliṭu l-ṭabīʿiyyāt*) as he acknowledges in *al-Samāʿ al-ṭabīʿī* I.2.[190] In other words, Avicenna conceives of the first two book of Aristotle's *Physics* as a propaedeutic to the science of physics.

188 cf. Bertolacci, "The Doctrine of Material and Formal Causality," 141; *The Reception of Aristotle's* Metaphysics *in Avicenna's* Kitāb al-Šifāʾ, ch. 7, referring to *al-Qiyās* I.2, 13.14–17, and *al-Burhān* II.9, 178.8–179.13.

189 *al-Samāʿ al-ṭabīʿī* I.2, 13.3. In his *Risāla fī l-ağrām al-ʿulwiyya*, Avicenna calls the same method that "by way of positing and adherence" (*ʿalā sabīl al-waḍʿ wa-l-taqlīd*; *Risāla fī l-ağrām al-ʿulwiyya* 3, 43.14f.). In his *al-Išārāt wa-l-tanbīhāt*, Avicenna even specifically states that those sciences which have hypotheses and postulates should introduce them at the beginning as a kind of preface; cf. *al-Išārāt wa-l-tanbīhāt* I.9.3, 83.5f. The reason for that advice is made explicit in his *Dānešnāme-ye ʿAlāʾī*, where Avicenna recommends one imitate the practice employed by Euclid in his *Elements*; cf. *Dānešnāme-ye ʿAlāʾī* I.32, 143.8–146.5.

190 *al-Samāʿ al-ṭabīʿī* I.2, §10, 16.8.

While Avicenna's *al-Samāʿ al-ṭabīʿī* contains four books, we may say that it consists of two parts.[191] There is first a propaedeutic covering all that which has to be presupposed for the composition of demonstrative syllogisms, the demonstration of knowledge, and, ultimately, the attainment of the science of physics in full. This is the first book of *al-Samāʿ al-ṭabīʿī* and it presents – but does not establish – the principles of natural things as hypotheses and postulates, corresponding to the contents of *Physics* I–II. The three remaining books, then, form the second part which is primarily an investigation of motion. It includes a study of motion itself as well as important related matters, in particular, place and time – this is book II. It is followed by an investigation of the subject which undergoes motion, i.e., the natural body being a continuous quantity, thereby, dealing with its non-atomic composition as well as the ways in which infinity may or may not be applicable to it and to its motion, and on the rectilinear motions due to its having a nature – this is book III. There is finally a miscellaneous book IV on various aspects of the motions of the natural body, including the numerical unity of motion; the contrary nature of motion and rest; and accidental, forced, and natural motion. In other words, Avicenna's *al-Samāʿ al-ṭabīʿī* contains a work on physics that is preceded by a long propaedeutic, which, strictly speaking, has "nothing to do with natural philosophy."

If it is correct to claim that the first book of Avicenna's *al-Samāʿ al-ṭabīʿī* is above all a highly elaborate preface to the actual physical elaboration on the essential feature of nature, i.e., motion, it can further be seen why almost all of Avicenna's great *summae* of philosophy, his *al-Šifāʾ*, *al-Naǧāt*, *ʿUyūn al-ḥikma*, *Dānešnāme-ye ʿAlāʾī*, *al-Hidāya*, *al-Ḥikma al-ʿArūḍiyya*, and *al-Ḥikma al-mašriqiyya*, introduce their sections on physics with at least a brief remark on these methodological underpinnings and the hierarchical structure of the scientific enterprise.[192] The order and structure of all these great works follows the Aristotelian division of the sciences which we have seen Avicenna transforming into a genuine division of labour among the sciences. Only his late *al-Išārāt wa-l-tanbīhāt* are strikingly different in that, although they examine principles, postulates, and hypotheses in their first logical part, they do not provide a comparable explanatory note at the beginning of its second part. The reason for this

191 q.v. also fn. 8 above, 4.

192 Admittedly, the methodological remark in the physics of Avicenna's *al-Hidāya* is all too brief and consists of merely two words marking the principles of physics as being "posited in" the science of physics (*yūḍaʿu fīhi*; *al-Hidāya* II.1, 135.2). Yet, this may have been enough for a rather untechnical compendium as *al-Hidāya*. After all, even in this work, Avicenna has already explained his method more fully in the preceding logical sections. Regarding *al-Ḥikma al-ʿArūḍiyya*, I was not able to find a corresponding passage in the logical sections of this work. There may be different reasons for this, among them the bad condition of the single manuscript containing the work, the dubious form of its edition, and the fact that the introduction to the sections on natural philosophy (which is a less complete version of the one contained in *al-Naǧāt*) already outlines the theoretical background in a concise manner. Thus, a corresponding section in the logic of *al-Ḥikma al-ʿArūḍiyya* may either be lost or never have existed.

seems to be obvious. Since Avicenna dispenses with the Aristotelian division of the sciences in his *al-Išārāt wa-l-tanbīhāt* altogether, he can easily pass over any such prefatory remark, and arrange the philosophical material in an entirely different and unprecedented order. All the other major works, however, make explicit the methodology of his scientific approach, sometimes relatively briefly as in Avicenna's *'Uyūn al-ḥikma*:

> كلّ واحد من العلوم الجزئية وهي المتعلّقة ببعض الأمور والموجودات يقتصر المتعلّم فيه أن يسلّم أصولاً ومبادئَ تتبرهن في غير علمه وتكون في علمه مستعملة على سبيل الأصول الموضوعة. والطبيعي علم جزئي فله أصول موضوعة فنعدّها عدّاً ونبرهن عليها في الحكمة الأولى.
>
> In each of the particular sciences, and these are those concerned with some of the things and existents, the student is content with accepting fundamentals (*uṣūlan*) and principles (*mabādi'a*) which are demonstrated (*tatabarhanu*) in a science other than his and which are employed in his science as hypotheses (*al-uṣūl al-mawḍū'a*). Natural [philosophy] is a particular science and, thus, has hypotheses (*uṣūl mawḍū'a*), whose number we enumerate and which we demonstrate in first wisdom (*al-ḥikma al-ūlā*). (*'Uyūn al-ḥikma* II.2, 17.12–15)

Sometimes the exposition is a bit more elaborate, as in *al-Naǧāt*:

> وللعلوم أيضاً مبادئ وأوائل من جهة ما يُبرهَن عليها وهي المقدّمات التي تُبرهِن ذلك العلم ولا تتبرهن فيه إمّا لبيانها وإمّا لعلوها عن أن تتبرهن في ذلك العلم بل إنّما تتبرهن في علم آخر. والعلم الطبيعي من تلك الجملة. وليس ولا على واحد من أصحاب العلوم الجزئية إثبات مبادئ علمه ولا إثبات صحّة المقدّمات التي تبرهن بها ذلك العلم بل بيان مبادئ العلوم الجزئية على صاحب العلم الكلّي وهو العلم الإلهي والعلم الناظر فيما بعد الطبيعة وموضوعه الموجود المطلق والمطلوب فيه المبادئ العامّة واللواحق العامّة. فلنضع المبادئ الكلّية للعلم الطبيعي الذي هو واحد من العلوم الجزئية وضعاً.
>
> Moreover, the [particular] sciences also have principles and primitives (*mabādi' wa-awā'il*) with regard to that which is demonstrated on their basis. They are the premisses which demonstrate this science[193] but which are not demonstrated[194] in it either because of their obviousness or their being [too] exalted to be demonstrated in this science. Instead they are demonstrated[195] only in another science. Natural philosophy belongs to this group [of particular sciences]. It is not up to one of the proponents of a particular science to establish (*iṯbāt*) the principles of his science[196] nor to establish the soundness of the premisses through which this science is demonstrated (*bihā tabarhana ḏālika l-'ilm*),[197] rather proving the principles of a particular science is up to the

---

193 One is tempted to suggest *allatī ⟨bihā⟩ tabarhana ḏālika l-'ilm*, as below in this quotation, instead of *allatī tubarhinu ḏālika l-'ilm*.

194 Reading *tatabarhanu* with al-Kurdī, Fakhry, and 'Umayra for *t-b-r-h-n* in Dānešpažūh, who mentions *tatabarhanu* as a reading in "another manuscript."

195 Reading *tatabarhanu* with al-Kurdī, Fakhry, and 'Umayra for *t-b-r-h-n* in Dānešpažūh, who mentions *tatabarhanu* as a reading in "another manuscript."

196 Reading *mabādi' 'ilmihī* with Dānešpažūh for *mabādi' mawḍū' 'ilmihī* in al-Kurdī, Fakhry, and 'Umayra.

197 Reading *tabarhana* with Dānešpažūh for *y-b-r-h-n* in al-Kurdī, Fakhry, and 'Umayra.

> proponent of the universal science, and this is the divine science and the science investigating what is after nature (*fī mā baʿd al-ṭabīʿa*). Its subject-matter is absolute existence and what is sought in it are the general principles and general concomitants. So, let us lay down the universal principles as posits (*fa-l-naḍaʿu l-mabādiʾ al-kulliyya … waḍʿan*) for natural philosophy, which is one of the particular sciences. (*al-Naǧāt* II.1, 189.13–190.8)[198]

The theoretical background presupposed by these statements is distributed over several chapters of *al-Burhān* of Avicenna's *al-Šifāʾ*, where they are meticulously discussed. They are also found in an abbreviated form in the logical sections of his other compendia. In this chapter, I tried to touch upon this background insofar as it pertains to our understanding of Avicenna's discussion of principles in *al-Samāʿ al-ṭabīʿī* and the methodological foundation of that work as a whole. It is all too clear that further studies devoted to Avicenna's logic, and above all his *al-Burhān*, are necessary before we can form an adequate understanding of Avicenna's complex theory of scientific methodology.[199] Meanwhile, I would like to conclude this chapter with a proof showing that Avicenna is also capable of putting an intricate methodological feature in a form that is both brief and to the utmost degree intelligible, as he does in this comparatively succinct note from the *Dānešnāme-ye ʿAlāʾī*, which contains all necessary information about the status of principles within natural philosophy:

و هر چه از اصول بایست مر علم طبیعی را و مر علم ریاضی را اندر علم برین گفته آمد.

> All that which is required with regard to principles in natural philosophy and in mathematics has already been stated in metaphysics. (*Dānešnāme-ye ʿAlāʾī* III.1, 2.10)[200]

By now, we have come to know some of the important aspects of Avicenna's methodology as it pertains to his *al-Samāʿ al-ṭabīʿī*, to other parts of his *al-Šifāʾ*, and to his philosophical thought as a whole. In recourse to Philoponus' own engagement

---

198 cf. *al-Naǧāt* II.1, 197.14f.; cf. also the corresponding passages in *al-Ḥikma al-ʿArūḍiyya* II.1, 113.9–16, 117.3–5.

199 Moreover, it will be the task of even more research to determine whether – and if so, for what reasons and to what extent – Avicenna abandoned this theory in his more mature works, as their apparent departure from the traditional ordering of the sciences may indicate. While *al-Ḥikma al-mašriqiyya* (and also already *Dānešnāme-ye ʿAlāʾī*) treats metaphysics before physics but after logic, the late *al-Išārāt wa-l-tanbīhāt* no longer uphold any real distinction between the sciences at all and discuss philosophy *as such*, following a first part devoted to logic (in which, among other things, Avicenna nonetheless – and one is tempted to ask why – elaborates on the traditional divisions of the sciences and the hierarchical method of principles that are proven in one science and employed in another as hypotheses and postulates). For a description of these works and their structure, cf. Gutas, *Avicenna and the Aristotelian Tradition*; for the new structure of Avicenna's *al-Išārāt wa-l-tanbīhāt*, cf. also McGinnis, "Pointers, Guides, Founts and Gifts."

200 That Avicenna here writes that the principles *have already* been stated in metaphysics is insofar appropriate for his *Dānešnāme-ye ʿAlāʾī*, as in this work, Avicenna reverses his usual order of exposition and treats metaphysics before the physics, as he states in *Dānešnāme-ye ʿAlāʾī* II.2, 8.7–10; cf. also Gutas, *Avicenna and the Aristotelian Tradition*, 118.

with the first chapter of Aristotle's *Physics* and with its delicate relation to *Posterior Analytics* I.2, I expounded Avicenna's *mode of instruction* and showed that the key terms to his philosophical – one may even be tempted to say "didactic" – agenda are *taʿlīm* ("teaching") and *taʿallum* ("learning"). While these two terms have their roots in certain passages of Aristotle's logical works, just as much as in Avicenna's biography and his social milieu, it emerged that the methodology which these terms encapsulate determines the way in which Avicenna develops the scientific topics he is about to discuss and the manner in which he approaches the contributions of his predecessors. His method affects the composition and structure of his *al-Samāʿ al-ṭabīʿī* in particular, and his own conception of philosophical enterprise in general, as he advances literally "from the universals to the particulars," thus dispensing with everything that may disturb his overall demonstrative procedure.[201]

Having thus come to know the methodological foundation of Avicenna's *al-Samāʿ al-ṭabīʿī*, let me now proceed to the actual content of that work and, first, examine Avicenna's account of the principles of natural things as well as its historic background in Aristotle's *Physics* and the late ancient commentary tradition.

201 This is also the reason for why Avicenna almost entirely dispenses with an investigation of the opinions of the Presocratics which, after all, was an essential part of Aristotle's method in the first book of the *Physics*. I shall analyse Avicenna's attitude towards these doxographic elements in Aristotle's works in a future publication.

3 The Subject-Matter of Physics

The subject-matter of physics, according to Avicenna, is "the sensible body insofar as it is subject to change" (*al-ğism al-maḥsūs min ğiha mā huwa wāqiʿ fī l-taġayyur*).[1] One might think that this an unfortunate formulation, as it appears that throughout his *al-Samāʿ al-ṭabīʿī*, Avicenna almost exclusively speaks of "natural things" (*al-umūr al-ṭabīʿiyya*) or "natural bodies" (*al-ağsām al-ṭabīʿiyya*) but no longer of "the sensible body."[2] Yet, it should be clear that a sensible body which is subject to change is precisely what a "natural body" or a "natural thing" amounts to.[3] Avicenna is not concerned with mathematical and purely intelligible bodies but with those bodies which exist in extra-mental reality and which, thus, are perceptible by sense.[4] Moreover, it is these bodies which are subject to change, as they either come-to-be and perish, undergo alteration, grow and diminish, or move with regard to place or position.[5]

Nonetheless, it is a significant detail that Avicenna introduces the subject-matter of physics in a way which already indicates a distinction between the sensible body as such (i.e., insofar as it is a body) and the sensible body as natural (i.e., insofar as it is subject to change). This distinction is particularly appropriate for Avicenna's

1 *al-Samāʿ al-ṭabīʿī* I.1, §1, 7.7f.; cf. *al-Ilāhiyyāt* I.2, §2, 10.6–8; *al-Nağāt* II, preface, 189.9f. ≈ *al-Ḥikma al-ʿArūḍiyya* II.1, 113.7f.; *ʿUyūn al-ḥikma* II.1, 17.1f.; *Dānešnāme-ye ʿAlāʾī* II.2, 5.15–6.3; *al-Hidāya* II.1, 134.4–6; *al-Ḥikma al-mašriqiyya* III, 2.7f.; cf. also *al-Samāʿ al-ṭabīʿī* III.1, §1, 177.4–12. Avicenna's explicit focus on bodies echoes Aristotle's statement in *De caelo* I.1 (somewhat similarly repeated in III.1) that "the science of nature" is concerned with "bodies and magnitudes as well as their properties and motions, and further with the principles of such substances" (*Cael.* I.1, 268a1–4); cf. *Phys.* III.4, 202b30–36; *Cael.* III.1, 298a27–b5; *Met.* K.4, 1061b28–32; cf. also *Met.* Γ.3, 1005a33–b2; E.1, esp. 1025b7–28 and 1026a27–32; Z.11, 1037a13–16; cf. further the remarks by Falcon in *Aristotle and the Science of Nature*, 31–54; "The Subject Matter of Aristotle's Physics."

2 Exceptions are *al-Samāʿ al-ṭabīʿī* II.8, §2, 124.7; III.3, §§1–2, 184.5, 185.1–4; cf. also his dialectic discussion concerning the existence of place in *al-Samāʿ al-ṭabīʿī* II.5, §2, 111.15–112.3, which relies on the notion of "sensible substance" (*ğawhar maḥsūs*). Avicenna does not pick up on this terminology when he begins to set out his own account.

3 I take "natural body" to mean all bodies which have a nature. This understanding of natural bodies includes artefacts as well as "natural" objects in the strict sense (both animate and inanimate). There is a nature in a statue and in a cake just as much as there is a nature in a stone and in a horse. This is evident in light of the fact that all these things have a natural tendency to move downwards. So, all things in which one can find a nature being a principle of motion, are natural things – and these are precisely the things which are sensible and which are such as to undergo motion and change.

4 It has been suggested, albeit neither convincingly nor with any evidence, that "in choosing 'sensible body' Avicenna likely has in mind the first division in Porphyry's tree" (Houser, "Avicenna and Aquinas's *De principiis naturae*, cc. 1–3," 582). This suggestion is all the more unconvincing, as in Porphyry's tree "sensible" does not denote an aptness for being perceived but a capacity for perception. Plants are classified as "insensible" bodies, not because they are invisible but because they have traditionally been taken as having no sensation.

5 For Avicenna's account of positional motion as a fifth kind of change, q.v. below, 340ff.

https://doi.org/10.1515/9783110546798-004

exposition of the principles of natural things in *al-Samāʿ al-ṭabīʿī*, as his whole account relies on a systematic distinction between corporeal existence, on the one hand, and its susceptibility to motion and change, on the other. In fact, with this formulation, Avicenna marks a first, and not merely accidental, difference between his treatment of principles and that of Aristotle in the *Physics*.[6]

Aristotle derives the three principles of natural things in the first book of his *Physics* through an inquiry into the notion of change or motion (κίνησις, *ḥaraka*). He, first, investigates Presocratic notions of principles in *Physics* I.2–4 and, on that basis, affirms in chapter I.5 that "the principles must be contraries," because any motion is governed by contraries or, more precisely, occurs within a range which is bounded by contraries.[7] In *Physics* I.6, then, Aristotle realises that two contraries alone are insufficient for explaining motion and that an additional third thing is required: an underlying subject (ὑποκείμενον, *mawḍūʿ*) on which the contraries act or which changes from one contrary to the respective other.[8] Despite the fruitful results of these earlier chapters, Aristotle announces a new investigation of "coming-to-be in general" (περὶ πάσης γενέσεως, *fī l-kawn ʿāmmatan*), in order to settle the question about the number of principles definitively. This investigation is carried out in chapter I.7.[9] The result of Aristotle's investigation in this chapter is that there is, first, the underlying object which, he states, is "one in number but two in form" (τὸ μὲν ὑποκείμενον ἀριθμῷ μὲν ἕν, εἴδει δὲ δύο, *al-mawḍūʿ wāḥid bi-l-ʿadad iṯnān bi-l-ṣūra*). Second, however, there is also "the privation or contrary which is accidental" (ἡ δὲ στέρησις καὶ ἡ ἐναντίωσις συμβεβηκός, *al-ʿadam wa-l-taḍādd humā min nawʿ al-aʿrāḍ*).[10] Aristotle exemplifies this with the notion of the unmusical man who becomes musical. The unmusical man as the underlying thing is *one* subject undergoing the motion. Yet, that man is characterised as "unmusical" and, therefore, is *two* in form: he is a single man, but he is also unmusical and considered under that additional formal aspect of being unmusical. The envisaged motion, then,

---

6 In addition, it is clear that the historical setting of Avicenna's expositions is altogether different from that of Aristotle's investigation, because Avicenna does not have to argue against the Eleatic challenge of denying the existence of motion as such.

7 *Phys.* I.5, 189a9f.; cf. *Phys.* I.5, 188b21–26; cf. also Bogen, "Change and Contrariety in Aristotle."

8 *Phys.* I.6, 189a21–26.

9 *Phys.* I.7, 189b30–32, tr. by Hardie/Gaye, modified; q.v. above, 56. According to a recent interpretation of Kelsey and of Ebrey, Aristotle's intention in *Physics* I.6 is to "systematically undermine" the arguments given in the preceding chapter I.5 (Kelsey, "The Place of I 7 in the Argument of *Physics* I," 182, 186, 191, 206; Ebrey, *Aristotle's Motivation for Matter*, 32). With their claim, both Kelsey and Ebrey elaborate on a remark made by William Charlton that the prominent chapter I.7, far from being a superfluous restatement of the results achieved in I.5 and I.6, resolves what he called a "mild antinomy" between these two chapters (his comments in *Physics*, 67). While this claim certainly is appealing – and although it is also true that *Physics* I.7 is not a redundant recapitulation – I do not follow the readings offered by Kelsey and by Ebrey, as Aristotle nowhere seems to deliberately, let alone "systematically," start out to undermine his own previous arguments.

10 *Phys.* I.7 190b23–27.

leads that man from being unmusical to its contrary, viz., being musical, which is a state from which the man was hitherto deprived. The precise number of principles, then, is somewhat imprecisely given by Aristotle as “in a way two but in another way three.”[11] Aristotle, however, is satisfied and concludes as follows:

> πόσαι μὲν οὖν καὶ τίνες εἰσὶν αἱ ἀρχαί, ἐκ τούτων θεωρείσθωσαν.
>
> وبهذا ينبغي تحديد عدد المبادئ وطبيعتها.
>
> From this, then, let it now be investigated how many and what the principles are. (*Phys.* I.7, 191a21f.)

The central notion of Aristotle’s analysis is change or motion, and the principles are established on the basis of an investigation of that phenomenon. In fact, the first result achieved in *Physics* I.5 is that the principles must include a pair of contraries, precisely because every *motion* is delimited by two contraries: one from which the motion begins and one towards which it is directed. Aristotle’s investigation can, therefore, be characterised as an inquiry into the natural body insofar as it is precisely this: a natural body, i.e., a body which is subject to change.

By contrast, Avicenna’s exposition in *al-Samāʿ al-ṭabīʿī* I.2 follows a different route. He does not arrive at his account of principles through an inquiry into change. In fact, Avicenna – as I have argued in the preceding chapter – does not even *inquire* into anything.[12] Instead, he puts forth the principles of natural things through the common notion of corporeality, because natural bodies are, first and foremost, corporeal.[13] The more particular notion of change and motion is brought into the discussion only later, and even there, it does not serve as an *explanans* of said principles, as in Aristotle, but as an *explanandum*, as we shall see.[14] Thus, although it is true that Avicenna follows Aristotle in accepting matter, form, and privation as the fundamental principles of natural things, he does not follow his predecessor’s strategy for establishing them. It is, then, this departure from Aristotle that is already noticeable in Avicenna’s introduction of the subject-matter of physics as “the sensible body insofar as it is subject to change,” as it contains an indication that Avicenna separates the corporeality of the physical world from the phenomenon of motion within the physical world. In fact, only little later, Avicenna makes this distinction explicit, effectively decoupling the investigation of motion and change from the investigation of that which undergoes motion and change by announcing the following:

---

11 *Phys.* I.7, 190b29f. It should be noted that the search for the precise number of principles is nothing other than the guiding question for most of the first book of the *Physics* and is introduced already in the first sentence of *Physics* I.2 at 184b15–20; cf. also *Phys.* I.6, 189a11f., 189b27–29; I.7, 190b29f., 191a21f.

12 q.v. above, 75ff.

13 cf. McGinnis, “Making Something of Nothing,” 554.

14 q.v. below, 201ff.

لكنّ هذا الجسم الطبيعي من حيث هو جسم طبيعي له مبادئ ومن حيث هو كائن وفاسد بل متغيّر بالجملة له زيادة في المبادئ.

However, this natural body insofar as it is a natural body has principles (*lahū mabādiʾ*), and insofar as it comes-to-be and perishes, and, indeed, simply is subject to change, it has additional principles (*lahū ziyāda fī l-mabādiʾ*). (*al-Samāʿ al-ṭabīʿī* I.2, §3, 13.13f.)

This distinction gives rise to two separate analyses: one which considers the essential constituents of the natural body that belong to it precisely insofar as it is a body, viz., matter and form, and another which is an additional or accidental examination of whatever is required for accounting for this body's engagement with change and motion.[15] So, Avicenna will, first, teach about the former, viz., the principles of the natural body insofar as it is a body, before advancing to any additional principle that pertains to the natural body insofar as it is in motion. This is nothing but a clear realisation of his own agenda: to begin with what is most common and to proceed to what is more particular. In the following analysis, I shall follow the direction of Avicenna's instruction in this regard and, first, focus on the account of corporeality and the essential principles of body, before turning my attention to the additional principle of privation that is required to explain motion and change.

3.1 Body, Substance, and Corporeality

In the first line of *al-Samāʿ al-ṭabīʿī* I.2, Avicenna announces that he "will enumerate" (*sanaʿudduhā*) the principles that belong to natural things (*al-umūr al-ṭibāʿiyya*).[16] A natural thing is immediately identified as a natural body (*al-ǧism al-ṭabīʿī*), which is said to be a substance (*al-ǧawhar*).

That natural bodies are substances is well established. For Avicenna, the defining characteristic of a substance is that "it is not in a subject at all" (*lā yakūnu fī mawḍūʿ*

15 Avicenna's distinction may have its roots in a differentiatiοn found in earlier commentaries on the *Physics*. Simplicius, for example, writes that "all natural things have elements and principles, two *per se*, form and matter, and in an accidental sense also privation." A little later, he adds that it is "one thing to seek the principles and elements of natural things from which, as primary ingredients, they are *per se* … and another to seek the principles of change" (*In Phys.*, 216.6–8, 30–34, tr. by Mueller). In turn, John Philoponus, while discussing the relation between matter and privation, draws a distinction between what is a being and a principle *per se* (matter), and what is so merely *per accidens* (privation); cf. *In Phys.*, 161.4–20.

16 Somewhat surprisingly, Avicenna uses here in the first sentence of *al-Samāʿ al-ṭabīʿī* II.1, and only here, the expression *al-umūr al-ṭibāʿiyya* instead of the more common *al-umūr al-ṭabīʿiyya*. Even though the latter is attested in Ms. Leiden or. 4, the former is found in Ms. Leiden or. 84 and has been retained by all modern editors, Zāyid, Āl Yāsīn, and McGinnis. On the whole, however, it must be said that the use of the singular *ṭibāʿ* as an apparently synonymous alternative to *ṭabīʿa*, while not frequent in Avicenna, does not seem to be entirely uncommon either.

al-battata).[17] He recognises four kinds of substances: matter, form, their composite, and soul (and *a fortiori* intellect).[18] Of these four kinds of substances, the only relatively uncontroversial case is the composite of matter and form, viz., body.[19] Such bodies are individuals (*al-šaḫṣiyyāt*) and have their occurrence in concrete reality (*al-ḥuṣūl fī l-aʿyān*) as independent objects which do not subsist in anything else. They are not in a subject (*lā fī mawḍūʿ*) and are, for that precise reason, substances. This is what Avicenna, in agreement with Aristotle's *Categories*, calls "primary substance" (*al-ǧawhar al-awwal*).[20]

Animate bodies have a soul, and some ensouled bodies even have an intellect. It is a difficult question whether the animate body, in which the soul exists, is a subject for the soul or not. If it were a subject, and if the soul would exist in a body as in a subject, then the soul could not be a substance according to the above-stated definition. Avicenna is determined to settle this potentially troublesome question right at the beginning of his complex treatment of soul in his *al-Nafs* and establishes, in chapter I.3, "that soul belongs to the category of substance" (*anna l-nafs dāḫila fī maqūlat al-ǧawhar*).[21] He concludes the discussion with the result, already established in the first chapter, that the soul is a perfection *for* a subject (*kamāl li-mawḍūʿ*) but is not *in* a subject.[22] The soul is, thus, a substance and not an accident.[23]

---

17 *al-Ilāhiyyāt* II.1, §2, 57.11; cf. *al-Maqūlāt* I.3, 23.3; I.6, 46.8–11; *al-Nafs* I.1, 8.20f.; *al-Naǧāt* IV.1.3, 497.1; *ʿUyūn al-ḥikma* III.1, 48.5f.; *Dānešnāme-ye ʿAlāʾī* II.3, 9.13–15; *Kitāb al-Ḥudūd*, §42, 24.1–8; cf. *Cat.* 2, 1a20–1b6; 5, 2a11–19; *Met.* Δ.8, 1017b13f.; cf. also the discussion in *Met.* Z.3, esp. 1029a7–9.

18 cf. *al-Ilāhiyyāt* II.1, §§8–10, 59.13–60.14; *al-Naǧāt* IV.1.3, 497.6–14; IV.1.8, 512.7–9; *ʿUyūn al-ḥikma* III.1, 48.7–12; *Dānešnāme-ye ʿAlāʾī* II.3, 10.11–14; cf. also *Met.* Z.10, 1035a1–4; Λ.4, 1070b10–15; *De an.* II.1, 412a6–22; cf. further Hyman, "Aristotle's First Matter," 398–400; A. D. Stone, "Avicenna"; Richardson, "Avicenna and Aquinas on Form and Generation," 256f.; Benevich, "Fire and Heat."

19 I say "relatively," because even in this case we have to worry about the ontological status of artefacts, an issue which cannot be discussed here.

20 *al-Maqūlāt* III.2, 95.15–96.7; cf. *Categories* 5, 2a11–14, 3a7–9; *Met.* Z.2, 1028b8–15.

21 *al-Nafs* I.3, 22.2.

22 *al-Nafs* I.3, 26.4f.; cf. *al-Nafs* I.1, 10.11–19.

23 cf. *al-Nafs* I.1, 9.13–16; 3, 23.8–10; *al-Naǧāt* II.6.9–10; *al-Ḥikma al-ʿArūḍiyya* II.6 (?), 158.10 ; *ʿUyūn al-ḥikma* II.16, 46.1f.; *Dānešnāme-ye ʿAlāʾī* III.37, 101.2f; *al-Hidāya* II.8, 217.7–220.6; *al-Ḥikma al-mašriqiyya* III.24, 136.3–138.11; *al-Išārāt wa-l-tanbīhāt* II.3.5, 121.19–121.10; cf. also Alexander of Aphrodisias, *Quaestiones* I.8; 17; cf. further *Quaestiones* I.26; q.v. fn. 34 below, 118. The famous argument about the "flying man" in *al-Nafs* I.1 does not itself prove the substantiality of the soul but primarily indicates that the human intellective soul is immaterial and independent from the body. This is later properly proven in *al-Nafs* V.2, 187.6–190.16, thus establishing that the human intellective soul is a substance; cf. *al-Nafs* I.3, 22.3–5. In chapter I.3, however, Avicenna focuses on the animal and vegetative souls, as these require a separate treatment due to their more intimate relation to the body and, thus, their less apparent substantiality. Still, the "flying man" as well as other considerations from *al-Nafs* I.1 provide Avicenna with concrete material to substantiate his argument now in chapter I.3 that the animal and the vegetative souls, too, do not exist in the body as in a subject, thus passing the test for being a substance; cf. Hasse, *Avicenna's* De Anima *in the Latin West*, 85f.

A difficulty similar to the one about the substantiality of the soul also affects the status of form.[24] Since form inheres in matter and seems to exist in matter as in a subject, it is *prima facie* rather difficult to see how form can be a substance. This is all the more troublesome, because Avicenna not infrequently calls matter a "subject" (*mawḍūʿ*). His ultimate reasons for doing so, presumably, lie in the fact that Aristotle did the same, for, having established the underlying thing (τὸ ὑποκείμενον, *al-mawḍūʿ*) as one of the three principles of change, he identifies matter as the "primary underlying thing" (τὸ πρῶτον ὑποκείμενον, *al-mawḍūʿ al-awwal*) out of which things come-to-be and which, once the thing has come-to-be, serves as a non-accidental constituent of that thing.[25] In this regard, matter clearly seems to be an underlying subject that receives forms. This raises the question of how form could itself be substance, if it is said to exist in a subject.

To answer this worry, Avicenna distinguishes in *al-Ilāhiyyāt* II.1 between a "substrate" (*al-maḥall*) and a "subject" (*al-mawḍūʿ*).[26] The expression "subject" signifies "something which comes to subsist through itself and through its specificity (*bi-nafsihī wa-nawʿiyyatihī qāʾiman*), and which, thereupon, may by itself become a cause through which something [else] can subsist in it."[27] By "something [else]," Avicenna means an accident. An accident is such that it is unable to subsist by itself and which requires a subject to subsist in.[28] This subject, of course, does subsist by itself as an independent entity. On the other hand, the expression "substrate" denotes "everything in which something [else] inheres (*yaḥilluhū šayʾ*) and which comes-to-be in a certain state through that thing."[29] A little later, Avicenna specifies that a substrate is something which "subsists in actuality only by being rendered subsistent through whatever inheres in it" (*bi-taqwīm mā ḥallahū*).[30] Accordingly, the major difference between a subject and a substrate is that a subject is capable of existing on its own, whereas a

---

24 On the relation between matter and form, cf. A. D. Stone, "Simplicius and Avicenna on the Essential Corporeity of Material Substance," 77–79; Belo, *Chance and Determinism in Avicenna and Averroes*, 63–65; McGinnis, "Making Something of Nothing," fn. 14, 555; cf. also Rahman, "Essence and Existence in Ibn Sīnā," 3–9; Lizzini, "The Relation between Form and Matter."

25 *Phys.* I.9, 192a31f. For Aristotle's understanding of matter as the underlying subject of generation, cf. also the discussion in *De generatione et corruptione* I.3 and II.1. Yaḥyā ibn ʿAdī quotes the passage from *Physics* I.9 explicitly as a definition of matter and provides a literal commentary on it; cf. *Maqāla fī l-mawǧūdāt*, 170.16–171.10. The notion of prime matter in Aristotle's philosophical system is the subject of intense discussion. The essential readings on this topic include H. R. King, "Aristotle without *prima materia*"; Solmsen, "Aristotle and Prime Matter"; Robinson, "Prime Matter in Aristotle"; Charlton, "Prime Matter" as well as the appendices by Charlton and Williams in *Physics* and *De generatione et corruptione*, respectively.

26 *al-Ilāhiyyāt* II.1, §7, 59.1–14.; cf. *al-Naǧāt* IV.1.3, 496.5–497.14; *Kitāb al-Ḥudūd*, §28, 16.6–13; §31, 18.4–7; §43, 24.9–13; cf. also *Dānešnāme-ye ʿAlāʾī* II.3, 9.13–15; II.8, 26.5–27.2.

27 *al-Ilāhiyyāt* II.1, §7, 59.1f.

28 cf. *al-Maqūlāt* I.6, 46.11–13.

29 *al-Ilāhiyyāt* II.1, §7, 59.3.

30 *al-Ilāhiyyāt* II.1, §7, 59.11.

substrate is not and, instead, requires something to be rendered subsistent by it.[31] Thus, a subject exists prior to its being qualified through "something [else]," but a substrate does not, as it only comes-to-be when "something [else]" inheres in it. This is further borne out in a long discussion in *al-Maqūlāt* I.3, in which Avicenna investigates what "to be said of a subject" (*yaqālu ʿalā mawḍūʿ*) and "to exist in a subject" (*yūǧadu fī mawḍūʿ*) mean. There, Avicenna asserts:

فلا تكون الهيولى موضوعةً للشيء الذي يُسمّى صورة لأنّها صفة خارجية مقوّمة للهيولى شيئاً بالفعل.

So, matter is not a subject for the thing which is called form, because it is an external attribute constituting matter as a thing in actuality (*muqawwima li-l-hayūlā šay'an bi-l-fiʿl*). (*al-Maqūlāt* I.3, 19.12f.)

On this account, matter is not a subject for form, because before form came to inhere in matter, matter itself did not exist in actuality. What does not actually exist can hardly be a subject for something else. Thus, far from being a *subject*, which is something real by itself through which other things can subsist, Avicenna presents matter as a *substrate* which is in itself incapable of independent existence and which requires form, in order to be. As Avicenna frequently emphasises in his works, neither matter nor form is capable of existing without the other.[32] Both substances exist only together in tandem. It is important to realise that there never was nor will there ever be matter without form. Likewise, there never was nor will there ever be form without matter. From all eternity, matter was enformed and form was enmattered, so that there never was a moment in which matter as such could have been a subject for form to take up its residence.[33] Avicenna's distinction between a substrate and a subject is, thus, designed to divide between subjects which can and do exist, and in which other forms and accidents can come to inhere, on the one hand, and substrates which do not exist as such but which, nonetheless, are an underlying component of corporeal reality insofar as they have been rendered subsistent through form, on the other. In consequence,

---

31 The discussion in *al-Naǧāt* IV.1.3 frames the difference between a substrate and a subject in a similar manner. There, a *maḥall* is a genus term that contains two species: one which is capable of independent existence and one which is not. Avicenna, then, calls the former *mawḍūʿ* and the latter *hayūlā* (496.11–15).

32 This is particularly true of matter but also pertains to form in the same way; cf. *al-Ilāhiyyāt* II.3–4, 72.4–89.15; *al-Samāʿ al-ṭabīʿī* I.2, §5, 14.12–14; I.10, §6, 49.18–50.5; *al-Naǧāt* IV.1.3, 497.15–498.5; IV.1.6–7, 502.8–512.5; *ʿUyūn al-ḥikma* III.2, 48.21–49.12; *Dānešnāme-ye ʿAlāʾī* II.8, 24.3–28.4; *al-Hidāya* III.1, 235.4–237.3; *al-Ḥikma al-mašriqiyya* III.1, 3.20–22; *al-Išārāt wa-l-tanbīhāt* II.1.16.

33 At the same time, there never was a moment when matter was created, as it has always been existing. Nonetheless, matter has been "created absolutely," i.e., trough *ibdāʿ*, as Avicenna explains in *al-Ilāhiyyāt* IV.2, §9, 266.9–15; cf. *al-Ilāhiyyāt* VIII.3, §§5–8, 342.1–343.5; *al-Išārāt wa-l-tanbīhāt* II.5.9, 153.5–8; *Kitāb al-Ḥudūd*, §104, 42.12–43.2.

form deserves to be called a substance, because it does not exist in a subject. It merely exists in matter, and matter, as we have seen, is not a subject in the true sense.[34]

Yet, it must be said that Avicenna rarely employs the term *al-maḥall* ("substrate") as a designation for matter. Instead, we find the term *mawḍūʿ* ("subject"). Moreover, Avicenna explicitly addresses this ambiguity and explains his equivocal application of the term with what almost seems to be an apology:

ومن جهة أنّها بالفعل حاملة لصورة فتُسمّى في هذا الموضع موضوعاً لها وليس معنى الموضوع هاهنا معنى الموضوع
الذي أخذناه في المنطق جزءَ رسمٍ للجوهر فإنّ الهيولى لا تكون موضوعاً بذلك المعنى البتّة.

> From the perspective that it [sc. matter] is actually the bearer of a form (*ḥāmil li-ṣūra*), it is called in this context (*fī hāḏā l-mawḍiʿ*) a subject for it, yet the meaning of "subject" here (*hāhunā*) is not the meaning of "subject" which we have adopted in logic as part of the description of substance, for matter is by no means a subject in that meaning. (*al-Samāʿ al-ṭabīʿī* I.2, §6, 14.15–15.1, tr. by McGinnis, modified)[35]

Although Avicenna does not use the term *maḥall* here, it is telling that in the same context, only a few words earlier, he explained that matter is "never separated from form as something subsisting through itself" – and this, as we have just seen, is precisely the feature which, in Avicenna's *al-Ilāhiyyāt* II.1, distinguishes between a substrate and a subject.[36] Since Avicenna's use of the term "subject" as a designation of matter must be taken *cum grano salis* as a commonplace inherited from the philosophical tradition, form, even though it must exist in matter, fulfils the condition of not being in a subject, after all, and is just as much a substance as the soul and the concrete body are.

Finally, matter itself must be accepted as a substance, because matter also does not exist in a subject.[37] Avicenna clarifies this in *al-Ilāhiyyāt* II.2:

والجوهرية التي لها ليس تجعلها بالفعل شيئاً من الأشياء بل تُعدّها لأن تكون بالفعل شيئاً بالصورة. وليس معنى
جوهريتها إلّا أنّها أمر ليس في موضوع.

---

34 Avicenna's explanation is certainly inspired by Alexander of Aphrodisias who, for example in his *Questiones*, explicitly addressed the same question twice; cf. *Quaestiones* I.8, 17; cf. also *Quaestiones* I.26. The central thrust of Alexander's argumentation is that "it is not possible for anything to be in prime matter as a subject, because such matter is not even a subject in actuality in the first place but rather requires form for being in existence" (*Quaestiones* I.17, 30.2–4, tr. by Sharples, modified); cf. M. Rashed, *Essentialisme*, 42–52.

35 cf. *al-Ḥikma al-mašriqiyya* III.1, 4.6f.

36 The terminological distinction between *mawḍūʿ* and *maḥall* is, nonetheless, present in Avicenna's *al-Samāʿ al-ṭabīʿī*; cf., for example, his account of substantial change in *al-Samāʿ al-ṭabīʿī* II.3, where he differentiates between a subject in the sense of a "real and actually subsisting subject as a species which is receptive of accidents" and a substrate (*maḥall*) by which he means matter (*al-Samāʿ al-ṭabīʿī* II.3, §4, 99.17–100.3).

37 cf. Aristotle's explicit formulation in *Metaphysics* Z.3, 1029a7–10, and his reservation at *Phys.* I.9, 192a3–6; cf. also Buschmann, *Untersuchungen zum Problem der Materie bei Avicenna*, ch. 5; Belo, *Chance and Determinism in Avicenna and Averroes*, 65.

> The substantiality which belongs to it [sc. matter] does not make it actually some thing; it rather prepares it for becoming actually a thing through form. The meaning of its substantiality is nothing other than that it is something which is not in a subject. (*al-Ilāhiyyāt* II.2, §21, 67.17–68.2)[38]

The reason for why matter is a substance is that there is nothing else underlying matter in which it exists as in a subject. There is no matter for matter and there is nothing in which matter itself inheres. Thus, matter is one of the four kinds of substance in Avicenna's ontology.[39]

---

38 cf. *Dānešnāme-ye ʿAlāʾī* II.3, 10.4–6; *Kitāb al-Ḥudūd*, §30, 17.10–18.2; §43, 24.9–13; cf. also *al-Samāʿ al-ṭabīʿī* I.2, §4, 14.4–9; *al-Ḥikma al-mašriqiyya* III.1, 3.17–20; *al-Nafs* I.3, 26.9f. The description of matter which Avicenna provides in §30 of his *Kitāb al-Ḥudūd* is odd. First, he says that matter "is a substance whose actual existence occurs only through the reception of the corporeal form due to a potentiality in it to receive forms," whereas a little later he states "the meaning of my calling it a substance is that its existence occurs to it in actuality through itself." This second remark led Arthur Hyman to maintain that, for Avicenna, first matter "is a substance in the sense of an 'abode,' a 'subject,' and something 'having existence in virtue of itself'" – which is incorrect. One would have to consult the manuscripts of the *Kitāb al-Ḥudūd* and see whether the text of Goichon's edition ought to be emended.

39 In the notes that accompany his translation of the metaphysics of Avicenna's *Dānešnāme-ye ʿAlāʾī*, Morewedge justifies his translation of the Persian noun *gūne* as "aspect" instead of "kind" by making the entirely unfounded claim that "ibn Sīnā does not place substratum-matter into the category of substances in any other passage of his *opera*" (n. 7, 114). In light of much evidence to the contrary, this claim is surprising, as Morewedge himself refers to a passage in Avicenna's *al-Ilāhiyyāt* in which we read that "substance is said of what is separable, of body, of matter, and of form" (*al-Ilāhiyyāt* III.1, §1, 93.5f.); cf. also Buschmann's complaint in *Untersuchungen zum Problem der Materie bei Avicenna*, 31–34. Another unsatisfactory claim has been advanced by Belo who maintains that for Avicenna, "prime matter is not really a substance." Matter, she writes, "is not a substance in any positive sense" and enjoys "a purely negative sense of substantiality"; cf. also Goichon's similar remark about matter being substance in a sense that is "tout négatif" in *La distinction de l'essence et de l'existence*, 437. Belo's reasons for this claim are that matter "does not exist as a particular physical substance"; that it "is neither a primary substance nor a secondary substance, i.e., a universal"; and that its substantiality consists merely in not "inhering in something else" (*Chance and Determinism in Avicenna and Averroes*, 65). This claim is unfounded. Admittedly, it could be supported by references, for example, to *al-Maqūlāt* I.6, in which Avicenna asserts that in addition to not being in a subject at all, substance is that which is "subsistent alone" (*qāʾim waḥdahū*; *al-Maqūlāt* I.6, 46.11). However, anyone who wishes to discredit matter's claim to substantiality on this ground, or claims that matter "is not really a substance," owes us at least an explanation for why form's substantiality remains unblemished even though form is just as unable to be "subsistent alone" as matter is. While there certainly are other reasons that may justify the consideration of form as substance, we should take Avicenna's wording at face value and accept that matter fulfils the primary condition for being a substance – and that it, accordingly, is a substance – without speaking of "a purely negative sense of substantiality" and without making matter a substance (but "not really"); cf. also *al-Naǧāt* IV.1.8, 512.12f., where Avicenna orders the four kinds of substances on the basis of their respective claim to *existence* (and *not* to substantiality) as follows: separate substance (i.e., soul and intellect), then form, then body, and then matter. All in all, Avicenna does not display any reluctance in calling matter a substance that could warrant even the moderate assertion that he only "begrudgingly acknowledges that there is a sense in which matter can be called a substance" (McGinnis, "Making Something of Nothing," fn. 14, 555). To the contrary, it is more the case

Returning to the subject-matter of natural philosophy, and to the intention to analyse it insofar as it is a body, Avicenna writes the following:

> فنقول إنّ الجسم الطبيعي هو الجوهر الذي يمكن أن يفرض فيه امتداد وامتداد آخر مقاطع له على قوائم وامتداد ثالث مقاطع لهما جميعاً على قوائم. وكونه بهذه الصفة هو الصورة التي بها صار جسماً وليس الجسم جسماً بأنّه ذو امتدادات ثلاثة مفروضة فإنّ الجسم يكون موجوداً جسماً وثابتاً وإنّ غيّرت الامتدادات الموجودة فيه بالفعل.
>
> So, we say that the natural body is the substance in which it is possible to demarcate (*yumkinu an yafruḍa*) a dimension, and another dimension intersecting it in a right [angle], and a third dimension intersecting them both together in a right [angle]. Its being along this description is the form through which it becomes a body (*al-ṣūra allatī bihā ṣāra ğisman*). However, body is not a body insofar as it has (*bi-annahū ḏū*) the three demarcated dimensions (*imtidādāt ṯalāṯa mafrūḍa*), for body does exist and remain as a body, even when the dimensions that exist in it are actually changed. (*al-Samāʿ al-ṭabīʿī* I.2, §2, 13.4–7, tr. by McGinnis, modified)[40]

Here, Avicenna provides an account of his understanding of corporeality. According to him, the corporeality of a given body is not identical with its having a concrete set of dimensions. A body may change its dimensions, it may grow and diminish, it may become wide or narrow, it may change its shape – but it will remain a body throughout. In other words, the corporeality of a body remains unchanged regardless of any quantitative transformation the body may suffer. The concrete dimensional specification of a given body certainly accounts for this body's magnitude (*miqdār*), and makes it fall under the category of quantity (*bāb al-kamm*), but it does not account for its corporeality (*ğismiyya*) nor does it define the essence of body (*māhiyyat al-ğism*).[41] A natural body, then, *has* (*ḏū*) a certain size specified through its three-dimensional shape or figure, but this is not what it is in consideration of its being a body, for body as such is neither already specified nor does it depend on any such dimensional specification. A body as such is only "a substance in which it is possible to demarcate" three dimensions, as Avicenna writes.

that Avicenna – as often – proudly advocates what might seem to some to be a rather counterintuitive doctrine. If substance is that which is not in a subject at all, then matter has to be accepted as being a substance.

40 cf. *al-Maqūlāt* III.4, 113.9–11; *al-Ilāhiyyāt* II.2, §§5–7, 63.4–17; *al-Naǧāt* IV.1.4, 498.7–499.2; *Dānešnāme-ye ʿAlāʾī* II.4, 12.10–14.7; *al-Hidāya* II.1, 135.2–6; *al-Ḥikma al-mašriqiyya* III, 2.11–16.

41 Avicenna famously illustrates this with the picture of a block of wax or a candle which changes its shape without losing its corporeality; cf. *al-Samāʿ al-ṭabīʿī* I.2, §2, 13.8f.; *al-Maqūlāt* III.4, 114.5–11; *al-Ilāhiyyāt* II.2, §§8–10, 64.1–15; *Dānešnāme-ye ʿAlāʾī* II.4, 13.9–14.2; *al-Hidāya* II.1, 135.4–6. As has been shown by Menn and Wisnovsky, it was subject to debate in the philosophical milieu immediately preceding Avicenna whether body is a substance or a quantitative accident; cf. the remarks in their introduction to Ibn ʿAdī, *On Whether Body is a Substance or a Quantity*, esp. 6–19. Avicenna's answer consists in distinguishing the absolute body as the substantial compound of matter and corporeal form together with its indefinite three-dimensional extensionality from the concrete body with its determinate and accidental set of dimensions.

It is striking that Avicenna almost always describes the essence of body in identical terms using the verb *faraḍa* to specify the relation between the dimensions and the body as a substance. Accordingly it is essential to understand precisely what Avicenna means when he writes that body is that "in which it is possible to demarcate" (*allaḏī yumkinu an yafruḍa fīhi*) three dimensions. This is all the more necessary, as the notion of body in Avicenna's philosophy has been the source for confusion and misinterpretation. As will be shown, Avicenna's conception of body relies on the notions of continuity, extension, and divisibility, so that body as such is a continuous substance which is indeterminately extended into three dimensions and which, for this reason, is essentially divisible. Moreover, body is a substantial composite of an incorporeal and receptive matter, on the one hand, and of a "corporeal form" (*ṣūra ǧismiyya*), on the other. It is precisely this corporeal form which is the principle and source of corporeality – i.e., of extension, continuity and, in one sense at least, divisibility.

The basic concept of body as a substance which is corporeal – i.e., continuous, extended, and divisible – is that which all concrete bodies have in common and which Avicenna sometimes calls the "absolute body" or "body absolutely" (*ǧism muṭlaqan*).[42] In short, it is an unqualified yet enmattered instance of the essence of body (*māhiyyat al-ǧism*).[43] It is the simple substantial composite of matter and corporeal form. Since natural bodies are concrete instances of the concept of an absolute body, a precise understanding of how Avicenna characterises body in general will provide us with an understanding of how he conceives of natural bodies in particular, and will ultimately reveal his understanding of matter and form as the principles of the natural body insofar as it is a body.[44]

---

42 e.g., *al-Samāʿ al-ṭabīʿī* I.2, §16, 18.5.

43 *al-Maqūlāt* III.4, 113.6.

44 I shall not engage with the absurd Marxist interpretations of Avicenna which describe him as a spearhead of the "Aristotelian left wing," arguing that he contributed greatly to the conception of an active – and not merely passively mechanistic – matter (Bloch, *Avicenna und die aristotelische Linke*, 44f.: "Also läuft die Aristotelische Linksrichtung, über die Umbildung der Stoff-Form-Beziehung, deutlich einer als aktiv begriffenen – und nicht nur mechanistisch begriffenen – Materie zu."); or characterise Avicenna's conception of the world in terms of a "materialistic pantheism" (Tisini, *Die Materieauffassung in der islamisch-arabischen Philosophie des Mittelalters*, 79: "Seine eigene Weltauffassung liegt also in der Richtung eines materialistischen Pantheismus."); or speak of Avicenna's "attempt at a pantheistic enhancement of matter along the lines of Proclus" (Ehlers, "Aristoteles, Proklos und Avicenna über philosophische Probleme der Mathematik," 92: "Diese, am modernen Problembewußtsein gemessen, vereinfachte Sicht ist bedingt durch seinen Versuch einer pantheistischen Aufwertung der Materie, und das verband ihn mit Proklos."); cf. Buschmann's direct engagement with Bloch's view in her book *Untersuchungen zum Problem der Materie bei Avicenna*, esp. ch. 8.

Absolute Body and Extensionality

Saying that for Avicenna, the absolute body is essentially extended may seem to be a mere triviality. Why should body not be extended? What should corporeality mean if not extension? Yet, the view that, according to Avicenna, body is not extended has dominated those publications which have so far discussed the topic – or, more precisely, those published in English.

We read, for example, in Harry Wolfson's meritorious study of *Crescas' Critique of Aristotle* the following: "According to Avicenna the corporeal form is a certain predisposition in prime matter for the assumption of tridimensionality." Wolfson proceeds by contrasting Avicenna's account with that of Abū Ḥāmid al-Ġazālī (d. 505/1111), for whom the corporeal form "is not a predisposition in matter for tridimensionality but rather the cohesiveness or massiveness of matter in which tridimensionality may be posited."[45] In turn, Averroes (d. 595/1198) is said to have disagreed with both, as he "identifies the corporeal form with tridimensionality itself but he distinguishes between indeterminate and determinate tridimensionality," and it is only the former which "constitutes the corporeal form."[46] Thus, according to Wolfson, Avicenna and al-Ġazālī differ from Averroes in that they do not conceive of body as such as indeterminately three-dimensionally extended. Additionally, Avicenna differs from al-Ġazālī in that he does not identify the essence of body with continuity (*ittiṣāl*) as the latter does.[47] Later in his book, Wolfson repeats his claim and tries to justify his reading not primarily

---

45 Wolfson in Crescas, *Crescas' Critique of Aristotle*, 101. It should be noted that "cohesiveness" and "cohesion" is Wolfson's (and later also Hyman's) rendering of the Arabic term *ittiṣāl*, which I shall translate as "continuity." Wolfson seeks to justify his translation later in his notes; cf. *Crescas' Critique of Aristotle*, n. 18, 579f.

46 Wolfson in Crescas, *Crescas' Critique of Aristotle*, 101; cf. also Wolfson's later remark in his notes: "It will also be gathered from our subsequent discussion that this 'cohesion' or 'mass' was conceived by Avicenna and Algazali as something which by itself is not tridimensional but which is capable of becoming tridimensional" (n. 18, 579f.).

47 It is interesting in this regard to mention that Wolfson notes that Hasdai Crescas, whose work he is translating and commenting upon in his study, had a confused understanding of Avicenna's and al-Ġazālī's doctrine and their difference from Averroes. Crescas writes the following: "It behooves you to know that Avicenna, Algazali, and those who follow them are of the opinion that the distinction of matter and form obtains in every body, including also the celestial spheres. For believing that the corporeal form is nothing but the continuity of the three dimensions, intersecting each other at right angles, they reason as follows: since continuity must be something different from the thing continuous, seeing that the latter may become divided whereas the former may not, there must exist a substratum capable of receiving both the continuity and the division. Reason therefore decrees that in every body there must be two essential principles, namely, matter and form" (Crescas, *Crescas' Critique of Aristotle* X.II, 260.5–11, tr. by Wolfson). According to Wolfson, this is a confused combination of al-Ġazālī's and Averroes' doctrine without any trace in Avicenna: "By combining these two statements it is not clear which of these two views he (sc. Crescas himself) meant to espouse. Nor is there anything in his statement to include or to exclude the view of Avicenna." As shall become clear, Crescas was almost entirely right about Avicenna, at least as far as the brevity of his statement allows.

on the basis of an analysis of Avicenna's own texts but of the criticism in Averroes' treatise *De substantia orbis*, of some reports by Jewish philosophers from Andalusia, in particular those of Moses Narboni (d. after 1362) and Isaac Abravanel (d. 1508), and of the testimony found in the *Kitāb al-Milal wa-l-niḥal* of Muḥammad ibn ʿAbd al-Karīm al-Šahrastānī (d. 548/1153).[48]

Arthur Hyman follows Wolfson in every detail and writes that although Avicenna and Averroes both argued for a corporeal form, they "disagreed about its definition."[49] Mentioning al-Ġazālī, Hyman states that he "identified the 'corporeal form' with 'continuity.'"[50] Avicenna, on the other hand, presented the corporeal form as "a predisposition for receiving the three dimensions – but a form which differs from the dimensions themselves."[51] His view is, finally, contrasted with that of Averroes:

> The alternative rejected by Avicenna was accepted by Averroes. Observing that all bodies are divisible by the substantial forms inhering in them, Averroes posited divisibility as the primary characteristic of all bodies. But to be divisible, a body had to possess three-dimensionality ... For Averroes "indeterminate three-dimensionality" was identical with the "corporeal form."[52]

In summary, Averroes is said to have conceived of body as such in terms of an indeterminate extension in three dimensions. Body, then, is essentially extended. Avicenna's conception of body, by contrast, is not extended, because the form of corporeality in Avicenna's account merely provides the *predisposition for becoming* extended in three dimensions.

The view presented by Wolfson and Hyman in unison about Avicenna is also maintained in a more recent study by Abraham Stone. He argues that Avicenna's description of body "cannot be taken as referring to body as quantitative – i.e., to either the determinate or the indeterminate dimensions."[53] So, for Stone, Avicenna's account of corporeality does not entail extension – not even indeterminate extension.

Perhaps the most recent repetition of this interpretation has been published by Sarah Pessin. Explicitly relying on Wolfson, Hyman, and Stone, she writes that "corporeity is seen as the form that brings to matter its 'disposition' and its 'preparedness' to take on three-dimensionality ... [it is] that which *allows for* the *ittiṣāl* ('cohesiveness,'

---

48 cf. Wolfson in Crescas, *Crescas' Critique of Aristotle*, n. 18, 582–590. It is to be said that no consistent picture emerges from the combination of these divergent sources.

49 Hyman, "Aristotle's First Matter," 386.

50 Hyman, "Aristotle's First Matter," fn. 4, 335.

51 Hyman, "Aristotle's First Matter," 386 and 403.

52 Hyman, "Aristotle's First Matter," 403; cf. also the similar remarks in the notes to his translation and study of Averroes' *De substantia orbis*, 30f., as well as fn. 7, 41, and fn. 66, 63–65. Like Wolfson, Hyman bases his understanding of Avicenna partly on the polemics of Averroes and the reports given by Narboni and Abravanel, even though he also takes recourse to Avicenna's own works, in particular *al-Samāʿ al-ṭabīʿī*, *al-Ilāhiyyāt*, and the *Kitāb al-Ḥudūd*.

53 A. D. Stone, "Simplicius and Avicenna on the Essential Corporeity of Material Substance," 101.

'continuity,' 'connection,' or 'continuum') of bodies ... [Avicenna's] particular conception of corporeal form ... provides an alternative to the views of al-Ghazālī and Ibn Rushd."[54]

This interpretation of Avicenna is inadequate. In fact, Avicenna's true position approximates very much that of Averroes as presented by Hyman and Wolfson. Thus, the major difference between Avicenna and Averroes does not lie in the fact that they disagreed about whether or not body as such is extended but that they disagreed about whether the corporeal form is a substantial form or only accidental.[55]

What is most surprising in all this is that Hyman refers to Amélie-Marie Goichon's earlier study *La distinction de l'essence et de l'existence* with the following words: "This discussion is especially valuable for its numerous references to the sources and because it shows ... that the textual evidence supports Averroes' interpretation of Avicenna."[56] In other words, Hyman claims that Goichon's discussion lends credibility both to Averroes' presentation of Avicenna's thought and to Hyman's (as well as Wolfson's) own reading of Avicenna. In Goichon's monograph, however, we read the following:

> D'après l'ensemble de ces renseignements, la forme de corporéité apparaît donc comme une forme substantielle qui ne donne au corps aucune autre propriété constitutive que d'avoir trois dimensions, et de pouvoir être divisé, elle ne spécifie aucunement la matière.[57]

Hyman also refers to the fourth volume of Pierre Duhem's *Le système du monde* as providing "helpful discussions of Avicenna's and Averroes' accounts of 'first matter' and the 'corporeal form.'"[58] Looking into Duhem's book, we read that "Avicenna did not commit the confusion ... of which he was accused by Averroes here," i.e., in *De substantia orbis*.[59] Instead, Duhem asserts:

> Mais ce qui est très vrai, c'est que, pour Ibn Sinâ, les dimensions non-terminées, c'est que la divisibilité, par lesquelles la *Hyle* est un corps étendu en longueur, largeur et profondeur, ne sont dans la *Hyle* que par une première forme, qui est la forme corporelle.[60]

The overall picture which results from the available secondary literature is nothing short of a mess. It is entirely unclear what Avicenna's doctrine really amounts to and it

---

54 Pessin, "Forms of Hylomorphism," 199, emphasis added: "allows for."

55 cf. Hasse, "Influence of Arabic and Islamic Philosophy on the Latin West," ch. 4. It has to be noted that it exceeds the scope of this current study to analyse whether Wolfson and Hyman presented a faithful picture of the respective positions of al-Ġazālī and Averroes, and to investigate why Averroes misrepresented Avicenna's position in his *De substantia orbis*.

56 Hyman in fn. 66, 65 of Averroes, *De substantia orbis*.

57 Goichon, *La distinction de l'essence et de l'existence*, 431f.

58 Hyman, "Aristotle's First Matter," fn. 51, 395.

59 Duhem, *Le système du monde* IV, 543: "Avicenne n'a pas commis cette confusion entre les dimensions non-terminées et les dimensions terminées dont il semble qu'Averroès l'accuse ici."

60 Duhem, *Le système du monde* IV, 543.

is especially uncertain whether he considered body as such to be extended or merely predisposed for becoming extended. In the following, it will be shown that Avicenna thought of the absolute body as essentially extended.[61] Moreover, the position attributed to al-Ġazālī – whether justifiably or not – aptly conforms to Avicenna, too: the form of corporeality is nothing but continuity which, in turn, means nothing other than divisibility and extension. In fact, as has already been remarked, the position attributed to Averroes himself – whether correctly or not – does not differ much from how Avicenna conceived of body, for body is continuous, and continuity entails divisibility, and divisibility requires extension.

The interpretation of Avicenna's account of corporeality as a "predisposition for the assumption" of the three dimensions, as it is found in Wolfson's and Hyman's studies as well as in more recent publications, has its roots not only in later reports of Avicenna's doctrine, such as those by Averroes, Narboni, and Abravanel, but also in the works of Avicenna himself, in particular those which make up his *al-Šifāʾ*, such as *al-Maqūlāt*, *al-Samāʿ al-ṭabīʿī*, and *al-Ilāhiyyāt*. Wolfson, for example, explicitly refers to Maximilian Horten's German translation of Avicenna's *al-Ilāhiyyāt* from 1907.[62] In this work, Avicenna's *al-Ilāhiyyāt*, we find the following assertion:

> الجسم هو الجوهر الذي يمكنك أن تفرض فيه بعداً كيف شئت ابتداء فيكون ذلك المبتدأ هو الطول. ثمّ يمكنك أن تفرض أيضاً بعداً آخر مقاطعاً لذلك البعد على قوائم فيكون ذلك البعد الثاني هو العرض، ويمكنك أن تفرض فيه بعداً ثالثاً مقاطعاً لهذين البعدين على قوائم تتلاقى الثلاثة على موضع واحد.
>
> Body is the substance in which it is possible for you to demarcate (*yumkinuka an tafruḍa*) a dimension in whatever manner you wish to begin. That with which you begin is "length." Then, it is possible for you to demarcate also another dimension intersecting that [first] dimension perpendicularly. So, this second dimension is "breadth." And it is possible for you to demarcate in it a third dimensions intersecting these two dimensions perpendicularly, the three meeting in one point. (*al-Ilāhiyyāt* II.2, §5, 63.5–9)

The formulations from *al-Šifāʾ* which describe the essence of body are marked by the fact that they all modify the verb *faraḍa* through the verb *amkana* ("to be possible").[63] Presumably, then, "predisposition," as we find it in the secondary literature, is an attempt to render the meaning of *amkana*, whereas "assumption" translates *faraḍa*, so that Avicenna's phrase *yumkinu an yafruḍa* (which could be read as "to be possible to assume") is conveyed into English as the"predisposition for the assumption" of three dimensions in the substance called "body." On this reading, body is merely something which *can become* extended once it has assumed the three dimensions, and which in itself is not extended but merely predisposed for becoming extended. It will now be

---

61 Investigating Avicenna's views on the impossibility of the interpenetration of two bodies, McGinnis arrived at the same conclusion; cf. "A Penetrating Question," 61.

62 cf. Wolfson in Crescas, *Crescas' Critique of Aristotle*, 583

63 cf. *al-Maqūlāt* III.4, 113.9–11; *al-Samāʿ al-ṭabīʿī* I.2, §2, 13.5; *al-Ilāhiyyāt* II.2, §5, 63.5, 9.

shown that this reading misrepresents the intention of Avicenna's account of body and that it does not harmonise with the statements contained in his other works.[64]

First, the modification achieved through *amkana* does not justify talking of a mere predisposition for the action described by *faraḍa*. That Avicenna describes body as that in which it is *possible* to assume three dimensions does not mean that the body as such is not extended, i.e., it does not mean that it is only potentially extended and will become actually extended once it has acquired concrete dimensions. It is much rather the case that the very reason that it is possible for us to assume the three dimensions at all is that the body as such is already extended. If it were not already extended we could not *find* three dimensions in it. In other words, we would be unable to identify three distinct dimensions in the body if it were not already extended in all possible directions. This reading gains further support by the detail that in the above passage from *al-Ilāhiyyāt*, Avicenna makes it clear that it is a possibility that pertains to "you": "it is possible for you" (*yumkinuka*).[65] Consequently, the possibility in question is not a possibility of a predisposition on the part of the body. To the contrary, the body is already such that it is now possible *for you* to demarcate up to three dimension in it. Since the body is already three-dimensionally extended, it is now possible for us to find and to identify in the body these three dimensions. If Wolfson's and Hyman's interpretation of Avicenna were right, the possibility and predisposition would have to belong to the body, i.e., it would have to be possible *for the body* to assume and to take on three dimensions. Instead, we should understand the modification achieved through the verb *amkana* as if it were already true, and as if it were simply right to say, that body is extended indeterminately, so that it is, because of this, now possible for us to find and to identify in the body these three dimensions. This, in fact, is exactly what we read in the formulations in Avicenna's *al-Hidāya* and *al-Naǧāt*. Having introduced the subject-matter of physics as the sensible body insofar as it is subject to change, Avicenna writes in his *al-Hidāya*:

---

64 It is a relevant detail that the English verb "to assume" basically encompasses two meanings: a body may assume three dimensions in the sense that it *takes on* or *acquires* three dimensions. This is reminiscent of how Hyman presents Avicenna's theory, for he describes the corporeal as "having a predisposition for *receiving* the three dimensions" ("Aristotle's First Matter," 386, 403, emphasis added). In this sense, the body would, first, be deprived of the three dimensions and, then, i.e., after the assumption, would have become three-dimensional. This, however, is not what is meant by the Arabic verb *faraḍa*, which corresponds to another meaning of the English term "to assume," viz., one signifying a mental operation. One can assume three dimensions in body, because body as such is already extended in such a way that enables one to perform the mental operation of assuming in it up to three perpendicular dimensions. This will become more clear below. For now, let it suffice that *faraḍa* describes a mental operation and simply cannot mean "to assume" in the sense of "to acquire," "to take on," or "to receive." This makes it so easy to misinterpret Avicenna's intention when conversing in English about a body's "predisposition to assume three dimensions."

65 *al-Ilāhiyyāt* II.2, §5, 63.5, 9.

جسمية هذا الجسم هو كونه بحيث يصحّ فيه فرض أبعاد ثلاثة متقاطعة على حدّ مشترك بقوائم. وأمّا قدره المعيّن في الطول والعرض والثخن فلوازم لصوره التي لا يتبدّل بتبدّلها في شمعة واحدة وهي كمّيته وبها يقدّر.

The corporeality of this body is its being such that it is true to demarcate in it (*kawnuhū bi-ḥayṯu yaṣiḥḥu fīhi farḍ*) three dimensions intersecting perpendicularly in one common point.[66] As for its particular size in length, breadth, and depth, these are concomitants to the forms of it [sc. the body]; it [sc. the body] does not undergo transformation through a transformation of them [as may happen] in one [piece of] wax and they [sc. the concrete sizes in length, breadth, and depth] are its quantity through which it is measured. (*al-Hidāya* II.1, 135.2–6)

We see that it is already "true" (*yaṣiḥḥu*) that we assume or demarcate the three dimensions in the substance called "body." They are already there – it is just that they have not yet been identified. A body as such is extended, yet its indeterminate extension is not yet recognised in terms of three separate dimensions, like a blank sheet of paper is already extended even before we have identified two dimensions by drawing a coordinate system on it.[67]

What is also clearly recognisable in this passage is the contrast between the particular measures of a natural body's length, breadth, and depth (through which that body has its concrete size and quantity) and that same body's corporeality (which consists in its "being such that it is true to demarcate in it" three perpendicular dimensions). This reads as if Avicenna attempts to differentiate between determinate dimensions, due to their particular sizes, and indeterminate extension, due to the body's corporeality. At least one must acknowledge the contrast, indicated by the particle *wa-ammā*, between the dimensions which are truly demarcated in the body and their *particular* sizes.

The same formulation can be found in *al-Naǧāt*:

بل الجسم إنّما هو جسم لأنّه بحيث يصحّ أن يفرض فيه أبعاد ثلاثة كلّ واحد منها قائم على الآخر.

Rather, body is body only because it is such that it is true to demarcate in it (*li-annahū bi-ḥayṯu yaṣiḥḥu an yafruḍa fīhi*) three dimensions, each one of them being perpendicular on the other. (*al-Naǧāt* IV.1.4, 499.1f.)

So, there are passages in Avicenna's oeuvre which, compared to the passages in his *al-Šifā'*, are identically structured and which are apparently meant to convey the same understanding of what body and corporeality mean. Yet, these passages lack the only verb that could really justify speaking of a "predisposition," as Hyman and Wolfson

66 Even more literally translated, Avicenna's wording in the *al-Hidāya* should read: "The corporeality of this body is its being such that in it the demarcation of three dimensions intersecting perpendicularly in one common point is true."

67 It is another crucial aspect of Avicenna's theory that the coordinate system we may draw on the sheet of paper, in order to identify two dimensions, can be drawn *in any manner we like* (*kayfa ši'ta*; *al-Ilāhiyyāt* II.2, §5, 63.5). In other words, we do not have to follow the direction of the sheet's edges but can draw the coordinate system on the sheet in any angle we wish, as long as the two dimensions are rectilinear *to each other*. This will be explained in more detail shortly.

do, by replacing *yumkinu* ("to be possible") with *yaṣiḥḥu* ("to be true"). Consequently, body is body only because it is already true that we can find these dimensions in body. Body must be essentially extended, for otherwise we could not single out and identify three dimensions in its indefinite extension.

The second point that needs to be rectified is the reading of *farada* along the lines of "assumption." To translate *farada* as "to assume" is not uncommon and the noun *farḍ* often means "assumption."[68] So, one could indeed take the expression "to assume" as indicating that the dimensions are not yet existent in such a manner that there is not even an extension that could be marked out by the three dimensions. Accordingly, we would only be able to assume that there are three dimensions (because they are not really there, for if they were there, we would not longer merely have to assume them).

This reading is only half-correct and overall misses Avicenna's point. It is certainly true that the three dimensions called length, breadth, and depth are not already there – but only because they have not yet been identified. In other words, it has not yet been brought to our attention that there are three, and only three, dimensions in the body, i.e., in body as such and, thus, in every body. As Avicenna emphasises, we can identify the dimensions in any manner we wish (*kayfa šiʾta*).[69] What this means is that if we consider a bare body that is extended, then we can identify a first dimension, but it is irrelevant how we do this and where to start. We can take the distance from the soles of my feet to the top of my head and call it "length," but we can also take the distance from my back to my chest as length or, in fact, the slanted distance from the little toe of my left foot to my right ear. Irrespective of what line we draw and what direction or angle it may have, what is important is only that whichever line we have chosen in this already extended body, we can always identify a second dimension which crosses the first one perpendicularly and, finally, a third one crossing both perpendicularly. What is absolutely impossible, however, is to find more dimensions than three, regardless of how they have been construed. If we pay attention to the perpendicularity of the lines, then we can draw a up to – and not more than – three lines in each and every body. This is precisely Avicenna's point:

> ولا يمكنك أن تفرض بعداً عمودياً بهذه الصفة غير هذه الثلاثة. وكون الجسم بهذه الصفة هو الذي يشار لأجله إلى الجسم بأنّه طويل عريض عميق.
>
> It is not possible for you to demarcate a perpendicular dimension along this account other than these three. The body's being along this description is that due to which body is referred to as long, wide, and deep. (*al-Ilāhiyyāt* II.2, §§5–6, 63.9–11)

---

68 q.v. also fn. 64 above, 126.

69 *al-Ilāhiyyāt* II.2, §5, 63.5.

Avicenna intends to explain why body is commonly said to be that which is long, wide, and deep.[70] According to him, however, body is not that which is said to be long, wide, and deep due to its being so-and-so long, so-and-so wide, and so-and-so deep. For him, corporeality means to be three-dimensionally extended but not to *have* the three dimensions of "length," "breadth," and "depth."[71] It is rather the case that body is that in which one can identify up to, and not more than, three dimensions. These dimensions can be identified and demarcated in body, precisely because body is already extended in as many dimensions as possible – and this means in "not more than three" dimensions (*lā yumkinu an yakūna fawqa ṯalāṯa*), as he puts it in *al-Naǧāt*.[72] Body as such has three-dimensions and, thus, is essentially three-dimensional, but the dimensions have not yet been demarcated.

In my analysis, I relied on English expressions such as "to show," "to identify," and "to demarcate," instead of the more commonly used "to assume," in order to render the Arabic verb *faraḍa*. That this choice is entirely justified clearly emerges both from Lane's Arabic-English dictionary and from Avicenna himself. According to Lane, *faraḍa* means "to make a mark" in something and "to notch" something. It, thus, seems as if the meaning of "to assume" derives from the action of leaving a mark on something insofar as we can assume something only so long as it has not yet been carved in stone, i.e., when it is still only marked and when it is still not fully concrete and determinate. Thus, what Avicenna seems to mean with this verb is not that we are able only to *assume* three dimensions, because they do not exist or because the body is not even extended. To the contrary, what Avicenna wants to say is that we are able to make a mark – in fact, *three* marks – in any body, because body is extended in such a way that it is true that we *can* make three marks by which we identify or demarcate three perpendicular dimensions. We are able to notch any body, such that we find in it one dimension, and another, and a third. It is in this light that I have translated the passages from Avicenna's works: body is that substance of which it is true to say that we can demarcate and identify three separate dimensions in it, simply because body is such that it provides the required "room" for our doing so. Without an extended room, we could not even identify three dimensions. Thus, far from being unextended and from providing a mere predisposition for the assumption of three dimensions, body as such – i.e., the absolute body being the common concept of body that is shared by all particular bodies – is indeterminately extended: it is extended but (i) without having concrete measures and (ii) without even having length, breadth, and depth already identified as dimensions in it.

---

70 This is a common definition of body since antiquity; cf. *Leg.* VII, 817e7; *Tim.* 53c5f.; Euclid, *Elements* XI, def. 1; *Cael.* I.1, 268a8; *Met.* Δ.131020a11–14, to name just a few passage from the classical period.
71 cf. the above-quoted passage from *al-Samāʿ al-ṭabīʿī* I.2, §2, 13.6f.: "body is not a body insofar as it has (*bi-annahū ḏū*) the three demarcated dimensions, for body does exist and remain as a body, even when the dimensions that exist in it are actually changed."
72 *al-Naǧāt* IV.1.4, 499.2f.; cf., again, *Cael.* I.1, 268a7–10.

This understanding of the verb *farada* is confirmed by Avicenna's Persian work *Dānešnāme-ye ʿAlāʾī*. There, he uses – just as he did in the works from his *al-Šifāʾ* – modal modifications, viz., the verbs *tavānestan* ("to be able") and *šāyīdan* ("to be possible"), and combines them with verbs that are obviously meant to be equivalent in meaning to the Arabic *farada*. So, we can derive his very own understanding of *farada* from the meaning of the Persian words he himself used when he composed the *Dānešnāme-ye ʿAlāʾī*. In its section on metaphysics, then, we read the following:

> جوهر مرکّب از مادّت و صورت جسم است و جسم آن جوهر است که توانی اندر وی درازی نمودن و درازی دیگر چون رسم چلیپا بر آن درازی پیشین ایستاده که میل ندارد هیچ گونه بیك سو.
>
> A substance composed of matter and form is a body, and body is that substance in which you are able to show (*tavānī ... namūdan*) one length and another length as in the figure of a cross, standing on that previous length not inclining to any side. (*Dānešnāme-ye ʿAlāʾī* II.4, 11.4–6)

Having explained laboriously that he intends the two dimensions to intersect one another perpendicularly, Avicenna resumes the account thus:

> پس جسم آن بود که چون درازیی بنهی اندر وی درازیی دیگر یابی برنده ورا بقائمه و درازی سوّم بر آن هر دو درازی بر قائمه ایستاده هم بر آن نقطه که برینش پیشین بروی بود، و هر چه اندر وی این سه درازی بشاید نهادن برین صفت و جوهر بود آن را جسم خوانند ... و جسم بدان جسم است که شاید که این سه چیز اندر وی بنمایی باشارت و مفروض.
>
> So, body is that which, when you lay (*benihī*) one length in it, you find (*yābī*) another length intersecting it perpendicularly and a third length, being perpendicular to the first two, also crossing that [same] point through which the first two lengths went. All that in which it is possible to lay (*bešayād nehādan*) these three lengths according to this description, and which is a substance, is called "body" ... Body is a body insofar as it is possible that you show (*šayād ke ... benamāyī*) these three things in it by pointing out and demarcation (*be-ešārat-o mafrūḍ*). (*Dānešnāme-ye ʿAlāʾī* II.4, 12.10–13.7)

In these passages, we are offered a number of expressions that transfer the Arabic *yumkinu an yafruḍa* into Persian. In particular, Avicenna uses verbs such as *namūdan* ("to show" or "to indicate"), *yabīdan* ("to find"), and *nehādan* ("to put" or "to lay"), in order to convey the meaning of *faraḍa*. These verbs all suggest that bodies are essentially extended, such that we can find, show, and lay out three dimensions in them.[73] There is, first, the extension of body in which we, second, demarcate three dimensions. That these terms are meant to be equivalent to *faraḍa* is further borne out by the fact that Avicenna, in a subsequent passage in the *Dānešnāme-ye ʿAlāʾī*, even employs the verbal noun that corresponds with the Arabic verb *faraḍa*, saying that concrete bodies may change with respect to their three actual dimensions, but they do not differ or change in that it "is possible to demarcate" (*šayād be-farḍ kardan*) the three dimensions in

73 cf. also *Dānešnāme-ye ʿAlāʾī* II.8, 24.3f.

them, thus confirming that he was all along talking about that very action which he describes with the verb *faraḍa* in his Arabic works.[74]

Thus, what Avicenna means by *faraḍa* here is not so much "to assume" something non-existent – and it surely is not "to receive" something hitherto lacking – but to find and to show, to notch and to demarcate, to identify and to reveal what is already there in an unidentified way. Therefore, what Avicenna intends in those contexts which employ the verb *faraḍa* is to bear out the fact that extension essentially belongs to body and that it is such that its extension can be divided into as many as three dimensions.[75]

What is more, his *Dānešnāme-ye ʿAlāʾī* provides the same comparison between the indeterminate extensionality that belongs to bodies as such and the determinate dimensions that belong to particular existing bodies we know from the above-quoted passage from Avicenna's *al-Hidāya* – and we find this comparison again in his *al-Naǧāt*:

فالجسم من حيث هو هكذا هو جسم وهذا المعنى منه هو صورة الجسمية. وأمّا الأبعاد المتحدّدة التي تقع فيه فليست صورة له بل هي من باب الكمّ. وهي لواحق لا مقوّمات، وله صورة جسمانية لا تزول عنه وله مع ذلك أبعاد يتحدّد بها نهاياته وشكله.

So, body insofar as it is such [i.e., insofar as it is true to demarcate in it three dimensions] is a body. This meaning which belongs to it is the form of corporeality (*ṣūrat al-ǧismiyya*). The determinate dimensions that pertain to it are not the form that belongs to it and, instead, belong to the category of quantity; they are concomitants (*lawāḥiq*) but not constituents (*muqawwimāt*). [Accordingly, body] has a corporeal form which does not vanish from it and, together with this, it has three dimensions through which[76] its limit and shape are determined. (*al-Naǧāt* IV.1.4, 499.5–9)[77]

What this paragraph adds to our understanding of Avicenna's conception of corporeality is that it introduces two metaphysically meaningful terms, viz., "concomitant" (*lawāḥiq*, sg. *lāḥiq*) and "constituent" (*muqawwimāt*, sg. *muqawwim*). The difference between a constituent and a concomitant is in that, while both are necessary for their subject, the former is "inside" (*dāḫil*) the essence of the subject and the latter "outside" (*ḫāriǧ*).[78] What is more, constituents are described as "parts" of the essence insofar as

74 *Dānešnāme-ye ʿAlāʾī* II.4, 13.14–14.2; cf. the use of *mafrūḍ* already in the above quotation.

75 It should be clear that Avicenna's deliberate word choice also reflects his intention to guarantee the unity of body. That is to say, by mentally *assuming* three dimensions in body, we merely identify its length, breadth, and depth – without, however, actually *splitting* the body lengthwise, breadthwise, and depthwise. This is further explains why Avicenna uses a "weak" verb such as *faraḍa*, describing a mental operation, in his account of body.

76 Reading *yataḥaddidu bihā nihāyatuhū* with Fakhry, ʿUmayra, and al-Kurdī for *yataḥaddidu nihāyatuhū* in Dānešpažūh.

77 In the previous chapter of *al-Naǧāt*, Avicenna seemed to align the corporeal form with the (indeterminate) extensions (*al-aqṭār*) and states that matter cannot be devoid of the corporeal form, because without it – i.e., without extensionality – it would be indivisible; cf. *al-Naǧāt* IV.1.3, 497.15–498.4.

78 This is made clear in the logic of *al-Ḥikma al-mašriqiyya*, published as *Manṭiq al-Mašriqiyyīn*, I.6, 13.19–14.2; cf. *al-Ḥikma al-mašriqiyya* I.10–11, 17.8–19.14. This terminology reoccurs also in three

the essence comes to be, i.e., is constituted, through the constituents.[79] A concomitant, by contrast, is a necessary accident following from – and, thus, being outside – the essence of its subject. Thus, when Avicenna, here, states that the determinate extensions are concomitants but not constituents (*hiya lawāḥiq lā muqawwimāt*), he describes them as accidents that necessarily belong to any existing body, even if they do not belong to the essence of body, i.e., even if "body as such" does not require determinate extension. Nonetheless, "body as such" is constituted through the form of corporeality. Corporeality, then, is a necessary part of the essence of body. Now it becomes clear that Avicenna's intention in discussing the absolute body is an attempt to define the core of the essence of bodies, i.e., their constituents, precisely without talking about their concomitants. It is these constituents which entail extension and divisibility, and not concomitants such as the three determinate dimensions.

Corporeality, then, entails extensionality. To be a body means to be extended and the absolute body must be regarded as an indeterminately extended substance. Above I said that Avicenna's conception of body relies not only on the notion of extension but also on the notions of continuity and divisibility. Having understood the absolute body as an extended substance, we can now turn to the idea of continuity, which will illuminate Avicenna's conception of the corporeal form, and to the feature of divisibility, which will help us comprehend his understanding of matter.

Continuity and Divisibility

In *al-Maqūlāt* III.4, when discussing quantity, and in *al-Ilāhiyyāt* II.2, when investigating corporeal substance, as well as in *al-Naǧāt* IV.1.4, when establishing matter, Avicenna spells out more fully what he means by the "absolute body." He first denies that a body as such has any actual line existing in it.[80] A line, for example, could have been specified through motion, as when the sphere revolves around an axis, or through determinate, i.e., concrete, dimensions, which would specify the diameter of a cube.[81] Both motion and concrete dimension, however, are accidental but not essential for body as such. Thus, the essence of body does not rely on having an actual line. Moreover, an absolute body does not even have a surface, because it is not essentially limited – in fact, body as such is not even finite. To the contrary, we conceptualise body without all these and other accidental additions to the essence of body. The bare

important quotations provided below from *al-Maqūlāt* III.4, 113.2–6; *al-Samāʿ al-ṭabīʿī* I.2, §6, 15.6; and *al-Ilāhiyyāt* VI.1, §3, 258.2.

79 cf. *al-Ḥikma al-mašriqiyya* I.15, 27.19.

80 His account in *al-Naǧāt* adds that there is not even an actual point in a body insofar as it is a body; cf. *al-Naǧāt* IV.1.4, esp. 498.8–10.

81 cf. *al-Ilāhiyyāt* II.2, §3, 61.16–62.2, where Avicenna particularly speaks of motion being the cause of a sphere's axis; cf. also *al-Ilāhiyyāt* III.4, §2, 111.7–112.2.

meaning of "body" dispenses with points, lines, surfaces, and even with finitude (but, as we have seen, not with extensionality).[82] This conception of the absolute body is well encapsulated in *al-Maqūlāt* III.4:

فنقول: يجب أن تعلم أنّ كلّ جسم فهو متناه ولكن حدّ الجسم من حيث هو جسم غير حدّ الجسم المتناهي، من حيث هو متناه. والتناهي يلزم كلّ جسم بعد ما تقوّم حدّ الجسمية جسماً. ولذلك قد يُعقَل الجسم جسماً ولا يُعقل تناهيه ... فالتناهي ليس داخلاً في ماهية الجسم فالسطح ليس جزء حدّ للجسم.

So, we say: It is necessary that you know that every body is finite, yet the definition of body insofar as it is body is not the definition of the finite body[83] insofar as it is finite. Finitude follows upon every body after (*ba'da*) the definition of corporeality is constituted as body. For that reason, body may be conceived as body without its finitude being conceived (*qad yu'qalu l-ğism ğisman wa-lā yu'qalu tanāhiyatuhū*) ... So, finitude is not internal to the essence of the body (*fa-l-tanāhī laysa dāḫilan fī māhiyyat al-ğism*), and so the surface is not a part of a definition of body (*ḥadd al-ğism*). (*al-Maqūlāt* III.4, 113.2–6)[84]

From what Avicenna writes, we can derive an idea about what body as such is *not*: it is not finite, it does not have a surface or a line, and, as we already know, it has no determinate dimensions that would delimit it as a particular magnitude with a specific shape. None of these aspects belongs to body as such but are exclusive traits of concrete bodies due to the species forms and individual accidents which they have acquired.

Yet, in addition to what body is not, Avicenna elsewhere also reveals his positive account of its essence. Most importantly, corporeality means "continuity" (*ittiṣāl*), as Avicenna emphasises in his discussion in *al-Ilāhiyyāt* II.2:

فالجسمية بالحقيقة صورة الاتّصال القابل لما قلناه من فرض الأبعاد الثلاثة.

So, corporeality, in reality, is the form of the continuity (*ṣūrat al-ittiṣāl*) which is receptive of what we have said in terms of the demarcation of the three dimensions. (*al-Ilāhiyyāt* II.2, §9, 64.6f.)[85]

---

82 cf. A. D. Stone, "Simplicius and Avicenna on the Essential Corporeity of Material Substance," 100f.; McGinnis, "A Penetrating Question," 59.

83 Reading *al-ğism al-mutanāhī* with Ms. Leiden or. 4 for *al-ğism wa-l-mutanāhī* in Qanawātī/al-Ḫuḍayrī/al-Ahwānī/Zāyid.

84 cf. *al-Ilāhiyyāt* II.2, §3, 62.2–7; *al-Nağāt* IV.1.4, 498.7–499.11; *Lettre au vizir Abū Sa'd*, 9.2–7, 12.5–7, 13.11–14.

85 cf. *al-Ilāhiyyāt* II.2, §§27–29, 70.1–71.9; *al-Nağāt* IV.1.4, 500.9f. Here, a general note of caution is in order: the absolute body does not exist. No one has ever perceived an absolute body nor will there ever be an absolute body in existence as such. For Avicenna, the absolute body is a construct; it signifies the most fundamental conceptual level of corporeal reality. It is the concept in which all bodies share invariably and with regard to which no body differs or exceeds another; cf. *al-Maqūlāt* III.4, 113.13–114.4; *al-Samā' al-ṭabī'ī* I.1, §7, 9.20; I.2, §2, 13.4–10; *al-Ilāhiyyāt* II.2, §9, 64.8–11; §29, 71.3–5; III.4, §2, 111.15; *al-Nağāt* IV.1.5, 501.6; *Dānešnāme-ye 'Alā'ī* II.4, 13.15–14.2; *al-Ḥikma al-mašriqiyya* III.2.18–20; *al-Išārāt wa-l-tanbīhāt* II.1.7, 92.19–93.5. Leaving aside the notion of mathematical body, it is clear that the bodies that do exist are natural bodies, i.e., concrete bodies such as stones and humans. These are corporeal, because they all contain corporeality on the most basic level of their formal determination. A human

If corporeality precisely means continuity and if continuity is exactly what we were discussing when we characterised body as that substance in which one can demarcate three dimensions, then continuity is precisely that which makes a body such that one can demarcate these dimensions. In other words, being continuous boils down to being extended. The primary feature of corporeality, then, is the continuity of indeterminate extensionality without the need for finitude, lines, points, surfaces, motions, dimensions, and measures.

In addition to extension and continuity, there is yet a third feature that belongs to the absolute body as such, viz., divisibility. Avicenna states several times that bodies as such are divisible.[86] This can only mean that that which makes body a body is also that which makes body divisible. If corporeality is what makes body a body, and if corporeality is continuity, then, continuity entails divisibility. In fact, divisibility is even the most characteristic trait of continuity, even more so than extension. This is already clear through the fact that Avicenna usually defines continuity through divisibility. Acknowledging that continuity is an equivocal expression (*ism muštarak*), he distinguishes several kinds of continuity of which only one is said to be continuity in itself (*fī nafsihī*), i.e., continuity not by virtue of reference to something else (*lā*

being, for example is a rational animal, and an animal is an ensouled body, and so "body" is an essential part of human. Since only concrete bodies exist – i.e., since no absolute bodies do – Avicenna usually discusses the former and not the latter. Most of what Avicenna writes in his *al-Ilāhiyyāt*, *al-Samāʿ al-ṭabīʿī*, and *al-Maqūlāt*, as well as the corresponding passages in his other works, concerns existing things. So, when he writes in his *al-Maqūlāt* – which, after all, are his treatise on the categories, and the categories are a classification of *existing* things – that continuity is a specific difference (*faṣl*) that pertains to magnitudes (*maqādīr*, sg. *miqdār*) dividing the genus quantity (*kamm*) into continuous quantities and discontinuous quantities (*al-Maqūlāt* III.4, 116.4–14), then this does not entail that the absolute body itself is a magnitude in the category of continuous quantity, simply because it is also continuous. Magnitudes or measures are accidents, as Avicenna also establishes in *al-Ilāhiyyāt* III.4, which belong to existing substances and which determine their quantity. They are different from what body is as such and from the form of corporeality (cf. esp. *al-Ilāhiyyāt* III.4, §2, 111.7–112.2). Just because continuity is a specific difference for this kind of accident does not mean that the substantial composite of matter and corporeal form fails to be essentially continuous, merely because continuity is an accident. Instead, continuity is the primary feature of corporeality – it is nothing other than corporeality itself and tantamount to continuous extensionality, without thereby making the absolute body a quantity or a magnitude. It is just that those existing things which share in this feature – i.e., those existing things which are corporeal and, thus, continuous – are all magnitudes that can be measured and that belong to the category of continuous quantities. Moreover, when Avicenna states that a body is divisible only insofar as it has quantity (e.g., *al-Maqūlāt* III.4, 118.8f.; *al-Ilāhiyyāt* II.3, §§12–13, 77.7–9; III.2, §13, 100.16–101.3), this does not mean that the absolute body fails to be divisible. In fact, the continuity and corporeality inherent in the concept of the absolute body is what makes all bodies essentially divisible, as it provides divisibility in the first place. It is also clear that this passage in *al-Maqūlāt* III.4 discusses the sensible body (*hāḏā l-ǧism al-maḥsūs*; 118.5) which, of course, belongs to the category of continuous quantity (118.1).

86 cf. *al-Ilāhiyyāt* II.2, §12, 65.4; §18, 66.15f.; cf. also *al-Naǧāt* IV.1.3, 497.15–498.4; *ʿUyūn al-ḥikma* III.2, 28.14; cf. also Shihadeh, "Avicenna's Corporeal Form," 366f.; *Doubts on Avicenna*, 156, 160.

bi-qiyās ilā ġayrihī).[87] This meaning is characterised in *al-Samāʿ al-ṭabīʿī* III.2, which is the terminological prelude to Avicenna's rejection of atomism. There he writes:

ويقال متّصل للشيء في نفسه إذا كان بحيث يمكن أن تفرض له أجزاء بينها الاتّصال الذي بالمعنى الأوّل أيّ بينها حدّ مشترك هو طرف لهذا وذاك وهذا هو حدّ متّصل وامّا الذي يقال له منقسم إلى أشياء تقبل القسمة دائماً فهو رمسه.

> "Continuous" is said of something in itself if it is such that it is possible that you demarcate for it (*bi-ḥayṯu yumkinu an tafruḍa lahū*) parts between which there is the continuity in the first sense [mentioned above], i.e., between them is a shared boundary which is a limit for this and that. This [first sense] is the definition of "continuous" (*ḥadd muttaṣil*), whereas that which is said that it is divisible in things that are [themselves] always susceptible to division, [this] is its description (*rasmuhū*). (*al-Samāʿ al-ṭabīʿī* III.2, §10, 183.7–9)

What is essentially continuous without having to rely on something else, i.e., what is continuous in itself, is that in which one can determine mentally different parts or bits which are not separate from one another but which share a common border. Since the assumed border belongs equally to both parts, it is as if these two parts are formerly one, so that the border is merely assumed but does not really exist. This description matches Avicenna's account in *al-Maqūlāt*:

وذلك لأنّ حدّه أنّه الذي يمكن أن تفرض له أجزاء يجمع بينها حدّ مشترك هو نهاية لجزأين منها.

> This [i.e., this sense of continuity which is the continuous in itself without reference to something else] is so, because its definition is that it is that for which it is possible that you demarcate (*yumkinu an yafruḍa lahū*) parts between which they unite at a shared boundary which is a limit for two of these parts. (*al-Maqūlāt* III.4, 116.10f.)

Avicenna's account of continuity ultimately derives from Aristotle, in particular from *Categories* 6 as well as its reverberations in *Physics* V and VI.[88] The distinction between a relative and an absolute sense of continuity is present even in Aristotle, though it is not yet fully formulated.[89] Avicenna emphasises, however, that the meaning of continuity *per se* is that in which it is possible to demarcate or to assume parts that are not yet actual as individual parts whose likewise merely assumed borders are *not* merely assumed to be one and the same but are *actually* and *really* one and the same so long as the assumed division has not yet been actualised. A continuous magnitude is continuous in the strict sense only so long as it is divisible and not already divided.

87 *al-Samāʿ al-ṭabīʿī* III.2, §8, 182.1f.; cf. *al-Maqūlāt* III.4, 116.6–117.19; *al-Samāʿ al-ṭabīʿī* III.2, §§8–10, 182.1–183.11; *al-Ḥikma al-mašriqiyya* III.12, 41.9–18; *Lettre au vizir Abū Saʿd*, 42.12–44.12; cf. also A. D. Stone, "Simplicius and Avicenna on the Essential Corporeity of Material Substance," 102; McGinnis, "A Small Discovery," 9–11.

88 cf. *Cat.* 6, 5a1–6; *Phys.* V.3, 227a10–12; VI.1, 231a22.

89 cf. esp. *Physics* VI.1, 231a22–26.

It is potentially divided – and this is what "to be divisible" means: being potentially divided.

It is, moreover, striking that in characterising the continuous, Avicenna uses much the same terminology as in defining the essence of body. While body is that "in which it is possible to demarcate" (*yumkinu an yafruḍa fīhi*) three dimensions, continuity is that "for which it is possible to demarcate" (*yumkinu an yafruḍa lahū*) parts that have a common border. Since these parts must be extended, continuity not only entails divisibility, it also entails extension. Thus, body as such is nothing other than something which is essentially continuous in three dimensions. Corporeality means three-dimensional continuity, and continuity amounts to actual extension and potential divisibility, but it does not amount to concrete dimensions or any determinate extensionality. So, in the end, we have to understand essential continuity as being tantamount to extension, precisely because continuity means divisibility in the sense just outlined.[90] Something which is continuous is such that it can be thought of as consisting of parts which have a common limit but without actually being divided into these parts. Furthermore, these parts are required to be extended in one way or another, for if these parts were not extended they would be like a point and something continuous cannot consist of points, as Avicenna elsewhere argues.[91] Therefore, what is continuous is divisible and what is divisible requires extension.

We can now see that Avicenna's position approximates the one which Hyman attributed to Averroes. Hyman argued that for Averroes, bodies are essentially divisible and, thus, must be endowed with indeterminate three-dimensionality which, ultimately, is identified with the corporeal form.[92] This means nothing other than that the core conception of body is that it is extended, continuous, and divisible – and this is precisely what Avicenna thinks, too.

Apart from the corporeal form, which is a notion foreign to Aristotle, the conception endorsed by Avicenna closely corresponds with, and may, in fact, follow, the opening passage from Aristotle's *De caelo*:

> Συνεχὲς μὲν οὖν ἐστι τὸ διαιρετὸν εἰς ἀεὶ διαιρετά, σῶμα δὲ τὸ πάντῃ διαιρετόν. Μεγέθους δὲ τὸ μὲν ἐφ' ἓν γραμμή, τὸ δ' ἐπὶ δύο ἐπίπεδον, τὸ δ' ἐπὶ τρία σῶμα· καὶ παρὰ ταῦτα οὐκ ἔστιν ἄλλο μέγεθος διὰ τὸ τὰ τρία πάντα εἶναι καὶ τὸ τρὶς πάντῃ.
>
> والمتّصل هو المنفصل في أشياء قابلة بتفصيل قبولاً دائماً. والجرم هو المنفصل في جميع الأقطار. وأمّا العظم فما كان منه ذا بعد واحد فهو الخطّ وما كان ذا بعدان فهو السطح وما كان منه ذا ثلاث أبعد فهو الجرم. وليس شيء ممّا له عظم خارجاً عن هذا لأنّ الكلّ أيضاً يقال في الثلاثة والثلاثة محصورة في معنى كلّ.
>
> Now, what is continuous is that which is divisible into parts always capable of subdivision, and a body is that which is in every way divisible. A magnitude divisible in one way is a line, that in two

90 One may also say that actual division presupposes continuity just as concrete determinate dimensions presuppose extensionality.

91 cf. *al-Samāʿ al-ṭabīʿī* III.3, 187.2f.

92 q.v. above, 123.

> ways a surface, and that in three ways a body. Beyond these there is no other magnitude, because the three [dimensions] are all that there are, and that which is divisible in three is divisible in all. (*Cael.* I.1, 268a6–10, tr. by Stocks, modified)[93]

So, Avicenna's discourse on corporeality, and his views on what physics as a science is all about, leads us once more to the programmatic first lines of *De caelo*, in which Aristotle outlined his understanding of "the science of nature" as a science concerned with bodies, subsequently describing these bodies as continuous, divisible, and three-dimensional.[94] There is, furthermore, a striking resemblance between Avicenna's understanding of natural philosophy and how Neoplatonic commentators such as Simplicius (d. ~ 560) read Aristotle's text in *De caelo* I.1. In his commentary, Simplicius explains his views on Aristotle's conception of natural philosophy and the structure of the works covering this field of inquiry. The first of these works is the *Physics*, the second is *De caelo*. Since the former is said to discuss the principles required for any inquiry into natural things, and since the latter begins that inquiry, it is incumbent to understand the transition between these two works. The fact that the *Physics* provides the principles for an inquiry that is finally commenced in *De caelo* necessitates – on Simplicius' reading at least – that the *De caelo* is introduced by a methodological proem which properly defines this new investigation by introducing its proper subject-matter. This is what Simplicius sets forth when commenting on the first lines of Aristotle's *De caelo*:

> Τὸ προοίμιον τόν τε σκοπὸν τῆς πραγματείας διδάσκει καὶ τὴν τάξιν αὐτῆς, ὅτι πρὸς τὴν Φυσικὴν ἀκρόασιν συνεχής· ἐπειδὴ γὰρ ἐκείνη περὶ τῶν φυσικῶν ἀρχῶν ἦν, ἔδει μετ' ἐκείνην περὶ τῶν ἀπὸ τῶν ἀρχῶν λέγειν, ταῦτα δ' ἔστι τὰ σώματα προσεχῶς ... διὸ καὶ ἀπὸ τοῦ συνεχοῦς τὴν ἀρχὴν εὐθὺς τῆς διδασκαλίας ἐν τούτοις ποιεῖται, ὅπερ γένος τοῦ σώματός ἐστιν, καὶ περὶ τῆς τοῦ σώματος φύσεως, καθ' ὃ σῶμα, τὴν τελειοτάτην διδασκαλίαν εὐθὺς ἐν ἀρχῇ παραδίδωσι.
>
> The prologue sets out the scope of the treatise and its order, i.e., that it is continuing the *Physics*. Since the latter was concerned with the natural principles (περὶ τῶν φυσικῶν ἀρχῶν), it is necessary next to speak of what derives from the principles, and these things are in the first place bodies ... And that is why he begins his exposition in these books immediately with the continuous, which is precisely the genus of body (γένος τοῦ σώματός), and makes the most complete exposition of the nature of body insofar as it is body (περὶ τῆς τοῦ σώματος φύσεως, καθ' ὃ σῶμα), right at the outset. (Simplicius, *In Cael.*, 6.29–32, 5.23–26, tr. by Hankinson, modified)[95]

---

93 cf. *Phys.* V.3, 227a11–15; VI.1, 231a21–29; *Cael.* III.1, 298a27–b5; cf. also what appears to be a comment by Philoponus on *Physics* V.3, 227a10–13, preserved in the margins of Ms. Leiden or. 583, edited by Badawī in Aristotle, *al-Ṭabīʿa*, 545.14–546.2.

94 q.v. fn. 1 above, 111.

95 Recently, Falcon offered the same diagnosis as Simplicius, stating that "the *Physics* is best understood as a prologomenon to the science of nature, and that the actual science of nature begins only with the treatise *On the Heavens*" ("The Subject Matter of Aristotle's Physics," 432).

Simplicius' position in this passage illustrates two things. First, it agrees with several central aspects of how Avicenna understands the teaching he is carrying out in his *al-Samāʿ al-ṭabīʿī*, for example, that Avicenna is currently concerned precisely with an exposition of the natural body insofar as it is a body; that he, to that end, sets out the nature of body; that the nature of body is grounded in the concept of continuity which is a genus of body; and that this ought to be done right at the outset.

Second, however, it also indicates an important difference between the Peripatetic approach and the Avicennian. Simplicius argues that "at the outset" means "after the *Physics*," so that an investigation of body as such befits the beginning of the treatise on the heavens, i.e., he explains that this is what ought to be carried out *after* the principles have been established in a treatise called *Physics*. By contrast, Avicenna's intention is to begin the science of physics itself with such a discussion of corporeality. Thus, the Peripatetic seeks to establish the principles in physics, in order to be able to investigate the natural world of bodies afterwards, whereas Avicenna, having established them in metaphysics, sets them out in the course of expounding the natural world itself, beginning with the most common and proceeding to the more particular. This, as I have argued above in chapter two, is essential to Avicenna's method in *al-Samāʿ al-ṭabīʿī*: Avicenna does not investigate the principles or inquire into them, in order to establish them – what he does, instead, is to teach, to explain, and to elucidate. Consequently, he does not begin his treatise *on the heavens* with the notion of corporeality – he begins his treatise *on physics* with it.

The question raised by this situation, i.e., by the very facts that bodies are corporeal; that their corporeality consists in continuity, divisibility, and extension; and that their corporeality is not explained by the mere fact of their actual measure, is the following: what is that which accounts for this corporeality?

According to Avicenna, corporeality is due to what he calls the "corporeal form" (*al-ṣūra al-ǧismiyya*) or the "form of corporeality" (*ṣūrat al-ǧismiyya*). This form is the form "through which [the body] becomes a body" in the first place (*al-ṣūra allatī bihā ṣāra ǧisman*).[96] It contains the essence of body and gives rise to an absolute body once conjoined with matter. Avicenna's analysis of corporeality, however, so far only established the need that something does in fact account for corporeality, but it did not yet show (i) that there should be any matter in which the essence of body (i.e., the form of corporeality) exists nor (ii) that corporeality could not likewise be explained by matter alone, which would make the assumption of a corporeal form redundant. So, Avicenna is required to establish the existence of matter *and* to show that corporeality is not explained by matter itself. This is all the more pressing against the background of late

96 *al-Samāʿ al-ṭabīʿī* I.2, §2, 13.6; cf. *al-Maqūlāt* III.4, 115.4; *al-Ilāhiyyāt* II.2, §7, 63.13f.; §19, 67.8–13; *al-Naǧāt* IV.1.4, 499.1–6; *al-Hidāya* III.1, 234.3–235.2; *al-Ḥikma al-mašriqiyya* III, 2.18–20.

ancient developments of the concepts of matter and corporeality, which established an understanding of matter, precisely along these lines, as something already corporeal.[97]

The Source of Corporeality

In the *Categories*, Aristotle enumerates the ten different categories of being, the first of which is substance, the other nine being different kinds of accidents. The first of these accidents treated by Aristotle is quantity (τὸ πόσον, *al-kamm*) and its discussion follows immediately upon that of substance. This could be taken to suggest that, while substance is first among the ten categories, quantity is first among the nine *accidental* categories in the sense that it is the most fundamental accidental description that can be applied to substance.[98] This interpretation may receive further support by a famous argument in Aristotle's *Metaphysics*. There, in *Metaphysics* Z.3, Aristotle provides some evidence that may lead one to think that matter is in fact a substance. In order to show that matter serves as what he calls "the first subject" (τὸ ὑποκείμενον πρῶτον, *al-mawḍūʿ al-awwal*), Aristotle abstracts from a body everything that can be abstracted from it.[99] He writes:

> περιαιρουμένων γὰρ τῶν ἄλλων οὐ φαίνεται οὐδὲν ὑπομένον· τὰ μὲν γὰρ ἄλλα τῶν σωμάτων πάθη καὶ ποιήματα καὶ δυνάμεις, τὸ δὲ μῆκος καὶ πλάτος καὶ βάθος ποσότητές τινες ἀλλ' οὐκ οὐσίαι (τὸ γὰρ ποσὸν οὐκ οὐσία), ἀλλὰ μᾶλλον ᾧ ὑπάρχει ταῦτα πρώτῳ, ἐκεῖνό ἐστιν οὐσία. ἀλλὰ μὴν ἀφαιρουμένου μήκους καὶ πλάτους καὶ βάθους οὐδὲν ὁρῶμεν ὑπολειπόμενον, πλὴν εἴ τί ἐστι τὸ ὁριζόμενον ὑπὸ τούτων, ὥστε τὴν ὕλην ἀνάγκη φαίνεσθαι μόνην οὐσίαν οὕτω σκοπουμένοις.
> فإنّه إذا انتزعت سائر الأشياء لا نرى شيئاً باقياً والمنفعلات الآخر التي للأجسام وأفعالها والقوى وأيضاً الطول والعرض والعمق كمّية هي وليست جواهر لأنّ الكمّية ليست بجوهر بل الذي له هذه الأشياء بعينها بنوع أوّل هو

97 There has been an increasing interest in late ancient developments of the concepts of matter and body, especially in Simplicius and Philoponus. I shall confine myself here to mentioning the most important points inasmuch as they are related to Avicenna's treatment. For more detailed information, cf. Hyman, "Aristotle's First Matter"; Sorabji, "Prime Matter as Extension"; *Matter, Space, and Motion*, chs. 1–3; Wildberg, *John Philoponus' Criticism of Aristotle's Theory of Aether*, 204–221; Mueller, "Aristotle's Doctrine of Abstraction in the Commentators"; de Haas, *John Philoponus' New Definition of Prime Matter*; A. D. Stone, "Simplicius and Avicenna on the Essential Corporeity of Material Substance," esp. 90–99; Sorabji, *The Philosophy of the Commentators*, vol. II, chs. 17 and 18; Golitsis, *Les commentaires de Simplicius et de Jean Philopon à la* Physique *d'Aristote*, 127–139. An interesting paper by Shihadeh furthermore hints at a similar interpretation of matter in post-Avicennian philosophy, especially in the works of Abū l-Barakāt al-Baġdādī; cf. "Avicenna's Corporeal Form," 369f.

98 This certainly was the common view; cf. Ammonius, *In Cat.*, 54.15. Still, there was some discussion about whether quantity or rather quality ought to be considered first among the nine accidental categories; cf. Simplicius discussing, and apparently agreeing with, the argument advanced by the Neopythagorean Ps.-Archytas at *In Cat.*, 120.27–122.30, 155.33–159.8.

99 For the notion of "the first subject" (τὸ ὑποκείμενον πρῶτον), cf. *Met.* Z.3, 1029a1f.; cf. also *Phys.* I.9, 192a31f. The very same passage from *Metaphysics* Z.3 will become relevant again, when we turn to the discussion of place; q.v. below, 376ff.

الجوهر ولاكنّ إذا انتزع الطول والعرض والعمق لا نرى شيئاً يبقى ما خلا إن كان شيء ما الذي هذه تحدّه فإذا مضطرّ أن يرى الهيولى وحدها جوهراً الذين يفحصون هذا الفحص.

When all else is taken away evidently nothing [apart from matter] remains. For everything else are affections, effects, and capacities of bodies, while length, breadth, and depth are quantities and not substances. For a quantity is not substance; substance is rather that to which these belong primarily. But when length and breadth and depth are taken away, we see nothing left, except if there is something which is determined by these (ὁριζόμενον ὑπὸ τούτων, *šay' mā llaḏī hāḏihī tuḥadduhū*), so that to those who consider the question thusly matter alone must seem to be substance. (*Met.* Z.3, 1029a11–19, tr. by Ross, modified)[100]

It is apparently quantity which constitutes the last layer before we reach matter or, put differently, is the first layer of body. So, once we have stripped away all "affections, effects, and capacities of bodies," what remains is length, breadth, and depth together with the matter determined by these. Matter, then, would be "the first subject" (τὸ ὑποκείμενον πρῶτον), whereas quantified matter, i.e., matter together with the three dimensions, would seem to be a "second subject." This is precisely the reasoning of John Philoponus (d. 574) in his commentary on the first line of *Categories* 6:

ἐν τῇ φύσει τῶν πραγμάτων δευτέραν ἔχει τάξιν τὸ ποσόν· ἡ γὰρ πρώτη ὕλη, ὡς πολλάκις εἴρηται, ἀσώματος οὖσα καὶ ἀνείδεος καὶ ἀσχημάτιστος πρότερον ἐξογκωθεῖσα τὰς τρεῖς διαστάσεις δέχεται καὶ γίνεται τριχῇ διαστατόν, ὃ φησιν ὁ Ἀριστοτέλης δεύτερον ὑποκείμενον, εἶθ' οὕτως δέχεται τὰς ποιότητας καὶ ποιεῖ τὰ στοιχεῖα, ὥστε τρίτην τὸ ποιὸν ἐν τοῖς οὖσιν ἔχει τάξιν, τετάρτην δὲ τὰ πρός τι·

In the nature of things, quantity occupies the second rank, for, as has often been said, prime matter, which is without body, form, or shape before being given volume, receives the three dimensions (τὰς τρεῖς διαστάσεις δέχεται) and becomes three-dimensional (γίνεται τριχῇ διαστατόν). And so this, which Aristotle calls "second subject" (δεύτερον ὑποκείμενον), then receives qualities and constitutes the elements, so that quality has the third rank among the things that there are, and relations the fourth. (Philoponus, *In Cat.*, 83.13–19, tr. by Sorabji, modified)[101]

This has been called the "conventional view" or the "traditional theory" of matter and three-dimensionality.[102] This is also the theory to which Philoponus adheres in his commentary on the *Physics* and the one which he expounds at the beginning of the eleventh argument in his *De aeternitate mundi contra Proclum*.[103] According to his presentation in this work, there is a first substrate, which is incorporeal and unformed

100 cf. *Phys.* IV.2, 209b9–11; IV.7, 214a11–14; IV.8, 216b2–9; *De mem.* 1, 449b31–450a14; cf. also *Enn.* II.4.10, 28–31.

101 Sorabji, *Matter, Space, and Motion*, 24; cf. Ammonius, *In Cat.*, 54.4–7.

102 Sorabji, *Matter, Space, and Motion*, 10; de Haas, *John Philoponus' New Definition of Prime Matter*, 31.

103 According to Proclus' eleventh argument, the world is eternal, because matter does not come-to-be out of another earlier matter but, instead, is ungenerated and eternal. Moreover, matter exists for the sake of having form in it, so that whenever matter exists, form must exist with it. If, then, matter is eternal, it must also be eternally enformed. Since the enformation of matter gives rise to the existence

matter (πρώτην οὖν ὕλην καὶ ἁπλῶς εἶναι ὕλην φασὶν τὴν ἀσώματον ἐκείνην καὶ ἀνείδεον), and a second substrate, which is three-dimensionally extended unqualified body (δευτέρως δὲ τὸ τριχῇ διαστατόν τε καὶ ἄποιον σῶμα), before there are, as a third layer, the four elements (τρίτως δὲ καὶ προσεχέστερον τὰ τέσσαρα στοιχεῖα).[104] In Philoponus' discussion, the second quantitive layer is often said to be a form, so that the second substrate would be a composite of matter and form. This is especially apparent in a passage from his corollary on void in which Philoponus describes the second substrate as "the envolumed matter and unqualified body, which is composed out of matter and the form in the category of quantity" (ἡ ὀγκωθεῖσα ὕλη καὶ τὸ ἄποιον σῶμα, ὅπερ σύγκειται ἐξ ὕλης καὶ τοῦ κατὰ ποσὸν εἴδους).[105]

This has close affinities to the two fundamental material layers in the complex system of Proclus (d. 485), viz., the first substrate (or "matter") and the "second substrate" (or "qualityless body"), and is altogether similar to what we find in Plotinus (d. 270).[106] As for Plotinus, he differs from Aristotle on various points, yet still defending the Aristotelian account of an incorporeal matter against the Stoic challenge of a through and through corporeal reality. Matter is incorporeal (ἀσώματος), Plotinus argues, and, as all incorporeal things, without quantity (ἄποιον). By contrast, quantity is a form (δῆλον, ὅτι εἶδος ἡ ποσότης), just as qualities are.[107] Thus, body is a composite of matter and a quantitative form, not unlike the traditional view as expressed in Philoponus' writings.[108]

Central points of this understanding of matter, moreover, are reverberated early in the Islamic milieu. Already Abū Yaʿqūb ibn Isḥāq al-Kindī (d. ~ 256/870) presented quantity and quality as the two "primary and separate predicates of substance."[109]

---

of the world, the world is itself eternal due to an eternal and ungenerated matter which eternally is not without form.

104 Philoponus, *De aeternitate mundi contra Proclum* XI.2, 410.20–25; cf. Wildberg, *John Philoponus' Criticism of Aristotle's Theory of Aether*, 207–212; de Haas, *John Philoponus' New Definition of Prime Matter*, 21–26. The expression "second subject" does not occur in Aristotle. Nonetheless, it has been argued that the commentators conceived of it as a Peripatetic notion and that it may derive from Alexander, as some passages in Simplicius' commentary on the *De caelo* seem to suggest; cf. Wildberg, *John Philoponus' Criticism of Aristotle's Theory of Aether*, fn. 85, 211; de Haas, *John Philoponus' New Definition of Prime Matter*, fn. 77, 21f.; cf. also Ammonius, *In Cat.*, 54.6.

105 Philoponus, *In Phys.*, 687.32f.; cf. *In Phys.*, 225.11–16, 244.6–9.

106 For Proclus' theory, cf. *In Tim.* I, 387.12; *In Parm.* II, 33–37; cf. also the analyses by van Riel, "Proclus on Matter and Physical Necessity," esp. 240–247; Opsomer, "The Natural World," esp. 156f.; cf. also de Haas, *John Philoponus' New Definition of Prime Matter*, 91–99.

107 *Enn.* II.4.9, 6f.; cf. *Enn.* II.4.8, 23–25.

108 The major difference between Plotinus and the traditional Peripatetic view, however, would be that matter, for Plotinus, does not really enter into a composition with form but remains impassive and unaffected by form; cf. esp. *Enn.* III.6.16–18.

109 al-Kindī, *Risāla fī kammiyyat kutub Arisṭūṭālīs wa-mā yuḥtāǧu ilayhi fī taḥṣīl al-falsafa*, vol. 1, 370.11–13. This is similar to what Avicenna does in the *Dānešnāme-ye ʿAlāʾī* II.9, 28.6–29.9, even though in *al-Maqūlāt* II.5, 84.4–17, he presents a more complex division of the accidental categories, among

Yaḥyā ibn ʿAdī (d. 363/974), too, seems to subscribe to the traditional view in a complex debate about the substantiality of body, recently edited and translated by Stephen Menn and Robert Wisnovsky.[110] The Iḫwān al-Ṣafāʾ (fl. ~ 370/980) even distinguish explicitly between a first and a second matter, the first being prime matter, the second being quantified matter:

> وانبجس من النفس الكلّية جوهر آخر دونه في الرتبة يُسمّى الهيولى الأولى وأنّ الهيولى الأولى قبلت المقادير التي هي الطول والعرض والعمق فصارت بذلك جسماً مطلقاً وهو الهيولى الثانية.
>
> [Know that] from the universal soul flows another substance lower than it in rank which is called "first matter" (*al-hayūlā l-ūlā*). [You should also know] that first matter receives the magnitudes (*al-maqādīr*) that are length, breadth, and depth, and so, through this, becomes an absolute body (*ǧisman muṭlaqan*), which is the "second matter" (*al-hayūlā l-ṯāniyya*) (*Rasāʾil Iḫwān al-Ṣafāʾ* XXXIII.1, 35.12–36.2)[111]

It is clear that the second matter described here by the Iḫwān al-Ṣafāʾ corresponds conceptually to Philoponus' "second substrate" and is similar to Avicenna's "absolute body." It is a composite of matter and magnitude (or quantity); it is envolumed matter and, thus, qualityless body. In fact, it seems as if the expression *ǧism muṭlaq* denotes precisely this: body in an unqualified way, i.e., body as such.[112]

In another epistle, the Iḫwān al-Ṣafāʾ further describe the absolute body in similar terms as "having three dimensions" (*ḏū ṯalāṯat abʿād*), thus being an absolute, i.e., unqualified, instance of a body "to which one can point" (*ǧisman muṭlaqan mušāran ilayhi*). As it seems, the absolute body, as conceived by the Iḫwān al-Ṣafāʾ, is (unlike the absolute body in Avicenna) already particularised through the set of dimensions it has received, so that it is a concrete magnitude, i.e., has a concrete size, while still lacking qualities of any kind. Thereupon, the body receives a certain shape (*al-šakl*), which is said to be a quality (*al-kayfiyya*), thereby becoming a specific – as opposed to an absolute – body to which one can point (*ǧisman maḫṣūṣan mušāran ilayhi*). Finally,

---

other things, by adding the category of position to quantity and quality, and describing these three together as accidents conceptualised without reference to something external; cf. also P. Thom, "The Division of the Categories According to Avicenna."

110 cf. the remarks and references by Menn and Wisnovsky in their introduction to Ibn ʿAdī, *On Whether Body is a Substance or a Quantity*, esp. 16.

111 In al-Bustānī's edition of the *Rasāʾil Iḫwān al-Ṣafāʾ*, this passage is found in chapter XXXII.6, 187.9–12. As Walker explains in the introduction to his edition and translation, the textual transmission of what he calls epistles 32a, 32b, and 33 – and what al-Bustānī called epistles 32 and 33 – is confused.

112 It ought to be noted that the Iḫwān al-Ṣafāʾ frequently employ the expression *ǧism muṭlaq*, that they repeatedly differentiate between a first and a second substrate, and that they often talk about a corporeal form of length, breadth, and depth that inheres in prime matter before it receives other forms; cf., for example, *Rasāʾil Iḫwān al-Ṣafāʾ* XXXIV.1, 55.2–5; XXXV.6, 114.13–115.6; cf. also Wolfson in Crescas, *Crescas' Critique of Aristotle*, 580, 582.

matter is said to be like the one, quantity like the two, and quality like the three.[113] Since matter is also said to be a substance and called an ipseity (*al-huwiyya*), one cannot resist the impression that the Iḫwān al-Ṣafāʾ are alluding to the ten categories, presenting substance as the first, quantity as the second, and quality as the third category. This would not only harmonise with the late ancient understanding of qualityless body as a second substrate but would also indicate some Pythagorean overtones. Nicomachus of Gerasa (d. ~ 120), for example, is known for having identified the Aristotelian categories with Platonic forms which, then, were reduced to "the formal properties of number."[114] In an interesting way, this corresponds to the fact that the above quoted passage from the Iḫwān al-Ṣafāʾ is sometimes transmitted within – and always, at least, in the close vicinity of – their presentation of the principles of existing things "according to the opinion of Pythagoras" (*ʿalā raʾy fīṯāġūris*).[115]

What is clear from the above is that there are strong conceptual similarities between Simplicius' conception of the corporeal form, Plotinus' and Philoponus' talk of a quantitative form, al-Kindī's emphasis of quantity as a primary predicate, and the Iḫwān al-Ṣafāʾ's mention of the "absolute body."[116] Yet, it is also clear that their accounts differ

113 *Rasāʾil Iḫwān al-Ṣafāʾ* XV.3, 9.4–10.11; cf. Ps.-Plutarchus, *Placita Philosophorum*, 308a.4–9, Arabic translation in Aetius Arabus, *Die Vorsokratiker in arabischer Überlieferung*, 16.7–9. The expression *mušār ilayhi* is usually the Arabic form of Aristotle's τόδε τι, taken to describe a particular "determinate" individual. However, since the Iḫwān al-Ṣafāʾ call shape (*al-šakl*) – such as circular, triangular or rectangular shape – a quality (*al-kayfiyya*) and since quality follows upon quantity as the number three follows upon the number two, there seem to be two ways to interpret their account. The first is to understand the "absolute body" of the Iḫwān al-Ṣafāʾ, against my suggestion, as not yet having a concrete size by being endowed with a concrete set of dimensions, while nonetheless already being three-dimensionally extended in an indeterminate way; cf. also *Rasāʾil Iḫwān al-Ṣafāʾ* XXXV.6, 114.15–115.1, where they call the three dimensions an "intellectual form" (*ṣūra ʿaqliyya*). This would mean that their conception would broadly conform to that of Avicenna. According to a second interpretation, the Iḫwān al-Ṣafāʾ would think of shapes as directly determining and bringing about concrete qualities in a manner similar to what Plato described in the *Timaeus*, so that fire, for example, would be very sharp and acute, thus explaining why coming into contact with fire hurts. On this second interpretation, their conception of the absolute body would be different from that of Avicenna, as it would already have a concrete size but still no quality, as it would still be lacking a shape. How a body could have a size but no shape, however, would have to be investigated more properly, then. Both interpretations seem to have their respective merits.

114 O'Meara, *Pythagoras Revived*, 17.

115 cf. Walker's remarks about the textual transmission of what he calls epistles 32a, 32b, and 33 in his introduction as well as the chapter headings of epistle 32a in his edition and of 32 in al-Bustānī's edition.

116 It should also be noted that Simplicius explicitly uses the expression τὸ σωματικὸν εἶδος ("the corporeal form") in his commentaries on the *Physics* and *De caelo* – the very same expression we find in Avicenna as *al-ṣūra al-ǧismiyya*; cf. Simplicius, *In Phys.*, 230.27; *In Cael.*, 279.23. As already mentioned, it is usually assumed that Simplicius' commentaries were not translated into Arabic, so that there could not have been a direct influence on Avicenna. This view is currently subject to debate and requires further investigation; q.v. above 34. Even without an Arabic translation of Simplicius' commentaries,

from Avicenna's understanding in at least one important respect. Whereas Avicenna maintains that the corporeal form does not invest the matter with a concrete accidental set of dimensions but with an indeterminate substantial extensionality in which one can identify three dimensions, his Greek and Arabic predecessors conceived of the corporeal quantitative form as that which provides the body with concrete accidental dimensions, thus following the traditional theory of matter as developed on the basis of Aristotle's argument from *Metaphysics* Z.3, which describes the second substrate as a composite precisely of matter and concrete accidental quantity.

This traditional theory is also the one which Philoponus, after his presentation at the beginning of *De aeternitate mundi contra Proclum* XI, refutes and replaces with a new theory of matter, at around the same time as his contemporary Simplicius likewise rethought the traditional understanding of prime matter.[117] According to this new theory, matter is itself extended, albeit in an indeterminate way. Accordingly, the Philoponus who rows with Proclus on the question of the eternity of the world tends to speak of matter as "the three-dimensional" (τὸ τριχῇ διαστατόν):

> ὥστε οὐ κωλύσει εἶναι πρώτην ὕλην τὸ τριχῇ διαστατὸν τὸ εἰδοπεποιῆσθαι αὐτὸ καὶ μὴ εἶναι ἀνείδεον· αὐτὸ γὰρ τὸ ἐναντίον ὁ λόγος ἔδειξεν, ὡς οὐδὲν ἐνδέχεταί τι τῶν ὄντων πάντη πάντων εἶναι ἀνείδεον. εἰδοπεποιημένον δὲ λέγοντες τὸ τριχῇ διαστατὸν οὐ σύνθετον αὐτό φαμεν ἀλλ' ἁπλούστατον· οὐ γὰρ ἐξ ὑποκειμένου καὶ εἴδους ἐστίν, ἀλλ' αὐτὸ ἁπλοῦς τίς ἐστιν ὄγκος ἐν τούτῳ αὐτῷ τὸ εἶναι ἔχον καὶ τοῖς λοιποῖς ἅπασιν ὑποκείμενον. ἀλλ' οὐδὲ τὸ τριχῇ διεστάναι συνθέσεώς τινα ἡμῖν παρέχει ἔννοιαν ... δέδεικται δέ, ὅτι οὐδὲ ἄλλο τι τῷ τριχῇ διαστατῷ ὑπόκειται, ἀλλ' αὐτό ἐστιν ὑποβάθρα πάντων, δῆλον ἄρα, ὡς ἁπλούστατόν ἐστιν καὶ ὕλη πάντων ἐξ οὐδενὸς τὴν σύνθεσιν εἰληφός. τούτων οὕτως ἐχόντων καὶ αὐθυποστάτου τοῦ τριχῇ ὄντος διαστατοῦ, μηδεμιᾶς δ' ἐπ' αὐτοῦ μεταβολῆς θεωρουμένης, οὐδεὶς ἄρα ἔστιν λόγος ὁ κατασκευάζειν δυνάμενος, ὡς ὕλη τις ἀσώματος τοῖς φυσικοῖς ὑπόκειται σώμασιν, ἀλλ' εἰς αὐτὸ ἀνάγκη τὰ φυσικὰ ἀναλύεσθαι τό, εἰς ὃ ἔσχατον, εἴτε ὑποκείμενόν τις πρῶτον εἴτε ὕλην αὐτὸ λαλεῖν βούλοιτο· οὐδὲν γὰρ περὶ τῶν ὀνομάτων φιλονεικήσωμεν.
>
> And so its being invested with form and not formless will not prevent the three-dimensional from being prime matter (εἶναι πρώτην ὕλην τὸ τριχῇ διαστατόν). In fact, the argument has shown the exact opposite, that nothing of all the things there are can be entirely formless. But when we say that the three-dimensional is invested with form, we do not mean that it is composite but that it is most simple (ἁπλούστατον). It does not consist of substrate and form but is itself a kind of

---

Avicenna could well have became acquainted with the idea indirectly or through other sources. For some information on Arabic, Hebrew, and Latin discussions of the Avicennian notion, cf. Wolfson in Crescas, *Crescas' Critique of Aristotle*, 579–590; Hyman, "Aristotle's First Matter"; Hasse, "Influence of Arabic and Islamic Philosophy on the Latin West," ch. 4.

117 On the development of Philoponus' views on prime matter, cf. esp. Sorabji, *Matter, Space, and Motion*, ch. 2; Wildberg, *John Philoponus' Criticism of Aristotle's Theory of Aether*, 204–221; de Haas, *John Philoponus' New Definition of Prime Matter*; for Simplicius' account, cf. Simplicius, *In Phys.*, 227.23–233.3; cf. also Sorabji, *Matter, Space, and Motion*, ch. 1; on the difference between Philoponus' and Simplicius' accounts, and for a correction of earlier interpretations according to which Philoponus and Simplicius adhered to the same (or even a similar) account, cf. Golitsis, *Les commentaires de Simplicius et de Jean Philopon à la* Physique *d'Aristote*, 127–139.

> simple volume, having its being in this itself, and a substrate for everything else. In fact, being three-dimensional does not even convey any notion of composition for us (συνθέσεώς ... ἔννοιαν) ... It has been shown that nothing else underlies the three-dimensional and that, rather, it is itself the foundation for all things. So, it is clear that it is most simple and the matter of all things, not having been composed from anything. If this is so, and if the three-dimensional is self-subsistent (αὐθυποστάτου), and if no change can be observed in it, then there is no argument (οὐδεὶς ... λόγος) that can establish that a kind of incorporeal matter underlies physical bodies, but physical things must be analysed down to whatever is the last level [possible], whether one prefers to call it "first substrate" or "matter," for we shall not squabble over names. (Philoponus, *De aeternitate mundi contra Proclum* XI.7, 428.1–25, tr. by Share, modified)[118]

As we can see, Philoponus does not mind speaking of matter as being endowed with form as long as this endowment is not taken to imply any sort of composition. The "substrate for everything else" has a three-dimensional form, but this does mean that it is composed, because this is just what that substrate is: three-dimensional extension.

What Philoponus says is governed by his conviction that "there is no argument that can establish that a kind of incorporeal matter underlies physical bodies." It is, therefore, unreasonable – and methodologically questionable – simply to assume the existence of something even below the three-dimensional. If corporeal things can only be analysed down until one has reached the three-dimensionally extended substratum, then this must be accepted as the most basic level of physical reality. Since it is also not scientific to quarrel about the mere names of things, it is irrelevant whether we should call this basic level "prime matter" or "first substrate." Thus, the three-dimensional substratum, which underlies all change, is the most fundamental level of corporeal reality that our scientific efforts are able to reach and must, therefore, be accepted as the underlying "substrate for everything else."[119]

This claim is central to what may be Philoponus' most important argument for establishing prime matter as an extended substance in section eight of *De aeternitate mundi contra Proclum* XI.[120] He argues that matter must be essentially three-dimensional, and, thus, actually be a body, because otherwise one could not account for the divisibility of wholes into parts.[121] If corporeal things are to be divisible, then there must be something that allows for that divisibility. This, however, cannot be due to the forms inhering in matter, because forms are by nature incorporeal and nothing incorporeal can be divided. Divisibility must consequently be due to the subject of these forms, which is the three-dimensionally extended underlying qualityless body.[122] This un-

---

118 cf. Philoponus' remarks in his discussion of place in the *Physics*, which seem to pre-shadow his later development (*In Phys.*, 520.18–24); cf. also Simplicius' interesting report in his *In Cael.*, 135.26–30 (= *De aeternitate mundi contra Aristotelem*, frgm. 72).

119 cf. Philoponus, *De aeternitate mundi contra Proclum*, XI.2–4.

120 cf. de Haas' analysis of the argument in *John Philoponus' New Definition of Prime Matter*, 115–120.

121 The question is raised explicitly at Philoponus, *De aeternitate mundi contra Proclum* XI.8, 436.16–24 and 437.7f., the main part of the discussion being at 439.2–443.6.

122 Philoponus, *De aeternitate mundi contra Proclum* XI.8, 440.6–18.

derlying corporeal subject is precisely what Philoponus wants to identify with prime matter. So, he needs to rule out the traditional view that this underling subject is itself a composition of an *incorporeal* prime matter which, due to a quantitative form, comes to be corporeal. In his discussion, Philoponus shows that matter itself must be actually corporeal, because it is impossible for it to change in such a way as to become corporeal out of being incorporeal.

The details of his involved argument do not concern us here.[123] What is important, though, is that Philoponus denies that matter must be incorporeal and that he argues for this conclusion on the basis of divisibility. Matter must be that which accounts for the possibility of dividing wholes into parts, and so must itself be corporeal.[124] The reason this is important is that Avicenna will demonstrate precisely on the basis of the divisibility of wholes into parts that more or less the exact opposite is true: there must be incorporeal prime matter as the substrate of corporeal form. Consequently, Avicenna does nothing other than to counter Philoponus' above-quoted claim that "there is no argument that can establish that a kind of incorporeal matter underlies physical bodies."[125]

It is a difficult question to what extent Avicenna is directly reacting to Philoponus in this regard. On the one hand, Philoponus' *De aeternitate mundi contra Proclum* was translated and known in Arabic.[126] In fact, the work is even mentioned in the epistolary exchange between Avicenna and Abū Rayḥān al-Bīrūnī (d. 440/1048).[127] There is no reason for why we should think Avicenna did not know that work or assume that he would not have read it. Having said this, even if we assume that Avicenna had access to, and knew, Proclus' arguments as well as Philoponus' rebuttal (which appears to be a justified assumption), he does not appear to refer directly to this discussion or attack any philosophical opponent in a direct way. Although Avicenna appears to have been proud of his argument – it is, after all, reproduced in almost all his major works virtually without alteration – one might be inclined to think that Avicenna would have savoured his victory over Philoponus more sardonically had he intended his argument to be a direct reply to him. In any case, it is certainly conspicuous and noteworthy that Avicenna, just like Philoponus before him, argues on the basis of the divisibility of wholes into parts, in order to establish precisely what Philoponus claimed to be non-existent and invalid, viz., an incorporeal prime matter underlying physical reality. As a result, the simplest answer might be that Avicenna is not directly arguing against any

---

123 The argument has conveniently be outlined by de Haas in *John Philoponus' New Definition of Prime Matter*, esp. 118–120. Despite de Haas' analysis, it is still difficult to identify the required premisses and to retrace all the necessary steps in Philoponus' text.

124 cf. de Haas, *John Philoponus' New Definition of Prime Matter*, 120.

125 Philoponus, *De aeternitate mundi contra Proclum* XI.7, 428.20–22, tr. by Share; cf. XI.3, 413.20f., 413.27–414.5.

126 q.v. above, 29, 31.

127 cf. Avicenna and al-Bīrūnī, *al-As'ila wa-l-ağwiba*, 52.1f.

unnamed opponent, but that he places his own proof for the existence of incorporeal prime matter within a broader tradition of argument that primarily builds on the notion of divisibility. This assumption is all the more reasonable, as Simplicius, too, rethought the traditional view of matter as incorporeal, in order to explain such features as extensionality and divisibility.[128] So, we find in the works of the two most important late ancient Greek commentators similar considerations leading them both to abandon the traditional view of matter and to settle for an account that, despite all differences, describes matter as extended or outright corporeal. Finally, we find a related debate in the Arabic tradition before Avicenna, as the recently edited dispute between Yaḥyā ibn ʿAdī, his younger brother Ibrāhīm ibn ʿAdī, and an unnamed opponent shows.[129]

That Philoponus and Simplicius took recourse to the notion of divisibility is hardly surprising, though. It is plausible to believe that among the primary reasons for why the notion of divisibility was at the heart of such discussions of matter surely was that division is the only affection which a qualityless body is able to suffer. In other words, division is an affection of body insofar as it is body. One might also say that division is one of the very few phenomena which affect corporeality as such – and if we intend to provide a satisfactory account of corporeality, we must be able to explain first and foremost this phenomenon. The late ancient tradition of argument diverged from Aristotle's original way of establishing matter in *Physics* I.7, which relied on the qualitative changes of a man becoming musical or some other concrete thing changing from black to white. All Aristotle established there was the existence of an underlying thing (τὸ ὑποκείμενον, *al-mawḍūʿ*) generally. The notion of matter was introduced only a little later, and Aristotle explicitly admitted that matter is reached only by way of analogy (κατ' ἀναλογίαν, *bi-l-naẓīr*).[130] It is, thus, preferable to regard Avicenna's argument for the existence of prime matter on the basis of the notion of divisibility and the corporeal form as a response to a late ancient (and early Arabic) tradition rather than an adaption of an argument that originally has been put forth by Aristotle.[131]

128 cf. Simplicius, *In Phys.*, 230.29–33, 514.4–515.6; cf. also de Haas, *John Philoponus' New Definition of Prime Matter*, 116. The Stoics, too, defended a similar position about matter, and Philoponus refers to their account implicitly in his commentary on the *Physics* (e.g., *In Phys.*, 520.18–24) and explicitly in his *De aeternitate mundi contra Proclum* XI.1, 410.1–3; XI.3, 413.24–414.5, in the latter passage even with approval (καλῶς). This is particularly interesting in light of Plotinus' strong criticism of Stoic doctrine; cf. *Enn.* II.4.8–12; VI.1.25–30; cf. also de Haas, *John Philoponus' New Definition of Prime Matter*, 100–114.
129 Ibn ʿAdī, *On Whether Body is a Substance or a Quantity*.
130 *Phys.* I.7, 191a8.
131 Thus, I do not think that "Avicenna adapts the traditional Aristotelian proof of prime matter from change, trading qualitative change for change in continuity" (Shihadeh, "Avicenna's Corporeal Form," 370). Besides, in "trading qualitative change for change in continuity" not much of Aristotle's original argument remains. Likewise, the mere fact that both arguments employ the same principle, viz., that contraries cannot act on each other, does not justify calling Avicenna's argument "just an adaptation," as Stone did ("Simplicius and Avicenna on the Essential Corporeity of Material Substance," 106).

So, what Avicenna provides in his works is an argument that turns on the notion of divisibility and establishes both above-mentioned *desiderata*: (i) a proof that matter exists as the primary underlying substrate and (ii) a demonstration that this matter is not corporeal or in any way able to explain corporeality by itself, i.e., without the need for a corporeal form, as Philoponus had eventually come to argue.

This is philosophically significant, because Avicenna is, indeed, able to provide an argument for the existence of prime matter. While Aristotle had to be content with merely pointing towards the existence of matter by way of analogy, and Plato famously by way of "bastard reasoning," Avicenna provides an actual proof for it. At the same time, this argument shows that matter is unable to account for both corporeality *and* divisibility. Whatever Philoponus has presented as matter, arguing that it cannot be shown to be composed of two separate factors and must, therefore, be accepted as the most basic level of corporeal reality, is demonstrated to be a composite of an incorporeal matter and an immaterial form. Moreover, Avicenna repeats his argument in most of his major works without substantial alteration, viz., in his *al-Ilāhiyyāt*, *al-Nağāt*, *ʿUyūn al-ḥikma*, *al-Hidāya*, and *al-Išārāt wa-l-tanbīhāt*.[132] The version contained in Avicenna's *al-Nağāt* runs as follows:

وأمّا الصورة الجسمية فلأنّها إمّا أن تكون نفس الاتّصال أو تكون طبيعة يلزمها الاتّصال حتّى لا تُوجَد هي إلّا والاتّصال لازم لها. فإن كانت نفس الاتّصال فقد يكون الجسم متّصلاً ثمّ ينفصل. فيكون هناك لا محالة شيء هو بالقوّة كلاهما. فليس ذات الاتّصال بما هو اتّصال قابل للانفصال لأنّ قابل الاتّصال لا يعدم عند الانفصال والاتّصال يعدم عند الانفصال. فإذاً شيء غير الاتّصال هو قابل للانفصال وهو بعينه قابل الاتّصال. فليس الاتّصال هو بالقوّة قابلاً للانفصال. ولا أيضاً طبيعة يلزمها الاتّصال لذاتها. فظاهر أنّ ههنا جوهر غير الصورة الجسمية هو الذي يعرض له الانفصال والاتّصال معاً وهو مقارن للصورة الجسمية وهو الذي يقبل الاتّحاد بصورة الجسمية فيصير جسماً واحداً بما يقوّمه أو يلزمه من الاتّصال الجسماني.

132 cf. *al-Ilāhiyyāt* II.2, §§18–19, 66.15–67.13; *al-Nağāt* IV.1.4, 500.9–501.4; *ʿUyūn al-ḥikma* III.2, 248.14–20; *al-Hidāya* III.1, 234.3–235.2; *al-Išārāt wa-l-tanbīhāt* II.1.6, 92.13–18. I was unable to find a corresponding passage in the *Dānešnāme-ye ʿAlāʾī* and *al-Ḥikma al-ʿArūḍiyya*, whereas the metaphysics of *al-Ḥikma al-mašriqiyya* is not known to be extant. Shihadeh calls the reasoning in Avicenna's *al-Ilāhiyyāt* "a little suspect" ("Avicenna's Corporeal Form," 372) and argues that the version found in *al-Nağāt* is "a developed version" of that in *al-Ilāhiyyāt* (374), whereas that in *al-Išārāt wa-l-tanbīhāt* "shifts" from an approach similar to that in *al-Ilāhiyyāt* to one more akin to that in *al-Nağāt* (375–378). I am not convinced that the argument in Avicenna's *al-Nağāt* is really "a developed version," compared to the argument in *al-Ilāhiyyāt*. Instead it seems to be merely less convoluted, i.e., more concise and to the point. Since I do not see a real difference between both versions, I also do not see how the argument in *al-Išārāt wa-l-tanbīhāt* could shift from one to the other. In fact, Shihadeh's meticulous analysis seems to be a bit over-determined. I also believe that much of the confusion that may make Avicenna's argument in *al-Ilāhiyyāt* appear "a little suspect" can be resolved by pointing to *al-Samāʿ al-ṭabīʿī* III.9, §3, 220.11–19, partially translated below, 152. Finally, the chances that the argument in *al-Nağāt* is, indeed, "a developed version," as Shihadeh claims, are slim in light of Gutas', admittedly somewhat rhetorical, remark that Avicenna's *al-Nağāt* is a "patchwork" of earlier materials and was "compiled … practically without composing a single line anew" (*Avicenna and the Aristotelian Tradition*, 116).

> [Without doubt], corporeal form [exists in a subject], because it is either[133] the continuity itself or a nature from which continuity follows, so that it does not exist unless continuity would follow from it. So, if it is the continuity itself (*nafs al-ittiṣāl*), then body may be continuous and, then, be divided. So, there is[134] without doubt a thing which is potentially both (*šay' huwa bi-l-quwwa kilāhumā*). So, continuity as such (*ḏāt al-ittiṣāl*), insofar as it is continuity, is not receptive (*qābil*) of division, because what is receptive of division does not vanish upon division, but continuity does vanish upon division. Therefore, a thing other than continuity is that which is receptive of division and this is the same [as that] which is receptive of continuity. So, continuity is not that which is potentially receptive of division nor would a nature from which continuity follows through itself [be receptive of division]. Thus, it is apparent that there is a substance other than the corporeal form (*ǧawhar ġayr al-ṣūra al-ǧismiyya*) which is that to which division and continuity happens alike, and it is conjoined to the corporeal form and that which receives unity through the form of corporeality. So, it becomes a single body through that which constitutes it or which follows from it in terms of corporeal continuity. (*al-Naǧāt* IV.1.4, 500.9–501.4)[135]

Avicenna begins with a description of the corporeal form as being either continuity itself or a nature which necessarily invests that in which it is with continuity.[136] The argument continues contrasting continuity (*al-ittiṣāl*) with division (*al-infiṣāl*). I decided to translate *infiṣāl* as "division" rather than "divisibility" or "discontinuity."[137] Both alternatives are viable translations of *infiṣāl* in various context but are misleading here for the following reasons. It would be erroneous to translate *infiṣāl* as "divisibility," because Avicenna would then wind up arguing that continuity cannot be receptive of divisibility, even though we have already seen that continuity precisely entails divisibility, for what is continuous can be divided. The translation of *infiṣāl* as "discontinuity" would have the seeming advantage that it would emphasise the contrary nature between *ittiṣāl* and *infiṣāl*. So, continuity and discontinuity would emerge as contraries in much the same way as black and white. A body could, then,

---

133 Reading *immā* with Fakhry, 'Umayra, and al-Kurdī for *ammā* in Dānešpažūh.

134 Reading *fa-yakūnu hunāka* with Fakhry, 'Umayra, and al-Kurdī for *fa-yakūnu* in Dānešpažūh.

135 The last clause ("So, it ... corporeal continuity") still puzzles me. It seems to refer back to the distinction at the beginning of the passage which described the corporeal form as being either "continuity itself or ... a nature from which continuity follows."

136 One should not read too much importance into this disjunction and question whether, and to what extent, Avicenna would in fact identify the corporeal form with continuity, as has been done by A. D. Stone, "Simplicius and Avicenna on the Essential Corporeity of Material Substance," 101–106. All Avicenna does here is to bring the corporeal form as much as possible into alignment with the notion of continuity. The corporeal form is the principle of continuity and there is nothing else apart from it, or in addition to it, that could make a body continuous. Of course, lines and surfaces are likewise continuous, although they do not consist of a corporeal form, which they would have to if the corporeal form were identical – in a strong sense – with continuity. So, there are reasons to hesitate, but the reasons are not relevant here in the context of establishing matter. The corporeal form is that which makes a body continuous, and so it is the principle of corporeal continuity; cf. also Avicenna's rather clear statement in *al-Samā' al-ṭabī'ī* III.9, §3, 220.17f., translated below.

137 This also means that the corresponding active participle *munfaṣil* has to be translated here as "divided," instead of "divisible" or "discontinuous."

be black and subsequently change to being white just as it can be continuous and change to being discontinuous through division.[138] This, however, is only seemingly an advantage. Upon closer investigation, it appears to be a rather misleading choice in the present context, because systematically, there is no contrary of "continuity." It is necessary for comprehending the argument fully, that no body ever was, is, or will be discontinuous. *Two* bodies can be discontinuous and the parts of one *aggregate* can be discontinuous, but there is not one single body which is discontinuous. Of course, if "division" is the preferred translation of *infiṣāl*, then one might object that likewise no single body ever was, is, or will be divided, at least when "to be divided" is taken to mean "to be in a state of division" rather than "to be receiving division." Yet, translating *infiṣāl* as "division" instead of "discontinuity" does not suggest that we are concerned with two contraries that can equally apply to one and the same object. If a body turns from black to white, the body as such remains in existence, whereas when a continuous body is divided, it ceases to be – with two new bodies coming into being. Thus, *ittiṣāl* and *infiṣāl* are precisely *not* two contraries in the same sense as black and white are, as they do not pertain to a common subject. Moreover, division is not an instance of qualitative change but one of substantial change, i.e., of coming-to-be and perishing.[139] Whereas continuity is due to a form, viz., the corporeal form, which we might also call the "form of continuity," as Avicenna does in *al-Ilāhiyyāt* II.2, division is precisely not due to a form, and there is no form which we could call "the form of division."[140] If anything at all, division is due to *two* forms, i.e., two distinct forms of continuity inhering in matter, resulting in two adjacent bodies, which in themselves, of course, are both essentially continuous, because each possesses the form of continuity. So, we might say that, loosely speaking, division is due to *two* corporeal forms, whereas continuity is due to one corporeal form.

In Avicenna's argument, the contrast between continuity and division is presented along the lines of the observed fact that a continuous body can and may be divided. Whatever is essentially continuous in itself, however, cannot be that which receives (*qābil*) division. If the corporeal form is the principle of corporeal continuity and is, in one way or another, "the continuity itself" (*nafs al-ittiṣāl*), then it cannot be that which receives the division, because it is destroyed through division and does not survive the process of division, so that one could say afterwards that, now, it has received the division. Instead, that which receives the division, and which is effectively divided, must be something apart from, or in addition to, the corporeal form which, as we have said, is continuity as such. This additional thing must be that which is equally apt to

138 This is how Shihadeh appears to conceive of the relation between *ittiṣāl* and *infiṣāl*. He consequently translates the terms as "continuity" and "discontinuity"; cf. "Avicenna's Corporeal Form," 368, 371.

139 This, in fact, is one further reason, why it is not correct to see Avicenna's argument as an adaptation of Aristotle's argument in *Physics* I.7, as the two arguments are systematically different, one being concerned with substantial change, the other with qualitative change.

140 On *al-Ilāhiyyāt* II.2 in this respect, cf. Lizzini, "The Relation between Form and Matter," 177.

receive continuity as well as division – it is what Avicenna calls "matter" (*hayūlā* or *mādda*), even though this appellation does not occur in the argument from *al-Naǧāt* itself.[141]

Thus, it seems as if matter is that which receives division, i.e., is that "to which division and continuity happens alike," as Avicenna wrote above. This, however, is only partly accurate, for there is a sense in which matter does, and another sense in which it does not, receive any division. It is systematically important to understand that for Avicenna, matter is not divisible.[142] All that matter is capable of is the reception of forms. So, if we want to make sense of a statement that matter is that which receives division or discontinuity, we need to translate that into a more precise terminology. One the one hand, then, it is clear that matter as such is neither divisible nor does it receive division, because matter as such is neither continuous nor extended. On the other hand, Avicenna claimed in the argument from *al-Naǧāt* that "what is receptive of division does not vanish upon division," so it would seem that body, likewise, cannot be that which is divisible, because division is, in fact, a form of substantial change through which one body ceases-to-be and two bodies come-to-be. Division happens when two forms occur where hitherto only one form was. Taken together, this seems to mean that it is *matter* which receives division (because it is matter which is stripped of its one form with two new forms of continuity coming to inhere in it), while it is *body* which is divisible (because only body is continuous and extended, even though

141 Among the terms most frequently used by Avicenna for referring to the concept of matter are *hayūlā* and *mādda*, the former being an Arabic loan word from the Greek ὕλη. Avicenna, however, does not usually draw a conceptual distinction between the two and employs them entirely interchangeably as synonyms. Alongside these, the term *ʿunṣur* is also sometimes employed for signifying matter, even though it may also refer to the elements, often being synonymous to the word *usṭuquss* ("element"), which is yet another loan word, this time from the Greek στοιχεῖον by way of the Syriac *esṭuḵsā*; for the Syriac lineage, cf. Daiber's remarks in Aetius Arabus, *Die Vorsokratiker in arabischer Überlieferung*, 18; Brock, "Greek Words in Syriac," 254; for *ʿunṣur* signifying prime matter, cf. Belo, *Chance and Determinism in Avicenna and Averroes*, 59, as well as the view reported in the name of Aristotle in Qusṭā ibn Lūqā al-Baʿlabakkī's Arabic version of Ps.-Plutarchus' *Placita Philosophorum* (Aetius Arabus, *Die Vorsokratiker in arabischer Überlieferung*, 5.7, 16.7) or that in the name of Plato in the *Muḫtaṣar waǧīz fī l-Usṭuqussāt ustuḫriǧu min kitāb Ǧālīnūs* 5, 70.3–8, a treatise attributed to Ḥunayn ibn Isḥāq which recently was edited and published by Langermann and Bos as "An Epitome of Galen's *On The Elements* Ascribed to Ḥunayn Ibn Isḥāq," together with the editors' comments in their introduction and synopsis. In *al-Samāʿ al-ṭabīʿī* I.2, Avicenna draws a distinction between *ʿunṣur* and *usṭuquss*, which probably stems from Galen, mediated through a Greek epitome of Galen's *De elementis ex Hippocratis sententia* in the Arabic translation of Ḥunayn ibn Isḥāq which was recently edited and translated by Walbridge; cf. *al-Samāʿ al-ṭabīʿī* I.2, §6, 15.1–5; Anonymous, *Ǧawāmiʿ Kitāb Ǧālīnūs fī l-ʿanāṣir ʿalā raʾy Ibuqrāṭ* 7, §28, 162.12–163.6. For an attempt to systematise Avicenna's terminology of matter in *al-Ilāhiyyāt*, cf. Bertolacci, "The Doctrine of Material and Formal Causality," 130; cf. also *al-Samāʿ al-ṭabīʿī* I.2, §6, 14.14–15.5; *al-Ḥikma al-mašriqiyya* 4.6–10; *Kitāb al-Ḥudūd*, §§30–35, 17.10–20.12.

142 This is, in fact, already clear in the light of the above analysis. If matter is by itself not extended, and if divisibility requires extension, matter is evidently indivisible. For a clear statement that matter lacks extension and magnitude, cf. *al-Išārāt wa-l-tanbīhāt* II.1.10, 94.10f.

no body survives the process of division). This is how division is to be understood in Avicenna.[143] Moreover, this is precisely what Avicenna describes in *al-Samāʿ al-ṭabīʿī* III.9:

> والأوّل لا يقبله المقدار لذاته البتّة لأن القابل يجب أن يبقى مع المقبول وذلك إذا عرض أبطل وجود المقدار الأوّل فإن المقدار الأوّل لم يكن إلّا ذلك الاتّصال المعيّن ليس شيئاً فيه ذلك الاتّصال المعيّن فانّ المقدار كما علمته مراراً هو نفس الاتّصال ليس الشيء المتّصل باتّصال فيه فإنّه إذا عرض الانفصال المفكّك أبطل المقدار الأوّل وأحدث مقدارين آخرين وحدث متّصلان محدودان آخران بالفعل بعد أن كانا بالقوّة.
>
> Now, the magnitude does not essentially receive the first [sc. discontinuity in the sense of "real division"] at all, because it is necessary that that which is receptive remains together with that which is received. When this [sc. real division] happens, the existence of the initial magnitude is eliminated, for the initial magnitude is nothing other than that determinate continuity and is not something in which that determinate continuity is, for magnitude, as you have learned repeatedly, is the continuity itself, not some continuous thing resulting from a continuity in it, for when the separating division happens, the initial magnitude is eliminated, and two different magnitudes are produced and two other delimited continuous things come to be actual after having been potential. (*al-Samāʿ al-ṭabīʿī* III.9, §3, 220.15–18, tr. by McGinnis, modified)

For Ayman Shihadeh, one of the reasons that Avicenna's reasoning in *al-Ilāhiyyāt* "seems a little suspect" is that the argument appears to establish matter as the subject of division, whereas it could be argued that the subject in question "can only be corporeal substance, rather than prime matter."[144] With this, Shihadeh points towards the interpretation, and in fact criticism, of Avicenna's first influential commentator Šaraf al-Dīn al-Masʿūdī (d. ~ 600/1204), who claimed in his critical remarks on Avicenna's *al-Išārāt wa-l-tanbīhāt* that the subject which, in Avicenna's argument, "serves as the recipient of accidental continuity and hence undergoes accidental change is not prime matter, but in fact body itself."[145] Avicenna's argument, however, appears to be less suspect, once we realise that al-Masʿūdī's intuition is correct insofar as it is, indeed, nothing other than the *body* which receives division, while it is nothing other than *matter* which receives two separate forms in the course of the division.[146]

---

143 One might also say that matter is only divisible *through* a corporeal form, i.e., insofar as it has become a body; cf. *al-Naǧāt* IV.1.3, 497.15–498.4; cf. also Shihadeh, "Avicenna's Corporeal Form," 371.

144 Shihadeh, "Avicenna's Corporeal Form," 372.

145 Shihadeh, "Avicenna's Corporeal Form," 379; cf. now also Shihadeh's remarks in his edition of al-Masʿūdī, *al-Mabāḥiṯ wa-l-sukūk ʿalā Kitāb al-Išārāt*.

146 On behalf of al-Masʿūdī, Shihadeh presents a further worry; cf. "Avicenna's Corporeal Form," 379. According to al-Masʿūdī, division is an accidental change in the category of quantity. Thus, for him, Avicenna's argument concerns an accidental change, even though an accidental change cannot establish the existence of matter. What Avicenna would need, if he wanted to demonstrate the existence of an incorporeal matter, is an argument that hinges on substantial change. This worry, however, can be dispelled by realising that for Avicenna, division is precisely *not* a change in the category of quantity as, for example, growth is. Instead, he would say that it is, indeed, a case of substantial

Above, I said that Avicenna had to show two things: (i) that there is any matter at all and (ii) that corporeality cannot be due to matter itself. The first point has just been demonstrated. Matter exists – indeed has to exist – if we want to make sense of, and understand, the phenomenon of the division of bodies. The second point is demonstrated almost by the same argument. Why is it that matter could not itself explain corporeality? It is the same reason: if matter itself were corporeal, matter would be continuity itself and, thus, necessarily unreceptive of division. So, if matter were corporeal, it could not be divided – in fact, *nothing* that in one way or another consists of matter could be divided. According to Avicenna, then, the argument of Philoponus, who argued that in order to comprehend division, we must conceive of matter as essentially corporeal, is unsuccessful, because Philoponus' matter – according to Avicenna's analysis – would be essentially indivisible, for it would have to be continuity itself, as it was argued to be corporeal and extended itself.

To be precise, Philoponus argued that our ability to investigate corporeal reality is limited, such that the utmost of what we can achieve is the demonstration that some corporeal subject underlies all change. What we cannot do is to show that this subject is itself a composite consisting of, for example, an incorporeal matter and an immaterial form. As long as we cannot provide sufficient proof that this subject is itself a composite, we have to accept it as a simple reality and must not quarrel about names, for irrespective of whether we call this subject "prime matter," "envolumed matter," or "absolute body," it is matter in the sense of the underlying subject of all change. Yet, Philoponus advanced the even stronger claim that this envolumed matter is not even a composite. It is no surprise, then, that he was doubtful whether there could be a demonstration that this subject is composed of two more basic principles – and this is exactly where Avicenna's argument steps in, showing that a simple subject cannot account for the phenomenon which it was intended to explain, viz., division.

Now, the subject-matter of physics, according to Avicenna, is the natural body. This body can be analysed in two primary perspectives: insofar as it is a body and insofar as it is subject to change. The former analysis reveals that the natural body insofar as it is body, i.e., insofar as it is a corporeal reality, is constituted by two fundamental principles. The first is the underlying matter which is in itself unextended and in no way already qualified other than by its being receptive of form. The second is the form which, at the most fundamental level of formal determination, is called "corporeal form," being tantamount to corporeal continuity as such. The combination of matter and corporeal form gives rise to what Avicenna sometimes calls an "absolute body,"

change. Consequently, "the continuity that passes away at the occurrence of discontinuity" is precisely not "an accident in the category of continuous quantity," as al-Masʿūdī writes, but the substantial continuity realised by the corporeal form inherent in the underlying matter. This being said, it is clear that the relation between the continuity of the absolute body, as presented in these passages, and the continuity that is a differentia of magnitudes of concrete objects, as it is mentioned in *al-Ilāhiyyāt* III.4 or *al-Maqūlāt* III.4, for example, deserves more attention; q.v. also the remarks in fn. 85 above, 133f.

being an hypothetical instance of the basic idea of body: it is the notion which all bodies share and with regard to which no body surpasses another. Thus, all bodies are equal in that they are corporeal – and this means that they are continuous, which means that they are extended, which means that they are divisible. By contrast, all bodies are not necessarily equal in their size, dimensions, colours, smells, relations, positions, and so on. Yet, all of them are such that one can identify and demarcate in them three – but not more than three – perpendicular dimensions. This is Avicenna's understanding of corporeality, and the corporeal form is its source and principle. Thus, matter and corporeal form emerge as the two principles of the subject-matter of physics when it is taken in its most fundamental sense, as they account for the sensible body plainly in its being a body:

فيكون الجسم جوهراً مركّباً من شيء عنه له القوّة ومن شيء عنه له الفعل. فالذي له به الفعل هو صورته والذي عنه بالقوّة هو مادّته، وهو الهيولى.

> Body, then, is a substance composed of something from which it has potentiality and something from which it has actuality. That through which it has actuality is its form (*ṣūratuhū*), and that from which it is potential is its matter (*māddatuhū*) – and this is *hayūlā*. (*al-Ilāhiyyāt* II.2, §19, 67.12f., tr. by Marmura, modified)

Having established matter and form as the two principles in which all natural bodies share, Avicenna will now investigate what it means to say that "all" natural bodies "share in" them, thus commencing a complex discussion on the commonality of matter and form that will further elucidate several important aspects about his conception of these two fundamental principles of corporeal reality.

3.2 Matter and Form as Common Principles

Avicenna describes matter and form as the principles (*mabādi'*, sg. *mabda'*) of natural things insofar as these things are corporeal. This is the broadest possible perspective on the natural world Avicenna could have adopted, because with this, he envisages what *constitutes* natural reality in the first place, before he proceeds to an account of what is *concomitant* to it by turning to the phenomenon of change and motion. It is in this vein that Avicenna concludes the outline of the principles of body insofar as it is a body in *al-Samāʿ al-ṭabīʿī* I.2:

فهذه هي المبادئ الداخلة في قوام الجسم.

> So, these [sc. matter and form] are the principles internal to the constitution of the body (*al-dāḫila fī qiwām al-ğism*). (*al-Samāʿ al-ṭabīʿī* I.2, §6, 15.6)[147]

147 cf. *al-Ilāhiyyāt* VI.1, §3, 258.1–5; *'Uyūn al-ḥikma* II.2, 17.16–18.

As principles of the natural body insofar as it is a body, matter and form are common to all natural bodies; and it is this commonality of principles that is one of Avicenna's main concerns in the first chapters of his *al-Samāʿ al-ṭabīʿī*. The question in what sense precisely matter and form are principles for natural bodies is a methodological question that will help Avicenna to define the scope of an investigation fitting for the science of physics and, in particular, to mark the boundaries between physics and metaphysics. So, he devotes an entire chapter, *al-Samāʿ al-ṭabīʿī* I.3, to the question "how the principles are common" (*fī kayfiyya kawn al-mabādiʾ muštaraka*).

It is beyond debate that principles are common in some sense. If principles are explanatory factors of a certain range of objects, then these principles are common to these objects, i.e., shared by them.[148] Thus, they equally apply to all objects within that range. In other words, if principles are premisses from which a science is demonstrated, then all – or at least: many – subjects of investigation within that science share a certain feature. More properly said, this feature is a premiss employed in the demonstrations within that discipline and, thus, a principle of the science which is concerned with those things that share this feature. Moreover, it is conventional to say that matter and form are principles of natural things, and that natural things share in the reality of the four causes. All this is even more evident when we are talking about "physics" in the Aristotelian sense of being the first of the natural sciences. I have already discussed in the preceding second chapter how Aristotle's *Physics* has been understood, especially by Philoponus, as a science concerned with that which is common to all natural things. I also showed that the Arabic philosophers before Avicenna, in particular al-Kindī and Abū Naṣr al-Fārābī (d. 339/950-51), often described the science of physics as being concerned with "the things that are common to all natural things" (*al-umūr al-ʿāmma li-ǧamīʿ al-ṭabāʾiʿ*) and that even Avicenna himself adopted this locution.[149]

Yet, for Avicenna, there is more to this. Although it is true that physics is concerned with what is common to all natural things, it is necessary, if we want to determine what it is that is common to all natural things, to know what "common" means – especially if "common" has two separate meanings, of which only one is relevant for the science of physics. In this regard, Avicenna clearly goes beyond his predecessors, as he seeks to determine more exactly from which point of view the principles of natural things belong to the realm of physics, i.e., ought to be investigated or taught in the science of physics, and in which way they pertain to the subject-matter of that science. In effect, he wants to specify what principles precisely we are currently talking about by distinguishing between two senses of "common": a "numerical commonality" and a "generic commonality," as I shall henceforth refer to them.

148 q.v. also above, 97ff.
149 q.v. above, 61, 67.

When Avicenna explicitly addresses the question "how the principles are common" in *al-Samāʿ al-ṭabīʿī* I.3, he actually returns to a distinction he had already introduced in the preceding chapter. There, in *al-Samāʿ al-ṭabīʿī* I.2, we read the following:

> والمشترك فيه هاهنا يعقل على نحوين. أحدهما أن يكون الفاعل مشتركاً فيه على أنّه يفعل الفعل الأوّل الذي يترتّب عليه سائر الأفاعيل كالذي يفيد المادّة الأولى الصورة الجسمية الأولى ... وتكون الغاية مشتركاً فيها بأنّها الغاية التي يؤمها جميع الأمور الطبيعية ... والنحو الآخر أن يكون المشترك فيه بنحو العموم كالفاعل الكلّي المقول على كلّ واحدة من الفاعلات الجزئية للأمور الجزئية والغاية الكلّية المقولة على كلّ واحدة من الغايات الجزئية للأمور الجزئية.
>
> The common (*al-muštarak fīhi*) here [i.e., in our discussion] is understood in two ways (*ʿalā naḥwayn*). One of them is that the agent (*al-fāʿil*) is common (*muštarakan fīhi*) in that it produces the first actuality from which all other actualities, like that which provides the first matter with the first corporeal form, follow ... and the end (*al-ġāya*) is common by that it is the end to which all natural things tend ... The other way that it is common is by way of generality (*bi-naḥw al-ʿumūm*), like the universal [predicate] "agent" is said of each one of the particular agents of particular things and the universal [predicate] *end* is said of each one of the particular ends of particular things. (*al-Samāʿ al-ṭabīʿī* I.2, §8, 15.11–17, tr. by McGinnis, modified)

Thereupon, Avicenna explains the two meanings further as follows:

> والفرق بين الأمرين أنّ المشترك بحسب المعنى الأوّل يكون في الوجود ذاتاً واحدةً بالعدد يشير العقل إليها بأنّها هي من غير أن يجوز فيها قولاً على كثيرين والمشترك بحسب المعنى الثاني لا يكون في الوجود ذاتاً واحدةً بل أمراً معقولاً يتناول ذواتاً كثيرةً تشترك عند العقل في أنّها فاعلة أو غاية فيكون هذا المشترك مقولاً على كثيرين.
>
> The difference between the two is that what is common (*al-muštarak*) in the first sense is in existence an entity that is one in number (*ḏātan wāḥidatan bi-l-ʿadad*), for which the intellect indicates that it is not such that it is possible for it to be said of many, whereas what is common (*al-muštarak*) in the second sense is not in existence a single entity but something intelligible (*amran maʿqūlan*) which applies to many entities (*yatanāwalu ḏawātan kaṯīran*) which share within the intellect in that they are agents or ends, and so what is common is predicated of many (*maqūlan ʿalā kaṯīrīn*). (*al-Samāʿ al-ṭabīʿī* I.2, §9, 16.1–4, tr. by McGinnis, modified)[150]

Avicenna's intention in distinguishing two senses of "common" may become clearer once we have considered his own examples. He mentions two principles of natural things to which the distinction applies, viz., agent and end. For Avicenna, saying that "agent" is a common principle for natural things has two meanings. On the one hand, it is a reference to God being *the Agent* which all natural things have in common. On the other hand, it is a reference to the fact that natural things are agents in themselves and produce a variety of effects, such that "agent" is also a common predicate attributed to many natural things. In like manner, saying that "end" is a common principle of natural things can be taken as referring to *the End* or as being merely a predicate describing the thing itself as an "end."

150 cf. *al-Ḥikma al-mašriqiyya* III.4, 8.17–9.1.

The question Avicenna is raising, then, is concerned with the way in which the principles are common to those natural things of which they are principles – and this means to ask whether *the Agent* and *the End* exist at all, so that it is meaningful to speak of *the Agent* and *the End* as principles of natural things, or whether "agent" and "end" are nothing but predicable characterisations of things. Moreover, this question is raised in the context of discussing matter and form, so that the more immediately relevant question for Avicenna will be whether matter and form are principles of natural things as *the Matter* and *the Form* or only as "matter" and "form."

In the case of the agent, Avicenna's position is clear. *The Agent*, i.e., "agent" in the first – the numerical – sense of "common," does exist: it is God, the ultimate and numerically one Agent which produces "the first actuality from which all other actualities ... follow," as we just read. In this sense, *the Agent* is more than a mere principle of motion, i.e., it is more than all the other things that can be described as "agents." This distinction resonates with a remark in the sixth book of Avicenna's *al-Ilāhiyyāt*:

الفلاسفة الإلهيين ليسوا يعنون بالفاعل مبدأ التحريك فقط كما يعنيه الطبيعيون بل مبدأ الوجود ومفيده مثل البارئ للعالم. وأمّا العلّة الفاعلية الطبيعية فلا تفيد وجوداً غير التحريك بأحد أنحاء التحريكات فيكون مفيد الوجود في الطبيعيات مبدأ حركة.

The metaphysical philosophers do not mean by "agent" just the principle of bringing about motion, as the natural philosophers do, rather [they mean] the principle and provider of existence, like the Creator for the world (*al-bāri' li-l-'ālam*). The natural efficient cause, however, does not provide existence other than the producing of motion in one of the ways of producing motion. So, the provider of existence in natural philosophy is a principle of motion. (*al-Ilāhiyyāt* VI.1, §2, 257.133–16)[151]

Thus, the agent of metaphysics is the agent *par excellence*; it is the Giver of Existence, and the ultimate and numerically one principle of the world, viz., God, the Creator. The agents within the natural world, however, bestow existence only insofar as they produce the existence of a motion and, thereby, initiate the coming-to-be of their effects.[152] The same idea is found in *al-Samā' al-ṭabīʿī* when Avicenna states that *the Agent*, who is numerically common in the first sense, is "not natural" (*fa-lā yakūnu ṭabīʿiyyan*), i.e., is outside the scope of natural teaching and inquiry. It belongs to metaphysics to study *the Agent* as a principle of natural things, as Avicenna implicitly emphasises later.[153]

---

151 This remark is to be understood in the greater context of the subsequent discussion in *al-Ilāhiyyāt* VI.1, §§11–17, 261.5–263.18, in which Avicenna argues for *the Agent* as a sustaining cause of existence.

152 Incidentally, this appears to be a deeply Platonic idea, as it emulates Plato's well-known distinction between being and becoming, between what truly is and what merely comes-to-be, between the unchanging Forms and their changing representations – in brief: between existence and motion.

153 *al-Samā' al-ṭabīʿī* I.2, §10, 16.5f.; cf. *al-Samā' al-ṭabīʿī* I.10, §3, 49.1–5; *al-Ḥikma al-mašriqiyya* III.4, 8.13–16.

In like manner can we ask whether there is something like *the End* or whether natural things things just have various goals and ends or themselves are those ends for other things. Once again, it is plain that for Avicenna, *the End*, being numerically common in the first of the two senses, is a principle of natural things. It is, again, God, the Necessary Existent, who is that whom all beings strive to imitate and to return to. Like the investigation of *the Agent*, the inquiry into *the End* is properly carried out in metaphysics and is decidedly not the subject of any exposition in physics.[154]

Nonetheless, the terms "agent" and "end" also have a more relevant bearing on natural things in the second sense of *muštarak*, insofar as the predicates "agent" and "end" generally apply to natural things. The two terms "agent" and "end" describe how natural things can interact with one another so as to be causally responsible for a change or be the final ends of a change, respectively. On the whole, agent and end are not merely two principles of natural things in addition to matter and form; they are principles which are common in *both* ways distinguished by Avicenna, so that the terms "agent" and "end" signify not only a single, numerically one entity, viz., God being *the Agent* and *the End*, but also two general and distinctive functions of natural compounds. This latter function is explained by Avicenna in the following words:

وللجسم مبادئ أيضاً فاعلة وغائية. والفاعلة هي التي طبعت الصورة التي للأجسام في مادّتها فقُوِّمت المادّة بالصورة وقُوِّمت منهما المركّب ... والغائية هي التي لأجلها ما طبعت هذه الصور في المواد.

> The body has as principles also agent (*fā'ila*) and end (*ġā'iyya*). The agent is that which impresses the form that belongs to bodies into their matter, and so the matter is rendered subsistent (*quwwimat*) by the form and from them the composite is constituted (*quwwimat*), ... and the end is that for the sake of which these forms are impressed into the matters. (*al-Samā' al-ṭabī'ī* I.2, §7, 15.6–9)[155]

Yet, since agent and end are not constitutive of natural things as matter and form are, they are both "non-proximate" (*ġayr qarībayn*) principles, as Avicenna calls them.[156] Thus, the subject-matter of physics as such has two essential or proximate principles, viz., matter and form, as well as two further or non-proximate principles, viz., agent and end. Since the science of nature is concerned with explaining, and ultimately also understanding, natural bodies, the four principles that belong to them are explanatory of them and, thus, relevant for the science concerned with them.[157] The interplay of the four principles, i.e., the fact that natural bodies can be said to be or have matter, form, agent, and end, explains not only why these bodies are as they are but also what else they are capable of becoming or bringing about within the natural world. These

---

154 In addition to *al-Mabda' wa-l-ma'ād*, Avicenna's *al-Ilāhiyyāt* X.1 provides a concise statement on "the beginning and the return" (*fī l-mabda' wa-l-ma'ād bi-qawl muǧmal*), as the chapter heading has it.

155 cf. *al-Samā' al-ṭabī'ī* I.10, §3, 49.1–5; I.10, §10, 52.14–16; I.11, §3, 53.13–16; *al-Ḥikma al-mašriqiyya* III.4, 8.9f.; III.5, 12.8; cf. also, generally, the discussion in *al-Ilāhiyyāt* VI.

156 *al-Samā' al-ṭabī'ī* I.11, §3, 53.13.

157 cf. also *al-Samā' al-ṭabī'ī* I.9.

four principles are the four causes that pertain to natural things, so that everyone who comprehends their fourfold principal nature fully grasps their existence and acquires knowledge (*al-ʿilm*) of them, thus attaining the science (*al-ʿilm*) concerned with them.

That the science of physics focuses on the principles of natural things, i.e., that it focuses on these insofar as they are matter, form, agent, and end, reflects a prominent interpretation of the first line of Aristotle's *Physics*:

> Ἐπειδὴ τὸ εἰδέναι καὶ τὸ ἐπίστασθαι συμβαίνει περὶ πάσας τὰς μεθόδους, ὧν εἰσὶν ἀρχαὶ ἢ αἴτια ἢ στοιχεῖα, ἐκ τοῦ ταῦτα γνωρίζειν ... δῆλον ὅτι καὶ τῆς περὶ φύσεως ἐπιστήμης πειρατέον διορίσασθαι πρῶτον τὰ περὶ τὰς ἀρχάς.
>
> لما كانت حال العلم واليقين في جميع السبل التي لها مبادئ أو أسباب أو أسطقسّات إنّما يلزم من قبل المعرفة لهذه ... فمن بيّن أنّ في العلم بأمر الطبيعة أيضاً قد ينبغي أن نلتمس أوّلاً فيه تلخيص أمور مبادئها.
>
> Since knowledge and understanding is attained in any investigation in which there are principles, causes, and elements (ἀρχαὶ ἢ αἴτια ἢ στοιχεῖα, *mabādiʾ aw asbāb aw usṭuqussāt*) from an acquaintance with these ... it is clear that in the science of nature, too, we must first attempt to determine what relates to the principles. (*Phys.* I.1, 184a10–16)

There are further passages, in particular in his *Metaphysics*, in which Aristotle refers to principles, causes, and elements as that which ought to be investigated in science. In *Metaphysics* H.1, for example, he states that his current investigation is concerned with the principles, causes, and elements of substance, and he refers to his earlier statement in E.1 that every theoretical science is more or less concerned with these three things.[158] As to the question of whether he intends to equate these three terms with one another, using one as a synonym for the respective others, a remark in *Metaphysics* Λ.4 is particularly informative. Since the first half of *Metaphysics* Λ is concerned with sensible substance, i.e., with its principles and what it consists of, and since Aristotle intends to shift his attention in the remaining chapters of book Λ to non-sensible substances and especially to the First Principle, which he considers to be a mover of some sort, Aristotle introduces a distinction between a principle (ἀρχή, *al-mabdaʾ*), on the one hand, and an element (στοιχεῖον, *al-usṭuquss*), on the other. He equates elements with "internal causes" (τὰ ἐνυπάρχοντα αἴτια, *al-asbāb hiya al-mawǧūda ... fī llatī takūnu*) but remarks that the mover (τὸ κινοῦν, *al-muḥarrik*) is something "external" (ἐκτός, *min ḫāriǧ*), so that it cannot belong to the internal causes. Thus, it is clear, he writes, that "principle" and "element" are different, even though both are causes (δῆλον ὅτι ἕτερον ἀρχὴ καὶ στοιχεῖον, αἴτια δ' ἄμφω, *fa-ẓāhir anna l-mabdaʾ wa-l-usṭuquss humā ġayrān wa-humā kilāhumā muḫtalifān*).[159] The difference is precisely in the fact that although elements are principles, they must be internal, whereas not all principles

158 cf. *Met.* E.1, 1025b3–7; H.1, 1042a5f.; cf. also *Met.* α.1, 982a1–3; Λ.1, 1069a18f., 25f.

159 *Met.* Λ.4, 1070b22–26. The Arabic version in the textus of Averroes' commentary is defective, providing *muḫtalifān* for αἴτια. The *altera versio in margine*, supplied by Bouyges in the apparatus, faithfully gives *fa-bayyin anna l-awwal wa-l-usṭuquss āḫar wa-āḫar wa-kilāhumā ʿilal*.

have to be internal. On that basis we may assume that at the beginning of his *Physics*, Aristotle does not intend the three terms "principles," "causes," and "elements" to be mere synonyms either but that, at least, the term "elements" is meant to denote a more restricted number of principles, viz., those that are internal to the subjects of investigation. Thus, there is reason to believe that matter and form are properly called "elements," because they are the internal constituents of sensible substances, whereas other principles, and especially moving principles, have to be considered as "external."[160]

Alexander of Aphrodisias (fl. ~ 200), in his commentary on the discussion of principles in *Metaphysics* Δ.1, makes Aristotle's distinction more explicit by elaborating upon the terms ἐνυπάρχοντος ("immanent" or "internal") and μὴ ἐνυπάρχοντος or ἐκτός ("external"), which we have just seen Aristotle using in distinguishing the material and the efficient principle.[161] In some ways, this distinction concurs with the Platonic contrast between true causes and auxiliary causes, which we can find in the *Phaedo*, the *Timaeus*, and the *Politicus*.[162] It is, thus, by no means surprising that for the late-ancient Platonists, this very distinction was an established aspect of Aristotle's (and Plato's) causal theory, and even a good example for the apparent agreement between Aristotle's and Plato's theories.[163] In his comments on the opening lines of the *Physics*, Philoponus makes use of that distinction, in order to explain the "principles, causes, and elements" of which Aristotle spoke, and provides the following elaborative interpretation:

> ἔστι δὲ τὸ μὲν τῆς ἀρχῆς ὄνομα καθολικώτερον (φέρεται γὰρ καὶ ἐπὶ τοῦ εἴδους καὶ ἐπὶ τῆς ὕλης καὶ ἐπὶ τοῦ ποιητικοῦ καὶ τελικοῦ καὶ τῶν λοιπῶν), τὸ δὲ αἴτιον καὶ τὸ στοιχεῖον μερικώτερά ἐστι, τὸ μὲν αἴτιον ἐπὶ τῶν κεχωρισμένων τοῦ ἀποτελέσματος ἀρχῶν τῆς τε ποιητικῆς καὶ τῆς τελικῆς καὶ ἐπὶ τῆς παραδειγματικῆς τε καὶ ὀργανικῆς, τὸ δὲ στοιχεῖον ἐπὶ τῶν συγκατατεταγμένων φέρεται ἀρχῶν, τοῦ εἴδους λέγω καὶ τῆς ὕλης, ἃ καὶ μέρος τοῦ ἀποτελέσματος γίνεται.
>
> The term "principle" (τὸ ... τῆς ἀρχῆς ὄνομα) is more general (καθολικώτερον), for it is applied to form and to matter and to the efficient and final causes and the rest. "Cause" (τὸ ... αἴτιον) and "element" (τὸ στοιχεῖον), however, are more particular (μερικώτερά). "Cause" is applied to the principles which are separate (τῶν κεχωρισμένων ... ἀρχῶν) from the product, the efficient

160 cf. also Aristotle's use of ἐνυπάρχοντος in *Physics* II.3, 194b23 as well as *Metaphysics* Δ.1, 1013a4–10; 2, 1013a24–26, and its contrast to ἐκτός in *Metaphysics* Δ.1, 1013a19f.; cf. further Bertolacci, "The Doctrine of Material and Formal Causality," 147f.; Wisnovsky, "Towards a History of Avicenna's Distinction between Immanent and Transcendent Causes," 61.

161 cf. Alexander of Aphrodisias, *In Met.*, 347.7–9, 348.9–24.

162 cf. *Phd.* 99a4–b6; *Tim.* 46c7–e6; *Plt.* 281d11–e10.

163 This can be witnessed in Proclus, *Institutio theologica*, prop. 75. Wisnovsky further refers to Plutarchus of Athens, Syrianus, Ammonius, and Asclepius of Tralles for similar interpretations ("Towards a History of Avicenna's Distinction between Immanent and Transcendent Causes," 49). Interesting is also Wisnovsky's reference to the Latin extract of al-Fārābī's lost commentary on the Aristotle's *Physics*, in which we find the following classification: *materia et forma (que due sunt intra rem) et agens at finis (que due sunt extra rem)* (*Distinctio super Librum Aristotelis de naturali auditu*, 475.7–8).

principle and the final principle as well as to the paradigmatic and the instrumental, whereas "element" is applied to immanent principles (τῶν συγκατατεταγμένων ... ἀρχῶν), I mean form and matter, which become part of the product. (Philoponus, *In Phys.*, 7.32–8.5, tr. by Osborne, modified)[164]

As is clear from his statement, Philoponus regards ἀρχή ("principle") as the "more general" genus term encompassing both αἴτια and στοιχεῖα. Whereas αἴτιον ("cause") comprises the external efficient and final causes, στοιχεῖον ("element") represents the internal material and formal causes.[165]

The distinction was also known to Avicenna.[166] In *al-Ilāhiyyāt* VI.1, for example, Avicenna divides the four causes that pertain to bodies into those which are "internal to its constitution and part of its existence" (*dāḫilan fī qiwāmihī wa-ǧuzʾan min wuǧūdihī*) and those which are not.[167] Here, Avicenna's expression *dāḫilan fī qiwām* seems to correspond to Aristotle's ἐνυπάρχοντος. Similarly, he describes the efficient and the final cause in his *al-Naǧāt* as the "two essential external principles" of natural things (*sababān ḫāriǧān ... bi-ḏāt*).[168] This is also how he distinguishes between the four causes later in the metaphysics of *al-Naǧāt*, where he divides the principles into those that are "like a part" of the thing (*kāna ka-l-ǧuzʾ*) and those that are "not like a part" (*lam yakun ka-l-ǧuzʾ*).[169]

---

164 cf. Philoponus, *In Phys.*, 5.16–6.17, 241.3–27; cf. also Simplicius, *In Phys.*, 3.16–18, 10.25–11.15, 259.3–9, 316.21–28.

165 The Neoplatonic (or Middle Platonic) paradigmatic and instrumental causes, which Philoponus mentioned, are not relevant to our present concern. According to Wisnovsky, they are absent from Avicenna's *al-Šifāʾ* as well as his *ʿUyūn al-ḥikma*, *Dānešnāme-ye ʿAlāʾī*, *al-Naǧāt*, and *al-Išārāt wa-l-tanbīhāt*, and occur only in his early works *al-Ḥikma al-ʿArūḍiyya* and *al-Hidāya*; cf. "Towards a History of Avicenna's Distinction between Immanent and Transcendent Causes," 66. However, already in *al-Ḥikma al-ʿArūḍiyya* (and also in *al-Naǧāt*), we even find Avicenna distancing himself from those who upheld these causes: "Some count the instruments (*al-ālāt*) among the causes, and the paradigms (*al-muṯul*), too, but these two are not in the natural things the way some claim" (*al-Ḥikma al-ʿArūḍiyya* II.1, 116.23f. ≈ *al-Naǧāt* II.1.1, 197.7f.). Interesting in this regard is also Avicenna's remark in *al-Ilāhiyyāt* VI.1, §3, 258.1, that "there is no cause beyond" the four already mentioned Aristotelian causes. For a first approach to the paradigmatic and instrumental causes, cf. Sorabji, *The Philosophy of the Commentators*, vol. II, ch. 6d; cf. also Karamanolis, "Porphyry, the First Platonist Commentator of Aristotle," 111f.; for the Arabic reception of the distinction between Plato's six and Aristotle's four causes, cf. Kraemer's remarks on Abū Sulaymān al-Siǧistānī in *Philosophy in the Renaissance of Islam*, 91–93; cf. also Ibn ʿAdī's account as translated in Périer, *Yaḥyā ben ʿAdī*, 101f.

166 cf. Jolivet, "La répartition des causes chez Aristote et Avicenne" and, correcting some of Jolivet's central claims, Wisnovsky, "Towards a History of Avicenna's Distinction between Immanent and Transcendent Causes."

167 *al-Ilāhiyyāt* VI.1, §3, 258.2; cf. *al-Samāʿ al-ṭabīʿī* I.2, §6, 15.6; *ʿUyūn al-ḥikma* II.2, 17.16–18.

168 *al-Naǧāt* II.1.1, 197.5f. ≈ *al-Ḥikma al-ʿArūḍiyya* II.2, 116.22; cf. also *Dānešnāme-ye ʿAlāʾī* II.15, 54.5, where Avicenna calls the efficient and the final cause *bīrūn* ("external").

169 *al-Naǧāt* IV.1.11, 518.8–519.11.

In *al-Samāʿ al-ṭabīʿī*, now, we find a passage which aptly captures Aristotle's idea from the first lines of *Physics* I.1, viz., that scientific knowledge of things can only be derived by acquiring knowledge of their "principles, causes, and elements," and which, at the same time, mirrors Philoponus' reading of that idea as expressed in the above quote from his commentary. There, in the first chapter of the first book of *al-Samāʿ al-ṭabīʿī*, we read the following:

فإن كان للأمور الطبيعية مبادئ وأسباب وعلل لم يتحقّق العلم الطبيعي إلّا منها فقد شُرِح في تعليم البرهان أنّه لا سبيل إلى تحقّق معرفة الأمور ذوات المبادئ إلّا بعد الوقوف على مبادئها والوقوف من مبادئها عليها فإنّ هذا النحو من التعليم والتعلّم هو الذي نتوصّل منه إلى تحقّق المعرفة بالأمور ذوات المبادئ.

> If, then, natural things have *mabādiʾ wa-asbāb wa-ʿilal*, natural knowledge cannot be ascertained other than through them. So, it has been explained in the teaching about demonstration that there is no way of ascertaining the knowledge of those things which have principles (*al-umūr ḏawāt al-mabādiʾ*) except after understanding their principles and understanding them from their principles, for this way from teaching and learning (*al-taʿlīm wa-l-taʿallum*)[170] is the one through which we arrive at the ascertainment of knowledge of things which have principles. (*al-Samāʿ al-ṭabīʿī* I.1, §1, 7.13–15)

At first, Avicenna's phrase *mabādiʾ wa-asbāb wa-ʿilal* might seem to be rather odd, because *sabab* (pl. *asbāb*) and *ʿilla* (pl. *ʿilal*) are two rather synonymous terms for "cause" – not only in Avicenna's writings but throughout the Graeco-Arabic translations and the ensuing philosophical tradition.[171] Yet, this impression vanishes immediately once they are considered and understood in the context of the distinction between internal and external causes, both of which can be called "principles," so that one of the two terms for "cause" may be more apt to express the idea of an internal cause, such as matter and form, while the other may apply more properly to external causes, such as agent and end. On the whole, we can notice an overall tendency in Avicenna to employ *ʿilla* preferably for the internal causes (such as matter and form), and *sabab* almost exclusively for the external and additional efficient and final causes. This is particularly true for Avicenna's *al-Samāʿ al-ṭabīʿī* but can also be witnessed in systematically different areas of his philosophy.[172] In his discussion of essential predication

170 As in the first quotation of this passage above, 64, I prefer reading *al-taʿlīm wa-l-taʿallum* with Mss. Leiden or. 4 and or. 84 for *al-taʿlīm aw al-taʿallum* in Zāyid, McGinnis, and Āl Yāsīn.

171 cf. Bertolacci, "The Doctrine of Material and Formal Causality," 130; cf. also Mahdi, *Ibn Khaldūn's Philosophy of History*, fn. 2, 63; Kennedy-Day, *Books of Definition in Islamic Philosophy*, 68–74.

172 Upon comparing Avicenna's uses of the two words for "cause" in his works, it appears that he generally prefers *ʿillā* as a technical term whenever he speaks of the four causes, especially when referring to them by combining a noun with a specifying adjective or participle, such as *al-ʿilla al-māddiyya*, *al-ʿilla al-ṣūriyya*, *al-ʿilla al-fāʿiliyya*, and *al-ʿilla al-ġāʾiya* for the material, formal, efficient, and final cause, respectively. In contrast to this technical usage, he often employs *sabab* as a more general term for cause of all sorts, such as when there is some impeding factor (*al-sabab al-māniʿ*), when there was some prior cause (*al-sabab al-mutaqaddim*), or when he uses *bi-sabab* in the lexical

in *al-Burhān* II.2, for example, Avicenna likewise appears to reserve the term *ʿilla* for internal constituents, i.e., matter and form, when he writes that every constituent is a cause (*kull muqawwim ʿilla*).[173] If there happens to be an occurrence of *sabab* in the same context, then it is clear that Avicenna is referring with this term to an external cause.[174]

This tendency to distinguish *ʿilla* as an internal cause from *sabab* as an external cause can also be warranted on etymological grounds. Whereas *sabab* stems from an expression for a rope used to tie the tent-pole securely to a peg in the ground, often signifying an external means to a specific end, *ʿilla* as a term for "cause" is a loan word from the Syriac *ʿelltā* whose Arabic cognate originally signified a disease or a defect, generally implying that a subject is afflicted by something or exhibits some malady from within.[175]

---

sense of "on account of" or "due to." As far as I can see, there is no occurrence in his *al-Ilāhiyyāt* or his *al-Naǧāt*, where Avicenna uses, for example, *al-sabab al-ṣūriyya* or *al-sabab al-ġāʾiya*. In my preliminary survey of Avicenna's terminology for "causes," I could find only one occurrence of *sabab fāʿil* in *al-Naǧāt* IV.2.37, 677.4; cf. also *al-Naǧāt* IV.2.37, 677.13. In Avicenna's *al-Samāʿ al-ṭabīʿī*, however, the term *sabab* is comparably much more frequent than in *al-Ilāhiyyāt* or *al-Naǧāt*. Moreover, it is even used when speaking of the four causes in a technical way. Yet, it is never used for the formal cause and only once for the material cause (*al-sabab al-māddī*). On the other hand, *ʿillā* is usually used for the material and formal cause but less often for the efficient and final cause. In general, we may say that *sabab* is almost never used for the internal material and formal cause but often for the external efficient and final cause, whereas *ʿilla* is more common for the internal material and formal cause but slightly less so for the external efficient and final cause. It is in this regard also noteworthy that the common expression *sabab min ḫāriǧ* ("cause from the outside") occurs throughout Avicenna's works, while we never find *ʿilla min ḫāriǧ*.

173 *al-Burhān* II.2, 129.11.

174 cf. *al-Burhān* II.2, 128.1. Let it be noted that a comparable distinction between *ʿilla* and *sabab* was upheld in an entirely different intellectual context. Pines gestured towards the ninth/fifteenth century Zaydī Muʿtazilite Aḥmad ibn Yaḥyā ibn al-Murtaḍā, who in his *al-Baḥr al-zaḫḫār* distinguishes between *al-fāʿil*, as an intentionally and voluntarily acting agent; *al-ʿilla*, as a cause effecting an attribute in the thing; and *sabab*, as a cause bringing about some other thing (*Studies in Islamic Atomism*, 38, referring to Schreiner, *Studien über Jeschuʿa Ben Jehuda*, fn. 1, 27). Thiele has shown that al-Murtaḍā took over this classification of causes from the earlier sixth/twelfth century Muʿtazilite al-Ḥasan al-Raṣṣāṣ, whose understanding can, again, be traced back to the fourth/tenth century and in particular to Abū Hāšim al-Ǧubbāʾī; cf. *Theologie in der jemenitischen Zaydiyya*, 101–104. Admittedly, the metaphysical framework of the Muʿtazilite conception is different from the one with which we are concerned in Philoponus' Neoplatonism and Avicenna's philosophy. A comparison between the two cases nonetheless suggests that both distinguish conceptually between *ʿilla* and *ʿsabab*, and that they do so on the basis of conceiving of an *ʿilla* in terms of a cause responsible for an effect within something, whereas *sabab* is taken to have a more outward direction, either having an effect on something different or on something in relation to some other thing; cf. also Thiele's example of *kawn* being both an *ʿilla* and a *sabab* in different respects in his *Theologie in der jemenitischen Zaydiyya*, 104.

175 cf. Walzer, "Gedanken zur Geschichte der philosophischen Terminologie," 108; van Ess, *Theologie und Gesellschaft*, vol. 3, 76; Endreß, "The Language of Demonstration," 232; Pormann, *The Oriental Tradition of Paul of Aegina's* Pragmateia; Thiele, *Theologie in der jemenitischen Zaydiyya*, 102.

If all this is right, then *ʿilal* is more suitable to express causes in the sense of στοιχεῖα than *asbāb* is. Since Avicenna, as I have noted, was aware of the Platonist distinction between internal and external causes, and since we have seen that Philoponus' commentary offers a reading of the opening remarks of Aristotle's *Physics* along the same lines, it is reasonable to believe that Avicenna's otherwise puzzling phrase *mabādiʾ wa-asbāb wa-ʿilal* must be interpreted in such a way that takes the principles (*mabādiʾ*) to be a more universal genus term for external (*asbāb*) and internal causes (*ʿilal*).[176] Avicenna can, thus, link his discussion of the two principles of natural things insofar as they are bodies (viz., matter and form) with his discussion of the four causes that are responsible for the internal constitution of these things as well as for their coming-to-be and their accidental changes. Moreover, the distinction between internal and external causes may also be related to Avicenna's cautious differentiation between two ways in which principles can be said to be "common," for it is only the external principles which can be said to be common in both senses, as we shall see.[177]

Accordingly, there are four principles – and that is: four causes – of natural things. Of these, we could see that Avicenna describes those two external ones as outright "common" in both meanings of the term. However, what about the commonality of the two more relevant, because internal and constitutive, principles matter and form? How common are they or, more precisely put, in what sense are they common? As in the case of agent and end, Avicenna makes it clear that it is important to ascertain precisely in which sense, if not in both, matter and form pertain to the subject-matter of physics, and devotes an entire chapter to it, viz., chapter I.3. Unfortunately, though, he withheld his answer to that question, so that it is now up to his reader to discern his views on matter and form as common principles of natural things. There are, nonetheless, clear indications as to his true position, which have so far been overlooked in the available secondary literature.

176 In this context, Lettinck pointed out that Avicenna may have used a translation of Aristotle's *Physics* different from that by Isḥāq ibn Ḥunayn, because Isḥāq ibn Ḥunayn faithfully translated Aristotle's phrase as *mabādiʾ aw asbāb aw usṭuqussāt*. This circumstance could, so Lettinck, account for Avicenna's divergence from the Aristotelian text (*Aristotle's* Physics *and its Reception in the Arabic World*, 97; "Problems in Aristotle's Physics I, 1," 97). While it is certainly true that Avicenna knew other translations than the one by Isḥāq ibn Ḥunayn, his choice of words here does not seem to be due to his reading from a different translation. It is less likely that a translator would render ἀρχαὶ ἢ αἴτια ἢ στοιχεῖα as *mabādiʾ wa-asbāb wa-ʿilal* than that Avicenna interpreted it that way. Taking στοιχεῖα as *ʿilal* in light of the Platonist distinction between internal and external causes is only a small step for a systematic reader like Avicenna but a broad interpretative jump for a translator, especially with viable alternatives like *arkān, basaʾiṭ*, and *ʿanāṣir*, that could have conveyed the idea of "element" more faithfully into the Arabic language – even if one wanted to avoid a perfectly matching (and already well-established) Graecism such as *usṭuqussāt*. A systematic doctrinal reason for Avicenna's odd phrase, like the one here proposed, is, thus, more likely than Lettinck's idea about a quotation from a translation other than Isḥāq ibn Ḥunayn's. On the question of which translation of Aristotle's *Physics* Avicenna used and knew, q.v. above, 37ff.

177 This may merely be a coincidence; if it is, however, it is certainly a striking one at that.

The Commonality of Form and Matter

The question in what sense matter and form are common to natural things as principles is relevant for, at least, two reasons. First, it will tell us how much and in what way Avicenna adheres to the doctrine of the "second substrate" which the commentators found in Aristotle and which has been expounded above. Second, we will learn to what extent supralunary and sublunary bodies have the same matter, and where matter actually comes from.[178]

Form

Form could be common to natural bodies in the way *the Form* would be common as one single and unique formal principle which is shared by all corporeal things or it could be common only insofar as corporeal things simply exhibit formal features, so that there are "forms" in the world. In the terminology introduced above, the former would constitute a "numerical commonality," whereas the latter would be a "generic commonality." Among the plurality of forms, Avicenna states, only the form of corporeality stands out in that it could perhaps be a form that satisfyies the conditions for numerical commonality.[179] After all, the corporeal form is the only form that is common to all natural bodies, because all natural bodies are corporeal. So, if there were something like *the Form*, then it would have to be *the Corporeal Form*.

In order to ascertain whether or not the corporeal form is numerically common, Avicenna suggests something like a litmus test to resolve the matter: if the form of corporeality were common in this sense, then the corporeal form of a certain amount of water which is about to be transformed into air would be one and the same as the form of corporeality of the corresponding amount of air after the water had been turned into air through excessive heat.[180] Consequently, there would be an underlying substance, i.e., the absolute body being composed of matter and the corporeal form, and this substance would undergo a change insofar as it was, first, characterised by the additional second form of water which, then, through the influence of excessive heat, was separated off and replaced by the likewise additional form of air. In this scenario, the underlying absolute body remains unaffected, as it consists of the same matter and the same corporeal form before as well as after the transformation. All that has happened is that one species form (viz., that of water) was replaced by another species form (viz., that of air).

This situation invites a well-known criticism by Averroes that what was supposed to be a substantial transformation is now revealed to be a mere accidental change.[181]

178 cf. *Met.* Λ.5, in which Aristotle raises similar questions as Avicenna does in the following.

179 cf. *al-Samāʿ al-ṭabīʿī* I.3, §3, 22.12f.

180 cf. *al-Samāʿ al-ṭabīʿī* I.3, §3, 22.13–23.1; *al-Ḥikma al-mašriqiyya* III.2, 6.4–10.

181 Averroes accused Avicenna of reducing all substantial change, as for example when water is transformed into air through excessive heat, to a mere instance of accidental change, because the

Moreover, it entails that natural things do not consist of one matter and one form alone (e.g., matter and the form of water), but that they, instead, consist of one matter and several forms (e.g., matter and the corporeal form plus the form of water), so that a complete substance would be the result of a multiplicity of forms inhering together in one matter or, alternatively, that one or more forms inhere in the "absolute body" or "second substrate" consisting of matter and the corporeal form.[182] This in itself would not be an absurdity, but it would commit Avicenna to a particular metaphysical theory.[183]

The secondary literature provides no clear view on these matters, i.e., neither on whether Avicenna would consider form to be common in sense of a numerical commonality nor on whether he would accept the idea of a multiplicity of forms.[184] In fact, most interpreters seem to agree that Avicenna would, in fact, allow such a multiplicity, so that a complete substance would consist of an unchanging "second substrate" (composed of matter and a corporeal form) together with one or more additional forms. Étienne Gilson, for example, writes the following about Avicenna:

---

underlying substance, i.e., the "absolute body" or "second substrate," remains as such unaffected in much the same way as any other substance remains as such unaffected when undergoing accidental change; cf. Hyman, "Aristotle's First Matter," 404f.

182 I shall not consider accidental forms that, indeed, additionally pertain to natural bodies.

183 On the whole, the test, as it is suggested by Avicenna, is somewhat puzzling. It is supposed to be a tool for determining whether the corporeal form is numerically common to all natural things in the way God is the single numerically one Agent common to all natural things. Avicenna's test, however, is merely concerned with the question of whether the water in this pot here has the same corporeal form as the air in the same pot after the water was transformed into air. Even if that would turn out to be true, the test would still not tell us anything about the more crucial question of whether the corporeal form of the water or the air in that pot is also the same corporeal form that exists in the water in the glass over there, or in the tree outside, in this book on the table, that human being over there or, ultimately, in *all* natural things. This, however, would have to be the case if we were speaking about *the Corporeal Form* which is numerically common to *all* natural things. Accordingly, Avicenna's test does not really fit the question it is supposed to illuminate. One way to respond to this concern is to assume that Avicenna might say that there clearly could not be a single numerically one *Corporeal Form* for all natural things if it is not even the case that the corporeal form of the water here in the pot is the same throughout the transformation of the water into air. If there is no form that is numerically common to only *two* substances, viz., this water and subsequently this air, then how could there be a numerically common form to *all* substances? Thus, if the test fails, and the corporeal form of the water is numerically different from the corporeal form of the air after the transformation, then we do not even need to worry about the bigger question about all natural things and their numerically common form. It seems that we need to take Avicenna's test along these lines – and only if we do, do we get a satisfactory answer.

184 It should be noted that whoever claims that form is numerically common must likewise accept the thesis of the multiplicity of forms. By contrast, a denial of form being numerically common does not also entail the denial of the multiplicity of forms, as the corporeal form of matter could be numerically different from the corporeal form of the air after the transformation, while still both water and air may consist of matter, a corporeal form, and the elemental form of water or air, respectively.

> The first and most universal of all physical forms is that which makes matter to be a body (*corpus*). It is called the form of corporeity (*forma corporeitatis*). This form is to be found in all bodies, together with other forms ... In doctrines where "corporeity" remains present under the higher forms (animality, rationality, etc.), the form of corporeity entails the plurality of forms in physical beings. Each being then is made up of matter plus at least two forms, that of corporeity and for instance that of animality.[185]

In like manner, Elisabeth Buschmann describes Avicenna's position as follows:

> Die Materie muss also zusätzlich zu der allgemeinen Form der Körperlichkeit eine der elementaren Formen (feurig, luftig, wässrig oder erdig) aufnehmen ... so ist das Entstehen und Vergehen der einzelnen elementaren Körper erklärt: eine Form muß der anderen weichen, das materielle Substrat mit der allgemeinen Form der Körperlichkeit aber wird dabei nicht vernichtet.[186]

Consequently, a given element would consist of matter, the corporeal form, and an additional elemental form. It is only these additional elemental forms which are exchanged during the transformation of elements, while the substantial core compound of matter and corporeal form remains throughout. Analogously, a horse would consist of matter joined by the forms of corporeality, animality, and horseness. Recently, the interpretation put forth by Gilson and Buschmann has been accepted by Catarina Belo and Bilal Ibrahim as well as Robert Pasnau, who wrote that "Avicenna's corporeal form, described above, marks him as a pluralist."[187]

Hyman, in somewhat less certain terms, writes that "Avicenna seems to have subscribed to the doctrine of the 'multiplicity of forms,' but how he understood this doctrine is not too clear."[188] Hyman cites Goichon's critical remarks against Aimé Forest in her study *La distinction de l'essence et de l'existence* for further evidence.[189] In a passage different from the one referred to by Hyman, Goichon quotes some text from Avicenna's *al-Ilāhiyyāt* IX.5 which, indeed, seems to suggest that the existence of a body is not complete through matter and the corporeal form alone but requires also another form joining the compound.[190] Earlier in her study, however, Goichon explicitly addressed the question about the two ways in which matter and form are common to natural things, i.e., the very question from Avicenna's *al-Samāʿ al-ṭabīʿī* with which we are presently concerned. Although she argues against the view that form is numerically

---

185 Gilson, *History of Christian Philosophy in the Middle Ages*, 193.

186 Buschmann, *Untersuchungen zum Problem der Materie bei Avicenna*, 52.

187 Pasnau, "Form and Matter," 644, referring back to the description given on 640; cf. Belo, *Chance and Determinism in Avicenna and Averroes*, 79f.; Ibrahim, "Theories of Matter," 355. It should also be noted that this became a widely held position among thinkers in the Latin middle ages; cf. Pasnau, *Metaphysical Themes 1274–1671*, ch. 25; Silva, *Robert Kilwardby on the Human Soul*.

188 Hyman, "Aristotle's First Matter," fn. 85, 404.

189 cf. Goichon, *La distinction de l'essence et de l'existence*, fn. 6, 435f.

190 cf. Goichon, *La distinction de l'essence et de l'existence*, 437f., referring to *al-Ilāhiyyāt* IX.5, §10, 413.13–16, which will be discussed below, 169ff.

common, she does not seem to problematise the related question about the plurality of forms within natural substances.[191]

Against the interpretation that Avicenna accepted the multiplicity-thesis, Stone reasonably points out that if Avicenna adhered to this doctrine, then the substantial form of "humanity," for example, would have to inhere in an already substantial subject consisting of matter together with the forms of corporeality and animality. Yet, this would be incompatible with Avicenna's repeated claim that forms, such as "humanity," are substances and that whatever is a substance does not exist in a subject. Thus, substantial forms cannot inhere in anything other than matter, for matter is not a subject, as we have already seen.[192] Therefore, Avicenna could not subscribe to the multiplicity of forms, because then only the first form to inhere in matter, viz., the form of corporeality, would be a substantial form, while all other forms would be accidents. This would not only go against the grain of Avicenna's metaphysics but would also, again, invite Averroes' objection that a multiplicity of forms would reduce any substantial transformation to a mere instance of an accidental change.

Recently, Kara Richardson also rejected the attribution of that doctrine to Avicenna on similar grounds as Stone arguing that such an interpretation would conflict with what she calls Avicenna's account of "hylomorphic unity."[193] Incidentally, Matteo Di Giovanni pointed out that the Latin Scholastics drew a contrast between Avicenna and Solomon ibn Gabirol (d. 1057-8) in such a way that "Ibn Sīnā was generally credited with the view that substantial form is one, whereas Ibn Gabirol ... was considered a supporter of the plurality thesis."[194] On the other hand, Di Giovanni's assertion seems to be more about how Thomas Aquinas (d. 1274) has drawn the line between Ibn Gabirol and Avicenna, for the Latin Avicennists usually adhered to the idea of a plurality of forms and were, thus, in opposition to Thomas on this matter.[195]

Unfortunately, all that Avicenna himself provides in answer to the question here in *al-Samāʿ al-ṭabīʿī* I.3 is that "the truth ... shall become clear in its [proper] place" (*wa-sayaẓharu laka l-ḥaqq ... fī mawḍiʿihī*) – without providing any indication of what

---

191 cf. Goichon, *La distinction de l'essence et de l'existence*, esp. 431–433.

192 cf. A. D. Stone, "Simplicius and Avicenna on the Essential Corporeity of Material Substance," 99f., referring to *al-Maqūlāt* I.6, 46.2; q.v. also above 114ff.

193 Richardson, "Avicenna and Aquinas on Form and Generation," fn. 26, 258.

194 Di Giovanni, "Substantial Form in Averroes's Long Commentary on the Metaphysics," 192. Di Giovanni further remarks that it is also not clear whether Averroes accepted or rejected the multiplicity of forms. Although he is traditionally taken to support the thesis, Hasse has recently provided "good reasons to dispute the historical association between Averroes and pluralism" (Di Giovanni, "Substantial Form in Averroes's Long Commentary on the Metaphysics," 193); cf. Hasse, "The Early Albertus Magnus." Other than that it seems that the Iḫwān al-Ṣafāʾ adhered to the multiplicity-thesis in their epistles, e.g., in XV.4, XVII.2, XXXIIa.2.

195 cf. Pasnau, *Metaphysical Themes 1274–1671*, ch. 25; Silva, *Robert Kilwardby on the Human Soul.*

that place might be.[196] In a note to his translation, Jon McGinnis suggests *al-Kawn wa-l-fasād* 14, in which Avicenna states his views about elemental transformation, and *al-Ilāhiyyāt* IX.5, which has already been hinted at by Goichon in support of her interpretation that Avicenna indeed adhered to the idea of a multiplicity of forms. In this latter chapter, we find Avicenna writing the following:

وبيّنّا أنّ الجسم لا يستكمل له وجود بمجرّد الصورة الجسمية ما لم تقترن بها صورة أخرى.

We have proven that existence does not become complete for the body through corporeal form alone, so long as no other form (*ṣūra uḫrā*) is conjoined to it (*taqtarinu bihā*). (*al-Ilāhiyyāt* IX.5, §10, 413.15f., tr. by Marmura, modified)

This is surely not the only passage where Avicenna seems to talk of some "other form" existing in matter in addition to the corporeal form. In fact, such talk is quite frequent in Avicenna, so that it is easy to find other straightforward passages, such as the following, which is taken from the physics of Avicenna's *al-Naǧāt*:

وفي مادّة الجسم الطبيعي صور أخر غير الصور الجسمية.

In the matter of the natural body are other forms (*ṣuwar uḫar*) different from the corporeal forms.[197] (*al-Naǧāt* II.1.1, 192.1 ≈ *al-Ḥikma al-ʿArūḍiyya* II.1, 114.15)[198]

Despite the passages just quoted, however, the evidence found in Avicenna's writings suggests that Avicenna rejected the idea of a multiplicity of forms, so that the passages in which Avicenna speaks of "other forms" existing in matter in addition to the corporeal form are loose locutions, employed by Avicenna for whatever reasons.[199]

196 *al-Samāʿ al-ṭabīʿī* I.3, §3, 23.2. The corresponding passage in *al-Ḥikma al-mašriqiyya* III.2, 6.4–10, omits even this unhelpful reference.

197 In the corresponding passage in *al-Ḥikma al-ʿArūḍiyya*, Avicenna writes *ṣuwar uḫar ġayr ṣuwar al-miqdār al-qaṭrī* ("other forms different from the forms of the dimensional magnitude") instead of *ṣuwar uḫar ġayr ṣuwar al-ǧismiyya*, which seems to imply that he refers to each of the three dimensions in a body as a form of a dimensional magnitude, which, in turn, may indicate that he generally employs the term "form" in a loose manner.

198 cf. *al-Samāʿ al-ṭabīʿī* I.2, §4, 14.1f.; *al-Hidāya* II.1, 135.8–136.2; *al-Išārāt wa-l-tanbīhāt* II.1.17, 98.8; *al-Ḥikma al-mašriqiyya* III.1, 4.1–3; III.2, 6.3f., mentioning "other forms" (*ṣuwar uḫar* and *sāʾir al-ṣuwar*) or "some forms" (*baʿḍ al-ṣuwar*) that pertain to matter in addition to the corporeal form; cf. also the way in which the question about *minima naturalia* is introduced in *al-Samāʿ al-ṭabīʿī* III.12, §1, 240.6–8.

199 One reason that springs to mind is that Avicenna may merely have wanted to emphasise his concept of the corporeal form as a concept of a *substantial* form which, were it to inhere in matter alone, would indeed render an absolute body subsistent as a substantial being. However, since the absolute body does not exist in the concrete world, there is never a body which consists exclusively of matter and the corporeal form. This means that the corporeal form – strictly speaking – does not exist in any body as what it is, i.e., as a corporeal form. In this regard it is striking that the passages in which Avicenna allows himself to speak loosely of a multiplicity of forms are all devoted to explaining the reality of things from a bottom-up perspective: there is first matter, then corporeality, then elemental forms. Discussing reality step-by-step may have compelled Avicenna to talking about matter as an

Apart from the fact that the multiplicity-thesis would commit Avicenna precisely to the objection mentioned by Averroes that any substantial change would be downgraded to a mere instance of accidental change, and also apart from Stone's reasonable warning that such a thesis would also downgrade what Avicenna explicitly calls substantial forms to mere instances of accidental forms, there are other reasons that support the interpretation that Avicenna is not committed to that thesis.

As mentioned, McGinnis hints at *al-Kawn wa-l-fasād* 14 as a possible target of Avicenna's reference that "the truth ... shall become clear in its [proper] place." In this chapter, Avicenna describes how matter needs to be properly prepared for the reception of a form from the Giver of Forms (*wāhib al-ṣuwar*), i.e., the Active Intellect.[200] Once the matter is in an appropriate state, a corresponding form emanates from the Giver of Forms to inhere in that matter. To my knowledge, Avicenna always speaks of only *one* form that is emanated and implanted into the matter, and not of several forms. Avicenna's discussion in *al-Kawn wa-l-fasād* 14 would be rather decisive for the question about the multiplicity-thesis, if we could preclude the possibility that Avicenna does not use "matter" here in an equivocal sense, i.e., if we could be certain that he means nothing but prime matter, because according to the multiplicity-thesis, the coming-to-be of an element would require (at least) two forms, viz., a corporeal form and an elemental form. However, we cannot be entirely certain, for in talking about the transformation of water into air, one could equivocally describe the water as the matter for the air, because it is the water that needs to be heated up and prepared, so that the water's matter – or its corporeal "second substrate" – lets go of its watery form and accepts the airy form. In a similar way, one can refer to blood and bone as the matter of the human body or the elements as the matter of composite bodies. Thus, Avicenna's discussion in *al-Kawn wa-l-fasād* 14, though promising, is not clear enough to decide the matter.

A more suitable passage is found in *al-Ilāhiyyāt* IX.5. We have just seen the same chapter providing material which seemed to suggest the multiplicity of forms, now it provides material indicating the opposite. Like *al-Kawn wa-l-fasād* 14, this passage explains how matter needs to be prepared for the acceptance of the form – singular –

independent feature (even though it does not exist as an independent thing), about corporeality being the first characteristic in matter (even though it does not exist as such), and about other more specific qualifications that complete the existence of water and air or human beings and horses (even though they are not to be conceived as separate, i.e., additional, forms). Thus, the passages discussed below, which bear out Avicenna's explicit denial of the idea of a multiplicity of forms, make it reasonable to assume that Avicenna used locutions such as *taqtarinu bi-* in the above passage from *al-Ilāhiyyāt* IX.5, precisely in order to clarify that the forms do not exist *separately* in matter but only in a unified, conjoined, manner i.e., as one single form and not as several single forms; q.v. also below, 172ff.

200 On the Giver of Forms and its role in Avicenna's ontology and cosmology, cf. Hasse, *Avicenna's* De Anima *in the Latin West*, 187–189; "Avicenna's 'Giver of Forms' in Latin Philosophy"; Janssens, "The Notions of *wāhib al-ṣuwar* and *wāhib al-ʿaql* in Ibn Sīnā"; Alpina, "Intellectual Knowledge, Active Intellect, and Intellectual Memory in Avicenna's *Kitab al-Nafs* and its Aristotelian Background."

being emanated from the Giver of Forms. Discussing once more how water needs to be warmed up, in order to prepare its matter for the airy form, Avicenna writes:

فإذا أفرط ذلك واشتدّت المناسبة اشتدّ الاستعداد فصار من حقّ الصورة النارية أن تفيض ومن حقّ هذه أن تبطل ولأنّ المادّة ليست تبقى بلا صورة فليس قوامها عن ما ينسب إليه من المبادئ الأولى وحدها بل عنها وعن الصورة.

If that [warming] becomes excessive and the appropriateness intense, the preparedness becomes intense, and so it becomes aright for the fiery form to emanate and aright for this [watery form] to cease. [This is] because the matter (*al-mādda*) does not remain without form, and so its subsistence is not due to what is attributed to the first principles alone but due to them and to the form. (*al-Ilāhiyyāt* IX.5, §§6–7, 412.15–413.1, tr. by Marmura, modified)[201]

In contrast to the passage in *al-Kawn wa-l-fasād* 14, where we could not be certain about whether the matter in question was actually prime matter or something else equivocally called "matter," here in this passage it is apparent that the term "matter" denotes prime matter, for only prime matter "does not remain without form." So, although this passage discusses and explains the very same phenomenon as the passage in *al-Kawn wa-l-fasād* 14, viz., the elemental transformation of water into air, it is more explicit in its concern with prime matter, as it states that the Giver of Forms implants *one* form into *prime* matter. So, when water is heated up, then there will be a point when the watery form ceases to be and when the underlying prime matter is in danger of going out of existence if not another form takes over the watery form's place. The same situation is also explained in *al-Ilāhiyyāt* VIII.1:

مثل الماء إنّما يصير هواء بأن تخلع عن هيولاه صورة المائية ويحصل لها صورة الهوائية.

For example, water becomes air only by the watery form being cast-off from its matter (*hayūlāhu*) and the airy form occurring to it. (*al-Ilāhiyyāt* VIII.1, §13, 330.6f., tr. by Marmura, modified)

Provided that Avicenna uses *hayūlā* here, precisely in order to refer to prime matter, as opposed to providing a reference to a possibly equivocal matter, the case is very clear: prime matter abandons its one watery form and takes on one airy form. Even if it were said that *hayūlā* could just as well as *mādda* be used in an equivocal sense, Avicenna explicitly maintains, somewhat later in the same book, that "the complete form of a thing is one (*al-ṣūra al-tāmma li-l-šay' wāḥida*) and that the multiple comes about from it by way of generality and specificity" (*'alā naḥw al-'umūm wa-l-ḫuṣūṣ*).[202] In the words of Amos Bertolacci, this means two things: first that "a particular horse has only the form of horseness," so that there is only *one* form existing in matter, and not a multiplicity; second, that "the forms of animality, corporality etc. belong to it in

201 cf. *al-Ilāhiyyāt* IX.5, §3, 410.14–411.4, where Avicenna also seems to speak about prime matter, even though this passage may, again, be taken to be not entirely decisive.
202 *al-Ilāhiyyāt* VIII.3, §4, 341.15f., tr. by Marmura.

so far as they are, respectively, the genus of its specific form, the genus of its genus and so on."[203] In consequence, Avicenna regards a natural substance as a compound, consisting of matter and of one single species form. It is on account of this species form that a particular horse is what it is, viz., a horse, and it is on account of this very same species form as well that this horse is also an animal and a body. Though the species form itself is one, it contains multiple layers of formal determination "by way of generality and specificity," as Avicenna writes. This harmonises well with another text in *al-Naǧāt*, in which Avicenna explains what is to be said as a proper answer to the question "what is something?" (*mā huwa?*). If we were to be asked "what is Zayd?," the accurate answer would be the following:

الإنسان ... فإنّه يشتمل على كلّ معنى مُفرَد ذاتي له مثل الجوهرية والتجسّم والتغذّي والنموّ والتوليد وقوّة الحسّ والحركة والنطق وغير ذلك.

[The answer would be] "man" ... for it contains (*yaštamilu*) every simple and essential meaning belonging to him, such as substantiality, becoming corporeal, nourishment, growth, and reproduction as well as the power of sense, motion, speech, and other things. (*al-Naǧāt* I.9, 13.3–5, tr. by Ahmed, modified)

What Avicenna describes here on a logical level about essential propositions, is expressed from a physical perspective in a passage from *al-Samāʿ al-ṭabīʿī* I.6. Discussing the relation of natural powers, on the one hand, and matter and form, on the other, Avicenna explains that although composite bodies comprise a variety of discrete powers, this variety is unified in one single form:

فكأنّ تلك القوّة جزء من صورتها وكأنّ صورتها تجتمع من عدّة معان فتتّحد كالإنسانية فإنّها تتضمّن قوى الطبيعة وقوى النفس النباتية والحيوانية والنطق. وإذا اجتمعت هذه كلّها نوعاً من الاجتماع أعطيت الماهية الإنسانية. وأمّا كيفية نحو هذا الاجتماع فالأولى أن يُبيّن في الفلسفة الأولى.

So, it is as if those powers are part of their form; it is as if their form is combined (*tuǧtamiʿu*) from a number of meanings, and so they are unified (*tattaḥidu*), just like "humanity," for it comprises the powers of nature, the powers of the vegetative and the animal soul, and reason.[204] If all of these are combined through some sort of combination (*nawʿan min al-iǧtimāʿ*), the essence of humanity obtains.[205] The manner of the way of this combination is more fitting for being proven in first philosophy. (*al-Samāʿ al-ṭabīʿī* I.6, §3, 3.9–12, tr. by McGinnis, modified)

Towards the end of this passage, Avicenna makes clear that he is currently engaged in a discussion of natural philosophy and not metaphysics, so that he does not have to go into the specifics of the underlying metaphysical theory he is alluding to. It

203 Bertolacci, "The Doctrine of Material and Formal Causality," 140.

204 Reading *al-nuṭq* with Mss. Leiden or. 4 and or. 84 as well as Zāyid for *al-nāṭiqa* suggested in McGinnis and Āl Yāsīn.

205 Reading *ʾuʿṭiyat* with Ms. Leiden or. 84 for *ʾa-ʿ-ṭ-t* in Ms. Leiden or. 4 as well as Zāyid, McGinnis, and Āl Yāsīn.

is, however, reasonable to assume that what Avicenna here alludes to as "some sort of combination" corresponds to the conjunction we have seen Avicenna mentioning above when he argued "that existence does not become complete for the body through corporeal form alone, so long as no other form (*ṣūra uḫrā*) is *conjoined* to it" (*taqtarinu bihā*).[206] Moreover, Avicenna reveals – in much the same way and vocabulary as we saw him doing in *al-Naǧāt* I.9 – that a thing may posses a number of powers, features, or attributes that are essential for it. Yet, all of these are combined and form a single unity, viz., its essence – and this essence is its form: a single form coming about through some sort of unifying combination. We may assume that this unifying combination arranges the different powers and attributes, as we have read above in *al-Ilāhiyyāt* VIII.3, "by way of generality and specificity" (*ʿalā naḥw al-ʿumūm wa-l-ḫuṣūṣ*).

In his *al-Nafs*, Avicenna addresses a related issue and provides a similar solution, ultimately arguing that the existence of multiple powers in the soul does not jeopardise the soul's unity. In *al-Nafs* I.3, for example, Avicenna explicitly mentions the thesis of the multiplicity of forms by saying that "between the remote subject and the soul are other forms which render it [sc. the remote subject] subsistent."[207] The remote subject, here, is matter. Only a little later, an objector raises a question by transferring the idea of a multiplicity of forms to a multiplicity of souls, asking for an answer about the ontological relation between the vegetative, the animal, and the intellective souls, on the on hand, and their matter, on the other.[208] This question is closely related to Stone's worry that if the underlying thing were already substance and, thus, a subject in the strict sense, then the souls – and most of all the "last" soul, i.e., the intellective soul – could not be substances, although it is precisely the intellective soul which is, most of all, a substance. Avicenna's response is related to, and uses similar terminology as, the just mentioned passage from *al-Ilāhiyyāt* VIII.3. He distinguishes the vegetative soul as it exists in plants but not in animals from the vegetative soul as a "general meaning (*al-maʿnā l-ʿāmm*) that is common to both the vegetative and the animal soul." Thus, the vegetative soul as a general meaning can be joined by a specific difference (*faṣl*), thereby becoming an animal soul.[209] That is to say that not two souls exist in an animal but one soul with a generic vegetative layer and a more specific animal layer which are differentiated "by way of generality and specificity," as Avicenna put it above in *al-Ilāhiyyāt* VIII.3, with each of these layers being responsible for providing various psychological powers to the underlying body. The whole discussion leads Avicenna to assert "that the soul is one and that [all] these powers are diffused from it into the organs."[210] This account of the unity of the soul extends even to the intellective soul itself, as Avicenna in *al-Nafs* V.1 maintains, for although we can discern two intellective

206 *al-Ilāhiyyāt* IX.5, §10, 413.15f., emphasis added; q.v. above 169ff.
207 *al-Nafs* I.3, 22.17.
208 *al-Nafs* I.3, 23.11–15.
209 *al-Nafs* I.3, 24.1–5.
210 *al-Nafs* I.3, 25.3.

powers in human beings, viz., the practical and theoretical intellect, "none of these is the human soul; rather, the soul is that thing which has these powers, while it is, as we have proven, an independent substance."[211]

Applying all this to our issue from *al-Samāʿ al-ṭabīʿī* I.3, it emerges that whatever plurality of powers or of formal determination a concretely existing thing may exhibit, it can still be formally one and does not have to be multiple – and that is when all its formal aspects inhere in matter not as separate forms but as a single form which is intrinsically differentiated by way of generality and specificity. Thus, the form of water, being one in itself, already includes the more general meaning of corporeality at its most basic formal level in addition to the what-it-means-to-be water at its more specific formal level. After all, water is a cold-wet *body*. If the water is, then, transformed into air through excessive heat, the form of water vanishes as a whole – and together with it its corporeal aspect. We may, thus, say that, in a manner of speaking, the underlying matter, when it loses its watery form, also loses its corporeal formal aspect, before it acquires a new form, viz., the airy form which brings with it a corporeal aspect as its own general component. After all, air is a hot-wet *body*.[212]

In consequence, the form of corporeality *in* the water is not one and the same as the form of corporeality *in* the air but is an integral general aspect *of* the water. If this is correct, then even the corporeal form fails the litmus test advanced by Avicenna, to determine its numerical commonality. Neither is the corporeal form of the water numerically the same as the corporeal form of the air after the transformation nor does it even exist as a separate form in the matter in addition to an equally separate watery or airy form. Thus, not only is the corporeal form not numerically common, it has also become clear that Avicenna, against the more widespread opinion, actually denies the multiplicity-thesis, as each and every natural thing consists of only one chunk of matter and only one form, even though his form contains several layers of formal determination "by way of generality and specificity."

Notwithstanding the lack of an explicit answer in *al-Samāʿ al-ṭabīʿī* I.3, some of what Avicenna writes there must be taken as a confirmation of the here advanced interpretation that form is common only in the generic sense, i.e., as something that is predicated of the many. For example, Avicenna describes form as follows:

وجميع ما يقال له إنّه صورة فهو الهيئة الحاصلة لمثل هذا الأمر المذكور والذي يحصل منهما أمر من الأمور بهذا النحو من التركيب.

211 *al-Nafs* V.1, 185.19f.; cf. Hasse, "The Early Albertus Magnus," 243f.

212 McGinnis arrives at the same conclusion by analysing Avicenna's *al-Burhān* I.10. He writes: "Three-dimensional body, then, does not function as some (pre-existing) subject to which being an animal is subsequently predicated, a position that Avicenna takes to be absurd. Quite the contrary, matter and form, or in our example three-dimensional body and animality, jointly constitute, and so cause, a specific kind of substance, namely, an animal ... Without the form of animality (or some other species form) no body would exist." (McGinnis, "Logic and Science," 176f.).

> All that about which it is said that it is form (*ṣūra*) is a disposition (*al-hay'a*) that occurs to an instance of this aforementioned thing [sc. the matter] and from which, together with it, a given thing comes-to-be by this way of composition. (*al-Samāʿ al-ṭabīʿī* I.3, §10, 25.9f., tr. by McGinnis, modified)[213]

This statement applies to all forms alike without distinguishing between species forms and the corporeal form. Being a statement of what "form" means within the context of physics, it speaks of form as a disposition which applies to, or is predicated of, other things and thereby resembles Avicenna's description of the second sense of "common," i.e., an intelligible object (*amran maʿqūlan*) applicable to many, because it is the proper expression for a certain disposition of its subject. Consequently, there is not one numerically single entity that is *the Form* or *the Corporeal Form*. When we perceive two human beings, we say of both that they are human, i.e., that they exhibit this very feature that makes them human and, at the same time, allows us to predicate "humanity" of them. The ontological status and the epistemological apprehension conform to one another. The same holds true of natural things insofar as they are corporeal. Two bodies insofar as they are bodies are rightly called "corporeal," because in each we can identify and demarcate three dimensions. We do not need to assume that the two bodies share in one and the same corporeal form nor that two human beings together share in a single form of humanity that is numerically one. Yet, they share the same numerically one Agent and the same numerically one End, even though they may additionally have their respective agents and ends – or be agents and ends – within the natural world: *the Agent* of a human being is God, the agents of a human being may be his or her parents, and the human being itself may be the agent of something else.

When we say "share," we properly convey into English what *muštarak* means in Arabic, viz., "shared." This is why *muštarak* is the adequate term for the numerical sense of "common," for we say *the Agent* is *muštarak* when there is only one single Agent which is *shared* by all created things. In particular with regard to form, it becomes evident that Avicenna's discussion of the two senses of "common" as a whole seems to contrast a somewhat Platonising view of principles with an Aristotelianising view. This may be indicated by the fact that *ištirāk* and *mušāraka* were the two preferred translations for Platonic μέθεξις ("participation") in the Arabic version of Aristotle's *Metaphysics*.[214] In effect, some Platonic overtones in the numerical sense of "common" as *muštarak* cannot be denied.

---

213 cf. *al-Samāʿ al-ṭabīʿī* I.2, §17, 18.9–12; *al-Ilāhiyyāt* VI.4, §9, 282.6–14; *al-Ḥikma al-mašriqiyya* III.2, 5.20f.

214 We find *ištirāk*, the verbal noun of the eighth form, at *Met.* A.6, 987b10, b13, and *mušāraka*, the verbal noun of the third form, at Z.6, 1031b18. It needs to be noted, however, that *ištirāk* is also commonly used to render μέθεξις in Porphyry's *Isagoge*, where it does not necessarily resonate with Platonic metaphysics, even though it often does; cf. Barnes' remarks in Porphyry, *Introduction*, e.g., 136–141.

The other Arabic expression Avicenna uses to denote something common is *ʿāmm*. This term is perhaps best translated into English here as "general" and, thus, expresses most aptly the second, i.e., generic, sense of "common." When we say "agent" is *ʿāmm*, then we say that being an agent is a general description of those things which exhibit a common disposition inasmuch as they exert some sort of agency.

When we recall how Avicenna introduced this distinction in *al-Samāʿ al-ṭabīʿī* I.2, §8, 15.11–17, we recognise that, first, he used *muštarak* in a broad sense as a genus term for both meanings, saying that what is *muštarak* can be understood in two ways. Then, he described numerical commonality as follows:

أحدهما أن يكون الفاعل مشتركاً فيه على أنّه يفعل الفعل الأوّل الذي يترتب عليه سائر الأفاعيل.

One of them is that the agent (*al-fāʿil*) is common (*muštarakan fīhi*) in that it produces the first actuality from which all other actualities follow (*al-Samāʿ al-ṭabīʿī* I.2, §8, 15.11f., tr. by McGinnis, modified)[215]

Accordingly, what is common in the first sense, i.e., the narrow sense of *muštarak*, is a single, numerically one entity in which (*fīhi*) other things share. This first sense is properly described through the term *muštarak*. It is striking that Avicenna's description of the second sense of "common" does not rely on the term *muštarak* but on a cognate of *ʿāmm*:

والنحو الآخر أن يكون المشترك فيه بنحو العموم كالفاعل الكلّي المقول على كلّ واحدة من الفاعلات الجزئية للأمور الجزئية.

The other way that it is common is by way of generality (*bi-naḥw al-ʿumūm*), as the universal [predicate] "agent" is said of each one of the particular agents of particular things. (*al-Samāʿ al-ṭabīʿī* I.2, §8, 15.16f., tr. by McGinnis, modified)

We see that Avicenna uses the adverbial construction *bi-naḥw al-ʿumūm* to qualify the second sense of "common." The noun *ʿumūm* is semantically related to the active participle *ʿāmm* which was used as the other word for "common" best translated as "general." Thus, what is generically common in the second sense is the general meaning, description, or predicate which is universally applicable to other things. Accordingly, agent and end are "common" also in the way the many agents and ends which we perceive in our everyday life can be connected by one common thread, precisely because they have a specific characteristic in common.

Regarding form, this means that form is not *muštarak* in the first, numerical, sense but, instead, is *ʿāmm*, i.e., general and common in the second sense. Not even the form of corporeality is one single entity. Quite to the contrary, it is just one of the many

215 More literally, one could translate *muštarakan fīhi* as "that in which there is sharing," instead of "common."

forms which exist in, and are predicated of, things.[216] A form is an accidental or a substantial disposition which a subject – be it a concrete composite or prime matter – has acquired through a process of change and it is through that acquisition of form that the subject came to be as it presently is.[217] It is in this sense that Avicenna states the general meaning of "form" as it is employed in the science of physics towards the end of *al-Samāʿ al-ṭabīʿī* I.2:

وقد جرّت العادة أن تُسمّى كلّ هيئة في هذا الموضع صورةً فلنسمّ كلّ هيئة صورة ونعني به كلّ أمر يحدث في قابل يصير له موصوفاً بصفة مخصوصة.

> It has become a custom to call every disposition in this context a "form" (*tusammā kull hay'a ... ṣūratan*), so let us, [too], call every disposition "form" and by that we mean all that which comes to be in a recipient (*al-qābil*) such that [the recipient] comes to have a description by a specific attribute (*bi-ṣifa maḫṣūṣa*). (*al-Samāʿ al-ṭabīʿī* I.2, §17, 18.11f., tr. by McGinnis, modified)[218]

This may not be the meaning of "form" that satisfies every metaphysician, but it is the meaning that suffices for physics and it is the general meaning in which Avicenna will use the term in his *al-Samāʿ al-ṭabīʿī*.[219]

Finally, there is one further passage in which Avicenna explicitly mentions the cessation of the corporeal form during a process of transformation. This passage ultimately confirms the here advanced interpretation that Avicenna rejects the idea of a multiplicity of forms inhering in matter and that he, consequently, likewise denies that there could be a form that is common in the numerical sense in which only *the Agent* and *the End* can be said to be common. This passage is part of Avicenna's account of nutrition and growth in *al-Kawn wa-l-fasād* 8. As nutrition involves the assimilation of food, i.e., the transformation of food into other substances such as blood and bone, it relies on substantial changes in the process of which one substance loses its form, so that its matter can acquire a new form. Furthermore, since nutrition leads to growth, it also relies on corporeality as such, for, in order to explain an increase in volume on part of the nourished, the food prior to its assimilation must be corporeal. During the process of digestion, then, the food, being potentially blood and bone, is assimilated by losing its form – including its "corporeal form" – thereafter acquiring a new one. This is explained by Avicenna as follows:

---

216 Here, I allowed myself, for didactic reasons, to use language that may suggest an adherence to the multiplicity-thesis. I am sure that Avicenna in certain contexts felt compelled to do the same, thus speaking of "other forms" in addition to the corporeal form without, however, intending to suggest any real existence of other forms in matter in addition to the corporeal form.

217 cf. *al-Samāʿ al-ṭabīʿī* I.3, §10, 25.9f., also quoted above, 174.

218 A similar definition of form can be found in *al-Nafs* I.1, 7.4–6.

219 For example, one might ask whether separate forms (*ṣuwar mufāriqa*), like the soul or the intellect, could adequately be subsumed under this definition of form; cf. *al-Naǧāt* IV.1.3, 497.13f. Yet, we need to keep in mind that we are presently reading a work on physics, not on metaphysics; cf. Avicenna's remark in *al-Samāʿ al-ṭabīʿī* I.6 quoted above, 172; q.v. also above, 81ff.

والغذاء الأوّل أعني التشبه بالقوّة هو جوهر لا محالة ... ويجب أن يكون جوهراً غير ممتنع عن أن يكون له مقدار طبيعي ... فلا يخلو إمّا أن يكون ذلك له بالفعل عند ما هو شبيه بالقوّة أو يكون بالقوّة. فإن كان بالقوّة فهو هيولى مجرّدة، ويستحيل قوامها إلّا مقارناً لصورة جسمانية .فهي إذن تكون مقارنة لصورة جسمانية وتلك الصورة الجسمية تزول عند قبولها هذه الصورة.

> Food primarily, I mean that which is potentially assimilated, is without doubt a substance ... It is necessary that it is a substance which does not abstain from having a natural magnitude ... So, it must be either that that belongs to it in actuality upon that which it is potentially alike or it is potential [altogether]. So, if it is potential [altogether], then it is bare matter, but its subsistence is impossible without being conjoined to a corporeal form. Therefore, then, it is conjoined to a corporeal form and this corporeal form vanishes upon its [sc. matter's] reception of this [other] form [i.e., the one to which it is assimilated] (*wa-tilka l-ṣūra al-ğismiyya tazūlu ʿinda qubūlihā hāḏihī l-ṣūra*). (*al-Kawn wa-l-fasād* 8, 145.3–8)[220]

The particularities of this passage need to be understood in its greater context, which we cannot presently discuss in detail. What is relevant, though, is that Avicenna cautiously describes how he thinks assimilation and digestion work. This assimilation either pertains to substances which are actually something else (e.g., bread) and only potentially that into which they are assimilated (e.g., blood and bone), or they are altogether potential. This second alternative may strike us as absurd, because, as Avicenna remarks, what is fully potential is prime matter, and it does not seem to happen that we eat and digest prime matter. The important point, however, is that *even if* it were purely potential, it would have to have a corporeal form, because otherwise the prime matter which is digested here would not even have subsistence, i.e., it would be nonexistent. So, it must have a corporeal form and be a substance. In the process of assimilation, then, the prime matter does not simply receive the form of blood or bone *in addition to* the corporeal form it already possesses, as would be the case if Avicenna were to adhere to the multiplicity of forms – no, even the bare matter first has to get rid of the corporeal form through which it subsists, before it can receive another form so as to be assimilated to the body that is nourished by it.

Thus, Avicenna's litmus test regarding the numerical commonality of form ultimately fails. The corporeal form of water does not remain when the water is transformed into earth. If form is not common in the sense of being numerically one in this particular case, how could it, then, be common universally in all cases, i.e., for all bodies. Consequently, form is only generically common. This also means that Avicenna adheres only to a limited extent to the idea of a second substrate as it is known from the Greek commentators on Aristotle. Although he argues that body is the result of a corporeal form and a non-corporeal matter, and although he uses terminology that is similar to Simplicius' τὸ σωματικὸν εἶδος, the "absolute body" in Avicenna does not serve as a substrate insofar as a substrate is considered to be something underlying something

220 cf. *al-Nafs* I.5, 32.6f.

else. The absolute body in Avicenna could only be said to underlie other accidental, or perhaps even substantial, qualifications if it were to exist as realised in the things. As has been shown, however, the corporeal form is not a separate form existing in matter but is a formal aspect that is a part of a complete species form, such as the form of "humanity" or the form of "water." What exists, therefore, are substances whose only substrate is prime matter, and it is in this prime matter that the species form inheres. There is no intermediate "second substrate" that could in any true sense of the word said to be "real," so that it could function in any true sense of the word as a "substrate."

Matter

However, what about matter? If *the Form* does not exist as a perfectly common principle, is there at least something like *the Matter*? Is there a single underlying prime mater that is the substrate of all things, as the analysis of the commonality of form may seem to suggest? Avicenna, once more, offers a test by which he intends to resolve the question. This time, he asks whether there is one single matter (*hayūlā wāḥida*), a numerically common material, for all corporeal things, i.e., for the heavenly unchanging bodies as well as for all those terrestrial ones under constant alteration?[221]

Avicenna's test is a particular application of a well known general puzzle posed by Aristotle as the tenth (or eleventh) ἀπορία in *Metaphysics* B.[222] There Aristotle asked whether the perishable and imperishable things share the same principles. Applying this question to the concept of matter, Alexander directly raised the question of whether the heavenly bodies consist of the same matter as the terrestrial ones.[223] On the one hand, if all bodies share the same kind of prime matter, then all bodies would seem to be equally perishable. On the other hand, if there are different kinds of prime matter, then these kinds would have to differ through some adjoining *differentia* and would no longer be simple but themselves composite. This, in turn, raises the original question

221 *al-Samāʿ al-ṭabīʿī* I.3, §2, 22.2. Apart from the historical context explained in the following analysis, Avicenna's discussion of the commonality of matter is, without doubt, akin to his important distinction between "genus" and "matter" in *al-Burhān* I.10 ≈ *al-Ilāhiyyāt* V.3 which, in turn, is a reaction to Ibn ʿAdī's *Šarḥ maʿānī maqālat al-Iskandar al-Afrūdīsī fī l-farq bayna al-ǧins wa-l-mādda*, commenting on Alexander's *Quaestiones*, q. II.28, whose discussion, again, has its roots in Aristotle's remarks in *Metaphysics* Δ.28, 1024b6–9 and Z.12, 1038a3–9; cf. Benevich, "The Priority of Natures against the Identity of Indiscernibles"; cf. also the interpretation in McGinnis, "Logic and Science," 173–178. That Alexander's discussion in *quaestio* II.28 provided one of the motivations for Avicenna's discussion of the commonality of matter is particularly borne out by the fact that Alexander, too, discusses the commonality of matter in this *quaestio* (esp. 78.11–25).

222 cf. *Met.* B.1, 996a2–4; B.4, 1000a5–1001a3; cf. also *Met.* K.2, 1060a27–36. It is the tenth puzzle discussed in book B, but it is the tenth or eleventh puzzled mentioned in the book's first chapter, depending on whether 995b20–25 is counted as a separate puzzle.

223 cf. Sorabji, *Matter, Space, and Motion*, 14f. The question is all the more interesting, as Aristotle himself has not given a clear view on whether the heavenly bodies consist of matter at all. Symptomatic in this regard is Aristotle's remark in *Metaphysics* H.4, 1044b7f.

again, as one can now ask whether the two kinds of composite matter share a single underlying non-composite prior matter.[224]

As in Avicenna's test about the commonality of form, the test now offered for matter *prima facie* does not really seem to be appropriate for answering the question.[225] Already Alexander's discussion showed that the question about whether the heavenly bodies consist of the same matter as the sublunary ones can easily, and perhaps even more naturally, be understood as a question about whether the bodies in the universe consist of the same *kind* of matter. Thus, the test seems to be concerned with generic, rather than numerical, commonality.

On a different note, the idea of a single and numerically one prime matter for all bodies could well be said to be an implausible, if not altogether insane, position to adhere to in the first place. Why should anyone think that the matter of the Sun is numerically identical with the matter of oneself, for example? An adequate analysis of Avicenna's discussion, thus, needs to achieve three things. It, first, needs to find a way to appreciate the seemingly implausible position of there being only one numerically single matter. Second, it needs to find a way that the test offered by Avicenna can, indeed, resolve the question. Finally, it needs to establish Avicenna's own opinion regarding the commonality of prime matter. The following discussion will establish these three points in this order.

The history of Greek philosophy witnessed different strategies for approaching the question raised by Alexander about whether or not the heavenly bodies have the same matter as the sublunary ones. It is apparent that the key aspect of the question lies in the fact that the heavens are usually seen to be incorruptible and unchangeable, whereas the natural world below the moon is precisely characterised by coming-to-be and change. At the same time, though, matter is said to be the underlying subject of all physical reality. How, then, is the fundamentally different behaviour of the two realms to be explained if they together share the same underlying material principle?

For Philoponus, the situation is rather convenient, as he came to deny the belief that the heavenly realm is characterised by incorruptibility anyway. Rejecting the Aristotelian idea of a divine and eternal fifth element, Philoponus simply "accepted the logic of Alexander's reasoning with pleasure," as Sorabji put it, and endorsed the view that, indeed, all bodies are equally perishable, because they are equally composed of the same materials.[226] For him, there is only one kind of matter which is the underlying substate for the four elements, so that all corporeal things consist of a certain mixture of the very same elements being *per se* equally corruptible. This position had the further advantage of being in harmony with Plato's position. As Philoponus writes in his *De aeternitate mundi contra Proclum*, "Plato clearly said that the celestial bodies

224 cf. Alexander of Aphrodisias, *Quaestiones*, q. I.15; cf. also q. I.10.

225 q.v. fn. 183 above, 166.

226 Sorabji, *Matter, Space, and Motion*, 15; cf. Philoponus' position *apud Simplicium*, *In Cael.*, 135.21–23; cf. also M. Rashed, "The Problem of the Composition of the Heavens."

are mostly constituted out of fire," whereas the position of Aristotle, who "is trying to deny [that], does not seem to me to have any force."[227] Thus, in Philoponus, we find someone who argues that there is one kind of matter throughout the universe, so that there is no distinction in terms of corruptibility and aptitude for change between the respective realms above and below the moon. Whether or not the commonality in kind for Philoponus also implies a commonality in number is not clear. Plato, at any rate, could be read along these lines, as I shall mention shortly.

In contrast to Philoponus, most other philosophers are interested in keeping this distinction between the celestial and the terrestrial realms. Alexander, for example, defends the corporeal simplicity of the heavenly bodies with a surprising move: he argues that they lack a material substrate altogether.[228] The forms of the heavenly bodies are not enmattered, i.e., they do not have a material substrate, and so are not subject to change and corruption. Alexander's position appears to have had an influence on Averroes' understanding of the immaterial nature of celestial bodies. At any rate, Averroes reports Alexander's position in his middle commentary on *De caelo*, referring to Alexander's comments on *Metaphysics* Λ.[229] According to the evidence found in Averroes, Themistius (d. ~ 385) shared Alexander's position. What is more, Abū Bišr Mattā ibn Yūnus (d. 328/940) and his disciple al-Fārābī likewise defend a fundamental difference between the celestial and the terrestrial realm. Abū Bišr claims that matter is that which is "susceptible to affection" (*yaqbalu al-ta'ṯīr*), so that the Sun – and, as may be assumed, the other celestial bodies, too – cannot be said to have matter (*laysa lahū hayūlā*), even though he admits that it must have something similar to matter (*lāki-*

227 Philoponus, *De aeternitate mundi contra Proclum* XIII.14, 517.7–11, tr. by Wilberding. Theophrastus, Aristotle's successor as the head of the Lyceum, likewise already emphasised the importance of fire as involved in the composition of the celestial bodies and, generally, as the active principle within the dynamics of the universe. In fact, he regarded the universe as a single unified system to be explained by the same set of rules, governing both celestial and terrestrial phenomena. This is evinced by his conviction that meteorological matters clearly cross any assumed boundary between the celestial and the terrestrial realm as well as from his understanding of Aristotle's *De caelo* as a treatise that investigates both realms together, as was reported by Simplicius *via* Alexander; cf. frgms. 143 and 169 in Theophrastus, *Sources for his Life, Writings, Thought and Influence*, 196 and 334, reported by Simplicius in his commentaries *In Phys.*, 20.17–26, and *In Cael.*, 1.8–10, respectively; cf. also Steinmetz, *Die Physik des Theophrastos von Eresos*, esp. 149f., 158–168. Theophrastus' position regarding celestial matter is less clear. It may well be, as Steinmetz forcefully argues, that Theophrastus rejected aether as the eternal fifth element of which the celestial bodies are composed and, instead, argued for (pure) fire to constitute their substance. Unlike Philoponus, however, Theophrastus regarded the universe as eternal nonetheless.

228 cf. Alexander of Aphrodisias, *In Met.*, 22.2–3, 169.18–19, 375.37–376.1; *De mixtione* 13, 229.6–9; cf. also Alexander's remarks in his discussion of the puzzle raised in *Metaphysics* B (*In Met.*, 223.2–5); cf. further Sorabji, *Matter, Space, and Motion*, fn. 69, 42; Falcon, *Aristotle and the Science of Nature*, 107f.

229 cf. Averroes, *Talḫīṣ al-Samā' wa-l-'ālam*, 183.12–17, translated in Janos, *Method, Structure, and Development in al-Fārābī's Cosmology*, 214; cf. Endreß, "Averroes' *De Caelo*," 36f., referring to a similar discussion in Alexander's *Maqāla fī l-qawl fī mabādi' al-kull*.

nna lahū šibh bi-l-hayūlā).[230] In some of al-Fārābī's works, then, we find him arguing that the sublunary realm is both characterised by change and associated with matter, whereas the supralunary realm is eternal and unchanging due to its association with a kind of matter that is entirely unlike the matter of the perishable sublunary realm. In his *Mabādiʾ ārāʾ ahl al-madīna al-fāḍila* and his *al-Siyāsa al-madaniyya* (a. k. a. *Mabādiʾ al-mawǧūdāt)*, however, he emphasises the immateriality of the heavenly bodies altogether, thus contrasting their matterless eternity with the composite nature of the entire sublunary realm.[231] With Alexander, Themistius, Abū Bišr, al-Fārābī, and Averroes, then, we find some philosophers who were interested in a fundamental distinction between the two realms and who achieved this distinction by banishing matter from the celestial realm altogether.

Finally there is the group of those thinkers who both regarded matter as the substrate for all kinds of bodies, while at the same time trying to defend the fundamental difference between the heavenly and the sublunary realm. It is among the thinkers in this group that we shall find the claim that there is a single and numerically one matter for all corporeal things – at least this is what Plotinus seems to have argued. For Plotinus, matter is generated from the activity of soul. When soul turns to itself, i.e., away from the One and away from reality, it walks towards non-existence and makes (ποιεῖ) an image of itself, something which is non-existent and indefinite, unintelligent and dark, without reason and far away from reality. This is matter, into which soul sinks.[232] Moreover, it is also the matter for the entire sensible cosmos, i.e., for both celestial and terrestrial bodies. The reason for why bodies below the moon are, nonetheless, subject to change and corruption, whereas their celestial counterparts are not, is explained through the claim that the sublunary souls were unable to master their matter as effectively as (οὐχ ὁμοίως κρατοῖτο ... ὡς) the celestial souls.[233] What explains the celestial incorruptibility, then, is not a difference in matter but a different quality of control on behalf of the soul upon the matter.

So far, all this would be in line with a matter that is common in kind only.[234] Yet, Plotinus' account of matter also heavily relies on the notion of impassibility (ἀπάθεια). Matter is entirely impassive and, as such, remains unaffected by any mastering of soul

230 Abū Bišr's comment in Aristotle, *al-Ṭabīʿa* II.7, 139.7–10.

231 cf. Janos, *Method, Structure, and Development in al-Fārābī's Cosmology*, 214f., where Janos also quotes from Averroes' commentary on Aristotle's *De caelo*. In explaining the different views that al-Fārābī held in his works, Janos argues for a developmental account according to which al-Fārābī first upheld, but later abandoned, the view that the celestial bodies were composites of matter and form; cf. Janos, *Method, Structure, and Development in al-Fārābī's Cosmology*, ch. 3, esp. 215–222; on the relation between Abū Bišr and al-Fārābī, cf. Janos, "Active Nature and Other Striking Features," 145–147.

232 *Enn.* III.9.3, 7–16; cf. *Enn.* III.4.1. I follow the interpretation of O'Brien, in particular in its revised form that was put forth in a recent series of articles with the title"Plotinus on the Making of Matter" in response to earlier challenges to his reading, esp. by Phillips, "Plotinus on the Generation of Matter."

233 *Enn.* II.1.5, 8–14; cf. also James Wilberding's comments in *Plotinus' Cosmology*.

234 Incidentally, it is so far, in its result, also close to Avicenna's account, as will be seen.

or any inherence of form. Plotinus explicitly describes matter as a "non-participant" (μὴ μετέχον) and asks how such a thing could nonetheless participate and, thus, bear a form or a soul. His answer is that it is a mere illusion (ἐφαντάσθη) that there is such an interaction or participation, whereas matter in reality does not perceive anything and remains entirely unaffected.[235] The matter of the sensible cosmos is, in fact, a decorated corpse (νεκρὸν κεκοσμημένον) and its shape is just a phantom (εἴδωλον).[236] A matter which remains impassible is not in any true sense of the word differentiated by forms inhering in it. There are merely different forms inhering in one and the same matter, so that all we get is an underlying barely existent, negative, evil, and indefinite matter which, being the result of the activity of soul, is common to all things in the strong numerical sense.

Moreover, in this conception, Plotinus certainly incorporates several aspects of Plato's characterisation of matter. Plato has described matter or space (χώρα) as the "wetnurse of becoming" (γενέσεως τιθήνην), as a "receptacle" (ὑποδοχήν) wherein things enter (εἰσιόντα), and as a "malleable stuff" (ἐκμαγεῖον) which is shaped by things (διασχηματιζόμενον).[237] Although there is, among scholars, no consensus about how we should understand Plato's account of the receptacle, it can be interpreted as something underlying which is through and through one, and in which things and forms can come to appear or inhere without it itself undergoing much of a transformation.[238] Consequently, Avicenna's discussion of whether or not matter is common to all bodies in the strong numerical sense can be appreciated more fully, when we regard it as a reaction to such a Platonist conception of matter. Thus, his discussion has a distinctive Platonic ring to it, in much the same way as his discussion of the commonality of form had.[239]

It appears that the view of there being only one single prime matter which is equally shared by all natural things is by no means implausible. To the contrary, given certain metaphysical commitments, in particular about the impassibility of matter (as in Plotinus) or about the nature of the receptacle (as in Plato), it emerges as a viable, even reasonable, position.

What is more, there is also yet another sense in which matter can be said to be numerically one for all bodies. There are some Neoplatonists who take matter as numerically common insofar as it is the singular product of a single source. Just as Plotinus, Porphyry (d. ~ 305) regards matter as the product of soul, whereas Proclus (and prob-

235 *Enn.* III.6.14, 21–28.

236 *Enn.* II.4.5, 16–22.

237 *Tim.* 52d4f., 49a5f., 51a5, 50c2–6.

238 For various was to interpret Plato's concept of χώρα, cf. Algra, *Concepts of Space in Greek Thought*, ch. 3; cf. also the recent discussion in Sattler, "A Likely Account of Necessity."

239 q.v. above, 175.

ably also Simplicius) sees the unlimitedness of the One as the source of all matter.[240] So, for them, matter is *in principle* one in number, because it originated from one single source in one single act as one single matter. Irrespective of whether and how this single matter is diversified later on, the idea of a matter being numerically one because of its procession from one single source is the key for understanding Avicenna's test case for the commonality of matter. If the matter of two things proceeded from two distinct sources, then these two things simply cannot share in a matter that is one and the same, i.e., numerically common to both of them. Consequently, if one were to demonstrate that the matter of the heavens originated from a different source than the matter of the sublunary realm, then this would be a sufficient reason to reject the idea of a matter that is numerically common to all bodies. Thus, if we understand Avicenna's question of whether all bodies have the same matter as a question about whether the matter for all bodies originated from one or more sources, then we can realise how his question, indeed, can constitute a test case for the commonality of matter. Should it turn out that the matter of the celestial bodies originated from a different source than the matter of the sublunary bodies, i.e., if they do *not* have a common source as the just-mentioned Neoplatonists maintained, then matter also cannot be common in the numerical sense.

Incidentally, this understanding of Avicenna's test about the commonality of *matter* is entirely analogous to how, as I have shown above, one should conceive of Avicenna's test for the commonality of *form*: there, Avicenna suggested to answer the bigger question about the commonality by solving a smaller question about the multiplicity of forms, because the denial of the multiplicity-thesis entails the denial of a form that is numerically common. Here, in the case of matter, a demonstration of the fact that sublunary matter has a different source than supralunary matter entails the denial of a numerically one matter shared by all bodies. So, if we can determine Avicenna's position about the generation of supralunary and sublunary matter, then the bigger, and more relevant, issue about the commonality of matter can be solved as well.

This, then, brings us to the third point: what, in fact, is Avicenna's position about the generation of matter? Does all matter proceed from one and the same source or are there different sources for numerically different matters? Moreover, if there are different sources, is all matter still one in kind, i.e., at least common in the generic sense? Again, if that would turn out to be the case, then how does Avicenna account

240 For Porphyry, cf. the long quotation provided by Proclus in his commentary on the *Timaeus* (*In Tim.* I, 439.29–440.15) as well as Adamson's remarks on that quotation in "One of a Kind," 348–350. For Proclus, cf. *Institutio theologica*, §92; *Theologia Platonica*, III, 32.15–23; cf. also the remarks by Opsomer in "Proclus vs Plotinus on Matter (*De mal. subs.* 30-7)," esp. 173f., referring to de Haas, *John Philoponus' New Definition of Prime Matter*, fn. 93, 80f. According to a passage in Proclus' *In Tim.*, it is more precisely universal nature which brings about matter through its participation in the One; cf. *In Tim.* I, 386.16–18; cf. also Lernould, "Nature in Proclus," 97f. For Simplicius, cf. *In Cael.*, 135.23–25 as well as the remarks by Sorabji in *Matter, Space, and Motion*, 15.

for the incorruptibility of the celestial bodies or does he, perhaps, ultimately agree with Philoponus that all body is equally corruptible?

Unfortunately, Avicenna's own position is somewhat difficult to determine on the basis of his *al-Samāʿ al-ṭabīʿī*, and there is, again, no scholarly consensus on the question. In fact, the discussion at times seems to mingle two separate issues. Above we have seen Stone providing a good argument for why Avicenna should not be considered an adherent to the multiplicity-thesis. Later in his article, Stone argues that the heavenly bodies, just like their terrestrial counterparts, have a corporeal form, for otherwise they could not be bodies at all. This also means that they are, in principle, just as corruptible as terrestrial bodies, because they are principally composed of the same components, viz., matter and form. According to Stone, "[t]he same argument ... which establishes that celestial and sublunar bodies share a common form, also serves to show that they have a common matter."[241] In order to confirm his thesis, Stone quotes a passage from *al-Samāʿ al-ṭabīʿī* I.3 but, for some reason, ends his quotation before Avicenna declares that what he just said is "far-fetched (*baʿīd*) in light of what will become clear later."[242] The situation in Stone is already unclear to some degree, because we have just seen that the denial of the multiplicity-thesis entails the denial of form being numerically common. So, when Stone emphasises that all bodies "share a common form" as well as "a common matter," it is clear, in light of Stone's argument for Avicenna's denial of the multiplicity-thesis, that the adjective "common" in his expression of "common form" must be taken in the *generic* sense of commonality, whereas Stone's reference to the "common matter" relies on an argument which Avicenna uses in discussing why matter could be taken to be "common" in the *numerical* sense. Thus, the analogy drawn by Stone between a "common form" and a "common matter" is misleading, as he uses the term "common" in an equivocal manner.

---

241 A. D. Stone, "Simplicius and Avicenna on the Essential Corporeity of Material Substance," 108.
242 *al-Samāʿ al-ṭabīʿī* I.3, §2, 22.8f., tr. by McGinnis, modified: *fa-in kāna ka-ḏālika – wa-baʿīd [!] an yakūna ka-ḏālika ʿalā mā sayataḍḍaḥu baʿda – fa-sayakūnu ḥīnaʾiḏin hayūlā muštarak bi-hāḏā l-waǧh.* Perhaps Stone either did not understand the adjective *baʿīd* or was confused by Dominicus Gundisalvi's Latin translation, in which we find the following: *Cum ergo sic fuerit (immo postquam [!] sic est, sicut postea apparebit), tunc erit hyle communis secundum hunc modum.* (For the identification of Gundisalvi as the translator of the majority of Avicenna's *al-Samāʿ al-ṭabīʿī* from Arabic into Latin, cf. now Hasse and Büttner, "Notes on Anonymous Twelfth-Century Translations of Philosophical Texts.") It seems that Gundisalvi translated the Arabic *baʿīd* through a hendiadys using both *immo* and *postquam*, hoping that a sensible reader would be able to gather the correct meaning. That this hope was, at least, partly in vain (or perhaps not at all) is indicated by the fact that Thomas' disciple Aegidius Romanus explicitly refers to the first book of Avicenna's *al-Samāʿ al-ṭabīʿī* in support of the view that the heavenly bodies are incorruptible not because of a special kind of matter – in fact, "the matter is essentially the same here and there," as Aegidius writes – but because the supralunary, as opposed to the sublunary, forms do not have a contrary; cf. Grant, "Celestial Matter," fn. 51, 170. This, in fact, harmonises well with Avicenna's own position, as we shall see, but it can only be derived from the text of *al-Samāʿ al-ṭabīʿī* by disregarding, neglecting, or misunderstanding the force of the adjective *baʿīd*.

This also means that we need to distinguish between two questions. On the one hand, Avicenna is well-known for having argued that all bodies, sublunary and supralunary bodies alike, are composed of matter and form. Among his reasons for this is the fact that all of them are corporeal and corporeality comes about through a form inhering in matter. Wolfson, for example, remarked that for Avicenna, as well as Maimonides, "the distinction of matter and form is to be found in all material substance, translunar as well as sublunar. The celestial substance, known as the fifth element, is … composed of matter and form as are the four sublunar elements."[243] Wolfson contrasts this position with the view put forth by Averroes, for whom the heavenly bodies are not hylomorphic compounds of matter and form. Hyman, in a similar way, lists in his introduction to Averroes' treatise *De substantia orbis* the many differences between terrestrial and celestial matter which Averroes had worked out, and claims that Avicenna has been "insisting on the similarity between celestial and terrestrial substances."[244] Yet, the fact that for Avicenna, celestial as well as terrestrial bodies are composites of matter and form does not also mean that, regarding form, they all share the same numerically one corporeal form, but that they all independently have a corporeal form. Regarding matter, then, saying that all bodies have matter does not mean that they all share the same numerically one matter, but that they all have their independent matters. So, while it is clear that Avicenna maintains that *all* corporeal reality consists of form and matter, it is less clear whether he would say that they all consist of *one and the same* form and matter. These are two separate issues which require separate answers. Moreover, we have also seen that numerical oneness is the characteristic feature of the first sense of commonality and Avicenna emphasises this once more when he, in his discussion of the commonality of matter, raises the question of whether there is one single matter (*hayūlā wāḥida*) that is the common material for all corporeal things, i.e., in both the heavens and the terrestrial realm.[245]

Recently, Damien Janos sought to contrast al-Fārābī's view with that of "Ibn Sīnā and Ibn Rushd [who] develop a theory whereby prime matter and the corporeal form are at the basis of all corporeal existents, including the celestial bodies."[246] As confirmation, Janos refers to Stone's article as well as to Wolfson's and Hyman's studies. While it is not clear how Janos' understanding of Averroes could derive from Wolfson's and Hyman's studies, it is clear that he tries to characterise al-Fārābī as an exception to the general view that there is no fundamental difference between heavenly and terrestrial bodies. As already mentioned, Janos argues that al-Fārābī's position consisted in either denying matter of celestial bodies altogether or by attributing to them a special kind of matter, so that either way the heavens are fundamentally different from sublunary bodies insofar as they, and only they, are essentially incorruptible. So, while al-Fārābī's and Avicenna's

---

243 Wolfson in Crescas, *Crescas' Critique of Aristotle*, 103.

244 Averroes, *De substantia orbis*, 33.

245 *al-Samāʿ al-ṭabīʿī* I.3, §2, 22.2.

246 Janos, *Method, Structure, and Development in al-Fārābī's Cosmology*, 232.

accounts differ insofar as Avicenna, but not al-Fārābī, allows for all bodies to consist of matter and form, it is, nonetheless, clear that al-Fārābī and Avicenna agree in that there is a fundamental distinction between the sublunary realm (which is characterised by coming-to-be, perishing, change, and rectilinear motion) and the supralunary realm (which is eternal, unchanging, and engaging in circular motion).[247] Yet, it still remains unclear how, on Avicenna's theory, the latter claim about the incorruptibility of the heavens relates to, and harmonises with, the former about the assumed, even though still "far-fetched," commonality of matter.

So, let us no turn to the test case that Avicenna devises for the question about the commonality of matter. This test case is introduced with the observation that some bodies are susceptible to coming-to-be and perishing (*qābila li-l-kawn wa-l-fasād*), whereas some are not. Avicenna continues as follows:

فإذا كان كذلك لم يكن لها هيولى مشتركة على النحو الأوّل من النحوين المذكورين فإنّه لا يكون هيولى واحدة تارةً تقبل صورة الكائنات الفاسدة وتارةً تقبل صورة ما لا يفسد في طباعه ولا له كون هيولانى فإنّ ذلك مستحيل ... اللهمّ إلّا أن يُجعل طبيعة الموضوع التي لصورة ما لا يفسد والموضوع لصورة ما يفسد طبيعة واحدة في نفسها صالحة لقبول كلّ صورة إلّا أنّ ما لا يفسد قد عرض أن قارنته الصورة التي لا ضد لها، فيكون السبب في أنّها لا تكون ولا تفسد من جهة صورتها المانعة لمادّتها عمّا في طباعها لا من جهة المادّة المطبوعة. فإن كان كذلك وبعيد أن يكون كذلك على ما سيتّضح بعد فسيكون حينئذ هيولى مشتركة بهذا الوجه.

If it is like this [sc. that some bodies are imperishable, while others are not], then there is no matter common in the first of the two aforementioned ways[248] [i.e., the numerical sense], for there is no single matter (*hayūlā wāḥida*) which sometimes is susceptible to the corruptible form of things that come-to-be, while sometimes being susceptible to the form of what neither corrupts in its nature nor has a material coming-to-be, for that is impossible (*fa-inna ḏālika mustaḥīl*) ... [Thus, matter is not numerically common to all natural things] unless (*'allāhumma 'illā*) the nature of the subject which belongs to some form that does not corrupt and the subject belonging to some form that does corrupt is made[249] a single nature which in itself is suited for receiving any form, except that what does not corrupt[250] happened to have been conjoined to a form which has no contrary, and so the cause for [the fact] that it neither comes-to-be nor passes away is due to its form preventing the matter from what is in its [sc. the matter's] nature, not[251] due to the somehow disposed matter.[252] So, if it is like this – and it is far-fetched (*ba'īd*) that it is like this in light of what will become clear later – then, in this case, there would be a matter common in this way. (*al-Samā' al-ṭabī'ī* I.3, §2, 22.1–9)

247 This is argued for, from a different perspective, in Avicenna's *al-Samā' wa-l-'ālam* 2–3.

248 Reading *al-naḥwayn al-maḏkūrayn* with Mss. Leiden or. 4 and or. 84 as well as Zāyid for *al-naḥwayn* in McGinnis and Āl Yāsīn.

249 Reading *yuǧ'ala* with Ms. Leiden or. 84 for *naǧ'ala* in McGinnis and Āl Yāsīn.

250 Reading *mā lā yafsudu* with Mss. Leiden or. 4 and or. 84 as well as McGinnis and Āl Yāsīn for *mā yafsudu* in Zāyid.

251 Reading *lā* with Mss. Leiden or. 4 and or. 84 as well as McGinnis and Āl Yāsīn for *illā* in Zāyid.

252 Suggesting to read *al-mādda al-maṭbū'a* against *al-mādda al-muṭāwi'a* in Mss. Leiden or. 4 and or. 84 as well as Zāyid, McGinnis, and Āl Yāsīn.

The thrust of this argument is clear. If there are both kinds of things, i.e., those which are susceptible to coming-to-be and perishing as well as those which are not, then there cannot be a single matter underlying both kinds of things, because such a matter would as such both be and not be susceptible to coming-to-be and perishing. Since this, however, is simply impossible (*fa-inna ḏālika mustaḥīl*), there is no single matter which is numerically common and shared by all natural things. This first part of the passage suggests that the difference between things that come-to-be and things that do not must be due to a difference in their matter (as opposed to their form). In a second step, Avicenna focuses on a possible alternative explanation which accounts for the difference between perishable and imperishable things not through a difference in their matter but through a difference in their form. Thus, there *could* be one single matter shared by both perishable and imperishable things, if things of the latter category, but not those of the former, were conjoined to an imperishable form, i.e., to a form that has no contrary. If that were the case, then "there would be a matter common in this way." All this is fairly easy to comprehend.

What is troubling here is that Avicenna claims that this alternative explanation is "far-fetched" or "unlikely" (*baʿīd*), as he will explain to us later. The reason for why this is troubling is twofold: first, it is, as so often, unclear what passages he is referring to, so that we are unable to verify Avicenna's position on the question about the commonality of matter through an independent reading of the account he here promises to give elsewhere. Yet, one might assume that what Avicenna tells us here is sufficient, for he makes it unmistakably clear that he deems the alternative interpretation "far-fetched" and "unlikely." This means that Avicenna himself tells us that there is, in fact, no numerically common material, because the imperishable nature of the heavenly bodies is actually not due to their imperishable form, which would have been such as to have no contrary, so that we might infer that it is, indeed, due to a difference in their matter as compared to the matter of the sublunary bodies. Unfortunately, however, this is in direct contradiction to what he tells us in other places, where his opinion is precisely this: the heavenly bodies consist of matter and a form, and it is this form which prevents the matter from taking on a different form, thus rendering the heavenly bodies incorruptible. This is made clear, for example, in a passage from Avicenna's *al-Nağāt* which is almost identical to a passage in his *al-Ilāhiyyāt*:

وهذا بيّن وأيضاً فإنّه إمّا أن يكون غير قابل للتشكيلات والتفصيلات كالفلك فيكون لصورة ما صار كذلك لأنّه بما هو جسم قابل لها وإمّا أن يكون قابلها بسهولة أو بعسر وأيش كان فهو على إحدى الصور المذكورة في الطبيعيات.

This [that the matter of bodies is not the source of any positive characteristic] is clear also, for either it [sc. the body] is not susceptible to acts of forming and dividing (*ġayr qābil li-l-taškīlāt wa-l-tafṣīlāt*) like the sphere (*ka-l-falak*),[253] and so it is because of some form [that] it became such – since insofar as it is a body it is susceptible to these, being susceptible to these[254] either with

253 The corresponding passage in Avicenna's *al-Ilāhiyyāt* omits the reference to the sphere.

254 Suggesting to read *qābilahā* for *qābilahumā* in Fakhry, ʿUmayra, al-Kurdī, and Dānešpažūh.

> ease or with difficulty. Whatever it may be,[255] then, it is one of the forms mentioned in natural philosophy. (*al-Naǧāt* IV.1.7, 508.12–509.3 ≈ *al-Ilāhiyyāt* II.3, §16, 78.17–79.3)[256]

Before this passage, Avicenna has explained the phenomenon of rarefaction and condensation (*al-taḫalḫul wa-l-takāṯuf*) through the fact that matter can be smaller or greater depending on certain characteristics that are not due to matter itself but to the forms inhering in it, be that substantial or accidental forms.[257] Likewise, a body does not have a natural place due to its matter. In fact, it does not even have this place due to its being a body but due to its being a *specific* body.[258] These and all other characterisations are due to forms that matter is merely capable of receiving. Analogously, matter is also not accountable for a body's capacity – or incapacity – for any sort of change, including division which, as we have seen, results in substantial change. If, then, a body lacks the capacity to undergo change and alteration, such as in the case of the celestial sphere, this lack is not due to its matter but due to the form inhering in its matter. Thus, all bodies may very well have the same matter, for the only matter that exists is the one which is nothing but a passive underlying thing for forms to inhere.

Even though the passage in *al-Ilāhiyyāt* which corresponds to the above quote from *al-Naǧāt* omits any reference to the sphere, Avicenna elsewhere in *al-Ilāhiyyāt* remarks the following:

> وثانياً أنّ طبيعة الجسمية التي لها لا يكون مستحيلاً عليها ذلك وإنّما يستحيل ذلك عليها من حيث صورة تنوّعها ونحن لا نمنع ذلك ويجوز أن يقارن الجسمية شيء يجعل ذلك الجسم قائماً نوعاً لا يقبل القسمة ولا الإتّصال بغيره وهذا قولنا في الفلك.
>
> Second, the nature of corporeality which belongs to them [sc. the indivisible atoms] is not what makes that [sc. division] impossible for them; that is only impossible for them insofar as the form specifies them – and we do not oppose that, as it is possible that something is conjoined to corporeality which makes that body subsistent as a species which is not susceptible to division (*naw'an lā yaqbalu al-qisma*) nor to continuity through something else, and this is what we assert about the sphere. (*al-Ilāhiyyāt* II.2, §17, 66.9–13)

Even though this passage is taken from a dialectical context in which Avicenna discusses critically the indivisibility of atoms, he reveals that he is not at all opposed to the very idea of indivisible bodies, for even he, despite being a stout adversary of atomism, allows for indivisible bodies, because the spheres are such. The spheres are physically indivisible not on account of their corporeality (or their matter) but on account of their form, which renders them subsistent as "a species which is not susceptible to division." The heavenly bodies, then, do not suffer change, as their forms preclude any capacity

---

255 Reading *wa-'ayša* (a contraction of *wa-ayy šay'*) with Dānešpažūh for *wa-ayyan mā* in Fakhry, 'Umayra, and al-Kurdī. The corresponding passage in Avicenna's *al-Ilāhiyyāt* reads *wa-kayfa mā*.
256 cf. *Dānešnāme-ye 'Alā'ī* II.8, 27.10–13.
257 The discussion, again, corresponds to the material in *al-Ilāhiyyāt* II.3, §§13–15, 77.8–78.14.
258 q.v. below, 351ff.

or aptitude to undergo change, which they naturally would have on account of their material and corporeal nature.

The same doctrine, is also put forth by Avicenna in his *al-Išārāt wa-l-tanbīhāt*:

> والهيولى قد لا تخلو أيضاً عن صور أخر وكيف ولا بدّ من أن يكون إمّا مع صورة توجِب قبول الانفكاك والالتئام والتشكّل بسهولة أو بعسر أو مع صورة توجِب امتناع قبول تلك وكلّ ذلك غير الجرمية وكذلك لا بدّ له من استحقاق مكان خاصّ أو وضع خاصّ متعيّنين وكلّ ذلك غير مقتضى الجرمية العامّة المشتركة فيها.
>
> Matter may also not be free from other forms – and how [could it be]? There is no escape from its being either with a form that necessitates the reception of fragmentation, conjunction, and shaping with ease or with difficulty, or with a form that necessitates the impossibility of that reception (*imtināʿ qubūl tilka*). All of this, however, is different from corporeality.[259] Likewise, there is no escape [for body] from deservedly having a specific place or specific position, both of which are particular [to it]. None of this is required by the shared common corporeality. (*al-Išārāt wa-l-tanbīhāt* II.1.17, 98.8–13)[260]

Again, Avicenna makes bodies essentially susceptible to change and division but allows for cases in which this capacity is prevented by a specific form which renders any such change impossible. It is fair to assume that here, too, Avicenna has in mind the heavenly bodies.

Finally, there is also an intriguing detail in Avicenna's *al-Ḥikma al-mašriqiyya*. The first chapter of the section on natural philosophy is devoted to the notion of matter. This chapter is, in its entirety, a compilation of quotations from *al-Samāʿ al-ṭabīʿī* I.2, I.3, and I.10. There is only one single sentence that is new. This new sentence follows upon a quotation from *al-Samāʿ al-ṭabīʿī* I.2, in which Avicenna states that with regard to the universal and absolute nature of matter "it is as if it (*ka-innahā*) is a genus for two species" (*ǧins li-nawʿayn*), because matter can receive two different specific kinds of forms after being constituted by the corporeal form as the absolute body.[261] Thereupon, he adds a new sentence, in order to specify what these two so-called "species" of material existents are:

> فأحد النوعين يختصّ بقبول صورة الأفلاك والكواكب والثاني يختصّ بقبول صور الكائنات والفاسدات.
>
> One of the two "species" is marked by its reception of the form of the spheres and planets, and the second is marked by its reception of the forms of the generable and corruptible things. (*al-Ḥikma al-mašriqiyya* III.1, 4.3f.)

Again, it is the apparently incorruptible forms of the celestial bodies that are contrasted with the explicitly corruptible forms of the sublunary bodies that inhere equally in

---

259 Reading *ġayr al-ǧirmiyya* with Forget for *ġayr muqtaḍā l-ǧirmiyya* in Dunyā.

260 It is to be noted that in his *al-Išārāt wa-l-tanbīhāt*, Avicenna often uses *girm* as a synonym for *ǧism* ("body"), whereas in his other works, he usually reserves *ǧirm* for celestial bodies. Thus, his use of *ǧirm* in this passage does not have a bearing on whether, or if so in what way, he refers to celestial bodies.

261 *al-Ḥikma al-mašriqiyya* III.1, 4.1 = *al-Samāʿ al-ṭabīʿī* I.2, §4, 14.6.

one and the same kind of matter, so that the same matter could be regarded as the underlying genus for two types of material existents: incorruptible and corruptible bodies. Afterwards, Avicenna continues with quoting from *al-Samāʿ al-ṭabīʿī* I.2, stating that matter is equally common to all forms whatsoever.[262] That is to say, the above new sentence is an interjection that interrupts what otherwise would have been continuous quotation from *al-Samāʿ al-ṭabīʿī*, apparently added to clarify that matter is, indeed, one in kind for all bodies.[263]

All this, and in particular the last passage from *al-Ḥikma al-mašriqiyya* together with the information that its chapter on matter is nothing but a compilation of quotations from *al-Samāʿ al-ṭabīʿī*, confronts us with the difficult situation that in his *al-Samāʿ al-ṭabīʿī*, Avicenna explicitly calls a certain philosophical position "far-fetched" or "unlikely," which he elsewhere, and consistently in several works, maintains. One easy solution is to regard the interjection *wa-baʿīd an yakūna ka-ḏālika ʿalā mā sayataḍḍaḥu baʿda* – and an interjection is what it is – to originally have been a marginal note which found its way into the text. Another solution would be to take the adjective *baʿīd* not as denying the idea about form being the cause for the incapacity of the heavenly bodies to undergo change but as denying that this by itself inevitably renders matter common in the numerical sense. Yet another solution would be to allow Avicenna to have changed his mind or, while writing *al-Samāʿ al-ṭabīʿī*, not even to have yet made up his mind on the question at hand. Finally, one might try to think that Avicenna originally wrote a word different from *baʿīd* which subsequently was corrupted during the transmission of the text. All four attempts to resolve the tension are dissatisfying, however. For one thing, the text is very explicit about what he is denying and about the fact the Avicenna is in fact denying it, as opposed to leaving the question open. Moreover, solutions about the assumption of marginal notes and textual corruption are always easy to make but, in the current state of research, difficult to prove.[264]

---

262 *al-Ḥikma al-mašriqiyya* III.1, 4.1 ≈ *al-Samāʿ al-ṭabīʿī* I.2, §4, 14.7.

263 All this conforms well to another passage at the end of the same chapter in *al-Ḥikma al-mašriqiyya*. There, after a long quotation from *al-Samāʿ al-ṭabīʿī* I.10, Avicenna returns to drawing on chapter I.3 and writes that "this common nature is something resulting from absolute creation" (*hāḏihī l-ṭabīʿa al-muštaraka mutaʿalliqa bi-l-ibdāʿ*; *al-Ḥikma al-mašriqiyya* III.1, 5.16 ≈ *al-Samāʿ al-ṭabīʿī* I.3, §2, 22.9f.). The reason that this is illuminating is that this passage from *al-Samāʿ al-ṭabīʿī* I.3 is the sentence that immediately follows upon the central passage of this discussion in which Avicenna states that it would be "far-fetched" if there would be a "matter common in this way," i.e., common to both incorruptible and corruptible bodies. Apparently, while this was a worry within the context of *al-Samāʿ al-ṭabīʿī*, here in *al-Ḥikma al-mašriqiyya*, Avicenna dismisses the worry altogether and merely picks up the conclusion that a "matter common in this way" – i.e., "this common nature" (*hāḏihī l-ṭabīʿa al-muštaraka*) – does, indeed, exist and came-to-be through "absolute creation" (*bi-l-ibdāʿ*). Thus, in *al-Ḥikma al-mašriqiyya*, Avicenna discusses matter as if this entire problem was not there, and he does so by compiling his account from various passages in *al-Samāʿ al-ṭabīʿī*, which is at least suggestive that his account in *al-Samāʿ al-ṭabīʿī* actually conforms with the account he later presents in *al-Ḥikma al-mašriqiyya*.

264 For what it is worth, neither the two manuscripts from Leiden nor any of the three editions of the Arabic text I am using indicate anything in this direction.

This tension cannot be solved and must remain a puzzle. What can be resolved, however, is whether Avicenna thinks that matter is numerically common. There are two answers to this question. The first is that if Avicenna, at least while writing the first book of his *al-Samāʿ al-ṭabīʿī*, really deems it "far-fetched" that the incorruptibility of the heavenly bodies is due to their form, then he must take it as being due to their matter. Thus, the matter of the celestial bodies is fundamentally different from the matter of the sublunary bodies. Since no single matter can be susceptible to change at one time and not susceptible to change at another, we must conclude that on this view matter cannot be common as a numerically one entity, for there are clearly two kinds of matters in the universe.[265] Therefore, according to this first answer, matter fails the test Avicenna devised for determining whether it is common in the numerical sense. In other words, if we follow the actual wording in the first book of *al-Samāʿ al-ṭabīʿī*, and accept the alternative theory as "far-fetched," then we must conclude that matter is not numerically common as a single matter for all corporeal things.

The second answer is that if, as is borne out by other passages in his writings, Avicenna actually thinks that the incorruptibility of the heavenly bodies is due to their form, so that both the supralunary as well as the sublunary bodies could consist of the same kind of matter, then matter is already shown to be at least generically common. Whatever is generically common may be, but does not have to be, also numerically common, because numerical oneness requires not only an identity in kind but moreover also a numerical identity. As already noted, two things can be numerically identical if they came-to-be as one and the same thing, i.e., if they have the same origin in the same respect. If, however, two things that are identical in kind differ in their respective origin, then they must be numerically distinct. Thus, one way to find out whether the heavenly and the terrestrial bodies share the same single numerically one matter is to inquire into Avicenna's position about the origin of prime matter in general or of sublunary prime matter in particular.

Fortunately, Avicenna's position on *this* point is much easier to determine. In her monograph on "the problem of matter in Avicenna," Buschmann highlights that Avicenna endorses the view that the existence of sublunary matter is due to the Active Intellect.[266] One of the main intentions of Buschmann's study is to argue against the Marxist interpretation of Avicenna's supposed materialism put forth by such writers

---

265 In this case, though, Avicenna would have to answer the question due to what these two matters differ and how they can differ without being also composite of an even more fundamental matter and a distinguishing feature. This would, obviously, beg the original question raised by Alexander of which Avicenna certainly was aware which, in turn, might indicate that Avicenna does, after all, not think that the universe consist of two different kinds of prime matter. For him, the very idea of *prime* matter precludes the idea of there being more than one kind of it (let alone the idea of being composite).
266 Buschmann, *Untersuchungen zum Problem der Materie bei Avicenna*, esp. ch. 7.

as Ernst Bloch.[267] The Marxist reading relies heavily on the assumption that matter is an uncreated and eternal, even independent, entity. Against this, Buschmann points to one of her main sources, Avicenna's *Dānešnāme-ye ʿAlāʾī*, and in particular to the penultimate chapter of its section on metaphysics. This chapter is concerned with investigating the cosmological and ontological underpinnings of sublunary bodies, i.e., those bodies that are characterised by their "being susceptible to coming-to-be and corruption" (*paḏīrande-ye kawn-o fasādand*). In it, Avicenna draws a distinction between heavenly bodies and sublunary bodies, stating that they are undoubtedly different (*šakk nīst ke īn ǧesmhā moḫtalef bovand*). Moreover, he maintains that the sublunary bodies have a common matter (*māddat īšān moštarak bovad*).[268] He continues by writing that the realisation of a particular sublunary body is the result of a particular interplay of a plurality of factors which prepared the matter for the acceptance of a form. Nonetheless, their matter *qua* matter must have originated from one single source, because it is a common sublunary matter. Incidentally, this source is the very same source from which also the form emanates once the matter has been sufficiently prepared by that particular interplay of factors. In identification of the source of both matter and form, Avicenna writes the following:

> پس هر چند که از این مفارق مادّت آید، هم صورتی از این مفارق باید که موجود آید تا این مادّت بفعل بود.
> پس مادّت از وی تنها بود، و لیکن بفعل بودن وی بصورت بود.
>
> Thus, although the matter comes from this separate [intellect] (*īn mofāreq*), a form must also come into existence from this separate [intellect], so that this matter is in actuality. Thus, the matter is alone from this [sc. the separate intellect], whereas its being in actuality is due to the form. (*Dānešnāme-ye ʿAlāʾī* II.56, 158.7–12)

According to Buschmann, this text provides clear evidence in refutation of the thesis of the uncreatedness of matter in Avicenna.[269] Thus, according to the *Dānešnāme-ye ʿAlāʾī*, the matter of all sublunary bodies has its origin in the Active Intellect and, thus, cannot be numerically identical with the matter of the heavenly bodies, since the coming-to-be of sublunary matter is essentially posterior to the coming-to-be of the matters of the heavenly bodies.

Avicenna presents this theory not only in his *Dānešnāme-ye ʿAlāʾī*, it is also prominent in his *al-Ilāhiyyāt* and his *al-Išārāt wa-l-tanbīhāt*. Supporting Buschmann's analysis, Belo rightly points towards *al-Ilāhiyyāt* IX.5 and argues that "[m]atter originates as the last effect of the emanative process" and is "wholly subordinate to higher principles."[270]

---

267 cf. Bloch, *Avicenna und die aristotelische Linke*; cf. also Tisini, *Die Materieauffassung in der islamisch-arabischen Philosophie des Mittelalters*; q.v. fn. 44 above, 121.

268 This will be discussed more fully in what follows.

269 Buschmann, *Untersuchungen zum Problem der Materie bei Avicenna*, 57: "Dieser Text leistet mehr als die Widerlegung der These von der Ungeschaffenheit der Materie bei Avicenna."

270 Belo, *Chance and Determinism in Avicenna and Averroes*, 74, 84, referring especially to *al-Ilāhiyyāt* IX.5, §1, 410.4–6; §8, 412.7f.; cf. also Lizzini, "The Relation between Form and Matter," 183f.

Belo concludes her analysis, writing that "[m]atter is that which characterises the world of generation and corruption and distinguishes it from the celestial world."[271]

Already before, and unbeknownst to, both Buschmann and Belo, Goichon in 1937, followed by Herbert Davidson in 1972, pointed out that according to Avicenna, matter comes-to-be from the Active intellect.[272] Both refer to a statement in the final *išāra* of the sixth *namaṭ* in Avicenna's *al-Išārāt wa-l-tanbīhāt* which very succinctly restates the position we have just seen Avicenna expound in the penultimate chapter of the metaphysics of his earlier *Dānešnāme-ye ʿAlāʾī*, viz., that matter comes-to-be from the Active intellect and that other factors were contributing to its preparation, so that only once all causes have been considered together it can be explained why things originated as they did:

> فيجب أن تكون هيولى العالم العنصري لازمة عن العقل الأخير ولا يمتنع أن يكون للأجرام السماوية ضرب من المعاونة فيه ... وأمّا الصور فتفيد أيضاً من ذلك العقل.
>
> So, it is necessary that the matter of the elemental world (*hayūlā l-ʿālam al-ʿunṣurī*) is a result (*lāzima*) of the last intellect, even though nothing prevents the heavenly bodies from having some kind of assistance (*ḍarb min al-muʿāwana*) in it ... As for the forms, they, too, emanate from that intellect. (*al-Išārāt wa-l-tanbīhāt* II.6.42, 175.1–4)

This is by and large the same account as that given in *Dānešnāme-ye ʿAlāʾī* II.56. Arguably the most fascinating passage in this regard, however, is to be found in Avicenna's *al-Ilāhiyyāt* from *al-Šifāʾ* at the very beginning of the tenth and final book. There, he describes the emergence of all things from the divine First Principle (a process which he calls *mabdaʾ*) and depicts the beginning of their return to it (a process which he calls *maʿād*):

> فالوجود إذا ابتدأ من عند الأوّل لم يزل كلّ تال منه أدون مرتبة من الأوّل ولا يزال ينحط درجات. فأوّل ذلك درجة الملائكة الروحانية المجرّدة التي تُسمّى عقولاً. ثمّ مراتب الملائكة الروحانية التي تُسمّى نفوساً وهي الملائكة العملة. ثمّ مراتب الأجرام السماوية، وبعضها أشرف من بعض إلى أن يَبلَغ آخِرها. ثمّ بعدها يبتدئ وجود المادّة القابلة للصورة الكائنة الفاسدة، فيلبس أوّل شيء صور العناصر. ثمّ يتدرج يسيراً يسيراً فيكون أوّل الوجود فيها أخس وأدون مرتبة من الذي يتلوه. فيكون أخس ما فيه المادّة ثمّ العناصر ثمّ المركبات الجمادية، ثمّ النباتات. وأفضلها الإنسان، وبعده الحيوانات، ثمّ النبات. وأفضل الناس مَن استكملت نفسه عقلاً بالفعل ومحصلاً للأخلاق التي تكوّن فضائل عملية. وأفضل هؤلاء هو المستعد لمرتبة النبوّة ... وهذا هو الموحى إليه. وكما أنّ أوّل الكائنات من

271 Belo, *Chance and Determinism in Avicenna and Averroes*, 89; cf. Davidson, *Alfarabi, Avicenna, and Averroes, on Intellect*, 47, 76f., 82. The last quotation from Belo's study sounds as if she wanted to claim that the matter of the heavenly realm is not merely numerically different from the matter in the sublunary realm, which, for Avicenna, clearly would be false. I am not sure if it was Belo's intention to claim this.

272 Goichon, *La distinction de l'essence et de l'existence*, 237; fn. 1, 243; Davidson, "Alfarabi and Avicenna on the Active Intellect," 154f. Davidson later repeated his interpretation in *Alfarabi, Avicenna, and Averroes, on Intellect*, 76. This later study was used also by Belo.

الابتداء إلى درجة العناصر كان عقلاً ثمّ نفساً ثمّ جرماً، فههنا يبتدئ الوجود من الأجرام، ثمّ تحدب النفوس، ثمّ عقول. وإنّما تفيض هذه الصور لا محالة من عند تلك المبادئ.

So, existence, when it commences from the First, always was [such that] all that which succeeds from Him was lower in rank and it continues to be degenerating in degrees. So, the first of these is the degree of the spiritual angels denuded [of matter] that are called "intellects." Thereupon are the ranks of the spiritual angels called "souls," and they are the productive angels. Thereupon are the ranks of the celestial bodies, of which some are nobler than others, until the last of these is reached. Thereupon, after these, commences the existence of matter receptive of the generable and corruptible forms (*yabtadi' wuǧūd al-mādda al-qābila li-l-ṣūra al-kā'ina al-fāsida*). It [sc. existence], first of all, takes on the forms of the elements. Thereupon, it proceeds little by little, such that the first existence in it [sc. the order of existence] is baser and lower in rank than the one that follows it. So, the basest of what is in it is matter, then are the elements, then the inanimate compounds, and then the plants. The most excellent is the human being and, below it, the animals, and then the plants. The most excellent of people is he whose soul is perfected as an intellect in act and who attains the morals that bring forth practical virtues. The most excellent of these is he who is prepared for the rank of prophethood ... and this is the one to whom revelation is given. Just as it is that the first of the things coming-to-be, from the commencement to the rank of the elements, had been intellect, then soul, and then body, so here [in the world below the moon] existence begins from bodies, then souls originate, and then intellects. These forms undoubtedly emanate only from these principles. (*al-Ilāhiyyāt* X.1, §§1–3, 435.6–436.4, tr. by Marmura, modified)

Avicenna describes a downward process from the First Principle to the intellects, to the celestial souls, to the celestial bodies, and finally to the matter of the sublunary realm. Thereupon begins a second process, this time in an upward direction, from the matter to the elements, to plants, to animals, to humans, and ultimately to the prophet, whose intellect is so powerful that it comes into contact with the heavenly intellects and, thus, with God. This completes the circle of *mabda'* and *ma'ād*.[273]

This depiction of *mabda'* and *ma'ād* here in the final book of Avicenna's *al-Ilāhiyyāt* is highly reminiscent of al-Fārābī's descriptions of emanation in his *al-Siyāsa al-madaniyya* (a. k. a. *Mabādi' al-mawǧūdāt*) and his *Mabādi' ārā' ahl al-madīna al-fāḍila*.[274] In the latter treatise, al-Fārābī writes, among other things, the following:

فيلزم عن الطبيعة المشتركة التي لها وحود المادّة الأولى المشتركة لكلّ ما تحتها.

Thus, there follows from the nature which is common to the them [sc. the celestial bodies] the existence of prime matter which is common to everything below them. (al-Fārābī, *Mabādi' ārā' ahl al-madīna al-fāḍila* 8, 134.9–10, tr. by Walzer, modified)[275]

Thereupon, al-Fārābī continues by describing how the elements originate, how their less complex compositions give rise to minerals and their more complex compositions

273 For Avicenna's account of prophethood, cf. Gutas, "Avicenna: *De Anima* (V 6)"; Hasse, *Avicenna's* De Anima *in the Latin West*, 154–165.

274 cf. also Davidson, *Alfarabi, Avicenna, and Averroes, on Intellect*, 47f., 82.

275 cf. al-Fārābī, *al-Siyāsa al-madaniyya* (a. k. a. *Mabādi' al-mawǧūdāt*), 54.12–14, 55.3–5, 63.2f.; cf. also al-Fārābī, *Risāla fī l-'aql*, 33.14–35.3.

to plants; that they are succeeded by irrational animals; and that, at last, man comes-to-be as the final result.[276] Two things are particularly noteworthy here: first, that matter comes to be through the heavenly bodies, so that there is a distinction between the supralunary heavens and the sublunary realm; second, that the sublunary matter is common to all *sublunary* things. Both points are central for Avicenna's discussion in *al-Samāʿ al-ṭabīʿī*.

Within this schema, adopted from al-Fārābī, it is evident that the bodies of the celestial spheres are prior to the matter which is common to the bodies below the moon, they even may provide "some kind of assistance" in its production, as Avicenna writes in *al-Išārāt wa-l-tanbīhāt* and indicates in the *Dānešnāme-ye ʿAlāʾī*. There is, then, no way there could be one common matter which is numerically one for all bodies alike, because regardless of whether the matter within the universe as a whole is one in kind, it certainly is not one in number, as the sublunary matter had a different origin than the matters of the celestial bodies.

Thus, irrespective of whether we take it as "far-fetched" that the incorruptibility of the heavenly bodies is due to their form or not, in either case, matter – just as form – fails the test for being common in the first, numerical, sense. Although all bodies, celestial and terrestrial bodies alike, are composed of matter and form, they do not share the same numerically one matter. Nonetheless, Avicenna, like al-Fārābī, emphasises that the matter of the sublunary world is still common to all sublunary bodies. This is already hinted at by a parenthetical remark in the discussion in *al-Samāʿ al-ṭabīʿī* I.3:

بل ربّما جاز أن تكون الهيولى المشتركة لمثل الأجسام الكائنة الفاسدة التي يتكوّن بعضها من بعض ويفسد بعضها من بعض كما سنبيّن من حال الأربعة التي تُسمّى الاسطقسات:

> Rather it may be possible that a common matter belongs to such things like the bodies which come-to-be and corrupt, and which come-to-be out of one another and corrupt into one another, just as we shall prove for the state of the four which are called "elements." (*al-Samāʿ al-ṭabīʿī* I.3, §2, 22.3f.)[277]

Accordingly, Avicenna does not deny that there may be a numerically common matter for sublunary bodies – indeed, all sublunary matter in principle originated from one and the same source, viz., the Active intellect – even though there is certainly no numerically common matter for *all* bodies.[278] So, although the sublunary matter is subsequently diversified and made multiple through the influence of the heavenly bodies

276 cf. al-Fārābī, *Mabādiʾ ārāʾ ahl al-madīna al-fāḍila* 8, 136.9–140.16; cf. also al-Fārābī, *al-Siyāsa al-madaniyya* (a. k. a. *Mabādiʾ al-mawǧūdāt*), 62.11f.

277 cf. *Dānešnāme-ye ʿAlāʾī* II.48, 135.14–136.1; *al-Išārāt wa-l-tanbīhāt* II.2.20, 115.14f.

278 What is more, Avicenna also maintains that there is not even a numerically common matter for all celestial bodies, for each of the celestial body has its own matter which is essentially and numerically distinct from any other. This is both explicitly stated in *Dānešnāme-ye ʿAlāʾī* II.48 and particularly clear from the viewpoint of the emanative schema as presented, for example, in *al-Ilāhiyyāt* IX.4, §12, 406.11–407.4, according to which every intellect brings forth the matter and the form of corresponding

and, ultimately, the inherence of different forms in different chunks of matter, it is one single matter in the same sense as there is one single matter – yet both supralunary and sublunary – in the cosmological systems of Plotinus, Porphyry, and Proclus, even though Avicenna is not committed to the impassibility of matter as it was advanced by Plotinus. Thus, for Avicenna, the matter of this drop of water is still numerically distinct from the matter of another drop of water. Yet, both matters are the same in kind and originated from the same source. They may even reunite again and form one larger drop of water or, once reunited, may separate again.[279]

Realising this provides important evidence in support of my understanding that matter as such, i.e., *all* matter, is common only in the second, generic, sense. Already in *al-Samāʿ al-ṭabīʿī* I.2, Avicenna said that the investigation of an agent that is common to all things absolutely, i.e., numerically common in the way God is *the Agent* (as well as *the End*), is not the task of the natural philosopher but of the metaphysician. However, if there were also an agent that is common to the things in the sublunary realm, then the examination of this common principle would belong to the science of physics, even though its investigation would collapse into discovering the full meaning of the term "agent" – and that is into an investigation of the *generic* commonality of the predicate "agent." That is to say that in metaphysics, we inquire into God and examine *the Agent* in its numerical commonality, i.e., as it is shared as a single entity by the totality of natural things. If, on the other hand, we inquire into an agent which is shared by a less total group of existents, such as only those existing below the moon, then the investigation of the commonality of this less universal agent collapses into an examination of the second, generic, sense of commonality.[280] Indeed, Avicenna describes such an investigation as follows:

> ووجه ذلك البحث أن يتعرّف حال كلّ ما هو مبدأ فاعلي لأمر من أمور الطبيعية أنّه كيف قوّته وكيف تكون نسبته إلى معلوله ... وغير ذلك وأن يبرهن عليه. فإذا فعل ذلك فقد عرف طبيعة الفاعل العامّ المشترك للطبيعيات بهذا النحو إذ عرف الحال التي تخصّ ما هو فاعل في الطبيعيات.
>
> The way of that investigation (*al-baḥṯ*) is that one comes to know the state of all that which is an efficient principle [i.e., an agent] for some natural thing about how its power is and how it is related to its effect ... and the like, and that one demonstrates [all this]. If one does that, then one

sphere through two separate acts of intellection. Thus, the matter of each sphere differs from that of any other sphere as it has its origin in a numerically different intellective act of a numerically different intellect.

279 Having said this, it is also clear that there never was a moment in which the Active Intellect emanated the whole of sublunary matter, so that there was a moment in which a single numerically common sublunary matter existed. Avicenna's universe exists from all eternity, and so its matter was from all eternity diversified. I am merely claiming that the idea of a numerically common sublunary matter is not adverse to the philosophical system of Avicenna, even thought the idea of a numerically common matter for *all* corporeal reality definitely is. Thus, the sublunary matter is, in principle at least, numerically common.

280 cf. *al-Samāʿ al-ṭabīʿī* I.2, §§10–11, 16.5–18.

> will have learned the nature of the general "agent" (*al-fāʿil al-ʿāmm*) shared by the natural things (*al-muštarak li-l-ṭabīʿiyyāt*) in this sense, since he will [have] learned the state which is specific to that which is an agent among natural things. (*al-Samāʿ al-ṭabīʿī* I.2, §11, 16.13–15)[281]

What is striking here is that Avicenna uses the term *al-ʿāmm* to describe this sense of commonality, which is the very same word we have seen him reserving for the second, generic, sense of commonality. Moreover, Avicenna writes that this investigation will lead one to knowing the specific state of that, whatever it may be, which is in the state of being an agent – i.e., this investigation demonstrates what it means to be an agent, thus revealing the nature of the universal and generically common predicate "agent."

If we transfer this situation to our current question about matter, it becomes clear that if there is a common matter that is shared by all sublunary things, i.e., a sublunary prime matter which is (in principle at least) numerically common to all sublunary things, then the investigation of this matter really is only about ascertaining the meaning of the universal predicate "matter" which is generically attributed as a common feature to all material things. In other words, any investigation about something that is numerically common not to an absolute totality but to a sub-totality – as, in the case of matter, not to *all* bodies but to all *sublunary* bodies – is an investigation of generic commonality despite the fact that it is numerically common to that sub-totality. Therefore, matter is, on the whole, generically common to all material existents (supralunary and sublunary alike) despite the fact that it is, in principle at least, numerically common only to all sublunary existents.

This harmonises very well with the fact that, somewhat later in the same discussion about the commonality of principles, Avicenna characterises matter as a common, i.e., generic, description for a certain function, in much the same way as we have seen him describing form.[282] Avicenna writes the following:

> فلجميع ما يقال إنّه هيولى طبيعةً تشترك في معنى أنّها أمر من شأنه أن يحصل له أمر آخر في ذاته بعد أنّ لا يكون له وهو الذي يكون منه الشيء وهو فيه لا بالعرض. فربّما كان هو بسيطاً وربّما كان مركّباً بعد البسيط كالخشب للسرير وربّما كان الحاصل له صورة جوهرية أو هيئة عرضية.
>
> All that about which it is said that it is matter (*hayūlā*) has a nature (*ṭabīʿa*) which shares in the meaning (*taštariku fī maʿnan*) that it is something which is in itself such that another factor could occur to it after not having belonged to it and is that from which something comes-to-be and is in [that thing] non-accidentally. Sometimes it is simple, and at other times it is composite after having been simple, such as the wood that belongs to the bed. It is also something that might acquire a substantial form or an accidental disposition. (*al-Samāʿ al-ṭabīʿī* I.3, §10, 25.6–8, tr. by McGinnis, modified)[283]

281 cf. *al-Ḥikma al-mašriqiyya* III.4, 9.2–4.

282 q.v. above, 174f.

283 cf. *al-Samāʿ al-ṭabīʿī* I.10, §5, 49.13–16; I.14, §17, 74.15–75.1; *al-Ilāhiyyāt* VI.4, §8, 281.16–282.5; *al-Ḥikma al-mašriqiyya* III.1, 4.11–15; cf. also Belo, *Chance and Determinism in Avicenna and Averroes*, 44, 57–61, referring to *al-Mubāḥaṯāt*, §170, a passage which in a particularly clear way describes matter as

The first thing we recognise in this general description of matter is that Avicenna describes the generically common as that which "shares in [a] meaning" (*taštariku fī maʿnan*). Thus, Avicenna uses the term *muštarak* – which I have argued to be specific for that which is numerically common – even for what is presently argued to be only *ʿāmm*, i.e., common in the generic sense. Yet, Avicenna does clearly not say that all natural things share in a single matter – he merely claims that whatever is material shares in one common meaning or description, which is that of having the capacity of acquiring some formal factor and of being the underlying thing "from which" things come to be through that acquisition. Thus, it is the meaning (*maʿnan*) which is one and shared, albeit not the matter itself.[284] Avicenna's use of *muštarak* here does not undermine the claim that matter is only generically common but confirms it, because it introduces terminology which precisely resembles how Avicenna describes that second, generic, sense of commonality: something is common "by way of generality" like a universal which is predicated of a number of things which, in turn, *share in the meaning* of that universal predicate.

Further, it makes no difference whether that which we describe as "matter" is something simple or composite.[285] We accurately call prime matter by the name "matter" just as much as "the wood that belongs to the bed," for both share in that common meaning of being something that is essentially receptive of form. Having said this, there is only one kind of prime matter in all corporeal reality, i.e., in the celestial and the terrestrial bodies – and this is the matter which is ready to receive forms.

Avicenna's cosmological system is, therefore, united. There is only *one* physics and this physics explains the reality of both the heavens and the earth. Both realms are governed by the same principles, i.e., they fundamentally consist of the same kind of matter and of the same kinds of form: all matter is such as to receive form – all form is such as to inhere in matter. The only difference is that Avicenna allows for some forms to separate more easily from their underlying matter as others, with the result that there are even a few forms which do not separate from their matter at all – and these are the forms of the heavenly bodies, such as the form of the Moon and the form of the Sun. This must not be taken as an occult aspect of Avicenna's physics. To the contrary, it is simply straightforward. It is already known that some forms adhere more strongly to their underlying matter than others do. The form of water, for example, separates easily from matter, whereas the form of earth does not. This explains why it is so easy to transform water into air by merely heating it up, whereas earth is not

pure receptivity. An especially striking passage is also *al-Ilāhiyyāt* II.2, §21, 68.5, in which Avicenna describes the "assumed" (*tuẓannu*) form that belongs to matter *qua* matter, viz., receptivity.

284 Likewise, two human beings share in one meaning of "humanity," but their form of humanity is not *numerically* one and the same, even though it is one and the same in account.

285 Incidentally it is in these cases all the more clear that a simple prime matter and a composite secondary matter are not numerically identical even though they, again, "share in" one and the same meaning, viz., the meaning of "matter."

so easily transformed into any other element. Likewise can we turn wood quickly into ash, but we cannot turn stone quickly into ash or, in fact, into anything. It is, thus, only reasonable to assume that some forms separate more easily from their matter, and so Avicenna infers that there are even a couple of forms which do not leave their matter at all.[286] Yet, these forms are not a different kind of form, they are forms just like any other – in particular, they inhere in matter just as any other form does – even though they are at the extreme point of the range that describes the formal readiness for being separated from the underlying matter.[287] It is to be noted, here, that the celestial bodies precisely do not consist of "aether," the supposed fifth element which, in contrast to the four terrestrial elements, is incorruptible, unchangeable, and only capable of circular motion, as Aristotle famously argued in *De caelo* I.2–3 and as some scholars have claimed about Avicenna.[288] For example, Avicenna does not explain the circular motion of the heavens by taking recourse to fifth element or any material (immaterial?) substrate. In *al-Ilāhiyyāt*, IX.2, he very explicitly argues that the circular motion of the heavenly bodies is due to their soul, i.e., their form, and that every celestial body has an *own* individual – indeed: unique – soul or form. It is important to realise that for Avicenna, there is no "form of aether" alongside the four sublunary elemental forms of fire, air, water, and earth. Thus, neither do they consist of the same fifth element (even though they consist of the same kind of prime matter as do also all sublunary elements) nor is any such element required for explaining the circular motion or the incorruptibility of the celestial bodies.[289] There is, then, no aether in addition to fire, air, water, and earth in Avicenna's system, and the supralunary, celestial region is in no way different from the sublunary, terrestrial realm in terms of its constitution and the physical laws that govern its behaviour and existence. Thus, not only does Avicenna's account of matter secure a unified physics that governs both realms of natural bodies, i.e., corruptible and incorruptible ones, his account of forms likewise guarantees the same result, because all forms are alike in that they are forms; they merely differ in their readiness to leave their matter.

---

286 Yet, it remains doubtful if Avicenna is entitled to draw this last inferential step. Saying that some forms can be separated from their matter more easily than others is an assertoric claim about degrees. Saying that some forms cannot be separated from their matter at all is a modal claim about possibility.

287 This is most explicitly argued for in *al-Išārāt wa-l-tanbīhāt* II.1.17, which has been quoted above, 190; it is also expressed in *al-Naǧāt* IV.1.7, 508.12–509.3 ≈ *al-Ilāhiyyāt* II.3, §16, 78.17–79.3.

288 cf. M. Rashed, "The Problem of the Composition of the Heavens," 41; Arif, "Ibn Sīnā's Idea of Nature and Change," 112, 129; "The Universe as a System," 135f.; Dagli, "Ether," 209.

289 When Avicenna mentions aether (*al-aṯīr*) or a fifth body (*al-ǧism al-ḫāmis*) in his writings, which he admittedly does (however rarely), then he takes this to be a collective name for those bodies that are engaged only in circular motion, i.e., as a name for the bodies of the supralunary region. Thus, neither does the heavenly region as a whole nor each of the heavenly bodies consist of an element "aether"; each one of the heavenly bodies consists of a matter and a form, and this form is not the form of aether but one of the unique forms (or souls) of the celestial bodies: the form of the Moon (in case of the Moon), the form of the Sun (in case of the Sun), and so on.

By way of summary, natural things (*al-umūr al-ṭabīʿiyya*) have two essential and internal principles, which belong to them insofar as they are corporeal. These are matter and form. These two principles are common to things not by being a single entity which is numerically one and upon which all things depend equally but only as a general (*ʿāmm*) description for a certain function, disposition, or state within natural compounds. Moreover, natural things also have additional external principles, viz., agent and end, because all of them can – and most of them do – act on each other or serve as purposes and ends of such actions. Moreover, all of them depend in their existence on the Necessary Existent being their ultimate Agent and End, i.e., their truly common and numerically unique principle of existence. Yet, the investigation of this principle and of its numerical commonality is another story, a meta-physical story, better suited to be written in another book, viz., Avicenna's *al-Ilāhiyyāt*.

3.3 Change and an Additional Principle

Avicenna's main intention in the early chapters of *al-Samāʿ al-ṭabīʿī* is to provide a full picture of the subject-matter of physics, viz., the natural body, of its constitution, and of its internal essential and external accidental principles, viz., matter and form as well as agent and end, respectively. Apart from the fact that Avicenna proceeds "by way of postulation and positing," what is perhaps the most striking aspect of Avicenna's approach is that he discusses the principles of natural things not on the basis of an analysis of change, as Aristotle had done in *Physics* I.5–7, but through an examination of the notion of corporeality.[290] That is to say, Avicenna's earlier promise that the body "insofar as it comes-to-be and perishes, and, indeed, simply is subject to change, has additional principles" (*min ḥaytu huwa kāʾin fāsid bal mutaġayyir bi-l-ǧumla lahū ziyāda fī l-mabādiʾ*) has so far been – if at all – only peripherally relevant.[291] Yet, in the middle of the second chapter of the first book of *al-Samāʿ al-ṭabīʿī*, Avicenna picks this up again and writes the following:

وأمّا الجسم من جهة ما هو متغيّر أو مستكمل أو حادث كائن فإنّ له زيادة مبدأ.

> The body insofar as it is changeable (*mutaġayyir*) or perfectible (*mustakmal*) or generable and coming-to-be (*ḥādiṯ kāʾin*) has additional principles (*ziyādat mabdaʾ*). (*al-Samāʿ al-ṭabīʿī* I.2, §12, 16.18, tr. by McGinnis, modified)[292]

With this, Avicenna begins the presentation of "privation" (*ʿadam*), which seems to be required as a third principle once the natural body is considered not insofar as it is

290 For Avicenna's method and his procedure "by way of postulation and positing," q.v. above, 81ff.; for the difference between Avicenna's and Aristotle's approach, q.v. above 112f.

291 *al-Samāʿ al-ṭabīʿī* I.2, §3, 13.13f.

292 cf. *al-Ḥikma al-mašriqiyya* III.3, 7.1.

a body but insofar as it undergoes change.[293] With Avicenna turning to change, one might think that his approach would now be more in line with the one known from Aristotle's *Physics* with its focus on change. Yet, again, this is not the case. For Aristotle, the notion of change was a means to establish the three principles of natural things. Put differently, change served as an *explanans*, so that an inquiry into the notion of change explained the principles and established their number. For Avicenna, however, the notion of change does not establish the principles nor does it even establish privation as an additional principle. Instead, it is the notion of change that is to be explained and not the principles. It is the principles that explain change and make it intelligible as a phenomenon of the natural world. This means that change, for Avicenna, is an *explanandum* – and it is privation, together with matter and form, which does the job.

That privation is not established through an analysis of change is already apparent in the way in which Avicenna describes it. He writes the following:

فنجد القابل للتغيّر والاستكمال ونجد العدم ونجد الصورة كلّها محتاجاً إليه في أن يكون الجسم متغيّراً أو مستكملاً وهذا يتّضح لنا بأدنى تأمّل.

> So, we find that which is susceptible for change and perfection, we find the privation, and we find the form, each of these [three] being something required (*muḥtāǧan ilayhi*) for the body's being changing or perfecting – and this is clear to us by the slightest reflection (*yattaḍiḥu lanā bi-adnā ta'ammul*). (*al-Samāʿ al-ṭabīʿī* I.2, §14, 17.17–19)[294]

What Avicenna does here is to present privation as an intrinsically apparent factor in motion as it is experienced within the natural world. He has already shown that every body that *exists* consists of matter and form, now he adds that every body that *changes* also has a privation. A privation, for him, is a privative state, i.e., a lack on the side of the subject undergoing the change. It is this lack which is remedied through the change.

There are two kinds of privations just as there are two modes of accidental change. According to Avicenna, there is a distinction between change (*taġayyur*) and perfection (*istikmāl*) in addition to substantial change, i.e., generation and coming-to-be. Turning first to body insofar as it is changeable, Avicenna states that change requires three factors: (i) something which remains throughout the change and which is what is changing (*šay' ṯābit huwa mutaġayyir*); (ii) a state which existed and, then, did not exist anymore (*ḥāla kānat mawǧūda fa-ʿudimat*); and (iii) a state which previously did not exist and, then, existed (*ḥāla kānat maʿdūma fa-wuǧidat*).[295] To illustrate this, Avicenna provides an example which is not Aristotle's famous unmusical man who becomes

293 On privation in Avicenna, cf. also Belo, *Chance and Determinism in Avicenna and Averroes*, 72f.; McGinnis, "Making Something of Nothing," 557–565; Shihadeh, *Doubts on Avicenna*, 117.

294 The meaning of *muḥtāǧ ilayhi* will be discussed below, 207ff.

295 *al-Samāʿ al-ṭabīʿī* I.2, §12, 17.2f.; reading *fa-wuǧidat* with Mss. Leiden or. 4 and or. 84 as well as Zāyid for *wuǧidat* in McGinnis and Āl Yāsīn; cf. *al-Ḥikma al-mašriqiyya* III.3, 7.4–7.

musical but which reminds us of the contrary pair of black and white which was frequently mentioned in *Physics* I.4–6. If there is a white robe becoming black, Avicenna writes, then there is involved (i) a robe, (ii) the whiteness, and (iii) the blackness.[296] The robe is the object of change and is what remains throughout; the whiteness is the state (*ḥāla*) or attribute (*ṣifa*) which the object, first, had and, then, did not have anymore when the blackness occurred; and the blackness is the subsequent state which did not exist at first, i.e., when there was whiteness, but which, then, came-to-be, thereby replacing the whiteness.

These, then, are the three factors already mentioned in the above quote: a matter or recipient (*qābil*) which remains, a form (*ṣūra*) which is lost, and a privation (*ʿadam*) which is remedied through the acquisition of a new form. In this case, what is described as a privation refers to a form, viz., a form which the recipient lacked even though it is such as to acquire and to have it (*min šaʾnihī an yakūna lahū* or *min šaʾnihī an yaḥṣula lahū*) and which it, then, acquired through the process of change.[297] While the robe is still full of whiteness, it is the whiteness which we ought to call its form and it is the blackness which we ought to call its privation insofar as the robe in being white is deprived of the blackness which the robe is set to acquire.

One might ask why Avicenna does not employ Aristotle's much more prominent example of the unmusical man who becomes musical to explain accidental change but, instead, prefers a white robe turning black.[298] The answer to this is simple: for Avicenna, the case of a man who becomes musical is not a case of a change – it is a case of a *perfection* (*istikmāl*).[299] This is made clear by Avicenna's account of perfection:

296 It should be noted that the existing state (ii) and the privation (iii) do not necessarily have to be contraries as Belo writes (cf. *Chance and Determinism in Avicenna and Averroes*, 72). A robe could just as well change from white to blue or from green to yellow. It is more adequate, as McGinnis suggests, to think of privation as what he calls an "'other than' relation," so that the changing object posses some determinate factor which is *other than* what it is about to acquire through the change ("Making Something of Nothing," 559).

297 *al-Samāʿ al-ṭabīʿī* I.3, §4, 23.5–9; I.3, §10, 25.10f.; *al-Ilāhiyyāt* VII.1, §§6–8, 304.18–305.9; *al-Ḥikma al-mašriqiyya* III.3, 7.3. The same condition is also mentioned by Aristotle in *Categories* 10, 12a26–31, and distinguishes between mere negations and real privations, the former simply describe all that which the subject is not, the latter only what the subject truly can become; cf. McGinnis, "Making Something of Nothing," 558f.

298 In *Physics* I.5, Aristotle exemplifies the contraries and their involvement in change often through something changing from black to white as, for example, in the conclusion drawn at 188b21–26.

299 Avicenna's idea to differentiate between processes of change and those of perfection may have been influenced by Aristotle's remarks in *Physics* VII.3, esp. 246a10–b2 (α-version) as well as 246a29–b27 (β-version), where he claims that the acquisition of ones proper excellence (ἀρετή) in terms of states (ἕξεις) is not a case of alteration (ἀλλοίωσις) but is a completion or perfection (τελείωσις); cf. also *Physics* VII.3, 247a1–3 (α-version) as well as 246b27–20 (β-version). Isḥāq ibn Ḥunayn's Arabic translation of the β-version of *Physics* VII.3, 246b27–20, provides the verbs *tamma* and *istakmala* as well as the noun *kamāl*. A little later, then, Aristotle uses an example akin to the man who becomes musical when he states, in both versions, that "the original acquisition of knowledge is not a becoming or an

والمفهوم من كونه مستكملاً هو أن يحدث له أمر لم يكن فيه من غير زوال شيء عنه مثل الساكن يتحرّك فإنّه حين ما كان ساكناً لم يكن إلّا عادماً للحركة التي هي موجودة له بالإمكان والقوّة فلمّا تحرّك لم يزل منه شيء إلّا العدم فقط.

What is understood by its being perfectible (*mustakmalan*) is that it comes to have something that did not exist in it [before] without itself losing something from it (*min ġayr zawāl šay' ʿanhu*), for example something being at rest that [came to] be in motion, for as long as it was at rest it was nothing but being deprived of the motion which existed for it possibly or potentially, whereas when it came to be in motion, nothing was lost from it except the privation only. (*al-Samāʿ al-ṭabīʿī* I.2, §13, 17.6–8, tr. by McGinnis, modified)[300]

Unlike a robe which loses its whiteness, in order to acquire the blackness, thus changing its colour from white to black, the man and the moving thing do not lose anything except their state of being deprived of musicality or motion, respectively. An unmusical man who becomes musical would be a precise example of something gaining its "first perfection" (ἐντελέχεια πρώτη, *kamāl awwal*), because in acquiring knowledge, he realises his species-given potential to exert an intellectual activity. Avicenna's example of a thing's being moved is an apt example of something gaining its "second perfection" (ἐντελέχεια δευτέρα, *kamāl ṯānin*), i.e., the actual exercise of a given potential.[301] Conversely, a robe which is white is neither more nor less perfect than a black one. Turning white or black does not realise any potential of what it essentially means to be a robe, whereas acquiring knowledge (ἐπιστήμη, *ʿilm*) and ultimately exercising knowledge (θεωρεῖν, *naẓara*) are two perfections of what it means to be human.[302]

alteration" (*Phys.* 247b9f. (α-version), 247b22f. (β-version), tr. by Hardie/Gaye). In Avicenna's text, the term used is *mustakmal* ("perfected" or "perfectible"), a passive participle to the verb *istakmala*. On the complicated history of the Greek terms for perfection, completion, completeness, and actuality as well as its Arabic counterparts and its impact on Avicenna's philosophy in various regards, cf. Wisnovsky, *Avicenna's Metaphysics in Context*.

300 cf. *al-Ḥikma al-mašriqiyya* III.3, 7.7, which typically omits the example. Another example for a perfection is a boy who becomes a man as described by Avicenna in *al-Ilāhiyyāt* VIII.1, §12, 329.18–330.2.

301 Aristotle himself does not use these expressions, but he sets out the theory, which was widely adopted by his Greek and Arabic commentators, mainly in *De anima* II.5, esp. 417a21–417b2. Regarding Avicenna, one might object that he explicitly defined motion as the "first perfection," so that motion should not be a second but rather a first perfection. This objection, however, would rely on a crucial confusion. A train moving from A to B is in motion. Its state of being in motion somewhere between A and B is what Avicenna defines as motion in terms of a first perfection. This, however, is a first perfection *with regard to its being at B*, because it is on its way, so that the train's arrival at B is considered its second perfection. Motion as such, however, is an exercise of a capacity of things capable of motion. Thus, it is a second perfection *with regard to the train itself*, i.e., with regard to its very own capacity to be a moving object. In the same way, seeing and thinking, for example, are classified as second perfections of man. This is the reason for why Avicenna in *al-Nafs* I.1, 10.4–7, for example, mentions motion as an example of a second perfection, while he more properly defines motion as a first perfection in his discussion of motion in *al-Samāʿ al-ṭabīʿī* II.1, §3, 83.5; q.v. also below, 360f.

302 *De an.* II.1, 412a19–28; cf., again, *al-Nafs* I.1, 10.4–7 as well as *al-Madḫal* I.2, 12.7–10; *al-Ilāhiyyāt* I.1, §2, 3.11–4.6; I.3, §1, 17.8f.; cf. also Wisnovsky, *Avicenna's Metaphysics in Context*, 7f., esp. 120–127.

Like change, any perfection, be it a first or second perfection, involves three factors, so that whatever is undergoing perfection has (i) an essence that, first, existed deficiently and, then, came to be perfected (*ḏāt wuǧidat nāqiṣatan ṯumma kamalat*); (ii) something that occurred in it (*amr ḥaṣala fīhi*); and (iii) a privation that preceded it (*ʿadam taqaddamahū*).[303]

Finally, regarding processes of generation and coming-to-be, Avicenna mentions (ii) something that came to be (*amr hadaṯa*) and (iii) an antecedent privation (*ʿadam sabaqa*). Since the question of whether in cases of generation, there is also (i) some underlying substance which initially was connected with the privation (*ǧawhar kāna muqāranan li-ʿadam al-ṣūra al-kāʾina*) is a more difficult question, Avicenna only remarks that this discussion does not belong to physics and that "we will demonstrate it in first philosophy" (*nubarhinu ʿalayhi fī l-falsafa al-ūlā*).[304] This does not mean that Avicenna is hesitant on this question; it merely is a nice example of Avicenna's methodology of teaching and learning in action, as the proof of the existence of the underlying substance in generation, which would be prime matter, belongs to metaphysics, as we have already seen.[305]

Does all this mean that Avicenna accepts privation as a principle of natural things along, and on a par, with matter and form? Can we, accordingly, say that "body has privation" just as we can say "body has matter" or "body has form?" There is an ancient debate underlying this question, a debate about the status of privation as a principle.

This debate is related to Aristotle's own quest for determining the exact number of principles, which he carried out in the first book of the *Physics*. Initially, Aristotle asked whether the principles are "one or more [in number] and if more, then either finitely or infinitely [so], and if finitely more than one, then they are either two or three or four or some other number."[306] In chapter six, Aristotle could narrow down the available options, stating that the principles are "neither one nor more than two or three." Yet, he also confesses that "whether they are two or three is ... a question of considerable difficulty" (ἀπορίαν ἔχει πολλήν).[307] His own solution, as subsequently determined in *Physics* I.7, is that the principles are in a way two and in a way three.[308]

In his commentary, Philoponus trivialises the "considerable difficulty" asserting that Aristotle, in fact, "has already revealed the answer to this, that they [sc. the principles] are three: two contraries and one substrate." He argues that Aristotle merely wanted to raise an awareness of what Philoponus considers to be a minor side-issue, viz., whether privation ought to be counted as a principle by itself or not. Since privation is "not strictly a principle" (μὴ κυρίως οὔσης ἀρχῆς), as he writes, but only accidentally

---

303 *al-Samāʿ al-ṭabīʿī* I.2, §13, 17.8f; cf. *al-Ḥikma al-mašriqiyya* III.3, 7.8f.
304 *al-Samāʿ al-ṭabīʿī* I.2, §15, 17.20f.; *al-Ḥikma al-mašriqiyya* III.3, 7.16f.
305 q.v. above, 148ff.
306 *Phys.* I.2, 184b15–20.
307 *Phys.* I.6, 189b27–29, tr. by Hardie/Gaye, modified.
308 cf. *Phys.* I.7, 190b29f.

so (κατὰ συμβεβηκός), as already Aristotle stated, we may arrive at a total sum of two or three principles depending on our preference for including or excluding accidental principles in our calculation.[309]

Simplicius, on the other hand does not take the ἀπορία of *Physics* I.6 as lightly as his contemporary Philoponus. Instead, he agrees with Aristotle that "in this matter is much difficulty" (καὶ περὶ ταῦτά ἐστιν ἡ πολλὴ ἀπορία), and particularly in the questions "whether contraries are principles in the same way" and what it means to be an accidental principle. Simplicius finds himself in disagreement with Alexander who, we are told, conceived of privation as a quality (ποιότης) and, thus, as some sort of form (εἶδός τι). This, however, is problematic, says Simplicius, suggesting that we should distinguish between two kinds of privations, one of which is opposite to a possession (ἀντικειμένη τῇ ἕξει), the other being opposite to form (ἀντικειμένη τῷ εἴδει).[310] He relates the first of these to the tenth chapter of Aristotle's *Categories*, quoting a passage in which it is said that "for privation and possession ... it is impossible for change into one another to occur."[311] So, the basic feature of a privation as an opposite to a possession is that the possession may change into the privation, whereas the privation cannot change back into the possession, just as a blind person cannot come to be sighted again, as one of the examples in the *Categories* runs, or, perhaps analogously, as vinegar cannot come-to-be wine again, as *Metaphysics* H.5 has it.[312] The second pair of contraries, on the other hand, i.e., that whose opposition is between privation and form, allows for change into one another. Without providing an example, Simplicius describes this kind of privation as a "disabling of the form" (πήρωσις ... τοῦ εἴδους).[313] Since the notion of a privation is, from the viewpoint of Aristotle's *Categories*, a complex notion, it is, indeed, not an easy task to determine how privation in the *Physics* ought to be conceived. Aristotle's worry that it is a difficult question whether the principles are actually two or three is, according to Simplicius, entirely justified.

Nonetheless the difficult question receives its solution, Simplicius argues, insofar as it will be shown to be true (ἀληθὲς φανήσεται) that the number of principles are, in fact, *both* two and three.[314] He gives the following explanation:

> ἰστέον δὲ ὅτι ἄλλο ἐστὶν ὡς ἀρχὰς καὶ στοιχεῖα τῶν φυσικῶν ζητεῖν, ἐξ ὧν πρώτως ἐνυπαρχόντων ἐστὶ καθ' αὑτὸ καὶ μὴ κατὰ συμβεβηκός, καὶ ἄλλο μεταβολῆς ἀρχὰς ζητεῖν. καὶ κατὰ μὲν τὸ πρῶτον ἡ στέρησις κατὰ συμβεβηκὸς ἂν εἴη αἴτιον ὡς μὴ ἐνυπάρχον, κατὰ δὲ τὸ δεύτερον καθ' αὑτό.
>
> It should be understood that it is one thing to seek the principles and elements of natural things (ἀρχὰς καὶ στοιχεῖα τῶν φυσικῶν) from which, as primary ingredients (πρώτως ἐνυπαρχόντων),

309 Philoponus, *In Phys.*, 150.15–151.4; for privation as an accidental principle in Aristotle, cf. *Phys.* I.7, 190b27, 191a12–15; I.9, 192a3–6; cf. also Aristotle's discussion of privation in *Categories* 10.

310 Simplicius, *In Phys.*, 211.13–212.15.

311 *Cat.* 10, 13a31–36.

312 cf. *Metaphysics* H.5, 1044b34–1045a6.

313 Simplicius, *In Phys.*, 212.6f., tr. by Mueller.

314 Simplicius, *In Phys.*, 208.11–13.

> they are *per se* and not in an accidental sense, and another to seek the principles of change (μεταβολῆς ἀρχάς). For in terms of the first, privation would be a cause in an accidental sense (κατὰ συμβεβηκός), since it does not inhere, whereas in terms of the second, it would be a cause *per se* (καθ' αὑτό). (Simplicius, *In Phys.*, 216.30–34, tr. by Mueller, modified)[315]

In much the same way as Avicenna will do later, Simplicius distinguishes between two kinds of investigations. According to the first, which is directed towards internal principles or "primary constituents" (πρώτως ἐνυπαρχόντων), privation is only of little, if any, importance, as it does not constitute the natural thing but merely attaches to it as an accidental feature.[316] For the existence of a tree, then, it is irrelevant whether it is, at the same time, not-blossoming or not-straight grown or any other privative aspect that attaches to it by accident. In fact, there may be a large number of such accidental privations, none of which describes or accounts for, let alone constitutes, the existence of that very tree. The situation is different, however, when we investigate something which actually undergoes a change, because privation is an essential aspect of change and is a genuine *per se* cause towards what the thing (currently) is not (αἴτιον … εἰς τὸ μὴ εἶναι).[317] For a changing thing, then, privation is a cause both by its presence (κατὰ τὴν παρουσίαν) and by its absence (κατὰ τὴν ἀπουσίαν): once when it describes what the changing thing actually lacks (i.e., through the presence of the lack) and once when it ceases to pertain to the thing after the completion of the change (i.e., through the absence of the lack now).[318] In general, however, and with regard to the immediate relation between the thing itself and the privation, Simplicius states that although privation is a cause in change, it is always "a cause not by inhering but by not inhering" (μὴ τῷ ἐνυπάρχειν αἰτίαν εἶναι, ἀλλὰ τῷ μὴ ἐνυπάρχειν).[319]

Despite their different assessments as to whether or not Aristotle's ἀπορία describes a genuine difficulty, both Philoponus and Simplicius emphasise that privation is a principle in an accidental sense. Indeed, one could even doubt whether it should be called a principle at all, especially since Simplicius apparently saw the need to explain why Aristotle, who is supposedly in agreement with Plato, had included privation among the principles of change, while Plato had not – and, of course, Plato should be right.[320]

Avicenna was certainly aware of late ancient considerations, worries, and debates about privation such as these, because he directly addresses the question of whether

315 cf. Philoponus, *In Phys.*, 2.35–37, 161.4–20.

316 Simplicius' use of expressions derived from the verb ἐνυπάρχειν reflects the terminology Aristotle employed in discussing internal causes (or "elements") in the course of *Metaphysics* Λ.4; q.v. also above, 159f.

317 Simplicius, *In Phys.*, 216.34f.

318 Simplicius, *In Phys.*, 216.35–37.

319 Simplicius, *In Phys.*, 246.8–10.

320 Simplicius, *In Phys.*, 244.22–246.16.

or not privation ought to be called a principle. So, in *al-Samāʿ al-ṭabīʿī* I.2, he writes the following:

> فإنّ العدم شرط في أن يكون الشيء متغيّراً أو مستكملاً فإنّه لو لم يكن هناك عدم لاستحال أن يكون مستكملاً أو متغيراً ... فإذن المتغيّر والمستكمل يحتاج إلى أن يكون قبله عدم حتّى يتحقّق كونه متغيراً أو مستكملاً. والعدم ليس يحتاج في أن يكون عدماً إلى أن يحصل تغيّر أو استكمال ... فالعدم من هذا الوجه أقدم فهو مبدأ إن كان كلّ ما لا بدّ من وجوده للأمر أيّ وجود كان ليُوجَد شيء آخر من غير انعكاس مبدأ. وإن كان ذلك لا يكفي في كون الشيء مبدأ ولا يكون المبدأ كلّ ما لا بدّ من وجوده للأمر أيّ وجود كان بل ما لا بدّ من وجوده مع الأمر الذي هو له مبدأ من غير تقدّم ولا تأخّر فليس العدم مبدأ.
>
> So, indeed,[321] privation is a condition (*šarṭ*) for something's being changeable and perfectible, and so if there were no privation, it would be impossible that it is perfectible or changeable ... Therefore, what is changeable and perfectible requires that (*yuḥtāğu ilā*) prior to it is a privation, so that its being changeable or perfectible is realised. The privation in that it is a privation, however, does not require a change or a perfection to occur ... So, privation in this respect is prior (*aqdam*) and, thus, is a principle – if a principle is all that whose existence for something,[322] however the existence might be, is inevitable,[323] in order for something other than it to come-to-be, but not conversely (*min ġayr inʿikās*). If that is not sufficient[324] for something's being a principle, and a principle is not all that whose existence for something, however the existence might be, is inevitable but rather is that whose existence inevitably is together with the thing of which it is a principle without priority or posteriority, then privation is not a principle. (*al-Samāʿ al-ṭabīʿī* I.2, §14, 17.10–16)[325]

According to Avicenna here, privation is a condition (*šarṭ*) for change and perfection insofar as that which is changeable or perfectible is inevitably characterised by a certain privation, in order to be able to undergo a change or a perfection at all. In turn, privation is said not to require any change or perfection to happen, because something could be deprived of a certain attribute without ever acquiring this attribute. Accordingly, privation is not a cause for change to happen but a requirement for being changeable and perfectible in the first place. Consequently, then, there is no privation in what is unchangeable, as Avicenna explains in the physics of his *al-Nağāt* when he writes that "whatever is not preceded by a privation is eternal" (*azalī*).[326] Privation does not necessarily entail the occurrence of a change or a perfection, whereas change and perfection require a privation, because no change could happen without a preceding privation. Insofar as privation is something required prior to a change or a perfection, it

---

321 Reading *fa-ʾinna* with Mss. Leiden or. 4 and or. 84 as well as Zāyid for *iḏ* in McGinnis and *inna* in Āl Yāsīn.

322 Reading *wuğūdihī li-l-amr* with Ms. Leiden or. 4 as well as Zāyid for *wuğūdihī* in Ms. Leiden or. 84 as well as Āl Yāsīn and McGinnis.

323 Reading *kull mā lā budda* with Mss. Leiden or. 4 and or. 84 as well as Āl Yāsīn and McGinnis for *kull mā kāna lā budda* in Zāyid.

324 Reading *yakfī* with Mss. Leiden or. 4 and or. 84 as well as Zāyid for *y-f-y* in McGinnis and Āl Yāsīn.

325 cf. *al-Ḥikma al-mašriqiyya* III.3, 7.9–14.

326 *al-Nağāt* II.1.1, 196.1f. ≈ *al-Ḥikma al-ʿArūḍiyya* II.1, 116.9f.

is a necessary but not a sufficient condition for change and perfection. Since it explains the occurrence of change and makes change intelligible, it qualifies, in this sense at least, for being a principle. Yet, since privation by itself does not necessitate any change to occur, it cannot be said to be a positive feature of something considered as such. A freshly baked cake, for example, can be still deprived of being cold, as it comes hot out of the oven. Of course, then, the cake immediately starts to cool down, but it is not the privation, i.e., its being not-cold, which necessitates that change to occur. The change of cooling-down to the natural temperature of this cake is effected by the cake's inherent nature which produces an inclination to cool down by itself, as we shall see in the next chapter of this study. In other words, that change is explained by what the cake inherently and essentially *is* – not by what it non-inherently and accidentally *is not*. Still, of course, privation explains that change, as it makes clear that the cake is not-cold even though it is essentially such as to be cold – again, it makes the change of cooling down intelligible – but it does not bring that change about. Insofar as it explains change, privation could be considered as a principle, yet it is not a principle of the thing insofar as it is what it is, and only what it is can cause a change to happen. So, privation is not a principle in the sense of something "whose existence inevitably is together with the thing" (*lā budda min wuǧūdihī maʿa l-amr*). It is, therefore, not enough merely to point to some sort of a priority-posteriority-relation between a thing's change and a thing's privation for privation to be a principle. In fact, the whole point of privation, in one way or another, is to be *not* together with the thing of which it was supposed to be a principle – privation is to be characterised "not by inhering but by not inhering" in the thing, if we may call upon Simplicius' above quoted formulation – and so it is clear that privation right away per definition fails to be a principle in this sense.

As a result, privation may be a principle just as well as it may not. Even though this seems to be a classic stalemate, Avicenna offers a pragmatic riposte, as he states the following:

> ولا فائدة لنا في أن نناقش في التسمية فلنستعمل بدل المبدأ المحتاج إليه من غير انعكاس.
>
> We achieve nothing by quibbling over terminology, so in lieu of "principle," let us use "what is required – but not conversely" (*al-muḥtāǧ ilayhi min ġayr inʿikās*). (*al-Samāʿ al-ṭabīʿī* I.2, §14, 17.16f., tr. by McGinnis)

This passage does not mean that Avicenna does not care whether someone takes privation to be a principle or not. It means that he does not care *as long as* one understands the fundamental difference between the way in which matter and form are principles as opposed to the way in which privation might be considered a principle. Interestingly, this has been his agenda since the very beginning. Avicenna is concerned with explaining the principles of natural things, and he has already conversed about those which belong to natural things insofar as they are corporeal, viz., matter and form, which are always together with the things they constitute. It is for this reason that matter and form are principles in the fullest sense, i.e., in both of the two senses: they are principles insofar as they are "inevitable in order for something other to come-to-be," i.e., they fulfil the priority condition. At the same time, they are also principles "whose existence inevitably is together with the thing," i.e., they fulfil both the priority condition *and* the together condition.

Privation, in turn, only fulfils the priority condition, as it is required prior to any change as a necessary precondition for that change to occur. Regardless of whether or not we call privation a principle, it is clear that neither will there be any change without privation nor will any such change be intelligible. Thus, within the science of physics, Avicenna explains privation, as he did with matter and form, as a certain functional prerequisite: while matter was said to be simply that which is "capable of acquiring some other factor" and form that which is "a disposition that has been acquired by [matter]," so privation is only whatever the compound of matter and form is presently lacking, where it is precisely this lack which can be remedied through a process of change or perfection currently envisaged or already going on.[327] Thus, in this way, the existence of a privation is, in fact, inevitable for that process to come about.

Having said this, Avicenna, clearly inclines towards regarding privation as a much inferior principle to matter and form. It is more properly called a condition (*šarṭ*).[328] This emerges particularly from what Avicenna writes a few lines later in an interim summary of the current account. There, he seeks to differentiate between the two *formal* aspects that are involved in any change, viz., form and privation:

> والصورة تفارق العدم بأنّ الصورة ماهية بنفسها زائدة الوجود على الوجود الذي للهيولى والعدم لا يزيد وجوداً على الوجود الذي للهيولى بل يصحبه حال مقايسته إلى هذه الصورة إذا لم تكن موجودة وكانت القوّة على قبولها موجودة.

> Form is distinct from privation in that the form is an essence in itself (*māhiyya bi-nafsihā*) adding (*zāʾid*) existence to the existence which belongs to matter, whereas privation does not add (*lā yazīdu*) existence to the existence which belongs to matter but rather is [something which is] accompanied by a state that relates it to this form when it [sc. this form] is not existent, whereas the potential to receive it (*qubūlihā*) is existent. (*al-Samāʿ al-ṭabīʿī* I.2, §17, 18.13–15, tr. by McGinnis, modified)[329]

The question about the difference between the formal and the privative factor is a fair one and an answer to it is overdue. In the present passage, Avicenna suggest a clear hierarchy. Form, he says, is an "essence in itself" which contributes and adds to the matter by providing existential and essential concreteness to the matter. This is why

327 For the descriptions of matter and form, cf. *al-Samāʿ al-ṭabīʿī* I.3, §10, 25.6–10; q.v. also above, 174f., 198f.

328 McGinnis, "Making Something of Nothing," 558.

329 cf. *al-Ḥikma al-mašriqiyya* III.3, 8.1–4; cf. also Philoponus, *In Phys.*, 161.18–20, tr. by Osborne: "For the privation contributes nothing to the being and existence of the object, but only by its own absence does it collaborate towards the development of the object."

form is a constituent and, thus, a principle of the being of natural bodies insofar as they are bodies and are what they are. By contrast, privation does not add anything to existence but merely represents the lack of a form. In fact, it does not even exist as such but only insofar as it has a relation or correspondence to a form which the thing once had or is about to acquire. Thus, we can decidedly *not* say that "body has privation" in the same sense as we can say that "body has matter" and "body has form," because privation depends on the form of a body and exists only in relation to it or in contrast with it. It does not exist as such and exists only accidentally. It is a principle only when we conceive of principle along the lines of "what is required – but not conversely" (*al-muḥtāǧ ilayhi min ġayr in'ikās*).

The involvement of privation in change still remains an odd one, for privation is something which is not there, i.e., it is a factor of a natural thing's processes, precisely because this thing lacks that which it is deprived of. This is also the gist of Avicenna's more concise description of privation in *al-Naǧāt*, which states the following:

وكون العدم مبدأً هو لا بدّ منه للكائن من حيث هو كائن وله عن الكائن بدّ وهو مبدأ بالعرض لأنّ بارتفاعه يكون الكائن لا بوجوده.

> Privation's being a principle is [such that] it is inevitable[330] for that which comes-to-be insofar as it comes-to-be, whereas it is not inevitable for it to have that which comes-to-be. It is an accidental principle (*mabda' bi-l-'araḍ*), because through its elimination (*bi-rtifā'ihī*) something comes-to-be and not through its existence (*lā bi-wuǧūdihī*). (*al-Naǧāt* II.1.1, 196.6–8)

Furthermore, it is evident that privation is not common in the sense of numerical commonality but is only generically common, as Avicenna adds:

وأمّا العدم فواضح من حاله أنّه لا يجوز أن يكون من جملته عدم مشترك بهذا النحو الأوّل لأنّ هذا العدم هو عدم شيء من شأنه أن يكون. وإذا كان من شأنه أن يكون لم يبعد أن يكون فحينئذ لا يبقى هذا العدم. فحينئذ لا يكون مشتركاً.

> As for privation, it is clear (*wāḍiḥ*) from its state that it is not possible at all (*lā yaǧūzu ... min ǧumlatihī*) that there be a common privation in this first sense, because this privation is the privation of something that is such as to come-to-be (*min ša'nihī an yakūna*). If it is such as to come to be, then it is not unlikely that it will come-to-be. Thus, in that case privation does not remain, and so in that case it is not something common (*muštarak*). (*al-Samā' al-ṭabī'ī* I.3, §4, 23.5–7)[331]

---

330 A variant in Dānešpažūh's apparatus suggests reading *huwa annahū lā budda*, whereas Fakhry, 'Umayra, and al-Kurdī read *huwa li-annahū lā budda*.

331 Avicenna's clear and definite wording here in *al-Samā' al-ṭabī'ī* about the question of whether privation is generically or numerically common leaves no room for interpretation. Thus, structural considerations of the textual composition of *al-Samā' al-ṭabī'ī* I.2–3 may provide further confirmation for the above advanced interpretation that for Avicenna, matter and form are likewise only common in the generic sense: first, he shows that matter, form, and privation together fail to be common as a single entity in the numerical sense, before he, then, goes on to show that all of them are, nonetheless, common in the second, generic, sense.

Privation, thus, emerges as an accidental principle which is, just as the essential and constitutive principles matter and form, common in the generic sense of the word but not as a single, numerically one entity. Only agent and end are common in both senses of the term, as all natural things share in God as their single First Cause. This concludes Avicenna's account of those principles of natural things which, in his own terminology, "are most appropriately called 'principles'" (*allatī hiya aḥrā an tusammā mabādi'*).

We shall, now, turn to those which, according to Avicenna, "are most deservedly called 'causes'" (*allatī hiya awlā an tusammā 'ilalan*).[332]

332 It is clear that this, again, is a reference to the opening line of *Physics* I, in which Aristotle declared his intention to investigate the "principles, causes, and elements" of natural things; q.v. above, 162ff.

4 Nature and Power

The chapter in which Avicenna defines nature is extreme.[1] On the first pages, it provides a new approach to the subject at hand that is not to be found in Aristotle nor anywhere else before Avicenna. Surely, even this "new" approach is influenced by Aristotle, yet Avicenna's exposition must be credited with being as new and unprecedented as a Peripatetic account of the concept of nature could possibly be, even though he does not do much more than demonstrating his capacity for the subtle rearrangement and systematisation of materials borrowed from the ancients. In the remaining two-thirds of the chapter, then, Avicenna does something very unusual for him: he offers a literal commentary on Aristotle's definition of nature (φύσις, *ṭabīʿa*) at *Physics* II.1, 192b20–23, quoting the definition in full, displaying his approval, and discussing all the terms involved. Then, he quotes what seems to be a late ancient reworking of that definition, states his disagreement, and provides his grounds for rejecting it, once again in the form of a literal commentary.

The reason *al-Samāʿ al-ṭabīʿī* I.5 is extreme, therefore, is that it is, first, especially fresh in its approach and, then, exceptionally direct in its execution. I shall begin with the latter aspect, i.e., Avicenna's commentary on the Aristotelian definition of nature, and investigate how Avicenna engages with his predecessors and how he defends Aristotle's definition against unnecessary and corrupted additions. For that reason, it is required, first, to outline several important aspects of the Greek reception of Aristotle's account. I shall, then, proceed to analyse Avicenna's own approach to "nature," explain his definition, and show how his account not only deals with certain ambiguities in the accounts of his predecessors but also reacts to a certain interpretation that was predominant also among the Arabic intellectuals of his own time.

4.1 Nature, and Soul, in the Greek Philosophical Tradition

It is commonly known that most of the eight books of Aristotle's *Physics* have been composed as individual treatises and that it was not Aristotle himself who assembled them so as to form a larger work that came to be known by the name of *Physics*.[2]

1 There are only few earlier contributions concerned with Avicenna's account of nature or or with various aspects of it; cf. Brown, "Avicenna and the Christian Philosophers in Baghdad"; Hasnawi, "La dynamique d'Ibn Sīnā"; Macierowski and Hassing, "John Philoponus on Aristotle's Definition of Nature"; Verbeke, "La nature dans une perspective nouvelle"; Arif, "Ibn Sīnā's Idea of Nature and Change"; "The Universe as a System"; McGinnis, "Natural Knowledge in the Arabic Middle Ages"; Belo, "The Concept of 'Nature' in Aristotle, Avicenna and Averroes"; cf. now also Lammer, "Defining Nature"; McGinnis, "Ibn Sina's Natural Philosophy."

2 The transmission of Aristotle's works has been – and still is – the subject of numerous publications, e.g., Lord, "On the Early History of the Aristotelian Corpus"; Barnes, "Roman Aristotle"; Primavesi,

https://doi.org/10.1515/9783110546798-005

Naturally, this affects how the various books are read by modern interpreters as opposed to their late ancient and medieval predecessors, as well as how they interpret the relation, dependence, and coherence between and within these eight books. Some, for example, have diagnosed a certain abruptness in the transition between the first book of the *Physics*, in which Aristotle establishes matter, form, and privation as the principles of natural things, and the second book, in which he treats the concept of nature as a principle of motion, thus stressing the disparity between the two books and their intention and content. William Ross, for example, straightforwardly denies any "organic connexion between the two books."[3] Wolfgang Wieland similarly states that although the first two books share the intention to discuss nature, as professed already at the very beginning of *Physics* I.1, the discussion was immediately transformed into an inquiry of the principles of natural things rather than nature itself. This discussion was completed in the first book, so that the second book could commence an "entirely independent treatment," focusing on "nature as such."[4] William Charlton seems to agree with Ross' and Wieland's diagnosis, even though he feels compelled to advance the weaker claim that "Phys. I–II rather complement one another than form a continuous treatise."[5] On this reading, then, there is a strong disparity between the account – and perhaps even the notion – of principles in book one of the *Physics* and the examination of nature and the causes in book two.

Contrary to this interpretation, the late antique commentators generally tended to highlight the inner coherence of Aristotle's work and the rational structure of his composition by emphasising the complementary character of these two books. John Philoponus (d. 574), for example, states that although Aristotle intended the first book of the *Physics* to be a thorough examination of both matter and form, he ended up talking "a lot" (πολύν) about matter and discussed form only "briefly" (βραχέα), so that Aristotle's agenda in the second book was, then, to compensate for that imbalance by focusing on form.[6] Philoponus, then, writes the following:

> πρόκειται οὖν αὐτῷ ἐν τούτῳ τῷ βιβλίῳ περὶ τοῦ εἴδους διαλαβεῖν, ἀλλ' ἐπειδὴ τὸ εἶδος τὸ ἑκάστου ἡ φύσις ἐστὶν ἡ ἑκάστου ... διὰ τοῦτο βουλόμενος περὶ τοῦ εἴδους διδάξαι ζητεῖ τί ποτέ ἐστιν ἡ φύσις· ἐὰν γὰρ εὕρωμεν τί ἐστιν ἡ φύσις, εὑρηκότες ἂν εἴημεν τί ἐστι τὸ εἶδος.
>
> So, it is his [sc. Aristotle's] task in this book [sc. the second book] to delineate form (τοῦ εἴδους διαλαβεῖν), but since the form of each thing is the nature of each thing (τὸ εἶδος τὸ ἑκάστου ἡ φύσις ἐστὶν ἡ ἑκάστου) ... so, for this reason, wishing to teach about form, he inquires into what

"Ein Blick in den Stollen von Skepsis." Regarding the *Physics*, cf. esp. Ross' introduction in *Physics* as well as Brunschwig, "Qu'est ce que *la Physique* d'Aristote?"

3 Ross' comments in *Physics*, 499.

4 Wieland, *Die aristotelische Physik*, 231: "Das erste Physikbuch führte in sich selbst zu einem gewissen Abschluß ... Die Natur als solche ist dagegen im zweiten Physikbuch Thema der Untersuchung. Diese Untersuchung ist in Ansatz und Durchführung eine vollkommen selbstständige Abhandlung."

5 Charlton's introduction in *Physics*, xiii.

6 Philoponus, *In Phys.*, 194.4–16; cf. 339.5–10.

> nature actually is, for if we find what nature is, we shall find what form is. (Philoponus, *In Phys.*, 194.16–21, tr. by Lacey, modified)[7]

With this argument, Philoponus attempts to justify the systematic unity of Aristotle's work, which apparently was one of his major concerns.[8] Moreover, he also makes the philosophical claim that Aristotle's discussion of principles from the first book is continued in the second, so that nature emerges as one of the principles of natural things which has already been discussed, albeit not sufficiently, in the guise of "form." Since the nature of some thing is to be identified with its form, nature as a principle of motion and rest has been discussed in the first book already, albeit from a different perspective, as the counterpart of matter in the constitution of natural things and as the formal principle involved in any change.

In a somewhat different way, though essentially arguing for a similar conclusion, Simplicius maintains that it is appropriate and, in fact, required for Aristotle to speak of nature in book two, because the first book of the *Physics* was marked by an emphasis on artificial change, despite his announcement "to seek the common principles of *all* change" (κοινὰς ἀρχὰς πάσης ἐζήτει μεταβολῆς).[9] Consequently, the second book is meant to focus on natural change and to establish, on that basis, the notion of "nature" and to account for what is "by nature," what is "in accordance with nature," and what "has nature."[10]

There is some merit in regarding Aristotle's discussion of principles, which was begun in book one, as also comprising the contents of book two. For example, one may point to Aristotle's explicit definition of nature as a principle (ἀρχή) of motion and rest.[11] Since nature is undoubtedly a principle of *natural* things, it is plausible to conceive of nature as being, together with matter and form, among the most important principles of natural things that the science of physics has to investigate. In fact, in the discussion of nature in *Physics* II.1, Aristotle himself raises the question of whether nature ought to be identified with matter or rather with form, eventually concluding that "form is nature rather than matter."[12] Since "nature," "form," and "matter" appear to be closely related to each other, there may be no reason for not applying the same term ἀρχή equally to these three concepts, especially since Aristotle apparently, in one way or another, tries

---

7 cf. Philoponus, *In Phys.*, 195.13–19.

8 This is evinced by a number of statements throughout Philoponus commentary on the *Physics*, cf. *In Phys.*, 2.13–17, 194.4–20, 339.5–10, 346.4–8, 440.15–17, 704.11, 18, 715.3, 726.12, 760.28, 762.9, 861.7–9, 907.8–11. In the main, Simplicius (d. ~ 560) seems to agree with this approach; cf. Simplicius, *In Phys.*, 259.3–260.2.

9 Simplicius, *In Phys.*, 260.9–16, my emphasis. For an interesting and elaborate contemporary argument emphasising the dependence of *Physics* I.7 on the concept of nature as developed in book II.1, cf. Broadie, *Nature, Change, and Agency in Aristotle's* Physics, 12–27.

10 Simplicius, *In Phys.*, 260.16–19.

11 *Phys.* II.1, 192b14, 21.

12 *Phys.* II.1, 193a28–b12; cf. *Met.* Δ.4, 1015a3–11, 13–17; Z.17, 1041b27–31.

to assimilate nature with the principles of *Physics* I – he even mentions privation at the very end of chapter II.1, in an attempt to incorporate it into his reflections on nature.[13] In addition to that, one might also point towards Aristotle's programmatic opening in the very first lines of the *Physics*, where he stated his intention to investigate the "principles, causes, and elements" (ἀρχαὶ ἢ αἴτια ἢ στοιχεῖα) of natural things. Since the first book discussed matter and form as the constitutive "elements" of things, a discussion of "causes" has not yet been provided. The second book of the *Physics*, however, is well-known for doing precisely that: among establishing the four causes, it also examines causality more generally and establishes its importance for the science of nature. It may, thus, seem that the contents of the two books are closely related; that at the beginning of *Physics* II, Aristotle's discussion of principles is still ongoing; and that it is the concept of nature which serves as a link between the notion of form as a constitutive element and the notion of form as a cause of motion.

If nature is a cause and principle of motion in Aristotle's natural philosophy, it is not the only one. There is also soul (ψυχή), which Aristotle discusses and defines in his *De anima*. In the fourth chapter of the second book of that work, Aristotle writes the following:

> ἔστι δὲ ἡ ψυχὴ τοῦ ζῶντος σώματος αἰτία καὶ ἀρχή. ταῦτα δὲ πολλαχῶς λέγεται, ὁμοίως δ' ἡ ψυχὴ κατὰ τοὺς διωρισμένους τρόπους τρεῖς αἰτία· καὶ γὰρ ὅθεν ἡ κίνησις καὶ οὗ ἕνεκα καὶ ὡς ἡ οὐσία τῶν ἐμψύχων σωμάτων ἡ ψυχὴ αἰτία.
>
> والنفس علّة الجرم الحيّ. وهذا قول متصرّف على أوجه لأنّ النفس علّة على الثلاثة الأنحاء التي ذكرنا آنفاً وذلك أنّها علّة ابتداء الحركة ومن أخل ذلك كان الجرم وهي جوهر الأجسام ذوي الأنفس.
>
> The soul is the cause and principle (αἰτία καὶ ἀρχή, *'illa*) of the living body. As these things are spoken of in many ways, so the soul is spoken of as a cause in the three of the ways delineated: for the soul is a cause as the source of motion (ὅθεν ἡ κίνησις, *ibtidā' al-ḥaraka*), as that for the sake of which, and as the substance of ensouled bodies. (*De an.* II.4, 415b8–12, tr. by Shields)[14]

The fact that for Aristotle, soul is a principle of motion in much the same way as nature is, is historically significant, as we shall see, because it allows for a reading that aligns nature with soul, so that both concepts are taken as efficient causes responsible for the motion of natural bodies.

13 cf. *Phys.* II.1, 193b18–21.

14 Hicks, who is followed in Hamlyn's translation, reads ὅθεν ἡ κίνησις αὐτή. Ross, being followed by Shields, omits αὐτή, which seems to be lacking in the Arabic translation, too. The Arabic translation reported here, however, further misses καὶ ἀρχή in line 415b8. This translation is one of two Arabic versions that were available to Averroes when he was composing his long commentary on Aristotle's *De anima* and the only one extant today as Ms. 2450 at Aya Sofya, Istanbul. The other, lost translation seems to have reproduced the αἰτία καὶ ἀρχή faithfully, as we can gather from Averroes' commentary; cf. Taylor's remarks in Averroes, *Long Commentary on the* De Anima *of Aristotle*, lxxvi–lxxix, fn. 87, 145.

Moreover, we have just seen Aristotle characterising nature by means of an explicit reference to form. The same happens to soul, for in *De anima* II.1, Aristotle states the following:

> ἀναγκαῖον ἄρα τὴν ψυχὴν οὐσίαν εἶναι ὡς εἶδος σώματος φυσικοῦ δυνάμει ζωὴν ἔχοντος.
>
> فالنفس بالاضطرار جوهر كصورة جرم طبيعي له حياة بالقوة.
>
> It is necessary, then, that the soul is a substance as the form of a natural body which has life in potentiality. (*De an.* II.1, 412a19–21, tr. by Shields)

These passages, which identify both nature and soul with the form of their underlying body, and which make them a cause and principle for both that body and its motion, not only illustrate once more the intimate relation between some of the most important concepts of Aristotle's natural philosophy, they could also be regarded as an emphatic invitation to systematically equate the concepts of nature and soul.[15] Such a strategy is already found in Alexander of Aphrodisias (fl. ~ 200). According to Simplicius' report, Alexander wrote the following:

> σημειωτέον γάρ ... ὅτι καὶ τὴν ψυχὴν περιείληφε τῷ τῆς φύσεως λόγῳ, εἴπερ ἡ μὲν ψυχὴ κατ' αὐτὸν ἐντελέχειά ἐστιν σώματος φυσικοῦ ὀργανικοῦ, ἡ δὲ φύσις κυρίως καὶ πρώτως ἐν τοῖς ἁπλοῖς ἐστι σώμασι καὶ οὐ τοῖς ὀργανικοῖς.
>
> We should note ... that he [sc. Aristotle] included (περιείληφε) soul in his description of nature, since according to him the soul is the actuality of the natural body, while nature strictly and primarily resides in simple nonorganic bodies. (Alexander *apud* Simplicium, *In Phys.*, 268.18–21, tr. by Fleet, modified)[16]

With this, Alexander seems to recommend that as soul is to the animate body, so is nature to the inanimate body. This does not need to mean that the soul of an animate body simply is its nature, because obviously an animate body falls down like a stone not on account of its soul but of the corporeal nature of its underlying elemental composition. Nature and soul can still be seen as distinct principles, even though, on a conceptual level, they are both principles of the motions of their underlying bodies.[17]

---

15 Aristotle's discussion of form as substance and cause in *Metaphysics* Z.17 is also immediatly relevant here, in particular the last thought of that chapter, concluding the whole book, to the effect that in all natural things, nature is their substance, not as an element but as a principle (*Met.* Z.17, 1041b28–31).

16 cf. Alexander *apud* Simplicium, *In Phys.*, 1219.1–7, where Alexander calls soul "a more perfect nature" (τελειοτέρα γὰρ φύσις ἡ ψυχή); cf. also Alexander *apud* Simplicium, *In Cael.*, 380.29–381.2, 387.14 as well as the *Maqāla fī l-qawl fī mabādiʾ al-kull*, §§4–5, 44.4–46.4; §§16–23, 52.3–56.2; §96, 94.9–15 (ed. Genequand); cf. further Pines, "Omne quod movetur necesse est ab aliquo moveri," 44–47; Moraux, *Der Aristotelismus bei den Griechen*, vol. 3, 138.

17 Having said this, it apparently remained a problem for the Greek commentators to specifically pin down the difference between nature and soul. A particularly delicate case in this regard were the heavenly bodies; cf. Sorabji's remarks (and the many references given) in the introduction to Fleet's translation of Simplicius' commentary on *Physics* II.

That soul and nature are distinct principles, while nonetheless being related and conceptually similar, was also a common theme among Neoplatonists. It is generally accepted, for example, that Plotinus (d. 270) identifies nature with the external activity (ἐνέργεια ... ἐκ τῆς οὐσίας) of the world-soul. He even writes in *Enneads* III.8 that "what is called nature is a soul" (ἡ μὲν λεγομένη φύσις ψυχὴ οὖσα) and explains that it is "the offspring (γέννημα) of a prior soul with a stronger life."[18] In this, he was apparently followed by Porphyry (d. ~ 305).[19] Simplicius was aware of such readings and, in direct engagement with the above quotation from Alexander, rejected them altogether.[20] Philoponus, on the other hand, endorsed such a reading of Aristotle and reinterpreted Aristotle's definition of nature in light of his Neoplatonic conception of soul. We shall now see that Philoponus' commentary serves as an apposite example in which we find some Aristotelian ambiguities epitomised and typically resolved. As will be shown, Philoponus' account was immensely influential among Arabic intellectuals of the third/ninth and fourth/tenth centuries in and around Baġdād. Moreover, it is Avicenna who found fault with this conception, reacting to an entire tradition of aligning soul with nature.

Philoponus on Nature

According to Philoponus, as we have just seen, the task of the second book of Aristotle's *Physics* is to "delineate form." So, when Aristotle, towards the end of *Physics* II.1, lists three meanings of "nature," viz., that it can refer to the shape and form (ἡ μορφὴ καὶ τὸ εἶδος, *ḫilqa wa-ṣūra*), to the primary underlying matter (ἡ πρώτη ... ὑποκειμένη ὕλη, *al-hayūlā l-ūlā l-mawḍūʿa*), or to the process towards nature (ὁδός ... εἰς φύσιν, *ṭarīq ilā l-ṭabīʿa*), Philoponus' comments on this passage emphasise that it is, in fact, the form which should be taken as the primary meaning of nature:

> Τριχῶς οὖν τῆς φύσεως λεγομένης, τῆς μὲν πρώτης καὶ κυριώτατα τοῦ εἴδους, κατὰ δεύτερον δὲ λόγον τῆς ὕλης, καὶ τρίτον τῆς γενέσεως τῆς ἐπὶ τὸ εἶδος ... ἔστι γὰρ καὶ ἡ ὕλη ἀρχὴ κινήσεως καὶ

18 *Enn.* III.8.4, 15f. For Plotinus' account of nature, cf. generally *Enn.* III.8.2–4; IV.4.13; for his conception of "double activity," cf. *Enn.* V.4.2, 27–30; cf. also *Enn.* IV.3.7, 14f.

19 Pointing particularly towards Porphyry's *Sententiae ad intelligibilia ducentes* 8, 12, and 29, A. Smith writes that Porphyry "shares Plotinus' designation of the lowest manifestation of soul in the material as *physis*" and that he "seems to accord to *physis* the status almost of a hypostasis distinct from Soul" ("The Significance of 'Physics' in Porphyry," 32). Armstrong argued that Plotinus envisaged not three but five hypostasis, among which he counts nature; cf. Armstrong, *The Architecture of the Intelligible Universe in the Philosophy of Plotinus*, 86, 102, referring to *Enn.* V.2.1, 24–28. That this view is not tenable has been shown by Rist, *The Road to Reality*, 92–99. For Porphyry, cf. also Adamson, "*Porphyrius Arabus* on Nature and Art."

20 cf. Simplicius, *In Phys.*, 268.18–269.4; 287.7–17. It is a different question whether Simplicius' attempts to differentiate between nature and soul were successful; cf., again, Sorabji's remarks in the introduction to Fleet's translation of Simplicius' commentary on *Physics* II.

> ἠρεμίας ... καὶ τὸ εἶδος δὲ ἀρχή ἐστι κινήσεως καὶ ἠρεμίας ... καὶ ἡ ὁδός δ' ἡ ἐπὶ τὸ εἶδος δύναται λέγεσθαι ἀρχὴ κινήσεως καὶ ἠρεμίας.
>
> So, "nature" is said in three ways: the primary and strictest, however, is form (τῆς μὲν πρώτης καὶ κυριώτατα τοῦ εἴδους), according to a second account [it is] matter, and, third, the generation towards form ... For even matter is a principle of motion and rest ... and form, too, is a principle of motion and rest ... and the process towards form can be called a principle of motion and rest. (Philoponus, *In Phys.*, 211.20–34, tr. by Lacey, modified)[21]

With this, Philoponus seconds Aristotle's own conclusion that "shape then is nature" (ἡ ἄρα μορφὴ φύσις, *fa-l-ṭabīʿa iḏan ḫilqa*).[22] This comes as no surprise, for earlier in his commentary, as we have already seen, Philoponus declared that "the nature of each thing is nothing other than the form of each thing (οὐδὲν ἄλλο ἐστὶν ἢ τὸ ἑκάστου εἶδος) and the form of each thing is nothing other than the nature of each thing."[23] In this sense, nature is considered as a formal cause (εἰδικόν ... αἴτιον).

In addition to that, nature is also an efficient (ποιητικόν) and a final cause (τελικόν), so that everything which has a nature is capable of initiating motion, i.e., has in itself the source for its own motion, such as to proceed towards a specific end.[24] This, then, is the difference which marks the distinction, introduced by Aristotle in the first line of *Physics* II.1, between things that exist "by nature" (φύσει, *bi-l-ṭabīʿa*) and things that exist "through other causes" (δι' ἄλλας αἰτίας, *min qibal asbāb uḫar*), for only the former are able to bring about motion through themselves. Philoponus immediately likens this distinction from *Physics* II.1 to the differentiation between the animate (τὸ ἔμψυχον, *ḏī l-nafs*) and the inanimate (τοῦ ἀψύχου, *mā lā nafsa lahū*) in *De anima* I.2 – a differentiation which conveniently consists in the former's aptitude for *motion* and sensation (κινήσει τε καὶ τῷ αἰσθάνεσθαι, *bi-l-ḥaraka ... bi-l-ḥiss*).[25] This initiates a brief discussion of the relation between nature and soul, which Philoponus concludes by accepting that it is possible to say that soul is the nature of animals insofar as they are animals, because soul is the cause of the motion of the animal.[26]

So far, Philoponus signalled his agreement with Aristotle's concept of nature as a principle of motion. Now, however, he voices his explicit discontent with Aristotle's definition. According to Philoponus, the definition of nature, as given in *Physics* II.1,

---

21 All these meanings of "nature" appear also in *Metaphysics* Δ.4.

22 *Phys.* II.1, 193b18, tr. by Hardie/Gaye.

23 Philoponus, *In Phys.*, 194.18f., tr. by Lacey. Simplicius, too, accepts this inference and remarks that in the second book of the *Physics*, Aristotle "will demonstrate [nature] as being both form and efficient cause" (ἣν καὶ ὡς εἶδος καὶ ὡς ποιοῦν αἴτιον οὖσαν ἀποδείξει; *In Phys.*, 260.1f., tr. by Fleet). However, he explicitly situates nature in a metaphysical context by characterising it as an instrumental cause that is influenced by the heavens and the intelligible realm; cf. *In Phys.*, 314.9–14 as well as 223.16–19; cf. also Gerson, *Aristotle and Other Platonists*, 103, 109f.

24 Philoponus, *In Phys.*, 195.24–196.26; cf. also *In Phys.*, 317.14–22.

25 *De an.* II.2, 403b25–7; cf. Philoponus, *In Phys.*, 195.19–24.

26 cf. Philoponus, *In Phys.*, 197.13–18.

is wanting, as it merely concerns "the activity of nature" (τῆς ἐνεργείας τῆς φύσεως), while failing to explain "what nature is" (τί ἐστιν ἡ φύσις).[27] In an attempt to provide a more satisfactory definition, Philoponus expands Aristotle's original definition of nature in the following way:

> ἵνα οὖν καὶ τῆς οὐσίας αὐτῆς τὸν ὁρισμὸν ἀποδῶμεν, λεκτέον οὕτως, ὅτι ἐστὶν ἡ φύσις ζωὴ ἤτοι δύναμις καταδεδυκυῖα διὰ τῶν σωμάτων, διαπλαστικὴ αὐτῶν καὶ διοικητική, ἀρχὴ κινήσεως οὖσα καὶ ἠρεμίας "ἐν ᾧ ὑπάρχει πρώτως καθ' αὑτὸ καὶ οὐ κατὰ συμβεβηκός."
>
> In order to give a definition of its substance (τῆς οὐσίας αὐτῆς), we must say that nature is a life or a power (ζωὴ ἤτοι δύναμις) which has descended (καταδεδυκυῖα) into bodies, and which shapes and governs them (διαπλαστικὴ αὐτῶν καὶ διοικητική), being a principle of motion (ἀρχὴ κινήσεως) and rest [for that] "in which it is primarily (πρώτως), by itself and not by accident." (Philoponus, *In Phys.*, 197.34–198.1, tr. by Lacey, modified)

Philoponus' decision to blend his own words with a partial quotation of Aristotle's original definition indicates his confidence of having legitimately emended the otherwise imperfect formulation from the *Physics*. Clearly, though, what Philoponus has done amounts to much more than a simple rewording and is, in fact, a thorough Neoplatonic reworking. Describing φύσις as ζωή ("life") links nature to the Athenian's discussion of soul as life and as self-moved in Plato's *Laws* X.[28] It is also reminiscent of the relation between nature and life drawn by Proclus (d. 485) in his commentary on the *Timaeus*.[29] By using καταδεδυκυῖα, a perfect participle of the verb καταδύειν ("to go down," "to sink or plunge into"), Philoponus employs further psychological terminology which can be linked to the Neoplatonic interpretation of the fall of the soul in Plato's *Phaedrus* and which we find in Plotinus' depiction of the soul's allegedly unfortunate residence in the depths of the body.[30] Of particular relevance is also Plotinus' account of the soul's

---

27 Philoponus, *In Phys.*, 197.30f., tr. by Lacey.

28 *Leg.* X, 894a8–896a5. It is often suggested that Aristotle's nature in *Physics* II.1 should be read in light of an engagement with, or even as a reaction to, Plato's remarks on soul in *Laws* X, cf. Mansion, *Introduction a la Physique Aristotélicienne*, 82–105; Solmsen, *Aristotle's System of the Physical World*, 95–102; Wieland, *Die aristotelische Physik*, 240–247; Broadie, *Nature, Change, and Agency in Aristotle's* Physics, 209–214, fn. 24, 238.

29 cf. Proclus, *In Tim.* II, 139.25–140.1; cf. also Simplicius, *In Phys.*, 289.33. For Proclus' account of nature, cf. generally Martijn, *Proclus on Nature*, ch. 2; Lernould, "Nature in Proclus"; Opsomer, "The Natural World," 152f.

30 *Phdr.* 246d3–248e3; *Enn.* I.6.8, 14; cf. *Enn.* I.8.13, 23; cf. also Philoponus, *In An.*, 4.31; Proclus, *In Tim.* I, 10.24–26; II, 103.14–16; Proclus, *In Parm.* III, 794.3–11. The expression καταδεδυκυῖα διὰ τῶν σωμάτων may also be translated as "diffused throughout bodies" as McGuire does ("Philoponus on *Physics* ii 1," 247, fn. 11, 264f.; but cf. Macierowski and Hassing, "John Philoponus on Aristotle's Definition of Nature," 82, fn. 18, 95). Lacey also notes, somewhat vaguely, that καταδεδυκυῖα displays Stoic or Neoplatonic influence and that "*dunamis katadedukuia* is perfectly acceptable as a Neoplatonic phrase, with *katadedukuia* being used to refer to the descent of souls into bodies" (fn. 43, 148f., to his translation of Philoponus' commentary on the *Physics*). Macierowski and Hassing, however, assert that "[t]he sense of sinking or descending conveyed by καταδεδυκυῖα is … all that distinguishes Philoponus from

descent into body in *Enneads* IV.8 with its references to soul's powers of shaping and governing the corporeal world, all of which reappear in the Arabic Plotinus' *Uṯūlūǧiyā*.[31] Moreover, δύναμις here does not indicate a passive Aristotelian potency. To the contrary, Philoponus seems to use the term once again in a sense related to the *Phaedrus* and to Plato's depiction of soul as the "power" or "force" (δύναμις) of a chariot with its team of winged horses and its charioteer.[32] It is important to understand this Platonic analogy in the context of the dialogue, for just a few lines earlier, Socrates has shown the soul to be the immortal (ἀθάνατος) principle of motion (κινήσεως ... ἀρχή) on account of its being "the self-mover of itself" (τὸ αὐτὸ αὐτὸ κινοῦν).[33] Such a nature, described as a δύναμις, is active and alive, and, indeed, is ζωή ("life").[34]

Consequently, Philoponus' version of Aristotle's "nature" should not be taken in the passive sense of *Physics* II.1, in which nature is said to be "a certain principle or cause of *being* moved (κινεῖσθαι, *yataḥarraku*) and of *being* at rest" (ἠρεμεῖν, *yaskunu*), or of *Physics* VIII.4, in which it is remarked that nature is a principle "not of moving [something] or of causing but of *suffering*" motion (οὐ τοῦ κινεῖν οὐδὲ τοῦ ποιεῖν, ἀλλὰ

---

the Stoics in his emendation of the definition of nature" (Macierowski and Hassing, "John Philoponus on Aristotle's Definition of Nature," 85). In other respects, they acknowledge Stoic traits in Philoponus' comments and, like McGuire and Sorabji, refer to his description of the nature of a thing as δύναμιν φυσικὴν συνεκτικὴν τοῦ εἶναι ("a natural power that holds the being [of something] together") and his use of διαπλαστική ... καὶ διοικητική ("shaping ... and governing"); cf. McGuire, "Philoponus on *Physics* ii 1," 262f.; Sorabji, *Matter, Space, and Motion*, 242f.; Macierowski and Hassing, "John Philoponus on Aristotle's Definition of Nature," 82–86; cf. also de Haas, *John Philoponus' New Definition of Prime Matter*, 101. For a detailed analysis of Philoponus' account of the soul in his commentary on Aristotle's *De anima*, cf. Perkams, *Selbstbewusstsein in der Spätantike*, 30–148.

31 *Enn.* IV.8.5, esp. 24–35; *Kitāb Arisṭāṭālīs al-faylasūf al-musammā bi-l-yūnāniyya Uṯūlūǧiyā* 7, esp. 84.5–14.

32 *Phdr.* 246a6f. In *Enn.* VI.8.1, 11–14, Plotinus has also already remarked upon the latent ambiguity within such terms as δύναμις and δύνασθαι which, he writes, may signify either an active or a passive meaning.

33 *Phdr.* 245c5–246a2, esp. 245d6f.; cf. *Enn.* IV.7.6–9; cf. also Philoponus, *In An.*, 92.20–95.35, 114.17–23.

34 Simplicius rejects interpretations that conceive of soul as a δύναμις on the grounds that soul, far from being a δύναμις, has been defined as "the lowest [i.e., first] *actuality* of the living body" (ἡ ἐσχάτη ἐντελέχεια σώματος φυσικοῦ ὀργανικοῦ; *In Phys.*, 286.25f. emphasis added). Accordingly, soul cannot be a δύναμις in the same sense as nature is, because the δύναμις of nature is a passive power of being moved, as is shown in *Physics* VIII.4, 255b29–256a3 and *De caelo* IV.3, 311a9–12; cf. *In Phys.*, 287.26–288.16; 1217.10–1218.19; *In Cael.*, 387.12–19. One should also keep in mind the explicit contrast between φύσις and δύναμις which Aristotle set up in *De caelo* III.2, where the former is said to be "the principle of motion within a thing itself" (ἡ ἐν αὐτῷ ὑπάρχουσα κινήσεως ἀρχή) and the latter "the [principle of motion] in another" (ἡ ἐν ἄλλῳ; *Cael.* III.2, 301b17–19). The same distinction between φύσις and δύναμις is made in *Metaphysics* Θ.8, in which, however, φύσις is further said to be in the same genus as δύναμις – the genus being homonymously called "δύναμις" – on the grounds that both are a principle of motion. One may well assume that Aristotle's discussion and definition of δύναμις in *Metaphysics* Θ contributed to Philoponus' understanding of "nature" in *Physics* II.1. At any rate, this was certainly Avicenna's impression, as we shall see; q.v. below, 276f. For Aristotle's discussions of various senses of δύναμις, cf. also *Met.* Δ.12; Θ.1–9; cf., generally, Charlton, "Aristotelian Powers."

τοῦ πάσχειν, *lā li-an yuḥarrika aw yafʿala bal li-an yaqbala l-fiʿl*).[35] On the contrary, Philoponus' nature is an active force, a mover and efficient cause, which is directly responsible for the natural motions of the things through which it permeates, and which it forms and governs (διαπλαστικὴ ... καὶ διοικητική).[36] It is in this regard also telling that Philoponus replaced Aristotle's mediopassive infinitive κινεῖσθαι with the simple noun κινήσεως, thus making nature an (active) principle of motion, instead of a (passive) principle of being in motion.[37] Finally, Philoponus ties this understanding of nature, which pervades a body as a self-moving causal principle, to his Neoplatonic conception of soul as the living and essentially self-moving steersman of animate beings, declaring the following:

> δῆλον οὖν καὶ ἐντεῦθεν, ὅτι συμπεριλήψεται ὁ ὅρος καὶ τὴν τῶν ἐμψύχων φύσιν, ἥτις ἐστὶν ἡ ψυχή· ἡ γὰρ τῶν ἐμψύχων ζωὴ οὐδὲν ἄλλο ἐστὶν ἢ ψυχή.
>
> It is clear from this too that the definition [of nature] will also embrace (συμπεριλήψεται) the nature of the animate (τῶν ἐμψύχων φύσιν), which is the soul (ἡ ψυχή); for the life of animate things (τῶν ἐμψύχων ζωή) is nothing other than soul. (Philoponus, *In Phys.*, 198.6–8, tr. by Lacey)[38]

---

35 *Phys.* II.1, 192b21f.; VIII.4, 255b30f., tr. by Hardie/Gaye, modified, emphasis added; q.v. below, 236ff., 240ff.

36 cf. Proclus, *In Tim.* I, 11.17f.

37 Lang argues that Philoponus deliberately avoids the passive and medial verb form, which she regards as central for Aristotle examination of nature, as it shows that, for Aristotle, nature is primarily a principle of *being* moved: "Philoponus never uses Aristotle's infinitives to characterize nature; rather, he consistently relies on the more ambiguous noun form, which he interprets as an intrinsic mover" (*Aristotle's* Physics *and its Medieval Varieties*, 111; cf. also *Aristotle's* Physics *and its Medieval Varieties*, 97f., 100; *The Order of Nature in Aristotle's Physics*, 42–45). Her argument relies greatly on Aristotle's position in *Physics* VIII.4, 255b29–31. However, she has been criticised, among other things, for her "claims about Greek usage" by Gill in a review of her *The Order of Nature in Aristotle's Physics* (Gill, "Review of *The Order of Nature in Aristotle's Physics: Place and the Elements* by Helen S. Lang," 551f.). Regarding the possible meanings of Aristotle's infinitive κινεῖσθαι, Sorabji asserts that "the word *kineisthai* stands indifferently for the intransitive *being in motion* and for the passive *being moved*" (Sorabji, *Matter, Space, and Motion*, 220). Broadie argues that κινεῖσθαι "is passive as to its grammatical form, but not necessarily passive as to its meaning," and translates Aristotle's definition as "a principle and cause of change and stasis" (*Nature, Change, and Agency in Aristotle's* Physics, 163, 39;); cf. *Nature, Change, and Agency in Aristotle's* Physics, 204–207. Fritsche emphatically argues against Lang for an active reading of Aristotle's definition; cf. Fritsche, "Aristotle's Usage of ἀρχὴ κινήσεως ('principle of motion') and the Two Definitions of Nature"; cf. also the interesting contribution by Katayama, "Soul and Elemental Motion in Aristotle's *Physics* VIII 4."

38 Perhaps it would even be more precise to interpret Philoponus' συμπεριλήψεται here in such a way that nature emerges as the genus term for soul. Nature, then, would not be an "inanimate soul," but rather soul would be an "animate nature"; cf. Müller, *Naturgemäße Ortsbewegung*, 54f. A similar view is attributed to Alexander who, as we have seen, is said to have "included (περιείληφε) the soul in his description of nature"; q.v. above, 217; cf. Moraux, *Der Aristotelismus bei den Griechen*, vol. 3, 138; cf. also Philoponus, *In An.*, 114.24–28. For Platonic metaphors of the soul as steersman or ruler, cf. *Alc. I* 129e9–130c4; *Phdr.* 247c7f.; cf. also *De an.* II.1, 413a8f.

On this basis, Philoponus can easily claim nature to be somewhat identical with soul, for animate beings, i.e., plants, animals, and planets, surely have a nature insofar as they are bodies consisting of the elements or their combinations, yet insofar as they are ensouled, their animate nature reduces to their soul.[39] Inverting the argument, Philoponus, by the same token, can also assert that nature is nothing but the soul of the soulless, as it were, insofar as nature plays the part of soul in those things which actually lack soul, serving as their mover. As a result, all natural things, animate and inanimate alike, can be said to have an active inner principle of motion and rest.[40] In this, the outcome of Philoponus' commentary echoes the following assertion from Proclus' commentary on Plato's *Timaeus*:

> ἐξηρτημένη δὲ ἐκεῖθεν καὶ ἀπαιωρουμένη φοιτᾷ διὰ πάντων ἀκωλύτως καὶ πάντα ἐμπνεῖ· δι' ἣν καὶ τὰ ἀψυχότατα ψυχῆς μετέχει τινός.
>
> It [sc. nature] pervades all things unhindered and breathes life into them. Through it even the things most devoid of soul (τὰ ἀψυχότατα) partake of some kind of soul. (Proclus, *In Tim.* I, 11.24f., tr. by Tarrant, modified)

While Philoponus achieves his reworking of the definition of nature which was provided by Aristotle in *Physics* II.1 by importing into his discussion features which are foreign to Aristotle, there is one thing Philoponus does not do – and that is quote Aristotle himself. It is Aristotle who, in his *De partibus animalium*, underscores the intrinsic similarity between nature and soul in being movers:

> εἰ δὴ ταῦτα οὕτως, τοῦ φυσικοῦ περὶ ψυχῆς ἂν εἴη λέγειν καὶ εἰδέναι ... ἄλλως τε καὶ τῆς φύσεως διχῶς λεγομένης καὶ οὔσης τῆς μὲν ὡς ὕλης τῆς δ' ὡς οὐσίας. Καὶ ἔστιν αὕτη καὶ ὡς ἡ κινοῦσα καὶ ὡς τὸ τέλος. Τοιοῦτον δὲ τοῦ ζῴου ἤτοι πᾶσα ἡ ψυχὴ ἢ μέρος τι αὐτῆς. Ὥστε καὶ οὕτως ἂν λεκτέον εἴη τῷ περὶ φύσεως θεωρητικῷ περὶ ψυχῆς μᾶλλον ἢ περὶ τῆς ὕλης, ὅσῳ μᾶλλον ἡ ὕλη δι' ἐκείνην φύσις ἐστὶν ἤ περ ἀνάπαλιν.
>
> فإن كانت هذه الأشياء كما وصفنا فهو من عمل صاحب العلم الطباعي أن يقول ويعلم من حال النفس ما يمكن في القول ... وبنوع آخر الطباع يقال بنوعين وكذلك هو إمّا النوع الواحد فهو مثل الهيولى والنوع الآخر مثل الجوهر والطباع مثل المحرّك ومثل تمام وكلّ نفس حيوان مثل هذا أو جزء من أجزائها. فهو بين بمثل هذا المأخذ والتصنيف أنّه ينبغي أن ينسب النظر في حال النفس إلى صاحب الرأي الطباعي فإنّ النظر في حال النفس أعظم من النظر في الهيولى لأنّ الهيولى إنّما يقال طباعاً لحال النفس وليس يقال النفس طباعاً لحال الهيولى.
>
> If it is like this, then it is up to the natural philosopher to speak and know about the soul ... especially since the nature (τῆς φύσεως, *al-ṭibāʿ*) of something is spoken of and is in two ways: as matter and as substance. As substance it is both the mover (ἡ κινοῦσα, *al-muḥarrik*) and the end (τὸ τέλος, *tamām*), and it is the soul (ἡ ψυχή, *nafs*) – either all of it or some part of it – that is such in the animal's case. So, in this way, too, it will be requisite for the person studying nature to

39 cf. Philoponus, *In Phys.*, 197.13–18.

40 cf. Lang, *Aristotle's* Physics *and its Medieval Varieties*, 121; cf. also Wolff, *Fallgesetz und Massebegriff*, 72–79.

> speak about soul more than the matter, inasmuch as it is more that the matter is nature because of soul than the reverse. (*De part. anim.* I.1, 641a21–31, tr. by Lennox, modified)[41]

Aristotle is even more explicit about the close relation between nature and soul in *De generatione animalium*. Analysing the similarity between the soul which is active in full grown animals and plants, and that which is active in their respective seeds, Aristotle asserts that it is in principle the same kind of soul which is merely different in degree and, consequently, "greater" (μείζων) in the fully grown organisms. Thus, the power in the semen and the power in the mature animal or plant is one and the same, even though it is somehow less fully developed in the former case. In both cases, however, this power constitutes the organism's nature.[42] Thereupon, Aristotle states the following:

> εἰ οὖν αὕτη ἐστὶν ἡ θρεπτικὴ ψυχή, αὕτη ἐστὶ καὶ ἡ γεννῶσα· καὶ τοῦτ' ἔστιν ἡ φύσις ἡ ἑκάστου ἐνυπάρχουσα καὶ ἐν φυτοῖς καὶ ἐν ζῴοις πᾶσιν, τὰ δ' ἄλλα μόρια τῆς ψυχῆς τοῖς μὲν ὑπάρχει τοῖς δ' οὐχ ὑπάρχει τῶν ζώντων.
>
> فإن كانت هذه النفس المغذّية فهي المولّدة وهذا الطباع الذي هو في الشجر وجميع الحيوان فأمّا الأخر فأجزاء نفس فهو بيّن أنّها تكون في بعض الأجسام التي تعيس.
>
> If it is the nutritive soul, it is also the generative soul, and this is the nature of every [organism], existing in all animals and plants (καὶ τοῦτ' ἔστιν ἡ φύσις ἡ ἑκάστου ἐνυπάρχουσα καὶ ἐν φυτοῖς καὶ ἐν ζῴοις πᾶσιν, *wa-hāḏā l-ṭibāʿ allaḏī huwa fī l-šağar wa-ğamīʿ al-ḥayawān*), whereas the other parts of the soul exist in some living things and not in others. (*De gen. anim.* II.4, 740b36–741a3, tr. by Platt, modified)[43]

Another passage, this time as evidence for nature as an active force, can be found in *Metaphysics* Θ.8, which describes nature as a "power" (δύναμις, *quwwa*) and as "a principle of motion not, however, in something else but in the thing itself *qua* itself" (ἀρχὴ γὰρ κινητική, ἀλλ' οὐκ ἐν ἄλλῳ ἀλλ' ἐν αὐτῷ ᾗ αὐτό, *ibtidāʾ ḏū ḥaraka wa-lākin laysa fī āḫar bal fī ḏātihī bi-annahū ḏātuhū*).[44] Finally, this conception of an internal power for motion is described as being "always active":

---

41 Following this passage, Aristotle states that if the natural philosopher were to discuss all soul, then there would be "no philosophy left besides natural science" (*De part. anim.* I.1, 641a34–36); cf. *De part. anim.* I.1, 641b5–10; cf. also Broadie, "νοῦς and Nature in De Anima III," 168f.; Caston, "Aristotle on the Relation of the Intellect to the Body," 181–184. For insightful remarks regarding the character of the Arabic translation, cf. the remarks by Brugman and Lulofs in the introduction to their edition of the Arabic version of Aristotle's *De generatione animalium*, esp. 11–37, as well as Kruk's notes in her introduction to the Arabic *De partibus animalium*, esp. 24–31.

42 cf. *De gen. anim.* II.4, 740b29–36.

43 cf. also the analysis of Janos in "Active Nature and Other Striking Features," 157–160, who points towards *De generatione animalium* II.3, 736b34, which, in combination with 737a21f., describes the nature in the male semen as "causing the female matter to be productive" (γόνιμα, *yusayyiruhū muwāfiqan li-l-wilād*), "putting [it] into form" (συνίστησι, *qawwama*), and "moving it" (κινεῖ, *ḥarrakahū*).

44 *Met.* Θ.8, 1049b5–10, tr. by Ross, modified; cf. *Met.* Δ.12, 1019a15f.; *Cael.* III.2, 301b17–19.

μιμεῖται δὲ τὰ ἄφθαρτα καὶ τὰ ἐν μεταβολῇ ὄντα, οἷον γῆ καὶ πῦρ. καὶ γὰρ ταῦτα ἀεὶ ἐνεργεῖ· καθ' αὑτὰ γὰρ καὶ ἐν αὑτοῖς ἔχει τὴν κίνησιν.

والأشياء التي تتغيّر تتشبّه بالتي لا تفسد مثل الأرض والنار فإنّ هذه فاعلة لأنّ لها حركة بذاتها وفيها.

Imperishable things are imitated by those that are involved in change, for example, earth and fire, for these, too, are always active (ἀεὶ ἐνεργεῖ, *fā'ila*), as they have motion of themselves and in themselves. (*Met.* Θ.8, 1050b28–30, tr. by Ross, modified)

What Philoponus might have enjoyed about the passages in *De partibus animalium* and *De generatione animalium* is that they align the nature of a thing, in particular that of an animal, with its soul, more precisely with either the entire soul, i.e., including reason, or a part of it, i.e., to the exclusion of reason. Moreover, nature thusly aligned with soul is said to be a "mover" (κινοῦσα). Contrary to his terminology in the *Physics*, Aristotle uses an active participle to describe nature in his *De partibus animalium*, thus lending support to Philoponus' reading of nature as a living force which has motion in and of itself. This nature, then, is an "always active" δύναμις, just as Aristotle had said in *Metaphysics* Θ.

As will be seen, Philoponus' redefinition proved to be influential beyond immediate geographic, temporal, or linguistic boundaries, so much so that many of Avicenna's predecessors and contemporaries within the Arabic philosophical tradition shared his convictions and, in his wake, described nature as an active force that permeates, governs, and shapes the natural bodies within the universe. Avicenna, however, rejected Philoponus' efforts as both vain and false. His criticism appears to be a reaction not to Philoponus alone but to the entire tradition that accepted his redefinition either as a proper complement to or a better version of Aristotle's true definition of nature. In order to assess Avicenna's Peripatetic position and his critical stance towards Philoponus, we must now turn to his own interpretation of the definition of nature given by Aristotle in the second book of his *Physics*.

4.2 Avicenna's Commentary on *Physics* II.1, 192b20–23

At the end of his discussion of matter and form as the principles of the natural body in *al-Samā' al-ṭabī'ī* I.3, Avicenna declares that it is now "necessary that we occupy ourselves with those principles which are most deservedly called 'causes'" (*'ilalan*). In particular, "we should make known the efficient principle common to natural things (*al-mabda' al-fā'ilī l-muštarak li-l-ṭabī'iyyāt*) – and this is nature" (*wa-huwa l-ṭabī'a*).[45] After a brief chapter on Presocratic thoughts on principles (and the "foolish nonsense" (*al-safah wa-l-ġabāwa*) put forth by Parmenides and Melissus), Avicenna, indeed, turns to the concept of nature in *al-Samā' al-ṭabī'ī* I.5. There, he states the following:

45 *al-Samā' al-ṭabī'ī* I.3, §12, 25.15.

وقد حُدّت الطبيعة بأنّها مبدأ أوّل لحركة ما يكون فيه وسكونه بالذات لا بالعرض.

Nature has been defined (*qad ḥuddat*) as that it is a first principle (*mabdaʾ awwal*) for the motion of that in which it is and for [that thing's] rest, essentially and not accidentally. (*al-Samāʿ al-ṭabīʿī* I.5, §5, 31.6f.)[46]

The way in which Avicenna introduces this famous definition with an impersonal reference to someone else by whom nature "has been defined" in the past (*qad ḥuddat*) creates the impression that he is providing a direct quotation from one of his own Arabic copies of Aristotle's *Physics*. This impression is further strengthened by Avicenna's subsequent announcement that he intends to provide an explanation (*ibāna*) of the description of nature which is "taken from the First Master" (*maʾḫūḏ ʿan al-imām al-awwal*).[47] The explanation he is about to give is a word-by-word commentary on Aristotle's definition of nature. What is more, Avicenna supplements his discussion with what appears to be an equally direct quotation of some of Philoponus' remarks on that definition together with a repudiation of the relevant aspects of the latter's Neoplatonic reinterpretation. Prima facie, then, it may seem that Avicenna was working straight from the translation of Aristotle's *Physics* which has been produced by Qusṭā ibn Lūqā al-Baʿlabakkī (d. 300/912), because that translation, as far as we know, was the only one containing Philoponus' commentary on books I–IV. This impression notwithstanding, Avicenna's presumed quotation of Aristotle could just as well be a simple paraphrase, or a more or less accurate quotation from memory.[48]

Regardless of whether or not the above quoted definition of nature is an actual fragment from one of the Arabic translations of Aristotle's *Physics*, it provides us with an undistorted version of how Avicenna *understood* Aristotle's definition, i.e., it is a genuine reproduction of how Avicenna *would* quote Aristotle even if he may not have happened to have his own copy of the *Physics* at hand.[49] Moreover, whatever it is

46 cf. *al-Ḥikma al-mašriqiyya* III.4, 9.4f.

47 *al-Samāʿ al-ṭabīʿī* I.5, §5, 31.11f.

48 q.v. also fn. 122 above, 38.

49 It is interesting that Avicenna's version of Aristotle's definition here in *al-Samāʿ al-ṭabīʿī* differs from the definitions of nature in some of his other major works. In *ʿUyūn al-ḥikma*, for example, he states that "nature is a cause insofar as it is a principle for motion for that in which it is as well as a principle for its rest, essentially and not accidentally" (*al-ṭabīʿa sabab ʿalā annahū mabdaʾ li-ḥaraka li-mā hiya fīhi wa-mabdaʾ li-sukūnihī bi-l-ḏāt lā bi-l-ʿaraḍ*; *ʿUyūn al-ḥikma* II.2, 18.11; reading *li-mā* with Ǧabr and ʿĀṣī for *mā* in Badawī and *bi-mā* in al-Saqqā). Faḫr al-Dīn al-Rāzī, in his *Šarḥ ʿUyūn al-ḥikma*, immediately mentions that this definition "is quoted from the great and wise Aristotle and, maybe, the Šayḫ just repeated him" (*Šarḥ ʿUyūn al-ḥikma* II.2, 35.6–8). In *al-Naǧāt*, Avicenna writes that nature "is a principle essentially for [the bodies'] motions and their rests essentially and for the rest of their perfections which belong to them essentially" (*hiya mabdaʾ bi-l-ḏāt li-ḥarakātihā wa-sukūnātihā bi-l-ḏāt wa-li-sāʾir kamālātihā llatī lahā bi-ḏātihā*; *al-Naǧāt* II.1.1, 194.6f.). The corresponding passage in *al-Ḥikma al-ʿArūḍiyya*, gives a slightly, though remarkably, different version: nature "is a power permeating through the bodies, being a principle essentially for their motions essentially and their

Avicenna provides us with here, it differs significantly from the version we find in the translation of Isḥāq ibn Ḥunayn (d. 298/910–11), which reads as follows:

فتكون الطبيعة مبدأً ما وسبباً لأن يتحرّك ويسكن الشيء الذي هي فيه أوّلاً بالذات لا بطريق العرض.

ὡς οὔσης τῆς φύσεως ἀρχῆς τινὸς καὶ αἰτίας τοῦ κινεῖσθαι καὶ ἠρεμεῖν ἐν ᾧ ὑπάρχει πρώτως καθ' αὑτὸ καὶ μὴ κατὰ συμβεβηκός.

So, nature is some principle and cause for that a thing, in which it is primarily (πρώτως, *awwalan*), by itself, and not by way of accident, is in motion and is at rest. (*Phys.* II.1, 192b20–23)

The greatest difference between Avicenna's and Isḥāq ibn Ḥunayn's versions is that Avicenna speaks of a principle of *motion*, using the simple noun *ḥaraka* ("motion"), where Isḥāq ibn Ḥunayn accurately rendered Aristotle's mediopassive κινεῖσθαι by using a verb of the reflexive fifth stem, *yataḥarraku* ("it is moved" or "is in motion"). Another variance is that Avicenna displaced the adverb πρώτως, which qualified ὑπάρχει, and made it an adjective, thus turning the principle into a *first* principle of motion (*mabdaʾ awwal li-ḥaraka*). It is apparent that, if the definition reported by Avicenna is supposed to be a direct quotation from Aristotle, Avicenna is not quoting from Isḥāq ibn Ḥunayn's version. He is, however, probably also not quoting from any translation from Qusṭā, for Qusṭā rendered Aristotle's definition, when translating Ps.-Plutarchus' *Placita Philosophorum*, as follows:

إنّ الطبيعة على أرسطوطاليس مبدأ الحركة والسكون فيما ذلك فيه على الأمر الأوّل لا بعرض.

Ἔστιν οὖν κατὰ τὸν Ἀριστοτέλην φύσις ἀρχὴ κινήσεως καὶ ἠρεμίας, ἐν ᾧ πρώτως ἐστὶ καὶ οὐ κατὰ συμβεβηκός.

Indeed, nature, according to Aristotle, is the principle of motion and rest in that in which it is in a primary manner (πρώτως, *ʿalā l-amr al-awwal*) and not by accident. (Ps.-Plutarchus, *Placita Philosophorum*, 274a24–27)[50]

Admittedly, there are already in the Greek some differences between Aristotle's original and the version in Ps.-Plutarchus, which could lead to different Arabic translations. The first is the replacement of the original mediopassive infinitive κινεῖσθαι with the simple noun κινήσεως, which led Qusṭā to render it as *mabdaʾ al-ḥaraka*.[51] The second difference concerns the shift from ἐν ᾧ ὑπάρχει πρώτως in Aristotle to ἐν ᾧ πρώτως

rests essentially and for the rest of their essential perfections" (*hiya quwwa sāriya fī l-ağsām hiya mabdaʾ bi-l-ḏāt li-ḥarakātihā bi-l-ḏāt wa-sukūnātihā bi-l-ḏāt wa-li-sāʾir kamālātihā l-ḏātiyya*; *al-Ḥikma al-ʿArūḍiyya* II.1 115.18f.). I shall have to come back to the version in *al-Ḥikma al-ʿArūḍiyya* below, 274ff. Neither *al-Hidāya* nor the *Dānešnāme-ye ʿAlāʾī* nor the late *al-Išārāt wa-l-tanbīhāt* give a definition of nature that can be mapped onto Aristotle's wording, as far as I can see; cf., however, *Dānešnāme-ye ʿAlāʾī* III.2, 7.1f. Compared to the *ʿUyūn al-ḥikma*, *al-Ḥikma al-ʿArūḍiyya*, and *al-Nağāt*, the version in *al-Samāʿ al-ṭabīʿī* I.5 – and *al-Ḥikma al-mašriqiyya* III.4 – comes closest to Aristotle's original.

50 Aetius Arabus, *Die Vorsokratiker in arabischer Überlieferung*, 2.14f.

51 As has been noted already, Philoponus, too, altered Aristotle's definition the same way, as he replaced Aristotle's mediopassive infinitive with a simple noun.

ἐστί in Ps.-Plutarchus. Further differences are Ps.-Plutarchus' omission of τινός and καὶ αἰτίας as well as the lack of the qualification καθ' αὑτό. All these alterations are reflected in Qusṭā's Arabic. Yet, even with these differences in mind, there is one striking detail which suggests that the version found in Avicenna's *al-Samāʿ al-ṭabīʿī* did not directly derive from Qusṭā's translation of the *Physics* – and this is the very different handling of the adverb πρώτως. While in the translation of the *Placita Philosophorum*, we find πρώτως rendered as *ʿalā l-amr al-awwal*, Avicenna has *mabdaʾ awwal*. Again, if the version in Avicenna's *al-Samāʿ al-ṭabīʿī* is in fact a quotation, and if Qusṭā would have translated the definition he found in Aristotle's *Physics* – despite the noted minor differences – more or less the same way as he did with Ps.-Plutarchus' report in the *Placita Philosophorum*, then it is apparent that Qusṭā's version could not have been Avicenna's direct source just as it is equally clear that it could not have been Isḥāq ibn Ḥunayn's.[52]

What is primarily important for understanding Avicenna's interpretation of Aristotle's definition as such, is that the version we read in *al-Samāʿ al-ṭabīʿī* defines nature as a principle for "motion," and not for "being in motion" or "being moved." In other words, Avicenna's version of Aristotle's definition lacks any passive or medial connotation which Aristotle's original conception, especially when read in light of his discussion in *Physics* VIII.4, conveyed or at least did not rule out entirely. Consequently, it is an "active" definition of nature as a "principle of motion" which Avicenna endorses and defends in his subsequent comments.[53]

First, he clarifies that a natural thing does not have two competing aspects within itself, one trying to cause motion, the other striving to bring about rest. Instead, nature is a single principle for both motion and rest, such that it brings about "motion, if there is motion, or rest, if there is rest."[54] He also states that by "principle for motion" Aristotle wanted to signify an "efficient principle" (*mabdaʾ fāʿilī*) which causes motion not in itself, i.e., in the nature, but in another (*fī ġayrihī*), i.e., in the body in which it is.[55]

---

52 Qusṭā's translation of πρώτως as *ʿalā l-amr al-awwal* will become a crucial detail in the history of the reception of Aristotle's account of nature discussed below, 265ff. There, it will also be shown that Qusṭā's translation of the definition in Ps.-Plutarchus is, in fact, consistent with his translation of the definition as contained in Philoponus' commentary.

53 q.v. esp. below, 236ff.

54 *al-Samāʿ al-ṭabīʿī* I.5, §5, 31.8, tr. by McGinnis; cf. *al-Ḥikma al-mašriqiyya* III.4, 9.5–7; cf. also *al-Samāʿ al-ṭabīʿī* IV.9, §5, 302.8–17; q.v. below, 251f., 280ff.

55 *al-Samāʿ al-ṭabīʿī* I.5, §6, 13f. With this note, Avicenna is not confusing Aristotle's remarks about δύναμις and φύσις in *Metaphysics* Θ.8, where the former is described as "a principle of change in another thing or [in the thing itself] as other" (ἐν ἄλλῳ ἢ ᾗ ἄλλο) and the latter as "a principle of motion not, however, in something else but in [the thing] itself *qua* itself" (οὐκ ἐν ἄλλῳ ἀλλ' ἐν αὐτῷ ᾗ αὐτό; *Met.* Θ.8, 1049b5–10, tr. by Ross, modified); cf. *Met.* Δ.12, 1019a15f.; Θ.1, 1046a11; Λ.3, 1070a7f.; *Cael.* III.2, 301b17–19. Rather, Avicenna's formulation rightly emphasises that the object of nature's efficacy is not directed towards nature itself but towards the natural body in which it resides and in which it,

Next, Avicenna seeks to clarify the meaning of the qualification "first" (*awwal*), which marks nature as a "*first* principle." Regarding this qualification, Philoponus argued that πρώτως is required for differentiating between the rational soul and nature. He wrote the following:

> τὸ δὲ πρώτως προσέθηκε, διότι καὶ ἡ λογικὴ ψυχὴ κινεῖ τὸ ζῷον καὶ ἔστιν ἡ τοιαύτη ἀρχὴ τῆς κινήσεως οὐκ ἔξωθεν, ἀλλ' ἐν αὐτῷ τῷ κινουμένῳ, ἀλλ' οὐ πρώτως κινεῖ ἡ λογικὴ ψυχή, ἀλλὰ διὰ τῆς ἀλόγου, καὶ οὐδὲ αὕτη πρώτως κινεῖ τὸ ζῷον, ἀλλὰ τῷ τὴν φύσιν κινεῖν. αὕτη οὖν ἡ πρώτως κινοῦσα.
>
> He [sc. Aristotle] added "primarily," because the rational soul, too, moves the animal and is such a principle of motion not outside but in the moved itself. The rational soul, however, does not move primarily but through the irrational, and neither does this move the animal primarily but by moving [its] nature (τῷ τὴν φύσιν κινεῖν). So, this [i.e., the nature] is what primarily (πρώτως) causes motion. (Philoponus, *In Phys.*, 196.28–30, tr. by Lacey, modified)

Avicenna explicitly reports this explanation and rejects it vehemently:

> وقد ظنّ قوم أنّ النفس تفعل حركة الانتقال بتوسّط الطبيعة ولا أرى الطبيعة تستحيل محرّكةً للأعضاء خلاف ما توجبه ذاتها طاعة للنفس. ولو استحالت الطبيعة كذلك لما حدث الإعياء عند تكليف النفس إيّاها غير مقتضاها ولما تجاذب مقتضى النفس ومقتضى الطبيعة.
>
> Some have believed that the soul produces local motion through the intermediacy of nature (*bi-tawassuṭ al-ṭabīʿa*), but I do not think that the nature is transformed (*tastaḥīlu*) [so as to be] a mover for the limbs, obeying the soul contrary to what its self requires (*ḫilāf mā tūǧibuhū ḏātihā*). If the nature were transformed like that, then there would not occur any weariness when the soul imposes upon it what is not required by it (*ġayr muqtaḍāhā*) nor would there be any disagreement between what is required by soul and what is required by nature. (*al-Samāʿ al-ṭabīʿī* I.5, §6, 31.16–18)

It is important to understand that Avicenna does not criticise Philoponus' explanation of what πρώτως means. In fact, he seconds his predecessor's remark that "primarily" – or in Avicenna's case: "first" – means "proximately" (*qarīb*) and that this means "with no intermediary" (*lā wāsiṭa*).[56] Avicenna is also not in total disagreement with Philoponus' conception of animal motion, as he would certainly concur "that sight

then, causes motion "in [the thing] itself *qua* itself"; cf. *al-Naǧāt* II.2.2, 210.5–211.11. That Avicenna reads the definition of nature in terms of *Metaphysics* Θ is manifest, because he himself explicitly refers to this chapter in his criticism of Philoponus' reworking, as we shall see shortly. Moreover, Avicenna's familiarity with *Metaphysics* Θ has been demonstrated by Bertolacci, *The Reception of Aristotle's* Metaphysics *in Avicenna's* Kitāb al-Šifāʾ, 355f.

56 *al-Samāʿ al-ṭabīʿī* I.5, §6, 31.14; cf. *al-Ḥikma al-mašriqiyya* III.4, 9.7; Philoponus, *In Phys.*, 196.32f., 197.4. In fact, Avicenna's phrase *maʿnā qawlinā awwal ayy qarīb* may have its roots in Philoponus' assertion λέγω δὲ πρώτως τὸ προσεχῶς (196.32f). It may also be noted that Qusṭā used *ʿalā l-qawl al-aqrab*, with the elative of *qarīb*, to render κατὰ δὲ τὸ προσεχές (Ps.-Plutarchus, *Placita Philosophorum*, 390a2; Aetius Arabus, *Die Vorsokratiker in arabischer Überlieferung*, 51.7f). Simplicius offers a different understanding of πρώτως, possibly influenced by Themistius; cf. Simplicius, *In Phys.*, 266.33–268.12; Themistius, *In Phys.*, 36.2–37.2.

moves desire and this moves the natural capacities and these move the animal," as we read in Philoponus.[57] Yet, there are two major doctrinal points in Philoponus' commentary which deeply upset Avicenna.

The first is that "some" people allegedly maintained that nature is not only persuaded or bent but effectively "transformed" or "altered" (*tastaḥīlu*) by soul. This appears to be Avicenna's understanding of Philoponus' phrase that the rational soul moves the animal "by moving [its] nature" (τῷ τὴν φύσιν κινεῖν). The original phrase in Philoponus is already difficult to understand and modern interpreters are in disagreement about how it ought to be translated.[58] Avicenna clearly takes this phrase – or whatever he might have read in the Arabic translation of Philoponus' commentary – to mean that soul not only *moves* the animal's nature, but that it *changes* its nature. Accordingly, if nature is changed or transformed by soul, it would not only temporarily be silenced or trumped by soul, similar to what one imagines to happen when reason overrides desire, but would be forced to intrinsically act against itself, i.e., unnaturally, and would become a mere extension of soul's voluntary and sovereign agency. There would not even be any weariness anymore, resulting from nature's constant efforts to do what soul commands against its own intentions, because soul entirely transformed nature in such a way that, eventually, what is "required by soul" (*muqtaḍā l-nafs*) is also "required by nature" (*muqtaḍā l-ṭabīʿa*). Avicenna, however, frequently emphasises that nature cannot but act always "according to a single course" (*ʿalā nahğ wāḥid*).[59] Should it happen that a stone is thrown upwards against its nature, it is not its nature that is diminished through the violent upward motion but its natural inclination, as we shall see. For Avicenna, then, nature cannot be diminished or altered or transformed but is always active in the same manner. Consequently, it never does what is required by something else but is solely concerned with what is "required by nature." Thus, far from clarifying the systematic distinction between soul and nature, Philoponus' explanation of why Aristotle "added" the word πρώτως, as read by Avicenna, actually obscures that distinction and, together with it, the difference between involuntary natural motions (such as a stone's falling down) and voluntary "unnatural" motions (such as a bird's ascending to its nest), which is so crucial for Avicenna's own classification of the powers of natural bodies and the definition of nature.[60] If soul brings about motion

57 Philoponus, *In Phys.*, 196.33f., tr. by Lacey. Avicenna explicitly subscribes to this view in *al-Nağāt*, where he asserts that soul is a power which acts "through the intermediacy of the organs" (*bi-tawassuṭ al-ālāt*) of the natural body (*al-Nağāt* II.1.1, 194.9–14; reading *bi-tawassuṭ al-ālāt* with Fakhry, ʿUmayra, and al-Kurdī for *bi-l-ālāt* in Dānešpažūh); cf. esp. *al-Nafs* IV.4; cf. also *al-Ilāhiyyāt* VI.5, §7, 285.12–17; VIII.7, §11, 367.1–6; cf. further *ʿUyūn al-masāʾil*,§20, 63.18f., as well as Ruffus and McGinnis, "Willful Understanding," 179.

58 Lacey, apparently in line with Avicenna's understanding, translates "by moving [the animal's] nature," whereas Macierowski and Hassing propose "nature moves it [sc. the animal]" (Macierowski and Hassing, "John Philoponus on Aristotle's Definition of Nature," 89).

59 This is one of the main aspects of Avicenna's conception of nature, as will be shown below, 286ff.

60 q.v. below, 280ff.

by *changing* the nature of the underlying body, then a bird's ascending flight would be natural, because it is ultimately through its nature – albeit an altered and transformed nature – that the upward motion, instead of a downward fall, occurs.

The second point of fundamental disagreement is that Philoponus, in his comments, seems to assert that *all* motion that is issued by soul is caused through the mediation of such instruments as nature and the natural capacities. Avicenna, however, only agrees that *some* kinds of motion are merely mediately caused by soul, and refers to generation and growth as examples. These are brought about by soul "not primarily" (*lā awwalan*) but "by using the natures and qualities" (*bi-stiḫdām al-ṭabā'iʿ wa-l-kayfiyyāt*) as intermediaries, whereas local motion seems to be a proximate effect with no intermediary.[61] These remarks are relatively obscure, for it intuitively may seem unfitting for Avicenna to advance the following claim:

فإن كان للنفس متوسّط في التحريك فذلك في غير التحريكات المكانية بل في تحريك الكون والإنماء.

If the soul has some intermediary in producing motion, then that is not with regard to the production of local motion (*al-taḥrīkāt al-makāniyya*) but with regard to the production of generation and growth (*taḥrīk al-kawn wa-l-inmā'*). (*al-Samāʿ al-ṭabīʿī* I.5, §6, 32.2, tr. by McGinnis, modified)

This reads as if the only kind of motion which is directly and immediately caused by soul is local motion. Why, however, should local motion be caused without, but generation and growth with, intermediates? Avicenna himself suggests in the preceding sentence that the answer is that soul causes local motion by producing an inclination (*mayl*).[62] Why, however, we might ask, should soul not also cause generation and growth by producing an inclination for generation or growth? In other words, why does soul not generally bring about any kind of motion by producing proper "inclinations" for any kind of motion?[63] Avicenna does not provide an answer in his *al-Samāʿ al-ṭabīʿī* nor could I find one in his other works on physics. What he may have had in mind here is what he argues for in *al-Nafs* I.5 when he describes and enumerates the various faculties or powers of the soul. One of the powers of the animal soul is the power which causes local motion proximately, as it seems, by directly contracting the muscles and moving the sinews through its *own* motive powers, i.e., without any intermediaries:

---

61 *al-Samāʿ al-ṭabīʿī* I.5, §6, 32.4, tr. by McGinnis; cf. *al-Ḥikma al-mašriqiyya* III.4, 9.7–9. It may well be that this is what Philoponus had in mind when he wrote that soul moves the animal "by moving [its] nature" (τῷ τὴν φύσιν κινεῖν). So, the just explained first point of disagreement is either an unfair objection against Philoponus, because it accuses him of a position he did not actually hold, or it is an objection inspired by the wording of the Arabic translation of Philoponus' commentary at Avicenna's disposal, which may well have interpreted κινεῖν along the lines of "change" and "alteration," rather than "moving" or "using."

62 For more on *mayl*, q.v. below, 240ff.

63 Here, "inclinations" do not mean general preferences, such as someone's inclination to favour mozzarella sticks over chicken wings, but a direct drive within a particular situation that leads one to follow soul's intention.

وللنفس الحيوانية بالقسمة الأولى قوّتان: محرّكة ومدركة. والمحرّكة على قسمين: إمّا محرّكة بأنّها باعثة على الحركة وإمّا محرّكة بأنّها فاعلة ... وأمّا القوّة المحرّكة على أنّها فاعلة فهي قوّة تنبعث في الأعصاب والعضلات من شأنها أن تشنّج العضلات فتجذّب الأوتار والرباطات المتّصلة بالأعضاء إلى نحو جهة المبدأ أو ترخّيها أو تمدّها طولاً فتصير الأوتار والرباطات إلى خلاف جهة المبدأ.

The animal soul, in the first division, has two powers: a moving and a perceptive [power]. The moving [power] is of two [further] divisions: it is either moving by inciting (*bāʿiṯa*) [other powers to produce] motion or moving by producing (*fāʿila*) [motion] ... The moving power by producing is a power dispersed in the nerves and muscles such that it contracts the muscles, and so draws the tendons and ligaments attached to the organs towards their starting point or loosens them or stretches them out, so that the tendons and ligaments come to be at the opposite end of their starting point. (*al-Nafs* I.5, 33.9–20, tr. by McGinnis/Reisman, modified)[64]

On this account, local motion would be the direct result of the soul's moving power which directly effects the motion of the muscles and sinews. That is to say, it is the soul itself which is dispersed through the animal's body and which, residing with its motive powers in the body's "nerves and muscles," causes motion without any intermediate by simply moving these muscles. Other kinds of motion, like generation and growth, cannot be caused directly, i.e., not even by the corresponding powers of generation and growth, because the soul may be able to arouse sexual desire or increase an animal's blood flow, but it does not *cause* reproduction or growth itself; it merely makes the body reproduce or makes the body grow. These powers of soul are only able to "incite" or "motivate" (*bāʿiṯa*) the relevant organs responsible for reproduction and growth. Thus, local motion appears to be the only kind of motion that is caused directly by the soul, more precisely by the power that causes motion by effecting (*al-quwwa al-muḥarrika ʿalā annahā fāʿila*), while the other kinds of motion are due to the power that causes motion by inciting (*[al-quwwa] al-muḥarrika ʿalā annahā baʿiṯa*).

Another explanation for why local motion is the only kind of motion that soul is able to cause directly, and likewise why a soul's moving faculty can move the body without intermediary, may be that local motion – as opposed to generation, growth, and alteration – is on the whole a *voluntary* motion and, thus, has its roots nothing other than the volition (*irāda*) of the animal. It is, then, the involuntary motions of an animal which are caused by means, or through the intermediation, of other natural capacities. These involuntary motions include processes such as growth, nutrition, and organic development, but not local motion.[65] We can choose to move our bodies to go for a walk, but we usually cannot choose to grow or to digest or to age and go grey;

64 McGinnis and Reisman, *Classical Arabic Philosophy*, 180; cf. *al-Samāʿ al-ṭabīʿī* I.14, §11, 72.10–15; *al-Nafs* I.4, 30.7–9; *al-Ilāhiyyāt* VI.5.7; *al-Išārāt wa-l-tanbīhāt* II.3.25, 135.4–8; cf. also Gätje, "Zur Psychologie der Willenshandlungen in der islamischen Philosophie," 359.

65 Local motion is involved in growth – on Aristotle's and Avicenna's account of place – only insofar as something which changes its size also accidentally changes its place, but this is not relevant here.

we just do.[66] So, whereas Philoponus, in his commentary on *Physics* II.1, regards the question about how the soul moves the body as a question about a how the rational faculty of the soul (ἡ λογικὴ ψυχή) relates to its non-rational faculties (τῆς ἀλόγου) and how, in turn, these relate to the non-psychological but nonetheless natural faculties (τὴν φύσιν) of the animal's body, Avicenna, as we shall see shortly, introduces a novel distinction according to which he generally conceives of the motions which can arise from any natural body – animate or not – as classifiable into those that are voluntary and those which are not.[67]

Along these lines, Avicenna's understanding of the qualification "first" in Aristotle's definition of nature can be reconstructed as follows. Avicenna states that it is not true that the soul of an animal alters its nature. Moreover, it is imprecise to say that soul generally causes motion through the mediation of nature or the capacities of the organic body, because there is in fact one kind of motion which soul is able to enact directly, viz., local motion. These are the two points on which "some" people, including Philoponus, went wrong.[68] On the other hand, Avicenna concedes that other kinds of motion, such as generation and growth, are indeed effected through the various organs of the body or through the natural capacities of the animal. On Avicenna's interpretation, then, the definition "principle for the motion of that in which it is and for [that thing's] rest, by itself and not by accident" adequately describes *both* nature and soul, and so Aristotle was in need to disambiguate his description, if he wanted to provide a clear definition of nature. This was achieved by qualifying the "principle for motion" as a "*first* principle for motion," because it is only nature, but not soul, which always and essentially causes motion as "first," i.e., proximately and without any intermediaries.[69]

In effect, Avicenna arrives at a conclusion which, as has been noted, is not at variance with Philoponus' understanding of what πρώτως means in the context of *Aristotle's* definition, viz., to differentiate between soul and nature. Avicenna's criticism

---

66 Avicenna's notion of volition (*irāda*) is a painfully understudied subject. It is not entirely clear how he conceives of the relation between choice (*iḫtiyār*) and volition. He often seems to use the two terms interchangeably, which is an interesting – even though not altogether surprising – aspect, given that *irāda* usually relates to the Greek βούλησις, whereas *iḫtiyār* represents προαίρεσις; q.v. my remarks below, 293ff. For valuable information on the history of the two notions βούλησις and προαίρεσις, cf. esp. Sorabji, "The Concept of the Will from Plato to Maximus the Confessor"; M. Frede, *A Free Will*.

67 q.v. below, 280ff.

68 Philoponus could also have been Avicenna's exclusive target. The Arabic terms *qawm* (*al-Samāʿ al-ṭabīʿī* I.5, §6, 31.16) and *baʿḍ* (*al-Samāʿ al-ṭabīʿī* I.5, §5, 31.9; §7, 32.16) can be used to refer both to "some" people as well as to "one" person; but see the discussion below, 256ff.

69 Nature's direct mode of effecting motion does not only pertain to local motion but to all kinds of motion. A prominent example in Avicenna's works is the self-cooling of water, through which the water, having been heated up forcefully, returns to its natural temperature much like it also returns to its natural place through local motion. This will be mentioned and discussed repeatedly in what follows; q.v. esp. 250f.

only concerns *Philoponus'* theories about the relation between soul and nature, and their respective ways of bringing about motion and change. Incidentally, it was nothing other than an interest in the precise relation between soul and nature that motivated Avicenna's novel definition of nature, as we shall see.

Still commenting literally on the Aristotelian text, Avicenna turns to another part of the definition, viz., the qualification *mā yakūnu fīhi* ("that in which it is"). According to Avicenna, this phrase reflects Aristotle's original approach in *Physics* I.1 of dividing "things that exist" into those that exist by nature (φύσει) and those that exist "by other causes" (δι' ἄλλας αἰτίας).[70] In Aristotle, the latter category is not further specified and may, according to some interpreters, encompass quite a number of causes among which we find art (τέχνη), chance (αὐτόματον), luck (τύχη), but also Platonic agents like intellect (νοῦς) and necessity (ἀνάγκη) as well as psychological capacities like desire (ὄρεξις), choice (προαίρεσις), and thought (διάνοια), or simply force (βία).[71] Avicenna, though, only mentions art (*al-ṣināʿa*) and forcefully acting agents (*al-qāsirāt*) in contrast to "nature" (*al-ṭabīʿa*). For him, the difference between nature and these other causes is that only the former is a cause operating exclusively from within the object.[72] Avicenna devotes merely one single sentence to this distinction which, after all, was the starting point of Aristotle's argument.

Finally, Avicenna focuses on the last part of Aristotle's definition, viz., that nature is a principle for motion *bi-l-ḏāt lā bi-l-ʿaraḍ* ("essentially and not accidentally" or "by itself and not by accident").[73] This qualification is exemplified by Aristotle in the *Physics* through the image of a sick doctor curing himself. The self-healing doctor could be seen as a principle of motion that satisfies all the conditions that were so far stipulated for nature, because *he* is curing *himself* on the basis of the medical knowledge he

---

70 *Phys.* II.1, 192b8f.

71 cf., for example, the commentaries of Themistius and Simplicius as well as Wagner *ad loc.*

72 *al-Samāʿ al-ṭabīʿī* I.5, §6, 32.4f.; cf. *al-Ḥikma al-mašriqiyya* III.4, 9.10. This is also made evident in Avicenna's other compendia. In his *al-Hidāya*, for example, we find an explicit contrast between those principles of motion and rest which are from the outside (*min ḫāriǧ*) and those which are from the inside (*min dāḫil*). The latter category includes nature and different kinds of souls (*al-Hidāya* II.1, 138.5–139.6). In *al-Naǧāt*, Avicenna provides an interesting distinction between three kinds of principles for the natural body: a separate (*mufāriq*) principle for the continued existence of their being, viz., God; constituting principles, viz., matter and form, of which natural bodies are "composed" (*murakkaba min* and *taqawwama bi-*); and finally principles within the bodies, through which certain actions, motions, and processes are brought forth, and which are said to "permeate through the bodies" (*sāriya fī l-aǧsām*). This latter category includes nature as well as different kinds of souls (*al-Naǧāt* II.1.1, 190.11–195.4 ≈ *al-Ḥikma al-ʿArūḍiyya* II.1, 113.18–116.2); q.v. below, 274f. Most closely resembling the discussion of *al-Samāʿ al-ṭabīʿī*, in this respect, is the second chapter of the section on natural philosophy contained in Avicenna's *ʿUyūn al-ḥikma*. There, he distinguishes matter and form as constitutive (*muqawwim*) principles from two sorts of moving principles, viz., those effecting from the outside (*min sabab ḫāriǧ*) resulting in forced motion (*ḥaraka qasriyya*) and those effecting from within the body itself (*min sabab fī nafs al-ǧism*), such as soul and nature (*ʿUyūn al-ḥikma* II.2, 17.16–18.6).

73 *al-Samāʿ al-ṭabīʿī* I.5, §6, 32.5–15; cf. *al-Ḥikma al-mašriqiyya* III.4, 9.10–17.

has *within* himself. This, Aristotle states, would ignore the fact that the sick doctor cures himself merely accidentally, because it is not insofar as he is a doctor that he gets better but insofar as he is a sick patient, and so, likewise, it is not insofar as he is a sick patient that he exercises his medical knowledge but insofar as he is a doctor. Rather, it is as though the doctor cures himself merely insofar as he is someone else, i.e., insofar as he is a patient.[74] This has been the unanimous interpretation of that qualification throughout the centuries up until Avicenna. In fact, Aristotle himself explains the meaning of μὴ κατὰ συμβεβηκός this way, as Simplicius rightly remarks.[75]

Avicenna regards this explanation as insufficient or incomplete, for he claims that the two qualifications *bi-l-ḏāt* and *bi-l-ʿaraḍ* can each apply to both the mover and the moved. The present example of the self-curing doctor, however, only explains what is meant by the case of an accidental motion with regard to the mover. To be sure, it is not that Avicenna disagrees with Aristotle or his commentators on that part of the definition of nature, but he thought that some noteworthy aspects have so far been overlooked and is ready to supply them, in order to complete and systematise the picture. So, Avicenna provides the self-curing doctor, on whose interpretation he fully agrees with his predecessors, as an illustration of an accidental motion of the *mover*. What Avicenna means by an accidental motion with regard to the *moved* is depicted by the downward-directed fall of a bronze statue. In that case, the statue is merely accidentally moved downwards because of the essential natural motion of its material. It is the bronze which falls downwards, and so the bronze statue accidentally falls down as well. That we find the example of the statue in Themistius (d. ~ 385) but not in Simplicius or Philoponus – or Aristotle for that matter – is worth mentioning.[76]

Avicenna asserts that, by the same token, *bi-l-ḏāt* can also refer to the mover as well as to the moved. Thus, when nature causes a stone to fall rectilinearly down to the ground, nature does so essentially, i.e., through and by itself, without any other factor, force, or coercion interfering with its causation. The stone's nature, as a mover, has not been persuaded to cause the downward motion nor has nature itself been otherwise caused to make the stone fall. Nothing but the very nature itself is responsible and, in fact, nature cannot but do what it does whenever it is unhindered, as Avicenna emphasises:

74 This is also the crucial difference between δύναμις and φύσις in *Metaphysics* Θ.8, for there the former is distinguished from the latter exactly because it is "a principle of change in another thing or [in the thing itself] as other" (ἐν ἄλλῳ ἢ ᾗ ἄλλο; *Met.* Θ.8, 1049b5–10); cf. *Met.* Δ.12, 1019a15f.; Θ.1, 1046a11; Λ.3, 1070a7f.; *Cael.* III.2, 301b17–19. The doctor, thus, cures himself insofar as he is another, viz., his own patient, and accordingly possesses two δυνάμεις: that of acting and that of being acted upon.

75 Simplicius, *In Phys.*, 267.5–18; cf. also Themistius, *In Phys.*, 36.13–17; Philoponus, *In Phys.*, 197.19–28.

76 cf. Themistius, *In Phys.*, 36.2–5. Of course, Aristotle as well as Simplicius and Philoponus mention a statue, and the bronze of which as statues is made, but they do so in the context of discussing Antiphon's view that the matter of a thing should above all be regarded as its nature; cf. *Phys.* II.1, 193a9–30.

فيستحيل أن لا تحرّك إن لم يكن مانع حركة مباينة للحركة القاسرة.

So, it is impossible that it [sc. nature] does not cause motion, when there is nothing impeding a motion different from the forced motion. (*al-Samāʿ al-ṭabīʿī* I.5, §6, 32.7)

Conversely, the stone, as the moved object, is likewise not moved by something else other than its own nature, and so there is between the moved and the mover nothing other than an essential direct immediate causation.

The current additions to Aristotle's claim that nature is a "principle and cause ... by itself and not by accident" are a clear case where Avicenna plays out his strengths as an interpreter and commentator of Aristotle. While Philoponus and Simplicius simply repeated Aristotle's claim and explained his single example of the self-curing doctor, in order to elucidate why nature is not an accidental principle, Avicenna, presumably influenced by Themistius (or perhaps by Alexander), expands that simple remark to a systematic statement that distinguishes four perspectives on accidental and essential motion.

Yet, there is something else about Avicenna's understanding of Aristotelian nature that we can learn from his current remarks: Avicenna takes up a clear position about the "greatest difficulty" (μάλιστα δ' ἀπορεῖται) of *Physics* VIII.4.[77] In this chapter, Aristotle wrote the following:

ταῦτα δ' ἐστὶν ἃ τὴν ἀπορίαν παράσχοι ἂν ὑπὸ τίνος κινεῖται, οἷον τὰ κοῦφα καὶ τὰ βαρέα. ταῦτα γὰρ εἰς μὲν τοὺς ἀντικειμένους τόπους βίᾳ κινεῖται, εἰς δὲ τοὺς οἰκείους, τὸ μὲν κοῦφον ἄνω τὸ δὲ βαρὺ κάτω, φύσει· τὸ δ' ὑπὸ τίνος οὐκέτι φανερόν, ὥσπερ ὅταν κινῶνται παρὰ φύσιν. τό τε γὰρ αὐτὰ ὑφ' αὑτῶν φάναι ἀδύνατον· ζωτικόν τε γὰρ τοῦτο καὶ τῶν ἐμψύχων ἴδιον.

وهذه توقّف الشكّ إن كانت تحرّك عن شيء ما مثال ذلك الخفيفة والثقيلة وذلك أنّ هذه تحرّك إلى الموضعين المتقابلين قسراً وتحرّك إلى تخصّها أمّا الخفيفة فإلى فوق وأمّا الثقيل فإلى أسفل طبعاً. فأمّا أنّ عن شيء ما تحرّك فليس بظاهر فيها كما هو ظاهر إذا تحرّكت خارجاً عن طبعها وذلك أنّ القول بأنّها إنّما تحرّك هي من تلقائها محال بأنّ هذا المعنى إنّما هو للحيوان وهو شيء يخصّ ذوات الأنفس.

It is these cases that present a difficulty (ἀπορίαν, *al-šakk*) through what [something] is in motion (ὑπὸ τίνος κινεῖται, *tataḥārraku ʿan šayʾ mā*), [i.e., something] like the light and the heavy, for they are in motion towards [their] opposite places by force (βίᾳ, *qasran*) but towards their proper [places] – the light thing up and the heavy thing down – by nature (φύσει, *ṭabʿan*). However, through what [they are in motion] is no longer apparent (τὸ δ' ὑπὸ τίνος οὐκέτι φανερόν, *fa-amma anna ʿan šayʾ mā tataḥarraku fa-laysa bi-ẓāhir*) as it is when they are in motion against [their] nature (παρὰ φύσιν, *ḫāriǧan ʿan ṭabʿihā*). It is impossible (ἀδύνατον, *muḥāl*) to say that [their motion] is by themselves, for this is a characteristic of what has life (ζωτικόν, *li-l-ḥayawān*) and peculiar to ensouled [beings] (ἐμψύχων, *ḏawāt al-anfus*). (*Phys.* VIII.4, 255a1–7, tr. by Hardie/Gaye, modified)

77 *Phys.* VIII.4, 254b33.

This is a place where Aristotle is in trouble.[78] In *Physics* II.1, Aristotle's starting point for determining what nature is was to contrast natural things with artificial things. This allowed him to claim that the latter, as opposed to the former, "has no innate impulse to change (οὐδεμίαν ὁρμὴν ἔχει μεταβολῆς ἔμφυτον, *laysa fīhi mabdaʾ ġarīzī aṣlan li-l-taġayyur*) insofar as they are products of art."[79] Now, in *Physics* VIII, he has a different agenda, viz., to slowly approach the First Principle of motion and to establish it as an unmoved mover. In order to do so, Aristotle argues that every mover other than the Unmoved Mover must itself be moved by something else. This was demonstrated in a rather abstract fashion in *Physics* VII.1. Still, the issue is taken up once more in chapter VIII.4, now with a concrete focus on the motions of natural bodies. The reason for this is apparent: if nature is an internal principle and cause for motion by itself, as Aristotle's definition in *Physics* II.1 suggests, it would seem to be an exception to the rule that every mover other than the First Principle must be moved by something, for the nature of each natural thing brings about motion without itself being moved by something else. If already every stone or drop of water possesses an unmoved mover, then one could be tempted to ask, as Richard Sorabji did, "why the heavens also should not rotate solely because of their inner nature, unassisted by anything else."[80] If the motions of the heavenly bodies could be explained through the efficacy of their inner natures, one could easily dispense with the First Principle as the ultimate cause of motion. This dilemma is the reason for why Aristotle, now in *Physics* VIII.4, seeks to determine precisely "through what" (ὑπὸ τίνος, *ʿan šayʾ mā*) natural things are naturally moved, for in the present context of *Physics* VII–VIII, a simple reference to nature as a principle of motion in the sense of *Physics* II.1 is no longer an adequate answer. Thus, he states in *Physics* VIII.4 that although nature is certainly a principle of motion, it is only a principle of *suffering*, but not of causing, motion (οὐδὲ τοῦ ποιεῖν, ἀλλὰ τοῦ πάσχειν, *lā li-an ... yafʿala bal li-an yaqbala l-fiʿl*). The proper efficient causes from which a naturally moved object suffers its motion are said to be that which generated it (γεννήσαντος καὶ ποιήσαντος, *al-mukawwin aw al-fāʿil*), i.e., that which moved it away from its natural place, and that which removed the obstacle which so far prevented its natural return towards that place (τὰ ἐμποδίζοντα καὶ κωλύοντα λύσαντος, *al-muzīl li-l-ʿawāʾiq wa-l-mawāniʿ*).[81]

---

78 cf. Wolff, *Fallgesetz und Massebegriff*, 40f.; Furley, "Self-Movers," 165f.; Machamer, "Aristotle on Natural Place and Natural Motion," 382f.; Broadie, *Nature, Change, and Agency in Aristotle's* Physics, esp. 206f.; McGuire, "Philoponus on *Physics* ii 1," 241–246; Wildberg, *John Philoponus' Criticism of Aristotle's Theory of Aether*, 39–44; Sorabji, *Matter, Space, and Motion*, ch. 13; Gill, "Aristotle on Self-Motion," 261f.; Algra, *Concepts of Space in Greek Thought*, 208–217; Müller, *Naturgemäße Ortsbewegung*, 35–73; Katayama, "Soul and Elemental Motion in Aristotle's *Physics* VIII 4"; cf. also the useful summary of research positions in Müller, *Naturgemäße Ortsbewegung*, 19–35.

79 *Phys.* II.1, 192b18f., tr. by Hardie/Gaye, modified; cf. *Cael.* I.2, 268b14–16.

80 Sorabji, *Matter, Space, and Motion*, 219.

81 *Phys.* VIII.4, 255b30–256a2; cf. *Cael.* IV.3, 310a31f., 310b31–33, 311a9–12.

As we shall see shortly, Philoponus explicitly rejected Aristotle's answer in *Physics* VIII.4.[82] Yet, this was to be expected given his understanding of nature as a "life or a power" (ζωὴ ἤτοι δύναμις), i.e., as an active force that by itself effects motion. With his account, which construes nature as something analogous to soul, Philoponus fully embraced what we have just seen Aristotle calling an outright impossibility, viz., that natural things are in motion through themselves, for this, Aristotle said, "is a characteristic of life (ζωτικόν, *li-l-ḥayawān*) and peculiar to ensouled [beings]" (ἐμψύχων, *ḏawāt al-anfus*). As for Avicenna, his remarks on how to understand the qualification *bi-l-ḏāt* ("essentially") make it clear that he sided with Philoponus against the Aristotle of *Physics* VIII, for he asserted the following:

الطبيعة تحرّك لذاتها حين ما تكون بحال تحريك لا عن تسخير قاسر.

Nature causes motion (*tuḥarriku*) through itself (*li-ḏātihā*) whenever it is in a situation to cause motion (*bi-ḥāl taḥrīk*) and not from a forceful compulsion (*ʿan tasḫīr qāsir*). (*al-Samāʿ al-ṭabīʿī* I.5, §6, 32.6f.)[83]

This is not entirely unanticipated. We have already seen that Avicenna introduced nature as "the efficient principle common to natural things" (*al-mabdaʾ al-fāʿilī l-muštarak li-l-ṭabīʿiyyāt*).[84] We have also seen that his version of Aristotle's definition of nature does not reproduce the mediopassive infinitive κινεῖσθαι and simply marks nature as a "first principle for motion." He also already spoke about nature as being that which is responsible for *taḥrīk*, i.e., the production or causation of motion – and likewise, too, in the passage just quoted, in which he, more explicitly than before, employs unambiguous causal terminology (*tuḥarriku* and *taḥrīk*).[85] For him, nature is a power which *causes* motion and is, thus, a principle οὐδὲ τοῦ πάσχειν, ἀλλὰ τοῦ ποιεῖν, if I am allowed to reverse Aristotle's statement from *Physics* VIII.4, 255b30f. – a principle of causing, not of suffering, motion.[86] Moreover, it may be a significant detail

---

82 q.v. below, 240f.

83 *al-Ḥikma al-mašriqiyya* III.4, 9.11–13.

84 *al-Samāʿ al-ṭabīʿī* I.3, §12, 25.15; cf. *al-Ḥikma al-mašriqiyya* III.4, 8.19–9.3; cf. also *al-Ilāhiyyāt* VI.1, §6, 259.15, where Avicenna describes the nature of wood explicitly as an efficient principle for motion (*mabdaʾ fāʿilī li-l-ḥaraka*).

85 In *ʿUyūn al-ḥikma*, Avicenna uses the corresponding participle *muḥarrik* to describe nature as a "mover" (*ʿUyūn al-ḥikma* II.2, 18.4), whereas in the *Dānešnāme-ye ʿAlāʾī*, he describes nature as the most immediate cause (*sabab-e nazdīktar*) of motion and rest which "is from oneself" (*az ḫōdīš āyad*, *Dānešnāme-ye ʿAlāʾī* III.2, 7.1f.). Later in his *al-Samāʿ al-ṭabīʿī*, Avicenna also states that natural and voluntary motions can both commonly be described by saying that "motion is brought about of the moved's own accord" (*al-ḥaraka al-kāʾina min tilqāʾ al-mutaḥarrik*), and that is to say that it is not through something external (*al-Samāʿ al-ṭabīʿī* IV.9, §4, 301.18–302.1).

86 In their article about Philoponus' commentary in Aristotle's definition of nature, Macierowski and Hassing also remark on Avicenna's understanding of nature, stating that it constitutes a "[d]eviation from Aristotle in favor of an active internal principle of the natural motions of the elements" ("John Philoponus on Aristotle's Definition of Nature," 79). In order to support their claim, they quote a

that Avicenna's explanation of the meaning of Aristotle's expression "essential" or "by itself" – in Arabic: *bi-ḏāt* – reoccurs in Avicenna, slightly modified, in the claim that nature causes motion "on account, through, because of, or in virtue of itself" – in Arabic: *li-ḏātihā*.[87]

In addition to that, Avicenna also emphasises that nature is *always* active, i.e., it brings about motion "whenever it is in a situation to cause motion" (*ḥīna mā takūnu bi-ḥāl taḥrīk*). Above we could already see, in a quotation from the same paragraph, that Avicenna called it "impossible" for nature not to cause motion in the absence of any impediment. We shall continue to come across a number of remarks from various works of Avicenna that emphasise precisely the same point.[88]

Taking it all together, in his commentary on *Physics* II.1, 192b20–23, Avicenna interprets Aristotle's nature as an internal efficient principle which causes motion immediately from within the very thing in which it is and to the exclusion of any other influence. Most ink was spent on elucidating the meaning of the qualification "primary" or "first." One of the reasons for why this aspect appears as the central point of Avicenna's discussion, and perhaps also why Avicenna apparently seeks to distance himself from Philoponus in this regard, is that, ironically, this is the aspect where Philoponus' influence on Avicenna is most significant, because the direct and non-mediated effect of nature's agency on that thing in which it is is what both Philoponus and Avicenna call "inclination" (ῥοπή, *mayl*). It has long been suggested that Avicenna accepted Philoponus' ideas of inclination in natural motion and of impetus in forced motion, and incorporated them into his own system. It even has been asserted that

number of passages from Dominicus Gundisalvi's Latin translation of *al-Samāʿ al-ṭabīʿī*. Among these quotations is the following: "the power (*vis*) of a stone in its descent and its resting at the center ... is called nature." Macierowski's and Hassing's conclusion is certainly correct, yet they are wrong in founding part of their argument for Avicenna's understanding of nature as an active force on the Latin word *vis*. While *vis* renders the Arabic *quwwa*, it is more narrow in its meaning than its Arabic counterpart and unambiguously denotes a "force" and "power," thus certainly entailing an active connotation by itself. Even in phrases like "vis cognitiva" and "vis imaginativa," where *vis* signifies a "capacity," it is clear that *vis* is a "power" to think or to imagine and not so much a "potential." Conversely, the Arabic *quwwa* can mean "force" and "power," but is actually also a standard term for a potential and has, in this meaning, often been translated into Latin as *potentia*. Accordingly, Macierowski and Hassing's argument is correct only by accident, because they rely on Gundisalvi's Latin interpretation of *quwwa*. Had Gundisalvi translated in the present context *quwwa* as *potentia* and not as *vis*, Macierowski and Hassing could not claim – at least not on the basis of that quotation, that Avicenna deviated from Aristotle.

87 In Arabic manuscripts the two expressions *bi-ḏātihā* and *li-ḏātihā* differ only slightly. Yet, Mss. Leiden or. 4 and or. 84 clearly and unambiguously give *li-ḏātihā*, and the editions of Zāyid and Āl Yāsīn do so as well without providing a *varia lectio* in their respective apparatus.

88 cf. *al-Samāʿ al-ṭabīʿī* IV.9, §5, 302.8–17; IV.12, §1, 313.14–314.11; *al-Samāʾ wa-l-ʿālam* 2, 9.4–8; 9, 64.10–65.3; *al-Kawn wa-l-fasād* 6, 130.5–7.

"Avicenna's natural *mayl* is clearly the same as Philoponus' natural *rhopê*."[89] Whether this claim is true and how Avicenna incorporated the idea into his account of natural motion, shall now be seen.

4.3 Avicenna, and Philoponus, on Inclination

The term ῥοπή was used by Aristotle himself in his discussion of the void in *Physics* IV.8.[90] However, he decidedly refrained from considering ῥοπή as a mover. In other words, Aristotle ascribes to bodies different degrees of impulse or strength due to their respective heaviness or lightness, but he does never call this strength or impulse a mover or a principle of motion.[91]

As for Philoponus, he only once alludes to ῥοπή in his comments on Aristotle's definition of nature.[92] This brief passage, though, is extremely important, because in it, Philoponus explicitly rejects Aristotle's account of *Physics* VIII.4 that nature is a principle not of causing but of suffering motion and that the actual mover of a naturally moving object is not that object's nature but that which generated it as well as that which eventually removed the obstacle which has kept it from moving. In his commentary, Philoponus repudiates this position as follows:

---

89 Zimmermann, "Philoponus' Impetus Theory in the Arabic Tradition," 123; cf., however, Nony, "Two Arabic Theories of Impetus," 8f. In addition to these, there is a richness of studies devoted to the notion of *mayl*, e.g., Duhem, *Le système du monde* I, ch. 6, esp. 380–398; Pines, "Les précurseurs musulmans de la théorie de l'impetus"; "Etudes sur Aḥwad al-Zamān Abu'l-Barakāt al-Baghdādī"; "Un précurseur Bagdadien de la théorie de l'impetus"; "Omne quod movetur necesse est ab aliquo moveri"; Maier, *Die Vorläufer Galileis im 14. Jahrhundert*, 132–154; *Zwei Grundprobleme der Scholastischen Naturphilosophie*, 113–314; Wolff, *Fallgesetz und Massebegriff*, ch. 2; "Philoponus and the Rise of Preclassical Dynamics"; Hasnawi, "La dynamique d'Ibn Sīnā"; "La théorie avicennienne de l'*impetus*"; Sayılı, "Ibn Sīnā and Buridan on the Dynamics of Projectile Motion"; "Ibn Sīnā and Buridan on the Motion of the Projectile"; Sorabji, "John Philoponus," 7–13; M. Rashed, "Natural Philosophy," 295–302. Most of these focus on the concept as an explanatory model for projectile motion, since it is regarded as a precursor to the physical concept of inertia. While it is admitted that the idea of *mayl* and *impetus* as an acquired or impressed force is important for the history of science, often being discussed in comparison to John Buridan, Galileo Galilei, and Isaac Newton, it is regrettable that the related idea of a "natural *mayl*" and *inclinatio* as an innate tendency to fall (or rise), which is more relevant for our present concerns, has been quite overshadowed by this interest. Given the great number of individual studies, I shall limit my remarks on the pre-Avicennian history of the notion of ῥοπή to a minimum and focus on Avicenna's own conception.

90 *Phys.* IV.8, 216a13, 19.

91 cf. Zimmermann, "Philoponus' Impetus Theory in the Arabic Tradition," 121.

92 He does, however, refer to the idea frequently in his discussion of Aristotle's arguments against the void; cf. also his mention of the "natural impulse of the stone which has moved it downwards" (τήν τε φυσικὴν τοῦ λίθου ὁρμὴν τὴν ἐπὶ τὸ κάτω κινήσασαν) at *In Phys.*, 260.14f.; cf. also the other expressions listed by Wolff, *Fallgesetz und Massebegriff*, 82f.

τὰ μὲν φυσικὰ φαίνονται τῆς κινήσεως ἑαυτῶν καὶ τῆς ἠρεμίας τὴν ἀρχὴν ἐν ἑαυτοῖς ἔχοντα· τά τε γὰρ ζῷα ὅταν κινῆται οὐκ ἔξωθεν ὑπό τινος κινεῖται, ἀλλ' ἐν ἑαυτοῖς ἔχει τὸ κινοῦν, καὶ τὰ ἄψυχα δέ· οἷον οἱ λίθοι ἀφιέμενοι οὐχ ὑπὸ τοῦ ἀφιέντος ἐπὶ τὸ κάτω κινοῦνται (ἐκεῖνος γὰρ μόνον ἀφῆκεν), ἀλλ' ἡ ἐν αὐτοῖς φυσικὴ ῥοπὴ κατήνεγκεν αὐτούς· οὕτω καὶ τὸ πῦρ ἀφεθὲν κάτωθεν ὑπὸ τῆς ἐν αὐτῷ φύσεως ἠνέχθη ἐπὶ τὸ ἄνω· εἶτα ἐνεχθέντα εἰς τὰς οἰκείας ὁλότητας καὶ τοὺς οἰκείους τόπους ὑπὸ τῆς ἐν αὐτοῖς φύσεως ἠρεμεῖ.

Natural things clearly have in themselves the principle of their own motion and rest (τῆς κινήσεως ἑαυτῶν καὶ τῆς ἠρεμίας τὴν ἀρχὴν ἐν ἑαυτοῖς ἔχοντα), for animals when they move are not moved by something outside but have the mover in themselves (ἐν ἑαυτοῖς ἔχει τὸ κινοῦν), and so in inanimate things, for example, stones on being released are not moved downwards by the releaser (οὐχ ὑπὸ τοῦ ἀφιέντος) – for he has merely released them – but the natural inclination in them (ἡ ἐν αὐτοῖς φυσικὴ ῥοπή) brings them down. In this way fire, too, when released from [being] below, is brought upwards by the nature in it (ὑπὸ τῆς ἐν αὐτῷ φύσεως), and then, having being brought to their own masses and their own places, they are at rest by the nature in them (ὑπὸ τῆς ἐν αὐτοῖς φύσεως). (Philoponus, *In Phys.*, 195.24–32, tr. by Lacey, modified)[93]

Directly denying Aristotle's solution, Philoponus compares the motions of animate beings with those of inanimate objects and claims that both kinds have "the mover in themselves" (ἐν ἑαυτοῖς ἔχει τὸ κινοῦν), so that, in the end, *all* natural things invariably have the principle of their own motions and rests in themselves (τὴν ἀρχὴν ἐν ἑαυτοῖς ἔχοντα).[94] More precisely, Philoponus clearly calls soul a mover (τὸ κινοῦν) and aligns it with the natural inclination (φυσικὴ ῥοπή) within inanimate objects. Since we have already seen that nature, too, is a mover and that it is analogous to soul, Philoponus offers a sum total of three different concepts, viz., nature, soul, and inclination, all of which are said to be movers of the natural body. Towards the end of the above passage, he explicitly equates the natural inclination in stones (ἡ ἐν αὐτοῖς φυσικὴ ῥοπή) with the nature in fire (ὑπὸ τῆς ἐν αὐτῷ φύσεως), so that it appears that nature is nothing other than the inclination of natural things, being a mover primarily of inanimate bodies just as a soul is the mover of animate ones.[95] There does not seem to be a conceptual distinction between nature and soul, for both are movers, nor is there

93 While rejecting Aristotle's first point that the efficient cause of natural motion is the remover of the obstacle that so far prevented a natural body from engaging in natural motion, Philoponus does not, however, reject Aristotle's second point that that which generated the natural thing (γεννήσαντος καὶ ποιήσαντος) is the actual mover of a stone; q.v. above, 237. While Aristotle arguably wanted to signify with this second expression whatever, in one way or another, made the object be, occur, or turn up in an unnatural place, Philoponus argues, in his late work *De opificio mundi*, that it was God who, generating all things, created the heavy and the light by implanting natural inclination into natural things; cf. *De opificio mundi*, 28.26–29.5; cf. also *In Phys.*, 581.19–31; cf. further Wolff, *Fallgesetz und Massebegriff*, 81–86; Sorabji, *Matter, Space, and Motion*, 232f.

94 cf. Philoponus, *In An.*, 110.12–17; cf. also Pines, "Omne quod movetur necesse est ab aliquo moveri," fn. 137, 50. Philoponus' position here somewhat resembles Aristotle's remarks in *De caelo* III.2, 301a20–26, where Aristotle also uses the term ῥοπή.

95 In addition to these three movers, it is also clear that for Philoponus, a place is also an object of desire and, thus, exerts some δύναμις of its own as a desirable or even attractive position within the order that has been decreed by God; cf. Philoponus' rich discussion in passages such as *In Phys.*,

an actual distinction between the inclination and nature.[96] Nonetheless, it should be noted that Philoponus does not seem to deny that inanimate natural things, as opposed to animate ones, first have to be moved away from their unnatural place and, thereupon, have to be released, before their natural inclination can begin actively to "bring them down," as he writes.

Philoponus' tendency to not distinguish between nature and inclination may have been influenced by Alexander, who, probably, was the main source of inspiration for Philoponus' understanding of ῥοπή.[97] In the *Risālat al-Iskandar al-Afrūdīsī fī anna kull mā yataḥarraku fa-innamā yataḥarraku ʿan muḥarrik*, we find a highly interesting interpretation of Aristotle's proof of the principle that everything that is moved is moved by something else. According to this interpretation, Aristotle shows in *Physics* VIII, first, that everything that is in motion accidentally is moved by something else and, then, turns to those things which are in motion essentially. Those that are essentially in motion through some force can also easily be determined as being moved by something else. More interesting are those things which naturally engage in essential motion. About these, Alexander writes the following:

> ثمّ لمّا بيّن أنّ الأجسام الطبيعية والتي في الكون تجري هذا المجرى من أنّ جميع الأشياء التي تتحرّك بالطبع تتحرّك عن شيء وذلك أنّه يظهر من أمر ذوي الأنفس أنّهم تتحرّكون بالنفس المحرّكة التي يتحرّكها المتنفّسون من طريق ما هم متنفّسون المخالفة لمحرّكة الشيء المجتمع من كلّيهما يعني النفس والبدن. وكذلك يظهر من أمر الأجسام التي تتحرّك بالطبع بالميل الذي فيما أنّ مبدأ حركتها إنّما هو من الميل الموجود فيها الذي به من قبل وجوده لها تتحرّك بالطبع. وذلك أنّ الشيء الذي أخرجها من الثقل بالقوّة إلى الثقل بالفعل يخعلها على خلاف الحال التي كانت عليها أيضاً هو سبب حركتها بالفعل.
>
> Next, after that, he proved that the natural bodies and those which are in generation proceed along these lines [i.e., are also moved by something else], because it is that all things which are naturally in motion are in motion through a thing. That is because it is clear from the case[98] of [things] which have souls that they are in motion[99] by the soul (*bi-l-nafs*), [which is both] the mover (*al-muḥarrik*) through which ensouled things are in motion by way of their being ensouled

579.27–580.3, 581.18–31, 632.4–634.2; cf. also Simplicius, *In Phys.*, 600.30–38; cf. further Sorabji, *Matter, Space, and Motion*, 211–213; Algra, *Concepts of Space in Greek Thought*, 196f., and generally Sorabji, *The Philosophy of the Commentators*, vol. II, ch. 13e.

96 Müller, likewise, argues that Philoponus identifies φύσις and ῥοπή; cf. *Naturgemäße Ortsbewegung*, 54, 62, 66.

97 In turn, Alexander himself may have been influenced by even earlier figures such as Strato of Lampsacus and Boethus of Sidon, as Moraux noted; cf. *Alexandre d'Aphrodise*, 7f. Despite these forebears, Pines stated that Alexander's theory is "to a certain extent ... his personal contribution" ("Omne quod movetur necesse est ab aliquo moveri," 28); cf. also Wolff and Müller, who both emphasise the direct influence Alexander had on Philoponus; cf. Wolff, *Fallgesetz und Massebegriff*, 44; Müller, *Naturgemäße Ortsbewegung*, 66f.

98 Reading *min amr* with Ms. Carullah 1279 for *min* in Marmura and Rescher.

99 Reading *tataḥarrakūna* for *yataḥarrakūna* in Marmura and Rescher.

> [and] something different (*al-muḫālif*)[100] from the motion[101] of the thing composed[102] of both, i.e.,[103] of body and soul. Likewise,[104] it is clear from the case of bodies which are naturally in motion by the inclination (*bi-l-mayl*) which[105] is in them that[106] the principle of their motion is only (*innamā*) from the inclination existing in them by which,[107] and on account of its existence for them, they are naturally in motion. That is because the thing [whose] bringing them[108] from potential heaviness to actual heaviness puts them into a different state than they had been also is the cause of their actual motion. (*Risālat al-Iskandar al-Afrūdīsī fī anna kull mā yataḥarraku fa-innamā yataḥarraku ʿan muḥarrik*, Ms. Carullah 1279, 67r.15–19)[109]

At first, and in light of the last sentence of this passage, it appears that Alexander's understanding of how natural things are in motion is contrary to that of Philoponus and more in line with Aristotle – indeed, Alexander's explanation is overall similar to Aristotle's reasoning from *Physics* VIII.4.[110] He divides between animate and inanimate things, and states that the former are moved by their soul, which is both a mover (*al-muḥarrik*) and separate enough (*al-muḫālif*) to satisfy the condition that everything that is in motion is so through something else, as the body (*al-badan*) is in motion through its soul. Inanimate things, though not ensouled, are still in motion through something else, because they have been dislocated, i.e., moved away from their natural place, so that their potential weight has been actualised. Thus, unlike Philoponus, Alexander stresses more clearly the importance of an external agent who, first, displaced and, then, released the natural things. Once they have been released, however, Alexander, like Philoponus, emphasises that they are in motion by the inclination (*bi-l-mayl*) – "the natural inclination in them brings them down," as we can read in Philoponus, and it is "only from the inclination existing in them by which, and on account of its

100 Reading *al-muḫālif* with Ms. Carullah 1279 for *a-l-ṭ-ḫ-l-f* in Marmura and Rescher.

101 Reading *li-ḥaraka* for *li-ḥarraka* (?) in Marmura and Rescher. The manuscript, indeed, seems to indicate a *šadda* above the the second radical (*rāʾ*), but the scribe often appears to put a mark above the *rāʾ*, e.g., in *yaẓharu* and *amr* (76r16), to mention just two examples.

102 Suggesting to read *al-muǧtamaʿ* for *iǧtamaʿa* in Marmura and Rescher. The facsimile of Ms. Carullah 1279 provided by Marmura and Rescher certainly indicates an *alif* followed by *m-ǧ-t-m-ʿ*.

103 Reading *yaʿnī* with Ms. Carullah 1279 for *maʿnā* in Marmura and Rescher.

104 Reading *wa-ka-ḏālika* with Marmura and Rescher for *fa-ḏālika* in Ms. Carullah 1279.

105 Reading *allaḏī* with Ms. Carullah 1279 for *allatī* in Marmura and Rescher.

106 Reading *anna* with Marmura and Rescher (following a suggestion by Pines) for *min* in Ms. Carullah 1279; cf., however, the discussion in 111, 244.

107 Reading *bihī* with Ms. Carullah 1279 for *lahu* in Marmura and Rescher.

108 Reading *iḫrāǧuhā* with Ms. Carullah 1279 for *yuḥarrikuhā* in Marmura and Rescher; still something is missing here, it seems.

109 cf. Alexander of Aphrodisias, *Maqāla fī l-qawl fī mabādiʾ al-kull*, §5, 44.13–46.4; §16, 52.3–6 (ed. Genequand). Alexander attributes a similar argument also to Plato, perhaps referring to *Timaeus* 57e3–5, as Pines remarks; cf. *Risālat al-Iskandar al-Afrūdīsī fī anna kull mā yataḥarraku fa-innamā yataḥarraku ʿan muḥarrik*, Ms. Carullah 1279, 66v.27–30; cf. also Pines, "Omne quod movetur necesse est ab aliquo moveri," 25f.

110 For Aristotle's reasoning, q.v. above, 236f.

existence for them, they are naturally in motion," as Alexander has it. In the end, then, both accounts, different though they may be, together emphasise the significance of a natural inclination in explaining the natural motion of inanimate things. In other words, once the weight has been actualised, Alexander would agree that nature is by no means a principle of suffering but clearly one of causing motion.

As in Philoponus, then, it is not entirely clear whether and how Alexander would differentiate conceptually between the agency of soul and that of nature in their production of motion, and define the involvement of inclination in both cases, for all three are somehow said to be movers and responsible for motion. Thus, in a way, i.e., despite the noted differences, we get more or less the same result in Alexander as in Philoponus: there is no conceptual distinction between inclination and soul, nor is there an actual distinction between the inclination and nature.[111]

It should be mentioned that any systematic study of the Greek notion of ῥοπή in Alexander and Philoponus faces the intricate challenge that comes with a simple lack of a sufficiently reliable textual basis, barring the conclusive resolution of questions

---

111 Müller, likewise, argues that Alexander identifies φύσις and ῥοπή, and that he aligns soul and inclination; cf. *Naturgemäße Ortsbewegung*, 67, 70f., referring also to Alexander of Aphrodisias, *De anima libri mantissa*, 106.5–8, as well as Alexander *apud* Simplicium, *In Cael.*, 380.29–35. Pines has labelled Alexander's tendency to align the natural motions of inanimate bodies with those of animate bodies terrestrial and celestial alike as his "naturism" ("Omne quod movetur necesse est ab aliquo moveri," 42–48); cf. also Bodnár, "Alexander of Aphrodisias on Celestial Motions." Regarding Alexander, it ought to be noted that a different interpretation might be in order if the suggestion by Pines, followed by Marmura and Rescher, to emend *bi-l-mayl allaḏī fī-mā min mabdaʾ ḥarakatihā* to *bi-l-mayl allaḏī fī-mā anna mabdaʾ ḥarakatihā*, is rejected, for, then, the inclination would seem to derive *from* the principle of their motion, i.e., nature, and would, perhaps, have to be distinct from it. Though the reading of *anna* gives a more fluent Arabic text, Pines' claim that reading *min* results in a "hopelessly corrupt" text seems to be an exaggeration ("Omne quod movetur necesse est ab aliquo moveri," 42). The Arabic is coarse in any case. Upon reading *min*, one would have to translate: "Likewise, it is clear from the case of bodies which are naturally in motion by the inclination (*bi-l-mayl*) which is in them from (*min*) the principle of their motion; it is only (*innamā*) from the inclination existing in them through which, and on account of its existence for them, they are naturally in motion." In fact, reading *min*, instead of *anna*, may seem to be more in line with Alexander's position as put forth in his *Maqāla fī l-qawl fī mabādiʾ al-kull*. There, he writes that every natural body, animate or not, has "a principle and cause of motion" – viz., nature (*al-ṭabīʿa*) – and is moved by itself through a "desire" (*al-ištiyāq*) towards perfection. Alexander, then, writes that "this desire, which proceeds from the natural disposition, is inclination" (*hāḏā l-ištiyāq al-ṣādir ʿan al-tahayyuʾ al-ṭabīʿī huwa al-mayl*; §§4–5, 44.4–46.4 (ed. Genequand)). Thus, in this treatise, inclination undoubtedly is "from" (*ʿan*) nature and is not nature itself. Regarding Philoponus, it ought to be noted that Wildberg's investigation of Philoponus' theory suggests, in contrast to Simplicius' position, that natural bodies lose their inclination once they have reached their natural places; cf. *John Philoponus' Criticism of Aristotle's Theory of Aether*, 129f.; cf. also Simplicius, *In Cael.*, 65.7f. Wildberg further notes that Simplicius also criticises Themistius for having argued that the elements have an inclination only when they are not in their natural places; cf. Simplicius, *In Cael.*, 70.2–7; Themistius, *In Cael.*, 221.28–30 (lat.) Thus, just as in the case of Alexander, there is evidence which may suggest that Philoponus actually upheld a distinction between nature and inclination.

surrounding certain specifics of their theories, on the one hand, and the definite determination of Philoponus' dependence on his predecessor, on the other. Available studies on Alexander are mostly based on a small number of poorly transmitted Arabic translations of lost Greek texts supplied with testimonies from Themistius and Simplicius, whereas studies on Philoponus need to gather up bits and pieces from various writings, such as his commentaries on the first half of the *Physics* or the one on *De anima* as well as his late *De opificio mundi*. Accordingly, the above analysis, suggestive and cogent though it may be, can hardly claim to be decisive in all respects. What emerges nonetheless, and sufficiently, I think, is that the concepts of nature, soul, and inclination have notoriously been employed in ancient and late ancient accounts of natural motion without, however, there having been any perceptible attempt to differentiate between them in a systematic fashion. They are all somehow movers and principles, i.e., responsible for motion. Avicenna, as we shall see, addresses this issue, apparently trying to establish a clearer picture, in which he systematically differentiates these concepts from one another.

If, then, Alexander and Philoponus both either failed to provide a clear and systematic differentiation between the agency of nature, soul, and inclination, or were actually driven by an intention to unify them, and if, moreover, "Avicenna's natural *mayl* is clearly the same as Philoponus' natural *rhopê*," as has been argued by Zimmermann, we should be surprised to find the following statement in Avicenna:[112]

وإن عُنِيَ بذلك أنّ النفس يحدث ميلاً وبالميل تُحرّك فالطبيعة تفعل ذلك أيضاً على ما سيتّضح لك وكأنّ مثل هذا الميل ليس هو المحرّك بل أمر به تحرّك المتحرّك.

However, if it is meant by this that the soul brings about (*yaḥduṯu*) an inclination and produces motion through the inclination (*bi-l-mayl tuḥarriku*), then the nature does that as well, as shall be made clear to you. Indeed, it is as if this inclination is not a mover (*hāḏā l-mayl laysa huwa l-muḥarrik*) but something through which the moved is in motion (*amr bihī taḥarraka l-mutaḥarrik*).[113] (*al-Samāʿ al-ṭabīʿī* I.5, §6, 31.18–32.2, tr. by McGinnis, modified)

The context of this passage is Avicenna's above analysed discussion of Philoponus' claim that soul moves an animal only through the mediacy of that animal's nature.[114] Avicenna interprets Philoponus' claim in such a way that soul actually changes the underlying body's nature. Denying that this is the case, Avicenna proceeds to offer more amiable readings of Philoponus' contention, i.e., readings of his commentary that come closer to what he considers to be the truth than the first interpretation which he flatly dismissed. The present passage is such an amiable reading.[115] So, Avicenna

112 Zimmermann, "Philoponus' Impetus Theory in the Arabic Tradition," 123.

113 Reading *al-mutaḥarrik* with Ms. Leiden or. 84 and the apparatus in Zāyid for *a-l-m-ḥ-r-k* in Ms. Leiden or. 4 as well as Āl Yāsīn, Zāyid, and McGinnis; on this choice, q.v. fn. 117 below, 246f.

114 cf. Philoponus, *In Phys.*, 196.26–30; q.v. above, 229ff.

115 This is relevant, as it helps to interpret the conjunction "if" (*wa-in*) correctly; here, "if" introduces a clause which does not convey a counterfactual mood.

intends to say that one could absolve Philoponus, and everyone else hiding behind the term *baʿḍ* ("some"), from his criticism if his intention was just to say that "soul brings about an inclination and produces motion through the inclination," for this line of thought is, in fact, correct. In effect, Avicenna states that he is favourable to the now offered alternative interpretation, because it approximates what he regards to be the correct opinion. He, thus, accepts the proposition that the soul brings about a certain inclination and that soul causes motion precisely by bringing about an inclination. To this he adds that nature, in this respect, is similar to soul, for nature, too, causes motion by virtue of producing an inclination, "as shall be made clear to you" (*ʿalā mā sayattaḍaḥū laka*).[116]

Now, however, Avicenna sounds a note of caution: we must not take the inclination to be a mover (*muḥarrik*). Instead, Avicenna urges us to understand the concept of inclination as "something by virtue of which the moved is in motion" (*amr bihī taḥarraka l-mutaḥarrik*).[117] Natural inclination is, thus, not an instrument through which

116 McGinnis rightly refers to *al-Samāʿ al-ṭabīʿī* IV.12. Other relevant remarks and discussions are to be found in *al-Samāʿ al-ṭabīʿī* II.8, §15, 132.9–11; IV.8, §11, 294.10f.; §§16–18, 298.3–299.13; IV.10, §4, 307.7–16; IV.12, §1, 313.14–314.11; IV.14, §5, 326.6f.

117 Available editions of Avicenna's *al-Samāʿ al-ṭabīʿī* unanimously render this clause as what seems to be *amr bihī taḥarraka l-muḥarrik*, which would have to be translated as "something through which the mover is in motion." This is difficult to make sense of. Moreover, it merely states that through inclination only the mover is in motion but remains silent about whether or not the moved is affected, too. Of course, one can read the word as a passive participle (*al-muḥarrak*) instead of the identically written active participle (*al-muḥarrik*), but Avicenna also often uses – indeed: prefers – *mutaḥarrik* as a term for that which is in motion, and one may surmise that he does so, in order to avoid the ambiguity within the indiscernible Arabic word *muḥarrik/muḥarrak*. On that premiss, then, the texts transmitted by the modern editions suggest *muḥarrik*, which entails that the object in motion – despite Avicenna's foregoing assertion that nature effects motion not in itself but "in another" (*fī ġayrihī*) – has to be the mover itself, i.e., nature. McGinnis, who clearly reads *muḥarrik* ("mover"), tries to avoid that apparent contradiction by translating the clause as "something through which the mover produces motion." This, however, would require to read *yuḥarriku*, an active causative of the second stem, instead of *taḥarraka*, a reflexive medial of the fifth stem. Both readings are, again, identical in their undotted Arabic *rasm*, which may also be the reason for why Gundisalvi's Latin translation of Avicenna's *al-Samāʿ al-ṭabīʿī* provides *sed est res per quam movet motor*. Apparently Gundisalvi, just as McGinnis, read the text as *yuḥarriku l-muḥarrik*. This certainly avoids the just-mentioned contradiction and is an intuitive reading, in particular because Avicenna just wrote that "soul ... produces motion through the inclination" (*al-nafs ... bi-l-mayl tuḥarrika*). What may perhaps speak against it is that all editions so far, including that of McGinnis, as well as Ms. Leiden or. 4 render the verb as what seems to be *taḥarraka*, while clearly writing *muḥarrik*. An alternative would be to follow a variant reading for *al-muḥarrik* ("mover") that is offered by Zāyid in the apparatus to the Cairo edition and also attested in Ms. Leiden or. 84: *al-mutaḥarrik* ("moved"). On that reading, the sentence would have to be translated as "something through which the *moved* is in motion." Counterintuitive as this may seem at first glance, it achieves precisely what Avicenna seems to intend here, viz., to clarify that inclination is not a mover, even though soul and nature produce motion "through inclination" (*bi-l-mayl*). Against this suggestion, let it be noted that the same result could have been achieved by reading *taḥarraka l-muḥarrak* and a

nature causes motion but is something which manifests itself in the motion.[118] Put differently, natural motion is not caused *by* inclination, i.e., inclination does not cause motion. Instead, motion is caused by nature (even though through inclination), so that motion is but the "expression" or "manifestation" *of* the inclination once the object is unimpeded. When a stone is elevated up high, one can feel its inclination towards its natural place as weight pressing against one's palm. Once, however, the stone is unimpeded, it falls to the ground. This motion is nothing but the manifestation of the inclination that drives the stone to the ground just as the weight pressing against one's palm is a different manifestation of that same inclination. The stone's nature, however, is the exclusive mover of the stones' motion, because it is the direct cause of the inclination. Nature, then, causes inclination – and inclination can manifest itself in motion.[119]

We can find further evidence for this interpretation that the natural motion of a natural object is the manifestation of an inclination which is the direct effect of its internal nature. In fact, motion is only one of *three* possible manifestations of an inclination which derives from a thing's efficient principle of motion, be that an external principle of forced motion or an internal principle of natural motion:

i) There is the natural motion, which is the manifestation of a natural inclination provided that the stone is not at its natural place and, in addition to that, is unimpeded, so that it is actually in motion towards its natural place.

---

similar result by *yuḥarriku l-muḥarrik*. Moreover, one could argue that *mutaḥarrik* is a later emendation precisely in order to disambiguate the clause. Yet, it is also true that the reading *mutaḥarrik* bears all the good signs of a genuine *lectio difficilior*: it is attested by the manuscripts; it is, at first glance, obscure; it does, however, make much sense; and it conforms to Avicenna's usual terminology. Whatever reading one adopts, it must conform to what Avicenna wants to express here, and that is that inclination does *not* come to be a mover (*hāḏā l-mayl laysa huwa l-muḥarrik*), but that it is something "through which the moved is in motion" or something "through which the mover produces motion." As a final note, accepting the reading *mutaḥarrik* (or keeping with *muḥarrak*), one could also read the verb as *tuḥarriku* and consider nature, though somewhat remote in the sentence, to be the feminine subject of the verb and translate "something through which it [sc. nature] moves the moved."

118 In similar terms, Janos writes about Abū Naṣr al-Fārābī that the inclination of the heavenly spheres "merely *represents the medium* through which this causality [sc. the causality of the heavenly souls and intellects] operates" (Janos, "Moving the Orbs," 183f., emphasis added).

119 cf. *al-Samāʿ al-ṭabīʿī* IV.10, §4, esp. 307.9, 15f.; cf. also *al-Samāʿ al-ṭabīʿī* IV.9, §5, 302.8–13, which is examined below, 280ff. In much the same way is someone who throws a stone the sole mover of the stone's motion, even though the mover moves the stone by implanting a forced inclination into the stone. As Avicenna emphasises in *al-Samāʿ al-ṭabīʿī* II.8, §16, 132.15–18, it is the separate mover (*al-muḥarrik al-mufāriq*) who produces a forced motion, e.g., by throwing a stone upwards. This motion can continue to exists even without the separate mover being present, because the mover has implanted a "cause which sustains the motion" (*sabab yastabqī l-ḥaraka*) and which "has some influence on [the body]" (*yuʾaṯṯiru fīhi*). Thus, the forced inclination is not itself a moving cause – it is a sustaining cause. Thus, again, it is that the separate mover causes motion through an inclination, and Avicenna, once more, abstains from calling that inclination a *mover*. I cannot presently go into more detail about Avicenna's theory of forced motion.

ii) There is weight or resistance, which is the manifestation that is to be perceived upon attempting to keep the stone from moving towards its natural place or to move the stone (further) away from its natural place.
iii) There is pressure or impulse which is the manifestation that is to be perceived upon catching a stone which has been thrown forcefully, i.e., which successfully has been propelled away, from its natural place.

We see that mostly inclination comes along with motion, as in the cases of natural motion (i) and of forced motion (iii). In case (ii), however, inclination is related to rest.[120] In addition, Avicenna tells us that rest may also be related to the absence of inclination, for a stone, when it has arrived at its natural place and has come to rest there, effectively loses its inclination.[121] In effect, there are situations in which nature, inclination, and motion coincide, but there are also other situations in which nature and inclination exist without motion or even nature without either motion or inclination. It is, thus, important to keep these three aspects of Avicenna's natural dynamics conceptually distinct from one another. Neither can inclination be identified with motion, because a stone which is kept from returning to its natural place has an inclination but does not undergo motion; nor can inclination be equated with nature, for a stone which has

120 We find similar enumerations in other works, too; cf. *al-Samā' wa-l-ʿālam* 9, 64.10–65.3; *al-Išārāt wa-l-tanbīhāt* II.2.6, 109.8–17; *Dānešnāme-ye ʿAlā'ī* III.22, 53.4–54.6; cf. also *al-Samāʿ al-ṭabīʿī* IV.8, §16, 298.3–5; IV.14, §5, 326.6f. In *al-Samā' wa-l-ʿālam*, for example, Avicenna writes that to the heavy and the light belong three states: (a) the state of its actually being in the place to which it is directed, (b) the state of its unimpeded motion towards it, and (c) the state of its being at a halt and prevented from going further. Of these three, (b) corresponds with (i) in the above list, and (a) and (c) apply to (ii). Item (iii) in the above list is not treated in the enumeration in *al-Samā' wa-l-ʿālam* 9 which, however, is not surprising, as this chapter is concerned with the light and the heavy (*al-ḫafīf wa-l-ṯaqīl*), whereas (iii) is an instance of unnatural or forced *mayl*, i.e., an instance of *impetus* as opposed to *inclinatio*. Nonetheless, Avicenna briefly alludes to forced inclination (*mayl qasrī*) immediately after the enumeration (64.17). He, moreover, also refers to an inclination which actually leads to natural motion as *mayl mursal ʿāmil* ("unimpeded productive inclination") and to the inclination which we perceive as weight as *mayl mamnūʿ ʿan yakūna ʿāmilan* ("inclination prevented from being productive"; 65.3).

121 cf. *al-Samāʿ al-ṭabīʿī* I.6, §2, 34.12–35.7; IV.8, §11, 294.10f.; *al-Samā' wa-l-ʿālam* 9, 64.14–65.1, 68.17–69.2; *al-Ḥikma al-mašriqiyya* III.4, 11.11f.; cf. also *Kitāb al-Ḥudūd*, §75, 34.6f.; cf. further Zimmermann, "Philoponus' Impetus Theory in the Arabic Tradition," 122; Wisnovsky, *Avicenna on Final Causality*, 95f.; Lettinck, *Aristotle's* Physics *and its Reception in the Arabic World*, 666. At another passage, *al-Samā' wa-l-ʿālam* 2, 9.4–8, Avicenna relates that there are two meanings of "heavy" and "light": one meaning is that something is heavy or light, if it is such as to be in motion (*min šānihī annahū ... taḥarraka*) by an internal inclination *whenever* it is not at its natural location (*iḏa kāna fī ġayr al-ḥayyiz al-ṭabīʿī*). In this sense, things are always (*dā'iman*) heavy or light, because things are always "such as to be in motion," even if they are not actually moving. The second meaning is that a heavy or light thing is actually moving either upwards or downwards towards its natural place. So here, too, Avicenna unites actual motion, on the one hand, and potential motion and actual rest, on the other, within a single notion of nature, which turns out to be a rather complex principle for motion and rest. A similar distinction is repeated and discussed in *al-Samā' wa-l-ʿālam* 9, 65.4–9.

arrived at its natural place still has its nature but no longer has an inclination; nor is nature the same as motion, due to similar reasons.[122]

There is even more evidence. In *al-Ilāhiyyāt* IX, Avicenna investigates the causal relation between the First Principle and everything that follows it. A theme which is of pertinence to our present concern is the discussion of the motion of the heavens in *al-Ilāhiyyāt* IX.2.[123] On his way to establish the conclusion that the heavenly bodies are moved neither by an internal nature nor by an inhering intellect but through a soul, Avicenna sums up important points about his general theory of motion and causation, explicitly stating the following:

> وأيضاً فإن كلّ قوّة فإنّما تحرّك بتوسّط الميل والميل هو المعنى الذي يحسّ في الجسم المتحرّك وإن سكن قسراً أُحِسَّ ذلك الميل فيه يقاوم المسكّن مع سكونه طلباً للحركة. فهو غير الحركة لا محالة وغير القوّة المحرّكة لأن القوّة المحرّكة تكون موجودة عند إتمامها الحركة ولا يكون الميل موجوداً.
>
> Moreover, then, every power (*quwwa*) causes motion only through the mediation of inclination (*tuḥarriku bi-tawassuṭ al-mayl*). Inclination (*al-mayl*) is the meaning which is sensed (*al-maʿnā llaḏī huwa yuḥassu*) in the moving body. If it [sc. the body] comes to rest by force (*qasran*), that inclination in it is sensed resisting (*yuqāwimu*) that which puts [the body] to rest, seeking motion despite its rest. Thus, it is undoubtedly other than the motion and other than the moving power (*fa-huwa ġayr al-ḥaraka lā maḥāla wa-ġayr al-quwwa al-muḥarrika*), because the moving power exists when it completes the motion, whereas the inclination does not exist. (*al-Ilāhiyyāt* IX.2, §4, 383.4–7, tr. by Marmura, modified)

On the basis that every power, for example, a nature or a soul, causes motion through inclination, Avicenna explains that inclination ought not to be identified with either motion or nature.[124] First, a stone which is forcefully thrown by an external efficient

---

122 These distinctions are not always observed in contemporary scholarship on Avicenna's dynamics. Arif, for example, erroneously claims that Avicenna identifies "nature with soul as well as inclination in the case of animals ... and inanimate objects respectively," and states that "in both cases nature expresses itself in the thing's motion" ("The Universe as a System," 137). Belo, on the other hand, falsely stated that Avicenna "identifies nature specifically with the movement or natural tendency of natural elements and natural substances" ("The Concept of 'Nature' in Aristotle, Avicenna and Averroes," 50). In light of the present analysis, both interpretations must be judged as incorrect. There is an interesting further reason that nature cannot be identified with inclination: in forced motion, when a stone is thrown upwards, for example, the object acquires a forced inclination and, thereby, loses its natural inclination, even though it most certainly does not lose its nature. That a body loses its natural inclination when it acquires a forced inclination is made explicit by Avicenna when he denies that there can be two inclinations in one and the same body at *al-Samāʿ al-ṭabīʿī* IV.8, §18, 299.7–9; cf. also *al-Samāʿ al-ṭabīʿī* IV.8, §11, 294.11–295.1; *al-Išārāt wa-l-tanbīhāt* II.2.6, 109.9–11; cf. further Pines, "Omne quod movetur necesse est ab aliquo moveri," 51f.; Hasnawi, "La dynamique d'Ibn Sīnā," 104; Nony, "Two Arabic Theories of Impetus," 14f.

123 This discussion corresponds, almost literally, to *al-Naǧāt* IV.2.27–30, 617.13–636.8, and partially to *al-Mabdaʾ wa-l-maʿād* I.39–41, 52.21–54.23; cf. *al-Naǧāt* II.3.5–6, 277.4–281.6; cf. also *al-Išārāt wa-l-tanbīhāt* II.3.26, 135.9–15.

124 For nature and soul being called "powers," q.v. below, 280ff.

principle coming to rest by force when it is caught by someone who, then, feels the inclination as a resistance in his hand shows that inclination is different from the motion (*ġayr al-ḥaraka*). Second, a stone that came to rest at its natural place loses its inclination as its local motion has been completed, but it does not lose its moving power (*wa-ġayr al-quwwa al-muḥarrika*), i.e., its nature, as we already know.

From what we have seen so far, it becomes clear that in Avicenna's system, the primary function of nature is to account, through the concept of inclination, for the phenomenon of local motion, both the sublunary rectilinear motion of the four elements as well as the supralunary circular motion of the celestial bodies. Yet, it should be emphasised that nature is the efficient principle of *all* kinds of motion.[125] In the case of local motion, it produces natural inclination which we perceive as weight, while other effects of nature may be called by different names. Nonetheless, they all work in a way that is analogous to the inclination in local motion. This is what Avicenna expounds in *al-Kawn wa-l-fasād* 6:

> وقد بان ممّا سلف أنّ الطبيعة غير هذا الميل بل هي مبدأ لهذا الميل. وكذلك فاعلم أنّ الطبيعة غير الكيف المذكور بل هي مبدأه. وقد علمت أنّ الطبيعة ليست مبدأ للحركة المكانية والسكون فيها فقط بل هي مبدأ لجميع الحركات التي بالطبع والسكونات التي بالطبع .وكذلك فاعلم أنّ طبيعة الماء هي التي تغيّر الماء إلى هذا الكيف وتحفّظه عليه وأنّ تلك الطبيعة إذ لا اسم لها فيستعار لها من الفعل الصادر عنها اسم فتارةً تُسمّى ثقلاً وتارةً تُسمّى برودةً ورطوبةً فإنّها إذا أُعتبِر ما صدر عنها من الميل المهبط سُمّيت ثقلاً وإنّما هي مبدأ للثقل وإذا أُعتبِر ما يصدر عنها من الكيفية سُمّيت برداً وإنّما هي مبدأ البرد. وهذا كما يُسمّى قوّة في الإنسان نطقاً أو ضحكاً وإنّما هي مبدأ النطق والضحك.
>
> It is already clear from what preceded that nature is different from this inclination (*al-ṭabīʿa ġayr hāḏā l-mayl*) – indeed, it is the principle for this inclination (*mabdaʾ li-hāḏā l-mayl*). Likewise you should know that nature is different from the aforementioned quality – indeed, it is its principle. You have already known that nature is not only the principle for local motion and rest in them [sc. natural bodies][126] but is a principle for all motions which are naturally (*bi-l-ṭabʿ*) as well as rests which are naturally (*bi-l-ṭabʿ*). Likewise you should know that the nature of water is that which changes the water into this quality and preserves it there, and that, since there is no name for this nature, one borrows a name for it from the actuality which proceeds from it, and so it is sometimes called "heaviness" and sometimes "coldness" or "wetness," for if what proceeds from it in terms of a downward inclination (*al-mayl al-muhbiṭ*) is considered, [nature] is called "heaviness," although it only is the principle for the heaviness, and if what proceeds from it in terms of quality is considered, it is called "coldness," although it only is the principle for the

---

125 This is made explicit at *al-Samāʿ al-ṭabīʿī* I.5, §8, 33.8–34.3; IV.9, §4, 302.2–7; cf. *al-Ḥikma al-mašriqiyya* III.4, 9.17f., 10.19–11.6.

126 I am tempted to suggest reading *ʿanhā* for *fīhā*, meaning "the principle for local motion and rest from it [sc. motion]," as nature is sometimes defined, e.g., in al-Kindī, *Risāla fī ḥudūd al-ašyāʾ wa-rusūmihā*, §3, 165.6 = *Risāla fī l-asmāʾ al-mufrada*, §3, 210.5; the numbering in paragraphs follows al-Kindī, *The Philosophical Works of al-Kindī*, 297–311.

coldness. This is just like calling a power in man "intellect" or "laughter," although it only is the principle of intellect and laughter. (*al-Kawn wa-l-fasād* 6, 131.3–11)[127]

First, we are told, once more, that nature ought not to be identified with inclination but is decidedly different from it by being its principle.[128] Moreover, nature is also different from the qualities to which it gives rise, because it is precisely, again, the principle of such qualities.[129] So, besides causing water's downward motion through an inclination towards the proper place of water, the nature of water also brings about further effects, such as coldness and wetness. Water which has forcibly been heated, for example, cools down by itself, i.e., by its own nature. Once it has arrived at what one might call its natural temperature (in analogy to its natural place), it naturally keeps that temperature just as it naturally stays at its natural place. While we can call the effects of nature – direct effects, being nothing other than the manifestations of the inclination – with regard to local motion "heaviness" and "lightness," we can call them with regard to qualities such as temperature "hotness" or "coldness." Such names are not precisely names for the nature itself, for a thing's nature as such remains imperceptible – these are merely names for the sensible effects of nature and are only in a loose manner of speaking used to describe nature in want of a more proper term.[130]

Avicenna's main intention in his elaboration of nature insofar as it is a principle of motion is clarity; and clarity comes with distinction. Thus, despite the clear and strong influence which Alexander's and Philoponus' ideas about ῥοπή had on Avicenna's conception of *mayl*, Avicenna carefully differentiates between a number of notions which his predecessors either accidentally failed to distinguish or actively wanted to unite. This pertains, on the one hand, to the notions of nature, inclination, and natural motion, as we have seen. For Avicenna, nature is an internal principle which produces motion in that in which it is. Since this motion is produced immediately, the concept of inclination must not be conceived as an instrument through which nature causes motion, so that this instrument would emerge as the proximate mover of that motion. To the contrary, in causing motion, nature effects an inclination and this inclination manifests itself in motion. This, however, does also not mean that inclination is the same as motion, for not every inclination corresponds to motion. This becomes clearer

127 cf. *al-Samāʿ al-ṭabīʿī* I.6, §2, 34.14–35.7; IV.9, §5, 302.16f.; *al-Kawn wa-l-fasād* 6, 129.15–130.4; 130.13–16; *Dānešnāme-ye ʿAlāʾī* III.22, esp. 52.6–55.2; *al-Išārāt wa-l-tanbīhāt* II.2.5, 108.20–109.2; 23, 116.7–14.

128 The argument establishing this conclusion is found in the preceding lines at *al-Kawn wa-l-fasād* 6, 130.17–131.2.

129 Incidentally, since the nature of a body is precisely its form, it emerges that the qualities of a body must be different from its form, too. So, the form of water is not cold and wet, for these are only qualities that are caused by the water's form, i.e., the water's nature; cf. *al-Samāʿ al-ṭabīʿī* I.6, §2, 34.14–35.7; *al-Kawn wa-l-fasād* 6, 130.13–16.

130 That nature as such is imperceptible, is stated by Avicenna at *al-Samāʿ al-ṭabīʿī* I.6, §2, 34.14–35.1; cf. *al-Samāʿ al-ṭabīʿī* I.5, §2, 30.2f.; *Dānešnāme-ye ʿAlāʾī* III.22, 53.2f.; *al-Ḥikma al-mašriqiyya* III.4, 10.7–9, 11.10f.

in light of the fact that nature is a principle for both motion *and* rest, as it brings about both results through a single effect, viz., the inclination to be in, stay at, or return to a natural state.[131]

On the other hand, however, Avicenna's striving for clarity also pertains to the relation between soul and nature. It was already conspicuous that in commenting on the meaning of Aristotle's definition of nature in *Physics* II.1, and in his engagement with Philoponus' exegesis, Avicenna spent most time on explaining the precise meaning of the adjectival qualification *awwal* – an adverbial πρώτως in the Greek original – which, in his Arabic version, made nature a "first principle" of motion. He agreed with Philoponus that this qualification discerns between soul and nature, but he attacked his predecessor for having an altogether erroneous conception of their systematic difference. This shall remain the major theme in Avicenna's analysis. In the end, as we shall see, Avicenna will not only have provided a clear distinction between nature, inclination, and motion, he will also have sufficiently differentiated between soul and nature just as he will have successfully distanced himself from the preceding tradition.

Before turning to Avicenna's own understanding of nature and its distinction from soul, we need to put his discussion into its historical context, so that we can appreciate both the intent of his attack on the preceding tradition as well as the novelty of his own approach.

4.4 Bad Readings of Aristotle

The Meaning of Avicenna's Attack

Philoponus complained that Aristotle's definition only revealed "the activity of nature" (τῆς ἐνεργείας τῆς φύσεως) but failed to actually "indicate what nature is" (οὐκ ἔστι τοῦ τί ἐστιν ἡ φύσις σημαντικός). Thus, he felt compelled to revise that definition in such a way that it also included an account of nature's substance (τῆς οὐσίας αὐτῆς).[132] Avicenna reports this criticism as follows:

ثمّ بدا لبعض مَن ورد من بعد أن استقصر هذا الرسم وتوخّى أن يزيد عليه زيادة فقال إنّ هذا إنّما يدلّ على فعل الطبيعة لا على جوهرها فإنّه إنّما يدلّ على نسبتها الى ما يصدر عنها.

Then, it appeared to some who came afterwards (*li-baʿḍ man warada min baʿd*) that this description is inadequate[133] and they aspired to make an addition to it, and so they said that this indicates (*yadullu ʿalā*) only the nature's act (*fiʿl al-ṭabīʿa*), not its substance (*ǧawharihā*), for it indicates only its relation to what proceeds from it. (*al-Samāʿ al-ṭabīʿī* I.5, §5, 31.9f., tr. by McGinnis, modified)

131 The idea of a "return" will be discussed more fully below, 283ff.

132 Philoponus, *In Phys.*, 197.30–33, tr. by Lacey.

133 Reading *istaqṣara* with Mss. Leiden or. 4 and or. 84 for *yastaqṣī* in Zāyid and *istanqaṣa* in McGinnis and Āl Yāsīn.

The text provided by Avicenna contains elements which correspond directly to the wording in Philoponus' commentary: *fi'l al-ṭabīʿa* is consistent with τῆς ἐνεργείας τῆς φύσεως; *ǧawharihā* matches τῆς οὐσίας αὐτῆς, perfectly reproducing even the pronoun αὐτῆς; and *yadullu ʿalā* is very apt and not rarely used for rendering ἔστι ... σημαντικός. Still, the Arabic word *baʿḍ*, as well as the expression *qawm* which we find a little later, can refer to a single individual as well as to a group of people.[134] Consequently, we cannot be sure whether *baʿḍ man warada min baʿd* points to Philoponus alone or also to other commentators in the Greek and Arabic philosophical traditions. What we do know, however, is that neither Themistius nor Simplicius say anything in that direction, nor does Simplicius report Alexander to have criticised Aristotle's definition as deficient in this way. Likewise no such remarks can be found in the margins of Ms. Leiden or. 583 preserving Isḥāq ibn Ḥunayn's Arabic translation of Aristotle's *Physics* together with some comments from Baġdādī intellectuals.

Avicenna, then, provides a quotation of what seems to be Philoponus' reworked definition of nature. In the translation of Jon McGinnis, this definition reads as follows:

> إنّ الطبيعة قوّة سارية في الأجسام تفيد الصور والخلق هي مبدأ لكذا وكذا.
>
> [N]ature is a power permeating through the bodies that provides the forms and temperament, which is a principle of ... and so forth. (*al-Samāʿ al-ṭabīʿī* I.5, §5, 31.11, tr. by McGinnis)

The Greek of Philoponus' commentary renders the original version as follows:

> ἡ φύσις ζωὴ ἤτοι δύναμις καταδεδυκυῖα διὰ τῶν σωμάτων, διαπλαστικὴ αὐτῶν καὶ διοικητική, ἀρχὴ κινήσεως οὖσα καὶ ἠρεμίας "ἐν ᾧ ὑπάρχει πρώτως καθ' αὑτὸ καὶ οὐ κατὰ συμβεβηκός."
>
> Nature is a life or a power (ζωὴ ἤτοι δύναμις) which has descended (καταδεδυκυῖα) into bodies, and which shapes and governs them (διαπλαστικὴ αὐτῶν καὶ διοικητική), being a principle of motion (ἀρχὴ κινήσεως) and rest [for that] "in which it is primarily, by itself and not by accident." (Philoponus, *In Phys.*, 197.34–198.1, tr. by Lacey, modified)[135]

In the Arabic version given by Avicenna, one can, again, recognise several elements that correspond to Philoponus' Greek original. All of these have already been examined above: there is *quwwa* for δύναμις, a foreseeable translation, and *sāriya fī l-aǧsām* for καταδεδυκυῖα διὰ τῶν σωμάτων, a very nice translation, because the participle *sāriya* covers both connotations of the Greek, viz., that of "descending into" or "entering" and that of "pervading through."[136] The phrase *hiya mabdaʾ li-kaḏā wa-kaḏā* marks the transition from Philoponus' reworked definition to his repeated citation of the remaining words of Aristotle's original.

Some elements from Philoponus, however, are missing in Avicenna. There is, for example, no expression for ζωή ("life") nor for διοικητική ("governing"), and what is

134 The noun *baʿḍ* is found at *al-Samāʿ al-ṭabīʿī* I.5, §5, 31.9, and §7, 32.16; the noun *qawm* in §6, 31.16.
135 Philoponus' account of nature has been examined above, 218ff.
136 q.v. fn. 30 above, 220f.

even more confusing is the phrase which McGinnis translated as "that provides the forms and temperament," especially because there is nothing about "temperament" in Philoponus' commentary here or anywhere in the vicinity. To be sure, the Arabic term consisting of the article together with the three letters *ḫ-l-q* could be read as the singular noun *ḫulq*, which was frequently used for the Greek ἦθος and which, in fact, became a technical term for "temperament."[137] Here, however, it is a false friend, because the word in Avicenna's text is not a singular noun but, as also the preceding plural *ṣuwar* suggests, should be a plural. More precisely, it is the plural of the comparably less frequent noun *ḫilqa* and ought to be read *ḫilaq*.[138] This is still not entirely transparent, unless it is realised that *ḫilqa* is in fact a not entirely uncommon translation of μορφή and is attested in particular also in Isḥāq ibn Ḥunayn's translation of the *Physics*.[139] Together with the verb *tufīdu* ("to give, to bestow"), it is clear that the phrase *tufīdu l-ṣuwar wa-l-ḫilaq* is a verbose version of Philoponus' διαπλαστική. Accordingly, Avicenna's version of what seems to be Philoponus' reworked definition of nature should be translated as follows:

إنّ الطبيعة قوّة سارية في الأجسام تفيد الصور والخلق هي مبدأ لكذا وكذا.

> Nature is a power (*quwwa*) permeating through the bodies (*sāriya fī l-ağsām*), which gives forms and shapes (*tufīdu l-ṣuwar wa-l-ḫilaq*); it is a principle of ... and so forth. (*al-Samāʿ al-ṭabīʿī* I.5, §5, 31.11)

Incidentally, this translation agrees entirely with what we read in the Latin translation of Avicenna's *al-Samāʿ al-ṭabīʿī* that was produced by Dominicus Gundisalvi (d. ~ 1190):

> natura est virtus diffusa per corpora quae attribuit eis formas et figuras, et est principium sic et sic. (Avicenna, *Sufficientia: Liber primus naturalium* I.5, 79f.)[140]

Although Avicenna's version apparently lacks proper equivalents of ζωή and διοικητική, while at the same time offering a slightly verbose rendering of διαπλαστική, the general impression is warranted that what Avicenna reports here, and the definition which he reproduces, bears a close resemblance to Philoponus' original up to the point that one

---

137 Another possible reading would be *ḫalq*, which is one of the most common words for divine "creation" and God is frequently referred to with the Qurʾānic term *ḫāliq*, the Creator. Reading *ḫalq* makes no sense, obviously.

138 The editions by Āl Yāsīn and Zāyid provide in their apparatus the singular variant *ḫilqa* and even *al-ṣūra wa-l-ḫilqa* for the whole expression in singular.

139 cf. *Phys.* I.9, 192a13; II.1, 193a30, b4; II.8, 199a31; IV.2, 209b3; IV.4, 211b7. It is also used by Isḥāq ibn Ḥunayn in his translation of Themistius' paraphrase of *De anima*, e.g., at 39.16, 40.35, 89.30, 109.4, 111.17. Avicenna himself makes a distinction between *ḫilqa* and *šakl* in *al-Maqūlāt* V.1, 173.17–19, maybe inspired by Isḥāq ibn Ḥunayn's translation of μορφή as *ḫilqa* in *Categories* 8, 10a12.

140 That Gundisalvi was the Latin translator of the majority of Avicenna's *al-Samāʿ al-ṭabīʿī* was recently shown by Hasse and Büttner, cf. "Notes on Anonymous Twelfth-Century Translations of Philosophical Texts".

ought to consider the possibility that Avicenna provides a direct quotation from an Arabic translation of Philoponus commentary which he had at his disposal. The only known translation of Philoponus' comments on *Physics* II, as already noted, had been produced by Qusṭā.

A little later, Avicenna offers a recapitulation of all relevant aspects of Philoponus' redefinition, in order to refute them or, more precisely, to show their redundancy. In particular, he mentions the following:

معنى القوّة ... معنى السارية ... معنى التخليق والتشكيل ... معنى حفظ الخلق والأشكال.

the meaning of "power" (*al-quwwa*) ... the meaning of "permeating" (*al-sāriya*) ... the meaning of "shaping and figuring" (*al-taḫlīq wa-l-taškīl*) ... the meaning of "preservation of forms and figures" (*ḥifẓ al-ḫilaq wa-l-aškāl*). (*al-Samāʿ al-ṭabīʿī* I.5, §7, 32.18–33.1)

One can recognise many reoccurring elements in this passage, especially, *quwwa* and *sāriya*. Moreover, Avicenna, again, employs words derived from the root *ḫ-l-q*, even though he uses them in a manner that is slightly different from what he has done before, as he, in the present passage, dispenses with the verb *tufīdu*, instead using the nominal expression *al-taḫlīq wa-l-taškīl*, which itself bears a causative connotation so as to express the act of giving shape and form, i.e., of "moulding," "shaping," or "being formative," as διαπλαστική has been translated by Alan R. Lacey, J. Edward McGuire, and Edward M. Macierowski and Richard F. Hassing, respectively. Another difference is the introduction of the phrase *ḥifẓ al-ḫilaq wa-l-aškāl*, which seems to be similar to our previous *tufīdu l-ṣuwar wa-l-ḫilaq* only that, this time, the forms are not given but "preserved" (*ḥifẓ* or *ḥafaẓa*). This is consistent with Philoponus' repeated claims that nature is just as much a principle for motion as it is a principle for rest, because nature provides the universe with of "stability" (στάσις):

οὐ γὰρ μόνον κινήσεώς ἐστιν ἀρχὴ ἡ φύσις, ἀλλὰ καὶ στάσεως· κινεῖ μὲν γὰρ ἵνα εἰς τὸ εἶδος ἀγάγῃ, ἵστησι δὲ ἵνα φυλάξῃ ἐν τῷ εἴδει.

For nature is a principle not only of change but also of stability (στάσεως), as it moves [things], in order to bring them into [the state of possessing] the form, and halts [them], in order to preserve [them] in the form (φυλάξῃ ἐν τῷ εἴδει). (Philoponus, *In Phys.*, 196.13–15, tr. by Lacey, modified)

Nature, as is said, is not only responsible for the acquisition of forms and perfections but also for keeping them. A stone, for example, which has fallen to the ground remains there, because this is its natural place and its nature strives to stay in it. Accordingly, φυλάξῃ ἐν τῷ εἴδει corresponds well with Avicenna's *ḥifẓ al-ḫilaq wa-l-aškāl* ("the preservation of the forms and figures"); indeed, as Philoponus, Avicenna equates it with *taskīn*, i.e., the "production of rest." Moreover, *ḥafaẓa* was a term frequently used for translating φυλάττειν.[141]

141 cf. Isḥāq ibn Ḥunayn's translation of Aristotle's *Rhetoric* I.4, 1360a7, and II.23,1398b8, or Themistius' paraphrase of *De anima*, 53.25.

Once again, the suggested translation is in line with Gundisalvi's Latin translation of Avicenna's *al-Samāʿ al-ṭabīʿī* in which we read:

> intellectus virtutis ... intellectus formantis aut figurantis ... intellectus penetrantis ... intellectus custodiendi formas et figuras. (Avicenna, *Sufficientia: Liber primus naturalium* I.5, 132–136.)

What is still disconcerting is that we seem to be missing equivalents for ζωή and διοικητική. There are a number of options with varying degrees of cogency to explain this circumstance. Either Avicenna's own text just lacks these expressions or he forgot to add them or regarded them as irrelevant. It is also possible that he saw them as unnecessary repetitions of connotations that already found their expression in δύναμις and διαπλαστική, respectively. This is particularly possible in the case of διαπλαστική for which he offers not one but two expressions (*al-taḫlīq wa-l-taškīl*), so that one of them could be meant to cover, at least partially, the intention of διοικητική. However, there are clearly more suitable expressions for conveying the meaning of διοικητική, especially those derived from the root *d-b-r*, for example *mudabbir* ("governing"). Another possibility is that Avicenna's Arabic source text, from which he was quoting or paraphrasing, or which he was trying to remember when he composed *al-Samāʿ al-ṭabīʿī* I.5, lacked proper equivalents of these terms, or even that it suffered from damage. One could further imagine a misreading of the Greek text on behalf of the translator or a simple mistranslation or a deliberate conflation of the meanings of both terms, διαπλαστική and διοικητική.[142] Whatever the explanation, the aspect that nature is something alive which manages or governs the natural body, as Philoponus maintained, is entirely underrepresented in Avicenna's version.

The Target of Avicenna's Attack

The above reflections provide us with an understanding of the verbal meaning of the account of nature which Avicenna ascribes to *baʿḍ man warada min baʿd* ("some who came afterwards"). Yet, before Avicenna's refutation of it can be analysed as an attack on Philoponus, it is required to investigate whether the statement given by Avicenna really derives from Philoponus' commentary on the *Physics* or whether it has other sources, being directed to a different, or larger, set of people. This is all the more advisable as the text provided by Avicenna does not reflect *all* the aspects of Philoponus' original and, in particular, lacks two central notions of his redefinition. Moreover, what is the precise nature of Avicenna's engagement with this version? If, as

142 It might be worth mentioning the relative similarity between δι-οικητική and words derived from εἰκών. Even though it does not seem probable, a translator could have read διαπλαστική and διοικητική and, a little bit too quickly, interpret the first as "producing a πλάσμα" and the second as "producing an εἰκών" – a form and a figure.

Avicenna will state in the end, this version does not add to Aristotle's definition and is, above all, a redundant and void exaggeration, then why does he so fervently attack it?

As will be shown, Avicenna's criticism in *al-Samāʿ al-ṭabīʿī* I.5 is not only the result of a personal quarrel with Philoponus and his Neoplatonic redefinition. Rather, Avicenna was reacting to what may have been the most widespread rival notion of nature from the Stoics to Alexander, from Plotinus and Porphyry to Proclus, and from the Greek commentators up to the Arabic intellectuals of his own time. In other words, what superficially seems to be Avicenna's critical remark on a singular version of Philoponus' account of nature is more adequately understood as his full retort to a philosophical custom that kept on misunderstanding nature as a second-rate soul for almost one and a half millennia.

In order to reconstruct Avicenna's personal reading of this version we may first have a look at Abū Yaʿqūb ibn Isḥāq al-Kindī (d. ~ 256/870). Among his works is the well known *Risāla fī ḥudūd al-ašyāʾ wa-rusūmihā*, which provides numerous definitions of philosophical concepts. This treatise is extant in two versions. In one of them, published as the *Risāla fī l-asmāʾ al-mufrada*, we find the following definition:

حدّ الطبيعة من جهة التعليم أنّها مبدأ الحركة والسكون وحدّها من جهة الطباع أنّها القوّة المدبّرة للأجسام.

The definition of nature with regard to teaching (*min ǧihat al-taʿlīm*) is that it is the principle of motion and rest (*mabdaʾ al-ḥaraka wa-l-sukūn*). Its definition with regard to its character (*min ǧihat al-ṭibāʿ*) is that it is the governing power (*al-quwwa al-mudabbira*) belonging to bodies. (al-Kindī, *Risāla fī l-asmāʾ al-mufrada*, §117 [§87], 215.7f.)[143]

It is striking that al-Kindī provides not one but two apparently complementary definitions. The first defines nature, along Aristotelian lines, as a "principle of motion and rest."[144] From a different perspective, though, nature is more adequately defined as a "governing power" (*al-quwwa al-mudabbira*). One is immediately tempted to interpret this twofold definition as being directly inspired by Philoponus' own twofold definition, for he, too, presented the Aristotelian definition of "the activity of nature" (τῆς ἐνεργείας τῆς φύσεως) – viz., that it is a principle of motion – to which he added his own definition of "its substance" (τῆς οὐσίας αὐτῆς) – viz., that it is a governing power. The obvious questions, however, are when Qusṭā completed his translation of Philoponus' commentary on *Physics* II and when al-Kindī composed his treatise on the definitions of things, i.e., whether it was possible for al-Kindī to already have access to Qusṭā's translation.[145]

143 The numbering in paragraphs follows al-Kindī, *The Philosophical Works of al-Kindī*, 297–311.

144 It may well be that "with regard to teaching" (*min ǧihat al-taʿlīm*) explicitly means "with regard to *Aristotle's* teaching," for Aristotle is often referred to as "the first teacher" and his works as "the first teaching" (*al-taʿlīm al-awwal*).

145 We do not know either date. What we know, however, is that al-Kindī was probably born around 184/800 and Qusṭā around 205/820.

Yet, an acquaintance with Qusṭā's translation of Philoponus' commentary is not the only possible source for the way in which al-Kindī defines nature. Indeed, two further no less possible explanations spring to mind. Since we know that ʿAbd al-Masīḥ ibn Nāʿima al-Ḥimṣī (fl. ~ 215/830) translated the second half of Philoponus commentary on the *Physics* and that he was active as a translator in al-Kindī's circle, one could imagine that Ibn Nāʿima also translated (at least) a selection of the more important passages from Philoponus' commentary to books I–IV to supplement his full translation of the remaining four books, and that al-Kindī, supervising Ibn Nāʿima's activities, had access to this material and implemented some aspects of it into his own *Risāla fī ḥudūd al-ašyāʾ wa-rusūmihā*.

Another explanation would be to consider not Philoponus' commentary on the *Physics* but the Arabic Plotinus and Proclus materials as al-Kindī's source.[146] After all, al-Kindī was either personally involved in the redaction of these or at least close to those who were responsible for it.[147] So, when al-Kindī explains earlier in his treatise that nature is not only a principle of motion and rest but also "the first of the faculties of the soul" (*awwal quwwa min quwā l-nafs*), and when he, moreover, elsewhere writes that according to Socrates "nature is the handmaiden for soul, soul the handmaiden the intellect, and the intellect that of the creator," we are reminded of the ontology

146 A further option, yet one that can be neither proven nor disproven as it seems, is that al-Kindī's source is actually Porphyry, whose commentary on *Physics* I–IV was translated by Basīl; q.v. above, 11; cf. also Adamson, "*Porphyrius Arabus* on Nature and Art."

147 It is not evident to me why Janos, in his assessment of Abū Bišr Mattā ibn Yūnus' account of an "active nature," describes the materials from and surrounding the Arabic corpora of Plotinus and Proclus as a "red herring," thus undermining their value for understanding the formation of the idea of an active nature in the thought of Abū Bišr, in particular, and virtually everyone in the early Arabic tradition sharing this idea with Abū Bišr, in general ("Active Nature and Other Striking Features," 154). Janos accepts the influence Philoponus probably had on Abū Bišr while denying the influence of "the Arabic Neoplatonic texts" – by which he means the Arabic Plotinus and Proclus – as if their Greek originals did not have any bearing on the formation of Philoponus' thought and, moreover, as if Philoponus' works would not deserve to be called "Neoplatonic" themselves. Be this as it may, I am not convinced that it is meaningful to argue, as Janos does, that the strict distinction between soul and nature, which he observes in Abū Bišr, was decidedly absent from "the Arabic Neoplatonic texts," merely because it is a "common Neoplatonic stance ... that there is no corporeal entity in the sublunary world that is not somehow animated by the powers of Soul" (154f.). The very fact that, as Janos writes, "nature is subjected to Soul and is merely an instrument or intermediary through which Soul and the higher principles can exercise their activity" precisely means that nature is something *different* from soul by being its effect, result, or outward activity, or even an individual hypostasis or particular goddess. The admitted similarity in the Neoplatonic descriptions of soul and of nature merely underscores the conceptual difference *besides* their functional similarity. Much of the material that I shall present in the remainder of this section here testifies to a tradition of interpreting nature as a principle of motion that was equally common to the Greek and to the Arabic philosophical tradition. I do not see any reason for following Janos in his claim that the Arabic Plotinus and Proclus materials are a "red herring" and should not be taken into consideration when investigating the Arabic tradition of the concept of an active nature; q.v. also above, 223.

inherent in the Arabic Proclus materials.[148] In particular, we may think of assertions as those made by Ps.-Aristotle in the Procliana Arabica:

والعقل إذن رئيس جميع الأشياء تحته وممسّكها ومدبّرها كما أنّ الطبيعة تدبّر الأشياء التي تحتها بقوّة العقل وكذلك العقل يدبّر الطبيعة بالقوّة الإلهية.

Therefore, intellect is the leader of all the things under it, seizing them and governing them (*mudabbiruhā*), just as it is that nature governs (*tudabbiru*) the things which are under it [sc. nature] through the power of the intellect, and likewise intellect governs nature through the divine power (*bi-l-quwwa al-ilāhiyya*). (*Kitāb al-Īḍāḥ fī l-ḫayr al-maḥḍ li-Arisṭūṭālīs* 8, 12.3f.)[149]

Accordingly, even without access to a translation of the second book of Philoponus' commentary, al-Kindī may have had reason enough to provide a further definition of nature in addition to the one derived from Aristotle, viz., that of a power which "governs (*tudabbiru*) the things which are under it." This natural power is the extension of soul and intellect which, on their part, are extensions of the godhead. Thus, al-Kindī may very well have arrived at a similar conception of nature independently of Philoponus, even if not independently from their shared Neoplatonic framework.[150]

Half a century later, the situation may have changed, as Abū Bakr Muḥammad ibn Zakariyā' al-Rāzī (d. 313/925), in a treatise called *Maqāla fī-mā ba'd al-ṭabī'a*, directly mentions Yaḥyā al-Naḥwī, i.e., "John the Grammarian" or John Philoponus, and criticises the definition of nature he attributes to him.[151] According to Abū Bakr al-Rāzī's testimony, Philoponus claimed the following:

إنّ الطبيعة قوّة تنفذ في الأجسام وتدبّرها.

Nature is a power (*quwwa*) which permeates through (*tanfuḏu fī*) the bodies and governs them (*tudabbiruhā*). (Abū Bakr al-Rāzī, *Maqāla fī-mā ba'd al-ṭabī'a*, 118.1)

Abū Bakr al-Rāzī's testimony seems, first of all, to be correct, for this is how Philoponus prefers to define the substance of nature. However, it seems to complicate the overall picture of our investigation, because Abū Bakr al-Rāzī's version deviates practically in all important aspects from that in Avicenna's *al-Samā' al-ṭabī'ī*: where καταδεδυκυῖα is rendered as *sāriya fī* in Avicenna, it is *tanfuḏu fī* in Abū Bakr al-Rāzī; where Avicenna's version has something that seems to correspond to διαπλαστική, Abū Bakr al-Rāzī's

148 al-Kindī, *Risāla fī ḥudūd al-ašyā' wa-rusūmihā*, §3, 165.6 = "al-Kindī's 'On Definitions and Descriptions of Things,'" §3, 210.5f.; al-Kindī, *Mimmā naqalahū al-Kindī min alfāẓ Suqrāṭ*, 30.18f., tr. by Adamson/Pormann.

149 For similar materials in the Arabic Plotinus, cf. *Kitāb Arisṭāṭālīs al-faylasūf al-musammā bi-l-yūnāniyya Uṯūlūǧiyā* 7, esp. 84.5–14, drawing on *Enn.* IV.8.5, esp. 24–35.

150 The bipartition into a definition "with regard to teaching" and one "with regard to its character" still remains a somewhat Philoponian element in al-Kindī's text.

151 cf. also Peters, *Aristoteles Arabus*, 32; Genequand, "Quelques aspects de l'idée de nature d'Aristote à al-Ghazālī," 123; Kraemer, *Philosophy in the Renaissance of Islam*, 176; Lucchetta, *La natura e la sfera*, 35–37; Gannagé, "Philopon (Jean-)," 521; Adamson, "Abū Bakr al-Rāzī on Animals," fn. 51, 263f.

version remains silent; and where Abū Bakr al-Rāzī's provides a perfect translation for διοικητική (*tudabbiruhā*), Avicenna seems to remain silent.[152]

One might think that, just as al-Kindī, so Abū Bakr al-Rāzī, too, may have been influenced rather by the Arabic Proclus than the comments of Philoponus. However, Abū Bakr al-Rāzī explicitly refers to Philoponus by name (*qawl Yaḥyā al-Naḥwī*) and accurately describes his account, so that both the version of Abū Bakr al-Rāzī as well as the version of Avicenna are close enough to Philoponus' Greek original so as to allow for the possibility that either could be a direct, even though somewhat incomplete, quotation from an Arabic translation of the latter's commentary. At the same time, they clearly differ from each other enough, so that, should both be quotations in the strict sense, they could not possibly be drawn from a common source. If, then, as Francis Peters notes, Abū Bakr al-Rāzī really used Ibn Nāʿima's translation of the *Physics*, i.e., if he did not yet have access to that produced by Qusṭā, then we would have to entertain the idea again that an Arabic translation of parts or fragments – or even of the entirety – of Philoponus' commentary circulated in the third/ninth century even before Qusṭā could complete his version.[153] As far as we know, however, and this is not much, there has been only one translation of Philoponus' commentary on the second book of the *Physics*. Unless provided with further material, we need to draw the conclusion that of these two Arabic versions of Philoponus' definition of nature, viz., the one in Abū Bakr al-Rāzī and the one in Avicenna, not more than one may be a direct quotation – a direct quotation from Qusṭā's version, that is. In fact, as shall become clear shortly, there is reason to believe that Abū Bakr al-Rāzī, indeed, had access to, and was using, Qusṭā's translation. This, in turn, would entail that between al-Kindī and Abū Bakr al-Rāzī the situation really had changed, because the governing power in Abū Bakr al-Rāzī's treatise really is Philoponus' account of nature, whereas al-Kindī's definition is derived from other, though similar, Neoplatonic materials. Indeed, one does not require Philoponus to describe nature as a governing power as al-Kindī did.[154] Abū

152 With regard to Abū Bakr al-Rāzī, too, one may ponder whether he might have regarded the qualification that nature is something which "manages" or "governs" the bodies as already entailing some formative function, so that the aspect of διαπλαστική could be omitted. In any case, for Abū Bakr al-Rāzī's purposes, the definition is sufficient, because his criticism concerns only the idea that nature "permeates through the bodies," i.e., the aspect of καταδεδυκυῖα, and not its function as forming or governing the bodies in which it inheres.

153 Peters' evidence – the sole fact that Abū l-Faraǧ Muḥammad ibn Isḥāq al-Nadīm lists among Abū Bakr al-Rāzī's works one that is called *Kitāb Samʿ al-kiyān* – however, is not conclusive and seems to rest on the assumption that Ibn Nāʿima's work was the only translation with this title; cf. Peters, *Aristoteles Arabus*, 32, referring to Ibn al-Nadīm, *Kitāb al-Fihrist*, vol. I, 299.22 (ed. Flügel)/vol. II, 308.2 (ed. Sayyid); q.v. the discussion above, 12ff.

154 cf. also al-Kindī's own reference to Hippocrates whom he reports to have claimed that "nature has four meanings," of which one is "the governing power of the body" (al-Kindī, *Risāla fī ḥudūd al-ašyāʾ wa-rusūmihā*, §92, 179.13f.).

Bakr al-Rāzī, on the other hand, not only refers to Philoponus by name, he also gives an almost complete reproduction of his definition.

Three of the central ideas of Philoponus' definition are that nature is a power, that it pervades or permeates all natural bodies, and that it governs or manages them. All of these ideas are reminiscent of another thinker who preceded Philoponus, viz., Alexander. One of Alexander's works, which is preserved in Syriac and Arabic versions, is known by its Arabic title as *Maqālat al-Iskandar al-Afrūdīsī fī l-qawl fī mabādiʾ al-kull bi-ḥasab raʾy Arisṭāṭālis al-faylasūf*. In this treatise, Alexander likened nature and power, which pervade the universe, to a ruler, who governs a city:

وهذه الطبيعة والقوّة هما سبب اتّحاد العالم وانتظامه وبحسب ما يجري الأمر عليه في المدينة الواحدة التي لها مدبّر واحد مقيم فيها غير مفارق لها كذلك نقول إنّ قوّة ما روحانية تسري في جميع العالم وتربط بعضه ببعض ... وكان جميع الأشياء التي فيه إنّما تطلب الاتّصال بالشيء الذي هو غير متغيّر وتقصد الاتّحاد الهيولاني بما يدبّره ويسوسه ويحفظ عليه ترتيب ونظامه بقوّة روحانية تسري في جميع أجزاء.

> This nature and power (*al-ṭabīʿa wa-l-quwwa*), they are the cause of the unity of the world and its order. In consideration of that according to which things are in one city which has one ruler (*mudabbir*) residing in it [and] not being separate from it, we likewise say that a certain spiritual power permeates through the whole world (*quwwa mā rūḥāniyya tasrī fī ǧamīʿ al-ʿālam*) and holds its parts together ... and all things which are in it [sc. the world (in analogy to the city)] seek to be in contact with that which is unchanging, and aim at the material union with that which rules and governs it and which preserves its arrangement and order (*yudabbiruhū wa-yasūsuhū wa-yaḥfiẓu ʿalayhi tartībahū wa-niẓāmahū*) by a spiritual power which permeates through all of its parts (*bi-quwwa rūḥāniyya tasrī fī ǧamīʿ aǧzāʾihū*). (Alexander of Aphrodisias, *Maqāla fī l-qawl fī mabādiʾ al-kull*, §§128–129, 112.8–114.2 (ed. Genequand), tr. by Genequand, modified)[155]

In this passage, we see that Alexander describes nature as a power that "permeates" the body of the universe. The Arabic text gives the verbal expression *tasrī fī* which conforms to the participle *sāriya fī* we found in Avicenna, both words being derived from the first stem of the root *s-r-y*. Alexander's analogy of nature with a ruler allows him to describe nature further as something which "governs" the universe. This idea is preserved in Arabic by the verb *yudabbiruhū* which is identical with Abū Bakr al-Rāzī's *tudabbiruhā*, only differing with regard to the genus of the verb's subject and genus or number of its object. Moreover, the idea that nature also "preserves" the order and stability of the world is, as we could see, also one the main features in Philoponus' conception of nature as a principle for rest.

The overall idea expressed in this passage resonates with other passages in Alexander's works.[156] We find similar statements in his commentary on Aristotle's *Meteorologica*, his *De anima libri mantissa*, and his *De providentia*, the latter being preserved

155 cf. also *al-Samāʿ al-ṭabīʿī* I.7, §3, 39.6f., where Avicenna seems to refer to Alexander, as McGinnis rightly noted.

156 Pines, however, argues that the idea that a "spiritual power permeates through the whole world" suggests that the treatise is precisely *not* a genuine work of Alexander, because it conflicts with Alexan-

in Arabic under the title *Maqāla fī l-ʿināya*.[157] The passage in his *Maqāla fī l-ʿināya* is especially interesting, as it explicitly speaks of nature as a "divine power" (*al-quwwa al-ilāhiyya allatī sammaynāhā ... al-ṭabīʿa*). There is even a pseudo-Aristotelian source for calling God's power a "divine nature" (ἡ θεία φύσις, *al-ṭabīʿa al-ilāhiyya*) which "permeates all places" (ἐπὶ πᾶν διικνεῖσθαι, *nāfiḏ fī kull makān*) and "pervades through the whole world" (διὰ τοῦ σύμπαντος κόσμου διήκουσαν, *intašarat fī l-ʿālam kullihī*), viz., the treatise *De mundo* – in Arabic transmitted as *Risālat Arisṭūṭālīs ilā l-Iskandar fī ṣifat tartīb al-ʿālam al-maʿrūfa bi-l-ḏahabiyya*.[158] One of the Arabic versions of this treatise is transmitted together with other works translated by Qusṭā. Whether or not this suggests that this version was also translated by Qusṭā is difficult to decide.[159] The *De mundo*, insofar as it was attributed to Aristotle in antiquity, could even have served as an Aristotelian source for Alexander to justify the interpretation of nature as a power which permeates the universe. Moreover, Alexander's *Maqāla fī l-qawl fī mabādiʾ al-kull* as well as the pseudo-Aristotelian *De mundo* show that Philoponus' account of nature, and the background of his interpretation of *Physics* II.1, does not only have to have its roots in the *Enneads* of Plotinus and other Platonist writings, as has been shown above, he could just as much have been influenced by works (erroneously) attributed to Aristotle or works composed by earlier Peripatetics. Since Alexander's commentary on the *Physics* is not extant, we do not know how Aristotle's definition of nature was explained in that work. Nonetheless, assuming that Alexander expounded nature in his commentary in a similar fashion as he did in his other works, one could even speculate that Philoponus merely had to quote Alexander's commentary when he provided his redefinition of nature in the commentary on Aristotle's *Physics*.

Furthermore, Alexander's treatise *Maqāla fī l-qawl fī mabādiʾ al-kull* was translated into Arabic, where it had a lasting influence on some figures in the Arabic philosophical tradition, in particular, on a group of fourth/tenth-century Baġdād intellectuals with some of whom Avicenna pursued a rivalry. The group consisted of thinkers such as Abū l-Qāsim al-Kirmānī (fl. ~ 410/1020), Abū ʿAlī Aḥmad Miskawayh (d. 421/1030), and ʿAlī Abū Ḥayyān al-Tawḥīdī (d. 414/1023), and centred around the logician Abū Sulaymān al-Siǧistānī (d. ~ 374/985), a former student of Yaḥyā ibn ʿAdī (d. 363/974).[160] The latter used to be known as the author of the doxographical and biographical collection *Ṣiwān*

der's views in *De mixtione*; cf. Pines, "The Spiritual Force Permeating the Cosmos"; cf. also *De mixtione*, esp. 10, 223.6–224.27; 11, 226.24–34.

157 cf. Alexander of Aphrodisias, *In Meteor.*, 7.9–14; *De anima libri mantissa*, 172.17–23; *Maqāla fī l-ʿināya*, 18.12f., 19.6f. (ed. Thillet); cf. also Adamson, "*Porphyrius Arabus* on Nature and Art" and generally Sorabji, *The Philosophy of the Commentators*, vol. II, ch. 1b.

158 Ps.-Aristotle, *De mundo* 6, 398b20, 397b33, 398b8; cf. Janos, "Active Nature and Other Striking Features," 160f.; cf. also Macierowski and Hassing, "John Philoponus on Aristotle's Definition of Nature," 82–86; A. Smith, "The Reception of *On the Cosmos* in Ancient Pagan Philosophy," 126–128.

159 cf. Takahashi, "Syriac and Arabic Transmission of *On the Cosmos*," 159f.

160 cf. Reisman, "The Life and Times of Avicenna," 15f. For Alexander's influence on al-Siǧistānī, cf. Genequand's remarks in Alexander of Aphrodisias, *On the Cosmos*, 23f.

al-ḥikma, which has been preserved only in the form of later redactions, even though, in the meantime, al-Siǧistānī's authorship of the *Ṣiwān al-ḥikma* has convincingly been contested.[161] One of these redactions, the so-called *Muntaḫab Ṣiwān al-ḥikma*, has been published twice, once in 1979 by Douglas Dunlop and five years earlier by ʿAbd al-Raḥman Badawī together with three smaller but authentic treatises.[162] In one of these smaller treatises, al-Siǧistānī's *al-Maqāla fī l-muḥarrik al-awwal*, we find the following two definitions of nature:

فَمَن حدّ الطبيعة بأنّها مبدأ الحركة والسكون للشيء الذي هي فيه أوّلاً وبالذات لا بطريق العرض فذلك بحسب النظر الطبيعي. ومَن حدّها بأنّها قوّة تنفذ في الأجسام فتُعطيها التخلّق والتصوّر بالصور الخاصّة بواحد واحد منها فذلك بحسب النظر فيما بعد الطبيعة.

Someone defined nature as the principle of motion and rest for something in which it is primarily, by itself, and not by way of accident, and this, then, is [its definition] with regard to natural inquiry (*bi-ḥasab al-naẓr al-ṭabīʿī*). Someone defined it as a power which permeates through the bodies (*tanfuḏu fī l-aǧsām*), and so gives them shaping and formation (*fa-tuʿṭīhā l-taḫalluq wa-l-taṣawwur*) through specific forms for each one of them, and this, then, is [its definition] with regard to the inquiry into metaphysics (*bi-ḥasab al-naẓar fī-mā baʿd al-ṭabīʿa*). (al-Siǧistānī, *al-Maqāla fī l-muḥarrik al-awwal*, 376.10–13)[163]

The first definition, which is according to "natural inquiry" (*al-naẓr al-ṭabīʿī*), is almost a verbatim quote from Isḥāq ibn Ḥunayn's Arabic translation of the *Physics*. The only difference is that Isḥāq ibn Ḥunayn's fine rendering of κινεῖσθαι by *yataḥarraku* has been altered to the less accurate simple noun *ḥaraka*, which grammatically also prompts the subsequent nominalisation of *yaskunu* as *sukūn* – the same words we find in Qusṭā's translation of Ps.-Plutarchus and in Avicenna. In the second definition, i.e., that with regard to the "inquiry into metaphysics" (*al-naẓar fī-mā baʿd al-ṭabīʿa*), we

161 cf. al-Qāḍī, "*Kitāb Ṣiwān al-ḥikma*"; cf. also Reisman, *The Making of the Avicennan Tradition*, 166–185.

162 Badawī, *Muntaḫab Ṣiwān al-ḥikma wa-ṯalāṯ rasāʾil*; Dunlop, *The Muntaḫab Ṣiwān al-ḥikmah of Abū Sulaymān as-Sijistānī*. For contemporary studies, cf. al-Qāḍī, "*Kitāb Ṣiwān al-ḥikma*"; Kraemer, *Philosophy in the Renaissance of Islam*; for a detailed review of both editions, cf. Gutas, "The *Ṣiwān al-Ḥikma* Cycle of Texts."

163 cf. also Kraemer, *Philosophy in the Renaissance of Islam*, §6.4.4, 292. The first definition can also be found at the beginning of another treatise by al-Siǧistānī called *al-Maqāla fī anna l-aǧrām al-ʿulwiyya ḏawāt anfus nāṭiqa*, where it is interpreted as an active principle (367.3–6); cf. Kraemer, *Philosophy in the Renaissance of Islam*, §5.1.1, 278. Furthermore, the second definition is mentioned in yet another treatise called *al-Maqāla fī l-kamāl al-ḫāṣṣ bi-nawʿ al-insān*. Badawī's edition lacks the sentence but the edition produced by Küyel-Türker has it. The wording is identical, if one considers Küyel-Türker's footnote (al-Siǧistānī, *al-Qawl fī l-kamāl al-ḫāṣṣ bi-nawʿ al-insān*, 221.22); cf. Kraemer, *Philosophy in the Renaissance of Islam*, §7.4.3, 299. Another treatise which is perhaps partially attributable to al-Siǧistānī is called *Kalām fī mabādiʾ al-mawǧūdāt* and, likewise, contains the second definition in an identical wording (269.6–8); cf. Kraemer, *Philosophy in the Renaissance of Islam*, §8.4, 307; cf. generally Kraemer, *Philosophy in the Renaissance of Islam*, 173–177.

see two elements reoccurring. We recognise Abū Bakr al-Rāzī's *tanfuḏu fī*, as opposed to Avicenna's *sāriya fī*, but with *tuʿṭīhā l-taḫalluq wa-l-taṣawwur* we read also something that very closely approximates Avicenna's formulations *tufīdu l-ṣuwar wa-l-ḫilaq* and *al-taḫlīq wa-l-taškīl*. In other words, the second definition of nature in al-Siğistānī's *al-Maqāla fī l-muḥarrik al-awwal* conforms with both Abū Bakr al-Rāzī's and Avicenna's versions of Philoponus' definition. More precisely, it is al-Siğistānī's first half that corresponds with Abū Bakr al-Rāzī, while the second half agrees with Avicenna even in the detail that it lacks a proper equivalent of διοικητική. In addition to that, al-Siğistānī, just like al-Kindī before him, provides two definitions of nature and, thus, appears to imitate Philoponus' distinction between a definition of "the activity of nature" (τῆς ἐνεργείας τῆς φύσεως) and a definition of "its substance" (τῆς οὐσίας αὐτῆς).

In *al-Muqābasāt* of al-Tawḥīdī, a work of one of al-Siğistānī's closest companions, we also find a list of at least nine different meanings of the term *ṭabīʿa*, including the following two:

قال أبو سليمان أوضاً إملاء ... وأمّا بحسب النظر الطبيعي العامّ الذي يخصّ الفيلسوف الطبيعي فهو المعنى الذي حدّه أرسطوطاليس بأنّه مبدأ الحركة والسكون للشيء الذي هو فيه أوّلاً بالذات لا بطريق العرض ... بحسب النظر الفلسفي وحدّ الطبيعة هو المعنى الذي يقال إنّها حياة تنفذ في الأجسام فتُعطيها التخلّق والتصوّر بالصورة الخاصّة بواحد واحد منها، وكأنّها القوّة السارية من المبدأ الأوّل إلى جميع الأشياء المنفعلة بها والقابلة لها.

Abū Sulaymān said in dictation: ... With regard to the common natural inquiry (*bi-ḥasab al-naẓar al-ṭabīʿī l-ʿāmm*), which is characteristic for the natural philosopher, it [sc. nature] has the meaning which Aristotle defined as the principle of motion and rest for something in which it is primarily, by itself, and not by way of accident ... with regard to philosophical inquiry (*bi-ḥasab al-naẓar al-falsafī*), however, the definition of nature is the meaning which is said that it is life (*ḥayāt*) which permeates through the bodies (*tanfuḏu fī l-ağsām*), and so gives them shaping and formation (*fa-tuʿṭīhā l-taḫalluq wa-l-taṣawwur*) through a specific form for each one of them; it is like a power descending from the First Principle into all the things (*al-quwwa al-sāriya min al-mabdaʾ al-awwal ilā ğamīʿ al-ašyāʾ*)[164] capable of being affected by it and receptive for it. (al-Tawḥīdī, *al-Muqābasāt*, §79, 284.15–285.11)[165]

Apparently, al-Tawḥīdī was not only a close follower of his master but also an accurate reporter of his words. This passage, with very few and mainly marginal differences, is

164 Here I translate *sāriya ... ilā* as "descending into," even though before I translated *sāriya ... fī* as "permeating through." This seems to be both demanded by the context and indicated by the different preposition.

165 cf. also Kraemer, *Philosophy in the Renaissance of Islam*, 173. It is to be noted that al-Tawḥīdī further subdivides the Aristotelian notion into a material aspect of being in motion and rest, and a formal aspect of causing motion and rest, which reflects a general tendency to align Aristotle's nature with both the matter and the form of a thing, thus following Aristotle's own discussion in *Physics* II.1 culminating in his well-known verdict that "form is nature rather than matter" (*Phys.* II.1, 193a28–b12). Ibn ʿAdī follows a similar strategy, as he first quotes Isḥāq ibn Ḥunayn's translation of Aristotle's definition and then states that the meaning of "principle" comprises both a passive principle of receiving, viz., matter, and an active principle of acting, viz., form; cf. Ibn ʿAdī, *Maqāla fī l-mawğūdāt*, 269.9–12.

a rather precise copy of what we have found in al-Siǧistānī's *al-Maqāla fī l-muḥarrik al-awwal* and, again, seems to imitate Philoponus' distinction into the activity and the substance of nature. There are two significant differences, though. First, al-Tawḥīdī expands the meaning of the second definition such that nature not only "permeates through" (*tanfuḏu fī*) the bodies but also "descends into" (*al-sāriya ... ilā*) all the things from the first principle. Together, these two descriptions very adequately capture the bivalence encapsulated in the Greek term καταδεδυκυῖα, known from Philoponus. Second, according to al-Tawḥīdī's "philosophical inquiry" (*al-naẓar al-falsafī*), nature is not a *power*, as in al-Siǧistānī, but precisely is *life* (*ḥayāt*) which "permeates through the bodies" and gives them "shaping and formation." According to this fourth/tenth-century Baġdādī circle, then, nature is both "life" and "power" – just as nature is described as "a life or a power" (ζωὴ ἤτοι δύναμις) in Philoponus' original definition.

Finally, we find a very similar, yet again slightly different, definition in Ms. Marsh 539 from the Bodleian Library, Oxford. This highly valuably and interesting manuscript was recently edited and translated in full by Elvira Wakelnig as *A Philosophy Reader from the Circle of Miskawayh*. It is a systematically arranged collection of Arabic texts and fragments from a large number of sources of the history of philosophy from antiquity up to the fifth/eleventh century. Miskawayh, himself a companion of al-Siǧistānī, seems to have been a close associate of the actual compiler of the manuscript.[166] In it, we find a collection of five definitions of nature, the first two of which are as follows:

> وقال أرسطالس في السماع الطبيعي الطبيعة مبدأ حركة وسكون فيما فيه ذلك على الأمر الأوّل بالذات لا بالعرض ... قوله على الأمر الأوّل فصل بينه وبين النفس ... وقال الطبيعة حياة تنفذ في الأجسام فتفعل فيها التخلّق وتدبّرها وهي مبدأ حركة وسكون.
>
> Aristotle said in the *Physics*: Nature is a principle of motion and rest in that in which it is in a primary manner (*ʿalā l-amr al-awwal*), by itself and not by accident ... His saying "in a primary manner" distinguishes between it and soul ... [Someone] said: nature is life (*ḥayāt*) which permeates through (*tanfuḏu fī*) the bodies, and so effects in them shaping (*fa-tafʿalu fīhā l-taḫalluq*)[167] and governs them (*wa-tudabbiruhā*); it is a principle of motion and rest. (Ms. Marsh 539, §§70–71, 144.18–21, 146.5f.)[168]

The first definition, which is explicitly reported as Aristotle's, deviates from Isḥāq ibn Ḥunayn's translation more than those by al-Siǧistānī and al-Tawḥīdī. It corresponds, however, in all its aspects with Qusṭā's translation as found in the Arabic version of Ps.-Plutarchus' *Placita Philosophorum*.[169] The second definition bears clear signs of Philoponus and in fact is, finally, a version which contains almost all important

166 On all this, cf. the introductory remarks by Wakelnig in *A Philosophy Reader from the Circle of Miskawayh*, 1–59.

167 I suggest to emend the text from *fa-yufʿalu* to *fa-tafʿalu* and translate accordingly.

168 The paragraph, page, and line numbers follow Wakelnig's edition.

169 cf. Ps.-Plutarchus, *Placita Philosophorum*, 274a24–27; Aetius Arabus, *Die Vorsokratiker in arabischer Überlieferung*, 2.14f.; q.v. above, 227f.

elements of the redefinition he provided in his commentary on Aristotle's *Physics*: Nature is said to be life (ζωή, *ḥayāt*) which permeates through the bodies (καταδεδυκυῖα διὰ τῶν σωμάτων, *tanfuḏu fī l-ağsām*), gives them form (διαπλαστική, *tafʿalu fīhā l-taḫalluq*), and governs them (διοικητική, *tudabbiruhā*) – it even reproduces the way in which Philoponus blends his own reworked definition into Aristotle's own words (ἀρχὴ κινήσεως οὖσα καὶ ἠρεμίας, *wa-hiya mabdaʾ ḥaraka wa-sukūn*). In addition, the text of Ms. Marsh 539 also reports Philoponus' remark that Aristotle's qualification πρώτως (*ʿalā l-amr al-awwal*) is meant to distinguish between nature and soul, to which it adds – omitted in the above quotation – a condensed version of the explanation offered by Philoponus in his commentary, taking recourse to the same example that "sight moves desire, this moves the natural powers, and these move the animal" (ἡ ὄψις μὲν τὴν ὄρεξιν κινεῖ, αὕτη δὲ τὰς φυσικὰς δυνάμεις, αὗται δὲ τὸ ζῷον, *al-baṣar yuḥarriku l-ištiyāq wa-l-ištiyāq yuḥarriku l-quwā l-ṭabīʿiyya wa-l-quwā l-ṭabīʿiyya tuḥarriku l-ḥayy*).[170] The only missing element is that Philoponus regarded nature as "a life or a power" (ζωὴ ἤτοι δύναμις), whereas Ms. Marsh 539, just as the version in al-Tawḥīdī, only mentions "life." Nonetheless, for the first time we can hope to have been given nothing other than a direct quotation from an Arabic translation of Philoponus' commentary.

Since it has been shown already that the expression *ʿalā l-amr al-awwal* in the Aristotelian part of the above quotation is distinctive of Qusṭā, and since the definition of nature in the second part undoubtedly derives from Philoponus commentary on the *Physics*, it seems clear that the compiler of Ms. Marsh 539 worked from Qusṭā's translation of that commentary. Thus, the translation of *tanfuḏu fī* for καταδεδυκυῖα may also be distinctive for Qusṭā, just as the forms from the root *ḫ-l-q* for διαπλαστική together with those from *d-b-r* for διοικητική. Thus, this version of Philoponus' account of nature corresponds both with the wording from Avicenna's *al-Samāʿ al-ṭabīʿī* (*al-taḫalluq*) and with that from Abū Bakr al-Rāzī (*tanfuḏu fī, tudabbiruhā*), in the same way as the versions in al-Siğistānī and al-Tawḥīdī do, who were colleagues, if not friends, of Miskawayh and, thus, presumably also of the redactor of the compendium preserved in Ms. Marsh 539.

This situation leads to the following assumptions: first, Abū Bakr al-Rāzī really had access to Qusṭā's translation of Philoponus' commentary and in providing the latter's definition of nature follows Qusṭā's vocabulary, merely omitting the aspects of "life" and of "forming and shaping"; second, the circle around al-Siğistānī also had access to Qusṭā's translation and quoted from it, sometimes in a more complete manner than Abū Bakr al-Rāzī had done. Consequently, Philoponus' commentary was available in fourth/tenth-century Baġdād in the translation of Qusṭā. Third, Avicenna himself had access to this translation, as his knowledge of Philoponus and some similarities in his terminology indicate. Yet, he does not quote literally from his source, but merely

170 Philoponus, *In Phys.*, 196b33f.; Ms. Marsh 539, §70, 146.1f. I suggest to emend the text in both instances from *tuḥarriku* to *yuḥarriku* and translate accordingly.

reproduced Philoponus' definition from memory or paraphrased it, in a way that was sufficiently adequate for the purpose of refuting him.

What is more, one could continue now and give numerous references to other passages in works from among the same circle around al-Siǧistānī in which nature is described as a "divine power permeating through all bodies which it governs" (*al-ṭabīʿa ... quwwa ilāhiyya sāriya fī l-aǧsām kullihā tudabbiruhā*), as in Miskawayh's *al-Fawz al-aṣġar*, with its parallel passages in the *altera recensio* of the same work, in the anonymous *Kitāb al-Ḥikma*, and in a different passage from Ms. Marsh 539; or as a "divine power permeating the world below" (*quwwa ilāhiyya sāriya fī l-ʿālam al-suflī*), as in the *al-Taqrīr li-awǧuh al-taqdīr* of Abū l-Ḥasan Muḥammad ibn Yūsuf al-ʿĀmirī (d. 381/992); or to the Iḫwān al-Ṣafāʾ (fl. ~ 370/980) who, similar to al-Kindī, defined nature as "one of the powers of the universal heavenly soul," and described it as "permeating through all the bodies (*sāriya fī ǧamīʿ al-aǧsām*) which are below the sphere of the moon" and as that which is responsible for moving, bringing to rest, governing, completing, and perfect these bodies (*muḥarrika lahā wa-musakkina wa-mudabbira wa-mutammima wa-muballiġa*).[171] What is, however, peculiar only to the passages discussed above, and not to those to which I have just now briefly alluded, is that they transmit the definition of Philoponus *together with* the one from Aristotle's *Physics* as its explanation, modification, expansion, or – in one way or other at least – as a complement to Aristotle. In this respect, the figures whose passages I have discussed were not only "Kindians" and "philosophers in al-Kindī's tradition," each providing (at least) two definitions of nature, one Aristotelian and one Neoplatonic.[172] They all quoted Philoponus' definition verbatim, bearing witness to the fact that the prevalent understanding of Aristotle's concept of nature among Avicenna's contemporaries in fourth/tenth-century Baġdād was that which had been formulated by Philoponus as an actually critical enhancement of Aristotle's defective definition. Philoponus achieved his reworking on the basis of an idea which, as far as we know, gained authority through Alexander but which may ultimately go back to the Stoic theory of an all-pervading πνεῦμα as the operative principle within the natural world.[173] The companions of al-Siǧistānī, however, did not regard this concept of nature as contrary to Aristotle's original definition of nature as a principle of motion, as is shown by the fact that the critical remarks, which were a distinctive feature in Philoponus' commentary, are

---

171 Miskawayh, *al-Fawz al-aṣġar* II.10, 101.8–13; Ms. Marsh 539, §49, 120.11–13; al-ʿĀmirī, *al-Taqrīr li-awǧuh al-taqdīr*, 334.13.; Iḫwān al-Ṣafāʾ, *Rasāʾil Iḫwān al-Ṣafāʾ* X.1, 355.9–356.5; cf. Wakelnig's commentary on Ms. Marsh 539, §49, as well as her "A New Version of Miskawayh's *Book of Triumph*."

172 For the appellation "Kindians" and "philosophers in al-Kindī's tradition," cf. Adamson, "The Kindian Tradition"; Wakelnig, "Die Philosophen in der Tradition al-Kindīs."

173 It is to be noted that the pseudo-Aristotelian treatise *De mundo* has also distinctly Stoic traits without, however, being Stoic through and through; cf. Furley's remarks in his translation (Aristotle, *On Sophistical Refutations, On Coming-to-be and Passing Away, On the Cosmos*, 335–337) and, generally, J. C. Thom's introduction to *Cosmic Order and Divine Power*.

entirely absent from the Arabic sources examined above. They all agree that nature is an actively moving principle, which permeates the bodies and governs their directions, being responsible for their motion and their striving towards perfection. This principle deserves its place within their Neoplatonic cosmology. Nature thus conceived is a second-rate soul and arbiter between *there* and *here*, i.e., between the divine realm and the material world, governing the latter in accordance with the former.

Yet, the influence of the Neoplatonic understanding of nature, which was so well encapsulated in Philoponus' reworked definition, was even greater than that. It affected not only those philosophers which Avicenna already loathed, viz., the Neoplatonists of Baġdād – it also appealed to some Peripatetics of Baġdād. This emerges, in striking clarity, from some marginal comments preserved in Ms. Leiden or. 583, the already mentioned heavily annotated copy of Isḥāq ibn Ḥunayn's translation of the *Physics* from the study circle around Ibn ʿAdī. These comments are attributed to Abū Bišr Mattā ibn Yūnus (d. 328/940), who was Ibn ʿAdī's teacher, and concern Aristotle's remarks on the teleological character of nature, which is imitated by art and plainly perceptible in animals.[174] In Abū Bišr's comments, we read the following:

> هذه الطبيعة مبثوثة من قبل الخلّاق عزّ وجلّ في جميع الأشياء الطبيعية ... وأعني بالطبيعة الفعّالة ليس المادّة ولا الصورة لكن الطبيعة المبثوثة في المتكوّنات هي المكوّنة ...وهذه الطبيعة تكون في المنى ... إذا حصلت النفس كفّت الطبيعة عن التحريك وبعد ذلك تكون موجودة مدبّرةً ومولّدةً.
>
> This nature is disseminated on account of the Creator – strong and exalted is He – throughout all natural things (*mabṯūṯa ... fī ǧamīʿ al-ašyaʾ al-ṭabīʿiyya*) ... I mean by "active nature" (*bi-l-ṭabīʿa al-faʿʿāla*) neither matter nor form but the nature disseminated throughout things which come-to-be, being the generative [nature] ... This nature exists in the semen ... When the soul occurred [in the animal which is formed in the womb from the semen], nature stops the production of motion and, after that, exists as something governing and generating (*mudabbiratan wa-muwallidatan*). (Abū Bišr's comments in Aristotle, *al-Ṭabīʿa* II.8, 147.19, 151.4–11)[175]

In this comment on *Physics* II.8, Abū Bišr expounds the meaning of that nature to whose efficacy Aristotle attributes a teleological character. This nature, he writes, is something "disseminated through" (*mabṯūṯa ... fī*) the natural bodies which are subject to generation and corruption. Among Abū Bišr's main concerns is the explanation of the generative power that is present even in the semen of an animal before the existence of a soul which, then, takes over the task of completing, teleologically speaking, the

---

174 cf. *Phys.* II.8, 199a8–13, 20–30.

175 cf. Brown, "Avicenna and the Christian Philosophers in Baghdad"; Genequand, "Quelques aspects de l'idée de nature d'Aristote à al-Ghazālī"; Janos, "Active Nature and Other Striking Features"; Adamson, "*Porphyrius Arabus* on Nature and Art." Brown's paper is particularly interesting, as it draws a line to Avicenna's commentary on *Metaphysics* Λ, in which he directly attacked Abū Bišr. This attack, however, does not concern Abū Bišr's conception of nature; cf. Avicenna, *Commentaire sur le livre Lambda de la* Métaphysique, 55.111–117. Abū Bišr's remarks are also translated by McGinnis and Reisman in their *Classical Arabic Philosophy*, 125f., which omits the one line from page 147.

generation of the animal.[176] Nonetheless, nature continues to exist in the embryo and the completed animal as a "governing and generating" (*mudabbiratan wa-muwallidatan*) principle. The structure of Abū Bišr's conception of nature corresponds to that of Philoponus and those in the Arabic tradition who followed him as, for example, al-Siǧistānī, al-Tawḥīdī, and Miskawayh. What is more, Abū Bišr offers his comments explicitly as his explanation of *Aristotle's* conception. His remarks should, accordingly, not be taken as an independent elaboration of the meaning of nature, as it can be found in such works as the aforementioned *al-Fawz al-aṣġar* of Miskawayh, *al-Taqrīr li-awǧuh al-taqdīr* of al-ʿĀmirī, or the epistles of the Iḫwān al-Ṣafāʾ. That is to say, they are precisely not the bovine expressions of an individual who puts forth his own Neoplatonic nonsense – they are remarks on Aristotle by the hand of a renowned Peripatetic who meant to clarify, explicate, and complement Aristotle's definition of nature in a manner not unlike that present in the works of al-Kindī, al-Siǧistānī, al-Tawḥīdī, and the redactor of Ms. Marsh 539, all of whom quote Aristotle together with one or more other definitions, often specifically remarking upon their complementary character by making explicit the fact that one definition merely focuses on natural inquiry (*bi-ḥasab al-naẓr al-ṭabīʿī*) or teaching (*min ǧihat al-taʿlīm*) or nature's activity (τῆς ἐνεργείας τῆς φύσεως), while the other focuses on metaphysics (*bi-ḥasab al-naẓar fī-mā baʿd al-ṭabīʿa*) or nature's character (*min ǧihat al-ṭibāʿ*) or its substance (τῆς οὐσίας αὐτῆς), as al-Siǧistānī, al-Kindī, and Philoponus had it, respectively. This tradition treats Aristotle's and Philoponus' definitions as equal, i.e., as expounding one and the same principle from two different points of view.

What can be gathered as a result of the foregoing investigation is that Philoponus is certainly not the exclusive target of Avicenna's attack in *al-Samāʿ al-ṭabīʿī* I.5. The idea of an independent power or life which pervades through the entire universe and which governs the natural events both on the large and the small scale has been prominent at least since Alexander of Aphrodisias and, in fact, goes back to the Stoics. While the Stoics did not employ the notion of a "nature," they argued for a divine self-moving principle that penetrates the passive material, like a soul penetrates us, endowing it with shape and motion.[177] A strikingly analogous idea confronts us in Alexander's treatise *Maqāla fī l-qawl fī mabādiʾ al-kull*. In Plotinus' metaphysical system, nature occupies a similarly prominent place as the lowest of the higher principles, i.e., as the outwardly directed manifestation of the world-soul. This view is also confirmed by

176 The specific details of this theory, which are expounded by Janos, do not concern us here; cf. Janos, "Active Nature and Other Striking Features," 147–154.

177 cf. Galen, *Kitāb fī l-asbāb al-māsika*, ch. 1; Alexander of Aphrodisias, *De mixtione* 3, 216.4–217.1; cf. also Sorabji, *Matter, Space, and Motion*, 85 (with a number of references in fn. 26); cf. generally, Long and Sedley, *The Hellenistic Philosophers*, ch. 44; q.v. also fn. 30 above, 220f. Moreover, the apparent similarities between the Stoic account of an all-pervading πνεῦμα and the Neoplatonic account of a permeating power led Arif to the assertion that what Avicenna "rejects [is] the Stoic definition of nature as the power which permeates a body" ("Ibn Sīnā's Idea of Nature and Change," 114).

Porphyry and fully absorbed in Philoponus' commentary on the *Physics*. Together with some of Alexander's treatises – above all, his no-longer extant commentary on the *Physics* – and the materials from the Arabic Plotinus and Arabic Proclus, Philoponus' commentary was translated into Arabic, and henceforth circulated among, and had influence on, intellectuals around Baġdād in the fourth/tenth century, as is evinced not only by the passages we found in al-Siǧistānī and al-Tawḥīdī but also attested through Ms. Marsh 539 as well as other more independent writings of figures from among the same Neoplatonic circle. As we also know from various sources, Avicenna was often, to put it mildly, in disagreement with the respective views of some of these figures from Baġdād, among them the followers of al-Siǧistānī, viz., al-Kirmānī and Miskawayh, as well as Abū l-Faraǧ ʿAbd Allāh ibn al-Ṭayyib (d. 435/1043).[178] Moreover, the same conception of nature is also found in Abū Bišr's remarks preserved in the margins of Ms. Leiden or. 583 – a circumstance which demonstrates that the influence of the concept of nature which is so well expressed through the words of Philoponus also reached deeply into the Peripatetic circles in Baġdād, viz., the school of Ibn ʿAdī and Abū Naṣr al-Fārābī (d. 339/950-51). This means that Avicenna, who was certainly familiar also with Abū Bišr's thought, had not only to *reject* the Neoplatonic misconception of nature – he also had to *rectify* the Peripatetic understanding of it.

What we, then, read in Avicenna's *al-Samāʿ al-ṭabīʿī* is not a narrow blow aimed at Philoponus' attempt to emend the definition of nature that was provided by Aristotle, but a much broader attack on what certainly was one of the most prominent, if not outright prevailing, conceptions of nature in the philosophical circles of Avicenna's time. Avicenna's target, then, is not only Philoponus nor is it only the Greek and Arabic Neoplatonists – it is the entire virtually unified philosophical tradition from at least Alexander up to the Peripatetics in fourth/tenth-century Baġdād. As a final piece of evidence for this, we may look at an interesting passage in the *Kitāb al-Milal wa-l-niḥal* by Muḥammad ibn ʿAbd al-Karīm al-Šahrastānī (d. 548/1153), in which we read the following:

> ونقل ثامسطيوس عن أرسطوطاليس وأفلاطن وثاوفرسطيس وفرفريوس وفلوطرخيس وهو رأيه أنّ في العالم أجمع طبيعة واحدة عامّة وكلّ نوع من أنواع النبات والحيوان مختصّ بطبيعة خاصّة. وحدّوا الطبيعة العامّة بأنّها مبدأ الحركة في الأشياء والسكون فيها على الأمر الأوّل من ذواتها وهي علّة الحركة في المتحرّكات وعلّة السكون في الساكنات. زعموا أنّ الطبيعة هي التي تدبّر الأشياء كلّها في العالم حيوته ومواته تدبيراً طبيعياً وليست هي حيّة ولا قادرة ولا مختارة ولكن لا تفعل إلّا حكمةً وصواباً وعلى نظم صحيح وترتيب مُحكَم.

178 cf. Avicenna's letter "Memoirs of a Disciple from Rayy," translated in Gutas, *Avicenna and the Aristotelian Tradition*, 60–67. As recorded in *al-Mubāḥaṯāt*, Avicenna occasionally refers to al-Kirmānī as *māḏiġ li-l-ḫarāʾ* ("the shit-eater"; §96, 69.4) and to those unworthy to benefit from his *al-Išārāt wa-l-tanbīhāt* as "riffraff" and "gnats" (*al-raʿāʿ* and *hamāǧ*; §2, 39.1, and *al-Išārāt wa-l-tanbīhāt*, epilogue, 222.10); cf. also Reisman, *The Making of the Avicennan Tradition*, 166–185, 206 as well as Gutas, *Avicenna and the Aristotelian Tradition*, 429); cf. further Reisman, "Two Medieval Arabic Treatises on the Nutritive Faculties."

> The report of Themistius about Aristotle, Plato, Theophrastus, Porphyry, and Plutarch, is that it is his opinion that in the world in its entirety is a single common nature, and every species of plant and animal is distinguished by a specific nature. They defined the common nature as the principle of motion in the things and of rest in them in a primary manner (*ʿalā l-amr al-awwal*) from their essences (*min ḏawātihā*), being the cause of motion in those which are in motion and the cause of rest in those which are at rest. They claimed that nature is that which governs (*tudabbiru*) all things in the world – both alive and dead – through a natural governing, but [that nature] is not [itself] living nor potent nor voluntary but merely acts wisely and correctly and in accordance with sound reflection and careful ordering. (al-Šahrastānī, *Kitāb al-Milal wa-l-niḥal*, 343.15–344.2)

In this passage, al-Šahrastānī – much like al-Kindī, al-Siǧistānī, and others before him – provides a twofold, even though clearly unified, account of nature as both a universal and common principle of motion, and a governing power in the entire world. He attributes this account to a wide range of people, Platonists and Peripatetics alike, and even, once more recognisable through the expression *ʿalā l-amr al-awwal*, seems to draw on material that has once been translated by Qusṭā. It is this tradition and this conception of nature to which Avicenna reacts.

Having said this, it is equally clear that Philoponus remains Avicenna's primary target. First of all, Avicenna reports Philoponus' dissatisfaction with Aristotle's definition which, according to Philoponus, only indicated "the activity of nature" (τῆς ἐνεργείας τῆς φύσεως) but could not explain "what nature is" (τί ἐστιν ἡ φύσις). Moreover, it is this dissatisfaction of Philoponus which Avicenna used as an opportunity to engage with Philoponus' account in such detail and to show its redundancy. Second, the belief of "some people (*qawm*) ... that the soul produces local motion through the intermediacy of nature," which was mentioned by Avicenna in *al-Samāʿ al-ṭabīʿī* I.5, §6, 31.16, could be identified with a passage in the commentary of Philoponus in the immediate vicinity of his redefinition of nature. Third, we could link Abū Bakr al-Rāzī's explicit reference to Yaḥyā al-Naḥwī through the definitions provided by al-Siǧistānī and al-Tawḥīdī and those preserved in Ms. Marsh 539 to the wording in Avicenna's *al-Samāʿ al-ṭabīʿī*. Despite the fact, then, that Avicenna does not seem to have provided a direct quotation from his copy of Philoponus' commentary, his version is certainly derived from a Philoponian source. Moreover, Philoponus' reformulation of the definition of nature must have seemed to Avicenna to be the very epitome of that view which was so widely accepted by contemporaries of all sorts. For Avicenna, then, Philoponus' account serves as a peg on which to hang his rejection of the idea of nature as an independent and maybe even all-encompassing, semi-divine, soul-like principle.

It is, therefore, justified to analyse Avicenna's criticism on this conception of nature on the basis of the account given in Philoponus' commentary on *Physics* II.1, even though Philoponus surely was not Avicenna's exclusive target.

The Argument of Avicenna's Attack

Avicenna's behaviour in his engagement with Philoponus is a good example of a well-known feature of Avicenna's writing: he lacks academic exactitude in quoting and marking his sources. Moreover, his terminology shifts, for example, from *al-ṣuwar* ("forms") in paragraph five to *al-aškāl* ("figures") in paragraph seven, and the phrase *tufīdu l-ṣuwar wa-l-ḫilaq* ("to give the forms and shapes") reoccurs in a normalised form as *al-taḫlīq wa-l-taškīl* ("shaping and figuring"), while the remark about preserving the forms and figures, not mentioned at first, only appears in a later passage. All this advises the reader to regard Avicenna's formulations as a quote from memory or, altogether, as a paraphrase at his convenience, i.e., for the sake of his criticism of Philoponus and everyone who followed him. Yet, it is possible to acquire a clear picture of how Avicenna *understood* Philoponus' emendation of the Aristotelian formula, for he breaks down Philoponus' comments into four conceptual aspects. It is the following four aspects which, according to Avicenna's reading of Philoponus' account, were meant to accurately define the οὐσία, and not just the ἐνέργεια, of nature:

i) nature is a power (δύναμις, *quwwa*),
ii) nature permeates through the bodies (καταδεδυκυῖα διὰ τῶν σωμάτων, *sāriya fī l-ağsām*),
iii) nature gives forms (διαπλαστικὴ ... καὶ διοικητική, *al-taḫlīq wa-l-taškīl*), and
iv) nature preserves forms (φυλάξῃ ἐν τῷ εἴδει, *ḥifẓ al-ḫilaq wa-l-aškāl*).

These four aspects of Avicenna's understanding of Philoponus' commentary can be compared to Avicenna's interpretation of Aristotle's definition, which he set out in the form of a literal commentary, as could be seen above. This comparison reveals on what grounds Avicenna rejects Philoponus' emendation as *bāṭil* ("void"), for Avicenna takes Aristotle's conception of nature to comprise the following four essential features:

i) nature is a principle for motion,
ii) nature is in something,
iii) nature causes motion, and
iv) nature causes rest.

The first half of Avicenna's criticism, now, is that Philoponus, his good intentions notwithstanding, said exactly the same as Aristotle had done – he merely used different words. Avicenna intends to demonstrate this by explaining the meaning (*maʿnan*) of each of the four aspects of Philoponus' reformulation by identifying them with their corresponding feature of Aristotle's initial account. In particular, he states the following:

i) the meaning of "power" is nothing but "principle of producing motion that is in something" (*wa-laysa maʿnā l-quwwa illā mabdaʾ taḥrīk yakūnu fī l-šayʾ*),
ii) the meaning of "permeating" is nothing but "being in something" (*wa-laysa maʿnā l-sarayān illā l-kawn fī l-šayʾ*),

iii) the meaning of "shaping and figuring" is already included in "producing motion" (*wa-laysa maʿnā l-taḫlīq wa-l-taškīl illā dāḫilan fī maʿnā l-taḥrīk*), and
iv) the meaning of "preservation of shapes and figures" is already included in "producing rest" (*wa-laysa maʿnā ḥifẓ al-ḫilaq wa-l-aškāl illā dāḫilan fī al-taskīn*).[179]

According to Avicenna, then, Philoponus' contribution to the examination of nature as a principle of natural things was that he just restated what Aristotle had already said and that he, thus, "repeated many things for which there was no need" (*mukarriran li-ašyaʾ kaṯīra min ġayr ḥāǧa ilayhā*).[180] At this point, however, the following questions arise: since we have seen above precisely how much Philoponus reinterpreted Aristotle's definition to the effect that his rewording has been a thorough *reworking* in a strictly Neoplatonic fashion, how, then, could Avicenna claim that Philoponus' account is in essence identical to Aristotle's? Is this not a major misinterpretation of the essence of Philoponus' remarks on behalf of Avicenna?

Two points are to be made in answer to this question. The first is that, here, we can recognise, again, one of Avicenna's general strategies in his philosophical approach: a "deflationary strategy." In his investigation of matter and form, Avicenna already claimed – and, indeed, concluded his investigation on this note – that the basic meaning of matter is that of being "capable of acquiring some other factor" and that form analogously is nothing but "a disposition that has been acquired."[181] Moreover, regarding the intricate question of whether or not privation is a principle, he nonchalantly replied that we "achieve nothing by quibbling over terminology" and settled the matter easily, if perhaps not for everyone convincingly, by basically saying that it depends on how one wishes to define the term "principle."[182] We recognise the very same calmed-down attitude here in our present context, for Avicenna reduces the charged-up concepts in Philoponus' commentary to very simple and basic notions which are, then, identified with aspects of Aristotle's account: the power (δύναμις, *quwwa*) which in Philoponus' commentary was not to be taken along the lines of Aristotelian potency but was meant to be an active and invigorated force full of life (ζωή) comes to be a mere source, starting point, or principle for motion on Avicenna's reading; the term καταδεδυκυῖα (*sāriya*) which is central to Neoplatonic cosmology, assimilating the concept of nature with the Platonic self-moving soul, which is destined to fall and enter into the unpleasant material environment of the body, comes to be a mere in-

179 *al-Samāʿ al-ṭabīʿī* I.5, §7, 32.17–33.1, tr. by McGinnis, modified. Once again, Avicenna changes his terminology, when he, instead of using the active participle *sāriya*, now employs the noun *sarayān*.
180 In his *Kitāb al-Ḥudūd*, Avicenna also criticises Philoponus' definition on the grounds that it is circular and would amount to saying that "nature is a principle of change, which is a principle of change." This, as Avicenna adds, "is tautologous jabber" (*haḏayān*; *Kitāb al-Ḥudūd*, §36, 21.2–7.
181 *al-Samāʿ al-ṭabīʿī* I.3, §10, 25.6–10; q.v. above, 174f., 198f.
182 *al-Samāʿ al-ṭabīʿī* I.2, §14, 17.10–17; cf. *al-Ḥikma al-mašriqiyya* III.3, 7.9–14; q.v. above, 209; for a similar case, cf. *al-Samāʿ al-ṭabīʿī* I.6, §3, 35.12f.

dicator of position and a synonym for the inherence in something; the active tasks of shaping and governing the natural body (διαπλαστικὴ αὐτῶν καὶ διοικητική) come to be restatements of the mere fact that nature is involved in the production of motion, whereas, finally, the nature's almost conscious and deliberate striving, first, "to bring [the natural bodies] to the form" (εἰς τὸ εἶδος ἀγάγῃ) and, then, to "preserve [them] in the form" (φυλάξῃ ἐν τῷ εἴδει) comes to be a manner of speaking about nature's involvement in the production of rest. In the end, what is left of Philoponus' complex efforts is that nature is *nothing but* a principle for the motion and the rest of that in which it is – a statement identical with Aristotle's definition as it was provided by Avicenna in *al-Samāʿ al-ṭabīʿī* I.5.

Here, we can also witness a development in Avicenna's attitude. The first philosophical compendium Avicenna wrote is *al-Ḥikma al-ʿArūḍiyya*. In this work, Avicenna enumerated the three kinds of powers (*quwā*, sg. *quwwa*) which are inherent in natural bodies (*ġarazat fī l-aǧsām*):

فمنها قوى سارية في الأجسام تحفظ عليها كمالاتها من أشكالها ومواضعها الطبيعية وأفاعيلها.

> Among them are the powers permeating through the bodies (*quwā sāriya fī l-aǧsām*) which preserve for them their perfections in terms of their forms, their natural positions, and their actions. (*al-Ḥikma al-ʿArūḍiyya* II.1, 115.14f.)

The first of these powers is nature, which Avicenna subsequently described as follows:

وهذه القوى تُسمّى طبيعية وهي قوّة سارية في الأجسام هي مبدأ بالذات لحركاتها بالذات وسكوناتها بالذات ولسائر كمالاتها الذاتية.

> And these powers which are called "natural" are a power permeating through the bodies (*quwwa sāriya fī l-aǧsām*), being a principle essentially for their motions essentially and their rests essentially and for the rest of their essential perfections. (*al-Ḥikma al-ʿArūḍiyya* II.1, 115.18f.)

Here Avicenna's account of nature could hardly be more reminiscent of that in Philoponus, for he describes nature as "a power permeating through the bodies" (*quwwa sāriya fī l-aǧsām*), characterising it as one of the many powers which bring about motion and produce rest. Avicenna could even be said to reproduce Philoponus attitude of blending his own redefinition with Aristotle's original (δύναμις καταδεδυκυῖα διὰ τῶν σωμάτων ... ἀρχὴ κινήσεως οὖσα) – here in Avicenna's *al-Ḥikma al-ʿArūḍiyya* expressed as *quwwā sāriya fī l-aǧsām hiya mabdaʾ ... li-ḥarakātihā*.[183]

More than twenty-five years later, when Avicenna was composing his *al-Naǧāt*, he drew upon his earlier writings.[184] The section on natural philosophy is, by and large, literally taken from his earlier *al-Ḥikma al-ʿArūḍiyya*. The passage in *al-Naǧāt* which corresponds to the two above quotations from *al-Ḥikma al-ʿArūḍiyya* reads as follows:

183 Philoponus, *In Phys.*, 197.35.

184 Gutas asserts that "Avicenna ... compiled *The Salvation* [i.e., *al-Naǧāt*] practically without composing a single line anew" (*Avicenna and the Aristotelian Tradition*, 116).

فمنها قوى سارية في الأجسام تحفظ عليها كمالاتها من أشكالها ومواضعها الطبيعية وأفاعيلها ... وهذه القوى تُسمّى طبيعية وهي مبدأ بالذات لحركاتها وسكوناتها بالذات ولسائر كمالاتها التي لها بذاتها.

Among them are the powers permeating through the bodies (*quwā sāriya fī l-aǧsām*) which preserve for them their perfections in terms of their forms, their natural positions, and their actions ... And these powers which are called "natural" are a principle essentially for their motions and their rests essentially and for the rest of their perfections which belong to them essentially. (*al-Naǧāt* II.1.1, 194.2–7)

This is almost the same text as that in *al-Ḥikma al-ʿArūḍiyya*. There are only a handful of minor differences – and one major deviation: the omission of *quwwa sāriya fī l-aǧsām* in the definition of nature. I cannot think of a more reasonable explanation than that this had been the result of a deliberate decision on Avicenna's part. Avicenna himself may have been influenced by Philoponus' conception of nature in his earlier – even his earliest – writings. He himself may have embraced the Neoplatonic understanding of nature just as his contemporaries in Baġdād have done and, just like them, may have been convinced of the similarity of nature and soul, insofar as both are powers that permeate through the bodies (*quwā sāriya fī l-aǧsām*). Yet, he abandoned this position some time between 389/999, when he wrote *al-Ḥikma al-ʿArūḍiyya*, and 418/1027, when he composed *al-Naǧāt*. In between these years lies his work on *al-Samāʿ al-ṭabīʿī*, which was porbably completed around 412/1022, i.e., approximately twenty years after he had composed his first compendium *al-Ḥikma al-ʿArūḍiyya*.

Yet, Avicenna kept the description of *all* powers as permeating the body (*quwā sāriya fī l-aǧsām*) in his *al-Naǧāt* – i.e., he only adjusted the text, and deleted the notion of a permeating power, in the definition of nature. This is no inconsistency. To the contrary, it is in line with Avicenna's argument in *al-Samāʿ al-ṭabīʿī* that the meaning of "permeating" is nothing but "being in something" (*wa-laysa maʿnā l-sarayān illā l-kawn fī l-šayʾ*). Since both nature and soul are powers *in* the natural bodies, there is no reason for why he should have removed *sāriya fī l-aǧsām* in the first instance, where it invariably applies to all natural powers, i.e., to the various kinds of souls as well as to nature. It is, however, removed as a suitable definitional feature of nature. There is no single occurrence of the feature of permeating bodies, as far as I can see, in his accounts of nature in any of his other major works after *al-Ḥikma al-ʿArūḍiyya*.

There is a second point which requires mentioning, in order to answer the question of whether Avicenna did not greatly misinterpret Philoponus when he concluded that what Philoponus thought to have achieved was nothing more than what Aristotle had originally said. It is not so much the case that Avicenna could arrive at this conclusion because he misconstrued Philoponus' intention and argument, and did not notice how far away Philoponus actually was from Aristotle – it is the other way around: Avicenna did arrive at this conclusion, because he himself misconceived the Aristotelian concept of nature, and did not notice how far away Aristotle was from Philoponus. It could already be seen that the largest contrast between Aristotle and Philoponus is obtained by interpreting, on the one hand, Philoponus' nature as an active force (δύναμις) that is directly responsible for the downward motion of a natural object just as the self-moved soul is responsible for the movements of an animate object and, on the other hand, Aristotle's nature as a passive potential (δύναμις) "not of causing but of suffering motion" (οὐδὲ τοῦ ποιεῖν, ἀλλὰ τοῦ πάσχειν, *lā li-an ... yafʿala bal li-an yaqbala l-fiʿl*). This, though, is neither how Avicenna understood nature nor how he understood Aristotle's definition of nature. It is clear that Avicenna introduces nature already in *al-Samāʿ al-ṭabīʿī* I.3 as an "efficient principle" (*al-mabdaʾ al-fāʿilī*) which belongs to such principles which are properly called "causes" (*ʿilal*).[185] Even before Avicenna began his discussion of nature, even before he had written the first word of his first chapter on nature, he stated that nature is a cause which, as an efficient principle, brings about motion. Throughout *al-Samāʿ al-ṭabīʿī* I.5, then, it was constantly recognisable that Avicenna described motion in causal terms, for example, when he repeated his description of nature as a "efficient principle," when he said that nature "produces motion" (*tuḥarriku* or *taḥrīk*) and that it does so "proximately with no intermediary" (*qarīb lā bi-tawassuṭ*), when he declared that nature is a principle for motion "essentially" (*bi-l-ḏāt*), because it produces motion "through itself" (*li-ḏātihā*), and lastly when he provided a version of Aristotle's definition that did not reproduce the mediopassive connotation of κινεῖσθαι.[186] Once we have acknowledged that Avicenna interpreted Aristotle's nature already as an efficient principle that produces motion through itself, we can easily understand how he could regard Philoponus' commentary as having merely "repeated many things for which there was no need" (*mukarriran li-ašyaʾ kaṯīra min ġayr ḥāǧa*). Seen in this light, Philoponus' supposed emendation would appear to be *bāṭil* ("void"), indeed. In effect, Avicenna is not maintaining that Philoponus said almost exactly what Aristotle had said but, more precisely, that Aristotle had said exactly what Philoponus did and that, consequently, Philoponus' efforts were in vain.

However, there is yet another aspect in Philoponus' argument with which Avicenna disagrees much more profoundly. That is to say, there is something in there that is not just "void" but expressly "wrong" and "corrupted" (*fāsid*), as Avicenna also writes.[187] Avicenna remarks, albeit very briefly and not in the form of a fully developed argument, that Philoponus' use of "power" is not justifiable and is, in fact, ill-fitting on Aristotelian grounds. Apparently referring to *Metaphysics* Θ.8, Avicenna states the following:

القوّة التي جعلها كالجنس في رسم الطبيعة هي قوّة الفاعلة وإذا حُدّت حُدّت بأنّها مبدأ الحركة من آخر في آخر بأنّه آخر.

185 *al-Samāʿ al-ṭabīʿī* I.3, §12, 25.14f.

186 All this implies, as we have already seen, that Avicenna sides with Philoponus against Aristotle's account of *Physics* VIII.4; q.v. above, 236ff.

187 *al-Samāʿ al-ṭabīʿī* I.5, §7, 33.7f.

> The power which he [sc. Philoponus] made so as to be the genus in the description of nature is the active power (*al-quwwa al-fāʿila*); and if it is defined, then it is defined by that it is "the principle of motion from another in another insofar as it is another." (*al-Samāʿ al-ṭabīʿī* I.5, §7, 32.16f., tr. by McGinnis, modified)[188]

As already remarked upon above, Aristotle distinguished between φύσις and δύναμις in *Metaphysics* Θ.8 precisely by making the former an internal and the latter an external principle for the production of motion.[189] Aristotle further differentiated between an active δύναμις of acting (ποιεῖν) and a passive δύναμις of being acted upon (πάσχειν).[190] On Avicenna's reading, then, Philoponus made it abundantly clear that he did not mean nature to be that latter kind of a passive δύναμις but was talking about nature being an active power, i.e., as a power bringing about motion in something other. Thus construed, Philoponus' nature qualifies as something that is external to the thing it moves or, at least, has a relation to the thing it moves as something other (ἐν ἄλλῳ ἢ ᾗ ἄλλο) – it *pervades through* that which it moves, thus being ontologically separate. Ironically, a nature understood as an external active power and as depicted by Philoponus is no longer strictly speaking a φύσις in the sense of *Metaphysics* Θ.8 – it is a δύναμις.

Modern interpreters likewise detected in Philoponus' commentary "a reification of nature foreign to the Aristotelian understanding."[191] Philoponus, who took recourse to active attributes and characteristics, in order to spell out his understanding of the natural power, developed nature into a "thing." He said that nature was not only an active mover and force – it was also a substance (οὐσία) whose essence (τί ἐστιν) needed to be defined, and Aristotle had missed the opportunity to do precisely that.[192] Finally, Philoponus also likened nature to soul, which, indeed, is a substance to the degree that it is, for Philoponus even more so than for Aristotle, an independent entity. The relation of soul to body is much more complicated than the relation between nature and body. If Philoponus, however, construes nature on the basis of its analogy to soul, he also imports at least some of these complications. This is precisely the Neoplatonic baggage behind Philoponus' redefinition.

None of these features passed unnoticed by Avicenna. So, apart from the minor point of criticism that Philoponus' account of nature is *bāṭil*, because it simply replaced every single word of Aristotle's definition by another virtually synonymous expression, Philoponus also committed a much graver error, because he situated nature within a Neoplatonic ontology and cosmology. Thus, Avicenna surmises that Philoponus used "power" instead of "principle" to define nature, precisely because he wanted to

---

188 cf. *al-Samāʿ al-ṭabīʿī* I.10, §2, 48.14; *al-Ḥikma al-mašriqiyya* III.4, 8.10f.

189 *Met.* Θ.8, 1049b5–10; cf. also *Met.* Δ.12, 1019a15f.; Θ.1, 1046a11; Λ.3, 1070a7f.; *Cael.* III.2, 301b17–19.

190 *Met.* Θ.1, 1046a19–29; cf. Makins' remarks in Aristotle, *Metaphysics*, xxx–xxxvi, 23; Beere, *Doing and Being*, ch. 3.

191 Macierowski and Hassing, "John Philoponus on Aristotle's Definition of Nature," 82, 86.

192 It seems that Aristotle simply "missed" the opportunity to do that, precisely because he did not conceive of nature as a substance whose essence had to be defined.

"escape" (*haraba*) the implication that nature taken as a principle would always be related too closely to the thing of which it is a principle:

قد حسب أنّه إذا قال قوّة فقد دلّ على ذات غير مضافة إلى شيء.

He [sc. Philoponus] reckoned that when he said "power," he had indicated an entity (*ḏāt*) that is not related to a thing (*ġayr muḍāfa ilā šay'*). (*al-Samā' al-ṭabī'ī* I.5, §7, 33.5f., tr. by McGinnis, modified)

Avicenna, too, charges Philoponus with the "reification" of nature, because on his reading, Philoponus wanted nature to be an active and substantial entity governing and shaping all natural affairs. So, when Philoponus defined nature as a "power which permeates through the bodies and which gives forms and shapes," he tried to describe the influence which nature as a universal entity (*ḏāt*) that is independent from the thing it moves (*ġayr muḍāfa ilā šay'*) has on that thing. This understanding of Avicenna's reading of Philoponus, as has been said, is plausible against the background of the Neoplatonic tradition. It is also plausible when Alexander's influential *Maqāla fī l-qawl fī mabādi' al-kull* is taken into consideration, for there, a single nature is likewise an independent power, even one that pervades through the universe as a whole and governs it like the single ruler governs a city. Although Alexander asserted that this ruler is not separate (*ġayr mufāriq lahā*) from the city, the ruler is nonetheless not entirely part of the city, either, and merely "resides in it" (*muqīm fīhā*), because he surely does not govern himself, even though he governs everything else. On this account, nature transcends the universe and the sum total of bodies just like soul transcends the body and can, thus, reasonably be regarded as a cosmic and self-sufficient substance. Moreover, the ruler of the city resembles the steersman of a ship and, again, introduces Platonic overtones that harmonise with Philoponus' conception of nature as the soul of the soulless.[193]

It is important to note that, presently, we are talking about two different kinds of "nature": one that is universal which governs the universe as a whole, preserving its order, and one that is particular, belonging to a single thing. The definition of nature given by Aristotle in *Physics* II clearly concerns a particular nature. It is the nature of stone or the nature of water which exists *in* a particular stone or a particular drop of water, serving as a principle of the motion of *that* stone or drop. The Stoic idea of an all-pervading πνεῦμα, which may be behind Alexander's understanding of nature, and the Neoplatonic cosmology of nature as the ἐνέργεια of a world-soul, which is behind Philoponus' conception, try to combine both a universal and a particular nature,

193 q.v. above, 223. Both examples reappear in Avicenna's *al-Nafs* and help Avicenna to underscore the soul's separability from the body and to stress his preference for regarding soul as a perfection (*kamāl*) rather than a mere form (*ṣūra*); cf. *al-Nafs* I.1, 7.2–4; cf. also Gutas, "Philoponus and Avicenna on the Separability of the Intellect"; Wisnovsky, *Avicenna's Metaphysics in Context*, ch. 6; Hasse, "The Early Albertus Magnus," 240-243.

because the universal is taken to be *in* the particular objects, as it *pervades through* or has *descended into* them, both of which are connotations of καταδεδυκυῖα and *sāriya*. Avicenna, however, is not only eager to keep these two notions apart, he even argues explicitly and vigorously against the idea of a universal nature. He maintains that although there is a universal conception of nature – for example, when we speak of the universal nature of water – it has existence only in the conceptualisation of our minds (*fī l-taṣawwur*) and not in concrete external reality (*fī l-aʿyān*). We can surely conceptualise the universal nature of water. Yet, this nature only has concrete existence insofar as it belongs to particulars (*lā wuǧūd illā li-l-ǧuzʾī*).[194] In his rejection of the universal notion of nature, Avicenna returns to the notions of a principle which is "permeating" (*sāriya*) all the bodies of a species or even the universe as a whole and which is involved in the governing (*tadbīr*) of all these bodies or the universe. His verdict about these notions is clear:

وليس من هذا شيء يجب أن يُصغى إليه فإنّه لا وجود إلّا للقوى المختلفة التي في القوابل.

There is nothing in this that one should pay attention to, for there is no existence other than that belonging to the various powers which are in the recipients. (*al-Samāʿ al-ṭabīʿī* I.7, §3, 39.8f.)

Avicenna's criticism of the conception of nature which he associates with Philoponus should not only be understood as a rejection of a different interpretation on the meaning of Aristotle's account. It is a rejection of a different ontology and cosmology: there simply is no single universal principle which, as such, pervades and governs more than one body or even the whole plurality of the universe. A universal nature, Avicenna writes, has no existence (*lā wuǧūd li-l-ṭabīʿa bi-hāḏā l-maʿnā*) – "there is absolutely no nature which is one in essence permeating different bodies" (*wa-lā takūnu l-battata ṭabīʿa wāḥidat al-māhiyya sāriya fī l-aǧsām al-uḫrā*).[195]

Furthermore, Avicenna's rejection of a universal nature is to be read in light of his differentiation between two sense of common, which I have discussed in the preceding chapter.[196] As is clear, Avicenna abstains from describing nature as numerically common in the first sense of *muštarak*, because there is no numerically single nature common to, and shared by, all natural things as there is one single God, being the First Principle of existence for all things. Nonetheless, all natural things have their own nature, just as they have their own matter and their own form, so that nature is common in the second, the generic, sense, i.e., common to all natural things in the sense of *ʿāmm*.

---

194 *al-Samāʿ al-ṭabīʿī* I.7, §2, 39.1–5; cf. *al-Ḥikma al-mašriqiyya* III.4, 11.21–12.4.

195 *al-Samāʿ al-ṭabīʿī* I.7, §3, 40.3. It is against this background that one has to read – with great care – Avicenna's remarks in *al-Samāʿ al-ṭabīʿī* I.1, §§4–16, 8.13–12.18; I.7, §4, 40.9–11; *al-Ilāhiyyāt* VI.5, §§22–23, 289.17–291.7.

196 q.v. above, 154ff.

Philoponus' account of a universal nature shared by and governing all natural things – as well as the account of all those who in a similar manner came to advocate this idea, for example, Alexander, al-Siǧistānī, Miskawayh, Abū Bišr, and others – is not only void (*bāṭil*) but eventually also corrupted (*fāsid*). To say that nature is a "a power permeating through the bodies which gives forms and shapes" is but a gross error. Contrary to this understanding, Avicenna defends, once more, a deflationary strategy. His understanding of nature as a power means "nothing but 'principle of producing motion,'" where "motion" should be taken as referring to all kinds of motion there are, i.e., motion in the categories of quantity, quality, place, position, and substance.[197]

It is now time to proceed with an investigation of Avicenna's own approach to nature, which I have already promised to be "as new and unprecedented as a Peripatetic account of the concept of nature could possibly be."

4.5 Avicenna's Account of Nature and its Relation to Soul

Among the first things Avicenna observes about Aristotle's definition of nature is this:

أنّها مبدأ لكلّ أمر ذاتي يكون للشيء من الحركة إن كانت والسكون إن كان.

> It [sc. nature] is a principle for any essential affair (*amr ḏātī*) which belongs to a thing in terms of motion, if there is [motion], and rest, if there is [rest]. (*al-Samāʿ al-ṭabīʿī* I.5, §5, 31.8)[198]

One might take this to be a rather plain or minor aspect of the efficacy of nature. It certainly is a remark one could easily pass over, but for Avicenna, it is the echo of a crucial feature of the classification of natural powers and of the definition of one particular power, viz., nature (*ṭabīʿa*). With this remark, Avicenna clarifies that nature does not always just act or bring about motion, but that it equally serves as a cause for rest and stability. It also implies that nature is not only productive of local motion but is a principle for *any* essential *amr* that may occur to a natural thing and that can further be categorised as either "motion" (*ḥaraka*) or "rest" (*sukūn*) – be it local motion, alteration, growth, and so on. Moreover, it spells out that nature is responsible for some thing's essential affair *whenever* it occurs, so that if there is motion, i.e., an essential motion, then nature is its principle, just as it is the principle of rest, i.e., essential rest, whenever there is some. We may, thus, say that nature as an efficient principle of natural things is in a way both variable and invariable. It is variable insofar as it does not simply and constantly produce motion but, instead, gives rise to two entirely opposite effects. It may stop producing motion and begin producing rest instead, should

197 cf. *al-Samāʿ al-ṭabīʿī* I.5, §8, 33.8–34.3; IV.9, §4, 302.2–7; cf. *al-Ḥikma al-mašriqiyya* III.4, 9.17f., 10.19–11.6; for Avicenna's discussion of the various kinds of motion, cf. *al-Samāʿ al-ṭabīʿī* II.3, esp. §20, 107.15–18; q.v. below, 340ff.

198 cf. *al-Ḥikma al-mašriqiyya* III.4, 9.17f., 10.19f.

rest, given certain conditions, be a more appropriate *amr* than motion for the *šay'* in question. Yet, at the same time it is highly invariable, because nature does not seem to have much of a choice, for it is not up to nature to decide when to act and when to stop acting. Nature simply re-acts and has brought about motion (or rest) whenever there is motion (or rest).

Towards the end of *al-Samāʿ al-ṭabīʿī*, in the ninth chapter of the fourth book, Avicenna expands upon this conception of nature's efficacy and successfully merges the two descriptions of nature as both variable and invariable into a single account. There, he writes the following:

ويجب أن يُعلَم أنّ قولنا حركة طبيعية ليس نعني به أنّ الحركة تصدر البتّة عن الطبيعة والطبيعة بحالها التي لها فان الطبيعة ذات ثابتة قارّة وما يصدر عنها لذاتها فهو أيضاً ثابت قارّ قائم موجود مع وجود الطبيعة. والحركة التي هي الحركة القطعية تُعدَم دائماً وتتجدّد دائماً بلا استقرار والحركة التي حقّقناها لا محالة فإنها تقتضي ترك شيء. والطبيعة إذا اقتضت لذاتها ترك شيء فتقتضي لا محالة ترك شيء خارج عن الطبيعة. وإذا كان كذلك فما لم يعرض أمر خارج عن الطبيعة لم يعرض قصد ترك لها بالطبع. فإذن الحركة الطبيعية لا تصدر عن الطبيعة إلّا وقد عرضت حال غير طبيعية.

It is necessary to know that with our talk of natural motion we do not mean that motion proceeds in an absolute way (*al-battata*) from the nature and through nature's state which belongs to it, for nature is a stable, fixed entity (*ḏāt ṯābita qārra*) and whatever proceeds from it through [nature] itself, then, is also stable, fixed, subsisting, and existing together with the existence of the nature. The motion which is a traversal motion, however, constantly perishes and constantly is renewed without abiding (*tuʿdamu dā'iman wa-tataǧaddadu dā'iman bi-lā stiqrār*). The motion which we are [currently] investigating undoubtedly [does so as well], for it requires leaving something behind (*taqtaḍī tark šay'*). When the nature through itself requires leaving something behind, then it undoubtedly requires leaving behind something which is external to the nature (*šay' ḫāriǧ ʿan al-ṭabīʿa*). If it is like that, then whenever nothing external to the nature occurs, no intention for leaving [something] behind will naturally occur to it. Therefore, natural motion does not proceed from the nature unless an unnatural state (*ḥāl ġayr ṭābīʿīa*) has happened to occur. (*al-Samāʿ al-ṭabīʿī* IV.9, §5, 302.8–13, tr. by McGinnis, modified)[199]

This passage corresponds to the above remark from *al-Samāʿ al-ṭabīʿī* I.5. Here in chapter IV.9, Avicenna says of motion that it is something unstable and under constant renewal (*taǧaddud*).[200] Motion thus described cannot proceed from nature just as it is, because nature is best depicted in exactly opposite terms as stable and fixed (*ṯābita qārra*), i.e., as something which is constant and invariable. In other words, the effect of nature must remain one and the same throughout, because nature itself is stable and fixed, and invariably remains one and the same. As we have already seen above, this invariable effect is an inclination towards the natural state, and the natural state never changes and is invariably one and the same. This inclination and striving towards the

199 cf. *al-Ilāhiyyāt* IX.2, §1, 381.15–382.7.

200 This crucial feature will become important in Avicenna's account of time; q.v. below, 429ff.

natural state also implies that there has to be something which is left behind through the motion. So, every rectilinear motion – and, consequently, every natural motion – involves leaving something behind (*tark*). What is left behind must be an unnatural state. The only effect, then, which comes about through the nature of a thing is a striving to the thing's natural state from an unnatural state – and this striving results in either motion, if the thing is not yet at its natural state, or rest, if its natural place has been attained. It is this striving (*al-ṭalab*) either to get to or to stay at the natural state which Avicenna calls "natural inclination" (*al-mayl al-ṭabīʿī*). When something is inclined to something else, it strives and aims towards it and, having it as its goal, will attempt to get there without indirection and as quickly as possible or, upon having reached it, will try to stay there as long as possible. A heavy stone, for example, will try to resist through its weight any attempt at moving it away from its natural place just as a bowl of water will resist any heating and remain at its natural temperature, unless subjugated by a burning fire. As soon as the fire goes out, it will immediately start cooling again. Thus, not just any effect will result from nature through nature's power to strive but only one single and determinate motion, viz., that back to the natural state, or, alternatively, one single and determinate rest, viz., that in the natural state. The production of motion and the production of rest are, thus, one and the same thing: they are the two sides of the single coin of nature's striving.[201]

Moreover, this motion and rest do not come about under any circumstance whatsoever but only when the natural body is not situated in its natural state or when it precisely is, respectively. A stone has only one natural place and this is down. Whenever a stone is down, it is at rest and there is no need for it to be in motion. Whenever a stone is down and has been warmed up during a sunny day, it may spatially be at its natural place but not with regard to one of its qualities, viz., its temperature, and so during the night, the stone, while still being at its natural place in spatial terms, also cools down and returns to its natural state with regard to its temperature.[202] What Avicenna wants to emphasise is that nature is stable and fixed, because it is directed towards one thing and one thing only – and this is the natural state (*ḥāl ṭābīʿiyya*) in the respective categories of place, quantity, quality, or position of that thing in which it is:

فتكون غير الطبيعية تترك تركاً متوجّهاً إلى الطبيعية. فكلّ حركة طبيعية إذا لم تُعق فهي تنتهي إلى غاية طبيعية. ويستحيل إذا حصلت تلك الغاية أن يتحرّك المتحرّك بالحركة الطبيعية لأنّ الحركة ترك ما وهرب والغاية الطبيعية ليست متروكة ولا مهروباً عنها بالطبع. فكلّ حركة طبيعية إذن فهي لأجل طلب سكون إمّا في اين أو في كيف أو في كمّ أو في وضع.

---

201 cf. *ʿUyūn al-ḥikma* II.9, 29.3–6; *al-Naǧāt* II.2.3, 213.3–5 ≈ *al-Ḥikma al-ʿArūḍiyya* II.2.2, 124.10–12; *Dānešnāme-ye ʿAlāʾī* III.5, 12.6f.; *al-Hidāya* II.2, 173.7–12; *al-Išārāt wa-l-tanbīhāt* II.2.10, 111.11–14.

202 Avicenna seems to employ the term *ḥāl* ("state," "condition") in the above passage from *al-Samāʿ al-ṭabīʿī* IV.9 deliberately, in order to capture the meaning of nature as a principle for *any* kind of motion.

So it is what is not natural (*ġayr al-ṭabīʿiyya*) which it [sc. nature] leaves behind, leaving it behind as directed towards what is natural (*tarkan mutawağğihan ilā l-ṭabīʿiyya*). Thus, every natural motion, if unimpeded, terminates at a natural end (*ġāya ṭabīʿiyya*). It is impossible, once that end is realised, that the moved should undergo natural motion, because the motion is some leaving behind and fleeing (*li-anna l-ḥaraka tark mā wa-harab*), whereas the natural end is not something that is naturally left behind and fled from. So, every natural motion is, therefore, for the sake of seeking rest (*ṭalab sukūn*) either in a place, a quality, a quantity, or a position. (*al-Samāʿ al-ṭabīʿī* IV.9, §5, 302.14–17, tr. by McGinnis, modified)[203]

The terms that recur in Avicenna's descriptions of nature's efficacy are *tark* ("leaving behind, departing"), *ṭalab* ("desire, seeking"), and *harab* ("flight, fleeing"). It is these terms which represent the single uniform course of nature and designate nature as a stable, fixed entity (*ḏāt ṯābita qārra*), for nature does nothing but one thing: it strives to make the thing in which it is be in its natural state through seeking its natural state and, once unimpeded, returning to it by leaving behind its unnatural state and, once arrived at its natural state, producing rest. On that note, Avicenna can aptly epitomise his account in his *al-Naǧāt* along the following lines:

وكلّ حركة بالطبيعة فهي هرب بالطبع عن حال فكلّ ما كان كذلك فهو عن حالة غير ملائمة. فإذاً كلّ حركة بالطبيعة عن حالة غير ملائمة وهذه الحركة ينبغي أن تكون مستقيمة إن كانت في المكان لأنّ هذه الحركة لميل طبيعي وكلّ ميل طبيعي فعلى أقرب مسافة وكلّما كان على أقرب مسافة فهو على خطّ مستقيم.

Every motion by nature is a natural fleeing from a state (*harab bi-l-ṭabʿ ʿan ḥāl*). So, all that which is like that, then, is from an inadequate state (*ʿan ḥāla ġayr mulāʾima*). Therefore, every motion by nature is from an inadequate state and this motion requires that it is rectilinear (*mustaqīma*) if it is in [the category of] place, because this motion is due to a natural inclination (*li-mayl ṭabīʿī*) and every natural inclination, then, is along the shortest distance (*aqrab masāfa*), and all that is along the shortest distance is also along a rectilinear line (*ʿalā ḫaṭṭ mustaqīm*). (*al-Naǧāt* II.2.3, 213.3–7 ≈ *al-Ḥikma al-ʿArūḍiyya* II.2.2, 124.10–15)[204]

That natural motion is, and in fact cannot but be, rectilinear and straight, returning to the natural state as quickly as possible, is a claim which Avicenna would like to see extended to all kinds of motion. When he, in the present passage, seems to restrict it only to local motion, he does so only because the terms *mustaqīm* ("straight, rectilinear"),

---

203 cf. also *al-Samāʿ al-ṭabīʿī* IV.12, §1, 313.14–314.11; *al-Naǧāt* II.2.3, 212.7–214.6.

204 cf. *al-Naǧāt* IV.2.15, 578.4–580.2, which is for the most part a verbatim quote of *al-Mabdaʾ wa-l-maʿād* I.20, 27.22–28.15; cf. also *ʿUyūn al-ḥikma* II.9, 31.1–3; *Dānešnāme-ye ʿAlāʾī* III.5, 12.8–13.9; 13, 27.4–8; *al-Hidāya* II.2, 173.7–174.5; *al-Išārāt wa-l-tanbīhāt* II.2.10, 111.11–14; 14, 112.8–16; cf. further Philoponus, *In An.*, 65.34–38. It is remarkable that in the commentary on *De anima*, Philoponus adhered to a theory of natural motions that is contrary to the one developed in his commentary on the *Physics*; cf. Wolff, *Fallgesetz und Massebegriff*, 70–72, 79–81. This becomes especially apparent when *In An.*, 65.32–34, is compared to *In Phys.*, 195.24–29. Wolff remarks that this could be a reason for regarding the commentary on the *De anima* as antedating that on the *Physics* (Wolff, *Fallgesetz und Massebegriff*, 79f.); cf. also Sorabji's chronological table of Philoponus' works in Sorabji, *Philoponus and the Rejection of Aristotelian Science*, 81.

masāfa ("distance"), and *ḫaṭṭ* ("line") seem to fit best with spatial trajectory and projection. If these words would be semantically applicable to qualitative change, Avicenna would have no quarrel with describing the return of hot water to its natural cold temperature as a natural motion that covers the distance between hot and cold along a rectilinear line, because water, as is clear, cools down steadily and continuously, takes the quickest way possible, and does not halt, pause, or suddenly get warmer again just by itself.[205]

Moreover, ever since Aristotle, local motion was the paradigm for describing motion, as most features of motion are best observed in local motion. What is more, local motion is also most important and, in fact, is the primary sort of motion, for the motion that is truly first is the circular motion of the heavens.[206] In *al-Ilāhiyyāt* IX.2, Avicenna provides a long argument to establish that precisely because nature can only bring about a motion which is "along a rectilinear line," the motions of the heavens must be unnatural in the sense of not being the effect of an innate nature.[207] They are only

205 The terms "steadily" and "continuously" are not meant to imply a constant speed nor a constant acceleration and merely express the idea that the water does get colder without stopping or reversing its direction towards coldness. In the same way, a falling stone does not stop nor does it reverse its direction; it simply falls. The phenomena of speed and acceleration are different aspects which, however, have a subordinate role in Avicenna's theory and do not seem to be fully worked out. According to M. Rashed one ought "to distinguish sharply between the 'general' impulsion of a given body towards its natural place (*mayl*-1), and the 'concrete' impulsion of this body at a certain instant (*mayl*-2)" (M. Rashed, "Natural Philosophy," 297). However, it is not clear how M. Rashed's advice concurs with Avicenna's insistence that there are not two inclinations in one single natural object; cf. *al-Samāʿ al-ṭabīʿī* IV.8, §18, 299.7. Rather, it seems that we, once again, need to distinguish properly between the principle of the inclination, i.e., nature, and the inclination itself. Nature strives towards its natural place, thus producing one single inclination. This inclination can vary in intensity and the object may, thus, accelerate, because the distance between the object and its natural place constantly changes throughout the motion. This changing factor seems to account for the acceleration of speed in natural motions and changes. Although Nony has pointed towards an interesting remark in Avicenna's *al-Mubāḥaṯāt*, it seems that Avicenna owes us a full explanation of the phenomenon of acceleration; cf. Nony, "Two Arabic Theories of Impetus," 21f., referring to *al-Mubāḥaṯāt*, §677.

206 However, the primary kind of motion, for Avicenna, is no longer local motion but rather motion in respect of position (and not place); q.v. below 340ff.; cf. also McGinnis, "Positioning Heaven," 159.

207 Much of this discussion corresponds, literally, to *al-Naǧāt* IV.2.27–30, 617.13–636.8, and partially to *al-Mabdaʾ wa-l-maʿād* I.39–41, 52.21–54.23; cf. *al-Išārāt wa-l-tanbīhāt* II.3.26, 135.9–15. Even though Avicenna holds Alexander's *Maqāla fī l-qawl fī mabādiʾ al-kull* in high esteem, this argument is probably directed against Alexander, who called the soul of the animate bodies their nature and, thus, claimed the heavenly motions, which come about through a natural inclination due to the planets' souls, to be natural; cf. Alexander of Aphrodisias, *Maqāla fī l-qawl fī mabādiʾ al-kull*, §§16–23, 52.3–56.2 (ed. Genequand); Alexander *apud* Simplicium, *In Phys.*, 1219.1–11; cf. also Simplicius, *In Cael.*, 380.29–31, 387.14; Philoponus, *In An.*, 138.18–22; cf. further Pines, "Omne quod movetur necesse est ab aliquo moveri," 44f.; Wolfson, "The Problem of the Souls of the Spheres from the Byzantine Commentaries on Aristotle through the Arabs and St. Thomas to Kepler," esp. 72f.; Berti, "Il movimento del cielo in Alessandro di Afrodisia"; M. Rashed's remarks in Alexander of Aphrodisias, *Commentaire perdu à la*

equivocally called "natural," as he quickly adds.[208] Instead, Avicenna aims at showing "that the proximate mover of the heavens is neither a nature nor an intellect but a soul," as the title of the chapter has it.[209] In his discussion, he employs much of the same terminology we have encountered in the quotations from *al-Samāʿ al-ṭabīʿī* and *al-Naǧāt*, and above all once again describes natural motion as a *harab* from a non-natural state.[210]

The reason that nature is incapable of producing a circular motion is that on a circle there is no real natural state to which to return nor an unnatural state from which to flee. If there were, then the circular motion would come to rest once the natural state has been attained. Circular motion, however, is continuous and does not come to rest, and so the circular motion of the heavenly spheres cannot be due to their natures.[211] This is also affirmed by Avicenna in his *al-Samāʿ al-ṭabīʿī*:

فكلّ حركة لا تسكن فليست بطبيعية فالحركة المستديرة المتّصلة إذن لا تكون طبيعية وكيف تكون؟ ... فالحركة المستديرة تكون إمّا من أسباب من خارج وإمّا عن قوّة غير الطبع بل قوّة إرادية.

So, every motion that does not come to rest, then, is not natural (*laysat bi-ṭabīʿiyya*), and so the continuous circular motion is, therefore, not natural – how could it be? ... So, circular motion either results from[212] external causes or from an unnatural power – indeed, a volitional power (*quwwa irādiyya*). (*al-Samāʿ al-ṭabīʿī* IV.9, §6, 302.17–303.3, tr. by McGinnis, modified)[213]

In distinguishing circular motion from rectilinear motion, Avicenna also differentiates between nature and soul and, more precisely, between natural powers and volitional powers. The idea of volitional and non-volitional powers is one of the two keys to Avicenna's own account of nature, as will now be shown.

Physique *d'Aristote*, 126–140. A possible source of inspiration may have been the Ps.-Aristotelian *De mundo*; cf. also the discussion in Twetten, "Aristotelian Cosmology and Causality in Classical Arabic Philosophy and Its Greek Background," 319–324. Recently, Belo published the following either self-contradictory or incomprehensible assertion: "This [sc. nature as a power in natural bodies] *includes* the movements of the celestial spheres, or the movement of plants when they grow and the movements of animals (so *excluding* the celestial, the vegetative and the animal soul respectively)" ("The Concept of 'Nature' in Aristotle, Avicenna and Averroes," 50, emphasis added).

208 *al-Ilāhiyyāt* IX.2, §§3–4, 383.1–12 ≈ *al-Naǧāt* IV.2.28, 619.12–620.9 ≈ *al-Mabdaʾ wa-l-maʿād* I.40, 53.21–54.10.

209 *al-Ilāhiyyāt* IX.2, 381.15, tr. by Marmura. Some aspects of Avicenna's argument resemble what we read in Ps.-al-Fārābī's *ʿUyūn al-masāʾil*, esp. §10, 59.18–60.4; §17, 62.10–12.

210 *al-Ilāhiyyāt* IX.2, §2, 382.8–1 ≈ *al-Naǧāt* IV.2.27, 618.13–619.9; cf. *al-Mabdaʾ wa-l-maʿād* I.39, 53.14–18.

211 Aristotle himself showed that circles do not have any beginning or end point, or, more precisely, any point that is more worthy of being called a beginning or end; cf. esp. *De caelo* I.4.

212 Reading *min* with Mss. Leiden or. 4 and or. 84 as well as Zāyid for the emendation *ʿan* suggested in McGinnis and Āl Yāsīn.

213 Again and just like in *al-Ilāhiyyāt* IX.2, *al-Naǧāt* IV.2.28, and *al-Mabdaʾ wa-l-maʿād* I.40, Avicenna is quick to add that "nature" can be said in many more or less equivocal ways; cf. *al-Samāʿ al-ṭabīʿī* IV.9, §§7–8, 303.10–304.16.

The Fourfold Classification of Natural Powers

Avicenna begins his account of nature in *al-Samāʿ al-ṭabīʿī* I.5 with a general distinction between those acts and motions (*afʿāl wa-ḥarakāt*) of natural bodies which proceed from, and are necessitated by, external causes (*ʿan asbāb ḫāriğa*), on the one hand, and those which come to be from the bodies themselves (*li-anfusihā*) without any relation to a further cause foreign to the bodies (*sabab ġarīb*), on the other.[214] He, then, focuses on this latter group of internal, i.e., not externally effected and not extrinsically influenced, motions and draws two further distinctions:

ثمّ الذي يكون عن ذاتها لا من خارج فنحن في أوّل النظر نجوّز أن يكون بعضه لازماً طريقة واحدة لا ينحرف عنها وبعضه يكون متفنّن الطرائق مختلفة الوجوه. ومع ذلك فنجوّز أن يكون كلّ واحد من الوجهين صادراً بإرادة وصادراً لا عن إرادة.

> Further, that which is from themselves (*ʿan ḏātihī*) and not from without, upon immediate inspection[215] we allow some of it to be following a single course (*lāziman ṭarīqata wāḥidata*) from which it does not deviate and some others to be manifold in [their] courses[216] and diverse in [their] ways (*mutafannin al-ṭarāʾiq muḫtalifa al-wuğūh*). In addition to that, we allow that each of these two cases may be something which proceeds by volition (*bi-irāda*) or something which proceeds not from volition (*lā ʿan irāda*).[217] (*al-Samāʿ al-ṭabīʿī* I.5, §2, 29.11–13)[218]

So, of all those acts and motions that seem somehow to result from natural bodies themselves, some appear to be with and others without volition, while again of all those acts and motions some are invariable, uniform, and always the same, whereas others are manifold, diverse, and unpredictable. Now, the important point is that, observing natural motions, Avicenna adds the following:

أنّه من الظاهر أنّ المحرّك لا يصحّ أن يكون جسماً بما هو جسم إنّما يحرّك بقوّة فيه.

> It is obvious that the mover (*al-muḥarrik*) cannot rightly [be said to] be the body insofar as it is a body; it produces motion only through a power in [the body] (*innamā yuḥarriku bi-quwwa fīhi*). (*al-Samāʿ al-ṭabīʿī* I.5, §2, 30.5f., tr. by McGinnis, modified)

With this, Avicenna specifies more exactly what he meant above by motions which are from the bodies themselves (*ʿan ḏātihī*). If the motions and acts were from the bodies themselves as direct results of the natural body insofar as it is a body, then every body would behave the same way and there would be only one kind of motion instead of

---

214 *al-Samāʿ al-ṭabīʿī* I.5, §1, 29.4–11, cf. *al-Ḥikma al-mašriqiyya* III.4, 9.20–10.3.

215 Reading *al-naẓar* with Mss. Leiden or. 4 and or. 84, and Zāyid for *al-amr* in McGinnis and Āl Yāsīn.

216 Reading *mutafannin al-ṭarāʾiq* with Mss. Leiden or. 4 and or. 84 for *mufannin al-ṭarāʾiq* in McGinnis and Zāyid, and *al-ṭarāʾiq* in Āl Yāsīn.

217 Reading *lā ʿan irāda* with Mss. Leiden or. 4 and or. 84 as well as McGinnis and Āl Yāsīn for *illā ʿan irāda* in Zāyid.

218 cf. *al-Ḥikma al-mašriqiyya* III.4, 10.4–9.

the many kinds of motion which Avicenna has just distinguished.[219] Consequently, the motion must be due to another aspect, i.e., a feature *of* the body, one which is not due to corporeality itself but is something additionally belonging to body. Such an additional factor which is responsible for motion, however, is what is called a "power," for a power, as we could already see above, is, at least since Aristotle's *Metaphysics* Θ, a principle of motion. Thus, motion must come about through a power – or through powers – different from the body insofar as it is body.[220]

What powers, though, could be responsible for this variety of motions? In answering this, Avicenna takes recourse to the two distinctions he drew earlier and combines them so as to categorise within a single schema all those motions that do not come about through any sort of an external influence but truly are the result of something within the bodies themselves (*ʿan ḏātihī*).[221] In this schema, he enumerates the following kinds of powers:

i) a power which produces motion and change, and from which the act proceeds in a single manner without volition (*quwwa tuḥarriku wa-tuġayyiru wa-yaṣduru ʿanhā l-fiʿl ʿalā nahǧ wāḥid min ġayr irāda*),
ii) a power just like that but with volition (*maʿa irāda*),
iii) a power manifold in the production of motion, the act being without volition (*quwwa mutafannina al-taḥrīk wa-l-fiʿl min ġayr irāda*), and
iv) a power just like that but with volition (*maʿa irāda*).[222]

Avicenna, then, asserts that each of these four powers apply to and explain a number of phenomena in the natural world. Moreover, each has already been given a name:

> فالأوّل من الأقسام كما للحجر في هبوطه ووقوفه في الوسط ويُسمّى طبيعةً. والثاني كما للشمس في دورانها ... ويُسمّى نفساً فلكيةً. والثالث كما للنباتات في تكوّنها ونشوئها ووقوفها ... ويُسمّى نفساً نباتيةً. والرابع كما للحيوان ويُسمّى نفساً حيوانيةً.
>
> The first of [these] kinds is like what belongs to the stone in its falling and its stopping at the centre, and is called "nature" (*ṭabīʿatan*). The second is like what belongs to the Sun in its rotations ...

219 This claim must be read in light of Avicenna's distinction in *al-Samāʿ al-ṭabīʿī* I.2, §3, 13.13f., between principles that pertain to the natural body insofar as it is a body and those that pertain to it insofar as it is subject to change. This is most explicit in *Dānešnāme-ye ʿAlāʾī* II.2, 6.5–10; cf. also *al-Samāʿ al-ṭabīʿī* IV.12, §1, 313.14–314.11.

220 Avicenna's discussion here at the beginning of *al-Samāʿ al-ṭabīʿī* I.5 corresponds to the longer argument in *al-Ilāhiyyāt* IV.2, §§20–23, 179.4–181.10, which constitutes Avicenna's proof for the existence of nature; cf. also *ʿUyūn al-ḥikma* III.3, 49.17–50.12; *al-Naǧāt* IV.1.13, 526.1–529.2; *al-Ḥikma al-mašriqiyya* III.4, 9.20–10.12.

221 For the following, cf. *al-Nafs* I.1, 5.6–10; I.5, 32.7f.; II.3, 58.18–59.8; *ʿUyūn al-ḥikma* II.2, 18.2–6; *al-Naǧāt* II.1.1, 194.2–195.3 ≈ *al-Ḥikma al-ʿArūḍiyya* II.1, 115.14–116.1; *Dānešnāme-ye ʿAlāʾī* III.2, 6.9–7.5; *al-Hidāya* II.1, 139.1–6; *al-Ḥikma al-mašriqiyya* III.4, 10.4–16; *al-Išārāt wa-l-tanbīhāt* II.2.1, esp. 106.12; II.2.5; II.3.24–26; cf. also Ps.-al-Fārābī, *ʿUyūn al-masāʾil*, §13, 60.20–23.

222 *al-Samāʿ al-ṭabīʿī* I.5, §3, 30.7–9.

> and is called "celestial soul" (*nafsan falakiyyatan*). The third is like what belongs to plants in their generation, growth, and stopping [to grow further] ... and is called "vegetative soul" (*nafsan nabātiyyatan*). The fourth is like what belongs to animals and is called "animal soul" (*nafsan ḥayawāniyyatan*). (*al-Samāʿ al-ṭabīʿī* I.5, §3, 30.9–12, tr. by McGinnis, modified)

The movements of animals, rational and non-rational alike, involve volition and are, thus, characterised as manifold, diverse, and somewhat unpredictable. A horse may first drink and then eat or do it the other way around; moreover, it may turn left or right, it may go uphill or downhill, forwards or backwards, so that there is nothing uniform in its movement, i.e., the horse does not have a determined direction to go downhill or to turn right or to always eat before drinking. All these movements, of course, are movements of an animal insofar as it is the animal it is. A horse surely may have to *fall* downhill, due to the elemental composition of its body, but it surely does not have to *trot* downhill. Instead, as Avicenna remarks, "we find that animals through their volition act freely (*tataṣarrafu*) in their kinds of movements."[223]

The situation is different in the case of plants. Although plants grow in various directions – their roots go down, their leaves go up, their branches may be widely ramified – they do not "act freely" (*tataṣarrafu*) and decide, as it were, in which direction they intend to grow their roots.[224] So, both kinds of movements, i.e., those of animals and those of plants, have something in common insofar as they are not along a single determinate direction, yet they differ insofar as the former involves volition and the latter does not. The power governing the former kind of movement, then, is called "animal soul" (*al-nafs al-ḥayawāniyya*), whereas the latter is called "vegetative soul" (*al-nafs al-nabātiyya*).

The motion of the Sun, as well as that of other planets, by contrast, is not manifold, but is uniformly always the same, as the Sun travels in a perfect circle around the earth, moving at a fixed pace in a continuous motion. It is not to be expected that it will change its course anytime soon or shift its speed or alter its direction. In fact, such a change is even altogether impossible.[225] At the same time, Avicenna is eager to show that the planets' motion is not due to a nature. He argues for this at length in his metaphysics, as has already been mentioned. This discussion is foreshadowed in *al-Samāʿ al-ṭabīʿī* IV.9, as we have already seen. Unlike the animal soul, however, the celestial volition (*irāda*) always has only one intention, as it is invariably directed towards the same end, and so always follows the same course, whereas an animal may

223 *al-Samāʿ al-ṭabīʿī* I.5, §1, 29.8, tr. by McGinnis; cf. *al-Naǧāt* IV.1.2, 494.7f.; cf. also *Eth. Nic.* III.3, 1111a25f.; III.4, 1111b8–10.

224 In *al-Samāʿ al-ṭabīʿī* III.13, §8, 250.5–14, Avicenna argues that plants have only two natural directions, viz., up and down, and that animals are the only things that naturally also have a forward and a backward direction.

225 In these remarks, questions about epicycles, retrogradation, seemingly different speeds, and so on, are left out of consideration, obviously.

pursue various, and over time even opposed, ends. In contrast to the vegetative soul, however, it *wills* its motion, even though the motion it wills is always the same.[226]

Finally, there is yet another motive power which brings about a non-manifold, but also non-volitional, motion – and this is nature. Clearly, Avicenna regards nature as comparable to soul given that both soul and nature belong to the genus "power" insofar as they are both principles for motion.[227] In this, he could be said to follow the tradition of Alexander and Philoponus, who aligned nature with soul. Yet, Avicenna is more concerned with *distinguishing* nature from soul, rather than comparing or reducing one to the other. Nature, then, has only one single purpose that it fulfils, and it does not get to choose when and under which conditions it has to do so. It always, and constantly, drives its body back to its natural place, if we are talking about local motion, or to its natural states, if we consider qualitative or quantitative alteration, whenever that body is unimpeded and removed from its natural place or state.

Tab. 4.1: Avicenna's fourfold classification of natural powers.

	without volition	**with volition**
uniform	nature (e.g., in a stone)	celestial soul (e.g., in the Sun)
non-uniform	vegetative soul (e.g., in a tree)	animal soul (e.g., in a horse)

As before, Avicenna is quick to add that the other three kinds of powers may equivocally be called "natural," for the term "nature" may be applied to everything from which some act (*fiʿl*) proceeds – and so a spider may be said to weave "naturally" (*bi-l-ṭabʿ*). Yet, Avicenna states, it should be clear that there is only one nature in the strict sense:

لكنّ الطبيعة التي بها الأجسام الطبيعية طبيعية والتي نريد أن نفحص عنها هاهنا هي الطبيعة بالمعنى الأوّل.

However, the nature by which natural bodies are natural (*ṭabīʿiyya*) and that which we intend to examine here is the nature in the first sense. (*al-Samāʿ al-ṭabīʿī* I.5, §3, 30.15f., tr. by McGinnis, modified)

226 With regards to the celestial soul being one of the four natural powers, Avicenna may also have been influenced by Ptolemy. In the *Kitāb fī l-hayʾa al-musammā l-Iqtiṣāṣ*, an Arabic version of his *Planetary Hypotheses*, we read that Ptolemy explained the motion of the heavenly spheres by taking recourse to a "psychological power" (*quwwa nafsāniyya*; 40.23f.) – a term which also occurs in *al-Ilāhiyyāt* IX.2. Although Janos claims that Avicenna eventually opted for a different explanatory model, Ptolemy's passage could have contributed to Avicenna's uniform picture of natural causation which covers both terrestrial and celestial, inanimate and animate motion within a single fourfold schema; cf. also Janos, "Moving the Orbs," esp. 189f. This conforms nicely to the above claim that the fact that Avicenna considers both celestial and terrestrial bodies to consist of the same kind of prime matter bespeaks his intention to provide a unified physics for the entire universe; q.v. above, 200.

227 cf. also *al-Nafs* I.1, 6.14–18, 7.6–8.

To be sure, Avicenna draws upon previous materials, but the precise systematic character of his approach towards classifying natural powers seems to be entirely novel and unprecedented.[228] Some of the materials that form the backbone of his classification may stem from Aristotle's discussion of chance in *Physics* II.4–6, where chance is usually contrasted with nature.[229] In the brief discussion of chance in the *Rhetoric*, Aristotle asserts:

> φύσει δὲ ὅσων ἥ τ' αἰτία ἐν αὐτοῖς καὶ τεταγμένη· ἢ γὰρ ἀεὶ ἢ ὡς ἐπὶ τὸ πολὺ ὡσαύτως ἀποβαίνει.
> فأمّا التي تكون بالطبيعة فكلّ التي تكون العلّة فهنّ ثابتة راتبة وهنّ متّفقات لكنّ هذا إمّا دائماً وإمّا بالأكثر.
> Those things happen by nature which have a fixed (τεταγμένη, *ṯābita rātiba*) and internal cause; they take place uniformly (ὡσαύτως, *muttafiqāt*), either always or for the most part. (*Rhet.* I.10, 1369a35–b2, tr. by Roberts)[230]

Here, nature is understood as a stable and uniform principle which brings about natural results "always or for the most part," whereas chance does not. The beginning of the second book of the *Nicomachean Ethics* may also be relevant:

> οὐθὲν γὰρ τῶν φύσει ὄντων ἄλλως ἐθίζεται, οἷον ὁ λίθος φύσει κάτω φερόμενος οὐκ ἂν ἐθισθείη ἄνω φέρεσθαι, οὐδ' ἂν μυριάκις αὐτὸν ἐθίζῃ τις ἄνω ῥιπτῶν, οὐδὲ τὸ πῦρ κάτω, οὐδ' ἄλλο οὐδὲν τῶν ἄλλως πεφυκότων ἄλλως ἂν ἐθισθείη.

228 It is, thus, appropriate to regard the *ʿUyūn al-masāʾil* of Ps.-al-Fārābī as deriving from an Avicennian circle; cf. *ʿUyūn al-masāʾil*, §13, 60.20–23; q.v. above, 37. This being said, there certainly have been earlier and not entirely dissimilar attempts to provide a clear and systematic differentiation of the quality of actions brought about by inanimate objects, non-rational animals, humans, or God. One striking example in this regard is the third/ninth century Jewish-Christian back-and-forth convert and theologian Dāwūd ibn Marwān al-Muqammaṣ, who describes the action of fire and of animals such as the silk worm by saying that they can perform "always only one act" (*fiʿl wāḥid abadan*), which proceeds from their respective nature (*ṭabʿ fī ġarīza wa-ṭibāʿ*), in contrast to the free action of human beings on the basis of *iḫtiyār* (*ʿIšrūn maqālatan* 12, §§21–23, 271.5–273.9); cf. Stroumsa, "From the Earliest Known Judaeo-Arabic Commentary on Genesis." (I am grateful to Peter Tarras for bringing this work to my attention.) It is clear that notions such as the "nature" of inanimate as well as animate, human, and divine beings or as the "will," the "volition," and the "voluntary action" are complex; that they, as philosophical concepts, generated huge amounts of literature from among various religious and pagan contexts; and that many of them also influenced pre-Avicennian debates within Arabic and Islamic circles, thus probably also shaping Avicenna's views on them. Studying these notions and their development seems to be an almost insurmountable task. In the following, I shall limit myself to only few points predominantly from the Peripatetic tradition, in order to indicate certain aspects that quite *immediately* contributed to Avicenna's systematic classification of nature and soul, in order to show both that Avicenna's classification did not come out of nowhere and that it is novel in its specific application of the two distinctions between volitional and non-volitional as well as variable and invariable motions. Besides, all the following aspects certainly also informed the just-mentioned pre-Avicennian debates, thus constituting the common ground of developments of the conceptions of natural and voluntary actions in the history of philosophy and theology.

229 cf. also *Phys.* II.8, 198b34–36.

230 cf. *Rhet.* I.11, 1370a3–27; cf. also Wolfson, *The Philosophy of the Kalam*, 547f.

ومن هذا يتبيّن أنّه ليس شيئاً من الفضائل الخلقية يكون فينا بالطبع على حال من الأحوال ويعوّد أن يكون على خلافها مثال ذلك أنّ الحجر يهبط إلى أسفل بالطبع فلو أنّ رامياً رمى به إلى فوق مراراً لا تحصى كثيرة يريد بذلك أن يعوّده الحركة إلى فوق لمّا اعتاد عليه وكذلك النار لا تعتلد أن تحرّك إلى أسفل ولا شيء من الأشياء المطبوعة على حال من الأحوال حالاً غيرها.

Nothing that exists by nature is changed through habituation, as for example the stone, which by nature moves downwards, will not be habituated into moving upwards, even if someone tries to make it so by throwing it upwards ten thousand times, nor will fire move downwards, nor will anything else that is by nature some way (τῶν ἄλλως πεφυκότων, *šay' min al-ašyā' al-maṭbū'a*) be habituated into behaving in another. (*Eth. Nic.* II.1, 1103a19–23, tr. by Rowe, modified)

According to this passage, natural occurrences, as opposed to ethical behaviour and psychologically motivated action, are not only uniform but altogether unchangeable, necessarily and always following the same course. Aristotle's discussion in *Physics* V.4 may also have contributed to the distinction between uniform and non-uniform motion, since in this chapter, Aristotle, apart from mentioning heaviness and lightness (βαρύτης καὶ κουφότης, *al-ṯiql aw al-ḫiffa*) as well as circular and linear motion, asserts the following:

ἔστιν δὲ ἐν ἁπάσῃ κινήσει τὸ ὁμαλῶς ἢ μή· καὶ γὰρ ἂν ἀλλοιοῖτο ὁμαλῶς, καὶ φέροιτο ἐφ' ὁμαλοῦ οἷον κύκλου ἢ εὐθείας, καὶ περὶ αὔξησιν ὡσαύτως καὶ φθίσιν. ἀνωμαλία δ' ἐστὶν διαφορὰ ὁτὲ μὲν ἐφ' ᾧ κινεῖται ... ἡ δὲ οὔτε ἐν τῷ ὅ οὔτ' ἐν τῷ πότε οὔτε ἐν τῷ εἰς ὅ, ἀλλ' ἐν τῷ ὥς.

وفي كلّ حركة يكون الاستواء والخروج عن الاستواء فإنّه قد تستحيل باستواء الشيء بالسواء وقد تنتقل من قبل شيء على استواء مثل أن تنتقل على دائرة أو على خطّ مستقيم. وكذلك في باب النموّ النقص.

In every kind of motion there may be uniformity or not (τὸ ὁμαλῶς ἢ μή, *al-istiwā' wa-l-ḫurūǧ 'an al-istiwā'*), for there may be uniform alteration and locomotion in a uniform path, like in a circle or on a straight line, and likewise for growth and diminution. (*Phys.* V.4, 228b19–21, tr. by Hardie/Gaye, modified.)

In addition, Aristotle's colleague and successor Theophrastus of Eresus (d. ~ 287 BC) characterises the purposive character of natural traits in animals as being "always in accordance to a single state and a single pattern" (ἀεὶ κατὰ ταὐτὰ καὶ ὡσαύτως, *dā'iman 'alā ḥal wāḥida wa-'alā miṯāl wāḥid*).[231] The first of Avicenna's two distinctions, then, is an Aristotelian commonplace, as natural acts are generally characterised as uniformly and invariably proceeding in a single manner and according to a single course.

The second distinction, i.e., that between volitional motion and non-volitional motion, is more complex but ultimately also derives from Aristotelian material. In particular the notion of wish (βούλησις) is important in this context. In the *Nicomachean Ethics*, Aristotle writes that wish (βούλησις, *hawā*) and decision (προαίρεσις, *iḫtiyār*) are similar capacities of the human soul. One of their major differences, however, is that the former is concerned with the end (τοῦ τέλους, *li-ġāyat al-šay'*), while the latter

231 Theophrastus, *Metaphysics*, 10b20.

is concerned with what leads to the end (τῶν πρὸς τὸ τέλος, *li-mā yu'addī ilā l-ġāya).*[232] Later in book VI, Aristotle claims decision to be the efficient principle of action. The principle of decision, in turn, is "desire and reasoning to an end" (ὄρεξις καὶ λόγος ὁ ἕνεκά τινος).[233]

In *De motu animalium*, Aristotle argues in a similar way and explains what he means by "desire and reasoning to an end" in this context. There, in chapter six, Aristotle differentiates between inanimate things, which are moved by something else, and animate living beings, which are moved by themselves or, more precisely, by some of their psychological capacities.[234] He lists a number of such capacities, viz., thought, imagination, perception, decision, wish, spiritedness, and appetite, and concludes that these can all be reduced to "intellect and desire" (νοῦν καὶ ὄρεξιν). The notion of "intellect," here, does not refer to the human capacity of reasoning but is meant to cover the first three so-called discriminative capacities (κριτικά) of thought, imagination, and perception. It is important to note that non-human animals (with the notable exception of such animals as the grub) share in two of these three discriminative capacities and that imagination is said to be somewhat similar or analogous to opinion and belief (δόξα), with belief playing an important role in the theory of human action in both the *Nicomachean Ethics* and the *Eudemian Ethics*.[235] The last three of the listed capacities, viz., wish, spiritedness, and appetite, are all said to be desires (ὀρέξεις), with decision commonly (κοινόν) relying on both, i.e., the three capacities of "intellect" and those three of "desire."[236] As Aristotle makes clear in his further elaborations, it is desire which is the efficient cause of motion in animate beings.[237] In the ethical and the zoological works, in particular in the *Nicomachean Ethics* and the *De motu animalium*, βούλησις, being a desire, is a prominent ingredient of, and a necessary requirement for, the production of motion and action.

It is not clear, however, to what extent Aristotle's *Nicomachean Ethics* was an important source for Avicenna. The *De motu animalium*, on the other hand, quite

---

232 *Eth. Nic.* III.4, 1111b19–30; III.6, 1113a15; cf. *Eth. Eud.* II.10, 1226a6–17. Another important difference lies in the fact that wish can be directed towards impossible things or things outside of our reach, whereas decision cannot.

233 *Eth. Nic.* VI.2, 1139a31–33; cf. *Eth. Eud.* II.10, 1227a3–5. Most of the sixth book of the *Nicomachean Ethics* is not preserved in Arabic and the *Eudemian Ethics* was probably not translated.

234 cf. *De motu anim.* 4, 700a16. Aristotle's account here of the motion of inanimate things is entirely in line with his explanatory model from *Physics* VIII.4.

235 *De an.* III.3, 428a9–24; *Nicomachean Ethics* III.4, 1111b30–1112a13; *Eudemian Ethics* II.10, 1226a1–1226b9. That most animals have their share in some discriminative capacities is also made clear by Aristotle in *Historia animalium* VIII.1, where he writes that non-human animals are endowed with something at least analogous (τὰ δὲ τῷ ἀνάλογον διαφέρει) and similar (τοιαύτη) to the human capacities of τέχνη, σοφία, and σύνεσις, as Aristotle makes clear in *Historia animalium* VIII.1, 588a28–31; cf. also *Historia animalium* VIII.1, 588a18–21.

236 *De motu anim.* 6, 700b6–23.

237 cf. *De motu anim.* 6 700b23f., 701a1, 702.17–19, 703a4f.

surely was not, as there is no trace of an Arabic translation of that work, even though Averroes (d. 595/1198), for example, claims to have had some indirect knowledge of the treatise through Nicolaus of Damascus (d. ~ 20 BC).[238] The theory expounded in *De motu animalium*, however, has intimate relations to *De anima* III.9–11 and can, indeed, be regarded as complementary.[239] It is certainly Aristotle's *De anima*, then, which may have influenced Avicenna in his understanding of volitional as opposed to non-volitional motion.

In *De anima* III.9, Aristotle defines wish (βούλησις, *rawīya*) as a rational desire.[240] In *De anima* III.10, then, we read that intellect and desire (νοῦς καὶ ὄρεξις, *al-šahwa wa-l-ʿaql*) move the animal.[241] In particular, Aristotle remarks the following:

> νῦν δὲ ὁ μὲν νοῦς οὐ φαίνεται κινῶν ἄνευ ὀρέξεως (ἡ γὰρ βούλησις ὄρεξις, ὅταν δὲ κατὰ τὸν λογισμὸν κινῆται, καὶ κατὰ βούλησιν κινεῖται), ἡ δ' ὄρεξις κινεῖ καὶ παρὰ τὸν λογισμόν· ἡ γὰρ ἐπιθυμία ὄρεξίς τίς ἐστιν.
>
> العقل فإنّا لا نراه يحرّك بغير شهوة وذلك أنّ الروية أرب وشهوة وتحرّك العقل بالفكر فإنّما يتحرّك بالروية. وأمّا الشهوة فإنّما تحرّك بغير فكر لأنّ الشهوة إنّما هي ضرب من الشوق.
>
> Now, reason apparently does not initiate motion without desire (since wish is desire (ἡ γὰρ βούλησις ὄρεξις, *al-rawīya arab wa-šahwa*), and whenever something is moved in accordance with calculation (κατὰ τὸν λογισμόν, *bi-l-fikr*), it is also moved in accordance with wish), whereas desire also initiates motion opposed to calculation, for appetite is a kind of desire. (*De an.* III.10, 433a22–26, tr. by Shields, modified)[242]

In this passage, Aristotle depicts wish, again, as a capacity that is central to the psychological production of motion. In particular, wish is involved whenever the animal moves "in accordance with calculation" (κατὰ τὸν λογισμόν, *bi-l-fikr*). This seems to mean that any motion which does not blindly follow an appetite but is due to some resolution to act requires and emerges from wish. Conversely, one may assume that motions that are irrational, i.e., not due to deliberation or opinion, could be termed "natural."[243] Thus, for Aristotle, wish is a central notion for the action of human beings, because only human begins have rationality, and wish is a *rational* desire.

Now, the Greek term βούλησις, which I have translated here as "wish," has often been translated into Arabic as *irāda*. Alternative translations include *rawīya*, as in the

---

238 cf. Kruk's remarks in the introduction to Aristotle, *The Arabic Version of Aristotle's* Parts of Animals, 13; cf. also Peters, *Aristoteles Arabus*, 48; Gätje, "Zur Psychologie der Willenshandlungen in der islamischen Philosophie," 352.

239 Various interpretations have been advanced concerning the relation between the theories expressed in the two treatises; cf. Corcilius, *Streben und Bewegen*, esp. 243–249.

240 cf. *De an.* III.9, 432b3–6; cf. also *Top.* IV.5; cf. further Corcilius, *Streben und Bewegen*, 160.

241 *De an.* III.10, 433a9–20.

242 The Arabic version provided by the only known manuscript of an Arabic translation of Aristotle's *De anima*, viz., Ms. Istanbul, Aya Sofya 2450, diverges from the Greek in various details.

243 cf. esp. *Rhetoric* I.11, 1370a18–21.

above quotation from Aristotle's *De anima*, and the not too common *hawan*, as we have seen above in the third book of the *Nicomachean Ethics*.[244] This strongly suggests that what Avicenna uses as a discriminative feature in his account of natural powers, classifying them into those which are with volition and those which are not, is derived from Aristotle's account of βούλησις, for Avicenna uses the terms *irāda* and *rawīya* in the same contexts. In *al-Samāʿ al-ṭabīʿī* I.5, for example, he defines nature as a power from which the act proceeds *ʿalā nahǧ wāḥid min ġayr irāda* ("in a single manner without volition") and allows for an equivocal use of the term "nature" when it describes animal action that proceeds from the animal *min ġayr rawīya* ("without deliberation").[245] Having said this, it is apparent that the major difference between Aristotle's and Avicenna's understandings of βούλησις and *irāda* or *rawīya* is that Avicenna does not restrict it to rational animals alone. This fact cannot merely be explained by a shift of terminology initiated through ambiguous translations in the Graeco-Arabic translation movement. While this difference deserves a fuller investigation than I am able to provide here, it is clear that one crucial aspect of it is a more sophisticated approach to animal action as a whole, leading to a higher appreciation of animal faculties of perception and imagination as discriminative capacities (κριτικά), as they were already called by Aristotle in *De motu animalium*.[246] In this regard, Dag Nikolaus Hasse gestured towards several important passages in Aristotle's *De anima*, in which Aristotle describes the role of images (sg. φαντάσματος, *šayʾ yataḫayyalu … ʿan al-tawahhum*) for the soul's capacity of judgement and thinking.[247] However, it is not only rational animals for whose psychological activities images are important, animals generally are said to "do many things in accordance with them," both non-rational animals, which lack reason, and rational animals whose reason is "shrouded," as we read in *De anima* III.3.[248] That images serve an important part in the action of all kinds of animals is, according to Hasse, further promoted through the distinction between a rational and a perceptual kind of imagination, as in *De anima* III.11:

> ὅλως μὲν οὖν, ὥσπερ εἴρηται, ᾗ ὀρεκτικὸν τὸ ζῷον, ταύτῃ αὐτοῦ κινητικόν· ὀρεκτικὸν δὲ οὐκ ἄνευ φαντασίας· φαντασία δὲ πᾶσα ἢ λογιστικὴ ἢ αἰσθητική. ταύτης μὲν οὖν καὶ τὰ ἄλλα ζῷα μετέχει.

244 The Greek term προαίρεσις ("decision") is commonly translated as *iḫtiyār*, sometimes, however, also as *irāda*; cf. also Ullmann's rich analysis of the terminology employed in the Arabic translation in *Die Nikomachische Ethik des Aristoteles in arabischer Überlieferung*.

245 *al-Samāʿ al-ṭabīʿī* I.5, §3, 30.8, 13f.; cf. *al-Samāʿ al-ṭabīʿī* I.14, §11, 72.5, where we even find the full expression *ʿalā nahǧ wāḥid min ġayr rawīya*. In fact, the whole discussion in *al-Samāʿ al-ṭabīʿī* I.14 is marked by a frequent use of the term *rawīya*. Yet, the two notions are not synonymous for Avicenna as we shall see.

246 *De motu anim.* 6, 700b20.

247 *De an.* III.7, 431a14–17; cf. Hasse, *Avicenna's* De Anima *in the Latin West*, 141; cf. also Gätje, "Zur Psychologie der Willenshandlungen in der islamischen Philosophie," 359; cf. further Hasse, *Avicenna's* De Anima *in the Latin West*, 92–98.

248 *De an.* III.3, 429.4–8, tr. by Shields.

فالحيوان كما قيل شهواني في الجملة ومن هذا صار محرّكاً (...) بغير توهّم. وكلّ توهّم إمّا كان فكرياً أو حواسّياً. وسائر الحيوان ذو توهّم.

In general, as has been said, insofar as an animal is capable of desire, it is, in virtue of this, capable of moving itself, but it is not capable of desire without imagination (φαντασίας, *tawahhum*).[249] All imagination, however, is either rational or perceptual (λογιστικὴ ἢ αἰσθητική, *fikriyyan aw ḥawassiyyan*), and in this latter, then, the other animals have a share as well. (*De anima* III.11, 433b27–30, tr. by Shields, modified)[250]

What these passages from Aristotle's *De anima* have in common and what this current quotation shows is, as Hasse rightly states, that they prepare, and feed into, Avicenna's conception of *wahm* or *tawahhum* ("estimation") – here in the current passage used to render φαντασία ("imagination") – as one of the core powers of the animal soul and, moreover, one at the heart of Avicenna's theory of animal action:

والقوّة الإجماعية تبع للقوى المذكورة فإنّها إذا اشتدّ نزاعها أجمعت. وهي كلّها تتبّع أيضاً القوّة الوهمية وذلك أنّه لا يكون شوق البتّة إلّا بعد توهّم المشتاق إليه وقد يكون وهم ولا يكون شوق ... فالوهم له السلطان في حيّز القوى المدرِكة في الحيوانات والشهوة والغضب لهما السلطان في حيّز القوى المحرّكة وتتبّعهما القوّة الإجماعية ثمّ القوى المحركة التي في العضل.

The power of resolution (*al-quwwa al-iǧmāʿiyya*)[251] follows upon the aforementioned powers [sc. those of anger and desire], for if their tending towards something becomes stronger, the resolution [to act] is made. All of these [powers] follow upon the power of estimation (*al-quwwa al-wahmiyya*), and this is because there is no desire whatsoever unless after the estimation of what is desired (*illā baʿda tawahhum al-muštāq*), even though there may be estimation without desire ... The estimation has authority in the domain of the perceptual powers in the animals, whereas appetite and anger have authority in the domain of moving powers, but they both are followed by the power of resolution, and then by the moving powers in the muscle. (*al-Nafs* IV.4, 174.6–13)[252]

First of all, we witness here the central position taken up by the power of estimation (*tawahhum*). In addition to the perception of Avicenna's famous "connotational attributes," such as the hostility a lamb perceives in a wolf, the estimation also serves a different purpose more in line with what Aristotle attributed to φαντασία insofar

249 The Arabic text as edited by Badawī omits the Arabic for ὀρεκτικὸν δὲ οὐκ. This seems to be a scribal or an editorial error, rather than a translation error. The other Arabic translation, whose Latin version is found in the lemmata of Averroes great commentary on *De anima* was more complete; cf. Averroes, *Long Commentary on the* De Anima *of Aristotle*, 426.

250 cf. *De an.* III.11, 434a4–12.

251 Reading *al-quwwa al-iǧmāʿiyya* with Mss. Leiden or. 4 and or. 84 as well as Rahman and Bakoš for *al-quwā al-iǧmāʿiyya* in Qanawātī/Zāyid.

252 cf. *al-Nafs* I.4, 30.5–10; *al-Išārāt wa-l-tanbīhāt* II.3.25, 135.4–8; cf. also Hasse, *Avicenna's* De Anima *in the Latin West*, 139. For the notion of *igmāʿ*, cf. van Riet, "Recherches concernant la traduction arabo-latine du Kitāb al-Nafs d'Ibn Sīna"; Gätje, "Zur Psychologie der Willenshandlungen in der islamischen Philosophie"; for an analysis of human and divine action, cf. Ruffus and McGinnis, "Willful Understanding."

as it is the authoritative psychological power for perception and, thus, for the organisation of desires. In addition, it also constitutes the highest capacity for judgement in non-human animals on the basis of received or stored perceptions.[253] It is not too far-fetched to expect that for Avicenna, estimation contributes to non-human animal action in an analogous way as opinion and belief (δόξα) contribute to human action in Aristotle's theory, in particular in light of Avicenna's characterisation of the estimation as "opining" (*wa-hāḏā l-quwwa al-musammāt bi-l-mutawahhima wa-l-ẓānna*) in his early *Kitāb fī l-nafs ʿalā sunnat al-iḫtiṣār*.[254] His account of the power of estimation is either a further development or a clearer exposition of what was already present to some degree in Aristotle, as we have seen it above.[255]

What is more, Avicenna combines the Aristotelian emphasis on estimation and φαντασία with the new component of a power of resolution (*iǧmāʿ*). It is ultimately this power of resolution to act which distinguishes the *voluntary* motions initiated by animals – both human and non-human – from the *involuntary* motions initiated by plants and inanimate bodies, for it seems that only animals engage in decision-making. Surely, non-rational animals are not endowed with a practical intellect (*ʿaql ʿamalī*), and so their decision-making is not based on thought and reflection, yet even non-human animals possess a kind of non-rational judgement and deliberation on the basis of the powers of estimation and resolution. This harmonises well with the way in which Avicenna presented three kinds of sublunary souls in the first book of his *al-Nafs*, viz., the vegetative soul (*al-nafs al-nabātiyya*), the animal soul (*al-nafs al-ḥayawāniyya*), and the human soul (*al-nafs al-insāniyya*), asserting that the animal soul brings about motion "through volition" (*bi-l-irāda*), whereas the human soul is capable of doing so "through discursive decision" (*bi-l-iḫtiyār al-fikrī*).[256]

What Avicenna means more precisely by the voluntary action of a non-human animal on the basis of a non-rational form of deliberation can be spelled out, at least a bit more fully, through a reference to two further passages. We read in *al-Nafs* IV.4 that desires, which are required for initiating motion, can be weak (*ḍaʿīfan*) or strong (*yuštaddu*). Only if they are strong, however, do they "necessitate the resolution" (*yūǧibu al-iǧmāʿ*).[257] This may seem to be a triviality but it aptly explains the contrast in Avicenna's fourfold classification of natural powers between non-voluntary stones and plants, on the one hand, and voluntary animals and celestial bodies, on the other. Plants and stones do not initiate their motions only if the desire is strong enough, for a stone will always fall to the ground, even if it was released only one centimetre

253 cf. esp. Black, "Estimation (*wahm*) in Avicenna," 227; cf. also Gätje, "Zur Psychologie der Willenshandlungen in der islamischen Philosophie," 358f.

254 *Kitāb fī l-nafs ʿalā sunnat al-iḫtiṣār* 7, 359.21.

255 cf. Black, "Estimation (*wahm*) in Avicenna," n. 2, 245, referring to Rahman's notes in *Avicenna's Psychology*, 83.

256 *al-Nafs* I.5, 32.4–11; cf. also *al-Naǧāt* II.2.3, 214.5f.

257 *al-Nafs* IV.4, 172.13.

above the ground. Likewise, a plant will always grow its branches and roots, and not only if the desire for doing so is strong enough. In a word, plants do not "act freely" (*tataṣarrafu*) as animals do.[258]

By contrast, an animal does not blindly and immediately follow its appetite but may linger in the sunlight, even if it is already a bit thirsty (but not thirsty enough to get up and trot to the watering place). Moreover, animals may even decide whether first to drink or to eat, or whether to eat the apple or the carrot. That is to say, animals deliberate in a non-discursive and non-rational way over their likes and dislikes, and about whether to engage in motion and action or not. Thus, an act with "volition" (*irāda*) is intimately related with a "deliberation" (*rawīya*) of several alternatives, leading up to a resolution.

Now, both terms – *irāda* and *rawīya* – have been used to render Aristotle's βούλησις into Arabic, and we have already seen that Avicenna uses both terms in a similar way when he describes natural acts as being "without volition" (*min ġayr irāda*) as well as "without deliberation" (*min ġayr rawīya*). So, while volition and deliberation are both important as internal features that characterise animal action, they are not coextensive, as we learn from *al-Samāʿ al-ṭabīʿī* I.14. There Avicenna states that "deliberation ... is for determining the act that is chosen from among all the acts that could have been chosen."[259] To this he adds the following:

ولو كانت النفس مسلَّمة عن النوازع المختلفة والمعارضات المتفنّنة لكان يصدر عنها فعل يتشابه على نهج واحد من غير روية.

If the soul was spared the diverse likes (*al-nawāziʿ al-muḫtalifa*) and the manifold dislikes (*al-muʿāraḍāt al-mutafannina*), then a uniform act would proceed from it in a single manner without deliberation. (*al-Samāʿ al-ṭabīʿī* I.14, §11, 72.4f., tr. by McGinnis, modified)

So, we learn that deliberation (*rawīya*) is about choosing between various likes and dislikes, about making preferences, and about deciding what to do – this is precisely what animals are capable of doing but no plant and no inanimate body. We also learn, however, why both celestial souls and animal souls are, according to Avicenna's classification, alike in being "with volition" but different in whether their initiated acts proceed "in a single manner," as the heavenly motion is circular and entirely uniform. The reason for this difference, then, is that heavenly bodies have no alternative likes and dislikes that need to be pondered over. However, this does not make their act involuntary, because they still *decided* to imitate their intellect, thereby bringing about the uniform circular motion of their body, even though it makes clear that their act is not due to deliberation, given the lack of alternatives, the lack of likes and dislikes, and the lack of preferences. Animals, including humans, however, have preferences and multiple alternatives at their disposal, thus the motions their souls initiate are

258 *al-Samāʿ al-ṭabīʿī* I.5, §1, 29.8.
259 *al-Samāʿ al-ṭabīʿī* I.14, §11, 72.3f.

not uniform, because they are due to acts of deliberation or, in the case of humans, rational discursive decision.

It is clear that a full study of the psychological underpinnings and the concepts of *irāda*, *rawīya*, and *iğmāʿ* would be necessary to carve out further the details of Avicenna's theory of animal action. It is equally clear that such an investigation would have to do justice not only to Aristotelian sources but also to Hellenistic and late ancient pagan, Christian, and Jewish as well as early Islamic theories of action. It is in this regard interesting to see that Philoponus writes the following in his commentary on *De anima*:

> ὡς μὲν οὖν ποιητικὴ ἀρχή, ὅτι αὕτη κινεῖ τὸ ζῷον μόνῃ τῇ βουλήσει.
>
> [The soul is a principle] in the sense of an efficient principle, in that it moves the living being by means of its willing only (μόνῃ τῇ βουλήσει). (Philoponus, *In An.*, 25.31f., tr. by van der Eijk, modified)[260]

Here, Philoponus, likewise, does not distinguish between rational and non-rational animals, while describing the soul in general terms as an efficient cause of motion through nothing other than βούλησις.[261] There is also, once again, Alexander's treatise *Maqāla fī l-qawl fī mabādiʾ al-kull* in which Alexander contends that the heavenly spheres, which are animate and ensouled, are moved by "volition" (*irāda* and *iḫtiyār*).[262] It seems clear that Alexander's no longer extant Greek original of that passage contained βούλησις, which was translated by the Arabic translators as both *iḫtiyār* and *irāda*.[263] Alexander's suggestion is, furthermore, in line with what the Athenian said in Plato's *Laws* X where βούλεσθαι is prominently mentioned as one of the soul's acts responsible for the heavenly motion.[264]

What is more, it was a central dispute among the Peripatetic commentators whether or not nature and art are rightly said to be analogous. This question emerged as a consequence of several remarks made by Aristotle in the course of *Physics* II. The position which was taken up by Alexander and Porphyry, but which was contested by Simplicius and mitigated by Philoponus, was that nature was regarded as an irrational power (ἄλογος ... δυνάμις) without will, choice, or thought and in this respect differed from

260 cf. Philoponus, *In An.*, 138.4–8; cf. alsoWolff, *Fallgesetz und Massebegriff*, 72–79.

261 It is not clear, however, whether – and if so in what form – Philoponus' commentary on Aristotle's *De anima* was available in Arabic translation; cf. Aristotle, *The Arabic Version of Aristotle's* Parts of Animals, 13; Gutas, "Philoponus and Avicenna on the Separability of the Intellect," 129; cf. generally Arnzen's remarks in Anonymous, *Aristoteles'* De anima.

262 cf. Alexander of Aphrodisias, *Maqāla fī l-qawl fī mabādiʾ al-kull*, §§6–13, 46.4–50.11 (ed. Genequand); cf. Genequand's notes *ad loc.* For Alexander's claim that the heavenly spheres have soul, cf. Alexander of Aphrodisias, *Quaestiones*, q. I.1, 3.10–14; cf. also Bodnár, "Alexander of Aphrodisias on Celestial Motions"; cf. generally Sorabji, *The Philosophy of the Commentators*, vol. II, ch. 22e.

263 cf. also Genequand's remarks in Alexander of Aphrodisias, *On the Cosmos*, 6, 36.

264 *Leg.* X, 896e8–897b6.

art which did involve a rational activity. Most of these views were probably known to Muslim, Christian, and Jewish scholars of the fourth/tenth century, and especially those active in Baġdād, through the Arabic translations of Alexander's, Porphyry's, Simplicius', and Philoponus' commentaries on the *Physics* or the *De anima*, but also through individual treatises such as Alexander's *Maqāla fī l-ʿināya*.[265] Moreover, Alexander's and Porphyry's position was also quoted and discussed, and in fact severely criticised, by Abū Bakr al-Rāzī in his *Maqāla fī-mā baʿd al-ṭabīʿa*. There, Abū Bakr al-Rāzī chides Porphyry for having argued that nature acts without intellect, thought, or volition (*irāda*).[266] Finally, some aspects of Alexander's position in this matter also reappear in the margins of the famous Ms. Leiden or. 583.[267]

What all these passages evince is that specifically when formulating the two distinctions on the basis of which he establishes his fourfold classification of natural powers – i.e., the distinctions between between volitional and non-volitional as well as between uniform and manifold motions – Avicenna could draw on a variety of sources from within the Peripatetic curriculum which have been influential in the Arabic tradition. Avicenna's achievement in the classification of natural powers, however, does not only consist in making these distinctions explicit or in combining them and making them an integral part of his account of nature. Before he could do that he, first, had to conceive of them as systematically distinct from one another, so as to be able to yield such a fourfold schema. It seems that one could easily maintain that whatever acts proceed from an agent by virtue of volition are nothing other than acts that are manifold and diverse, because they are due to a will and not to a fixed and invariable power. Consequently, those acts that proceed without recourse to volition may, in turn, necessarily be those which cannot be manifold and, thus, are always the same and equal. Aristotle in *Metaphysics* Θ.2 and 5, for example, achieved a similar distinction between rational and non-rational powers (δυνάμεις, *quwan*) on the basis that only the former, but not the latter, are able to bring about multiple, or indeed contrary, effects:

> καὶ αἱ μὲν μετὰ λόγου πᾶσαι τῶν ἐναντίων αἱ αὐταί, αἱ δὲ ἄλογοι μία ἑνός, οἷον τὸ θερμὸν τοῦ θερμαίνειν μόνον ἡ δὲ ἰατρικὴ νόσου καὶ ὑγιείας.
>
> وجميع التي تكون مع كلمة هي للاضداد أيضاً ولكن ليس كأحدها لواحد مثل الحارّ للحرّ وأمّا الطبّ فللسقم والصحّة.
>
> And for all those [powers] which are with reason (μετὰ λόγου, *maʿa kalima*), the same [power] is for contrary effects, but non-rational [powers] are only for one [effect], for example, the hot is only for heating, but the medical art is of both disease and health. (*Met.* Θ.2, 1046b4–7)[268]

---

265 cf. Alexander of Aphrodisias, *Maqāla fī l-ʿināya*, 19.6–10 (ed. Thillet).
266 Abū Bakr al-Rāzī, *Maqāla fī-mā baʿd al-ṭabīʿa* 121.1f. The Greek and the Arabic context of this Peripatetic dispute is depicted and discussed in Adamson, "*Porphyrius Arabus* on Nature and Art."
267 cf. Giannakis, "Fragments from Alexander's Lost Commentary on Aristotle's *Physics*," esp. frgm. 2.
268 cf. *Met.* Z.7, 1032b1–6; Θ.2, 1046b18–21; Θ.5, 1047b35–1048a10.

Even though Aristotle is not contrasting volitional and non-volitional but rational and non-rational principles of motion, he achieves this contrast on a psychological level by aligning the psychologically superior with the causally variable. It may, therefore, be rather natural to maintain that the distinction between variable motions and invariable motions more or less amounts to – or collapses into – the distinction between volitional and non-volitional acts or, alternatively, to claim that the former division merely achieves for lifeless things what the latter does for animate things. Avicenna not only presents these distinctions, he also successfully establishes each of them as serving a different purpose, so that their combination yields a classification of four different powers which, together, comprise the whole range of acts and motions that the natural corporeal reality has to offer. On this basis, Avicenna can, in a systematic manner, interrelate and differentiate all powers of natural bodies within a single, comprehensive, and systematic schema.

Finally, it should be noted that Avicenna's classification does away with the strict fundamental difference between sublunary and supralunary motions by integrating the heavenly motions into the picture. The heavenly spheres are moved through a volitional power, viz., the celestial soul, which, nonetheless, brings about only a uniform circular motion, just as animals are moved by a volitional power, viz., the animal soul, which, however, brings about manifold and non-uniform motions. That Avicenna harmonises the sublunary and the supralunary dynamics is also apparent in the fact that the concept of inclination (*mayl*) applies to sublunary motion just as it applies to supralunary motion.[269]

Avicenna's Definition of Nature

Along the way, Avicenna has presented and established his very own definition of nature. Of course, nature is an internal principle for motion and rest, as Aristotle had defined it. More properly and more adequately, however, nature is defined as follows:

قوّة تحرّك وتغيّر ويصدر عنها الفعل على نهج واحد من غير إرادة.

> a power which produces motion and change, and from which the act proceeds in a single manner without volition. (*al-Samāʿ al-ṭabīʿī* I.5, §3, 30.7f., tr. by McGinnis, modified)

A proper definition supplies a genus term (*ǧins*) with a proper difference (*faṣl*) and indicates the essence (*māhiyya*) or reality (*ḥaqīqa*) of that which is defined.[270] Nature, then, is to be found in the genus "power" (*quwwa*). Like every power, it brings about motion and change. It is, however, distinguished from other powers by being such that

269 Again, this is in line with my above analysis of Avicenna's account of prime matter, which in a similar way unifies the physics of celestial bodies with the physics of terrestrial ones; q.v. above, 200.
270 For a concise statement on definitions, cf. *al-Naǧāt* I.139–140, esp. 151.5–10.

it brings about motion "in a single manner without volition" (*ʿalā nahǧ wāḥid min ġayr irāda*). This is how Avicenna defines nature and how he prefers to speak about it.[271]

Of course, Avicenna is a Peripatetic and, thus, frequently mentions an Aristotelian definition of nature. Yet, he usually does so *after* having established his own account. In fact, Avicenna appears to give a general preference to his own definition. This strategy is especially recognisable in the sections on natural philosophy from his *al-Šifāʾ*, *al-Naǧāt* (as well as *al-Ḥikma al-ʿArūḍiyya*), and *ʿUyūn al-ḥikma*. In the latter work, for example, we see Avicenna, first, providing an inference to his fourfold classification:

وكلّ جسم يتحرّك فحركته إمّا من سبب خارج وتُسمّى حركة قسرية وإمّا من سبب في نفس الجسم إذ الجسم لا يتحرّك بذاته. وذلك السبب إن كان محرّكاً على جهة واحدة على سبيل التسخير فيُسمّى طبيعة وإن كان محرّكاً حركات شتّى بإرادة أو غير إرادة أو محرّكاً حركة واحدة بإرادة فيُسمّى نفساً.

Every body is in motion, and so its motion is either due to an external cause – and is called "forced motion" – or due to a cause in the body itself (*fī nafs al-ǧism*), since the body is not in motion [just] by itself. If this cause moves along one single direction by way of compulsion (*ʿalā ǧiha wāḥida ʿalā sabīl al-tasḫīr*), then it is called "nature," whereas if it produces diverse motions through volition (*muḥarrikan ḥarakāt šattā bi-irāda*) or [does so] not through volition, or [if it] moves a single motion through volition, then it is called "soul." (*ʿUyūn al-ḥikma*, II.2, 18.2–6)

A little later, almost *en passant* between the four causes and the definition of motion, Avicenna briefly also supplies Aristotle's definition:

الطبيعة سبب على أنّه مبدأ لحركة لما هي فيه ومبدأ لسكونه بالذات لا بالعرض.

Nature is a cause insofar as it is a principle for motion for that[272] in which it is as well as a principle for its rest essentially and not accidentally. (*ʿUyūn al-ḥikma* II.2, 18.11)

The account in Avicenna's *ʿUyūn al-ḥikma* reproduces very nicely all the major points of his discussion in *al-Samāʿ al-ṭabīʿī*: Avicenna distinguishes between externally forced and internally caused motions; he states that motion is not due to the body alone insofar as it is a body; he adds his distinction between motions which are along a single course and those which are manifold; finally, he also adds the distinction between volitional and non-volitional motion (which he here prefers to call compulsive motion (*ʿalā sabīl al-tasḫīr*)).[273] Taken as a whole, this inference yields a contrast of nature with

271 In *al-Samāʿ al-ṭabīʿī*, Avicenna twice refers back to a definition of nature (*ḥadd al-ṭabīʿa*) he has given, cf. *al-Samāʿ al-ṭabīʿī* I.5, §9, 34.3; I.6, §3, 35.14. That this present account constitutes his proper definition of nature does not entail that the accounts he gave of the three kinds of souls – the vegetative, the animal, and the celestial soul – are necessarily proper definitions, too. What is a true specific difference (*faṣl*) for the definition of nature, viz., the distinctions of whether the motion proceeds in a single manner and whether it proceeds with or without volition, may just as well only be a *proprium* (*ḫāṣṣa*) for the three kinds of souls. In general, the definition of soul is a more difficult matter, as is borne out by the difficulties in understanding Avicenna's reflections in *al-Nafs* I.1.

272 Reading *li-mā* with Ǧabr and ʿĀṣī for *mā* in Badawī and *bi-mā* in al-Saqqā.

273 cf. *al-Naǧāt* II.1.1, 194.5f.

three kinds of souls, viz., animal, vegetative, and celestial souls. In *al-Hidāya* and the *Dānešnāme-ye ʿAlāʾī*, Avicenna even completely dispenses with Aristotle's definition and only provides his own classification.

As always, the case with Avicenna's *al-Išārāt wa-l-tanbīhāt* is different, for they seem to lack a definition of nature altogether. The closest we get to a statement of the essence of nature is in *al-Išārāt wa-l-tanbīhāt* II.2.4, a brief *išāra* on the nature of the elements:

الجسم البسيط هو الذي طبيعته واحدة ليس فيه تركيب قوى وطبائع. والطبيعة الواحدة تقتضي من الأمكنة والأشكال وسائر ما لا بدّ للجسم أن يلزمه واحداً غير مختلف فالجسم البسيط لا يقتضي إلّا شيئاً غير مختلف.

The simple body is that whose nature is one (*ṭabīʿatuhū wāḥida*) [and] in which there is no composition of [multiple] powers and natures. The single nature requires from the places and figures and of all that which inevitably belongs to bodies that something which is one and not diverse (*wāḥidan ġayr muḫtalif*) follows from it [sc. the body]. Thus, the simple body requires nothing but a thing which is not diverse. (*al-Išārāt wa-l-tanbīhāt* II.2.4, 108.16–19)

In this brief note, Avicenna reminds us that the nature of an element like earth, water, air, or fire is singular and simple, and that from such a nature only a singular effect proceeds, i.e., a singular effect in each category that necessarily belongs to body, like place, shape, and qualities such as temperature, for example. Thus, water has a single nature which requires from an amount of water one thing with respect to place, viz., its being at its natural place. With regard to its temperature, it also requires only one thing, viz., its being cold. Should the water not be at its natural place or have its natural temperature, the nature of the element water still demands one thing and one thing alone, i.e., its being in its natural state. Its nature seeks to attain this through a single and uniform effect, viz., its direct return to its natural state. Conversely, should the water already be there, or finally arrive there, its nature, again, requires one thing and one thing only, viz., its being in its natural state. So, it is most evident in the cases of the simple elements that the nature of an element simply "is identical with its form" (*bi-ʿaynihī ṣūratihī*), as Avicenna explained in *al-Samāʿ al-ṭabīʿī* I.6.[274] Perhaps the most appropriate and complete passage to that effect is in *al-Kawn wa-l-fasād* 6:

فينبغي لنا أن نصرّح ... أنّ كلّ واحد من الاسطقسّات له صورة جوهرية بها هو ما هو ويتبع هذه الصورة الجوهرية كمالات من باب الكيف ومن باب الكمّ ومن باب الأين. فيتخصّص كلّ جسم منها ببرد أو حرّ من جهة تلك الصورة ويبس ورطوبة من جهة المادّة المقترنة بالصورة وبقدر من الكمّ طبيعي وبحركة طبيعية وسكون طبيعي. فتكون تلك الصورة يفيض عنها في ذات ذلك الجسم قوى بعضها ممّا لها بالقياس إلى المنفعل كالحرارة والبرودة الطبيعيتين وبعضها بالقياس إلى الفاعل للشكل كاليبوسة والرطوبة الطبيعيتين وبعضها بالقياس إلى الأجسام المكتنفة له كالحركة والسكون الطبيعيين.

274 *al-Samāʿ al-ṭabīʿī* I.6, §2, 34.10f.; cf. *al-Naǧāt* II.1.1, 195.3f. ≈ *al-Ḥikma al-ʿArūḍiyya* II.1, 116.1f.; *Dānešnāme-ye ʿAlāʾī* III.22, 53.2f.

> So, it is required from us that we explain ... that each of the elements has a substantial form through which it is what it is. [From] this substantial form follow perfections in the category of quality, in the category of quantity, and in the category of place. Thus, each body of these is specified by cold and heat because of that form, [by] wetness and dryness because of the matter conjoined with the form, by a natural size in terms of quantity, and by a natural motion and a natural rest. So, from that form [a number of] powers emanate into the being of that body, some of which are those which belong to it with regard to what is passive (such as natural heat and cold), some of which with regard to what is active of the shape (such as natural wetness and dryness), some of which with regard to the bodies enclosing it (such as natural motion and rest). (*al-Kawn wa-l-fasād* 6, 129.15–130.4)[275]

Other natural objects may consist of a combination of the elements, such as earth and air, and so the nature of natural objects that are not simple bodies is the result of the combination of the respective natures of their components. This is why a block of wood floats on top of the water, because it consists of enough upward-directed air (and maybe also a little fire) to counterbalance the downward-directed nature of its other component earth. This does not mean that wood, being composed of multiple ingredients, consists of multiple natures and multiple forms, and so has multiple natural effects, one effect from each nature. Rather, it is the case that once the right components have been mixed together in an adequate way, wood comes-to-be from them. These initial components, however, contained enough air and fire in addition to earth and water, so that the single wooden nature – resulting from this composition – likewise has only one single natural state in the categories that belong to it: it has a natural place, it has a natural temperature, it has natural capacities to ignite and to burn, and so on. Thus, wood is like the simple elements singular in both nature and form.[276] So, inanimate natural objects have one power, i.e., one nature and form. It is more complicated with animate composites, such as a horse or a man, in which multiple powers are present, i.e., not only the various powers of the soul but also the power of its underlying body. In these cases, it is the the combination (*al-iǧtimāʿ*) of all these powers that provides the essence "humanity": the powers of nature as well as the powers of the vegetative and the animal soul, and reason (*quwā l-ṭabīʿa wa-quwā l-nafs al-nabātiyya wa-l-ḥayawāniyya wa-l-nuṭq*).[277] Thus, in these cases, we need to

275 For the common Aristotelian distinction between passive and active qualities, cf. *De gen. et corr.* II.2, 329b22–33; *Meteor.* IV.1 378b10–26; cf. also Avicenna's complex discussion in *al-Samāʾ wa-l-ʿālam* 1, esp. 3.14–17; cf. further Gill, *Aristotle on Substance*, 80–82; Hansberger, "Ticklish Questions," esp. 152–156.

276 cf. *al-Samāʿ al-ṭabīʿī* I.6, §3, 35.7–10; IV.12, §7, 318.14–16; *al-Samāʾ wa-l-ʿālam* 1, 1.7–5.6. This is in harmony with the above interpretation that form is common not in the numerical sense of *muštarak* but in the generic sense of *ʿāmm*, so that Avicenna does not adhere to the "multiplicity of form," as some interpreters claimed, but regards "the complete form of a thing to be one" (*al-ṣūra al-tāmma li-l-šayʾ wāḥida*), as he writes in *al-Ilāhiyyāt* VIII.3, §4, 341.15f., tr. by Marmura; q.v. above, 165ff.

277 *al-Samāʿ al-ṭabīʿī* I.6, §3, 35.10f.; cf. *al-Naǧāt* I.9, 13.3–5; *al-Ḥikma al-mašriqiyya* III.4, 11.15–21; q.v. also above, 172ff.

distinguish between a thing's nature and a thing's complex form in that the former is only a part of the latter – at least if we want to express ourselves rigorously.[278]

We can see that even despite the fact that Avicenna's *al-Išārāt wa-l-tanbīhāt* do not offer a definition of nature, they contain an accurate description of the singular nature of the simple elements which conforms entirely with the more explicit account in *al-Samāʿ al-ṭabīʿī*, as it, ultimately, relies on the unique features Avicenna attributed to nature concordantly in all his philosophical compendia: that it is invariable and always the same (and by implication, since the elements lack any psychological capacities, that it is also without volition).

It happens only in his philosophical dictionary *Kitāb al-Ḥudūd* that Avicenna exclusively lists Aristotle's definition instead of his own. However, this may be due to the nature of this work. In its introductory remarks, Avicenna relates that his students begged him to write down a work in which he should list the definitions of philosophical concepts. He laments the difficulty and, to his mind, the inappropriateness of such an undertaking, as it is "almost an impossible task for man" (*ka-l-amr al-mutaʿaḏḏir ʿala l-bašar*).[279] Avicenna's reluctance is primarily motivated by methodical reasons, though. We may assume that, since his own definition of nature is only fully understandable in the context of a longer elaboration on the classification of the natural powers, i.e., since it is difficult to grasp its full meaning when it is given in the form of a brief catch phrase without the relevant context and without any reference to soul, Avicenna might have had good reason not to give his definition in the *Kitāb al-Ḥudūd* but to provide Aristotle's instead. Aristotle's definition, unlike his own, is very accessible and perfectly meets the requirements that a book on definitions – at least in the eyes of Avicenna – may stipulate. Aristotle's version seems to be the preferable definition for a general book that he wrote for his students, in particular since they may anyway have been more interested in the historically influential notion of nature which had come down to them.[280] So, it is understandable that Avicenna uses only Aristotle's definition in the *Kitāb al-Ḥudūd*, that he puts forth his own definition in brief systematic treatises like *Dānešnāme-ye ʿAlāʾī* and *al-Hidāya*, but that he mentions and discusses both definitions in his longer elaborations *al-Naǧāt* (and *al-Ḥikma al-ʿArūḍiyya*) as well as *al-Šifāʾ*. After all, we should not forget that Avicenna actively endorses Aristotle's definition and defends it against Philoponus' superfluous distortion.

---

278 Once more, Avicenna remarks that one may be allowed to use the term "nature" in a less strict sense and say that "the nature of each thing is its form" (*ʿasā an takūna ṭabīʿa kull šayʾ ṣūratahū*; *al-Samāʿ al-ṭabīʿī* I.6, §3, 35.13). Yet, Avicenna is quick to add that he prefers to use the term as he himself defined it.

279 *Kitāb al-Ḥudūd*, §3, 1.4.

280 It is this circumstance which further explains, why Avicenna even lists the influential definition of Philoponus in the *Kitāb al-Ḥudūd*, even though he rejects it, as we have seen, while not adding his own.

What, then, is the precise relation between Aristotle's and Avicenna's definitions of nature? Both definitions are in their core account congruent with one another. Whereas Aristotle defined nature as a "first principle for the motion of that in which it is," it is a "power which produces motion" in Avicenna. The meaning of "first" is covered by the fact that it actively and directly "produces motion," and the meaning "principle for the motion," as we have been told repeatedly, is nothing other than that of a "power." That nature is something "in" the thing is, moreover, achieved by the first of the distinctions Avicenna has drawn in *al-Samāʿ al-ṭabīʿī* I.5, viz., that between those acts and motions of natural bodies which proceed from external causes (*asbāb ḫāriǧa*) as opposed to those which come to be from the bodies themselves (*li-anfusihā*). Nature and the three kinds of souls belong to this latter group. The qualifications "by itself and not by accident" which Aristotle added could also be seen as more or less covered by Avicenna's understanding of a non-volitional uniform internal "power," even though he does not state that explicitly.

However, it should also not be forgotten that there is one crucial aspect of Aristotle's definition that is ambiguous – ambiguous on Avicenna's understanding, that is.[281] Above, Avicenna argued that soul is able to effect local motion directly and without any intermediate.[282] Thus, it is possible to define the motive power of soul, which is dispersed through the nerves of muscles of an animal's body, simply by adopting Aristotle's definition of nature as a "first principle for the motion of that in which it is and for [that thing's] rest, essentially and not accidentally." For Avicenna, this is a severe and intolerable ambiguity. To be sure, Avicenna, as we have seen above, agrees with Philoponus that Aristotle added πρώτως or *awwal* precisely in order to be able to draw the distinction between nature and soul. According to Avicenna, this attempt was unsuccessful, as no adverb like πρώτως and no adjective like *awwal* could achieve this, because the motive power of the soul is, in fact, a first or primary principle of motion. Moreover, we have also seen that Avicenna severely criticised what he took to be Philoponus' understanding of the actual relation between nature and soul. We also saw that the entire philosophical tradition before Avicenna up to, and including, his own contemporaries relied heavily on a comparison, sometimes even identification, of soul and nature. Avicenna, however, is interested in classifying

---

281 It is in this respect conspicuous that Avicenna calls both Aristotle's and Philoponus' definitions only a description (*rasm*); cf. *al-Samāʿ al-ṭabīʿī* I.5, §5, 31.9, 12; cf. also *al-Samāʿ al-ṭabīʿī* I.5, §7, 32.17. Moreover, in both his *al-Samāʿ al-ṭabīʿī* and *al-Ḥikma al-mašriqiyya*, Avicenna calls the Aristotelian definition of nature "generic" (*ka-l-ǧinsiyya*), apparently referring to the distinction between concepts and definitions either "*qua* matter" or "*qua* genus" as developed in *al-Burhān* I.10 and *al-Ilāhiyyāt* V.3 (*al-Samāʿ al-ṭabīʿī* I.5, §9, 3434.3f.; *al-Ḥikma al-mašriqiyya* III.4, 9.18f.). For the significance of this distinction and its historical context, cf. McGinnis, "Logic and Science," 173–178; Benevich, "The Priority of Natures against the Identity of Indiscernibles." As Avicenna indicates a little later in his *al-Ḥikma al-mašriqiyya*, it is only *his* definition of nature that denotes its essence and reality (*ḥaqīqatihā*; III.4, 9.19f.)

282 q.v. above, 229ff.

natural powers systematically and to *discern* their respective sphere of influence. A Neoplatonic definition of nature and soul, i.e., one which regards nature as a second-rate soul or as the external activity of the world-soul, is absolutely useless for any such cause. This, then, is precisely the reason that Avicenna steers away from the attempt to define nature by means of an unclear and blurred nature-soul dichotomy, and introduces the novel combination of distinctions between uniform and manifold motions which are either with or without volition. The result is clear and unambiguous: the motive capacity of the soul may, like nature, produce motion "primarily" but, unlike nature, it does so through volition.

In effect, the two distinctions between "with volition" and "without volition," and between "uniform" and "manifold," are the proper specific difference by which the genus "power" can be described and distinguished so as to yield four different categories of powers, of which one is nature, while the other three are different types of soul. On the basis of all we have seen in this chapter, it is absurd to assert that Avicenna's classification of the natural powers "blurs the distinction, evident within ordinary experience, between living things and non-living things," as has first been claimed by James Weisheipl, who was followed in this by Macierowski and Hassing.[283] This view must be regarded as a severe misjudgement. Avicenna does not blur the distinction between living and non-living things – Avicenna *saves* the distinction, and he does so with a novel, unprecedented, and Peripatetic account of natural powers that categorises inanimate as well as three kinds of animate beings, viz., plants, planets, and animals.

This concludes my analysis of Avicenna's account of nature, which Avicenna introduced as the efficient principle common to natural bodies. Since Avicenna denies the existence of a universal nature, we must understand the commonality of nature not long the lines of *muštarak*, i.e., as a single numerically one principle common to all natural bodiess, but along the lines of *ʿāmm*, as a general principle that belongs to each and every natural body individually. As such it constitutes an additional principle of the natural body not insofar as it is body but insofar as it is subject to change. The notion of change and motion is crucial and central to any philosophical examination of the natural world, as it is accepted as the paradigm characteristic of the material world. While I shall not present an analysis of motion myself, I shall discuss in detail the two most important features of natural bodies insofar as they are subject to motion, viz., place and time. Since every natural body seems to have a place and since every natural body's motion has some time, an analysis of these two features is essential for a satisfactory understanding of Avicenna's system of natural philosophy.

283 cf. Weisheipl, "Aristotle's Concept of Nature," 146f.; "The Concept of Nature," 20f.; Macierowski and Hassing, "John Philoponus on Aristotle's Definition of Nature," 81; cf. also the absurd claim by Arif that "in the case of animals ... nature is identified with soul as well as inclination" ("The Universe as a System," 137).

5 Putting Surface Back into Place

Avicenna's account of place is underrated. It is also understudied (arguably as a result of being underrated) and, consequently, it has also not been adequately understood, neither as an aspect of Avicenna's thought nor in its significance within the history of philosophy – and so it has continued to be underrated.[1]

This situation can be illustrated with the help of two quotations. The first is a typical assessment of the Arabic, and in particular the Avicennian, contribution to the philosophical understanding of the concept of place. It was made by Pierre Duhem and reads, in its English translation by Roger Ariew, as follows:

> One should not expect to find the depth and originality of thought of Damascius and Simplicius in the work of the Arabic philosophers; with respect to the nature of place and its immobility they mostly limited themselves to commenting upon Aristotle's doctrines, making use of the reflections by Alexander of Aphrodisias and Themistius, with varying degrees of success. They hardly ever mentioned Joannes Philoponus's theory except in order to reject it summarily, and they appear not to have bothered with Damascius's theory which Simplicius developed ... Avicenna defined place in the same manner as al-Kindi, that is, in the same manner as Aristotle.[2]

Apart from the fact that Duhem, who published the first volume of his *Le système du monde* more than a century ago, had even less knowledge about which works exactly were translated into Arabic than we have nowadays, and also apart from his apparent admiration for Damascius (d. after 538) and Simplicius (d. ~ 560), whose theories may not have have been translated at all and, thus, simply could not have been bothered with, his assessment that Avicenna merely followed Abū Yaʿqūb ibn Isḥāq al-Kindī (d. ~ 256/870) who merely followed Aristotle, is too simplistic.[3] What is more, in light of the results of the following analysis, Duhem's claim that Avicenna "hardly ever mentioned Joannes Philoponus's theory," and that he rejected it only "summarily," while not funny, sounds like a joke.

Leaving aside Duhem's remark about the depth and the originality of Arabic philosophers, which is not too simplistic but simply offensive, one might come to Duhem's defence by mentioning the possibly narrow range of available texts in translation, and

1 Among the few publications which touch upon aspects related to Avicenna's account of place are al-ʿIrāqī, *al-Falsafa al-ṭabīʿiyya ʿinda Ibn Sīnā*, 260–299; Duhem, *Medieval Cosmology*; Bäck, "Ibn Sina on the Individuation of Perceptible Substances"; Jeck, "Zenons Aporie des Topos"; Verbeke, "Notions centrales de la physique d'Avicenne"; Arif, "The Universe as a System"; Maróth, "Averroes on the Void"; cf. also the valuable contributions by McGinnis, "A Penetrating Question"; "Positioning Heaven"; "Avoiding the Void."

2 Duhem, *Medieval Cosmology*, 140; for the French original, cf. *Le système du monde*, vol. 7, 159.

3 Duhem's judgement about al-Kindī derives from al-Kindī's account in his *Liber de quinque essentiis*, 27.15–31.21; cf. *Risāla fī ḥudūd al-ašyāʾ wa-rusūmihā*, §19, 167 (= §18 in al-Kindī, *Risāla fī l-asmāʾ al-mufrada*).

https://doi.org/10.1515/9783110546798-006

the perhaps limited quality of what was available to him, when he wrote his immense *Le système du monde*.[4] One might even say that there is some limited truth in Duhem's statement insofar as there are undeniable, striking similarities between Avicenna's and Aristotle's approach to place that *prima facie* may warrant the assertion that Avicenna by and large followed Aristotle. Both philosophers, for example, introduce a number of requirements which they believe any successful definition of place must satisfy, before they enumerate the probable candidates of which one, in the end, turns out to be correct. They even both arrive at practically the same definition of place, as is immediately apparent upon comparing Aristotle's well-known definition of place as "the limit of the containing body at which it is in contact with the contained body" with the one Avicenna provided in his *al-Naǧāt* that place is "the limit of the containing [body] in contact with the limit of the contained [body]."[5]

Yet, the apparent similarities notwithstanding, it is evident that anyone who is satisfied with thinking that Aristotle thought the same about place as al-Kindī and Avicenna has a naive understanding of the history of philosophy and overlooks the fact that even if the Arabic philosophers accepted Aristotle's definition of place, they might have had specific reasons for doing so – reasons which deserve to be investigated. As it happens, this is nowhere as true as with regard to the philosophical concept of place, for it is outright momentous within the history of philosophy that the Arabic philosophers adhered to the Aristotelian doctrine at all – for that was a doctrine which, having come under attack already in antiquity, has been abolished entirely in the sixth century. The fact that Avicenna accepts Aristotle's account does not render his own engagement with place boring or unoriginal; to the contrary, it makes it all the more exciting, because after the sixth century, i.e., after John Philoponus (d. 574) had destroyed Aristotle's theory in his famous *Corollarium de loco*, there seemed to be no reason left for adhering to it anymore.[6] As will be seen, however, Avicenna developed Aristotle's account so massively and carefully, that it could withstand and overcome each single one of Philoponus' objections. If Philoponus' *Corollarium de loco* constitutes the greatest attack on Aristotle's account, Avicenna's *al-Samāʿ al-ṭabīʿī* contains its greatest defence.

While Duhem's assertion shows that the significance of Avicenna's account of place within the history of philosophy has been plainly overlooked, a second quotation will illustrate how Avicenna's efforts in developing a satisfying theory have been misunderstood and carelessly neglected. In an article by Udo Reinhold Jeck on Arabic and Latin discussions of Zeno's puzzle about place, we find a brief two-page section on Avicenna's discussion in *al-Samāʿ al-ṭabīʿī*. This section begins with the following words:

4 Duhem seems to have relied on Carra de Vaux's 1900 monograph on Avicenna and, like Carra de Vaux, refers primarily to Avicenna's *al-Naǧāt* and *ʿUyūn al-ḥikma* but not to his *al-Samāʿ al-ṭabīʿī*.

5 *Phys.* IV.4, 212a6–6a; *al-Naǧāt* II.2.10, 244.8f.

6 Philoponus' corollary is inserted into his commentary on the *Physics* at 557.7–585.4.

> Auch Avicenna beschäftigte sich im fünften Kapitel der Sufficientia mit der Philosophie des Ortes. Seine Analyse gliedert sich in drei größere Abschnitte: Er untersuchte zunächst die Argumente jener Philosophen, die die Existenz des Ortes lehrten bzw. verneinten (Kap. 5), zählte dann die differenten Meinungen der Denker über den Ort auf (Kap. 6) und schloß seine Untersuchung mit der Destruktion verschiedener Theorien zum Ort ab (Kap. 7). Danach ging er zur Erforschung des Vakuums über und folgte mit dieser Anordnung dem vierten Buch der Physik des Aristoteles.[7]

With this bewildering outline of Avicenna's discussion of place, Jeck suggests that Avicenna himself had not much to say about place in his *Sufficientia* (i.e., in the Latin translation of *al-Samāʿ al-ṭabīʿī*), apart from listing earlier arguments for and against the existence of place in chapter five, recounting various ancient theories about its essence in chapter six, and rejecting those he considered to be false in chapter seven. This is all Avicenna had to say about place, apparently, for after these three chapters, he turned his attention to the next topic: the investigation of the void, thus following Aristotle's order of inquiry in the *Physics*.

Surely, to list, to recount, and to reject theories advanced by earlier intellectuals about certain topics can be, and often is, a valuable part of doing philosophy and an important contribution to the scientific endeavour of understanding reality. So, maybe one should not be too captious with Jeck's statements, as he clearly acknowledges these efforts. After all, Jeck's primary interest was in the history and reception of Zeno's paradox, and that is fair enough.[8] This task certainly can be accomplished without first having to scrutinise the three chapters Avicenna is said to have written about the subject of place before dealing with the next subject, viz., the void. It simply was not Jeck's primary interest to investigate Avicenna's account of place, and so he may be excused for not having realised that for Avicenna, the investigation of the void constitutes an important part of, instead of being merely the next topic after, the inquiry into place.

What is disappointing, though, is that the interest in Avicenna's philosophy of place, as displayed in Jeck's article, was apparently so limited that Jeck did not even bother to survey the contents of the 1508 edition of Avicenna's Latin *Sufficientia*, which is the referenced source for his outline quoted above, with any desirable amount of attention. Had he turned just two leaves, or checked the appended alphabetical list of contents, he would have learned that the very next chapter, chapter II.9, is announced as *de certificando quid sit locus* – thus being yet another chapter on place which, it must be noted, is itself almost as long as chapters five, six, and seven taken together.[9]

---

7 Jeck, "Zenons Aporie des Topos," 430f.

8 Jeck's monograph *Aristoteles contra Augustinum* has a similar agenda and traces views about the relation between time and soul throughout the history of philosophy. His investigation devotes some considerable attention to the texts of Avicenna and Averroes, and examines their views on this question. Yet, this attention primarily serves Jeck's overall interest in the writings of the Latin thinkers in the thirteenth century and their knowledge of the opinions expressed in the Greek commentaries, i.e., opinions which reached them, in part, through Arabic works translated into Latin.

9 Avicenna, *Opera*, 31r, 110v.

In short, what Jeck missed was that Avicenna's extensive discussion of place does not comprise only three chapters but five, that Avicenna did not simply proceed to an investigation about the void after having dealt with place, and that he did precisely *not* follow the structure of Aristotle's *Physics*.

What is nonetheless true is that much of Avicenna's discussion is concerned with various earlier opinions about place. In fact, as a whole, it is driven by a commitment to defending the troubled account of place which Aristotle had presented in *Physics* IV.1–5 against numerous objections. What needs to be realised, now, is that *although* the discussion in *al-Samāʿ al-ṭabīʿī* considerably draws upon earlier theories, Avicenna's engagement with his predecessors must be appreciated as a major break with a long tradition of opposing Aristotle on the subject of place – and it is nothing other than this ninth chapter of the second book, the one which Jeck overlooked, in which most of the magic happens.

Of course, Avicenna was not the first to return to Aristotle's definition. Among his Greek predecessors we find Alexander of Aphrodisias (fl. ~ 200) and Themistius (d. ~ 385), who promoted Aristotle's account. Moreover, some Peripatetics from Baġdād, among them Yaḥyā ibn ʿAdī (d. 363/974) and Abū Naṣr al-Fārābī (d. 339/950-51), and also already al-Kindī and the Iḫwān al-Ṣafāʾ (fl. ~ 370/980), defended Aristotle's reasoning of *Physics* IV.1–5 against certain objections, as we shall see.[10] Even the Muʿtazilites from Baġdād argued, against their brothers from Baṣra, that place ought to be conceived as a surface, i.e., effectively along the lines of Aristotle.[11] Yet, from among the testimonies that are known to be extant, Avicenna's discussion of place remains by all means the most comprehensive, the most rigorous, and the most ingenious vindication of the Aristotelian position.

In order to demonstrate this, I shall begin with a brief outline of Aristotle's account as well as some central themes of the ancient and late ancient discontent with it. I shall compare Avicenna's approach to the definition of place with that of Aristotle and analyse how Avicenna developed and clarified the Aristotelian notion. Thereupon, I shall turn to his active defence of the Aristotelian position against the popular rival conception of space. I shall, first, show what notion of space Avicenna received and, second, explain how he argues that space is both entirely non-existent and altogether not required to explain certain phenomena in the natural world. My intention in all this is to demonstrate that Avicenna's cleverly articulated account of place constitutes a significant development within the history of natural philosophy and must no longer be underrated, understudied, or misunderstood.

---

10 Maróth erroneously asserted that both al-Fārābī and Avicenna rejected Aristotle's accounts of void and place, and followed the Neoplatonists in accepting the existence of a three-dimensional independent extension; cf. "Averroes on the Void," 15–19. Likewise inaccurate is Bäck's remark that "[b]y space ... Ibn Sina, like Philoponus and early Islamic philosophers, has a remarkable modern notion of a featureless continuum" ("Ibn Sina on the Individuation of Perceptible Substances," 30).

11 cf. Dhanani, *The Physical Theory of Kalām*, 66–68.

5.1 A Troubled Account of Place

Aristotle's Strategy

The basic idea of Aristotle's investigation of place in *Physics* IV.1–5 can be recounted quickly.[12] As usual in the *Physics*, Aristotle begins by asking whether place exists, how it exists, and, if it exists, what it is. *That* place exists is nothing Aristotle worries too much about. In fact, he considers the existence of place to be borne out by various natural phenomena. Replacement (ἡ ἀντιμετάστασις, *al-istibdāl*), for example, is for him one clear indicator that there is something like place, for if the water in a jug is replaced by air, then the place in which the water used to be, i.e., the place inside the jug, is now occupied by air.[13] This shows not only that places exist but suggests that places exist as something over and above the bodies that are in place (τι ... παρὰ τὰ σώματα, *mā ġayr al-ağsām*).[14] A second indication for the existence of place is the fact that natural simple bodies or elements move towards certain places: earth and water move downwards to the centre, whereas fire and air move upwards to the periphery, away from the centre. So, at least the places "above" and "below" seem to have some reality to themselves, which suggests that places generally have a reality.[15] All in all, it

---

12 For more detailed expositions of Aristotle's investigation as a whole, or of various aspects of it, cf. A. E. Taylor, *A Commentary on Plato's Timaeus*, 664–677; H. R. King, "Aristotle's Theory of *τόπος*"; Mendell, "Topoi on Topos"; Zekl, *Topos*; Jammer, *Concepts of Space*, 17–22; Mariña, "The Role of Limits in Aristotle's Concept of Place"; Algra, *Concepts of Space in Greek Thought*, ch. 4–5; Casey, *The Fate of Place*, 50–71; Lang, *The Order of Nature in Aristotle's Physics*; Dean-Jones, "Aristotle's Understanding of Plato's Receptacle"; Morison, *On Location*; Fritsche, "Aristotle on Space, Form, and Matter"; "Aristotle on χώρα in Plato's *Timaeus*"; Bostock, "A Note on Aristotle's Account of Place." For an assessment of Aristotle's remarks on the category of "where?" in the *Categories* and the seeming incompatibility with his account of place in the *Physics*, cf. esp. Mendell, "Topoi on Topos"; cf. also Morison, *On Location*, 57. Due to the relatively broad public interest in "theories of space," some of the contributions listed here target a broader audience and should be considered as falling into the category of popular science books or contemporary philosophy, esp. the books by Jammer and Casey. Others, though professing to offer a scientific exposition of Aristotle's account of place, are confused and baffling, and, on the whole, cannot be recommended, e.g., the book by Lang which, according to Gill's review, "is a disappointment." Gill's dissatisfaction is shared by Morison and Cohen. Yet, the book has also been praised as "the best book on Aristotle's treatment of the physical world to appear in recent years" (Miller's review). McGinnis, too, commended it as a "careful analysis" ("Positioning Heaven," fn. 24, 149).

13 *Phys.* IV.1, 208b1f.

14 *Phys.* IV.1, 208b28.

15 That "above" and "below" exist, however, does not mean that "above" and "below" are independently existing places. It is incorrect to say that fire naturally moves to the above. It would be more correct to say that "above" is that where fire naturally moves to. The places "above" and "below" do not independently have a reality to themselves as the proper places for fire and earth – they are real, but only *insofar as* fire moves up (and eventually is up) and earth moves down (and eventually is down). In other words, it is not the case that if there were no "above" and "below," there would be no natural motion. It is rather the case that if there were no natural motion, there would be no "above"

seems that for Aristotle, it would be just as ridiculous to demand a proper proof for the existence of place as it is for the existence of nature, because both are borne out by the indubitable reality of natural motion.[16]

The question of *what* – as opposed to whether – place is is more demanding. In chapter IV.4, Aristotle states that there are four potential candidates: form, matter, a three-dimensional extension, and the two-dimensional inner surface of the containing body.[17] One may ask, and commentators have done so, how this list could possibly be exhaustive, and why there are only these four and not more or other candidates available. The question is crucial insofar as Aristotle proceeds by elimination – a type of argument which yields a convincing result only if all options (or all reasonable options) apart from one are shown to be absurd, so that the remaining option automatically emerges as true. If a process of elimination operates on the basis of an incomplete list, it is bound to be dissatisfactory (even though its result may not necessarily be wrong). However, starting the sentence that introduces the four options with the adverb σχεδόν, Aristotle himself seems to indicate that the list is not absolutely exhaustive in the sense of including every possible option whatsoever. Surely, there are many other things place could be which Aristotle did not consider: for example, place might be a corporeal light, as in Proclus (d. 485); or a relation, as according to some interpreters in Theophrastus of Eresus (d. ~ 287 BC); or a fixed set of coordinates, as some might perhaps say today.[18] Yet, since Aristotle eventually claims that his analysis determined the nature of place with "necessity" (ἀνάγκη, *fa-wāǧib*), it is clear that, at least, *he*

and "below"; cf. Broadie, *Nature, Change, and Agency in Aristotle's* Physics, 104f.; cf. also Morison, *On Location*, 4. That Aristotle, in *Physics* IV.1, calls upon Hesiod and quotes a passage to insinuate that place or space (ὁ τόπος ... καὶ ἡ χώρα, *al-makān wa-l-mawḍiʿ*) is something that exists independently of, and even prior to, bodies, should be regarded as a concession to the dialectical character of the first chapter. In a similar way should we treat Aristotle's dialectical assertion that places seem "to have a some sort of power" (ἔχει τινὰ δύναμιν, *lahū ... quwwatan mā*); cf. Algra, *Concepts of Space in Greek Thought*, 200–203. Consequently, place is decidedly not a "principle of order," as Lang argues, not even "in respect to the category of 'where,'" nor is it a "constitutive principle of the cosmos [and] of what is contained" or "acting as a determinative principle" or "a single principle that determines the cosmos as a whole" (*The Order of Nature in Aristotle's Physics*, 39, 100–102, 161, 270); cf. also Lang's earlier analysis in *Aristotle's* Physics *and its Medieval Varieties*, ch. 3. For other views, in particular about the question of whether or not – and if so in what way – place has a power, cf. Machamer, "Aristotle on Natural Place and Natural Motion"; Sorabji, *Matter, Space, and Motion*, ch. 11 and 12; Matthen, "Why Does the Earth Move to the Center?," to name only a few contributions.

16 cf. *Phys.* II.1, 193a3f.

17 *Phys.* IV.4, 211b6–9. Lang argues that the fourth option, which Aristotle eventually affirms, must not be understood as a two-dimensional surface. Instead, she claims that "place is unique: it is three-dimensional but not a body, a limit but not a surface" (*The Order of Nature in Aristotle's Physics*, 72). What she means with this, though, remains unclear. Moreover, it seems that matter is precisely a candidate for place because it is some sort of extension, whereas form is a candidate, because it is a limit – just like a surface; cf. *Phys.* IV.2, 209b1–3, 6f.; cf. also *Cael.* IV.4, 312a12f.

18 For Proclus, cf. Simplicius' long report in his corollary of place (*In Phys.*, 611.25–612.35) as well as Proclus, *In Remp.*, vol. 2, 196.24–30, 198.4–15; *In Tim.*, vol. 1, 138.21–25, 161.1–3, 162.4–8; cf. also Sorabji,

regards his selection of the four candidates as appropriate and his decision to proceed with an argument by elimination as justified.[19] Moreover, most ancient and late ancient interpreters of Aristotle agreed with him on this.[20]

The place of a body, then, has to be either its form or its matter or an overlapping three-dimensional extension or the two-dimensional inner surface of the containing body. Aristotle is quick in eliminating matter and form. Already in the very first lines of his investigation, Aristotle noted that places are something beyond or distinct from the bodies that are in place (τι ... παρὰ τὰ σώματα, *mā ġayr al-ağsām*).[21] Aristotle's conception of matter and form as the constitutive principles of a natural body, however, cannot satisfy this condition, and so neither matter nor form can be the place of a natural body constituted by them.[22]

His reason for rejecting matter and form is all the more comprehensible once it is understood that Aristotle's interest in the nature of place in the *Physics* derives from his interest in motion. The primary kind of motion, however, is local motion or change

---

Matter, Space, and Motion, 109–118; Schrenk, "Proclus on Space as Light"; "Proclus on Corporeal Space"; Griffin, "Proclus on Place as the Luminous Vehicle of the Soul"; for Theophrastus, cf. frgm. 149 in Theophrastus, *Sources for his Life, Writings, Thought and Influence*, 304f., again reported by Simplicius (*In Phys.*, 639.13–22). As Sambursky and Jammer argued, it was Theophrastus who, in opposition to Aristotle, developed a relational account of place; cf. Sambursky, *The Physical World of Late Antiquity*, 2, 6; *The Concept of Place in Late Neoplatonism*, 12f.; Jammer, *Concepts of Space*, 23; cf. also Steinmetz, *Die Physik des Theophrastos von Eresos*, 156f. In the meantime, more moderate interpretations of Theophrastus' relation to Aristotle's definition of place appeared; cf. esp. Sorabji, *Matter, Space, and Motion*, 202–204; Algra, *Concepts of Space in Greek Thought*, 231–248; Morison, "Did Theophrastus Reject Aristotle's Account of Place?"

19 *Phys.* IV.4, 212a5.

20 Themistius accepts Aristotle's list of options as well as the validity of his argument by elimination; cf. *In Phys.*, 112.25–28. Simplicius explicitly raises the question whether or not the list is exhaustive. He stresses that for Aristotle's argumentation it would be better if it were, and provides a justification of why it, indeed, is; cf. *In Phys.*, 571.31–572.8. His explanation mirrors the one advanced by his earlier contemporary Philoponus; cf. *In Phys.*, 547.20–29. It is clear that both Simplicius and Philoponus themselves have to justify the validity of Aristotle's method of proceeding by elimination, for otherwise they could not derive their own position – which is also one of the four alternatives – from rejecting Aristotle's; cf. Philoponus, *In Phys.*, 567.31–568.1. The same is true of Avicenna, whose justification of Aristotle's four candidates follows a similar idea, even though he ultimately develops and enlarges the list, as we shall see; cf. *al-Samāʿ al-ṭabīʿī* II.6, §2, 115.7–11; on Philoponus and Avicenna, q.v. below, 329ff. Among contemporary interpreters, Hussey is altogether sceptical about the adequacy of Aristotle's list of options; cf. his comments in Aristotle, *Physics*, *ad* 211b5. Aristotle's choice has been defended in recent times by Morison and by McGinnis; cf. Morison, *On Location*, 104f.; McGinnis, "Positioning Heaven," fn. 3, 142f.

21 *Phys.* IV.1, 208b28; cf. IV.2, 209a22–32; IV.3, 210b27–31.

22 Since Aristotle's argument against identifying place with matter relies on his own conception of matter, it is not clear to what extent Plato's understanding of space and matter is vulnerable to Aristotle's criticism.

of *place*.[23] Thus, if we want to understand local motion, we need to know what it is that changes when something engages in local motion.[24] If place were something that inseparably belongs to the thing in place, as that thing's form and matter do, then nothing could ever engage in local motion as long as "to engage in local motion" means precisely "to change place." Since nothing can change, or leave behind, its own matter or its own form (except by undergoing substantial change), nothing could ever change its place. Instead, wherever something is, it would be at the same place as it already was, just as it would consist of the same matter and the same form it already had.[25] Thus, when Aristotle lists a number of axiomatic requirements at the beginning of *Physics* IV.4, in order to begin his final attempt to determine what place is, he reaffirms his earlier claim that place must "not be anything [pertaining] to the object" (μηδὲν τοῦ πράγματος, *laysa bi-šay' min ḏālika l-amr*) and that it must be capable of being left behind by it (ἀπολείπεσθαι ἑκάστου, *yaḫlū min šay' šay' min ǧihāt*) and separable from it (χωριστόν, *yufāriquhū*).[26] As further requirements, he adds that place must also contain that which is in place, that it must not be greater or smaller than the thing in place, and that it must be able to explain the natural motion of the elements to places that are "up" or "down."[27]

What remain as viable candidates for place are the overlapping three-dimensional incorporeal extension equal to the body and the surrounding surface containing the

---

23 e.g., *Phys.* IV.1, 208a31f.; VIII.7, 260a26–29; cf. also the recent study by Odzuck, *The Priority of Locomotion in Aristotle's* Physics. It should be noted that, for Avicenna, local motion is no longer the primary kind of motion. The primary kind of motion is rather circular motion, which Avicenna categorises as motion in respect of position (and not place); cf. McGinnis, "Positioning Heaven," 159. Avicenna's position needs to be understood in contrast to a superficially similar, though systematically different, claim made by Aristotle who also emphasised in *Physics* VIII.9, 265a13, the primacy of circular motion: "that circular motion is the primary kind of local motion is clear" (Ὅτι δὲ τῶν φορῶν ἡ κυκλοφορία πρώτη, δῆλον, *wa-min al-bayyin anna l-ḥaraka dawran awwal aṣnāf al-naqla*). While for both Aristotle and Avicenna, circular motion emerges as the primary kind of all motion, Aristotle classifies it *among* local motion – and not as a distinct kind *besides* local motion, as Avicenna does. For Avicenna's position, q.v. below 340ff.

24 cf. Aristotle's explicit claim at *Physics* IV.4, 211a12f.

25 cf. *Phys.* IV.2, 210a2f.; cf. also *al-Samāʿ al-ṭabīʿī* II.5, §2, 112.3–6; *al-Naǧāt* II.2.10, 233.10–13 ≈ *al-Ḥikma al-ʿArūḍiyya* II.2.8, 133.20–22; *Dānešnāme-ye ʿAlāʾī* III.6, 14.8–10.

26 Suggesting to read in the Arabic *yufāriquhū* instead of *tufāriquhū/tafāraqahū* as in Badawī at *Physics* IV.4, 211a3; cf. also *Phys.* IV.3, 210b27–31.

27 *Phys.* IV.4, 210b34–211a6. One is inclined to say that Aristotle commits the fallacy of a *petitio principii* when he first stipulates the condition that place must be something which contains that which is in place and, then, concludes that place is precisely the inner limit of the containing body, because it seems that this condition simply rules out the third candidate for place, viz., the extension, because it seems that no extension really contains the body occupying it. The late ancient commentators, however, did not see it that way. We find both Philoponus and Simplicius discussing this issue and, eventually, accepting the condition, arguing that it can also satisfactorily – or even better – be met by the idea of an extension; cf. Philoponus, *In Phys.*, 539.24–16, 588.28–589.18; Simplicius, *In Phys.*, 565.8–12, 604.13–25, 607.25–608.22. Their arguments, however, do not seem to exempt Aristotle from the accusation entirely.

body. Aristotle's rejection of the third candidate, i.e., the extension, is more complicated, in particular because it is more brief than clear.[28] Commentators have advanced a number of different interpretations of the Aristotelian text. On the whole, Aristotle claims that if place were an extension, two absurd results would follow: first, there would exist an actually infinite number of places; and second, place would have to be considered as capable of being in motion itself, so that it, too, would require a place, which, again, leads to an infinite number of coinciding places.[29] Having thus eliminated three candidates from a justifiably exhaustive list of four, Aristotle writes:

> εἰ τοίνυν μηδὲν τῶν τριῶν ὁ τόπος ἐστίν, μήτε τὸ εἶδος μήτε ἡ ὕλη μήτε διάστημά τι ἀεὶ ὑπάρχον ἕτερον παρὰ τὸ τοῦ πράγματος τοῦ μεθισταμένου, ἀνάγκη τὸν τόπον εἶναι τὸ λοιπὸν τῶν τεττάρων, τὸ πέρας τοῦ περιέχοντος σώματος <καθ' ὃ συνάπτει τῷ περιεχομένῳ>.
>
> فإذ كان المكان ليس هو واحداً من الثلاثة لا صورةً ولا هيولى ولا بعداً لأنّه إن كان بعداً فقد يجب أن يكون هاهنا بعد ما آخر غير بعد الأمر المنتقل فواجب أن يكون المكان هو نهاية الباقي من الأربعة وهو نهاية الجسم المحيط وهو نهاية الجسم المحتوي تماسّ عليها ما يحتوي عليه.
>
> If, then, place is none of the three – neither the form nor the matter nor some ever existing extension that is different from the [extension] of the thing which changes place – place necessarily is what remains of the four:[30] the limit of the containing body at which it is in contact with the contained body. (*Phys.* IV.4, 212a2–6a, tr. by Hardie/Gaye, modified)[31]

After having identified place as the inner surface of the containing body by way of eliminating all other available options, Aristotle endeavours also to provide positive confirmation for his conclusion by showing that his account of place not only meets all the requirements he stipulated at the beginning of *Physics* IV.4 but also avoids or overcomes the puzzles he listed in chapter one that hitherto made it difficult to see what place is.[32] Thus, for Aristotle, the final conclusion that place is the inner surface of the containing body is not simply the only remaining alternative but is an actually satisfactory account that grew out of a dialectical argument by elimination.

---

28 Morison even asserts: "These lines are almost certainly corrupt in several places" (*On Location*, 122). One reason for why Aristotle is so brief here may be that he is already looking ahead to his more thorough rejection of the void in *Physics* IV.6–9. Since the conception of the void has strong similarities to the present conception of place as an extended three-dimensional space, he may have allowed himself to be brief here.

29 cf. *Phys.* IV.4, 211b19–25; cf. also the interpretation of Alexander *apud* Simplicium, *In Phys.*, 576.30–577.1, and the remarks by M. Rashed on *scholium* 54 in Alexander of Aphrodisias, *Commentaire perdu à la* Physique *d'Aristote*, 208–210; q.v. further below, 369.

30 Suggesting to read in the Arabic *huwa nihāyat al-bāqī* for *huwa nihāyat al-ǧism al-bāqī* in Badawī.

31 According to Ross, the phrase καθ' ὃ συνάπτει τῷ περιεχομένῳ is not contained in any Greek manuscript used by Bekker but is present in the Arabic-Latin version as well as the sixteenth century Basel editions of Aristotle's works; cf. also Qusṭā's Arabic version of Ps.-Plutarchus' *Placita Philosophorum* (Aetius Arabus, *Die Vorsokratiker in arabischer Überlieferung*, 20.4f.).

32 cf. esp. *Phys.* IV.4, 212a21–30; IV.5, 212b22–213a11.

Criticism from Early on

There is no other concept of Aristotle's natural philosophy that found so many opponents and so few supporters as place. Pupils, followers, and commentators usually accepted the theory that natural bodies consist of a material and a formal component, that they behave according to a certain way that is natural to them, that they undergo motion, and that their motion has a certain numerical relation to the time of their motion. Hardly anyone, especially in the Greek tradition, has ever agreed that place is the inner limit of the containing body.[33]

It is interesting, in this regard, to compare the attitudes displayed by Philoponus and Simplicius in their two critical corollaries on place. Whereas the former writes in a trenchant tone that brims with self-assurance, the latter submissively apologises that he begs to disagree and humbly recommends one re-investigate the idea of place as a three-dimensional extension which, it seems to him, is "worthy of more extended consideration," hoping that "Aristotle would countenance [his] daring."[34] In the end, however, it must be said that many of the objections Philoponus and Simplicius raise against Aristotle's theory, despite the difference in tone, are alike in several respects.

One major objection to Aristotle's account of place has been advanced by Aristotle himself. Although he also presented an answer to it, scholars still regard it as "the most perplexing dilemma in Aristotle's doctrine of place."[35] Moreover, it is one of the five objections used by Philoponus to show the invalidity and defectiveness of Aristotle's definition of place.[36] This objection concerns the apparent incompatibility between two of Aristotle's core conditions of place. On the one hand, place has been defined as a limit which "is in contact" (συνάπτει, *tamāssa*) with the body in place.[37] On the other hand, Aristotle later added that place must be "unmoving" (ἀκίνητον, *ġayr al-mutaḥarrika*).[38]

---

33 As already mentioned, notable exceptions include Alexander and Themistius.

34 Simplicius, *In Phys.*, 601.7–13, tr. by Urmson.

35 Grant, "The Medieval Doctrine of Place," 59; cf. also Sorabji, *Matter, Space, and Motion*, 187. Morison seems to actively trivialise the objection and lists it as one of the "standard objections," thus implying that it is simply a common objection rather than a troublesome issue (*On Location*, 154f.).

36 cf. Philoponus, *In Phys.*, 564.14–565.1.

37 *Phys.* IV.4, 212a6.

38 *Phys.* IV.4, 212a20. It is crucial here to distinguish two senses of "unmoving." When Aristotle argues that place must be unmoving, he does not claim that place could not be moved. If there is water in the jug and if, on his account, the inner surface of the jug serves as the water's place, then of course we can move the jug from one room to another together with the water and the water's place. The place of the water would always be "in the jug where the jug's inner surface is in contact with the water," whereas the jug's place changes from being here in this room to being there in that room. When Aristotle argues that place must be unmoving, he does not argue against this sense. What he wants to emphasise is only that place must be something stable, i.e., something that can be determined and identified. If a boat is moored in a streaming river, so that its place, being the inner surface of the river's water touching

It is easy to see how these two conditions can run afoul of each other. If we consider a boat on a still lake, we can nicely establish, on the basis of Aristotle's definition, the boat's place as the immediately adjacent layer of water that is in contact with the boat's hull. The boat, then, is where this layer of water touches the hull.[39] When the boat starts moving, it is precisely this layer of water which begins to change. Thus, the boat engages in local motion, as it is always in contact with different parts of the water, changing its place again and again. Once the boat has stopped moving, it will be in contact with a different layer of water, now being at a different place. In this scenario, Aristotle's definition reveals its obvious merits.

What, however, is the place of a boat which is itself unmoving, because it is, for example, moored in a streaming river? In this case, the limit which is in contact with that which is in place is itself in motion, as the water streams around the boat's hull. The place, being the inner limit of the surrounding body, would constantly be changing not due to a motion of the boat but due to the motion of the water. Further scenarios spring to mind: what is the place of a boat that is carried off downstream? What is the place of a boat when it is itself moving full speed ahead in addition to being carried off downstream?

In the first case of a boat moored in a streaming river, Aristotle finds himself on a sticky wicket. The boat itself does not seem to be moving or to change its place, even though its place, i.e., the limit of the surrounding body, is changing constantly. The second case is no less embarrassing, as the limit, i.e., the water layer which touches the boat, seems to be unchanging (provided that the water layer which touches the boat equally moves together with the boat), yet the boat surely is moving downstream and, thus, seems to be changing its place.[40] In the third case, then, the place of the

---

the boat's hull, is in flux, it cannot be determined or identified as a place, because it does not remain but incessantly slips away. Aristotle's criterion is designed to forestall this latter situation, not to deny the former; cf. also Morison, *On Location*, 148–162, for a discussion of the term ἀκίνητος in Aristotle's account of place.

39 Aristotle remains silent about the fact that only part of the boat is in contact with water, while the other part of the boat is in contact with air. Apparently, Aristotle's example of a boat on a river, which we are about to discuss, is construed from a somewhat aerial perspective, so that the boat is considered as if it were a two-dimensional drawing and its place a one-dimensional line touching the rim of the boat. Corporeal reality, however, is three-dimensional and most objects that exist in the natural world are in contact with more than one surrounding substance. A boat, as we said, usually touches both water and air, and land animals for the most part touch both earth and air. Aristotle, however, talks of place as if place is the *one* inner surface of the *one* surrounding body (e.g., when he defines place at *Phys.* IV.4, 212a6–6a as τὸ πέρας τοῦ περιέχοντος σώματος <καθ’ ὃ συνάπτει τῷ περιεχομένῳ>). The Greek commentators did not greatly elaborate on that point or lament Aristotle's lack of precision; cf. Themistius, *In Phys.*, 119.9–11; Philoponus, *In Phys.*, 592.24f.; Simplicius, *In Phys.*, 586.15–20. We shall see later how Avicenna responds to this, and how he improves upon Aristotle's understanding of the notion of "surface" in this regard; q.v. below, 347ff.

40 This is how Algra reconstructs Aristotle's argument; cf. *Concepts of Space in Greek Thought*, 224. Algra, moreover, attributes this reading also to "Alexander, Themistius, Simplicius and Philoponus."

boat changes not for one but for two reasons: first, because the river flows, and second, because the boat itself is in motion. On account of what, then, can we say that the boat is changing its place? Moreover, how do we generally distinguish between a *moving* boat whose place changes on a flowing river and a *moored* boat whose place changes on a flowing river?

One ironic result of these scenarios is that although Aristotle intended to investigate place, in order to understand the phenomenon of local motion within the natural world, the definition he established appears to be plausible and coherent only as long as we consider the place of an unchanging body within unchanging surroundings. As soon as we introduce local motion together with common, every-day conditions of natural reality, for example, the wind in the air and the flow of a river, his definition falters. Since most objects within the natural world are either in flowing water or in windy air, Aristotle's account of place is in danger of being no more than an hypothetical construct which has close to no explanatory strength in the situations provided by the reality of the natural world, as it is unable to distinguish a moving boat on a river from a moored boat on a river – that is to say: Aristotle's account fails even to explain the fundamental difference between local motion and rest.

Before we draw any conclusions as to the inadequacy of Aristotle's account of place, we should see how he responds to this objection, given that he himself raised it. Towards the end of *Physics* IV.4, i.e., after his definition of place, Aristotle envisages the situation in which a moving object moves within surroundings that are in motion:

> διὸ ὅταν μὲν ἐν κινουμένῳ κινῆται καὶ μεταβάλλῃ τὸ ἐντός, οἷον ἐν ποταμῷ πλοῖον, ὡς ἀγγείῳ χρῆται μᾶλλον ἢ τόπῳ τῷ περιέχοντι. βούλεται δ' ἀκίνητος εἶναι ὁ τόπος· διὸ ὁ πᾶς μᾶλλον ποταμὸς τόπος, ὅτι ἀκίνητος ὁ πᾶς. ὥστε τὸ τοῦ περιέχοντος πέρας ἀκίνητον πρῶτον, τοῦτ' ἔστιν ὁ τόπος.
>
> ولذلك متى كان ما هو داخل متحرّك تحرّك وتبدّل في متحرّك مثل السفينة تسير في النهر فمنزلة المحيط حينئذ عنده منزلة الإناء لا منزلة المكان. وواجب أن يكون المكان غير متحرّك ولذلك إن كان ولا بدّ فالنهر بأسره أولى بأن يكون مكاناً لأنّ كلّه غير متحرّك. فنهاية الخطّ إذا غير المتحرّكة الأولى هي المكان.
>
> So, when something moves within something moving and changing,[41] like a boat on a river, then what surrounds plays the part of a vessel (ἀγγείῳ, *al-inā'*) rather than that of place. Place, however, should be unmoving (ἀκίνητος εἶναι ὁ τόπος, *al-makān ġayr mutaḥarrik*). Thus, it is rather the

Aristotle's own words allow for two interpretations, viz., a boat which is itself moving (due to wind or oarsmen) on a flowing river as well as a boat that is merely carried off downstream like flotsam. Themistius' wording follows closely that of Aristotle. It would, thus, be precipitant to attribute to him one view to the exclusion of the other, as Algra does; cf. *In Phys.*, 118.28f. Simplicius, by contrast, compares the boat to a piece of wood which "moves together with that in which it is" (συγκινεῖσθαι αὐτῷ τὸ ἐν ᾧ ἐστιν; *In Phys.*, 583.21). Philoponus, in the same vein, speaks of a boat which "moves together with the flow" (συγκινεῖται γὰρ τῷ ῥεύματι; *In Phys.*, 586.13f.). Finally, Alexander, according to Simplicius, seems to allow for that same interpretation; cf. Alexander *apud* Simplicium, *In Phys.*, 584.2–5.

41 Suggesting in the Arabic to emend to *taḥarraka* instead of *yataḥarraka* as in Badawī and, subsequently, to read *tabaddala* instead of *y-b-d-l*.

> whole river that is place, because as a whole it is unmoving, so that this is place: the first unmoving limit of what contains (τὸ τοῦ περιέχοντος πέρας ἀκίνητον πρῶτον, *fa-nihāyat al-ḫaṭṭ iḏa ġayr al-mutaḥarrika al-awlā hiya l-makān*). (*Phys.* IV.4, 212a16–21, tr. by Hardie/Gaye, modified)

As Aristotle argues, the water of the river functions as a vessel rather than as a place for the boat. The boat is in the water as in a vessel and the water is in the river as in a place. Thus, the place of the boat is supposed to be the river and not the water, for place is something unmoving and the nearest unmoving surrounding is not the water but the river. In this case, however, we seem required to abandon the condition that place is "the limit of the surrounding body at which it is *in contact* with the surrounded body."[42] This is what Richard Sorabji called the "standard interpretation" according to which Aristotle modified his original account of place by replacing the condition of immediate contact with the condition of being unmoving. Sorabji also adds that this interpretation is unsatisfactory, because it does not seem that Aristotle, in fact, wanted to abandon the contact-condition, in particular because he would also have had to abandon the condition that the proper place of a body is exactly as great as the body which it contains. After all, a river is not only greater than the boat but may also contain more than one boat as well as a couple of animals, all of which would be together in the same place.[43] In his commentary proper, Philoponus considers this result to be unproblematic, for he makes use of Aristotle's distinction between the "proper place" of something, which contains only this thing, and its "common place," which may contain other things as well. On that basis, he writes nonchalantly that if the river serves as the place for the boat, then place "is obviously not place in the primary sense, but common place."[44]

---

42 *Phys.* IV.4, 212a6–6a, tr. by Hardie/Gaye, modified, emphasis added. On the conflict between the two conditions, cf. Simplicius, *In Phys.*, 584.15–25, as well as Ross' comments in *Physics*, *ad* 212a20f.; cf. also Algra, *Concepts of Space in Greek Thought*, 226; Morison, *On Location*, 157.

43 cf. Sorabji, *Matter, Space, and Motion*, 188; cf. also Algra, *Concepts of Space in Greek Thought*, 226; Grant, "The Medieval Doctrine of Place," 59f.

44 Philoponus, *In Phys.*, 586.19, tr. by Algra; cf. Ross' comments in *Physics*, 57. In order to understand Philoponus' remark here, we need to keep in mind that although Philoponus does not accept Aristotle's account at all, he nonetheless expounds (and sometimes even defends) the Aristotelian theory in the course of his commentary outside his critical corollary. Thus, the issue that the place of a boat on a river is only a common, not a proper, place is unproblematic for Philoponus only in terms of expounding Aristotelian orthodoxy, and is probably an interpretation put forth by Ammonius in his lectures on the *Physics*, recorded by Philoponus. In terms of what constitutes the true doctrine about place, however, Philoponus would probably say that the issue is deeply problematic, as he generally argues that Aristotle's definition of place is fundamentally flawed and that it does not correspond to the reality we observe and experience. Having said this, Philoponus surprisingly does not make use of the issue about the river being merely a boat's common place in his refutation. In this regard, one should also mention Verrycken's contested thesis that the corollary is a later insertion into Philoponus' earlier written commentary on the *Physics*, thus reflecting a later, much more critical, stage in his philosophical development; q.v. fn. 93 above, 30.

In response to Aristotle's modification that makes place the first unmoving limit of a surrounding body, one of his pupils, Eudemus of Rhodes (d. ~ 300 BC), referred to the heavens as the ultimate reference point, because the heavens do not change their place, as their parts merely revolve.[45] Eudemus' idea is still popular today among interpreters. Edward Hussey, for example, resorts to the immobility of the universe as did, rather recently, Benjamin Morison, who defended Aristotle's account with reference to the immobility of the universe as a whole. In doing so, Morison tried to save all three conditions, viz., that place is unmoving, that it contains only one thing, and that it is in contact with that thing, arguing that "*x*'s proper place is the inner limit of *x*'s surroundings, where this is understood in the first place as being the inner limit of the universe where it is in contact with *x*."[46] Eudemus', Hussey's, and Morison's solutions seem to transform Aristotle's account – to some degree at least – into a relational account, where the place of a body is defined ultimately through its relation to certain remote bodies which are fixed, thus serving as a reference point. One could, for example, define place as a relation to certain unmoving geographical or astronomical positions.[47]

There is still, after more than two and a half millennia of discussion and interpretation, no consensus on the question of how we ought to interpret Aristotle's definition of place as the unmoving though contiguous inner surface of the surrounding body nor is it clear whether Aristotle is in fact able to provide a satisfactory solution to the boat-on-the-river issue on the basis of his conviction that place must be the surface of the surrounding body. David Bostock recently published a critical note on Morison's attempt to save the account through a reference to the immobility of the universe, whereas Hussey, immediately after suggesting this solution, expressed his scepticism as to whether any such reference could "rescue" Aristotle. Keimpe Algra, finally, is entirely pessimistic and entertains the possibility that Aristotle "did not actually think over all problems [and] simply added the immobility requirement without working out a more specific and technical account of immobility."[48]

There is even greater trouble on a cosmic scale. Since the Aristotelian universe relies on the reality of natural motion, i.e., on the reality that natural bodies move to their natural places, it also relies on natural places. Yet, with Aristotle's definition, we

45 cf. Algra, *Concepts of Space in Greek Thought*, 248–258.

46 Morison, *On Location*, 161; for his argumentation, cf. esp. 154–161; for recent criticism of his argumentation, cf. Bostock, "A Note on Aristotle's Account of Place"; cf. also Hussey's remarks in Aristotle, *Physics*, *ad* 212a14.

47 Indeed, it does not seem to be impossible, nor would it be altogether un-Aristotelian, to develop Aristotle's definition into an relational account on the basis of his own condition that place must be an unmoving limit. For a survey of possible solutions that either develop this idea further or take a different path, cf. Sorabji, *Matter, Space, and Motion*, ch. 11; Algra, *Concepts of Space in Greek Thought*, 224–260 ; cf. also Sorabji, *The Philosophy of the Commentators*, vol. II, ch. 13a.

48 Algra, *Concepts of Space in Greek Thought*, 228.

would have to assert that there exist almost no natural places that deserve the name "place." Upon the assumption that Aristotle would, in fact, transfer his account of place to his understanding of natural places, the natural place of fire would seem to be the inner surface of the sphere of the moon. That sphere, however, is in constant motion. If place must be unmoving, the sphere of the moon cannot be the place of fire. Something similar holds for water, for if the place of water is the inner limit of air and if air is always in motion due to wind, and if there is always at least some slight breeze, then the surface of the air cannot be the place of water. It is in this spirit that Philoponus voices the following complaint in his corollary:

> ἐμοῦ γὰρ ἑστηκότος καὶ μὴ μετακινουμένου ὁ περιέχων με τόπος, λέγω δὴ ἡ ἐπιφάνεια τοῦ ἀέρος καθ' ἣν ἅπτεταί μου, οὐχ ἡ αὐτὴ μένει, ἀλλὰ κινεῖται τοῦ ἀέρος κινουμένου, καὶ ἄλλοτε ἄλλο περιέχει με τοῦ ἀέρος μέρος ... ὥστε εἰ μηδέν ἐστιν ἀκίνητον πλὴν τῆς γῆς, ἀδύνατον ἄρα τὸν τόπον ἀκίνητον εἶναι, κἂν τὸ περιεχόμενον ἀκίνητον ᾖ. εἰ οὖν ... ἀκίνητον δεῖ εἶναι τὸν τόπον, τὸ δὲ πέρας τοῦ περιέχοντος οὐκ ἀκίνητον ... οὐκ ἄρα πέρας τοῦ περιέχοντος ὁ τόπος ἐστίν.
>
> For if I stand still and do not move around, the place that surrounds me – I mean the surface of the air by virtue of which it is in contact with me – does not remain the same but moves as the air moves, and now one, now another part of the air contains me ... So, if nothing is unmoving except the Earth, it is impossible that place be unmoving, even if that which is contained be unmoving. Thus, if ... place must be unmoving, and the limit of the container is not unmoving ... it follows that place is not the limit of the container. (Philoponus, *In Phys.*, 564.20–565.1, tr. by Furley, modified)[49]

In his own corollary on place, Simplicius raises the same question.[50] From this situation, as well as from some other implications that follow from the condition that place must be unmoving, he eventually draws the following conclusion:

> ὥστε ἢ τὸ ἀξίωμα σαλεύειν ἀνάγκη τὸ λέγον ἀκίνητον εἶναι τὸν τόπον ἢ μὴ λέγειν τόπον ἁπλῶς τὸ πέρας τοῦ περιέχοντος.
>
> It is necessary either to loosen up the postulate that says that place is unmoving or else simply not to say that place is the limit of the container. (Simplicius, *In Phys.*, 607.8f., tr. by Urmson, modified)

It is clear that neither Philoponus nor Simplicius would, in fact, like to loosen up this postulate, as their own conceptions of place – or better: space – *can* accommodate it. What Simplicius really recommends here is to withdraw from Aristotle's definition. If, however, Aristotle's definition is retained, then the criterion that place must be unmoving should perhaps be reconsidered and, given the difficulties it generates not

---

49 There is also a possible additional dilemma about the natural place of earth, for according to the definition of place in *Physics* IV, the natural place of earth should be the inner surface of the water (where earth is in contact with water) or air (where it is in contact with air); cf. *Phys.* IV.5, 212b20–22. Yet, in *De caelo* II.14, 296b6–25, it has been established that the natural place of earth is the centre of the universe – and not any airy or watery surface. Philoponus and Simplicius both complain about this ambiguity, the latter even with a direct reference to that passage in the *De caelo*; cf. Philoponus, *In Phys.*, 592.11–22; Simplicius, *In Phys.*, 606.1–16.

50 cf. Simplicius, *In Phys.*, 603.28–604.5.

only for the definition of place as such but for the conception of the natural world as a whole, eventually even be abandoned. Unfortunately, this would also bereave Aristotle from his only solution to the boat-on-the-river issue. We need to wait for Avicenna before we are offered a new solution to this famous dilemma.[51]

There are further issues that surround the notion of a surface or limit. Since this notion is the centrepiece of Aristotle's definition, any problem with this notion is also a problem for his concept of place. Philoponus mentions two such related issues:

> εἰ γὰρ τὸ ἐν τόπῳ ὂν οὐδὲν ἄλλο ἐστὶν ἢ τὸ σῶμα, καὶ οὐ κατὰ ἄλλο τί ἐστιν ἐν τόπῳ ἢ καθὸ σῶμά ἐστι, τὸ δὲ ἐν τῇ ἐπιφανείᾳ τοῦ περιέχοντος ὂν οὐ καθὸ σῶμά ἐστιν ἐν αὐτῇ ἐστι (τὸ μὲν γὰρ σῶμα τριχῇ ἐστι διαστατόν, ἐν δὲ τῇ ἐπιφανείᾳ καθὸ τοιαύτη ἐστὶν οὐ δύναται εἶναι τὸ τριχῇ διαστατόν), οὐκ ἄρα ἐπιφάνειά ἐστιν ὁ τόπος ... ἔτι εἰ δεῖ τὸν τόπον ἴσον εἶναι τῷ ἐν τόπῳ (τοῦτο γὰρ ἓν τῶν κοινῶν ἐστι περὶ τοῦ τόπου ὁμολογημάτων), οὐκ ἂν εἴη ἡ ἐπιφάνεια τόπος· πῶς γὰρ ἂν ἐπιφάνειαν σώματι ἴσην εἶναι ἐνδέχεται; ... ἀδύνατον δὲ ἐπιφάνειαν ἴσην σώματι εἶναι, ἐπεὶ μηδὲ γραμμὴν ἐπιφανείᾳ μηδὲ σημεῖον γραμμῇ· ἀδύνατον ἄρα τὸν τόπον ἐπιφάνειαν εἶναι.
>
> If what is in place is nothing other than body, and it is not in place by virtue of anything other than its being body (καθὸ σῶμά), but what is in the surface of the container is not in it by virtue of being body (for body is extended in three dimensions and whatever is so extended cannot be in a surface as such), it follows that place is not a surface ... Furthermore, if place must be equal (ἴσον) to what is in place (this is one of the things commonly agreed about place), the surface could not be place; for how can there be a surface equal to a body? ... [I]t is impossible for a surface to be equal to a body, since neither can a line equal a surface nor a point equal a line. So it is impossible that place be a surface. (Philoponus, *In Phys.*, 563.27–564.14, tr. by Furley)

These are another two of the five objections which Philoponus advances against Aristotle's account in his corollary on place.[52] The basic idea of these two is very simple: something that is three-dimensional is different from something that is two-dimensional.[53] The first objection employs this basic idea by arguing that a body that is in a place is so insofar as it is a body (καθὸ σῶμά), i.e., insofar as it is a three-dimensional entity. A body occupies some place, because its length, breadth, and depth must be accounted for such that all parts of a body in all their dimensions can be said to be somewhere. Among all the features of a body, there is none that requires a place other than its quantity. It is its quantity that needs to be in place, and not its qualities, for example. Its quantity, however, is extended into three dimensions. If this is the feature of a body that requires placement, then that which answers to that requirement must be capable of doing so. What is capable of providing a place for a three-dimensionally extended body, Philoponus argues, must itself be three-dimensionally extended, for otherwise the body would not as a whole, i.e., with all its dimensions, and in its entirety,

51 q.v. below, 356ff.

52 Both objections will be reoccurring in the Arabic tradition in the letter which Ibn Abī Saʿīd al-Mawṣilī wrote to Ibn ʿAdī as well as in the latter's response; q.v. below, 349f.

53 cf. also the similar worries in Simplicius, *In Phys.*, 604.13–25.

i.e., with all its parts, be in place. Since a surface is merely two-dimensional, it does not meet the respective requirements and, thus, fails to be a place for the body.[54]

Philoponus' second objection turns Aristotle against himself. At the beginning of *Physics* IV.4, Aristotle stipulated, among other things, that a place must be "neither smaller nor greater" (μήτ' ἐλάττω μήτε μείζω, *laysa bi-aṣġar wa-lā aʿẓam minhu*) than the body of that which is in place.[55] In brief it must be "equal" (ἴσον), as Philoponus has it. This formulation is appropriate, because Aristotle himself argued in the *Categories* that equality and inequality (τὸ ἴσον τε καὶ ἄνισον, *musāwiyan wa-ġayr musāwin*) are peculiar characteristics of quantities.[56] Yet, as has just been said, something two-dimensional is different from, and so arguably not "equal" to, something three-dimensional. Consequently, a place of a body could not be equal to the body in place, if place were conceived as a two-dimensional surface merely surrounding that body. Philoponus supports this claim with further, geometrical examples: a point does not equal a line and a line does not equal a surface, and so a surface does not equal a body.[57] In the light of this, Aristotle's idea that a surface can serve as the place for a body and that it, in an appropriate sense, can be called "neither smaller nor greater" than the body seems to fall apart.[58]

In the sixth century, when Philoponus was composing his commentary on the *Physics*, the central idea behind these objections was already more than eight hundred years old and a classic issue for the Aristotelian theory. We know this objection, which Philoponus developed and split into two separate arguments, from a small list of ἀπορίαι found in Simplicius' commentary on the *Physics*, where it is attributed to Theophrastus:

> ἰστέον δὲ ὅτι καὶ ὁ Θεόφραστος ἐν τοῖς Φυσικοῖς ἀπορεῖ πρὸς τὸν ἀποδοθέντα τοῦ τόπου λόγον ὑπὸ τοῦ Ἀριστοτέλους τοιαῦτα· ὅτι τὸ σῶμα ἔσται ἐν ἐπιφανείᾳ, ὅτι κινούμενος ἔσται ὁ τόπος, ὅτι οὐ πᾶν σῶμα ἐν τόπῳ (οὐδὲ γὰρ ἡ ἀπλανής), ὅτι ἐὰν συναχθῶσιν αἱ σφαῖραι, καὶ ὅλος ὁ οὐρανὸς

54 That a body is in place by virtue of its volume and three-dimensional extension becomes a commonplace among philosophers after Aristotle in both the Greek and Arabic traditions, as we shall see. In fact, it even has its roots in one of Aristotle's own arguments in *Physics* IV.8, in particular in Themistius' version of the argument; q.v. below, 371ff. and fn. 202 below, 373.

55 *Phys.* IV.4, 211a1f.; cf. *Phys.* IV.1, 209a27–29.

56 cf. *Cat.* 6, 6a26–35.

57 As Simplicius states in his corollary, if Aristotle were right, then a point would be as great as a body – "[w]hat could be more absurd than that?" (*In Phys.*, 604.35f., tr. by Urmson).

58 The formulation of this objection on the basis of the notion of equality may go back at least to Proclus, whom Simplicius reports to have claimed that "place must be equal (ἴσον) to what is in the place" (Proclus *apud* Simplicium, *In Phys.*, 611.36, tr. by Urmson). For Proclus, however, the equality condition had a peculiar, and even stronger, connotation, as it was meant to establish that place or space is actually body, for otherwise it could not be equal to body; cf. Proclus *apud* Simplicium, *In Phys.*, 611.36–612.1; cf. also Sorabji, *Matter, Space, and Motion*, 109–118, as well as the interpretation by Schrenk, "Proclus on Corporeal Space," 158–162, criticising Sorabji. In Proclus' *Institutio physica* I, def. 6, we get what seems to be an Aristotelian version of the equality condition.

οὐκ ἔσται ἐν τόπῳ, ὅτι τὰ ἐν τόπῳ ὄντα μηδὲν αὐτὰ μετακινηθέντα, ἐὰν ἀφαιρεθῇ τὰ περιέχοντα αὐτά, οὐκέτι ἔσται ἐν τόπῳ.

However, it is to be known that Theophrastus, too, in his *Physics*, raises difficulties against the account of place given by Aristotle, such as the following: (i) that body will be in a surface; (ii) that place will be moving; (iii) that not all body will be in a place – for [the sphere of] the fixed stars will not; (iv) that if the spheres are taken together, even the whole heaven will not be in a place; (v) that the things in place, though they themselves remain unmoved, will no longer be in place when those which surround them are removed (ἀφαιρεθῇ). (Theophrastus *apud* Simplicium, *In Phys.*, 604.5–11, tr. by Urmson, modified)

This list of difficulties is well-known. It is one of a handful of fragments that testify to Theophrastus' views on place.[59] There is good reason to think that these ἀπορίαι bear witness to his critical stance towards Aristotle's theory.[60] We have just come across the first difficulty raised by Theophrastus in an elaborated form in Philoponus: "body will be in a surface," i.e., something three-dimensional will be "in" or "contained by" or "equal to" something two-dimensional. The second difficulty is an abstract formulation of the boat-on-the-river issue, alluding to Aristotle's criterion that place must be unchanging and to the problems plaguing any attempt to preserve this criterion within the natural world, in which the physicist inevitably encounters moving surroundings and revolving limits both in the sublunary and the supralunary sphere. The third and the fourth difficulties are two formulations of yet another classic issue of the Aristotelian account. Since the universe is finite, having outside of its limit neither void nor anything at all, it lacks a surrounding body, so that, consequently, both the outermost sphere and the universe as a whole seem to have no place. Philoponus constantly reproaches Aristotle for this absurdity and his faithful followers, such as Alexander and Themistius, for their feeble attempts to find a remedy.[61]

Finally, there is the fifth difficulty in Theophrastus' list. It introduces the idea of surroundings that not only are in motion, as in the second difficulty and the boat-on-the-river issue, but are altogether "removed" (ἀφαιρεθῇ). The idea of surroundings that are removed is so odd that interpreters are unsure in what way it ought to be read.[62] It is also so interesting that Avicenna discusses a strikingly similar objection:

وقالوا أيضاً إنّ المكان يجب أن يكون شيئاً لا يتحرّك بوجه ولا يزول ونهايات المحيط قد تتحرّك بوجه ما وتزول.

They [sc. those who claim that place is an extension] also said that it is necessary that place is something that does not move in any way (*lā yataḥarraku bi-wağhin*) nor disappear (*wa-lā yazūlu*), yet the limits of the surrounding may move in some way or disappear. (*al-Samāʿ al-ṭabīʿī* II.6, §7, 116.9f.)

59 cf. frgms. 146–149 in Theophrastus, *Sources for his Life, Writings, Thought and Influence*, 302–305.

60 Whether or not Theophrastus himself developed a rival theory of place is a different matter; q.v. the references given in fn. 18 above, 313.

61 q.v. below, 334ff.

62 For three interpretations, cf. Sorabji, *Matter, Space, and Motion*, 197f.; Morison, "Did Theophrastus Reject Aristotle's Account of Place?," 85–87; Algra, *Concepts of Space in Greek Thought*, 236.

We must be careful not to overstate this brief passage. Avicenna simply may have intended *yazūlu* to mean the result of *yataḥarraku*, so that the objector would claim that limits often seem to move away (and when they have moved away, they would also have disappeared), even though, according to Aristotle, they should not be in motion at all (let alone disappear). In his later reply to this issue, Avicenna seems to address precisely this point, as he writes that place surely does not move essentially (*bi-ḏātihī*), yet there is nothing fundamentally wrong with a place that moves accidentally (*bi-l-ʿaraḍ*), as a jar's inner limit certainly is a place and can move accidentally when the jar is moved essentially.[63] Yet, the Arabic verb *zāla/yazūlu*, which occurs in the passage in which Avicenna introduces the objection, and which is absent from his reply, is more often used in the sense of something's perishing and abating into non-existence. This existential connotation would seem to suggest a reasoning that is strikingly close to the one expressed in Theophrastus' fragment (despite already mentioned issues in interpreting this fragment in the first place).

It is difficult to assess whether or not Avicenna's passage, and its similarity to Theophrastus' fragment, is more than simply an interesting coincidence; a decisive answer will require more research into the transmission of Theophrastus' works into Arabic.[64] What is certain, though, is that most of Avicenna's long discussion of place in *al-Samāʿ al-ṭabīʿī* is driven by a desire to engage with the long tradition of opposing, and even ridiculing, Aristotle's account of place, of which we caught a glimpse in this section. From this engagement, Avicenna emerges as a zealous and steady defender of the Aristotelian theory. Yet, it is not just that Avicenna picked up Philoponus' commentary and went through all the critical remarks and possible alternative views about place contained therein. Instead, he drew on a variety of different sources, ranging from Aristotle's *Physics* and Philoponus' commentary to unidentified Neoplatonic material and Muʿtazilī theological discourses.[65] Thus, it cannot be ruled out that Avicenna, at one point in his career, had some direct or mediated knowledge of Theophrastean material, too – neither, however, can it be proven at the present stage of research.

Overall, Avicenna's vindication of Aristotle's account falls into two parts: first, improving on the Aristotelian notion of place as a surface, so that it can defy the criticism levelled against it for centuries; and second, countering the alternative notion of place as a three-dimensional extension underlying corporeal reality with new arguments, in order both to disprove that notion and to demonstrate the superiority of the Aristotelian account. The following two sections deal with these two aspects, respectively. It will,

---

63 *al-Samāʿ al-ṭabīʿī* II.9, §13, 143.5–7; cf. also *al-Samāʿ al-ṭabīʿī* II.9, §6, 139.4–10.

64 In this regard, cf. Gutas, "The Life, Works, and Sayings of Theophrastus in the Arabic Tradition"; Theophrastus, *Sources for his Life, Writings, Thought and Influence*, 11–13, and his remarks in Theophrastus, *On First Principles* (known as his *Metaphysics*), 75–92; q.v. also above, 20.

65 Incidentally, discussions of place and its relevance for natural motion among Muʿtazilites may also have provided a context in which the disappearance of place (*zawāl al-makān*) is discussed; cf. Ibn Mattawayh, *al-Taḏkira*, X.9, 484.10f. (ed. Luṭf/ʿŪn)/XI.22, 274.10–12 (ed. Gimaret).

first, be shown how Avicenna elaborates on the notion of surface in the list of potential candidates for what place might be. This includes an inquiry into the outermost sphere as well as the questions of whether it can be said to have a place and how it could engage in motion, even if it may lack a place. My findings will demonstrate how Avicenna expands Aristotle's method and his argumentative *approach* towards defining place as a surface, integrating it into the changed setting of the intellectual milieu of the fourth/tenth and early fifth/early eleventh centuries. Furthermore, we shall also see how Avicenna develops Aristotle's *definition* itself both by clarifying the central notion of "surface" and by warding off three further major objections including the well-known issue about the place of a body located in changing surroundings, such as in the case of a boat on a river. In the end, Avicenna will have provided good arguments against four of the five objections which Philoponus has advanced against Aristotle's account in his corollary on place and all of the ἀπορίαι in Theophrastus. Second, I shall investigate the ancient notion of a three-dimensional extension or space, in particular as it was received by Avicenna. As will become clear, Avicenna not only provides new arguments against the existence of any such notion but, moreover, employs his new understanding of place as a surface to demonstrate the superiority of the Aristotelian account, thus making the assumption of a three-dimensional space superfluous.

5.2 Clarifying Aristotle's Troubled Account of Place

The Notion of Surface in the List of Candidates

Having mentioned in *al-Samāʿ al-ṭabīʿī* II.5 a number of arguments regarding the existence of place, both for and against, together with a promise to reject the latter, Avicenna begins chapter six with a dichotomy between two common notions of place:

> إنّ لفظة المكان قد يستعملها العامّة على وجهين. فربّما عنوا بالمكان ما يكون الشيء مستقرّاً عليه ثمّ لا يتميّز لهم أنّه هو الجسم الأسفل أو السطح الأعلى من الجسم الأسفل إلّا أن يتزعزعوا يسيراً عن العامّية فيتخيّل بعضهم أنّه هو السطح الأعلى من الجسم الأسفل دون سائره، وربّما عنوا بالمكان الشيء الحاوي للشيء ... وبالجملة ما يكون فيه الشيء وإن لم يستقرّ عليه وهذا هو الأغلب عندهم.
>
> The term "place" is commonly used by the people in two ways. So, sometimes they mean by place that on which the thing rests (*mustaqirran ʿalayhi*), but then they do not distinguish whether it is the body underneath (*al-ğism al-asfal*) or the outside surface (*al-saṭḥ al-aʿlā*) of the body underneath, unless they have broken with common opinion a little, and so some of them imagine that it is the outside surface of the body underneath without the rest [of the body]. At other times they mean by place something containing the thing (*al-šayʾ al-ḥāwī li-l-šayʾ*) ... and, in general, that in which the thing is (*ma yakūnu fīhi l-šayʾ*), even if it is not resting on it – and this is the more dominant [view] among them. (*al-Samāʿ al-ṭabīʿī* II.6, §1, 114.13–115.2, tr. by McGinnis, modified)[66]

66 cf. *al-Ḥikma al-mašriqiyya* III.9, 25.18–22.

The first of these two options was common among Muʿtazilī theologians and is attested, for example, through the *Maqālāt al-islāmiyyīn* of Abū l-Ḥasan al-Ašʿarī (d. 324/935-36). In this work, we read that two common views about what the place of something is were that which "carries it and upon which it rests" (*yuqilluhū wa-yaʿtamidu ʿalayhi*) as well as that which "prevents it from falling" (*mā yamnaʿu min al-huwīy*).[67] Two similar, and in essence identical, expressions can be found in *al-Taḏkira fī aḥkām al-ǧawāhir wa-l-aʿrāḍ* of the Muʿtazilite Abū Muḥammad ibn Mattawayh (d. 469/1076), who writes that something which is alive and characterised by independent action has a place which "carries it and upon which it stays" (*yuqilluhū wa-yaṯbutu ʿalayhi*), whereas something that is characterised by weight inevitably has something which "prevents its weight from bringing it down" (*yamnaʿu ṯiqlahū min al-nuzūl fīhi*).[68]

Reading Avicenna's first approximation to the topic against the background of current theological theories is particularly appropriate in light of independent evidence that Avicenna was aware of kalām conceptions of place and even directly engaged with some of the theologians of his time. In a treatise known as the *Risāla li-baʿḍ al-mutakallimīn ilā l-Šayḫ fa-aǧābahum*, Avicenna is asked by an unknown interlocutor to explain "what this extension (*wusʿa*) is which accommodates all things ... and which some call *faḍāʾ*, and some *makān* and *markaz*, and which the mutakallimūn call *ǧiha* and *ḥayyiz*, and which the Muʿtazila calls *muḥāḏāt*."[69] The interlocutor, then, quotes briefly from Avicenna's older contemporary ʿAbd al-Ǧabbār ibn Aḥmad al-Hamadānī (d. 415/1025), a famous Muʿtazilite from Baṣra and teacher of Ibn Mattawayh, whom Avicenna himself will mention later in his reply. It is known that the Baṣrī branch of Muʿtazilism avowed the existence of the void and criticised the conception of place as a two-dimensional surface.[70] In his response, Avicenna attacks their terminology and reproaches the Baṣrī Muʿtazilites for their belief in the existence of the void which he blames on a misguided judgement of the imaginative faculties: since air cannot visually be perceived and lacks colour as well as other qualities which usually accompany

---

67 al-Ašʿarī, *Maqālāt al-islāmiyyīn*, 442.10, 13.

68 Ibn Mattawayh, *al-Taḏkira*, I.2, 52.3–5 (ed. Luṭf/ʿŪn)/11.10f. (ed. Gimaret); cf. Ibn Mattawayh, *al-Taḏkira*, X.9, 484.3f. (ed. Luṭf/ʿŪn)/XI.21, 274.2–4 (ed. Gimaret); cf. also Dhanani, *The Physical Theory of Kalām*, 70f. According to Avicenna, such a notion of place is derived from the simple parlance of the common man; cf. *al-Samāʿ al-ṭabīʿī* II.6, §16, 118.2f. Moreover, the Muʿtazilī understanding may have had a further theological dimension in the context of early discussions of God's place and throne (*kursī* or *ʿarš*). If God's throne is that upon which God is, and if His throne is His place, then His place might just be that upon which He is. Van Ess interestingly remarks that one of the Hebrew appellations of God in early Judaism was *māqōm* ("place") (*Theologie und Gesellschaft*, vol. 4, 409); cf. in this regard also Philo of Alexandria, *De somniis*, 218.11–21; Sambursky, *The Physical World of Late Antiquity*, 4.

69 Avicenna, *Risāla li-baʿḍ al-mutakallimīn ilā l-Šayḫ fa-aǧābahum*, 155.5–7. Gutas lists the treatise in his "inventory of Avicenna's authentic works" as "*R. fī l-Wusʿa* (GP 4)," stating that "there seems to be no doubt about its authenticity"; cf. also Pines, *Nouvelles etudes sur Aḥwad al-Zamān Abu-l-Barakāt al-Baghdādī*, 51–54; Dhanani, "Rocks in the Heavens?!"

70 cf. Dhanani, *The Physical Theory of Kalām*, 62–71.

bodies, the imagination (*wahm*) conceives of air not as a body but as yet extended, and from this impression derives the notion of empty unoccupied space (*faḍā'*).[71] As it appears from his discussion, Avicenna is well-acquainted with spatial conceptions prevalent in his times. We also see that these various conceptions were subject of debate, otherwise Avicenna would not have been asked about these matters by his interlocutor, and that he took a critical stance towards the mutakallimūn, perhaps even actively engaging with them in a debate.[72]

It is, therefore, at first rather surprising that the Muʿtazilī conception of place as a surface, which Avicenna mentioned at the beginning of *al-Samāʿ al-ṭabīʿī* II.6, appears to harmonise with Avicenna's own Aristotelian view that place is a surface. As Avicenna mentions, some of those who considered place to be that upon which something rests emphasised that it is more proper to say that place is only the *surface* of the supporting body (to the exclusion of the rest of the body), because it is precisely this surface (and not the whole body) upon which a placed thing rests. Yet, it is clear that Avicenna's terminology draws attention to the fact that such a surface is an *outside* surface (*al-saṭḥ al-aʿlā*).[73] So, although it is true that this Muʿtazilī conception contains a clear reference to the idea of place as a surface, this surface is not a surface *in which* something may be placed but a surface *on which* something may be placed. Place thus conceived does not contain or surround the thing which rests on it but merely supports or carries it and prevents it from falling down. By contrast, Avicenna emphasises that the second conception of place signifies that which contains other things (*al-šay' al-ḥāwī li-l-šay'*) and that *in which* other things are (*ma yakūnu fīhi l-šay'*). It emerges, then, that according to Avicenna's initial presentation, the relevant difference between the two conceptions of place is not that one apparently alludes to a surface and the other does not. It is rather the case that according to the first, a placed thing cannot be said to be *in* its place or to be *contained by* its place, for it merely rests *upon* it or is *on*

---

71 Avicenna, *Risāla li-baʿḍ al-mutakallimīn ilā l-Šayḫ fa-aǧābahum*, esp. 158.25–159.11; cf. also *al-Samāʿ al-ṭabīʿī* II.6, §11, 117.1–5. Avicenna's diagnosis resembles Aristotle's criticism of Anaxagoras' attempts to disprove the existence of the void through experiments with wineskins and devices such as the clepsydra ("water-thief"). According to Aristotle, all Anaxagoras achieved was to show that air is actually something (ἐπιδεικνύουσι γὰρ ὅτι ἐστίν τι ὁ ἀήρ, *yadhabūna ʿalā anna l-hawā' šay' mā*; *Physics* IV.6, 213a25f.). We might say, then, that Anaxagoras attempted to disprove the void but actually misconceived air, while the Baṣrī Muʿtazilites tried to prove the void but likewise misconceived air. This is also al-Fārābī's verdict; cf. al-Fārābī, *Maqāla fī l-ḫalā'*, 16.1–3.

72 For the debate among Muʿtazilī theologians on the nature of place, cf. the statement by Abū ʿAbd Allāh Muḥammad ibn Muḥammad al-Šayḫ al-Mufīd in his *Awā'il al-maqālāt fī l-maḏāhib wa-l-muḫtārāt*, 43.16–44.2, hinted at by Dhanani, *The Physical Theory of Kalām*, 67.

73 Avicenna seems to play with words here. While the preposition *ʿalā* ("upon") has been used to describe place as that "upon which" (*ʿalayhi*) something rests by al-Ašʿarī and Ibn Mattawayh as well as by Avicenna himself, he uses the elative *aʿlā* ("higher, uppermost") of the same root to qualify the surface. It is clear that it signifies the uppermost surface of the body, i.e., the surface on the outside, "upon which" something rests (hence my decision to translate *al-saṭḥ al-aʿlā* as "*outside* surface").

top of it – or even: is *outside* of it – whereas place in the second sense is that which *contains* something and that *in which* something can be or come-to-be.[74]

Besides being the more dominant view, as Avicenna writes, it is also this second conception which has been developed further by the philosophers.[75] We are told that they established a number of attributes (*awṣāf*, sg. *waṣf*) which ought to belong to that which eventually will be identified with place. They stipulated, for example, that place must be something in which things can be and from which things can depart (*yufāriquhū*) as well as something which accommodates only the one thing it contains and, finally, something which can "receive" things (*yaqbalu … ilayhi*).[76] It is apparent that this list of requirements concerns exclusively what Aristotle has called a body's "proper place" in contrast to its "common place."[77] A proper place is that in which no other body is, which is exactly as great as that body, and which is that body's "first" or "primary" place. According to Avicenna, then, these philosophers agreed upon a number of requirements and set out to develop further the second, more dominant, conception of a thing's proper place. This, however, is where their consensus came to an end. Avicenna writes:

فلمّا أرادوا أن يعرفوا ماهية هذا الشيء وجوهره فكأنّهم قسموا في أنفسهم، فقالوا إنّ كلّ ما يكون خاصّاً بالشيء
ولا يكون لغيره فلا يخلو إمّا أن يكون داخلاً في ذاته أو يكون خارجاً عن ذاته. فإن كان داخلاً في ذاته فإمّا

74 It should be noted that al-Aš'arī's description of the first conception of place allows for things to be placed *in* such a place, too: *makān al-šay' mā yuqilluhū wa-ya'tamidu 'alayhi wa-yakūnu l-šay' mutamakkinan fīhi* (*Maqālāt al-islāmiyyīn*, 442.10). Yet, this may well be an explicit attempt to respond to the slight embarrassment that if place is that on which something rests, then, strictly speaking, things cannot be *in* their places, so that al-Aš'arī's source felt the need to add a remark to clarify that this conception still – somehow – allows referring to places with the preposition "in," as is common in ordinary speech. In other words, the fact that al-Aš'arī's report contains this clarification may indicate nothing other than the fact that there was, indeed, something that ought to be clarified. As will become clear, Avicenna favours the second conception, for only it can really satisfy the requirement, stipulated later in chapter nine, that place must be "that in which (*allaḏī fīhi*) the body alone exists."

75 cf. *al-Samā' al-ṭabī'ī* II.6, §2, 115.4–6; *al-Ḥikma al-mašriqiyya* III.9, 26.1–3.

76 This set of four requirements resembles the one elaborated by Aristotle at the beginning of *Physics* IV.4; q.v. above, 314. Since Avicenna here does not seem to distinguish between the requirement that place must not be anything that pertains to the object (μηδὲν τοῦ πράγματος, *laysa bi-šay' min ḏālika l-amr*) and the one that it must be separable from the object (χωριστόν, *yufāriquhū*), we can say that the list presented in *al-Samā' al-ṭabī'ī* contains all six requirements Aristotle has enumerated – with one exception: Aristotle mentioned that every place must have an above and a below (πάντα τόπον ἔχειν τὸ ἄνω καὶ κάτω, *kull makān fa-lahū fawq wa-asfal*), so that every body by nature moves to, and remains in, its proper place (φέρεσθαι φύσει καὶ μένειν ἐν τοῖς οἰκείοις τόποις, *yantaqilu bi-l-ṭab' wa-yalbaṯu fī makānihī l-ḫāṣṣ bihī*; *Physics* IV.4, 211a3–5). Avicenna, on the other hand, omits any reference to natural motion and to the power a place is often said to exert upon natural bodies. Elsewhere, he alludes to natural motion, cf. *al-Samā' al-ṭabī'ī* II.5, §8, 114.4–7; cf. also the list of requirements in *Dānešnāme-ye 'Alā'ī* III.6, 13.11–14.3. It seems that Avicenna's positive account in *al-Samā' al-ṭabī'ī* is overall rather sparing with references to natural places, to natural motion, and to the power of place.

77 cf. *Phys.* IV.2, 209a32f.

ان يكون هيولاه وإمّا أن يكون صورته. وإن كان خارجاً عن ذاته ويكون مع ذلك يساويه ويخصّه فهو إمّا نهاية سطح يلاقيه ويشغل بمماسّته ولا يماسّه غيره إمّا محيط وإمّا محاط مستقرّ عليه أيّهما اتّفق وإمّا أن يكون بعداً يساوي أقطاره فهو يشغله بالاندساس فيه.

When they intended to find out the essence of this thing [sc. place] and its substance, it was as if they became split among themselves. So, they said that whatever is proper to something (*ḫāṣṣan bi-l-šay'*) and to nothing other than it must be either (a) internal to the thing itself (*dāḫilan fī ḏātihī*) or (b) extrinsic to the thing itself (*ḫāriğan ʿan ḏātihī*). So, if it is (a) internal to the thing itself, then it is either (a1) its matter (*hayulāhu*) or (a2) its form (*ṣūratahū*), but if it is (b) extrinsic to the thing itself but still equals it and is proper to it, then it is either (b1) a limit of a surface which is in contact with it (*nihāyat saṭḥ yulāqīhu*), is occupied through its being in contact with it, and is not in contact with something other than it ([and which is] either something surrounding (*muḥīṭ*) or something surrounded on which it rests (*muḥāṭ mustaqirr ʿalayhi*), whichever of the two it may happen to be); or (b2) an extension which equals its [sc. the thing's] dimensions (*buʿdan yusāwī aqṭārahū*), and so is something it occupies by entering it. (*al-Samāʿ al-ṭabīʿī* II.6, §2, 115.6–11, tr. by McGinnis, modified)

There seem to be, then, four alternatives for what a proper place could be: it is either a body's (a1) matter or (a2) form, or (b1) a surface in contact with it or (b2) an extension equal to it. Avicenna's justification for these four alternatives closely resembles those which Philoponus and Simplicius provided in their commentaries in support of Aristotle's list of candidates for place. Philoponus, for example, wrote:

ὅτι δὲ ἀδύνατον παρ' ἕν τι τούτων ἄλλο τι εἶναι τὸν τόπον, ἔστιν ἐκ διαιρέσεως κατασκευάσαι οὕτως. τὸ κατὰ τόπον μεταβάλλον, ἢ κατά τι τῶν ἐν αὐτῷ μεταβάλλει ἢ κατά τι τῶν περὶ αὐτό· εἰ μὲν οὖν κατά τι τῶν ἐν αὐτῷ μεταβάλλει, ἢ κατὰ τὴν ὕλην πάντως μεταβάλλει ἢ κατὰ τὸ εἶδος, εἰ δὲ κατά τι τῶν περὶ αὐτό, ἢ κατὰ τὸ διάστημα τὸ μεταξὺ τῶν περάτων τοῦ περιέχοντος ἢ κατὰ τὰ αὐτὰ τὰ πέρατα·

That it is impossible for place to be anything other than one of these, can be established on the basis of a division, as follows. What changes with respect to place, does so either (a) with respect to something in itself (κατά τι τῶν ἐν αὐτῷ) or (b) with respect to something external to it (κατά τι τῶν περὶ αὐτό). If it changes with respect to something in itself, at all events it changes either (a1) with respect to matter (κατὰ τὴν ὕλην) or (a2) with respect to form (κατὰ τὸ εἶδος). If it changes with respect to something external, it does so either (b2) with respect to the extension (κατὰ τὸ διάστημα) in between the limits of the container or (b1) with respect to these limits themselves (κατὰ τὰ αὐτὰ τὰ πέρατα). (Philoponus, *In Phys.*, 547.20–26, tr. by Algra, modified)[78]

This interpretation of Aristotle's list of candidates was common in the Arabic tradition also prior to Avicenna, for we find a very similar enumeration in the following marginal note from Ms. Leiden or. 583, which is attributed to "Yaḥyā and Abū ʿAlī," arguably Philoponus and Abū ʿAlī ibn al-Samḥ (d. 418/1027):

وإنّما وجب أن يكون المكان لا يخلو من هذه الأقسام الأربعة فإنّه إذا اختلف مكان الشيء فإمّا أن يكون اختلافاً في نفس الشيء أو فيما يلي الشيء الذي اختلف مكانه. فإن كان اختلافاً في نفس الشيء فإمّا أن يكون في هيولاه

78 cf. Simplicius, *In Phys.*, 571.31–572.8; q.v. also fn. 20 above, 313.

أو في صورته وإن اختلف فيما يليه فإمّا أن يكون اختلاقاً في البعد الذي يظنّ أنّ الجرم يشغله أو في نهاية المحيط بالجرم.

It is necessary that place must be among these four divisions only, for[79] if the place of a thing changes, then, there is a change either (a) in the thing itself (*fī nafs al-šay'*) or (b) in something adjacent (*fī-mā yalī*) to the thing which changes its place. So, if there is a change (a) in the thing itself, then it is either (a1) in its matter (*hayulāhu*) or (a2) in its form, and if it changes (b) in what is adjacent to it, then there is a change either (b2) in the dimension which the body is thought to occupy or (b1) in the limit of that which contains the body. (Philoponus' and Ibn al-Samḥ's comment in Aristotle, *al-Ṭabīʿa* IV.4, 312.14–313.3)

The three passages from Avicenna, Philoponus, and the margins of Ms. Leiden or. 583 clearly follow the same idea, viz., that Aristotle presents a basic distinction between what pertains to the body and what does not pertain to it, and that in each horn of the distinction there are two candidates, one that is some sort of limit and another that is some sort of extension.[80] Following this, Avicenna provides the rationales that led his predecessors to favour one or the other of the four candidates. Some people claimed that place is matter, because matter is that which is susceptible to successive replacement (*qābil li-l-taʿāqub*).[81] Others who maintained that place is form claimed that form is the only containing limit that is truly "first" or "primary" (*awwal*).[82] Others again, confidently defended the view that place is nothing but "fixed and natural extensions" (*abʿādan mafṭūratan ṯābitatan*) which can successively be occupied by bodies – a position which, for Avicenna, arguably struck some Platonic notes, as will be seen.[83] In addition to providing positive arguments in support of their own view,

79 Suggesting to read *fa-innahū* for *annahū* in Badawī.

80 From the fact that the explanation for Aristotle's list of four potential candidates for place which is given by Philoponus is almost identical (even in its wording) to the one in Simplicius together with a very similar explanations in Ms. Leiden or. 583 and in Avicenna's *al-Samāʿ al-ṭabīʿī*, one is inclined to assume that this way of justifying Aristotle's list of candidates was either a common strategy from the sixth century onwards (for we do not find anything comparable in Themistius) or that it may go back to an earlier source such as Alexander's commentary (despite the lack of a comparable passage in Themistius). Yet, I could find nothing similar attributed to either Alexander or Themistius in the fragments and testimonies provided in Simplicius' commentary on the *Physics* nor in the marginal notes of Ms. Leiden or. 583 nor in the *scholia* of Alexander published by M. Rashed. It may also be noted that the wording in Ms. Leiden or. 583 seems to display a somewhat greater conformity to the wording in Simplicius' than to that in Philoponus' commentary, especially because of the use of the verb *yalī* which corresponds so well to Simplicius' προσεχῶς.

81 *al-Samāʿ al-ṭabīʿī* II.6, §3, 115.11. This reason derives from what Aristotle wrote at *Physics* IV.4, 211b29–212a2, where he presented matter as the subject of replacement, i.e., of the successive participation in different forms, so that what once was water, may now be air. In *Physics* IV.2, Aristotle already had presented a different reason, arguing that matter is that which remains when one strips away all qualities from a body. This is the reason for why, according to Aristotle, Plato identified matter and place.

82 *al-Samāʿ al-ṭabīʿī* II.6, §3, 115.11f.

83 q.v. below, 385f.

this last group of thinkers also "specifically addressed" those who defended place as a surface (*yuḫāṭibūna ḫāṣṣatan aṣḥāb al-suṭūḥ*) and attacked their position with a number of objections, whose enumeration occupies the remainder of chapter six in the second book of *al-Samāʿ al-ṭabīʿī*.[84]

It is worthwhile to investigate more closely how Avicenna presents option (b1) that place is a surface, since Aristotle's account – and his own – is along these lines. I also just said that it seems as if Avicenna presents four potential candidates for the essence of place, thus following Aristotle, and that he provided practically the same justification as Philoponus and Simplicius for why there are these four options. On closer inspection it emerges, however, that Avicenna's list of candidates is richer than that of Aristotle or those of his Greek predecessors. Recognising this is crucial for understanding how Avicenna developed and clarified Aristotle's account of place. So, we have just seen that Avicenna describes the fourth option as follows:

... نهاية سطح يلاقيه ويشغل بمماسّته ولا يماسّه غيره إمّا محيط وإمّا محاط مستقرّ عليه أيّهما اتّفق.

> ... a limit of a surface which is in contact with it, is occupied through its being in contact with it, and is not in contact with something other than it ([and which is] either something surrounding (*muḥīṭ*) or something surrounded on which it rests (*muḥāṭ mustaqirr ʿalayhi*), whichever of the two it may happen to be (*ayyuhumā ttafaqa*)). (*al-Samāʿ al-ṭabīʿī* II.6, §2, 115.9f.)

In focusing on the notion of "surface" as a *contacting* surface, Avicenna does two things. First, he directly responds to developments in the Muslim intellectual milieu. As we could see above, Avicenna explicitly characterised the conception of place which al-Ašʿarī reported in the name of his Muʿtazilite predecessors as an *outside* surface (*al-saṭḥ al-aʿlā*), i.e., as a surface that does not contain or surround the object in place but rather belongs to something which itself is surrounded by that very surface upon which the object in place rests. I also noted above that it may seem as if Avicenna would have to find favour with this conception simply because it relies – no less than Aristotle's account – on the notion of a contacting surface. Now, it becomes clear that this impression was justified, as Avicenna fully integrates the Muʿtazilite conception into the discussion. If place must be, above all, a surface that is in contact with that which is in place, then a (Muʿtazilī) *outside* surface, i.e., the outer surface of that on which what is in place rests (*muḥāṭ mustaqirr ʿalayhi*), is no less viable a candidate as is the idea of an (Aristotelian) *inside* surface, i.e., the inner surface of that which surrounds or contains (*muḥīṭ*) that which is in place. In determining the essence of place, it is, thus, incumbent upon Avicenna to decide, and to be clear about, which of these two surfaces ought to be identified as a thing's place. With there being two

84 *al-Samāʿ al-ṭabīʿī* II.6, §4, 115.15f. The remark that those who defended place as an extension also vehemently attacked the account of place as a surface tallies with Philoponus' overall attitude in his commentary on place, as he was both a defender of that view and the fiercest critic of Aristotle. This could be a clue indicating that Avicenna once more has primarily – even though not exclusively – Philoponus in mind when he prepares his defence of Aristotle's concept of place; q.v. also below, 355.

different kinds of surfaces, Avicenna's list of potential candidates for the essence of places grows to five.[85]

Second, Avicenna also reacts to developments in the late ancient tradition of commenting on Aristotle. Since the notion of a contacting surface, as such, can refer to two kinds of surfaces, it is intrinsically ambiguous. Exposing this ambiguity gives Avicenna the opportunity to expand the argumentative *approach* that led Aristotle to his account as well as some of his followers astray when they, struggling with the question about the place of the outermost sphere, ultimately accepted simply *any* contacting surface as place, regardless of whether it is a surrounding or a surrounded surface.[86] It is – once more – incumbent upon Avicenna to decide, and to be *very* clear about, which kind of surface ought to be identified with a thing's place. Facing both new ideas from his Muslim fellows as well as bad ideas from his Peripatetic peers, Avicenna does not present only four viable candidates of which one must be place nor does he present five – instead, he presents *six* of them: there are matter, form, extension, and there are three kinds of a surface in contact with the thing in place:

- the outer surface of a surrounded body (on which the thing in place rests), as the Muʿtazilites claimed;
- the inner surface of a surrounding body (in which a thing in place is), as Aristotle claimed; and
- simply any contacting surface "whichever of the two it may happen to be" (*ayyuhumā ttafaqa*), as prominent Peripatetics confusedly claimed, as shall be seen.

In the following chapter, *al-Samāʿ al-ṭabīʿī* II.7, Avicenna consequently refutes four of these six positions. This is already apparent from the heading of that chapter:

في نقض مذهب مَن ظنّ أنّ المكان هيولى او صورة أو أيّ سطح ملاق كان أو بعد.

> On refuting the teaching of those who believe[87] that place is matter or form or whatever surface that is in contact or an extension.[88] (*al-Samāʿ al-ṭabīʿī* II.7, 118.13f.)

Apparently, Avicenna follows Aristotle in rejecting the idea that place is matter, form, or an extension.[89] In addition, he also maintains that place must be *either* the outside

85 cf. also Faḫr al-Dīn al-Rāzī's explicit enumeration of "five" (*ḫamsa*) different teachings about place in *al-Mabāḥiṯ al-mašriqiyya* II.1.1.17, vol. 1, 332.17.

86 The issue about the place and the motion of the outermost sphere together with some of the solutions offered by prominent Peripatetics will be discussed shortly; q.v. below, 334ff.

87 Reading *ẓānna* with Mss. Leiden or. 4 and or. 84 as well as Zāyid for *qāla* in McGinnis and Āl Yāsīn.

88 Reading *buʿd* with Mss. Leiden or. 4 and or. 84 for *buʿdan* in McGinnis, Zāyid, and Āl Yāsīn.

89 Avicenna's reasons against place being either matter or form resemble those offered by Aristotle in *Physics* IV.2, 209b17–210a13, most of which come down to the idea that if place were matter or form, then motion, and in particular local motion would seem to be inexplicable, as nothing would seem to be able to move by changing its place. This is also the gist of his argument later in *al-Samāʿ al-ṭabīʿī* II.9, §1, 137.5–10, where matter and form are ruled out due to their inability to satisfy the condition

surface of the surrounded body *or* the inside surface of the surrounding body; it cannot be just *any* contacting surface whatsoever. This may seem to be rather negligible point, yet, as we shall see now, there is a systematic reason for why Avicenna deems it necessary to bring this circumstance to our attention and to devote his own attention to the notion of a contacting surface, in order to clarify what exactly is meant by it.

According to Aristotle's account, everything is in place by means of its surrounding body. This account is satisfactory only for as long as there actually is a surrounding body. If we were to find only one body which does not have any surroundings, i.e., a body which is not contained by any other body, then we would be entitled to question either the entire idea of defining the place of a body by means of what is outside that body or would have to accept the irritating consequence that there is a body that has no place at all. This is exactly the issue the Greek commentators had to face with regard to the place of the universe as a whole and with the place of the outermost sphere in particular. Since the Aristotelian universe is spatially finite, there is nothing outside the outermost sphere, i.e., there is neither void nor anything else. Consequently, the outermost sphere does not seem to have a place, thereby entailing that the universe as a whole cannot be said to have a place. This very issue is known already from Theophrastus and Eudemus, two of Aristotle's own pupils, and was briefly mentioned above as the third of the five ἀπορίαι reported by Simplicius in the name of Theophrastus.[90]

Various solutions have been advanced in defence of Aristotle. It is common to most of them – with the notable exception of Alexander – that they attempt to find a way in which one can, after all, claim that the outermost sphere has, in fact, a place rather than embracing the discomforting conclusion that it does not.[91] Perhaps the most popular attempt can be found in Themistius:

> οὐ πάντα δὲ ἐν τόπῳ τὰ μόρια (οὐδὲ γὰρ ἅπαντα περιέχεται), οὐδὲ ἡ ἔξω σφαῖρα, ἀλλ' αὕτη κατὰ μὲν τὸ ἐντὸς εἴη ἂν ἐν τόπῳ (ἅπτεται γὰρ τῆς τοῦ Κρόνου καὶ οἷον περιέχεταί πως), κατὰ δὲ τὸ ἔξω παντελῶς ἀμοιροῖ τόπου.

---

that place must be separable from that which is in place; q.v. below, 345. In *al-Samāʿ al-ṭabīʿī* II.9, §9, 140.8–10, Avicenna adds that arguing for matter to be place on the grounds that both matter and place are the subject of replacement is inconclusive, as it misses out on an essential premiss – one which Avicenna refuses to accept – within its logical structure. I shall investigate his reasons against place as an extension below, 367ff.

90 As fragment 146 states: ὅτι οὐ πᾶν σῶμα ἐν τόπῳ (οὐδὲ γὰρ ἡ ἀπλανής) (Theophrastus *apud* Simplicium, *In Phys.*, 604.8); for Eudemus, cf. Eudemus *apud* Themistium, *In Phys.*, 119.27–120.3 (= Eudemus *apud* Simplicium, *In Phys.*, 595.9–15); cf. also Sorabji, *Matter, Space, and Motion*, 194–196; Algra, *Concepts of Space in Greek Thought*, 235f., 252–258; Morison, *On Location*, 166–169. It is also among the concerns addressed in the correspondence between Ibn Abī Saʿīd and Ibn ʿAdī; q.v. below, 349f. Moreover, it is discussed in a comment attributed to Ibn ʿAdī in the margins of Ms. Leiden or. 583; cf. Aristotle, *al-Ṭabīʿa* IV.5, 334.8–335.8. Avicenna explicitly mentions this issue (without an explicit reference to the outermost sphere) in *al-Samāʿ al-ṭabīʿī* II.6, §9, 116.12f., and provides his solution in II.9, §15, 144.3–19; q.v. fn. 118 below, 342.

91 For Alexander's position, q.v. below, 339f.

> But not all [the heavens'] parts are in place (for not all are contained) nor is the outer sphere; instead, it is in place in respect of what is on its inner side (for it is in contact with the [sphere] of Saturn and is, in a way (πως), surrounded), whereas in respect of its outer side, it entirely lacks any place. (Themistius, *In Phys.*, 121.1–4, Todd, modified)

Themistius acknowledges the embarrassing situation that the outermost sphere does not have a surrounding body which contains it and provides a place for it. This, though, is not an issue, he says, because the outermost sphere is, "in a way" (πως), surrounded by the sphere of Saturn. Since the sphere of Saturn is in contact with the outermost sphere and delimits it from the inside, it can adequately be called the place of the outermost sphere. Themistius, apparently, was content with making an exception to Aristotle's general claim that place must be the inner limit of the surrounding body and made the sphere of Saturn an outer limit of the surrounded body.

Themistius' solution was prominent within the Aristotelian philosophical tradition. Even Philoponus, who in his corollary on place attacks Themistius vehemently, recommends his solution outside his critical corollary as the most reasonable way to deal with the situation in Aristotle, even if the convex surface of the sphere of Saturn only provides the outermost sphere with a place in an analogous way (κατὰ ἀναλογίαν).[92] In addition, we find also a version of Themistius' reasoning in Abū Bakr Muḥammad ibn Bāǧǧa (d. 533/1139), where this way of placing the outermost sphere is no longer the exception but has become the rule for all circular bodies. In consequence, the outermost sphere is no longer in place merely "in a way" (πως) or in an analogous way (κατὰ ἀναλογίαν) but regularly.

According to Ibn Bāǧǧa's assessment in his commentary on the *Physics*, Aristotle is right in that the place of a body is a surface. However, since bodies can be divided into those which move rectilinearly and those which move in a circle, two different kinds of surface are relevant as the places of bodies in general. Natural bodies moving rectilinearly have their places in the inner concave surface of the body surrounding them, just as Aristotle explained. Celestial bodies moving in a circle, however, are in place by the outer convex surface of the surrounded body around which they are rotating:

> فالمكان إذاً ضرورةً هو البسيط القريب المُطيف بالجسم فإن كان الجسم ذا أبعاد مستقيمة كان الجسم المحيط خارجاً عنه وإن كان كرّة طبيعية تامّة الإحاطة كان بسيط الجسم المُطيف داخلاً فيها.
>
> Thus, place is, therefore, necessarily the proximate surface encompassing the body. So, if the body has rectilinear dimensions, it [sc. place] is the surrounding body outside of it (*ḫāriǧan ʿanhu*), but if it is a completely circular natural sphere, it [sc. place] is the surface of the encircling body inside of it (*dāḫilan fīhā*). (Ibn Bāǧǧa, *Šurūḥāt al-Samāʿ al-ṭabīʿī* IV.4, 688.8–11 (ed. Lettinck))[93]

---

92 Philoponus, *In Phys.*, 594.14–19, 602.22–24.

93 cf. Lettinck, *Aristotle's* Physics *and its Reception in the Arabic World*, 296f.

On the whole, then, Ibn Bāǧǧa argues that the place of a body is both the inner surface of the surrounding body (in the case of bodies moving rectilinearly) and the outer surface of the surrounded body (in the case of circular bodies). The reason why Ibn Bāǧǧa's account is relevant for our analysis of Avicenna is that Averroes (d. 595/1198), who provides a detailed outline of Ibn Bāǧǧa's position in *commentum* 43 of the fourth book of his *Commentarium magnum in Aristotelis Physicorum*, asserts in Michael Scotus' Latin translation that "it seems to me that what Ibn Bāǧǧa reported is the opinion of al-Fārābī " (*videtur mihi quod hoc, quod narravit Avempace, est opinio Alfarabii*). Moreover, Averroes explicitly mentions that this solution was put forth in response to Philoponus (*contradicentem quaestionibus Ioannis*).[94] Thus, what we get in Ibn Bāǧǧa's commentary is the same (or at least a relatively similar) solution to the problem about the place of the outermost sphere that Avicenna's predecessor al-Fārābī formulated in response either to Philoponus' criticism of Aristotle's insufficient definition of place or to Philoponus' attack on Themistius' attempt to solve the issue by making a one-time exception. Should the latter be true, then al-Fārābī may, indeed, have been driven by a intention to develop Themistius' appealing solution systematically. This seems to be a plausible assumption, for al-Fārābī's developed solution can, indeed, overcome the central complaint which Philoponus levelled against Themistius' argument. Philoponus develops his complaint as follows:

> διό τινες τῶν ἐξηγητῶν τόπον εἶναί φασι τῆς ἀπλανοῦς τὴν κυρτὴν τῆς τοῦ Κρόνου σφαίρας ἐπιφάνειαν, ἄντικρυς πάντα τὰ κοινὰ περὶ τοῦ τόπου ἀναιροῦντες ὁμολογήματα, ἅπερ αὐτὸς ὁ Ἀριστοτέλης ἔθετο, ἔξωθεν εἶναι τὸν τόπον τοῦ ἐν τόπῳ καὶ περιέχειν αὐτό, καὶ ἴσον εἶναι τὸν τόπον τῷ ἐν τόπῳ ... εἰ γὰρ ἡ Κρονία σφαῖρα κατὰ τὴν κυρτὴν ἐπιφάνειαν τόπος ἐστὶ τῆς ἀπλανοῦς, κατ' αὐτὴν δὲ πάλιν τὴν ἐπιφάνειαν περιεχομένην ὑπὸ τῆς ἀπλανοῦς ἐν τόπῳ ἐστὶν ἐκείνη, τὸ αὐτὸ ἄρα (ἡ τοῦ Κρόνου λέγω σφαῖρα) κατὰ τὸ αὐτὸ (τὴν κυρτὴν ἑαυτῆς ἐπιφάνειαν) καὶ τόπος ἐστὶ τῆς ἀπλανοῦς καὶ ἐν τόπῳ ἐστὶν ἐκείνῃ. καὶ πῶς ἂν τὸ αὐτὸ καὶ τόπος εἴη ἄλλου καὶ τόπον ἐκεῖνο αὐτὸ ἔχοι, οὗ τόπος ἐστί; ... διὰ τοῦτο γοῦν οἱ οὕτω λέγοντες τὴν ἀπλανῆ ἐν τόπῳ τὰς κοινὰς περὶ τοῦ τόπου ἐννοίας ἀναιροῦσιν.
>
> So, some of the exponents say that the place of the sphere of the fixed stars is the convex surface of the sphere of Saturn, openly abolishing all the commonly agreed assumptions about place, posited by Aristotle himself, that place is outside that which is in place and that it contains it and that place is equal to that which is in place ... for if the sphere of Saturn in respect of its convex surface is the place of the sphere of fixed stars but again in respect of that same surface, which is contained by the fixed sphere, is in that as in place, it follows that the same thing, namely the sphere of Saturn, in the same respect, namely its convex surface, both is the place of the fixed sphere and also is in that as in place. And how could the same thing both be the place of something and have as its place that very thing whose place it is? ... In this way, then, those who say the sphere of fixed stars is in place in this manner abolish the common conceptions about place. (Philoponus, *In Phys.*, 565.21–566.7, tr. by Furley, modified)

94 Averroes, *Commentarium magnum in Aristotelis Physicorum*, 142rB; cf. also Lettinck, *Aristotle's* Physics *and its Reception in the Arabic World*, 307; M. Rashed's notes in Alexander of Aphrodisias, *Commentaire perdu à la* Physique *d'Aristote*, 46f.

The main point of Philoponus' strident criticism is that allowing the sphere of Saturn to be the place of the outermost sphere would result in an absurd circle: the outermost sphere would, as the regular inner limit of the surrounding body, be the place for the sphere of Saturn. In turn, the sphere of Saturn would, as the irregular outer limit of the surrounded body, be the place of the outermost sphere. Thus, both spheres would contain each other, which would also mean that both spheres are in one and the same respect place and placed – a consequence which, according to Philoponus, is absurd.[95] Therefore, he suggests that if place is a surface, then one has to accept that the heavens simply cannot be in a place in any respect – which, however, leads to a further and no less troublesome question, viz., how the outermost sphere could be moving if it is not in a place.

It has been commonplace since Aristotle to distinguish between four kinds of motion: substantial change, qualitative change, quantitative change, and local motion.[96] As the heavenly spheres move and revolve around in a circle, their motion is neither substantial nor qualitative nor quantitative. It, thus, appears to be a local motion. Local motion, however, is a change of place. If the outermost sphere lacks a place, there is nothing it could change. So, in order to be able to engage in local motion, it is, first, required to have a place.[97] However, even if it had a place, one could still say that the outermost sphere does not engage in local motion, because it does not seem to change or leave its place in any way. In light of this, Philoponus advances the following diagnosis:

> ταύτης δὲ τῆς συγχύσεως αἴτιον γέγονε τὸ ὁρίσασθαι τὸν τόπον πέρας εἶναι τοῦ περιέχοντος, καθὸ περιέχει τὸ περιεχόμενον.
>
> The cause of this confusion is the definition of place as the limit of the surrounding body in respect to which it surrounds the surrounded. (Philoponus, *In Phys.*, 567.5–7, tr. by Furley, modified)

Avicenna knows the issue well, and fundamentally disagrees with Philoponus' assessment. In fact, Avicenna recasts the whole discussion, in order to anticipate – and avoid – the problems around the place of the outermost sphere right from the outset. As the debates between Themistius and Philoponus as well as between al-Fārābī, Ibn Bāǧǧa, and Averroes show, it had become necessary to address the idea of an outside surface as a possible candidate for place. Not only did some Muʿtazilites defend a similar view of place; some Peripatetics, and most notably Themistius and al-Fārābī, also allowed in extreme or special cases for place to be the outer surface of the inner body (as opposed to the inner surface of the outer body). So, what Themistius did,

95 cf. Philoponus, *In Phys.*, 566.3–6; cf. also *In Phys.*, 565.1–9. It should be noted that this consequence no longer follows on al-Fārābī's (and Ibn Bāǧǧa's) understanding of place, for there, the place of the sphere of Saturn would be the outer surface of the next inner sphere, viz. that of Jupiter.

96 cf. *Phys.* III.1, 200b33f.; cf. also *Phys.* V.1, 225a30–32, 225b5–9.

97 cf. Philoponus, *In Phys.*, 566.34–567.2.

according to Avicenna's understanding, was to abolish the relation between place and that which is in place, and to define place, in one instance, as whatever surface is in contact with the body in place.[98] Such a surface could either be a containing (*muḥīṭ*) surface on the inside of a surrounding body or a contained (*muḥāṭ*) surface on the outside of a surrounded body. This, however, entails the consequence that a single body could have two places (*fa-yalzamuhum an yaǧʿalū li-l-ǧism al-wāḥid makānayn*), although a single thing in place should only have one place (*wa-anna li-l-mutamakkin al-wāḥid makānan wāḥidan*).[99] In essence, Avicenna's dissatisfaction here strongly resembles that of Philoponus, as expressed in the above quotation.

Although al-Fārābī's solution was more robust and not vulnerable to this criticism, Avicenna must have disliked it, too, as it introduces a moment of unnecessary ambiguity into Aristotle's definition. Yes, al-Fārābī, or Ibn Bāǧǧa at least, argued that the place of every body is the surface which surrounds it, but the notion of that *surrounding* surface is loosened, so that even next inner bodies can be said to "surround" the outer bodies. This means, for example, that Saturn should be said to be surrounded by Jupiter and not by the outermost sphere – which would seem to be a rather odd result, to say the least. So, even though al-Fārābī's idea is more systematic, insofar as it does not merely constitute an *ad hoc* solution for a singular problematic case but accounts for the place of *all* circular bodies, it is unacceptable to Avicenna that place, on the whole, may simply be *any* surface that fits: inside surface, outside surface – "whichever of the two it may happen to be" (*ayyuhumā ttafaqa*).[100]

Since the notion of an outside surface, then, was apparently not only endorsed by the Muʿtazilites in general but also accepted by prominent Peripatetics in certain problematic or special cases, Avicenna deemed it necessary to disambiguate the notion of surface, in order to dissociate Aristotle's correct definition of place from both the inadequate Muʿtazilī account and the confused notion of his Peripatetic predecessors who confounded two distinct notions of surface, having been misled by the issues about the place and the motion of the outermost sphere.[101]

This brings us to the second aspect of Avicenna's understanding of the issue: the solution. Directly addressing Aristotle's followers, Philoponus wrote in his corollary on place:

---

98 In his letter to Ibn ʿAdī, Ibn Abī Saʿīd complains in the same spirit that allowing the sphere of Saturn to be the place of the outermost sphere would reverse the definition of place and make place a contained, rather than a containing, surface; cf. Ibn ʿAdī, *Kitāb Aǧwiba Bišr al-Yahūdī ʿan masāʾilihī*, 317.10: *fa-yakūnu l-amr fī l-makān bi-l-ʿaks al-maḥwiy lā l-ḥāwī*; q.v. also below, 349f.

99 *al-Samāʿ al-ṭabīʿī* II.7, §2, 119.3–6.

100 We shall find Avicenna later arguing that inner bodies generally have no bearing on an outer body's place; q.v. below, 347ff.

101 Avicenna explicitly states that those who reverted to an outside surface – i.e., people such as Themistius and al-Fārābī (as well as Philoponus outside his corollary) – were actually forced to do so, "because they did not understand the motion of the celestial sphere" (*al-Samāʿ al-ṭabīʿī* II.7, §2, 119.6–8).

> ὅθεν ἀποδοῦναι βουλόμενοι πῶς ἂν ἡ ἀπλανὴς κινοῖτο κατὰ τόπον μὴ οὖσα ἐν τόπῳ, πάντα κυκῶσι μᾶλλον ἢ λέγουσί τι σαφὲς καὶ πεῖσαι δυνάμενον· ἀρνήσασθαι μὲν γὰρ τὸ μὴ κατὰ τόπον κινεῖσθαι τὴν ἀπλανῆ οὐ δύνανται (οὐδὲ γὰρ οὐδὲ πλάσασθαι δύνανται τίνα ἂν κινοῖτο κίνησιν).
>
> Hence, when they try to explain how the sphere of the fixed stars could move in place when it is not in place, they throw everything into confusion rather than say anything clear and persuasive. For they cannot deny that the [outermost] sphere moves in place, because they cannot even make up a story about what [other] kind of motion it would have. (Philoponus, *In Phys.*, 565.12–16, tr. by Furley)

From Philoponus' perspective, his accusation that the defenders of Aristotle, as well as Aristotle himself, "could not even make up a story" for the motion of the heavenly spheres that is in accordance with Aristotle's definition of place is entirely justified. Themistius' solution was unacceptable for reasons we already know, whereas Aristotle devoted only a meagre handful of words to the issue, stating that "the whole will be moved in one sense, but not in another, for as a whole it does not change its place at once, though it will be moved in a circle, for this place is the place of its parts."[102] These words certainly do contain some material, even material relevant for Avicenna's solution, but it seems that Alexander was the only one in the history of philosophy who was more or less fully satisfied with it. He is reported by Simplicius to have said the following:

> ἢ ἄλλο ἐστί, φησὶν Ἀλέξανδρος τὸ κατὰ φορὰν καὶ ἄλλο τὸ κατὰ περιφοράν, τὸ μὲν ἐπ' εὐθείας καὶ ὅλον τόπον ἐκ τόπου μεταβαῖνον, τὸ δὲ κύκλῳ καὶ ἐν τῷ αὐτῷ φερόμενον κατὰ μόρια κινεῖται. διὸ οὐδ' ἐν τόπῳ ἐστὶν ὅλον, ὅτι μηδὲ κινεῖται κατὰ τόπον ὅλον.
>
> Alexander says that perhaps local motion and rotation are different, one being in a straight line and wholly exchanging one place for another, the other being in a circle and motion in the same place with only the parts changing its place. So it [sc. the universe] is not in a place as a whole, because it does not change place as a whole. (Alexander *apud* Simplicium, *In Phys.*, 580.12–16, tr. by Urmson, modified)[103]

It is apparent that Alexander's remarks, which probably were available to Avicenna, are important for Avicenna's solution.[104] Yet, Alexander clearly missed the opportunity to investigate the notion of rotation further, and "to classify it properly and to determine its characteristics," as Paul Moraux noted.[105] While Alexander remained firm in his claim that the motion of the outermost sphere is not local motion according to place, Simplicius is justified in asking in return what motion it should be, then, for it clearly is not motion according to substance, quality, or quantity, either (δῆλον γὰρ ὅτι οὔτε

---

102 *Phys.* IV.5, 212a34–212b1.

103 cf. further reports by Simplicius, *In Phys.*, 589.4–8, 595.20–22, 602.31–35; cf. also Moraux, *Der Aristotelismus bei den Griechen*, vol. 3, 153.

104 This has already been noted by McGinnis, "Positioning Heaven," esp. 147f., 157.

105 Moraux, *Der Aristotelismus bei den Griechen*, vol. 3, 153: Alexander "bemüht sich auch nicht, die Kreisbewegung einzuordnen und in ihrer Eigenart zu definieren."

κατ' οὐσίαν ἐστὶν οὔτε κατὰ ποσὸν οὔτε κατὰ ποιόν).[106] Moreover, one of Simplicius' most convincing arguments against any solution which treats the outermost sphere as an exception – i.e., solutions such as those offered by Aristotle, Alexander, and Themistius – consists in asking why it is, then, that all other spheres nonetheless have places and are said to move according to place (even though they do not really change their places), whereas the outermost sphere does not have a place and is not said to move according to place, despite that all spheres are, or should be, alike in their motion.[107] In other words, why should the explanation for the motion of the outermost sphere be in any way different from that of the remaining spheres, if all spheres move in a circle? Such solutions provide nothing other than a *dissociation arbitraire*, as Marwan Rashed asserted about Alexander.[108] Although Avicenna's solution to the issue of the place and the motion of the outermost sphere seems to be inspired by Alexander's insistence that the outermost sphere neither is in a place nor moves according to place, it is not vulnerable to any concern so far mentioned.

Earlier in his *al-Samāʿ al-ṭabīʿī*, in chapter II.3, Avicenna analysed the relation between motion and the categories. There, he argued that the outermost sphere does not undergo local motion and, thus, does not require a place, because its motion does not involve a change of place. Accordingly, we can safely accept the only seemingly absurd implication of Aristotle's account of place that the outermost sphere does not have a place due to the fact that there is nothing outside the outermost sphere that could be its place.[109] The outermost sphere, Avicenna argues, does not change its place (even if it had one), nor does it need or, indeed, have one. Embracing Aristotle's definition with all its consequences, Avicenna suggests that the motion of the outermost sphere is not a motion with respect to the category of place but a motion with respect to the category of position, i.e., it is a positional motion (*al-ḥaraka al-waḍʿiyya*).[110] Avicenna writes in *al-Samāʿ al-ṭabīʿī* II.3:

106 Simplicius, *In Phys.*, 595.17f. Simplicius effectively turns Aristotle against himself and emphasises that Aristotle himself classified rotation as local motion; cf. *In Phys.*, 602.21–28, quoting from *Physics* VIII.8, 261b28f.; *In Phys.*, 603.7f., quoting from *De caelo* I.2, 268b17f. At *In Phys.*, 595.16, Simplicius directly asks "what kind of motion revolution is" (ποία τῶν κινήσεών ἐστιν ἡ κυκλοφορία) and subsequently adds that Alexander "clearly says that this motion is not [one with respect to] place ... which, however, it is [supposed to] be, he does not say." Responding to Alexander's suggestion, Simplicius, again, refers to the just-mentioned passage from the *De caelo*, thus dismissing Alexander's remark.

107 Simplicius, *In Phys.*, 591.1–4.

108 M. Rashed, "Alexandre d'Aphrodise et la 'magna quaestio,'" 317. Again, it seems that a similar worry may have inspired al-Fārābī and Ibn Bāǧǧa to develop a solution which does not merely aim at finding an arbitrary exception for the motion of the outermost sphere and, instead, to provide a systematic account for the places and the motions of all spheres.

109 cf. *Phys.* IV.5, 212b8–10, 14, 20–22.

110 cf. *al-Samāʿ al-ṭabīʿī* II.3, §§13–16, 103.8–105.13; *al-Naǧāt* II.2.1, 206.6–207.8 ≈ *al-Ḥikma al-ʿArūḍiyya* II.2, 121.12–22; *ʿUyūn al-ḥikma* II.2, 19.2; *Dānešnāme-ye ʿAlāʾī* III.3, 7.10–8.3; III.5, 12.6–13.2; *al-Hidāya* II.1, 137.2–4; *al-Ḥikma al-mašriqiyya* III.7, 19.18–21.5; *al-Išārāt wa-l-tanbīhāt* II.2.3, 108.7–9; 11; cf. Hasnawi, "La dynamique d'Ibn Sīnā," 106; M. Rashed, "Alexandre d'Aphrodise et la 'magna quaestio,'" 302–345;

وأمّا كيفية وجود الحركة في الوضع فهو أنّ كلّ مستبدل وضع من غير أن يفارق بكلّيته المكان بل بأن تتبدّل نسبة أجزائه إلى أجزاء مكانه وإلى جهاته. فهو متحرّك في الوضع لا محالة لأنّ مكانه لم يتبدّل بل يتبدّل وضعه في مكانه والمكان هو الأوّل بعينه.

The way that motion exists with respect to position is that the whole [of something] changes its position without leaving the place with its entirety (*min ġayr an yufāriqa bi-kulliyyatihī l-makān*). Rather, it is that the relation of its parts to the parts of its place and to its sides changes. So, it is without doubt in motion with respect to position, because its place does not change; rather its position in its place changes (*makānahū lam yatabaddalu bal yatabaddalu waḍʿuhū fī makānihī*), while the place is the same as it was at first. (*al-Samāʿ al-ṭabīʿī* II.3, §14, 104.2–4, tr. by McGinnis, modified)[111]

A little later in the same paragraph, Avicenna explicitly addresses the issue of the outermost sphere and states that whatever engages in positional motion either has a place and does not change it, while its parts change their position, or does not have a place, and so, *a fortiori*, does not change it, while its parts nonetheless change their position to each other:

فإنّه إمّا أن يكون كالفلك الأعلى الذي ليس في مكان بمعنى نهاية الحاوي الشامل المساوي الذي إيّاه نعني بالمكان وإمّا أن يكون في مكان لكنّه لا يفارق كلّية مكانه بل إنّما تتغيّر عليه نسبة أجزائه إلى أجزاء مكانه التي يلقاها.

So, either it is like the outermost celestial sphere (*ka-l-falak al-aʿlā*), which is not in a place in the sense of the limit of the containing [thing] which exactly surrounds [what it contains] (*laysa fī makān bi-maʿnā nihāyat al-ḥāwī l-šāmil al-musāwī*) – which is what we mean by "place" – or it is in a place but does not leave the whole of its place, whereas only the relation of its parts to the parts of its place with which it is in contact are changing for it.[112] (*al-Samāʿ al-ṭabīʿī* II.3, §14, 104.11–13, tr. by McGinnis, modified)[113]

---

his notes in Alexander of Aphrodisias, *Commentaire perdu à la* Physique *d'Aristote*, 46–49; McGinnis, "Positioning Heaven"; Arif, "The Universe as a System," 144f.; cf. also Algra's footnotes 204 and 205 in his translation of Philoponus' commentary on *Physics* IV.1–5. One should also not forget that a similar suggestion was made by Eudemus, which is discussed by Algra in *Concepts of Space in Greek Thought*, 255–257; cf. also Philoponus, *In Phys.*, 593.25–594.10, 603.18f.; Iḫwān al-Ṣafāʾ, *Rasāʾil Iḫwān al-Ṣafāʾ* XV.12, 32.7–34.2. Recently, M. Rashed hinted at yet another possible source for Avicenna, viz., the commentary on Aristotle's *De generatione et corruptione* attributed to the Imāmite scholar and theologian Abū Muḥammad al-Ḥaṣan ibn Mūsā al-Nawbaḫtī, in which motion is allowed to take place in *all* categories, and not only in four as in Aristotle or five as in Avicenna; cf. al-Nawbaḫtī (?), *Commentary on Aristotle* De generatione et corruptione, 99f. On a different note, Faḫr al-Dīn claims that the idea of positional motion was already in place before Avicenna; cf. *al-Mabāḥiṯ al-mašriqiyya*, II.1.5.14, vol. 1, 701.12–14. As evidence, he refers to the *ʿUyūn al-masāʾil*, which he explicitly attributes to al-Fārābī; cf. *ʿUyūn al-masāʾil*, §12, 60.16f. Apparently already at the time of Faḫr al-Dīn, in the sixth/twelfth century, this pseudepigraphic compendium was thought to be by al-Fārābī; q.v. above, 37.

111 cf. *al-Ḥikma al-mašriqiyya* III.7, 19.18f.

112 Reading *allatī yalqāhā* with Mss. Leiden or. 4 and or. 84 as well as McGinnis and Āl Yāsīn for *allaḏī talqāhā* in Zāyid.

113 cf. *al-Ḥikma al-mašriqiyya* III.7, 20.5–7.

According to Avicenna, the outermost sphere does not change its place, because it does not have a place. Nonetheless, it engages in motion, viz., rotation.[114] Rotation, then, is a change in the position which the respective parts and segments of the sphere have to each other. In the same sense, a spinning top may not change its place, although it certainly engages in motion, as its parts and segments revolve around the centre and, thereby, change their positions within the whole.[115]

Recently, Morison argued that Aristotle could have answered the objection about the motion and the place of the outermost sphere by providing a fully developed account of rotation. There would be "no difficulty," Morison writes, "that the outer sphere has no place, because rotation is obviously change of place in respect of the parts of something," and so "Aristotle's account of place can ... meet the objection that according to him the outer sphere of the universe has no place, and yet rotates."[116] What Avicenna did was precisely to develop this line of thought even more rigorously than Morison, because he argues for rotation to be a fifth kind of motion in addition to the four known kinds, viz., substantial change, qualitative change, growth, and local motion.[117]

For Avicenna, then, it is as reasonable to say that the outermost sphere does engage in motion as it is unproblematic to claim that it does not have a place.[118] In fact, there is no problem at all, once one has understood properly how the outermost sphere moves – and this is a motion in the category of position which does not require having a place. Thus, Avicenna is the first who can "provide a story," as Philoponus put it, and answer Simplicius' question as to what kind of motion rotation is, if it is apparently none of the four kinds available.

---

114 cf. *Physics* IV.5, 212a31–212b1.

115 The example of the spinning top is borrowed from Plato; cf. *Rep.* IV, 436d3–e7.

116 Morison, *On Location*, 168f.; cf. Algra, *Concepts of Space in Greek Thought*, fn. 142, 185.

117 For a more detailed exposition of Avicenna's account of positional motion, cf. McGinnis, "Positioning Heaven," who likewise points to Algra's and Morison's suggestions in succession of Avicenna. One could also link Avicenna's account of positional motion with his views about shellfish and more generally with his claim that all animals, besides having the sense of touch, are also able to move voluntarily, as is expressed in his psychological writings, e.g., Avicenna, *al-Nafs*, II.3, 58.18–59.8. With Avicenna's account of positional motion in mind, one can substantiate Hasse's claim that the motion of the shellfish is precisely not a kind of local motion but is rather a positional motion brought about through contraction and dilation; cf. Hasse, *Avicenna's* De Anima *in the Latin West*, 93–95; cf. also Hall, "Intellect, Soul and Body in Ibn Sīnā," 85.

118 cf. Avicenna's argumentation in *al-Samāʿ al-ṭabīʿī* II.9, §15, 144.3–19, where he specifically addresses the objection, outlined in II.6, §9, 116.12f., that place should be an extension, because if place were a surface, not every body could be in a place, whereas if it is an extension, then every body could be in a place. This objection is known from Theophrastus' list of ἀπορίαι where it is claimed "that not all body will be in a place – for the [sphere of] the fixed stars will not" (ὅτι οὐ πᾶν σῶμα ἐν τόπῳ (οὐδὲ γὰρ ἡ ἀπλανής). Avicenna argues, first, that the objection fails, because it is simply untrue that every body is in place (for the outermost sphere is not); and second, that even if every body were in place it would not follow that place would have to be an extension.

Two aspects of Avicenna's solution are particularly significant. First, it is not an *ad hoc* attempt to find a singular exception for a special case. In a way, Avicenna does not even acknowledge that the case of the outermost sphere is special at all. Admittedly, the outermost sphere is peculiar insofar as it does not have a place – but for Avicenna, this is nothing other than a petty *datum* already openly recognised by Aristotle and accepted by Alexander.[119] It is nothing to worry about and certainly nothing which would require any modification in, let alone revision of, Aristotle's account of place. The outermost sphere, and the universe as a whole, just does not have a place, but this is entirely acceptable, because it does not have a surrounding body. Thus, it is not necessary to treat it in any special way and make it an exception to the rule, as especially Themistius did, when he argued that the place of the outmerost sphere – and *only* of this sphere – was the surface of the next inner body surrounding it "in a way" (πως) from the inside.

Second, Avicenna's solution dismantles the above-mentioned objection by Simplicius, who precisely complained about the *dissociation arbitraire* within Alexander's and Themistius' solutions that if the place and the motion of the outermost sphere is treated as an exception, we forfeit the inner unity of a consistent explanation for the places and the motions in the entire celestial region.[120] If all spheres change their places by moving around in a circle, why, then, is not every sphere in a place and moving according to the same account as all the others? As we have just seen, Avicenna argues that positional motion can occur both for those bodies which do not have a place (as the outermost sphere) *as well as* for those bodies which do have a place (as all other spheres). Thus, for Avicenna, *all* celestial spheres move with respect to position or, put negatively, *none* of them moves according to place, even though all spheres, except for the outermost sphere, have a place – a place that can entirely be accounted for without any modification of the Aristotelian definition by taking recourse to the inner limit of the body surrounding it from the outside.

Taking it all together, Avicenna's understanding of this supposed issue is both universal and uniform, because it dispenses with *ad hoc* exceptions just as much as it forgoes any modification in the Aristotelian account of place – developing the Aristotelian understanding of motion instead. It becomes clear that Avicenna is an unconditional believer in the explanatory strength and universal adequacy of Aristotle's definition of place.

Ultimately, what this discussion of the issue of the place of the outermost sphere has brought to light is that the Aristotelian condition that place must be in contact with the thing in place can, indeed, be satisfied by *three* different kinds of surfaces, so that, as already mentioned, place could equally be the outside surface of a body upon which

---

119 cf. *Phys.* IV.5, 212b8–10, 14, 20–22; Alexander *apud* Simplicium, *In Phys.*, 580.15f.; cf. also Moraux, *Der Aristotelismus bei den Griechen*, vol. 3, 153.

120 cf. Simplicius, *In Phys.*, 591.1–4; M. Rashed, "Alexandre d'Aphrodise et la 'magna quaestio,'" 317.

some thing may rest, as some Muʿtazilites argued; the inner surface of the surrounding body which contains some other body, as Avicenna understands Aristotle's position; or simply any contacting surface however it might be (be that an outside or an inner surface), as especially Themistius and al-Fārābī, and even Philoponus (outside his corollary), have allowed in one or more cases.

It is only against this background that we can understand why Avicenna regards it as crucial to clarify – and to rectify – the Aristotelian approach by disambiguating the notion of surface, by explaining the condition that the surface must be in contact with that which is in place, and by enlarging the Aristotelian list of four candidates to a total of six.[121] What remains to be done is to decide which of these six options is correct. Avicenna passes his verdict in the final chapter on place, *al-Samāʿ al-ṭabīʿī* II.9.

Avicenna begins this final chapter with a reduced list of requirements. While Aristotle had stipulated six such requirements at the beginning of *Physics* IV.4, Avicenna has mentioned four examples of attributes which philosophers commonly ascribed to place in *al-Samāʿ al-ṭabīʿī* II.6.[122] Now, in chapter II.9, he offers only two basic axiomatic requirements on whose basis the essence of place is to be determined. He writes the following:

فإذاً كان المكان هو الذي فيه الجسم وحده ولا يجوز أن يكون فيه معه جسم آخر غيره إذ كان مساوياً له وكان يستجدّ ويفارق والواحد منه تتعاقب عليه عدّة متمكّنات. وكانت هذه الصفات كلّها أو بعضها لا تُوجَد إلّا لهيولى أو صورة أو بعد أو سطح ملاقٍ كيف كان.

> Therefore, (i) place is that in which the body alone exists (and it is not possible that another body that is different from it is together with it in it, since [place] is equal to it);[123] and (ii) it can be entered anew and departed from, and in one [place] a number of things in place can succeed [one another]. These attributes – whether all or some – exist only on account of a matter or a form or an extension or a contacting surface (however it might be). (*al-Samāʿ al-ṭabīʿī* II.9, §1, 137.5–7, tr. by McGinnis, modified)[124]

---

121 We find an explicit confirmation of this interpretation at the end of *al-Samāʿ al-ṭabīʿī* II.6. There, Avicenna returns to the initial distinction he made in the opening lines of the chapter about two common conceptions of place; q.v. above, 326f. First, he mentions, and briefly dismisses, the idea that place is that on which someone sits, i.e., the outside surface. Second, he refers to a "contacting ... surface however it might be" which has been used, Avicenna continues, to account for the place and the motion of the outermost sphere, explaining that this entails that things are reciprocally in place by containing one another. Finally, he refers to a third option, viz., the "containing surface," which is the notion he promises to "verify later," i.e., in chapter II.9, after having "falsified these [other] schools," first, i.e., in chapters II.7–8. With these words, he concludes the chapter; cf. *al-Samāʿ al-ṭabīʿī* II.6, §§16–17, 118.2–10.

122 q.v. above, 314 and 329, respectively.

123 Reading *kāna musāwiyan lahū* with McGinnis and Āl Yāsīn for *kāna musāwiyan* in Zāyid, *huwa musāwin* in Ms. Leiden or. 4, and *kāna musāwin* in Ms. Leiden or. 84.

124 cf. *al-Ḥikma al-mašriqiyya* III.9, 26.11–14. The same two requirements are found at the beginning of the discussion on place in *al-Hidāya* II.1, 151.5f.; both conditions are also confirmed at the beginning and the end of the chapter on place in *al-Naǧāt* II.2.10, which is almost identical to the chapter contained in *al-Ḥikma al-ʿArūḍiyya* II.2.8, of which the latter half is not extant, though.

With the first requirement, Avicenna once again confirms that he is interested in the proper place of something, i.e., the one place which only belongs to one body and to no other body at the same time. This place is equal to the body (*musāwiyan lahū*), i.e., it is neither greater nor smaller than the body. The second reiterates that place must be something in which several bodies can be at different times, so that one body which has left a place can be succeeded by another body which occurs in that place. This second requirement also emphasises that one of the reasons for investigating the essence of place – and for Aristotle even the primary reason – is that understanding place is relevant for understanding local motion, for local motion, it seems, is a change precisely of place. A body changes its place when it separates itself from its earlier place and comes to be in another.

The possible candidates for what place is, as enumerated here, are four. The fourth candidate – "a contacting surface (however it might be)" – should be understood as containing all three sub-options: just simply any contacting surface or a contacting outside surface or a contacting inside surface.[125] That place cannot be just any contacting surface has been established earlier by showing that this would result in the unbearable situation that many bodies would be at two different places at the same time.[126] Matter and form are also ruled out as viable candidates, because they cannot satisfy one of the two requirements. Although Avicenna does not specify which one, it is obvious that he refers to the second, as no body can depart from, and leave behind, its own matter or its own form (without undergoing substantial change, in which case it would cease to be the same body).[127] If place must be separable from the body which is in place, and if matter and form are essentially inseparable from the body they constitute, then neither could possibly also constitute the body's place.

The next option, that place is an extension, is ruled out, because such an extension simply does not exist (*wa-l-buʿd lā wuǧūda lahū*), regardless of whether this extension is empty – and so is void – or is always filled, being something which merely underlies and penetrates through the existing bodies. Avicenna has devoted most of the earlier chapter seven and the entire chapter eight to disproving the existence of an extension, and I shall discuss some of his arguments below.[128]

Thereupon, Avicenna turns to the non-containing surface (*al-saṭḥ ġayr al-ḥāwī*), which is the fifth candidate on Avicenna's list. This is an outside surface, i.e., a surface

---

125 Avicenna's brief discussion in *al-Hidāya* is confined to presenting only two options: place is either the surface of the containing body or an extension equal in size to the interpenetrating extensions of the body in place; cf. *al-Hidāya* II.1, 151.6f.

126 cf. *al-Samāʿ al-ṭabīʿī* II.7, §2, 119.3–6; q.v. also above, 338.

127 This is the same reason provided by Aristotle in *Physics* IV.2, 209b22–28; cf. *Phys.* IV.4, 211b36–212a2; cf. also the reasons given against matter and form as candidates for place in *al-Naǧāt* II.2.10, 233.10–13 ≈ *al-Ḥikma al-ʿArūḍiyya* II.2.8, 133.20–22; *Dānešnāme-ye ʿAlāʾī* III.6, 14.4–10; *al-Ḥikma al-mašriqiyya* III.9, 26.13–22.

128 q.v. below, 367ff.

which does not enclose or contain or surround the body in place but is one on which the body rests and which supports it and prevents it from falling, as al-Ašʿarī and Ibn Mattawayh put it. Avicenna is rather quick with this candidate and merely writes:

والسطح غير الحاوي ليس بمكان ولا حاوٍ منه إلّا الذي هو نهاية الجسم الشامل.

The non-containing surface is not place. No [surface] is something that contains except that which is the limit of the surrounding body (*nihāyat al-ğism al-šāmil*). (*al-Samāʿ al-ṭabīʿī* II.9, §1, 137.8)

Here the argumentative weight is on the notion of the limit of the *surrounding* – in contrast to a surrounded – body (*al-ğism al-šāmil*). It is clear that Avicenna's reason for rejecting this candidate is that a non-containing outside surface of a surrounded body does not satisfy the first requirement insofar as an outside surface neither really contains a body nor can it be said to contain only *one* body. An outside surface, by its very definition, is not "closed." If it were enclosing the body in place, it would be an inner surface and would envelop the body on all its sides. Since a non-containing surface is, therefore "open," it does not adequately delimit the body's place and, thus, is prone to "contain" more than one body (provided that "containing" is an applicable description at all). Since Avicenna by now has provided arguments against five of the six available options, the remaining sixth option – which is also the only option which exist *and* satisfies both requirements – must be what place is:

فالمكان هو السطح الذي هو نهاية الجسم الحاوي لا غير.

So, place is[129] the surface which is the limit of the containing body (*nihāyat al-ğism al-ḥāwī*) – and nothing else. (*al-Samāʿ al-ṭabīʿī* II.9, §1, 137.8f.)[130]

With this, Avicenna has established Aristotle's conclusion. He did so by expanding the scope of Aristotle's method and the argumentative *approach*, reacting to developments that postdate Aristotle's efforts. In particular, he sought to clarify the notion of surface which Aristotle employed, first, in order to establish an enlarged list of candidates; and second, in order to decide clearly, and without leaving room for ambiguity or exceptions, which of these comes down as correct. However, Avicenna is not yet done with clarifying the notion of surface. It will now be seen how he also emends and defends the Aristotelian *definition*.

129 Reading *huwa* with Mss. Leiden or. 4 and or. 84 as well as Zāyid for *huwa huwa* in McGinnis and Āl Yāsīn.

130 cf. *al-Nağāt* II.2.10, 244.8f.; *al-Hidāya*, II.1, 155.3; *Dānešnāme-ye ʿAlāʾī* II.11, 24.9–11; *ʿUyūn al-ḥikma* II.7, 26.4f.; *al-Ḥikma al-mašriqiyya* II.9, 26.9–11, 16; cf. also the discussion in *al-Maqūlāt* III.4, 119.14–120.16. The single manuscript preserving the text of *al-Ḥikma al-ʿArūḍiyya* lacks a couple of folia, and so breaks off in the middle of the discussion of void before reaching the definition of place. Avicenna's *ʿUyūn al-ḥikma*, on the other hand, discusses place only in passing stating that "the place of the body is not a dimension in which it is, as you know, but is the surface of something which, being in contact with it, contains it, and so it [sc. the body] is in it" (*ʿUyūn al-ḥikma* II.7, 26.4f.).

The Notion of Surface in the Definition of Place

Above I complained in a side remark that Aristotle speaks of the surface of a body as if every body were contained by only one surrounding substance in such a way that the surface that functions as the body's place were a homogenous surface.[131] He asks, for example, whether the water of a river or the river itself is the appropriate place for a boat. What, however, about the adjacent air? Is not more than half of the boat in contact with air rather than with water? In reality, most bodies are contained by at least two substances which only together surround and enclose the body in place. Is place, then, a composite of the inner surfaces of all these substances? A horse's place, for example, would most of the time be composed of the surfaces of earth and air, and a crocodile's place would often be a combination of the surfaces of earth, water, and air, whereas at work, many people's places are a combination of the surfaces of a chair, a carpet, a desk, some air, and even some pencil. Avicenna addresses this issue immediately after having established the essence of place and states that "place may happen to be a single surface, but it also may happen to be a number of surfaces from which a single surface is made up."[132] Avicenna inquires more into this issue:

> ويجب أن ننظر هذا إذا كان ماء مثلاً في جرّة وفي وسط الماء شيء آخر يحيط به الماء وقد علمنا أنّ مكان الماء هو السطح المقعّر من الجرّة فهل هو وحده مكانه أو هو والسطح المحدّب الظاهر من الجسم الموجود في الماء مجموعين مكان الماء؟
>
> It is necessary that we think about this: when water, for example, is in a jar and in the midst of the water (*fī wasaṭ al-mā'*) is something else which the water encloses, and when we have come to know that the place of the water was the concave surface of the jar, then is it alone its place or is it and[133] the outward convex surface of the body which exists in the water both together the place of the water? (*al-Samā' al-ṭabī'ī* II.9, §3, 137.14–138.1)[134]

Following this question, Avicenna distinguishes two cases and, apparently, drew two pictures in his autograph of *al-Samā' al-ṭabī'ī*, which he labeled "here" (*hāhunā*) and

---

131 q.v. fn. 39 above, 317.

132 *al-Samā' al-ṭabī'ī* II.9, §2, 137.11; cf. *al-Ḥikma al-mašriqiyya* III.9, 26.22. Avicenna may be influenced by Themistius who, although in a different context, explains that sublunary bodies are contained either by three elements, viz., earth, water, and air, as in the case of rocks in a riverbed, or by only two of them, viz., earth and air or water and air, as in the case of walkers or swimmers; cf. *In Phys.*, 119.8–11. Philoponus picks up on this and adds that some are also contained by only one, viz., air or water or earth, as in the case of birds and fish and some things deep inside the earth; cf. *In Phys.*, 591.25–592.11. In his commentary on the *Categories*, Ammonius similarly speaks of the "parts of place" (τὰ τοῦ τόπου μόρια) that need to "unite" (συνάπτει) so as to form a continuous boundary to serve as the place for a continuous body (*In Cat.*, 58.21–26).

133 Reading *aw huwa wa-l-saṭḥ* with Mss. Leiden or. 4 and or. 84 as well as McGinnis and Āl Yāsīn for *aw huwa l-saṭḥ* in Zāyid.

134 cf. *al-Ḥikma al-mašriqiyya* III.9, 27.3–6.

"there" (*hunāka*).[135] Using my own examples for clarification, Avicenna's picture "here" (*hāhunā*) represents a bowl of water with a cork floating on top in the midst of the water (*fī wasaṭ al-mā'*), then, the place of the water is the sum of all its adjacent surfaces: the flat surface of the air on top, the convex surface of the cork, and the concave surface of the bowl. These three surfaces together make up one single thing, i.e., one combined surface, which serves as the place of the water.

The other picture "there" (*hunāka*), however, represents an identical bowl of water, this time not with a cork floating on the water but with a fish swimming *inside* the water (*fī dāḫil al-mā'*). In that case, the place of the water is *not* the sum of all its adjacent surfaces, argues Avicenna, for there the air on top, the concave surface of the bowl, and the outside surface of the fish inside the water do not make up a *single* surface.[136] Instead, there are two surfaces: the single combined surface of the air and the bowl *as well as* the outside convex surface of the fish inside the water. Relevant for the place of the water, however, is only the former, i.e., only the single combined surface of the air and the bowl make up the place of the water regardless of whether there is a fish inside the water. Put differently, the water is always at the same place regardless of whether or not something is swimming inside the water, underneath its surface. Should, however, there be a cork floating on the water, instead of a fish swimming inside the water, then the place of the water would be the surface of the air together with the surface of the bowl *and* the convex surface of the part of the cork which is in contact with the water, for in this case there is, in fact, a single surface that can be combined from these three surfaces. With this, Avicenna concludes that the place of a body is the combination of all the surfaces that are in contact with it on all its sides *under the condition that* one single thing comes-to-be from their combination:

فيشبه أن يكون حيث يحصل من الجملة واحد فإنّ الجملة تكون مكاناً واحداً وتكون الأجزاء أجزاء المكان ولا يكون شيء منها مكاناً للكلّ وحيث لا يحصل لا يكون.

So, it seems that insofar as from the combination a single [thing] occurs (*ḥayṯu yaḥṣulū min al-ǧumla wāḥid*), the combination truly is a single place and the parts would be the place's parts, but none of them would [by itself] be a place for the whole, and inasmuch as no [single thing] comes to be, it is not [the thing's place]. (*al-Samāʿ al-ṭabīʿī* II.9, §3, 138.7–9, tr. by McGinnis, modified)[137]

---

135 McGinnis' first drawing is the same as, according to Āl Yāsīn's edition, the one in Ms. Cairo, Maktabat al-Azhar al-Šarīf, Beḫīt 331 falsafa and similar to the one in Zāyid's edition. More helpful, however, seems to be the drawing which can be found in Ms. Leiden or. 84, on folio 340r, and, according to Āl Yāsīn's edition, in Ms. Oxford Pococke 125.

136 My interpretation is based on the observation that Avicenna seems to distinguish between an object "in the midst of the water" (*fī wasaṭ al-mā'*) and an object "inside the water" (*fī dāḫil al-mā'*). While the latter is *immersed in* water, having water on all its sides, like a fish deep in the sea or a submerged submarine, the former is merely *floating on* the water having water around but not on top of it, like a boat or a cork floating on the water.

137 cf. *al-Ḥikma al-mašriqiyya* III.9, 27.14–16. There is a problem in the transmission of the text of the last clause: Zāyid has *lā yaḥṣulu*, McGinnis and Āl Yāsīn have *lā yaʾtalifuhū*, Ms. Leiden or. 84 has what

Avicenna's current point is surely more than mere pedantry, as Avicenna appears to combine the exegesis and refinement of Aristotle with some criticism of Themistius' and al-Fārābī's solutions to the dilemma of the place of the outermost sphere, for they, indeed, have argued that the place of that sphere would be the convex surface of something *inside* the sphere, i.e., the convex surface of the next inner sphere of Saturn.[138] What Avicenna is presently denying, however, is precisely that the convex surface of something inside could have any bearing whatsoever on a thing's place.

Still, this clarification remains a detail compared to the other, severe issues that plagued the Aristotelian account of place as a contacting surface right from the start. Looking at Theophrastus' list of ἀπορίαι, again, the first item is the issue "that body will be in a surface" (ὅτι τὸ σῶμα ἔσται ἐν ἐπιφανείᾳ). As has already been mentioned, this brief and in itself not very telling concern formed the basis not for one but for two of Philoponus' five objections against Aristotle's definition. In Avicenna, we not only find a direct response to these two objections, we shall also find a clear indication that Avicenna used Philoponus' commentary when he defended Aristotle's account.

To recall, Philoponus argued, first, that a body is in place by virtue of nothing other than its being a body (οὐ κατὰ ἄλλο τί ἐστιν ἐν τόπῳ ἢ καθὸ σῶμά). Since body is three-dimensionally extended, it is in place precisely by virtue of its being three-dimensionally extended. On that basis, Philoponus claimed that a surface, being merely two-dimensional, simply cannot accommodate a body adequately in all its three dimensions and, thus, fails to be a proper place for the body. In a second argument, he states that place must be "equal" to that which is in place (δεῖ τὸν τόπον ἴσον εἶναι τῷ ἐν τόπῳ). This was his interpretation of Aristotle's commonly agreed condition that place must neither be greater nor smaller than, i.e., must be equal to, that which is in place. Yet, if place is a surface and that which is in place is a body, then we would get the disturbing result that a surface would be equal to a body, although it is beyond discussion that a point is not equal to a line nor a line to a surface nor a surface to a body, for otherwise a point would eventually be equal to a body, too.[139]

The same objections have also been discussed by commentators writing in Arabic. There is not only a brief marginal gloss attributed to "Yaḥyā and Abū ʿAlī" in Ms. Leiden or. 583 discussing the first claim that body is in place by virtue of its three-dimensionality, there is also a direct discussion of both objections in the letter that Ibn Abī Saʿīd al-Mawṣilī (fl. fourth/tenth century) addressed to Yaḥyā ibn ʿAdī.[140] In this letter, we read the following:

---

seems to be *lā yaḥṣulu yaʾtalifu*, and Ms. Leiden or. 4 has *lā yaḥṣulū* with a marginal note adding what seems to be *yaʾtalifu*. Despite the differences, the sense clearly is that when there is no combination (*lā yaʾtalifu*) and no single combined thing comes-to-be (*lā yaḥṣulu*), it is not a place for the thing.

138 q.v. above, 335ff.

139 Philoponus, *In Phys.*, 563.27–564.14; cf. Simplicius, *In Phys.*, 603.35f.; q.v. above, 322ff.

140 For the marginal gloss in Ms. Leiden or. 583, cf. Aristotle, *al-Ṭabīʿa* IV.4, 313.16f.

أحدها أ يكون المكان مساوياً لما هو فيه لا أصغر منه ولا أعظم. ونهاية الحاوي ليس هو بهذه الصفة لأنّه ذو بعدين فقط لأنّه بسيط وما فيه أعني الجسم ذو ثلاثة أبعاد. فما في المكان إذاً على هذا السبيل أعظم من المكان. فعرفني، أيّدك الله، كيف تسلم لنا المساواة في نهاية الحاوي فإنّي أنا ما أرى ذلك يطرد.

> One of them [sc. one of the requirements listed by Aristotle] was that place is equal (*musāwiyan*) to what is in it, and neither smaller than it nor greater (*lā aṣġar minhu wa-lā aʿẓam*).[141] Yet, the limit of what contains [does] not [fit] this description, because it has only two dimensions, because it is a surface (*basīṭ*), whereas what is in it, i.e., the body, has three dimensions. Thus, that which is in place is, therefore, in this way greater than the place. So, let me know – may God aid you – how the equality of the limit of the containing can be accepted by us, for I do not see this [objection] be driven away. (Ibn Abī Saʿīd *apud* Ibn ʿAdī, *Kitāb Ağwiba Bišr al-Yahūdī ʿan masāʾilihī*, 316.14–317.4)

It is clear that Ibn Abī Saʿīd's first concern corresponds to Philoponus' *second objection* about the equality of place and that which is in place. Sadly, Ibn ʿAdī's attempt at answering it does not seem to help much in driving that objection away.[142] In a subsequent question, Ibn Abī Saʿīd worries about the outermost sphere and specifically asks whether or not it can have a place at all without violating either Aristotle's definition or his claim that outside the universe there is neither void nor anything else (*lā ḫalāʾa wa-lā malāʾa*).[143] In his reply, Ibn ʿAdī states that the source of that problem is the belief that every body is in a place because of its corporeality (*al-ʿilla ... ğismiyyatihā*).[144] Although Ibn Abī Saʿīd's second question concerns the place of the outermost sphere, Ibn ʿAdī's response uses the terminology of Philoponus' *first objection* about body's being in place by virtue of its corporeality. Thus, we find both of Philoponus' objections occurring in the correspondence between Ibn ʿAdī and Ibn Abī Saʿīd.

Like Avicenna, as we shall see, Ibn ʿAdī explicitly denies that every body is in place because of its corporeality and tries to defend Aristotle's definition against Ibn Abī Saʿīd's two Philoponian worries.[145] This is in accord with Ibn ʿAdī's general statement in his *Maqāla fī l-mawğūdāt* that place is what Aristotle had said it is: "the internal surface of the containing body equalling the external surface of the contained body."[146] Yet, it remains unclear how he would have solved the issues – and even whether he himself knew how they could be solved.[147]

---

141 Aristotle's list of requirements were mentioned above, 314.

142 In his brief response, Ibn ʿAdī merely seems to say that "equality" (*al-musāwāt*) is a word indicating a relation between two or more things and that this relation can only be understood, once one has fully discerned each of the relata with regard to their quantity, so that one thing can be said to be equal to another (Ibn ʿAdī, *Kitāb Ağwiba Bišr al-Yahūdī ʿan masāʾilihī*, 331.10–13).

143 Ibn ʿAdī, *Kitāb Ağwiba Bišr al-Yahūdī ʿan masāʾilihī*, 317.5–15.

144 Ibn ʿAdī, *Kitāb Ağwiba Bišr al-Yahūdī ʿan masāʾilihī*, 331.14f.

145 Ibn ʿAdī, *Kitāb Ağwiba Bišr al-Yahūdī ʿan masāʾilihī*, 332.1f.

146 Ibn ʿAdī, *Maqāla fī l-mawğūdāt*, 273.15f.

147 On the discussion between Ibn Abī Saʿīd's and Ibn ʿAdī on place, cf. also Pines, "A Tenth Century Philosophical Correspondence," 106–110; M. Rashed, "Alexandre d'Aphrodise et la 'magna quaestio,'" 328–330.

Roughly half a century later, Avicenna reports the two Philoponian objections in his *al-Samāʿ al-ṭabīʿī* as follows:

وقالوا أيضاً إنّ كون الجسم في مكان ليس بسطحه بل بحجمه وكميته فيجب أن يكون ما فيه بجسميته مساوياً له. فيكون بعداً ولأنّ المكان مساو للمتمكّن والمتمكّن جسم ذو ثلاثة أقطار فالمكان أيضاً ذو ثلاثة أقطار.

They [sc. those who claim that place is an extension] also said that a body's being in place is not by means of its surface but by means of its volume and quantity (*bi-ḥağmihī wa-kammiyyatihī*). So, it is necessary that what is in it[148] by means of its corporeality must be equal (*musāwiyan*) to it. So, it is an extension and is so, because place is equal to that which is in place, and that which is in place is a body having three dimensions, and so place also has three dimensions. (*al-Samāʿ al-ṭabīʿī* II.6, §6, 116.7–9, tr. by McGinnis, modified)

We see that Avicenna's passage contains aspects from both of Philoponus' objections, but presents them together as what appears to be one and the same worry. First, a body is said to be in place by means of its volume and quantity (*bi-ḥağmihī wa-kammiyyatihī*), i.e., by virtue of its being a body (καθὸ σῶμά) and by having a volume (ᾗ ὄγκον ἔχει). Second, place must be equal (ἴσον, *musāwiyan*) to that which is in place, so that if that which is in place is three-dimensional, place likewise must be three-dimensional.

The objection as such has a strong intuitive appeal. It is not the body's surface which requires a place, but the body itself. Aristotle's definition, however, seems to provide – in some sense at least – only the body's surface with a place, for only its surface is, in the truest sense of the word, in direct contact with the surrounding body, whereas all other parts of the body, which are not in contact with the surrounding body, are either not in place at all or only derivatively so.

Having presented Philoponus' two objections together, as if they were one, Avicenna prepares his twofold response three chapters later in *al-Samāʿ al-ṭabīʿī* II.9. First, he criticises his opponent's argument as inconclusive, stating that the central premiss of the objection simply fails to establish the intended conclusion. The way Avicenna sees things, the central premiss is an entirely innocent claim, and so he does not hesitate to accept it, because he is convinced that this claim neither harms nor even affects his own account in any way. By accepting this claim, he effectively disarms his opponent:

وأمّا الحجّة التي بعد هذا فجوابها أنّ قول هذا القائل إنّ الجسم يقتضي المكان لا بسطحه بل بجسميته، إن عنى به أنّ الجسم بسطحه وحده لا يكون في مكان بل إنّما يكون في المكان بجسميته أو عنى أنه لأنّه جسم يصلح أن يكون في مكان، فالقول حقّ وليس يلزم منه أن يكون مكانه جسماً فإنّه ليس يجب إذا كان أمر يقتضي حكماً ما أو إضافة إلى شيء ما بسبب وصف له أن يكون المقتضى بذلك الوصف.

The response to the argument after this one is that the assertion of this person who said that body requires (*yaqtaḍī*) place not by means of its surface but by means of its corporeality (*lā bi-saṭḥihī bal bi-ğismiyyatihī*) – whether he means by it that (a) the body is not in place by means

148 Reading *yakūna mā fīhi* with Mss. Leiden or. 4 and or. 84 as well as Zāyid and Āl Yāsīn for *yakūna fīhī* in McGinnis.

> of its surface alone but is in place only by means of its corporeality (*innamā yakūnu fī l-makān bi-ǧismiyyatihī*) or whether he means that (b) it is so, because it is a body of which it is correct to say that it is in a place – so, the assertion is true (*fa-l-qawl ḥaqq*), but it does not follow from it (*wa-laysa yalzamu minhu*) that [a body's] place is a body, for it is not necessary that if something requires some status or relation to some thing on account of a description it has that that which is required is [itself something governed] by that [very same] description. (*al-Samāʿ al-ṭabīʿī* II.9, §12, 142.8–11, tr. by McGinnis, modified)

Avicenna grants that a body which is in a place is so on account of its being a body, of its being three-dimensionally extended, and of its having a volume. Accordingly, every body which has a place, does not have that place because of its qualities, such as its colour and smell, or because of its surface. A body in place, Avicenna agrees, is in place "not by means of its surface but by means of its corporeality" (*lā bi-saṭḥihī bal bi-ǧismiyyatihī*). In short, Avicenna accepts that "body requires place ... by means of its corporeality" (*al-ǧism yaqtaḍī l-makān ... bi-ǧismiyyatihī*) in the sense that everything which has a place requires or has its place because of its corporeality.

What he does not accept, though, is that the claim that "body requires place ... by means of its corporeality" (*al-ǧism yaqtaḍī l-makān ... bi-ǧismiyyatihī*) means that *every* body is in a place, so that everything which has corporeality would also have a place because of its corporeality. This is something that does not come out very clearly in the present passage but which must be understood in the greater context of Avicenna's position. We have already seen that the body of the outermost sphere (just as the universe as a whole) does not have a place, even though it is corporeal. So, Avicenna does not want to say that body as such needs to have a place because of its corporeality, so that "being a body" would entail "having a place." He merely accepts the converse, i.e., that "having a place" entails "being a body," for whatever is in place requires that place because of its corporeality. In other words, if a body has a place, then it surely is the body which is in place and not the surface – this is the way in which Avicenna allows himself to approve of his opponent's premiss.

A second claim which Avicenna does not accept is the general, even though unstated, premiss that whatever is required by something because of a certain description or attribute must itself have that very attribute. In other words, there is no reason for why place would have to be three-dimensional, simply because that which is in place is three-dimensional. Avicenna provides examples: it is incorrect to claim that if a body, insofar as it is corporeal, requires some principles, that these principles are themselves corporeal. It is also apparently unsound to assert that if an accident by being an accident requires a subject, that this subject itself is an accident. This, however, would have to be the case if it were universally true that whatever is required by something insofar as this something is governed by a certain description must itself be governed by that very same description. The opponent missed his chance to support or specify this hidden premiss, and Avicenna feels certain that his counter-examples are convincing enough to show that it is doubtful whether this premiss could, in fact, be substantiated. Consequently, the opponent's desired conclusion is just as unreasonable as his hidden premiss is unjustified. The fact that a body requires a place on account of its being three-dimensionally extended does not entail that place, too, must be three-dimensionally extended. At least, the opponent owes us a justification for this unstated premiss; at worst, his whole argument collapses.

Having provided reasons against Philoponus' argument, which expose the argument as inconclusive as long as the hidden premiss remains unproven, Avicenna, in a second step, returns to his role of being an exponent of the Aristotelian doctrine and rebuts the allegation that a two-dimensional surface can only in an inadequate way be the place of a three-dimensional body:

وبالجملة أنّه ليس إذا كان بجسميته يقتضي المكان يجب أن يلاقي بجميع جسميته المكان ... وبالجملة فإنّه غير مسلّم أنّ الجسم يقتضي لجسميته مكاناً إلّا بمقدار ما يسلّم أنّه بجسميته يقتضي حاوياً. ومعنى القولين جميعاً إنّ جملة الجسم المأخوذ كشيء واحد يوصف بأنّه في مكان أو في حاو وليس كون الشيء بكلّيته في شيء هو كونه ملاقياً له بكلّيته فإنّا نقول إنّ جميع هذا الماء وجملته في هذه الجرّة ولا نعني به أنّ جملته ملاقية للجرّة.

On the whole, it is not the case that if [the body] is by means of its corporeality such as to require a place, that it is necessary[149] that it is with the whole of its corporeality in contact with the place ... [Likewise] on the whole, it is not acceptable that the body requires a place because of its corporeality unless to the extent[150] it is [also] accepted that by means of its corporeality it requires something containing (*ḥāwiyan*). The sense of both assertions together is that the whole of the body is taken as one thing (*ma'ḫūḏ ka-šay' wāḥid*) which is described as being in a place or in a container, but something's being in its entirety in another is not [tantamount to] its being in contact with it in its entirety, for we say that all of this water and its whole is in the jar, but not do we mean by this that its whole is in contact with the jar. (*al-Samā' al-ṭabī'ī* II.9, §12, 142.14–143.3)

It is important to understand that Avicenna does not deny that bodies have a volume or an extension. He is also far from denying Aristotle's condition that place must be in contact with the thing in place. What he denies, though, are two things: first, he does not accept that every body has a place because of its corporeality. This would be true, he writes, only if it were also true that every body must have something containing it because of its corporeality. There is nothing, however, within the meaning of corporeality that would require its being contained by something else. What is corporeal, as we have learned, is simply something that is continuous, extended, and divisible – but it is not necessarily something contained.[151] The second point Avicenna does not accept is that a body, in order to count as a thing in place and, thus, in order to be in place, must fulfil the contact-condition *in its entirety*. Instead, it is entirely

149 Reading *yağibu* with Ms. Leiden or. 84 as well as Zāyid for *yalzamu* in Ms. Leiden or. 4 as well as McGinnis and Āl Yāsīn.

150 Reading *illā bi-miqdār mā* with Mss. Leiden or. 4 and or. 84 as well as McGinnis and Āl Yāsīn for *illā miqdār mā* in Zāyid.

151 Again, this is particularly clear in the greater context of Avicenna's understanding of the natural cosmos and his position about the place of the outermost sphere. For the notion of corporeality as being continuous, extended, and divisible, q.v. above, 122ff.

sufficient for a body to be in place *as a whole* – and in order to be in place as a whole, it is sufficient that the body, taken as a whole, i.e., as a single thing (*maʾḫūḏ ka-šayʾ wāḥid*), is in contact with place through its surface, because the surface defines and delimits the whole. What the whole of the body requires, in order to be in place, is not that there be an extension that runs alongside the body, extending together with the body's volume in three dimensions and accommodating the body *in its entirety* (as Philoponus said). Rather, what the whole of body (when it is a body which is in place) requires is something which provides *the whole of* the body with a place by containing it (*ḥāwiyan*).

As an example, Avicenna takes recourse to the well-known image of water in a jar. The water is in the jar as a whole. For Avicenna, then, it would be absurd and surreal to ask for the place of every "piece" of the water of the whole. A continuous homoeomerous body, lacking actual parts, is precisely in its place as a whole. The "pieces" of the water do not need to be in a place, because they do not exist separately and, instead, belong to the whole of the water. Since there are no actual parts of water, there is only the water which, as a whole, is contained by the jar and which is in contact with the jar in such a way that the place of the water is nothing but the inner surface of the jar which contains the water. Moreover, the same also holds true for non-homoeomerous bodies, for although non-homoeomerous bodies have actual parts and may not be wholes as such, they can, nonetheless, be *taken* as a single thing (*maʾḫūḏ ka-šayʾ wāḥid*) and, thus, be considered as wholes. Or even take aggregates, such as sand or a mix of sugar and salt, which have even less unity than non-homoeomerous bodies. These, too, can be *taken* as a single thing and be said to be *as a whole* in a jar. In this sense, also non-homoeomerous bodies and aggregates can have a place as a whole, while each of its parts has a place on its own.[152]

In the end, not only does Philoponus' objection fail to establish its intended conclusion, it is also from a systematic point of view an undue criticism, as Aristotle's position proves to be fairly well capable of explaining the ways in which wholes and parts are – or are not – in their respective places. So, from Avicenna's point of view, the present objection is doubly silly, because neither was Philoponus capable of establishing that place must be three-dimensional due to the fact that the body is in place through its being a body (καθὸ σῶμά) nor did he reveal any weakness in Aristotle's account.

152 cf. also Avicenna's response at *al-Samāʿ al-ṭabīʿī* II.9, §14, 143.8–144.2, to an objection he reported at II.6, §8, 116.10–12, and which can be found in Philoponus' corollary on place; cf. *In Phys.*, 571.18f. The objection was that a place can be said to be empty or full, but a surface cannot. Avicenna replies that this objection is not scientific as it is advanced merely on the basis of common parlance. Yet, even so, if one takes it seriously, it emerges that people usually say a cask or a jar is empty or full but do not say anything about whether the *extension* within the cask and the jar is empty or full. In fact, common parlance eventually even supports the view that place is a surface, for the common man believes that something is full when it "surrounds something solid on its inside such that it is in contact with it on every side" (*al-Samāʿ al-ṭabīʿī* II.9, §14, 143.11f., tr. by McGinnis, modified).

Above we have seen that from Theophrastus' single concern "that body will be in a surface," Philoponus extracted two objections. We have also seen that in Avicenna's outline in *al-Samāʿ al-ṭabīʿī* II.6, the two objections are again presented together as if they are one. Presenting both objections together is appropriate, because they, indeed, seem to be similar or even variations of one and the same line of thought. In chapter II.9, however, Avicenna adds the following brief remark, in order to address the second objection explicitly:

وأمّا الحجّة التي بعد هذه المبنية على مساواة المكان والمتمكّن فقد فرغ عن جوابها.

> As for the argument which is after this (*al-ḥuǧǧa allatī baʿda haḏihī*) [and which] relied on the equality (*musāwāt*) of place and that which is in place, its answer has [also] been accomplished. (*al-Samāʿ al-ṭabīʿī* II.9, §12, 143.4, tr. by McGinnis, modified)

This line is telling in two ways: first, it shows that Avicenna thinks that the same answer that invalidates Philoponus' first objection, also adequately rebuts the second one. In addition, it is interesting that here, Avicenna explicitly refers to "the argument which is after this" (*al-ḥuǧǧa allatī baʿda haḏihī*), even though in his presentation in chapter II.6, there is no "argument after this," as we have seen, because he presented both arguments together. He even presented the two as if the one followed from the other, which seems to underscore the intrinsic relation between to two. In his earlier presentation, then, there was only *one* argument. Avicenna's expression "after this" (*baʿda haḏihī*) three chapters later is, thus, not meaningful in the context of his own discussion in *al-Samāʿ al-ṭabīʿī*, because there simply was no argument "after this" in his presentation in chapter II.6 that "relied on the equality of place and that which is in place." Instead, the expression "after this" is only meaningful in the context of Philoponus' original corollary, in which the second objection really follows upon the other and in which both objections are in fact separated and presented as *two* distinct, even though surely related, issues of the Aristotelian account. With the expression "after this" here in *al-Samāʿ al-ṭabīʿī* II.9, Avicenna cannot refer to his own presentation but must have meant to refer to the order and succession of arguments in a source text containing the objections as two distinct issues. Assuming that this source text was an Arabic version of Philoponus' commentary, it emerges that the brief expression "after this" can be taken as a clear indication that Avicenna was working with Philoponus' commentary, and even that he must have been working *from* it.[153]

153 Another, even though less straightforward, indication that Avicenna, in much of his discussion of place in *al-Samāʿ al-ṭabīʿī*, draws quite directly on Philoponus' commentary, and in particular on his corollary, is his remark in chapter II.6 that those who considered place to be a three-dimensional extension tried to establish their claim also by specifically addressing those who defend the view that place is a surface (*yuḫāṭibūna ḫāṣṣatan aṣḥāb al-suṭūḥ*; §4, 115.15f.). So, Avicenna was aware that those who argued for an extension explicitly polemicised against Aristotle. As I remarked above, being polemical and assertive are features that are especially specific to Philoponus' corollary, whereas other

Being Unmoved: A Boat on the River and a Bird in the Air

We have so far been looking at Avicenna's responses to issues that arise from Aristotle's claim that place, being a surface, must be in direct contact with that which is in place. The condition of immediate contact is only one of two central qualifications of the Aristotelian notion of place. The second condition, which Aristotle added a little later, requires that place must also be essentially unmoving. Consequently, place is not only "the limit of the containing body at which it is in contact with the contained body."[154] Place is also the following:

> ὁ τοῦ περιέχοντος πέρας ἀκίνητον πρῶτον.
>
> فنهاية الخطّ إذا غير المتحرّكة الأولى.
>
> The first unmoving limit of what contains. (*Phys.* IV.4, 212a20)

As mentioned above, it proved to be considerably difficult to retain both conditions, especially when envisaging the very situation which led Aristotle to introducing that second condition, that place must be entirely unmoving, viz., the situation when the surroundings of the body whose place is to be determined are themselves in motion, like in the case of a boat on a streaming river, for in this situation, the place of the body is changing not because of any local motion of the body but simply because the surroundings themselves are in motion.[155]

It should be recalled that most commentators agreed – and still agree – with Aristotle that place must be unmoving.[156] If we were to allow place to be moving, we seem to jeopardise the applicability of the account of place to the concept it was originally designed to explain, viz., local motion. If local motion is a change of place, and if to engage in local motion means to have been at one place and to be later at another place, then it seems that place is required to be unmoving, for otherwise one could not identify *one* place as opposed to *another* nor could one distinguish between something's being engaged in local motion and its being at rest. So, interpreters who tended to accept the immobility requirement considered the possibility that Aristotle might have intended to abandon the (earlier stated) condition that place must be in contact with the object which is in place, at least in those cases in which this object is located within surroundings that are themselves in motion, such as the streaming river that surrounds the boat. On this understanding, then, the river bank would be a

---

major works, such as Simplicius' own corollary, were written in a dismissive and apologetic, even though no less critical, style; q.v. above, 316.

154 *Phys.* IV.4, 212a6–6a, tr. by Hardie/Gaye, modified

155 q.v. above, 316ff.

156 For the meaning of "unmoving" in Aristotle's account of place, q.v. fn. 38 above, 316f.; for Philoponus' justification, cf. *In Phys.*, 584.16–25.

viable candidate to serve as an unmoving – even though not contacting – place for the moored boat. The boat would, thus, be "in the river" instead of "in the water."

On the other hand, critical commentators such as Philoponus and Simplicius preferred to retain both requirements. Their own positions, that place is not a surface but a three-dimensional extension or space, can easily accommodate both, as the extension was considered to be unmoving in itself and to be penetrating through the body, thus being through and through in contact with the body.[157]

Avicenna, now, is one of the few – possibly even the first – to have decided that it would be more advantageous to dismiss the second requirement that place must be unmoving and to retain only the first that place must be in contact with that which is in place. His solution to the boat-on-the-river dilemma is appealing and original, even though by abandoning the requirement that place must be unmoving, Avicenna also abandons what may be called Aristotle's "literal" position. What is more, his solution builds on his own account of motion. Nonetheless, Avicenna's view of philosophy as a universal endeavour entails that he corrects, and improves upon, his predecessors whenever possible. The questions of whether place should be in contact or unmoving and how the place of something in a changing environment should be determined are clearly occasions where Avicenna seizes this possibility, as there is actually something in Aristotle's account that could do with some improvement.

When Avicenna begins to report the objections raised by those who claim place to be an extension against those who maintain that it is a surface, the first objection he mentions is analogous to Aristotle's boat-on-the-river example. He writes the following:

> إن كان المكان سطحاً يلقى سطح الشيء فتكون الحركة هي مفارقة سطح متوجّهاً إلى سطح آخر. فالطائر الواقف في الهواء والحجر الواقف في الماء وهما يتبدّلان عليه وهو يفارق سطحاً إلى سطح يجب أن يكون متحرّكاً. وذلك لأنّ ما يجعلونه مكانه يتبدّل عليه. فإن كان ساكناً فسكونه في أيّ مكان إذ من شرط الساكن أن يلزم مكانه زماناً إذ الساكن قد يصدق عليه هذا القول. فإذ ليس يلزمه السطح فما الذي يلزمه سوى البعد الذي شغله الذي لا ينزع ولا يتبدّل بل يكون دائماً واحداً بعينه.
>
> If place is a surface which is in contact with the surface of a thing, then motion would be to leave a surface, advancing towards another surface. Thus, the bird sitting still in the air (*al-wāqif fī l-hawā'*) and the rock lying firm in the water (*al-wāqif fī l-mā'*) – with both [the air and the water] being in change around [the bird and the rock, respectively] – would leave a surface for a surface, [and so] it would be necessary [to say] that it is in motion (*yağibu an yakūna mutaḥarrikan*). That is because what they have made its [sc. the bird's and the rock's] place is changing around it. So, if it is at rest, then in which place is its rest (*fa-sukūnuhū fī ayy makān*)? [The question arises] since a condition for that which is at rest is that it adheres to its place for a time (*an yalzama makānahū zamānan*) (and this statement is sometimes adequate (*qad yaṣduqu*) for that which is at rest). So, since the surface does not adhere to it, that which adheres to it is equal to the extension which it occupies and which is neither disturbed nor changing but persisting as one and the same. (*al-Samā' al-ṭabī'ī* II.6, §4, 115.16–116.3, tr. by McGinnis, modified)

157 I shall investigate their positions more fully below, 367ff.

The examples adduced by Avicenna are different from the one we know from Aristotle's *Physics*. He is not talking about a boat on a river but about a rock in water and a bird in the air. Avicenna also makes it clear that both the bird and the rock are not undergoing local motion themselves but remain still and firm (*al-wāqif*), whereas Aristotle did not explicitly say that.[158] We should, perhaps, image the bird as sitting on the branch of a tree and the rock as lying on the riverbed with windy air blowing around the former and streaming water washing around the latter.[159] The place of the bird, viz., the adjacent air (together with the bark of parts of the branch), and that of the rock, viz., the adjacent water (together with the surface of parts of the riverbed), are both constantly changing around the bird and the rock (*yatabaddalān ʿalayhi*), respectively. If place were a surrounding surface, the bird and the rock could not be said to be at rest, because rest is the opposite of motion and we know that there is motion, when one surface is replaced by another, whereas we know that there is rest, when an object remains in one place, i.e., adheres to one surface, for more than merely one instant. So, the bird and the rock would both be in motion, even though we have explicitly said that they are at a halt (*al-wāqif*).

On the whole, the objection claims that an account of place which conceives of place as the inner surface of the containing body fails to explain why the bird and the rock are actually at rest, and how their current situation can be distinguished from a situation in which the bird actually flies away and the rock finally gets carried off downstream.

Avicenna's solution is simple and introduces a novel twist, something nobody before him seems to have realised, perhaps because it was too obvious. According to his interpretation, the real issue concerns what it means for an *object* to be at rest, rather than the question whether or not that objects' *surroundings* are at rest, as it was

---

158 As it appears, the usual interpretation among ancient and late ancient commentators was to consider the boat to be carried off downstream; q.v. fn. 40 above, 317f. Nowadays, the usual interpretation is that of a moored boat; e.g., Sorabji, *Matter, Space, and Motion*, 188–191.

159 Another possibility for the bird example would be to think of a seagull, which stays steady against the wind; q.v. my remarks in fn. 178 below, 364f. In any case, the source of these examples in Avicenna is not clear. McGinnis suggests Galen as a potential origin for the bird-example but remarks in a footnote that Galen used the example in a quite different context. In fact, Galen is concerned with a bird who neither ascends nor descends in the air, and so may, indeed, have envisaged a hummingbird or a seagull; cf. Galen, *De motu musculorum* I.8, 402.12–403.10. There are more possible sources. Themistius, for example, mentions "stones protruding from rivers" (*In Phys.*, 119.10, tr. by Todd). Philoponus, on the other hand, refers to air in general when he declares that on Aristotle's account, there are hardly any surfaces that deserve the name "place," because most surfaces are in constant motion, like the air which surrounds us; cf. *In Phys.*, 564.20–23. A little later, though, he refers to birds (and fish) in a different context; cf. *In Phys.*, 591.7–9. Moreover, the Iḫwān al-Ṣafāʾ, when discussing place and void, explicitly refer twice to "the fish in the sea and the bird in the air," like Philoponus – yet, they do so not in the context of an objection (*Rasāʾil Iḫwān al-Ṣafāʾ* XVI.5, 81.6; cf. XV.10, 27.2). Indeed, picturing a situation that involves air and wind may seem to be the most obvious and immediate way to develop the objection, even more obvious than water and a river with a boat on it.

traditionally discussed. As a consequence, the issue is not about whether an object changes its place but about whether – and how – it is at rest. In fact, Avicenna does not hesitate to accept the inescapable result that for the bird, the rock, and the boat, there is a change of place. How could there not be a change of place, when place depends on the containing body and when this body is in motion? If place is the inner surface of the containing body and if the containing body is in constant change, with the result that its inner surface, which is in contact with the object in place, is itself in constant change, then the place of the object simply must constantly be changing. This is a fact that cannot be explained away and which has to be accepted:

وأمّا الحجّة التي لأصحاب البعد المبنية على وجود البسيط مستبدلاً والمتمكّن غير مستبدل مكانه وليس هناك شيء يبقى ثابت إلّا البعد فنقول إنّا لا نسلّم أنّ المتمكّن غير مستبدل مكانه بل هو مستبدل بمكانه إلّا أنّه ليس بمتحرّك ولا ساكن.

About the argument which belongs to those who advocate the extension [which is] based on the existence of a surface (*al-basīṭ*) as changing and that which is in place as not changing its place and where there is nothing that remains stable other than the extension, we say that we do not accept that that which is in place is not changing its place (*lā nusallimu inna l-mutamakkin ġayr mustabdil makānahū*). Rather, it is changing its place – however, it is [also] neither in motion nor is it at rest (*huwa mustabdil bi-makānihī illā annāhu laysa bi-mutaḥarrik wa-lā sākin*). (*al-Samāʿ al-ṭabīʿī* II.9, §10, 140.14–16)

Here, in a first step Avicenna enters, with only one brief remark, new territory. It is not the case that we should discard the requirement that place must be in contact with the objects in place, in order to find a way that provides even the boat or the bird or the stone with a place. The requirement that ought to be abandoned is the claim that place is something unmoving, because any object that is placed in unstable and changing surroundings certainly changes its place. Yet, the fact that the bird's place is changing is irrelevant for the solution to the problem, for the problem is not concerned with whether or not the *surrounding body* is in motion (e.g., the air) but with whether or not the *surrounded body* is in motion (e.g., the bird).[160]

So, what about the bird, then? Is it in motion or is it at rest? In order to answer this, Avicenna states that the bird is neither in motion nor at rest. If we want to appreciate this at first rather surprising answer, we need to understand what it means for something to be at rest. So, Avicenna approaches the notion *sākin* ("something at rest") thus:

أمّا أنّه ليس بساكن فلأنّه ليس عندنا في مكان واحد زماناً اللهمّ إلّا أن نعني بالساكن لا هذا بل الذي لا تتبدّل نسبته من أمور ثابتة فيكون ساكناً بهذا المعنى أو الذي لو خلّي وحاله وترك عليه مكانه حفظ ذلك المكان ولم يستبدل به من نفسه وكان حافظاً لمكان واحد. ونحن لا نريد الآن بالساكن لا الأوّل لا هذا فإن أردنا أحد المعنيين كان ساكناً.

160 cf. also Verbeke, "Notions centrales de la physique d'Avicenne," 45*.

> As for its not being at rest (*annahū laysa bi-sākin*), this is because for us it is not in a single place for a period of time (*fī makān wāḥid zamānan*),[161] unless we mean by "something at rest" not this[162] but that which does not change its relation to certain stable things, and so is at rest in this sense, or that which, even if[163] it were to vacate and depart it and leave it,[164] it would keep its place as that place and would not have changed it on its own account and would be something which keeps a single place. We, however, do not presently (*al-ān*) mean by "something at rest" either the first or this, for if we intended one of the two meanings, it would [indeed] be at rest. (*al-Samāʿ al-ṭabīʿī* II.9, §10, 140.16–141.1)

Three chapters earlier, in *al-Samāʿ al-ṭabīʿī* II.6, Avicenna affirmed that in the context of this objection, the condition for something's being at rest is that it is "in a single place for a period of time" (*fī makān wāḥid zamānan*).[165] He also said that this condition "is sometimes adequate" (*qad yaṣduqu*) for what is said to be at rest. Here in chapter II.9, he once more emphasises that "presently" (*al-ān*), i.e., in the context of that objection, to be at rest is used in this very sense. For the sake of refuting the objection, we could simply say that "to be at rest" means something else – and Avicenna offers two alternatives which at once would repudiate the objection – but not only would that be too easy and question-begging, it would also be plainly wrong on Avicenna's count. Instead, Avicenna says, we need to accept that "presently," i.e., in the context of the objection, the bird is not at rest, because it is in no place for longer than merely an instant. Thus, we have to accept both that the bird constantly changes its place and that, for the very same reason, it cannot be said to be at rest.

The meaning of "to be at rest," then, is in some cases, and the present objection is such a case, to be in a single place for a period of time. What, however, is the meaning of "to be at rest" as such, i.e., *not* within the framework of the objection? What does it actually and properly mean? Avicenna has answered this question earlier in *al-Samāʿ al-ṭabīʿī* II.4, the final chapter on motion, immediately before he set off his presentation of place. There, he discussed the contrary nature between motion (*al-ḥaraka*) and rest (*al-sukūn*). He confirmed that motion and rest are opposites and even contraries. Motion has been defined by Aristotle by the following statement:

> ἡ τοῦ δυνάμει ὄντος ἐντελέχεια, ᾗ τοιοῦτον, κίνησίς ἐστιν.
>
> الحركة هي كمال ما بالقوّة بما هو كذلك.
>
> The perfection of what is potentially, as such (ᾗ τοιοῦτον, *bi-mā huwa ka-ḏālika*), is motion. (*Phys.* III.1, 201a10f.)

161 Reading *zamānan* with Mss. Leiden or. 4 and or. 84 for *zamān* in McGinnis, Āl Yāsīn and Zāyid. Other passages support this reading: *al-Samāʿ al-ṭabīʿī* II.4, §1, 108.9, 11; II.6, §4, 116.2.

162 Reading *hāḏā* with Mss. Leiden or. 4 and or. 84 as well as McGinnis and Āl Yāsīn for *m-ḏ-ā* in Zāyid.

163 Reading *aw allaḏī law* with Mss. Leiden or. 4 and or. 84 as well as McGinnis for *aw allaḏī* in Āl Yāsīn and *wa-llaḏī law* in Zāyid.

164 Reading *wa-taraka ʿalayhī* with Mss. Leiden or. 4 and or. 84 as well as Āl Yāsīn and Zāyid for *wa-taraka ʿalā* in McGinnis.

165 cf. *al-Samāʿ al-ṭabīʿī* II.6, §4, 116.1f.

Avicenna accepts this definition but, as so many interpreters before him, had to find a satisfying reading of what "as such" (ᾗ τοιοῦτον, *bi-mā huwa ka-ḏālika*) means. His choice is reflected in the way in which he himself defines motion in *al-Samāʿ al-ṭabīʿī* II.1. There, he writes the following:

فالحركة كمال أوّل لما هو بالقوّة من جهة ما هو بالقوّة.

> So, motion is a first perfection (*kamāl awwal*) belonging to what is potentially with regard to what is potentially. (*al-Samāʿ al-ṭabīʿī* II.1, §3, 83.5)[166]

Presently, I cannot fully go into the details concerning the differences between Aristotle's and Avicenna's definition.[167] What is important for us, now, are two points. The first is that for Avicenna, motion is a state that belongs to the object that is in motion. It is a state of a first perfection. To give an example: when we are in Munich and plan a trip from Munich to Berlin, then we are potentially in Berlin but actually in Munich. When we are already on our way, being on a train from Munich to Berlin, then we are still only potentially in Berlin. Nonetheless, in this second case, the (second) potentiality which belongs to us while we are on the move is different from the (first) potentiality which belonged to us before we actually began our journey in the moment the train started to move. So, there was a first potentiality, while we were still in Munich planing our trip or waiting for the train to depart, and there is now a second potentiality, while we are actually on our way somewhere in between Munich and Berlin. In both cases we are not actually in Berlin – and, thus, are only potentially in Berlin – but in the second case, we are in a state of actualising our potentiality to actually be in Berlin, i.e., we are *on the move* or we *are* going to Berlin. This second potentiality, then, is actually a first perfection which will eventually be completed by a second perfection, viz., our actually *being* in Berlin, once the train stops, having actually arrived in Berlin. For Avicenna, then, motion is a perfection – a *first* perfection – i.e., an actualised state of being *on the move*. It is a form that belongs to a subject *when it is undergoing motion* – and this is what he calls "the form of motion" (*ṣūrat al-ḥaraka*).[168]

The second point that is important for us now is that this definition of motion is reaffirmed by Avicenna three chapters later in *al-Samāʿ al-ṭabīʿī* II.4 in his discussion of motion and rest. In this chapter, the question is not so much "what is motion?," for Avicenna has already answered that motion is a positive state that belongs to the thing which is undergoing motion. The question is rather, "what is rest?" Given that rest is

166 cf. *al-Naǧāt* II.2.1, 204.14 ≈ *al-Ḥikma al-ʿArūḍiyya* II.1, 120.21f.; *ʿUyūn al-ḥikma* II.2, 18.12; *al-Hidāya* II.1, 138.1; *al-Ḥikma al-mašriqiyya* III.7, 15.8f.

167 There is, however, good secondary literature available on this issue, esp. Hasnawi, "La définition du mouvement dans la *Physique* du *Shifāʾ* d'Avicenne"; Wisnovsky, *Avicenna's Metaphysics in Context*; McGinnis, "A Medieval Arabic Analysis of Motion at an Instant"; for a quick overview, cf. McGinnis, "Avicenna's Natural Philosophy," 71–75; Ahmed, "The Reception of Avicenna's Theory of Motion in the Twelfth Century," 216–225.

168 *al-Samāʿ al-ṭabīʿī* II.1, §6, 84.9–19.

the contrary of motion, we get two options: either rest is also a positive state, i.e., a "possession" (*qunya* or *malaka*) that belongs to a subject and is contrary to the state of being in motion or rest is not a positive state but merely the "privation" and "absence" (*ʿadam*) of motion.[169] The difference between the two is that if rest is a "possession," then it is something a subject can actually *have*, but if rest is a "privation," then it is not something belonging to a subject, because the subject could only *lose* motion but not really *have* or *acquire* rest. Avicenna also adds that the first option of rest as a "possession" would mean that rest amounts to "occurring in a single place for a period of time" (*ḥuṣūl fī makān wāḥid zamānan*).[170] In this sense, then, a resting subject could positively be said to occur in a single place for a period of time, rather than merely lacking motion. Eventually, Avicenna discovers that it is impossible to establish the contrary nature of motion and rest if rest were a "possession," and concludes that rest is simply the privation of motion (*fa-l-sukūn ʿadam al-ḥaraka*).[171]

It is important for appreciating Avicenna's current discussion about rest and its relation to motion in its historical context, and to understand Avicenna's motivation for arguing against the idea that rest can be a possession, i.e., a positive attribute belonging to the concrete object, insofar as this object remains in the same place for more than one moment. Aristotle himself was not clear about rest. In his *Physics* we find two kinds of statements. On the one hand, he wrote that rest is the contrary of motion and even its privation.[172] On the other hand, Aristotle also claimed elsewhere that what it means for an object to be at rest is precisely to stay in one place for a period of time.[173] This is also how Proclus defined rest in his *Institutio physica*.[174] More importantly, however, this is how the Muʿtazilites generally understood rest within the framework of their atomist conception of space, time, and the corporeal reality on the whole, for they claimed rest to be nothing other than a positive attribute belonging to the object – an attribute of being in the same place for more than one moment.[175] It is important to realise that on the basis of the Muʿtazilī atomist ontology, rest is not simply the privation of motion but is a positive attribute, just as much as its opposite, viz., motion, is. Thus, Avicenna's discussion in *al-Samāʿ al-ṭabīʿī* II.4 is important both for mending an aspect of Peripatetic natural philosophy as well as for dissociating himself from the ontology of Muʿtazilī kalām.

---

169 The distinction between a possession and a privation is ultimately inspired by Aristotle's discussion of privation, possession, and contrariety in *Categories* 10.

170 *al-Samāʿ al-ṭabīʿī* II.4, §1, 108.9.

171 *al-Samāʿ al-ṭabīʿī* II.4, §6, 111.1; cf. also II.4, §5, 110.16f.

172 cf. *Phys.* V.2, 226b15f.; VIII.8, 264a27f.; cf. also *Cat.* 14, 15b1.

173 cf. *Phys.* VI.8, 239a26.

174 cf. Proclus, *Institutio physica* I, def. 6; cf. also *Institutio physica* I, prop. 18.

175 cf. in particular the account of the Muʿtazilite Ibn Mattawayh in his *al-Taḏkira*, X, 432.4f. (ed. Luṭf/ʿŪn)/XI, 237.3f. (ed. Gimaret); for further references, cf. Frank, *Beings and Their Attributes*, 101f.; Dhanani, *The Physical Theory of Kalām*, 51.

If we now come back to the issue about the place and the rest of a bird in the air, we see that the notion of "rest" employed in the objection is not what rest, according to Avicenna, actually means. For him, rest is only a privation of motion, i.e., the privative state that an object is in when it lacks the form of motion. The objection, however, employs rest in a different sense, viz., the kalām sense of rest as a possession of a positive attribute. It is in *this* sense that we "presently" have to assert that the bird is not at rest.[176] This, though, is not the end of the story, for we have seen Avicenna saying that the bird is not in motion, either: "it is neither in motion nor is it at rest" (*annāhu laysa bi-mutaḥarrik wa-lā sākin*).[177] Having explained in what sense the bird and the rock and the boat are not at rest, Avicenna goes on to explain why they are not in motion:

> وأمّا أنّه ليس بمتحرّك فلأنّه ليس مبدأ الاستبدال منه والمتحرّك بالحقيقة هو الذي مبدأ الاستبدال منه وهو الذي الكمال الأوّل لما بالقوة فيه من نفسه حتّى أنّه لو كان سائر الأشياء عنده بحالها لكان حاله يتغيّر.
>
> As for its not being in motion (*annahū laysa bi-mutaḥarrik*), this is because the principle of change does not pertain to it (*fa-li-annahū laysa mabda' al-istibdāl minhu*), whereas that which is in motion really is that to which the principle of change pertains and this is the first perfection belonging to what is potentially in it from itself (*al-kamāl al-awwal limā bi-l-quwwa fīhi min nafsihī*), so that if everything else were [to remain in the same] state, then its state would [nonetheless] be changing. (*al-Samā' al-ṭabī'ī* II.9, §10, 141.1f.)

As Avicenna explains, the difference between a bird sitting still on a branch and a bird flying through the air, and the difference between a rock lying firm on the riverbed and a rock being carried downstream, and finally also the difference between a moored boat on a river and a boat travelling on a river is not that there is no change of place in one situation, whereas in the other situation there is. The crucial difference, instead, is the elemental fact that in all of these three cases, the object is, first, not in motion and, then, is in motion – and "to be in motion" means that the object actually has the form of motion and, thus, *is engaging* in motion.

As I remarked above, and as we can now see, for Avicenna, the objection turns on whether or not the *object* is in motion, rather then whether or not its *surroundings* are – and this, Avicenna argues, can easily be determined: if the object has the form of motion pertaining to it, then yes, it is undergoing motion, but if the form does not pertain to it, i.e., if it lacks the form of motion, then no, it is not undergoing motion. So, the bird sitting on a branch in windy air, the rock on a riverbed, and the moored boat on a river, they all do not move, because they do not have what Avicenna presently calls the principle of change (*mabdā' al-istibdāl*) and which he explicitly identifies

---

176 Since Avicenna showed in *al-Samā' al-ṭabī'ī* II.4 that the meaning of rest as a "possession" is not the proper opposite of motion, he can here, in *al-Samā' al-ṭabī'ī* II.9, claim that a bird in the air is neither in motion nor at rest. Since the current meaning of rest is not the opposite of motion, this statement is not self-contradictory.

177 *al-Samā' al-ṭabī'ī* II.9, §10, 140.16.

with motion being the first perfection belonging to what is potential and, thus, with the form of motion. The bird, the rock, and the boat are, properly speaking, at rest.[178]

Therefore, the objection fails to establish the extension, or one of the other candidates, as the proper essence of place by criticising the Aristotelian notion of surface, because there is nothing that Aristotle's account of place, as understood by Avicenna, fails to explain. Those who claim that place is an extension, i.e., Neoplatonists such as Simplicius and Philoponus, can assert that the bird stays at the same place, because it always occupies the same extension, whereas those who claim that place is that which prevents heavy objects from falling, i.e., Muʿtazilites such as Ibn Mattawayh, can claim that the bird stays on the same branch for more than one moment. For these groups, it is easy to distinguish between motion and rest, here, because motion means to change one's place, but the bird does not change its place, thus being at rest. Avicenna, by contrast, argues that the bird's place certainly changes, because the air surrounding the bird changes, and so the bird cannot be said to be "at rest" in one sense. Yet, the bird is certainly not in motion, either, as it is "sitting still in the air" (*al-wāqif fī l-hawāʾ*) and, thus, lacks the form of motion – which, in turn, entails that the bird is at rest in the proper sense of the word as established in *al-Samāʿ al-ṭabīʿī* II.4. The bottom line of Avicenna's argument, then, is that if place is a surrounding surface, one is by no means incapable of distinguishing between motion and rest, as the objection claims, as long as rest is understood in its proper sense. Consequently, there is no need for abandoning the Aristotelian definition of place.

In order to support his solution, Avicenna states that we should not be surprised to read that there are things which are neither in motion nor at rest. In fact, this is very common in the natural world even in other cases:

فليس بواجب أن يكون الجسم لا محالة ساكناً أو متحرّكاً فإنّ للجسم أحوالاً لا يكون فيها ساكناً ولا متحرّكاً في المكان. من ذلك أنّ لا يكون له مكان، ومن ذلك أن يكون له مكان ولكن ليس له ذلك المكان بعينه في زمان ولا هو المبدأ في مفارقته، ومن ذلك أن يكون له مكان وهو له بعينه زماناً ولكنّ أخذناه فيه لا في زمان بل من حيث هو في آن فيكون الجسم حينئذ لا ساكناً ولا متحرّكاً.

178 This is also the reason that Avicenna's example of the bird does not seem to be referring to a hummingbird, which is capable of staying at one place in the air, yet only by rapidly beating its wings. The hummingbird, then, clearly is very much engaging in motion, in order to remain at the same place. The seagull, on the other hand, is a more difficult example. One might say that it is actually engaging in motion due to its weight and that it is merely not moving, because the wind caught in its wings forcefully keeps it up. However, it is clear from Avicenna's account of inclination that the natural downward inclination through the weight of the seagull is actually nullified through the wind, so that the seagull would not be engaging in motion and would actually appear to lack the form of motion; q.v. fn. 122 above, 249. Due to the difficulty involved in the seagull example, I resorted to the example of a bird sitting still on the branch of a tree which has the two further advantages of being more analogous to Avicenna's other example of a rock lying firm on the riverbed and more similar to Philoponus' objection at *In Phys.*, 564.20–23.

> So, it is not necessary that body must be either at rest or in motion, for there are certain situations for body in which it is neither at rest nor in motion with regard to place (*mutaḥarrikan fī l-makān*). Among them is (i) that it does not have a place; among them is also (ii) that it does have a place but has neither that same place for some time nor the principle for leaving it; and among them is also (iii) that it does have a place and that it [even] has the same [place] for some time, yet we are considering it [sc. the body] in it [sc. its place] not during [that] time but with regard to its being in an instant, and so the body,[179] in this case, is neither at rest nor in motion. (*al-Samāʿ al-ṭabīʿī* II.9, §10, 141.4–7)

This passage provides three situations in which a body may be neither in motion nor at rest, the second being the one we have been talking about already: a body which has a place that is changing constantly, even though the body lacks the form of motion on account of which it could be said to be leaving its place itself. The first situation is that of the outermost sphere, which does not have a place and, thus, cannot be at rest in the sense which is "presently" relevant in the context, i.e., it cannot be said to remain in a place for a period time. Nonetheless, it would be foolish to infer from this that the outermost sphere is "in motion with regard to place" (*mutaḥarrikan fī l-makān*), because we have already learned that the outermost sphere is precisely not undergoing local motion but is rotating, i.e., is engaged in positional motion. So, it is neither at rest nor does it move locally. The third situation is that a body may have a place and may, indeed, remain at that same place for a period of time, yet we are not considering this body in its being at that place during that time but merely in one single instant. In this instant, then, the body is surely not in motion, because it does not have the form of motion; nor does it change its place, because it "has the same [place] for some time"; nor even is it at rest in the sense of being in the same place for more than one instant (as the "presently" employed meaning of "to be at rest" would have it), because it is precisely considered in only one single instant.[180] Thus, Avicenna's initial claim that the bird and the rock and the boat are neither in motion nor at rest (*laysa bi-mutaḥarrik wa-lā sākin*) is not as strange and implausible as it may have seemed at first sight. To the contrary, it is a viable solution to what both Edward Grant and Richard Sorabji called "the most perplexing dilemma" in Aristotle's doctrine of place. It, moreover, harmonises with other aspects of Avicenna's natural philosophy such as the motion of the outermost sphere and the possibility of motion at an instant.[181]

We must conclude that Avicenna's solution to this problem – and in fact his whole account of place – is in the highest degree systematic, original, and (in a sense) rigorously Aristotelian. It is systematic, because it corresponds very well with important

---

179 Reading *fī ān fa-yakūnu l-ǧism* with Mss. Leiden or. 4 and or. 84 as well as McGinnis and Āl Yāsīn for *fī ān al-ǧism* in Zāyid.

180 In a footnote to his translation, McGinnis notes that Avicenna, as opposed to Aristotle, accepts that there could also be motion at an instant (cf. fn. 17, 207). Avicenna argued for this in *al-Samāʿ al-ṭabīʿī* II.1; cf. McGinnis, "A Medieval Arabic Analysis of Motion at an Instant."

181 cf. Grant, "The Medieval Doctrine of Place," 59; cf. also Sorabji, *Matter, Space, and Motion*, 187.

positions Avicenna has established elsewhere in his *al-Samāʿ al-ṭabīʿī*. It is original, because Avicenna, far from blindly following Aristotle as Duhem claimed, enters new territory when he attempts to solve issues that have troubled the Aristotelian account from its very beginning. Two major examples in this regard were the place of the outermost sphere and the place of a boat on a river. Avicenna is also alert to the implications of an account of place that makes place a surface. Not only does he disambiguate the notion of surface between internal and external surfaces, he also clarifies the notion of an internal surface when he shows that it can consist of several surface-parts which, taken together, form a single place. He also explains how place can be a surface even though every body which is in a place is so precisely by means of its being a body and why it is not absurd to think of a two-dimensional place being equal to a three-dimensional body.

On the whole, this means nothing less than that Avicenna has addressed and rejected four of the five objections with which Philoponus had repudiated Aristotle's account of place being a surface.[182] In addition to that, he has resolved all five issues which already Theophrastus had enumerated against his own teacher's definition and which may well have been a source of inspiration for Philoponus.

Of course, in the end, Avicenna follows and accepts Aristotle's position, and his overall argument, like Aristotle's, proceeds by elimination, because he affirms the one option which has not been shown to be false. No one can deny the strong similarities between Aristotle's and Avicenna's accounts and strategies. Yet, it is foolish to assert that this alone warrants the claim that we "should not expect to find the depth and originality of thought of Damascius and Simplicius in the work of the Arabic philosophers."[183] Avicenna follows Aristotle, not because he was an incompetent philosopher, unable to make up his mind of his own, but because he was smart enough to find appropriate reasons for doing so. It is not a sign of philosophical incapacity to be an Aristotelian – and an Aristotelian is exactly what Avicenna is with regard to place: he accepts Aristotle's definition not only as it is but with all its consequences, i.e., all those consequences which for hundreds of years have been said to effectively disable the definition. Avicenna is very rigorous in this regard, even though he clearly abandons what one might call Aristotle's "literal" position by claiming that place does not have to be unmoving and by importing his own developed account of motion.

For Avicenna, then, Aristotle's position is correct both because of its explanatory strength and because it is the only option on the list of candidates that proved to be viable: matter and form are clearly far from being acceptable as candidates for the essence of place, and the only possibly suitable alternative to conceiving of place as a surface is that place might be an extension, whose major flaw, according to Avicenna,

182 In Avicenna's *al-Samāʿ al-ṭabīʿī*, there is no trace of Philoponus' fifth and final objection which, however, is somewhat odd in itself.

183 Duhem, *Medieval Cosmology*, 140.

is that it simply does not exist. The Peripatetic tradition before Avicenna was deterred by the obvious objections to Aristotle's account of place, those objections which were already conveniently enumerated by Theophrastus. Some attempts to rectify the definition were advanced, for example, by Themistius. On the whole, however, to most thinkers, Aristotle's definition seemed to be plainly inadequate – and it was precisely this inadequacy which encouraged them to look for an alternative to Aristotle's troubled definition and to eventually adopt one of the candidates which Aristotle had originally dismissed: a three-dimensional extension which underlies the corporeal world. We shall now see how Avicenna deals with this rival conception.

5.3 Eliminating Void and Space

The central discriminative feature between place in the Aristotelian sense and place in the sense of an extension is the nature of the relation assumed between place and body. For Aristotle and Avicenna, the place of a body depends on the body – or, more precisely, it depends on *two* bodies: one which is in place and another which provides the place. Consequently, if these bodies are removed or annihilated, place ceases to be.[184] If, on the other hand, place is conceived as an extension, it is considered to be independent of the body in place – indeed, independent of all corporeal reality – such that if the body is removed, place continues to exist. On this conception, place is merely occupied by bodies. Yet, it is even more than that: place as an extension is something on which the body in place depends, rather than the other way around. If there were no extension, a body could not be in place; and perhaps it could not even be.

The idea of place as an extension is, in a very clear sense, the exact metaphysical opposite to the Aristotelian conception of place as an accident of body. Place as an extension, which we also might like to call "space," is a feature of the world and a substance in itself. The central question, then, that divides between the followers of Aristotle and the followers of space is whether or not such an additional thing is required – and if we say that it, indeed, is required, we need to be able to specify *for what* it is required.

With this, we encounter a further discriminative feature between the two camps. When Aristotle asks about a body's place, he inquires into an aspect of this body with the particular intention of understanding what it is that changes, once this body begins to engage in local motion. It is important to understand that Aristotle does not want to know where to find his keys. He is not interested in finding the precise location of a corporeal object. He only seeks to understand what this feature of the physical world is that changes when bodies engage in the most fundamental kind of motion, viz., local

184 q.v. the ἀπορία about place being altogether removed in Theophrastus and possibly also in Avicenna, mentioned above, 324f.

motion, because there is, apparently, something that changes during local motion and which makes local motion intelligible as a species of change. He asks: what changes when corporeal things move? – and his answer is: the surface where the surrounding body is in contact with the thing-in-motion.

The adherents of space, on the other hand, are driven by a different agenda. Of course, place as an extension is likewise capable of providing an answer to the question of what changes when corporeal things move. Their answer is that a body, as long as it is moving, overlaps again and again with other segments of the three-dimensionally extended space that permeates all physical reality. So, both conceptions of place are, in theory, able to explain local motion. Yet, the adherents of space also want to provide an answer to a metaphysical question: what is that wherein things are? What is that which provides any corporeal thing with a place to be ? – or: what is that substance which receives bodies, while remaining separate from them? Their answer, of course, is that there exists a separate three-dimensional extension over and above the corporeal extension of bodies, something like an independent space wherein things are and come-to-be.

The most important point to keep in mind for what follows is that a rigorous Aristotelian would deny that this question is a question worth asking, so that the answer given by the adherents of space is not an answer worth giving.

The following investigation will begin with a brief presentation of Aristotle's arguments against space and void as they are known from his *Physics*. Following this, I shall analyse how critics such as Philoponus developed their notion of space further by engaging with Aristotle's arguments, in order to grasp the position Avicenna is about to refute. Accordingly, we shall, first, investigate how Avicenna conceived of space as a three-dimensional extension and, then, come to understand how he argued against it.

Extension as Void and Space in and after Aristotle

Aristotle alludes to the conception of place as an extension for the first time in the *Physics* in a passage in chapter IV.1. There, he mentions that those who believe in the void imagine it as a place without a body.[185] This prompts a quotation from Hesiod which seems to suggest that first of all there was Chaos representing a spatial extension in which things subsequently were created – a view with strong similarities to the understanding of pre-cosmic space in Plato's *Timaeus*. In his revised list of candidates in *Physics* IV.4, then, Aristotle presents this conception as "some extension between the

185 cf. *Phys.* IV.1, 208b25–27; cf. also *Phys.* IV.6, 213a17–19; IV.7, 213b31, 33; 214a12, 16f.; IV.8, 214b17f. Incidentally, this is also a definition among Arabic philosophers prior to Avicenna, such as al-Kindī and ʿAlī Abū Ḥayyān al-Tawḥīdī; cf. al-Kindī, *Kitāb fī l-falsafa al-ūlā*, 21.19f. (ed. R. Rashed/Jolivet); al-Tawḥīdī, *al-Muqābasāt*, §84, 290.4f.

extremities" (ἢ διάστημά τι τὸ μεταξὺ τῶν ἐσχάτων, *buʿd mā fī-mā bayna l-ġayāt*).[186] A few lines later, he refers to this conception as "that in between" which, he says, seems to be "something" and, more precisely, "an extension … over and above the body which may be subject to replacement" (τὸ μεταξὺ εἶναί τι δοκεῖ διάστημα, ὡς ὄν τι παρὰ τὸ σῶμα τὸ μεθιστάμενον, *ẓunna bihī buʿd mā fī-mā bayna l-ġāyāt wa-annahū šayʾ siwan al-ǧism allaḏī qad yantaqilu*).[187] Finally, Aristotle also describes it as "some extension which is natural and static" (τι διάστημα τὸ πεφυκὸς καὶ μένον, *buʿdan mā mafṭūran lābiṯan*).[188]

We can gather that this extension is first of all limited by the extremities that limit the body. Aristotle is, thus, not talking about a vast space which permeates the whole universe but about a particular extension which corresponds to the particular corporeal extension of a body being exactly as great as that body. This reflects Aristotle's interest in what he has called a thing's proper (ἴδιος, *ḫāṣṣ*) or primary (πρώτῳ, *awwal*) place, as opposed to its common (κοινός, *ʿāmm*) place.[189] This extension is occupied by only one single body. Although it is co-extensive with the body it contains, it is independent and has its existence apart from it. It is a place for a body, albeit a place with a distinct reality.

Aristotle rejects this conception of place in *Physics* IV.4 on the grounds that it would pave the way for an actual infinity of coinciding places. Interpreters agree that this, at least, must be the intended conclusion of Aristotle's argument. How the argument as such is supposed to work, however is subject to debate.[190] What is striking is that this is all Aristotle has to say about this conception of place in his discussion in *Physics* IV.1–5. Already Themistius, who emphatically defends Aristotle's contention, railing against those who think that place is an extension, admits that Aristotle's arguments are rather obscure (ἀσαφέστερον), which is also the reason he felt compelled to advance his own arguments against the view.[191] Philoponus, too, criticises the overall quality of Aristotle's arguments against place as an extension within the context of the discussion of *Physics* IV.1–5:

186 *Phys.* IV.4, 211b7f.

187 *Phys.* IV.4, 211b16f.; cf. *Physics* IV.4, 212a3–5.

188 *Phys.* IV.4, 211b19f. I am not following Ross' conjecture to emend τι διάστημα τὸ πεφυκὸς καὶ μένον to τι [τὸ] διάστημα <καθ' αὑ>τὸ πεφυκὸς <εἶναι> καὶ μένον and, instead, keep the text as it also is in Philoponus, *In Phys.*, 549.1f., and Simplicius, *In Phys.*, 574.16, and as it is reflected in the Arabic translation by Isḥāq ibn Ḥunayn.

189 *Phys.* IV.2, 209a32f.

190 cf. *Phys.* IV.4, 211b19–25. There is not even an agreement about whether we are dealing with one, two, or three arguments; cf. the commentaries of Simplicius and Hussey *ad loc.*; cf. also Morison, *On Location*, 121–132, and the remarks by M. Rashed on *scholium* 54 in Alexander of Aphrodisias, *Commentaire perdu à la* Physique *d'Aristote*, 208–210.

191 cf. esp. Themistius, *In Phys.*, 116.10–12.

> ἀσαφὴς δὲ πάνυ ὁ τῶν λέξεων νοῦς, καὶ εἰ μὴ αὐτὸς ἐν τοῖς τοῦ κενοῦ λόγοις ἡρμήνευσεν ἑαυτόν, ἔμεινεν ἂν ἀνερμήνευτος·
>
> The meaning of his [sc. Aristotle's] words is very unclear (ἀσαφὴς δὲ πάνυ), and if he had not explained himself in his account of void, his meaning would have remained inexplicable (ἀνερμήνευτος). (Philoponus, *In Phys.*, 548.16–18, tr. by Algra)

Philoponus is right to refer to Aristotle's discussion of the void in *Physics* IV.6–9 as a place where Aristotle revisits the question about whether or not place should be understood as an extension. After all, Aristotle himself mentions place several times in the course of discussing void and, in particular, initiates his inquiry with the following words:

> Τὸν αὐτὸν δὲ τρόπον ὑποληπτέον εἶναι τοῦ φυσικοῦ θεωρῆσαι καὶ περὶ κενοῦ, εἰ ἔστιν ἢ μή, καὶ πῶς ἔστι, καὶ τί ἐστιν, ὥσπερ καὶ περὶ τόπου ... οἷον γὰρ τόπον τινὰ καὶ ἀγγεῖον τὸ κενὸν τιθέασιν οἱ λέγοντες, δοκεῖ δὲ πλῆρες μὲν εἶναι, ὅταν ἔχῃ τὸν ὄγκον οὗ δεκτικόν ἐστιν, ὅταν δὲ στερηθῇ, κενόν, ὡς τὸ αὐτὸ μὲν ὂν κενὸν καὶ πλῆρες καὶ τόπον, τὸ δ' εἶναι αὐτοῖς οὐ ταὐτὸ ὄν.
>
> وينبغي أن تعلم أن من حقّ صاحب الطبيعة أن يجعل نظره على هذا النحو الذي جرينا عليه في أمر المكان في أمر الخلاء ... فإنّ الذين يقولون بالخلاء يضعونه منزلة مكان ما وإناء ويُظنّ أنّه ملاء متى كان فيه الجمم الذي إيّاه يقبل ومتى عدمه كان خلاء حتّى يكون الخلاء والملاء والمكان معنى واحداً يعينه غير أن وجودها ليس واحداً.
>
> In the same way it must be supposed that it is up to the natural philosopher to inquire also about the void whether or not it exists, and how it exists, and what it is – just as about place ... for those who hold that the void exists regard it as a sort of place (οἷον γὰρ τόπον τινὰ ... τιθέασιν, *yaḍaʿūnahā manzilat makān mā*) or vessel which is supposed to be filled when it contains the volume which it is capable of receiving, and void when it is deprived, as if void and being filled and place were the same thing, though their being is not the same. (*Phys.* IV.6, 213a12–19, tr. by Hardie/Gaye, modified)[192]

From this it seems as if the question of whether or not place is "some extension between the extremities," as we read in chapter four, belongs to the larger context of asking about the existence of the void, for the particular extension occupied by a body could be seen as being merely a part of a larger whole. This larger whole would be extension as such or simply space. It is clear that if that larger whole would not exist, a particular part of it, corresponding to the extension of a particular corporeal object, would likewise not exist. Aristotle explicitly states that those who defend the existence of the void make it a "sort of place" (τόπον τινά, *makān mā*).[193] The question raised here is whether there exists some simple extension over and above bodies, be it finite or infinite, be it filled or empty, which we have so far failed to recognise. Against this background, then, the discussion of the void in *Physics* IV.6–9 is a logical, even required, continuation of

---

192 For further information about Aristotle's discussion of the void in *Physics* IV.6–9, cf. Furley, "Aristotle and the Atomists on Motion in a Void"; Thorp, "Aristotle's *Horror Vacui*." Furley's article has been reprinted in his collection *Cosmic Problems*, which also contains other articles about conceptions of the void among Strato and the Epicureans; cf. also Sedley, "Two Conceptions of Vacuum."

193 *Phys.* IV.6, 213a16.

Aristotle's inquiry into place. So, while Aristotle's rejection of place as an extension in his discussion of place is marked by a paucity of arguments, his refutation of the void is extensive. This is particularly true of his objections against the possibility of motion in a void which, according to Philoponus, "are the most beautiful [and] have snared nearly everyone by their persuasiveness" – everyone except Philoponus himself, of course.[194]

Finally, there is yet another argument with which Aristotle completes his refutation of the existence of the void. Dwelling on this argument, and in particular on its background and the history of its reception, will reveal how space and void have been conceived in the philosophical tradition after Aristotle – which is immediately relevant, because it is this understanding of space and void which was translated into Arabic and ultimately rejected by Avicenna.

Moreover, Aristotle's argument itself is particularly interesting, as it has been used by both opponents and adherents of the void in equal measure.[195] In contrast to the arguments that involve motion, this argument does not intend to demonstrate that assuming the existence of the void results in intractable absurdities but to furnish proof that the void is actually redundant, superfluous, and useless.[196]

Aristotle begins by announcing that he will consider the void in itself (καθ' αὑτό, *fī nafsihī*).[197] The void as such, extending itself into the three dimensions, would permeate (διεληλυθέναι, *yanfuḏu* and διῄεσαν, *yasriyān*) throughout any body that is placed in it.[198] If we considered a wooden cube, for example, then the void would stretch throughout the cube in all its dimensions, and go through all its parts and points, such that the body and the void permeating it would be equal in size. Aristotle makes the

---

194 Philoponus, *In Phys.*, 675.18–20 In his introduction to Furley's translation of Philoponus' *Corollaries on Place and Void*, 10f., Sorabji provides a convenient outline of Aristotle's arguments about the impossibility of motion in void and of Philoponus' rebuttal. Philoponus introduced the idea that every object requires *some* time to traverse a certain distance, and that there is a further amount of *extra-time* to be added if the motion takes place in a medium that offers resistance to the motion, so that a motion through water requires more extra-time to be added than a motion traversing an equal distance through air. The central twist in Philoponus argument is that a motion through the void would, contrary to Aristotle, still require *some* time – but it would not require some extra-time to be added, because void is a medium with zero resistance (and, thus, zero extra-time). Quite surprisingly, the idea of an extra-time is nowhere mentioned or discussed by Avicenna, as far as I can see, which means that we do not know whether Avicenna knew Philoponus' argument, whether he was aware of its strengths, and how he would have rejected it.

195 The argument itself has been analysed by McGinnis, "A Penetrating Question," tracing its history from Aristotle via Themistius and Philoponus to Avicenna. In addition to this, Sorabji, *Matter, Space, and Motion*, ch. 2, provides insightful remarks about the context of the argument in Philoponus; cf. also Wieland, "Zur Raumtheorie des Johannes Philoponus," 118–123; de Haas, *John Philoponus' New Definition of Prime Matter*, 31–36.

196 cf. Philoponus, *In Phys.*, 686.31–35.

197 *Phys.* IV.8, 216a26.

198 *Phys.* IV.8, 216a35, 216b2.

observation that the magnitude of the body differs from all its other accidents insofar as it cannot be separated from it in any way. We can abstract from any given body – at least in thought – its colour, weight, temperature, as well as all other accidental features, but we cannot strip away its magnitude and extension. That is to say that even without all other accidental attributes, a body would still have its extension, it would still occupy the same amount of the assumed void, and it would still be at that same place or position. Thus, Aristotle asks the following:

τί οὖν διοίσει τὸ τοῦ κύβου σῶμα τοῦ ἴσου κενοῦ καὶ τόπου;

فماذا ليت شعري يكون الفرق بين جرم المكعّب وبين الخلاء أو المكان المساوي له؟

How, then, will the body of the cube differ from the equal [amount of] void or place? (*Phys.* IV.8, 216b9f., tr. by Hardie/Gaye)

For Aristotle, there is no way of distinguishing the corporeal extension of the body from the assumed incorporeal extension of the void. As long as the body exists, its corporeal extension will occupy the incorporeal extension of the void. Thus, the incorporeal extension of the void will never exist as such, i.e., unoccupied by the body. What, then, is the explanatory import of this supposed void extension? What does it contribute to our understanding of the body which it is said to occupy? Why should we regard it as an existing reality, if it is never – neither *in abstracto* nor *in concreto* – extensionally different from the magnitude of the body?[199]

Aristotle continues that if there really were two separate extensions at the same place, one belonging to the body and one belonging to the void, then why should there not be even more extensions in addition to these two? Why, in fact, should there not be any – perhaps even an infinite – number of co-existing and co-extensive extensions? This, Aristotle claims, is absurd and impossible (ἄτοπον καὶ ἀδύνατον, *šaniʿ muḥāl*), so that he concludes the following:

ὥστ' εἰ τοῦ τόπου μηδὲν διαφέρει, τί δεῖ ποιεῖν τόπον τοῖς σώμασιν παρὰ τὸν ἑκάστου ὄγκον, εἰ ἀπαθὲς ὁ ὄγκος; οὐδὲν γὰρ συμβάλλεται, εἰ ἕτερον περὶ αὐτὸν ἴσον διάστημα τοιοῦτον εἴη.

فإن كان لا فرق بين هذا وبين المكان أصلاً فما الحاجة إلى أن نجعل للأجسام مكاناً سوى حجم كلّ واحد منها إذا كان الحجم لا يقبل التأثير؟ فإنّه لا درك في أن يكون حوله بعد آخر بهذه الصفة مساو له.

Therefore, if this [sc. the body's extension] differs in no respect from its place, why need we assume a place for bodies over and above the volume of each, if their volume be conceived of as free from attributes? It contributes nothing to the situation if there is an equal extension attached to it as well. (*Phys.* IV.8, 216b13–16, tr. by Hardie/Gaye, modified)

It is important for understanding the history of the argument to realise that Aristotle does not – at least not explicitly – say that two extensions cannot coincide, as Sorabji

199 Hussey refers to similar argumentative strategies by Aristotle against the existence of Platonic forms and numbers; cf. his comments in Aristotle, *Physics*, *ad* 216a23.

has noted.[200] Thus, for Aristotle, the assumption of an underlying void is primarily absurd, because it is scientifically inadequate and without value – it is itself void, as he famously asserts (τὸ λεγόμενον κενὸν ὡς ἀληθῶς κενόν, *ẓahara min amrihī annahu bi-l-ḥaqīqa ḫalāʾ*).[201] In addition, however, it is also implausible, because there seems to be no limit to the number of possible extensions overlapping at the same spot – and we have already seen above that this is one of Aristotle's primary reasons against place as an extension.[202]

Themistius develops the argument further, because he senses another absurdity entailed, but not yet fully exposed, by the argument. He summarises the argument in its logical form as follows:

> εἰ σῶμά ἐστιν ἐν ἐκείνῳ, διάστημά ἐστιν ἐν διαστήματι ... εἰ δὲ διάστημα ἐν διαστήματι, καὶ σῶμα ἐν σώματι ἔσται· ἐπεὶ γὰρ κατὰ μόνους τοὺς ὄγκους τὰ σώματά ἐστιν ἐν τόπῳ, καὶ κατ' οὐδὲν ἄλλο τῶν ὑπαρχόντων, εἰ δυνατὸν τὸν ὄγκον ἐν ὄγκῳ εἶναι, τά γε ἄλλα συμβεβηκότα οὐδὲν κωλύει τὸ σῶμα ἐν σώματι εἶναι. ἀλλὰ μὴν ἄτοπον σῶμα ἐν σώματι εἶναι· ἀδύνατον ἄρα καὶ σῶμα ἐν κενῷ εἶναι·
>
> If a body is in [the void], then an extension is in an extension ... But if an extension is in an extension, then a body will also be in a body (εἰ δὲ διάστημα ἐν διαστήματι, καὶ σῶμα ἐν σώματι ἔσται), for since bodies are in place only by virtue of their volumes, and not by virtue of any other of their properties, then if the volume can be in a volume, the other incidental properties certainly do not prevent a body from being in a body. However, it is absurd for a body to be in a body. Therefore, a body also cannot be in a void. (Themistius, *In Phys.*, 134.25–31, Todd, modified)[203]

In his version of the argument, Themistius makes use of the by now familiar claim that bodies are in place by virtue of their volumes, i.e., by virtue of their three-dimensionality and extension. Since the question is precisely about whether extensions are allowed to be in, i.e., to penetrate in such a way as to overlap with, other extensions and since, further, bodies are in place precisely by virtue of their extension, Themistius argues that anyone who allows for the extension of a body to coincide with the extension of empty space would also have to allow for two bodies to coincide with one another. Yet, two bodies cannot possible interpenetrate, from which he infers that it is impossible

---

200 cf. Sorabji, *Matter, Space, and Motion*, 76f.

201 *Phys.* IV.8, 216a26f.

202 q.v. above, 369. This interpretation is also found in Themistius (*In Phys.*, 135.5–7) and Simplicius (*In Phys.*, 682.1f., 16–18) as well as in Philoponus, as we shall see shortly. Moreover, this is also how Aristotle's argument reappears in al-Tawḥīdī's *al-Muqābasāt*. Reporting what Abū Sulaymān al-Siǧistānī has said about the void, al-Tawḥīdī reproduces Aristotle's argument – together with Themistius' and Philoponus' thesis that a body occupies its place only by virtue of its three dimensions – in order to disprove the existence of the void by accusing its adherents of an infinite regress; cf. *al-Muqābasāt*, §84, 290.14–17; cf. also Kraemer, *Philosophy in the Renaissance of Islam*, 184–186.

203 Simplicius draws on, and effectively reproduces, Themistius' version of the argument in his own commentary; cf. Simplicius, *In Phys.*, 682.2–8.

for *any* two extensions, i.e., extensions of whatever sort, to interpenetrate, so that also no body could ever coincide with, and be in, void space.[204]

Themistius' argument is clearly more straightforward than Aristotle's. For him the idea of an extended body being located in an extended space is not only uninformative, as it does not contribute to our understanding of the three-dimensionality of corporeal objects, but is plainly impossible as such. That is to say, we do not need to assume an infinite number of coinciding extensions for the argument to result in an impossibility – two extensions are enough.

In Philoponus' commentary on the *Physics*, we find Aristotle's argument expounded along the lines of Themistius' reading:

> εἰ δύο διαστήματα ὅμοια ἐχώρησαν δι' ἀλλήλων, καὶ πλείονα δηλονότι δυνατὸν χωρῆσαι. τοῦτο δὲ ἀδύνατον· εἰ γὰρ διάστημα ἐν διαστήματι δυνατὸν χωρῆσαι, καὶ σῶμα ἐν σώματι χωρῆσαι δυνατόν· κατ' οὐδὲν γὰρ ἄλλο τὰ σώματα ἐν τόπῳ ἐστὶν ἢ κατὰ τοὺς ὄγκους· εἰ οὖν δυνατὸν ὄγκον ἐν ὄγκῳ εἶναι, τά γε ἄλλα συμβεβηκότα οὐδὲν κωλύει τὸ σῶμα ἐν σώματι εἶναι. ἀλλὰ μὴν τοῦτο ἀδύνατον· οὐδ' ἄρα σῶμα ἐν κενῷ δυνατὸν εἶναι·
>
> If two similar extensions passed through one another, it is clearly also possible for even more to pass through. This, however, is impossible, for if it is possible for an extension to pass through an extension, it is also possible for a body to pass through a body (σῶμα ἐν σώματι χωρῆσαι δυνατόν), for in no other way are bodies in a place than by virtue of their volumes (κατ' οὐδὲν γὰρ ἄλλο τὰ σώματα ἐν τόπῳ ἐστὶν ἢ κατὰ τοὺς ὄγκους). If, therefore, it is possible for a volume to be in a volume, its other accidents in no way prevent the body from being in a body. But that is impossible, and so neither is it possible for a body to be in a void. (Philoponus, *In Phys.*, 666.15–21, tr. by Huby, modified)[205]

As can be seen, Philoponus follows Themistius' understanding of Aristotle's argument. Of course, he accepts the claim that bodies are in place by virtue of their volumes (κατὰ τοὺς ὄγκους).[206] After all, this was already the basis for one of his central arguments against Aristotle's definition of place as a surface as discussed above.[207] Yet, he disagrees with his predecessor on whether the argument sufficiently demonstrates that

204 McGinnis argues that Themistius here invokes the principle that "body is whatever is three-dimensional" and that "three-dimensionality is a necessary and sufficient condition for being a body." On that basis, he reconstructs Themistius' argument as claiming that space, having three-dimensions, is in fact a body and would, thus, coincide and penetrate the body located in space; cf. McGinnis, "A Penetrating Question," 51f. This seems to go too far. All Themistius says here is that if extensions could be allowed to coincide, then bodies would also have to be allowed to coincide. This is also how Sorabji reads the argument in *Matter, Space, and Motion*, 76. Whether or not Themistius draws on Alexander in the present argument is difficult to establish, but cf. McGinnis, "A Penetrating Question," fn. 9, 51f.

205 cf. the similar exposition in Philoponus' corollary on void at *In Phys.*, 686.35–687.14, as well as his own affirmation at Philoponus, *In Phys.*, 689.7–11; q.v. also below, 374ff.

206 cf. also Iamblichus *apud* Simplicium, *In Phys.*, 639.24f. (= part of frgm. 90 in Iamblichus, *In Platonis dialogos commentariorum fragmenta*): πᾶν σῶμα ᾗ σῶμα ὑπάρχει ἐν τόπῳ ἐστί.

207 q.v. above, 322ff.

the void is useless and superfluous (μάτην).[208] In fact, Philoponus uses the very same line of thought to refute Themistius' (and Aristotle's) argument and to substantiate his own claim that the place of bodies is an independently existing, three-dimensional extension which is always filled with bodies, even though considered in itself it is void.[209]

The central claim in Philoponus' argument is that the void is not a body. Since that is so, the assumption of a body coinciding with the void is not on a par with the absurd assumption of a body coinciding with another body, as Themistius' version of Aristotle's argument had it. In fact, Philoponus agrees with his predecessors that no body could ever penetrate or pass through any other body. Yet, there is nothing that prevents the three-dimensional material extension of a body from coinciding with the three-dimensional immaterial extension of the void. If, following Aristotle's line of reasoning, we remove from a body all its accidents, it would still remain as a body, i.e., as "envolumed matter" (ἡ ὀγκωθεῖσα ὕλη) or "unqualified body" (τὸ ἄποιον σῶμα), Philoponus writes.[210] In other words, a body deprived of all accidents is still a piece of matter qualified by a quantity which provides it with a definite three-dimensional corporeal extension.[211] The void, on the other hand, is an extension, too, but it is not a *material* extension, as Philoponus explains:

> τὸ δὲ κενὸν οὐ σύγκειται ἐξ ὕλης καὶ εἴδους· οὐδὲ γάρ ἐστι σῶμα, ἀλλὰ ἀσώματον καὶ ἄυλον, καὶ χώρα μόνη σώματος. εἰ τοίνυν τοῦ μὲν σώματος ἀφαιρεθεισῶν τῶν ποιοτήτων οὐδὲν ἧττον σῶμα τὸ καταλειπόμενον, τὸ δὲ κενὸν οὐκ ἔστι σῶμα, οὐδέποτε συμβήσεται σῶμα ἐν σώματι εἶναι, εἰ ἐν τῷ κενῷ ὡς ἐν τόπῳ εἴη τὸ σῶμα.
>
> [T]he void is not composed of matter and form, for it is not a body at all, but bodiless and matterless (ἀσώματον καὶ ἄυλον, καὶ χώρα μόνη σώματος) – space without body. So, if what remains when all the qualities are removed from body is nevertheless body, and the void is not a body, it will never be the case that body is in body, if the body is in the void as in a place. (Philoponus, *In Phys.*, 687.34–688.2, tr. by Furley)

In essence, Philoponus argues that while it is certainly true that no material extension can pass through another material extension, there is nothing that prevents a material extension (such as body) to pass through an *immaterial* extension (such as void or place).

---

208 Philoponus, *In Phys.*, 686.30–689.25.

209 This is the canonical definition of Philoponus' notion of place or space, which he reiterates again and again throughout his corollaries on place and void.

210 Philoponus, *In Phys.*, 687.32f., tr. by Furley.

211 q.v. above 140ff., where I also briefly discussed how Philoponus' views developed over time. The following discussion of the void clearly belongs to a time where Philoponus had not yet arrived at his final view about envolumed matter.

Philoponus' argument further entails a rejection of an understanding of body that defines it as whatever is three-dimensionally extended.[212] This rejection was explicitly formulated in the course of his discussion of place, in particular in his corollary, where he wrote the following:

> οὐδὲ γὰρ τὸ τριχῇ διαστατὸν εὐθὺς καὶ σῶμα, οὐδὲ τοῦτον ὅρον εἶναι τοῦ σώματος παραδεξόμεθα· τὸ μὲν γὰρ σῶμα ἄλλο τι ὂν οὕτως ἐστὶ τριχῇ διαστατόν.
>
> For, what is extended in three dimensions is not automatically a body; we shall not accept that this is the definition of body, since it is by virtue of being something else that body is extended in three dimensions. (Philoponus, *In Phys.*, 561.5–8, tr. by Furley)

A little later he emphasises once more that "three-dimensionality is not the definition of body" (οὐκ ἄρα τὸ τριχῇ διαστατὸν σώματός ἐστιν ὅρος).[213] Since for Philoponus, place is an incorporeal and immaterial three-dimensional space which, though essentially void, is always filled with body, he is required to decouple the notion of three-dimensionality from the notion of body. In fact, what Philoponus does is abstract the notion of a three-dimensionally extended space from the notion of body. Once again, one of Aristotle's own arguments serves as the basis for his reasoning.

In *Metaphysics* Z.3, Aristotle provides an argument that seems to suggest that matter is substance.[214] At the heart of this argument, Aristotle proposes to abstract from a body everything that can be abstracted from it, in order to arrive at what he calls "the first subject" (τὸ ὑποκείμενον πρῶτον, *al-mawḍūʿ al-awwal*). This subject, it seems, is that of which all the abstracted affections had been predicated. Moreover, this subject may be a good candidate for substance, because substance has been said to be "that which is not predicated of a subject, but of which all else is predicated" (τὸ μὴ καθ' ὑποκειμένου ἀλλὰ καθ' οὗ τὰ ἄλλα, *lā allaḏī ʿalā mawḍūʿ bal allaḏī ʿalayhi al-āḫar*).[215] Aristotle, then, reasons as follows:

> περιαιρουμένων γὰρ τῶν ἄλλων οὐ φαίνεται οὐδὲν ὑπομένον· τὰ μὲν γὰρ ἄλλα τῶν σωμάτων πάθη καὶ ποιήματα καὶ δυνάμεις, τὸ δὲ μῆκος καὶ πλάτος καὶ βάθος ποσότητές τινες ἀλλ' οὐκ οὐσίαι (τὸ γὰρ ποσὸν οὐκ οὐσία), ἀλλὰ μᾶλλον ᾧ ὑπάρχει ταῦτα πρώτῳ, ἐκεῖνό ἐστιν οὐσία. ἀλλὰ μὴν

---

212 This, indeed, is a definition offered by Aristotle at the beginning of *De caelo* (cf. esp. *Cael.* I.1, 268a7f.). It has the considerable disadvantage that it does not provide any help in distinguishing between mathematical bodies and solids, on the one hand, and natural bodies and concrete objects, on the other; cf. in this regard Euclid's definition of mathematical solids in *Elements* XI, def. 1. Consequently, Aristotle's definition from *De caelo* I.1 ought to be understood within the context of the work and especially with regard to its formulation *at the very beginning* of that work, i.e., as establishing the science of nature (Ἡ περὶ φύσεως ἐπιστήμη) as being concerned with the natural body, i.e., a body having a nature; cf. also Falcon, *Aristotle and the Science of Nature*, ch. 2, esp. 38.

213 Philoponus, *In Phys.*, 561.22f., tr. by Furley.

214 The argument already has been discussed above in a different context; q.v. 139ff.

215 *Met.* Z.3, 1029a8f.

ἀφαιρουμένου μήκους καὶ πλάτους καὶ βάθους οὐδὲν ὁρῶμεν ὑπολειπόμενον, πλὴν εἴ τί ἐστι τὸ ὁριζόμενον ὑπὸ τούτων, ὥστε τὴν ὕλην ἀνάγκη φαίνεσθαι μόνην οὐσίαν οὕτω σκοπουμένοις.

فإنّه إذا انتزعت سائر الأشياء لا نرى شيئاً باقياً والمنفعلات الآخر التي للأجسام وأفعالها والقوى وأيضاً الطول والعرض والعمق كمّية هي وليست جواهر لأنّ الكمّية ليست بجوهر بل الذي له هذه الأشياء بعينها بنوع أوّل هو الجوهر ولاكنّ إذا انتزع الطول والعرض والعمق لا نرى شيئاً يبقى ما خلا إن كان شيء ما الذي هذه تحدّه فإذا مضطرّ أن يرى الهيولى وحدها جوهراً الذين يفحصون هذا الفحص.

When all else is taken away evidently nothing [apart from matter] remains. For everything else are affections, effects, and capacities of bodies, while length, breadth, and depth are quantities and not substances. For a quantity is not substance; substance is rather that to which these belong primarily. But when length and breadth and depth are taken away, we see nothing left, except if there is something which is determined by these, so that to those who consider the question thus matter alone must seem to be substance. (*Met.* Z.3, 1029a11–19, tr. by Ross, modified)[216]

This passage aptly captures the fundamental difference between Aristotle and Philoponus in their conceptions of void and space. For Aristotle, that which remains when everything possible has been stripped away is still material – it is either matter itself or an abstract, i.e., unqualified, body.[217] This, however, is something with which Philoponus agrees only partially. He, too, ties body to matter and argues that when we remove from a body all accidents and qualities, what remains is an unqualified body. In fact, if we were also to remove the matter, then the form of the body would vanish, too, so that the body would instantly cease to be.[218] Thus far, Philoponus agrees with Aristotle. In an earlier passage, however, Philoponus already went one step further than Aristotle:

Σκόπει δὲ καὶ ὧδε. εἰ μηδέν ἐστιν ἕτερόν τι διάστημα παρὰ τὰ ἐγγινόμενα σώματα τὸ δεχόμενον αὐτά, ὑφέλωμεν κατ' ἐπίνοιαν τὰ μεταξὺ σώματα καὶ ἴδωμεν εἰ τῷ ὄντι οὕτως ἔχει. ἆρ' οὖν εἰ ἐπινοήσωμεν τὰ ἐντὸς τοῦ οὐρανοῦ σώματα μὴ ὄντα, γῆν λέγω καὶ ὕδωρ καὶ ἀέρα καὶ πῦρ, τί λοιπὸν τὸ μεταξὺ κατελείπετο ἢ διάστημα κενόν; ἦν γὰρ δηλονότι εὐθείας ἀπὸ τοῦ κέντρου ἐπὶ τὴν περιφέρειαν πανταχόθεν ἐκβαλεῖν· τὸ οὖν δι' οὗ τὰς εὐθείας ἐκβάλλομεν τί ἄλλο ἐστὶν ἢ διάστημα κενὸν τριχῇ διαστατόν; καὶ μή τις λεγέτω, ὅτι ἀδύνατος ἡ ὑπόθεσις ... ὁ γοῦν Ἀριστοτέλης ... τὰ σώματα χωρίσας πάσης ποιότητος καὶ παντὸς εἴδους οὕτως αὐτὰ καθ' αὑτὰ θεωρεῖ. καὶ τῆς ὕλης δὲ οὕτως εἰς ἔννοιαν ἐρχόμεθα πᾶν εἶδος αὐτῆς χωρίσαντες καὶ γυμνὴν αὐτὴν καθ' αὑτὴν θεώμενοι. οὐ γὰρ ἄτοπον ὑποθέσεσι χρῆσθαί τισιν, εἰ καὶ ἀδύνατοι εἶεν, πρὸς ἄλλων ἐπίσκεψιν·

Consider the following. If there is no distinct extension receiving them, over and above the bodies that come to be in it, let us in thought (κατ' ἐπίνοιαν) remove the bodies in the middle and see if it is really so. So then, if we think of the bodies within the heaven as not being there – I mean

216 cf. *Phys.* IV.2, 209b9–11; IV.7, 214a11–14; IV.8, 216b2–9; *De mem.* 1, 449b31–450a14; cf. also *Enn.* II.4.10, 28–31.

217 We would arrive at prime matter, if all that can possibly by taken away includes the three dimensions, as the first clause suggests. However, it may be that nothing really remains if the three dimensions were in fact taken away, in which case all that can possibly be taken away excludes the three dimensions – with the result that we would arrive at matter plus a definite extension, i.e., an unqualified body; q.v. also the argument from *Physics* IV.8 discussed above, 371ff.

218 Philoponus, *In Phys.*, 688.2–35.

> earth, water, air, and fire – what would remain in the middle but an empty extension (τί λοιπὸν τὸ μεταξὺ κατελείπετο ἢ διάστημα κενόν)? For it was plainly possible to extend straight lines from the centre to the circumference everywhere: so what is it through which we draw the lines but empty extension extended in three dimensions? Let no one say that the hypothesis is impossible ... Aristotle himself ... studies bodies in and of themselves by separating them from all quality and all form; and we arrive at a conception of matter by separating all form from it (πᾶν εἶδος αὐτῆς χωρίσαντες) and studying it naked, all by itself (γυμνὴν αὐτὴν καθ' αὐτήν). It is not absurd to use hypotheses even if they are impossible, for examination of other things (οὐ γὰρ ἄτοπον ὑποθέσεσι χρῆσθαί τισιν, εἰ καὶ ἀδύνατοι εἶεν, πρὸς ἄλλων ἐπίσκεψιν). (Philoponus, *In Phys.*, 574.13–575.3, tr. by Furley)[219]

This is a complex passage. Put simply, Philoponus does nothing more than to specify what it really means when people, among them Aristotle, say that void is place deprived of body.[220] More precisely, Philoponus suggests that we could consider the entire universe and remove – at least in thought (κατ' ἐπίνοιαν) – all bodies within the heavenly sphere, in order to study the void space that is left once the bodies have been removed. It is clear that Philoponus' argument is meant to counter those who deny that there exists something like an underlying extension in which bodies are or come-to-be. Addressing those who remain sceptical, he asks: what is that which remains if we removed everything inside the heavens? Of course, he immediately supplies an answer: it would be an empty spatial extension which is such that we can draw perpendicular lines in it, thereby demonstrating that this extension is three-dimensional.[221]

219 cf. the similar argument in Sextus Empiricus, *Adversus physicos* II.12; cf. also Grant, *Much Ado about Nothing*, fn. 67, 276. Several interpreters have drawn attention to the passage in Philoponus and to his method of arguing on the basis of an impossible hypothesis. Wieland and, in particular, Martin have hinted at Eudemus as a precursor for Philoponus' present method, the latter even calling it an "Eudemian procedure," while the former mentions Eudemus as an opponent of such a procedure; cf. Wieland, "Zur Raumtheorie des Johannes Philoponus," fn. 15, 123; Martin, "Non-reductive Arguments from Impossible Hypotheses in Boethius and Philoponus"; cf. also Sedley, "Philoponus' Conception of Space"; Kukkonen, "Ibn Sīnā and the Early History of Thought Experiments." Kukkonen also refers to Simplicius' criticism of Philoponus' argument at Simplicius, *In Phys.*, 1334.26–34. Themistius objected in a similar way to Galen, as we shall see.

220 q.v. fn. 185 above, 368; cf. also Simplicius, *In Phys.*, 657.5f.

221 It is noteworthy that Philoponus mentions the possibility that we can draw lines within this empty space. He seems to depict void in analogy to mathematical space. In this regard, Wieland cited a passage from Themistius' paraphrase of the *Physics* devoted to Aristotle's remarks about mathematical bodies from *Physics* IV.1, 208b22–25. There, Themistius stated that we conceive of mathematical bodies by imagining place together with them (τόπον αὐτοῖς συμφανταζόμεθα). This harmonises with Aristotle's immediately following remark, in the words of Themistius, that "those who introduce the void introduce it as place; that is, we conceive of the void, if it exists, as simply place stripped of body" (τόπος σώματος ἐστερημένος; *In Phys.*, 103.18–26). From this, Wieland inferred that Themistius considers here two separate mental operations: first, abstracting the mathematical body and, second, deriving place or space from that abstracted mathematical body. This is noteworthy insofar as Wieland further shows how Philoponus can actually dispense with keeping these two operations apart and that he treats the realm of natural entities as analogous to the realm of mathematical ones. As a result, Philoponus

Philoponus legitimates his argument with an explicit reference to Aristotle's method of studying matter "naked [and] all by itself" (γυμνὴν αὐτὴν καθ' αὑτήν) by "separating all form from it" (πᾶν εἶδος αὐτῆς χωρίσαντες). This is precisely the above argument from *Metaphysics* Z.3.[222] Of course, it is impossible to remove all body within the heavenly sphere, in order to study the void – but no more impossible than removing all accidents from body, in order to study matter: "It is not absurd to use hypotheses even if they are impossible, for examination of other things," Philoponus claims.

Whether or not conceiving of something impossible is admitted, in order to demonstrate something else, is a much disputed question.[223] Philoponus' approach leads us to a final aspect of his late ancient conception of void and of space, for it resembles an earlier argument which Galen (d. ~ 216) advanced in favour of the void and which was criticised, in turn, by Themistius. In one of his rare excursus that disrupt the flow of his paraphrase of Aristotle's *Physics*, Themistius writes:

> Ἀλλ' ὑποθώμεθα ἐξαιρεθέντος τοῦ ὕδατος μηδὲν ἕτερον εἰσρυῆναι σῶμα. μένει τοίνυν μεταξὺ τῆς ἐπιφανείας διάστημα κεχωρισμένον. ἀλλ' ἄλογος ἡ ὑπόθεσις, ὦ σοφώτατε Γαληνέ (αὐτὸ γὰρ ὑποτίθεται ὃ ζητοῦμεν) ... πλάττεις σεαυτῷ καὶ ἀναζωγραφεῖς, ὃ βούλει εἶναι διάστημα κεχωρισμένον, οὐχ ὅτι ὑπάρχει δεικνύεις. ὅλως τε οὐδὲν δυνατὸν ἐννοεῖς ... καὶ γὰρ οὕτως μόνον καταλιπεῖν βουλήσεται διάστημα, ἐν ᾧ τὰ σώματα νῦν ἐστι, τηνικαῦτα δὲ οὐκ ἔσται. ἀλλ' οὔτε τοῦτο δυνατὸν οὔτε ὃ βούλεται ὁ Γαληνός· διάστημα γὰρ ἄνευ σώματος ἀμήχανον ὑποστῆναί ποτε, ἀλλὰ θᾶττον ἂν ὁ χαλκὸς συμπέσοι τῆς κοίλης ἐπιφανείας ἢ δίχα σώματος μείνειεν· τὸ γὰρ κενὸν ὅτι κενὸν ὄντως ἐστίν, εὐθὺς ἐπιδειχθήσεται.
>
> But let us hypothesise that when the fluid was removed [from a vessel], no other body flowed in: a separate extension therefore remains within the surface [of the vessel]. But the hypothesis is illogical, all-wise Galen, for it hypothesises the very object of our inquiry ... you fabricate for yourself a picture of just what you want – that a separate extension exists – without proving that it exists. In general terms, you conceive of something impossible[224] ... In fact, this is the only way that [Galen] will get his wish to leave an extension in which there are bodies now, but not at another time. But this is impossible, and not what Galen intends: for an extension can never manage to subsist without a body – instead, the bronze that forms the hollow surface [of a vessel] would sooner implode than remain without body. (Themistius, *In Phys.*, 114.7–21, tr. by Todd)

That this discussion from Themistius' paraphrase is directly related to the argument in Philoponus is shown by the fact that Philoponus, immediately after his argument about

---

abstracts in one single operation the notion of space from the existence of natural bodies; cf. Wieland, "Zur Raumtheorie des Johannes Philoponus," 120. For the notion of abstraction in Aristotle and his commentators, cf. also Mueller, "Aristotle's Doctrine of Abstraction in the Commentators."

222 Simplicius likewise moved seamlessly from Aristotle's argument about the wooden cube in the *Physics*, to the assertion that bodies are in place solely by virtue of their dimensions, to the abstraction argument from *Metaphysics* Z.3, and back to the wooden cube in the developed version of Themistius; cf. Simplicius, *In Phys.*, 681.14–682.8.

223 cf., again, Martin, "Non-reductive Arguments from Impossible Hypotheses in Boethius and Philoponus"; Kukkonen, "Ibn Sīnā and the Early History of Thought Experiments."

224 Following Todd's emendation to read οὐδὲν for οὔτε in Schenkl's text.

the removal of all body within the heavenly sphere, turns to Themistius' present point about the vessel imploding due to the removal of what it hitherto contained. He even discusses whether or not in reality the heavens would collapse once the interior bodies were actually removed as his thought experiment supposes.[225] Thereupon, Philoponus criticises Themistius for charging Galen with having committed a *petitio principii*.[226] By explicitly defending Galen, Philoponus also defends the validity of his own thought experiment, which is analogous to that offered by Galen and through which he wanted to derive a notion of void space. Yet, he clarifies that this space cannot exist by itself empty devoid of body (καθ' αὑτὸ εἶναι κενὸν σώματος), for Philoponus is convinced, siding with Aristotle, that *void* space does not exist.[227]

Indeed, it is an indispensable aspect of Philoponus' understanding of the void that he thinks that the void is always and completely filled with body. There is never, nor could there ever be, a truly empty void. The idea of a void entirely filled with corporeal substance is nothing other than Philoponus' understanding of a space which permeates through all corporeal reality. This also explains why Philoponus consistently uses the term "void" (τό κενόν) interchangeably with the terms "space" (χώρα), "place" (τόπος), and "extension" (διάστημα).[228] Moreover, this is perfectly in line with Philoponus' own characterisation of the Galen-inspired argument as an "impossible," though nonetheless helpful, hypothesis to derive the proper notion of that extension which is known as place, or space, or void:

> οὐδὲ γὰρ τοῦτο λέγομεν, ὅτι μένει ποτὲ τὸ διάστημα τοῦτο κενὸν σώματος, ἀλλ' ὅτι ἐστὶ μὲν ἕτερον πάντων τῶν ἐμπιπτόντων σωμάτων, οὐδέποτε μέντοι κενὸν γίνεται σώματος, καὶ διὰ τοῦτο ἡ ἀντιμετάστασις τῶν σωμάτων καὶ ἡ τοῦ κενοῦ βία, ἵνα μὴ μείνῃ κενὸν σώματος τὸ τοπικὸν διάστημα.
>
> For we do not say that this extension ever remains empty of body, but that it is different from all the bodies that come to be in it, even though it never comes to be empty of body; and for this reason there is the replacement of bodies (ἡ ἀντιμετάστασις τῶν σωμάτων) and the force of the void (ἡ τοῦ κενοῦ βία), so that place-extension may never remain empty of body. (Philoponus, *In Phys.*, 579.5–9, tr. by Furley, modified)[229]

It is this actual impossibility of the existence of truly void space that is also behind Philoponus' frequent mention of the "force of the void" (ἡ τοῦ κενοῦ βία). He elaborates on this idea while explaining a number of phenomena that can be witnessed when experimenting with water-filled clepsydrae held up high in the air without water dripping out of its holes at the bottom or with pipes that, once air has been sucked out of them, make the water rise upwards against its own nature. In brief, there are

225 Philoponus, *In Phys.*, 575.14–576.12.

226 Philoponus, *In Phys.*, 576.12–577.9.

227 Philoponus, *In Phys.*, 576.24.

228 cf. Philoponus, *In Phys.*, 563.20f.; cf. also Sedley, "Philoponus' Conception of Space," 141.

229 Philoponus, *In Phys.*, cf. 569.7–10.

various phenomena, and in particular those surrounding compression and expansion, rarefaction and condensation, "whose cause is nothing other than the force of the void" (ούτου δὲ ἡ αἰτία οὐδεμία ἄλλη ἢ ἡ τοῦ κενοῦ βία), as Philoponus asserts.[230]

Consequently, Philoponus combines the conceptual possibility of the void as such with the actual impossibility of its real existence.[231] Nature, then, always prevents a void from forming by not allowing the water to drip out of a clepsydra or by forcing the water upwards in a pipe against its own nature, thereby filling the space which was in imminent danger of becoming vacuous. These phenomena, Philoponus asserts, cannot be explained on the basis of Aristotle's concept of place as the inner surface of the containing body:

> εἰ οὖν ἐπιφάνειά ἐστιν ὁ τόπος, καὶ μὴ ἔστι τι διάστημα τῷ ἰδίῳ λόγῳ κενόν, τίς ἐστιν ἡ ἐν τῇ φύσει δύναμις ἐπὶ τὸ παρὰ φύσιν κινοῦσα πολλάκις τὰ σώματα, ἵνα μὴ κενὸν γένηται, μηδενὸς ὄντος ἐν τῷ παντὶ διαστήματος τοῦ κινδυνεύοντος κενοῦ γενέσθαι;
>
> Now, if place is a surface, and there is no extension that is empty by its own definition, what power is it in nature that often moves bodies in the direction contrary to nature, so that a void may not occur, if there is in the universe no extension that is at risk of becoming void? (Philoponus, *In Phys.*, 572.2–6, tr. by Furley)

To sum up, we have seen that Aristotle discusses at least two different conceptions of space. There is the limited or particular space which is supposed to permeate through a particular body and which is a rival account for place. The place of a body is simply the three-dimensional extension that corresponds with, even though being separate from, the corporeal extension of the body. This particular space, however, is part of a larger continuum which, as void space, allegedly pervades the entire universe. Although Aristotle's arguments against limited space are very brief, he extensively rebuts the conception of void space by appealing to the impossibility of motion in the void and to the fact that the notion of space which is always filled by a corresponding body is essentially superfluous and redundant.

Philoponus, then, turns the tables. He argues that it is not the account of place as an extension that is troubled by insurmountable absurdities but Aristotle's own conception of place as a surface. In addition, he argues that Aristotle's reasons against place as an extension are unconvincing. He also shows that the requirements which, according to Aristotle, any successful account of place has to meet, can in fact be met by the conception of place as an extension – perhaps even better than by Aristotle's own conception of place as a surface.[232] So, Philoponus, just as Aristotle, proceeds by elimination: of the four candidates for place, viz., matter form, extension, and surface, two are obviously false (matter and form, as has been shown by Aristotle already), whereas the fourth, place as a surface, has now been disproven by Philoponus. Thus,

230 Philoponus, *In Phys.*, 569.28.
231 cf. Sedley, "Philoponus' Conception of Space."
232 Philoponus, *In Phys.*, 586.25–589.18, 598.3f.

the remaining option must be what place is – and this is an extension, which Philoponus further characterises in his corollaries on place and on void as an immaterial and incorporeal, three-dimensional extension which, in itself, is devoid of all body but which, in fact, is always filled by body. This understanding of place is not only superior to Aristotle's conception, Philoponus claims, it is also better able to account for the well-known natural phenomena that people have observed in carrying out experiments devised for proving the existence of the void (even though what these phenomena actually suggest in the end is the *impossibility* of an empty space, thus, demonstrating the "force of the void" as an operative power within nature).

In all this, Philoponus is one among many thinkers who were genuinely dissatisfied with Aristotle's take on the subject of place. As early as Theophrastus, thinkers advanced puzzles and arguments against Aristotle's conception and as early as Strato of Lampsacus (d. ~ 269 BC) we see the view that place is not a surface but an extension always occupied by body.[233] The predominant idea was that place must be three-dimensional, because the body which is said to be in place is also three-dimensional and that underlying all corporeal reality was a powerful extension responsible both for location and the well-known phenomena which someone like Philoponus attributed to the "force of the void." The complex history of space which has been outlined above provides us with an apt picture of the direct enemy of Avicenna's own Aristotelian conviction of what constitutes the essence of place – a conviction he is required to defend not only by developing the notion of surface but also by actively arguing against this most predominant of all rival conceptions, for his analysis of place, just as much as those of Aristotle and Philoponus, proceeds by way of elimination. So, Avicenna can truly vindicate the Aristotelian definition only by demonstrating that the three-dimensional extension is, after all, no viable candidate for place.

The Concept of Place as an Extension in *al-Samāʿ al-ṭabīʿī*

In *al-Samāʿ al-ṭabīʿī* II.6, when Avicenna lists the available options for the essence of place, he mentions the view that place might be "an extension which equals its [sc. a body's] dimensions (*buʿdan yusāwī aqṭārahū*), and so is something it [sc. the body] occupies by entering it."[234] Shortly afterwards, he spells out this notion in more detail:

ومنهم مَن زعم أنّ المكان هو الأبعاد فقال إنّ بين غايات الإناء الحاوي للماء أبعاداً مفطورةً ثابتةً وأنّها يتعاقب عليها الأجسام المحصورة في الإناء.

233 cf. Simplicius, *In Phys.*, 601.22–24, 618.23–25; cf. also Sambursky, *The Physical World of Late Antiquity*, 3; Daiber, "Fārābīs Abhandlung über das Vakuum," 40f.; Furley, "Strato's Theory of the Void."

234 *al-Samāʿ al-ṭabīʿī* II.6, §2, 115.10f.; cf. *al-Ḥikma al-mašriqiyya* III.9, 26.4f.

Some among them claim that place is the extensions (*al-makān huwa l-abʿād*). They say that between the extremities of the vessel (*bayna ġāyāt al-inā'*) containing the water are fixed and natural extensions (*abʿādan mafṭūratan ṯābitatan*) and that the bodies limited by the vessel succeed one another in it. (*al-Samāʿ al-ṭabīʿī* II.6, §4, 115.12f.)

Avicenna adds that the thinkers upholding this view distinguished themselves by specifically attacking the Aristotelian theory that place is a surface (*yuḫāṭibūna ḫāṣṣatan aṣḥāb al-suṭūḥ*).[235] Moreover, we are told that these people derived their notion of place as a stable and natural extension by means of analysis (*taḥlīl*) and removal (*rafʿ*), i.e., by mentally removing one feature after another from a given body, in order to represent to the mind, and subsequently to study, whatever remains once the abstractive process has come to an end:

وقالوا أيضاً إنّ الأمور البسيطة إنّما يؤدّي إليها التحليل وتوهّم رفع شيء شيء من الأشياء المجتمعة معاً وهماً. فالذي يبقى بعد رفع غيره في الوهم هو البسيط الموجود في نفسه وإن كان لا ينفرد له قوام. وبهذا السبب عرفنا الهيولى والصورة والبسائط التي هي آحاد في أشياء مجتمعة. ثمّ إذا توهّمنا الماء أو غيره من الأجسام مرفوعاً غير موجود في الإناء لزم من ذلك أن يكون البعد الثابت بين أطرافه موجوداً وذلك أيضاً موجود عندما تكون هذه موجودة معه.

They also say that simple things are brought about only through analysis (*al-taḥlīl*) and the imagination of the removal (*tawahhum rafʿ ... wahman*) of each and every thing from the composed objects together. Thus, that which remains after the removal of what is other than it in the imagination (*allaḏī yabqā baʿda rafʿ ... fī l-wahm*) is a simple existent in itself (*al-basīṭ al-mawǧūd fī nafsihī*) which, even if it does not [exist] in isolation, has subsistence. In this way, we recognise matter, form, and simple [bodies], which [normally] are singular parts in composite objects. Moreover, if we imagine water or some other body as removed and inexistent in the vessel, it follows from that that the fixed extension between its limits (*al-buʿd al-ṯābit bayna aṭrāfihī*) exists and that, furthermore, that [extension] exists whenever these [things] exist together with it. (*al-Samāʿ al-ṭabīʿī* II.6, §5, 116.3–7)

Having presented further arguments advanced by these people in support of their view, Avicenna states:

لكنّ أصحاب البعد على مذهبين منهم مَن يحيل أن يكون هذا البعد يبقى فارغاً لا مالئ له بل يوجب أنّه لا يتخلّى عن مالئ البتّةً إلّا عند لحوق مالئ ومنهم مَن لا يحيل ذلك بل يجوز أن يكون هذا البعد خالياً تارةً ومملوءاً تارةً وهم أصحاب الخلاء.

However, the advocates of the extension are of two schools (*ʿalā maḏhabayn*), among which are those who deny that this extension remains unoccupied without something filling it, instead requiring that it is not left behind by what fills it at all, unless with something that subsequently fills it, as well as those who do not deny that, instead allowing that this extension is sometimes void and sometimes full – and these are the advocates of the void. (*al-Samāʿ al-ṭabīʿī* II.6, §11, 116.16–18)[236]

---

235 *al-Samāʿ al-ṭabīʿī* II.6, §4, 115.15f.

236 cf. *al-Naǧāt* II.2.10, 233.13–15 ≈ *al-Ḥikma al-ʿArūḍiyya* II.2.8, 133.22–24; *Dānešnāme-ye ʿAlāʾī* III.6, 14.11–15.10; *al-Ḥikma al-mašriqiyya* III.9, 26.7–9.

These passages are in many respects informative, and specifically and carefully single out for further critical inspection the very notion of space we have seen Philoponus developing in the preceding section.

First, Avicenna presents space and void, in accordance with Aristotle's description in the *Physics*, as "some extension between the extremities" (ἢ διάστημά τι τὸ μεταξὺ τῶν ἐσχάτων, *buʿd mā fī-mā bayna l-ġayāt*).[237] This correlates with the intention to discuss the place of body insofar as this place contains nothing else apart from that one body. Thus, the extension in question is spread out in between the limits of the body and is entirely equal to the body in terms of size in all three dimensions. If we are considering water in a vessel, then the inner surface of the vessel, which is in contact with the water's outer surface, is the limit of the water whose place, on this conception, is the extension permeating throughout the water, itself being limited by the inner surface of the vessel. Thus, Avicenna writes, "between the extremities of the vessel" (*bayna ġāyāt al-ināʾ*) is not only the water contained by the vessel but also some extensions (*abʿād*). The term *buʿd* (pl. *abʿād*) is a common translation for the Greek διάστημα and signifies an extension or an interval. Used in the plural, it often signifies the three dimensions of length, breadth, and depth. When Avicenna writes about this conception of place or space, he often uses either the plural *abʿād* ("the [three] extensions") or simply the singular *buʿd* as what seems to be an abstract noun in the sense of "the [three-dimensional] extension."

Moreover, Avicenna characterises these extensions as *mafṭūra* and *ṯābita*. The participle *mafṭūr* is unusual and, at first, it is also not clear what it means here in this context. In fact, Avicenna rarely uses the term – when he does, however, as here in the course of discussing space, it often qualifies the noun *buʿd*, which may suggest that it is a technical term that commonly accompanies that noun under a specific conception of it.[238] In his edition of Avicenna's *al-Samāʿ al-ṭabīʿī*, Saʿīd Zāyid writes in the above quoted passage from *al-Samāʿ al-ṭabīʿī* II.6, §4, 115.13, *maqṭūra* instead of *mafṭūra*, even though he surprisingly decided to retain *mafṭūr* in other similar instances later in the text. Jon McGinnis devotes a footnote in his translation to discussing the two alternatives.[239] He convincingly argues that *mafṭūra* should be accepted, because the twelfth-century Latin translation by Dominicus Gundisalvi (d. ~ 1190) speaks of *spatia infinita permanentia*. McGinnis suspects that *infinita* has been corrupted from an original *insita*. This argument is convincing, especially in consideration of the fact that *infinita*, when written in an abbreviated form, may closely resemble *insita* in Latin manuscripts. The ultimate reason that establishes that *mafṭūra* is beyond doubt the correct reading, however, emerges from Aristotle's *Physics*, for there we have seen Aristotle talking about "some extension which is natural and static" (τι διάστημα τὸ

---

237 *Phys.* IV.4, 211b7f.

238 cf. esp. Avicenna's use of the term in *al-Samāʿ al-ṭabīʿī* II.7, §§8–9, 122.10, 11, 123.1.

239 cf. fn. 5, 164.

πεφυκὸς καὶ μένον, *buʿdan mā mafṭūran lābiṯan*).[240] This phrase is close to the one found in Avicenna. Thus, *mafṭūra* is not only the correct reading, we now also know what it means: it describes the extension as something which just is or has being. It is not dependent on a body, in order to be, but naturally is and exists by itself as something over and above the bodies which may or may not occupy it. The participle *ṯābita* – which incidentally is palaeographically as well as semantically strikingly close to the Arabic Aristotle's *lābiṯa* – then describes these dimensions as unchanging, stable, and indiscriminate in themselves, thus, corresponding to the Greek Aristotle's μένον.[241]

Second, in the above passage from *al-Samāʿ al-ṭabīʿī* II.6, Avicenna explains how those who conceive of place as "the fixed extension between [a body's] limits" (*al-buʿd al-ṯābit bayna aṭrāfihī*) derived their notion in the first place.[242] They did so by abstraction and analysis, i.e., by mentally removing from a given object one aspect after another, in order to arrive at a simple and bare – or: "naked" (γυμνήν), as we read in Philoponus – notion of an underlying feature of that object. This process has been used, Avicenna tells us, in order to establish the notion of, for example, matter. It is certainly no mere coincidence that this was precisely the purpose of the abstraction argument in Aristotle's *Metaphysics* Z.3, which also served as the explicit model for Philoponus' own argument to derive the concept of space as an underlying feature of corporeal reality. Avicenna was, consequently, not only working from, and implicitly referring to

240 *Phys.* IV.4, 211b19f. Interestingly, a similar expression also appears in the *Kitāb al-Taʿrīfāt* of ʿAlī ibn Muḥammad al-Sayyid al-Šarīf al-Ǧurǧānī. There, al-Ǧurǧānī writes that "the void according to Plato is the natural dimension" (*al-ḫalāʾ huwa l-buʿd al-mafṭūr ʿinda Aflaṭūn*; 105.8). It is not entirely clear how this information reached al-Ǧurǧānī nor what it is supposed to refer to in Plato, for Plato is not known for having accepted the existence of void in the sense of empty space; cf. esp. *Tim.* 58a4–b5. A natural assumption would be to take al-Ǧurǧānī as referring to Plato's account of χώρα in the *Timaeus*. Of course, Plato's doctrine of χώρα in the *Timaeus* is enigmatic and controversial, and there is no consensus among interpreters on what it actually amounts to; cf. esp. Algra's discussion in *Concepts of Space in Greek Thought*, ch. 3. On one account, Plato identified χώρα with matter. The earliest evidence for this reading is Aristotle; cf. *Phys.* IV.2, 209b6–17. Another reading of Plato's *Timaeus*, however, takes χώρα to be space or even empty space. If that is right, then we can see how Plato could be said to have claimed space to be a dimension that naturally exists as independent from the bodies which occur in it and which may occupy parts of it. What is interesting, here, is that the Arabic tradition – at least as exemplified by al-Ǧurǧānī – apparently categorised Plato as someone who defended the view that space is an independently existing three-dimensionally extended magnitude which in itself is empty and undifferentiated, i.e., an extension which underlies the spatially finite world, in which bodies come-to-be, and which bodies can occupy, instead of taking heed of Aristotle's remark that for Plato, place was actually matter. If the expression which Avicenna uses here for place as an underlying three-dimensional extension is a technical term of Platonic provenance, then it would seem that for Avicenna, the conception of place as space or void is ultimately derived from a Platonic perspective of the natural world – a perspective such as the one adopted in Philoponus' corollary on place; cf. also Simplicius, *In Phys.*, 537.19–22. Finally, this would also mean that for Avicenna, too, Plato was not primarily someone who identified space with matter, as Aristotle's accusation has it.

241 q.v. Avicenna's use of *ṯābit* and *qārr* in his account of time below, 440.

242 *al-Samāʿ al-ṭabīʿī* II.6, §5, 116.6f.

Philoponus' commentary on the *Physics*, while he was preparing his defence of the Aristotelian account of *place*, as we have seen; Avicenna presently also introduces the concept of the three-dimensional and independent *space* in a manner that matches the strategy that is characteristic of Philoponus.

This impression is confirmed by the actual argument presented by Avicenna: the imagination is said to remove one aspect after another from an envisaged object until that which remains in the imagination (*allaḏī yabqā baʿda rafʿ … fī l-wahm*) is no more than a simple thing that exists in itself (*al-basīṭ al-mawǧūd fī nafsihī*). Thus, if we envisage a vessel that contains some water, and if we imagine only the removal of the water without there occurring any replacement of the water by air – and without anything else that might happen were we to perform the current operation not in our imagination but in concrete reality – then the notion we are able to derive from this removal is that of a fixed extension existing between the limits of the vessel (*al-buʿd al-ṯābit bayna aṭrāfihī*) which usually, normally, and in reality always exists as occupied by bodies.

On the whole, the thought experiment which Avicenna presents here on behalf of the proponents of place as space is analogous to the one attributed to Galen, criticised by Themistius, and defended and reformulated by Philoponus, in which the notion of space is established by removing "in thought" (κατ' ἐπίνοιαν) or imaginatively (*wahman*) everything within certain boundaries (whether these are a jar as in Galen, Themistius, and Avicenna or the outermost heavenly sphere as in Philoponus) under the condition that these boundaries do not collapse despite the absence of what they hitherto contained and that nothing else, be that air or any other corporeal substitute, enters the now vacant space.

Finally, Avicenna explains that those who believe that place is a naturally existing and static three-dimensional extension fall into two camps: those who actually allow such extension to be devoid of any body, thus affirming the actual existence of empty space, i.e., void, and those who, while affirming its existence as a fundamental feature of reality, do not allow space to be empty.

The former position is characteristically atomistic. According to the Greek atomists and the Baṣrī branch of Muʿtazilism, bodies are composed of atoms which exist in empty space.[243] Between one atom (or atomic compound) and another may be a gap that is occupied by nothing at all. The arguments presented in favour of their position often include those which we already know from Aristotle's *Physics* about the compression and expansion of bodies; about cups that, although completely filled with ashes, can still absorb water without overflowing; about casks of wine that cannot only contain the wine but also additionally the wineskins; about the impossibility for natural bodies to absorb nutrition and to grow were there no void spaces; and, finally, about the

243 The Muʿtazilites from Baṣra affirmed the existence of void spaces within or between atomic compounds against their brothers from Baġdād; cf. Dhanani, *The Physical Theory of Kalām*, 73.

impossibility to move in an absolute plenum.[244] The second position, in turn, is clearly no other than the one presented, developed, and advocated, with his usual aplomb, by Philoponus.

What we see here is that Avicenna follows Aristotle's strategy in expanding the scope of his discussion. Both first mention the notion of space as something which is supposed to exist between the extremities and limits of a single body and which, thus, serves as a candidate of that body's place. This conception is called a διάστημα πεφυκός or *buʿd mafṭūr*. The examination of this notion, however, leads to a discussion of the void conceived as a spatial concept underlying not only that single body but the whole universe, i.e., the entirety of bodies, and no longer necessarily confined to whatever is between any limits at all. Avicenna discusses the notion of a *buʿd mafṭūr* in detail in *al-Samāʿ al-ṭabīʿī* II.7. Once it has been introduced as a concept of the three-dimensional space of one body, the notion is not dropped before Avicenna concludes the chapter with the words that "this is what we say in refutation of the existence of this natural extension" (*fī ibṭāl wuǧūd hāḏā l-buʿd al-mafṭūr*).[245] In the following chapter II.8, then, Avicenna immediately embarks on a long discussion and refutation of the void (*al-ḫalāʾ*), being the three-dimensional space supposedly containing all bodies. While presenting new arguments, he also from time to time refers back to the arguments he used to refute the *buʿd mafṭūr*. After that, he returns with chapter II.9 to his discussion of place and the verification (*taḥqīq*) of its essence (*māhiyya*).

From this, it is altogether evident that for Avicenna, the analysis of the void is an indispensable part of the discussion of place, as the void just is the greater context of any analysis of place, if conceived as an extension. In fact, the void considered as a *buʿd mafṭūr* is – and since Aristotle had been – one of the prominent candidates for place. Moreover, it is the very candidate which has gained support and momentum during the preceding one-and-a-half millennia of philosophical history and, in particular, in the sixth century with Philoponus.

This, then, is the reason Avicenna clearly departs from the structure of Aristotle's *Physics*, as he integrates his full discussion on the void into his general discussion of place.[246] It is only after the list of all six available candidates for the essence of place has been set up *and* all five false candidates have been refuted – i.e., after the void has been

---

244 cf. *Phys*. IV.6, 213b2–22; *al-Samāʿ al-ṭabīʿī* II.6, §§12–15, 117.8–118.2; *al-Ḥikma al-mašriqiyya* III.10, 30.19–31.12.

245 *al-Samāʿ al-ṭabīʿī* II.7, §9, 123.1.

246 Although the term *ḫalāʾ* dominates the discussion of void in *al-Samāʿ al-ṭabīʿī* II.8, we also occasionally come across the terms *buʿd* and *makān*, both of which are apparently used in a similar, if not synonymous, sense. This indicates, again, that for Avicenna the greater part of chapter II.7 and the entire chapter II.8 works with one and the same concept, approached and refuted from different angles and perspectives. Moreover, it mirrors Philoponus terminology, who likewise uses the terms for "space" (χώρα), "place" (τόπος), "void" (τό κενόν), and "extension" (διάστημα) interchangeably, as has already been noted; q.v. above, 380.

shown to be non-existent, and matter and form as well as two kinds of surfaces have been shown to be implausible – that Avicenna begins to present the correct account of place and to develop the notion of a surface, as has been shown above, in order both to establish his own definition and to reaffirm Aristotle's. All this must be understood as one great investigation, culminating in the sophisticated account of *al-Samāʿ al-ṭabīʿī* II.9, containing the final word on place.

Moreover, this indicates that the discussion of space and void is not only indispensable for Avicenna's discussion of place but that it is at the very heart of it – and this impression holds true not only for his *al-Samāʿ al-ṭabīʿī* but also for his other major works. If we look into the chapter on place in *al-Naǧāt* (chapter II.2.10, 233.5–244.10), which is almost identical to the extant parts of the discussion of place in *al-Ḥikma al-ʿArūḍiyya* (chapter II.2.8, 133.15–137.16), we see that Avicenna briefly introduces the subject, and rejects matter and form as viable candidates. He then engages in an extensive rejection of the void culminating in the claim that "the void is absolutely non-existent (*al-ḫalāʾ ġayr mawǧūd aṣlan*) and is just as its name," i.e., void.[247] The case is similar in *al-Ḥikma al-mašriqiyya*, which rarely mentions matter and form as candidates for place, and instead focusses on the idea of space as the main competitor to the correct view of place as the surface of the containing body in contact with the contained body.[248] The concept of void is, then, discussed and rejected in a subsequent chapter that is twice as long as the chapter on place. In his *al-Hidāya*, then, Avicenna does not even mention matter and form as potential candidates for place, and begins his rebuttal of space and void immediately after one single line of introduction. The discussion ends, after three pages, again with one single line stating that "therefore, place is the inner surface of what contains which is in contact with what is contained."[249] The same situation is found in the *Dānešnāme-ye ʿAlāʾī*, in which the discussion of place spans six chapters: a brief introductory chapter and a brief conclusion – with four long chapters on the void in between.[250] Avicenna's *ʿUyūn al-ḥikma* is even more striking in this regard, for it dispenses with an inquiry into the concept of place altogether and *only* offers a comprehensive refutation of void which is followed by a rejection of atomism.[251] This chapter, then, is concluded with one line stating that "the place of the body is not a dimension in which it is, as you know, but is the surface of something which, being in contact with it [sc. the body], contains it, and so it [sc. the body] is in it."[252]

247 *al-Naǧāt* II.2.10, 243.12f.; cf. *Physics* IV.8, 216a26f.

248 cf. *al-Ḥikma al-mašriqiyya* III.9, 26.3–11. In fact, in light of the way in which Avicenna develops his argumentation there, it is quite unexpected that he suddenly mentions matter and form at all; cf. *al-Ḥikma al-mašriqiyya* III.9, 26.14, 20f.

249 *al-Hidāya*, II.1, 151.6f., 155.3.

250 cf. *Dānešnāme-ye ʿAlāʾī* III.6–11, 13.11–25.9.

251 cf. *ʿUyūn al-ḥikma* II.6, 23.2–24.15; II.7, 24.17–26.5.

252 cf. *ʿUyūn al-ḥikma* II.7, 26.4f.

Apparently the reason for all this is that Avicenna's primary interest was in refuting the existence of the void, for once that is accomplished, place can no longer be a three-dimensional extension that subsists by itself, because any such extension would be essentially identical with the void, and the void has been shown to be non-existent. With this, the decision about place has been made, as there is only one real alternative left, viz., place as the inner surface of the surrounding body.

From a historical perspective, it needs to be noted that for Aristotle, the main challenge in discussing place and void had been to argue against the doctrines of the early Greek atomists, in particular those put forward by Democritus and Leucippus, and that subsequently his results had to compete with the upcoming current of Epicureanism. By contrast, Avicenna, in addition to having been aware of the Ancient debate, had to face not only the atomism propagated by the Baṣrī branch of Muʿtazilism and the emerging school of the Ašʿarites, both of whom allowed for actual void spaces within atomic compositions.[253] He may also have had to deal with certain currents among contemporaneous scientists, such as al-Ḥasan ibn al-Ḥasan ibn al-Hayṯam (d. after 430/1040), who rigorously analysed the notion of place just to conclude that a surface does not deserve to be called "place," and, finally, to fend off Philoponus' attacks on Aristotelian physics.[254] In addition, we find the Baġdādī Muʿtazilites, who considered place to be a surface containing the body in place and, though subscribing to atomism, denied the existence of void spaces, objecting to their Baṣrī brothers with Peripatetic arguments.[255] Furthermore, there is also the doctrine of absolute place, i.e., space, commonly associated with the name of Abū Bakr Muḥammad ibn Zakariyāʾ al-Rāzī (d. 313/925). It is not entirely clear where Abū Bakr al-Rāzī, an atomist himself, is to be located within this debate and whether he could be said to have been an ally to any of the other groups. From the known fragments about his doctrine of place, it is also not clear whether he would allow absolute space to exist without body occupying it. Yet, the examples he provides at least seem to entertain the possibility that it could.[256] Having said this, Philoponus' examples also somehow rely on the idea that void could exist in actuality, even though it never does. There is no reason for why Abū Bakr al-Rāzī would not have adhered to a similar view. While it is certain that Philoponus was the

---

253 cf. Dhanani, *The Physical Theory of Kalām*, 67, 73. Dhanani translates from the *Awāʾil al-Maqālāt* by al-Šayḫ al-Mufīd, in which the position of the Baṣrī Muʿtazilites about the existence of empty spaces is also attributed to further groups, such as the Materialists, the Determinsts, and the Anthropomorphists (*al-ḥašwiyya wa-l-ahl al-ğabar wa-l-tašbīh*).

254 For al-Ḥasan ibn al-Hayṯam, cf. his *Risāla fī l-makān*, esp. 5.17–21, which has been edited twice, once as part of his *Mağmūʿ al-rasāʾil* and once critically by R. Rashed in his *Les mathématiques infinitésimales*, vol. 4; cf. also El-Bizri, "In Defence of the Sovereignty of Philosophy"; R. Rashed, "Le concept de lieu."

255 cf. also Daiber, "Fārābīs Abhandlung über das Vakuum," 37f.

256 cf. Abū Bakr al-Rāzī, *al-Qawl fī l-qudamāʾ al-ḫamsa*, 199.1–3; cf. also Pines' analysis of his position and the criticism of it by Avicenna's contemporary Nāṣer-e Ḫosrow in *Studies in Islamic Atomism*, 54–57, appx. B; cf. also Pines, "Etudes sur Aḥwad al-Zamān Abu'l-Barakāt al-Baghdādī," fn. 83, 20; Adamson, "From al-Rāzī to al-Rāzī."

major opponent envisaged in Avicenna's rejection of space, of void, and of place as an extension, it is unclear whether or not Avicenna was also arguing specifically against Abū Bakr al-Rāzī's doctrine.[257]

Thus, with regard to place, space, and void, there are four different parties involved: (i) the Muʿtazilites from Baṣra together with the Ašʿarites and the Greek atomists (and perhaps Abū Bakr al-Rāzī); (ii) the Muʿtazilites from Baġdād; (iii) figures such as Philoponus and al-Ḥasan ibn al-Hayṯam (and perhaps Abū Bakr al-Rāzī); and (iv) Aristotle and his followers, in particular Themistius, al-Kindī, and al-Fārābī, as well as Avicenna.

This is roughly the intellectual climate at the time of Avicenna. There is a richness of possible positions as well as a variety of both arguments for and objections against them, on which Avicenna can draw and with which he is confronted. Above, we have already seen him engaged with Baṣrī Muʿtazilites and their doctrine of empty space in the *Risāla li-baʿḍ al-mutakallimīn ilā l-Šayḫ fa-ağābahum*.[258] There he explicitly named ʿAbd al-Ğabbār as well as Hesiod, Pythagoras, Democritus, and Leucippus as proponents of various views that involve the existence of empty space.[259] In his more comprehensive works of philosophy, however, Avicenna is reluctant to provide any names, even though his discussion in *al-Samāʿ al-ṭabīʿī* seems to be directed at all varieties of accepting the existence of void spaces within the universe.[260] Still, it is by all means Philoponus who looms largest in Avicenna's refutation of an independently existing extension as becomes evident when Avicenna explicitly selects his account as the primary target of his critique in *al-Samāʿ al-ṭabīʿī* II.7:

وأمّا القائلون بأنّ المكان هو البعد الثابت بين أطراف الحاوي فنخصّ الذين يُحيلون منهم خلو هذا البعد عن المتمكّن.

As for those who claim that place is the fixed extension between the limits of what contains, we shall single out those of them who deny [that] this extension [could] be without that which is in place. (*al-Samāʿ al-ṭabīʿī* II.7, §3, 119.9f., tr. by McGinnis, modified)[261]

---

257 On the whole, we seem to lack the textual basis for analysing the relation between Avicenna and Abū Bakr al-Rāzī in this regard more fully.

258 q.v. above, 327f.

259 cf. Avicenna, *Risāla li-baʿḍ al-mutakallimīn ilā l-Šayḫ fa-ağābahum*, 156.20; 157.7, 10, 11; Ülken, the editor of the treatise, failed to recognise Leucippus and suggested Lucretius instead. Hesiod is certainly mentioned due to Aristotle's remark at *Physics* IV.1, 208b29–33.

260 That is to say, Avicenna does not seem to discuss the claim, shared by the Pythagoreans and the Stoics, that there is void outside the heavens, presumably, because it is disproven by so many other aspects of his natural philosophy; cf. esp. *al-Samāʿ al-ṭabīʿī* III.8, §4, 214.3–10; cf. also McGinnis, "Avoiding the Void," 83–87. The issue is mentioned, however, in his *al-Samāʾ wa-l-ʿālam*, for example, in the course of denying that the world is actually egg-shaped or lenticular, stating that if that were true, the positional motion of the outermost sphere would have to occur in an existing void; cf. *al-Samāʾ wa-l-ʿālam* 3, 21.11–15.

261 cf. *al-Ḥikma al-mašriqiyya* III.10, 27.18f.; cf. also Janssens, "Ibn Sīnā," 86. That Philoponus is Avicenna's main target is also clear from the fact that Avicenna argues vehemently against the so-called "force of the void," which is essential (even if not exclusive) to Philoponus theory. Others, such as the Baġdādī Muʿtazilites sought to defend their conceptions of the world as entirely filled with bodies that

Clearly, though, Avicenna was not the first within the Arabic tradition to oppose the late ancient criticism against Aristotle that was nowhere as poignantly expressed as in Philoponus' corollaries on place and void. We have already seen Ibn ʿAdī at least claiming that Aristotle's position is correct, even though he apparently failed to show how one could defend Aristotle's account against the known objections. We have also seen that al-Kindī put forth the Aristotelian definition as the true understanding of place. More influential on Avicenna, though, was arguably al-Fārābī. Although most of al-Fārābī's works on physics are not known to be extant, we have seen, through the testimony of Ibn Bāǧǧa and Averroes, how he solved the issue about the place and the motion of the outermost sphere. Even though his solution was not adopted by Avicenna, it is clear that it shaped his understanding of the notion of surface and contributed to Avicenna's enlarged list of candidates. Additionally, there is one work in which al-Fārābī firmly argues against the notion of void space, disproving the experiments commonly adduced for establishing both its actual existence and its power or force, viz., his *Maqāla fī l-ḫalāʾ*. This treatise is interesting in its own regard and we may assume that either it or similar discussions in al-Fārābī's lost works on natural philosophy, including his commentary on Aristotle's *Physics*, have influenced Avicenna's own position considerably, thus aiding his general cause of defending Aristotle. Yet, the influence of this particular treatise on Avicenna remains limited. For one thing, the treatise is rather short and has a narrow focus, as its exclusive aim is in providing an explanation of the mechanism behind experiments with so-called clepsydrae that does not rely on the existence of the void. That is to say, al-Fārābī's treatise as such constitutes neither a discussion of place nor a refutation of space as place nor really a refutation of the existence of void. Instead, it envisages an experiment that was commonly discussed in the Arabic tradition by philosophers and theologians alike, and had already been discussed by scientists and intellectuals for many centuries before.[262] This experiment supposedly shows that the existence of the void needs to be assumed if the observed phenomenon is to be explained. Against this, al-Fārābī argues that the experiment can be accounted for even without assuming the existence of the void. As we shall see, in *al-Samāʿ al-ṭabīʿī*, Avicenna basically offers the same explanation as al-Fārābī, but he systematically combines it with his general account of place and his apparent concern with defending the notion of surface. It, thus, seems that Peripatetics between the fourth/tenth and fifth/eleventh century such as al-Fārābī and Avicenna have found a new way to respond to the powerful idea of the "force of

---

surround and contain one another, and of place as a two-dimensional surface surrounding the body in place by using precisely those phenomena which Philoponus ascribed to the "force of the void" against their colleagues from Baṣrā, who like Philoponus advocated the existence of space but unlike him allowed for genuinely void spaces, thus denying the "force of the void"; q.v. also below 406ff.

262 For the inner-Muʿtazilī debate between Baṣrī and Baġdādī mutakallimūn, cf. Dhanani, *The Physical Theory of Kalām*, 74, 81; for a brief exposition of their Greek precursors, cf. Daiber, "Fārābīs Abhandlung über das Vakuum."

the void" which was so vehemently defended by Philoponus.[263] Moreover, since their response essentially relies on Aristotelian hylomorphism, it could not be appropriated by the Muʿtazilī atomists from Baṣra in their own denial of the arguments about the "force of the void" (or nature's abhorrence of void) against their brothers from Baġdād. So, within the larger context of the great battle between hylomorphism and atomism, the argument devised by al-Fārābī and Avicenna may additionally have served a further purpose, viz., the general defence and effective rehabilitation of Aristotelian natural philosophy as an explanatory model even for the phenomena of space and place within the corporeal reality of nature – a project which Avicenna definitely pursued in his elaborations on place, as we have already seen.

Having said this, Avicenna's overall strategy in refuting the final candidate for the essence of place, viz., the extension which subsists naturally as an independent and fundamental feature of reality, is the same as Aristotle's: the void is void.[264] That is to say, for Avicenna, it is "absolutely nothing" (*lā šayʾa al-battata*).[265] This also applies to everything that is essentially void but actually always filled with body, as Philoponus argued. Thus, any extension we might like to conceive as permeating corporeal objects, any void these objects might be thought to occupy, and any space that might be said to be that which receives all corporeal reality is superfluous, non-explanatory, vain, void, and uncalled for. What is more, Avicenna will also add that it is – for all these reasons – nothing other than non-existent. Since Avicenna's argument to that conclusion has already been analysed with great care by McGinnis, I shall keep my own presentation at a minimum and focus more on the historical and systematic background, instead of the details of the argument as such.[266] Afterwards, I shall turn my attention to the just-mentioned experiment and to Avicenna's explanation of it, which seeks to demonstrate not that the void is non-existent but that it is simply not required. As will be seen, Avicenna not only successfully rebuts Philoponus' notion of the "force of the void," he also develops al-Fārābī's earlier solution by emphasising once more the hitherto neglected advantages of the Aristotelian notion of place as a surface.

Metaphysical Arguments against the Void

Avicenna demonstrates the non-existence of space and void as an extension underlying all corporeal reality through a vehement attack on the above-mentioned abstraction

263 I would, therefore, like to counter Daiber's claim that al-Fārābī's contribution was not original or innovative ("Fārābīs Abhandlung über das Vakuum," 43: "Fārābīs Beitrag ist somit nicht originell"); q.v. below, 414ff.

264 cf. *Phys.* IV.8, 216a26f.

265 q.v. fn. 288 below, 401.

266 For these details, cf. McGinnis, "A Penetrating Question," esp. 57–69; cf. also the related argument discussed in McGinnis, "Logic and Science."

argument, which Philoponus developed on the basis of Themistius' criticism of an argument devised by Galen in response to the famous thought experiment carried out by Aristotle himself in *Metaphysics* Z.3. The central question posed in Avicenna's critique is whether or not there really is an independent extension in addition, i.e., over and above, the corporeal extension of the body in place.

This same question was raised already by Aristotle in *Physics* IV.8.[267] Aristotle answered in the negative, stating that the assumption of a separate extension in addition to the body's extension is unnecessary and paves the way for allowing any number of extensions to coincide, which he considered absurd. Themistius added that two extensions simply cannot coincide, for otherwise two bodies could coincide as well, which, as even Philoponus agreed, is impossible. Philoponus, in turn, countered both claims by emphasising that there is nothing impossible in a material, corporeal extension penetrating an immaterial, incorporeal extension. For him, what precludes two bodies from penetrating each other is not the fact that both are extended in three dimensions but the fact that bodies consist of matter. Yet, since space or void is immaterial, there is nothing that keeps a body from coinciding with the void and from taking on a part of the void as its place, so that wherever a body is located there are two extensions, one belonging to the body and one belonging to its place which is considered to be a part of the void containing all corporeal reality.

There are two aspects that need to be recognised in Philoponus' response. The first is that Philoponus maintains that there are, indeed, two different extensions existing, of which he identifies one as the material extension belonging to body and the other as the immaterial extension belonging to space. The second point is that he claims that what keeps two extensions from interpenetrating is their materiality, such that two bodies cannot coincide, whereas body body and space can.

In response to the first aspect, Avicenna states the following:

وقد علم أنّ الأمور المتّفقة في الطباع التي لا تتنوّع بفصول في جوهرها لا تتكثّر في هوياتها، إنّما تتكثّر بتكثّر الموادّ التي تحملها. وإذا كانت المادّة لها واحدة لم تتكثّر البتّة فلا يكون بعدان.

It has been known that things agreeing in nature which are not divided into species by differences in their substance are not multiple in their beings; they are multiple only through the multiplicity of the matters to which they apply. If the matter for them is one, they are not multiple in any way, and so there are not two intervals. (*al-Samāʿ al-ṭabīʿī* II.7, §8, 122.13–15)[268]

As McGinnis has noted, Avicenna is employing here a certain doctrinal component that, though not formulated by Aristotle himself, had become commonplace among Peripatetics, viz., that the principle of individuation and of the multiplicity of things

---

267 q.v. above, 371ff.

268 cf. *al-Ḥikma al-mašriqiyya* III.10, 28.17–19.

that are identical in species is matter.[269] If two or more things share in one and the same formal account, they are distinguished in their concrete existences only through the fact that the same form and the same accidents inhere in, or apply to, differently located chunks of matter. Since three-dimensional extension of the body and the supposedly corresponding three-dimensional extension are with regard to its formal account equal, they require different matters, in order to be individuated and to be distinguishable from one another. Philoponus, however, maintained that one of the two extensions in question precisely lacks matter. It, thus, also lacks the only thing which could have individuated it and distinguished it from the extension that belongs to the body.

For Avicenna, then, the case is clear: there is, and can be, only one extension, viz., the one inhering in matter – and this is the corporeal extension of the body. Even if there were a second extension over and above the first, it could not be identified due to its own supposed immaterial nature, so that, again, we only get one extension, viz., the one inhering in matter – and this is the corporeal extension of the body.

Rebutting the second aspect of Philoponus' reasoning, viz., that it is actually matter which keeps two extensions from interpenetrating and not their extensionality, is apparently an exercise dear to Avicenna's heart, for we find numerous passages throughout his major works in which he elaborates on this point.[270] In all these passages, Avicenna sets out to determine what it is that keeps two bodies from interpenetrating. In *al-Naǧāt* and *al-Ḥikma al-ʿArūḍiyya*, for example, he distinguishes three options: the interpenetration of two bodies is prevented either because of (a) the materiality of the two bodies, (b) the fact that each body is a combination of matter and extension, or (c) their extensionality as such, i.e., irrespective of their materiality.[271] This tripartition is reminiscent of a marginal gloss found in Ms. Leiden or. 583 on Aristotle's Arabic *Physics*. That gloss is attributed to Ibn al-Samḥ and likewise defends Aristotle's argument from chapter IV.8 about the absurdities involved in coinciding extensions by analysing what it is that effectively prevents the interpenetration of bodies. As Ibn al-Samḥ writes, the impossibility of interpenetration is not due to matter (*li-mādda*) nor is it due to the combination of matter and the extensions (*li-maǧmūl al-mādda wa-l-abʿād*); instead, it is due to the extension itself (*li-buʿd*).[272] On the whole, the argument in *al-Naǧāt* and *al-Ḥikma al-ʿArūḍiyya* is very similar to the brief remark in Ibn al-Samḥ's gloss.

---

269 As an early Peripatetic source, McGinnis refers to Alexander's *Maqāla fī l-qawl fī mabādiʾ al-kull*, §86, 86.16–88.5 (ed. Genequand). For further studies on matter as the principle of individuation in Avicenna, cf. Bäck, "The Islamic Background"; Pickavé, "On the Latin Reception of Avicenna's Theory of Individuation"; Black, "Avicenna on Individuation, Self-Awareness, and God's Knowledge of Particulars."

270 cf. *al-Samāʿ al-ṭabīʿī* II.7, §§4–7, 120.8–122.9; cf. *al-Naǧāt* II.2.10, 237.14–241.4 ≈ *al-Ḥikma al-ʿArūḍiyya* II.2.8, 135.18–137.4; *ʿUyūn al-ḥikma* II.11, 23.3–12; *Dānešnāme-ye ʿAlāʾī* III.7, 16.11–18.10; *al-Hidāya*, II.1, 152.1–9; *al-Ḥikma al-mašriqiyya* III.10, 28.9–11; *al-Išārāt wa-l-tanbīhāt* II.1.31, 104.11–14.

271 cf. *al-Naǧāt* II.2.10, 238.3–5 ≈ *al-Ḥikma al-ʿArūḍiyya* II.2.8, 135.22–24.

272 Ibn al-Samḥ's comments in Aristotle, *al-Ṭabīʿa*, 383.5–19; cf. Lettinck, *Aristotle's* Physics *and its Reception in the Arabic World*, 331f.

In addition, Avicenna is able to link his remarks about the interpenetration of bodies systematically with his own conception of matter, which I discussed earlier.[273] Avicenna often argues that matter as such is not located, i.e., it is not distinguished with regard to its position (*al-waḍʿ*) and location (*al-ḥayyiz*).[274] It only becomes accidentally distinguished by taking on a form and receiving a concrete set of dimensions. In fact, as has already been stressed, all that matter does is be receptive of form. In itself, it is nothing concrete and fully indeterminate, but it can take on a form, such as a corporeal form, i.e., a three-dimensional extensionality, as well as accidents, such as those in the category of quantity, i.e., a concrete set of dimensions.[275] With regard to place, void, and the impossibility of the interpenetration of bodies, this means that something that is as passive, indeterminate, and receptive as matter cannot *by itself* prevent the interpenetration of bodies, because matter as such is not even extended. Thus, Avicenna writes:

> لكنّ جملة الجسم تمانع مداخلة جسم آخر فهو بسبب أنّ في أجزائه ما يمنع ذلك فإنّه ليس كلّ جزء منه غير مانع لذلك. إذ ليست الهيولى سبباً يمنع ذلك ولا سبب فعل خاصّ وانفعال خاصّ فبقى أن تكون طبيعة البعد لا تحتمل التداخل.
>
> Rather, the whole body (*ǧumlat al-ǧism*) opposes the interpenetration of another body, and so[276] it is due to the fact that in its parts is something which prevents this, for[277] not every part of it does not prevent this. Since the material is not a cause which prevents that (*iḏ laysat al-hayūlā sababan yamnaʿu ḏālika*), neither as a cause for a specific [case of] acting nor for a specific [case of] being acted upon, it remains that it is the nature of the dimension that does not suffer interpenetration. (*al-Samāʿ al-ṭabīʿī* II.7, §7, 122.6–8)

Accordingly, if matter alone is not the cause that prevents two bodies from coinciding, and if it must be something that pertains to the bodies, then the cause preventing one body from moving into another must be the fact that bodies as such are extended – due to the corporeal form, on a universal level, and their individual quantitative accidents, on a particular level. From all this, it emerges that extensionality as such, i.e., the corporeal form as it inheres in matter, is not only the reason for why bodies are extended objects at all, as we have learned in the first book of *al-Samāʿ al-ṭabīʿī*; it is also here, in the second book, the reason for why two bodies cannot interpenetrate. If, then, according to Philoponus, the void is a pure extension, then it should be impossible for void to coincide with the extension of a body just as it is for any two extensions, for

273 q.v. above, 111ff.; cf. also McGinnis, "A Penetrating Question," 59–63.

274 cf. *al-Naǧāt* II.2.10, 239.6f. ≈ *al-Ḥikma al-ʿArūḍiyya* II.2.8, 136.14f.; *al-Išārāt wa-l-tanbīhāt* II.1.14, 97.6–10.

275 q.v. above, 122ff.

276 Reading *fa-huwa bi-sabab* with Mss. Leiden or. 4 and or. 84 as well as Zāyid for *bi-sabab* in McGinnis and as suggested by Āl Yāsīn.

277 Reading *fa-innahū* with Ms. Leiden or. 84 as well as Zāyid for *wa-annahū* in Ms. Leiden or. 4 as well as McGinnis and Āl Yāsīn.

example, two bodies. What has become apparent now is that Avicenna followed, and defended, the argument that we have seen above being put forth by Themistius.[278]

Apart from the fact, then, that Avicenna would argue that there are no immaterial extensions, even if there were, it would not matter whether or not one of the two extensions is immaterial, as Philoponus claimed, for materiality is not the reason interpenetration is impossible, as materiality as such is not a cause for anything. Consequently, it is absolutely impossible for void to exist over and above the bodies, because a void conceived as being essentially extended cannot coincide with, or permeate through, an essentially extended body. Further, if the void, as Philoponus argued, only exists together with body, i.e., if the void is not able to exist unoccupied by itself and is always filled with body, then the void, considered as an extension between the limits of a body, does not exist.

On the whole, this means that Philoponus' entire strategy of drawing a distinction between material and immaterial extensions, which may have seemed to be a congenial move at first glance, is revealed to be dissatisfying on two counts: neither is it possible to identify that immaterial extension as different from that belonging to the body nor is it true that materiality is what keeps bodies from interpenetrating.

This result brings us to Avicenna's criticism of the abstraction argument itself. Like his predecessors in both the Arabic and Greek philosophical traditions, Avicenna emphasises that the apparently well-known abstraction argument relies on the activity of the imagination (*tawahhum*). However, he adds a novel twist to the criticism of his predecessors by reinterpreting the value of imaginative abstraction processes and thought experiments in general.

Themistius, for example, charged Galen with "fabricating" (πλάττεις) for himself the existence of a separate extension without providing independent proof for its existence.[279] In the Arabic tradition preceding Avicenna, we find al-Kindī and the Iḫwān al-Ṣafā', both of whom accepted Aristotle's definition of place, argue against the existence of the void along the same lines.[280] In the epistles of the Iḫwān al-Ṣafā', now, we find a particularly fitting discussion:

> واعلم أنّ الذين قولوا إنّ المكان هو الفضاء إنّما نظروا إلى صورة الجسم. ثمّ انتزعوا من الهيولى بالقوّة الفكرية وصوّروها في نفوسهم وسمّوها الفضاء وإذا نظروا إليها وهي في الهيولى سمّوها المكان. وهذا يدلّ على قلّة معرفتهم أيضاً بجوهر النفس وكيفية معارفها.
>
> Know that those who have said that place (*al-makān*) is space (*al-faḍā'*) only investigated the form of body. Then, they removed it from the matter through the cogitative power, represented it

278 q.v. above, 373f.; cf. also the discussion in al-Fārābī's *Maqāla fī l-ḫalā'*, esp. 5.4–6.8, 8.14–9.10 (referring to pages and lines of the edited text). There, al-Fārābī likewise exploits the assumption that whatever is three-dimensional is also a body, so that the idea of space as permeating the corporeal extension of body would result in the existence of two bodies at the same place.

279 Themistius, *In Phys.*, 114.7–21.

280 For al-Kindī, cf. his al-Kindī, *Kitāb fī l-falsafa al-ūlā*, 21.13–23 (ed. R. Rashed/Jolivet).

> in their souls, and called it "space," whereas, when they investigated it while it is in the matter, they called it "place." This also shows the paucity of their comprehension of the soul's substance (*qillat ma'rifatihim ... bi-ğawhar al-nafs*) and of the mode of its acts of comprehension. (*Rasā'il Iḫwān al-Ṣafā'* XV.11, 28.7–11, tr. by Baffioni, modified)

Here, too, we find the same reference to an abstractive process through which one is allegedly able to derive the three-dimensional notion of space and place. This process, however, is immediately criticised, as it merely indicates that those who reason along these lines have a deficient grasp of the soul and its operations, and about what it can and cannot accomplish. Later in their work, in the context of arguing against the existence of a void inside or outside the universe, the Iḫwān al-Ṣafā' supply exactly that information about the soul and its powers which their opponents lacked:

> واعلم بأنّ الوهم قوّة من قوى النفس وهي تتخيّل ما له حقيقة وما لا حقيقة له. فلا ينبغي أن تحكم على متخيّلاتها أنّها حقّ أو باطل إلّا بعد ما شهد لها إحدى القوى الحساسة أو يقوم عليها برهان ضروري أو يقضي بها العقل.
>
> Know that the imagination (*al-wahm*) is one of the powers of the soul and it is that which imagines (*tataḫayyalu*) [both] what has reality and what does not have reality. Thus, it is required that you judge about its imaginations whether they are true or false only after one of the faculties of sensation has testified for them or necessary demonstration has established them or intellect has determined them. (*Rasā'il Iḫwān al-Ṣafā'* XVI.6, 82.9–83.4, tr. by Baffioni, modified)

Apparently, then, Avicenna was not the first to have blamed the view that there exists a separate extension over and above the bodies on a misconception of the imagination. Both Themistius and the Iḫwān al-Ṣafā' marked in identical contexts the gap between imagining something to exist and demonstrating that it really does exist. The problem, though, is that Philoponus was well aware of that criticism. Already at the beginning of his commentary on the discussion of the void in Aristotle's *Physics* IV.6, Philoponus wrote the following:

> Κἂν γὰρ μὴ ὑπάρχῃ τὸ κενὸν μηδὲ ἔχῃ τινὰ φύσιν ἐν τοῖς οὖσιν, ἀλλ' οὖν ἐπειδὴ ὅλως περιφαντάζεται αὐτὸ ἡ διάνοια, δεῖ εἰπεῖν τί ποτε εἶναι αὐτὸ ὑπονοοῦσιν οἱ τῶν ὄντων αὐτὸ εἶναι λέγοντες, καὶ τί αὐτῷ ὑπάρχειν ἢ μή, οἷον ὅτι δοκεῖ διάστημα εἶναι καὶ τόπος ἐστερημένος σώματος καὶ οἷον ἀγγεῖον μηδὲν ἔχον. καὶ γὰρ περὶ τραγελάφου, καίπερ οὐκ ὄντος ἐν ὑποστάσει, ὅμως ζητήσειέ τις, τί ποθ' ἡ φαντασία περὶ αὐτοῦ ὑπονοεῖ.
>
> For even if the void does not exist and does not have any nature among things that are, yet since the mind has very imaginative ideas about it, one ought to say whatever it is that those who say that it is among the things that are suppose that it is, and what characteristics it has or does not, such as that it appears to be an extension and a place devoid of body and like a vessel with nothing in it. For someone could also ask about a goatstag, although it does not exist in reality, what the imagination conceives about it. (Philoponus, *In Phys.*, 612.6–12, tr. by Huby)

In fact, not only was Philoponus aware of claims that indicated that what can be imagined does not, by itself, have to have any bearing on reality – in particular when what is imagined is actually impossible; he was also ready to counter such claims. His thought experiment about removing all interior bodies inside the heavenly sphere is, of course, actually impossible. This is why such a thought experiment needs to be carried out in the imagination or "in thought" (κατ' ἐπίνοιαν), as Philoponus wrote.[281] On that basis, we have seen him claiming above that "it is not absurd to use hypotheses, even if they are impossible, for examining other things."[282] In fact, Aristotle himself did the same thing, when he, in *Metaphysics* Z.3, set out to investigate matter by means of a thought experiment that consisted in abstracting from a body everything, even its form, until he arrived at matter, which, in reality, cannot subsist without form but which, now, has been made available for representation to the mind. So, Philoponus could justifiably ask why it should be that one thought experiment is allowed and another forbidden, when both deal with essentially impossible hypotheses by investigating something that cannot exist by itself and require the imaginative apparatus of the human soul to carry out such an investigation.

This claim of Philoponus is countered by Avicenna in *al-Samāʿ al-ṭabīʿī* II.9. Avicenna argues that there is, in fact, a clear reason that some imaginative processes of abstraction are allowed, while others are not. Avicenna states:

وأمّا ما ذكروا من حديث التحليل فإنّ التحليل ليس على وجه الذي ذكروا بل التحليل هو إفراد واحد واحد من أجزاء الشيء الموجود فيه. فإنّ التحليل يدلّ على الهيولى بأنّه يبرهن أنّ هناك صورة وأنّها لا تقوم بذاتها بل لها مادّة. فيبرهن أنّ في هذا الشيء الآن صورة ومادّة. وأمّا البعد الذي يدعونه فهو شيء ليس ثبوته على هذا القبيل. وذلك لأنّ البعد إنّما يثبت في الوهم عند رفع المتمكن وإعدامه.

As for what they mentioned about the account of analysis (*al-taḥlīl*), analysis is not the way they said. Instead, analysis is an isolation (*ifrād*) of one after another of the parts of a thing existing in it. Thus, analysis indicates the matter by demonstrating that there is a form and that it does not subsist by itself but, rather, has a matter. So, it demonstrates that in this thing now is a form and a matter. The extension, however, which they posit, is something whose affirmation is not in this way. That is because the extension is affirmed only in the imagination upon the removal of that which is in place and its elimination (*ʿinda rafʿ al-mutamakkin wa-iʿdāmihī*). (*al-Samāʿ al-ṭabīʿī* II.9, §11, 141.8–11, tr. by McGinnis, modified)

According to Avicenna, the two mental processes – i.e., that of Aristotle for determining matter and that of Galen and Philoponus for determining space – are fundamentally different. For Aristotle, it was possible to establish the existence of matter through an affirmation of form, i.e., by investigating a concrete object, isolating its features, realising that there is a form which does not subsist without matter, thus establishing matter as the required counterpart of form. This mental process, then, is more an analysis (*al-taḥlīl*) than an abstraction, as it dissolves the concrete object into its various parts and, by attentively considering these parts, recognises their features and implications.[283] Thus, by realising that a concrete object consists of a form, together

281 Philoponus, *In Phys.*, 574.14, tr. by Furley.

282 Philoponus, *In Phys.*, 575.2f, tr. by Furley, modified.

283 cf. the more detailed analysis in McGinnis, "A Penetrating Question," 64–67.

with the implication that a form requires matter, in order to subsist, we can establish the reality of matter. This process of analysis does not involve *removing* the various parts of the concrete object, or in any way *eliminating* them – it merely *isolates* them, for if one were to eliminate the form of a thing, then the thing would necessarily cease to be, and there would be nothing left to analyse.

An underlying extension, however, cannot be reached through a process of analysis, Avicenna claims. Instead, as Philoponus proposed, one has to eliminate the concrete object, in order to be able to – perhaps – affirm the existence of an independent extension. So, as a first point, Avicenna stresses that there is a fundamental difference between both approaches. We might ask, however, why the difference matters at all. Could one not simply establish the existence of the extension by removing the thing as Philoponus suggested? Avicenna's reply is that, in order to do so, further assumptions need to be made, such as stipulating the condition that the surrounding limits do not collapse and are preserved. This is made explicit in the following:

> وأمّا وجود بعد ما معيّن التقدير فإنّما يكون في الوهم تبعاً لعدم جسم بشرط حفظ الأجسام المُطيفة به التي كانت تقدّر البعد المحدود.
>
> The existence of a certain extension that determines the measure follows in the imagination only due to an elimination of body under the condition (*bi-šarṭ*) of preserving the bodies surrounding it which measure the determined extension. (*al-Samāʿ al-ṭabīʿī* II.9, §11, 141.18f.)[284]

In other words, if we want to affirm in our imagination the existence of an extension by removing a body from a container, for example, some water in a vessel or the interior bodies inside the heavenly sphere, then this is only possible upon the further condition that – contrary to what would actually happen in concrete reality – the surrounding bodies are preserved and do not collapse and implode. In short: we would require a ballon which, upon the removal of air, remains in its inflated shape. This further condition, though, is counterfactual and contrary to nature, as – again – even Philoponus and his fellows did not grow tired of mentioning: empty space does not exist devoid of bodies. Thus, Avicenna argues, it is not enough simply to eliminate the body in question; we also have to assume that what usually follows upon such an elimination is prevented from happening. This further assumption, though, may jeopardise the validity of the whole thought experiment, for there is nothing that guarantees that by adding this further assumption we have not fabricated our own false results:

> فما يُدريه أنّ هذا التوهّم ليس فاسداً حتّى لا يكون تابعه محالاً وهل صحيح أنّ هذا الفرض ممكن حتّى يكون ما يتبعه غير محال؟

---

284 Similarly, we have seen Themistius arguing that the bronze sphere in Galen's example "would sooner implode than remain" once the water it hitherto contained would be removed (Themistius, *In Phys.*, 114.19f., tr. by Todd).

> How could one know that this imagination is not corrupt (*fāsidan*), such that what follows upon it is absurd, and whether it is correct [to say] that this assumption is possible, such that what follows upon it is not absurd? (*al-Samāʿ al-ṭabīʿī* II.9, §11, 142.1f., tr. by McGinnis, modified)

If the opponent, now, were to admit that he cannot establish the existence of an independent extension through a process of elimination and removal without adding a further questionable assumption, he might still ask why it should not be possible to establish it on the basis of what, according to Avicenna, is an instance of "analysis" (*taḥlīl*), rather than of elimination and removal (*rafʿ*). That is to say: why should it be so difficult to establish the existence of an extension by way of isolation (*ifrād*) and selective attention, just as in the case of matter? Avicenna would have welcomed such a question, for he does have an answer waiting, which is his ultimate reason for why Philoponus' account on the whole is nothing but false.

If we were to analyse the situation by way of isolating certain features and by directing our explicit attention to one feature to the exclusion of others, we would be able to establish that, without any doubt, there is an extension. Indeed, Avicenna does not deny that there is a real and existing extension between the interior surface of a vessel (as in Galen's example) or inside the heavenly sphere (as in Philoponus' example). Of course there is – but this extension *belongs to the contained body*.[285] Consequently, the result of an analysis, as Avicenna explained it in *al-Samāʿ al-ṭabīʿī* II.9, brings us back to the very beginning, i.e., to the affirmation that there, indeed, exists an extension between the boundaries of a vessel, viz., the very extension of the body contained by the vessel, as argued for in *al-Samāʿ al-ṭabīʿī* II.7.[286] So, analysis shows us that there is an extension between these two limits – but it does not show us that this extension is an independent extension *apart from* or *in addition to* the one belonging to the body, just as in Aristotle's thought experiment, matter is not shown to be capable of independent existence either.

It may seem that Avicenna's argumentation moved in a circle. Yet, that is not the case. It is rather that his opponent's argumentation went in a circle, as he still cannot

285 cf. *al-Burhān* I.6, 72.7–11.

286 It should perhaps be noted that it is by no means inadequate to analyse Avicenna's thoughts on place, space, and void by piecing together various bits of arguments from different chapters. In fact, Avicenna's own discussion requires us to do precisely this, for he not rarely introduces problems and arguments to which he returns two more times, so that he, first, raises an issue in one chapter, discusses the alternative solutions critically in another, and, finally, provides his own solution in yet another. This is a situation that is peculiar to his discussion of place in *al-Samāʿ al-ṭabīʿī* II.5–9 and arguably due to the fact that here, more than anywhere else, Avicenna is concerned with the critical material objecting to Aristotle's account he received. Indeed, Avicenna himself, in his *al-Ḥikma al-mašriqiyya*, condenses his treatment of the various issues of space and void in precisely the same manner as I do here, too, i.e., by piecing together various bits from different chapters of *al-Samāʿ al-ṭabīʿī*: materials both from *al-Samāʿ al-ṭabīʿī* II.6, where he presented the issue, and from chapter II.9, where he presented his solution; cf. esp. *al-Ḥikma al-mašriqiyya* III.10, 30.19–31.23.

provide any reason that there should be a second additional extension over and above the extension of the body, and so his opponent finds himself confronted with the initial issue from which we departed. It is his opponent, then, who is required to explain the principle which individuates the independent extension and according to which we can distinguish the two supposed extensions in the first place. As we have already seen, however, Philoponus cannot identify his two overlapping extensions as distinct from another, because one of these otherwise equal extensions is immaterial and, thus, lacks the principle of individuation. In the final analysis, there is only one extension between any boundary – and that is an extension inhering in matter, i.e., the extension of the very body between these boundaries.

A related argument can be found in *al-Samāʿ al-ṭabīʿī* II.8. With this chapter, Avicenna proceeds to a new topic: discussing the void as such, i.e., no longer as an extension confined by the limits of a body but in itself.[287] This means that he is now turning to questions such as: what is the void? Is it something? Can it be something, at all? He begins with the remark that void cannot simply be said to be nothing, for if it were truly and absolutely nothing, then "there would be no dispute between us and them" (*fa-laysa hāhunā munāzaʿa baynanā wa-baynahum*), because everyone would agree that the void simply is not. Yet, this is not what "they," i.e., the proponents of the void, claim, for they assert that the void is something, some existent, even a quantity. It is also said that it is a substance and, moreover, that it has an active power (*quwwa faʿʿāla*). Yet, none of this, Avicenna states, can be predicated of what is purely a no-thing (*wa-hāḏihī l-aḥwāl lā tuḥmalu l-battata ʿalā l-lā-šayʾ al-ṣirf*).[288] Thus, he will engage with their claims in one very long chapter in his *al-Samāʿ al-ṭabīʿī*, viz., chapter II.8.

Following these first remarks about what the void really is supposed to be, Avicenna begins with an investigation of the metaphysics and the logic behind the attempt to provide a satisfactory definition of the void. His argument has been analysed by McGinnis in an article devoted to the relation between logic and science in the works

---

287 cf. also the recent article by Celeyrette, "Le vide chez Avicenne," which is hardly more than an outline of the arguments contained in *al-Samāʿ al-ṭabīʿī* II.8 with close to no historical – not to mention philosophical – analysis.

288 *al-Samāʿ al-ṭabīʿī* II.8, §1, 123.7–13; cf. *Dānešnāme-ye ʿAlāʾī* III.8, 19.8f. In this respect, the discussion in *al-Naǧāt* and *al-Ḥikma al-ʿArūḍiyya* is most informative. There, Avicenna states that the void cannot be a no-thing and, then, begins meticulously to construct the void on the basis of his opponents' conception: he infers that it must be a quantity (*kamm*) and, indeed, both divisible and continuous. Next, he argues that it must also have position (*waḍʿ*) and, finally, shows that it must be three-dimensionally specified. Thus, the void, if it were to exist, could not be purely nothing – it would have to be "a quantity having position and three dimensions" or a "magnitude through itself." On this basis, then, Avicenna begins to deconstruct the void again and to show its absurdity (*al-Naǧāt* II.2.10, 234.1–236.8 ≈ *al-Ḥikma al-ʿArūḍiyya* II.2.8, 133.24–135.1). Maróth mistakes Avicenna's remarks at the beginning of *al-Samāʿ al-ṭabīʿī* II.8, 123.7f., as an affirmation of the existence of the void by Avicenna. Consequently, he also mistakes the subsequent discussion as an attempt to attain "a good definition of the void" ("Averroes on the Void," 17).

of Avicenna.[289] McGinnis shows how, for Avicenna, logic can serve as a tool in science and how there can be a bridge between universal knowledge, on the one hand, and the investigation of concrete particulars, on the other. For Avicenna, this bridge is the essence in itself, i.e., the essence providing us with the bare definition of something as a statement about what something is without any recourse to its existential status. This is what Avicenna often exemplifies by talking about horseness, which is the essence (*māhiyya*) of a horse, i.e., that which is instantiated either in a concrete horse as a particular thing or in our intellect as a universal when we think about horses.[290] This also implies that in the absence of such an essence, there is no bridge between what we are capable of thinking and what is capable of existing. Thus, if we are unable to define something, fruitlessly having exerted all efforts in finding a definition, then that which we were trying to define may simply not be existent. If something is shown to have no essence, it cannot have existence either, because there is no essence of it that could be instantiated in the world.

In the first paragraphs of *al-Samāʿ al-ṭabīʿī* II.8, Avicenna shows that any attempt to define the void – on the assumption that it is something that can be defined, i.e., on the just-mentioned assumption that it is not a mere no-thing (*al-lā-šayʾ*) – is an endeavour to no end. Eventually, then, the intelligible "void" will emerge as a "vain intelligible" (*maʿqūlan mafrūġan*).[291] The reason for this is that something that exists requires a specific difference that distinguishes it from something else from among the same assumed genus. Since both void and body would be among the genus of extended beings, we must identify a difference between them. Moreover, the difference must be a positive statement.[292] Thus, we cannot state that the difference between the void and a body is that the void is an immaterial extension, because the difference "immateriality" is a feature that has *no* correspondent in concrete reality, as it does not refer to anything that is, being precisely a reference to something that is not.[293]

What may be added to this is that, historically, Avicenna's argument is a continuation of a tendency already attributed to Aristotle by Alexander. According to Simplicius' report, Alexander remarked that in the discussion of the void, Aristotle adopted a methodological approach that was different from his usual approach in examining other physical concepts, such as time:

---

289 cf. McGinnis, "Logic and Science."

290 One of the canonical passages is *al-Ilāhiyyāt* V.1, §4, 196.6–16; cf. esp. Wisnovsky, *Avicenna's Metaphysics in Context*, ch. 7–9; Bertolacci, "The Distinction of Essence and Existence in Avicenna's Metaphysics"; Benevich, "Die 'göttliche Existenz.'"

291 *al-Samāʿ al-ṭabīʿī* II.8, §3, 125.12. For vain forms and intelligibles in Avicenna's psychology and ontology, cf. Michot, "Avicenna's 'Letter on the Disappearance of the Vain Intelligible Forms After Death'"; "'L'épître sur la disparition des formes intelligibles vaines après la mort' d'Avicenne"; Black, "Avicenna on the Ontological and Epistemic Status of Fictional Beings"; Druart, "Avicennan Troubles."

292 cf. *al-Madḫal* I.13, 78.15–18.

293 cf. McGinnis, "Logic and Science," 178–181.

> σημειωτέον δέ ... ὅτι ἐπὶ μὲν τοῦ κενοῦ ὃ ἔμελλε δείξειν μὴ ὂν εἶπεν ἀρχόμενος τοῦ περὶ αὐτοῦ λόγου, τί σημαίνει τοὔνομα, ἐπὶ δὲ τοῦ χρόνου, ὅς ἔστιν ὁμολογουμένως, τίς ἡ φύσις ζητεῖ·
>
> One must point out that on the subject of the void, which he [sc. Aristotle] was about to show to be non-existent, he said at the beginning of its discussion what the word (τοὔνομα) means, but on the subject of time, which unquestionably exists, he inquired into its nature (ἡ φύσις). (Alexander *apud* Simplicium, *In Phys.*, 696.3–6, tr. by Urmson, modified).

Apparently for the void, an investigation into its essence would be a waste of time, for there is no essence that could be defined, because what is not such as to exist at all does not have an essence. So, according to Alexander, Aristotle confined himself to merely explaining the meaning of the word used for what is assumed to be the void – and indeed, at *Physics* IV.7, 213b30f., Aristotle voices his explicit intention to discuss the meaning of the term "void" (τί σημαίνει τοὔνομα, *al-maʿnā llaḏī yadullu ʿalayhi hāḏā l-ism*). Thus, on this line of reasoning, whatever has no existence, has no essence and cannot be defined. This is also what we read in Ibn ʿAdī's *Maqāla fī l-mawǧūdāt*:

> الخلاء قد بيّن أرسطوطالس في المقالة الرابعة من كتابه في السماع الطبيعي أنّه ليس بموجود وما ليس بموجود لا يمكن أن يكون له حدّ إذ كان الحدّ هو قول يدلّ على ما هو المحدود والخلاء ليس هو بموجود فلا اسم له.
>
> Aristotle has proven in the fourth book of his *Physics* that the void is not existent – and it is impossible for that which is not existent to have a definition, since a definition is a statement which points towards that[294] which is defined, but the void is not existent, and so does not have a name. (Ibn ʿAdī, *Maqāla fī l-mawǧūdāt*, 374.1–4)

For Avicenna, clearly, this idea cuts both ways: not only do things that cannot exist not have a definition, it is also that those things that cannot have a definition do not exist. It is, therefore, reasonable to believe that Avicenna made explicit what he found more or less implicit in the preceding philosophical tradition. Systematically, however, Avicenna's logico-metaphysical analysis at the beginning of *al-Samāʿ al-ṭabīʿī* II.8 serves as the counterpart to his earlier "physical" argument in II.7 that there is no way to distinguish between the extension belonging to a body and the supposedly existing extension that additionally pervades that body. In other words, neither is there any ground for distinguishing the two extensions with regard to their instantiation in the real world nor can we distinguish them with regard to their definition.

Having added more details about the nature of internal and external differences and their relation to species, and about what all that means for a successful definition of a thing in *al-Samāʿ al-ṭabīʿī* II.8, §4, 125.12–126.6, Avicenna writes the following, in order to conclude his present discussion and to focus on arguments more akin to his actual intention here in *al-Samāʿ al-ṭabīʿī*, viz., the investigation of the void with physical arguments:

> وكأنّا أمعنّا الآن في غير النظر الذي من غرضنا أن نتكلّم فيه وهو النمط الأشبه بالكلام الطبيعي.

294 Suggesting to read *ʿalā mā* for *ʿalayhi mā* in Ḫalīfāt.

> It is as if we, now, were fully engaged in an investigation that is different from what our intention of discussion actually was about, which in its modus is more similar to physical argumentation (*bi-l-kalām al-ṭabīʿī*). (*al-Samāʿ al-ṭabīʿī* II.8, §5, 126.7)[295]

It is precisely this "physical argumentation" to which we shall now also turn. In so doing, my primary focus shall be on one argument which, from a historical and philosophical perspective, is perhaps the most important of all those which Avicenna presents in *al-Samāʿ al-ṭabīʿī* II.8. This argument supplies the above metaphysical considerations about the non-existence of the void with physical reasons for why we do not need the void to explain commonly observed natural phenomena.

Physical Arguments against the Void

Many of the "physical" arguments against the existence of the void which Avicenna presents in *al-Samāʿ al-ṭabīʿī* II.8 are known from Aristotle's *Physics* IV.8–9. Most of them, first, assume the actual existence of empty space and, then, try to conceive of how the motion of corporeal things could be possible within such an empty space. With his arguments, Aristotle wanted to counter the allegation that motion would be impossible if there were no void. In fact, he argued, the exact opposite is true, viz., that any motion is impossible if it had to occur in void.[296]

In the greater part of *al-Samāʿ al-ṭabīʿī* II.8, Avicenna elaborates and expands upon Aristotle's original arguments in what seems to be an attempt to explain as exhaustively as possible what in Aristotle was often rather brief and succinct. In all this, however, he follows the strategy of Aristotle. There cannot be any natural rectilinear motion in the void, because the void altogether lacks any differentiation with the result that there is simply no reason that a natural body would have a tendency to move in one direction rather than in another, because any direction would seem to be just as good as any other. In fact, the void, were it to exist, would not even have any direction.[297]

---

295 Apparently, this statement marks a digression. Yet, it is not so clear where the digression began. McGinnis seems to imply that the whole argument spanning from *al-Samāʿ al-ṭabīʿī* II.8, §§2–4, 123.13–126.6, is in fact the digression in question, which would make the whole argument an alien element within Avicenna's otherwise rather "physical" investigation of the void; cf. McGinnis, "Logic and Science," 181–186. However, it seems more reasonable to think that Avicenna intended to call only the material in *al-Samāʿ al-ṭabīʿī* II.8, §4, 125.12–126.6, a digression. If that is right, then we get an argument in paragraphs two and three which argues that the void is a "vain intelligible," followed by a real digression about the nature of species-making differences in definitions which, indeed, exceeds the realm of physical considerations in paragraph four, before he turns to the really "physical" arguments beginning with paragraph five.

296 *Phys.* IV.8, 214b28–31, 216a23f.

297 *al-Samāʿ al-ṭabīʿī* II.8, §§9–10, 127.19–130.2; cf. *Phys.* IV.8, 214b32–215a1, 215a6–14; cf. also *ʿUyūn al-ḥikma* II.6, 23.13–24.15; *Dānešnāme-ye ʿAlāʾī* III.9, 20.7–21.4; *al-Hidāya* II.1, 153.4–6; *al-Ḥikma al-mašriqiyya* III.10, 29.13–16.

The same argument also shows that, just as there can be no motion in the void, there can be no rest in it either.[298]

To this, Avicenna adds an intriguing argument about the impossibility of a circular motion in the void.[299] Moreover, natural motions of natural bodies vary in speed in accordance with the density of the traversed medium. Since the void as a medium has no density, the comparison of the speed of a natural motion in the void to that in other media leads to absurd results.[300]

Likewise, since there is no natural motion in the void, there can be no forced motion, either, for if the mover of a forced motion intrinsically belongs to the moving thing, then this situation is actually the same as that of a natural (or voluntary) motion, in which the mover, likewise, belongs to the moving thing. So, forced motion in a void, just as natural motion in a void, would vary in intensity and speed depending on the moving power, and so would suffer from all the already known problems associated with natural motion in the void.[301] If, however, forced motion were due not to an intrinsic mover but to an external cause, it could not be conceived how a featureless and undifferentiated void could be said to exert any influence on the moving body by either sustaining the motion or impeding it.[302]

On the whole, it may seem that by turning to "physical" arguments, Avicenna also addresses a new group of opponents. Whereas before, he singled out the position adopted by Philoponus that the void is always and completely filled with bodies, he

298 *al-Samāʿ al-ṭabīʿī* II.8, §7, 127.1f.; §10, 130.2; §19, 134.3–6; cf. *Phys.* IV.8, 215a19–22; cf. also *al-Naǧāt* II.2.10, 241.8 ≈ *al-Ḥikma al-ʿArūḍiyya* II.2.8, 137.7f.; *ʿUyūn al-ḥikma* II.6, 24.6f.; *Dānešnāme-ye ʿAlāʾī* III.9, 21.2f.; *al-Hidāya* II.1, 153.4f.; *al-Ḥikma al-mašriqiyya* III.10, 29.11f.

299 *al-Samāʿ al-ṭabīʿī* II.8, §8, 127.3–18; cf. *al-Samāʿ al-ṭabīʿī* III.8, §4, 214.3–10; *al-Naǧāt* II.2.10, 241.12–242.8 ≈ *al-Ḥikma al-ʿArūḍiyya* II.2.8, 137.9–16; *al-Ḥikma al-mašriqiyya* III.10, 29.16–30.5; cf. also McGinnis, "Avoiding the Void." As McGinnis convincingly argues, Avicenna was not only systematically required to add an argument about circular motion, he was also attentive enough to recognise this need and smart enough set it up. The corresponding argument in the edition of *al-Ḥikma al-ʿArūḍiyya* is incomplete due to missing folia in the manuscript. In *al-Naǧāt* II.2.10, 242.9–243.13, Avicenna adds a further argument that draws on impossible implications of a spatially finite void.

300 *al-Samāʿ al-ṭabīʿī* II.8, §§11–14, 130.3–132.6; cf. *Phys.* IV.8, 215a24–216a26; cf. also *ʿUyūn al-ḥikma* II.6, 24.8–15; *Dānešnāme-ye ʿAlāʾī* III.9, 21.6–22.10; *al-Hidāya* II.1, 154.1–155.2; *al-Ḥikma al-mašriqiyya* III.10, 30.6–18. All in all, Avicenna's argumentation here seconds Aristotle's line of thought and, surprisingly, shows no signs of Philoponus' celebrated refutation of it; q.v. fn. 194 above, 371.

301 *al-Samāʿ al-ṭabīʿī* II.8, §15, 132.7–13; cf. *Phys.* IV.8, 215a1–6; cf. also *ʿUyūn al-ḥikma* II.6, 24.7f.; *Dānešnāme-ye ʿAlāʾī* III.9, 21.2f.; *al-Hidāya* II.1, 153.5f.

302 *al-Samāʿ al-ṭabīʿī* II.8, §§16–18, 132.13–134.3; cf. *Phys.* IV.8, 215a14–19; VIII.10, 266b27–267a20; cf. also *al-Samāʿ al-ṭabīʿī* IV.14. Avicenna's argument is involved and complex, and certainly deserves more attention than I am presently able to give it here, as it would require a full investigation of Avicenna's theory of projectile motion, which, despite some valuable contributions, still has not been studied sufficiently; cf. Sayılı, "Ibn Sīnā and Buridan on the Dynamics of Projectile Motion"; Nony, "Two Arabic Theories of Impetus"; cf. also Zimmermann, "Philoponus' Impetus Theory in the Arabic Tradition"; Sorabji, *Matter, Space, and Motion*, ch. 14–15.

now is dealing with the implications of an atomist conception of the world according to which corporeal objects move around in void space and according to which corporeal objects actually consist, to a greater or lesser degree, of interstitial void spaces. After all, this was also Aristotle's motivation in the corresponding discussion in the *Physics* on which Avicenna's own discussion relies. Having said this, it is clear at the same time that Avicenna never completely loses sight of Philoponus throughout his discussion. This is primarily due to the fact that Philoponus' position is somewhat ambivalent. On the one hand, he accepts Aristotle's conclusion that the void does not exist in actuality. On the other hand, he is famous for having successfully rebutted Aristotle's arguments to that conclusion. The reason for this ambivalence is that he, indeed, accepts that there is no void space – but only because all void space is always actually filled with body. Void or space is the underlying room for bodies, but it does not exist without them. So, for Philoponus, Aristotle was right to reject the existence of an empty void as an unoccupied extension, but he was not right to reject the idea of a space that is by definition void but in reality always occupied by bodies. So, although with the above arguments, Avicenna seemed to turn his attention to attempts at establishing the existence of the void from an atomist perspective, as atoms move not only through void but also into void interstices, he is still concerned with Philoponus' account, because in the final analysis, for Philoponus, too, bodies move through, and exist in, the void, even though in reality, this void is always filled.[303]

With *al-Samāʿ al-ṭabīʿī* II.8, §20, 134.6, then, Avicenna turns his attention to a prominent argument which relies on those phenomena which people such as Philoponus explained through the "force of the void." Avicenna writes the following:

وقد بلغ من غلوّ القائلين بالخلاء في أمره أن جعلوا له قوّة جاذبة أو محرّكة ولو بوجه آخر حتّى قالوا إنّ سبب احتباس الماء في الأواني التي تُسمّى سرّاقات الماء وانجذابه في الآلات التي تُسمّى زرّاقات الماء إنّما هو جذب الخلاء وأنّه

303 However, one may also argue that Avicenna already began to envisage the atomist conception of the void in the first line of *al-Samāʿ al-ṭabīʿī* II.8, when he explicitly addressed the "proponents of the void" (*al-qāʾilūn bi-l-ḫalāʾ*). This would mean that the entire discussion of the impossibility of defining a void, carried out in the same chapter, would likewise have been directed against them and not primarily against Philoponus. Although it certainly is true that Avicenna's specific focus on Philoponus' position, which was made explicit in *al-Samāʿ al-ṭabīʿī* II.7, §3, 119.9f., when Avicenna announced and singled out for discussion the position that the void is always filled, ends with the conclusion of chapter II.7, and although he specifically envisages with the first line of II.8 a new target, viz., "the proponents of the void," it is apparent that not all of his current arguments depend on the actual existence of unoccupied void spaces in the world. Indeed, some arguments, such as that about the impossibility of defining the void, bear upon the rejection of the conceptual possibility of the void, which doubtlessly was defended by Philoponus, whereas other arguments, such as that to which we shall turn now, rely on what Philoponus called the "force of the void" and presuppose, the actual non-existence of the void. Since Avicenna explicitly attributes this argument to the "proponents of the void," it seems that within Avicenna's refutation, Philoponus (who affirms the "force of the void" and denies empty space) belongs to these proponents just as much as the Baṣrī Muʿtazilites do (who deny the "force of the void" and affirm empty space).

يجذب أوّل شيء الأكثف ثمّ الألطف. وقال آخرون بل الخلاء محرّك للأجسام إلى فوق وأنّه إذا تخلخل الجسم بكثرة خلاء يداخله صار أخف وأسرع حركة إلى فوق.

The proponents of the void (*al-qā'ilīn bi-l-ḫalā'*) have reached the point of exaggeration in its case when they attributed to it an attractive or moving power (*quwwa ǧāḏiba aw muḥarrika*), even if [this time] in another sense, so that they claimed that the cause for the water's being retained in the vessels which are called clepsydrae (*sarrāqāt al-mā'*) and its being attracted into the instruments which are called pipes (*zarrāqāt al-mā'*) is only the attraction of the void (*ǧaḏb al-ḫalā'*), and that it, first, attracts what is denser and, then, what is more subtle. Others said, instead, [that] the void is a mover for the bodies [moving them] upwards and that, when there is a rarefaction of body by much void entering it, it becomes lighter and moves upward more quickly. (*al-Samā' al-ṭabī'ī* II.8, §20, 134.6–9, tr. by McGinnis, modified)[304]

What Avicenna describes here are two examples in which the void is said to have an influence on natural bodies. In the first, the void attracts other bodies. This is a well-known phenomenon and often demonstrated with an ancient device called clepsydra or "water-thief" (sg. κλεψύδρα, *sarrāqat al-mā'*).[305] The clepsydra can be described as a vessel with a hole on top and a perforated base. Once immersed in water, it fills with water. If the hole on top is now blocked and the clepsydra raised above the water, the water is retained in the device, and only drips out when the top hole is no longer blocked, allowing air to stream in. One way to explain this phenomenon is to assume that there is a natural force belonging to the space occupied by the water inside the clepsydra which prevents the formation of an *empty* space. If water were to drip out of a clepsydra despite the top hole being blocked, such that no air is allowed to enter, a void would form inside the clepsydra. Since there can be no void, the water must be retained forcefully inside the clepsydra so long as the top hole is blocked. This force is precisely what we have seen Philoponus calling the "force of the void."[306]

A variant of the clepsydra experiment is described later in *al-Samā' al-ṭabī'ī* II.9. There, Avicenna uses the term *al-qārūra*, which seems to be more a normal flask or phial rather than a specific device with a perforated base as the clepsydra.[307] Nonetheless, such a simple phial can be used for a similar experiment in which one sucks air out of the phial, whereupon its mouth is being closed and the phial turned over and immersed in water. Once the mouth is re-opened under water, water enters the phial, the question now being why it does. One common answer, again, is that this is due to a void which was actually formed inside the phial through the sucking and which nature

304 cf. *Dānešnāme-ye 'Alā'ī* III.10, 23.2–24.6.

305 Avicenna uses the common term *sarrāqat al-mā'*, a literal translation of "water-thief" in seeming tandem with the more obscure but almost identical expression *zarrāqat al-mā'*. McGinnis is puzzled by this and devotes a footnote to a discussion of the terms. In an almost identical passage in Faḫr al-Dīn's *al-Mabāḥiṯ al-mašriqiyya*, the editor of that work, al-Baġdādī, suggests to read *zarāfat al-mā'* (fn. 1, vol.1, 358); cf. also Pines, *Studies in Islamic Atomism*, 151–153.

306 q.v. above, 380f.

307 cf. *al-Samā' al-ṭabī'ī* II.9, §§20–21, 145.16–147.13; *al-Ḥikma al-mašriqiyya* III.10, 31.11–23.

subsequently tries to eliminate by attracting water into the phial to fill the vacant space. According to another answer, the sucking only created the *risk* of an actual void (κινδυνεύει γενέσθαι κενόν), which was subsequently overcome through the water being pulled upwards by the force of the void.[308]

The second example mentioned in the above passage does not rely on any experiment with a device such as the clepsydra or the phial; it merely describes the case of interstitial void spaces used to explain why light things move upwards more readily than heavy things do. Since light things are said to contain more void spaces, they are lighter than other bodies with less void spaces. Especially within an atomistic physics, this explains why light bodies rise through heavier ones (e.g., air through water) and heavy bodies fall through light ones (e.g., stones through water). The same interstitial void spaces are also employed to explain phenomena such as condensation and rarefaction which, in turn, are related to the clepsydra experiments.[309] Hero of Alexandria (d. ~ 70), for example, explained pneumatic forces with the help of a certain tension or elasticity (εὐτονία) of the air due to interstitial void spaces.[310]

Avicenna mentions and discusses these examples twice in his investigation of place in *al-Samāʿ al-ṭabīʿī*: once in chapter eight, where he primarily argues that the assumption of an actually existing void does not help to explain the natural phenomena, and once in chapter nine, when he provides his own analysis of them and shows how they can be explained even without assuming the void.[311] In fact, at the end of chapter eight, he already hints at his own solution stating that examples that involve clepsydrae and phials are only possible because of two essential features of the natural world: the impossibility of the existence of the void *and* the necessity that the surfaces of bodies adhere to one another (*li-aǧl imtināʿ wuǧūd al-ḫalāʾ wa-wuǧūb talāzum ṣafāʾiḥ al-aǧsām*).[312] Both features are essential not only to the natural world but also to the Aristotelian physics of place so laboriously defended by Avicenna.

Experiments with water and air inside or outside of phials, clepsydrae, and pipes often in combination with heating and cooling were common not only in ancient and late ancient times but also among scientists in the Islamic world. Moreover, the related use of hot cupping glasses is a well-attested medical procedure in both Antiquity and the Middle Ages, just as the cracking of bottles when exposed to either intense heat or freezing cold was a familiar phenomenon. It is, thus, not surprising that scientist for

308 Philoponus, *In Phys.*, 570.16–18; cf. *In Phys.*, 572.5f.

309 Aristotle mentioned these and other examples in *Physics* IV.6 and IV.9; cf. also *al-Samāʿ al-ṭabīʿī* II.6, §§12–15, 117.8–118.2; *al-Ḥikma al-mašriqiyya* III.10, 30.19–31.11.

310 cf. Daiber, "Fārābīs Abhandlung über das Vakuum," 39. By the time of Hero, the concept εὐτονία and its application in explaining mechanical phenomena already had a long history; cf. Berryman, *The Mechanical Hypothesis in Ancient Greek Natural Philosophy*, esp. 191–197.

311 cf. *al-Samāʿ al-ṭabīʿī* II.8, §§20–25, 134.6–136.10; II.9, §§17–22, 145.6–148.1.

312 *al-Samāʿ al-ṭabīʿī* II.8, §25, 136.4.

centuries have been engaged in finding a suitable explanation of their observations.[313] Among these scientists, it is already Strato, for example, who uses the explicit expression of an "attractive power" (τὴν ἑλκτικὴν δύναμιν) in this context.[314] One should also mention Abū Bakr al-Rāzī, who, as we are told by Faḫr al-Dīn al-Rāzī (d. 606/1210), tried to prove the existence of void and absolute space by experimenting with clepsydrae and the above-mentioned pipes.[315] Faḫr al-Dīn explicitly mentions the expression *quwwa ǧāḏiba* ("attractive power") being attributed to the void by Abū Bakr al-Rāzī – the same expression that was employed by Avicenna in the above quotation and that obviously corresponds to terminology already in use in the third century BC.

In the following, I shall investigate two explanations Avicenna offers for these phenomena, one stemming from his youthful correspondence with Abū Rayḥān al-Bīrūnī (d. 440/1048) and the other from his mature *al-Samāʿ al-ṭabīʿī*. I shall compare his early account with that provided by the Muʿtazilites from Baġdād together with its criticism by both al-Bīrūnī and the Muʿtazilites from Baṣra, and his revised account with the solution offered by al-Fārābī in his *Maqāla fī l-ḫalāʾ*. These comparisons will reveal that Avicenna changed his mind about how these phenomena are to be explained, probably in response to criticism; how he was influenced by al-Fārābī's treatise; and, finally, how he developed his predecessor's solution further.

It was early in Avicenna's career that he engaged in an exchange of letters with his contemporary al-Bīrūnī, who mentions his discussions (*muḏākarāt*) with "the excellent young man Abū ʿAlī al-Ḥusayn ibn ʿAbd Allāh ibn Sīnā" in his *al-Āṯār al-bāqiya ʿan al-qurūn al-ḫāliya*.[316] According to its editor Eduard Sachau, al-Bīrūnī's work was completed in 390/1000, so that his correspondence with Avicenna would have to have taken place before that year.[317] This would mean that the exchange occurred more than twenty years before Avicenna was composing his *al-Samāʿ al-ṭabīʿī*.

As the sixth of his second bunch of questions, al-Bīrūnī asks Avicenna why he thinks water rises up in a phial (*al-qārūra*) after air has been sucked out of it and it has been immersed in water if there were no void in the world to explain this phe-

---

313 Particularly relevant in this regard are the already mentioned Hero as well as his third century BC predecessors Strato, Ctesibios, and Philo of Byzantium; cf. generally Berryman, *The Mechanical Hypothesis in Ancient Greek Natural Philosophy*. It is to be noted that Philo's works on pneumatics were available in Arabic, while Hero was at least known by name; cf. Daiber, "Fārābīs Abhandlung über das Vakuum," fn. 45, 44; cf. also Grant, *Much Ado about Nothing*, ch. 4.

314 Strato *apud* Simplicium, *In Phys.*, 663.4–7.

315 cf. al-Rāzī, *al-Mabāḥiṯ al-mašriqiyya* II.1.1.20, vol. I, 357.22–358.2.

316 al-Bīrūnī, *al-Āṯār al-bāqiya ʿan al-qurūn al-ḫāliya*, 257.4f.

317 cf. Sachau's introduction in al-Bīrūnī, *al-Āṯār al-bāqiya ʿan al-qurūn al-ḫāliya*, xxiv. Gutas, who follows Sachau's dating, also considers, and dismisses, a suggestion made by Yaḥyā Mahdavī about a possible later dating of al-Bīrūnī's response to the first set of answers; cf. Gutas, *Avicenna and the Aristotelian Tradition*, 449f.; cf. also Moḥaqqeq's remarks in his introduction to the edition of Avicenna and al-Bīrūnī, *al-Asʾila wa-l-aǧwiba*, viif.

nomenon.[318] The implication is that the void apparently would be able to account for the observed facts if it just were granted existence. The example in al-Bīrūnī's question, thus, does not directly concern the experiments with clepsydrae but is more akin to those which involve the supposed formation of an actual void (or the risk of such a formation) inside phials, as described above. Avicenna's answer to al-Bīrūnī's question is as follows:

> ليس ذلك لأجل الخلاء لكنّ العلّة في ذلك أنّ القارورة إذا مصّصتها وامتنع خروج الهواء عنها لامتناع الخلاء حرّك المصّ الهواء الذي فيها على تتابع حركات قسرية. والحركات المتتابعة القسرية تُحدِث حرارة وسخونة تُحدِث في الهواء انفشاشاً وأذا انفشّ هواء القارورة طلب مكاناً أوسع فمن الضرورة أنّ بعدضه يخرج وما يتّسع له الزجاجة يبقى. فإذا أصابته برودة الماء تكاثف وانقبض وأخذ مَوضِعاً اقلّ وكان وقوع الخلاء ممتنعاً دخل الماء القارورة على نسبة الانقباض الذي حدث في الهواء المنفشّ عند مماسّة الجسم البارد.
>
> This is not due to the void (*laysa ḏālika li-aǧl al-ḫalāʾ*); rather, the cause for this is that if you suck it [sc. the phial] and if it is impossible for air to get out of it due to the impossibility of the void, then the sucking moved the air which is inside of it through uninterrupted forceful motions. The uninterrupted forceful motions bring about (*tuḥdiṯu*) warmth and heat (*ḥarāra wa-suḫūna*), which brings about an expansion (*infišāšan*)[319] in the air – and when the air in the phial expands, it seeks a wider place, and so it is necessary that some of it [sc. the air] gets out, while whatever the flask [can] accommodate remains [in it]. So, when you lower it (*aṣābtahū*) into the coldness of the water (*burūdat al-māʾ*), it is condensed and contracted, taking up lesser space. However, the occurrence of void is impossible, [and so] water enters the phial in the [same] ratio as the contraction which happens in the [hitherto] expanded air upon contact with the cold body [of the water]. (*al-Asʾila wa-l-aǧwiba*, 47.8–48.3)

Straightforwardly denying that the void is the cause of the described phenomenon, Avicenna asserts that the "warmth and heat" (*ḥarāra wa-suḫūna*) which the sucking produced is solely responsible, for this heat caused the air in the phial to expand a little, so that eventually some warm air leaked out of, or was sucked away from, the phial. If the phial's mouth is then blocked, and the phial turned over and immersed in "the coldness of the water" (*burūdat al-māʾ*), nothing would happen at first after the mouth has been re-opened, i.e., no water would enter the phial. It is only after the air in the phial has been cooled down by "the coldness of the water" now surrounding the phial that the cold air inside the phial is condensed and reduced in volume, so that, finally, water enters the phial to the extent the cooled air condenses. According to the young Avicenna, then, it is the warming due to the sucking and the subsequent

318 Avicenna and al-Bīrūnī, *al-Asʾila wa-l-aǧwiba*, 47.5–7; cf. also the related questions, number ten of the first and number seven of the second bunch of questions.

319 The term *infišāš*, found both in the edition of Moḥaqqeq/Nasr and in Ms. Leiden or. 184, 85v16, is perplexing. The context seems to dictate translating it along the lines of "expansion." Strohmaier suggests *intifāš* (cf. al-Bīrūnī, *In den Gärten der Wissenschaft*, fn. 70, 252), which seems unlikely in light of the recurrent use of word forms from the same root as *infišāš* in the remaining bits of Avicenna's answer. I am grateful to Paul Hullmeine for sharing his copy of the manuscript with me.

cooling by the water together with the air's expansion and condensation caused by the change in temperature which explains why the water enters the phial after it has been sucked and immersed in water. This means that the sucking proper is not itself responsible – it is only the change in temperature induced by the sucking together with the corresponding change in volume. So, Avicenna continues by expanding his theory along these lines and claims that we could likewise also have *blown* into the phial (instead of sucking on it) or just warmed it up:

ألّا ترى أنّك لو لم تمصّ بل اتيت بالفعل المضادّ للمصّ وهو النفخ ونفخت في القارورة نفخاً متّصلاً متتابعاً حتّى أسخن حركات النفخ هواء القارورة ثمّ أكببتها على الماء عملت هذا العمل بعينه. وذلك مجرّب وكذلك لو أسخنت القارورة عملت هذا عمل. وهذا كفاية في الجواب.

Do you not see that if you did not suck but instead carried out the act contrary to sucking, viz., blowing, and blew into the phial continuously and uninterruptedly, so that the motions of the blowing would heat the air of the phial, thereupon turning it over into the water, the very same would happen? That is something that has been tested methodically (*muğarrab*). Likewise, if you heated the phial, this would happen, too. This is sufficient as an answer. (*al-As'ila wa-l-ağwiba*, 48.3–7)

With this astonishing passage, Avicenna emphasises once more that it is only the change in temperature through "warmth and heat" which is actually responsible, regardless of whether we suck on the phial or blow into it, because in either case we would get the same result – viz., that of air entering once the coldness of the water has counteracted the heat – just as if we had simply heated up the phial without sucking or blowing.

While it seems that Avicenna is right in claiming that in natural substances we find an interrelation of temperature and volume, made evident by the cracking of bottles in winter, and while he may certainly think of medical treatments that involve, for example, hot cupping glasses, it is by no means clear whether it is really possible to warm up the air inside a phial sufficiently merely by sucking on or blowing into it, despite Avicenna's assurance that he has acquired his knowledge through *tağriba* ("methodic experience"), of which the corresponding term *muğarrab* is the passive participle.[320]

Incidentally, al-Bīrūnī was not impressed by this answer, for he writes the following back to Avicenna:

أمّا قولك ذلك مجرّب فأنّي جرّبته ففعل ضدّ الفعل أيضاً وهو أنّ الهواء خرج من القارورة بتقبقبه ولم يدخله شيء من الماء البتّة. وانكسر منّي قوارير تسع في ماء جيحون.

320 On the notion of *tağriba*, q.v. above, 46ff. Moreover, it is interesting to note that there are numerous phenomena of attraction of substances that are immediately relevant for the science of medicine, so that the so-called "force of the void" was an everyday principle employed in the theory, and observable in the practice, of medicine; cf. esp. the discussion in Adamson, "Galen on Void."

> As for your assertion that this is something that has been tested methodically (*muğarrab*), I did, indeed, test it methodically (*ğarrabtuhū*), but the result was the opposite of [your] result, as the air *went out* of the phial due to its swelling but nothing of the water entered it. I shattered [so many] phials of mine, enough to contain[321] the water of the Oxus river! (al-Bīrūnī, *al-As'ila wa-l-ağwiba*, 58.8–10)

It seems that al-Bīrūnī is genuinely startled by Avicenna's theory that blowing into a phial would eventually lead to water entering it, once it has been immersed in water. He describes the opposite result that if some extra air is blown into the phial, and if presumably the phial is with its mouth blocked immersed in water, then all that can be observed once the mouth is no longer blocked is that the inside air bulges out of the phial, being enlarged or "swollen" due to the now released extra air, with no water entering whatsoever.

What al-Bīrūnī's response, despite its amusing rhetoric, neglected altogether is the central reason at work in Avicenna's theory, namely that blowing and sucking ultimately result in a change of temperature of the air inside the phial. It is this neglect which Avicenna's disciple Abū Saʿīd Aḥmad ibn ʿAlī al-Maʿṣūmī (d. 430/1038) criticises when he formulates his response in Avicenna's name:

> وأمّا تجربتك القارورة فلأنّك لم تجرّبها على الوجه كما يجب وهو أن ينفخ فيها إلى أن يحمى الهواء. ثمّ يكبّها على الماء من غير أن يُغطى رأسها حتّى يخرج فضل تزايد الهواء بالإحماء منها. ثمّ إذا صادمت البرودة ما بقي جمعته وصار أقلّ ممّا كان فيه ودخلها الماء حينئذ.
>
> As for your methodic experience with the phial, so this was because you did not test it methodically the way it needs to be done, and this is that one blows into it until (*ilā an*) the air is hot. Then, it is turned over into the water without its mouth being covered, so that the surplus of the heat-induced increase of the air (*faḍl tazāyud al-hawā' bi-l-iḥmā'*) gets out of it. Then, when the coldness hits upon what remained [in the phial], it pulls it [sc. the air] together and it becomes less than it was in it [sc. the phial], in which case water enters it. (al-Maʿṣūmī, *al-As'ila wa-l-ağwiba*, 86.1–5)

This response by al-Maʿṣūmī is suggestive in two ways. First, it emphasises yet another time that the actually relevant detail is the "heat-induced" expansion, as he somewhat comically recommends to al-Bīrūnī that he should keep on blowing into the phial until, finally, the inside air has been warmed up sufficiently. Only then is it possible to observe the phenomenon described by Avicenna and restated here by al-Maʿṣūmī in a slightly revised form that we see, first, air coming out of the phial due to the continuing increase of the air's volume and, second, water entering the phial after the coldness of the water reduced the temperature of the air, thus also reducing its volume. It should be noted, again, that Avicenna and al-Maʿṣūmī, of course, are right that an increase of temperature comes along with an increase of volume, the question is whether this is something that can really be observed so easily by warming the air inside the phial merely by sucking or blowing, instead of heating it properly by fire or sunlight.

---

321 Suggesting to read *tasaʿu* for *yasaʿu* in Moḥaqqeq/Nasr.

This brings me to the second way in which al-Maʿṣūmī's response is suggestive. According to Dimitri Gutas, al-Maʿṣūmī "was known as the scientist among Avicenna's pupils."[322] His expertise apparently ranged from astronomy, as Gutas states, to medicine, because it was allegedly al-Maʿṣūmī who read, during Avicenna's evening sessions, from his teacher's *al-Qānūn fī l-ṭibb*.[323] It is, thus, reasonable to assume that Avicenna's theory that it is heat that is the decisive factor in explaining the observed phenomenon is, indeed, derived from his own expertise as a physician and his knowledge of treatments with heated cupping glasses and similar devices. It is in this regard fitting that the Baġdādī Muʿtazilites likewise referred to cupping glasses as well as to clepsydrae and phials in support of their contention that the void cannot exist.[324] About the phial, Ibn Mattawayh reports the following argument on their behalf:

قالوا إنّا نمصّ الهواء من القارورة فإذا قلبناها على الماء دخلها الماء مع أنّ من حقّه النزول. فإذا صعد إليها فلا بدّ من علّة وهي استحالة الخلاء في العالم لأنّا بإخراج الهواء من القارورة قد أحميناها بما فعلنا فيها من النفس ومن شأن الحارّ أن تخفّ حركته تسرع. والهواء الحارّ يخرج من القارورة فلا بدّ من شيء يخلفه وهو الماء. ولو لا ذلك لم يصحّ تصاعد الماء إليها.

They say that we suck air out of a phial (*al-qārūra*) and if we, then, turn it over into water, water enters [by ascending] despite that it should more appropriately have descended. So, if it rises in it [sc. the phial], it is inevitably due to a cause, and this is the impossibility of the void in the world (*istiḥālat al-ḫalāʾ fī l-ʿālam*), because by getting the air out of the phial, we have warmed it through what we effected in it from our breath (*qad aḥmaynāhā bi-mā faʿalnā fīhā min al-nafas*), and what is hot is such as to rush in its motion and to speed up. With hot air getting out of the phial, it is inevitable that something substitutes it in return, and this is water. If it were not for that, it would not be true [to say] that water rises in it. (Ibn Mattawayh, *al-Taḏkira*, I.30, 120.15–121.2 (ed. Luṭf/ʿŪn)/50.4–7 (ed. Gimaret))

In the words of Ibn Mattawayh, the Muʿtazilites from Baġdād employed the same example and the same explanation against their brothers from Baṣrā, in order to refute their belief in the actual existence of void spaces within the world. Here, too, the actual cause of the observed phenomenon is the change of temperature produced through the act of sucking and the warmth of the breath.

The Baṣrī Muʿtazilites responded by denying that anything warm could have entered the phial, if the act in question was sucking (*al-maṣṣ*).[325] On the one hand, their response is surprising, because the Baġdādī argument, at least as translated

322 Gutas, *Avicenna and the Aristotelian Tradition*, 97.

323 cf. al-Bayhaqī, *Tatimmat Ṣiwān al-ḥikma*, 62.7 (published as *Taʾrīḫ ḥukamāʾ al-islām*); cf. also Gohlman's footnote to his translation of Avicenna's autobiography (Avicenna and al-Ǧūzǧānī, *Sīrat al-šayḫ al-raʾīs*, fn. 71, 128); Gutas, *Avicenna and the Aristotelian Tradition*, 97.

324 For their arguments about cupping glasses and clepsydrae, cf. Ibn Mattawayh, *al-Taḏkira*, I.30, 121.10–12, 122.14–17 (ed. Luṭf/ʿŪn)/50.13f., 51.6–8 (ed. Gimaret); cf. also Dhanani, *The Physical Theory of Kalām*, 76–80.

325 Ibn Mattawayh, *al-Taḏkira*, I.30, 121.3 (ed. Luṭf/ʿŪn)/50.8 (ed. Gimaret).

above from Ibn Mattawayh's *al-Taḏkira*, did not mention any warm air *entering* the phial.[326] On the other hand, it is interesting, because the Baṣrīs immediately add that it would "only" (*innamā*) be possible for something warm to enter the phial, if there were some *blowing* (*al-nafḫ*) into the phial, as we have seen Avicenna recommending, too.[327] What is more, the Muʿtazilites from Baṣra employ the very same experiment, together with their rejection of the explanation offered by the Baġdādīs, as one of their own arguments in support of the existence of void and empty space, because for them, the experiment does nothing other than to demonstrate that even humans have the capacity to evacuate space.[328]

Given the inner-Muʿtazilī debate and the fact that we find the same arguments recurring in both the Muʿtazilites and Avicenna, together with the further fact that with al-Bīrūnī we have yet another intellectual who was interested in the question and familiar with the answers figures such as Avicenna, al-Maʿṣūmī, and some of the Muʿtazilites would give, we can safely assume that there was an ongoing debate in the fourth/tenth century in philosophical, scientific, and theological circles precisely about how these phenomena ought to be explained. Moreover, all parties involved so far were additionally also aware of criticism of their respective argumentation. Additionally, Avicenna may also have been aware of a further shortcoming of his theory, viz., that even though his theory might well explain what happens in a phial or a cupping glas, it certainly cannot explain the mechanism of a clepsydra, where there is no heat, warmth, breath, or anything hot involved. Against this background, it is not surprising, first, that al-Fārābī, too, weighed in on the matter, arguably reacting to his Muʿtazilī contemporaries; and second, that more than twenty years after his correspondence with al-Bīrūnī, i.e., while composing his *al-Samāʿ al-ṭabīʿī*, Avicenna by and large abandoned his earlier account and adopted an explanatory model that is much more in line with the proposal of al-Fārābī to which he, nonetheless, adds a highly significant detail, as we shall see.

Now, al-Fārābī's *Maqāla fī l-ḫalāʾ* offers an investigation specifically of the phial experiment. According to the introduction of the treatise, this experiment has been adduced by a certain party (*qawm*) in support of their claim that the void exists (*anna l-ḫalāʾ mawǧūd*). Following these remarks, al-Fārābī describes carefully the procedure.

---

326 We find this depiction of the argument, however, in Abū Rašīd Saʿīd ibn Muḥammad al-Nīsābūrī's *Kitāb al-Masāʾil*, in which we read that hot air *entered* the phial from the breath (*al-hawāʾ al-ḥārr allaḏī daḫala fī l-qārūra min nufus al-insān*, 33.12 (ed. Biram)/54.3f. (ed. Ziyāda/Sayyid)). Judging from their response in both the *Kitāb al-Masāʾil* and Ibn Mattawayh's *al-Taḏkira*, this is also how the Baṣrī Muʿtazilites have understood the argument and reacted to it; cf. also the paraphrase by Dhanani, who writes that "as a result of the sucking, hot air from our breath enters the flask" (*The Physical Theory of Kalām*, 78). Yet, this is not how Ibn Mattawayh's presentation, as translated above, is to be read, which is much closer to the answer given by Avicenna in his correspondence with al-Bīrūnī.

327 Ibn Mattawayh, *al-Taḏkira*, I.30, 121.4 (ed. Luṭf/ʿŪn)/50.8f. (ed. Gimaret).

328 cf. al-Nīsābūrī, *Kitāb al-Masāʾil*, 27.15–19 (ed. Biram)/49.15–18 (ed. Ziyāda/Sayyid); cf. also Dhanani, *The Physical Theory of Kalām*, 85f.

He writes that one third of the air contained in the phial is supposed to be sucked out before its mouth has been blocked. Thereupon, he examines the nature of this one-third section in the phial which hitherto contained air and which now no longer contains air, as the air has been removed. With the help of two arguments, he forces his adversaries to admitting that this one-third section must be three-dimensional, having length, breadth, and depth. Thus, this one third section cannot be absolutely nothing but must be a body, because it is something three-dimensional.[329] What we do not know, however, is what body it is.[330]

Subsequently, al-Fārābī offers the following options. The body taking up one third of the space inside the phial either always has been occupying this space or came to occupy it following the act of sucking the air out. The first option is absurd, because this would mean that two bodies have been occupying the same place. If, consequently, the second option is true, "then this body is either air (*hawāʾ*) or water diffused in air" (*māʾ šāʾiʿ fī l-hawāʿ*).[331] The second alternative is quickly dismissed, and al-Fārābī concludes that the body that occupies this one-third section in the phial must be air.[332] This brings him to what is, on his analysis, the most important question of all: what happened to the air and why does it, instead of preventing the water from entering the phial, attract the water into it (*ḏātuhū yaǧḏibu al-māʾ ilayhi*).[333]

Instead of answering these questions right away, al-Fārābī inserts an import excursus on the warming and cooling of natural substances. His intentions, however, are

329 cf. also McGinnis' suggestion to emend the edition and the translation of Sayılı/Lugal in "Arabic and Islamic Natural Philosophy and Natural Science," fn. 8.

330 al-Fārābī, *Maqāla fī l-ḫalāʾ*, 2.3–7.6, 8.11–14.

331 al-Fārābī, *Maqāla fī l-ḫalāʾ*, 9.7.

332 It is not entirely clear what al-Fārābī meant when he wrote here that the body in question may be "water diffused in air" (*māʾ šāʾiʿ fī l-hawāʿ*). First of all, al-Fārābī has not made clear that at the present stage of the experiment, the phial already is immersed in water. If, however, this is what we need to picture, then it remains unclear how water could have entered the phial, if the phial's mouth is still blocked. Is it that he describes the situation in that split second in which we have already removed the finger from the phial's mouth but water has not yet entered? Or is he merely logically excluding all options that, now that the phial is immersed in water with its mouth still blocked, the body in question could only be from one of the two adjacent substances, viz., air and water (obviously excluding the glass of the phial). Moreover, what does he mean by water "diffused" in air? He states that it has already been said that this option is false (*wa-lā yumkinu an yakūna māʾan šāʾiʿan fī l-hawāʾ ka-mā qulnā*; 9.8f.), but it is not obvious what he is referring to. Is the state of water being diffused in air impossible because this, too, leads to the absurd situation of two bodies occupying the same place? Since al-Fārābī is likely arguing against Muʿtazilī proponents, one may also think of the Baġdādī account of the related mechanism behind the cupping glass, for they explain that the flesh of the finger blocking the phial's mouth is drawn into the glass by becoming mixed (*muḫtaliṭ* in al-Nīsābūrī, *muḫāliṭa* in Ibn Mattawayh) with the air in the glass (al-Nīsābūrī, *Kitāb al-Masāʾil*, 31.19 (ed. Biram)/52.20f. (ed. Ziyāda/Sayyid); Ibn Mattawayh, *al-Taḏkira*, I.30, 121.16 (ed. Luṭf/ʿŪn)/50.16f. (ed. Gimaret)); cf. Dhanani, *The Physical Theory of Kalām*, 76. Perhaps it is this "mixture" of the two adjacent substances which al-Fārābī means when he writes that water may be diffused in air in this one-third section of the phial.

333 al-Fārābī, *Maqāla fī l-ḫalāʾ*, 9.10f.

different from those of Avicenna in his correspondence with al-Bīrūnī. Far from explaining the interrelation of temperature and volume, al-Fārābī asserts that the heating and cooling of a natural substance either occurs by adding to it, or bringing it in contact with, something hotter or colder, respectively, or it happens by itself (*bi-nafsihā*).[334] In other words, if we heat water on a stove and turn of the stove, the water can cool down by itself, i.e., without something cold having to be added to it. Natural substances, then, have a natural state with respect to temperature, a state to which they will return by themselves after any forceful increase or decrease in temperature has come to an end. This being established, al-Fārābī maintains that precisely this is also the case "with things which become greater and smaller."[335] Thus, becoming greater and smaller either occurs by adding some other body to and removing a portion from it, respectively, or it happens by itself – and among those bodies where this is possible, al-Fārābī adds, "is air, for it may become bigger in greatness (*fī ʿiẓam azyad*) up to whatever magnitude without adding to it another [body's] greatness from the outside."[336] It is important to understand, though, that the air which changes its volume and "greatness" always remains one and the same air (*huwāʾan wāḥidan bi-ʿaynihī*), it merely changes its volume sometimes due to force and sometimes due to its nature (*bi-ṭibāʿihī*), just as a stone may move upwards by force but always returns to its natural place on account of its nature.[337] On this basis, al-Fārābī presents the following important insight:

> كذلك الهواء إذا ازداد عظمه قسراً فإنّ الممسّك له على العظم الذي صار إليه قسراً ما دام مقارناً له يقف على ذلك العظم. فإذا فارقه الممسّك له على ذلك العظم رجع إلى عظمه الطبيعي.
>
> Likewise, when the greatness of air is increased forcefully, then, indeed, for as long as that which holds it at the greatness which it forcefully was made to have is associated with it it stays at that greatness. However, if, then, that which holds it at that greatness separates from it, it returns to its natural greatness (*ilā ʿiẓamihī l-ṭabīʿī*). (al-Fārābī, *Maqāla fī l-ḫalāʾ*, 13.10–13)

With this, al-Fārābī has now all the ingredients for his explanation of the phenomenon of the phial. First of all, he emphasises that inside the phial is only air and no void. Then, he states that when one third of the air inside the phial is sucked out, the remaining two-thirds of air are forcefully and unnaturally expanded, so as to occupy now the whole of the phial. As long as the phial's mouth remains blocked, the air remains unnaturally expanded. Once it is immersed in water, however, and the mouth is re-opened, the air – through its own nature – reduces to its natural volume, thus withdrawing from the one third it was forced to occupy unnaturally, so that the now adjacent water will enter the phial and occupy as much of it as air has been sucked out of it. The ultimate cause

334 al-Fārābī, *Maqāla fī l-ḫalāʾ*, 10.3–11.2.
335 al-Fārābī, *Maqāla fī l-ḫalāʾ*, 11.6f.
336 al-Fārābī, *Maqāla fī l-ḫalāʾ*, 12.12–14.
337 al-Fārābī, *Maqāla fī l-ḫalāʾ*, 13.4–10.

for the observed phenomenon, then, is the nature (*ṭibāʿ*) in natural substances and not some mysterious force or the void.[338]

The explanation provided by al-Fārābī is systematic insofar as it combines an account of condensation and rarefaction with the explanation of the experiment with phials and clepsydrae on the basis of his general acceptance of hylomorphism. In both cases, the substance inside the device – air in the phial and water in the clepsydra – counteracts or tries to avoid any unnatural increase of volume. Thus, air inside a phial attracts the water, in order to *regain* its natural volume, whereas the water in a clepsydra does not drip out, in order to *retain* its natural volume. There is no void anywhere in the world; all there is is the continuity of matter inhabited by forms.[339] So, what al-Fārābī's adversaries mistook for the void was nothing other than air.[340] On the whole, then, al-Fārābī's intention in writing this treatise was to support the Aristotelian contention that all the experiments people devised to prove the existence of the void merely proved the existence of air, which they subsequently confuse with the void.[341]

In addition, we see that al-Fārābī employs heat in a different way than the Muʿtazilites from Baġdād did, and as Avicenna and al-Maʿṣūmī will do in their response to al-Bīrūnī. For him heating and cooling is simply an example of a change of temperature which may be unnatural or natural, used for expanding the well-known theory of natural motion in the category of place to motions in other categories, such as quality and quantity. Not only do natural substances have natural places which explain their local motions to these places, they also have natural qualitative as well as quantitative states, such that *any* accidental change against the nature of a given substance brings about a natural tendency or inclination to return to that state, be that a stone's local motion back to its natural place or the cooling down of hot soup or the contraction of freezing water. What remains unclear is whether al-Fārābī would also accept the interrelation of temperature and volume.

Turning now to Avicenna's second explanation, the one he puts forth in his *al-Samāʿ al-ṭabīʿī*, we should recall right away that Avicenna agrees with al-Fārābī on natural places, temperatures, and volumes. We have already seen in the investigation of his account of nature and inclination that he explicitly extends the scope of nature's activity to *all* kinds of natural motion.[342] For Avicenna, the volume of a body is an accidental state just as its temperature. In other words, its concrete quantity is an

338 cf. al-Fārābī, *Maqāla fī l-ḫalāʾ*, 14.5–10, 15.3–11. Although what al-Fārābī explains here is close to our modern understanding of density, being the relation between weight and volume, I shall abstain from using this modern term and, instead, follow al-Fārābī's and Avicenna's terminology, who speak of "volume" (*ḥaǧm*) as well as "greatness" (*ʿiẓam*) and "smallness" (*ṣiġar*).

339 cf. al-Fārābī, *Maqāla fī l-ḫalāʾ*, 14.17–15.3, 16.1f.

340 cf. al-Fārābī, *Maqāla fī l-ḫalāʾ*, 16.2f.

341 q.v. fn. 71 above, 328.

342 cf. esp. *al-Kawn wa-l-fasād* 6, 131.3–11, translated and discussed above, 250f.

accident, just as its qualities are, and can be subject to change. One and the same body, i.e., one and the same composite of matter and form, can be hot and cold or great and small. For Avicenna, this means that all characteristics imposed on a body through its quantitative determinations are systematically analogous to its qualitative determinations. An object is a chunk of matter together with its form which determines its essential as well as its accidental behaviour. Just as water and air have a natural place, so they also have a certain natural temperature and a certain natural volume. Its natural place, temperature, and volume are determined through its form or nature. Thus, a body could simply reside in an unnatural place (which would induce an inclination to return to its natural place), or have an unnatural temperature (which would induce an inclination to return to its natural temperature), or an unnatural volume (which would induce an inclination to return to its natural volume). In addition, if a body is at its natural place, temperature, or volume, force is required to subdue its inclination for retaining what is natural. This is precisely what al-Fārābī was expounding in his treatise, and it is also what Avicenna immediately mentions when he finally approaches the experiments with phials, pipes, and clepsydrae in *al-Samāʿ al-ṭabīʿī* II.9. There, he writes the following:

فكما أنّه يجوز أن يسخن ويبرد ويكون منه ما هو طبيعي ومنه ما هو قسري فكذلك الحال في العظم والصغر. وإذا كان هذا جائزاً لم يكن كلّ انتقاص جزء من جسم يوجب أن يبقى الباقي على حجمه الأوّل حتّى يكون إذا أخذ جزء من هواء مالئ للقارورة يجب أن يبقى الباقي على حجمه فيكون ما وراءه خلاء.

So, just as it is possible that it [sc. a natural body] heats up and cools down – and this could be both natural and forced – the same situation, then, [obtains] regarding greatness and smallness (*fī l-ʿiẓam wa-l-ṣiġar*). If this is possible, then not every diminution of some part of a body requires that the rest retains its original volume (*ḥağmihī al-awwal*), such that if some part of the air filling the phial is taken away, the rest has to retain[343] its volume, so that what is left behind it would be a void. (*al-Samāʿ al-ṭabīʿī* II.9, §20, 146.1–4)[344]

With this passage, Avicenna steals the thunder of his opponents. Taking refuge to the void and its supposed force is not the only way to account for the observed phenomena. Indeed, it is by no means necessary to assume the existence of the void if it is accepted that natural bodies can be forced to change their volume against their nature so as to take up more space than they naturally would have occupied. Avicenna argues that if there is one litre of air in a phial and if one third of it is sucked out, the consequence is not that the phial is, then, filled with two-thirds of air occupying two thirds of the phial together with one third of void occupying one third of the phial. Instead, when one third of air is sucked out of the phial, the remaining two-thirds of air will have to make

343 Reading *yabqā l-bāqī* with Mss. Leiden or. 4 and or. 84 as well as Zāyid for *yabqā* in McGinnis and Āl Yāsīn.

344 cf. *al-Ilāhiyyāt* II.3, §14, 77.14–6; IX.5, §10, 413.15–414.5; *al-Nağāt* II.3.13, 299.9–302.26 (partially corresponding to *al-Ḥikma al-ʿArūḍiyya* II.3, 148.17–149.8); *al-Ḥikma al-mašriqiyya* III.10, 31.15.

up for the missing third and, as a result, will be unnaturally enlarged such as to fill the whole phial. This is entirely in line with his own account of nature and inclination, and with the explanation offered in al-Fārābī's *Maqāla fī l-ḫalāʾ*.

Yet, Avicenna goes beyond al-Fārābī when he combines the theory of natural volumes with the Aristotelian conception of place as a surface, because he emphasises that it is only due to the outer surface of the air in the phial adhering to the inner surface of the phial that the air behaves like an elastic band does when one end of it is attached to one side of a room and when someone pulls its other end in the opposite direction, thus stretching it to a size it would not have attained through its own nature but only through the activity of a forcefully acting agent. This is what Avicenna explains in the following passage:

> وإذا كان اقتطاع ذلك الجزء منه لا يمكن أو ينبسط انبساطاً يصير الباقي في حجمه الأوّل لامتناع وقوع الخلاء ووجوب الملاء وكان هذا الانبساط ممكناً وكان للقاسر قوّة تُحوج إلى خروج هذا الممكن إلى الفعل بجذبه إيّاه في جهة ولزوم سطحه لما يليه في جهة ... وصار بعض ما انبسط واقفاً خارج القارورة وهو الممصوص وبقي الباقي ملء القارورة ضرورةً قد ملأها منبسطاً لضرورة الجذب الماصّ بقدر القارورة.
>
> If the removal of that part of it is not possible unless (*aw*)[345] there is an expansion [such that] the remaining rest becomes its original volume,[346] because of the impossibility of the occurrence of the void and the necessity that [everything] is filled – and this expansion is possible – and if the agent acting by force has the power required for bringing this possibility into actuality through his attraction of it to one side, while its surface adheres (*luzūm saṭḥihī*) to what is adjacent to its [other] side ... then part of what expanded will reach[347] the outside of the phial – and this is what has been sucked out – and the rest will necessarily[348] remain filling the phial, having been expanded due to the necessity of the sucking attraction through the length of the phial. (*al-Samāʿ al-ṭabīʿī* II.9, §20, 146.6–11, tr. by McGinnis, modified)[349]

According to Avicenna's understanding, what happens inside the phial is that the air is forcefully, i.e., unnaturally, enlarged. Throughout the process, the air does nothing but strive for retaining its natural volume inside the phial and to stick to its *place* – and its place is the inner surface of the containing body (in this case the phial) which is in contact with the outer surface of the contained body (in this case the air). The reason it is difficult and exhausting to suck the air out of the phial is the same reason it is difficult and exhausting to lift a heavy stone: doing this means to counter-act the

---

345 For *aw* meaning "unless" when followed by a verb in the subjunctive mood, cf. Fischer, *Grammatik des klassischen Arabisch*, §411.

346 Reading *ḥağmihī* with Ms. Leiden or. 4 and Zāyid for for *ḥagm* in Ms. Leiden or. 84 as well as McGinnis and Āl Yāsīn.

347 Reading *wāqifan* with Ms. Leiden or. 4 and Zāyid for *wāqiʿan* in Ms. Leiden or. 84 as well as McGinnis and Āl Yāsīn.

348 Reading *al-qārūra ḍarūratan* with Mss. Leiden or. 4 and or. 84 as well as Zāyid for *al-qārūra* in McGinnis and Āl Yāsīn.

349 cf. *al-Ḥikma al-mašriqiyya* III.10, 31.18–22

nature of a natural body and to perceive its inclination (*mayl*) first-hand.[350] If, then, the forcefully acting agent succeeds in overcoming the natural inclination of the air to retain its volume, some parts of the air are moved outside the phial, thus prompting the remaining parts inside to expand against their nature. If the phial, whose mouth was subsequently blocked with a finger, is then immersed in water, and if, further, the finger covering its mouth is removed, one can witness how some water is sucked into the phial through the force of the inclination that belongs to the unnaturally expanded air, whose nature is actively striving to bring it back to its natural volume, so that, once the air returned to its natural volume and its natural quantitative state (*ʿāda ilā qiwāmihī*), we find some water having been attracted into the phial now making up for the missing parts of the original amount of air.

The notion of the surface enters the picture, when we realise that once the phial's mouth has been blocked, part of the surface of the unnaturally enlarged air was in immediate contact with part of the surface of the finger, while the rest of the air's surface still adhered to the inner surface of the phial. The air's inclination, however, was not able to pull the rather solid body of the finger inside the phial. Thus, it had to remain in its unnaturally enlarged state. When, however, upon re-opening the phial's mouth, the surface of the air came in contact, and adhered to (*luzūm*), the surface of the water, it could overcome the inclination belonging to the water and attract the rather fluid body of the water unnaturally upwards into the phial. The attractive force at work here is, thus, revealed to be the natural body's inclination to retain its natural volume by adhering to its natural place being nothing other than the inner surface of the containing body which is in contact with the outer surface of the contained body.

Understanding Avicenna's mature account from his *al-Samāʿ al-ṭabīʿī* concerning the mechanism behind such an experiment with phials allows us to establish three historically significant results about the philosophical and scientific history of place, space, and the void. The first result contextualises Avicenna's solution within the late ancient debate and, in particular as a response to Philoponus. In his corollary on place, Philoponus self-confidently asked "what on earth" (τί δήποτε) would happen if there, inside the clepsydra, were "no extension that is distinct from the body [and] void in its own definition?" Moreover, he exclaimed, the force which we are observing in these experiments could hardly be attributed to a surface, for "no one in his right mind ... would call a surface filled or void," and it is precisely the danger of something getting empty or void that is the real cause for the phenomenon.[351] Against this, it has already been noted in which sense Avicenna argues that a surface can, indeed, be said to be full or empty.[352] Now, we have additionally witnessed how Avicenna explains "what on earth" it is that happens inside devices such as a clepsydra: it is the Aristotelian notion

350 q.v. esp. above, 247f.

351 Philoponus, *In Phys.*, 571.9–19, tr. by Furley, modified.

352 cf. *al-Samāʿ al-ṭabīʿī* II.9, §14, 143.8–144.2; q.v. fn. 152 above, 354.

of place as a contacting surface at work together with a strong sense of the hylomorphic unity of a body as the explanatory background for condensation and rarefaction and of the body's nature serving as a cohesive power striving to preserve the body in all aspects as it is.

Incidentally it is this very same point, viz., Avicenna's emphasis on the notion surface as an indispensable factor in the proposed explanation, which also – and this is the second result – sets off Avicenna's account from that of his predecessor al-Fārābī. Evidently, Avicenna was indebted to the way in which al-Fārābī, first, sets out the problem, then, provides an excursus on the heating and cooling of natural substances, and, finally, applies the fruits of that excursus to the problem, for Avicenna follows al-Fārābī's structure in his own explanation.[353] What is new with Avicenna, though, is that he ultimately explains the "attractive power" with the help of the notion of a surface. There was one passage in al-Fārābī's treatise, in which he hinted at the mutual contact between bodies (*hiya mutamāssa*).[354] In another passage, he mentioned the "adhesion" (*taʿalluq*) of water to air (using a different expression than Avicenna).[355] There is also one singular mention of the notion of surface (*saṭḥ*) in the more relevant parts of his treatise.[356] Yet, is it fundamentally clear that al-Fārābī did not incorporate the notion in his own explanation of the observed phenomenon.[357]

So, Avicenna clearly developed al-Fārābī's solution further – and he did so in a way entirely in line with the strategy we have seen him pursuing throughout his entire investigation of place. Not only does he resurrect Aristotle's definition of place and defend it as a coherent conception in detail; he also implements his contentions in his arguments for disproving space and void in such a way that it is ironically the allegedly ridiculous idea of place as a surface that ultimately explains why water stays in a clepsydra, why one can make water move upwards through pipes against its natural downward tendency, and why water enters a phial after some air has been sucked out. It is clear beyond doubt that for Avicenna, there really was not a single reason that Aristotle's definition of place as a surface should be abandoned – to the contrary, given the tenor of his responses, it seems that all the criticism he had read in ancient and late ancient sources and commentaries only provided him with more and more

---

353 cf. especially the first lines of his account in *al-Samāʿ al-ṭabīʿī* II.9, §20, 145.16–146.3; *al-Ḥikma al-mašriqiyya* III.10, 31.13–15.

354 al-Fārābī, *Maqāla fī l-ḫalāʾ*, 14.17.

355 al-Fārābī, *Maqāla fī l-ḫalāʾ*, 15.15.

356 al-Fārābī, *Maqāla fī l-ḫalāʾ*, 5.8.

357 That is to say, he does not do it here in the small treatise on the void. However, he may have done so in his lost commentary on the *Physics*. In addition, a reference to Aristotle is apporpriate, who in the *De caelo* describes how air can attract water "when its surface becomes one" (ὅταν γένηται τὸ ἐπίπεδον ἕν; *Cael.* IV.5, 312b9f.), i.e., one with the surface of the air, as Simplicius will clarify later; cf. *In Cael.*, 723.17–32; cf. also Themistius' remarks on the same passage in response to Alexander which, in turn, are discussed by Averroes in his *Commentum magnum super libro De celo et mundo*, comm. 39, 126–142, as mentioned by Grant (*Much Ado about Nothing*, 78).

reason for accepting Aristotle's position, because there is nothing that can explain all the puzzling phenomena more adequately and convincingly than a nicely developed account of place as a surface.

As a third result, we can now assess and ascertain a clear development in Avicenna's thought leading from his early account in the correspondence with al-Bīrūnī to his new explanation in *al-Samā' al-ṭabī'ī*. It is evident that Avicenna changed his mind on the issue, because in his mature explanation, he did not once mention that the act of sucking leads to a change of the air's temperature in the phial or that heat in any way brings about a change in volume. Sure, heat was mentioned but, following al-Fārābī, only as an example of an unnatural change of temperature subsequently counteracted by the nature, so that the unnaturally heated body cools down by itself. That is to say, heat was not mentioned as the cause of an expansion of volume. This, however, used to be the core of Avicenna's, and al-Ma'ṣūmī's, earlier explanation in their correspondence with al-Bīrūnī.

In order to understand why Avicenna changed his mind, we need to recall the following points. First, there apparently was a debate going on in the fourth/tenth century precisely about this issue in theological, scientific, and philosophical circles. Second, Avicenna was aware of some criticism of his theory, viz., the criticism that reached him from al-Bīrūnī.[358] Third, there is no reason to believe that he was not aware of more criticism, viz., the criticism of the Baṣrī Mu'tazilites against their brothers from Baġdād, who agreed with Avicenna on this, as we have seen. This point gains further support through Avicenna's *Risāla li-ba'ḍ al-mutakallimīn ilā l-Šayḫ fa-aǧābahum*, documenting his engagement with the Mu'tazilī doctrines of space and void. Fourth, it has also been remarked that Avicenna may have realised that his earlier explanation was incapable of explaining *all* phenomena, for it cannot account for experiments in which no heat or any change of temperature is involved, such as those with clepsydrae. Finally, Avicenna's predecessor al-Fārābī also wrote a specific treatise on the void, offering an new explanation of the phenomena which does not rely on a heat-induced change of volume and which, thus, was not vulnerable to all this criticism. Against this background it is not surprising that Avicenna, at one point having become aware of either al-Fārābī's explanation or similar accounts put forth by other philosophers and scientists who participated in the fourth/tenth-century debate, abandoned his earlier and evidently insufficient theory. It is, thus, reasonable for Avicenna to adopt a different theory such as the one we have seen at work in al-Fārābī's treatise. With this, however, Avicenna is now no longer able to account for the paradigm case which probably had motivated him in his early theory in the first place, viz., the case of hot cupping glasses as it was used in medical treatments which al-Fārābī's model, as it was adopted by Avicenna, does not cover, as that model does not rely on the interrelation of

---

358 For another case in which Avicenna seems to have changed his mind after al-Bīrūnī's criticism, cf. Hasse, *Avicenna's* De Anima *in the Latin West*, 108–113.

temperature and volume. Accordingly, we might at first be surprised that Avicenna now in *al-Samāʿ al-ṭabīʿī* II.9 also asks what would happen if we *blew* into the phial instead of sucking air out, because it reminds us of his earlier theory which we thought he had abandoned; yet, in the final analysis, his question demonstrates that he has a bigger goal in mind and that he is aiming at a theory which accounts for *all* phenomena. So, in *al-Samāʿ al-ṭabīʿī* II.9, Avicenna describes the experiment that we already know from his correspondence with al-Bīrūnī, where neither the experiment nor the proposed theory behind it struck us as particularly convincing, with the following words:

> ونحن إذا نفخنا في القارورة ثمّ أكبناه على الماء خرجت منها ريح كثرية يبقبق منها الماء ثمّ عاد الماء فدخل فيها.
>
> When we blow into the phial and, then, turn it over into the water, much vapour gets out of it and bubbles up from the water before the water came back and entered it. (*al-Samāʿ al-ṭabīʿī* II.9, §21, 146.12f.)

Apparently Avicenna is still confident that this experiment works as he depicts it; maybe it does. At any rate, the observation he describes obviously cannot be explained by the solution he just gave for the previous phenomenon of water being attracted into the phial after sucking some air out of it. So, if a phial is entirely filled with air, and if we force more air into it, then, following Avicenna's mature theory, the air inside the phial is unnaturally condensed. Once we stop blowing into the phial, the unnaturally condensed air in the phial strives to return to its natural volume, and so the added extra air is expelled and leaves the phial. This can best be witnessed under water, where we see air coming out of the phial in bubbles. However, once the extra air got out, i.e., once the air inside the phial returned to its natural volume which fills the phial entirely, why should now water enter the phial, if the phial is completely filled with air? This, however, is exactly what Avicenna describes. So, Avicenna has to deal here with a double phenomenon: the bubbling of air out of the phial *and* the subsequent entering of water into the phial. Accordingly, Avicenna also needs a double explanation. This is precisely what he provides a little later:

> بقي أنّ السبب فيه التجاء الهواء إلى حجم أصغر للانضغاط فإذا زال انبسط إلى حجمه. ولأجل أنّ هناك سبباً آخر يقتضي حجماً أكبر وهو التسخّن والتلطّف بقسر تحريك النفخ إن كان ممنوعاً عن مقتضاه بالضغط الذي يكثّفه أشدّ من تلطيف هذا وقد زال العائق فاقتضى السخونة العارضة أن يصير الهواء أعظم حجماً من الحجم الذي كان قبل النفخ. ومن أجل أنّ تلك السخونة عرضية بهذا وتزول وينقبض الهواء إلى الحجم الذي اقتضته طبيعته لو لم تكن تلك السخونة فيعود الماء فيدخل لاستحالة وقوع الخلاء. فلهذا ما نشاهد من المنفوخ بالقوّة أوّلاً تتبقبق منه هواء يخرج ثمّ يأخذ في جذب الماء إلى نفسه كما لو سدّ فم القارورة بأصبع وسخنت بنار حارّة لا تكسّرها ثمّ أكبّت على الماء عرض أوّلاً تبقبق ثمّ امتصاص منها للماء.
>
> It remains that the cause of it is that the air seeks refuge in a smaller volume because of being compressed and then, when [the compression] ceases, it expands to its [original] volume. Yet, because there is another cause (*sababan āḫar*) which requires a greater volume, namely, becoming hot and rarefied (*al-tasaḫḫun wa-l-talaṭṭuf*) due to the force of causing the motion of blowing

> (*bi-qasr taḥrīk al-nafḫ*), if[359] it [sc. the air] is prevented from what it requires because of the pressure which condenses it being stronger than the rarefaction of this,[360] and [if further] the obstacle ceases, then the accidental heat requires that the air becomes in volume greater than the volume which was before the blowing. Because that heat is accidental (*ʿaraḍiyya*) to this and ceases, the air contracts to the volume that its nature required had there not been that heat, and so the water comes back and enters due to the impossibility of the occurrence of the void. It is because of this that what we observe regarding that which was vigorously inflated (*al-manfūḫ bi-l-quwwa*) is, first, that air bubbles out of it, getting out, and, then, it starts to attract water into itself – just as when the mouth of the phial is blocked by a finger and you heat it with a hot fire (*bi-nār ḥārra*) without shattering it and, then, turn it over into the water, it first happens to bubble, and then there is sucking from it of water [into the phial]. (*al-Samāʿ al-ṭabīʿī* II.9, §21, 147.7–13)

The first sentence restates his mature theory as adopted from al-Fārābī. With the second sentence he importantly points to yet "another cause" (*sababan āḫar*) involved. This other cause likewise leads to a change in volume, viz., heat (*tasaḫḫun*) leading to rarefaction (*talaṭṭuf*). The reason that heat and rarefaction are also involved in the experiment is that we not only blew once or twice in the phial but exerted much effort to blow into it vigorously (*bi-l-quwwa*). So, we really laboured long and hard to force (*bi-qasr*) some extra air into the phial. Thus, our engagement with blowing into the phial (*taḥrīk al-nafḫ*) leads to two results: (i) there is now more air in the phial than there had been before and (ii) the air inside the phial is now hot or warm, at least warmer than before. Normally, the increase in temperature would require an increase in volume, i.e., a rarefaction; here, however, we blew into the phial, which leads to the opposite, viz., a condensation. Thus, the hot air cannot expand as it would, because "the pressure which condenses" the air, i.e., our rigorous blowing, "is stronger than the rarefaction." If, now, the phial is turned over and immersed in water, we observe that, first, the extra

359 Reading *in kāna* with Ms. Leiden or. 84 as well as McGinnis and Zāyid for only *kāna* in Ms. Leiden or. 4 and Āl Yāsīn.

360 The structure of this first half of the sentence is not entirely clear, in particular inasmuch as it is not evident whether "the force of causing the motion of blowing" explains (i) why there was some "becoming hot and rarefied" or rather (ii) why the air "is prevented from what it requires." If the second, then the translation would read: "Yet, because there is another cause (*sababan āḫar*) which requires a greater volume, namely, becoming hot and rarefied (*al-tasaḫḫun wa-l-talaṭṭuf*), if due to the force of causing the motion of blowing it [sc. the air] is prevented from what it requires..." Against this, I decided in favour of the first option, primarily for two reasons. First, because it is subsequently the fact that "the pressure which condenses it [is] stronger than the rarefaction of this" which explains why the air "is prevented from what it requires." Second, it seems that the reason for why there is some "becoming hot and rarefied" is precisely the *vehemence* of the forceful blowing; it is because we blew so heavily into the phial that the air became warm. This not only makes sense, but is reaffirmed in the following and, furthermore, also in line with the earlier recommendation of al-Maʿṣūmī that al-Bīrūnī has to "blow into [the phial] *until* (*ilā an*) the air is hot." Finally, Gundisalvi also seems to have understood the text this way, for he translated that passage as follows: *Et quia est ibi alia causa propter quam debet habere maiorem quantitatem, quae est calefactio et tenuitas propter constrictionem motus sufflationis, idea non potuit esse quantum debeat esse propoter densationem constringentem, quae habet maiorem vim quam tenuitas huius* (Avicenna, *Sufficientia: Liber primus naturalium* II.9, 85–89).

air we blew into the phial gets out and bubbles up. This is the al-Fārābī-inspired first half of the explanation of the double phenomenon. Once the extra air got out, the heat of the inside air is no longer "prevented from what it requires," viz., expansion and rarefaction. Thus, even *more* air gets out as the inside air can now expand due to the increased temperature. In sum, then, there is now less air filling the whole phial than there had been even before we blew into it. If, due to the coldness of the water, the inside air then begins to cool down, it also begins to decrease in volume again. Yet, since there is less air filling the phial than before and since the air additionally also returns to its natural volume, it retreats, so as to no longer occupy the entire phial, making room for the adjacent water to enter. The water, with its surface in contact with the retreating surface of the air, is attracted through the surface-tension and pulled inside the phial. This is the still-valid youthful explanation of Avicenna for the second half of the double phenomenon: "first, that air bubbles out of it, getting out, and, then, it starts to attract water into itself."

While we may still be uncertain whether mere blowing, vigorously or not, is enough to heat the air inside the phial sufficiently to witness the phenomenon, Avicenna is entirely justified in not letting go of his earlier explanation *entirely*, because, of course, there is an interrelation between temperature and volume in natural substances, and he knows it – and he makes it explicit when he mentions in the last sentence that the same happens when the phial is heated on a "hot fire" (*bi-nār ḥārra*), just as is done with hot cupping glasses in medicine. On the whole, Avicenna can now explain experiments that involve (a) clepsydrae, phials (with sucking), and pipes (i.e., cases of negative pressure) as well as (b) cracking bottles in winter or in a fire, phials (with blowing), and cupping glasses (i.e., cases of temperature-dependent volume change), by combining his earlier justified conviction about heat and volume with al-Fārābī's new theory. The most important detail in all this, however, is that Avicenna no longer uses his earlier theory to explain the experiments in category (a), which means that he, indeed, abandoned his earlier model here, even though he did not abandon it completely.

Taking it all together, Avicenna's achievement lies not in devising the very argument as such which, according to him, refutes what has perhaps been the most prominent and most successful experiment for, allegedly, demonstrating the "force of the void." The argument as such was known to him presumably through al-Fārābī. Yet, Avicenna successfully, and more so than al-Fārābī, combines a number of core elements of his physics. What ultimately explains the mechanisms behind clepsydrae and other devices is a complex interplay of a number of important elements of his physical theory which have been established throughout his *al-Samāʿ al-ṭabīʿī* as this study has shown. There is (i) corporeality as a foundational feature of corporeal bodies; (ii) matter as the principle that, once specified through a form, is pure and passive receptivity of any quantitative, qualitative, and specific determination; (iii) nature as an active force within natural bodies that organises them in accordance with what they are, i.e., preserving their unity, keeping them at their place, holding their proper temperature, and retaining their assigned volumes in proportion to their underlying matter; and, finally, (iv) place as the inner surface of the containing body which is in contact with the outer surface of the contained body. Moreover, all this makes it, once more, abundantly clear that we are still concerned with a discussion of *place* and that the refutation of the void is nothing but a crucial and important component within Avicenna's discussion of that concept. Only after the extension – be it void or filled – as a candidate for place has been demonstrated to be non-existent, the correct definition of place as a surface can fully be embraced.

In this sense, then, it should now have become sufficiently clear why there is no extension over and above the body, regardless of whether we call that extension space or void: first of all, there exists only the extension that belongs to the body. Since the void is supposed to be always filled, there are no grounds for another additional extension. In fact, the argument which was supposed to make known what the void is by imagining an impossible situation is a deception, resting upon a faulty and illicit understanding of what abstraction and analysis actually amounts to. That there is no separate extension over and above the bodies is, second, also borne out by the fact that every attempt to define the void fails. There is, then, nothing that corresponds to the assumed three-dimensional immaterial extension. It has no essence; what has no essence cannot be instantiated; and what cannot be instantiated does not exist in concrete reality. Third, Avicenna provides ample material in support of Aristotle's arguments against the possibility of motion in an assumed void, so ample that he perhaps did not even have to address the most famous of Philoponus' counter-arguments directly.[361] Finally, there is also no way in which the void could be said to have an attractive influence on bodies. We must conclude, then, that there is no extension, no void, no space in any form, because conceiving of space is a mistake of the imagination; because it has no meaning and, thus, no definition; because it makes motion impossible; and because it is not required to explain the behaviour of natural bodies. The void is nothing, it is itself void – just as Aristotle has argued one-and-a-half thousand years earlier. As a result, the inner surface of the containing body is the only remaining option for the essence of place – i.e., the only option from the initial list of candidates which is neither incoherent nor non-existent, and which can easily account for all relevant natural phenomena experienced in the world.

In all this, i.e., in establishing the essence of place and rejecting the existence of void and space, Avicenna was at his most Aristotelian. He accepted the Aristotelian position with all its allegedly inconsistent consequences and improved upon the details of the definition. Moreover, he rejected any idea of an extension which purportedly exists independently from the body both with Aristotelian arguments and with arguments he either devised himself or carried to a further level. It is, therefore, necessary to agree with Duhem that "Avicenna defined place ... in the same manner as Aristotle"

---

361 q.v. fn. 194 above, 371.

– at least as long as we take “manner” to refer to the literal wording of the definition itself and not to the approach towards or the details about it. Nonetheless, Avicenna’s position is by no means uninteresting. There are two primary reasons for this. First, because it is interesting to see the ways in which he clarifies so many crucial details surrounding the definition and, in particular, the notion and the explanatory strength of a surface. Second, because he was the first to provide a full account in support of Aristotle’s definition *after* it was destroyed and ripped to pieces by such ingenious Neoplatonists as Philoponus. After Philoponus, it became excruciatingly difficult to be an Aristotelian regarding place. Moreover, Avicenna often appeared, sometimes with the help or earlier Arabic Peripatetics, to react against other rival conceptions of his own day, especially those brought forward by the Baṣrī branch of Muʿtazilism. Against both camps, the Neoplatonists and the Muʿtazilites, Avicenna kept his Aristotelian stance and defended his account in a great battle which, on the outset, already seemed to be lost but which, in the end, he seems to have won.

With Avicenna’s account of place being perhaps the *most* Aristotelian aspect within Avicenna’s natural philosophy, I shall now to turn a concept regarding which Avicenna appears, in one important respect at least, to be at his *least* Aristotelian – the concept of time.

6 Time and Temporality in the Physical World

There is no part of Avicenna's *al-Samāʿ al-ṭabīʿī* that is as well studied as his discussion of time. Yet, the effective outcome in terms of actual publications in western languages is surprisingly slender, for the two longest studies, the doctoral dissertations of Yegane Shayegan (submitted in 1986) and Jon McGinnis (submitted in 1999), remain unpublished to this day.[1] Shayegan does not seem to have published any material from her doctoral dissertation in the form of separate articles as McGinnis has done.[2] There is, moreover, a chapter on Avicenna's account of time on the basis of the Latin translation of *al-Samāʿ al-ṭabīʿī* in the German monograph *Aristoteles contra Augustinum* by Udo Reinhold Jeck, published in 1994.[3] Jeck investigates the relation between time and soul, and discusses some relevant passages in the Aristotelian text and the late ancient commentaries, before he turns to Avicenna and Averroes, and finally to the Latin tradition in the thirteenth century. In Arabic scholarly literature, the topic "time" likewise raised the interest of a number of scholars who examined the temporal theories of Avicenna and of his Greek and Arabic predecessors, in particular Plato, Aristotle, Plotinus (d. 270), and Abū Bakr Muḥammad ibn Zakariyāʾ al-Rāzī (d. 313/925).[4]

Aristotle's discussion of time in *Physics* IV.10–14 has likewise received a large share of attention, of which the two books by Ursula Coope and Tony Roark are just the most recent larger additions to a long list of articles and monographs that have been published in the previous decades.[5] As often, the vast and complex developments achieved in late antiquity have less frequently been the subjects of investigation.[6]

1 Shayegan, *Avicenna on Time*; McGinnis, *Time and Time Again*.

2 cf. esp. McGinnis, "Ibn Sīnā on the Now"; cf. also McGinnis, "The Topology of Time"; "For Every Time There is a Season"; "Time to Change." Shayegan's translation of chapters II.11–12, however, have been reprinted recently in Nasr and Aminrazavi, *An Anthology of Philosophy in Persia*, 292–302. Another important article that deserves to be mentioned is Mayer, "Avicenna against Time Beginning."

3 Jeck, *Aristoteles contra Augustinum*, 103–113.

4 cf. ʿĀtī, *al-Zamān fī l-fikr al-Islāmī*; ʿAbd al-Mutaʿāl, *Taṣawwur Ibn Sīnā li-l-zamān*; Šalaq, *al-Zamān fī l-fikr al-ʿarabī wa-l-ʿālamī*; cf. also al-ʿIrāqī, *al-Falsafa al-ṭabīʿiyya ʿinda Ibn Sīnā*.

5 Coope, *Time for Aristotle*; Roark, *Aristotle on Time*; cf. further, to name only some of the more important or more recent contributions, von Leyden, "Time, Number, and Eternity in Plato and Aristotle"; Conen, *Die Zeittheorie des Aristoteles*; Hintikka, *Time & Necessity*; Miller, Jr., "Aristotle on the Reality of Time"; Annas, "Aristotle, Number and Time"; Owen, "Aristotle on Time"; Broadie, *Nature, Change, and Agency in Aristotle's* Physics; "Aristotle's Now"; Seeck, "Zeit als Zahl bei Aristoteles"; Rudolph, *Zeit, Bewegung, Handlung*; Bolotin, "Aristotle's Discussion of Time"; Bostock, "Aristotle's Account of Time"; Inwood, "Aristotle on the Reality of Time"; Coope, "Why Does Aristotle Say that There Is no Time without Change?"; Roark, "Why Aristotle Says There Is no Time without Change"; "Aristotle's Definition of Time Is not Circular"; Bowin, "Aristotle on the Order and Direction of Time"; Trifogli, "Change, Time, and Place"; Loughlin, "Souls and the Location of Time"; Falcon, "Aristotle on Time and Change"; Harry, *Chronos in Aristotle's Physics*.

6 Nonetheless, there are a number of publications which in various ways are instructive; cf. Clark, "The Theory of Time in Plotinus"; Callahan, *Four Views of Time in Ancient Philosophy*; Sambursky, *Physics of*

https://doi.org/10.1515/9783110546798-007

As before, I shall take recourse to Aristotle and his commentators only insofar as it is conducive to our understanding of Avicenna's discussion of time.[7] Unlike Shayegan and McGinnis, however, I intend to approach this topic not in the form of a running commentary, which would mean following Avicenna's order of exposition. Instead, I shall proceed thematically and explore the two main questions about time: the question of what time is and the question of whether it is. My analysis will be concluded by a brief examination of the relevance of the concept of the now (τὸ νῦν, *al-ān*) for Avicenna's philosophy of time. As I hope to show elsewhere in more detail, the now has been essentially misunderstood and its relevance for the existence of time has been greatly exaggerated in the secondary literature. Once the precise nature of time's existence is understood, along the lines of my analyses here, the position of the now within Avicenna's account of time needs to be reconsidered.

One of the main results of the following analysis is that Avicenna's account of time is more complex than interpreters have so far registered. In order to unravel this complexity, and to grasp Avicenna's doctrine of time in full, I shall proceed by way of a close examination of the Arabic text, revisiting and analysing a number of central

---

the Stoics; *The Physical World of Late Antiquity*; O'Neill, "Time and Eternity in Proclus"; Sambursky and Pines, *The Concept of Time in Late Neoplatonism*; Sonderegger's comments in Simplicius, *Über die Zeit*; Sharples' comments in Alexander of Aphrodisias, *On Time*; Sorabji, *Time, Creation and the Continuum*; A. Smith, "Soul and Time in Plotinus"; Steel, "The Neoplatonic Doctrine of Time and Eternity"; McGinnis, "For Every Time There is a Season"; Mesch, *Reflektierte Gegenwart*; Beierwaltes' comments in Plotinus, *Über Ewigkeit und Zeit*; Adamson, "Galen and al-Rāzī on Time"; Baracat, "Soul's Desire and the Origin of Time in the Philosophy of Plotinus"; Chase, "Time and Eternity from Plotinus and Boethius to Einstein."

7 Moreover, I shall not make use of McTaggart's distinction between an A-series and a B-series of time nor shall I talk of dynamic and static conceptions of time as is common to contemporary studies even of historical approaches. Even if one were convinced that such distinctions can help to shed light on ancient, late ancient, and medieval accounts of time, they do not seem to be a necessary prerequisite for an adequate understanding and, quite frankly, introduce a foreign element into what already and by itself is a rich and sophisticated framework for the investigation of time, an element, I may add, which by and large distracts from the autochthonous distinctions which the historical inquiry into temporal reality established in the two-and-a-half millennia before McTaggart's famous article. Instead of differentiating between a dynamic A-series and a static B-series, philosophers in the Peripatetic tradition divided opinions about time into categories such as substance and accident. To this they added further subcategories such as corporeal and incorporeal substances, substances which may or may not be subject to constant renewal, accidents of accidents, and various sorts of accidental relations. In other words, these philosophers developed their own terminology by which they approached the treatment of the philosophical concept of time. Admittedly, some of the historical categories resemble contemporary positions of a dynamic or static A or B-series, yet they emerged within a fundamentally different conception of reality and cannot – maybe even ought not – be related or compared with their modern distant relatives. For two examples of post-Avicennian discussions of time which illustrate the aforementioned division into different types of substances and accidents, cf. Lammer, "Time and Mind-Dependence in Sayf al-Dīn al-Āmidī's *Abkār al-afkār*"; Adamson and Lammer, "Fakhr al-Dīn al-Rāzī's Platonist Account of the Essence of Time."

passages which have not been read with the appropriate amount of attention and rigour. In the end, it is by means of highlighting certain details, recommending a different terminology, and translating some sentences anew that we shall be able to understand and appreciate the complexity of Avicenna's position adequately.

6.1 A New Approach to an Old Definition

Aristotle is famous for having drawn an explicit distinction between the questions of whether time is and of what time is, stating his intention first to treat the former and thereupon the latter.[8] Avicenna, in turn, scrapped this distinction to some degree. Although he acknowledges the value of both questions, along with the need to answer them both, he seems to have succumbed to the singular peculiarity of the subject of time which makes it impossible to discuss the two questions entirely separate from one another. In this sense, Avicenna states his intention to investigate the essence of time (*māhiyyat al-zamān*), claiming that it is "from there" (*min hunāka*) that the existence of time (*wuǧūduhū*) shall also become clear to us.[9] Consequently, we find the relevant materials for answering both questions within a single discussion of time's definition and essence conducted in chapter eleven of the second book of *al-Samāʿ al-ṭabīʿī*.[10]

According to McGinnis, this chapter is divided into two parts: "It first offers a proof for the reality of time and then undertakes an analysis of the nature or essence of time."[11] This, however, does not seem to be convincing, not least because we have just seen Avicenna declaring his intention, *first*, to discuss the essence, but not the existence, of time, so that the existence shall, *then*, become clear from this – this is the reverse layout compared to what McGinnis suggested. Although some of what Avicenna establishes in the first paragraphs of chapter eleven, indeed, entails or indicates the real existence of time, his arguments clearly answer to the purpose of establishing the definition of time as the magnitude of motion and of providing an account of its essence as that which through itself is before and after. It is only towards the end of the chapter that Avicenna, on this basis, demonstrates the existence of time by means of an argument which will reoccur in his later *al-Išārāt wa-l-tanbīhāt*, where it has, for

8 cf. *Phys.* IV.10, 217b31f.

9 *al-Samāʿ al-ṭabīʿī* II.10, §13, 154.12f.

10 In the preceding tenth chapter, Avicenna recounts various attempts at proving and disproving the existence of time as well as at establishing its essence. Some of these attempts will be taken up again and resolved in chapter thirteen, the last chapter of the second book. Chapter twelve is devoted to an explanation of the now and does not provide, in my opinion at least, materials relevant for answering either question.

11 McGinnis, *Time and Time Again*, 210. Despite occasional disagreement, the following study is in many ways heavily indebted to McGinnis' work – and, in particular, his unpublished dissertation – on Avicenna's account of time. I am grateful to him for kindly having shared a copy of his dissertation with me.

centuries, been taken to do precisely that: answering the question of whether time exists. It is, therefore, advisable to follow Avicenna's own words and read the first paragraphs of chapter eleven as an argument pointing out what – and not whether – time is.

The heart of Avicenna's investigation of time's essence is an analysis of various observable situations that involve motion. In essence, he compares objects which move at different speeds in their possibilities to traverse longer or shorter distances in more or less time. All these aspects – speed, distance, time, and possibility – are central to Avicenna's argumentation, and no one before Avicenna has investigated their interconnection in an attempt to define the essence of time. However, they have been investigated together in a different context and for a different purpose.

Among Aristotle's major concerns in *Physics* VI is the exposition of motion (and change) in light of its continuous nature. Thus, Aristotle investigates in chapter VI.2 in what way the distance traversed by a motion and the time required for doing so are likewise continuous.[12] He begins this investigation by proving his claims that "the faster of two things traverses a greater magnitude in an equal time, an equal magnitude in less time, and a greater magnitude in less time, in conformity with the definition sometimes given of the faster."[13]

Commenting on this passage, Simplicius (d. ~ 560) informs us that Alexander of Aphrodisias (fl. ~ 200) raised a puzzle about Aritsotle's argument in *Phys.* VI.2 in light of certain remarks Aristotle had made earlier in chapter IV.14 about the connection between time and the motion, in particular the motion of the outermost sphere.[14] Alexander enquired how Aristotle could ask about the time of a slower or faster motion if time belongs only to the motion of the outermost sphere and if that sphere does not vary in its speed, and so simply is never faster or slower but always equal in speed. Both of the answers Alexander offered contain references to a "possibility" (δύναμις) inherent in moving objects to move faster or slower.[15] Bodies simply have a possibility to move faster and slower, even if they do not make use of this possibility. This terminology is taken up by John Philoponus (d. 574) in his own comments on *Physics* VI, which are partially preserved in the margins of Ms. Leiden or. 583. There, we read how "Yaḥyā and Abū ʿAlī" – i.e., most probably Philoponus and Abū ʿAlī ibn al-Samḥ (d. 418/1027) – outlined and explained Aristotle's contention that motions at different speeds traverse greater or lesser distances. After this outline, we read the following:

كلّ حركة فهي في زمان وكلّ زمان فيمكن أن تكون فيه حركة وكلّ متحرّك فيمكن أن يكون أسرع ويمكن أن يكون أبطأ. فكلّ زمان يمكن أن تكون فيه حركة سريعة ... أمّا بيان على أنّ كلّ حركة فهي في زمان فهو أنّ الحركة

12 q.v. also fn. 53 below, 444f.

13 *Phys.* VI.2, 232a25–27.

14 We shall come back to this below, 454ff., 497ff.

15 cf. Simplicius, *In Phys.*, 941.23–942.18.

إنّما تكون من حيث إلى حيث وهي فيما بينهما تُوجَد. فلا بدّ أن يُتصوّر مع الحركة ابتداء وانتهاء ووسط وهذا هو معنى الماضي والحاضر والمستقبل وهذه هي أقسام الزمان فكلّ حركة إذن فهي في زمان.

> Every motion, then, is in time, and in every time, then, it is possible (*fa-yumkinu*) that motion [occurs], and for every moving thing, then, it is possible that it is faster and it is possible that it is slower. Thus, in every time it is possible that a fast motion [occurs] ... The proof that every motion is in time is that motion is only from some here to some there, and it is in what is between these two that it [sc. motion] exists. Inevitably, then, a beginning, an end, and a middle (*ibtidāʾ wa-ntihāʾ wa-wasaṭ*) is conceptualised with every motion. This is the meaning of past, present, and future, and these are the parts of time, so every motion is, therefore, then, in time. (Philoponus' and Ibn al-Samḥ's comment in Aristotle, *al-Ṭabīʿa* VI.2, 624.2–11)

In his comment, Philoponus clearly draws on Alexander and speaks of a moving thing's general possibility to move faster or slower. On this basis, he emphasises that motion occurs in time and that time, consisting of past, present, and future, extends between the beginning of a motion and its end (*ibtidāʾ wa-ntihāʾ*). All this implies that the continuous extension of time, insofar as it belongs to the continuous motion, corresponds to the continuous distance that was traversed through the motion, thus corroborating Aristotle's general intention in *Physics* VI.2.

Insofar as Avicenna draws on this material from the commentary tradition on *Physics* VI – as will become sufficiently evident shortly – it is clear that his contribution does not lie in the fact that he, too, investigates the interplay between the speeds, distances, and times of moving objects (for this is credit goes to Aristotle) nor in the aspect that he, too, implements the notion of possibility into this investigation (for this is credit goes to Alexander, followed by Philoponus); instead, Avicenna's contribution consists precisely in his philosophical attitude towards disentangling himself from the rigidity of tradition and towards rearranging the available material, divested of its original purpose, in order to forge something new. In the case of time, then, Avicenna does not merely discuss this material but employs it as one of the most important pieces in his argumentation, as he decided to *begin* his investigation of the essence of time precisely with an analysis of different situations in which moving objects traversing more or less distance move at higher or lower speeds, particularly focusing on their inherent possibility (*imkān*) to do so.

One of the situations which Avicenna mentions now in *al-Samāʿ al-ṭabīʿī* II.11 is that two moving objects which began their respective motions together (*maʿan*), i.e., at the same moment, and which also ended their motions together may, nonetheless, differ with regard to the distance they have covered in their motion. This, then, was due to a difference in speed (*al-buṭʾ wa-l-surʿa*), so that the faster moving object was able to traverse more distance than the slower object.[16]

16 Whenever Avicenna uses *surʿa* or *buṭʾ* independently without the other, he is referring to a certain "fastness" or "slowness," indicating a high or a low velocity, respectively, or a contrast between a faster

Fig. 6.1: A complete schema of Avicenna's analysis of motion at different speeds.

same moments	→ same speed	⟷	same distance	(a) *al-Naǧāt*$_1$
	→ different speed	⟷	different distance	(b) *al-Samāʿ al-ṭabīʿī*$_1$ *al-Naǧāt*$_3$
same speed	→ same distance	⟷	same moments	(c) *al-Naǧāt*$_1$
	→ different distance	⟷	different moments	(d) *al-Naǧāt*$_2$
same distance	→ same moments	⟷	same speed	(e) *al-Naǧāt*$_1$
	→ different moments	⟷	different speed	(f) *al-Samāʿ al-ṭabīʿī*$_2$

Another situation is also possible in which two moving objects began their respective motions together *and* traversed an equal distance, yet one of them reached the end of the distance before the other. So these two, having begun their motion together, did not finish it together in the same moment. Again, this would be due to a difference in speed.

These are the two cases Avicenna mentions in *al-Samāʿ al-ṭabīʿī*.[17] To this picture, he adds two more cases in *al-Naǧāt* (copied from *al-Ḥikma al-ʿArūḍiyya*).[18] There is, first, a situation in which two moving objects began and ended their motion together, and traversed an equal distance, because they traveled at the same speed. Yet, it could also be that two equally fast objects only ended, but did not begin, their motion together, with the result that they, again, traversed an unequal distance. Finally, Avicenna mentions also a situation already known from *al-Samāʿ al-ṭabīʿī*, in which two objects differed in speed, one being fast (*sarīʿ*) and the other slow (*baṭīʾ*), while nonetheless having begun and ended their motion together, so that they also differ with regard to the length of the traversed distance.

In themselves, the two accounts from *al-Samāʿ al-ṭabīʿī* and *al-Naǧāt* seem to be somewhat selective and it is not at all clear why or how Avicenna chose the respective set of examples presented in these two works.[19] In their combination, however, they

and a slower motion. Both words together (*al-buṭʾ wa-l-surʿa*), however, signify simply the velocity or speed of an object. Thus, I shall translate *al-buṭʾ wa-l-surʿa* always with the single word "speed."

17 cf. *al-Samāʿ al-ṭabīʿī* II.11, §1, 155.4–7.

18 cf. *al-Naǧāt* II.2.9, 225.4–9 ≈ *al-Ḥikma al-ʿArūḍiyya* II.2.7, 130.9–12.

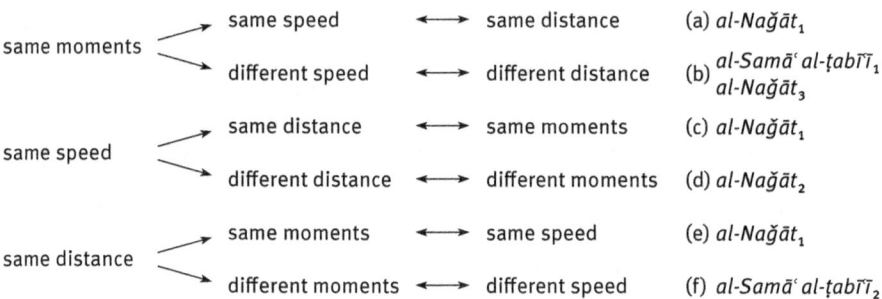

19 One may also consider the possibility of textual corruption in the transmission due to the high number of repetitive phrases within these examples. Other than that, it may be noted that Avicenna's *al-Hidāya*, the *ʿUyūn al-ḥikma*, and *al-Ḥikma al-mašriqiyya* do not compare objects moving at different speeds at all and merely provide the conclusion that, generally, there must be a possibility of going faster or slower that obtains between the beginning and the end of a motion. Avicenna's *al-Išārāt wa-l-tanbīhāt*, in turn, do not mention the possibility for motion at all, whereas the physics of the *Dānešnāme-ye ʿAlāʾī* lacks an account of time altogether. The only information about time in the *Dānešnāme-ye ʿAlāʾī* is a brief remark in its section on metaphysics, stating that time is "the magnitude of

result in the complete schema depicted above. As already mentioned, cases (a), (c), and (e) represent the first, and (d) the second example from *al-Naǧāt*; (b) is jointly the first example from *al-Samāʿ al-ṭabīʿī* and the third from *al-Naǧāt*; and (f) represents the second example from *al-Samāʿ al-ṭabīʿī*.

Following this, Avicenna writes in *al-Samāʿ al-ṭabīʿī* II.11:

ويكون في كلّ حال من الأحوال من مبتدأ كلّ حركة إلى منتهاها إمكان قطع تلك المسافة بعينها بتلك الحركة المعيّنة السرعة والبطء ... وإمكان قطع أعظم من تلك المسافة بالأسرع منها ... وإمكان قطع أقلّ منها بالأبطأ من تلك ... وإنّ ذلك لا يجوز أن يختلف البتّة. فقد ثبت بين المبتدأ والمنتهى إمكان محدود بالقياس إلى الحركة وإلى السرعة.

In each of these cases, there is from the starting of each motion to its ending (*min al-mubtadaʾ kull ḥaraka ilā muntahāhā*) a possibility (*imkān*) for traversing that very distance by that motion that is determined by a certain speed ... as well as a possibility for traversing more of that distance by a faster [motion] than it ... as well as a possibility for traversing less of that [distance] by a slower [motion] than that ... It is not possible to disagree with that at all. So, it is already established that between the starting and the ending is a determinate possibility relative to the motion and the velocity. (*al-Samāʿ al-ṭabīʿī* II.11, §1, 155.7–10)[20]

According to McGinnis, this argument constitutes Avicenna's proof for the existence of time, because it demonstrates the existence of a possibility for motion, and that possibility, he claims, is subsequently said to be a magnitude which, ultimately, is identified with time.[21] However, it is crucial not to jump to conclusions already. Neither here nor later – nor, in fact, anywhere – is Avicenna arguing that time is to be identified with this possibility (*imkān*).[22] Thus, the fact that he claims to be "already established" (*fa-qad ṯabata*) here in this passage, viz., the indisputable fact that there is a possibility between the moments of starting and ending a motion, does not amount to a proof of time's existence. Avicenna is also not treating the possibility as a "thing," "aspect," or "factor" that pertains to motion in addition to distance and speed without which we cannot fully understand or explain motion as it occurs in the world. All Avicenna does here is refer to distance as an aspect of motion alongside speed, while pointing out that it is not to be disputed that a moving thing, starting and ending its motion at certain non-identical moments, *could* traverse, i.e., has a possibility for traversing, a given distance at a given speed or a shorter distance at a lower speed or greater distance at a higher speed. The *imkān* is not a reified factor that belongs to the phenomenon

motion" (*zamān andāze-ye ǧonbaš ast*) whose investigation will be carried out in physics (*Dānešnāme-ye ʿAlāʾī* II.10, 32.15). Yet, no such investigation is to be found anywhere in its physics.

20 cf. *al-Naǧāt* II.2.9, 225.9–226.5 ≈ *al-Ḥikma al-ʿArūḍiyya* II.2.7, 130.13–20; *ʿUyūn al-ḥikma* II.8, 27.1–4; *al-Hidāya* II.1, 156.3–5; *al-Ḥikma al-mašriqiyya* III.11, 32.2–5.

21 cf. McGinnis, *Time and Time Again*, 232; *Avicenna*, 198; "The Ultimate Why Question," 70; "Arabic and Islamic Natural Philosophy and Natural Science," ch. 2.4; "Creation and Eternity in Medieval Philosophy," 75f.; q.v. fn. 47 below, 443.

22 There is only one passage, in Avicenna's *ʿUyūn al-ḥikma*, which seems to suggest otherwise. This passage, however, ought to be emended, as I shall argue in fn. 135 below, 470.

of motion in addition to distance and speed or the ratio of distance over speed – it is simply nothing more than the contingent fact that every moving object, in theory or practice, could move slower or faster but, then, would be bound to traverse less or more distance. Time is not a possibility for traversing a distance at a speed nor has time in any way already entered the picture of Avicenna's exposition.[23] All Avicenna so far wanted to achieve is to analyse motion and to hint at a number of indisputable facts: motion entails some sort of distance, motion entails some sort of speed, motion entails some sort of a moving object, and this object could have covered less or more distance had it travelled at a lower or higher speed – "it is not possible to disagree with this at all," as he writes.

Moreover, his depiction of these different situations, and his reference to a "possibility," corresponds entirely to what we have seen above from Alexander and Philoponus.[24] Analogous to his predecessors' use of δύναμις, Avicenna uses the word *imkān* as an expression for a contingent possibility *of the moving thing* and, more precisely, of the moving thing when considered as moving – or potentially moving – from a moment of starting its motion to a moment of ending it.[25] In turn, distance and speed are said to be additional interdependent factors of the motion that occurs between the starting and ending of that moving thing's motion. What Avicenna intends to examine next is the as yet indistinct notion of that which is between the "starting" (*mubtada'*) and "ending" (*muntahā*) of the motion, i.e., of that *wherein* the possibility for traversing a distance at a corresponding speed occurs – or, as Philoponus and Ibn al-Samḥ had it,

23 Note that Avicenna avoids the term "time" (*zamān*) as well as any other temporal notion at this stage of the argument altogether, presumably because he wants to avoid being charged with circular reasoning. His particular concern of providing a non-circular argument is explicitly stated in *al-Samā' al-ṭabī'ī* II.11, §3, 157.6f., where he fends off Galen's charge of circularity against Aristotle's definition. Thus, the terms for "starting" and "ending" (*mubtada'* and *muntahā*) should not be taken in a temporal way. These moments merely signify the beginning *of a motion* and not a determinate moment in a time (*waqt*) or a now (*ān*). As such, the "starting" and the "ending" belong to and describe the motion insofar as every motion *qua* motion has a beginning and an end (leaving aside circular motion). They are, thus, *kinetic*, and not temporal, notions. In *al-Naǧāt* and *al-Ḥikma al-'Arūḍiyya*, Avicenna chooses different terminology, and speaks of *aḫḏ* and *tark* to describe the start and the end of a motion. The reason for this change in terminology is unclear and most likely insignificant. It should be noted, however, that Avicenna's model for comparing moving objects in terms of their speed and the distance covered, viz., the ancient and late ancient comments on Aristotle's arguments in *Physics* VI.2 referred to above, often employ the notion of time. After all their discussion in book six *follows upon* the analysis of time in the fourth book of the *Physics*. That Avicenna altogether avoids the notion of time is, thus, clearly a deliberate move and shows that he employs the traditional material he received for a different purpose: *approaching* the concept of time.

24 However, in contrast to his predecessors Avicenna is careful not to mention "time" in this context and at this stage of his argument; q.v. also the preceding footnote.

25 cf. Philoponus' and Ibn al-Samḥ's comment in Aristotle, *al-Ṭabī'a* VI.2, 624.3: "for every moving thing, then, it is possible that it is faster and it is possible that it is slower" (*wa-kull mutaḥarrik fa-yumkinu an yakūna asra' wa-yumkinu an yakūna abṭa'*).

the "middle" between the "beginning" and the "end" (*ibtidā' wa-ntihā' wa-wasaṭ*) of the motion.[26]

Now, Avicenna argues that if a moving object, at a certain speed, did not cover the full distance but only half of it, then there also was only half a possibility to do so, i.e., there only was a possibility for traversing *half* of the distance at that speed (or, correspondingly, even less than half or more than half of it at a lower or higher speed, respectively). The same, of course, holds true of the second half of the distance, so that the motion over the entire distance could be taken as the combination of two motions each over one half of the distance to which two possibilities correspond, one for each of the two halves. Thus, both the traversed distance as a whole as well as the corresponding possibility are essentially quantifiable, i.e., divisible into more and less, as Avicenna argues in the following passage:

> فيكون الإمكان إلى النصف ومن النصف اتّساويان فكلّ واحد منهما نصف الإمكان المفروض أوّلاً. فيكون الإمكان المفروض أوّلاً منقسماً ... فنقول إنّ هذا الإمكان قد صحّ أنّه منقسم وكلّ منقسم فمقدار أو ذو مقدار، فهذا الإمكان لا يعرى عن مقدار.
>
> So, the possibility up to the halfway point and from the halfway point [to the end] are equal, and each one of them is half of the initially assumed possibility. Thus, the initially assumed possibility is divisible (*munqasiman*) ... So, we say that this possibility is rightly [said] to be divisible, and all that is divisible, then, is a magnitude or has a magnitude (*fa-miqdār aw ḏū miqdār*), and so this possibility is not devoid of (*ya'rā 'an*) magnitude. (*al-Samā' al-ṭabī'ī* II.11, §§1–2, 155.13–156.4, tr. by McGinnis, modified)[27]

It is important to keep in mind that a possibility as such is not a "thing," so that it itself could *be* a magnitude (*miqdār*). Possibilities merely endow some thing with various contingent options for moving from one location to another. The possibility of a certain object to cover a distance at a certain speed is not itself an extended magnitude just as any other possibility, such as the possibility of a green tomato to become red or the possibility of a boy to become a piano player, is likewise not extended. It is, thus, more correct to say that the possibility *pertains to* – or maybe even *occurs in* – a magnitude, viz., the magnitude between the moments of starting and ending a motion, than to say that it *is* a magnitude. What Avicenna shows, here, is that this possibility, though not a magnitude itself, nonetheless *has* a magnitude or is intrinsically related to a magnitude, so that this possibility is not "free from" or "devoid of" (*ya'rā 'an*) magnitude, as Avicenna himself puts it.

If a moving object covers only half of a given distance at a certain speed, then this affects the possibilities that obtain between the starting and ending of the motion, because they now also apply only to half of the distance. If an object has a certain possibility to traverse a given distance in its entirety at a certain speed, then it has only

---

26 Philoponus' and Ibn al-Samḥ's comment in Aristotle, *al-Ṭabī'a* VI.2, 624.10.

27 cf. *al-Ḥikma al-mašriqiyya* III.11, 32.8–11.

half of that possibility if it were to traverse only half of the distance at the same speed. Equipped with only half the possibility, a moving object is bound to end its motion at a different – if not to say: earlier – moment compared to the moment at which it would have ended its motion had it traversed the distance in its entirety. This is a result of Avicenna's previous analysis of motion which demonstrated that a difference in distance implies a difference either in speed or in the moments of starting and ending a motion. Since Avicenna remains silent about any change in the speed of the object, he seems to hint at a difference with regard to the moment of ending the motion. Thus, half of the traversed distance entails half of the possibility which, at the same speed, entails a different moment of ending.

Consequently, the gap between the moments of starting and ending a motion allows for more and less, i.e., it is susceptible to division, because the possibility that obtains between the starting and ending of a motion allows for more and less, i.e., is susceptible to division, and that possibility allows for more and less, because the covered distance allows for more and less, i.e., is susceptible to division. Everything which is susceptible to division either is or has a magnitude, as we are told. What Avicenna has established with this argument, then, is not that the possibility itself is a magnitude (even though he mentions this as an option) but that it is determined by a magnitude, because it obtains in a magnitude, viz., the magnitude of the interval between the starting and the ending of a motion. Therefore, the possibility "has" (*ḏū*) a magnitude or, as Avicenna will later say, it "occurs in" (*yaqaʿu fī*) a magnitude, so that a magnitude "belongs" to (*li-*) the possibility.[28]

In a next step, Avicenna attempts to identify this magnitude more precisely through a process of elimination. The magnitude in question may be the magnitude either of the distance (*al-masāfa*) or of the moving thing (*al-mutaḥarrik*), or it may be identical with motion (*al-ḥaraka*) or speed (*al-surʿa wa-l-buṭʾ*). Avicenna dismisses all these alternatives for obvious reasons.[29] If the magnitude in question were the magnitude of the distance, for example, then all moving objects that traverse the same distance would be equal in this magnitude regardless of their speed. If it were the magnitude of the moving thing, then smaller objects would, by default, be less in this magnitude than larger objects, regardless of their speed and the traversed distance. If it were the speed, then all objects moving at the same speed would be equal with regard to this magnitude regardless of the distance they have traversed. These examples become more evident once it is understood that this magnitude will eventually be identified as "time," and so, clearly, large objects do not, by default, take more time to traverse a distance than small objects, and so on. The fact that this magnitude will be identified with time

28 *al-Samāʿ al-ṭabīʿī* II.11, §5, 157.18; cf. *al-Ḥikma al-mašriqiyya* III.11, 33.19f.; cf. also *al-Samāʿ al-ṭabīʿī* II.11, §2, 156.10; *al-Ḥikma al-mašriqiyya* III.11, 32.16; q.v. also fn. 135 below, 470.

29 cf. *al-Samāʿ al-ṭabīʿī* II.11, §2, 156.4–11; *al-Naǧāt* II.2.9, 228.4–11 ≈ *al-Ḥikma al-ʿArūḍiyya* II.2.7, 131.17–23; *ʿUyūn al-ḥikma* II.8, 27.4–6; *al-Hidāya* II.1, 156.7–157.2; *al-Ḥikma al-mašriqiyya* III.11, 32.11–17; *al-Išārāt wa-l-tanbīhāt* II.5.4, 150.9f.

also explains why it cannot be motion itself (*nafs al-ḥaraka*), for Avicenna has already rejected claims of identifying time with motion in *al-Samāʿ al-ṭabīʿī* II.10, following Aristotle's arguments in *Physics* IV.10.[30] Avicenna concludes this line of reasoning with the following words:

> فقد ثبت وجود مقدار لإمكان وقوع الحركات بين المتقدّم والمتأخّر وقوعاً يقتضي مسافات محدودة ليس مقدار المتحرّك ولا المسافة ولا نفس الحركة.
>
> So, the existence of a magnitude is already established belonging to a possibility for the occurrence of motions (*wuǧūd miqdār li-imkān wuqūʿ al-ḥaraka*) between the prior and the posterior – an occurrence requiring definite distances, that is – which is neither the magnitude of the moving thing or of the distance nor is it motion itself. (*al-Samāʿ al-ṭabīʿī* II.11, §2, 156.10f.)[31]

In this conclusion, Avicenna, more distinctly than before, describes the magnitude as *belonging to* the possibility (*miqdār li-imkān*), instead of describing the possibility itself as a magnitude. He states that there is a possibility for the occurrence of motion and to this possibility belongs some still undetermined magnitude. It is not the possibility that will be identified with time but the magnitude in which it occurs and which belongs to it. The possibility is merely a possibility belonging to a (potentially) moving object for traversing a certain distance at a certain speed, i.e., for having a certain motion that traverses certain prior and posterior positions during that motion and, ultimately, covers some certain distance.

Avicenna continues the process of elimination asserting that the magnitude cannot be subsistent through itself (*qāʾiman bi-nafsihī*), because it is dependent upon a subject, and comes-to-be and perishes together with that subject.[32] Later in *al-Samāʿ al-ṭabīʿī* II.11, Avicenna elaborates further on this point and describes time as "material" (*māddī*), because it is something that originates and passes away (*ḥādiṯ wa-fāsid*) existing only together with the continuous renewal of some state (*taǧaddud ḥāl*).[33] Yet, the subject of the magnitude cannot be the matter (*mādda*) of the moving thing for a reason similar to that which already prevented it from being the magnitude of the moving thing. So, it must be one of its accidental formal dispositions (*hayʾāt*, sg. *hayʾa*).[34]

There are integral and non-integral dispositions. An example of an integral disposition (*hayʾa qārra*) is "being white."[35] If a thing has acquired an integral disposition,

---

30 cf. *Phys.* IV.10, 218b9–20. For a more detailed outline of Avicenna's process of eliminating the various alternatives, cf. McGinnis, *Time and Time Again*, 216–222.

31 cf. *al-Ḥikma al-mašriqiyya* III.11, 32.16f.

32 *al-Samāʿ al-ṭabīʿī* II.11, 156.11f.; cf. *al-Ḥikma al-mašriqiyya* III.11, 32.17f.

33 *al-Samāʿ al-ṭabīʿī* II.11, §6, 159.2–4, 9; cf. *al-Ḥikma al-mašriqiyya* III.11, 34.5–7, 12f. Similar remarks can be found in *al-Maqūlāt* III.4, 119.3–5; *al-Ilāhiyyāt* III.4, §18, 117.8–16; IX.1, §22, 380.6f.; *al-Naǧāt* II.2.9, 226.6–9 ≈ *al-Ḥikma al-ʿArūḍiyya* II.2.7, 130.21–23; *ʿUyūn al-ḥikma* II.8, 27.6f.; *Dānešnāme-ye ʿAlāʾī* II.11, 38.7–9; *al-Hidāya* II.1, 156.7–157.2; 160.2f.; *al-Išārāt wa-l-tanbīhāt* II.5.4–5, 150.5–151.1.

34 *al-Samāʿ al-ṭabīʿī* II.11, 156.13f.; cf. *al-Ḥikma al-mašriqiyya* III.11, 32.18–20.

35 *al-Samāʿ al-ṭabīʿī* II.11, 156.14f.; cf. *al-Ḥikma al-mašriqiyya* III.11, 32.20f.

then it has this disposition completely in such a way that there remains nothing of the disposition which is not yet fully realised in the thing. The precise meaning of the term *qārr* is paraphrased, and thereby explained, in *al-Ilāhiyyāt* III.4 as "that which occurs in existence with all its parts" (*ḥāṣil al-wuǧūd bi-ǧamīʿ aǧzāʾihī*).[36] By contrast, a non-integral disposition is a disposition which is never fully realised as a whole in the thing of which it is a disposition.

Avicenna quickly dismisses the first alternative: the disposition in question cannot possibly be a disposition that is stable or integral (*ṯābitan qārran*). Instead, it must be one which "has its being in becoming," if we are allowed to borrow a Neoplatonic phrase.[37] The magnitude, then, belongs to a non-integral disposition (*hayʾa ġayr qārra*), and the only non-integral disposition is motion – or rather the disposition of "being in motion" or of "currently undergoing motion," i.e., the disposition of having the form of motion.[38] This brings Avicenna to the desired conclusion:

فبقي أن يكون مقدار هيئة غير قارة وهي الحركة من مكان إلى مكان ... وهذا هو الذي نُسمّيه الزمان.

So, it remains that it [sc. this magnitude] is a magnitude of a non-integral disposition, and this is the motion from place to place ... and this is that which we call "time" (*allaḏī nusammīhi al-zamān*). (*al-Samāʿ al-ṭabīʿī* II.11, §2, 156.15–17, tr. by McGinnis, modified)[39]

---

36 *al-Ilāhiyyāt* III.4, §18, 117.9; cf. *al-Maqūlāt* III.4, 119.3–5.

37 Avicenna's understanding of *taǧaddud* and of *ġayr qārr*, indeed, seems to approximate the intent of the expression ἐν τῷ γίνεσθαι ἔχει τὸ εἶναι which we frequently find especially in the works of Philoponus and Simplicius but also in Olympiodorus, who regards it as a feature distinguishing between motion and time, conceiving of time as a somewhat stable eternity that is mapped out by an ever progressing motion; cf. Simplicius, *In Phys.*, 777.6; Philoponus, *In Phys.*, 735.24f.; Olympiodorus, *In Cat.*, 83.32–35; cf. also Ammonius, *In Cat.*, 59.12; Proclus, *Institutio theologica*, prop. 50, 48.28–30; cf. further Olympiodorus, *In Meteor.*, 146.15–23. An Arabic version of that Greek phrase ἐν τῷ γίνεσθαι ἔχει τὸ εἶναι is also found in Avicenna in *al-Samāʿ al-ṭabīʿī* II.13, §1, 167.4, where Avicenna sates that the "existence of [time] is by way of coming-to be" (*wuǧūduhū ʿalā sabīl al-takawwun*), even though the context is slightly different. Other than that, Avicenna's use of *ṯābit* may signal a reference to *Categories* 6, 5a26f., where Aristotle noted that the parts of time are not stable (ὑπομένει γὰρ οὐδὲν τῶν τοῦ χρόνου μορίων), which in Isḥāq ibn Ḥunayn's translation reads as *fa-innahu lā ṯabāta li-šayʾ min aǧzāʾ al-zamān*, with *ṯabāt* being the corresponding verbal noun to the participle *ṯābit*. In *ʿUyūn al-ḥikma* II.8, Avicenna clearly uses *ṯābit* as a synonym for *qārr* when he writes that the magnitude of the possibility, i.e., time, is "not fixed but renewed" (*ġayr ṯābit bal mutaǧaddid*); q.v. also below 469f. Incidentally, one is also reminded of Abū Bakr al-Rāzī's famous remark that the constant flow of time, being a self-subsisting substance, can be illustrated simply by saying: *ṭaf-ṭaf-ṭaf* (*al-Munāẓarāt bayna Abī Ḥātim al-Rāzī wa-Abī Bakr al-Rāzī*, 304.13); cf. also Pines, *Studies in Islamic Atomism*, 60; Kraemer, *Philosophy in the Renaissance of Islam*, 168f.

38 q.v. above 360ff.

39 cf. *al-Naǧāt* II.2.9, 228.1f. ≈ *al-Ḥikma al-ʿArūḍiyya* II.2.7, 131.14–16; *ʿUyūn al-ḥikma* II.8 27.6–10; *al-Hidāya* II.1, 157.1f.; *al-Ḥikma al-mašriqiyya* III.11, 32.21–23; *al-Išārāt wa-l-tanbīhāt* II.5.4, 150.10–13; II.5.5, 150.17–151.1.

What we have been told so far, then, is that there is a magnitude which accommodates the possibility for traversing certain distances at certain corresponding speeds, that this magnitude is the magnitude of a non-integral disposition which is motion, and that this magnitude of a non-integral disposition is what is called "time." Accordingly, time is the magnitude of motion. This already approximates the Aristotelian definition of time to some degree – what is missing is the notion of the prior and posterior (τὸ πρότερον καὶ ὕστερον, *al-mutaqaddim wa-l-muta'aḫḫir*), which is what Avicenna will now elaborate.

For Avicenna, the prior and posterior in motion is an inseparable and concomitant feature of motion:

وأنت تعلم أنّ الحركة يلحقها أن تنقسم إلى متقدّم ومتأخّر وإنّما يُوجَد فيها المتقدّم ما يكون منها في المتقدّم من المسافة والمتأخّر ما يكون منها في المتأخّر من المسافة.

> You know that it follows concomitantly upon motion (*al-ḥaraka yalḥaquhā*) that it is divisible into what is prior and what is posterior, and the prior only exists in it as that which belongs to it from the prior within the distance and the posterior as that which belongs to it from the posterior within the distance. (*al-Samāʿ al-ṭabīʿī* II.11, §3, 156.18–157.1)[40]

What is prior and what is posterior in a motion corresponds to, and derives from, certain positions within the distance. When a moving object during its motion passes first through one spatial position and then through another, there is in the motion first a prior state at which it passed through one position and then a posterior state at which it passed through the other. This makes motion a phenomenon essentially characterised by a direction from beginning to an end. By contrast, spatial distance in itself lacks such a direction, because its positions are not ordered in the way prior and posterior states in a motion are.[41] What is more, spatial positions co-exist with one another, whereas the prior in motion does not, and even cannot, exist together with the posterior. The condition that the prior cannot exist together with the posterior is what it means to be in motion, for whenever a moving object is in a prior state, the posterior states are not yet existent, while the prior states are no longer existent once

40 cf. *al-Ḥikma al-mašriqiyya* III.11, 32.24–33.1; cf. also *Phys.* IV.11, 219a14–19; q.v. also below, 462ff.

41 Avicenna's account of the prior and posterior of motion resembles in many respects modern interpretations of Aristotle's understanding of the relation between distance, motion, and time. Both Coope and Roark find strong reasons for claiming that Aristotle's account of time has its roots in a non-temporal, essential order or direction that derives from a feature that is intrinsic to motion. Roark's interpretation of Aristotle is at times a surprisingly accurate interpretation of Avicenna; cf. Coope, *Time for Aristotle*, 69–75; Roark, "Aristotle's Definition of Time Is not Circular"; *Aristotle on Time*, chs. 4–5; cf. also McGinnis' review of Roark's book, pointing out the same similarities between his interpretation and Avicenna's position ("Review of *Aristotle on Time: A Study of the* Physics by Tony Roark"); cf. further Bowin, "Aristotle on the Order and Direction of Time," who provides an interesting critique of Coope's suggestions as well as an interpretation why change is "intrinsically asymmetric by definition" (57), as Bowin writes.

the moving object is at a posterior state. The corresponding spatial positions, however, through which the moving object passed during its motion, already existed before the object passed through them and remained existent after it did. The impossibility of a prior state co-existing together with a posterior state is a specific feature (*ḫāṣṣiyya*) which Avicenna attributes to the prior and posterior of motion. This specific feature is not shared by their spatial counterparts.

Nonetheless, Avicenna stresses that what is prior and what is posterior in the motion are dependent upon the positions within the distance and as such are the direct result of the thing's motion *through* these positions, so that a motion is intrinsically characterised by prior and posterior states that correspond to, and derive from, certain traversed spatial positions. It is through a relation to these spatial positions that motion is differentiated into prior and posterior states, which are, then, "numbered" by motion's passage through these spatial positions, such that the moving object, *first*, moves through this position; *second*, through that position; *third*, through another position; and so on. It is through these, i.e., the prior and posterior, that motion receives its number and measure:

ويكونان معدودين بالحركة فإنّ الحركة بأجزائها تعدّ المتقدّم والمتأخّر. فيكون الحركة لها عدد من حيث لها في المسافة تقدّم وتأخّر ولها مقدار أيضاً بإزاء مقدار المسافة. والزمان هو هذا العدد أو المقدار فالزمان عدد الحركة إذا انفصلت إلى متقدّم ومتأخّر لا بالزمان بل في المسافة وإلّا لكان البيان تحديداً بالدور.

The two [sc. the prior and the posterior] are numbered by motion (*ma ʿdūdayn bi-l-ḥaraka*), for motion through its parts numbers what is prior and what is posterior.[42] So, motion has[43] a number (*lahā ʿadad*) insofar as the prior and the posterior belong to it in [view of] the distance, and it also has a magnitude (*wa-lahā miqdār*) paralleling the magnitude of the distance. Time is this number or magnitude (*hāḏā l-ʿadad aw al-miqdār*). Thus, time is the number of motion when it is differentiated into what is prior and what is posterior, not by time but with respect to the distance (*fa-l-zamān ʿadad al-ḥaraka iḏa nfaṣalat ilā mutaqaddim wa-muta'aḫḫir lā bi-l-zamān bal fī l-masāfa*), for otherwise the proof of the definition would be circular. (*al-Samāʿ al-ṭabīʿī* II.11, §3, 157.4–7, tr. by McGinnis, modified)[44]

42 This sentence might sound tautological, as Avicenna appears to be saying that "the prior and the posterior are numbered by motion, because motion numbers them." This, however, is not what Avicenna intends here. For him, motion is essentially that which has prior and posterior states, because any state within a motion is such that the moving object never was at that state before and, once it is at that state, never will be at that state ever again. Motion is essentially directed from a beginning to an end, and provides the prior and the posterior "through its parts." We, thus, need to read the sentence here with an emphasis on "through its parts," so that Avicenna says that "the prior and the posterior are numbered by motion, because it is *through its parts* that motion numbers them." This claim, then, is by no means tautological but a reminder of a crucial aspect of Avicenna's account of motion; cf. also *al-Samāʿ al-ṭabīʿī* II.12, §7, 165.4f., and *al-Ḥikma al-mašriqiyya* III.11, 37.23–38.1, which is discussed below, 460ff.

43 Reading *yakūnu* for *takūnu* in McGinnis, Zāyid, and Āl Yāsīn.

44 cf. *al-Ḥikma al-mašriqiyya* III.11, 33.3–6.

This passage is as close as Avicenna gets to Aristotle's canonical definition of time as "the number of motion in respect of the prior and posterior" (ἀριθμὸς κινήσεως κατὰ τὸ πρότερον καὶ ὕστερον, *ʿadad al-ḥaraka min qibal al-mutaqaddim wa-l-mutaʾaḫḫir*).[45] A few lines later, Avicenna clarifies again the relation between time, the magnitude, and the possibility:

> ومعلوم أنّ ذلك الشيء هو الذي يقع فيه إمكان التغييرات على النحو المذكور وقوعاً أوّلياً ويقع في غيره لأجله. فيكون ذلك الشيء هو المقدار المقدّر للإمكان المذكور تقديراً بذاته ويكون ما نحن فيه لا غيره. فنحن إنما كنّا جعلنا الزمان اسماً للمعنى الذي هو لذاته مقدار للإمكان المذكور ويقع فيه الإمكان المذكور وقوعاً أوّلياً.
>
> It is known that that thing [sc. time] is that in which the possibility for making changes, in the aforementioned manner, primarily occurs (*yaqaʿu fīhi imkān al-taġyīr ... wuqūʿan awwaliyyan*) and on account of which it occurs in something else.[46] So, that thing is the magnitude measuring (*al-miqdār al-muqaddir*) the aforementioned possibility essentially and it is that with which we are concerned, and with nothing else. So, we only have made "time" a name for the meaning which through itself is a magnitude for the aforementioned possibility (*isman li-l-maʿnā llaḏī huwa li-ḏātihī miqdār li-l-imkān*)[47] and in which the possibility primarily occurs. (*al-Samāʿ al-ṭabīʿī* II.11, §§4–5, 157.15–18, tr. by McGinnis, modified)[48]

These passages provide us with an understanding of Avicenna's definition of time and of its relation to the Aristotelian original. For Avicenna, time is first and foremost a name for a magnitude. The Arabic word *miqdār*, which I translate as "magnitude," can also mean "measure." It was employed by Graeco-Arabic translators primarily to render

---

45 *Phys.* IV.11, 219b1f.; cf. 220a24–26; cf. also *Phys.* IV.14, 223b21–23; VIII.1, 251b10–14; *Cael.* I.9, 279a14f.; II.4, 287a23–26; *De gen. et corr.* II.10, 337a22–25; *Met.* Λ.6, 1071b6–11.

46 It is difficult to understand what Avicenna means by *wa-yaqaʿu fī ġayrihī li-ağlihī*. Both suffixed masculine pronouns seem to refer to time, and so one ought to translate "and on account of [time] it [sc. the possibility] occurs in something other than [time]." The question, thus, is what is meant by "something other than time." One option, for example, is to say that this is distance, so that the possibility for changes occurs, mediated through time, also in distance, because the motion of things which have such a possibility occurs over a certain distance. A more promising option, however, is to understand *ġayrihī* as referring to the body of the moving thing, so that it is through time – in which the possibility primarily occurs – that the possibility occurs also in other things than time, viz., in the things which move. This is the interpretation adopted here. Other than that, another interesting option would be to take *ġayrihī* more generally in the sense of "something else," so that on account of time the possibility occurs also in other things that move. Thus, two moving objects can share one possibility when they move at the same time, for they both have the same possibility to traverse the same distance at the same speed in the same time.

47 In his translation, McGinnis inadvertently omits the words *li-l-maʿnā llaḏī huwa li-ḏātihī miqdār*, so that his text reads: "We ourselves have made time only a name for the possibility noted above and in which that possibility primarily occurs." This has fatal consequences insofar as it leads to a reading according to which Avicenna makes time a name *for the possibility*, instead of a name *for the magnitude in which* the possibility occurs.

48 cf. *al-Ḥikma al-mašriqiyya* III.11, 33.17–20; cf. also *al-Samāʿ al-ṭabīʿī* II.11, §5, 159.1f.; *al-Ḥikma al-mašriqiyya* III.11, 34.3–5.

μέτρον and μέγεθος, and will later often be translated by the Arabic-Latin translators as *mensura* and *quantitas*. In *Physics* IV.10–14, Aristotle's terminology oscillated between describing time as a number (ἀριθμός) and as a measure (μέτρον).[49] His descriptions of time, thus, found their way into Arabic through the words *miqdār* (used for translating both μέτρον and μέγεθος) and *ʿadad* (used for translating ἀριθμός) – this, at least, was the word choice of Isḥāq ibn Ḥunayn (d. 298/910–11) in his translation of the *Physics* and, arguably, also of Qusṭā ibn Lūqā al-Baʿlabakkī (d. 300/912) in his translation of the commentary of Philoponus.[50]

When I say that for Avicenna time is primarily a magnitude, I mean that he puts a stronger emphasis on the μέγεθος-aspect of time than on the μέτρον-aspect, with both aspects nonetheless being inherent in the Arabic noun *miqdār*.[51] Thus, when Avicenna makes time a *miqdār* that obtains between the starting and the ending of a motion, he regards time primarily as a magnitude, i.e., as an extension or interval spanning from one moment to another. Moreover, Avicenna's primary reason for claiming that the possibility either is or has a *miqdār*, as has been discussed above, is its essential divisibility – and this is a feature which Aristotle attributed to μέγεθος.[52] Avicenna also states that the *miqdār* of time is parallel to the *miqdār* of distance, which seems to be one of the places where he echoes Aristotle's remarks that time follows (ἀκολουθεῖ, *yatbaʿu*) motion which follows the μέγεθος of distance, as we have seen above.[53] As is

49 cf. *Phys.* IV.11, 221b2 and – only a few lines later – IV.12, 221b7; cf. also Annas, "Aristotle, Number and Time," 98; Coope, *Time for Aristotle*, chs. 5–6; Roark, *Aristotle on Time*, 109–112.

50 That Isḥāq ibn Ḥunayn used *miqdār* for μέτρον as well as μέγεθος is shown by his translations of *Physics* IV.11, 219a11f. (for μέγεθος) and of IV.12, 221b7 (for μέτρον). The translator of Philoponus' comments in the margins of Ms. Leiden or. 583, by all appearances Qusṭā, generally used, like Isḥāq ibn Ḥunayn, *ʿadad* for ἀριθμός and, at least in one extant passage *miqdār* for μέγεθος (*Phys.* IV.11, 219a11f.); cf. also Lettinck, *Aristotle's* Physics *and its Reception in the Arabic World*, 358. Whether Qusṭā also used *miqdār* for μέτρον can, though probable, not be verified with certainty; cf. also Daiber's glossary in Aetius Arabus, *Die Vorsokratiker in arabischer Überlieferung*, esp. #2124–2126, 2620.

51 Avicenna occasionally plays with words. He writes, for example, that time is "the magnitude measuring the … possibility" (*al-miqdār al-muqaddir li-l-imkān*), as we have just seen in *al-Samāʿ al-ṭabīʿī* II.11, §4, 157.16f; cf. *al-Ḥikma al-mašriqiyya* III.11, 33.18.

52 *al-Samāʿ al-ṭabīʿī* II.11, §2, 156.3f.; cf. *al-Ḥikma al-mašriqiyya* III.11, 32.10f.; cf. also *al-Samāʿ al-ṭabīʿī* III.9, §6, 221.10–222.1; cf. further *Phys.* IV.11, 219a11; VI.2, 232a23.

53 *al-Samāʿ al-ṭabīʿī* II.11, §3, 157.5f.; cf. *al-Ḥikma al-mašriqiyya* III.11, 33.4f.; cf. also *Phys.* IV.11, 219a10–21; 219b15f.; 219b22f.; 220a4–6; cf. further *Phys.* VI.1, 232a18–22; VI.2, 232b20–233a21, 233b19–33; VI.4, 235a18–24; *Met.* Δ.13, 1020a32; q.v. also the similar expression in Yaḥyā ibn ʿAdī 80 below, 453. Describing the relation between time, distance, and motion by means of the verb ἀκολουθεῖ is Aristotle's way of saying that distance, motion, and time conform to each other in structure. Since the distance is continuous and infinitely divisible, as opposed to being atomic, the motion which takes place along the distance is also continuous. Moreover, since time is nothing but the number of motion measuring its extension, it is likewise essentially continuous, because its motion, and ultimately the distance covered by the motion, are such; cf. also *Phys.* VI.1–2; cf. further Aristotle's critique of atomism in *De generatione et corruptione* I.2. It is also noteworthy that Avicenna does not employ the terminology of

clear, central aspects of Avicenna's understanding of *miqdār* within his discussion of time derive from Aristotle's conception of μέγεθος.

Moreover, Avicenna's understanding of *miqdār* in the discussion of time is a consequence of his general views about quantity, magnitude, and multiplicity as they are documented in his *al-Ilāhiyyāt*.[54] Within the discussion of the accidental nature of the categories in the third book of Avicenna's *al-Ilāhiyyāt*, we are told that *miqdār* belongs to the category of quantity (*kammiyya*), thus answering to the question "how much?" (*kamm*). Avicenna's account draws on Aristotle's remarks in *Categories* 6 and *Metaphysics* Δ.13, both of which are concerned with the category of "how much?" (ποσόν, *kamm*). At the end of *al-Ilāhiyyāt* III.4, Avicenna states:

فالكمّية بالجملة حدّها هي أنّها التي يمكن أن يُوجَد فيها شيء منها يصحّ أن يكون واحداً عادّاً.

On the whole, then, the definition of quantity (*al-kammiyya*) is that it is that in which it is possible to find something of it that can rightly [be said] to be a numbering unit (*wāḥidan ʿāddan*). (*al-Ilāhiyyāt* III.4, §21, 118.14f.)

Amos Bertolacci traces this definition of quantity back to a corresponding definition provided by Aristotle in *Metaphysics* Δ.13.[55] At the beginning of this chapter, we read the following:

Ποσὸν λέγεται τὸ διαιρετὸν είς ἐνυπάρχοντα ὧν ἑκάτερον ἢ ἕκαστον ἕν τι καὶ τόδε τι πέφυκεν εἶναι. πλῆθος μὲν οὖν ποσόν τι ἐὰν ἀριθμητὸν ᾖ, μέγεθος δὲ ἂν μετρητὸν ᾖ.
يقال كمّية الذي يتجزّأ في أشياء هي فيه ولكلّ واحد منها أو أحدها طبع أن يكون واحداً ما وهذا الشيء أيضاً.
ويقال كثرة كمّية الذي يعُدّ وعظم كمّية إذا كانت تُمسَح بمقدار ما.

Quantity (ποσόν, *kammiyya*) is said of that which is divisible into two or more constituent parts of which each is such that it is a unit and a this (ἕν τι καὶ τόδε τι, *wāḥidan mā wa-hāḏā l-šayʾ*). A quantity is a multiplicity (πλῆθος, *kaṯra*) when it is numerable (ἀριθμητόν, *allaḏī yuʿaddu*) but is a magnitude (μέγεθος, *ʿiẓam*) when it is measurable (μετρητόν, *tumsaḥu bi-miqdār mā*). (*Met.* Δ.13, 1020a7–10, tr. by Ross, modified)

Aristotle's explicit distinction between multiplicity and numerability, on the one hand, and magnitude and measurability, on the other, seems to reflect a similar division brought forward in *Categories* 6 between quantities that are discrete (διωρισμένον, *munfaṣil*) and those that are continuous (συνεχές, *muttaṣil*). The former includes such quantities as numbers and words (ἀριθμὸς καὶ λόγος, *al-ʿadad wa-l-qawl*), whereas the latter comprises lines, planes, bodies as well as time and place (γραμμή, ἐπιφάνεια, σῶμα, ἔτι δὲ παρὰ ταῦτα χρόνος καὶ τόπος, *al-ḫaṭṭ wa-l-basīṭ wa-l-ǧism wa-ayḍan*

Isḥāq ibn Ḥunayn's translation when he talks about the relation of distance, motion, and time, i.e., he does not use *tabaʿa* for Aristotle's ἀκολουθεῖν but *ṭābaqa*; q.v. above, 37ff.

54 q.v. also above, 122ff.

55 Bertolacci, *The Reception of Aristotle's* Metaphysics *in Avicenna's* Kitāb al-Šifāʾ, 342.

mimmā yaṭīfu bi-hāḏihī l-zamān wa-l-makān).[56] Although Aristotle defined time as a number in the *Physics*, his remarks in *Categories* 6 and *Metaphysics* Δ easily suggest to a well-read scholar such as Avicenna that time should be considered as a measurable magnitude instead of a numerable multiplicity.[57]

Avicenna accepts Aristotle's distinction between multiplicity and magnitude. Taking number as corresponding to multiplicity, he states that "multiplicity is nothing but a name for that which is composed of units" (*al-kaṯra laysat illā sman li-l-muʿallaf min al-waḥdāt*), with the result that in Avicenna, just as in Aristotle, we get a distinction between number and magnitude.[58] Yet, Avicenna seems to be less strict when it comes to distinguishing between the *acts* of numbering and measuring, as he writes the following:

المقدار كونه مقداراً هو أنّه بحيث يقدّر وكونه بحيث يقدّر هو كونه بحيث يُعَدّ وكونه بحيث يُعَدّ كونه بحيث أنّ له واحداً.

> Magnitude's being a magnitude (*miqdāran*) is insofar as it is measurable, and its being insofar as it is measurable is its being insofar as it is numerable, and its being insofar as it is numerable is to have a unit (*wāḥidan*). (*al-Ilāhiyyāt* III.1, §10, 96.2–4)

A magnitude, then, is something which is essentially measurable which means that one can apply a number to it once a certain unit has been determined or agreed upon. To be measurable means to be numerable and to be numerable means to be such as to have a unit. One might like to criticise Avicenna for having conflated two species of quantities which he, following Aristotle, elsewhere distinguishes from one another; after all, this passage speaks about magnitudes by means of numbers which, however, are multiplicities. Yet, Aristotle himself did something very similar in *Metaphysics* I.6 when he wrote the following:

---

56 *Cat.* 6, 4b20–25; cf. also Ross' comments in *Physics*, 323.

57 However, it has been argued that what Aristotle means by "number" and by "measure" in the *Physics* is not co-extensive and that the meanings of these terms ought to be distinguished from one another, with the result that defining time as the *number* of motion, instead of measure, was a deliberate decision on his part; cf. Conen, *Die Zeittheorie des Aristoteles*, 138–142; Sorabji, *Time, Creation and the Continuum*, 84–89; Coope, *Time for Aristotle*, chs. 5–6; cf. also Annas, "Aristotle, Number and Time"; Roark, *Aristotle on Time*, ch. 6. In any case, many interpreters, late ancient and modern alike, are and have been insensitive to the question whether or not number and measure are somewhat the same in Aristotle's account of time or, in fact, took it for granted that they are, given passages such as those listed by Annas in fn. 5, 98: "Time is the number of motion (221b2); the being of eternal things is not measured by time (b5); time is the measure of motion (b7); time is not motion but the number of motion (b11); time measures moving and resting things qua moving and resting (b16–7), since it measures the quantity of their motion and rest (b18–9); time is the measure of motion and rest (b22–3, cf. b25–6)."

58 *al-Ilāhiyyāt* III.3, §5, 105.14. On number, cf. *al-Ilāhiyyāt* III.3, §17, 110.3f.; III.5, esp. §§2–4, 119.6–120.8; cf. also Menn, "Avicenna's Metaphysics," 160f.

πολλὰ γὰρ ἕκαστος ὁ ἀριθμὸς ὅτι ἕνα καὶ ὅτι μετρητὸς ἑνὶ ἕκαστος ... τὸ δὲ πλῆθος οἷον γένος ἐστὶ τοῦ ἀριθμοῦ· ἔστι γὰρ ἀριθμὸς πλῆθος ἑνὶ μετρητόν.

〈...〉 واحد وأنّ كلّ واحد مكول لواحد ... وأمّا الكثرة فهي كجنس العدد فإنّ العدد كثرة مكولة بواحد.

For every number is many because it consists of units and because each is measurable by a unit (μετρητὸς ἑνί, *makūl li-wāḥid*) ... Multiplicity (πλῆθος, *kaṯra*) is like a genus of number, for number is a multiplicity measurable by a unit (πλῆθος ἑνὶ μετρητόν, *kaṯra makūla bi-wāḥid*). (*Met.* I.6, 1056b23–1057a4, tr. by Ross, modified)[59]

According to Avicenna, then, *miqdār* is one of two kinds under the genus term *kammiyya*.[60] It is continuous and signifies an amount or a size answering to the question "how much?" Moreover, it contains something that is or can serve as a unit, so that it, as a whole, is measurable insofar as these units can be numbered and counted. These features derive from Aristotle's account of μέγεθος, so that my above claim that Avicenna considers time first and foremost to be a magnitude, instead of a measure, is not only warranted on the grounds of certain considerations from within Avicenna's discussion of time in his *al-Samāʿ al-ṭabīʿī* but is also generally supported by his views about the nature of magnitudes which he expresses in his *al-Ilāhiyyāt* and which he derived from studying Aristotle's *Categories* and *Metaphysics*.

An example will illustrate how Avicenna conceives of time as a measurable magnitude. Let us take a bucket, for example. A bucket is a certain magnitude that can contain a certain amount of water. Thus, there is a certain volume that belongs to the bucket itself, providing it with an abstract number expressing its size. We may not yet know that number, and so may not know the exact size of the bucket and how much water it may contain, but we do know that it has a number which represents its volume. Moreover, this number can easily be determined by a process of measuring and numbering according to a given unit. The bucket's volume will ultimately be expressed by means of a concrete number and a unit such as "twenty times one litre," i.e., "twenty litres."[61] The numbering and measuring, then, is a derivative action derived from the volume of the bucket itself. The bucket has a magnitude, therefore it is measurable – and it has a measure, once it has been measured.

---

59 The Arabic translation by Usṭāṯ, as contained in Averroes commentary on the *Metaphysics*, seems to lack a formulation corresponding to πολλὰ γὰρ ἕκαστος ὁ ἀριθμὸς ὅτι.

60 It is interesting to note that Abū Yaʿqūb ibn Isḥāq al-Kindī likewise emphasised time as a quantity (*kammiyya*) repeatedly; cf. *Kitāb fī l-falsafa al-ūlā*, vol. 2, 31.10, 35.19f., 39.11, 81.22f.; cf. also Jolivet, "al-Kindī, vues sur le temps," 56f.

61 Instead of 20 litres, it could also be 20 000 cubic centimetres or 35,2 imperial pints. All these are different numbers, nonetheless they express the same volume or size. When I say "the bucket's volume has a number," then I do not mean a number in a sense that varies according to a chosen unit but in an abstract sense, i.e., in a sense in which 20 litres, 20 000 cubic centimetres, and 35,2 imperial pints all express *the same abstract number* of the size of the bucket. It is in this sense, that number and magnitude can mean the same thing.

A magnitude, then, is first and foremost a size or extension. Despite the essential measurability of a *miqdār*, Avicenna employs this term, in order to signify a magnitude, and only derivatively a measure.[62] Significant in this context is also a passage in *al-Maqūlāt* in which Avicenna seems to equate *imtidād* ("extension") with *miqdār*, thus, again, demonstrating his understanding of *miqdār* along the lines of μέγεθος.[63]

For Avicenna, then, time, defined as the "magnitude of motion" (*miqdār al-ḥaraka*), is primarily something like the "size" or the "extension" of a motion, spanning from its moment of starting to its moment of ending.[64] Having said this, Avicenna does not lose sight of the measuring aspect of time, for example, when he writes that time is "the magnitude measuring the aforementioned possibility essentially" (*al-miqdār al-muqaddir li-l-imkān ... bi-ḏātihī*) or when he emulates Aristotle's oscillating description of time as a number and as a measure by making time a "number or magnitude" (*al-ʿadad aw al-miqdār*), thereby highlighting also the numbering aspect – and, thus, the measuring aspect – of time.[65] Still, his primary understanding of time is that it is *that wherein* motion and possibilities for motion occur. This understanding of time appears to have its roots in a central remark by Aristotle himself:

> ἀλλὰ μὴν καὶ τὸν χρόνον γε γνωρίζομεν ὅταν ὁρίσωμεν τὴν κίνησιν, τῷ πρότερον καὶ ὕστερον ὁρίζοντες· καὶ τότε φαμὲν γεγονέναι χρόνον, ὅταν τοῦ προτέρου καὶ ὑστέρου ἐν τῇ κινήσει αἴσθησιν λάβωμεν. ὁρίζομεν δὲ τῷ ἄλλο καὶ ἄλλο ὑπολαβεῖν αὐτά, καὶ μεταξύ τι αὐτῶν ἕτερον· ὅταν γὰρ ἕτερα τὰ ἄκρα τοῦ μέσου νοήσωμεν, καὶ δύο εἴπῃ ἡ ψυχὴ τὰ νῦν, τὸ μὲν πρότερον τὸ δ' ὕστερον, τότε καὶ τοῦτό φαμεν εἶναι χρόνον· τὸ γὰρ ὁριζόμενον τῷ νῦν χρόνος εἶναι δοκεῖ·
>
> وإنّما نعرف الزمان أيضاً عند تحصيلنا الحركة بأن نحصّلها بالمتقدّم والمتأخّر. وحينئذ نقول إنّه قد كان زمان متى أحسسنا بالمتقدّم والمتأخّر في الحركة. وأمّا تحصيلها فإن نراهما مختلفين وأنّ بينهما شيئاً آخر غيرهما وذلك أنّا إذا رأينا بالذهن الطرفين مخالفين للوسط وحكمت النفس بالآنين أحدهما متقدّم والآخر متأخّر فحينئذ نقول إنّ هذا زمان فإنّ الذي يحدّ به الآن قد نظنّ أنّه زمان.
>
> But we apprehend (γνωρίζομεν, *naʿrifu*) time only when we mark off motion, marking it off by the prior and posterior. It is only when we have perceived the prior and posterior in motion that we say that time has passed. Now we mark off by taking them as other and other and some third thing as between them (μεταξύ τι αὐτῶν ἕτερον, *baynahumā šayʾan āḫar ġayrahumā*). When we conceive of (νοήσωμεν, *raʾaynā bi-l-ḏihn*) the limits as different from the middle (τοῦ μέσου, *al-wasaṭ*) and the soul pronounces (εἴπῃ ἡ ψυχή, *wa-ḥakamat al-nafs*) that the nows are two, one prior and one posterior, then it is that we say that there is time, for what is marked off[66] by the now is time, as it seems. (*Phys.* IV.11, 219a22–30, tr. by Hardie/Gaye, modified)

62 cf. also Bertolacci's and Lizzini's translation of *miqdār* as "estensione" as opposed to Marmura's consistent translation as "measure" in their translations of *al-Ilāhiyyāt* III.1, §10, 95.13–96.4.

63 *al-Maqūlāt* III.4, 119.6–10.

64 In his *Tahāfut al-falāsifa*, Abū Ḥāmid al-Ġazālī reproduces the Aristotelian-Avicennian account once as *qadr al-ḥaraka* ("the extent of motion"; 31.10) and subsequently as *imtidād al-ḥaraka* ("the extension of motion"; 33.10).

65 *al-Samāʿ al-ṭabīʿī* II.11, §4, 157.16f.; §3, 157.6; cf. *al-Ḥikma al-mašriqiyya* III.11, 33.18, 5.

66 Suggesting to read in the Arabic *yaḥuddu* instead of *naḥuddu* as in Badawī.

In the final sentence, Aristotle explains that what has been marked off by the now (τὸ γὰρ ὁριζόμενον τῷ νῦν, *allaḏī yaḥuddu bihī l-ān*) – or rather: by two nows – is time. With this, he identifies time with the interval between (μεταξύ τι, *baynahumā šay'an*) the nows, i.e., with that which is in the middle (τοῦ μέσου, *al-wasaṭ*) and which is different from the limits that mark it off. This language, reminiscent also of Philoponus' and Ibn al-Samḥ' terminology in their comment on *Physics* VI.2, presumably laid the foundation for Avicenna's analysis of motion on the basis of which he establishes time as a magnitude between the start and the end of a motion. Yet, we have seen that in his analysis, Avicenna avoids temporal terminology altogether, and so he abstains from writing that it is the *nows* which mark off that which is in between; after all, the now is a temporal notion.[67] What is more, Avicenna will argue later that the now is a result of the continuity of motion and a product of our imagination.[68] Thus, at the present stage of Avicenna's argument, any talk of the now would not only result in a circular reasoning, insofar as he would have used something that follows from time for establishing time in the first place, but would also jeopardise the concrete reality of time right from the start, insofar as he would have used something that exists only in the imagination for establishing time as something existing outside the mind in concrete reality. Thus, Avicenna resorts to expressions of motion, such as *mubtada'* ("beginning") and *muntahā* ("ending") in *al-Samāʿ al-ṭabīʿī*, as well as their equivalents *aḫḏ* and *tark* in *al-Naǧāt* and *al-Ḥikma al-ʿArūḍiyya*, as the terms that frame and delimit the magnitude which he identifies with time.[69] From the very start of his exposition, Avicenna presents time as that which obtains between two boundaries or, in other words, as a magnitude describing the size of a motion.

Avicenna may have found more inspiration in Philoponus, who commented on Aristotle's just quoted passage as follows:

> Τὸ πρότερον καὶ τὸ ὕστερον ὁρίζοντες, φησί, τὸ ἐν τῇ κινήσει, οὕτως εἰς ἔννοιαν τοῦ χρόνου ἐρχόμεθα ... ὅταν τοῦτο ὁρίσωμεν καὶ εἴπωμεν ἄλλο μὲν εἶναι τὸ νῦν ἐν ᾧ ἤρξατο ἡ κίνησις, ἄλλο δὲ ἐν ᾧ πέπαυται, τὸ μεταξὺ τούτων ἕτερον ὂν παρὰ τὰ ἄκρα τοῦτο εἶναί φαμεν τὸν χρόνον.
>
> In determining the prior and the posterior in motion, he [sc. Aristotle] says, we come to an awareness of time ... Whenever we mark this off and say that there is one now at which the motion began (τὸ νῦν ἐν ᾧ ἤρξατο ἡ κίνησις) and a different one at which it has ceased (ἐν ᾧ πέπαυται), that which is between these (τὸ μεταξὺ τούτων), being other than the extremes, is what we say is time. (Philoponus, *In Phys.*, 721.15–19, tr. by Broadie, modified)[70]

---

67 Later in *al-Samāʿ al-ṭabīʿī* II.13, i.e., after his investigation of the now in the preceding twelfth chapter, Avicenna explicitly seconds Aristotle's argumentation in a manner reminiscent of Philoponus, *In Phys.*, 721.15–19, quoted below; cf. *al-Samāʿ al-ṭabīʿī* II.13, §1, 167.4f.

68 cf. *al-Samāʿ al-ṭabīʿī* II.12; q.v. below, 515ff., for a brief account of the now in Avicenna's temporal theory.

69 q.v. fn. 23 above, 436.

70 cf. *al-Samāʿ al-ṭabīʿī* II.13, §1, 167.4f.

Elsewhere, Philoponus describes time as an "interval" or "dimension" (τὸ διάστημα), or like Aristotle as that which is "in between" (τὸ μεταξύ) and as the "middle" (*wasaṭ*) between the beginning and the end of a motion, as above in his comments on *Physics* VI.2.[71] Philoponus even writes the following:

> οὐ γὰρ ὁ αὐτῆς τῆς κινήσεως ἀριθμὸς χρόνος, ἀλλὰ τὸ τοῦ προτέρου ἐν αὐτῇ καὶ ὑστέρου διάστημα μεταξύ.
>
> Time, then, is not the number of motion itself but rather is the interval between the prior and posterior in it (τὸ τοῦ προτέρου ἐν αὐτῇ καὶ ὑστέρου διάστημα μεταξύ). (Philoponus, *In Phys.*, 731.23–25, tr. by Broadie, modified)

In particular this last passage shifts the conceptual weight from the notion of time as a number to that of time as a magnitude – the same shift we recognised in Avicenna. It is passages like these which shaped Avicenna's understanding of time as a magnitude.[72]

This passage in Philoponus' commentary is significant, for in asserting that time is more adequately said to be an "interval" (διάστημα), rather than a number of motion, Philoponus does nothing other than turn an Aristotelian definition of time into a Neoplatonic one. This is crucial both for understanding Avicenna's account as well as for assessing its position within the history of natural philosophy. So far, we have seen how Avicenna devised a novel strategy for deriving the definition of time from an analysis of various situations that involve moving objects, inspired by Aristotelian material from *Physics* VI.2. Moreover, it is clear that the definition he, then, provided – that "time is the number of motion when it is differentiated into what is prior and what is posterior" – is given in an entirely Aristotelian spirit, being almost literally the same as the one we find in *Physics* IV.11.[73] On these grounds, one could easily describe Avicenna's account as being entirely faithful to Aristotle. One might even trivialise the fact that Avicenna emphasised what I have called the μέγεθος-aspect of time, instead of the μέτρον-aspect, by stressing that Aristotle himself did not with utmost clarity distinguish number, measure, and magnitude from each other, on the one hand, and claiming that Avicenna's preference for the term *miqdār*, instead of *ʿadad* is merely terminologically motivated and, thus, negligible, on the other. Likewise, one might

---

71 Philoponus, *In Phys.*, 722.11, 737.27f.; Philoponus' and Ibn al-Samḥ's comment in Aristotle, *al-Ṭabīʿa* VI.2, 624.10; cf. also the above quotation from *Physics* IV.11, 219a22–30, which had τοῦ μέσου translated as *al-wasaṭ*.

72 In his discussion of time in the *Enneads*, Plotinus writes that "those who say that [time] is something belonging to motion [mean] that it is the interval of motion (ἢ διάστημα κινήσεως) or the measure" (μέτρον; *Enn.* III.7.7, 24f.). Armstrong's translation is incorrect, for he translates the first option as "the distance covered by the movement." This is not only wrong but genuinely dissatisfying, as it would identify the time of a motion with the *spatial* distance covered by that motion. Instead, what Plotinus is doing, here, is listing two views on motion that together bear witness to a firmly established distinction between, as I have called it, the μέγεθος-aspect and the μέτρον-aspect of time. We shall have to come back to Plotinus' discussion in what follows.

73 *al-Samāʿ al-ṭabīʿī* II.11, §3, 157.6; cf. *Phys.* IV.11, 219b1f., 220a24–26.

argue that the just quoted passages from Philoponus' commentary ought to be seen as nothing other than a straightforward Peripatetic exposition of Aristotle's discussion.[74] On this interpretation, however, we would miss out on an important development within the Greek and Arabic commentary tradition which contributed a great deal to a somewhat un-Aristotelian appreciation of Aristotle's definition of time.[75]

The Platonism of Time as a Magnitude

In a commentary on Aristotle's *Categories* attributed to Boethus of Sidon (fl. second half of the first century BC), we find an interesting reflection on the relation between time and motion through the notion of number. In this commentary, we read the following:

> ἀλλ' ἔστιν ἀριθμὸς ὁ μὲν ἀριθμῶν, ὁ δὲ ἀριθμούμενος. ζητητέον πῶς φαμεν τὸν χρόνον ἀριθμὸν κινήσεως, ἆρα ὡς ἀριθμοῦντα τὴν κίνησιν ἢ ὡς ὑπ' αὐτῆς ἀριθμούμενον. φαμὲν δὴ τὸν χρόνον ἀριθμεῖσθαι μὲν ὑπὸ τῆς πρώτης καὶ ἁπλῆς κινήσεως τῆς κυκλοφορικῆς, ἀνταριθμεῖν δὲ πάλιν αὐτήν. εἰ μὴ γὰρ ὑπὸ χρόνου ἡ τοιαύτη κίνησις, ὑπὸ τίνος ἀριθμηθείη ἄν; τὴν πρώτην οὖν καὶ κυριωτάτην τῶν κινήσεων τὴν κυκλοφορικὴν ὁ χρόνος μετρῶν κατ' ἐκείνην καὶ τὰς ἄλλας μετρεῖ, ὥστε τῆς μὲν κυκλοφορικῆς κινήσεως ἀριθμὸς ἔσται ὁ χρόνος καὶ ὡς ἀριθμῶν καὶ ὡς ἀριθμούμενος, τῶν δὲ λοιπῶν κινήσεων ὡς ἀριθμῶν μόνον οὐ μὴν καὶ ὡς ἀριθμούμενος· οὐ γὰρ τῆς ἐμῆς βαδίσεως ἀριθμὸς ἔσται ὁ χρόνος ὡς ἀριθμούμενος, ἀλλὰ μόνον ὡς ἀριθμῶν.
>
> However, one number numbers (ἀριθμῶν), another is numbered (ἀριθμούμενος). We should inquire how we say that time is the number of motion, whether as numbering the motion or as being numbered by it (ὑπ' αὐτῆς ἀριθμούμενον). Well, we say that time is numbered by the first and simple motion in a circle (ἀριθμεῖσθαι μὲν ὑπὸ τῆς πρώτης καὶ ἁπλῆς κινήσεως τῆς κυκλοφορικῆς), and numbers it in return (ἀνταριθμεῖν). For if such a motion were not numbered by time, by what would it be numbered? So time, which measures the primary and most proper motion which is that in a circle, measures the other [motions], too, by this, so that time will be the number of the motion which is in a circle both as numbering it and as being numbered, but of the remaining motions only as numbering but not also as being numbered. For time will not be the number of my walking as being numbered but only as numbering. (Boethus of Sidon (?), *Περὶ τῆς τοῦ ποτὲ κατηγορίας*, 21.8–20, tr. by Sharples, modified)[76]

Two things are relevant here. The first is that Boethus presents time as something which is *numbered by* motion. This is a surprising move for a Peripatetic, because Aristotle explicitly defined time as something which *numbers* motion. However, Boethus obviously takes advantage of – or is confused by – Aristotle's famous distinction between

74 Philoponus' remarks on *Physics* IV.10–14 as a whole have indeed been characterised by Sorabji as a "straight exposition, with little objection or defence of Aristotle" – quite unlike the rest of his commentary on the *Physics*, which does not spare with severe criticism and is full of major developments of Aristotelian doctrine; cf. Sorabji's notes in his introduction to Broadie's translation of Philoponus, *On Aristotle "Physics" 4.10–14*; q.v. also fn. 93 above, 30f.

75 cf. also my remarks in "Time and Mind-Dependence in Sayf al-Dīn al-Āmidī's *Abkār al-afkār*."

76 Sharples, *Peripatetic Philosophy 200 BC to AD 200*, 172; cf. also Huby, "An Excerpt from Boethus of Sidon's Commentary on the Categories?"

number as numbered (τὸ ἀριθμούμενον) and number as numbering (ᾧ ἀριθμοῦμεν).[77] Since Aristotle explained that time as the number of motion ought to be understood as actually being something numbered, Boethus feels justified to conclude that time is not only numbered, but even that it is numbered *by* motion (ὑπ' αὐτῆς ἀριθμούμενον). On that basis, Boethus claims that time is, first and foremost, something which is numbered by motion and, only secondarily, also "numbers it in return" (ἀνταριθμεῖν).

A second important aspect of Boethus' interpretation is that time is not numbered by just any motion but, primarily and exclusively, by the "first and simple motion," i.e., the uniform circular motion of the outermost sphere. We may, thus, assume that the motion of the outermost sphere somehow brings about time by numbering it, so that this time, being something numbered by that motion, then, numbers other motions as, for example, my walking from here to the park.

Interestingly, Boethus' views resonate well with those of Alexander. Although Alexander's commentary on Aristotle's *Physics* is not known to have survived in any language in any substantial form, we know much of his thoughts on time from what seems to be an independent treatise he wrote on that subject. The treatise is extant in an Arabic translation by Ḥunayn ibn Isḥāq (d. 260/873) from the Greek and a Latin translation by Gerard of Cremona (d. 1187) from the Arabic.[78] In this treatise, we read the following:

> وسنقول في الزمان على رأي الفيلسوف من غير أن نخالف شيئاً منه. فزعم أنّه بقول منطقي عدد حركة الفلك المشرقية ولغير ذلك فحدّه أنه مدّة تعدّها الحركة.
>
> We shall talk about time according to the opinion of the Philosopher without deviating from him in any respect. So, he maintains that, logically speaking,[79] it [sc. time] is the number of the westbound motion of the sphere and of what is other than this. Thus, its definition is that it is a duration which motion numbers (*mudda ta'udduhā l-ḥaraka*). (*Maqālat al-Iskandar al-Afrūdīsī fī l-zamān*, 20.12–14)

77 *Phys.* IV.11, 219b5–8. For the standard interpretation of this distinction, cf. Mendell, "Aristotle and Mathematics," ch. 10.3.

78 q.v. above, 23f.

79 It is not entirely clear what *bi-qawl manṭiqī* is supposed to mean. A promising thought is to assume an adverbial λογικῶς in the Greek original for Ḥunayn ibn Isḥāq's translation, so that the following definition is considered by Alexander to be merely verbal or conceptual and rather abstract. On the use of that expression in Aristotle, cf. Simplicius, *In Phys.*, 440.20–441.2; Ross' comments in *Physics*, *ad* 202a21; Pines, "Omne quod movetur necesse est ab aliquo moveri," 29; Frede's and Patzig's comments in Aristotle, *Metaphysik Z*, vol. 2, 59; Algra, *Concepts of Space in Greek Thought*, fn. 106, 164; Burnyeat, *A Map of* Metaphysics Z, ch. 5; for the use of the word in Alexander's commentary on the Metaphysics, cf. fn. 34, 96, in Madigan's translation to book III; for the use of the word and in Syrianus' commentary on the Metaphysics, cf. fn. 1, 119, in O'Meara and Dillon's translation to book III. Additionally, the word often seems to take on a pejorative connotation in the sense of "(merely) dialectically." Gerard of Cremona rendered the Arabic as "sermone dyalectico" and Sharples translated the expression from the Latin as "dialectically."

Both central aspects of Boethus' account are present in this brief passage. First, the dictum that time as a number of motion is understood in such a way that time is something which is numbered by motion. Alexander even goes one step further than Boethus and writes that time is a "duration which motion numbers" (*mudda taʿudduhā l-ḥaraka*). Second, the motion in question is precisely the circular motion of the outermost sphere, just as in Boethus. As is known, Alexander's treatises were very influential in their Arabic translation, and particularly so in fourth/tenth-century Baġdād. It is, therefore, not surprising to read in the *Maqāla fī l-mawǧūdāt* of Yaḥyā ibn ʿAdī (d. 363/974), again, something very similar:

> وأمّا الزمان فهو بحسب ما رسمه أرسطوطالس مدّة تعدّها الحركة بالمتقدّم والمتأخّر وهو يعني بالمدّة الامتداد الذي يضاد الحركة ويشار بها إليه. وذلك أنّ الزمان إنّما يُوجَد أوّلاً زماناً تامّاً للحركة ... فقد بيّن أرسطوطالس في المقالة الرابعة من السماع الطبيعي أنّه لو لم تكن حركة لم يكن زمان لأنّه لا سبيل إلى تصوّر زمان من دون تصوّر الحركة.
>
> Time, according to how Aristotle described it, is a duration which motion numbers (*mudda taʿudduhā l-ḥaraka*) by the prior and the posterior. What he means by "duration" is the extension (*al-imtidād*) which contrasts[80] motion and which is pointed at by it [sc. motion]. That is because time exists only primarily as a complete time because of motion ... So, Aristotle has proven in the fourth book of the *Physics* that if there were no motion, there would not be time, because there is no way for grasping time without grasping motion. (Ibn ʿAdī, *Maqāla fī l-mawǧūdāt*, 273.2–6)

In his remarks, Ibn ʿAdī follows Alexander in identifying time with a duration (*mudda*), emphasising in particular its extended character (*al-imtidād*) as a magnitude in contrast, or perhaps parallel, to (*yuḍāddu*) the extension of motion. Time, so understood, is measured by motion; put differently, motion emerges as the measure of time rather than time as the measure of motion, as Aristotle would have preferred. What is more, Ibn ʿAdī adds a little later that we learn about temporal notions such as "year" or "month" only "through measuring them by the motion of the Sun" (*bi-taqdīrihī bi-ḥarakat al-šams*). The notion of "day," however, is derived from the revolution of the outermost sphere (*al-falak al-aʿlā*).[81] This means that in Ibn ʿAdī, too, both aspects of Boethus' interpretation are present.

It is interesting that both Alexander and Ibn ʿAdī explicitly emphasise that they are following Aristotle. Alexander even assures that he intends to present Aristotle's

---

80 It is not entirely clear what Ibn ʿAdī intends with the verb *yuḍāddu* ("to be in contrast to") which usually has a strong adversative connotation. One thought would be simply to suggest reading *yuḍāfu* ("to be related to") for *yuḍāddu*, so that the extension would simply be related to the motion. However, in this case one would expect the preposition *ilā* with a pronoun to accompany the verb just as in the subsequent expression *yušāru bihā ilayhi*, where, however, *ilayhi* in the edition is marked (i.e., bracketed) as an emendation by the editor and, thus, likewise not attested by the manuscripts. Another, more promising, option is to understand *yuḍāddu* not in an adversative sense but simply as meaning "to be parallel to." In that case, Ibn ʿAdī's expression would basically be the same as Avicenna's expression *bi-izāʾ* in *al-Samāʿ al-ṭabīʿī* II.11, §3, 157.5 (and *al-Ḥikma al-mašriqiyya* III.11, 33.4f.).

81 Ibn ʿAdī, *Maqāla fī l-mawǧūdāt*, 273.8–12.

opinion "without deviating from him in any respect," whereas Ibn ʿAdī elsewhere asserts that the truth about time is what Aristotle said.[82] Indeed, it is true that both of the central aspects of their interpretation can be derived from a remark Aristotle made in *Physics* IV.14, the final chapter on time.[83] There, Aristotle stated that time is primarily related to the uniform and circular motion of the outermost sphere, which is the very motion through which time is measured (μετροῦνται ... ὁ χρόνος ταύτῃ τῇ κινήσει, *bi-hadihī l-ḥaraka taqaddara ... al-zamān*).[84] This passage must be read in its context and with an eye to the preceding chapters and in particular to those passages in which Aristotle explains the reciprocal relation between time and motion which allows us "not only to measure motion by time but also time by motion."[85] Taken in isolation, however, the passage in *Physics* IV.14 may give rise to a position entirely at odds with Aristotle's, viz., that time is not that which numbers or measures motion, as the canonical definition in *Physics* IV.11 demands, but rather that it is *motion* which numbers or measures time – and this is the position which we find in Boethus, Alexander, and Ibn ʿAdī.

What is more, Ibn ʿAdī elsewhere even explicitly contrasts time (*al-zamān*), which he calls "a duration which is numbered by motion as prior and posterior" (*mudda maʿdūda bi-l-ḥaraka mutaqaddimatan wa-mutaʾaḫḫiratan*), with eternity (*al-dahr*), which he calls "an unlimited and unnumbered duration" (*mudda ġayr maḥdūda wa-lā maʿdūda*).[86] This situation led Joel L. Kraemer to note that Ibn ʿAdī's alleged Peripatetic position "is surprising as it implies the concept of time ascribed by Galen to Plato," according to which time is a self-subsisting substance (*ǧawhar qāʾim bi-nafsihī*) and a

---

82 cf. Ibn ʿAdī, *Kitāb Aǧwiba Bišr al-Yahūdī ʿan masāʾilihī*, 332.3f.; q.v. the translation below, 457.

83 Chapter IV.14 of the *Physics* consists of a number of separate investigations. First, Aristotle discusses what it means to be "in time." Thereupon, he turns to the question of how time is related to soul. Next, he says that "one might well raise the question (ἀπορήσειε δ' ἄν τις) of what kind of change time is the number." Having ascertained that time is the same everywhere, he turns to locomotion and in particular to the circular motion of the outermost sphere, whose motion is "above all else" a measure. This is followed by a consideration of whether or not the number of sheep and dogs is the same or different. While bits of this chapter certainly follow some sort of plan (for example, from the question of which motion time is the number, first, to local motion; then, to circular motion; and, finally, to the sphere), it is difficult to find an overall agenda. It rather seems, that segments of chapter fourteen could be employed to substantiate certain claims and to follow up on certain aspects that have been established earlier in *Physics* IV.11–12. Hussey even claims that chapters thirteen and fourteen are "rag-bags containing bits and pieces never worked into the main discussions" together with "some parts of superseded versions [and] some notes containing second thoughts" (Hussey's comments in Aristotle, *Physics*, xxxviii). To what degree Hussey's strong contentions are justified is a different matter.

84 *Phys.* IV.14, 223b18–23.

85 *Phys.* IV.11, 220b14–16; a similar statement also immediately precedes that passage in *Physics* IV.14.

86 Ibn ʿAdī, *Maqāla fī l-mawǧūdāt*, 271.19–272.2; reading *mutaqaddimatan wa-mutaʾaḫḫiratan* for *mutaqaddimatin wa-mutaʾaḫḫiratin* in Ḫalīfāt. Note that the definition of time provided here is nothing but the *exact* opposite of Aristotle's original definition; cf. also *Maqāla fī l-mawǧūdāt*, 273.2f., which has been translated above.

duration (*al-mudda*) which is surveyed and measured by motion (*al-ḥaraka tamsaḥuhā wa-tuqaddiruhā*).[87] Indeed, when Ibn ʿAdī states that time is a duration measured by motion, he – as well as Alexander and Boethus – seems to have unwittingly, but effectively, *reversed* Aristotle's initial definition.

That this was a common Peripatetic confusion has already been noted by Plotinus seven hundred years before Ibn ʿAdī. In his *Enneads*, Plotinus sharply remarked that certain people, by which he apparently meant the Peripatetics (presumably including figures such as Boethus and Alexander), have a confused conception of the relation between motion and time. This confusion is itself due to an underlying and even more confused account of what it is in their definition that measures and what it is that is measured.[88] Plotinus' discussion of time is, moreover, marked not only by a critical, even if not altogether negative, engagement with the Aristotelian definition of time but also by a similar examination of the Stoic definition of time as an "interval of motion" (κινήσεως διάστημα).[89] Although elsewhere Plotinus opposed the Stoic tenet of making time a quantity, he nonetheless allowed time to reveal the size of motion (δήλωσιν τοῦ ὁπόση ἡ κίνησις).[90] In itself, however, he takes time to be the life of the soul which is revealed (δηλωθείς) and measured by the heavenly circuit (μετρούμενον ὑπὸ τῆς περιφορᾶς).[91] There is, then, no great conceptual difference between the Platonist account of Plotinus, on the one hand, and the alleged Peripatetic position advanced by Boethus, Alexander, and Ibn ʿAdī, on the other, for they all claim time to be measured

---

87 Kraemer, *Philosophy in the Renaissance of Islam*, 170; cf. also Adamson, "Galen and al-Rāzī on Time." Both Kraemer and Adamson refer to Ibn Abī Saʿīd al-Mawṣilī's testimony about Galen's position contained in his letter to Ibn ʿAdī, which will be discussed shortly (Ibn Abī Saʿīd *apud* Ibn ʿAdī, *Kitāb Ağwiba Bišr al-Yahūdī ʿan masāʾilihī*, esp. 318.1–319.8); cf. also Furlani, "Le 'Questioni filosofiche' di Abū Zakarīyā Yaḥyà b. ʿAdī"; Pines, "A Tenth Century Philosophical Correspondence," 110–114.

88 *Enn.* III.7.13, 9–18; cf. III.7.9, 1f., in which Plotinus voices his explicit preference for μέτρον over ἀριθμός as the key term in Aristotle's definition of time and subsequently engages in an examination of the notion of a measure.

89 cf. in particular von Arnim, *Stoicorum Veterum Fragmenta* I, §93; II, §§509–510; cf. also Long and Sedley, *The Hellenistic Philosophers*, §51. In his commentary on *Enneads* III.7, Beierwaltes also refers to the Neopythagorean definition of time of Ps.-Archytas, which was erroneously attributed to the Pythagorean Archytas of the fourth century BC, *apud* Simplicium, *In Phys.*, 786.12f. Ps.-Plutarchus, in turn, ascribes to Plato the view that time "is a moving image of eternity or the interval of the motion of the universe" (αἰῶνος εἰκόνα κινητὴν ἢ διάστημα τῆς τοῦ κόσμου κινήσεως, *miṯāl li-l-dahr mutaḥarrik aw buʿd li-ḥaraka al-ʿālam*; *Placita Philosophorum*, 318a.4f., with the Arabic translation by Qusṭā in Aetius Arabus, *Die Vorsokratiker in arabischer Überlieferung*, 20.12f.).

90 *Enn.* III.7.12, 43; cf. VI.1.5, 19; cf. also Beierwaltes' comments on the terms διάστασις and διάστημα at *Enn.* III.7.8, 23–30, 11, 41; 12.36–49.

91 *Enn.* III.7.12, esp. 40–52; 11, 43–62; 13, 1; cf. also Beierwaltes' comments in Plotinus, *Über Ewigkeit und Zeit*, 267f., 278–281; generally, 62–74; cf. further Mesch, *Reflektierte Gegenwart*, 239. Porphyry may have shared Plotinus' view in his *Sententiae ad intelligibilia ducentes*; cf. A. Smith, "The Significance of 'Physics' in Porphyry," 42f.

by motion – according to Harry Wolfson, "the correspondence of this definition with Plotinus' conception of time ... is so striking that it needs no further comment."[92]

In brief, it is the hallmark of an Aristotelian account of time that time is that which measures motion, whereas it is the hallmark of a Platonist or Neoplatonic account of time that time is that which motion measures (i.e., that time is a duration which is measured by motion). The reason why this is the hallmark of a Neoplatonic account of time is that this duration which is measured by motion is nothing other than the self-subsisting *substance* of eternity which Galen (d. ~ 216), reading Plato's *Timaeus*, has identified with time, whereas Aristotle's time, being the measure of motion, is an *accident*.[93] Moreover, according to the Neoplatonic understanding, time is universal: there is one time for all existents and all motion, so that time is that in which motions occur and in which things exist (analogous to the Neoplatonic understanding of place). Aristotle, however, claimed that time is a particular accident that belongs to each and every motion that occurs; every motion has its time. Consequently, it also belongs to the motion of the outermost sphere, but this does not make the time which as a number belongs to that primary motion a universal time. There is no universal time in Aristotle; time is particular (analogous to his understanding of place).[94]

Shifting the definition of time from the measure of motion to the duration or *magnitude* of motion means drifting into Platonist territory, especially when the relation between time and motion is reversed as well, so that it is no longer time which measures motion but motion which measures the extent of time. This shift has been prepared by Aristotle himself in two ways, both of which have already been mentioned. First, we find in *Physics* IV.14 a remark which explicitly states that time is measured by the revolution of the outermost sphere. As we have also seen, this remark is echoed by Boethus, Alexander, and Ibn ʿAdī in the above quoted passages. Second, we already know that Aristotle explained in another passage that the term "number," which he

---

92 Wolfson's comments in Crescas, *Crescas' Critique of Aristotle*, 655. Pines remarked in a similar manner that this account "agrees with the concepts of time held by both Plotinus and Proclus, and it is essentially identical with the definition that al-Bīrūnī reports in the name of [Abū Bakr] al-Rāzī" (*Studies in Islamic Atomism*, 59). His further claim that "[t]his definition of time is rejected by the Aristotelian *falāsifa*," however, must be modified in the light of the present analysis. For Abū Bakr al-Rāzī, q.v. fn. 99 below, 458.

93 cf. esp. Adamson, "Galen and al-Rāzī on Time," 7.

94 I do not intend to claim that Peripatetic such as Boethus, Alexander, and Ibn ʿAdī were following Plato or that they were Platonists in their conception of time. It is clear that they all think that they follow Aristotle, because they repeatedly emphasise, for example, that there is no time without motion. Moreover, they evidently deny that time ought to be viewed as a self-subsisting substance. For them, time is and remains an accident dependent upon motion (or the perception of motion), and so they are, and consider themselves to be, Peripatetics with regard to time. So, what I am arguing, instead, is that they have a confused understanding of what Aristotle's account amounts to – and that it is this confusion which led them adopt a theory which actually – inadvertently? – is on closer inspection more reminiscent of Plato than of Aristotle.

used in his definition of time, is ambiguous, and should be understood as "what is numbered" (τὸ ἀριθμούμενον) and not as "that by which we number" (ᾧ ἀριθμοῦμεν). So far we could only *suspect* that figures such as Boethus may have been led astray by that distinction. Within the Arabic tradition, however, there is actual *proof* that this well-meant clarification became a major source of confusion. This is made evident in a letter written by Ibn Abī Saʿīd al-Mawṣilī (fl. fourth/tenth century) to Ibn ʿAdī. Among other things, Ibn Abī Saʿīd requests an explanation of Aristotle's definition of time as what is numbered by motion (*al-zamān huwa maʿdūd al-ḥaraka*).[95] As we can see in his question, Ibn Abī Saʿīd incorporated the Aristotelian clarification that time is not so much that which numbers but rather that which is numbered (in Arabic expressed by the passive participle *maʿdūd*) into the definition of time which, now, no longer states that time is *ʿadad al-ḥaraka* ("the number of motion") but that it is *maʿdūd al-ḥaraka* ("that which is numbered of motion"). However, "that which is numbered of motion" is naturally understood as "that which is numbered *by* motion."[96] In his response, Ibn ʿAdī confirms to Ibn Abī Saʿīd that the correct definition of time is that of Aristotle, who said that time is *maʿdūd al-ḥaraka bi-l-mutaqaddim wa-l-mutaʾaḫḫir*, which Ibn ʿAdī explains as follows:

> والجواب عن الرابعة: الحقّ عندي ما قاله الحكيم في الزمان والصواب ما رآه فيه. وأمّا معناه في قوله إنّه معدود الحركة بالمتقدّم والمتأخّر فهو أنّه يُعَدّ بما نتصوّره النفس عند قسمتها حركة الفلك ... إلى ما تقدّم منها وما تأخّر ومساحتها إيّاها بهذين القسمين.
>
> The answer to the fourth [of your questions]: The truth, for me, is what the Sage has said about time and the correct view is what he thinks about it. As to what he meant when he said that [time] is "that which is numbered of motion (*maʿdūd al-ḥaraka*) by the prior and the posterior" is that it is that which is numbered (*yuʿaddu*) by what the soul grasps when dividing spherical motion ... into what of it is prior and what posterior, and when measuring it by these two divisions. (Ibn ʿAdī, *Kitāb Aǧwiba Bišr al-Yahūdī ʿan masāʾilihī*, 332.3–6)

This textual situation provided by the interpolation of *maʿdūd* into Aristotle's actual definition made it easy for Ibn ʿAdī to remain entirely unaware of the fact that he has positioned himself off the Aristotelian stance by presenting time as something measured by motion. In addition to that, Ibn Abī Saʿīd and Ibn ʿAdī were not the first to be confused about the situation. For one thing, there is already Alexander's Arabic treatise on time, which attributes this very account explicitly to Aristotle. Yet, even before Alexander there were other authoritative treatises – at least the one treatise by Boethus – in which the very same Aristotelian distinction between number as

95 Ibn Abī Saʿīd *apud* Ibn ʿAdī, *Kitāb Aǧwiba Bišr al-Yahūdī ʿan masāʾilihī*, 318.5–10.

96 This is further borne out by another passage in Ibn ʿAdī's treatise *Maqāla fī l-mawǧūdāt*, in which he adds the preposition *bi-*, thus defining time explicitly as "what is numbered *by* motion" (*maʿdūd bi-ḥaraka*; Ibn ʿAdī, *Maqāla fī l-mawǧūdāt*, 272.2, emphasis added); cf. also cf. Ibn ʿAdī, *On the Four Scientific Questions Concerning the Three Kinds of Existence*, §11, 80.22f.; cf. further al-Tawḥīdī and Miskawayh, *al-Hawāmil wa-l-šawāmil*, 31.16–18.

numbered and number as numbering led to the very same confusion about whether time is a number “as numbering the motion or as being numbered by it” which, in turn, led to the very same result that time was said to be numbered *by* motion – just as Ibn ʿAdī explained it a thousand years later. Yet, Ibn ʿAdī went one step further than Boethus, because in his *Maqāla fī l-mawǧūdāt*, he made time a *duration* which is numbered by motion, whereas Boethus did not mention any duration. Nonetheless, Ibn ʿAdī was in good company, notably Abū Yaʿqūb ibn Isḥāq al-Kindī (d. ~ 256/870), the Iḫwān al-Ṣafāʾ (fl. ~ 370/980), and Abū ʿAlī Aḥmad Miskawayh (d. 421/1030), for they all agreed that time is a duration numbered by motion (*mudda taʿudduhā l-ḥaraka*), thus repeating verbatim the formulation that can be found in the Arabic translation of Alexander’s treatise on time.[97] The description of time as a duration measured or numbered by motion is even more significantly Platonic, as it appears in Ibn Abī Saʿīd’s letter as an explicit description of Plato’s account of time. It is Plato who is reported to have claimed that “time is substance – by which he means a ‘duration’ (*mudda*) which is merely surveyed and measured by motion.” This at least, Ibn Abī Saʿīd adds, is what Alexander has reported about Plato’s position in his treatise against Galen, in which he also said that Plato’s position is more or less the same as that of Galen, viz., that time is a self-subsisting substance which exists independently of any motion.[98]

Against this background, and despite the fact that Boethus certainly was one – maybe the first but certainly not the only – precursor, it seems evident that it was Alexander’s treatise which was primarily responsible for expanding a somewhat un-Aristotelian, if not already Platonic, current into a Peripatetic mainstream.[99] It is reas-

---

97 cf. al-Kindī, *Kitāb fī l-falsafa al-ūlā*, vol. 2, 31.23f.; al-Kindī, *Risāla fī ḥudūd al-ašyāʾ wa-rusūmihā*, §18, 167.6 (= §17 in al-Kindī, *Risāla fī l-asmāʾ al-mufrada*); Iḫwān al-Ṣafāʾ, *Rasāʾil Iḫwān al-Ṣafāʾ* XV.13, 43.6f.; al-Tawḥīdī, *al-Muqābasāt*, §91, 313.10; al-Tawḥīdī and Miskawayh, *al-Hawāmil wa-l-šawāmil*, 31.5; Nāṣer-e Ḫosrow, *Ketāb-e Ǧāmʿ al-ḥikmatayn* 5, 90.18–91.1; cf. also again Kraemer, *Philosophy in the Renaissance of Islam*, 170; additionally for al-Kindī, q.v. above fn. 60, 447.

98 Ibn ʿAdī, *Kitāb Aǧwiba Bišr al-Yahūdī ʿan masāʾilihī*, 318.10–319.1.

99 A further consequence of this reading is that it could cast new light on Abū Bakr al-Rāzī’s account of absolute and relative time. It is usually said that Abū Bakr al-Rāzī combines a Neoplatonic understanding with an Aristotelian understanding of time by speaking of a (Neoplatonic) absolute time, which is an eternal duration, and an (Aristotelian) relative time, which is a segment of that eternity measured by a corresponding motion. This supposedly Aristotelian relative time, however, clearly is again “something measured by motion” (*mā qaddarathu l-ḥāraka*) and not something which *measures* motion, as an Aristotelian account would require it (Abū Bakr al-Rāzī, *al-Qawl fī l-qudamāʾ al-ḫamsa*, 198.12f., 18f.). So, what Abū Bakr al-Rāzī really provides is a thoroughly Neoplatonic account of time that involves an eternal duration which is in itself unmeasured but which can be measured by motion and a finite segment of that duration which has been singled out and measured by a particular motion – the former came to be known as “absolute time” and the latter as “relative time.” It is, however, worth mentioning here that Abū Bakr al-Rāzī may himself also have been unaware that his account of “relative” time is actually rather un-Aristotelian, i.e., just as unaware as Alexander, al-Kindī, the Iḫwān al-Ṣafāʾ, Ibn ʿAdī, Miskawayh, and all the others were regarding their own accounts; cf. Abū Bakr al-Rāzī’s reference to Aristotle in *al-Munāẓarāt bayna Abī Ḥātim al-Rāzī wa-Abī Bakr al-Rāzī*, 304.4f.

onable to believe that this treatise, due to Alexander's reputation as a formidable Peripatetic and exceptional expositor of Aristotle's doctrines, enjoyed supreme authority, especially once translated into Arabic. It seems that as long as a definition of time did not include the all too clearly Platonic catch-phrase *ǧawhar qāʾim bi-nafsihī wa-mustaqill bi-ḏātihī* ("self-subsisting and essentially independent substance"), a Peripatetic would consider himself as being on firm ground and entirely in line with *Physics* IV.10–14, even though, on closer inspection, his account should more adequately be characterised as either confused or (Neo-)Platonic.

A case in point, in this regard, is al-Kindī. In his *Kitāb fī l-falsafa al-ūlā*, he intends to show that time is necessarily finite. It suits his argumentation, then, that time is a quantity (*kammiyya*), because his previous argument has just established that all quantities are necessarily finite, so time is, too.[100] A few lines later, he elaborates a bit more on time and its finitude, explaining that time is the duration of the body of the whole (*zamān ǧirm al-kull aʿnī muddatahū*), and provides the definition of time, stating that "time is only the number of motion (*ʿadad al-ḥaraka*), i.e., it is a duration which motion numbers" (*mudda taʿudduhā l-ḥaraka*), so that there is no time without motion.[101] Certainly, al-Kindī has his own agenda here and is arguing for the creation of the world. His assertions regarding the nature of time, nonetheless, reveal both the existence of a genuine confusion within the early Arabic reception of Greek philosophy *and* that people were unconscious of that confusion, and indiscriminately combined Aristotelian and Platonic material.

In the Arabic tradition, Abū Sulaymān al-Siǧistānī (d. ~ 374/985) was one of the few – maybe the first – who after Plotinus detected this confusion and criticised its adherents. Once again, we find his testimony preserved in *al-Muqābasāt* of ʿAlī Abū Ḥayyān al-Tawḥīdī (d. 414/1023):

> أملى علينا أبو سليمان فقال: ... والزمان هو عدد حركة الفلك المشرقي بالتقديم والتأخير. قال: ومن الناس مَن قال إنّه مدّة تعدّها الحركة. وهذا الحدّ توهّم أن الحركات كالكيال للمعنى المفهوم من اسم الدهر وليس هذا معنى الزمان على الحقيقة وجوده إنّما هو في عدد الحركة معدودة ليس هو الدهر وإنّما هو الحركة.
>
> Abū Sulaymān dictated to us and said: ... Time is the number of the motion of the diurnal sphere by means of the priority and posteriority. He said: Among people are some who say that it is a duration which motion numbers (*mudda taʿudduhā l-ḥaraka*). This definition assumes that the motions are like a measurer for the meaning which is understood by the term eternity (*li-l-maʿnā l-mafhūm min ism al-dahr*), but this is not the meaning of time in reality whose existence is only in the number of motion, [and] what is numbered is not eternity but only motion. (al-Tawḥīdī, *al-Muqābasāt*, §73, 278.8, 16–19)

The core of al-Siǧistānī's criticism, as reported by his closest companion al-Tawḥīdī, is precisely that if we take time to be a duration measured by motion, we align time with

100 al-Kindī, *Kitāb fī l-falsafa al-ūlā*, vol. 2, 31.10.
101 al-Kindī, *Kitāb fī l-falsafa al-ūlā*, vol. 2, 31.22–25.

eternity (*dahr*) and adopt a Platonic, Plotinian, or Neoplatonic conception on which an eternal time is mapped out by the heavenly motions. This, however, is not what time means (*laysa hāḏā maʿnā l-zamān*), al-Siǧistānī observes. Time is not something that is numbered by motion but something by which motion is numbered. What is, moreover, interesting is that al-Tawḥīdī is the same person who had requested from Miskawayh an explanation of what time and place are, and who received from him the very answer which al-Siǧistānī criticises.[102]

Returning to Avicenna, it is evident that Avicenna's understanding of time as a magnitude, and his entire discussion of time as such, must be understood against this background, i.e., in light of the common reformulation of Aristotle's definition of time as a duration which is measured by motion, as it was advanced by influential and authoritative Peripatetics such as Alexander and Ibn ʿAdī. Avicenna's strong emphasis on magnitude in *al-Samāʿ al-ṭabīʿī* II.11 also explains why his account, in comparison to Aristotle's, is conspicuously sparing with references to measurement and numbering. The reason for the apparently subordinate significance of the numbering aspect of time is the derivative status of that aspect. Motion surely does have a number, but only because it has a magnitude, i.e., "insofar as the prior and posterior belong to it with respect to distance." Thus, time indeed is the number of motion, but only insofar as motion is "differentiated into what is prior and posterior ... with respect to the distance."[103] Time numbers motion, because, being the magnitude of a motion traversing a distance, it indicates its size and duration. Time, however, is numbered by motion and through motion's own essential differentiation into what is prior and what is posterior. The aspect of numbering, then, is a result of the existence of magnitude together with the numerical application of the prior and posterior states of the motion on its magnitude and is, as such, *derivative* of the notion of magnitude. Time, then, is a magnitude – and the notion of magnitude has a certain Neoplatonic, or at least a distinctly un-Aristotelian, shade to it.

This is also what Avicenna tells us in one of the rare passages in which he, indeed, accommodates the idea of time as a number and measure. This passage is found in *al-Samāʿ al-ṭabīʿī* II.12, i.e., in his chapter on the now. There, he is concerned with an aspect similar to that in the above translated passages from Aristotle and Philoponus in which we were told how we apprehend time by marking off prior and posterior states between different nows.[104] So, Avicenna, indeed, mentions the idea of time as a number and measure, but he does so by emphasising the reciprocal nature of the numbering

102 cf. al-Tawḥīdī and Miskawayh, *al-Hawāmil wa-l-šawāmil*, 31.5, 16–18; cf. also Kraemer, *Philosophy in the Renaissance of Islam*, 170; cf. further *al-Muqābasāt*, §91, 313.10, which contains a list of philosophical terms and their definition apparently compiled by al-Tawḥīdī from various sources where time is defined in the same manner as "a duration which motion numbers and whose parts are fixed" (*mudda taʿudduhā l-ḥaraka ṯābita al-aǧzāʾ*).

103 *al-Samāʿ al-ṭabīʿī* II.11, §3, 157.5f.; cf. *al-Ḥikma al-mašriqiyya* III.11, 33.5.

104 cf. *Phys.* IV.11, 219a22–30; Philoponus, *In Phys.*, 721.15–19; q.v. above, 448ff.

process in a manner similar to Boethus, Alexander, and especially Ibn ʿAdī. In this passage, Avicenna writes the following:

فالحركة تعدّ الزمان على أنّها تُوجِد عدد الزمان وهو المتقدّم والمتأخّر والزمان يعدّ الحركة بأنّه عدد لها نفسها.

> Thus, motion numbers time in that it makes time's number exist, and this is the prior and posterior, whereas time numbers motion in that it is the number that belongs to it [sc. motion] itself. (*al-Samāʿ al-ṭabīʿī* II.12, §7, 165.4f., tr. by McGinnis, modified)[105]

Here, time is presented as the number belonging to motion *itself*. This apparently means that motion, insofar as it occurs between a moment of starting and a moment of ending, has a magnitude, and this magnitude is nothing other than time indicating the size of the motion which, of course, can be numbered. The magnitude, then, is numbered by the motion, because motion provides the units for measuring time when it is differentiated by the prior and posterior. As we have seen above, Avicenna describes in his *al-Ilāhiyyāt*, and similarly in his *al-Maqūlāt*, a magnitude as that which is measurable, which means that it is numerable, which, in turn, means that it has something that is one, i.e., such as to be used as a unit, by which the whole can be numbered.[106] So, Avicenna, too, argues that motion numbers time insofar as it is responsible for the ordered series of prior and posterior states within the motion which occur over a traversed distance and which serve as units for counting and numbering time, thus providing time with its number. In addition, as we shall see later, the ultimate reference, for Avicenna, is the motion of the outermost heavenly sphere, which completes one revolution every twenty-four hours.[107] From its motion, we derive the notions of days, hours, minutes, as well as months and years by means of the mutual correspondence between motion, distance, and time.

The correspondences between distance, motion, and time as well as between earlier and later spatial positions, prior and posterior kinetic states, and temporal moments of before and after, in turn, go back to the idea that distance, motion, and time conform to each other so that time's being the magnitude of motion "parallels" (*bi-izāʾ*) the magnitude of distance which is traversed by the motion.[108] Again, we have to conclude that the core of Avicenna's concept of time is the notion of a magnitude – and not so much that of a measure or number, as it was in Aristotle's *Physics*. Avicenna's account so far displayed certain undeniably strong similarities, in particular, to the account provided in Ibn ʿAdī's *Maqāla fī l-mawǧūdāt* and to the position adopted in Ibn ʿAdī's correspondence with Ibn Abī Saʿīd.[109] Just as Ibn ʿAdī's theory is not free

---

105 cf. *al-Ḥikma al-mašriqiyya* III.11, 37.23–38.1; cf. also *al-Samāʿ al-ṭabīʿī* II.12, §8, 165.8–14; *al-Ḥikma al-mašriqiyya* III.11, 38.5–11; cf. further *Phys.* IV.11, 220b14–26; IV.14, 223b15f.

106 cf. esp. *al-Ilāhiyyāt* III.1, §10, 96.2–4; q.v. above, 446.

107 q.v. below, esp. 492ff.

108 *al-Samāʿ al-ṭabīʿī* II.11, §3, 157.5; cf. *al-Ḥikma al-mašriqiyya* III.11, 33.4f.

109 Whether, and if so, to what extent, Avicenna was influenced by Ibn ʿAdī in his conception of time, is difficult to assess as long as we lack a textual basis providing a more detailed elaboration on

from unintentional Neoplatonic elements, Avicenna's doctrine cannot be said to be entirely devoid of them, either.[110]

Above we have seen that Avicenna defined time as the magnitude of motion when motion is differentiated into the prior and posterior. My analysis so far has focused on the aspect that time is a magnitude, highlighting the Neoplatonic implications and connotations of that characterisation. I shall now examine more closely how he conceives of "the prior and posterior." This will reveal the great complexity of Avicenna's account as a whole and lead us to an understanding of what time is in its essence.

6.2 The Before and After

Above Avicenna announced that he was careful not to provide a definition of time that is circular (*wa-illā li-kāna l-bayān taḥdīdan bi-l-dawr*).[111] With his remark, he reacts to a certain criticism of Aristotle's definition that is not only common among contemporary interpreters. The first known charge of circularity against Aristotle's definition of time was levelled by Galen, and is reported by both Themistius (d. ~ 385) and Simplicius:

> Γαληνῷ δὲ οὐ προσεκτέον οἰομένῳ τὸν χρόνον ἀφορίζεσθαι δι' αὐτοῦ· πολλὰ γὰρ ἐξαριθμησάμενος σημαινόμενα τοῦ προτέρου τε καὶ ὑστέρου τὰ μὲν ἄλλα οὐκ ἐφαρμόζειν φησὶ τῷ ὁρισμῷ, τὸ κατὰ χρόνον δὲ μόνον, ὥστε εἶναι τὸν χρόνον ἀριθμὸν τῆς κινήσεως κατὰ χρόνον.
>
> We must not align ourselves with Galen in his belief that time is defined through itself (ἀφορίζεσθαι δι' αὐτοῦ), for after fully listing numerous significations of "prior" and "posterior," he says that none coincide with the definition [of time] except the one in respect of time, so that time is the number of motion in respect of time (εἶναι τὸν χρόνον ἀριθμὸν τῆς κινήσεως κατὰ χρόνον). (Themistius, *In Phys.*, 149.4–7, tr. by Todd, modified)[112]

Galen's quarrel with Aristotle's definition of time is that he does not see how τὸ πρότερον καὶ ὕστερον, being a central element in that definition, could be understood without already entailing a hidden or apparent reference to time. If we cannot help understanding τὸ πρότερον καὶ ὕστερον in temporal terms, then time, since it is the number of motion κατὰ τὸ πρότερον καὶ ὕστερον, would have been defined by means of a reference to temporal notions and, thus, through itself (δι' αὐτοῦ). Despite Themistius' and Simplicius' attempts to defend Aristotle's definition against such criticism, the core of Galen's position was widely accepted by contemporary interpreters of the twentieth

---

time from the hands of Ibn ʿAdī. What clearly emerged in this chapter, however, is that Avicenna was certainly influenced by the same *tradition* of understanding time as Ibn ʿAdī had been.

110 q.v. below, 509ff.

111 *al-Samāʿ al-ṭabīʿī* II.11, §3, 157.6f.; q.v. above, 442.

112 cf. Simplicius, *In Phys.*, 718.13–18; cf. also Sorabji, *The Philosophy of the Commentators*, vol. 2, ch. 11a.

century.[113] More recent expositors of Aristotle's temporal theory, however, turned away from Galen and provided various strategies to absolve Aristotle from this accusation.[114] Alluding to this charge of circularity, Avicenna writes:

والذي ظنّ بعض المنطقيين أنّه وقع في هذا البيان دور إذ لم يفهم هذا فقد ظنّ غلطاً.

What some of the logicians (*ba'ḍ al-manṭiqiyyīn*) believed is that a circle occurs in this proof, [but] since they did not understand this [definition] (*lam yafhum hāḏā*), they believed wrongly. (*al-Samā' al-ṭabī'ī* II.11, §3, 157.7, tr. by McGinnis, modified)

As before in the discussion of nature, Avicenna does not tell us whether we ought to understand *ba'ḍ* as "one" or "some."[115] In addition to that, we do not know who these logicians were – or who this logician was – who believed that Aristotle's explanation of time amounts to a *petitio principii.*

In his dissertation as well as in his translation of Avicenna's *al-Samā' al-ṭabī'ī*, McGinnis rules out quite a number of possible candidates from within the Arabic tradition, in particular Avicenna's Baġdādī predecessors such as Abū Bišr Mattā ibn Yūnus (d. 328/940), Abū Naṣr al-Fārābī (d. 339/950-51), Ibn 'Adī, Ibn al-Samḥ, and al-Siǧistānī, who has been given the epithet *al-mantiqī*.[116] There are two other potential candidates whom McGinnis did not consider: al-Ḥasan ibn Suwār ibn al-Ḫammār (d. after 407/1017), a student of Ibn 'Adī, and his own student Abū l-Faraǧ 'Abd Allāh ibn al-Ṭayyib (d. 435/1043). Given Avicenna's general critical attitude against these contemporaries together with the fact that Ibn al-Ṭayyib commented at least the later part of the *Physics*, he appears to qualify for having been a potential target of Avicenna's straightforward and brief remark here.[117] Yet, there seems to be no way to confirm this suggestion unless further textual evidence comes to light.[118]

This leaves us with another famous logician as the most likely – but not necessarily exclusive – referent of Avicenna's criticism: Galen. One might think that he does not qualify to be called *ba'ḍ al-manṭiqiyyīn* as it would, perhaps, be an odd choice on

113 Most well-known are the points of criticism voiced in Annas, "Aristotle, Number and Time," fn. 11, 101; Corish, "Aristotle's Attempted Derivation of Temporal Order from That of Movement and Space"; Owen, "Aristotle on Time," 24f.; Sorabji, *Time, Creation and the Continuum*, 86; cf. also Seeck, "Zeit als Zahl bei Aristoteles."

114 cf. Roark, "Aristotle's Definition of Time Is not Circular"; *Aristotle on Time*, chs. 4–5; Coope, *Time for Aristotle*, ch. 4; Bowin, "Aristotle on the Order and Direction of Time."

115 q.v. above, 256ff.

116 cf. McGinnis, *Time and Time Again*, fn. 21, 227f.; fn. 6, 232, to his translation.

117 For Avicenna's critical attitude towards Ibn al-Ṭayyib, cf. Ferrari's remarks in Ibn al-Ṭayyib, *Tafsīr Kitāb al-Maqūlāt*, 23–25; Gutas, *Avicenna and the Aristotelian Tradition*, 59–67, esp. 61–65. For Ibn al-Ṭayyib's comments on the *Physics*, q.v. above, 17ff.

118 In his *Tafsīr Kitāb al-Maqūlāt*, Ibn al-Ṭayyib briefly notes that "time is associated with the divine things (*al-umūr al-ilāhiyya*) and this is so, because it is the enumeration of their motions" (*iḥṣā' li-ḥarakātihā*; 14, 199.24f.). It is fair to assume that the "divine things" refer to the heavenly bodies. We may tentatively assume, perhaps, that Ibn al-Ṭayyib accepted Aristotle's definition more or less.

Avicenna's behalf to pick, of all the possible descriptions available for referring to Galen, that of him being a logician – and that while discussing time, i.e., a subject of natural philosophy. Yet, one should likewise not forget that Galen levelled his critique, which by the way concerns the formal validity of the proposed definition of time, in an extensive work known as *On Demonstration*. This work, though no longer extant as far as we know, had been translated, at least partially, into Arabic and was available to Christian and Muslim scholars in Baġdād.[119] If Avicenna knew the work, he would probably have been well aware of the criticism to which he is alluding here in *al-Samāʿ al-ṭabīʿī* II.11. Since the criticism is part of a work which predominantly, even if not exclusively, was devoted to logical matters, there is no reason why Avicenna should not refer to its proponent as *baʿḍ al-manṭiqiyyīn*. Since we know for a fact that Galen was the prime expositor of this line of criticism against the Aristotelian definition of time and since he expressed his views in a logical work known in Arabic with the title *Fī l-burhān* and since, finally, there is no reason to believe that Avicenna was ignorant of that work, it appears to be almost certain that it was Galen whom Avicenna criticised for not having understood the Aristotelian definition sufficiently.

In any case, Avicenna considers the definition of time he provided to be in essence identical to that of Aristotle, for otherwise it would not potentially be vulnerable to the same line of criticism. Thus, for Avicenna, the analysis of motion, the discussion of the possibility (*imkān*) for motion, and the identification of time with a magnitude serves the single purpose of establishing and confirming Aristotle's definition:

فالزمان عدد الحركة إذا انفصلت إلى متقدّم ومتأخّر لا بالزمان بل في المسافة.

Thus, time is the number of motion when it is differentiated into what is prior and what is posterior (*ilā mutaqaddim wa-mutaʾaḫḫir*), not by time but with respect to the distance (*lā bi-l-zamān bal fī l-masāfa*). (*al-Samāʿ al-ṭabīʿī* II.11, §3, 157.6, tr. by McGinnis, modified)[120]

Avicenna's addition that "what is prior and what is posterior" (*mutaqaddim wa-mutaʾaḫḫir*) should not be taken as referring to time but to distance is the reason why his – and Aristotle's – definition effectively evades the charge of circularity. In other words, he advises us to conceive of the prior and the posterior not as temporal notions. The logician who accused Aristotle of circular reasoning did not understand the subtleties of that definition of time and, thus, was wrong in accusing Aristotle.[121] A few words later, though, we read – in the translation of Shayegan – the following remark:

وهذا الزمان هو أيضاً لذاته مقدار لما هو في ذاته ذو تقدّم وتأخّر لا يُوجَد المتقدّم منه مع المتأخّر كما قد يُوجَد في سائر أنحاء التقدّم والتأخّر.

119 q.v. above, 21f.

120 cf. *al-Naǧāt* II.2.9, 231.4f. ≈ *al-Ḥikma al-ʿArūḍiyya* II.2.7, 132.20f.; *ʿUyūn al-ḥikma* II.8, 27.10f.; *al-Hidāya* II.1, 158.1–3; *al-Ḥikma al-mašriqiyya* III.11, 33.5f.; *al-Išārāt wa-l-tanbīhāt* II.5.5, 150.17–151.1.

121 q.v. also below, 508f.

> This time is also a measure in its own right for (*lammā*)[122] it is that which *qua* itself possesses priority and posteriority (*taqaddum wa-taʾaḫḫur*), and the prior and the posterior do not co-exist in time as they do in other modes of priority and posteriority. (*al-Samāʿ al-ṭabīʿī* II.11, §4, 157.7–9, tr. by Shayegan)

On Shayegan's translation, Avicenna claims that time is that which *qua* itself possesses priority and posteriority. In this crucial point, her translation agrees with the one published by McGinnis, whose translation of the same sentence reads as follows:

> Moreover, this time is that which is essentially a magnitude owing to what (*li-mā*) it is in itself, possessing [the states] of being earlier and later (*taqaddum wa-taʾaḫḫur*), the later part of which does not exist together with what is earlier, as might be found in other types of [things that might] be earlier and later. (*al-Samāʿ al-ṭabīʿī* II.11, §4, 157.7–9, tr. by McGinnis)

Among the minor differences between these two translations are McGinnis' decision to render *miqdār* as "magnitude" and *taqaddum wa-taʾaḫḫur* along the lines of "earlier" and "later," whereas Shayegan opted for "measure" as well as "prior" and "posterior."[123] A more severe divergence between McGinnis' and Shayegan's translations is that McGinnis interpreted the particle between *miqdār* and *huwa* as *li-mā* ("owing to what"), whereas Shayegan read it as *lammā* ("for").

These differences notwithstanding, on both translations time is said to possess the prior and posterior "*qua* itself" or "essentially." However, if that were right, we should wonder how Avicenna would ever be able to escape the charge of circularity as he just has declared. If time is the number of motion when differentiated into the prior and posterior and if time is what essentially possesses the prior and posterior – i.e., if "prior" and "posterior" are essentially temporal terms – then Galen's objection cannot be escaped, as the definition is hopelessly circular. How could Avicenna have advised us not to take the prior and the posterior as temporal notions if they are precisely temporal notions?

This issue is even more apparent in the commentary provided in McGinnis' dissertation, in which we read several remarks such as the following:

> the distinction between "prior" and "posterior" are accounted for by appealing to distinctions within spatial magnitude. Hence, Ibn Sīnā tells us, the account of time is not circular ... Time is something that must be essentially prior and posterior in the strongest possible sense, i.e., its priority and posteriority cannot be found together as with spatial magnitude ... this priority and posteriority are not essential to a given spatial magnitude ... time essentially possesses priority and posteriority; for a before time cannot be together with an after time ... time is essentially before

---

122 Since my now following discussion concerns in part whether one should read here *lammā* or *li-mā*, and since it will be shown that Shayegan's decision to read the former was wrong, I leave the *mīm* here without a *šadda*.

123 I have already mentioned my reasons for translating *miqdār* as "magnitude" and shall continue to translate *mutaqaddim* and *mutaʾaḫḫir* as "prior" and "posterior."

> and after ... time must possess priority and posteriority essentially, *while everything else possesses them on account of time* ... time must be before and after essentially.[124]

What we are told, here, is the following: the prior and posterior in the definition of time refers to the distance covered by a motion. This is said to be the reason that Avicenna's definition of time is not circular. Yet, the distance does not essentially have priority and posteriority, whereas time essentially possesses priority and posteriority. Whatever does not essentially have the prior and posterior – distance, for example, and presumably also motion – depends on something which essentially has the prior and posterior, such as time, in order to become prior and posterior. So, the priority and posteriority in distance is due to time, when something moves over a given distance in a certain amount of time, being "here" before being "there." In the definition of time, Avicenna declared that the priority and posteriority refers to distance and not to time, but since distance derived its priority and posteriority from time, the definition eventually does rely on the priority and posteriority in time. Moreover, the expression "prior and posterior" is used interchangeably with "before and after," and so time can be said to be essentially prior and posterior or, if one prefers, before and after.[125]

In response to this rather unfortunate situation, a few things need to be clarified. In his discussion of time, Aristotle used the Greek expression τὸ πρότερον καὶ ὕστερον, which has been translated by interpreters as either "prior and posterior" or "before and after" or "earlier and later." Aristotle's expression was rather consistently rendered in Arabic as *al-mutaqaddim wa-l-muta'aḫḫir* and is so used by Arabic philosophers including Avicenna. Aristotle explained the meaning of prior and posterior in general terms in *Categories* 12. There, he listed five meanings of πρότερον, all of which turn up in a similar way in the final chapter of Avicenna's *al-Maqūlāt*, chapter VII.4, which corresponds largely to Aristotle's *Categories* 12–14.[126]

In *al-Maqūlāt* VII.4, we are told that there are several ways in which something could be *mutaqaddim* and *muta'aḫḫir*: there is, first, that which is prior by time (*al-mutaqaddim bi-l-zamān*); second, that which is prior by nature (*al-mutaqaddim bi-l-ṭabʿ*); third, that which is prior in order absolutely (*al-mutaqaddim fī l-martaba ʿalā l-iṭlāq*); fourth, that which is prior by eminence (*al-mutaqaddim bi-l-šaraf*); and fifth, that

---

124 McGinnis, *Time and Time Again*, 227–231, emphasis added.

125 That McGinnis does not distinguish between "prior and posterior" and "before and after" is particularly apparent in the following quotation: "Although Ibn Sīnā does not consider this question, one may complain that time possesses priority and posteriority because motion is essentially before and after. Thus it is motion that rightly should be called essentially before and after, while time is only so on account of the motion" (McGinnis, *Time and Time Again*, 229). It is also apparent in his later published translation, where he avoids the pair "prior and posterior" but employs "earlier and later" as well as "before and after" sometimes interchangeably; cf. especially his translation of *al-Samāʿ al-ṭabīʿī* II.12, §7, 165.2–5.

126 cf. also *Met.* Δ.11, 1018b9–1019a14.

which is prior by causality (*al-mutaqaddim bi-l-ʿilliyya*).[127] Thus, the expression "prior and posterior" is equivocal and may be taken to form a genus with five species. One of these species, then, is the priority with regard to order absolutely:

وأمّا الثالث فهو المتقدّم في المرتبة على الإطلاق وهو الشيء الذي تنسب إليه أشياء أخرى فيكون بعضها أقرب منه وبعضها أبعد.

The third is that which is prior in order absolutely (*ʿalā l-iṭlaq*) and this is something to which other things are related, and so some of them are closer to it and others are more remote. (*al-Maqūlāt* VII.4, 266.7f.)

By means of the characterisation "absolutely" (*ʿalā l-iṭlaq*) Avicenna wanted to make it clear that the priority of something that is prior in order is not due to any intrinsic feature or any further qualification that makes it prior as such or posterior as such to other things, as is the case in the other four kinds of priority. A king is prior by eminence, because he is the King. The reason for his priority over his servants lies in himself or in the fact that he simply is king. Likewise, the number one is prior to the number two, because the existence of twoness entails the prior existence of oneness.[128] There is no way to reverse the order between numbers one and two or between the king and his servants. However, a certain bus stop between my home and my office may be prior to another bus stop when I am on my way to work, but it surely is posterior when I am on my way back home. There is, then, no intrinsic existential or essential entailment involved in the priority in order absolutely. What is prior in order is so because of an external feature or perspective. All this is made clear by the following:

والمتقدّم بالمرتبة ليس يجب له بذاته أن يكون متقدّماً بل بحسب اعتبار النسبة المذكورة ولذلك قد ينقلب الأقدم فيصير أشد تخلّفاً.

It is not necessary for that which is prior by order to be prior by itself (*bi-ḏātihī*), [and so it is] that it is prior rather with regard to the consideration of the aforementioned relation and, because of that, what is earlier (*aqdam*) may be reversed so that it becomes more remote (*ašadd taḫallufan*). (*al-Maqūlāt* VII.4, 266.12f.)

Accordingly, what is prior in order is not essentially prior but only prior on account of the relation mentioned in the previous quotation. Although things which are prior and posterior in order form a certain sequence and are not entirely at random, the direction of that sequence can change, so that what used to be prior from one point of view becomes posterior from another. This becomes particularly clear with the following example. Everyone who engages in a direct journey from Munich to Berlin will have to pass by Nuremberg and Leipzig, i.e., one will have to pass by Nuremberg, *first*, and only, *then*, by Leipzig. In other words the structure of the distance is due to

---

127 *al-Maqūlāt* VII.4, 265.16–269.12; cf. *Dānešnāme-ye ʿAlāʾī* II.14., 50.13f.

128 *al-Maqūlāt* VII.4, 266.2–6.

the relation that obtains between the spatial positions. In our example, the structure follows the order Munich–Nuremberg–Leipzig–Berlin. This structure is inalienable and cannot change. What can change, however, is the direction of that sequence, as one can likewise travel the other way from Berlin by Leipzig and Nuremberg to Munich. So, distance provides some sort of ordering or relation of its parts, but it does not provide an essential ordering or direction. Instead, it is motion which ordains this direction, but the direction of motion is a different kind of prior and posterior extraneous to the prior and posterior in order, as I have already mentioned.[129]

With that in mind, we are not surprised to be told by Avicenna that the prior in place (*makān*) and position (*waḍʿ*), on which my example relies, indeed belongs to the kind of priority that is a priority "in order absolutely."[130] We may safely assume that the prior and posterior "within the distance" (*fī l-masāfa*), to which Avicenna refers in the definition of time as that according to which motion is differentiated and with reference to which time is the magnitude of motion, is nothing other than the prior and posterior in place, thus belonging to the species of what is prior in order absolutely. The motion of an object that traverses a given distance derives the order of its motion from the order of the spatial positions within the distance, but it traverses the distance in a direction which is specified through its own motion. This direction is not due to distance as such; it is due to the fact that the moving object has determined one spatial position as a starting point and the other position as an endpoint for its motion, thus traversing the prior and posterior within the distance in that specific direction.

A different kind of priority and posteriority discussed in *al-Maqūlāt* VII.4 is that with regard to time. Aristotle labeled the temporal sense as the "first and foremost" (πρῶτον μὲν καὶ κυριώτατα) sense of what is prior and posterior.[131] Avicenna refrains from any such qualification. For him, the temporal sense is just the first of the five senses enumerated in the chapter:

فالوجه الأوّل من التقدّم هو الذي يكون بالزمان فانّ الأكبر سناً أقدم من الأحدث.

> The first way of priority is that which is by time (*allaḏī yakūnu bi-l-zamān*), for he who is advanced in years is prior than the youngster. (*al-Maqūlāt* VII.4, 266.1)

If something is said to be prior or posterior without further qualification, it can be so in any of the five mentioned senses. It could be prior by nature, order, eminence, causality, or time. Its precise sense would have to be determined by the context or by an explicit qualification, like, for example, in *al-Ilāhiyyāt* III.10 where Avicenna's enumerates various kinds of relatives saying that the relative in the category of "when?" is the prior and the posterior (*fī l-mattā ka-l-mutaqaddim wa-l-mutaʾaḫḫir*) and, towards the end

129 q.v. above, 441f.; cf. also Bowin, "Aristotle on the Order and Direction of Time."
130 *al-Maqūlāt* VII.4, 266.13–267.2.
131 *Cat.* 12, 14a26f. In *Met.* Δ.11, 1019a1–14, Aristotle considers the prior and posterior κατὰ φύσιν καὶ οὐσίαν, and not that κατὰ χρόνον, as the most basic sense of prior and posterior.

of the chapter, explicitly addresses "the prior and posterior in time" (*al-mutaqaddim wa-l-mutaʾaḫḫir fī l-zamān*.[132] Accordingly, the prior and posterior by time is just one species of the genus "prior and posterior" among others.

Returning to Avicenna's discussion of time in *al-Samāʿ al-ṭabīʿī*, one cannot but recognise that he uses the expression *al-mutaqaddim wa-l-mutaʾaḫḫir* ("the prior and posterior") as well as *al-qabl wa-l-baʿd* ("the before and after"). He also uses the nouns *taqaddum* and *taʾaḫḫur* ("priority" and "posteriority") in the sense of the former, and derives the abstracta *qabliyya* and *baʿdiyya* ("beforeness" and "afterness") from the latter. What I am arguing, now, is that when Avicenna states that time is that which through itself has the before and after as well as that from which all other things derive their beforeness and afterness, then he uses *al-qabl wa-l-baʿd* as a shorthand for *al-mutaqaddim wa-l-mutaʾaḫḫir bi-l-zamān*.[133] In other words, *al-qabl wa-l-baʿd* are intrinsically temporal notions, signifying the prior and posterior with respect to time. By contrast, when he defines time as that which is a magnitude of motion when the latter is differentiated into what is prior and posterior not temporally but spatially (*lā bi-l-zamān bal fī l-masāfa*), then he clearly speaks of a priority and posteriority that is different from the before and after, i.e., he speaks of a priority and posteriority that is precisely not temporal and which is in no way derived from time. If it were temporal or derived from time, the definition of time would, indeed, be circular, because one of its central elements would be defined through time, and that despite Avicenna's explicit claim that he is able to avoid said charge of circularity.[134] Thus, in addition to the temporal pair "before and after," Avicenna uses the non-temporal pair "prior and posterior." Consequently, whenever Avicenna speaks of something being *before or after*, he describes the situation in temporal terms, but when he speaks of something being *prior or posterior* to some other thing, he does not. At least, we would hope that Avicenna maintains this distinction throughout his discussion of time – and, indeed, we see that he does so in *al-Samāʿ al-ṭabīʿī* just as well as in his other major works.

In *al-Naǧāt*, Avicenna does not make great use of either pair, but the discussion of time in his *ʿUyūn al-ḥikma* relies heavily on *qabl* and *baʿd*, in particular in the introductory statements about time. A little later, when Avicenna approaches time's definition, he states:

---

132 *al-Ilāhiyyāt* III.10, §4, 153.4; III.10, §22, 159.15–17.

133 Avicenna's claim that time is that which through itself has the before and after as well as that from which all other things derive their beforeness and afterness will be discussed below, 473ff.

134 Of course, it could be objected that the order of positions in a motion presupposes time and, more fundamentally, that motion as such cannot be understood without any reference to time and temporality. This, however, would severely misunderstand Avicenna's account of motion, because motion is as such intrinsically ordered by what is prior and posterior. To be prior and posterior is what it means to be in motion. The idea, there, precisely is that no reference to temporality is involved. Moreover, this supports my above contention that terms such as "starting" (*mubtadaʾ* and *aḫḏ*) and "ending" (*muntahā* and *tark*), which Avicenna uses at the beginning of his account of time, likewise, are kinetic terms and decidedly not temporal; q.v. fn. 23 above, 436.

وهذا الإمكان ومقداره غير ثابت بل متجدّد كما أنّ الابتداء بالحركة للحركة غير ثابت ولو كان ثابتاً لكان موجوداً للسريع والبطيء بلا اختلاف. فهذا اذن هو المقدار المتصّل على ترتيب القبليات والبعديات على نحو ما قلنا وهو متعلّق بالحركة وهو الزمان وهو مقدار الحركة في المتقدّم والمتأخّر الذين لا يثبت أحدهما مع الآخر لا مقدار المسافة ولا مقدار المتحرّك.

> This possibility and its magnitude[135] is not fixed but renewed,[136] just as the kinetic beginning of motion is unfixed. If it were fixed, then it would exist for the fast and the slow without difference. This, therefore, is the continuous magnitude along the order of the beforenesses and afternesses (*ʿalā tartīb al-qabliyyāt wa-l-baʿdiyyāt*), as we have said, and it is dependent upon motion (*mutaʿalliq bi-l-ḥaraka*) and it is time being the magnitude of motion with respect to what is prior and posterior (*al-mutaqaddim wa-l-mutaʾaḫḫir*) of which one does not remain together with the other; it is not the measure of the distance nor of the moved. (*ʿUyūn al-ḥikma* II.8, 27.6–11)

Among the things Avicenna tells us in this passage is that time is a magnitude that is ordered by beforeness and afterness, that it is dependent upon motion, and that it is the magnitude of motion in terms of what is prior and posterior. What is remarkable here is that Avicenna uses both expressions, the before and after as well as the prior and posterior, together only a few words apart from each other. He does not take them to be synonymous nor does he simply switch the terminology from one to the other, merely because this is the terminology traditionally used for an Aristotelian definition of time. Instead, he deliberately employs both, and when he mentions the prior and posterior, he does so, because he wants to refer to an aspect that is different from that expressed by the before and after. As has been noted, the before and after describes the order that applies to *time*: time as a continuous magnitude is essentially ordered by what is before and what is after, and that is what time essentially is. The prior and posterior, on the other hand, describe the order that applies to *motion*: motion is differentiated by what is prior and posterior, because that is what motion is.[137] So, we get time, the continuous magnitude which is ordered by what is before and what is after when motion is differentiated by what is prior and what is posterior. Of course, there is an intrinsic connection between the before and after, on the one hand, and the prior and posterior, on the other – and this is one of the reasons that Avicenna writes that time is dependent upon motion (*mutaʿalliq bi-l-ḥaraka*) – but there is no compelling reason that the before and after should be identical with the prior and posterior here

---

135 Reading *wa-miqdāruhū* with ʿĀṣī, al-Saqqā, and Ms. Istanbul Ahmet III 3268 for *miqdār* in Ülken, Badawī, and al-Ǧabr. Ülken's, Badawī's, and al-Ǧabr's reading results in a text which states that "this possibility is an unfixed magnitude" and, thus, claims that time is identical with the possibility. I have argued, however, that the possibility is not a magnitude but only *has*, pertains to, or *occurs in* a magnitude. Ülken, Badawī, and al-Ǧabr, then, are three further interpreters who misunderstood the relation between time and the possibility for motion.

136 Recognise that Avicenna here uses *ṯābit* as a synonym for what he calls *qārr* in *al-Samāʿ al-ṭabīʿī*; q.v. fn. 37 above, 440.

137 In addition to that, there are also earlier and later positions within the distance, because the distance, too, is ordered, even though it lacks an intrinsic direction, as we have seen above, 466f.

in this passage from the *'Uyūn al-ḥikma*. To the contrary, the fact that Avicenna uses both expressions, applying one to time and the other to motion, suggests nothing other than that they signify two strictly different aspects of reality.

Once the fundamental difference between the prior and posterior, on the one hand, and the before and after, on the other, has been recognised, many passages in *al-Samā' al-ṭabī'ī* II.11 become more meaningful and clear, and reveal an interesting, yet complex, theory of time. On this interpretation, time does not, and simply cannot, possess the "prior and posterior" essentially. The only passage anywhere in Avicenna's works that *seemingly* claims that the prior and posterior belong to time essentially is the one that has been quoted above in Shayegan's and in McGinnis' translation. In the discussions of time in his other works, as well as in the rest of *al-Samā' al-ṭabī'ī*, he does neither equate the concept of prior and posterior with that of before and after nor does he ever say that the prior and posterior belongs to time.[138] All he ever says is that the before and after belongs to time, and that time is a magnitude of motion when differentiated into what is prior and posterior, as we have just seen in the *'Uyūn al-ḥikma*. If we want to understand why Avicenna claims that the definition of time he proposes avoids the charge of circularity, we must understand what it means for him that motion is differentiated into what is prior and posterior (*al-mutaqaddim wa-l-muta'aḫḫir*) in the present context. For that reason, the sentence quoted above in the translations of Shayegan and McGinnis is crucial, as it precisely states the relation between the prior and posterior, on the one hand, and time, on the other. Since both translations invite the charge of circularity, rather than avoid it, I shall offer a different translation, which reads as follows:

وهذا الزمان هو أيضاً لذاته مقدار لما هو في ذاته ذو تقدّم وتأخّر لا يُوجَد المتأخّر منه مع المتقدّم كما قد يُوجَد في سائر أنحاء التقدّم والتأخّر.

> This time is also through itself (*li-ḏātihī*) a magnitude for that (*li-mā*) which in itself (*fī ḏātihī*) has a priority and posteriority (*taqaddum wa-ta'aḫḫur*) of which the posterior does not exist together with the prior as what may be found in other types (*fī sā'ir al-anḥā'*) of priority and posteriority. (*al-Samā' al-ṭabī'ī* II.11, §4, 157.7–9)[139]

On my reading, time does not in itself posses priority and posteriority but is the magnitude *for that which* in itself possesses priority and posteriority – and this, as Avicenna has already explained and as I have already noted, is motion as it occurs over a distance.

---

138 There is one further passage in Avicenna's *al-Samā' al-ṭabī'ī*, in which he describes the prior and posterior as "parts of time" (*aǧzā' al-zamān*; *al-Samā' al-ṭabī'ī* II.12, §7, 165.1f.); cf. *al-Ḥikma al-mašriqiyya* III.11, 37.19. This may sound problematic, at first, but is resolved by paying close attention to the context of the passage and to the fact that time, nonetheless, is the magnitude *of motion* with motion being that which is essentially characterised by the prior and posterior. In fact, nowhere in this passage does Avicenna say that the prior and posterior are temporal notions. If anything, this passage bears out that they are kinetic notions.

139 cf. *al-Hidāya* II.1, 157.3–158.1; *al-Ḥikma al-mašriqiyya* III.11, 33.7–9.

In fact, Avicenna told us that it is an inseparable feature of motion to be divisible into what is prior and what is posterior.[140] Thus, motion is that which has in itself a priority and posteriority, which it derives from a traversal over certain earlier and later positions in a distance. This priority and posteriority intrinsic to motion is such that what is prior cannot exist together with what is posterior, just as a moving thing cannot be both here and there but is either here or there. In distance, however, the situation is different, because the earlier and later spatial positions which correspond to the prior and posterior states of motion surely can exist together, just as "here" and "there" can. So, in motion they cannot, but "in other types (*fī sāʾir al-anḥāʾ*) of priority and posteriority," such as the priority and posteriority in number or distance, they can.[141]

In effect, what Avicenna tells us, here, is nothing new compared to what he has already told us before when he claimed that time is the magnitude of motion: time is that which through itself is a magnitude for motion, with motion being that which in itself has a priority and posteriority of which the posterior does not exist together with the prior. There is no word about time essentially possessing the prior and posterior – and this for good reason, "for otherwise the definition would be circular," as he wrote only one line above.[142]

Thus, what Shayegan and McGinnis did not fully convey in their translations is the correct meaning of *li-mā*. Shayegan misread it as *lammā*, thus treating the following clause as a justification for the claim that time is a magnitude at all. By contrast, McGinnis took *li-mā huwa fī ḏātihī* to mean that time is a magnitude "owing to what it is in itself" and that it, as such, possesses priority and posteriority.[143] Both readings are grammatically justifiable. The only reading that can avoid the charge of circularity and make Avicenna's account sensible, however, is to translate *miqdār li-mā huwa fī ḏātihī ḏū* as "magnitude for that which in itself has" priority and posteriority. Accordingly, Avicenna states that the definition of time is valid, because the prior and posterior by

140 Avicenna explicitly states: "You know that it follows concomitantly upon motion that it is divisible into what is prior and posterior, and the prior only exists in it as that which belongs to it from the prior within the distance and the posterior as that which belongs to it from the posterior within the distance" (*al-Samāʿ al-ṭabīʿī* II.11, §3, 156.18–157.1); q.v. above, 441ff.; q.v. also above, 360ff.

141 Avicenna employs the numerical priority of the number one over the number two in his remarks on time in *al-Išārāt wa-l-tanbīhāt* II.5.4, 150.5–13. In *al-Maqūlāt* VII.4, he calls this kind of priority "the prior by nature" (*al-mutaqaddim bi-l-ṭabʿ*). As Mayer remarked in his article about the account of time in *al-Išārāt wa-l-tanbīhāt*, "Avicenna here is simply speaking about coexistent numerable things and not speaking of numbers as such" ("Avicenna against Time Beginning," 126).

142 *al-Samāʿ al-ṭabīʿī* II.11, §3, 157.6f.

143 It ought to be noted that in the translation published by McGinnis, he follows the misleading punctuation established by Āl Yāsīn's edition of the text. In the translation provided in his unpublished dissertation ten years earlier, he followed Zāyid's edition and translates the sentence differently and more correctly: "Moreover, this time is essentially a magnitude of what in its essence possesses priority and posteriority, of which the prior part does not exist with the posterior, as might be found in the rest of the types of priority and posteriority" (McGinnis, *Time and Time Again*, 204).

which motion is differentiated is not a temporal priority and posteriority nor is it in any way derived from a temporal priority or posteriority. It is, rather, a priority and posteriority in distance (*lā bi-l-zamān bal fī l-masāfa*), when the distance is traversed by a moving thing. This is, perhaps most explicitly stated in *al-Samāʿ al-ṭabīʿī* II.13, where Avicenna writes that "the continuity of motion is only because of the continuity of distance, and because of distance's continuity, it becomes a cause for existence of priority and posteriority in motion" (*yaṣīru ʿilla li-wuǧūd taqaddum wa-taʾaḫḫur fī l-ḥaraka*).[144]

So far, Avicenna's examination of time in *al-Samāʿ al-ṭabīʿī* II.11 relied on the notions of "magnitude" and of "what is prior and posterior" (*al-mutaqaddim wa-l-mutaʾaḫḫir*). Now, however, his terminology changes and he begins to use the notions "before" (*qabl*) and "after" (*baʿd*), signalling that he no longer talks about the definition of time as a magnitude of the motion with its prior and posterior states which correspond to certain positions in a distance. Instead, he begins to examine what time is in its essence and through itself, for time is essentially the before and after, thus providing the notions of "before" and "after," which, as I have said, must be understood as temporal notions in contrast to the prior and posterior, which must not so be understood. Accordingly, Avicenna writes the following:

> وهذا هو لذاته يكون شيء منه قبل شيء وشيء منه بعد شيء، وتكون سائر الأشياء لأجله بعضها قبل وبعضها بعد وذلك لأنّ الأشياء التي يكون فيها قبل وبعد ... إنّما تكون كذلك لا لذواتها بل لوجودها مع قسم من أقسام هذا المقدار فما طابق منها جزءاً هو قبل قيل له إنّه قبل وما طابق جزءاً هو بعد قيل له إنّه بعد.
>
> Of this [sc. time], through itself (*li-ḏātihī*) something is before another and something is after another, whereas of everything else some are before and some are after on account of it (*li-aǧlihī*). That is because[145] the things in which there is a before and an after (*qabl wa-baʿd*) ... are not such because of themselves but only because of their existence together with one of the parts[146] of this magnitude. So, whatever of them conforms[147] to a part which is before is said to be "before"

---

144 *al-Samāʿ al-ṭabīʿī* II.13, §3, 169.3f.; cf. *al-Samāʿ al-ṭabīʿī* II.13, §4, 169.13f., *al-Ḥikma al-mašriqiyya* III.11, 40.8f.; q.v. also below, 504f. Avicenna's solution to the issue has strong similarities with the ways in which recent expositors of Aristotle try the save him from Galen's charge of circularity; cf., in particular, Roark's argument about "kinetic positions" (or: "kinetic cuts") and his interpretation of Aristotle's definition of motion in "Aristotle's Definition of Time Is not Circular," 306–312; *Aristotle on Time*, chs. 4–5; cf. also Coope, *Time for Aristotle*, ch. 4; Bowin, "Aristotle on the Order and Direction of Time." In his review to Roark's book *Aristotle on Time*, McGinnis likewise emphasised the strong similarity between Roark's interpretation of motion and time in Aristotle, and Avicenna's account of these philosophical concepts; cf. "Review of *Aristotle on Time: A Study of the* Physics by Tony Roark."

145 Reading *wa-ḏālika li-anna* with Mss. Leiden or. 4 and or. 84 as well as Zāyid for *li-anna* in McGinnis and Āl Yāsīn.

146 Reading *qism min aqsām* with Mss. Leiden or. 4 and or. 84 as well as McGinnis and Āl Yāsīn for *qismīn min aqsām* in Zāyid.

147 Reading *fa-mā ṭābaqa* with Mss. Leiden or. 4 and or. 84 as well as McGinnis and Āl Yāsīn for *fī-mā yuṭābiqu* in Zāyid.

> and whatever conforms[148] to a part which is after is said to be "after." (*al-Samāʿ al-ṭabīʿī* II.11, §4, 157.9–12, tr. by McGinnis, modified)[149]

In this passage, Avicenna explains what time is and how other things derive their temporality, i.e., their beforeness and afterness, from time. Time, he begins, is that of which some parts are before and some parts are after, and that this is so through time itself (*li-ḏātihī*). All other things, however, derive their beforeness and afterness from time, i.e., they are not before and after through themselves but only insofar as they correspond or conform (*ṭābaqa*) to what is before or after in the magnitude we call time. For example, we can say that the outbreak of the Peloponnesian War is "before" and Abū Muslim's raising the black banners, which is often taken to mark the beginning of the ʿAbbāsid Revolution, is "after," *only because* the moment of the former corresponds to a period of time which is before that period of time to which the moment of the latter corresponds.[150] Both the outbreak of the Peloponnesian War and Abū Muslim's raising the black banners are individually before or after the respective other, each through its own "vertical relation to" a part of time but not through a "horizontal relation between" themselves. Time, then, is what endows other things with a "before" or an "after," because it itself is that which provides these temporal aspects, regardless of whether these things may also posses the non-temporal "prior" and "posterior" due to a motion in which they are currently engaged.[151] Generally speaking, things are before and after insofar as they correspond to various periods which through time itself are ordered as before and after.[152]

Fig. 6.2: A vertical relation of things to time.

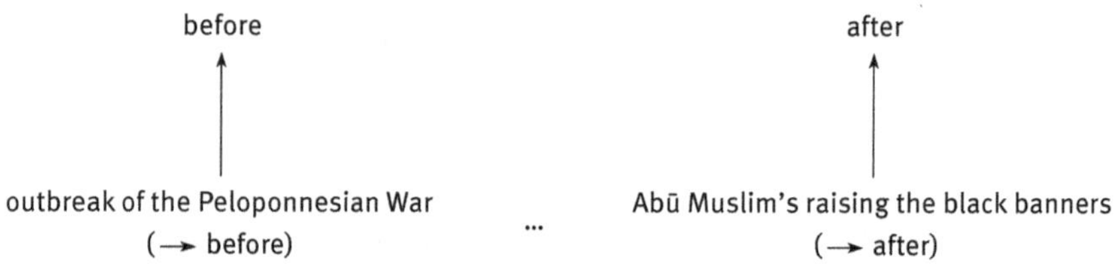

148 Reading *wa-mā ṭābaqa* with Mss. Leiden or. 4 and or. 84 as well as McGinnis and Āl Yāsīn for *wa-mā yuṭābiqu* in Zāyid.

149 cf. *al-Ḥikma al-mašriqiyya* III.11, 33.9–13.

150 cf. Watt, *The Formative Period of Islamic Thought*, 151f.; Nagel, "Das Kalifat der Abbasiden," 101.

151 For example, a tomato's state of being green is prior to that same tomato's state of being red through the tomato's being engaged in the motion of ripening. Still, the state of being green is also before and that of being red after individually through their correspondence to a before and an after part of time, respectively; q.v. the diagrams below, 482f.

152 cf. also Jeck, *Aristoteles contra Augustinum*, 111.

For Avicenna, the essence of time is defined as the magnitude of motion or, more precisely, as the magnitude of the circular motion of the outermost sphere, as we shall learn later.[153] There is, however, more to be said about time's essence than merely that time is the magnitude of motion, and this is that time is the essential bearer of the before and after, i.e., time is that on account of which other things are called "before" and "after." Elaborating on times' essence, Avicenna continues his investigation as follows:

وهذا الشيء ليس يكون قبل وبعد لأجل شيء آخر لأنّه لو كان كذلك لكان القبل منه إنّما صار قبلاً لوجوده في قبل شيء آخر فيكون ذلك الشيء أو شيء آخر ينتهي إليه التدريج آخِرَ الأمر هو لذاته ذو قبل وبعد.

> This thing [sc. time] is not before and after on account of some other thing, because if it were so, then its before (*al-qabl minhu*) would only become a before[154] through its existence in the before of some other thing, and so *that* thing – or something else at which the regress eventually ends – would have through itself a before and after. (*al-Samāʿ al-ṭabīʿī* II.11, §4, 157.13–15, tr. by McGinnis, modified)[155]

Avicenna's intention is to establish that there is necessarily something which is the essential bearer of before and after, that this is time, and that time as such cannot be before and after on account of something else. To that end, he devises a dialectical thought experiment. If time were before and after on account of something else, then this would mean that this other thing is essentially before and after, in which case this other thing would have to be time, whereas the former so-called "time" would only derivatively be before and after. If, however, this other thing were again only before and after on account of some further thing, then it would be this further thing which is essentially before and after, and would more appropriately be called time, and so on. Although this dialectical regress could go on and on, it must come to an end at some point, at which we reach something which really and essentially is before and after, for otherwise there would be no before and after, i.e., no temporal priority and posteriority, whatsoever in this world.

Although it is clear that Avicenna regards this regress, whether finite or infinite, as absurd, his primary aim is not to establish the absurdity of this line of reasoning as such. Instead, he intends to establish that it does not matter whether the first of these things is essentially before and after or the fifth or the five-hundredth. His claim is that at one point or another, there must be something that essentially provides the

---

153 q.v. below, 492ff. In fact, however, Avicenna has already made this explicit in *al-Samāʿ al-ṭabīʿī* I.11 when, right after determining that time is the magnitude of an non-integral disposition, he identified the non-integral disposition with motion and, more precisely "positional motion" (*al-ḥaraka al-waḍʿiyya*; §2, 156.16). On Avicenna's account of positional motion as the motion proper to the outermost sphere, q.v. above 340ff.

154 Reading *qablan* with Mss. Leiden or. 4 and or. 84 as well McGinnis and Āl Yāsīn for *qablahā* in Zāyid.

155 cf. *al-Ḥikma al-mašriqiyya* III.11, 33.14–16.

beforeness and afterness – and this is what ought to be called time. On this basis, Avicenna intends to forge a connection between this account of time as the essential bearer of before and after with the previously established definition of time as the magnitude of motion:

ومعلوم أنّ ذلك الشيء هو الذي يقع فيه إمكان التغييرات على النحو المذكور وقوعاً أوّلياً ويقع في غيره لأجله. فيكون ذلك الشيء هو المقدار المقدّر للإمكان المذكور تقديراً بذاته ويكون ما نحن فيه لا غيره. فنحن إنما كنّا جعلنا الزمان اسماً للمعنى الذي هو لذاته مقدار للإمكان المذكور ويقع فيه الإمكان المذكور وقوعاً أوّلياً. فبين من هذا أن هذا المقدار المذكور هو بعينه الشيء الذي هو لذاته يقبل إضافة قبل وبعد بل هو بنفسه منقسم إلى قبل وبعد.

It is known that that thing [sc. time] is that in which the possibility for making changes, in the aforementioned manner, primarily occurs and on account of which it occurs in something else. So, that thing is the magnitude measuring the aforementioned possibility essentially and it is that with which we are concerned, and with nothing else. So, we only have made "time" a name for the meaning which through itself is a magnitude for the aforementioned possibility and in which the possibility primarily occurs. Thus, it is clear from this that this aforementioned magnitude is the same thing as that which through itself receives the relation of before and after (*li-ḏātihī yaqbalu iḍāfat qabl wa-baʿd*) or, rather, which by itself[156] is divisible into before and after (*bi-nafsihī munqasim ilā qabl wa-baʿd*). (*al-Samāʿ al-ṭabīʿī* II.11, §§4–5, 157.15–158.1, tr. by McGinnis, modified)[157]

Continuing his thought experiment, Avicenna claims that whatever it is that is essentially before and after, be it the first, fifth, or five-hundredth instance, it is that about which we have been talking all along: it is that magnitude wherein the possibility for change and motion occurs. Since we call this magnitude time, and since, further, the essential bearer of the before and after is that magnitude, it follows that what is essentially before and after is nothing other than time. Therefore, time not only is a magnitude for motion; this magnitude is also that by virtue of which other things are before and after, because it itself, as a magnitude, has the before and after essentially, being through itself divisible into what is before and what is after.

Parts of this passage have already been quoted above when I discussed time as a magnitude.[158] Here I have presented it once more, because in this passage Avicenna's thoughts about what time is come together in the form of an interim conclusion. What I mean by "interim conclusion" is that Avicenna's argument, having provided us with a definition of time (the magnitude of motion) and an account of what time essentially is (that which is before and after through itself), has already started to shift towards another question, viz., the question about the existence of time. Avicenna has already warned us that one cannot discuss the essence of time and its existence apart from

156 Reading *bi-nafsihī* with Mss. Leiden or. 4 and or. 84 as well as Zāyid for *nafsuhū* in McGinnis and Āl Yāsīn.

157 cf. *ʿUyūn al-ḥikma* II.8, 26.8f.; *al-Hidāya* II.1, 157.3–158.1; *al-Ḥikma al-mašriqiyya* III.11, 33.17–21.

158 q.v. above, 443.

each other when he wrote that he will, first, investigate the essence of time (*māhiyyat al-zamān*), because the existence of time (*wuǧūduhū*) shall become clear to us "from there" (*min hunāka*).[159] In other words, a full understanding of time's essence will also provide the means for answering the question about time's existence. I shall, now, also shift my attention towards the existence of time. This will both conclude the account of time's essence and demonstrate time's existence.

6.3 Continuity and the Cause of Time

Some of the most pressing questions at the moment are the following: how does the before and after of time come about, and is the before and after really conceptually separate from the prior and posterior? If the before and after were not separate, one could question the existence of time as such, arguing that all that exists is the prior and posterior states of things due to their motion and that the before and after is just a synonymous way of talking about the prior and posterior. So, we need to answer the questions: does time exist? Why does it exist? What explanatory gap is time supposed to fill? These are the questions which Avicenna is about to answer in the second half of *al-Samāʿ al-ṭabīʿī* II.11.

Now, the long paragraph five of chapter eleven, in the numbering provided by McGinnis' translation, can be subdivided into five parts:

i) Some introductory remarks that belong to what I have just called an "interim conclusion."[160]
ii) A statement of what it means for a thing to be "before" (and implicitly also "after").[161]
iii) A statement of what it means for a thing to be "prior" (and implicitly also "posterior").[162]
iv) An argument rounding up what has been established in (ii) and (iii), that neither beforeness nor priority belong to a thing through itself.[163]
v) A proof for the existence of time as that which provides beforeness and afterness.[164]

After all this, Avicenna provides a brief conclusion, and proceeds to the sixth and final paragraph of the chapter, in which he establishes time's dependence upon motion, thus concluding the discussion.

---

159 *al-Samāʿ al-ṭabīʿī* II.10, §13, 154.12f.; q.v. above, 431f.
160 cf. *al-Samāʿ al-ṭabīʿī* II.11, §5, 157.17–158.1.
161 cf. *al-Samāʿ al-ṭabīʿī* II.11, §5, 158.1–5.
162 cf. *al-Samāʿ al-ṭabīʿī* II.11, §5, 158.5–7.
163 cf. *al-Samāʿ al-ṭabīʿī* II.11, §5, 158.7–9.
164 cf. *al-Samāʿ al-ṭabīʿī* II.11, §5, 158.9–159.1.

Beginning his argumentation, Avicenna emphasises that since time receives the relation of before and after through itself (*li-ḏātihī yaqbalu iḍāfat qabl wa-baʿd*) and is itself divisible into before and after (*bi-nafsihī munqasim ilā qabl wa-baʿd*), it cannot be before without relation (*lā bi-l-iḍāfa*).[165] What Avicenna seems to argue, here, is that time does not exist simply as such, always being in the same state, i.e., it cannot have a beforeness without also having some related afterness. Accordingly, time is precisely not some wholly invariable substance which exists independently of everything else or a container in which other things and motions can occur; it is not an indeterminate and unnumbered eternity which is revealed and numbered by motion.[166] Avicenna will later emphasise and clarify time's ontological dependence upon motion.[167] So, instead of time being intrinsically invariable and independent, Avicenna argues for the opposite: time is essentially structured by the before and after, and dependent upon motion. That is to say, despite being essentially structured by the temporal states of before and after, time requires for its existence that concrete objects are themselves in certain states now, and subsequently in other states. In other words, time's existence as something which is before and after through itself requires the priority and posteriority of the motion of a concrete object. It is only through motion, i.e., through a thing in different states, that time can exist as having the before and after through itself. Avicenna argues as follows:

ولست أعنى بهذا أنّ الزمان يكون قبل لا بالإضافة بل أعنى أنّ الزمان لذاته تلزمه هذه الإضافة وتلزم سائر الأشياء بسبب الزمان فإنّ الشيء إذا قيل له قبل، وكان ذلك الشيء غير الزمان فكان مثل الحركة والإنسان وغير ذلك، كان معناه أنّه موجود مع شيء هو بحال تلك الحال يلزمها إذا قيست إلى حال الآخر إن كان الشيء بها قبلٌ لذاته أيّ يكون هذا اللزوم له لذاته.

165 *al-Samāʿ al-ṭabīʿī* II.11, §5, 157.18–158.2.

166 cf. Avicenna's subsequent remark that "time is not something which subsists by itself" (*al-zamān laysa mimmā yaqūmu bi-ḏātihī*) just a little later in *al-Samāʿ al-ṭabīʿī* II.11, §6, 159.3, which seems to be directed against a Platonist account of time as, for example, in Galen; cf. *al-Samāʿ al-ṭabīʿī* II.11, §2, 156.11; *al-Ḥikma al-mašriqiyya* III.11, 32.17f., 34.5–7. It is here that Avicenna keeps the Platonism of his conception of time as a magnitude in check and remains a Peripatetic insofar as time, as we shall see, entirely comes-to-be through – and, thus, depends on – motion. It is this aspect which also distinguishes his account from the confused understanding of Ibn ʿAdī, for example, who, as we have seen, claimed allegiance to Aristotle while comparing time with the unlimited and unnumbered eternity of *dahr*. Admittedly, Ibn ʿAdī also said that "if there were no motion, there would not be time," as we have already seen (*Maqāla fī l-mawǧūdāt*, 273.5f.); q.v. above, 453. Yet, for him, the existence of motion is an *epistemological* condition, as he states that "there is no way for *grasping* time without grasping motion" (*Maqāla fī l-mawǧūdāt*, 273.6, emphasis added). So, one could well assume that even without motion, there would still be the eternal *dahr*, being the unlimited duration of eternity that is merely revealed and measured by motion – just as Plato and Plotinus, for example, believed, too; q.v. also al-Siǧistānī's criticism discussed above, 459f. On Avicenna's Platonism of time, q.v. below, 509ff. On the conception of *dahr* in Islamic thought, cf. also Tamer, *Zeit und Gott*, esp. ch. 3.

167 q.v. below, esp. 492ff.

> By this [i.e., by time's receiving the relation of before and after through itself], I do not mean that time could be before without relation (*lā bi-l-iḍāfa*).[168] Rather, I mean that this relation necessarily belongs (*talzamuhū*) to time through itself (*li-ḏātihī*) and it necessarily belongs to other things because of time, for the thing (*al-šay'*) when it is said to have a before – and that thing is not time but is, then, something like a motion or a human or something other than that – its meaning [i.e., the meaning of the thing's being said to have a before] is that it exists together with something (*šay'*) being in a state (*huwa bi-ḥāl*), where it necessarily belongs[169] to that state (*tilka l-ḥāl*), when it is correlated with another state (*qīsat ilā ḥāl al-āḫar*) – if the thing (*al-šay'*) is in it – a before through itself (*qabl li-ḏātihī*), i.e., this necessary belonging (*al-luzūm*) belongs to it [i.e., time] through itself. (*al-Samā' al-ṭabī'ī* II.11, §5, 158.1–5)

This is a very complex, if not to say obscure, sentence, which not only grammatically allows different readings but which also invites various misunderstandings. In the main, my translation follows the French translation which Jules Janssens provided in the footnotes to the edition of the twelfth-century Latin translation of Avicenna's *al-Samā' al-ṭabī'ī* achieved by Dominicus Gundisalvi (d. ~ 1190).[170] The reason this sentence is so difficult to understand seems to be that Avicenna combines and mixes – or even confounds – two different but interrelated aspects of his understanding of time: that time is that which is before and after through itself, and that it comes-to-be through motion. In short, as I said, time is precisely not invariable and independent.

Avicenna's argument, then, seems to be the following: compelled to explain what it means for time to be before and after through itself, he considers, first, what it means for a thing other than time, i.e., for a concrete motion or a concrete object such as a human being or just anything that can occur in time, to be said to have a before.[171] The meaning

168 Mayer disregarded the double negation of the sentence and translated: "I do not mean by this that time has a before by dint of a relation" ("Avicenna against Time Beginning," 128).

169 Reading *yalzamuhā* with Zāyid for *talzamuhā* in McGinnis and Āl Yāsīn.

170 cf. Avicenna, *Sufficientia: Liber primus naturalium*, vol. 2, fn. 2, 327: "le sens en est (*kāna ma'nāhu*) que c'est existant (*annahu mawjūd*) avec une chose (*ma'a shay'*) qui est dans un état (*huwa bi-ḥāl*) tel que, lorsque cet état (*tilka l-ḥāl*) est comparé à l'état de l'autre (*idhā qīsat ilā ḥāl al-ākhar*), il implique nécessairement (*yalzamuhā*), si la chose est à cause de lui [sc. cet état-là] (*in kāna l-shay' bihā*), un avant par soi-mê me (*qabl li-dhātihi*), c'est-à-dire que cette implication nécessaire lui appartient par soi-même (*ayy yakūnu hādhā l-luzūm lahu li-dhātihi*)." Gundisalvi himself understood the sentence differently, and the differences have been noted in the same footnote. In this context, cf. also Janssens, "The Latin Translation of the Physics," 524. Another syntactical construal is provided by Shayegan's translation who read *tilka l-ḥāl yalzamuhā … an* ("that state … implies that") instead of *tilka l-ḥāl yalzamuhā … in*. McGinnis, apart from minor differences, took the last *qabl* to be the predicate of the verb *kāna*, in which case, however, one would expect it to be in the accusative (*qablan*). Finally, it must be said that one cannot exclude the possibility that the sentence is corrupt in one way or another.

171 Janssens suggested, comparing the Arabic text with Gundisalvi's Latin translation, to read *sukūn* for *insān* ("The Latin Translation of the Physics," 524). I think this reading ought to be rejected. Avicenna is talking about things that are in time and which derive their beforeness and afterness from time. Thus, he refers to concrete things or phenomena, and not to the absence of such phenomena, as would be the case if we read *sukūn*. On the whole, I doubt that Avicenna would say that rest can be "in time" in the same sense as a man or a motion can be said to be "in time."

of this (*maʿnāhu*), i.e., the meaning of a concrete thing's being characterised by a before, is that this concrete thing exists together with something else (*maʿa šayʾ*). This other, grammatically indeterminate "something" (*šayʾ*), I believe, is to be distinguished from the concrete, grammatically determinate "the thing" (*al-šayʾ*), insofar as the latter signifies the concrete thing in time, while the former denotes time itself in which or with which (*maʿa*) the concrete thing exists. So, what it means for the concrete thing to have a before is to be together with something (viz., time), where this something (viz., time) is in a certain state (*huwa bi-ḥāl*). What is to be said about that state (*tilka l-ḥāl*) of that something (viz., time) is that to it belongs a before through this something itself (*qabl li-ḏātihī*), i.e., this state of time has or is a before through time itself.

Now, however, Avicenna introduces an important qualification – indeed, a qualification which he already introduced in the first lines of the passage when he wrote that "I do not mean that time could be before without relation" (*lā bi-l-iḍāfa*). It is this assertion which Avicenna intends to explain here. Apparently, then, time is not such as *simply* to have a before through itself. For time to have a before through itself something else is required – a relation – and, indeed, time is intrinsically characterised by such a relation: a relation of what is before *to* what is after. Along these lines, then, Avicenna introduces the qualification that to this state (of time) in which the concrete thing is belongs the before *only if* this state (of time) is correlated to another, subsequent state (of time) in which the concrete thing subsequently is, too. Thus, the concrete thing is, first, with (*maʿa*) this state (of time) and, then, with another state (*ḥāl al-āḫar*) – and the former state can be a before only if the concrete thing subsequently is also with the other state.[172] Thus, in order for time to have a state that is before through time itself, a concrete thing is required which is itself in different states, so as to be with one temporal state and subsequently with another temporal state. In other words, what is required is a concrete thing undergoing motion. When there is such a concrete thing undergoing motion, then it is in or with different states of time, and then – and only then – is the one state a before and the other state an after through time itself, so that only if there is the motion of a concrete thing, can time necessarily have its relation

172 It is not clear why Avicenna used the *iḍāfa*-construction *ḥāl al-āḫar* ("the state *of* something other"), which is supported by the two editions and both Leiden manuscripts, and not *al-ḥāl al-uḫar* or *ḥāl uḫar* ("another state"), which would seem to be what he wants to express. The interpretation and reading advanced here gains further support from a parallel passage in which Avicenna explains why the Flood is in the past and the Resurrection in the future. There, he writes: "It is necessary that together with this there is another condition and that is something which through itself is such that of it some thing is that which is the past itself or the future itself, so that its nature is something which, if correlated with another thing (*qīsat ilā amr āḫar*), is through itself past and future" (*al-Samāʿ al-ṭabīʿī* II.10, §11, 154.1–3). In addition, it is also unclear whether we should read *ḥāl al-āḫar* ("another state" or "the state of something other") or rather *ḥāl al-āḫir* ("a later state" or "the state of something later"). Other or later, Avicenna seems to explain that this state is one of the other, subsequent states in which the thing can be and, at one point, will be (*in kāna al-šayʾ bi-ḥāl*).

of before and after through itself – i.e., only then is it that this necessary belonging (*al-luzūm*) belongs to it [i.e., time] through itself, as Avicenna puts it.[173]

As we can see, Avicenna's conception of time as essentially being that which through itself is before *and* after has far-reaching implications for its existence. In fact, as has been noted and as we have seen, Avicenna appears to mark out his own position against other possible conceptions of time, by warning us that time should not be taken to exist absolutely independently in an invariable and uniform state. Avicenna is too much a Peripatetic to abandon the essential dependence of time on motion. Time is, after all, considered to be an accident of motion – indeed, it is its magnitude – and, thus, ontologically subordinate to motion. So, he sees the need to explain why time is subordinate to motion, even though motion or things in motion are themselves dependent upon time for receiving their temporal qualifications as before and after, as his account implies. Indeed, this complex situation calls for some explanation, and so Avicenna tries to clarify that "before and after through itself" does not mean that time is without any outside help before and after. Time can be before and after through itself only if there is motion. Yet – and this is the crucial detail – this, in turn, does not mean that time receives the before and after from motion, or from something else, either. What Avicenna means by *li-ḏātihī* in this context is that whenever certain concrete things are (or at least one certain thing is) in motion so as to be in different prior and posterior states, then time exists and *through itself* is before and after. Thus, time depends on motion for its existence but not for its being divisible into before and after, for it is essentially, i.e., "through itself," divisible into the before and after.

173 A most pertinent issue in the interpretation of this sentence is the determination of the correct referent of the masculine pronoun in the penultimate occurrence of the expression *li-ḏātihī*. The referent cannot be the state (*ḥāl*), which has been clearly marked by Avicenna as feminine throughout the sentence (e.g., through the pronoun *tilka*). This leaves us with *qabl*, *al-šay'*, *šay'*, and, though somewhat remote, *zamān* as possible masculine referents. To say that the pronoun refers to the concrete thing (*al-šay'*), while grammatically possible, contradicts Avicenna's own assertion in the first lines that concrete things are before and after "because of time" and not through themselves – otherwise there would be no need for time. To say, alternatively, that the before belongs to the state through the before itself (*qabl*) seems to be circular. The best option, then, is to take the pronoun to refer to the indeterminate *šay'*, which, as I have argued, should be interpreted as itself referring, or standing for, time (*zamān*). This must be the correct reading, because the following clause *hāḏā l-luzūm lahū li-ḏātihī* clearly refers to time – again through masculine pronouns. On this reading the sentence as a whole begins by saying that the relation between before and after belongs to time through itself and ends by saying that this necessary belonging belongs to time through itself – two statements which seem to be congruent. This issue about the correct referent of the pronoun, then, provides further support for the contention that one has to distinguish the grammatically indeterminate *šay'* from the grammatically determinate *al-šay'*, for otherwise the passage's conclusion would be incomprehensible or circular. Āl Yāsīn's apparatus notes the variant *li-ḏātihā*, which should probably be dismissed as an emendation by a scribe who intended to remedy the complex situation by making a reference to the only feminine noun available, viz., the state (*ḥāl*), so that a before belongs to the state through itself.

Fig. 6.3: A vertical relation of a thing's states to time.

As an analogy, we can imagine having a green light bulb installed in a room.[174] Upon turning the switch, the light bulb fills the room with green light. That the light is green is due to the light bulb itself, but that there is light at all is due to a certain condition that has to obtain first, viz., somebody turning the switch. If we imagine ourselves standing in the darkened room while turning the switch, the light bulb goes on and emits green light that not only fills the room but also makes us be coloured in green. We derive our greenness from something which through itself, i.e., as a result of its very own essence, provides the greenness, even though it does not provide it independently, requiring us to turn the switch.

In a similar way is time before and after through itself, whereas a concrete human being is before and after only through time. The before and after is the green colour of the lit light bulb, and we are the concrete object that is said to be "before" and "after." We will be green if, and only if, there obtains a certain condition, just as there will be time if, and only if, there is a certain difference between two states, i.e., when there is motion. The green light depends upon that condition for its existence, but it does not depend upon that condition for its being green. By analogy, time, for Avicenna, depends on motion for its *being*, but it does not depend on anything for its being *before and after*, because it is before and after through itself (*li-ḏātihī*), i.e., time – when it has being – always is before *and* after.[175]

Apart from the implicit claim that time comes-to-be through motion, in particular through the prior and posterior states in motion (without, however, the before and after coming-to-be through or deriving from the prior and posterior), we are told here that the before and after does not belong to concrete things on their own account but belongs to them through time. Thus, a thing is before or after when it has a certain

---

174 This analogy is to be taken *cum grano salis*. For one thing (among others), one should disregard the fact that there may be other green light bulbs or other things that could turn objects green.

175 Later in the same paragraph, Avicenna will employ the term *qiyās* as a synonym of *iḍāfa* speaking of time as that which is "before and after through itself, even if it is by relation" (*bi-l-qiyās*). We have also just seen him using the passive verb *qīsat*, deriving from the same root as *qiyās*, along the same lines. This is not the only passage where Avicenna is mixing, or even confounding, terminology, which makes it particularly difficult for his interpreters to gather a firm understanding of his already complex theory. In these intricate passages, Avicenna's Arabic becomes increasingly vexed and his thought evermore difficult to unravel.

Fig. 6.4: A horizontal relation between a thing's states in time.

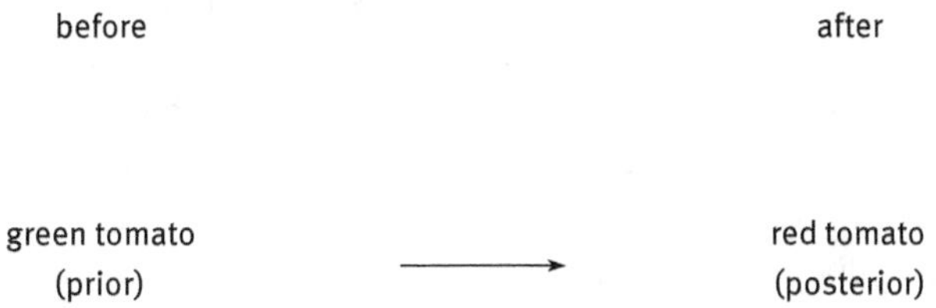

relation to time or, as in the above passage, when it is "with" time. This kind of relation is what I have called above a thing's *vertical relation to* time.[176]

The prior and posterior, Avicenna argues next, likewise does not belong to concrete things through themselves. Instead, a thing is prior or posterior when there is a *horizontal relation between* it and another thing (or between different accidental states of one thing):

فالمتقدّم تقدّمه أنّه له وجود مع عدم شيء آخر لم يكن موجوداً وهو موجود. فهو متقدّم عليه إذا اعتبر عدمه وهو معه إذا اعتبر وجوده فقط.

> So, the priority of what is prior is that it has a certain existence together with the non-existence of some other thing which has not existed, whereas it [sc. the prior thing] has existed. Thus, it is prior to it [sc. the other thing] when its [sc. the other thing's] non-existence is considered, but it is together with it [sc. the other thing] only when its [sc. the other thing's] existence is considered. (*al-Samāʿ al-ṭabīʿī* II.11, §5, 158.5f., tr. by McGinnis, modified)

Something is said to be "prior" when we consider its existence together with the non-existence of something else which has not existed previously. In addition, it is "together" (*maʿa*) with it, when we consider both things as existent at a posterior moment. Consequently, the prior and posterior states of a thing, like the before and after of a thing, come-to-be through a relation – this time, though, the relation obtains *between* these objects (or between different states of one and the same object). I have called this relation a *horizontal relation between* things.[177] Due to such a horizontal relation, different things or states can be said to be prior or posterior, while it is due to such things' vertical relation to time that they can be said to be before or after.

Avicenna concludes this discussion by saying that neither priority nor beforeness is a meaning (*maʿnan*) that belongs to the concrete object (*ḏāt*) through itself.[178] Both descriptions are something additional to the thing. This is further evinced by the fact

---

176 This "vertical relation" is depicted in Fig. 6.3 as well as in Fig. 6.2 above, 474.

177 This "horizontal relation" is depicted in Fig. 6.4.

178 I do not think that the fact that Avicenna uses a singular noun (*maʿnan*) jeopardises in any way my reading that priority and beforeness are two distinct concepts. In fact, my reading is dictated by the overall argument Avicenna pursues in the whole paragraph as outlined above: he focuses on beforeness, turns to priority, and concludes that neither attaches to the concrete thing through it itself.

that the very same thing may at the same time be before one thing and after another, just as it could simultaneously be prior to one thing and posterior to another, just as the red state of a tomato is both prior to its rotten state and posterior to its green state. If these descriptions belonged to the thing through itself, it would have to be itself both before and after or both prior and posterior at the same time, which is not only impossible but "absolutely impossible as such" (*al-battata stiḥālatan li-ḏātihī*), as Avicenna informs us emphatically.[179] The concrete thing, then, remains or persists (*yabqā*), while different, and even contrary, descriptions may apply, or be attributed, to it. Time, however, cannot remain or persist but, as we have been told before, is such that its parts are ceaselessly before and after one another – time is just what is before and after, constantly shifting (much like motion is just what is prior and posterior, constantly shifting).[180]

This is also the reason that terms such as *taqaḍḍin* or *taṣarrum* ("elapsing") and *taǧaddud* ("renewal") as well as negative attributes such as *ġayr qārr* or *ġayr ṯābit* ("non integral" or "unstable") are so relevant not only for characterising motion but also time.[181] This is noticeable in Avicenna and perhaps even more in the discussions of time in later thinkers from within the Avicennian tradition.[182] As it appears, the nature of time as something under constant elapsing and renewal indicates two central aspects. First, it shows the intimate relation between time and motion – or, more precisely, the *dependence* of time on motion. As has just been shown, time requires elapsing and renewal for its being. Without motion and without any difference in a thing's states, i.e., without there being a prior state which elapsed and a different posterior state coming newly into being, there would be no time. In a very real sense, time depends on the priority and the posteriority of motion; and this means that time requires and depends on *taqaḍḍin* and *taǧaddud*. This also spells out once more why, and in what sense, time is an accident – viz., the magnitude – of motion. This brings us to the second aspect, for the parts of that magnitude, i.e., the parts of time, are themselves characterised by constant elapsing and renewal. Just as what is prior cannot exist together with what is posterior in motion, so the before cannot co-exist with the after in time. Time, being the magnitude of motion, is itself subject to elapsing and renewal just as motion is. Time, then, is intrinsically characterised by constantly being before and after "through itself." Whenever time is, it is, on account of its very own self, in progress and constantly evolving. The parts of time, i.e., the parts of the magnitude of motion, are just as motion itself non-integral and unstable, and "have their being in becoming," as one might put it.[183]

---

179 *al-Samāʿ al-ṭabīʿī* II.11, §5, 158.8f.

180 cf. *al-Samāʿ al-ṭabīʿī* II.11, §4, 157.7–10; cf. *al-Ḥikma al-mašriqiyya* III.11, 33.7–10.

181 q.v. fn. 33 above, 439.

182 cf. Adamson and Lammer, "Fakhr al-Dīn al-Rāzī's Platonist Account of the Essence of Time"; Lammer, "Time and Mind-Dependence in Sayf al-Dīn al-Āmidī's *Abkār al-afkār*."

183 cf. *al-Samāʿ al-ṭabīʿī* II.13, §1, 167.4; q.v. fn. 37 above, 440.

Time's Existence

It is on this basis – i.e., on the basis of the now established understanding of what time is in its essence – that Avicenna can demonstrate the existence of time, thus making good on his promise from the beginning that after an investigation of the essence of time (*māhiyyat al-zamān*), it is "from there" (*min hunāka*) that the existence of time (*wuğūduhū*) shall also become clear to us.[184] He states:

وأمّا نفس الشيء الذي هو قبل وبعد لذاته وإن كان بالقياس فلا يجوز أن يبقى هو بعينه فيكون بعد بعد ما كان قبل فإنّه ما جاء المعنى الذي به الشيء بعد إلّا بطل ما هو به قبل والشيء ذو هذا الأمر هو باقٍ مع بطلان الأمر القبل. وهذا الأمر لا يجوز أن يكون نسبةً إلى عدم فقط أو إلى وجود فقط، فإن نسبة وجود الشيء إلى عدم الشيء قد يكون تأخراً كما يكون تقدماً وكذلك في جانب الوجود بل هو نسبة إلى عدم مقارن أمراً آخر إذا قارنه كان تقدماً وإن قارن غيره كان تأخراً والعدم في الحالين عدم وكذلك الوجود ... وهذا الأمر هو زمان أو نسبة إلى زمان فإن كان زماناً فذلك ما نقوله.

As for the very thing which is before and after through itself, even if it is [only] by relation (*bi-l-qiyās*),[185] it is not possible that it remains the same as it is, and so [what is] "after" is after what was "before," for the meaning through which something is after does not come about (*mā ğā'a*) unless that through which it was before has perished, while the thing having this qualification [as either before or after] (*hāḏā l-amr*) remains despite the perishing of the qualification [as] before (*al-amr al-qabl*). It is not possible that this qualification [as either before or after] is a relation[186] to a non-existence alone (*'adam faqaṭ*) or to an existence alone, for the relation of the existence of the thing to the non-existence of the thing could be a posteriority just as it could be a priority (and likewise in the case of existence). It is rather a relation[187] to a non-existence as associated (*'adam muqāran*) with another qualification [as either before or after]. When it [i.e., the non-existence] is associated with it [i.e., with a qualification as before], it [i.e., the non-existence] is a priority, and when it is associated with some other [qualification], it is a posteriority, while the non-existence in both states is [just] non-existence (and likewise for existence) ... This qualification [as either before or after] is time or some relation to time. So, if it is time, then that is what we say. (*al-Samā' al-ṭabī'ī* II.11, §5, 158.11–17)[188]

This sentence is again extremely intricate, and it seems as though Avicenna struggled to put down into words what he thought to be the correct view.[189] His terminology is messy and confusing. He talks about the very thing (*nafs al-šay'*) which is before and

184 *al-Samā' al-ṭabī'ī* II.10, §13, 154.12f.; q.v. above, 431f.
185 q.v. fn. 175 above, 482.
186 Reading *nisba* with Mss. Leiden or. 4 and or. 84, McGinnis, and Āl Yāsīn for *nisbatuhū* in Zāyid.
187 Reading *nisba* with Mss. Leiden or. 4 and or. 84, and Zāyid for *nisbatuhū* in McGinnis and Āl Yāsīn.
188 cf. *al-Ḥikma al-mašriqiyya* III.11, 33.23–34.3.
189 McGinnis regards this passage as "a response to a potential objection ... that existence and nonexistence are sufficient conditions to explain priority and posteriority" and, as it seems, attaches only little importance to it (*Time and Time Again*, 236–238). On my reading, this passage is one of the most important and complex passages in the entire chapter, and aims at establishing the existence of time rather than merely brushing off a potential objection.

after through itself, viz., time; about a meaning (*al-ma'nā*) through which some thing is before or after, viz., the meanings of before and after provided by time; about said thing (*al-šay'*) which through this meaning is before or after, viz., a concrete object; about a thing (*al-šay'*) which has a qualification as before or after and which remains, viz., the concrete object again, which once is before and then after; and about the qualification (*al-amr*) which this thing has, viz., the before and the after that are attributed to the thing and come-to-be and pass away. The concrete object is, further, envisaged through its non-existence (*'adam*) before it came-to-be and its existence (*wuǧūd*) after it came-to-be. We are, furthermore, reminded that the non-existence and the existence here are just nothing but simple non-existence and existence, i.e., a state at which the concrete thing was not and a state at which the concrete thing was, respectively.

Avicenna's argument is that a thing may have non-existence and may have existence, and that these two states may succeed each other, so that a thing may first be non-existent, then exist, and then may be non-existent again. Neither the thing itself nor its states of non-existence and existence can account for any temporal qualification as before or after or for any order as prior and posterior. This is in line with what we have already been told earlier, viz., that concrete things or states are in themselves neither before and after nor prior and posterior.[190] So, any qualification of a concrete thing as before or after must be derived from something other than the thing itself, other than its non-existence, and other than its existence. Thus, a naked relation of a concrete thing to its bare non-existence alone (*nisba ilā 'adam faqaṭ*) is not enough to establish a thing's beforeness and to qualify it as before.

From this, it is clear that the states of non-existence and existence in this passage are not related to each other as certain states within a continuous motion are related to each other. Avicenna is decidedly not talking, for example, about a heating process that transforms ice into water and water into air, so that there would be the non-existence of water (together with the existence of ice), then the existence of water, and then, again, the non-existence of water (together with the existence of air). If that were what Avicenna has in mind, then the subsequent states of non-existence and existence would already be ordered and, thus, would already be prior and posterior to each other, as they have their part within the framework of a certain motion, in this case that of a heating process. In the above passage, however, the states of non-existence and existence are not related and Avicenna asks how they can be ordered, where "to be ordered" means to be arranged in a sequence of priority and posteriority. Since this sequence and order is precisely what we are looking for, and since motion is itself determined by such a sequence and order, the states to which Avicenna refers in this passage cannot be concrete states within a motion but are independent states of non-existence and existence.

190 cf. esp. *al-Samā' al-ṭabī'ī* II.11, §5, 158.7–9.

The situation we have to envisage could, perhaps, be exemplified by considering the non-existence of Avicenna (at the time of Aristotle), the existence of Avicenna (on New Years Eve in the year 1000), and the non-existence of Avicenna (now in our time).[191] In this example, the three states are not connected with each other but are independent and not parts of a continuous motion. Since these states provide nothing that could determine their order and succession – and that means: since a relation to the non-existence of Avicenna alone (*faqaṭ*) does not establish the priority of the one non-existence over the state of existence or the other state of non-existence – we either must admit that there is no such order, and that, consequently, we are incapable of both establishing and comprehending the priority of one event or state over another event or state, or acknowledge that there is, in fact, a framework that provides such a – we may daresay – *temporal* order.

So, what is required in the example about the non-existent Avicenna, the existent Avicenna, and the again non-existent Avicenna is something additional – and this is either time itself, which qualifies the states directly, or something else which in turn has a relation to time, thus mediating its own direct qualification to Avicenna's existential states. In either case, the states of non-existence and existence would have a certain (mediated or direct) relation to time and would, thus, be temporally qualified as being before or after, so that the first period of non-existence was prior to the second period of non-existence and prior to the period of existence, while the second period of non-existence was posterior both to the first period of non-existence and to the period of existence. So, we get the *horizontal relation between* two independent states of non-existence of which one non-existence is prior to the other, because each non-existence has its own direct or mediated *vertical relation to* a time which is before and a time which is after, respectively.

In other words, independent concrete *things* derive their qualification as before and after when their *states* of existence or non-existence – or in fact any other state such as being white, wearing clothes, taking a nap – are horizontally ordered as prior and posterior. This horizontal order comes about through the vertical relation of these independent states to time or through the mediation of something else which itself has an intrinsic relation to time. Through the direct or mediated relation with the before and after of time, states of existence and non-existence come to be characterised as before or after individually and, therefore, ordered as prior and posterior to one another,

---

191 The information in brackets is added to make the example more comprehensible. By adding this information, however, the states of non-existence and existence are already associated with other events which we take to have some temporal location. Since Avicenna intends to derive such a temporality, he himself emphasised that the existence and the non-existence he is talking about are existence and non-existence "alone" (*faqaṭ*), i.e., existence and non-existence precisely without any such association. The same goes for temporal copulae such as "is" and "was."

so that the things that are associated with these states of existence and non-existence derive their beforeness and afterness through these states' relation to time.[192]

The brief version of all this is that even individual and entirely independent states are prior and posterior to each other, because they are embedded in time; and concrete things are qualified as before or after, because they are in one of these states or another.

Avicenna's argument asserts that we can explain neither beforeness and afterness nor priority and posteriority fully without some additional thing that is essentially before and after, and through a (direct or mediated) vertical relation to which other things and their states can derive their horizontal order as being prior or posterior to other things and their states.[193] This is Avicenna's proof for the existence of time. Time is that which is required if we want to make sense of priority and posteriority, and beforeness and afterness, because there is nothing else that could account for these. This is the explanatory gap time is supposed to fill, and so time exists.

This argument bears a strong resemblance to another argument by Avicenna which for roughly eight-hundred years has been taken to do precisely what I have just claimed: demonstrate the existence of time. This argument is contained as the fourth chapter of the fifth *namaṭ* in Avicenna's *al-Išārāt wa-l-tanbīhāt*. It has been analysed, alongside its commentaries by Faḫr al-Dīn al-Rāzī (d. 606/1210) and Naṣīr al-Dīn al-Ṭūsī (d. 672/1274), in a skilfully detailed article by Toby Mayer.[194]

Mayer reports that Naṣīr al-Dīn has argued that Avicenna designed chapter four as a *tanbīh* ("reminder") for what he considers to be a clear (*ẓāhir*) fact, viz., time's existence or being (*anniyya*), whereas chapter five constitutes an *išāra* ("pointer") to a much more obscure (*ḫafīy*) topic, viz., time's essence (*māhiyya*).[195] However, "framing the discussion thus is stilted," says Mayer, emphasising that the debate between Faḫr al-Dīn and Naṣīr al-Dīn, which he aims to reconstruct in his article, "is, more accurately, about time's *pre*-existing" than about time's existing.[196] This, though certainly true, is itself somewhat stilted, it seems. The question about the pre-eternity of time is, of course, a widely ramified and most delicate philosophical and theological issue. It is hardly surprising that the ensuing debate between Faḫr al-Dīn and Naṣīr al-Dīn focusses on this contested problem, even more so since Naṣīr al-Dīn believes, as we have just

---

192 McGinnis asserts in a similar manner that "x is prior to y because (1) x exists when y does not exist and (2) x exists congruent with some thing that is before the existence of y; and this something is either time itself, which is essentially before and after, or something that receives its beforeness and afterness because it is related to time" (*Time and Time Again*, 237f.).

193 As already mentioned, this current argument is about independent states. Things and states may, however, also be part of a single motion, in which case they would already be ordered as prior and posterior. I shall address the interplay between motion and time below, 510ff.

194 Mayer, "Avicenna against Time Beginning."

195 al-Ṭūsī, *Ḥall muškilāt al-Išārāt*, vol. 3, 72.8–10.

196 Mayer, "Avicenna against Time Beginning," 125; cf. also Faḫr al-Dīn's own note that the chapter was concerned with the question whether or not there belongs to time a beginning and an end (*Šarḥ al-Išārāt wa-l-tanbīhāt* II.5.5, vol. 2, 402.1f. (ed. Naǧafzādeh)).

seen, that the question about the existence of time deserves nothing more than a quick "reminder," because it is clear in itself that time exists. Indeed, the existence of time has for hundreds of years been taken for granted, and so Aristotle's neglect to provide an answer to the sceptical doubts about the existence of time which he mentioned in *Physics* IV.10 has been condoned by the Greek and Arabic philosophical tradition.[197] Since both Naṣīr al-Dīn and Faḫr al-Dīn agree that time exists, the existence of time is hardly a contentious topic, and so these two post-Avicennian intellectuals battled over more controversial ground, viz., the pre-eternity of time.

In addition, any question about the pre-existence of time is also a question about its existence. Thus, despite Mayer's claim that it is somewhat stilted to say that chapter four of the fifth *namaṭ* of Avicenna's *al-Išārāt wa-l-tanbīhāt* is about the existence of time, much of Faḫr al-Dīn's critical arguments are designed to precisely undermine Avicenna's claim that the before and after are in an existential sense "real," so that Avicenna's strategy to infer the reality of time on the basis of the reality of the before and after is likewise demolished. Mayer says so himself towards the end of his article, arguing that the first part of Faḫr al-Dīn's critique is "destroying the basis on which time is inferred," even though, of course, Faḫr al-Dīn uses this as a spring board for his much more theologically relevant contention that Avicenna's argument also fails to demonstrate the pre-eternity of time.[198] Consequently, Naṣīr al-Dīn's assertion that chapter four is concerned with an argument in favour of time's existence is correct, even though Faḫr al-Dīn's criticism, as well as his general agenda in his commentary on *al-Išārāt wa-l-tanbīhāt*, turns this harmless chapter into a divisive issue about eternity and pre-existence.

Be that as it may, the chapter from Avicenna's *al-Išārāt wa-l-tanbīhāt* which has justifiably been said to contain an argument for the existence of time bears a strong resemblance to the last passage we have looked at from *al-Samāʿ al-ṭabīʿī*; it runs as follows:

> تنبيه: الحادث بعد ما لم يكن له قبل لم يكن فيه ليس كقبلية الواحد التي هي على الاثنين التي قد يكون بها ما هو قبل وما هو بعد معاً في حصول الوجود بل قبلية قبل لا يثبت مع البعد. ومثل هذا ففيه أيضاً تجدّد بعدية بعد قبلية باطلة. وليست تلك القبلية هي نفس العدم فقد يكون العدم بعد ولا ذات الفاعل فقد يكون قبل ومع وبعد فهو شيء آخر لا يزال فيه تصرّم وتجدّد على الاتّصال. وقد علمت أنّ مثل هذا الاتّصال الذي يوازي الحركات في المقادير لن يتألّف من غير منقسمات.
>
> Reminder: That which originates (*al-ḥādiṯ*) after not having been has a before in which it was not and which is not like the beforeness of the [number] one which it [has] over the [number] two by which what is before and what is after may occur together in actual existence (*maʿan*

197 cf. Lammer, "Time and Mind-Dependence in Sayf al-Dīn al-Āmidī's *Abkār al-afkār*."
198 Mayer, "Avicenna against Time Beginning," 140.

> *fī ḥuṣūl al-wuğūd*). It is rather the beforeness of a before[199] which does not remain (*yaṯbutu*)[200] together with the after.[201] Like this, then, in it is also a renewal of an afterness after a perishing beforeness. That beforeness is neither the non-existence itself, for non-existence may be after, nor the agent itself, for it may be[202] before and together and after. Thus, it[203] is something else in which elapsing and renewal[204] do not vanish continuously. You have already known that what is like this continuity which corresponds to the motions over [spatial] magnitudes is not composed of indivisibles. (*al-Išārāt wa-l-tanbīhāt* II.5.4, 150.5–13)[205]

As in the last passage quoted from *al-Samāʿ al-ṭabīʿī* above, Avicenna's argument here turns on a certain concrete thing which comes-to-be (*al-ḥādiṯ*), passing from non-existence into existence. We are also told that the non-existence alone is not capable of explaining the beforeness of the non-existence, because the non-existence – being nothing other than non-existence – could likewise occur after the existence, just as Avicenna was non-existent at the time of Aristotle and is also non-existent now at our own time. In addition, Avicenna singles out the type of beforeness he is currently interested in as that type which entails elapsing and renewal, thus signalling that he is not talking about a priority by nature, order, eminence, or causality, for in all these cases the things are not constantly renewed, so that something which is prior can, and in some cases must, exist together with that which is posterior, like the number one which can exist together with the number two despite its priority over the number two. Here, Avicenna metaphorically described the priority of the number one as a "beforeness" (*qabliyya*), even though beforeness and afterness apply strictly speaking only to temporal priority and posteriority. So, the beforeness under consideration is a beforeness that cannot persist like the concrete thing described by that beforeness can do.

The argument as such is very much like what has already been discussed. The non-existence of a thing cannot be described as before through the thing itself, nor through the non-existence of the thing, nor through the agent responsible for the thing's passing from non-existence to existence. Thus, the beforeness in question must be "something else" (*šay' āḫar*) which is essentially characterised by elapsing and renewal, and which is also continuous (*ʿalā ttiṣāl*) and eternal (*lā yazālu*).[206] What Avicenna adds to his argument is something which has also already been noted several

---

199 Reading *qabliyya qabl* with Forget and Dunyā for *qabliyyatuhū qabl* in al-Zārʿī.

200 Reading *yaṯbutu* with Forget for *taṯbutu* in Dunyā and al-Zārʿī.

201 An alternative translation would render *lā yaṯbutu* (or: *lā yuṯbatu*) as "is not affirmed [in its existence]."

202 Reading *yakūnu* with Forget and al-Zārʿī for *takūnu* in Dunyā.

203 Reading *huwa* with Forget and Dunyā for *hiya* in al-Zārʿī. I take it that the gender of the pronoun is due to the following masculine *šay'* even though its implied referent is the feminine *tilka l-qabliyya*.

204 Reading *taṣarrum wa-tağaddud* with Forget for *tağaddud wa-taṣarrum* in Dunyā and al-Zārʿī.

205 cf. *al-Hidāya* II.1, 157.3–6; cf. also *Phys.* VIII.1, 251b10–12.

206 The last two characterisations of time may have further spurred Faḫr al-Dīn to begin a discussion on the eternity, rather than the existence, of time.

times before in both Avicenna and Aristotle: the continuity of beforeness and afterness, which – as we are informed in the following chapter, *al-Išārāt wa-l-tanbīhāt* II.5.5, is nothing other than time – corresponds to the distance over which motion occurs and is, for this very reason, non-atomic in structure and essentially continuous, just as motion and distance are.

This brief chapter of Avicenna's *al-Išārāt wa-l-tanbīhāt*, then, is nothing other than a highly condensed version of the full argument in *al-Samāʿ al-ṭabīʿī* II.11. As such, it is hardly comprehensible for anyone who has not read Avicenna's other works. We are able to see, however, that what the argument does is establish the *existence* of time as the ultimate *explanans* of beforeness and afterness on the basis of time's essence as that which essentially is before and after through itself. It is now apparent that Avicenna's prediction that the existence of time will become clear from its essence turned out to be correct. Before Avicenna could demonstrate the existence of time, he had to establish time as that which through itself is before and after – and he could do this only after having shown that it is, in fact, the magnitude of motion when motion is differentiated into what is prior and posterior because of the intimate relation between motion's prior and posterior, on the one hand, and time's before and after, on the other.

So, we have seen that concrete things and their states are, as such, incapable of accounting for any qualification as either before and after or prior and posterior. There is only one way how a thing or a state can become before or after, and this is through a (direct or mediated) relation to time, because time is through itself before and after. Things or states which are related to time, then, derive their temporality as before or after from time. In essence, Avicenna argues that the temporality of things and states does not come from anything other than time – and since the temporality of things is a fact, time exists.[207]

By contrast, there are two ways in which a state or a thing can come to be prior or posterior to another state or thing. One of these is through time: if one state has a relation to time and has derived its temporality as before while another state is likewise related to time and has derived its temporality as after, then both states have become part of an ordered sequence in which the before-state is prior to the after-state.[208]

---

207 The reality of temporality is a prominent and highly controversial topic in the discussions on the eternity and the creation of the world in the post-Avicennian tradition, as is clear from the second argument of the first discussion of al-Ġazālī's *Tahāfut al-falāsifa* as well as from the debate on the meanings of "beforeness" and "priority" in sixth/twelfth-century intellectuals such as Muḥammad ibn ʿAbd al-Karīm al-Šahrastānī and Abū l-Barakāt al-Baġdādī, among others; cf. Lammer, "Two Sixth/Twelfth-Century Hardliners on Creation and Divine Eternity"; cf. also Lammer, "Eternity and Origination in the Works of Sayf al-Dīn al-Āmidī and Athīr al-Dīn al-Abharī."

208 As examples, I mentioned Avicenna's non-existence (preceding his existence which, in turn, likewise preceded his non-existence after his death) as well as the Peloponnesian War (preceding the ʿAbbāsid Revolution).

The second way is that a qualification of two states as prior or posterior can come about through motion, because motion is such that parts of it are prior and others posterior. Since motion is intrinsically ordered, and contains prior and posterior states, these states, which are an essential aspect of the motion, are already related to each other with regard to priority and posteriority, even though they depend on time for their respective temporal qualification as before or after.[209]

One question has not yet been answered but has been merely alluded to: if things derive their qualification as before and after from time; and if states can be ordered as prior and posterior, because one state has been qualified as before and the other as after – if, in other words, time is the cause for a thing's qualification as before and after, just as it can be the cause for a thing's qualification as prior and posterior – what, then, is the cause of time and how is it that time, being that which is through itself before and after, comes into existence?

The Cause of Time's Existence

There is one particularly clear statement in Avicenna's works about what it is that brings about – and, thus, is the cause of – the existence of time. We find this statement in the *'Uyūn al-ḥikma*. There Avicenna writes:

الحركة علّة حصول الزمان والمحرّك علّة علّة الزمان فالمحرّك علّة الزمان ولا كلّ محرّك بل محرّك مستديرة ... فإذن الحركة المُوجِبة للزمان نفسانية إرادية فالنفس علّة وجود الزمان.

> Motion[210] is the cause for the occurrence of time (*al-ḥaraka 'illat ḥuṣūl al-zamān*) and the mover is the cause of the cause of time (*wa-l-muḥarrik 'illat 'illat al-zamān*). Thus, the mover is the cause of time, yet not every mover but [only] the mover of circular [motion] (*muḥarrik mustadīra*) ... [Circular motion, however, is due to soul] ... Therefore, the motion that gives rise to time (*al-mūǧiba li-l-zamān*) is due to soul and voluntary (*nafsāniyya irādiyya*). Thus, the soul is the cause of the existence of time (*fa-l-nafs 'illat wuǧūd al-zamān*). (*'Uyūn al-ḥikma* II.8–9, 28.17–29.7)[211]

This passage contains two essential claims entailing a conclusion: first, circular motion is the cause for the occurrence (*ḥuṣūl*), i.e., the actual existence, of time; second, soul is the cause for circular motion. Therefore, soul is the cause of the cause of the actual existence of time.

The claim that soul is somehow responsible for the existence of time goes back to Plato but is more prominent, and even infamously so, in the last chapter of Aristotle's

209 As examples, I mentioned a heating process in which ice turns into water which subsequently turns to air as well as the ripening process of a green tomato turning into a red tomato.

210 I follow the punctuation as it is in texts of 'Āṣī and al-Saqqā, in which the word *al-ḥaraka* starts a new sentence. The editions of Ülken, Badawī, and al-Ǧabr lack punctuation here.

211 cf. *al-Samā' al-ṭabī'ī* III.9, §6, 222.6–8; *al-Ta'līqāt*, 142.17 (ed. Badawī)/§764, 424.1 (ed. Mousavian).

discussion of time in *Physics* IV.[212] There, Aristotle asked "how time can be related to the soul" (πῶς ποτε ἔχει ὁ χρόνος πρὸς τὴν ψυχήν, *kayfa layta šiʿrī ḥāl al-zamān ʿinda l-nafs*) and, after a brief investigation into the matter, asserted the following:

> ἀδυνάτου γὰρ ὄντος εἶναι τοῦ ἀριθμήσοντος ἀδύνατον καὶ ἀριθμητόν τι εἶναι, ὥστε δῆλον ὅτι οὐδ' ἀριθμός ... εἰ δὲ μηδὲν ἄλλο πέφυκεν ἀριθμεῖν ἢ ψυχὴ καὶ ψυχῆς νοῦς, ἀδύνατον εἶναι χρόνον ψυχῆς μὴ οὔσης, ἀλλ' ἢ τοῦτο ὅ ποτε ὂν ἔστιν ὁ χρόνος, οἷον εἰ ἐνδέχεται κίνησιν εἶναι ἄνευ ψυχῆς.
>
> فنقول إنّه إذا العادّ غير موجود لا محالة فالذي يُعَدّ أيضاً غير موجود ... وإن كان ليس شيء من شأنه أن يعدّ سوى النفس ومن النفس العقل فغير ممكن أن يكون الزمان موجوداً إذا لم تكن نفس موجوداً اللهمّ إلّا من قبل ذلك الشيء الذي متى كان موجوداً كان الزمان موجوداً من غير أن يكون نفس.
>
> For if it is impossible that there is something that numbers, it is impossible that there is something that is numerable ... If, however, nothing but soul – and of soul intellect – is such as to be able to number, it is impossible that time exists if there is no soul, even though that, whatever it is by being which time is, may exist, for example, if it is possible that motion is without soul. (*Phys.* IV.14, 223a22–28)

While modern expositors "have looked askance at" this Aristotelian passage, as David Bostock put it, their ancient forebears almost universally gave their consent.[213] Simplicius and Themistius mention only Boethus as a critic of Aristotle in this regard, rejecting their predecessor's argument that just as things remain perceptible even in the absence of a perceiver, so time surely remains numerable even in the absence of soul.[214]

---

212 cf. *Phys.* IV.14, 223a16–29; cf. also *Tim.* 47a1–7. Contemporary interpretations of the Aristotelian passage are often critical, even dismissive; cf. Sorabji, *Time, Creation and the Continuum*, ch. 7; Hussey's appendix A in Aristotle, *Physics*, esp. 180–184; Wieland, *Die aristotelische Physik*, ch. 18; Wagner's comments in *Physikvorlesung*, *ad loc.*; Loughlin, "Souls and the Location of Time."

213 Bostock, "Aristotle's Account of Time," fn. 7, 169.

214 cf. Boethus *apud* Themistium, *In Phys.*, 160.26–28; Simplicius, *In Phys.*, 759.18–20, 766.17–19; cf. generally Sorabji, *The Philosophy of the Commentators*, vol. 2, ch. 11d. It is to be noted that Themistius' attitude towards Aristotle's argument and the criticism advanced by Boethus is not entirely clear. In his paraphrase of the *Physics*, Themistius states that Boethus made an error (σφάλλεται δέ) and accepts Aristotle's argument, whereas in his paraphrase of the *De anima*, he maintains that, by making time the result of the ἐπίνοια ("conception") of the human mind, Alexander was "wrong and unfaithful to Aristotle" (οὐκ ὀρθῶς οὐδὲ ἑπομένως Ἀριστοτέλει), because he did not grant time "its own real existence" (*In Phys.*, 120.15–21, tr. by Todd); cf. Simplicius, *In Phys.*, 765.19–766.33. For this reason, Sorabji lists Themistius together with Boethus as one of two critics of Aristotle's position in *Phys.* IV.14; cf. Sorabji, *The Philosophy of the Commentators*, vol. 2, ch. 11d. This tension in Themistius' position towards Aristotle and against Boethus and Alexander can be resolved by distinguishing "number" from "numerable." Following Aristotle's claim that "that, whatever it is by being which time is," may still exist in the absence of the human soul, most commentators (including Philoponus and Simplicius) argued that in the absence of the human soul, time retains its *number* but is no longer *numerable*, as nothing is able to number time anymore. Boethus, however, argued that this line of reasoning is unjustified, because time always remains *numerable*, even if no human soul exists. Themistius counters Boethus' argument by maintaining that although time's number is independent from the human soul,

Interestingly, most ancient commentators did not just endorse Aristotle's reasoning but also expanded its implication. Themistius, having rebutted Boethus' objection to Aristotle's claim that the numerable does not exist in the absence of something capable of numbering, remarks further:

> μᾶλλον δὲ οὐδὲ κίνησιν εἶναι δυνατὸν ἄνευ ψυχῆς· ἀρχὴ μὲν γὰρ πάσης κινήσεως ἡ κυκλοφορία· ὑπὸ γὰρ ταύτης ἀλλοιοῦται τὰ πάθη τὰ σωματικὰ καὶ αὔξει καὶ φθίνει, αὕτη δὲ ὑπὸ νοῦ καὶ κατ' ὄρεξιν.
> In fact, there cannot even be motion without soul, for the principle of every motion is the circular motion (ἡ κυκλοφορία), for through it the bodily affections are altered and grow and diminish, but this is through intellect and in accordance with desire (ὑπὸ νοῦ καὶ κατ' ὄρεξιν). (Themistius, *In Phys.*, 161.5–7, tr. by Todd, modified)

The same explanation is advanced by Philoponus who expounds the Aristotelian text along the same lines:

> ἐνδείκνυται ὅτι καὶ ἡ κίνησις ἀναιρεῖται τῆς ψυχῆς ἀνῃρημένης.
> He [sc. Aristotle] indicates that motion, too, is removed when soul is removed. (Philoponus, *In Phys.*, 775.19, tr. by Broadie, modified)

Simplicius agrees as well, and scents a harmony between Aristotle and "our leader" (τῷ σφετέρῳ καθηγεμόνι), viz., Plato, whom he reports as having declared that the soul is the "the source and principle of motion" (πηγὴ καὶ ἀρχὴ κινήσεώς).[215]

It emerges that, where Aristotle gave one reason for why there cannot be time if there were no soul, the late ancient commentators and expositors provided *two* reasons: first, it is that numbering, being an act of the soul, obviously requires soul, so that time, being the *numbered aspect* of motion, likewise requires soul; second, since all motion is ultimately due to soul, viz., the soul of the heavenly sphere, all motion is due to soul, so that time, being the numbered aspect *of motion*, likewise requires soul. For both reasons, we can find a source which even predates Themistius and which gained prominence in its Arabic translation – it is, once again, Alexander's treatise on time, in which we read the following:

---

its being numerable is not. By contrast, he interpreted Alexander's statements as claiming that not even time's *number* exists without the human conception. Thus, Themistius takes a middle position between Boethus and Alexander. This middle position is also adopted by Philoponus and Simplicius in their commentaries, as they claim that time's number exists, even though it is no longer numerable if there were no soul, thus endorsing the overall thrust of Aristotle's argument. Consequently, neither should Themistius be grouped together with Boethus as a critic of Aristotle, nor should it be said that Philoponus and Simplicius "reject the mind-dependence of time" that Aristotle had argued for, as Trifogli wrote ("Averroes's Doctrine of Time and its Reception in the Scholastic Debate," fn. 3, 57; cf. *Oxford Physics in the Thirteenth Century*, 219–221). Nonetheless, it is true that Philoponus and Simplicius used their Platonic account of number to explain (or develop) Aristotle's argument, as Trifogli noted; cf. also Annas, "Aristotle, Number and Time"; Hussey's appendix in *Physics*, 176–184.

215 Simplicius, *In Phys.*, 761.5–9; *Phdr.* 245c9.

ونقول إنّه لو بطلت النفس التي تعدّ الحركات بطل الزمان. ولو بطلت النفس لم يتحرّك الفلك ولو لم يتحرّك لبطلت الحركات كلّها لأنّها علّة الحركات كلّها.

We say that if the soul, which numbers motion, were abolished, then time would be abolished, and if the soul were abolished (*wa-law baṭalat al-nafs*), then the sphere would not be moved, and if it were not moved, then all motion would be abolished (*la-baṭalat al-ḥarakāt kulluhā*), because it[216] is the cause of all motion (*ʿillat al-ḥārakāt kullihā*). (*Maqālat al-Iskandar al-Afrūdīsī fī l-zamān*, 22.2–4)

This argument of Alexander is also attested in Greek by Simplicius in his commentary on the *Physics*:

εἰ μέντοι μὴ δύναται κίνησις ἄνευ ψυχῆς εἶναι, οὐ μόνον ὁ χρόνος ἀλλὰ καὶ ἡ κίνησις ἀναιρεθήσεται ψυχῆς μὴ οὔσης· εἰ γὰρ ἡ κυκλοφορία, ἐξ ἧς καὶ αἱ ἄλλαι κινήσεις καὶ αἱ μεταβολαὶ τὸ εἶναι ἔχουσιν, ὑπὸ νοῦ καὶ κατ' ὄρεξίν ἐστιν, ὡς ὁμολογεῖ καὶ Ἀλέξανδρος, ἀναιρουμένης ψυχῆς ἀναιροῖτο ἂν πᾶσα κίνησις ... ὥστε καὶ τῆς κατὰ γένεσιν μεταβολῆς αἰτία ἐστὶν ἡ κυκλοφορία· καὶ αἱ κατὰ ἀλλοίωσιν δὲ καὶ κατὰ αὔξησιν καὶ μείωσιν μεταβολαὶ ἀπ' ἐκείνης.

If, however, it is not possible for there to be motion without soul, not only time but also motion will be abolished when soul is not, for if the cyclic motion (ἡ κυκλοφορία), from which all other motions and changes have their existence, is through intellect and in accordance with desire (ὑπὸ νοῦ καὶ κατ' ὄρεξίν),[217] as Alexander also agrees, then if soul were abolished, all motion would be abolished (ἀναιρουμένης ψυχῆς ἀναιροῖτο ἂν πᾶσα κίνησις) ... Cyclic motion is the cause of that change in terms of generation, and the changes in terms of alteration and growth and diminution are also from it. (Simplicius, *In Phys.*, 760.14–25, tr. by Urmson, modified)

Upon comparison of Simplicius' text with the Arabic of Alexander's treatise as well as the Greek of Themistius' paraphrase, we have good reason to believe that either Simplicius drew upon both an earlier Greek text of Alexander and that of Themistius, or that Themistius drew upon Alexander without acknowledging his source, for Simplicius shares with Themistius the phrase ὑπὸ νοῦ καὶ κατ' ὄρεξίν ἐστιν, which Simplicius even explicitly attributes to Alexander (ὡς ὁμολογεῖ καὶ Ἀλέξανδρος), and with Alexander the argument that "if soul were abolished, all motion would be abolished" (ἀναιρουμένης ψυχῆς ἀναιροῖτο ἂν πᾶσα κίνησις, *wa-law baṭalat al-nafs ... la-baṭalat al-ḥarakāt kulluhā*).[218]

The argument we found in Avicenna's *ʿUyūn al-ḥikma* is tantamount to the second of the two reasons which Alexander, and with him apparently the entire Greek commentary tradition, offered in support of Aristotle's contention that there cannot be time

216 Suggesting to read *li-annahā* instead of *li-annahū* as in Badawī.

217 Reading ὑπὸ νοῦ with manuscript F and Schenkl's edition of Themistius' paraphrase, for ὑπὸ νοῦν in Diels' edition of Simplicius' commentary.

218 This line may even be a genuine fragment of Alexander's lost commentary on the *Physics*; cf. also the remarks by M. Rashed on *scholium* 203 in Alexander of Aphrodisias, *Commentaire perdu à la* Physique *d'Aristote*.

without soul.[219] This argument is Avicenna's main reason for why there could not be time in the absence of soul. In fact, it is even his *only* reason. As I have emphasised above, Avicenna's account of the essence of time rarely employs, and even actively trivialises, any terminology that would underscore the idea of time as the *number* of motion, instead promoting the idea of time as a magnitude. The same strategy is at play here with regard to the existence of time, for we see Avicenna disregarding Aristotle's contention that time relies on the noetic activity of numbering and counting in favour of the commentators' argument that without soul, there would be no circular motion and without circular motion, there would be no motion at all. This is also apparent in *al-Samāʿ al-ṭabīʿī* II.12, in which Avicenna argues that "the soul numbers" (*al-nafs ... taʿuddu*) the ten-ness of ten people, but it does so "through the people" (*bi-l-insān*), because "people through their existence are the cause of their number" (*al-nās li-wuǧūdihim hum asbāb wuǧūd ʿadadihim*), and so it is "through their existence that the ten-ness exists."[220] Therefore, the number of some people or stones does not rely on the numbering activity of a soul for its existence, because ten stones are ten stones through themselves, i.e., even in the absence of any soul. Accordingly, the number of motion exists even in the absence of any soul, as well.[221] This, in turn, provides further support for my above contention that Avicenna differentiates between the μέγεθος-aspect of time (which is independent from any noetic activity of the human soul) and the μέτρον-aspect (which is not), and harmonises well with Avicenna's general emphasis throughout his investigation of time precisely on the former, i.e., the μέγεθος-aspect, making time a *magnitude* of motion, for the magnitude of a motion does exist together with the motion as its quantitative concomitant, so that there is no mental activity required for the magnitude of motion to come to be.[222] It is, thus, clear that for Avicenna, time could exist even in the absence of any numbering activity of a (human) soul, even though it could not exist in the absence of soul absolutely, for without a (celestial) soul there would not be any motion, and consequently there would not be any magnitude of motion.[223]

---

219 cf. also Pines, *Studies in Islamic Atomism*, fn. 46, 57f.

220 *al-Samāʿ al-ṭabīʿī* II.12, §8, 165.5–8; cf. *al-Ḥikma al-mašriqiyya* III.11, 38.1–4.

221 cf. *al-Ilāhiyyāt* III.4, §2, 111.7–112.2; §17, 117.7–10; III.5, §§2–4, 119.6–120.8; cf. also Philoponus, *In Phys.*, 770.3–771.3; Simplicius, *In Phys.*, 765.19–766.33; cf. further Menn, "Avicenna's Metaphysics," 160f.

222 Even though mental activity is required if one wanted to *represent* the magnitude of motion as an integral whole in our mind or, of course, if that magnitude were to be numbered and measured.

223 Jeck's claim that according to Avicenna, time exists even in the absence of an individual soul is only partially correct (*Aristoteles contra Augustinum*, 111: "Avicenna spricht es nicht explizit aus, aber nach seinem Entwurf einer die Natur ordnenden Weltzeit existiert auch dann Zeit, wenn keine individuelle Seele vorhanden ist."). Jeck's claim is the result of his interpretation that Avicenna defended a "world-time," which exists outside and apart from soul ("eine außerseelische absolute Weltzeit"). As we have seen, it is true that Avicenna devalues the numbering activity of the human soul and that he does not integrate the numbering-argument we know from Aristotle's *Physics* IV.14 into his own line of thought, even though the argument had been employed by the Greek commentators. Yet, we have also seen that

We have already come across Avicenna's lengthy argumentation in *al-Ilāhiyyāt* IX.2, which has been reused word for word in *al-Naǧāt* IV.2.27–30 and partially in *al-Mabdaʾ wa-l-maʿād* I.39–41, that "the proximate mover of the heavens is neither a nature nor an intellect but a soul." There, it is established that the circular and eternal motion of the heavens is due to soul and, as we now have been told in *ʿUyūn al-ḥikma*, it is their motion, and in particular the motion of the outermost sphere, which is the cause of time. This is also the gist of an argument in *al-Naǧāt* II.2.9. There, Avicenna remarks that time, which he has defined as "the magnitude that belongs to the circular motion" (*al-miqdār li-l-ḥaraka al-mustadīra*), is not created through a temporal creation (*ġayr muḥdaṯ ḥudūṯan zamāniyyan*). Even less so is motion created and, even less again, circular motion, because this type of motion is continuous and eternal. For that matter, the being (*huwiyya*) of this magnitude, viz., time, is due to circular motion.[224] Moreover, time belongs primarily to only one circular motion (*awwalan li-šayʾ minhā*) and secondarily to all other motions, which, then, are measured in accordance (*bi-l-muṭābaqa*) with that one motion.[225]

The overall aim of the argument, once more, is reminiscent of the last chapter of the fourth book of Aristotle's *Physics*:

> εἰ οὖν τὸ πρῶτον μέτρον πάντων τῶν συγγενῶν, ἡ κυκλοφορία ἡ ὁμαλὴς μέτρον μάλιστα, ὅτι ὁ ἀριθμὸς ὁ ταύτης γνωριμώτατος. ἀλλοίωσις μὲν οὖν οὐδὲ αὔξησις οὐδὲ γένεσις οὐκ εἰσὶν ὁμαλεῖς, φορὰ δ' ἔστιν. διὸ καὶ δοκεῖ ὁ χρόνος εἶναι ἡ τῆς σφαίρας κίνησις, ὅτι ταύτῃ μετροῦνται αἱ ἄλλαι κινήσεις καὶ ὁ χρόνος ταύτῃ τῇ κινήσει.
>
> وإذ كان المقدار الأوّل به تقدّر الأشياء كلّها التي من جنس واحد فأحقّ الحركات بأن تكون المقدّر الحركة على الاستدارة المستوية لأنّ عدد هذه الحركة أعرف الأعداد. وليست حركة الاستحالة بمستوية ولا حركة النموّ ولا حركة التكوّن. فأمّا النقلة فقد تكون مستوية. ولذلك قد يظنّ بالزمان أنّه حركة الكرّة من قبل أنّ بهذه الحركة تقدّر هذه الحركات الباقية والزمان.
>
> If, now, what is first is the measure of all things of the same kind, then uniform circular motion is above all else the measure, because the number of this is the best known (γνωριμώτατος, *aʿraf*). Now, neither alteration nor increase nor coming into being can be uniform, but locomotion can be. This is why time is thought to be the motion of the sphere, because the other motions are measured by this one, and time by this motion. (*Phys.* IV.14, 223b18–23, tr. by Hardie/Gaye, modified)

Avicenna accepts a further second argument, viz., that soul is the cause of time's existence, because soul is the cause of the motion of the outermost sphere of the heavens. Thus, Avicenna does not defend a "world-time" which exists outside and apart from *any* individual soul, even though he defends what we could call a "world-time" which exists outside and apart from the numbering activity of the *human* soul (but not apart from soul as such). We shall come back to Jeck's interpretation, when we consider the Neoplatonic implications of Avicenna's account below, 509ff.

224 For the relation between *mawǧūd* and *huwiyya*, in particular in Avicenna's metaphysical discourse, cf. Bertolacci, "Some Texts of Aristotle's *Metaphysics* in the *Ilāhīyāt* of Avicenna's *Kitāb al-Šifāʾ*."

225 *al-Naǧāt* II.2.9, 230.9–232.1 ≈ *al-Ḥikma al-ʿArūḍiyya* II.2.7, 132.16–133.2; cf. *al-Samāʿ al-ṭabīʿī* II.13, §3, 168.9–169.1; *ʿUyūn al-ḥikma* II.8, 28.3–5; *al-Hidāya* II.1, 160.2–153.6; *al-Ḥikma al-mašriqiyya* III.11, 39.15–40.2.

That Aristotle introduces this contention here towards the end of his entire discussion is somewhat unexpected, for with this, he suddenly thrusts his own definition into a new direction. Up to this point, Aristotle merely spoke about time as the number of motion, and one was inclined to take it that by "motion" he meant "particular motion," i.e., each and every instance of motion. In this sense, there are various motions individually occurring in the universe and each of these occurs for some time; for example, a road trip from Munich to Berlin may take six hours, while a flight from Munich to Berlin may take only one hour. It is not entirely clear why Aristotle suddenly feels the need to provide a more universal grounding for time. To be sure, it is not surprising from a philosophical point of view, for without a universal temporal framework, a notion such as simultaneity remains incomprehensible and particular times of individual processes could not be coordinated or even compared with one another.[226] This is the reason for why Aristotle in many of his works alludes to the heavenly motion and its intimate relation to time.[227] What is surprising, though, is that Aristotle plants this essential piece of doctrine somewhere within the final, rather miscellaneous, chapter after his actual discussion of time.[228]

This afterthought from *Physics* IV.14 was influential in the subsequent philosophical tradition. We have already seen how it was integrated in the accounts of time put forth by Boethus, Alexander, and Ibn ʿAdī.[229] In addition, many philosophers even integrated this afterthought from *Physics* IV.14 into the canonical definition of time given in *Physics* IV.11 and, consequently, "quoted" Aristotle's definition of time as "the number of the motion of the sphere."[230] This is particularly true of the Arabic philosophical tradition and may once more be explained through the authority of Alexander as the prime expositor of Peripatetic doctrine, for in his treatise on time we read the following:

ونقول إنّ الزمان إنّما صار عدد حركة الفلك دون غيرها من الحركات لأنّه لا حركة أسرع منها وإنّما يُعَدّ الشيء ويُذرَع ويُكال بما هو أصغر منه.

226 cf., however, *Physics* IV.12, 220b5f.

227 cf. *Phys.* VIII.1, 251b10–14; *Cael.* II.4, 287a23–26; *De gen. et corr.* II.10, 337a22–25; *Met.* Λ.6, 1071b6–11.

228 q.v. also fn. 83 above, 454.

229 q.v. above, 451ff.

230 This definition may be given with or without an explicit reference to the prior and posterior; cf. Aetius Arabus, *Die Vorsokratiker in arabischer Überlieferung*, 20.14 (this Aristotelian definition is not found in the Greek of Ps.-Plutarchus' *Placita Philosophorum*); al-Kindī, *Kitāb al-Kindī fī l-ibāna ʿan al-ʿilla al-fāʿila al-qarība li-l-kawn wa-l-fasād*, 220.11; Iḫwān al-Ṣafāʾ, *Rasāʾil Iḫwān al-Ṣafāʾ* XV.13, 43.6; al-Fārābī (?), *Kitāb al-Ǧamʿ bayna raʾyay al-ḥakīmayn Aflāṭun al-ilāhī wa-Arisṭāṭālīs*, 63.18–64.1; Ibn Suwār ibn al-Ḫammār, *Maqāla fī anna dalīl Yaḥyā al-Naḥwī ʿalā ḥadaṯ al-ʿālam awlā bi-l-qabūl min dalīl al-mutakallimīn aṣlan*, 247.10f.; al-Tawḥīdī, *al-Muqābasāt*, §73, 278.16f.; Ms. Marsh 539, §8, 66.30f. (the paragraph, page, and line numbers follow Wakelnig's edition); Averroes, *Faṣl al-maqāl*, 38.1; Nāṣer-e Ḫosrow, *Ketāb-e Ǧāmʿ al-ḥikmatayn* 5, 90.18–91.1; *Resāle-ye ḥekmatī*, 584.2; al-Rāzī, *al-Maṭālib al-ʿāliya min al-ʿilm al-ilāhī* V.4, 51.5; cf. also the more recent formulation in al-Zarkān, *Faḫr al-Dīn al-Rāzī wa-ārāʾuhū*, 452.

> We say that time is only (*innamā*) the number of the motion of the sphere (*ʿadad ḥarakat al-falak*) and not of any other motion, because there is no motion faster than it and something is numbered, measured, and compared only by what is smaller than it. (*Maqālat al-Iskandar al-Afrūdīsī fī l-zamān*, 21.1–3)[231]

In *Physics* IV.14, Aristotle's reason that the motion of the sphere should above all be the reference for time was that it is that whose number is "best known" (γνωριμώτατος, *aʿraf*). Alexander, however, provides a reason precisely for why the number of that motion is "best known," viz., because it is the fastest of all motions. With this, Alexander imports a principle that Aristotle had formulated in *Metaphysics* I.1 – and elsewhere in *De caelo* II.4 – where we read that motions are known "by the simple motion and the fastest" (τῇ ἁπλῇ κινήσει καὶ τῇ ταχίστῃ, *fī l-ḥaraka al-mabsūṭa wa-l-sarīʿa*), and so in astronomy, Aristotle continues, it is the motion of the heavens (τὴν κίνησιν ... τοῦ οὐρανοῦ, *ḥaraka al-samāʾ*) which is the principle and measure, because it is most uniform and swift.[232] So, it seems that Alexander may have found an apt justification for why that piece of doctrine at the end of Aristotle's discussion of time actually provides the most adequate understanding of time.

The subsequent tradition, then, followed Alexander apparently unanimously in defining time as the number of the motion of the outermost sphere. One may surmise that the explicit reference to the motion of the heavens may have had the further advantage of bringing Aristotle's definition of time in an ever more harmonious congruence with Plato's account, for in the *Timaeus*, Plato had written the following:

> εἰκὼ δ' ἐπενόει κινητόν τινα αἰῶνος ποιῆσαι, καὶ διακοσμῶν ἅμα οὐρανὸν ποιεῖ μένοντος αἰῶνος ἐν ἑνὶ κατ' ἀριθμὸν ἰοῦσαν αἰώνιον εἰκόνα, τοῦτον ὃν δὴ χρόνον ὠνομάκαμεν.
>
> So, he [sc. the Demiurge] took thought to make a moving likeness of eternity (εἰκὼ ... κινητόν τινα αἰῶνος) and, at the same time that he ordered the heavens, he made, of eternity that remains in unity (μένοντος αἰῶνος ἐν ἑνί), an eternal likeness moving according to number (κατ' ἀριθμὸν ἰοῦσαν αἰώνιον εἰκόνα) – that to which we have given the name "time." (*Tim.* 37d5–7, tr. by Cornford, modified)[233]

All this has become a Peripatetic commonplace in both the Greek and the Arabic tradition, and so it is no surprise that we read, for example, in the *Institutio physica* of Proclus (d. 485) that "time is the number of the motion of the heavenly bodies" (Χρόνος ἐστὶν ἀριθμὸς κινήσεως οὐρανίων σωμάτων) nor is it a surprise to find traces of the same idea in Avicenna.

It has, then, become clear that for Avicenna, time is not only ultimately caused by soul, we also learned that it is specifically due to the soul that moves the outermost

231 This claim can be found frequently in Alexander's brief treatise, e.g., at 20.7–8, 13, 21.23–22.1.

232 *Metaphysics* I.1, 1053a8–12; cf. *Cael.* II.4, 287a23–26.

233 cf. the corresponding passage in the Arabic version of Galen's paraphrase of the *Timaeus* (*Compendium Timaei Platonis*, 8.6–9); for a translation, cf. Adamson, "Galen and al-Rāzī on Time," 6.

heavenly sphere in a uniform, equal, and – most importantly – circular motion. This motion, then, is what brings about the existence of time. Yet, how exactly does this happen? What is it about the eternal, circular motion of the outermost sphere that brings about a magnitude which is the before and after through itself, viz., time?

Already in the tenth chapter of the second book of *al-Samāʿ al-ṭabīʿī*, i.e., before his actual discussion of time, Avicenna hinted at the preeminent status of the outermost sphere. Although this chapter is devoted to a report, and rejection, of previous views and various disagreements about the subject of time, Avicenna thought that it would be "appropriate (*awlā*) for us, first, to point out time with regard to existence."[234] Then, he engages with arguments that time is either the same as motion or the same as the motion of the sphere, or that it even is the very sphere itself. He rejects all these claims with arguments we know from Aristotle, asserting that, for example, motion cannot be identical with time, because motion can be faster and slower, whereas time cannot.[235] For Avicenna, these are "the early views before the maturity of wisdom" (*qabla naḍǧ al-ḥikma*).[236] Upon this, he adds the following:

وحكم الحركة الأولى الفلكية هذا الحكم بعينه فإنّها يصحّ أن يقال فيها إنّها أسرع الحركات لأنّها تقطع مع قطع الحركة الأخرى أعظم ... وهذه المعية تدلّ على أمر غير الحركتين بل تدلّ على معنى ينسبان كلتاهما إليه ويتساويان فيه ويختلفان في المسافة. وذلك المعنى ليس ذات أحدهما لأنّ الثاني لا يشارك الآخر في ذاته ويشاركه في الأمر الذي هما فيه معاً. ويمكن من هذا الموضع أن يظهر فساد قول مَن جعل الأوقات أعراضاً تُوقَّت لأغراض.

The judgement about the first spherical motion is the same as this one, and so it is correct to say about it that it is the fastest of motions, because it covers, [compared] with the traversal of another motion, a larger [distance] ... This togetherness (*al-maʿiyya*) [between two motions] points towards something different from the two motions (*amr ġayr al-ḥarakatayn*) and, indeed, points towards a meaning (*maʿnan*) to which both of them are related and with respect to which the two are equal, while differing in [view of] the distance [they have traversed]. That meaning is not the essence of one of the two [motions], because the second [motion] does not itself share in the other [motion], but it shares in something in which both [motions] are [sharing] together. From this vantage point, it is possible to see the falsity (*fasād*) of the assertion of him who made moments (*awqāt*) certain events appointed as moments (*tuwaqqatu*) for [other] events. (*al-Samāʿ al-ṭabīʿī* II.10, §§9–10, 152.17–153.4, tr. by McGinnis, modified)

What Avicenna tells us, here, is that, in order to account for the simultaneity of occurring motions, we require something in addition to these motions. If we were to say that the cock crowed when the sun rose over the horizon, then we could not understand the "when" which conjoins both events in our sentence without a reference to some coordinating principle that explains the simultaneity and togetherness (*al-maʿiyya*) inherent in the conjunction "when." So, the "when" points toward a framework not unlike a timeline on which we, first, pin the crowing cock and, second, the rising sun,

---

234 *al-Samāʿ al-ṭabīʿī* II.10, §7, 151.19.

235 cf. *al-Samāʿ al-ṭabīʿī* II.10, §§8–9, 152.1–17; *Phys.* IV.10, 218b9–20.

236 *al-Samāʿ al-ṭabīʿī* II.10, §8, 152.11.

just so that we realise that they are in some way "together" (*maʿan*), because one is actually pinned on top of the other (as opposed to one being pinned after the other, which would illustrate that one event is before the other rather than pointing out their simultaneity).

Mentioning the heavenly sphere seems to be a deliberate decision on Avicenna's part for two reasons. One reason is Avicenna's engagement with earlier claims that identified time with motion, among which we find those ancient views already discussed by Aristotle. Yet, it is also apparent that Avicenna additionally targets another earlier, but not ancient, conception of time, i.e., one that arose within the Islamic milieu and which became the most widespread rival notion of his time. This position is one also reported by Abū l-Ḥasan al-Ašʿarī (d. 324/935-36) in his *Maqālāt al-islāmiyyīn*, where it is ascribed to the Muʿtazilite theologian Abū ʿAlī al-Ǧubbāʾī (d. 303/915-16):

واختلفوا في الوقت ... وقال قائلون: الوقت هو ما تُوقّته للشيء. فإذا قلت: آتيك قدوم زيد فقد جعلت قدوم زيد وقتاً لمجيئك. وزعموا أنّ الأوقات هي حركات الفلك لأنّ الله عزّ وجلّ وقّتها للأشياء، هذا قول الجبّائي.

> [People] differ about time (*al-waqt*) ... Some say: "Time is whatever you appoint as the time for something (*mā tuwaqqituhū li-l-šayʾ*). So, when you say 'I come to you when Zayd arrives,' then you have made the arrival of Zayd a time for your own coming." They claim that the times (*al-awqāt*) are the motions of the sphere (*al-awqāt hiya ḥarakāt al-falak*), because God – strong and exalted is He – appointed them as moments for the things. This is the assertion of al-Ǧubbāʾī. (al-Ašʿarī, *Maqālāt al-islāmiyyīn*, 443.1–6)

In al-Ǧubbāʾī's account, times – or perhaps better: "moments" (*awqāt*, sg. *waqt*) – are concurrences of events.[237] When one makes Zayd's arrival the moment for one's own arrival, then the concurrence of both people's arrival is *the time* of their joint arrival. Thus, if someone else were to ask: "When did you arrive?," then the answer "We arrived when Zayd did" is sufficiently precise and accurate. It might prove to be more intricate, though, if one were to go on and ask: "Well, and when did Zayd arrive?" The position put forth in al-Ašʿarī's testimony suggests a possible answer even to this question. Since we are told that God has decreed that the heavenly motions be times and moments for events and happenings that occur on the earth, one could settle the matter definitively by saying "Zayd arrived when the sun had reached its highest point – and we arrived when he did." According to al-Ǧubbāʾī, then, temporality is a mixture of the notion of

237 It is not so clear how one should best translate the term *waqt* in these contexts. On the one hand, it seems to be appropriate to translate it simply as "moment." On the other hand, the term *zamān*, which in philosophical contexts is commonly used for "time," much less frequently seems to occur in kalām discussions, in which we nonetheless find similar temporal phenomena being discussed with recourse to the notion *waqt*. On the whole, then, it appears that the concept of *waqt* in kalām texts is analogous to the concept of *zamān* in philosophical texts (while of course being embedded in an entirely different metaphysical framework). At any rate, a *waqt* designates the "time spot" or "moment" of an existent or an event in the temporal grid of kalām atomist ontology; cf. also Wolfson, *The Philosophy of the Kalam*, ch. 6; McGinnis, "The Topology of Time"; Dhanani, *The Physical Theory of Kalām*.

concurrence, on the one hand, and the claim that time, in the final analysis, is identical with the motion of the sphere, on the other.[238]

For Avicenna, though, this position is confused, as it entails a non-acknowledged reference to something different from both sublunary and concurring heavenly events: “what is understood by the togetherness is undoubtedly not what is understood by either” but is something in addition to them – and this “something” (*amr*), then, or this “meaning” (*maʿnan*), is time. Both events may happen in time, but neither of them is time. Thus, Avicenna takes the concurrence of events, which is so essential to al-Ǧubbāʾī’s position, for no more than a pointer that hints towards the existence of time as well as a clarification that, whatever time is, it undoubtedly must be something different from motion, and so cannot be the motion of the sphere itself.

The critical engagement with previous doctrines, and in particular with the one attributed to al-Ǧubbāʾī, is one reason that Avicenna, in this context, alludes to the heavenly motion. The second reason is that for Avicenna, as well, the heavenly motion is essential for understanding the existence of time. Although Avicenna does not mention the heavenly motion again anywhere in the discussion of time in chapter eleven or the account of the now in chapter twelve, he does return to the subject of the circular motion of the heavenly sphere in chapter thirteen, when he sets out for a “solution of the doubts raised about time,” as the chapter title has it, and in particular those doubts that are concerned with its existence.[239] There, Avicenna reminds the reader that it has been demonstrated to us (*tabarhana lanā*) that time is dependent upon motion (*mutaʿalliq bi-l-ḥāraka*) and that it is a disposition of it (*hayʾa lahā*). Yet, he immediately restricts this claim by saying that time does not depend (*lā yataʿallaqu*) upon motions that have a beginning and an end (*ibtidāʾ wa-ntihāʾ*):

> نعم إذا وُجِد الزمان بحركة على صفة يصلح أن يتعلّق بها وجود الزمان تُقدَّر بها سائر الحركات وهذه الحركة حركة يصحّ عليها الاستمرار ولا يتحدّد لها بالفعل أطراف.
>
> Indeed, when time exists by a motion having a certain description (*bi-ḥaraka ʿalā ṣifa*), it is correct [to say] that the existence of time is dependent upon it and that the rest of the motions will be measured by it. This motion is a motion of which it is true [to say that it has] uninterrupted permanence (*al-istimrār*) and that it is not actually determined by limits (*lā yataḥaddadu lahā bi-l-fiʿl aṭrāf*). (*al-Samāʿ al-ṭabīʿī* II.13, §2, 168.7–9)[240]

With this statement, Avicenna answers an obvious question, perhaps the same question which prompted Aristotle to introduce the motion of the outermost sphere as the ultimate motion of which time is the number. This question asks whether there exist

238 cf. also van Ess, *Theologie und Gesellschaft*, vol. 3, 242f.

239 There is one exception: in *al-Samāʿ al-ṭabīʿī* II.11, §2, 156.16, when Avicenna identified time as the magnitude of motion, he *en passant* specified motion as “positional motion” (*al-ḥaraka al-waḍʿiyya*); cf. *al-Ḥikma al-mašriqiyya* III.11, 32.22f.

240 cf. *al-Ḥikma al-mašriqiyya* III.11, 39.12–14.

multiple, perhaps even infinitely many, times: to each and every motion that happens anywhere one individual time. This would leave us with a vast number of uncoordinated times whose actual relation to one another is far from being clear.[241] Avicenna's answer to this is that there is one motion that is special in such a way that all other motions are ultimately measured by this motion *and* the time which comes-to-be from it. Yet, saying this instantly provokes a new and obvious objection:

فإن قال قائل: أرأيت إن لم تُوجَد تلك الحركة لكان يفقد الزمان حتّى تكون حركات أخرى غيرها بلا تقدّم ولا تأخّر؟

So, if it is said: "Do you think, if that motion did not exist, that then[242] time would be lost, so that other motions different from it would be without priority and posteriority?" (*al-Samāʿ al-ṭabīʿī* II.13, §3, 168.9f., tr. by McGinnis, modified)[243]

Avicenna answers this objection with a twofold strategy. First, he argues that without "this motion," viz., the circular motion of the outermost sphere, there would not be any other motion at all, because any subsequent circular as well as sublunar rectilinear motion could not exist in the absence of this first circular motion. Avicenna refers to a subsequent discussion, probably in *al-Samāʿ al-ṭabīʿī* III.14 or *al-Samāʾ wa-l-ʿālam* 4, in which he will explain that the directions of natural – and that is: rectilinear – motions are determined by a body at the periphery which moves in a circular motion, thus specifying the direction and the extremities of up and down.[244] Without this circular motion, there would not be any directionality nor any natural motion and, therefore, also no forced motion and, ultimately, no motion at all.[245]

So, Avicenna argues that without a circular motion, no other motion could occur in time, because there would be no other *motion*. In the second part of his reply, he argues that this is also true, because without a circular motion there would be no *time*:

فالزمان إذن وجوده متعلّق بحركة واحدة يقدّرها ويقدّر أيضاً سائر الحركات التي يستحيل أن تُوجَد دون حركة الجسم الفاعل بحركته للزمان ... وذلك كالمقدار الموجود في جسم يقدّره ويقدّر ما يحاذيه ويوازيه.

241 This will become one of Faḫr al-Dīn's most favourite objections against all accounts that make time supervenient on motion, such as the ones by Aristotle, Avicenna, and Abū l-Barakāt; cf. Adamson and Lammer, "Fakhr al-Dīn al-Rāzī's Platonist Account of the Essence of Time."

242 Reading *la-kāna* with Mss. Leiden or. 4 and or. 84 as well as Zāyid for *a-kānā* in McGinnis and Āl Yāsīn.

243 cf. *al-Ḥikma al-mašriqiyya* III.11, 39.15f. It is clear that the objection is formulated from an entirely un-Avicennian perspective, thus also using un-Avicennian vocabulary.

244 cf. *al-Samāʿ al-ṭabīʿī* III.14, §§1–7, 251.4–255.6; *al-Samāʾ wa-l-ʿālam* 4, 26.13f.; 28.8–11; cf. also *Cael.* I.2, 268b11–269b17; II.4, 286b10–287b21; IV.1, 307b28–308a33.

245 As Avicenna admits, this is not evident by itself, because we may be deceived to imagine a finite rectilinear motion without any circular motion. Yet, he writes, we are not concerned with what can and cannot be imagined or supposed but with what is correct in existence (*fī-mā yaṣiḥḥu fī l-wuǧūd*; *al-Samāʿ al-ṭabīʿī* II.13, §3, 168.16f.); cf. *al-Ḥikma al-mašriqiyya* III.11, 39.23f.

> So, the existence of time, therefore, is dependent upon a single motion (*muta'alliq bi-ḥaraka wāḥida*) which it [sc. time] measures and, also, the rest of the motions whose existence would be impossible without the motion of the body which, through its motion, is productive of time (*ḥarakat al-ǧism al-fā'il bi-ḥarakatihī li-l-zamān*)[246] ... That is like the magnitude existing in some body that measures [both] it and whatever is parallel and juxtaposed to it. (*al-Samā' al-ṭabī'ī* II.13, §3, 168.18–169.1, tr. by McGinnis, modified)[247]

Time is dependent upon one single motion.[248] This motion is the one without which all other motions could not exist. As we have just been told, this one motion is the motion which gives all motions their direction. Thus, the motion in question is the circular motion of the outermost sphere, whose body, Avicenna adds, produces time through its motion (*al-fā'il bi-ḥarakatihī li-l-zamān*), as he writes here in *al-Samā' al-ṭabī'ī*, and preserves time (*yaḥfaẓu al-zamān*), as he remarks in *al-Samā' wa-l-'ālam*.[249] It is this motion which is the cause of the existence of time, while soul is the cause for this motion thereby being the cause of the cause of time (*'illat 'illat al-zamān*), as Avicenna put it in the *'Uyūn al-ḥikma*.[250] The magnitude and measure of this motion, i.e., its time, is that against which other motions are measured by means of juxtaposition, i.e., by comparison and by "holding" them against it. This is similar to what we do, when we want to know the size of a box, and take a yardstick and hold it against the sides of the box as parallel as possible, in order to get an exact result. The motion of the outermost sphere is the infinite yardstick of time and other motions happen against this background, thus being parallel and juxtaposed to a segment of the infinite temporal magnitude of this eternal motion. Avicenna proceeds:

والحركة اتّصالها ليس إلّا لأنّ المسافة متّصلة ولأنّ اتّصال المسافة يصير علّة لوجود تقدّم وتأخّر في الحركة تكون الحركة بهما علّة لوجود عدد لها هو الزمان.

> The continuity of motion is only because of the continuity of distance, and because of distance's continuity, it becomes a cause for the existence of priority and posteriority in motion (*yaṣīru 'illa li-wuǧūd taqaddum wa-ta'aḫḫur fī l-ḥaraka*); through these, the motion is a cause for the existence of number which belongs to it – and this is time. (*al-Samā' al-ṭabī'ī* II.13, §3, 169.3f., tr. by McGinnis, modified)[251]

---

246 Reading *li-l-zamān* with Mss. Leiden or. 4 and or. 84 as well as Zāyid for *al-zamān* in McGinnis and Āl Yāsīn.

247 cf. *al-Ḥikma al-mašriqiyya* III.11, 39.24–40.2.

248 cf. the brief remark in Ps.-al-Fārābī's *'Uyūn al-masā'il*, §15, 91.17f.

249 *al-Samā' wa-l-'ālam* 4, 28.8f.; cf. *al-Išārāt wa-l-tanbīhāt* II.6.16, 165.1f.

250 *'Uyūn al-ḥikma* II.8, 28.18; q.v. above, 492.

251 cf. *al-Samā' al-ṭabī'ī* II.13, §4, 169.13f., *al-Ḥikma al-mašriqiyya* III.11, 40.8f.; cf. also *al-Samā' al-ṭabī'ī* II.12, §8, 165.8f.: "If there were no motion *qua* what it makes within the distance in terms of limiting points of priority and posteriority, there would exist no number to time" (tr. by McGinnis, modified); cf. further Themistius, *In Phys.*, 145.24–146.27.

In order to understand this passage about the coming-to-be of time, we need to remind ourselves of the Aristotelian principle that motion follows (ἀκολουθεῖ, *yatbaʿu*) distance and that time, in turn, follows motion.[252] In the above passage, Avicenna employs this principle and states that the continuity of a traversed distance is what guarantees that the motion which occurs over this distance is likewise continuous. This, however, is not all. As we said, the prior and posterior positions within the distance are ordered but lack direction. When a motion occurs over an ordered distance, motion adopts the prior and posterior positions, endows them with directionality by designating one position as a beginning and one position as an end, and, passing over the distance, becomes itself essentially ordered by what is prior and what is posterior. The prior and posterior of motion, thus, is the result of two things: first, the positions within a continuous distance; and second, the directionality instituted by a motion that passes over these positions from a beginning to an end, with the result that a moving thing is essentially such that its being at one spatial position is prior to its being at another spatial position. It is the continuous motion over a continuous distance which "becomes a cause for existence of priority and posteriority in motion" (*yaṣīru ʿilla li-wuǧūd taqaddum wa-taʾaḫḫur fī l-ḥaraka*).

In addition, by virtue of the prior and posterior, the motion also is the cause of time. Time was defined as the magnitude of motion when motion is differentiated into the prior and posterior. Motion has a magnitude which maps all the prior and posterior states of a motion in relation to a distance. Without motion, there would be no *magnitude of motion*, and it is this magnitude which is time. This has already been the theme of a passage quoted above, in which Avicenna wrote – in a fashion reminiscent of Boethus, Alexander, and especially Ibn ʿAdī – that "motion numbers time in that it makes time's number exist, and this is the prior and posterior."[253] What is more, without the prior and posterior of motion there would be no *number of motion*, and it is this number which is time. The prior and posterior of motion correspond not only to certain earlier and later positions within the distance, they correspond also to before and after moments of time. Yet, it would be incorrect to say that for Avicenna, the before and after of time is caused by the prior and posterior of motion, as we have seen.[254] What we must say is that time as such is that which "through itself" (*li-ḏātihī*) is ordered by the before and after, but it could not be that which through itself is the before and after if there were no motion that is essentially differentiated by the prior and posterior. As a magnitude, time is the result of the motion over a distance which, through its prior and posterior states, caused the existence of the magnitude of motion which is time. Consequently, it is on account of motion's essential ordering by what is

252 q.v. fn. 53 above, 444f.

253 *al-Samāʿ al-ṭabīʿī* II.12, §7, 165.4f.; cf. *al-Ḥikma al-mašriqiyya* III.11, 37.23–38.1; q.v. above, 460.

254 q.v. above, 481f.

prior and posterior that time comes-to-be as that which is through itself the before and after.[255]

The cause for the existence of time is, thus, motion – precisely: that of the outermost sphere – insofar as it is essentially ordered, or differentiated, by the prior and the posterior, i.e., insofar as it occurs over a continuous distance. This is Avicenna's position, and he expends considerable effort in making this as clear as possible. In fact, there may be no place anywhere in Avicenna's philosophical works where he is so insistent and adamant as here in *al-Samāʿ al-ṭabīʿī* II.13 regarding the cause for the existence of time, for he repeats his position over and over again just to ensure that everyone understands it, as the following compilation of passages illustrates:

> وأمّا اتّصال الزمان فعلته القريبة اتّصال الحركة بالمسافة لا اتّصال المسافة وحدها فإنّ اتّصال المسافة وحدها ما لم تكن حركة موجودة لا تُوجِب اتّصال الزمان وحدها ... بل يجب أن تكون علّة الزمان اتّصال المسافة بتوسّط الحركة ... وليس هذا الاتّصال علّة لصيرورة الزمان متّصلاً بل لايجاد الزمان فإنّه ليس الزمان شيئاً يعرض الاتّصال الخاصّ به بل هو نفس ذلك الاتّصال ... نقول إنّ اتّصالاً هو سبب لوجود اتّصال لا أنّه سبب لصيرورة ذلك الشيء اتّصالاً فإنّه اتّصال بذاته ... ونقول إنّا نجعل الاتّصال المسافي سبباً للزمان ولكنّ لا مطلقاً بل من حيث صار لحركة.
>
> The proximate cause of the continuity of time is the continuity of motion through the distance (*ittiṣāl al-ḥaraka bi-l-masāfa*) and not the continuity of the distance alone, for as long as there is no motion, the continuity of distance does not necessitate the continuity of time ... Indeed, it is necessary that the cause of time[256] is the distance through the intermediacy of the motion (*al-masāfa bi-tawassuṭ al-ḥaraka*) ... This continuity is not the cause of time's becoming continuous but for making time exist,[257] for time is not something to which a specific continuity just accidentally happens, rather, it is itself that continuity ... [Quite generally] we say that a continuity is a cause for the existence of a continuity, but not that it is a cause for that thing's becoming a continuity, for it is by itself a continuity ... We say that we make the spatial continuity a cause for time, yet not absolutely but only insofar as [it] becomes [a cause] through motion. (*al-Samāʿ al-ṭabīʿī* II.13, §§4–5, 169.13–170.10, tr. by McGinnis, modified)

The remote cause for the existence time, as we already know, is soul. The proximate cause (*ʿillatuhū l-qarība*), however, is motion over a distance or, alternatively, a distance when traversed by motion. Distance alone, despite being more fundamental than motion and time, insofar as it is that upon which both motion and time follow (ἀκολουθεῖ, *yatbaʿu*) or that to which they conform (*yuṭābiqu*), cannot cause the existence of time, for only motion and distance together bring about an ordered sequence of priority and posteriority. It is the continuity of distance, mediated through a motion occurring over

---

255 Other than that, the prior and posterior of motion also numbers the motion insofar as it provides the unit through which the motion can be measured; cf. *al-Samāʿ al-ṭabīʿī* II.12, §7, 164.16–165.5; *al-Ḥikma al-mašriqiyya* III.11, 37.13–38.1; cf. also cf. *Phys.* IV.11, 219a22–30; Philoponus, *In Phys.*, 721.15–19.

256 Reading *ʿillat al-zamān* with Mss. Leiden or. 4 and or. 84 as well as Zāyid for *ʿillat ittiṣāl al-zamān* in McGinnis and Āl Yāsīn.

257 Reading *li-iğād* with McGinnis and Āl Yāsīn for *li-ttiḥād* in Zāyid.

it, that is the cause for "making time exist" (*ʿilla … li-iğād al-zamān*).[258] In the above passages we see that Avicenna even corrects himself to be ever more articulate. When he writes that distance and motion are the cause for the continuity of time, he does not mean that they merely cause time's continuity, while its existence may be caused by something else. It is rather so that they cause the existence of time as continuous, for time is essentially continuous, i.e., it is continuous as soon as it exists and does not require an additional cause for becoming continuous. Finally, when Avicenna feels that he could not make it any clearer, he almost pleadingly addresses the reader and provides a conclusion:

> فافهم الآن أنّ اتّصال المسافة من حيث هي للحركة علّة لوجود ذات الزمان الذي هو بذاته متّصل أو اتّصال لا أنّه علّة لكون ذات الزمان متّصلاً فذلك أمر لا علّة له. فبهذا يصحّ أنّ الزمان أمر عارض للحركة وليس بجنس ولا فصل لها ولا سبب من أسبابها بل أمر لازم لها يقدّر جميعها.
>
> Do understand now that the continuity of distance insofar as it is through motion a cause for the existence of the essence of time (*ʿillat wuğūd ḏāt al-zamān*),[259] which is by itself continuous or a continuity, is not a cause for time's essence being continuous, for that is something that has no cause (*lā ʿilla lahū*)! So, by this, it is true [to say] that time is something that happens through motion and is neither its genus nor a difference for it nor one of its causes. It is rather something concomitant to it which measures[260] its [sc. motion's] entirety. (*al-Samāʿ al-ṭabīʿī* II.13, §5, 170.11–13, tr. by McGinnis, modified)[261]

Time, being ontologically subordinate to motion while at the same time providing all motion (other than the motion of the outermost sphere) with a single unified temporal framework, comes into existence through the prior and posterior of a motion that occurs over a continuous distance, viz., the eternal circular uniform motion of the outermost sphere. This view resembles closely a remark we find in Themistius' paraphrase of Aristotle's *Physics*. The context of this remark is Themistius' criticism of Galen's objection that Aristotle's definition of time is circular, because one supposedly cannot understand τὸ πρότερον καὶ ὕστερον without recourse to time and temporality, as Galen argued.[262] Themistius counters Galen's objection as follows:

> ἀλλ' ἰστέον, ὅτι τὸ πρότερον καὶ τὸ ὕστερον ἐν κινήσει οὐ διὰ τὸν χρόνον τὸ μὲν πρότερόν ἐστιν, τὸ δὲ ὕστερον, ἀλλὰ αὐτὸ μᾶλλον ποιεῖ τὸ ἐν χρόνῳ πρότερον καὶ ὕστερον, γίνεται δὲ ἐκ τοῦ κατὰ μέγεθος καὶ τὴν θέσιν, παρ' οὗ καὶ τὸ συνεχὲς ἔχει· καὶ τοῦτο διαρρήδην φησὶν Ἀριστοτέλης· τὸ δὴ πρότερον τε καὶ ὕστερον ἐν τόπῳ πρῶτόν ἐστιν, ἐνταῦθα μὲν τῇ θέσει· ἐπειδὴ δὲ ἐν τῷ μεγέθει, ἀνάγκη καὶ ἐν κινήσει.

---

258 cf. also *al-Ilāhiyyāt* III.4, §2, 111.7–112.2.

259 Reading *ʿillat wuğūd ḏāt al-zamān* with Mss. Leiden or. 4 and or. 84 as well as Zāyid for *ʿillat wuğūd al-zamān* in McGinnis and Āl Yāsīn.

260 Reading *yuqaddiru* with McGinnis and Āl Yāsīn for *bi-qadr* in Zāyid.

261 cf. *al-Samāʿ al-ṭabīʿī* III.9, §§6–7, 221.10–222.18.

262 q.v. above, 462ff.

> One must understand that the prior and the posterior in motion is not through time one prior and the other posterior but rather itself produces the prior and posterior in time (ἀλλὰ αὐτὸ μᾶλλον ποιεῖ τὸ ἐν χρόνῳ πρότερον καὶ ὕστερον) – it is generated from [the prior and posterior] according to magnitude and position through which it also has continuity. This is said so explicitly by Aristotle: "The prior and posterior, then, is primarily in place and there it is through position. Since it is in the magnitude, it is necessarily also in motion." (Themistius, *In Phys.*, 149.7–13)[263]

Here, Themistius distinguishes the prior and posterior in motion (ἐν κινήσει) from the prior and posterior in time (ἐν χρόνῳ) making the former a cause for the latter. This comes close to Avicenna's later distinction between the prior and posterior (which is in motion) and the before and after (which is in time). Galen, however, argued that the prior and posterior is primarily in time. Responding to Galen, both Themistius and Avicenna blame him for not having understood the definition properly.[264] What apparently escaped Galen's attention is the intimate relation Aristotle has ascribed to motion, on the one hand, and the prior and posterior, on the other:

> ἔστι δὲ τὸ πρότερον καὶ ὕστερον ἐν τῇ κινήσει ὅ μέν ποτε ὂν κίνησις [ἐστιν]· τὸ μέντοι εἶναι αὐτῷ ἕτερον καὶ οὐ κίνησις.
>
> وأيضاً فإنّ المتقدّم والمتأخّر في الحركة أمّا من جهة ما هما في وقت ما فإنّهما حركة وأمّا في الآنية فإنّهما شيء آخر غير الحركة.
>
> The prior and posterior in motion are that, whatever it is by being which motion is; yet its being is different and is not motion. (*Phys.* IV.11, 219a19–21)[265]

The immediate context of this passage attributes the prior and posterior primarily to place (ἐν τόπῳ πρῶτόν ἐστιν, *awwalan fī l-makān*) and derivatively to time (καὶ ἐν χρόνῳ ἔστιν, *wa-fī l-zamān ayḍan*). Nonetheless, the prior and posterior is a vital and indispensable feature for motion, because motion occurs over spatial distance. In this way, the prior and posterior is assimilated and adopted by motion and, thereby, becomes "that, whatever it is by being which motion is" (ὃ μέν ποτε ὂν κίνησις [ἐστιν], *min ǧiha mā humā fī waqt mā … ḥaraka*).[266] Themistius took this to mean that the prior

263 cf. *Phys.* IV.11, 219a14–18. My translation follows Urmson, who translates from Simplicius' quotation of Themistius' paraphrase (718.19–22), instead of Todd, who takes τὸ ἐν χρόνῳ πρότερον καὶ ὕστερον to be the subject, and not the object, of ποιεῖ. Both Todd and Urmson, however, have a different understanding of the quotation from Aristotle. Moreover, Hussey translated ἐνταῦθα μὲν τῇ θέσει as "there, it is by convention," which, though of course possible, does not seem to be right.

264 It is interesting to note the similarity between Themistius' use of ἰστέον here and Avicenna's expression *lam yafhum hāḏā* in *al-Samāʿ al-ṭabīʿī* II.11, §3, 157.7.

265 cf. also *Phys.* IV.11, 219b21–25.

266 For Ross' reasons to excise ἐστιν, cf. his comments in *Physics*, *ad loc.* I shall not engage in a discussion about the precise meaning of Aristotle's phrase ὃ δέ ποτε ὄν ἐστι. For various views about this, cf. Coope's discussion in the appendix of her book *Time for Aristotle*, 173–177, and the remarks by McGinnis in his dissertation *Time and Time Again*, 161f. as well as the comments by Themistius (*In Phys.*, 150.3–7), Simplicius (*In Phys.*, 712.24–26, 721.30f.), and Philoponus (*In Phys.*, 721.26f., 726.27f.); cf.

and the posterior belongs to motion as such, so that motion, through the prior and the posterior, produces (ποιεῖ) time. Avicenna, as we now have come to know, thinks along the same lines.[267] Motion is, as it were, the prior and posterior itself, just as time is the before and after itself. This is what Galen did not understand, this is why the definition of time is not circular, and this is also how motion causes the existence of time – and all this has its roots in Aristotle's *Physics*.[268]

We have also already come to know that it is not just each and every motion that brings about time, such that there would be as many times as there are motions each having its own particular time. It is the circular motion of the outermost sphere which brings about time through its even and eternal revolution at the circumference. It is *its* prior and posterior that causes time to exist. All motions are compared with *this* motion and, thus, are measured by the time *this* motion produces. Avicenna states that there is a difference between saying that "time is a magnitude for all motion" (*al-zamān miqdār li-kull ḥaraka*) and saying that "its being depends on all motion" (*anniyyatuhū mutaʿalliqa bi-kull ḥaraka*) – and it is, of course, the former which is correct, as Avicenna explains.[269] Time, then, is the *single* magnitude by which each and every motion's extension can be measured. This measurement, as has been noted, is achieved through juxtaposition. It is because all motions happen in parallel to the one eternal motion of the outermost sphere, as it were, that all motions have a magnitude or share a part of the infinite magnitude produced by the outermost sphere. Time depends on motion for its existence, but it does not depend on all motions – still, time is a single magnitude for all motions.

6.4 Avicenna's Neoplatonic Peripateticism

It is apparent, now, that Avicenna argues for a universal time, i.e., for a single time which is common to all motions, which encompasses all motions, and which coordinates all motions. This time is through itself the before and after, i.e., it is the ultimate source for temporal notions that characterise states, motions, and events as "before" or "after," thus making their successive order intelligible. There is no state, motion, or event that is through itself characterised as "before" or "after," for example, there is nothing

now also the remarks by M. Rashed in his commentary on al-Nawbaḫtī (?), *Commentary on Aristotle* De generatione et corruptione, 80–85, and his reference to Philoponus, *In Gen. et corr.*, 63.15f.

267 Themistius clearly influenced Avicenna's understanding of motion in more than one way; cf. Hasnawi, "La définition du mouvement dans la *Physique* du *Shifāʾ* d'Avicenne," §5; Wisnovsky, *Avicenna's Metaphysics in Context*, 52f.; cf. also Janssens, "Ibn Sīnā," 85; cf. further Themistius, *In Phys.*, 145.24–146.27; q.v. above 360ff.

268 cf. also the similar discussion with regard to Aristotle in Roark, "Aristotle's Definition of Time Is not Circular"; *Aristotle on Time*, chs. 4–5.

269 *al-Samāʿ al-ṭabīʿī* II.13, §2, 167.15–168.9.

within the state of non-existence that belonged to Avicenna at the time of Aristotle that distinguishes it temporally from the state of non-existence that belongs to Avicenna now at our own time. He is just as non-existent back then as he is now. Likewise, there is nothing within the Peloponnesian War that essentially renders it as "before" nor is there anything within the ʿAbbāsid Revolution that makes it "after." A state or a motion or an event is "before," only because it has a *vertical relation to* time or, more precisely, to a *part* of time.[270] This part is essentially anchored in the infinite duration of time and has its firm position within the order of time. It is, thus, intrinsically characterised as "before" or "after." Through the relation which the state or the motion has to this part of time, it becomes itself qualified, in a derivative way, as "before" or "after." Once it has been qualified as "before" or "after," i.e., once it has a relation to one or another part of time, it is temporally located and through this relation becomes *horizontally related* to other states or events as well. For example, the state of non-existence that belonged to Avicenna at the time of Aristotle can now be said to be "prior to" the state of non-existence that now belongs to Avicenna at our own time, because the former state is related to one part of time (a before-part), while the latter is related to another part of time (an after-part). Likewise is the Peloponnesian War prior to the ʿAbbāsid Revolution, because it happened at a time which is before that of the ʿAbbāsid Revolution. Consequentially, time is that which is through itself before and after, and that through which everything else comes to be "before" and "after" *as well as* ordered as "prior" and "posterior."

The infinite duration of time, which is through itself ordered by what is before and what is after, is a magnitude. This magnitude belongs to the circular motion of the outermost sphere, which is the proximate cause of the existence of time. If there were no soul that moved the outermost sphere, there would be no motion of the outermost sphere nor would there be any other motion, and so there would also be no time. Time is ontologically dependent upon motion as one of its concomitant accidents. It comes-to-be through the motion of the outermost sphere and supervenes on that motion as its magnitude. In short: it is the epiphenomenon of one single eternal all-encompassing motion.

Motion itself is structured by what is prior and posterior. Thus, every motion contains parts that are prior or posterior to other parts. For that reason is it an essential fact that the outbreak of the Peloponnesian War was prior to the capitulation of Athens, but it is not an essential fact that the outbreak of the Peloponnesian War is prior to the Abū Muslim's raising the black banners. These, as I have said above, are unrelated or independent events and, thus, require their own vertical relation to time, in order to become ordered as prior and posterior to one another, even though their own respective parts are themselves structured by what is prior and posterior insofar as they belong to

270 Talking about the "parts" of time does, of course, not mean that time is discontinuous and actually composed of parts.

the event we call the Peloponnesian War or the ʿAbbāsid Revolution, respectively.[271] Motion, then, is essentially prior and posterior – and it is this characteristic of motion which ultimately also brings about the existence of time as that which is essentially before and after.

Since the motion of the outermost sphere is infinite, the magnitude it produces is likewise infinite, having no beginning and no end. For this reason, the magnitude which is produced by the circular motion of the sphere is an infinite extension that is eternally structured by what is before and what is after. This essential structure by the before and after consists in time's being subject to constant elapsing and renewal (*taqaḍḍin* and *taǧaddud*). Time evolves, i.e., it has its being in becoming, and is precisely not stable or integral (*ṯābit*, *qārr*), and so does not exist together with all of its parts. Time, then, is such that in it before, and after, and after again succeed one another infinitely, as long as there is the motion of the outermost sphere, whose constant revolution over prior, and posterior, and again posterior states and positions eternally creates time as the evolving magnitude of the eternal revolution of the outermost sphere. Every other motion that occurs, occurs within, or against the background of, this magnitude and, thus, is temporally located in the above-mentioned sense. Every state of a motion is *qua* motion prior or posterior to other parts of that motion. Since the essential characteristic of motion, viz., the prior and posterior, causes the existence of time, anything that is in motion is also in time: "Some thing is in time by having the meaning of prior and posterior to it ... this [i.e., the prior and posterior] belongs to motion on account of its substance" (*min tilqāʾ ǧawharihā*).[272] The states of a motion, then, are by themselves prior and posterior, and correspond to the before and after of time, deriving their own characterisation as "before" or "after" from time.

Interpreters might like to criticise Avicenna for having offered not one but two definitions of time and to question their compatibility. Shayegan, for example, remarked that "Avicenna operates with two definitions of time in the *Physics* of the *Healing*, one is Aristotelian and the other is his personal definition of time." She labels "his personal definition of time" as "non-Aristotelian" and concludes that "Avicenna acts as a commentator of Aristotle before proceeding to the elaboration of his own theory."[273] There is some truth in this interpretation. After all, Avicenna's account in *al-Samāʿ al-ṭabīʿī* II.11 yields two results: first, it establishes and confirms time as the magnitude of motion and, second, it develops time as that which through itself is before and after. However, far from questioning the compatibility of these "two definitions," as Shayegan called them, it has emerged in the present study that the salient point of Avicenna's analysis is precisely that they ought to be taken as complementary and as amounting, or contributing, to the same account. For Avicenna, time is the magnitude

271 q.v. above, 487f.

272 *al-Samāʿ al-ṭabīʿī* II.13, §6, 170.14–16; cf. *al-Ḥikma al-mašriqiyya* III.11, 40.14–16.

273 Shayegan, *Avicenna on Time*, 12–15. Shayegan may not have meant this to be a criticism.

of motion which spans from the first moment of a motion to its last. This magnitude is that extension in which there are numerous possibilities of covering more distance at higher speeds or less distance at a lower speeds. That magnitude wherein the possibility for changes occurs is "that which we call 'time'" (*allaḏī nusammīhi al-zamān*).[274] This account in itself, however, is incomplete, for it fails to elucidate the temporal order of before and after which we experience in reality and which even structures our reality. Responding to this, Avicenna adds, first, that time primarily is the infinite magnitude of the motion of the outermost sphere and, second, that it through itself contains parts which are in succession to one another, so that some are "before" and others are "after." That is to say, the before and after is a necessary and inseparable concomitant of the essence of time; this is why time is that which through itself, i.e., by virtue and on account of its own essence, is before and after. Insofar as things or events are related to the parts of this primary time, they derive their own temporality from time and come-to-be described as before and after themselves. As a result, time is a magnitude of motion which is through itself before and after.

As it seems, this twofold conception of time attempts to conjoin two historically opposing models, of which we may call one the "Aristotelian model" and the other the "Neoplatonic model." In fact, the most remarkable achievement of Avicenna's temporal theory is that it gets the best of both worlds, the Neoplatonic and the Aristotelian.

As I have described above, Avicenna's philosophy emerges after even rigidly Peripatetic authors such as Boethus, Alexander, and Ibn ʿAdī, presumably inadvertently, departed from Aristotelian territory and ventured into the Platonic lands. What they took to be a definition of time derived from the *Physics* itself was in truth close to being the reverse. The time which they conceived as a duration numbered by motion (*mudda taʿudduhā l-ḥaraka*) is what a thorough Platonist would identify not with an accident of motion but with a substance that subsists independently of motion (*ǧawhar qāʾim bi-nafsihī wa-mustaqill bi-ḏātihī*) and which is measured out by the motion of the outermost sphere.[275] Plotinus and al-Siǧistānī were among the few who recognised the odd position the Greek and Arabic Peripatetics were occupying. Like most of his predecessors, Avicenna seems to have *not* been aware of the Neoplatonic hues to a purportedly Aristotelian conception. To the contrary, the clear shift from regarding time as the measure or "number of motion" (ἀριθμὸς κινήσεως), as Aristotle did, to regarding it as the magnitude of motion (*miqdār al-ḥaraka*), as Avicenna does, bears witness either to his oblivious acceptance of his predecessors' misunderstanding or,

274 *al-Samāʿ al-ṭabīʿī* II.11, §2, 156.17; cf. *al-Ḥikma al-mašriqiyya* III.11, 32.23.

275 The expression *ǧawhar qāʾim bi-nafsihī wa-mustaqill bi-ḏātihī* is the very catch-phrase of a Platonic account of time. Boethus, Alexander, and Ibn ʿAdī would have denied that their accounts are Platonic in any way, claiming that their duration, nonetheless, is an accident of motion rather than a self-subsisting substance. Yet, treating motion as the measure of time rather than time as the measure of motion reverses the Aristotelian idea. The result seems to be that their accounts of time are either Platonic or incoherent.

at least, to a clear influence on him by his predecessors, above all Alexander and Ibn ʿAdī. It is the number or measure of motion which *measures* the motion, but it is the extension or magnitude of motion which *is measured by* motion.

A philosopher who regards himself as standing in the Neoplatonic tradition would argue that time, like space, is a universal or necessary condition of motion. Indeed, it is fundamental to the degree that it is almost a necessary existent, and a rival to the unique status of the First Principle.[276] Time exists ontologically prior to motion and serves as a precondition and prerequisite for the occurrence of motion. There cannot be motion without time just as there cannot be a located object without space in which it could be placed. On this account, time and space are two necessary and primary conditions for every body, every change, and every event.

Avicenna does not regard himself as standing in that tradition. He is a Peripatetic and does not accept time and place as necessary or as fundamentally primary. Without there being a body, there would be no place for that body, and so, likewise, without there being motion, there would be no time, as the existence of time depends upon motion. So, motion is the cause for the existence of time, instead of time being a necessary prerequisite for the occurrence of motion. Yet, this does not invalidate the compatibility of his "two definitions of time" – it merely makes his temporal theory considerably more complex than so far recognised by previous interpreters, precisely because Avicenna, inadvertently or not, attempts to combine two apparently incompatible conceptions of time, one Aristotelian and the other Neoplatonic. On Avicenna's understanding, then, time comes to be through motion and exists because of motion. Consequently, we can say that motion produces time. This, however, means nothing other than that motion – and, more precisely, the motion of the outermost sphere – produces that which is through itself before and after, i.e., this one motion is responsible for bringing about, and causing, the existence of a magnitude which is intrinsically and essentially structured by what is before and what is after. This creature of motion, in turn, is responsible for bestowing, or providing, the before and after to those things which are related to it. Thus, time depends on, and is posterior to, motion in terms of existence, but motions depend on time, and are posterior to, time in terms of their temporality, i.e., in terms of their having a temporal position. Motion, after all, occurs *in* time; and time, after all, numbers and measures motions.

What made it possible for Avicenna to combine the Aristotelian model, in which time is dependent upon and measures a pre-existing and eternal motion, with the Neoplatonic model, in which motions depend upon and measure a universal and eternal time, is the infamous remark by Aristotle towards the end of his account in *Physics* IV.14 that the "uniform circular motion is above all else the measure" of motion, so that time can be "thought to be the motion of the sphere, because the other motions

276 As can be witnessed in the discussions of time in the works of Faḫr al-Dīn, cf. Adamson and Lammer, "Fakhr al-Dīn al-Rāzī's Platonist Account of the Essence of Time."

are measured by this one, and time by this motion."[277] This must be the textual basis which inspired Alexander to present Aristotle's definition of time – "without deviating from him in any respect," as he wrote – as "the number of the westbound motion of the sphere," while at the same time claiming that time is the "duration which motion numbers."[278] When Aristotle initially defined time as the number of motion, he defined a time as a *particular* number that belongs to a *particular* motion. Every motion has a number indicating its time, and time is just that number that indicates the duration of a motion. The time which is "above all else" (μάλιστα) the measure of the motion of the outermost sphere, however, serves as a *universal* motion, because it measures all other motion as well as time.

Avicenna, like so many before him, accepts this interpretation – and it is this interpretation which allows him to fuse the Aristotelian model, on which time is produced by motion, with the Neoplatonic model, on which time is a universal feature of reality. If time is the magnitude of motion and if this magnitude is above all else produced by the motion of the outermost sphere (and if this time of the outermost sphere's motion is, consequently, a universal rather than a particular time), then the time which is created by the never-beginning and never-ending motion of the sphere is the universal temporal framework that bestows beforeness and afterness to everything else, can be measured out and compared by means of other motions, and exists as an unceasing all-encompassing temporal magnitude in which all things come-to-be, pass away, change, and move. On this account, it is not just that time is "above all else" the measure of the sphere, as Aristotle had it; much rather is it the case that time, indeed, has become and is nothing but the magnitude of the motion of the sphere, that it is infinite and eternal, and that it can be measured by other motions – this, to a serious degree, is akin to the Neoplatonic conception.

I am not claiming that Avicenna's account of time is Neoplatonic. What I do claim is that his account is a Neoplatonic Peripateticism. Of course, Avicenna opposes the fundamental trait of any Neoplatonic conception of time, viz., that time is a self-subsisting substance. For him, time is and remains an accident of motion. This, then, is also the final arbiter that makes Avicenna's account Peripatetic: time is an epiphenomenon of motion and does explicitly *not* subsist independently as a Platonist would have it. Nonetheless, his time, being guarded and preserved by the eternal and circular motion of the outermost sphere, has the same explanatory *function* within the cosmos as the self-subsisting time of the Platonist has. Though Avicenna's account is Peripatetic, it has a distinctive Neoplatonic trait that must not be overlooked. This is why I labelled his account a "Neoplatonic Peripateticism" instead of a "Peripatetic Neoplatonism": it is and remains a Peripateticism at heart, but with a distinctive Neoplatonic mark.

277 *Phys.* IV.14, 223b18–23, tr. by Hardie/Gaye, modified; q.v. above 497ff.
278 Alexander of Aphrodisias, *Maqālat al-Iskandar al-Afrūdīsī fī l-zamān*, 20.12–14.

Within the overall Peripatetic physics that is contained in Avicenna's *al-Samāʿ al-ṭabīʿī*, his discussion of time may be the least Peripatetic section, even though Avicenna seems to be following Aristotle closely. Yet, the undetected Neoplatonic overtones in centuries worth of writing about time and reading Aristotle by philosophers who considered themselves to be firmly embedded in Peripateticism also creeped into Avicenna's own understanding of time. He does not seem to have been aware of the fact that his final product was an interesting, not to say intriguing, mixture of Neoplatonic and Aristotelian material. What he certainly was aware of, though, is that he himself struggled with getting his own complex understanding down on paper. The most important passages that were discussed in the above analysis were also the most demanding ones (and also those which previous scholarship only inadequately took into consideration). Avicenna's Arabic in these passages became increasingly vexed and difficult up to the point that he seems to have been unsure in deciding which terminology he ought to choose for expressing his thoughts. We witnessed him switching between *maʿnā* and *amr*, *šayʾ* and *ḏāt*, *iḍāfa* and *qiyās*, when talking about things that exist in time, are described by time, or have a relation to time. In other words, precisely in those passages in which the Neoplatonism of his account of time came into contact – or into conflict – with his Peripateticism, i.e., where he investigates how moving things which have time are temporally located in time, he lost his grip a bit and became slightly fuzzy in his writing – not necessarily because he was himself confused, but because he struggled with putting his complex theory down on paper: the terms he had to avail himself, in order to express aptly the abstract conception of time he had set in his mind, seem to have "crumbled in his mouth like mouldy fungi," as the German poet Hugo von Hofmannsthal famously described the crisis of language at the turn of the nineteenth to the twentieth century in his fictitious letter of Lord Chandos to Francis Bacon. Yet, it is my sincere hope that the above analysis was able to resolve some of Avicenna's more demanding passages in what otherwise, once adequately appreciated, constitutes a rather clear account of a fundamental feature of physical reality.

6.5 The "Flowing Now" in Avicenna's Account of Time

I have now provided a full explanation of Avicenna's conception of time. I have described how Avicenna arrived at his conception, how he analysed the motion of bodies moving at different speeds and established time as a magnitude of motion on that basis, and also how his definition relates to that found in Aristotle's *Physics*. I have provided materials from various treatises of Aristotle's ancient, late ancient, and early Arabic commentators, in order to show how they understood the account of time developed in the *Physics* and how their interpretations influenced Avicenna's own view on what time is. I have offered readings of a number of complex statements in *al-Samāʿ al-ṭabīʿī* that have proven to be central to the understanding of what it means to be before and after in contrast to what it means to be prior and posterior. Moreover, I have explained what the cause of time is and how it comes into existence. I also touched upon the relation between time and the heavenly motions and, thus, also upon its relation to eternity.

Nothing essential seems to be missing from this presentation of Avicenna's account of time, even though I almost entirely left out a full chapter of Avicenna's investigation, viz., the twelfth chapter of the second book: Avicenna's chapter on the "now" (*al-ān*). This is especially surprising given that this chapter has unanimously been considered to be a very important piece within Avicenna's doctrine in general and no less than crucial for the existence of time in particular. In fact, it is the established opinion that for Avicenna, time is the product of a "flowing now." This, at least, is what we are told by Muḥammad ʿĀṭif al-ʿIrāqī, Yegane Shayegan, Jon McGinnis, ʿAlāʾ al-Dīn Muḥammad ʿAbd al-Mutaʿāl, and Toby Mayer.[279] The most elaborate exposition of this reading is to be found in chapter eight of McGinnis' impressive doctoral dissertation from 1999, which was published slightly modified as an article called "Ibn Sīnā on the Now" in the same year. McGinnis' overall thesis is that there are certain passages in Aristotle's *Physics* that have influenced especially Alexander and Philoponus in such a way that they came to argue that time is generated by a flowing now and that Avicenna, in turn influenced by reading Alexander's and Philoponus' commentaries, likewise argued that the now "produces time ... through its flow."[280]

In brief, the idea of a flowing now is that the now is a moment or instant which is always present. Since each moment which once was "now" has been a different moment, while still having been once a present now, the now could be seen as constantly moving and developing, so that it is both always the same (because it is always present) and always different (because it always marks a different moment). The moving now, then, is not unlike the second hand on a watch, which, likewise, is always the same, even though it constantly moves on, always marking another – further – position in time. The idea that time is the result of such a flowing now, or that it is itself nothing but that flow, accounts for two powerful features of our common experience of time. On the one hand, time seems to be something which incessantly progresses forth. The now as both always the same and always different captures this intuition very well. On the other hand, we often visualise the extent of time by means of a timeline. This line both illustrates the continuous nature of time and helps us understand what we mean when we say that we waited for "five minutes" or walked for "one hour." On the whole, then, it is quite plausible to say that the incessantly passing nature of time together with our strong sense of the present as well as the belief that time can be expressed – or expresses itself – in quantities is aptly portrayed by the idea that time is generated through the constant motion of an ever present temporal moment in analogy

279 cf. al-ʿIrāqī, *al-Falsafa al-ṭabīʿiyya ʿinda Ibn Sīnā*, 249–254; Shayegan, *Avicenna on Time*, 188–212; McGinnis, "Ibn Sīnā on the Now," 97–106; ʿAbd al-Mutaʿāl, *Taṣawwur Ibn Sīnā li-l-zamān*, 232–235; Mayer, "Avicenna against Time Beginning," 142f.

280 cf. esp. McGinnis, *Time and Time Again*, chs. 5–6; cf. also McGinnis, "Ibn Sīnā on the Now," 98f.

to a drawn line which can be said to be the product of the moving point; a prominent image also mentioned by Aristotle in his *De anima*.[281]

Instead of providing a full investigation of the concept and the status of the now within Avicenna’s discussion of time in general and of the relevance of the “flow of the now” for the existence of time in particular – something which I am planning to provide elsewhere – I shall now point towards five reasons that show that the now is a subordinate concept in Avicenna’s temporal theory and actually irrelevant for the realisation of both the existence and the essence of time.[282] In short, contrary to the consensus in the secondary literature, time, for Avicenna, is *not* the product of a “flowing now.”

The first of these reasons is that there simply is no passage anywhere in Avicenna’s major writings that explicitly states that time is the product of a flowing now. Of course, there are a number of passages on which interpreters relied so far in attributing this view to Avicenna. All these passages, however, have to be read carefully and need to be expounded attentively in light of their context – both the particular contexts of these passages and the systematic context within Avicenna’s natural philosophy. Most of all, however, these passages should not be misrepresented. One striking example of an inappropriate treatment of Avicenna’s text is to be found in al-ʿIrāqī’s monograph *al-Falsafa al-ṭabīʿiyya ʿinda Ibn Sīnā*. There, we read the following:

يذهب فيلسوفنا إلى أنّ الآن إذا استمرّ في متقدّم الحركة ومتأخّرها أحدث الزمان.

> Our philosopher holds the view that the now (*al-ān*), when it remains through the prior and posterior of motion, produces (*aḥdaṯa*) time. (al-ʿIrāqī, *al-Falsafa al-ṭabīʿiyya ʿinda Ibn Sīnā*, 251)[283]

Although this passage is, in part, one of the many unacknowledged quotations from Avicenna’s *al-Samāʿ al-ṭabīʿī* which al-ʿIrāqī silently incorporates into his own text, it not merely gives a wrong impression; it is plainly false. In fact, in Avicenna’s original, “the now” (*al-ān*) is not even the subject of the verbs *istamarra* (“to remain”) and *aḥdaṯa* (“to produce”). So, what does Avicenna really say in passages such as the one al-ʿIrāqī was drawing on and which incidentally is the passage which most strongly seems to suggest Avicenna’s adherence to the idea of the flowing now? The answer is simple: Avicenna talks about the thing-in-motion (*al-muntaqil*) precisely *when* it is in motion, i.e., he discusses the concrete object that is borne along during its motion in such a way that it “remains through the prior and posterior” of its own motion. Accordingly, it is this concrete moving object which “produces time” when it is such as to be moving. The above passage belongs to Avicenna’s investigation of whether there really is “in

281 cf. *De an.* I.4, 409a3–6.

282 I am currently working on a detailed investigation of the matter with the tentative title “Revisiting Avicenna’s Account of the Now.”

283 cf. al-ʿIrāqī, *al-Falsafa al-ṭabīʿiyya ʿinda Ibn Sīnā*, 253.

time something – namely, the now – which flows."[284] A more complete quotation from *al-Samāʿ al-ṭabīʿī* provides the following text as Avicenna's answer to this question:

فإن كان لهذا الشيء وجود فهو وجود الشيء مقروناً بالمعنى الذي حقّقنا فيما سلف أنّه حركة من غير أخذ متقدّم ولا متأخّر ولا تطبيق ... كونه ذا ذلك المعنى الذي سمّيناه الآن إذا استمرّ في متقدّم الحركة ومتأخّرها أحدث الزمان. فنسبة هذا الشيء إلى المتقدّم والمتأخّر هي في كونه آناً وهو في نفسه شيء يفعل الزمان ويعدّ الزمان بما يحدث إذا أخذنا آنا من حدود فيها.

If existence belongs to this thing (*fa-in kāna li-hāḏā l-šay' wuǧūd*), then it is the existence of the thing as connected (*maqrūnan*) with the meaning which we have earlier verified as motion without taking what is prior and what is posterior and what is simultaneous ... [So], its being something that has that meaning which we called the now (*kawnuhū ḏā ḏālikā l-maʿnā llaḏī sammaynāhu l-ān*), when it remains through the prior and posterior of motion (*istamarra fī l-mutaqaddim al-ḥaraka wa-muta'aḫḫirihā*), produces time (*aḥdaṯa l-zamān*). The relation of this thing to the prior and posterior, then, is in its being a now (*fī kawnihī ānan*)[285] and this is in itself something which makes time and numbers time (*wa-huwa fī nafsihī šay' yafʿalu l-zamān wa-yaʿuddu l-zamān*) through what comes-to-be when we take a now from among the limiting points in them [sc. the prior and posterior]. (*al-Samāʿ al-ṭabīʿī* II.12, §6, 164.12–16)[286]

It is clear from this passage that Avicenna does not merely ask whether there is some flowing now that exists by itself and produces time on its own through its flow. What he asks, instead, is that if we talk about a flowing now, as some of his predecessors, in particular Alexander and Philoponus, have done, what, then, is the meaning of such talk? The meaning is that in using the expression of a flowing now, we are actually referring to the concretely existing thing that is "connected with the meaning which we have earlier verified as motion." That is to say, what we are talking about is the concrete object that is currently in motion *insofar* as its is currently in motion by having that which Avicenna calls the "form of motion," for the "form of motion" is, indeed, the meaning which was "earlier," viz., in *al-Samāʿ al-ṭabīʿī* II.1, verified as motion.[287] There, he argued that the form of motion is a real feature that belongs to a moving object when it is undergoing motion. In every instant of the motion of a moving object, this object can be said to be presently undergoing motion. Thus, it is actually the thing-in-motion insofar as it is bearing the form of motion to which we refer when we talk about the flowing now. Incidentally, the overall vocabulary in these two discussions, i.e., that about motion and that about the now, is similar – as is the idea behind them: if we consider the thing-in-motion inasmuch as it is undergoing motion, i.e., inasmuch as it develops during its motion by covering all the the intermediary stages between beginning and end, then we can take the thing-in-motion as a limiting point that

284 *al-Samāʿ al-ṭabīʿī* II.12, §6, 164.4–6.

285 Āl Yāsīn and McGinnis read *fī* here, which is omitted in Zāyid and not attested in Mss. Leiden or. 4 and or. 84; it does not seem to affect the meaning of the text.

286 cf. *al-Ḥikma al-mašriqiyya* III.11, 37.9–13.

287 q.v. above, 360f.

"flows" from the beginning of the motion to its end, being now here and now there without ever remaining at one of the intermediary points for more than one instant; it is, then, that we can also say that this thing-in-motion, by having the form of motion and being at these instantaneous intermediary positions, "has that meaning which we called the now," as the above passage from *al-Samāʿ al-ṭabīʿī* II.12 states.[288] In a way, then, the concrete object can be said to have a now by performing its motion and by occurring at all the instantaneous moments of that motion, so that, by proceeding from the beginning to the end, it "remains through the prior and posterior of motion." It is in this sense that it, viz., the thing-in-motion, "produces time" (*aḥdaṯa l-zamān*), with time being nothing other than the magnitude of that motion in which all the possibilities for different higher or lower speeds obtain.

In other words – and this is now the second reason which I wanted to point out – the above passage harmonises well with what we have already come to know, viz., that time comes into existence through the motion of a concrete object, ultimately and most precisely through the circular motion of the outermost sphere. There is, then, no need to take recourse to the idea of a flowing now, in order to account for the existence of time. All that is needed for time to exist is a moving body, especially the moving body of the outermost sphere; and when this body is in motion, i.e., is "connected with the meaning which we have earlier verified as motion," it brings about a magnitude that accompanies that motion and indicates its quantity, and this is the time of the motion, which in the case of the outermost sphere serves as the universal time for the whole cosmos.

The third reason, then, is that once it has been understood that this is Avicenna's answer regarding the existence of time, we can accept without restriction what Avicenna himself tells us about the ontological status of the now. As a result, our account is in no way plagued by what has been the primary issue in earlier interpretations asserting that time, for Avicenna, was the product of a flowing now. This issue concerned the ontological status of the now as something imagined *vis-à-vis* the ontological status of time as a real feature of concrete reality. Whenever Avicenna speaks about the now, he never fails to emphasise that it is something "imagined" (*mutawahhim*). For example, when he begins his account of the now as a division (*faṣl*) and connector (*wāṣil*) of time, i.e., as that which is between what is past and what is future, he states that the now is "by no means existent" (*laysa mawǧūd al-battata*) but, instead, is something "whose existence is only insofar as the imagination imagines it" (*innamā wuǧūduhū ʿalā an yatawahhamuhū l-wahm*).[289] Likewise, when Avicenna subsequently introduces the flowing now, he states that "another now with another description *might be imagined*" (*qad yutawahhamu*).[290] With his repeated assertions that the now is

288 cf. esp. *al-Samāʿ al-ṭabīʿī* II.1, §6, 84.11–13; *al-Ḥikma al-mašriqiyya* III.7, 16.3–8.

289 *al-Samāʿ al-ṭabīʿī* II.12, §1, 160.5f.

290 *al-Samāʿ al-ṭabīʿī* II.12, §5, 163.12, emphasis added.

always something imagined, Avicenna emphasises the ontological dependence of the now as an indivisible point upon the magnitude to which it belongs *when* it is imagined as belonging to it. This is also the gist of the following passage:

ولأنّ الزمان كما قلنا مقدار وهو متّصل محاذ لاتّصال الحركات والمسافات فله لا محالة فصل متوهّم وهو الذي يُسمّى الآن.

> Because time, as we said, is a certain magnitude (*miqdār*) which is continuous, paralleling the continuity of motions and distances, it inevitably (*lā maḥāla*) has an imagined division (*faṣl mutawahhim*) and this is what is called "the now" (*al-ān*). (*al-Samāʿ al-ṭabīʿī* II.11, §6, 159.15f., tr. by McGinnis, modified)[291]

Since time is a magnitude, it can be divided just as any magnitude can. Such divisions could be actual, resulting in the destruction of the divided object together with the generation of two smaller objects, or they could be conceptual, i.e., "imagined," having no real effect on the magnitude as it exists in the concrete world. Time, as Avicenna explicitly states cannot actually be divided, even though it can be divided conceptually by stipulating points in it through an act of the imagination.[292] This is what we do when we represent time in our minds as an extended reality and think, for example, about what we have done at *this* moment as opposed to what we have done at *that* moment: we mentally impose instantaneous points or moments *onto* a magnitude that is essentially continuous, i.e., a magnitude that is essentially such as to allow for any such imposition. Given the now's ontological dependence on time as a magnitude, it is already clear that the now cannot bring about, and cause, the existence of the very magnitude on which it itself belongs ontologically. The now being an instantaneous, momentary point that is imagined in the continuous, infinitely divisible magnitude of time is, in its own existence as something imagined, dependent upon the prior existence of that magnitude. There can be no now without time existing – how, then, could the existence of time be dependent upon the flow of a now? Indeed, the now is even epistemologically dependent upon time, as Avicenna states that "the now is known from the knowledge of time."[293]

That the now is essentially something that is imagined and merely conjectural is often acknowledged by modern interpreters despite their claim that Avicenna accepts the notion of the flowing now as the immediate cause of time's existence.[294] This is also why most of them try to evade the very issue that emerges from this situation: how is it possible that the now, despite being merely imagined and by no means actual, brings

---

291 cf. *al-Naǧāt* II.2.9, 231.4–8 ≈ *al-Ḥikma al-ʿArūḍiyya* II.2.7, 132.20–23; *al-Ḥikma al-mašriqiyya* III.11, 34.20f.

292 cf. *al-Samāʿ al-ṭabīʿī* II.12, §1, 160.7.

293 *al-Samāʿ al-ṭabīʿī* II.12, §1, 160.4.

294 e.g., Shayegan, *Avicenna on Time*, 205; McGinnis, *Time and Time Again*, 286f.; "Ibn Sīnā on the Now," 100f.; Mayer, "Avicenna against Time Beginning," 142.

about, and causes, the actual and not merely conjectural reality of time? Toby Mayer's assertion that although "an extramental now in act results in intractable problems ... Avicenna prefers not to consign the now simply to mental status – given that it generates time" is a case in point, as it seems to surrender to confusion out of the conviction that it simply must be the now which produces time. The now is not extramental, as Mayer admits, but it is not mental either, as he feels to be compelled to state – yet, what is it, then? According to McGinnis, "[t]he flowing now is not conceived as some actual entity or object in its own right; nonetheless, it is a real state belonging to that which is borne along." So, McGinnis, too, admits that the now is not really and actually something that exists but some aspect of the thing-in-motion. This, in fact, is quite right – but would it not then be more accurate to say that it is precisely the thing-in-motion *qua* having the form of motion that produces time, as has been outlined above? Consequently, if we abandon the interpretation according to which Avicenna considered time to be generated by a flowing now, this problem is resolved, as we can accept the now as what Avicenna tells us it is, viz., something "imagined," while time acquires real existence through the real motion of the existing body of the outermost sphere.

The fourth reason that time cannot be the product of a flowing now is that the now, much like a point, is essentially something indivisible. Yet, Avicenna agrees with Aristotle that what is indivisible is not capable of motion. Thus, the now cannot produce time through its flow, because it cannot flow in the first place. In *al-Samāʿ al-ṭabīʿī* III.6, Avicenna discusses the question "whether it is possible for something which has no parts to be in motion."[295] He, first, analyses one of Aristotle's arguments to that conclusion, criticising it as unconvincing, before adding another argument which "satisfies us," as he writes.[296] According to this second argument, the reason that something indivisible without parts cannot move is that it does not have a position that belongs to it by itself. Since it does not have a proper position, it cannot move from one position to another. If indivisibles do engage in motion, they do so accidentally, i.e., insofar as they belong to something else – a one-, two-, or three-dimensional magnitude – which itself engages in motion. That is to say that here, too, we have to realise once more that indivisible parts, such as a point and the now, depend on the magnitude to which they belong and on which they have been stipulated. Indivisibles generally have no concrete reality by themselves. Avicenna, thus, seconds Aristotle's conclusion from the *Physics* that it is "not possible for that which has no parts to be in motion or to change in any way."[297]

This brings me to the fifth and final reason. The idea of the flowing now as that which produces the magnitude of time through its flow is intrinsically tied to the analogy

295 *al-Samāʿ al-ṭabīʿī* III.6, §7, 206.13.
296 *al-Samāʿ al-ṭabīʿī* III.6, §8, 207.10.
297 *Phys.* VI.10, 240b30f., tr. by Hardie/Gaye.

of the moving point as that which produces the magnitude of a line through its motion. However, a point cannot *really* produce a line, as Avicenna argues in *al-Ilāhiyyāt* III.4. In this chapter, we read the following:

> والذي يقال إنّ النقطة ترسم بحركتها الخطّ فإنّه أمر يقال للتخيّل ولا إمكان وجود له لا لأنّ النقطة لا يمكن أن تفرض لها مماسّة متنقلة ... لكنّ المماسّة لمّا كانت لا تثبت وكان لا يبقى الشيء بعد المماسّة إلاّ كما كان قبل المماسّة فلا تكون هناك نقطة بقيت مبدأ خطّ بعد المماسّة ولا يبقى امتداد بينها وبين أجزاء المماسّة لأنّ تلك النقطة إنّما صارت نقطة واحدة كما علمت في الطبيعيات بالمماسّة لا غير. فإذا بطلت المماسّة بالحركة فكيف تبقى هي نقطة؟ وكذلك كيف يبقى ما هي مبدأ له رسماً ثابتاً؟ بل إنّما ذلك في الوهم والتخيّل فقط.
>
> That which is said that the point draws a line through its motion, is a matter said for the imagination and has no possibility of [concrete] existence (*amr yaqālu li-l-taḫayyul wa-lā imkāna wuǧūd lahū*), not because one could not assume for it [sc. the point] a contact that locally moves [steadily with it] ... but, since the contact is not stable and [since] after contact the thing does not remain, except just as it was before the contact, so neither would there be a point that remains as the starting point of a line after the contact nor would there remain an extension (*imtidād*) between it and the parts of contact, because that point became only one single point through the contact and nothing else, as you have learned in natural philosophy. So, if the contact ceases through motion, then how would it remain a point? Likewise, how could that which is a starting point for it remain as a stable drawing? Rather, this is something that exclusively belongs only to the imagination and fancy (*innamā ... fī l-wahm wa-l-taḫayyul faqaṭ*). (*al-Ilāhiyyāt* III.4, §11, 115.5–12, tr. by Marmura, modified)

In this passage, Avicenna is adamant that any assertion about a point producing a line through its flow has relevance only and exclusively (*innamā*, *faqaṭ*) for our imagination (*al-wahm wa-l-taḫayyul*). It has no bearing whatsoever on real existence and concrete reality (*wuǧūd*). As Avicenna has emphasised earlier during his discussion of motion, motion does not have concrete existence as an extended reality.[298] Surely, a point that is in motion can be in contact with a corresponding spatial point within the distance, yet any such contact as well as the actuality of any such spacial point with which the moving point was in contact ceased to exist as soon as the contact with it ceased. There is, then, no line that can be produced by a point, for a point merely actualises that point with which it currently is in contact. Of course the entire motion can be presented in our minds as an extended reality spanning from its moment of beginning to its end, but this is precisely something which can be apprehended only in our imagination. In fact, whenever we employ any such talk of points in a line or distance, we presuppose the real existence of such a distance as a continuous magnitude, because only then can we stipulate and imagine a point in contact with one of the points on the line moving along this line. The same pertains to the now and time. There must be time, first, before we can talk about any such moment *in time*. This, then, is precisely what

---

298 cf. esp. *al-Samāʿ al-ṭabīʿī* II.1, §5, 83.19–84.8.

Avicenna argues in the passage immediately following upon the above quotation from *al-Ilāhiyyāt* III.4:

وأيضاً فإنّ حركتها تكون لا محالة وهناك شيء موجود تكون الحركة عليه أو فيه وذلك الشيء قابل لأن يتحرّك فيه فهو جسم أو سطح أو بعد في سطح أو بعد هو خطّ. فتكون هذه الأشياء موجودة قبل حركة النقطة فلا تكون حركة النقطة علّة لأن توجِد هي.

> Moreover, [the point's] motion is [i.e., occurs] without doubt, and there is an existing thing on which or in which motion occurs (*šay' mawǧūd … 'alayhi aw fīhi*). This thing is receptive to having motion take place in it, and so it is a body or a surface or a dimension in a surface or a dimension which is a line. Thus, these things exist before the point's motion (*haḏihī l-ašyā' mawǧūda qabla ḥarakat al-nuqṭa*), and so the point's motion is not a cause for making these exist. (*al-Ilāhiyyāt* III.4, §11, 115.12–15, tr. by Marmura, modified)

This passage emphasises once more what has already been stated. The point as an indivisible limit of a distance ontologically (and epistemologically) presupposes the existence of that distance. Unless a line were already to exist, one could not imagine a point moving along it – and unless time were already existent, one could not imagine a now flowing through it. Time and distance exist "before" the now's and the point's motion, respectively, as Avicenna puts it here. Thus, again, time cannot be the real product of a flowing now

The above points show that Avicenna defends a coherent view in both his physics and metaphysics on the basis of his understanding of continuous magnitudes and their imagined divisions. Above all, he is consistent in emphasising that no such division could in anyway be said to bring about, and to produce, that magnitude of which it is a division – and that we, whenever we resort to such talk, retreat to our imagination.

All this is to say that the flowing now is wholly irrelevant for either establishing the existence of time or for defining time in terms of its essence. It is for this reason that we should consider Avicenna's twelfth chapter of the second book of *al-Samā' al-ṭabī'ī*, devoted to an investigation of the now, as an appendix to the actual discussion of time accomplished in the preceding eleventh chapter. Not only is it that the now follows in both its being and its conception from the existence and the essence of time, respectively, also the discussion of the now follows upon that of the discussion of time, because it, too, depends on the latter.

Nonetheless, the now is not entirely without value within Avicenna's discussion, in particular it is not without a *didactic* value, as the now is a powerful symbol that serves the purpose of making comprehensible the reality of time as a continuous magnitude which is essentially structured by the before and after. Thus, Avicenna adds chapter twelve "on the explanation of the now," as the chapter heading has it, as a didactic chapter intended for all those who still have trouble understanding – or mentally representing – what time is. In this chapter, then, he provides the means to ease the mind troubled by the admittedly opaque and explicitly "tenuous existence" (*aḍ'af fī l-wuǧūd*) of time.[299] Once more, then, Avicenna emerges as a capable teacher in his *al-Samāʿ al-ṭabīʿī* – a book which, as we have seen, was specifically designed to teach physics in its most accomplished form.

299 *al-Samāʿ al-ṭabīʿī* II.13, §1, 166.14–16; cf. *Phys.* IV.10, 217b32f.

Conclusion

In this study, I analysed the core concepts of Avicenna's physics. The central text of my investigation was *al-Samāʿ al-ṭabīʿī*, in which Avicenna presents his most detailed and extensive treatment of natural things. Additionally, I provided further references to passages in his other major works or employed these passages, in order to contextualise my discussions and to substantiate my interpretations. Moreover, I also examined various texts from the preceding Greek and Arabic philosophical traditions, because Avicenna's philosophy can only be adequately described in full and appreciated in detail against the background of ancient, late ancient, and early Arabic scientific developments. It is precisely Avicenna's engagement with his predecessors which demonstrates the originality of his thought, the rigour of his analysis, and, ultimately, the strength of his philosophical reasoning. If my investigation of "the elements of Avicenna's physics" was successful, then I was able to provide a convincing outline of

- Avicenna's philosophical method,
- his thoughts on matter, form, and corporeality,
- his views on nature as a dynamic principle of motion,
- his understanding of the place of bodies, and
- his conception of time within the natural world.

However, in addition to that, I hope that this study also revealed different facets of Avicenna's personality as a philosopher, as a thinker, and as a writer within the history of philosophy and science.

In the second chapter, for example, we became acquainted with *Avicenna the Systematiser*, who devises a complex system of interdependent sciences, being related with each other through their principles, questions, and subject-matters. Within this complex architecture, physics takes up the second most elevated position, only surpassed in commonality and importance by metaphysics. The science of physics provides the central ideas, the most important notions, and the crucial elements that lay the foundation to any further first-hand investigation of the objects that immediately surround us within the natural world. My analysis has shown that, in contrast to Aristotle, Avicenna's works do not document his inquiry into the natural world but, instead, follow the requirements of "teaching and learning." It is these two notions which epitomise Avicenna's approach in his major works – above all, those works which form his *al-Šifāʾ* – and represent his personal views on how reality should be conceived, how it should be reproduced in writing, and how it should be unpacked didactically.

What is more, the method of "teaching and learning" corresponds not only to the biographical information about how, when, and why Avicenna composed his *al-Šifāʾ*, but also to his own personal understanding of *science* as a universal endeavour and his conception of the philosophical procedure recommended by Aristotle in the

https://doi.org/10.1515/9783110546798-008

Posterior Analytics. It was shown that the style, the structure, and the argumentative layout of his *al-Samāʿ al-ṭabīʿī* is nothing other than the rigorous application of these methodological underpinnings to the concrete situation of teaching natural philosophy to his disciples and readers. In presenting the principles of natural things "by way of postulation and positing," Avicenna ultimately follows Aristotle's advice of *Physics* I.1 to proceed "from the universals to the particulars" in a way hitherto unprecedented within the history of philosophy.

In the third chapter, then, we met *Avicenna the Peripatetic*, who does not follow the Aristotelian method in establishing the principles of natural things through an investigation of change, but who, nonetheless, fundamentally accepts and systematically develops the Aristotelian truth that concrete objects are composed of the constitutive principles matter and form. The resulting philosophical theory is intriguing and systematic. Focusing on the natural body, first, in its fundamental respect of being a body, Avicenna explains that a body as such is a three-dimensionally extended substance. For him, being corporeal means nothing other than being extended in such a way that it is possible to identify up to three distinct and perpendicularly intersecting dimensions. Being extended, moreover, means being essentially continuous, which, in turn, entails being essentially divisible. Thus, Avicenna's account of the corporeality of natural bodies intrinsically relies on the three notions of extensionality, continuity, and divisibility. The principle of this threefold meaning of corporeality is what Avicenna calls "corporeal form," inhering in an underlying substrate called "matter." It is the union of an incorporeal matter and a corporeal form which gives rise to the essentially extended and continuous substance of body. Moreover, Avicenna demonstrates the existence of this underlying matter on the basis of an argument which intrinsically relies precisely on the notion of divisibility and continuity, i.e., on the idea of the corporeal form as inherent in prime matter. In doing so, he does not merely develop and explain his own theory but engages critically with late ancient arguments which conceived of matter as already corporeal and denied the possibility of proving the existence of an incorporeal matter altogether.

Avicenna's adherence to the idea of a corporeal form as the most fundamental form of body, however, does not commit him to the thesis of the multiplicity of forms, i.e., the ontological thesis according to which concrete objects are constituted through the inherence of two or more forms in one underlying matter. Much to the contrary, it emerged that concrete objects only have one form, where it is this one form which contains all formal determinations in a unified manner "by way of generality and specificity." A human being, for example, does not exist of matter together with the forms of corporeality, of animality, and of rationality; a human being consists only of *one* matter and of *one* form, viz., that of humanity, which makes this human being a rational animate body.

My analysis has also shown that Avicenna presents a fundamentally unified physics in which all bodies – eternal celestial and corruptible terrestrial bodies alike – are governed by the same principles, because they all do not only consist of form and matter but consist of *the same kind* of matter that is distinguished and diversified through different kinds of forms, all of which contain corporeality as their most general and most common formal component. For Avicenna, matter is simply the essentially receptive and not further qualified substrate for form, whereas form is nothing other than a disposition inhering in matter. Thus, matter and form are principles which pertain to all natural beings and are, for that reason, common to all of them. Yet, their commonality is not of a numerical kind, as only God can be said to be "numerically common" to all existent things. Instead, matter and corporeal form are "generically common" precisely insofar as they fulfil a specific function in the natural world, viz., to be receptive of form and to be inherent in matter, respectively.

In addition to his universal analysis of corporality, Avicenna also considers the natural body from a more restricted perspective, viz., insofar as it is subject to change. Change, he argues, is explained through the additional aspect of privation, which signifies the body only insofar as it lacks a certain form which it is intrinsically such as to acquire. Privation is itself not a principle on equal terms with, and in addition to, the constitutive principles of form and matter; still it functions as a necessary prerequisite for change and motion. As such, privation depends on the two universal principles matter and form, because these constitute what the natural thing is in its *being*, whereas privation only illustrates what a natural thing could *become* on the basis of what it already is.

In chapter four, we were introduced to *Avicenna the Attacker*, who does not just seize John Philoponus' new definition of nature but who takes it up with an entire tradition of, as he would say, misrepresenting the true meaning of nature. Taking his departure from a quotation of Aristotle's definition of nature, Avicenna plays out his strengths as a competent commentator both by providing new insights and by displaying an acute awareness of intricate issues in previous interpretations. According to his diagnosis, Aristotle and Philoponus treated the (for him) crucial distinction between nature and soul with less care as would have been necessary. Aristotle was not able to explain why the motive faculty of the animal soul should not be defined with the very same words as those he used for defining nature. Philoponus, in turn, ruined his initially correct understanding of why nature is a "primary" or "first" principle of motion through his subsequent idea according to which a body's nature is subjugated to the sovereign command of its soul with the result that soul was actually capable of altering the underlying nature, which, again, blurred the distinction between the agency of nature and that of soul.

Despite this disagreement, Avicenna fundamentally accepts Philoponus' interpretation that Aristotle's nature must be understood as an active principle involved in the production of motion, instead of being a passive principle of being moved. This is also apparent in his account of inclination, which he adopts from Alexander of Aphrodisias and Philoponus. However, it was shown that Avicenna considers the idea of inclination to have been rather poorly developed by his predecessors, especially because their accounts, again, failed to draw a clear line, this time between nature, its corresponding inclination, and its effect (i.e., either motion or rest). In Avicenna's theory, however, it is a natural body's nature which brings about an ever identical effect: its inclination for being at rest in its natural place or state. This entails that upon forcefully moving that body away from its natural place its nature still effects only one identical effect, viz., the inclination to be in its natural place. Yet, it is this inclination which manifests itself either in what we perceive as weight, when we try to move the body even further away from its natural place, or in a motion back towards its natural place, once we have released the body. Thus, for Avicenna, nature, inclination, and motion are intertwined but ultimately distinct.

The same urge for clarity and distinction is also present in Avicenna's own classification of natural powers. Systematically differentiating between voluntary and involuntary motions as well as between uniform and manifold motions, Avicenna defines nature as "a power which produces motion and change, and from which the act proceeds in a single manner without volition." In addition to this, Avicenna also describes three types of soul as powers that likewise produce motion and change but from which only one single act proceeds with volition (as in the case of the celestial soul) or from which several acts proceed either with or without volition (as in the case of the animal soul and the vegetative soul, respectively).

Ultimately, my analysis showed that Avicenna seizes the opportunity to attack Philoponus' account of nature, not because of his own personal or singular dissatisfaction with what he found in his predecessor's commentary on the *Physics*, but because it all too aptly epitomises a theory of natural agency that was widely accepted by Greek and Arabic Neoplatonic and Peripatetic intellectuals up to his own time as a complement, or even a rival, to Aristotle's original definition. For Avicenna, that understanding of nature was a superfluous – and actually unsuccessful – attempt to improve upon Aristotle's words as well as a severe distortion of Aristotle's actual intention, because it conceives of nature along the lines of an independent power which merely permeates the bodies it governs. This, as Avicenna asserts, is an account of a universal nature, which has no place either in his conception of physics nor in his ontology.

In his philosophical investigation of place, then, we discovered *Avicenna the Defender*. Again, Avicenna takes it up with an entire tradition. This time, however, he does not so much have to attack a philosophical opponent but to defend the Aristotelian notion of place, which was discredited and ridiculed already by the earliest followers of Aristotle and, then, by almost all of his Greek commentators. This tradition of arguing against Aristotle's account of place found its culmination once more in the writings of Philoponus and was even applied, under different circumstances, by some Muʿtazilites in the theological tradition of Islam. Consequently, Avicenna faces both the shattered and the distorted fragments of a philosophical concept. My examination brought to light how Avicenna's careful and meticulous analysis of the core idea of Aristotle's definition – the idea of a surface – gradually restores the definition in three steps. First, Avicenna improves upon Aristotle's *approach* of defining place by investigating the central notion of "surface." This was not only necessary because of the common

Mu'tazilite understanding of place as the surface upon which something rests, but also because a number of Peripatetics, notably Themistius and Philoponus, had a confused understanding of that notion, as they applied it invariably to an outside surface as well as to an inside surface, in order to overcome a common objection to Aristotle's account, viz., that it, purportedly, cannot account for the place of the outermost sphere and, ultimately, fails to explain its circular motion. Against this, Avicenna argues that the outermost sphere does not have a place, even though it still engages in motion, however, not a motion in the category of place but in the category of position. In consequence, we saw that Avicenna rigorously emphasises that the idea of place must be conceived as the inner surface of the containing body and cannot be a Mu'tazilite outside surface or simply any surface whatsoever.

In a second step, he turns to the actual *definition* and sets out to making it more robust. In particular, Avicenna applies a new strategy for solving what may have been the greatest puzzle to Aristotle's theory, viz., the question of how to conceive of a body's place when that body itself is located in unstable surroundings. This puzzle was specifically troublesome for Aristotle, because he himself had raised it but, according to his commentators, was found unable to solve it. Avicenna's reply constitutes a novel analysis of the underlying issue. As we have seen, Avicenna argues that one should stop focusing on the unstable surroundings and finally investigate whether the body itself is in motion or at rest. He accepts the only seemingly absurd consequence that the body's place is in constant motion, while demonstrating that this does by no means nullify the distinction between the body's motion and rest, for motion and rest are explained through the presence or absence of the "form of motion" in the body – and this form pertains to the body irrespective of whether its surroundings are in motion or at rest. Avicenna's analysis brings to light two central aspects of his philosophical reasoning: he is independent enough to disagree with Aristotle, because he rejects the condition that place must be unmoving, and confident enough not only to accept but also to argue for results that have been credited for centuries as absurd or insane or both.

Finally, we have seen how Avicenna employs what he defends as a viable account of place in his rejection of the most widespread alternative theory of place, viz., place as an independent three-dimensional space that is void in itself but always filled with body. He argues that this idea of space is invalid for various reasons: it does not exist, it abolishes all possibility of motion, and it cannot have any influence on bodies. Ultimately, it is the notion of a surface which celebrates its return in the explanation of the mechanisms behind such devices as the clepsydra, thus repudiating the hitherto prevalent idea of the "force of the void." In all this, then, Avicenna does not only defend Aristotle's arguments for place as a surface, he also defends (and develops) Aristotle's arguments against place as an extension.

Finally, we have witnessed *Avicenna the Synthesiser*, who devises an novel strategy for deriving the essence of time on the basis of an analysis of different motions with different speeds. For Avicenna, time is not the number of motion but the "*magnitude* of motion." This magnitude corresponds and conforms to motion, thus indicating the measurable size of that motion. As I have shown, however, the idea of understanding time along the lines of a magnitude or duration has strong Platonist overtones and a long historic pedigree. Ever since Plato, who formulated the theory of a stable eternity which is imitated by time as the merely moving image of that eternity, it was possible to conceive of motion as the measure of time. Ever since Boethus of Sidon in the second century BC, this idea was mistaken as an Aristotelian idea, despite the fact that Aristotle defined time as the measure of motion. This understanding not only reversed the original idea that was expressed in the *Physics*, but also paved the way for the further idea of time being nothing other than the result of a now which constantly flows through eternity, as is demonstrated by Alexander's brief treatise on time, in which Alexander presented time, purportedly, "without deviating from [Aristotle] in any respect" as a duration measured by motion and created by the flowing now. One may surmise that it was ultimately through Alexander that this understanding became a Peripatetic commonplace. Moreover, it was welcomed and positively received by those commentators who generally intended to harmonise Plato's philosophy with that of Aristotle. It is, consequently, hardly surprising to find the same theory expressed in Philoponus' commentary.

According to my analysis, Avicenna shares only certain parts of this doctrine, in particular by integrating the notion of a magnitude into his account of time. Furthermore, he distinguishes between what is prior and posterior and what is before and after, and conceives of time, in accordance with the latter, as that which is "through itself before and after," so that all things in time ultimately derive their temporality, i.e., their individual qualification as being before or being after, from time. He also argues that the motion of the outermost sphere is the cause for the existence of time. Given that this motion is an eternal motion, the result of Avicenna's theory is the existence of an infinite magnitude which is intrinsically structured by the before and after. This infinite magnitude, then, is time. It is, finally, against the background of this time that other particular motions occur. The particular times of these particular motions, in turn, are segments or portions of the eternal time produced by the never-ending revolution of the sphere. In other words, they are magnitudes which themselves have been measured out by the individual motions to which they each apply as their magnitude. Thus, what Avicenna does is to unify Aristotle's idea of time as an epiphenomenon of motion with the Platonist idea of time as a magnitude or duration. In consequence, Avicenna devises a theory of time which accomplishes something that is almost impossible: the complete – even though complex – harmony of two utterly contradictory accounts. It is here that we perceived Avicenna as a capable synthesiser, who labours (and actually struggles) to put down into words what he conceives as a complicated amalgamation of outright Aristotelian and unnoticed un-Aristotelian elements, when we saw him constantly rephrasing certain passages, changing his terminology, and trying to be evermore adequate in his formulations.

Finally, he appends a further chapter to his account of time in which he expounds the now and also discusses the image of the flow of a now – not, however, to reveal the essence of time or to demonstrate its existence, for that has already been accomplished in the preceding chapter. Instead, Avicenna employs the flowing now as a didactic means for his students who still may have had trouble understanding the complexity of his temporal theory. The flowing now, imagined as a temporal point pertaining to a thing-in-motion, can be mentally represented as producing the extension of the magnitude of time, just as a moving point could be said to draw out a line. This, however, is neither what time is nor how time comes into being. The now is, generally, something which results *from* time or, to be more precise, from the continuity of time, which is ultimately safeguarded by time's own existential dependence on the motion of the outermost sphere and its essential characterisation as that which is "through itself before and after."

Taking it all together, this study contains an analysis of the fundamentals of Avicenna's natural philosophy. It demonstrates the resourcefulness of his writings, the abundance of materials contained in his works, and the diligence in his argumentation, thus providing a decidedly affirmative answer to the question that I raised in the introduction whether "Avicenna's natural philosophy is as rich and innovative as his logic and his metaphysics already proved to be." At times, my study suggests and establishes more correct or adequate interpretations as those which could so far be found in the secondary literature on Avicenna. More often, however, it examines certain topics and concepts for the first time in detail in a western language. My overall methodical intention was to understand Avicenna through a careful analysis of the text of his works together with an investigation of the philosophical developments in the preceding Greek and Arabic traditions. In this sense, my results put Avicenna's philosophy in its historical context of the Aristotelian tradition, while at the same time positioning his natural philosophy within its systematic context of his own philosophy as it is expressed in all his major works.

Bibliography

Primary Sources

Manuscripts

Alexander of Aphrodisias. *Risālat al-Iskandar al-Afrūdīsī fī l-radd ʿalā Ǧālīnūs fī-mā ṭaʿana bihī ʿalā Arisṭū fī anna kull mā yataḥarraku fa-innamā yataḥarraku ʿan muḥarrik*. Ms. Carullah 1279. Istanbul: Süleymaniye Kütüphanesi, 66v–69r. Published as a facsimile in Alexander of Aphrodisias. *The Refutation of Alexander of Aphrodisias of Galen's Treatise on the Theory of Motion*. Edited, translated, and annotated, with an introduction, by Nicholas Rescher and Michael E. Marmura. Islamabad: Islamic Research Institute, 1965.

Alexander of Aphrodisias. *Risālat al-Iskandar al-Afrūdīsī fī l-radd ʿalā Ǧālīnūs fī-mā ṭaʿana bihī ʿalā Arisṭū fī anna kull mā yataḥarraku fa-innamā yataḥarraku ʿan muḥarrik*. Ms. arab. 794. El Escorial: Real Biblioteca del Monasterio de San Lorenzo, 60r–69v. Published as a facsimile in Alexander of Aphrodisias. *The Refutation of Alexander of Aphrodisias of Galen's Treatise on the Theory of Motion*. Edited, translated, and annotated, with an introduction, by Nicholas Rescher and Michael E. Marmura. Islamabad: Islamic Research Institute, 1965.

Anonymous. Ms. Marsh 539. Oxford: Bodleian Library. Published by Elvira Wakelnig, editor, translator, commentator, and introduction. *A Philosophy Reader from the Circle of Miskawayh*. Cambridge: Cambridge University Press, 2014.

Aristotle. *al-Samāʿ al-ṭabīʿī*. In: *Šarḥ al-Samāʿ al-ṭabīʿī*. Ms. or. 583. Leiden: Universiteitsbibliotheek. Published as Aristotle. *al-Ṭabīʿa. Tarǧamat Isḥāq ibn Ḥunayn maʿa šurūḥ Ibn al-Samḥ wa-Ibn ʿAdī wa-Mattā ibn Yūnus wa-Abī Faraǧ ibn al-Ṭayyib*. Edited, with an introduction, by ʿAbd al-Raḥmān Badawī. 2 vols. Cairo: al-Dār al-Qawmiyya li-l-Ṭibāʿa wa-l-Našr, 1964.

Aristotle. *Kitāb fī l-nafs*. Ms. 2450. Istanbul: Aya Sofya. Published in ʿAbd al-Raḥmān Badawī, editor, annotator, and introduction. *Arisṭūṭālīs fī l-nafs – "al-Ārāʾ al-ṭabīʿiyya" al-mansūb ilā Flūṭarḫus – "al-Ḥāss wa-l-maḥsūs" li-Ibn Rušd – "al-Nabāt" al-mansūb ilā Arisṭūṭālīs*. Cairo: Maktabat al-Nahḍa al-Miṣriyya, 1954.

Aristotle. *Kitāb Rīṭūrīkā li-Arisṭūṭālīs*. Ms. ar. 2346. Paris: Bibliothèque nationale de France.

Avicenna. *al-Ḥikma al-mašriqiyya*. Ms. Vollers 796. Leipzig: Universitätsbibliothek.

Avicenna. *Kitāb al-Šifāʾ*. Ms. or. 4. Leiden: Universiteitsbibliotheek.

Avicenna. *Kitāb al-Šifāʾ*. Ms. or. 84. Leiden: Universiteitsbibliotheek.

Avicenna. *Kitāb ʿUyūn al-ḥikma*. Ms. 3268. Istanbul: Ahmet III. Published as a facsimile by Yaḥyā Mahdawī and Moǧtabā Mīnowī, eds. *Kitāb ʿUyūn al-ḥikma*. With an introduction by Moǧtabā Mīnowī. Entešārāt-e Dānešgāh-e Tehrān 208. Tehran, 1954.

Avicenna and Abū Rayḥān al-Bīrūnī. *al-Asʾila wa-l-aǧwiba*. Ms. or. 184. Leiden: Universiteitsbibliotheek, 65v–86v.

Published Works

Aetius Arabus. *Die Vorsokratiker in arabischer Überlieferung*. Edited, translated, and commented, with an introduction, by Hans Daiber. Veröffentlichungen der Orientalischen Kommission 33. Wiesbaden: Franz Steiner Verlag, 1980.

Alexander of Aphrodisias. *Praeter commentaria scripta minora*. Edited by Ivo Bruns. Supplementum Aristotelicum II.2. Berlin: Verlag Georg Reimer, 1892.

https://doi.org/10.1515/9783110546798-009

Alexander of Aphrodisias. *Commentaire perdu à la* Physique *d'Aristote (Livres IV–VIII). Les scholies byzantines*. Edited, translated, and commented, with an introduction, by Marwan Rashed. Commentaria in Aristotelem graeca et byzantina. Quellen und Studien 1. Berlin and Boston: Walter de Gruyter, 2011.

Alexander of Aphrodisias. *De anima libri mantissa*. Edited and commented, with an introduction, by Robert W. Sharples. Peripatoi. Philologisch-historische Studien zum Aristotelismus 21. Berlin and New York: Walter de Gruyter, 2008.

Alexander of Aphrodisias. *De mixtione*. In: Alexander of Aphrodisias. *Praeter commentaria scripta minora*. Edited by Ivo Bruns. Supplementum Aristotelicum II.2. Berlin: Verlag Georg Reimer, 1892, 213–238.

Alexander of Aphrodisias. *De mixtione*. Edited, translated, and commented by Robert B. Todd. In: Todd, Robert B. *Alexander of Aphrodisias on Stoic Physics. A Study of the De mixtione with Preliminary Essays, Text, Translation and Commentary*. Philosophia antiqua. A Series of Monographs on Ancient Philosophy 28. Leiden: E. J. Brill, 1976, 108–173.

Alexander of Aphrodisias. *De motu et tempore*. Edited by Gabriel Théry. In: Théry, Gabriel. *Autour du décret de 1210*. Vol. 2: Alexandre d'Aphrodisias. Aperçu sur l'influence de sa noétique. Bibliotheque Thomiste 7. Le Saulchoir Kain: Revue des sciences philosophiques et théologiques, 1926, 92–97.

Alexander of Aphrodisias. *Die durch Averroes erhaltenen Fragmente Alexanders zur Metaphysik des Aristoteles*. Edited, translated, and annotated, with an introduction, by Jakob Freudenthal. In collaboration with Siegmund Fränkel. Berlin: Verlag der königlichen Akademie der Wissenschaften, 1885.

Alexander of Aphrodisias. *Épitre* des Principes du Tout *selon l'opinion d'Aristote le Philosophe*. Translated by ʿAbd al-Raḥmān Badawī. In: Badawī, ʿAbd al-Raḥmān. *La transmission de la philosophie grecque au monde arabe*. Études de philosophie médiévale 56. Paris: Librairie philosophique J. Vrin, 1968, 121–139.

Alexander of Aphrodisias. *In Aristotelis* Metaphysica *commentaria*. Edited by Michael Hayduck. Commentaria in Aristotelem graeca I. Berlin: Verlag Georg Reimer, 1891.

Alexander of Aphrodisias. *In Aristotelis* Metereologicorum *libros commentaria*. Edited by Michael Hayduck. Commentaria in Aristotelem graeca III.2. Berlin: Verlag Georg Reimer, 1899.

Alexander of Aphrodisias. *Le Commentaire d'Alexandre d'Aphrodise aux "Seconds Analytiques" d'Aristote*. Edited, translated, and annotated by Paul Moraux. Peripatoi. Philologisch-historische Studien zum Aristotelismus 13. Berlin and New York: Walter de Gruyter, 1979.

Alexander of Aphrodisias. *Maqālat al-Iskandar al-Afrūdīsī fī l-qawl fī mabādiʾ al-kull bi-ḥasab raʾy Arisṭāṭālis al-faylasūf*. In: *Arisṭū ʿinda l-ʿarab. Dirāsa wa-nuṣūṣ ġayr manšūra*. Edited and annotated, with an introduction, by ʿAbd al-Raḥmān Badawī. Dirāsāt Islāmiyya 5. Kuwait: Wakālat al-Maṭbūʿāt, ²1978, 253–277.

Alexander of Aphrodisias. *Maqālat al-Iskandar al-Afrūdīsī fī l-zamān*. In: *Šurūḥ ʿalā Arisṭū mafqūda fī l-yūnāniyya wa-rasāʾil uḫrā. Commentaires sur Aristote perdus en grec et autres épitres*. Edited, with an introduction, by ʿAbd al-Raḥmān Badawī. Recherches publiées sous la direction de l'Institut de Lettres Orientales de Beyrouth. Nouvelle série A. Langue arabe et pensée islamique. Tome 1. Beirut: Dār al-Mašriq, 1971, 19–24.

Alexander of Aphrodisias. *Maqālat al-Iskandar al-Afrūdīsī yaqtaṣṣu wa-yubayyinu fīhā raʾy Dīmuqrāṭīs wa-Abīqūruš wa-sāʾir aḥdāṯ al-falāsifa al-bāqīn fī l-ʿināya*. Edited, translated, and annotated, with an introduction, by Hans-Jochen Ruland. In: Ruland, Hans-Jochen. "Die arabischen Fassungen von zwei Schriften des Alexander von Aphrodisias. Über die Vorsehung und Über das liberum arbitrium." PhD thesis. Saarbrücken: Universität des Saarlandes, 1976, 1–106.

Alexander of Aphrodisias. *On Aristotle's "Metaphysics" 2 & 3*. Translated and annotated by William E. Dooley and Arthur Madigan. Ancient Commentators on Aristotle. Ithaca: Cornell University Press, 1992.

Alexander of Aphrodisias. *On the Cosmos*. Edited, translated, and commented, with an introduction, by Charles Genequand. Islamic Philosophy and Theology. Texts and Studies 44. Leiden, Boston, and Cologne: Brill, 2001.

Alexander of Aphrodisias. *On Time*. Translated and annotated, with an introduction, by Robert W. Sharples. In: *Phronesis* 27.1 (1982), 58–81.

Alexander of Aphrodisias. *Quaestiones*. In: Alexander of Aphrodisias. *Praeter commentaria scripta minora*. Edited by Ivo Bruns. Supplementum Aristotelicum II.2. Berlin: Verlag Georg Reimer, 1892, 1–116.

Alexander of Aphrodisias. *Quaestiones 1.1–2.15*. Translated and annotated, with an introduction, by Robert W. Sharples. Ancient Commentators on Aristotle. Ithaca: Cornell University Press, 1992.

Alexander of Aphrodisias. *Quaestiones 2.16–3.15*. Translated and annotated, with an introduction, by Robert W. Sharples. Ancient Commentators on Aristotle. Ithaca: Cornell University Press, 1994.

Alexander of Aphrodisias. *The Refutation of Alexander of Aphrodisias of Galen's Treatise on the Theory of Motion*. Edited, translated, and annotated, with an introduction, by Nicholas Rescher and Michael E. Marmura. Islamabad: Islamic Research Institute, 1965.

Alexander of Aphrodisias. *Traité de la Providence (Περὶ προνοίας). Version arabe de Abū Bishr Mattā ibn Yūnus*. Edited and translated, with an introduction, by Pierre Thillet. Paris: Éditions Verdier, 2003.

al-ʿĀmirī, Abū l-Ḥasan Muḥammad ibn Yūsuf. *A Muslim Philosopher on the Soul and its Fate. al-ʿĀmirī's* Kitāb al-Amad ʿalā l-abad. Edited, translated, and commented, with an introduction, by Everett K. Rowson. American Oriental Series 70. New Haven: American Oriental Society, 1988.

al-ʿĀmirī, Abū l-Ḥasan Muḥammad ibn Yūsuf. *al-Taqrīr li-awǧuh al-taqdīr*. In: al-ʿĀmirī, Abū l-Ḥasan Muḥammad ibn Yūsuf. *Rasāʾil Abī l-Ḥasan al-ʿĀmirī wa-šaḏarātuhū l-falsafiyya*. Edited and annotated, with an introduction, by Saḥbān Ḫalīfāt. Manšūrāt al-Ǧāmiʿa al-Urduniyya. Amman: al-Ǧāmiʿa al-Urduniyya, 1988, 303–341.

Ammonius. *In Aristotelis Categorias commentarius*. Edited by Adolf Busse. Commentaria in Aristotelem graeca IV.4. Berlin: Verlag Georg Reimer, 1895.

Ammonius. *On Aristotle's "Categories."* Translated and annotated by S. Marc Cohen and Gareth B. Matthews. Ancient Commentators on Aristotle. Ithaca: Cornell University Press, 1991.

Anonymous. *Aristoteles'* De anima. *Eine verlorene spätantike Paraphrase in arabischer und persischer Überlieferung. Arabischer Text nebst Kommentar, quellengeschichtlichen Studien und Glossaren*. Edited, translated, and commented, with an introduction, by Rüdiger Arnzen. Aristoteles Semitico-Latinus 9. Leiden, New York, and Cologne: Brill, 1998.

Anonymous. *Ǧawāmiʿ Kitāb Ǧālīnūs fī l-ʿanāṣir ʿalā raʾy Ibuqrāṭ*. In: *The Alexandrian Epitomes of Galen. Vol. I: On the Medical Sects for Beginners, The Small Art of Medicine, On the Elements According to the Opinion of Hippocrates*. Edited, translated, and annotated, with an introduction, by John Walbridge. Islamic Translation Series. Provo: Brigham Young University Press, 2014, 131–186.

Aristotle. *al-Aḫlāq. Tarǧamat Isḥāq ibn Ḥunayn*. Edited, with an introduction, by ʿAbd al-Raḥmān Badawī. Kuwait: al-Dār al-Qawmiyya li-l-Ṭibāʿa wa-l-Našr, 1979.

Aristotle. *al-Ḫiṭāba. al-Tarǧama al-ʿarabiyya al-qadīma*. Edited, with an introduction, by ʿAbd al-Raḥmān Badawī. Cairo: Maktabat al-Nahḍa al-Miṣriyya, 1959.

Aristotle. *al-Maqāla al-ūlā min Kitāb al-Samāʿ al-ṭabīʿī. Naql Isḥāq ibn Ḥunayn wa-taʿlīq Abī ʿAlī al-Ḥasan ibn al-Samḥ*. Edited by Wilhelm Kutsch and Khalil al-Georr. In: *Mélanges de l'Université Saint-Joseph* 39 (1963), 266–312. Reprint in Fuat Sezgin, ed. *Aristotle in the Arabic Tradition. Text and Studies III.* Parva naturalia, De partibus animalium, Physica, Metaphysica *and* Ethica. In

collaboration with Mazen Amawi, Carl Ehrig-Eggert, and Eckhard Neubauer. Islamic Philosophy 99. Frankfurt am Main: Institute for the History of Arabic-Islamic Science, 2000.
Aristotle. *al-Naṣṣ al-kāmil li-manṭiq Arisṭū*. Edited, with an introduction, by Farīd Ǧabr. 2 vols. Beirut: Dār al-Fikr al-Lubnānī, 1999.
Aristotle. *al-Ṭabīʿa. Tarǧamat Isḥāq ibn Ḥunayn maʿa šurūḥ Ibn al-Samḥ wa-Ibn ʿAdī wa-Mattā ibn Yūnus wa-Abī Farağ ibn al-Ṭayyib*. Edited, with an introduction, by ʿAbd al-Raḥmān Badawī. 2 vols. Cairo: al-Dār al-Qawmiyya li-l-Ṭibāʿa wa-l-Našr, 1964.
Aristotle. *Ars rhetorica*. Edited by Rudolf Kassel. Berlin and New York: Walter de Gruyter, 1976.
Aristotle. *Ars rhetorica. The Arabic Version*. Edited and commented, with an introduction, by Malcolm Cameron Lyons. 2 vols. Cambridge: Pembroke College, 1982.
Aristotle. *Categoriae et Liber de interpretatione*. Edited by Lorenzo Minio-Paluello. Scriptorum classicorum bibliotheca oxoniensis. Oxford: Clarendon Press, 1949.
Aristotle. *De anima*. Edited, translated, and annotated, with an introduction, by Robert Drew Hicks. Cambridge: Cambridge University Press, 1907.
Aristotle. *De anima*. Edited and commented, with an introduction, by William David Ross. Oxford: Clarendon Press, 1961.
Aristotle. *De anima. Books II and III*. Translated and annotated, with an introduction, by David W. Hamlyn. With an afterword by Christopher Shields. Clarendon Aristotle Series. Oxford: Clarendon Press, 1993.
Aristotle. *De anima*. Translated and commented, with an introduction, by Christopher Shields. Clarendon Aristotle Series. Oxford: Clarendon Press, 2016.
Aristotle. *De caelo*. Edited, with an introduction, by Donald J. Allan. Oxford Classical Texts. Oxford: Clarendon Press, 1936.
Aristotle. *De generatione animalium*. Edited by Hendrik Joan Drossaart Lulofs. Oxford Classical Texts. Oxford: Clarendon Press, 1965.
Aristotle. *De generatione et corruptione*. Translated and annotated, with an introduction, by Christopher John Fards Williams. Clarendon Aristotle Series. Oxford: Clarendon Press, 1982.
Aristotle. *De la génération et la corruption*. Edited, translated, and annotated, with an introduction, by Marwan Rashed. Collection des universités de France. Paris: Les Belles Lettres, 2004.
Aristotle. *De motu animalium*. Edited, translated, and commented, with an introduction, by Martha C. Nussbaum. Princeton: Princeton University Press, 1978.
Aristotle. *Ethica Nicomachea*. Edited by Ingram Bywater. Oxford: Clarendon Press, 1894.
Aristotle. *Ethica Nicomachea*. Edited by Richard Walzer and Jean Mingay. Oxford: Clarendon Press, 1991.
Aristotle. *Fī l-samāʾ wa-l-Āṯār al-ʿulwiyya*. Edited, with an introduction, by ʿAbd al-Raḥmān Badawī. Dirāsāt Islāmiyya 28. Cairo: Maktabat al-Nahḍa al-Miṣriyya, 1961.
Aristotle. *Generation of Animals. The Arabic Translation Commonly Ascribed to Yaḥyā ibn al-Biṭrīq*. Edited, with an introduction, by Jan Brugman and Hendrik Joan Drossaart Lulofs. Publications of the "De Goeje Fund" 23. Leiden: E. J. Brill, 1971.
Aristotle. *Histoire des animaux*. Edited, translated, and annotated, with an introduction, by Pierre Louis. 3 vols. Collection des universités de France. Paris: Les Belles Lettres, 1964–1969.
Aristotle. *Kitāb fī l-nafs*. In: *Arisṭūṭālīs fī l-nafs – "al-Ārāʾ al-ṭabīʿiyya" al-mansūb ilā Flūṭarḫus – "al-Ḥāss wa-l-maḥsūs" li-Ibn Rušd – "al-Nabāt" al-mansūb ilā Arisṭūṭālīs*. Edited and annotated, with an introduction, by ʿAbd al-Raḥmān Badawī. Cairo: Maktabat al-Nahḍa al-Miṣriyya, 1954, 1–88.
Aristotle. *Les parties des animaux*. Edited, translated, and annotated, with an introduction, by Pierre Louis. Collection des universités de France. Paris: Les Belles Lettres, 1956.
Aristotle. *Manṭiq Arisṭū*. Edited, with an introduction, by ʿAbd al-Raḥmān Badawī. 3 vols. Dirāsāt Islāmiyya 7. Kuwait and Beirut: Wikālat al-Maṭbūʿāt and Dār al-Qalam, 1980.

Aristotle. *Metaphysics*. Edited and commented, with an introduction, by William David Ross. 2 vols. Oxford: Clarendon Press, 1924.

Aristotle. *Metaphysics*. Translated by William David Ross. In: Aristotle. *The Complete Works of Aristotle. The Revised Oxford Translation*. Edited by Jonathan Barnes. Vol. 2. 2 vols. Bollingen Series 71.2. Princeton: Princeton University Press, [6]1995, 1552–1728.

Aristotle. *Metaphysics. Books B and K 1–2*. Translated and commented, with an introduction, by Arthur R. Madigan. Clarendon Aristotle Series. Oxford: Clarendon Press, 1999.

Aristotle. *Metaphysics. Book Θ*. Translated and commented, with an introduction, by Stephen Makin. Clarendon Aristotle Series. Oxford: Clarendon Press, 2006.

Aristotle. *Metaphysics A*. Edited, with an introduction, by Oliver Primavesi. In: *Aristotle's* Metaphysics *Alpha. With an Edition of the Greek Text by Oliver Primavesi*. Proceedings of the 18th Symposium Aristotelicum. Edited by Carlos Steel. Symposium Aristotelicum. Oxford: Oxford University Press, 2012, 385–516.

Aristotle. *Metaphysik Z*. Edited, translated, and commented, with an introduction, by Michael Frede and Günther Patzig. 2 vols. Munich: C. H. Beck, 1988.

Aristotle. *Meteorologicorum libri quattuor*. Edited by Francis Howard Fobes. Cambridge: Harvard University Press, 1919.

Aristotle. *Nicomachean Ethics*. Translated by Christopher Rowe. With a commentary by Sarah Broadie. With an introduction by Sarah Broadie and Christopher Rowe. Oxford and New York: Oxford University Press, 2002.

Aristotle. *On Coming-to-be and Passing-away. De generatione et corruptione*. Edited and commented, with an introduction, by Harold H. Joachim. Oxford: Clarendon Press, 1922.

Aristotle. *On Sophistical Refutations, On Coming-to-be and Passing Away, On the Cosmos*. Edited and translated by Edward Seymour Forster and David Furley. Loeb Classical Library 400. Cambridge and London: Harvard University Press, 1955.

Aristotle. *On the Heavens*. Edited and translated by William Keith Chambers Guthrie. Loeb Classical Library 338. Cambridge and London: Harvard University Press, 1939.

Aristotle. *On the Parts of Animals I–IV*. Translated and commented, with an introduction, by James G. Lennox. Clarendon Aristotle Series. Oxford: Clarendon Press, 2001.

Aristotle. *Physics*. Edited and commented, with an introduction, by William David Ross. Oxford: Clarendon Press, 1936.

Aristotle. *Physics. Books III and IV*. Translated and annotated, with an introduction, by Edward Hussey. Clarendon Aristotle Series. Oxford: Clarendon Press, 1983.

Aristotle. *Physics. Books I and II*. Translated and commented, with an introduction, by William Charlton. Clarendon Aristotle Series. New impression with supplementary material. Oxford: Clarendon Press, 1992.

Aristotle. *Physics*. Translated by Robert P. Hardie and Russell K. Gaye. In: Aristotle. *The Complete Works of Aristotle. The Revised Oxford Translation*. Edited by Jonathan Barnes. Vol. 1. 2 vols. Bollingen Series 71.2. Princeton: Princeton University Press, [6]1995, 315–446.

Aristotle. *Physics*. Translated by Robin Waterfield. With an introduction and annotations by David Bostock. Oxford World's Classics. Oxford and New York: Oxford University Press, 1996.

Aristotle. *Physics. Book VIII*. Translated and commented, with an introduction, by Daniel Graham. Clarendon Aristotle Series. Oxford: Clarendon Press, 1999.

Aristotle. *Physics VII*. Edited, translated, and annotated, with an introduction, by Robert Wardy. In: Wardy, Robert. *The Chain of Change. A Study of Aristotle's* Physics *VII*. Cambridge Classical Studies. Cambridge: Cambridge University Press, 1990.

Aristotle. *Physikvorlesung*. Translated and annotated, with an introduction, by Hans Wagner. Aristoteles. Werke in deutscher Übersetzung 11. Berlin: Akademie Verlag, [5]1995.

Aristotle. *Posterior Analytics*. Translated and commented, with an introduction, by Jonathan Barnes. Clarendon Aristotle Series. Oxford: Clarendon Press, ²1993.

Aristotle. *Prior Analytics*. Translated and commented, with an introduction, by Robin Smith. With annotations by Robin Smith. Indianapolis: Hacket Publishing Company, 1989.

Aristotle. *Prior and Posterior Analytics*. Edited and commented, with an introduction, by William David Ross. Oxford: Clarendon Press, 1949.

Aristotle. *The Arabic Version of Aristotle's* Parts of Animals. *Book XI–XIV of the* Kitāb al-Ḥayawān. Edited, with an introduction, by Remke Kruk. Aristoteles Semitico-Latinus 2. Amsterdam and Oxford: North-Holland Publishing Company, 1979.

Aristotle. *The Arabic Version of the* Nicomachean Ethics. Edited by Anna Akasoy and Alexander Fidora. Translated and annotated, with an introduction, by Douglas M. Dunlop. Aristoteles Semitico-Latinus 17. Leiden and Boston: Brill, 2005.

Aristotle. *The Complete Works of Aristotle. The Revised Oxford Translation*. Edited by Jonathan Barnes. 2 vols. Bollingen Series 71.2. Princeton: Princeton University Press, ⁶1995.

Aristotle. *Topica et Sophistici elenchi*. Edited by William David Ross. Oxford Classical Texts. Oxford: Clarendon Press, 1970.

Aristotle. *Über Werden und Vergehen*. Translated and annotated, with an introduction, by Thomas Buchheim. Aristoteles. Werke in deutscher Übersetzung 12.IV. Berlin: Akademie Verlag, 2010.

Ps.-Aristotle. *Aqwāl al-šayḫ al-yūnānī*. In: *Aflūṭīn ʿinda l-ʿarab*. Edited, with an introduction, by ʿAbd al-Raḥmān Badawī. Dirāsāt Islāmiyya 20. Cairo: Maktabat al-Nahḍa al-Miṣriyya, 1955, 184–194.

Ps.-Aristotle. *Aristotelis qui fertur libellus* De mundo. *Accedit capitum V, VI, VII interpretatio syriaca ab Eduardo König Germanice versa*. Edited by William Laughton Lorimer. Nouvelle collection de textes et de documents publiée sous le patronage de l'Association Guillaume Budé. Paris: Les Belles Lettres, 1933.

Ps.-Aristotle. *Kitāb al-Ḥaraka*. Edited by Elvira Wakelnig. URL: http://www.ancientwisdoms.ac.uk/folioscope/sawsTexts:HME5683.KHar.saws01.

Ps.-Aristotle. *Kitāb al-Īḍāḥ fī l-ḫayr al-maḥḍ li-Arisṭūṭālīs*. In: *al-Aflāṭūniyya al-muḥdaṯa ʿinda l-ʿarab*. Edited, with an introduction, by ʿAbd al-Raḥmān Badawī. Kuwait: Wakālat al-Maṭbūʿāt, ²1977, 3–33.

Ps.-Aristotle. *Kitāb Arisṭāṭālīs al-faylasūf al-musammā bi-l-yūnāniyya Uṯūlūǧiyā*. In: *Aflūṭīn ʿinda l-ʿarab*. Edited, with an introduction, by ʿAbd al-Raḥmān Badawī. Dirāsāt Islāmiyya 20. Cairo: Maktabat al-Nahḍa al-Miṣriyya, 1955, 1–164.

Ps.-Aristotle. *On the Cosmos*. Translated by Johan C. Thom. In: *Cosmic Order and Divine Power*. Edited by Johan C. Thom. Scripta antiquitatis posterioris ad ethicam religionemque pertinentia 23. Tübingen: Mohr Siebeck, 2014, 20–57.

Ps.-Aristotle. *Risāla fī l-ʿilm al-ilāhī*. In: *Aflūṭīn ʿinda l-ʿarab*. Edited, with an introduction, by ʿAbd al-Raḥmān Badawī. Dirāsāt Islāmiyya 20. Cairo: Maktabat al-Nahḍa al-Miṣriyya, 1955, 165–183.

Ps.-Aristotle. *Risālat Arisṭūṭālīs ilā l-Iskandar fī ṣifat tartīb al-ʿālam al-maʿrūfa bi-l-ḏahabiyya*. Edited, translated, and commented, with an introduction, by David Alan Brafman. In: Brafman, David Alan. "The Arabic *De mundo*. An Edition with Translation and Commentary." PhD thesis. Durham: Duke University, 1985.

al-Ašʿarī, Abū l-Ḥasan. *Maqālāt al-islāmiyyīn wa-ḫtilāf al-muṣallīn. Die dogmatischen Lehren der Anhänger des Islam*. Edited, with an introduction, by Hellmut Ritter. Bibliotheca islamica 1. Beirut: Klaus Schwarz Verlag, ⁴2005.

Averroes. *Commentarium magnum in Aristotelis Physicorum*. In: *Aristotelis opera cum Averrois commentariis*. Vol. 4. Venice: Apud Junctas, 1562–1574.

Averroes. *Commentum magnum super libro De celo et mundo Aristotelis*. Edited by Francis James Carmody and Rüdiger Arnzen. 2 vols. Recherches de Théologie et Philosophie Médiévales. Bibliotheca 4. With a preface by Gerhard Endreß. Leuven: Peeters, 2003.

Averroes. *De substantia orbis. Critical Edition of the Hebrew Text*. Edited, translated, and commented by Arthur Hyman. Medieval Academy Books 96. Cambridge and Jerusalem: The Medieval Academy of America, The Israel Academy of Sciences, and Humanities, 1986.
Averroes. *Die entscheidende Abhandlung und die Urteilsfällung über das Verhältnis von Gesetz und Philosophie. Arabisch – Deutsch*. Translated and commented, with an introduction, by Franz Schupp. Philosophische Bibliothek 600. Hamburg: Felix Meiner Verlag, 2009.
Averroes. *Long Commentary on the* De Anima *of Aristotle*. Translated and annotated, with an introduction, by Richard C. Taylor. In collaboration with Thérèse-Anne Druart. Yale Library of Medieval Philosophy. New Haven and London: Yale University Press, 2009.
Averroes. *Mittlerer Kommentar zu Aristoteles'* De generatione et corruptione. Edited and commented, with an introduction, by Heidrun Eichner. Abhandlungen der Nordrhein-Westfälischen Akademie der Wissenschaften 111. Paderborn: Ferdinand Schöningh, 2005.
Averroes. *Tafsīr Mā baʿd al-ṭabīʿa*. Edited, with an introduction, by Maurice Bouyges. 4 vols. Bibliotheca arabica scholasticorum. Série arabe V–VII. Beirut: Dār al-Mašriq, 1938–52.
Averroes. *Talḫīṣ al-Samāʾ wa-l-ʿālam*. Edited and annotated, with an introduction, by Ǧamāl al-Dīn al-ʿAlawī. Fez: Kulliyyāt al-Ādāb, 1984.
Avicenna. *Abhandlung über die Teile der Geisteswissenschaften (Risāla fī aqsām al-ʿulūm al ʿaqliyya)*. Translated, with an introduction, by Roland Pietsch. In: *Spektrum Iran. Zeitschrift für islamisch-iranische Kultur* 24.3 (2011), 5–26.
Avicenna. *al-Burhān min Kitāb al-Šifāʾ. De demonstratione ex libro "Alchifāʾ."* Edited and annotated, with an introduction, by ʿAbd al-Raḥmān Badawī. Dirāsāt Islāmiyya 18. Cairo: Maktabat al-Nahḍa al-Miṣriyya, 1954.
Avicenna. *al-Ḥikma al-mašriqiyya. al-Ṭabīʿiyyāt*. Edited by Ahmet Özcan. In: Özcan, Ahmet. "İbn Sīna'nın el-Hikmetu'l-Meşrikiyye adlı eseri ve tabiat felsefesi." PhD thesis. Istanbul: Marmara Üniversitesi, 1993.
Avicenna. *al-Išārāt wa-l-tanbīhāt*. Edited, with an introduction, by Muǧtabā al-Zārʿī. Qom: Būstān-e Ketāb, ²2008.
Avicenna. *al-Išārāt wa-l-tanbīhāt maʿa šarḥ Naṣīr al-Dīn al-Ṭūsī*. Edited by Sulaymān Dunyā. 4 vols. Ḏaḫāʾir al-ʿarab 22. Cairo: Dār al-Maʿārif, ³1983.
Avicenna. *al-Mabdaʾ wa-l-maʿād*. Edited by ʿAbd Allāh Nūrānī. Selsele-ye Dāneš-e Īrānī 36. Tehran: Institute of Islamic Studies, McGill University, Tehran Branch, 1984.
Avicenna. *al-Maqūlāt. Commentary on Aristotle's* Categories. Translated and annotated, with an introduction, by Allan Bäck. Analytica Liber Conversus. Munich: Philosophia Verlag, 2016.
Avicenna. *al-Mubāḥaṯāt*. Edited and annotated, with an introduction, by Moḥsen Bīdārfar. Qom: Entešārāt-e Bīdār, 1992.
Avicenna. *al-Naǧāt fī l-ḥikma al-manṭiqiyya wa-l-ṭabīʿiyya wa-l-ilāhiyya*. Edited by Muḥyī al-Dīn Ṣabrī al-Kurdī. Cairo: Maṭbaʿat al-Saʿāda, ²1938.
Avicenna. *al-Naǧāt fī l-manṭiq wa-l-ilāhiyyāt*. Edited and annotated, with an introduction, by ʿAbd al-Raḥmān ʿUmayra. Beirut: Dār al-Ǧīl, 1992.
Avicenna. *al-Naǧāt min al-ġaraq fī baḥr al-ḍalālāt*. Edited, with an introduction, by Moḥammad Taqī Dānešpažūh. Tehran: Entešārāt-e Dānešgāh-e Tehrān, 1985.
Avicenna. *al-Samāʿ al-ṭabīʿī min Kitāb al-Šifāʾ*. Edited, with an introduction, by Ǧaʿfar Āl Yāsīn. Beirut: Dār al-Manāhil li-l-Ṭibāʿa wa-l-Našr wa-l-Tawzīʿ, 1996.
Avicenna. *al-Šifāʾ. al-Manṭiq. al-Muǧallad 1: al-Madḫal*. Edited by Ǧurǧ Šiḥāta Qanawātī, Maḥmūd Muḥammad al-Ḫuḍayrī, and Aḥmad Fuʾād al-Ahwānī. With an introduction by Ibrāhīm Madkūr. With a preface by Taha Ḥusayn Bāšā. Cairo: al-Maṭbaʿa al-Amīriyya, 1952.
Avicenna. *al-Šifāʾ. al-Manṭiq. al-Muǧallad 5: al-Burhān*. Edited, with an introduction, by Abū l-ʿAlā ʿAfīfī. With a preface by Ibrāhīm Madkūr. Cairo: al-Maṭbaʿa al-Amīriyya, 1956.

Avicenna. *al-Šifāʾ. al-Manṭiq. al-Muǧallad 2: al-Maqūlāt*. Edited by Ǧurǧ Šiḥāta Qanawātī, Maḥmūd Muḥammad al-Ḫuḍayrī, Aḥmad Fuʾād al-Ahwānī, and Saʿīd Zāyid. With an introduction by Ibrāhīm Madkūr. Cairo: al-Hayʾa al-ʿĀmma li-Šuʾūn al-Maṭābiʿ al-Amīriyya, 1959.

Avicenna. *al-Šifāʾ. al-Ilāhiyyāt*. Edited by Ǧurǧ Šiḥāta Qanawātī, Saʿīd Zāyid, Muḥammad Yūsuf Mūsā, and Sulaymān Dunyā. With an introduction by Ibrāhīm Madkūr. 2 vols. Cairo: al-Hayʾa al-ʿĀmma li-Šuʾūn al-Maṭābiʿ al-Amīriyya, 1960.

Avicenna. *al-Šifāʾ. al-Manṭiq. al-Muǧallad 4: al-Qiyās*. Edited by Saʿīd Zāyid. With an introduction by Ibrāhīm Madkūr. Cairo: al-Hayʾa al-ʿĀmma li-Šuʾūn al-Maṭābiʿ al-Amīriyya, 1964.

Avicenna. *al-Šifāʾ. al-Ṭabīʿiyyāt. al-Muǧallad 2–4: al-Samāʾ wa-l-ʿālam, al-Kawn wa-l-fasād, al-Afʿāl wa-l-infiʿālāt*. Edited by Maḥmūd Qāsim. With an introduction by Ibrāhīm Madkūr. Cairo: Dār al-Kitāb al-ʿArabī li-l-Ṭibāʿa wa-l-Našr, 1969.

Avicenna. *al-Šifāʾ. al-Ṭabīʿiyyāt. al-Muǧallad 6: al-Nafs*. Edited by Ǧurǧ Šiḥāta Qanawātī and Saʿīd Zāyid. With an introduction by Ǧurǧ Šiḥāta Qanawātī. With a preface by Ibrāhīm Madkūr. Cairo: al-Hayʾa al-Miṣriyya al-ʿĀmma li-l-Kitāb, 1975.

Avicenna. *al-Šifāʾ. al-Ṭabīʿiyyāt. al-Muǧallad 1: al-Samāʿ al-ṭabīʿī*. Edited by Saʿīd Zāyid. With a preface by Ibrāhīm Madkūr. Cairo: al-Hayʾa al-Miṣriyya al-ʿĀmma li-l-Kitāb, 1983.

Avicenna. *al-Ṭabīʿiyyāt min ʿUyūn al-ḥikma*. In: Avicenna. *Tisʿ rasāʾil fī l-ḥikma wa-l-ṭabīʿiyyāt wa-fī āḫirihā qiṣṣat Salāmān wa-Absāl*. Edited, with an introduction, by Ḥasan ʿĀṣī. Cairo: Dār al-ʿArab, [2]1989, 2–38.

Avicenna. *al-Taʿlīqāt*. Edited by ʿAbd al-Raḥmān Badawī. al-Maktaba al-ʿArabiyya 130. Cairo: al-Hayʾa al-Miṣriyya al-ʿĀmma li-l-Kitāb, 1973.

Avicenna. *al-Taʿlīqāt*. Edited and annotated, with an introduction, by Seyyed Hossein Mousavian. Maǧmūʿe-ye Āṯār 1. Tehran: Moʾassese-ye Pažūhešī-ye Ḥekmat-o Felsefe-ye Īrān, 2013.

Avicenna. *Avicenna's Psychology. An English Translation of* Kitāb al-Najāt, *Book II, Chapter VI with historico-philosophical Notes and Textual Improvements on the Cairo Edition*. Translated and annotated, with an introduction, by Fazlur Rahman. London: Oxford University Press, 1952.

Avicenna. *Book of Definitions*. Translated by Kiki Kennedy-Day. In: Kennedy-Day, Kiki. *Books of Definition in Islamic Philosophy. The Limits of Words*. London and New York: RoutledgeCurzon, 2003, 98–114.

Avicenna. *Commentaire sur le livre Lambda de la* Métaphysique d'Aristote (chaiptres 6–10). *Šarḥ Maqāla al-lām (faṣl 6–10) min Kitāb Mā baʿd al-ṭabīʿa li-Arisṭūṭālīs (min Kitāb al-Inṣāf)*. Edited, translated, and annotated, with an introduction, by Marc Geoffroy, Jules Janssens, and Meryem Sebti. Études musulmanes 43. Paris: Vrin, 2014.

Avicenna. *Dānešnāme-ye ʿAlāʾī. Resāle-ye manṭeq*. Edited by Moḥammad Moʿīn and Moḥammad Meškāt. Selsele-ye Entešārāt-e Anǧoman-e Āṯār-e Mellī 12. Tehran: Entešārāt-e Anǧoman-e Āṯār-e Mellī, 1952.

Avicenna. *Dānešnāme-ye ʿAlāʾī. Ṭabīʿiyyāt*. Edited by Moḥammad Meškāt. Selsele-ye Entešārāt-e Anǧoman-e Āṯār-e Mellī 13. Tehran: Entešārāt-e Anǧoman-e Āṯār-e Mellī, 1952.

Avicenna. *Dānešnāme-ye ʿAlāʾī. Elāhiyyāt*. Edited by Moḥammad Moʿīn. Selsele-ye Entešārāt-e Anǧoman-e Āṯār-e Mellī 15. Tehran: Entešārāt-e Anǧoman-e Āṯār-e Mellī, 1952.

Avicenna. *De Anima (Arabic Text). Being the Psychological Part of Kitāb al-Shifāʾ*. Edited by Fazlur Rahman. Cairo: al-Hayʾa al-ʿĀmma li-Šuʾūn al-Maṭābiʿ al-Amīriyya, 1959.

Avicenna. *Deliverance. Logic*. Translated and annotated by Asad Q. Ahmed. With an introduction by Tony Street. Studies in Islamic Philosophy. Karachi: Oxford University Press, 2011.

Avicenna. *Die Metaphysik Avicennas enthaltend die Metaphysik, Theologie, Kosmologie und Ethik*. Translated and annotated by Maximilian Horten. Halle and New York: Verlag Rudolph Haupt, 1907.

Avicenna. *Ibn Sina Risâleleri*. Edited and annotated, with an introduction, by Hilmi Ziya Ülken. 2 vols. İstanbul Üniversitesi Edebiyat Fakültesi. Yayınlarından 552. Ankara: Türk Tarih Kurumu Basımevi, 1953.

Avicenna. *Kitāb al-Hidāya*. Edited and annotated, with an introduction, by Muḥammad ʿAbduh. Cairo: Maktabat al-Qāhira al-Ḥadīṯa, ²1974.

Avicenna. *Kitāb al-Išārāt wa-l-tanbīhāt. Le livre des théorèmes et des avertissements publié d'après les mss. de Berlin, de Leyde et d'Oxford*. Edited by Jacques Forget. Leiden: E. J. Brill, 1892.

Avicenna. *Kitāb al-Maǧmūʿ aw al-Ḥikma al-ʿArūḍiyya*. Edited, with an introduction, by Muḥsin Sāliḥ. Beirut: Dār al-Hādī li-l-Ṭibāʿa wa-l-Našr wa-l-Tawzīʿ, 2007.

Avicenna. *Kitāb al-Naǧāt fī l-ḥikma al-manṭiqiyya wa-l-ṭabīʿiyya wa-l-ilāhiyya*. Edited, with an introduction, by Majid Fakhry. Beirut: Dār al-Afāq al-Ǧadīda, 1985.

Avicenna. *Kitāb fī l-nafs ʿalā sunnat al-iḫtiṣār*. Edited, translated, and annotated, with an introduction, by Samuel Landauer. In: Landauer, Samuel. "Die Psychologie des Ibn Sīnā." In: *Zeitschrift der Deutschen Morgenländischen Gesellschaft* 29 (1876), 335–418.

Avicenna. *Kitāb ʿUyūn al-ḥikma*. Edited by Muwaffaq Fawzī al-Ǧabr. With an introduction by Muḥammad al-Ǧabr. Damascus: Dār al-Yanābīʿ, 1996.

Avicenna. *Kitāb ʿUyūn al-ḥikma wa-yuštamilu ʿalā ṯalāṯat funūn al-manṭiqiyyāt wa-l-ṭabīʿiyyāt wa-l-ilāhiyyāt*. In: Avicenna. *Ibn Sina Risâleleri*. Edited and annotated, with an introduction, by Hilmi Ziya Ülken. Vol. 1. 2 vols. İstanbul Üniversitesi Edebiyat Fakültesi. Yayınlarından 552. Ankara: Türk Tarih Kurumu Basımevi, 1953, 1–55.

Avicenna. *Le livre de science*. Translated and annotated, with an introduction, by Mohammad Achena and Henri Massé. 2 vols. Traductions de textes persans publiées sous le patronage de l'Association Guillaume Budé. Paris: Les Belles Lettres, ²1986.

Avicenna. *Les sciences physiques et métaphysiques selon la Risālah fī Aqsām al-ʿulūm d'Avicenne. Essai de traduction critique*. Translated and annotated, with an introduction, by Yahya Michot. In: *Bulletin de philosophie médiévale* 22 (1980), 62–73.

Avicenna. *Lettre au vizir Abū Saʿd*. Edited, translated, and annotated, with an introduction, by Yahya Michot. Sagesses musulmanes 4. Beirut: Les Éditions al-Bouraq, 2000.

Avicenna. *Liber primus naturalium. Tractatus primus de causis et principiis naturalium*. Edited by Simone van Riet. With an introduction by Gérard Verbeke. Avicenna Latinus. Louvain-la-Neuve and Leiden: Éditions Peeters and E. J. Brill, 1992.

Avicenna. *Liber primus naturalium. Tractatus secundus de motu et de consimilibus*. Edited by Simone van Riet, Jules Janssens, and André Allard. With an introduction by Gérard Verbeke. Avicenna Latinus. Brussels: Académie Royale de Belgique, 2006.

Avicenna. *Libro della guarigione. Le cose divine*. Translated and annotated, with an introduction, by Amos Bertolacci. Classici del Pensiero 53. Turin: Utet Libreria, 2008.

Avicenna. *Livre des définitions*. Edited, translated, and annotated by Amélie-Marie Goichon. Mémorial Avicenne 6. Cairo: Publications de l'Institut Français d'Archéologie Orientale du Caire, 1963.

Avicenna. *Livre des directives et remarques. Kitāb al-ʾIšārāt wa l-tanbīhāt*. Translated and annotated, with an introduction, by Amélie-Marie Goichon. Collection d'œuvres arabes de l'Unesco. Beirut and Paris: Commission Internationale pour la traduction des chefs d'œuvres and J. Vrin, 1951.

Avicenna. *Manṭiq al-Mašriqiyyīn wa-l-Qaṣīda al-muzdawiǧa fī l-manṭiq*. Edited by Muḥibb al-Dīn al-Ḫaṭīb and ʿAbd al-Fattāḥ al-Qatlān. Cairo: al-Maktaba al-Salafiyya, 1910.

Avicenna. *Metafisica. La* scienza delle cose divine (al-ilāhiyyāt) *dal* Libro della Guarigione (Kitāb al-Šifāʾ). *Con testo arabo e latino*. Edited by Olga Lizzini and Pasquale Porro. Translated and annotated, with an introduction, by Olga Lizzini. With a foreword by Pasquale Porro. Il pensiero occidentale. Milano: Bompiani, ²2006.

Avicenna. *Muḫtaṣar al-awsaṭ fī l-manṭiq. al-Qāṭīġūriyās ayy al-Maqūlāt*. Edited, with an introduction, by Alexander Kalbarczyk. In: Kalbarczyk, Alexander. "The *Kitāb al-Maqūlāt* of the *Muḫtaṣar al-awsaṭ fī l-manṭiq*. A Hitherto Unknown Source for Studying Ibn Sīnā's Reception of Aristotle's *Categories*." In: *Oriens* 40.2 (2012), 305–354.

Avicenna. *Opera. In lucem redacta ac nuper quantum ars niti potuit per canonicos emendata*. Venice: Bonetus Locatellus for Octavianus Scotus, 1508.

Avicenna. *Remarks and Admonitions. Part One. Logic*. Translated and annotated, with an introduction, by Shams C. Inati. Medieval Sources in Translation 28. Toronto: Pontifical Institute of Medieval Studies, 1984.

Avicenna. *Remarks and Admonitions. Physics and Metaphysics*. Translated and annotated, with an introduction, by Shams C. Inati. New York: Columbia University Press, 2014.

Avicenna. *Risāla fī aqsām al-ʿulūm al-ʿaqliyya*. In: Avicenna. *Tisʿ rasāʾil fī l-ḥikma wa-l-ṭabīʿiyyāt wa-fī āḫirihā qiṣṣat Salāmān wa-Absāl*. Edited, with an introduction, by Ḥasan ʿĀṣī. Cairo: Dār al-ʿArab, ²1989, 104–118.

Avicenna. *Risāla fī l-ağrām al-ʿulwiyya*. In: Avicenna. *Tisʿ rasāʾil fī l-ḥikma wa-l-ṭabīʿiyyāt wa-fī āḫirihā qiṣṣat Salāmān wa-Absāl*. Edited, with an introduction, by Ḥasan ʿĀṣī. Cairo: Dār al-ʿArab, ²1989, 39–59.

Avicenna. *Risāla fī l-ḥudūd*. In: Avicenna. *Tisʿ rasāʾil fī l-ḥikma wa-l-ṭabīʿiyyāt wa-fī āḫirihā qiṣṣat Salāmān wa-Absāl*. Edited, with an introduction, by Ḥasan ʿĀṣī. Cairo: Dār al-ʿArab, ²1989, 71–102.

Avicenna. *Risāla li-baʿḍ al-mutakallimīn ilā l-Šayḫ fa-ağābahum*. In: Avicenna. *Ibn Sina Risâleleri*. Edited and annotated, with an introduction, by Hilmi Ziya Ülken. Vol. 2. 2 vols. İstanbul Üniversitesi Edebiyat Fakültesi. Yayınlarından 552. Ankara: Türk Tarih Kurumu Basımevi, 1953, 155–159.

Avicenna. *The* Metaphysica *of Avicenna (Ibn Sīnā). A Critical Translation-commentary and Analysis of the Fundamental Arguments in Avicenna's* Metaphysica *in the* Dānish Nāma-i ʿalāʾī (The Book of Scientific Knowledge). Translated and commented, with an introduction, by Parviz Morewedge. Persian Heritage Series 13. London: Routledge & Kegan Paul, 1973.

Avicenna. *The Metaphysics of* The Healing. *A Parallel English-Arabic Text*. Edited, translated, and annotated, with an introduction, by Michael E. Marmura. Islamic Translation Series. Provo: Brigham Young University Press, 2005.

Avicenna. *The Physics of* The Healing. *A Parallel English-Arabic Text*. Edited, translated, and annotated, with an introduction, by Jon McGinnis. Islamic Translation Series. Provo: Brigham Young University Press, 2009.

Avicenna. *The* Physics *of the* The Book of Scientific Knowledge. Translated and commented by Jamila Jauhari. In: Jauhari, Jamila. "The Physics of Avicenna. A Translation and Commentary upon the Physics Proper of the 'Tabiy'yat' of Avicenna's 'Danish Nana-i [sic!] Alai.'" PhD thesis. University of Pennsylvania, 1988.

Avicenna. *Tisʿ rasāʾil fī l-ḥikma wa-l-ṭabīʿiyyāt wa-fī āḫirihā qiṣṣat Salāmān wa-Absāl*. Edited, with an introduction, by Ḥasan ʿĀṣī. Cairo: Dār al-ʿArab, ²1989.

Avicenna. *ʿUyūn al-ḥikma*. Edited, with an introduction, by ʿAbd al-Raḥmān Badawī. Ḏikrā Ibn Sīnā 5. Cairo: al-Maʿhad al-ʿIlmī l-Faransī li-l-Āṯār al-Šarqiyya, 1954.

Avicenna and Abū Rayḥān al-Bīrūnī. *al-Asʾila wa-l-ağwiba*. Edited, with an introduction, by Mahdi Moḥaqqeq and Seyyed Hossein Nasr. Šōrā-ye ʿĀlī-ye Farhang-o Honar. Markaz-e Moṭālaʿāt-o Hamāhangī-ye Farhangī 9. Tehran: Čāpḫane-ye Moʾassese-ye Entešārāt-o Čāp-e Dānešgāh-e Tehrān, 1973.

Avicenna and Abū Rayḥān al-Bīrūnī. *Ğawāb sitta ʿašara [sic!] masʾalatan li-Abī Rayḥān wa-Ağwibat masāʾil saʾala anhā Abū Rayḥān*. In: Avicenna. *Ibn Sina Risâleleri*. Edited and annotated, with an introduction, by Hilmi Ziya Ülken. Vol. 2. 2 vols. İstanbul Üniversitesi Edebiyat Fakültesi. Yayınlarından 552. Ankara: Türk Tarih Kurumu Basımevi, 1953, 2–36.

Avicenna and Abū Rayḥān al-Bīrūnī. *Ibn Sīnā – al-Bīrūnī Correspondence I–VIII*. Translated by Rafik Berjak and Muzaffar Iqbal. In: *Islam & Science* 1–5 (2003–07).

Avicenna and Abū ʿUbayd al-Ǧūzǧānī. *The Life of Ibn Sina. Sīrat al-šayḫ al-raʾīs*. Edited, translated, and annotated, with an introduction, by William E. Gohlman. Studies in Islamic Philosophy and Science. Albany: State University of New York Press, 1974.

Badawī, ʿAbd al-Raḥmān, editor and introduction. *Aflūṭīn ʿinda l-ʿarab*. Dirāsāt Islāmiyya 20. Cairo: Maktabat al-Nahḍa al-Miṣriyya, 1955.

Badawī, ʿAbd al-Raḥmān, editor and introduction. *al-Aflāṭūniyya al-muḥdaṯa ʿinda l-ʿarab*. Kuwait: Wakālat al-Maṭbūʿāt, ²1977.

Badawī, ʿAbd al-Raḥmān, editor, annotator, and introduction. *Arisṭū ʿinda l-ʿarab. Dirāsa wa-nuṣūṣ ġayr manšūra*. Dirāsāt Islāmiyya 5. Kuwait: Wakālat al-Maṭbūʿāt, ²1978.

Badawī, ʿAbd al-Raḥmān, editor, annotator, and introduction. *Arisṭūṭālīs fī l-nafs – "al-Ārāʾ al-ṭabīʿiyya" al-mansūb ilā Flūṭarḫus – "al-Ḥāss wa-l-maḥsūs" li-Ibn Rušd – "al-Nabāt" al-mansūb ilā Arisṭūṭālīs*. Cairo: Maktabat al-Nahḍa al-Miṣriyya, 1954.

Badawī, ʿAbd al-Raḥmān, editor, annotator, and introduction. *Muntaḫab Ṣiwān al-ḥikma wa-ṯalāṯ rasāʾil*. Tehran: Entešārāt-e Bunyād-e Farhang-e Īrān, 1974.

Badawī, ʿAbd al-Raḥmān, editor and introduction. *Šurūḥ ʿalā Arisṭū mafqūda fī l-yūnāniyya wa-rasāʾil uḫrā. Commentaires sur Aristote perdus en grec et autres épitres*. Recherches publiées sous la direction de l'Institut de Lettres Orientales de Beyrouth. Nouvelle série A. Langue arabe et pensée islamique. Tome 1. Beirut: Dār al-Mašriq, 1971.

Barhebraeus. *Butyrum sapientiae, Physics*. Edited, translated, and commented, with an introduction, by Jens Ole Schmitt. Aristoteles Semitico-Latinus 20. Leiden and Boston: Brill, [forthcoming].

al-Bayhaqī, ʿAlī ibn Zayd Ẓahīr al-Dīn. *Taʾrīḫ ḥukamāʾ al-islām*. Edited by Muḥammad Kurd ʿAlī. Damascus: Maṭbaʿat al-Taraqqī, 1946.

al-Bīrūnī, Abū Rayḥān. *al-Āṯār al-bāqiya ʿan al-qurūn al-ḫāliya. Chronologie orientalischer Völker*. Edited, with an introduction, by Eduard Sachau. Leipzig: F. A. Brockhaus, 1878.

al-Bīrūnī, Abū Rayḥān. *In den Gärten der Wissenschaft. Ausgewählte Texte aus den Werken des muslimischen Universalgelehrten*. Translated and annotated, with an introduction, by Gotthard Strohmaier. Leipzig: Reclam, 1988.

al-Bīrūnī, Abū Rayḥān. *Risāla li-l-Bīrūnī fī fihrist kutub Muḥammad ibn Zakariyāʾ al-Rāzī*. Edited by Paul Kraus. Paris: Maisonneuve, 1936.

Boethus of Sidon (?). *Περὶ τῆς τοῦ ποτὲ κατηγορίας*. In: Aristotle. *Organon graece*. Edited and commented, with an introduction, by Theodor Waitz. Vol. 1. 2 vols. Leipzig: Hahn, 1844–1846, 19–23.

Crescas, Hasdai. *Crescas' Critique of Aristotle. Problems of Aristotle's* Physics *in Jewish and Arabic Philosophy*. Edited, translated, and annotated, with an introduction, by Harry A. Wolfson. Harvard Semitic Series 6. Cambridge: Harvard University Press, 1929.

Dunlop, Douglas M., editor and introduction. *The Muntaḫab Ṣiwān al-ḥikmah of Abū Sulaymān as-Sijistānī*. Near and Middle East Monographs 4. The Hague, Paris, and New York: Mouton Publishers, 1979.

Euclid. *The Thirteen Books of the Elements*. Translated and commented, with an introduction, by Thomas L. Heath. 3 vols. Cambridge: Cambridge University Press, ²1926.

al-Fārābī, Abū Naṣr. *al-Manṭiq ʿinda l-Fārābī*. Edited by Rafīq al-ʿAǧam and Majid Fakhry. 4 vols. al-Maktaba al-Falsafiyya. Beirut: Dār al-Mašriq, 1986.

al-Fārābī, Abū Naṣr. *Alfārābī's philosophische Abhandlungen*. Translated, with an introduction, by Friedrich Dieterici. Leiden: E. J. Brill, 1892.

al-Fārābī, Abū Naṣr. *Alfārābī's philosophische Abhandlungen aus Londoner, Leidener und Berliner Handschriften*. Edited, with an introduction, by Friedrich Dieterici. Leiden: E. J. Brill, 1890.

al-Fārābī, Abū Naṣr. *Distinctio super Librum Aristotelis de naturali auditu*. Edited by Alexander Birkenmajer. In: Birkenmajer, Alexander. "Eine wiedergefundene Übersetzung Gerhards von Cremona." In: *Aus der Geisteswelt des Mittelalters*. Studien und Texte Martin Grabmann zur

Vollendung des 60. Lebensjahres von Freunden und Schülern gewidmet. Edited by Albert Lang, Joseph Lechner, and Michael Schmaus. Beiträge zur Geschichte der Philosophie und Theologie des Mittelalters. Supplementband 3.1. Münster: Aschendorfsche Verlagsbuchhandlung, 1935, 475–481.

al-Fārābī, Abū Naṣr. *Halâ Üzerine Makalesi. Article on Vacuum.* Edited and translated, with an introduction, by Necati Lugal and Aydın Sayılı. Türk Tarih Kurumu Yayınlarından XV. Seri 1. Ankara: Türk Tarih Kurumu Basımevi, 1951.

al-Fārābī, Abū Naṣr. *Iḥṣā' al-ulūm.* Edited, with an introduction, by ʿUṯmān Amīn. Cairo: Maktabat al-Anǧilū l-Miṣriyya, ³1968.

al-Fārābī, Abū Naṣr. *Kitāb al-Burhān.* In: al-Fārābī, Abū Naṣr. *al-Manṭiq ʿinda l-Fārābī.* Edited by Rafīq al-ʿAǧam and Majid Fakhry. Vol. 4. 4 vols. al-Maktaba al-Falsafiyya. Beirut: Dār al-Mašriq, 1986, 19–96.

al-Fārābī, Abū Naṣr. *Kitāb al-Ḥurūf. Book of Letters.* Edited and annotated, with an introduction, by Muhsin Mahdi. Recherches publiées sous la direction de l'Institut de Lettres Orientales de Beyrouth. Série I. Pensée arabe et musulmane. Tome 46. Beirut: Dār al-Mašriq, 1969.

al-Fārābī, Abū Naṣr. *Kitāb al-Mūsīqā l-kabīr.* Edited and annotated, with an introduction, by Ġaṭṭās ʿAbd al-Malik Ḫašaba and Maḥmūd Aḥmad al-Hifnī. Cairo: Dār al-Kātib al-ʿArabī li-l-Ṭibāʿa wa-l-Našr, 1967.

al-Fārābī, Abū Naṣr. *Kitāb al-Siyāsa al-madaniyya al-mulaqqab bi-Mabādi' al-mawǧūdāt.* Edited and annotated, with an introduction, by Fawzī Mitrī Naǧǧār. Beirut: Dār al-Mašriq, ²1993.

al-Fārābī, Abū Naṣr. *Maqāla fī aġrāḍ al-ḥakīm fī kull maqāla min al-kitāb al-mawsūm bi-l-ḥurūf wa-huwa taḥqīq ġaraḍ Arisṭūṭālīs fī Kitāb Mā baʿd al-ṭabīʿa.* In: al-Fārābī, Abū Naṣr. *Alfārābī's philosophische Abhandlungen aus Londoner, Leidener und Berliner Handschriften.* Edited, with an introduction, by Friedrich Dieterici. Leiden: E. J. Brill, 1890, 34–38.

al-Fārābī, Abū Naṣr. *On the Perfect State. Abū Naṣr al-Fārābī's* Mabādi' ārā' ahl al-madīna al-fāḍila. Edited, translated, and commented, with an introduction, by Richard Walzer. Oxford: Clarendon Press, 1985.

al-Fārābī, Abū Naṣr. *Political Regime, Nicknamed Principles of the Existence. Plato the Divine and Aristotle.* In: al-Fārābī, Abū Naṣr. *The Political Writings. Volume II. "Political Regime" and "Summary of Plato's Laws."* Translated and annotated, with an introduction, by Charles E. Butterworth. Agora Editions. Ithaca and London: Cornell University Press, 2015, 29–94.

al-Fārābī, Abū Naṣr. *Risāla fī-mā yanbaġī an yuqaddama qabla taʿallum al-falsafa.* In: al-Fārābī, Abū Naṣr. *Alfārābī's philosophische Abhandlungen aus Londoner, Leidener und Berliner Handschriften.* Edited, with an introduction, by Friedrich Dieterici. Leiden: E. J. Brill, 1890, 49–55.

al-Fārābī, Abū Naṣr. *Risālat fī' l-ʿaql.* Edited, with an introduction, by Maurice Bouyges. Bibliotheca arabica scholasticorum. Série arabe. Beirut: Dār al-Mašriq, ²1983.

al-Fārābī, Abū Naṣr. *The Political Writings. Volume II. "Political Regime" and "Summary of Plato's Laws."* Translated and annotated, with an introduction, by Charles E. Butterworth. Agora Editions. Ithaca and London: Cornell University Press, 2015.

al-Fārābī, Abū Naṣr. *Über die Wissenschaften. De scientiis.* Nach der lateinischen Übersetzung Gerhards von Cremona. Edited, translated, and annotated, with an introduction, by Franz Schupp. Philosophische Bibliothek 568. Hamburg: Felix Meiner Verlag, 2005.

al-Fārābī (?), Abū Naṣr. *L'armonia delle opinioni dei due sapienti, il divino Platone e Aristotele.* Edited, translated, and commented, with an introduction, by Cecilia Martini Bonadeo. Greco, arabo, latino. Le vie del sapere 3. With a preface by Gerhard Endreß. Pisa: Edizioni Plus, 2008.

al-Fārābī (?), Abū Naṣr. *The Harmonization of the Two Opinions of the Two Sages. Plato the Divine and Aristotle.* In: al-Fārābī, Abū Naṣr. *The Political Writings. Selected Aphorisms and Other Texts.* Translated and annotated, with an introduction, by Charles E. Butterworth. Studies in Islamic Philosophy 3. Karachi: Oxford University Press, 2005, 125–167.

Ps.-al-Fārābī, Abū Naṣr. *'Uyūn al-masā'il*. In: al-Fārābī, Abū Naṣr. *Alfārābī's philosophische Abhandlungen aus Londoner, Leidener und Berliner Handschriften*. Edited, with an introduction, by Friedrich Dieterici. Leiden: E. J. Brill, 1890, 56–65.

Galen. *Compendium Timaei Platonis alioquorumque dialogorum synopsis quae extant fragmenta*. Edited, with an introduction, by Paul Kraus and Richard Walzer. Plato Arabus 1. London: The Warburg Institute, 1951.

Galen. *De elementis ex Hippocratis sententia*. Edited, translated, and commented, with an introduction, by Phillip De Lacy. Corpus medicorum graecorum V 1.2. Berlin: Akademie Verlag, 1996.

Galen. *De motu musculorum*. In: Galen. *Opera omnia*. Edited by Karl Gottlob Kühn. Vol. 4. Leipzig: Karl Knobloch, 1821–1833, 367–464.

Galen. *Kitāb fī l-asbāb al-māsika*. In: Galen. *De partibus artis medicativae, De causis contentivis, De diaeta in morbis acutis secundum Hippocratem libellorum versiones Arabicas. De partibus artis medicativae, De causis contentivis libellorum editiones alterius*. Edited by Malcolm Lyons, Diethard Nickel, Jutta Kollesch, and Gotthard Strohmaier. Translated, with an introduction, by Malcolm Lyons. Corpus medicorum graecorum. Supplementum orientale II. Berlin: Akademie Verlag, 1969, 52–73.

al-Ġazālī, Abū Ḥāmid. *Tahafot al-falasifat*. Edited, with an introduction, by Maurice Bouyges. Bibliotheca arabica scholasticorum. Série arabe II. Beirut: Imprimerie Catholique, 1927.

al-Ġazālī, Abū Ḥāmid. *The Incoherence of the Philosophers. A Parallel English-Arabic Text*. Edited, translated, and annotated, with an introduction, by Michael E. Marmura. Islamic Translation Series. Provo: Brigham Young University Press, [2]2000.

al-Ǧurǧānī, 'Alī ibn Muḥammad al-Sayyid al-Šarīf. *Kitāb al-Ta'rīfāt. Definitiones*. Edited and annotated by Gustav Flügel. Leipzig: Wilhelm Vogel, 1845.

Ḥāǧǧī Ḫalīfa. *Kašf al-ẓunūn 'an asāmī l-kutub wa-l-funūn. Lexicon bibliographicum et encyclopaedicum a Mustafa Ben Abdallah Katib Jelebi dicto et nomine Haji Khalfa celebrato compositum*. Edited by Gustav Flügel. 7 vols. Leipzig: Oriental Translation Fund of Great Britain and Ireland, 1835–58.

Nāṣer-e Ḫosrow (?). *Resāle-ye ḥekmatī*. In: Nāṣer-e Ḫosrow. *Dīvān-e aš'ār. Moštamel ast bar Rawšanā'īnāmeh, Sa'ādatnāmeh, qaṣā'ed-o moqaṭṭa'āt*. Edited by Moǧtabā Mīnowī. With an introduction and commentary by Ḥasan Taqīzādeh. With annotations by 'Alī Akbar Dehḫodā. In collaboration with Naṣr Allāh Taqavī. Entešārāt-e Mo'īn, [2]2001, 583–594.

Ḥunayn ibn Isḥāq. *On his Galen Translations. A Parallel English-Arabic Text*. Edited and translated, with an introduction, by John C. Lamoreaux. Eastern Christian Texts. With an appendix by Grigory Kessel. Provo: Brigham Young University Press, 2016.

Ḥunayn ibn Isḥāq. *Risāla ilā 'Alī ibn Yaḥyā fī ḏikr mā turǧima min kutub Ǧālīnūs bi-'ilmihī wa-ba'ḍ mā lam yutarǧam. Über die syrischen und arabischen Galen-Übersetzungen*. Edited and translated, with an introduction, by Gotthelf Bergsträßer. Abhandlungen für die Kunde des Morgenlandes XVII.2. Leipzig: Deutsche Morgenländische Gesellschaft, 1925.

Iamblichus. *In Platonis dialogos commentariorum fragmenta*. Edited, translated, and commented, with an introduction, by John M. Dillon. Leiden: E. J. Brill, 1973.

Ibn Abī Uṣaybi'a. *'Uyūn al-anbā' fī ṭabaqāt al-aṭibbā'*. Edited by August Müller. 2 vols. Cairo: al-Maṭba'a al-Wahbiyya, 1882.

Ibn 'Adī, Yaḥyā. *Kitāb Aǧwiba Bišr al-Yahūdī 'an masā'ilihī*. In: Ibn 'Adī, Yaḥyā. *Maqālāt Yaḥyā ibn 'Adī al-falsafiyya*. Edited and annotated, with an introduction, by Saḥbān Ḫalīfāt. Manšūrāt al-Ǧāmi'a al-Urduniyya. Amman: al-Ǧāmi'a al-Urduniyya, 1988, 314–336.

Ibn 'Adī, Yaḥyā. *Maqāla fī l-mawǧūdāt*. In: Ibn 'Adī, Yaḥyā. *Maqālāt Yaḥyā ibn 'Adī al-falsafiyya*. Edited and annotated, with an introduction, by Saḥbān Ḫalīfāt. Manšūrāt al-Ǧāmi'a al-Urduniyya. Amman: al-Ǧāmi'a al-Urduniyya, 1988, 266–274.

Ibn 'Adī, Yaḥyā. *Maqāla fī tabyīn wuǧūd al-umūr al-'āmmiyya wa-l-naḥw allaḏī 'alayhi takūnu maḥmūla wa-l-naḥw allaḏī taḫruǧu bihī min an takūna maḥmūla*. In: Ibn 'Adī, Yaḥyā. *Maqālāt*

Yaḥyā ibn ʿAdī al-falsafiyya. Edited and annotated, with an introduction, by Saḥbān Ḫalīfāt. Manšūrāt al-Ǧāmiʿa al-Urduniyya. Amman: al-Ǧāmiʿa al-Urduniyya, 1988, 148–159.

Ibn ʿAdī, Yaḥyā. *Maqālāt Yaḥyā ibn ʿAdī al-falsafiyya*. Edited and annotated, with an introduction, by Saḥbān Ḫalīfāt. Manšūrāt al-Ǧāmiʿa al-Urduniyya. Amman: al-Ǧāmiʿa al-Urduniyya, 1988.

Ibn ʿAdī, Yaḥyā. *On the Four Scientific Questions Concerning the Three Kinds of Existence*. Edited, translated, and annotated, with an introduction, by Stephen Menn and Robert Wisnovsky. In: *MIDEO. Mélanges de l'Institut Dominicain d'Études Orientales du Caire* 29 (2012), 73–96.

Ibn ʿAdī, Yaḥyā. *On Whether Body is a Substance or a Quantity*. Edited, translated, and annotated, with an introduction, by Stephen Menn and Robert Wisnovsky. In: *Arabic Sciences and Philosophy* 27.1 (2017), 1–74.

Ibn ʿAdī, Yaḥyā. *Šarḥ maʿānī maqālat al-Iskandar al-Afrūdīsī fī l-farq bayna al-ǧins wa-l-mādda*. In: Ibn ʿAdī, Yaḥyā. *Maqālāt Yaḥyā ibn ʿAdī al-falsafiyya*. Edited and annotated, with an introduction, by Saḥbān Ḫalīfāt. Manšūrāt al-Ǧāmiʿa al-Urduniyya. Amman: al-Ǧāmiʿa al-Urduniyya, 1988, 280–292.

Ibn al-Hayṯam. *Maǧmūʿ al-rasāʾil*. Hyderabad: Maṭbaʿa Dāʾira al-Maʿārif al-ʿUṯmāniyya, 1938.

Ibn al-Hayṯam. *Qawl fī l-makān*. Edited and translated by Roshdi Rashed. In: Rashed, Roshdi. *Les mathématiques infinitésimales du IXe au XIe siécle*. Vol. 4. 5 vols. London: al-Furqān Islamic Heritge Foundation, 1996–2006, 666–685.

Ibn al-Hayṯam. *Risāla fī l-makān*. In: Ibn al-Hayṯam. *Maǧmūʿ al-rasāʾil*. Hyderabad: Maṭbaʿa Dāʾira al-Maʿārif al-ʿUṯmāniyya, 1938. Chapter 5.

Ibn al-Qifṭī, ʿAlī ibn Yūsuf. *Taʾrīḫ al-ḥukamāʾ*. Edited by Julius Lippert and August Müller. With an introduction by Julius Lippert. Leipzig: Dieterich'sche Verlagsbuchhandlung, 1903.

Ibn al-Ṭayyib, Abū l-Faraǧ ʿAbd Allāh. *Tafsīr Kitāb al-Maqūlāt. Der Kategorienkommentar von Abū l-Faraǧ ʿAbdallāh ibn aṭ-Ṭayyib. Text und Untersuchungen*. Edited and commented, with an introduction, by Cleophea Ferrari. Aristoteles Semitico-Latinus 19. Leiden and Boston: Brill, 2006.

Ibn Bāǧǧa, Abū Bakr Muḥammad. *Šurūḥāt al-Samāʿ al-ṭabīʿī*. Edited, with an introduction, by Maʿan Ziyāda. Beirut: Dār al-Kindī and Dār al-Fikr, 1978.

Ibn Bāǧǧa, Abū Bakr Muḥammad. *Šurūḥāt al-Samāʿ al-ṭabīʿī*. Edited by Paul Lettinck. In: Lettinck, Paul. *Aristotle's* Physics *and its Reception in the Arabic World. With an Edition of the Unpublished Parts of Ibn Bājja's* Commentary on the Physics. Aristoteles Semitico-Latinus 7. Leiden, New York, and Cologne: E. J. Brill, 1994, 681–747.

Ibn Suwār ibn al-Ḫammār, al-Ḥasan. *Maqāla fī anna dalīl Yaḥyā al-Naḥwī ʿalā ḥadaṯ al-ʿālam awlā bi-l-qabūl min dalīl al-mutakallimīn aṣlan*. In: *al-Aflāṭūniyya al-muḥdaṯa ʿinda l-ʿarab*. Edited, with an introduction, by ʿAbd al-Raḥmān Badawī. Kuwait: Wakālat al-Maṭbūʿāt, ²1977, 243–247.

Ibn Zurʿa, ʿĪsā. *Manṭiq Ibn Zurʿa*. Edited by Ǧīrār Ǧīhāmī and Rafīq al-ʿAǧam. Silsilat ʿIlm al-Manṭiq. Beirut: Dār al-Fikr al-Lubnānī, 1994.

Iḫwān al-Ṣafāʾ. *On the Natural Sciences. Epistles 15–21*. Edited, translated, and annotated, with an introduction, by Carmela Baffioni. With a foreword by Nader El-Bizri. Epistles of the Brethren of Purity. Oxford: Oxford University Press, 2013.

Iḫwān al-Ṣafāʾ. *Rasāʾil Iḫwān al-Ṣafāʾ*. Edited, with an introduction, by Buṭrus al-Bustānī. 4 vols. Beirut: Dār al-Ṣādir, 1957.

Iḫwān al-Ṣafāʾ. *Sciences of the Soul and Intellect. Part I: Epistles 32–36*. Edited and translated, with an introduction, by Paul E. Walker, Ismail K. Poonawala, David Simonowitz, and Godefroid de Callataÿ. With a foreword by Nader El-Bizri. Epistles of the Brethren of Purity. Oxford: Oxford University Press, 2015.

al-Kindī, Abū Yaʿqūb ibn Isḥāq. *Kitāb al-Kindī fī l-ibāna ʿan al-ʿilla al-fāʿila al-qarība li-l-kawn wa-l-fasād*. In: al-Kindī, Abū Yaʿqūb ibn Isḥāq. *Rasāʾil al-Kindī l-falsafiyya*. Edited and annotated, with an introduction, by Muḥammad ʿAbd al-Hādī Abū Rīda. Vol. 1. 2 vols. Cairo: Dār al-Fikr al-ʿArabī, 1950–1953, 214–237.

al-Kindī, Abū Yaʿqūb ibn Isḥāq. *Liber de quinque essentiis*. In: al-Kindī, Abū Yaʿqūb ibn Isḥāq. *Rasāʾil al-Kindī l-falsafiyya*. Edited and annotated, with an introduction, by Muḥammad ʿAbd al-Hādī Abū Rīda. Vol. 2. 2 vols. Cairo: Dār al-Fikr al-ʿArabī, 1950–1953, 9–35.

al-Kindī, Abū Yaʿqūb ibn Isḥāq. *Livre d'al-Kindī sur la Philosophie Première à al-Muʿtaṣim bi-llah*. In: al-Kindī, Abū Yaʿqūb ibn Isḥāq. *Oeuvres philosophiques et scientifiques d'al-Kindī*. Edited, translated, and annotated by Roshdi Rashed and Jean Jolivet. Vol. 2. 2 vols. Islamic Philosophy, Theology and Science. Texts and Studies 29. Leiden, Boston, and Cologne: Brill, 1996–1998, 1–117.

al-Kindī, Abū Yaʿqūb ibn Isḥāq. *Mimmā naqalahū al-Kindī min alfāẓ Suqrāṭ*. Edited by Majid Fakhry. In: Fakhry, Majid. "al-Kindī wa-l-Suqrāṭ." In: *al-Abḥāṯ* 16 (1963), 23–34.

al-Kindī, Abū Yaʿqūb ibn Isḥāq. *Rasāʾil al-Kindī l-falsafiyya*. Edited and annotated, with an introduction, by Muḥammad ʿAbd al-Hādī Abū Rīda. 2 vols. Cairo: Dār al-Fikr al-ʿArabī, 1950–1953.

al-Kindī, Abū Yaʿqūb ibn Isḥāq. *Risāla fī ḥudūd al-ašyāʾ wa-rusūmihā*. In: al-Kindī, Abū Yaʿqūb ibn Isḥāq. *Rasāʾil al-Kindī l-falsafiyya*. Edited and annotated, with an introduction, by Muḥammad ʿAbd al-Hādī Abū Rīda. Vol. 1. 2 vols. Cairo: Dār al-Fikr al-ʿArabī, 1950–1953, 165–180.

al-Kindī, Abū Yaʿqūb ibn Isḥāq. *Risāla fī kammiyyat kutub Arisṭūṭālīs wa-mā yuḥtāǧu ilayhi fī taḥṣīl al-falsafa*. In: al-Kindī, Abū Yaʿqūb ibn Isḥāq. *Rasāʾil al-Kindī l-falsafiyya*. Edited and annotated, with an introduction, by Muḥammad ʿAbd al-Hādī Abū Rīda. Vol. 1. 2 vols. Cairo: Dār al-Fikr al-ʿArabī, 1950–1953, 363–384.

al-Kindī, Abū Yaʿqūb ibn Isḥāq. *Risāla fī l-asmāʾ al-mufrada*. Edited by Félix Klein-Franke. In: Klein-Franke, Félix. "al-Kindī's 'On Definitions and Descriptions of Things.'" In: *Le Muséon. Revue d'études orientales* 95.215 (1982), 210–216.

al-Kindī, Abū Yaʿqūb ibn Isḥāq. *The Philosophical Works of al-Kindī*. Translated and annotated, with an introduction, by Peter Adamson and Peter E. Pormann. Studies in Islamic Philosophy. Oxford and New York: Oxford University Press, 2012.

Long, Anthony A. and David Sedley, eds. *The Hellenistic Philosophers*. 2 vols. Cambridge, New York, and Melbourne: Cambridge University Press, 1987.

Maimonides, Moses. *Dalālat al-ḥāʾirīn*. Edited, with an introduction, by Hüseyin Atay. Ankara Üniversitesi İlâhiyat Fakültesi yayınları 93. Ankara: Ankara Üniversitesi, 1974.

al-Masʿūdī, Šaraf al-Dīn Muḥammad ibn Masʿūd. *al-Mabāḥiṯ wa-l-šukūk ʿalā Kitāb al-Išārāt*. Edited, with an introduction, by Ayman Shihadeh. In: Shihadeh, Ayman. *Doubts on Avicenna. A Study and Edition of Sharaf al-Dīn al-Masʿūdī's Commentary on the* Ishārāt. Islamic Philosophy and Theology. Texts and Studies 95. Leiden and Boston: Brill, 2016, 193–288.

Ibn Mattawayh, Abū Muḥammad. *al-Taḏkira fī aḥkām al-ǧawāhir wa-l-aʿrāḍ*. Edited and annotated, with an introduction, by Sāmī Naṣr Luṭf and Fayṣal Budayr ʿŪn. Cairo: Dār al-Ṯaqāfa, 1975.

Ibn Mattawayh, Abū Muḥammad. *al-Taḏkira fī aḥkām al-ǧawāhir wa-l-aʿrāḍ*. Edited and annotated, with an introduction, by Daniel Gimaret. 2 vols. Cairo: al-Maʿhad al-ʿIlmī l-Faransī li-l-Āṯār al-Šarqiyya, 2009.

McGinnis, Jon and David C. Reisman, eds. *Classical Arabic Philosophy. An Anthology of Sources*. Indianapolis: Hacket Publishing Company, 2007.

Miskawayh, Abū ʿAlī Aḥmad. *al-Fawz al-aṣġar. Le petit livre du salut*. Edited, with an introduction, by Sāliḥ ʿUdayma. Translated and annotated by Roger Arnaldez. Fondation nationale pour la traduction, l'établissement des textes et les études. Tunis: Maison arabe du livre, 1987.

al-Muqammaṣ, Dāwūd ibn Marwān. *Twenty Chapters. ʿIšrūn maqālatan*. Edited, translated, and annotated, with an introduction, by Sarah Stroumsa. Library of Judeo-Arabic Literature. Provo: Brigham Young University Press, 2016.

Ibn al-Nadīm. *Kitāb al-Fihrist.* Edited and annotated, with an introduction, by Ayman Fu'ād Sayyid. 4 vols. London: al-Furqān Islamic Heritge Foundation, ²2014.

Ibn al-Nadīm. *Kitāb al-Fihrist.* Edited by Gustav Flügel and Johannes Roediger. With annotations by Gustav Flügel and August Mueller. 2 vols. Leipzig: Verlag von F. C. W. Vogel, 1871–72.

Nāṣer-e Ḫosrow. *Ketāb-e Ǧām' al-ḥikmatayn. Le livre réunissant les deux sagesses ou Harmonie de la philosophie grecque et de la théosophie ismaélienne.* Edited, with an introduction, by Henry Corbin and Moḥammad Mo'īn. Ganǧīne-ye neveštehā-ye Īrānī 3. Tehran: Instītū Īrān-o Farānse, 1953.

Nasr, Seyyed Hossein and Mehdi Aminrazavi, eds. *An Anthology of Philosophy in Persia. From Zoroaster to 'Umar Khayyām.* Edited by Mohammad Reza Jozi. Vol. 1. London and New York: I.B.Tauris and The Institute of Ismaili Studies, 2008.

al-Nawbaḫtī (?), al-Ḥasan ibn Mūsā. *Commentary on Aristotle* De generatione et corruptione. Edited, translated, and commented by Marwan Rashed. Scientia graeco-arabica 19. Berlin and Boston: Walter de Gruyter, 2015.

al-Nīsābūrī, Abū Rašīd Sa'īd ibn Muḥammad. *al-Masā'il fī l-ḫilāf bayna l-baṣriyyīn wa-baġdādiyyīn.* Edited, with an introduction, by Ma'an Ziyāda and Riḍwān al-Sayyid. Beirut: Ma'had al-inmā' al-'arabī, 1979.

al-Nīsābūrī, Abū Rašīd Sa'īd ibn Muḥammad. *Kitāb al-Masā'il fī l-ḫilāf bayna l-baṣriyyīn wa-baġdādiyyīn. Die atomistische Substanzlehre aus dem Buch der Streitfragen zwischen Basrensern und Bagdadensern.* Edited, translated, and annotated, with an introduction, by Arthur Biram. Leiden: Brill, 1902.

Olympiodorus. *In Aristotelis* Meteora *commentaria.* Edited by Wilhelm Stüve. Commentaria in Aristotelem graeca XII.2. Berlin: Verlag Georg Reimer, 1900.

Olympiodorus. *Prolegomena et in Categorias commentarium.* Edited by Adolf Busse. Commentaria in Aristotelem graeca XII.1. Berlin: Verlag Georg Reimer, 1902.

Pacius, Julius. *Aristotelis Naturalis auscultationis libri VIII cum graecis tam excusis quam scriptis codicibus accurate contulit, latina interpretatione auxit et commentariis illustravit.* Frankfurt am Main: Marnius et Aubrius, 1596.

Philo of Alexandria. *De somniis.* Edited by Paul Wendland. In: Philo of Alexandria. *Opera quae supersunt.* Edited by Leopold Cohn, Paul Wendland, and Siegfried Reiter. Vol. 3. 7 vols. Berlin: Verlag Georg Reimer, 1896–1930, 204–306.

Philoponus, John. *Against Aristotle on the Eternity of the World.* Translated and annotated by Christian Wildberg. Ancient Commentators on Aristotle. London: Duckworth, 1987.

Philoponus, John. *Against Proclus'* On the Eternity of the World *12–18.* Translated and annotated by James Wilberding. Ancient Commentators on Aristotle. Ithaca: Cornell University Press, 2006.

Philoponus, John. *Against Proclus'* On the Eternity of the World *9–11.* Translated and annotated by Michael Share. Ancient Commentators on Aristotle. Ithaca: Cornell University Press, 2010.

Philoponus, John. *Corollaries on Place and Void.* With Simplicius. *Against Philoponus on the Eternity of the World.* Translated and annotated by David Furley and Christian Wildberg. Ancient Commentators on Aristotle. London: Duckworth, 1991.

Philoponus, John. *De aeternitate mundi contra Proclum.* Edited by Hugo Rabe. Leipzig: Teubner, 1899.

Philoponus, John. *De opificio mundi. Libri VII.* Edited by Walter Reichardt. Scriptores sacri et profani 1. Leipzig: Teubner, 1897.

Philoponus, John. *De opificio mundi. Über die Erschaffung der Welt.* Translated and annotated, with an introduction, by Clemens Scholten. 3 vols. Fontes christiani 23. Freiburg: Herder, 1997.

Philoponus, John. *In Aristotelis* Analytica posteriora *commentaria cum anonymo in librum II.* Edited by Maximilian Wallies. Commentaria in Aristotelem graeca XIII.3. Berlin: Verlag Georg Reimer, 1909.

Philoponus, John. *In Aristotelis* Categorias *commentarium.* Edited by Adolf Busse. Commentaria in Aristotelem graeca XIII.1. Berlin: Verlag Georg Reimer, 1898.

Philoponus, John. *In Aristotelis* De anima *libros commentaria*. Edited by Michael Hayduck. Commentaria in Aristotelem graeca XV. Berlin: Verlag Georg Reimer, 1897.
Philoponus, John. *In Aristotelis libros* De generatione et corruptione *commentaria*. Edited by Girolamo Vitelli. Commentaria in Aristotelem graeca XIV.2. Berlin: Verlag Georg Reimer, 1897.
Philoponus, John. *In Aristotelis* Physicorum *libros quinque posteriores commentaria*. Edited by Girolamo Vitelli. Commentaria in Aristotelem graeca XVII. Berlin: Verlag Georg Reimer, 1888.
Philoponus, John. *In Aristotelis* Physicorum *libros tres priores commentaria*. Edited by Girolamo Vitelli. Commentaria in Aristotelem graeca XVI. Berlin: Verlag Georg Reimer, 1887.
Philoponus, John. *On Aristotle "Physics" 1.4–9*. Translated and annotated by Catherine Osborne. Ancient Commentators on Aristotle. London: Duckworth, 2009.
Philoponus, John. *On Aristotle "Physics" 2*. Translated and annotated by Alan R. Lacey. Ancient Commentators on Aristotle. London: Duckworth, 1993.
Philoponus, John. *On Aristotle "Physics" 4.1–5*. Translated and annotated by Keimpe Algra and Johannses van Ophuijsen. Ancient Commentators on Aristotle. London: Bristol Classical Press, 2012.
Philoponus, John. *On Aristotle "Physics" 4.10–14*. Translated and annotated by Sarah Broadie. Ancient Commentators on Aristotle. London: Bristol Classical Press, 2011.
Philoponus, John. *On Aristotle "Physics" 4.6–9*. Translated and annotated by Pamela Huby. Ancient Commentators on Aristotle. London: Bristol Classical Press, 2012.
Philoponus, John. *On Aristotle "Physics" 5–8*. With Simplicius. *On Aristotle on the Void*. Translated by Paul Lettinck and James O. Urmson. With annotations by Paul Lettinck, James O. Urmson, and Peter Lautner. Ancient Commentators on Aristotle. London: Duckworth, 1994.
Philoponus, John. *On Aristotle "Posterior Analytics" 1.1–8*. Translated and annotated by Richard McKirahan. Ancient Commentators on Aristotle. London: Duckworth, 2008.
Philoponus, John. *On Aristotle "Posterior Analytics" 1.19–34*. Translated and annotated by Owen Goldin and Marije Martijn. Ancient Commentators on Aristotle. London: Bristol Classical Press, 2012.
Philoponus, John. *On Aristotle "Posterior Analytics" 1.9–18*. Translated and annotated by Richard McKirahan. Ancient Commentators on Aristotle. London: Bristol Classical Press, 2012.
Philoponus, John. *On Aristotle's "Coming-to-Be and Perishing" 2.5–11*. Translated and annotated by Inna Kupreeva. Ancient Commentators on Aristotle. Ithaca: Cornell University Press, 2005.
Philoponus, John. *On Aristotle's "On the Soul" 1.1–2*. Translated and annotated by Philip J. van der Eijk. Ancient Commentators on Aristotle. Ithaca: Cornell University Press, 2005.
Philoponus, John. *On Aristotle's "On the Soul" 1.3–5*. Translated and annotated by Philip J. van der Eijk. Ancient Commentators on Aristotle. Ithaca: Cornell University Press, 2006.
Philoponus, John. *On Aristotle's "Physics" 1.1–3*. Translated and annotated by Catherine Osborne. Ancient Commentators on Aristotle. Ithaca: Cornell University Press, 2006.
Philoponus, John. *On Aristotle's "Physics" 3*. Translated and annotated by Mark J. Edwards. Ancient Commentators on Aristotle. Ithaca: Cornell University Press, 1994.
Plato. *Complete Works*. Edited by John M. Cooper. In collaboration with Douglas S. Hutchinson. Indianapolis: Hacket Publishing Company, 1997.
Plato. *Plato's Cosmology. The* Timaeus *of Plato*. Translated and commented, with an introduction, by Francis Macdonald Cornford. London and New York: Kegan Paul, Trench, Trubner & Co., Harcourt, Brace, and Company, 1937.
Plato. *Platonis Opera*. Edited by John Burnet. 5 vols. Oxford Classical Texts. Oxford: Clarendon Press, 1900–07.
Plotinus. *Enneads*. Edited by Paul Henry and Hans-Rudolph Schwyzer. Translated by Arthur Hilary Armstrong. 6 vols. Loeb Classical Library 440–445 and 468. Cambridge and London: Harvard University Press, 1966–88.

Plotinus. *Plotini opera*. Edited by Paul Henry and Hans-Rudolph Schwyzer. 3 vols. Museum Lessianum. Series philosophica 33–35. Paris, Brussels, and Leuven: Desclée de Brouwer and Brill, 1951–73.

Plotinus. *Plotinus' Cosmology. A Study of* Ennead *II.1 (40)*. Edited, translated, and commented, with an introduction, by James Wilberding. Oxford: Oxford University Press, 2006.

Plotinus. *Über Ewigkeit und Zeit. Enneade III 7*. Edited, translated, and commented, with an introduction, by Werner Beierwaltes. Klostermann RoteReihe 36. ⁵2010.

Ps.-Plutarchus. *Περί των αρεσκόντων φιλοσόφοις φυσικών δογμάτων*. In: *Doxographi graeci*. Edited by Hermann Diels. Berlin: Verlag Georg Reimer, 1879, 267–444.

Porphyry. *Fragmenta*. Edited by Andrew Smith. In collaboration with David Wasserstein. Bibliotheca scriptorum Graecorum et Romanorum Teubneriana. Stuttgart and Leipzig: Teubner, 1993.

Porphyry. *Introduction*. Translated and commented, with an introduction, by Jonathan Barnes. Clarendon Later Ancient Philosophers. Oxford: Clarendon Press, 2003.

Porphyry. *Sentences*. Edited and translated by Luc Brisson and John Dillon. With a commentary by Unité propre de recherche no. 76 du CNRS. 2 vols. Histoire des doctrines de l'antiquité classique 33. Paris: Librairie philosophique J. Vrin, 2005.

Porphyry. *Sententiae ad intelligibilia ducentes*. Edited by Erich Lamberz. Bibliotheca scriptorum Graecorum et Romanorum Teubneriana. Leipzig: Teubner, 1975.

Proclus. *Commentary on Plato's* Timaeus. *Book 1: Proclus on the Socratic State and Atlantis*. Translated and annotated, with an introduction, by Harold Tarrant. Vol. 1. Cambridge: Cambridge University Press, 2007.

Proclus. *In Platonis Parmenidem commentaria*. Edited by Carlos Steel and Leen van Campe. 3 vols. Oxford Classical Texts. Oxford: Oxford University Press, 2007–09.

Proclus. *In Platonis Rem publicam commentarii*. Edited by Wilhelm Kroll. 2 vols. Bibliotheca scriptorum Graecorum et Romanorum Teubneriana. Leipzig: Teubner, 1899–1901.

Proclus. *In Platonis Timaeum commentaria*. Edited, with an introduction, by Ernst Diehl. 3 vols. Bibliotheca scriptorum Graecorum et Romanorum Teubneriana. Leipzig: Teubner, 1903–06.

Proclus. *In primum Euclidis Elementorum librum commentarii*. Edited by Gottfried Friedlein. Leipzig: B. G. Teubner, 1873.

Proclus. *On the Eternity of the World (de Aeternitate Mundi)*. Edited, translated, and commented, with an introduction, by Helen S. Lang and Anthony D. Macro. Argument I Translated from the Arabic by Jon McGinnis. Berkeley, Los Angeles, and London: University of California Press, 2001.

Proclus. *The Elements of Theology*. Edited, translated, and commented, with an introduction, by Eric R. Dodds. Oxford: Clarendon Press, ²1963.

Proclus. *Théologie platonicienne*. Edited by Henri Dominique Saffrey and Leendert Gerritt Westerink. 6 vols. Collection des universités de France. Paris: Les Belles Lettres, 1968–1997.

Proclus. *Zwanzig Abschnitte aus der* Institutio theologica *in arabischer Übersetzung*. Edited and commented, with an introduction, by Gerhard Endreß. Beiruter Texte und Studien 10. Wiesbaden: Franz Steiner Verlag, 1973.

Proclus. *Στοιχείωσις φυσική*. *Institutio physica*. Edited, translated, and commented by Albert Ritzenfeld. Bibliotheca scriptorum Graecorum et Romanorum Teubneriana. Leipzig: Teubner, 1912.

Ptolemy. *Kitāb fī l-hay'a al-musammā l-Iqtiṣāṣ*. Edited, translated, and commented by Bernard R. Goldstein. In: Goldstein, Bernard R. "The Arabic Version of Ptolemy's Planetary Hypotheses." In: *Transactions of the American Philosophical Society. New Series* 57.4 (1967), 3–55.

al-Rāzī, Abū Bakr. *al-Munāẓarāt bayna Abī Ḥātim al-Rāzī wa-Abī Bakr al-Rāzī*. In: al-Rāzī, Abū Bakr. *Rasā'il falsafiyya ma'a qiṭa' baqiyat min kutubihī l-mafqūda*. Edited and annotated by Paul Kraus. Ǧāmi'at Fu'ād al-Awwal. Kulliyyat al-Ādāb 22. Cairo: Maṭba'at Būl Bārbīh, 1939, 291–316.

al-Rāzī, Abū Bakr. *al-Qawl fī l-qudamā' al-ḫamsa*. In: al-Rāzī, Abū Bakr. *Rasā'il falsafiyya ma'a qiṭa' baqiyat min kutubihī l-mafqūda*. Edited and annotated by Paul Kraus. Ǧāmi'at Fu'ād al-Awwal. Kulliyyat al-Ādāb 22. Cairo: Maṭba'at Būl Bārbīh, 1939, 191–216.

al-Rāzī, Abū Bakr. *Kitāb al-Sīra al-falsafiyya*. In: al-Rāzī, Abū Bakr. *Rasā'il falsafiyya ma'a qiṭa' baqiyat min kutubihī l-mafqūda*. Edited and annotated by Paul Kraus. Ǧāmi'at Fu'ād al-Awwal. Kulliyyat al-Ādāb 22. Cairo: Maṭba'at Būl Bārbīh, 1939, 97–111.

al-Rāzī, Abū Bakr. *Maqāla fī-mā ba'd al-ṭabī'a*. In: al-Rāzī, Abū Bakr. *Rasā'il falsafiyya ma'a qiṭa' baqiyat min kutubihī l-mafqūda*. Edited and annotated by Paul Kraus. Ǧāmi'at Fu'ād al-Awwal. Kulliyyat al-Ādāb 22. Cairo: Maṭba'at Būl Bārbīh, 1939, 113–134.

al-Rāzī, Abū Bakr. *Rasā'il falsafiyya ma'a qiṭa' baqiyat min kutubihī l-mafqūda*. Edited and annotated by Paul Kraus. Ǧāmi'at Fu'ād al-Awwal. Kulliyyat al-Ādāb 22. Cairo: Maṭba'at Būl Bārbīh, 1939.

al-Rāzī, Faḫr al-Dīn. *al-Mabāḥiṯ al-mašriqiyya fī 'ilm al-ilāhiyyāt wa-l-ṭabī'iyyāt*. Edited, with an introduction, by Muḥammad al-Mu'taṣim bi-llāh al-Baġdādī. 2 vols. Beirut: Dār al-Kutub al-'Ilmiyya, 1990.

al-Rāzī, Faḫr al-Dīn. *al-Maṭālib al-'āliya min al-'ilm al-ilāhī*. Edited by Aḥmad Ḥiǧāzī al-Saqqā. 9 vols. Beirut: Dār al-Kitāb al-'Arabī, 1987.

al-Rāzī, Faḫr al-Dīn. *Šarḥ al-Išārāt wa-l-tanbīhāt*. Edited, with an introduction, by 'Alī Reḍā Naǧafzādeh. 2 vols. Selsele-ye Entešārāt-e Hamāyeš-e Bayna al-Melalī-ye Qorṭoba-o Eṣfahān 26–27. With a preface by Mahdī Moḥaqqeq. Tehran: Anǧoman-e Āṯār-o Mafāḫer-e Farhangī, 2005.

al-Rāzī, Faḫr al-Dīn. *Šarḥ 'Uyūn al-ḥikma*. Edited, with an introduction, by Aḥmad Ḥiǧāzī al-Saqqā. 3 vols. Cairo: Maktabat al-Anǧilū l-Miṣriyya, 1986.

al-Šahrastānī, Muḥammad ibn 'Abd al-Karīm. *Kitāb al-Milal wa-l-niḥal. Book of Religious and Philosophical Sects*. Edited by William Cureton. London: Society for the Publication of Oriental Texts, 1846.

Sambursky, Samuel, editor, translator, annotator, and introduction. *The Concept of Place in Late Neoplatonism*. Publications of the Israel Academy of Sciences and Humanities. Section of Humanities. Jerusalem: The Israel Academy of Sciences and Humanities, 1982.

Sambursky, Samuel and Shlomo Pines, editors, translators, annotators, and introduction. *The Concept of Time in Late Neoplatonism*. Publications of the Israel Academy of Sciences and Humanities. Section of Humanities. Jerusalem: The Israel Academy of Sciences and Humanities, 1971.

al-Šayḫ al-Mufīd, Abū 'Abd Allāh Muḥammad ibn Muḥammad. *Awā'il al-maqālāt fī l-maḏāhib wa-l-muḫtārāt*. Edited by Mehdī Moḥaqqeq. With an introduction by Martin J. McDermott. Selsele-ye Dāneš-e Īrānī 41. Tehran: Entešārāt-e Mo'assese-ye Moṭāla'āt-e Eslāmī, 1993.

Sextus Empiricus. *Against the Ethicists (Adversus mathematicos XI)*. Translated and commented, with an introduction, by Richard Bett. Oxford: Clarendon Press, 1997.

Sextus Empiricus. *Against the Physicists*. Translated and annotated, with an introduction, by Richard Bett. Cambridge: Cambridge University Press, 2012.

Sharples, Robert W., ed. *Peripatetic Philosophy 200 BC to AD 200. An Introduction and Collection of Sources in Translation*. Cambridge: Cambridge University Press, 2010.

al-Siǧistānī, Abū Sulaymān. *al-Maqāla fī anna l-aǧrām al-'ulwiyya ḏawāt anfus nāṭiqa*. In: *Muntaḫab Ṣiwān al-ḥikma wa-ṯalāṯ rasā'il*. Edited and annotated, with an introduction, by 'Abd al-Raḥmān Badawī. Tehran: Entešārāt-e Bunyād-e Farhang-e Īrān, 1974, 367–371.

al-Siǧistānī, Abū Sulaymān. *al-Maqāla fī l-kamāl al-ḫāṣṣ bi-naw' al-insān*. In: *Muntaḫab Ṣiwān al-ḥikma wa-ṯalāṯ rasā'il*. Edited and annotated, with an introduction, by 'Abd al-Raḥmān Badawī. Tehran: Entešārāt-e Bunyād-e Farhang-e Īrān, 1974, 377–387.

al-Siǧistānī, Abū Sulaymān. *al-Maqāla fī l-muḥarrik al-awwal*. In: *Muntaḫab Ṣiwān al-ḥikma wa-ṯalāṯ rasā'il*. Edited and annotated, with an introduction, by 'Abd al-Raḥmān Badawī. Tehran: Entešārāt-e Bunyād-e Farhang-e Īrān, 1974, 372–376.

al-Siǧistānī, Abū Sulaymān. *al-Qawl fī l-kamāl al-ḫāṣṣ bi-naw' al-insān*. Edited by Mübahat Küyel-Türker. In: Küyel-Türker, Mübahat. "Le traité inédit de Siǧistānī sur la perfection humaine." In: *Pensamiento. Revista de investigación e Información filosófica* 25 (1969), 207–223.

al-Siǧistānī (?), Abū Sulaymān. *Kalām fī mabādi' al-mawǧūdāt*. Edited by Gérard Troupeau. In: Troupeau, Gérard. "Une traité sur les principes des êtres attribué a Abū Sulaymān al-Siǧistānī." In: *Pensamiento. Revista de investigación e Información filosófica* 25 (1969), 259–270.

Simplicius. *Against Philoponus on the Eternity of the World*. With Philoponus. *Corollaries on Place and Void*. Translated and annotated by Christian Wildberg and David Furley. Ancient Commentators on Aristotle. London: Duckworth, 1991.

Simplicius. *Corollaries on Place and Time*. Translated by James O. Urmson. With annotations by Lucas Siorvanes and James O. Urmson. Ancient Commentators on Aristotle. London: Duckworth, 1992.

Simplicius. *In Aristotelis* Categorias *commentarium*. Edited by Karl Kalbfleisch. Commentaria in Aristotelem graeca VIII. Berlin: Verlag Georg Reimer, 1907.

Simplicius. *In Aristotelis* De caelo *commentaria*. Edited by Johan Ludvig Heiberg. Commentaria in Aristotelem graeca VII. Berlin: Verlag Georg Reimer, 1894.

Simplicius. *In Aristotelis* Physicorum *libros quattuor posteriores commentaria*. Edited by Hermann Diels. Commentaria in Aristotelem graeca X. Berlin: Verlag Georg Reimer, 1895.

Simplicius. *In Aristotelis* Physicorum *libros quattuor priores commentaria*. Edited by Hermann Diels. Commentaria in Aristotelem graeca IX. Berlin: Verlag Georg Reimer, 1882.

Simplicius. *On Aristotle "Categories" 5–6*. Translated and annotated by Frans A. J. de Haas and Barrie Fleet. Ancient Commentators on Aristotle. London: Duckworth, 2001.

Simplicius. *On Aristotle "Categories" 7–8*. Translated and annotated by Barrie Fleet. Ancient Commentators on Aristotle. London: Duckworth, 2002.

Simplicius. *On Aristotle "On the Heavens" 1.1–4*. Translated and annotated, with an introduction, by Robert J. Hankinson. Ancient Commentators on Aristotle. London: Duckworth, 2002.

Simplicius. *On Aristotle on the Void*. With Philoponus. *On Aristotle "Physics" 5–8*. Translated by James O. Urmson and Paul Lettinck. With annotations by James O. Urmson, Peter Lautner, and Paul Lettinck. Ancient Commentators on Aristotle. London: Duckworth, 1994.

Simplicius. *On Aristotle "Physics" 1.3–4*. Translated and annotated by Pamela Huby and Christopher Charles Whiston Taylor. Ancient Commentators on Aristotle. London: Bristol Classical Press, 2011.

Simplicius. *On Aristotle "Physics" 1.5–9*. Translated and annotated by Han Baltussen, Michael Atkinson, Michael Share, and Ian Mueller. Ancient Commentators on Aristotle. London: Bristol Classical Press, 2012.

Simplicius. *On Aristotle "Physics" 2*. Translated and annotated by Barrie Fleet. Ancient Commentators on Aristotle. London: Duckworth, 1997.

Simplicius. *On Aristotle "Physics" 4.1–5, 10–14*. Translated by James O. Urmson. With annotations by Richard Sorabji and James O. Urmson. Ancient Commentators on Aristotle. London: Duckworth, 1992.

Simplicius. *On Aristotle's "Physics" 6*. Translated and annotated by David Konstan. Ancient Commentators on Aristotle. Ithaca: Cornell University Press, 1989.

Simplicius. *Über die Zeit. Ein Kommentar zum Corollarium de tempore*. Translated and commented, with an introduction, by Erwin Sonderegger. Göttingen: Vandenhoeck & Ruprecht, 1982.

Simplicius (?). *In Aristotelis* De anima *commentaria*. Edited by Michael Hayduck. Commentaria in Aristotelem graeca XI. Berlin: Verlag Georg Reimer, 1882.

al-Šīrāzī, Ṣadr al-Dīn Muḥammad. *Conception and Belief in Ṣadr al-Dīn al-Shirāzī (ca 1571–1635). al-Risāla fī l-taṣawwur wa-l-taṣdīq*. Translated and commented, with an introduction, by Joep Lameer. Tehran: Iranian Institute of Philosophy, 2006.

Sorabji, Richard, ed. *The Philosophy of the Commentators, 200-600 AD. A Sourcebook*. 3 vols. Ithaca: Cornell University Press, 2005.

Syrianus. *On Aristotle "Metaphysics" 2 & 3*. Translated and annotated by Dominic O'Meara and John Dillon. Ancient Commentators on Aristotle. London: Duckworth, 2008.

al-Tawḥīdī, ʿAlī Abū Ḥayyān. *al-Muqābasāt*. Edited and annotated, with an introduction, by Ḥasan al-Sandūbī. Kuwait: Dār Suʿād aṣ-Ṣabbāḥ, ²1992.

al-Tawḥīdī, ʿAlī Abū Ḥayyān. *Kitāb al-Imtāʿ wa-l-muʾānasa*. Edited and annotated, with an introduction, by Aḥmad Amīn and Aḥmad al-Zayn. 3 vols. Cairo: Lağnat al-Taʾlīf wa-l-Tarğama wa-l-Našr, 1939–44.

al-Tawḥīdī, ʿAlī Abū Ḥayyān and Abū ʿAlī Aḥmad Miskawayh. *al-Hawāmil wa-l-šawāmil*. Edited, with an introduction, by Aḥmad Amīn and Aḥmad Ṣaqr. Cairo: Maṭbaʿat Lağnat al-Taʾlīf wa-l-Tarğama wa-l-Našr, 1951.

Themistius. *An Arabic translation of* Themistius [sic!] Commentary *on Aristoteles [sic!]* De Anima. Edited, with an introduction, by Malcolm Cameron Lyons. Oriental Studies 2. Oxford: Cassirer, 1973.

Themistius. *Analyticorum posteriorum paraphrasis*. Edited by Maximilian Wallies. Commentaria in Aristotelem graeca V.1. Berlin: Verlag Georg Reimer, 1900.

Themistius. *Commentum super Librum posteriorum*. Edited, with an introduction, by J. Reginald O'Donnell. In: O'Donnell, J. Reginald. "Themistius' Paraphrasis of the Posterior Analytics in Gerard of Cremona's Translation." In: *Medieval Studies* 20 (1958), 239–315.

Themistius. *In Aristotelis* De anima *paraphrasis*. Edited by Richard Heinze. Commentaria in Aristotelem graeca V.3. Berlin: Verlag Georg Reimer, 1999.

Themistius. *In Aristotelis* Physica *paraphrasis*. Edited by Heinrich Schenkl. Commentaria in Aristotelem graeca V.2. Berlin: Verlag Georg Reimer, 1900.

Themistius. *In libros Aristotelis* De caelo *paraphrasis. Hebraice et latine*. Edited by Samuel Landauer. Commentaria in Aristotelem graeca V.4. Berlin: Verlag Georg Reimer, 1902.

Themistius. *On Aristotle "On the Soul."* Translated and annotated by Robert B. Todd. Ancient Commentators on Aristotle. London: Duckworth, 1996.

Themistius. *On Aristotle "Physics" 1–3*. Translated and annotated by Robert B. Todd. Ancient Commentators on Aristotle. London: Bristol Classical Press, 2012.

Themistius. *On Aristotle "Physics" 5–8*. Translated and annotated by Robert B. Todd. Ancient Commentators on Aristotle. London: Duckworth, 2008.

Themistius. *On Aristotle's "Physics" 4*. Translated and annotated by Robert B. Todd. Ancient Commentators on Aristotle. Ithaca: Cornell University Press, 2005.

Theophrastus. *Meteorology*. Edited, translated, and annotated, with an introduction, by Hans Daiber. In: Daiber, Hans. "The *Meteorology* of Theophrastus in Syriac and Arabic Translation." In: *Theophrastus. His Psychological, Doxographical, and Scientific Writings*. Edited by William W. Fortenbaugh and Dimitri Gutas. Rutgers University Studies in Classical Humanities 5. New Brunswick and London: Transaction Publishers, 1992, 166–293.

Theophrastus. *On First Principles* (known as his *Metaphysics*). Edited, translated, and commented, with an introduction, by Dimitri Gutas. Philosophia antiqua. A Series of Studies on Ancient Philosophy 119. Leiden and Boston: Brill, 2010.

Theophrastus. *Sources for his Life, Writings, Thought and Influence. Vol. I: Life, Writings, Various Reports Logic, Physics, Metaphysics, Theology, Mathematics*. Edited and translated by William W. Fortenbaugh, Pamela M. Huby, Robert W. Sharples, and Dimitri Gutas. Philosophia antiqua. A Series of Studies on Ancient Philosophy 54. Leiden, New York, and Cologne: E. J. Brill, 1992.

al-Ṭūsī, Naṣīr al-Dīn. *Ḥall muškilāt al-Išārāt*. In: Avicenna. *al-Išārāt wa-l-tanbīhāt maʿa šarḥ Naṣīr al-Dīn al-Ṭūsī*. Edited by Sulaymān Dunyā. 4 vols. Ḏaḫāʾir al-ʿarab 22. Cairo: Dār al-Maʿārif, ³1983.

al-Ṭūsī, Naṣīr al-Dīn. *Šarḥ al-Išārāt wa-l-tanbīhāt*. Edited and annotated by Āyatollāh Ḥasan-zādeh al-Āmolī. 3 vols. Falsafe-ye Eslāmī 45. Qom: Būstān-e Ketāb, ³2012.

von Arnim, Hans, ed. *Stoicorum Veterum Fragmenta*. 4 vols. Leipzig: Teubner, 1903–24.

Wakelnig, Elvira, editor, translator, commentator, and introduction. *A Philosophy Reader from the Circle of Miskawayh*. Cambridge: Cambridge University Press, 2014.

Walbridge, John, editor, translator, annotator, and introduction. *The Alexandrian Epitomes of Galen. Vol. I: On the Medical Sects for Beginners, The Small Art of Medicine, On the Elements According to the Opinion of Hippocrates*. Islamic Translation Series. Provo: Brigham Young University Press, 2014.

Secondary Sources

ʿAbd al-Mutaʿāl, ʿAlāʾ al-Dīn Muḥammad. *Taṣawwur Ibn Sīnā li-l-zamān wa-uṣūluhū l-yūnāniyya*. Alexandria: Dār al-Wafāʾ li-Dunyā l-Ṭibāʿa wa-l-Našr, 2003.

Adamson, Peter. "Abū Bakr al-Rāzī on Animals." In: *Archiv für Geschichte der Philosophie* 94 (2012), 249–273.

Adamson, Peter, ed. *Classical Arabic Philosophy. Sources and Reception*. Warburg Institute Colloquia 11. London and Turin: The Warburg Institute, 2007.

Adamson, Peter. "From al-Rāzī to al-Rāzī. Platonist Views of Time and Place in the Islamic World." In: *On What There Was. Time and Space*. Edited by Aurélien Robert and Cecilia Trifogli. Turnhout: Brepols, [forthcoming].

Adamson, Peter. "Galen and al-Rāzī on Time." In: *Medieval Arabic Thought*. Essays in Honour of Fritz Zimmermann. Edited by Rotraud Hansberger, Muhammad Afifi al-Akiti, and Charles Burnett. Warburg Institute Studies and Texts 4. London and Turin: The Warburg Institute and Nino Aragno Editore, 2012, 1–14.

Adamson, Peter. "Galen on Void." In: *Philosophical Themes in Galen*. Edited by Peter Adamson, Rotraud Hansberger, and James Wilberding. Supplement to the Bulletin of the Institute of Classical Studies 114. London: Institute of Classical Studies, 2014, 197–211.

Adamson, Peter, ed. *Interpreting Avicenna. Critical Essays*. Cambridge: Cambridge University Press, 2013.

Adamson, Peter. "On Knowledge of Particulars." In: *Proceedings of the Aristotelian Society. New Series* 105 (2005), 273–294.

Adamson, Peter. "One of a Kind. Plotinus and Porphyry on Unique Instantiation." In: *Universals in Ancient Philosophy*. Edited by Riccardo Chiaradonna and Gabriele Galluzzo. Seminari e convegni 33. Pisa: Edizioni della Normale, 2013, 329–351.

Adamson, Peter. "*Porphyrius Arabus* on Nature and Art. 463F Smith in Context." In: *Studies on Porphyry*. Edited by George Karamanolis and Anne Sheppard. London: Institute of Classical Studies, 2007, 141–163.

Adamson, Peter. "*Posterior Analytics* II.19. A Dialogue with Plato?" In: *Aristotle & the Stoics Reading Plato*. Edited by Verity Harte, Mary Margaret McCabe, Robert W. Sharples, and Anne Sheppard. Supplement to the Bulletin of the Institute of Classical Studies 107. London: Institute of Classical Studies, 2010, 1–19.

Adamson, Peter. *The Arabic Plotinus. A Philosophical Study of the "Theology of Aristotle."* London: Duckworth, 2002.

Adamson, Peter. "The Kindian Tradition. The Structure Of Philosophy In Arabic Neoplatonism." In: *The Libraries of the Neoplatonists*. Proceedings of the Meeting of the European Science Foundation Network "Late Antiquity and Arabic Thought. Patterns in the Constitution of European Culture." (Strasbourg, 12th–14th Mar. 2004). Edited by Cristina D'Ancona. Philosophia antiqua. A Series of Studies on Ancient Philosophy 107. Leiden and Boston: Brill, 2007, 351–370.

Adamson, Peter, Han Baltussen, and Martin W. F. Stone, eds. *Philosophy, Science and Exegesis in Greek, Arabic and Latin Commentaries*. 2 vols. Supplement to the Bulletin of the Institute of Classical Studies 83.1–2. London: Institute of Classical Studies, 2004.

Adamson, Peter and Andreas Lammer. "Fakhr al-Dīn al-Rāzī's Platonist Account of the Essence of Time." In: *Philosophical Theology in Medieval Islam. The Later Ashʿarite Tradition*. Edited by Ayman Shihadeh and Jan Thiele. Islamicate Intellectual History. Studies and Texts in the Late Medieval and Early Modern Periods. Leiden and Boston: Brill, [forthcoming].

Adamson, Peter and Richard C. Taylor, eds. *The Cambridge Companion to Arabic Philosophy*. Cambridge: Cambridge University Press, 2005.

Aertsen, Jan A. "Avicenna's Doctrine of Primary Notions and its Impact on Medieval Philosophy." In: *Islamic Thought in the Middle Ages. Studies in Text, Transmission and Translation, in Honour of Hans Daiber*. Edited by Anna Akasoy and Wim Raven. Islamic Philosophy, Theology and Science. Texts and Studies 75. Leiden and Boston: Brill, 2008, 21–42.

Ahmed, Asad Q. "The Reception of Avicenna's Theory of Motion in the Twelfth Century." In: *Arabic Sciences and Philosophy* 26.2 (2016), 215–243.

Algra, Keimpe. *Concepts of Space in Greek Thought*. Philosophia antiqua. A Series of Studies on Ancient Philosophy 65. Leiden, New York, and Cologne: E. J. Brill, 1995.

Alpina, Tommaso. "Intellectual Knowledge, Active Intellect, and Intellectual Memory in Avicenna's *Kitab al-Nafs* and its Aristotelian Background." In: *Documenti e studi sulla tradizione filosofica medievale* 25 (2014), 131–183.

Alwishah, Ahmed and Josh Hayes, eds. *Aristotle and the Arabic Tradition*. Cambridge: Cambridge University Press, 2015.

Anagnostopoulos, Georgios. "Aristotle's Methods." In: *A Companion to Aristotle*. Edited by Georgios Anagnostopoulos. Chichester: Wiley-Blackwell, 2009, 101–122.

Angioni, Lucas. "Explanation and Definition in Physics I 1." In: *Apeiron. A Journal for Ancient Philosophy and Science* 34.4 (2001), 307–320.

Annas, Julia. "Aristotle, Number and Time." In: *The Philosophical Quarterly* 25.99 (1975), 97–113.

Arif, Syamsuddin. "Ibn Sīnā's Idea of Nature and Change." In: *Afkār. Journal of ʿAqīdah and Islamic Thought* 8 (2007), 111–139.

Arif, Syamsuddin. "The Universe as a System. Ibn Sīnā's Cosmology Revisited." In: *Islam & Science* 7.2 (2009), 127–145.

Armstrong, Arthur Hilary. *The Architecture of the Intelligible Universe in the Philosophy of Plotinus. An Analytical and Historical Study*. Cambridge: Cambridge University Press, 1940.

Arnzen, Rüdiger. "Plato's *Timaeus* in the Arabic Tradition. Legends – Testimonies – Fragments." In: *Il Timeo. Esegesi greche, arabe, latine*. Relazioni introduttive ai seminari della quinta "Settimana di Formazione" del Centro interunivesitario "Incontri di culture. La trasmissione dei testi filosofici e scientifici dalla tarda antichità al medioevo islamico e cristiano." (Pisa, Santa Croce in Fossabanda, 26th–30th Apr. 2010). Edited by Francesco Celia and Angela Ulacco. Pisa: Pisa University Press, 2012, 181–267.

Arnzen, Rüdiger. "Proclus on Plato's *Timaeus* 89e3–90c7." In: *Arabic Sciences and Philosophy* 23.1 (2013), 1–45.

Arzhanov, Yury and Rüdiger Arnzen. "Die Glossen in Ms. *Leyden or. 583* und die Syrische Rezeption der aristotelischen *Physik*." In: *De l'Antiquité tardive au Moyen Âge. Études de logique aristotélicienne et de philosophie grecque, syriaque, arabe et latine offertes à Henri Hugonnard-Roche*. Edited by Elisa Coda and Cecilia Martini Bonadeo. Études musulmanes 44. Paris: Vrin, 2014, 415–463.

ʿĀtī, Ibrāhīm. *al-Zamān fī l-fikr al-Islāmī. Ibn Sīnā – al-Rāzī al-ṭabīb – al-Maʿarrī*. Dirāsāt Falsafiyya. Beirut: Dār al-Muntaḫab al-ʿArabī li-l-Dirāsāt wa-l-Našr wa-l-Tawzīʿ, 1993.

Bäck, Allan. "Ibn Sina on the Individuation of Perceptible Substances." In: *Proceedings of the Patristic, Medieval, and Renaissance Conference* 14 (1989), 23–42.

Bäck, Allan. "The Islamic Background. Avicenna (b. 980; d. 1037) and Averroes (b. 1126; d. 1198)." In: *Individuation in Scholasticism. The Later Middle Ages and the Counter-Reformation, 1150–1650*.

Edited by Jorge J. E. Gracia. SUNY Series in Philosophy. Albany: State University of New York Press, 1994, 39–67.

Badawī, ʿAbd al-Raḥmān. *La transmission de la philosophie grecque au monde arabe*. Études de philosophie médiévale 56. Paris: Librairie philosophique J. Vrin, 1968.

Baltes, Matthias. *Die Weltentstehung des platonischen Timaios nach den antiken Interpreten*. 2 vols. Philosophia antiqua. A Series of Monographs on Ancient Philosophy 30, 35. Leiden: E. J. Brill, 1976–1978.

Baracat, José Carlos. "Soul's Desire and the Origin of Time in the Philosophy of Plotinus." In: *Literary, Philosophical, and Religious Studies in the Platonic Tradition*. Papers from the 7th Annual Conference of the International Society for Neoplatonic Studies. Edited by John F. Finamore and John Phillips. Academia Philosophical Studies 43. Sankt Augustin: Academia Verlag, 2013, 25–41.

Barnes, Jonathan. "An Introduction to Aspasius." In: *Aspasius. The earliest extant commentary on Aristotle's* Ethics. Edited by Antonina Alberti and Robert W. Sharples. Peripatoi. Philologisch-historische Studien zum Aristotelismus 17. Berlin and New York: Walter de Gruyter, 1999, 1–50.

Barnes, Jonathan. "Aristotle's Theory of Demonstration." In: *Phronesis* 14.2 (1969), 123–152.

Barnes, Jonathan. "Proof and the Syllogism." In: *Aristotle on Science. The "Posterior Analytics."* Proceedings of the 8th Symposium Aristotelicum. (Padua, 7th–15th Sept. 1978). Edited by Enrico Berti. Padua: Editrice Antenore, 1981, 17–59.

Barnes, Jonathan. "Roman Aristotle." In: *Philosophia Togata II. Plato and Aristotle in Rome*. Edited by Jonathan Barnes and Miriam Griffin. Oxford: Oxford University Press, 1997, 1–69.

Barnes, Jonathan, Malcolm Schofield, and Richard Sorabji, eds. *Articles on Aristotle*. Vol. 1: Science. London: Duckworth, 1975.

Bayer, Greg. "Coming to Know Principles in *Posterior Analytics* II 19." In: *Apeiron. A Journal for Ancient Philosophy and Science* 30.2 (1997), 109–142.

Beere, Jonathan. *Doing and Being. An Interpretation of Aristotle's* Metaphysics *Theta*. Oxford Aristotle Studies. Oxford: Oxford University Press, 2009.

Belo, Catarina. *Chance and Determinism in Avicenna and Averroes*. Islamic Philosophy and Theology. Texts and Studies 69. Leiden and Boston: Brill, 2007.

Belo, Catarina. "The Concept of 'Nature' in Aristotle, Avicenna and Averroes." In: *Kriterion. Revista de Filosofia* 56 (2015), 45–56.

Benevich, Fedor. "Die 'göttliche Existenz.' Zum ontologischen Status der Essenz qua Essenz bei Avicenna." In: *Documenti e studi sulla tradizione filosofica medievale* 26 (2015), 103–128.

Benevich, Fedor. "Fire and Heat. Yaḥyā b. ʿAdī and Avicenna on the Essentiality of Being Substance or Accident." In: *Arabic Sciences and Philosophy* 27.2 (2017), 237–267.

Benevich, Fedor. "The Priority of Natures against the Identity of Indiscernibles. Alexander of Aphrodisias, Yaḥyā b. ʿAdī, and Avicenna on Genus as Matter." In: *Journal of the History of Philosophy* ([forthcoming]).

Berryman, Sylvia. *The Mechanical Hypothesis in Ancient Greek Natural Philosophy*. Cambridge: Cambridge University Press, 2009.

Berti, Enrico. "Il movimento del cielo in Alessandro di Afrodisia." In: *La filosofia in età imperiale. Le scuole e le tradizioni filosofiche*. (Rome, 7th–9th June 1999). Edited by Aldo Brancacci. Elenchos 31. Naples: Bibliopolis, 2000, 227–243.

Berti, Enrico. "Les méthodes d'argumentation et de démonstration dans la 'Physique' (apories, phénomènes, principes)." In: *La physique d'Aristote et le conditions d'une science de la nature*. Actes du colloque organisé par le Séminaire d'Epistémologie et d'Histoire des Sciences de Nice. Edited by François de Gandt and Pierre Souffrin. Bibliothèque d'histoire de la philosophie. Nouvelle série. Paris: Vrin, 1991, 51–72.

Bertolacci, Amos. "Avicenna and Averroes on the Proof of God's Existence and the Subject-Matter of Metaphysics." In: *Medioevo. Rivista di Storia della Filosofia Medievale* 32 (2007), 61–97.
Bertolacci, Amos. "How Many Recensions of Avicenna's *Kitāb al-Šifāʾ*?" In: *Oriens* 40.2 (2012), 275–303.
Bertolacci, Amos. "On the Arabic Translations of Aristotle's *Metaphysics*." In: *Arabic Sciences and Philosophy* 15.2 (2005), 241–275.
Bertolacci, Amos. "Some Texts of Aristotle's *Metaphysics* in the *Ilāhīyāt* of Avicenna's *Kitāb al-Šifāʾ*." In: *Before and After Avicenna*. Proceedings of the First Conference of the Avicenna Study Group. Edited by David C. Reisman. In collaboration with Ahmed H. al-Rahim. Islamic Philosophy, Theology and Science. Texts and Studies 52. Leiden and Boston: E. J. Brill, 2003, 25–45.
Bertolacci, Amos. "The Distinction of Essence and Existence in Avicenna's Metaphysics. The Text and Its Context." In: *Islamic Philosophy, Science, Culture, and Religion. Studies in Honor of Dimitri Gutas*. Edited by Felicitas Opwis and David Reisman. Islamic Philosophy, Theology and Science. Texts and Studies 83. Leiden and Boston: Brill, 2012, 257–288.
Bertolacci, Amos. "The Doctrine of Material and Formal Causality in the 'Ilāhiyyāt' of Avicenna's 'Kitāb al-Šifāʾ.'" In: *Quaestio. Annuario di storia della metafisica* 2 (2002), 125–154.
Bertolacci, Amos. *The Reception of Aristotle's* Metaphysics *in Avicenna's* Kitāb al-Šifāʾ. *A Milestone of Western Metaphysical Thought*. Islamic Philosophy, Theology and Science. Texts and Studies 63. Leiden and Boston: Brill, 2006.
Birkenmajer, Alexander. "Eine wiedergefundene Übersetzung Gerhards von Cremona." In: *Aus der Geisteswelt des Mittelalters*. Studien und Texte Martin Grabmann zur Vollendung des 60. Lebensjahres von Freunden und Schülern gewidmet. Edited by Albert Lang, Joseph Lechner, and Michael Schmaus. Beiträge zur Geschichte der Philosophie und Theologie des Mittelalters. Supplementband 3.1. Münster: Aschendorfsche Verlagsbuchhandlung, 1935.
El-Bizri, Nader. "In Defence of the Sovereignty of Philosophy. al-Baghdādī's Critique of Ibn al-Haytham's Geometrisation of Place." In: *Arabic Sciences and Philosophy* 17.1 (2007), 57–80.
Black, Deborah L. "Al-Fārābī on Meno's Paradox." In: *In the Age of al-Fārābī. Arabic Philosophy in the Fourth/Tenth Century*. Edited by Peter Adamson. Warburg Institute Colloquia 12. London and Turin: The Warburg Institute and Nino Aragno Editore, 2008, 15–34.
Black, Deborah L. "Avicenna on Individuation, Self-Awareness, and God's Knowledge of Particulars." In: *Judeo-Christian-Islamic Heritage. Philosophical & Theological Perspectives*. Edited by Richard C. Taylor and Irfan A. Omar. Marquette Studies in Philosophy 75. Milwaukee: Marquette University Press, 2012, 255–281.
Black, Deborah L. "Avicenna on the Ontological and Epistemic Status of Fictional Beings." In: *Documenti e studi sulla tradizione filosofica medievale* 8 (1997), 425–453.
Black, Deborah L. "Avicenna's 'Vague Individual' and its Impact on Medieval Latin Philosophy." In: *Vehicles of Transmission, Translation, and Transformation in Medieval Textual Culture*. Edited by Robert Wisnovsky, Faith Wallis, Jamie C. Fumo, and Carlos Fraenkel. Turnhout: Brepols, 2011, 259–292.
Black, Deborah L. "Estimation (*wahm*) in Avicenna. The Logical and Psychological Dimensions." In: *Dialogue. Canadian Philosophical Review* 32 (1993), 219–258.
Black, Deborah L. "How Do we Acquire Concepts? Avicenna on Abstraction and Emanation." In: *Debates in Medieval Philosophy. Essential Readings and Contemporary Responses*. Edited by Jeffrey Hause. Key Debates in the History of Philosophy. New York and Abingdon: Routledge, 2014, 126–144.
Black, Deborah L. "Knowledge (*ʿilm*) and Certitude (*yaqīn*) in al-Fārābī's Epistemology." In: *Arabic Sciences and Philosophy* 16.1 (2006), 11–45.

Black, Deborah L. *Logic and Aristotle's* Rhetoric *and* Poetics *in Medieval Arabic Philosophy*. Islamic Philosophy and Theology. Texts and Studies 7. Leiden et al.: E. J. Brill, 1990.

Black, Deborah L. "Psychology. Soul and Intellect." In: *The Cambridge Companion to Arabic Philosophy*. Edited by Peter Adamson and Richard C. Taylor. Cambridge: Cambridge University Press, 2005, 308–326.

Bloch, Ernst. *Avicenna und die aristotelische Linke*. Frankfurt am Main: Suhrkamp, 1963.

Bodnár, István. "Alexander of Aphrodisias on Celestial Motions." In: *Phronesis* 42.2 (1997), 190–205.

Bogen, James. "Change and Contrariety in Aristotle." In: *Phronesis* 37.1 (1992), 1–21.

Boilot, Jacques-Dominique. "L'œuvre d'al-Beruni. Essai bibliographique." In: *MIDEO. Mélanges de l'Institut Dominicain d'Études Orientales du Caire* 2, 3 (1955, 1956), 161–256, 391–396.

Bolotin, David. "Aristotle's Discussion of Time." In: *Ancient Philosophy* 17.1 (1997), 47–62.

Bolton, Robert. "Aristotle's Method in Natural Science. *Physics* I." In: *Aristotle's* Physics. *A Collection of Essays*. Edited by Lindsay Judson. Oxford: Clarendon Press, 1991, 1–29.

Bolton, Robert. "Definition and Scientific Method in Aristotle's *Posterior Analytics* and *Generation of Animals*." In: *Philosophical Issues in Aristotle's Biology*. Edited by Allan Gotthelf and James G. Lennox. Cambridge: Cambridge University Press, 1987, 120–166.

Bos, Gerrit and Y. Tzvi Langermann. "An Epitome of Galen's *On The Elements* Ascribed to Ḥunayn Ibn Isḥāq." In: *Arabic Sciences and Philosophy* 25.1 (2015), 33–78.

Bostock, David. "A Note on Aristotle's Account of Place." In: Bostock, David. *Space, Time, Matter, and Form. Essays on Aristotle's* Physics. Oxford Aristotle Studies. Oxford: Clarendon Press, 2006, 128–134.

Bostock, David. "Aristotle on the Principles of Change in *Physics* I." In: Bostock, David. *Space, Time, Matter, and Form. Essays on Aristotle's* Physics. Oxford Aristotle Studies. Oxford: Clarendon Press, 2006, 1–18. Reprint of "Aristotle on the Principles of Change in *Physics* I." In: *Language & Logos*. Studies in Ancient Greek Philosophy presented to G. E. L. Owen. Edited by Malcolm Schofield and Martha C. Nussbaum. Cambridge: Cambridge University Press, 1982, 179–196.

Bostock, David. "Aristotle's Account of Time." In: *Phronesis* 25.2 (1980), 148–169. Reprint in *Space, Time, Matter, and Form. Essays on Aristotle's* Physics. Oxford Aristotle Studies. Oxford: Clarendon Press, 2006.

Bostock, David. *Space, Time, Matter, and Form. Essays on Aristotle's* Physics. Oxford Aristotle Studies. Oxford: Clarendon Press, 2006.

Bowin, John. "Aristotle on the Order and Direction of Time." In: *Apeiron. A Journal for Ancient Philosophy and Science* 42.1 (2009), 33–62.

Brentjes, Burchard, ed. *Avicenna – Ibn Sina. 980–1036*. Materialien einer wissenschaftlichen Arbeitstagung aus Anlaß der Millenniumsfeier für den großen tadshikischen Gelehrten. (Martin-Luther-Universität Halle-Wittenberg, 25th–26th Feb. 1980). 2 vols. Wissenschaftliche Beiträge 17. Halle: Martin-Luther-Universität Halle-Wittenberg, 1980.

Broadie, Sarah. "Aristotle's Now." In: *The Philosophical Quarterly* 34.135 (1984), 104–128.

Broadie, Sarah. *Nature, Change, and Agency in Aristotle's* Physics. *A Philosophical Study*. Oxford: Clarendon Press, 1982. Published as Sarah Waterlow.

Broadie, Sarah. "νοῦς and Nature in De Anima III." In: *Proceedings of the Boston Area Colloquium of Ancient Philosophy* 12 (1996), 163–176.

Brock, Sebastian. "Greek Words in Syriac. Some General Features." In: *Scripta Classica Israelica* 15 (1996), 251–262.

Bronstein, David. *Aristotle on Knowledge and Learning. The* Posterior Analytics. Oxford Aristotle Studies. Oxford: Oxford University Press, 2016.

Bronstein, David. "The Origin and Aim of *Posterior Analytics* II.19." In: *Phronesis* 57.1 (2012), 29–62.

Brown, H. Vivian B. "Avicenna and the Christian Philosophers in Baghdad." In: *Islamic Philosophy and the Classical Tradition*. Essays presented by his friends and pupils to Richard Walzer on his

Seventieth Birthday. Edited by Samuel Miklos Stern, Albert Hourani, and H. Vivian B. Brown. Oxford: Cassirer Publishers, 1972, 35–48.

Brunschwig, Jaques. "Qu'est ce que *la Physique* d'Aristote?" In: *La physique d'Aristote et le conditions d'une science de la nature*. Actes du colloque organisé par le Séminaire d'Epistémologie et d'Histoire des Sciences de Nice. Edited by François de Gandt and Pierre Souffrin. Bibliothèque d'histoire de la philosophie. Nouvelle série. Paris: Vrin, 1991, 11–40.

Burnyeat, Myles Fredric. *A Map of* Metaphysics *Z*. Pittsburgh: Mathesis Publications, 2001.

Burnyeat, Myles Fredric. "Aristotle on the Foundations of Sublunary Physics." In: *Aristotle's* On Generation and Corruption *I*. Proceedings of the 15th Symposium Aristotelicum. (Deurne, the Netherlands, 21st–28th Aug. 1999). Edited by Frans A. J. de Haas and Jaap Mansfeld. Oxford: Oxford University Press, 2004, 7–24.

Burnyeat, Myles Fredric. "*De anima* II 5." In: *Phronesis* 47.1 (2002), 28–90.

Buschmann, Elisabeth. *Untersuchungen zum Problem der Materie bei Avicenna*. Europäische Hochschulschriften. Reihe XX. Philosophie 38. Frankfurt am Main, Bern, and Las Vegas: Peter Lang, 1979.

Butler, Travis. "*Empeiria* in Aristotle." In: *Southern Journal of Philosophy* 41 (2003), 330–342.

Butorac, David D. and Danielle A. Layne, eds. *Proclus and his Legacy*. Millennium-Studien zu Kultur und Geschichte des ersten Jahrtausends n. Chr. Millennium Studies in the Culture and History of the First Millennium C.E. 65. Berlin and Boston: Walter de Gruyter, 2017.

Callahan, John F. *Four Views of Time in Ancient Philosophy*. Cambridge: Harvard University Press, 1948.

Capelle, Wilhelm. "Das Proömium der Meteorologie." In: *Hermes. Zeitschrift für klassische Philologie* 47 (1912), 514–535.

Casey, Edward S. *The Fate of Place. A Philosophical History*. Berkeley, Los Angeles, and London: University of California Press, 1997.

Caston, Victor. "Aristotle on the Relation of the Intellect to the Body. Commentary on Broadie." In: *Proceedings of the Boston Area Colloquium of Ancient Philosophy* 12 (1996), 177–192.

Celeyrette, Jean. "Le vide chez Avicenne." In: *La nature et le vide dans la physique médiévale*. Études dédiées à Edward Grant. Edited by Joël Biard and Sabine Rommevaux. Studia Artistarum. Etudes sur la Faculté des arts dans les Universités médiévales 32. Turnhout: Brepols, 2012, 101–117.

Cerami, Cristina. *Génération et substance. Aristote et Averroès entre physique et métaphysique*. Scientia graeco-arabica 18. Berlin and New York: Walter de Gruyter, 2015.

Cerami, Cristina. "Thomas d'Aquin lecteur critique du Grand Commentaire d'Averroès à *Phys*. I, 1." In: *Arabic Sciences and Philosophy* 19.2 (2009), 189–223.

Charlton, William. "Aristotelian Powers." In: *Phronesis* 32.3 (1987), 277–289.

Charlton, William. "Prime Matter. A Rejoinder." In: *Phronesis* 28.2 (1983), 197–211.

Chase, Michael. "al-Šahrastānī on Proclus." In: *Proclus and his Legacy*. Edited by David D. Butorac and Danielle A. Layne. Millennium-Studien zu Kultur und Geschichte des ersten Jahrtausends n. Chr. Millennium Studies in the Culture and History of the First Millennium C.E. 65. Berlin and Boston: Walter de Gruyter, 2017, 323–333.

Chase, Michael. "Time and Eternity from Plotinus and Boethius to Einstein." In: *ΣΧΟΛΗ* 8.1 (2014), 67–110.

Chiaradonna, Riccardo. "Le traité de Galien *Sur la démonstration* et sa postérité tardo-antique." In: *Physics and Philosophy of Nature in Greek Neoplatonism*. Proceedings of the European Science Foundation Exploratory Workshop. (Il Ciocco, Castelvecchio Pascoli, 22nd–24th June 2006). Edited by Riccardo Chiaradonna and Franco Trabattoni. Philosophia antiqua. A Series of Studies on Ancient Philosophy 115. Leiden and Boston: Brill, 2009, 43–77.

Chiaradonna, Riccardo and Franco Trabattoni, eds. *Physics and Philosophy of Nature in Greek Neoplatonism*. Proceedings of the European Science Foundation Exploratory Workshop. (Il Ciocco,

Castelvecchio Pascoli, 22nd–24th June 2006). Philosophia antiqua. A Series of Studies on Ancient Philosophy 115. Leiden and Boston: Brill, 2009.

Clark, Gordon H. "The Theory of Time in Plotinus." In: *The Philosophical Review* 53.4 (1944), 337–58.

Conen, Paul F. *Die Zeittheorie des Aristoteles*. Zetemata. Monographien zur klassischen Altertumswissenschaft 35. Munich: C. H. Beck, 1964.

Coope, Ursula. *Time for Aristotle*. Physics *IV.10–14*. Oxford Aristotle Studies. New York: Oxford University Press, 2005.

Coope, Ursula. "Why Does Aristotle Say that There Is no Time without Change?" In: *Proceedings of the Aristotelian Society. New Series* 101 (2001), 359–367.

Corcilius, Klaus. "Physik." In: *Aristoteles Handbuch. Leben – Werk – Wirkung*. Edited by Christof Rapp and Klaus Corcilius. Stuttgart and Weimar: J. B. Metzler, 2011. Chapter III.3, 75–84.

Corcilius, Klaus. *Streben und Bewegen. Aristoteles' Theorie der animalischen Ortsbewegung*. Quellen und Studien zur Philosophie 79. Berlin and New York: Walter de Gruyter, 2008.

Corish, Denis. "Aristotle's Attempted Derivation of Temporal Order from That of Movement and Space." In: *Phronesis* 21.3 (1976), 241–251.

D'Ancona, Cristina. "Al-Kindī et l'auteur du *Liber de causis*." In: *Recherches sur le Liber de causis*. Edited by Cristina D'Ancona. Études de philosophie médiévale 72. Paris: Librairie philosophique J. Vrin, 1995, 155–194.

D'Ancona, Cristina. "Avicenna and the *Liber de causis*. A Contribution to the Dossier." In: *Revista española de filosofía medieval* 7 (2000), 95–114.

D'Ancona, Cristina. "Greek Sources in Arabic and Islamic Philosophy." In: *The Stanford Encyclopedia to Philosophy*. Edited by Edward N. Zalta. Winter 2013 Edition. URL: http://plato.stanford.edu/archives/win2013/entries/arabic-islamic-greek/.

D'Ancona, Cristina. "La Teologia neoplatonica di 'Aristotele' e gli inizi della filosofia arabo-musulmana." In: *Entre Orient et Occident. La philosophie et la science gréco-romaines dans le monde arabe*. Edited by Richard Goulet and Ulrich Rudolph. Entretiens sur l'antiquité classique 57. Vandoeuvres: Fondation Hardt, 2011, 135–190.

D'Erlanger, Rodolphe. *La musique arabe*. 6 vols. Paris: Librairie orientaliste Paul Geuthner, 1930–1959.

Dagli, Caner. "Ether." In: *The Oxford Encyclopedia of Philosophy, Science, and Technology in Islam*. Edited by Ibrahim Kalin. Vol. 1. 2 vols. New York: Oxford University Press, 2014, 207–210.

Daiber, Hans. "Fārābīs Abhandlung über das Vakuum. Quellen und Stellung in der islamischen Wissenschaftsgeschichte." In: *Der Islam. Zeitschrift für Geschichte und Kultur des Islamischen Orients* 60 (1983), 37–47.

Daiber, Hans. "The *Meteorology* of Theophrastus in Syriac and Arabic Translation." In: *Theophrastus. His Psychological, Doxographical, and Scientific Writings*. Edited by William W. Fortenbaugh and Dimitri Gutas. Rutgers University Studies in Classical Humanities 5. New Brunswick and London: Transaction Publishers, 1992, 166–293.

Davidson, Herbert A. "Alfarabi and Avicenna on the Active Intellect." In: *Viator. Medieval and Renaissance Studies* 3 (1972), 109–178.

Davidson, Herbert A. *Alfarabi, Avicenna, and Averroes, on Intellect. Their Cosmologies, Theories of the Active Intellect, and Theories of Human Intellect*. New York and Oxford: Oxford University Press, 1992.

de Gandt, François and Pierre Souffrin, eds. *La physique d'Aristote et le conditions d'une science de la nature*. Actes du colloque organisé par le Séminaire d'Epistémologie et d'Histoire des Sciences de Nice. Bibliothèque d'histoire de la philosophie. Nouvelle série. Paris: Vrin, 1991.

de Haas, Frans A. J. *John Philoponus' New Definition of Prime Matter. Aspects of its Background in Neoplatonism and the Ancient Commentary Tradition*. Philosophia antiqua. A Series of Studies on Ancient Philosophy 69. Leiden, New York, and Cologne: Brill, 1997.

de Haas, Frans A. J. "Modifications of the Method of Inquiry in Aristotle's *Physics* I.1. An Essay on the Dynamics of the Ancient Commentary Tradition." In: *The Dynamics of Aristotelian Natural Philosophy from Antiquity to the Seventeenth Century*. Edited by Cees Leijenhorst, Christoph Lüthy, and Johannes M. M. H. Thijssen. Medieval and Early Modern Science 5. Leiden, Boston, and Cologne: Brill, 2002, 31–56.

Dean-Jones, Lesley. "Aristotle's Understanding of Plato's Receptacle and its Significance for Aristotle's Theory of Familial Resemblance." In: *Reason and Necessity. Essays on Plato's* Timaeus. Edited by Maureen R. Wright. London and Swansea: Duckworth and The Classical Press of Wales, 2000, 101–112.

Dhanani, Alnoor. "Rocks in the Heavens?! The Encounter between ʿAbd al-Ǧabbār and Ibn Sīnā." In: *Before and After Avicenna*. Proceedings of the First Conference of the Avicenna Study Group. Edited by David C. Reisman. In collaboration with Ahmed H. al-Rahim. Islamic Philosophy, Theology and Science. Texts and Studies 52. Leiden and Boston: E. J. Brill, 2003, 127–144.

Dhanani, Alnoor. *The Physical Theory of Kalām. Atoms, Space, and Void in Basrian Muʿtazilī Cosmology*. Islamic Philosophy, Theology and Science. Texts and Studies 14. Leiden: E. J. Brill, 1994.

Di Giovanni, Matteo. "Substantial Form in Averroes's Long Commentary on the Metaphysics." In: *In the Age of Averroes. Arabic Philosophy in the Sixth/Twelfth Century*. Edited by Peter Adamson. Warburg Institute Colloquia 16. London and Turin: The Warburg Institute and Nino Aragno Editore, 2011, 175–194.

Di Liscia, Daniel A., Eckhard Kessler, and Charlotte Methuen, eds. *Method and Order in Renaissance Philosophy of Nature. The Aristotle Commentary Tradition*. Aldershot and Brookfield: Ashgate, 1997.

Druart, Thérèse-Anne. "Avicennan Troubles. The Mysteries of the Heptagonal House and of the Phoenix." In: *Tópicos. Revista de filosofía* 42 (2012), 51–73.

Druart, Thérèse-Anne. "Le Traité d'al-Fārābī sur les Buts de la Métaphysique d'Aristote." In: *Bulletin de philosophie médiévale* 24 (1982), 38–43.

Duhem, Pierre. *Le système du monde. Histoire des doctrines cosmologiques de Platon à Copernic*. 10 vols. Paris: Hermann, 1913–1959.

Duhem, Pierre. *Medieval Cosmology. Theories of Infinity, Place, Time, Void, and the Plurality of Worlds*. Edited and translated by Roger Ariew. Chicago and London: The University of Chicago Press, 1985.

Dyke, Heather and Adrian Bardon, eds. *A Companion to the Philosophy of Time*. Blackwell Companions to Philosophy 52. Chichester: Wiley-Blackwell, 2013.

Ebrey, David. *Aristotle's Motivation for Matter*. PhD thesis. Los Angeles: University of California, 2007.

Ehlers, Dietrich. "Aristoteles, Proklos und Avicenna über philosophische Probleme der Mathematik." In: *Avicenna – Ibn Sina. 980–1036*. Materialien einer wissenschaftlichen Arbeitstagung aus Anlaß der Millenniumsfeier für den großen tadshikischen Gelehrten. Vol. 1: *Probleme der Philosophie*. (Martin-Luther-Universität Halle-Wittenberg, 25th–26th Feb. 1980). Edited by Burchard Brentjes. 2 vols. Wissenschaftliche Beiträge 17. Halle: Martin-Luther-Universität Halle-Wittenberg, 1980, 88–94.

Eichner, Heidrun. "al-Amidi and Fakhr al-Din al-Rāzi. Two 13th-Century Approaches to Philosophical Kalām." In: *Uluslararası Seyfuddîn Âmidî Sempozyumu Bildirileri. International Conference on Sayf al-Din al-Amidi Papers*. (Diyarbakır, 24th–26th Oct. 2008). Edited by Ahmet Erkol, Abdurrahman Adak, and Ibrahim Bor. Istanbul: Ensar Neşriyat, 2009, 333–345.

Eichner, Heidrun. "al-Fārābī and Ibn Sīnā on 'Universal Science' and the System of Sciences. Evidence of the Arabic Tradition of the *Posterior Analytics*." In: *Documenti e studi sulla tradizione filosofica medievale* 21 (2010), 71–95.

Eichner, Heidrun. "Dissolving the Unity of Metaphysics. From Faḫr al-Dīn al-Rāzī to Mullā Ṣadrā al-Šīrāzī." In: *Medioevo. Rivista di Storia della Filosofia Medievale* 32 (2007), 139–197.

Eichner, Heidrun. *The Post-Avicennian Philosophical Tradition and Islamic Orthodoxy. Philosophical and Theological* summae *in Context.* Habilitationsschrift. Halle-Wittenberg: Martin-Luther-Universität, 2009.

Endreß, Gerhard. "Alexander Arabus on the First Cause. Aristotle's First Mover in an Arabic Treatise Attributed to Alexander of Aphrodisias." In: *Aristotele e Alessandro di Afrodisia nella tradizione araba.* Atti del colloquio *La ricezione araba ed ebraica della filosofia e della scienza greche.* (Padua, 14th–15th May 1999). Edited by Cristina D'Ancona and Giuseppe Serra. Subsidia Mediaevalia Patavina 3. Padua: Il Poligrafo, 2002, 19–74.

Endreß, Gerhard. "Averroes' *De Caelo.* Ibn Rushd's Cosmology in his Commentaries on Aristotle's *On the Heavens.*" In: *Arabic Sciences and Philosophy* 5.1 (1995), 9–49.

Endreß, Gerhard. "Die griechisch-arabischen Übersetzungen und die Sprache der arabischen Wissenschaften." In: *Symposium Graeco-Arabicum.* Akten des zweiten *Symposium Græco-Arabicum.* (Ruhr-Universität Bochum, 3rd–5th Mar. 1987). Edited by Gerhard Endreß. Archivum graeco-arabicum 1. Amsterdam: B. R. Grüner, 1989, 103–145.

Endreß, Gerhard. "Die wissenschaftliche Literatur." In: *Grundriß der Arabischen Philologie.* Vol. 2: *Literaturwissenschaft.* Edited by Helmut Gätje. 3 vols. Wiesbaden: Dr. Ludwig Reichert Verlag, 1987, 400–506. Continued in: Gerhard Endreß. "Die wissenschaftliche Literatur." In: *Grundriß der Arabischen Philologie.* Vol. 3: *Supplement.* Edited by Wolfdietrich Fischer. 3 vols. Wiesbaden: Dr. Ludwig Reichert Verlag, 1992, 3–152.

Endreß, Gerhard. "Mattā b. Yūnus." In: *The Encyclopaedia of Islam. New Edition.* Vol. 6. 12 vols. Leiden: E. J. Brill, 1991, 844–846.

Endreß, Gerhard. "Reading Avicenna in the Madrasa. Intellectual Genealogies and Chains of Transmission of Philosophy and the Sciences in the Islamic East." In: *Arabic Theology, Arabic Philosophy. From the Many to the One.* Essays in Celebration of Richard M. Frank. Edited by James E. Montgomery. Orientalia Lovaniensia Analecta 152. Leuven: Peeters, 2006, 371–422.

Endreß, Gerhard. "The Cycle of Knowledge. Intellectual Traditions and Encyclopædias of the Rational Sciences in Arabic Islamic Hellenism." In: *Organizing Knowledge. Encyclopædic Activities in the Pre-Eighteenth Century Islamic World.* Edited by Gerhard Endreß. Islamic Philosophy, Theology and Science. Texts and Studies 61. With a preface by Abdou Filali-Ansary. Leiden and Boston: Brill, 2006, 103–133.

Endreß, Gerhard. "The Language of Demonstration. Translating Science and the Formation of Terminology in Arabic Philosophy and Science." In: *Early Science and Medicine* 7.3 (2002): *Certainty, Doubt, Error. Aspects of the Practice of Pre- and Early Modern Science. In Honour of David A. King.* Edited by Sonja Brentjes, Benno van Dalen, and François Charette, 231–254.

Endreß, Gerhard, Rüdiger Arnzen, and Yury Arzhanov. *Glossarium Graeco-Arabicum.* URL: http://telota.bbaw.de/glossga/.

Engberg-Pedersen, Troels. "More on Aristotelian Epagoge." In: *Phronesis* 24.3 (1979), 301–319.

Falcon, Andrea. *Aristotle and the Science of Nature. Unity without Uniformity.* Cambridge: Cambridge University Press, 2005.

Falcon, Andrea. "Aristotle on Time and Change." In: *A Companion to the Philosophy of Time.* Edited by Heather Dyke and Adrian Bardon. Blackwell Companions to Philosophy 52. Chichester: Wiley-Blackwell, 2013, 47–58.

Falcon, Andrea. "The Subject Matter of Aristotle's Physics." In: *ΣΩΜΑ. Körperkonzepte und körperliche Existenz in der antiken Philosophie und Literatur.* Beiträge zum IV. Internationalen Kongress der Gesellschaft für antike Philosophie. (Ludwig-Maximilians-Universität München, 7th–11th Oct. 2013). Edited by Thomas Buchheim, David Meißner, and Nora Wachsmann. Archiv für Begriffsgeschichte. Sonderheft 13. Hamburg: Felix Meiner Verlag, 2016, 423–436.

Fazzo, Silvia. “Alexandre d’Aphrodise contre Galien. La naissance d’une légende.” In: *Philosophie Antique* 2 (2002), 109–144.

Fazzo, Silvia. “L’Alexandre arabe et la génération à partir du néant.” In: *Perspectives arabes et médiévales sur la tradition scientifique et philosophique grecque. Actes du colloque de la SIH-SPAI (Société Internationale d’Histoire des Sciences et de la Philosophie Arabes et Islamiques).* (Paris, 31st Mar.–3rd Apr. 1993). Edited by Ahmad Hasnawi, Abdelali Elamrani-Jamal, and Maroun Aouad. Orientalia Lovaniensia Analecta 79. With a preface by Roshdi Rashed. Leuven and Paris: Peeters, 1997, 277–288.

Fazzo, Silvia and Mauro Zonta. “Towards a Textual History and Reconstruction of Alexander of Aphrodisias’s Treatise *On the Principles of the Universe*.” In: *Journal of Semitic Studies* 59.1 (2014), 91–116.

Fiori, Emiliano. “L’épitomé syriaque du *Traité sur les causes du tout* d’Alexandre d’Aphrodise attribué à Serge de Rešʿaynā. Édition et traduction.” In: *Le Muséon. Revue d’études orientales* 123.1–2 (2010), 127–158.

Fischer, Wolfdietrich. *Grammatik des klassischen Arabisch*. Porta linguarum orientalium. Neue Serie 11. Wiesbaden: Harrassowitz Verlag, [4]2006.

Fischer, Wolfdietrich and Helmut Gätje, eds. *Grundriß der Arabischen Philologie*. 3 vols. Wiesbaden: Dr. Ludwig Reichert Verlag, 1982–92.

Frank, Richard M. *Beings and Their Attributes. The Teaching of the Basrian School of the Muʿtazila in the Classical Period*. Studies in Islamic Philosophy and Science. Albany: State University of New York Press, 1978.

Frank, Richard M. “Some Fragments of Isḥāq’s Translation of the *De anima*.” In: *Cahiers de byrsa* 8 (1958–59), 231–251.

Frede, Dorothea. “Alexander of Aphrodisias.” In: *The Stanford Encyclopedia to Philosophy*. Edited by Edward N. Zalta. Summer 2013 Edition. URL: http://plato.stanford.edu/archives/sum2013/entries/alexander-aphrodisias/.

Frede, Michael. *A Free Will. Origins of the Notion in Ancient Thought*. Edited by Anthony A. Long. With a foreword by David Sedley. Berkeley, Los Angeles, and London: University of California Press, 2011.

Fritsche, Johannes. “Aristotle on Space, Form, and Matter (*Physics* IV:2, 209b17–32).” In: *Archiv für Begriffsgeschichte* 48 (2006), 45–63.

Fritsche, Johannes. “Aristotle on χώρα in Plato’s *Timaeus* (*Physics* IV:2, 209b6–17).” In: *Archiv für Begriffsgeschichte* 48 (2006), 27–44.

Fritsche, Johannes. “Aristotle’s Usage of ἀρχὴ κινήσεως (‘principle of motion’) and the Two Definitions of Nature in *Physics* II, 1.” In: *Archiv für Begriffsgeschichte* 52 (2010), 7–31.

Fritsche, Johannes. *Methode und Beweisziel im ersten Buch der “Physikvorlesung” des Aristoteles*. Monographien zur philosophischen Forschung 239. Frankfurt am Main: Verlag Anton Hain, 1986.

Furlani, Giuseppe. “Le ‘Questioni filosofiche’ di Abū Zakarīyā Yaḥyâ b. ʿAdī.” In: *Rivista degli studi orientali* 8 (1919–20), 157–162.

Furley, David. “Aristotle and the Atomists on Motion in a Void.” In: *Motion and Time, Space and Matter. Interrelations in the History of Philosophy and Science*. Edited by Peter K. Machamer and Robert G. Turnbull. Columbus: Ohio State University Press, 1976, 83–100.

Furley, David. *Cosmic Problems. Essays on Greek and Roman Philosophy of Nature*. Cambridge: Cambridge University Press, 1989.

Furley, David. “Self-Movers.” In: *Aristotle on Mind and the Senses*. Proceedings of the Seventh Symposium Aristotelicum. Edited by Geoffrey Ernest Richard Lloyd and Gwilym Ellis Lane Owen. Cambridge: Cambridge University Press, 1978, 165–179.

Furley, David. "Strato's Theory of the Void." In: *Aristoteles. Werk und Wirkung*. Paul Moraux gewidmet. Vol. 1: *Aristoteles und seine Schule*. Edited by Jürgen Wiesner. 2 vols. Berlin and New York: Walter de Gruyter, 1985–87, 594–609.

Gacek, Adam. *Arabic Manuscripts. A Vademecum for Readers*. Handbook of Oriental Studies. Section 1.The Near and Middle East 98. Leiden and Boston: Brill, 2009.

Galston, Miriam. "al-Fārābī on Aristotle's Theory of Demonstration." In: *Islamic Philosophy and Mysticism*. Edited by Parviz Morewedge. Studies in Islamic Philosophy and Science. Delmar: Caravan Books, 1981, 23–34.

Gannagé, Emma. "Philopon (Jean-). Tradition arabe." In: *Dictionnaire des philosophes antiques. Vol. Va: de Paccius à Plotin*. Edited by Richard Goulet. Paris: C. N. R. S. Éditions, 2012, 503–563.

Gätje, Helmut. "Simplikios in der arabischen Überlieferung." In: *Der Islam* 59.1 (1982), 6–31.

Gätje, Helmut. *Studien zur Überlieferung der aristotelischen Psychologie im Islam*. Annales Universitatis Saraviensis. Reihe Philosophische Fakultät 11. Heidelberg: Carl Winter Universitätsverlag, 1971.

Gätje, Helmut. "Zur Psychologie der Willenshandlungen in der islamischen Philosophie." In: *Saeculum. Jahrbuch für Universalgeschichte* 26.4 (1975), 347–363.

Genequand, Charles. "Quelques aspects de l'idée de nature d'Aristote à al-Ghazālī." In: *Revue de théologie et de philosophie* 116 (1984), 105–129.

Germann, Nadja. "Avicenna and Afterwards." In: *The Oxford Handbook of Medieval Philosophy*. Edited by John Marenbon. New York: Oxford University Press, 2012, 83–105.

Germann, Nadja. "How Can I Know? al-Fārābī on Teaching and Learning." In: *Knowledge and Education in Classical Islam*. Edited by Sebastian Günther. Leiden and Boston: Brill, [forthcoming].

Gerson, Lloyd. *Aristotle and Other Platonists*. Ithaca and London: Cornell University Press, 2005.

Giannakis, Elias. "Fragments from Alexander's Lost Commentary on Aristotle's *Physics*." In: *Zeitschrift für Geschichte der arabisch-islamischen Wissenschaften* 10 (1996), 157–187.

Giannakis, Elias. *Philoponus in the Arabic Tradition of Aristotle's* Physics. PhD thesis. University of Oxford, 1992.

Giannakis, Elias. "Proclus' Arguments on the Eternity of the World in al-Shahrastānī's Works." In: *Proclus and his Legacy*. Edited by David D. Butorac and Danielle A. Layne. Millennium-Studien zu Kultur und Geschichte des ersten Jahrtausends n. Chr. Millennium Studies in the Culture and History of the First Millennium C.E. 65. Berlin and Boston: Walter de Gruyter, 2017, 335–351.

Giannakis, Elias. "The Quotations from John Philoponus' *De aeternitate mundi contra Proclum* in al-Bīrūnī's *India*." In: *Zeitschrift für Geschichte der arabisch-islamischen Wissenschaften* 15 (2002–03), 185–195.

Giannakis, Elias. "The Structure of Abū l-Ḥusayn al-Baṣrī's Copy of Aristotle's *Physics*." In: *Zeitschrift für Geschichte der arabisch-islamischen Wissenschaften* 8 (1993), 251–258.

Gill, Mary Louise. "Aristotle on Self-Motion." In: *Aristotle's* Physics. *A Collection of Essays*. Edited by Lindsay Judson. Oxford: Clarendon Press, 1991, 243–265.

Gill, Mary Louise. *Aristotle on Substance. The Paradox of Unity*. Princeton: Princeton University Press, 1989.

Gill, Mary Louise. "Review of *The Order of Nature in Aristotle's Physics: Place and the Elements* by Helen S. Lang." In: *British Journal for the History of Science* 51.3 (2000), 549–557.

Gilson, Étienne. *History of Christian Philosophy in the Middle Ages*. New York: Random House, 1955.

Glasner, Ruth. *Averroes' Physics. A Turning Point in Medieval Natural Philosophy*. Oxford: Oxford University Press, 2009.

Goichon, Amélie-Marie. *La distinction de l'essence et de l'existence d'après Ibn Sīnā (Avicenne)*. Paris: Desclée de Brouwer, 1937.

Goichon, Amélie-Marie. *Lexique de la langue philosophique d'Ibn Sīnā (Avicenne)*. Paris: Desclée de Brouwer, 1938.

Golitsis, Pantelis. *Les commentaires de Simplicius et de Jean Philopon à la* Physique *d'Aristote. Tradition et innovation*. Commentaria in Aristotelem graeca et byzantina. Quellen und Studien 3. Berlin and New York: Walter de Gruyter, 2008.

Goulet, Richard, ed. *Dictionnaire des philosophes antiques. Vol. Va: de Paccius à Plotin*. Paris: C. N. R. S. Éditions, 2012.

Grant, Edward. "Celestial Matter. A Medieval and Galilean Cosmological Problem." In: *The Journal of Medieval and Renaissance Studies* 13 (1983), 157–186.

Grant, Edward. *Much Ado about Nothing. Theories of Space and Vacuum from the Middle Ages to the Scientific Revolution*. Cambridge: Cambridge University Press, 1981.

Grant, Edward. "The Medieval Doctrine of Place. Some Fundamental Problems and Solutions." In: *Studi sul XIV secolo. In memoria di Anneliese Maier*. Edited by Alfonso Maierù and Agostino Paravicini Bagliani. Storia e letteratura. Raccolta di studi e testi 151. Rome: Edizioni di storia e letteratura, 1981, 57–79.

Griffin, Michael. "Proclus on Place as the Luminous Vehicle of the Soul." In: *Dionysius* 30 (2012), 161–186.

Gutas, Dimitri. "Aspects of Literary Form and Genre in Arabic Logical Works." In: *Glosses and Commentaries on Aristotelian Logical Texts. The Syriac, Arabic and Medieval Latin Traditions*. Edited by Charles Burnett. Warburg Institute Surveys and Texts 23. London: The Warburg Institute, 1993, 29–76.

Gutas, Dimitri. *Avicenna and the Aristotelian Tradition. Introduction to Reading Avicenna's Philosophical Works*. Second, Revised and Enlarged Edition, Including an Inventory of Avicenna's Authentic Works. Islamic Philosophy, Theology and Science. Texts and Studies 89. Leiden and Boston: Brill, ²2014.

Gutas, Dimitri. "Avicenna: *De Anima* (V 6). Über die Seele, über Intuition und Prophetie." In: *Hauptwerke der Philosophie. Mittelalter*. Edited by Kurt Flasch. Interpretationen. Stuttgart: Reclam, 1998, 90–107.

Gutas, Dimitri. "Avicenna's Eastern ('Oriental') Philosophy. Nature, Contents, Transmission." In: *Arabic Sciences and Philosophy* 10.2 (2000), 159–180.

Gutas, Dimitri. "Certainty, Doubt, Error. Comments on the Epistemological Foundations of Medieval Arabic Science." In: *Early Science and Medicine* 7.3 (2002): *Certainty, Doubt, Error. Aspects of the Practice of Pre- and Early Modern Science. In Honour of David A. King*. Edited by Sonja Brentjes, Benno van Dalen, and François Charette, 276–289.

Gutas, Dimitri. "Greek Philosophical Works Translated into Arabic." In: *The Cambridge History of Medieval Philosophy*. Edited by Robert Pasnau and Christina van Dyke. Vol. 2. 2 vols. Cambridge: Cambridge University Press, 2010, 802–814.

Gutas, Dimitri. *Greek Thought, Arabic Culture. The Graeco-Arabic Translation Movement in Baghdad and Early ʿAbbāsid Society (2nd–4th/8th–10th centuries)*. New York: Routledge, 1998.

Gutas, Dimitri. "Intuition and Thinking. The Evolving Structure of Avicenna's Epistemology." In: *Aspects of Avicenna*. Edited by Robert Wisnovsky. Princeton: Markus Wiener Publishers, 2001, 1–38.

Gutas, Dimitri. "Medical Theory and Scientific Method in the Age of Avicenna." In: *Before and After Avicenna*. Proceedings of the First Conference of the Avicenna Study Group. Edited by David C. Reisman. In collaboration with Ahmed H. al-Rahim. Islamic Philosophy, Theology and Science. Texts and Studies 52. Leiden and Boston: E. J. Brill, 2003, 145–162.

Gutas, Dimitri. "Philoponus and Avicenna on the Separability of the Intellect. A Case of Orthodox Christian-Muslim Agreement." In: *Greek Orthodox Theological Review* 31.1–2 (1986), 121–129.

Gutas, Dimitri. "Platon. Tradition arabe." In: *Dictionnaire des philosophes antiques. Vol. Va: de Paccius à Plotin*. Edited by Richard Goulet. Paris: C. N. R. S. Éditions, 2012, 845–863.

Gutas, Dimitri. "The Empiricism of Avicenna." In: *Oriens* 40.2 (2012), 391–436.

Gutas, Dimitri. "The Life, Works, and Sayings of Theophrastus in the Arabic Tradition." In: *Theophrastus of Eresus. On His Life and Work*. Edited by William W. Fortenbaugh. Rutgers University Studies in Classical Humanities 2. New Brunswick and Oxford: Transaction Books, 1985, 63–102.

Gutas, Dimitri. "The *Ṣiwān al-Ḥikma* Cycle of Texts." In: *Journal of the American Oriental Society* 102.4 (1982), 645–650.

Gutas, Dimitri. "The Study of Avicenna. Status quaestionis atque agenda." In: *Documenti e studi sulla tradizione filosofica medievale* 21 (2010), 45–69.

Hadot, Ilsetraut. "The Life and Work of Simplicius in Greek and Arabic Sources." In: *Aristotle Transformed. The Ancient Commentators and Their Influence*. Edited by Richard Sorabji. Ithaca: Cornell University Press, 1990.

Hall, Robert E. "Intellect, Soul and Body in Ibn Sīnā. Systematic Synthesis and Development of the Aristotelian, Neoplatonic and Galenic Theories." In: *Interpreting Avicenna. Science and Philosophy in Medieval Islam*. Proceedings of the Second Conference of the Avicenna Study Group. (Mainz, 12th–13th Sept. 2002). Edited by Jon McGinnis. In collaboration with David C. Reisman. Vol. 56. Islamic Philosophy, Theology and Science. Texts and Studies. Leiden and Boston: Brill, 2004, 62–86.

Hamlyn, David W. "Aristotelian Epagoge." In: *Phronesis* 21.2 (1976), 167–184.

Hansberger, Rotraud. "Ticklish Questions. Pseudo-Proclus and Job of Edessa on the Workings of the Elemental Qualities." In: *Oriens* 42.1–2 (2014), 140–219.

Harry, Chelsea C. *Chronos in Aristotle's Physics. On the Nature of Time*. SpringerBriefs in Philosophy. Heidelberg et al.: Springer, 2015.

Hasnawi, Ahmad. "Alexandre d'Aphrodise *vs* Jean Philopon. Notes sur quelques traités d'Alexandre 'perdus' en grec, conservés en arabe." In: *Arabic Sciences and Philosophy* 4 (1994), 53–109.

Hasnawi, Ahmad. "Commentaire et démonstration. Brèves remarques sur la *Physique* du *Šifāʾ* d'Avicenne." In: *Le Commentaire entre tradition et innovation*. Actes du colloque international de l'Institut des Traditions Textuelles. (Paris and Villejuif, 22nd–25th Sept. 1999). Edited by Marie-Odile Goulet-Cazé. Bibliothèque d'histoire de la philosophie. Nouvelle série. Paris: Vrin, 2000, 509–519.

Hasnawi, Ahmad. "La définition du mouvement dans la *Physique* du *Shifāʾ* d'Avicenne." In: *Arabic Sciences and Philosophy* 11 (2001), 219–255.

Hasnawi, Ahmad. "La dynamique d'Ibn Sīnā (La notion d''inclination': *mayl*)." In: *Études sur Avicenne*. Edited by Jean Jolivet and Roshdi Rashed. Collection sciences et philosophie arabes. Paris: Les Belles Lettres, 1984, 103–123.

Hasnawi, Ahmad, ed. *La lumière de l'intellect. La pensée scientifique et philosophique d'Averroès dans son temps*. Actes du IVe colloque international de la SIHSPAI (Société Internationale d'Histoire des Sciences et de la Philosophie Arabes et Islamiques). (Córdoba, 9th–12th Dec. 1998). Ancient and Classical Sciences and Philosophy. With a preface by Roshdi Rashed. Leuven: Peeters, 2011.

Hasnawi, Ahmad. "La *Physique* du *Šifāʾ*. Aperçus sur sa structure et son contenu." In: *Avicenna and his Heritage*. Acts of the International Colloquium. (Leuven and Louvain-la-Neuve, 8th–11th Sept. 1999). Edited by Jules Janssens and Daniel De Smet. Ancient and Medieval Philosophy. De Wulf-Mansion Centre. Series 1.28. Leuven: Leuven University Press, 2002, 67–80.

Hasnawi, Ahmad. "La théorie avicennienne de l'*impetus*. Ibn Sīnā entre Jean Philopon et Jean Buridan." In: *Naẓẓarāt fī falsafat Ibn Sīnā wa-Mullā Ṣadrā al-Šīrāzī*. (Carthage, 22nd–24th Oct. 2013). Edited by Mokdad Arfa Mensia. Silsilat al-ʿUlūm al-Islāmiyya. Tunis: al-Maǧmaʿ al-Tūnisī li-l-ʿUlūm wa-l-Ādāb wa-l-Funūn, 2014, 25–42.

Hasnawi, Ahmad. "Le statut catégorial du mouvement chez Avicenne. Contexte grec et postérité médiévale latine." In: *De Zénon d'Élée à Poincaré*. Recueil d'études en hommage à Roshdi Rashed. Edited by Régis Morelon and Ahmad Hasnawi. Les cahiers du mideo 1. Louvain and Paris: Peeters, 2004, 607–621.

Hasnawi, Ahmad. "Un élève d'Abu Bišr Mattā b. Yūnus. Abū ʿAmr al-Ṭabarī." In: *Bulletin d'études orientales* 48 (1996), 35–55.
Hasper, Pieter Sjoerd and Joel Yurdin. "Between Perception and Scientific Knowledge. Aristotle's Account of Experience." In: *Oxford Studies in Ancient Philosophy* 47 (2014), 119–150.
Hasse, Dag Nikolaus. "Avicenna on Abstraction." In: *Aspects of Avicenna*. Edited by Robert Wisnovsky. Princeton: Markus Wiener Publishers, 2001, 39–72.
Hasse, Dag Nikolaus. *Avicenna's* De Anima *in the Latin West. The Formation of a Peripatetic Philosophy of the Soul, 1160-1300*. Warburg Institute Studies and Texts 1. London and Turin: The Warburg Institute and Nino Aragno Editore, 2000.
Hasse, Dag Nikolaus. "Avicenna's Epistemological Optimism." In: *Interpreting Avicenna. Critical Essays*. Edited by Peter Adamson. Cambridge: Cambridge University Press, 2013, 109–119.
Hasse, Dag Nikolaus. "Avicenna's 'Giver of Forms' in Latin Philosophy, Especially in the Works of Albertus Magnus." In: *The Arabic, Hebrew and Latin Reception of Avicenna's Metaphysics*. (Villa Vigoni in Loveno di Menaggio, Italy, 2nd–6th July 2008). Edited by Dag Nikolaus Hasse and Amos Bertolacci. Scientia graeco-arabica 7. Berlin and Boston: Walter de Gruyter, 2012, 225–249.
Hasse, Dag Nikolaus. "Influence of Arabic and Islamic Philosophy on the Latin West." In: *The Stanford Encyclopedia to Philosophy*. Edited by Edward N. Zalta. Fall 2008 Edition. URL: http://plato.stanford.edu/archives/fall2008/entries/arabic-islamic-influence/.
Hasse, Dag Nikolaus. "Plato arabico-latinus. Philosophy – Wisdom Literature – Occult Sciences." In: *The Platonic Tradition in the Middle Ages. A Doxographic Approach*. Edited by Stephen Gersh and Maarten J. F. M. Hoenen. In collaboration with Pieter Th. van Wingerden. Berlin and New York: Walter de Gruyter, 2002, 31–65.
Hasse, Dag Nikolaus. "The Early Albertus Magnus and his Arabic Sources on the Theory of the Soul." In: *Vivarium* 46 (2008), 232–252.
Hasse, Dag Nikolaus and Amos Bertolacci, eds. *The Arabic, Hebrew and Latin Reception of Avicenna's Metaphysics*. (Villa Vigoni in Loveno di Menaggio, Italy, 2nd–6th July 2008). Scientia graeco-arabica 7. Berlin and Boston: Walter de Gruyter, 2012.
Hasse, Dag Nikolaus and Amos Bertolacci, eds. *The Arabic, Hebrew, and Latin Reception of Avicenna's Physics and Cosmology*. (Villa Vigoni in Loveno di Menaggio, Italy, 26th–30th June 2013). Scientia graeco-arabica. Berlin and Boston: Walter de Gruyter, [forthcoming].
Hasse, Dag Nikolaus and Andreas Büttner. "Notes on Anonymous Twelfth-Century Translations of Philosophical Texts from Arabic into Latin on the Iberian Peninsula." In: *The Arabic, Hebrew, and Latin Reception of Avicenna's Physics and Cosmology*. (Villa Vigoni in Loveno di Menaggio, Italy, 26th–30th June 2013). Edited by Dag Nikolaus Hasse and Amos Bertolacci. Scientia graeco-arabica. Berlin and Boston: Walter de Gruyter, [forthcoming].
Hein, Christel. *Definition und Einteilung der Philosophie. Von der spätantiken Einleitungsliteratur zur arabischen Enzyklopädie*. Europäische Hochschulschriften. Reihe XX. Philosophie 177. Frankfurt am Main, Bern, and New York: Peter Lang, 1985.
Helmig, Christoph. *Forms and Concepts. Concept Formation in the Platonic Tradition*. Commentaria in Aristotelem graeca et byzantina. Quellen und Studien 5. Berlin and Boston: Walter de Gruyter, 2012.
Herzberg, Stephan. *Wahrnehmung und Wissen bei Aristoteles. Zur epistemologischen Funktion der Wahrnehmung*. Quellen und Studien zur Philosophie 97. Berlin and New York: Walter de Gruyter, 2011.
Hintikka, Jaakko. "Aristotelian Induction." In: *Revue internationale de philosophie* 34 (1980), 422–440.
Hintikka, Jaakko. *Time & Necessity. Studies in Aristotle's Theory of Modality*. Oxford: Clarendon Press, 1973.

Horstschäfer, Titus Maria. *"Über Prinzipien." Eine Untersuchung zur methodischen und inhaltlichen Geschlossenheit des ersten Buches der* Physik *des Aristoteles*. Quellen und Studien zur Philosophie 47. Berlin and New York: Walter de Gruyter, 1998.

Houser, Rollen E. "Avicenna and Aquinas's *De principiis naturae*, cc. 1–3." In: *The Thomist* 76.4 (2012): *Aquinas and the Arabs*, 577–610.

Huby, Pamela M. "An Excerpt from Boethus of Sidon's Commentary on the Categories?" In: *The Classical Quarterly* 31.2 (1981), 398–409.

Hugonnard-Roche, Henri. "Remarques sur la tradition arabe de l'*Organon* d'après le manuscrit Paris, Bibliothèque nationale, ar. 2346." In: *Glosses and Commentaries on Aristotelian Logical Texts. The Syriac, Arabic and Medieval Latin Traditions*. Edited by Charles Burnett. London: The Warburg Institute, 1993, 19–28.

Hugonnard-Roche, Henri. "Une ancienne 'édition' arabe de l'*Organon* d'Aristote. Problèmes de traduction et de transmission." In: *Les problèmes posés par l'édition critique des textes anciens et médiévaux*. Edited by Jacqueline Hamesse. Université Catholique de Louvain. Publications de l'Institut d'Études Médiévales. Textes, études, congrès 13. Louvain-la-Neuve: Brepols, 1992, 139–157.

Hyman, Arthur. "Aristotle's 'First Matter' and Avicenna's and Averroes' 'Corporeal Form.'" In: *Harry Austryn Wolfson Jubilee Volume*. On the Occasion of his Seventy-fifth Birthday. Vol. 1. 3 vols. Jerusalem: American Academy for Jewish Research, 1965, 385–406. Reprint in Arthur Hyman, ed. *Essays in Medieval Jewish and Islamic Philosophy. Studies from the Publications of the American Academy for Jewish Research*. New York: Ktav Publishing House, 1977.

Ibrahim, Bilal. "Theories of Matter." In: *The Oxford Encyclopedia of Philosophy, Science, and Technology in Islam*. Edited by Ibrahim Kalin. Vol. 2. 2 vols. New York: Oxford University Press, 2014, 352–355.

Inwood, Michael. "Aristotle on the Reality of Time." In: *Aristotle's* Physics. *A Collection of Essays*. Edited by Lindsay Judson. Oxford: Clarendon Press, 1991, 150–178.

al-ʿIrāqī, Muḥammad ʿĀṭif. *al-Falsafa al-ṭabīʿiyya ʿinda Ibn Sīnā*. Maktabat al-Dirāsāt al-Falsafiyya. Cairo: Dār al-Maʿārif, ²1983.

Jammer, Max. *Concepts of Space. The History of Theories of Space in Physics*. With a foreword by Albert Einstein. Mineola: Dover Publications, ³1993.

Janos, Damien. "'Active Nature' and Other Striking Features of Abū Bishr Mattā ibn Yūnus's Cosmology as Reconstructed from His Commentary on Aristotle's *Physics*." In: *Ideas in Motion in Baghdad and Beyond. Philosophical and Theological Exchanges between Christians and Muslims in the Third/Ninth and Fourth/Tenth Centuries*. Edited by Damien Janos. Leiden and Boston: Brill, 2015, 135–177.

Janos, Damien, ed. *Ideas in Motion in Baghdad and Beyond. Philosophical and Theological Exchanges between Christians and Muslims in the Third/Ninth and Fourth/Tenth Centuries*. Leiden and Boston: Brill, 2015.

Janos, Damien. *Method, Structure, and Development in al-Fārābī's Cosmology*. Islamic Philosophy, Theology and Science. Texts and Studies 85. Leiden and Boston: Brill, 2012.

Janos, Damien. "Moving the Orbs. Astronomy, Physics, and Metaphysics, and the Problem of Celestial Motion According to Ibn Sīnā." In: *Arabic Sciences and Philosophy* 21 (2011), 165–214.

Janssens, Jules. "'Experience' (*tajriba*) in Classical Arabic Philosophy (al-Fārābī – Avicenna)." In: *Quaestio. Annuario di storia della metafisica* 4 (2004), 45–62.

Janssens, Jules. "Ibn Sīnā. An Important Historian of the Sciences." In: *Uluslararası İbn Sīnā Sempozyumu Bildirileri*. (Istanbul, 22nd–24th May 2008). Edited by Mehmet Mazak and Nevzat Özkaya. Vol. 2. 2 vols. İstanbul Büyükşehir Belediyesi Kültür A.Ş. Yayınları, 2009, 83–93.

Janssens, Jules. "L'Avicenne latin. Un témoin (indirect) des commentateurs (Alexandre d'Aphrodise – Thémistius – Jean Philopon)." In: *Tradition et traduction. Les textes philosophiques et scien-*

tifiques grecs au Moyen Âge Latin. Hommage à Fernand Bossier. Edited by Rita Beyers, Jozef Brams, Dirk Sacré, and Koenraad Verrycken. Ancient and Medieval Philosophy. De Wulf-Mansion Centre. Series 1.25. Leuven: Leuven University Press, 1999, 89–105.

Janssens, Jules. "The Latin Translation of the Physics. A Useful Source for the Critical Edition of the Arabic Text?" In: *Oriens* 40.2 (2012), 515–528.

Janssens, Jules. "The Notions of *wāhib al-ṣuwar* (Giver of Forms) and *wāhib al-ʿaql* (Bestower of intelligence) in Ibn Sīnā." In: *Intellect et imagination dans la philosophie médiévale. Intellect and Imagination in Medieval Philosophy. Intelecto e imaginação na Filosofia Medieval*. Actes du XIe Congrès International de Philosophie Médiévale de la Société Internationale pour l'Étude de la Philosophie Médiévale (S.I.E.P.M.) (Porto, 26th–31st Aug. 2002). Edited by Maria Cândida Pacheco and José F. Meirinhos. Rencontres de Philosophie Médiévale 11. Turnhout: Brepols, 2006, 551–562.

Jeck, Udo Reinhold. *Aristoteles contra Augustinum. Zur Frage nach dem Verhältnis von Zeit und Seele bei den antiken Aristoteleskommentatoren, im arabischen Aristotelismus und im 13. Jahrhundert*. Bochumer Studien zur Philosophie 21. Amsterdam and Philadelphia: B. R. Grüner, 1994.

Jeck, Udo Reinhold. "Zenons Aporie des Topos, ihre Interpretation bei den griechischen Aristoteleskommentatoren, bei Averroes, Avicenna und im lateinischen Mittelalter." In: *Raum und Raumvorstellungen im Mittelalter*. Edited by Jan A. Aertsen and Andreas Speer. Miscellanea Mediaevalia 25. Berlin and New York: Walter de Gruyter, 1998, 419–436.

Jolivet, Jean. "al-Kindī, vues sur le temps." In: *Arabic Sciences and Philosophy* 3.1 (1993), 55–75.

Jolivet, Jean. "La répartition des causes chez Aristote et Avicenne. Le sens d'un déplacement." In: *Lectionum Varietates. Hommage à Paul Vignaux (1904-1987)*. Edited by Jean Jolivet, Zénon Kaluza, and Alain de Libera. Études de philosophie médiévale 65. Paris: Vrin, 1991, 49–65.

Judson, Lindsay, ed. *Aristotle's* Physics. *A Collection of Essays*. Oxford: Clarendon Press, 1991.

Kalbarczyk, Alexander. "The *Kitāb al-Maqūlāt* of the *Muḫtaṣar al-awsaṭ fī l-manṭiq*. A Hitherto Unknown Source for Studying Ibn Sīnā's Reception of Aristotle's *Categories*." In: *Oriens* 40.2 (2012), 305–354.

Kalin, Ibrahim, ed. *The Oxford Encyclopedia of Philosophy, Science, and Technology in Islam*. 2 vols. New York: Oxford University Press, 2014.

Karamanolis, George. "Porphyry, the First Platonist Commentator of Aristotle." In: *Philosophy, Science and Exegesis in Greek, Arabic and Latin Commentaries*. Edited by Peter Adamson, Han Baltussen, and Martin W. F. Stone. 2 vols. Supplement to the Bulletin of the Institute of Classical Studies 83.1–2. London: Institute of Classical Studies, 2004, 97–120.

Katayama, Errol G. "Soul and Elemental Motion in Aristotle's *Physics* VIII 4." In: *Apeiron. A Journal for Ancient Philosophy and Science* 44.2 (2011), 163–190.

Kaya, M. Cüneyt. "Şukûk alâ 'Uyûn. *'Uyûnu'l-mesâil*'in Fârâbî'ye Aidiyeti Üzerine." In: *İslam Araştırmaları Dergisi* 27 (2012), 29–67.

Kelsey, Sean. "The Place of I 7 in the Argument of *Physics* I." In: *Phronesis* 53.2 (2008), 180–208.

Kennedy-Day, Kiki. *Books of Definition in Islamic Philosophy. The Limits of Words*. London and New York: RoutledgeCurzon, 2003.

Kessler, Eckhard. "Method in the Aristotelian Tradition. Taking a Second Look." In: *Method and Order in Renaissance Philosophy of Nature. The Aristotle Commentary Tradition*. Edited by Daniel A. Di Liscia, Eckhard Kessler, and Charlotte Methuen. Aldershot and Brookfield: Ashgate, 1997, 113–142.

King, Daniel. "Alexander of Aphrodisias' *On the Principles of the Universe* in a Syriac Adaptation." In: *Le Muséon. Revue d'études orientales* 123.1–2 (2010), 159–191.

King, Hugh R. "Aristotle without *prima materia*." In: *Journal of the History of Ideas* 17.3 (1956), 370–389.

King, Hugh R. "Aristotle's Theory of *τόπος*." In: *The Classical Quarterly* 44.1–2 (1950), 76–96.

Klein-Franke, Félix. "al-Kindī's 'On Definitions and Descriptions of Things.'" In: *Le Muséon. Revue d'études orientales* 95 (1982), 191–216.

Koetschet, Pauline. "Galien, al-Rāzī, et l'éternité du monde. Les fragments du traité *Sur la démonstration*, IV, dans les *Doutes sur Galien*." In: *Arabic Sciences and Philosophy* 25.2 (2015), 167–198.

Konstan, David. "A Note on Aristotle *Physics* 1.1." In: *Archiv für Geschichte der Philosophie* 57.3 (1975), 241–245.

Kotwick, Mirjam Engert. *Alexander of Aphrodisias and the Text of Aristotle's* Metaphysics. California Classical Studies 4. Berkeley: Department of Classics, 2016.

Koutzarova, Tiana. *Das Transzendentale bei Ibn Sīnā. Zur Metaphysik als Wissenschaft erster Begriffs- und Urteilsprinzipien*. Islamic Philosophy, Theology and Science. Texts and Studies 79. Leiden and Boston: Brill, 2009.

Koutzarova, Tiana. "Wissenschaft als 'Genesung.' Avicennas Konzept einer Enzyklopädie von Wissenschaften." In: *Albertus Magnus und der Ursprung der Universitätsidee. Die Begegnung der Wissenschaftskulturen im 13. Jahrhundert und die Entdeckung des Konzepts der Bildung durch Wissenschaft*. Edited by Ludger Honnefelder. Berlin: Berlin University Press, 2011, 192–205.

Kraemer, Joel L. "A Lost Passage from Philoponus' *Contra Aristotelem* in Arabic Translation." In: *Journal of the American Oriental Society* 85.3 (1965), 318–327.

Kraemer, Joel L. *Humanism in the Renaissance of Islam. The Cultural Revival during the Buyid Age*. Leiden, New York, and Cologne: E. J. Brill, ²1992.

Kraemer, Joel L. *Philosophy in the Renaissance of Islam. Abū Sulaymān al-Sijistānī and his Circle*. Studies in Islamic Culture and History 8. Leiden: E. J. Brill, 1986.

Kraus, Paul. "Plotin chez les Arabes. Remarques sur un nouveau fragment de la paraphrase arabe des *Ennéades*." In: *Bulletin de l'Institut d'Égypte* 23 (1940–1941), 263–295.

Kraus, Paul. "Zu Ibn al-Muqaffaʿ." In: *Rivista degli Studi Orientali* 14 (1933), 1–20.

Kukkonen, Taneli. "Ibn Sīnā and the Early History of Thought Experiments." In: *Journal of the History of Philosophy* 52.3 (2014), 433–460.

Kutash, Emilie. "Commentary on Nikulin." In: *Proceedings of the Boston Area Colloquium of Ancient Philosophy* 18 (2003), 210–219.

LaBarge, Scott. "Aristotle on *empeiria*." In: *Ancient Philosophy* 26 (2003), 23–44.

Lagerlund, Henrik. "Singular Terms and Vague Concepts in Late Medieval Mental Language Theory or the Decline and Fall of Mental Language." In: *Intentionality, Cognition, and Mental Representation in Medieval Philosophy*. Edited by Gyula Klima. Medieval Philosophy. Texts & Studies. New York: Fordham University Press, 2015, 122–140.

Lameer, Joep. *al-Fārābī and Aristotelian Syllogistics. Greek Theory and Islamic Practice*. Islamic Philosophy and Theology. Texts and Studies 20. Leiden, Boston, and Cologne: E. J. Brill, 1994.

Lameer, Joep. "The *Organon* of Aristotle in the Medieval Oriental and Occidental Traditions." In: *Journal of the American Oriental Society* 116.1 (1996), 90–98.

Lammer, Andreas. "Defining Nature. From Aristotle to Philoponus to Avicenna." In: *Aristotle and the Arabic Tradition*. Edited by Ahmed Alwishah and Josh Hayes. Cambridge: Cambridge University Press, 2015, 121–142.

Lammer, Andreas. "Eternity and Origination in the Works of Sayf al-Dīn al-Āmidī and Athīr al-Dīn al-Abharī. Two Discussions from the Seventh/Thirteenth Century." In: *The Muslim World* 107.3 (2017), 432–481.

Lammer, Andreas. "Time and Mind-Dependence in Sayf al-Dīn al-Āmidī's *Abkār al-afkār*." In: *The Arabic, Hebrew, and Latin Reception of Avicenna's Physics and Cosmology*. (Villa Vigoni in Loveno di Menaggio, Italy, 26th–30th June 2013). Edited by Dag Nikolaus Hasse and Amos Bertolacci. Scientia graeco-arabica. Berlin and Boston: Walter de Gruyter, [forthcoming].

Lammer, Andreas. "Two Sixth/Twelfth-Century Hardliners on Creation and Divine Eternity. al-Šahrastānī and Abū l-Barakāt al-Baġdādī on God's Priority over the World." In: *Islamic Philosophy from the 12th till the 14th Century*. (Annemarie Schimmel Kolleg, University of Bonn, 24th–26th Feb. 2016). Edited by Stephan Conermann and Abdelkader Al Ghouz. Göttingen: Bonn University Press and V&R unipress, [forthcoming].

Lang, Helen S. *Aristotle's* Physics *and its Medieval Varieties*. SUNY Series in Ancient Philosophy. Albany: State University of New York Press, 1992.

Lang, Helen S. *The Order of Nature in Aristotle's Physics. Place and the Elements*. Cambridge: Cambridge University Press, 1998.

Langermann, Y. Tzvi. "From My Notebooks. On *tajriba/nissayon* ('Experience'). Texts in Hebrew, Judeo-Arabic, and Arabic." In: *Aleph* 14.2 (2014), 147–176.

Langermann, Y. Tzvi. "Islamic Atomism and the Galenic Tradition." In: *History of Science* 47.3 (2009), 277–295.

Lernould, Alain. "Nature in Proclus. From Irrational Immanent Principle to Goddess." In: *Neoplatonism and the Philosophy of Nature*. Edited by James Wilberding and Christoph Horn. Oxford: Oxford University Press, 2012, 68–102.

Lesher, James H. "Aristotle's Considered View of the Path to Knowledge." In: *El espíritu y la letra. Un homenaje a Alfonso Gómez-Lobo*. Edited by Marcelo D. Boeri and Nicole Ooms. Buenos Aires: Ediciones Colihue, 2012, 127–45.

Lettinck, Paul. *Aristotle's* Physics *and its Reception in the Arabic World. With an Edition of the Unpublished Parts of Ibn Bājja's* Commentary on the Physics. Aristoteles Semitico-Latinus 7. Leiden, New York, and Cologne: E. J. Brill, 1994.

Lettinck, Paul. "Problems in Aristotle's Physics I, 1 and their Discussion by Arab Commentators." In: *Journal for the History of Arabic Science* 10 (1994), 91–109.

Lizzini, Olga. "The Relation between Form and Matter. Some Brief Observations on the 'Homology Argument' (*Ilāhīyāt*, II.4) and the Deduction of *fluxus*." In: *Interpreting Avicenna. Science and Philosophy in Medieval Islam*. Proceedings of the Second Conference of the Avicenna Study Group. (Mainz, 12th–13th Sept. 2002). Edited by Jon McGinnis. In collaboration with David C. Reisman. Vol. 56. Islamic Philosophy, Theology and Science. Texts and Studies. Leiden and Boston: Brill, 2004, 175–185.

Lord, Carnes. "On the Early History of the Aristotelian Corpus." In: *The American Journal of Philology* 107.2 (1986), 137–161.

Loughlin, Tim. "Souls and the Location of Time in Physics IV 14, 223a16–223a29." In: *Apeiron. A Journal for Ancient Philosophy and Science* 44.4 (2011), 307–325.

Lucchetta, Giulio A. *La natura e la sfera. La scienza antica e le sue metafore nella critica di Rāzī*. Collana dell'Istituto di Filosofia dell'Università degli Studi di Chieti. Saggi 1. With a preface by Geoffrey E. R. Lloyd. Lecce: Milella, 1987.

MacCoull, Leslie S. B. and Lucas Siorvanes. "*PSI XIV* 1400. A Papyrus Fragment of John Philoponus." In: *Ancient Philosophy* 12.1 (1992), 153–170.

Machamer, Peter K. "Aristotle on Natural Place and Natural Motion." In: *Isis* 69.3 (1978), 377–387.

Machamer, Peter K. and Robert G. Turnbull, eds. *Motion and Time, Space and Matter. Interrelations in the History of Philosophy and Science*. Columbus: Ohio State University Press, 1976.

Macierowski, Edward M. and Richard F. Hassing. "John Philoponus on Aristotle's Definition of Nature. A Translation from the Greek with Introduction and Notes." In: *Ancient Philosophy* 8.1 (1988), 73–100.

Madelung, Wilferd. "Abū 'l-Ḥusayn al-Baṣrī." In: *The Encyclopaedia of Islam. New Edition*. Vol. 12. Supplement. 12 vols. Leiden: E. J. Brill, 2004, 25–26.

Mahdi, Muhsin. "Alfarabi against Philoponus." In: *Journal of Near Eastern Studies* 26.4 (1967), 233–260.

Mahdi, Muhsin. *Ibn Khaldūn's Philosophy of History. A Study in the Philosophic Foundation of the Science of Culture*. London: George Allen & Unwin Ltd., 1957.

Maier, Anneliese. *Studien zur Naturphilosophie der Spatscholastik*. Vol. 1: *Die Vorläufer Galileis im 14. Jahrhundert*. Storia e letteratura. Raccolta di studi e testi 22. Rome: Edizioni di storia e letteratura, 1949.

Maier, Anneliese. *Studien zur Naturphilosophie der Spatscholastik*. Vol. 2: *Zwei Grundprobleme der Scholastischen Naturphilosophie. Das Problem der intensiven Größe, die Impetustheorie*. Storia e letteratura. Raccolta di studi e testi 37. Rome: Edizioni di storia e letteratura, 31968.

Mansion, Augustin. *Introduction a la Physique Aristotélicienne*. Aristote. Traductions et Études. Louvain and Paris: Éditions de l'Institute Supérieur de Philosophie et Librairie philosophique J. Vrin, 21945.

Mariña, Jacqueline. "The Role of Limits in Aristotle's Concept of Place." In: *The Southern Journal of Philosophy* 31.2 (1993).

Marmura, Michael E. *Probing in Islamic Philosophy. Studies in the Philosophies of Ibn Sīnā, al-Ghazālī and Other Major Muslim Thinkers*. Binghamton: Global Academic Publishing, 2005.

Maróth, Miklós. "Averroes on the Void." In: *La lumière de l'intellect. La pensée scientifique et philosophique d'Averroès dans son temps*. Actes du IVe colloque international de la SIHSPAI (Société Internationale d'Histoire des Sciences et de la Philosophie Arabes et Islamiques). (Córdoba, 9th–12th Dec. 1998). Edited by Ahmad Hasnawi. Ancient and Classical Sciences and Philosophy. With a preface by Roshdi Rashed. Leuven: Peeters, 2011, 11–22.

Maróth, Miklós. "Das System der Wissenschaften bei Ibn Sina." In: *Avicenna – Ibn Sina. 980–1036*. Materialien einer wissenschaftlichen Arbeitstagung aus Anlaß der Millenniumsfeier für den großen tadshikischen Gelehrten. Vol. 2: *Wissenschaftsgeschichte*. (Martin-Luther-Universität Halle-Wittenberg, 25th–26th Feb. 1980). Edited by Burchard Brentjes. 2 vols. Wissenschaftliche Beiträge 17. Halle: Martin-Luther-Universität Halle-Wittenberg, 1980, 27–34.

Maróth, Miklós. "Der erste Beweis des Proklos für die Ewigkeit der Welt." In: *Acta antiqua Academiae Scientiarum Hungaricae* 30 (1982–1984), 181–189.

Maróth, Miklós. *Die Araber und die antike Wissenschaftstheorie*. Islamic Philosophy and Theology. Texts and Studies 17. Leiden: E. J. Brill, 1994.

Martijn, Marije. *Proclus on Nature. Philosophy of Nature and its Methods in Proclus' Commentary on Plato's* Timaeus. Philosophia antiqua. A Series of Studies on Ancient Philosophy 121. Leiden and Boston: Brill, 2010.

Martijn, Marije. "Proclus' Geometrical Method." In: *The Routledge Handbook of Neoplatonism*. Edited by Pauliina Remes and Svetla Slaveva-Griffin. Routledge Handbooks in Philosophy. Abingdon: Routledge, 2014, 145–159.

Martin, Christopher J. "Non-reductive Arguments from Impossible Hypotheses in Boethius and Philoponus." In: *Oxford Studies in Ancient Philosophy* 17 (1999), 279–302.

Matthen, Mohan. "Why Does the Earth Move to the Center? An Examination of Some Explanatory Strategies in Aristotle's Cosmology." In: *New Perspectives on Aristotle's* De Caelo. Edited by Alan C. Bowen and Christian Wildberg. Philosophia antiqua. A Series of Studies on Ancient Philosophy 117. Leiden and Boston: Brill, 2009, 119–138.

Mayer, Toby. "Avicenna against Time Beginning. The Debate between the Commentators on the *Ishārāt*." In: *Classical Arabic Philosophy. Sources and Reception*. Edited by Peter Adamson. Warburg Institute Colloquia 11. London and Turin: The Warburg Institute, 2007, 125–149.

Mazak, Mehmet and Nevzat Özkaya, eds. *Uluslararası İbn Sīnā Sempozyumu Bildirileri*. (Istanbul, 22nd–24th May 2008). 2 vols. İstanbul Büyükşehir Belediyesi Kültür A.Ş. Yayınları, 2009.

McGinnis, Jon. "A Medieval Arabic Analysis of Motion at an Instant. The Avicennan Sources to the *forma fluens/fluxus formae* Debate." In: *British Journal for the History of Science* 39.2 (2006), 189–205.

McGinnis, Jon. "A Penetrating Question in the History of Ideas. Space, Dimensionality and Interpenetration in the Thought of Avicenna." In: *Arabic Sciences and Philosophy* 16 (2006), 47–69.

McGinnis, Jon. "A Small Discovery. Avicenna's Theory of *Minima Naturalia*." In: *Journal of the History of Philosophy* 53.1 (2015), 1–24.

McGinnis, Jon. "Arabic and Islamic Natural Philosophy and Natural Science." In: *The Stanford Encyclopedia to Philosophy*. Edited by Edward N. Zalta. Winter 2013 Edition. URL: http://plato.stanford.edu/archives/win2013/entries/arabic-islamic-natural/.

McGinnis, Jon. *Avicenna*. Great Medieval Thinkers. New York: Oxford University Press, 2010.

McGinnis, Jon. "Avicenna's Natural Philosophy." In: *Interpreting Avicenna. Critical Essays*. Edited by Peter Adamson. Cambridge: Cambridge University Press, 2013, 71–90.

McGinnis, Jon. "Avicenna's Naturalized Epistemology and Scientific Method." In: *The Unity of Science in the Arabic Tradition. Science, Logic, Epistemology, and their Interaction*. Edited by Shahid Rahman, Tony Street, and Hassan Tahiri. Dordrecht, Boston, and London: Kluwer-Springer Academic Publishers, 2008.

McGinnis, Jon. "Avicennan Infinity. A Select History of the Infinite through Avicenna." In: *Documenti e studi sulla tradizione filosofica medievale* 21 (2010), 199–222.

McGinnis, Jon. "Avoiding the Void. Avicenna on the Impossibility of Circular Motion in a Void." In: *Classical Arabic Philosophy. Sources and Reception*. Edited by Peter Adamson. Warburg Institute Colloquia 11. London and Turin: The Warburg Institute, 2007, 74–89.

McGinnis, Jon. "Creation and Eternity in Medieval Philosophy." In: *A Companion to the Philosophy of Time*. Edited by Heather Dyke and Adrian Bardon. Blackwell Companions to Philosophy 52. Chichester: Wiley-Blackwell, 2013, 73–86.

McGinnis, Jon. "For Every Time There is a Season. John Philoponus on Plato's and Aristotle's Conception of Time." In: *KronoScope* 3.1 (2003), 83–111.

McGinnis, Jon. "Ibn Sīnā on the Now." In: *American Catholic Philosophical Quarterly* 73.1 (1999), 73–106.

McGinnis, Jon. "Ibn Sina's Natural Philosophy." In: *The Stanford Encyclopedia to Philosophy*. Edited by Edward N. Zalta. Fall 2016 Edition. URL: http://plato.stanford.edu/archives/fall2016/entries/ibn-sina-natural/.

McGinnis, Jon, ed. *Interpreting Avicenna. Science and Philosophy in Medieval Islam*. Proceedings of the Second Conference of the Avicenna Study Group. (Mainz, 12th–13th Sept. 2002). In collaboration with David C. Reisman. Vol. 56. Islamic Philosophy, Theology and Science. Texts and Studies. Leiden and Boston: Brill, 2004.

McGinnis, Jon. "Logic and Science. The Role of Genus and Difference in Avicenna's Logic, Science and Natural Philosophy." In: *Documenti e studi sulla tradizione filosofica medievale* 18 (2007), 165–187.

McGinnis, Jon. "Making Abstraction Less Abstract. The Logical, Psychological, and Metaphysical Dimensions of Avicenna's Theory of Abstraction." In: *Proceedings of the American Catholic Philosophical Association* 80 (2006): *Intelligence and the Philosophy of Mind*, 169–183.

McGinnis, Jon. "Making Something of Nothing. Privation, Possibility, and Potentiality in Avicenna and Aquinas." In: *The Thomist* 76.4 (2012): *Aquinas and the Arabs*, 551–575.

McGinnis, Jon. "Natural Knowledge in the Arabic Middle Ages." In: *Wrestling with Nature. From Omens to Science*. Edited by Peter Harrison, Ronald L. Numbers, and Michael H. Shank. Chicago: The University of Chicago Press, 2011, 59–82.

McGinnis, Jon. "Pointers, Guides, Founts and Gifts. The Reception of Avicennan Physics in the East." In: *Oriens* 41.3–4 (2013), 433–456.

McGinnis, Jon. "Positioning Heaven. The Infidelity of a Faithful Aristotelian." In: *Phronesis* 51.2 (2006), 140–161.

McGinnis, Jon. "Review of *Aristotle on Time: A Study of the* Physics by Tony Roark." In: *Philosophy in Review* 32.6 (2012), 518–520.

McGinnis, Jon. "Scientific Methodologies in Medieval Islam." In: *Journal of the History of Philosophy* 41.3 (2003), 307–327.

McGinnis, Jon. "The Topology of Time. An Analysis of Medieval Islamic Accounts of Discrete and Continuous Time." In: *The Modern Schoolman* 81 (2003), 5–25.

McGinnis, Jon. "The Ultimate Why Question. Avicenna on Why God Is Absolutely Necessary." In: *The Ultimate Why Question. Why is There Anything at All Rather Than Nothing Whatsoever?* Edited by John F. Wippel. Washington, D. C.: The Catholic University of America Press, 2011, 65–82.

McGinnis, Jon. *Time and Time Again. A Study of Aristotle and Ibn Sīnā's Temporal Theories*. PhD thesis. Philadelphia: University of Pennsylvania, 1999.

McGinnis, Jon. "Time to Change. Time, Motion and Possibility in Ibn Sīnā." In: *Uluslararası İbn Sīnā Sempozyumu Bildirileri*. (Istanbul, 22nd–24th May 2008). Edited by Mehmet Mazak and Nevzat Özkaya. Vol. 1. 2 vols. İstanbul Büyükşehir Belediyesi Kültür A.Ş. Yayınları, 2009, 251–257.

McGuire, J. Edward. "Philoponus on *Physics* ii 1. Φύσις, δύναμις, and the Motion of the Simple Bodies." In: *Ancient Philosophy* 5.2 (1985), 241–267.

Mendell, Henry. "Aristotle and Mathematics." In: *The Stanford Encyclopedia to Philosophy*. Edited by Edward N. Zalta. Winter 2008 Edition. URL: http://plato.stanford.edu/archives/win2008/entries/aristotle-mathematics/.

Mendell, Henry. "Topoi on Topos. The Development of Aristotle's Concept of Place." In: *Phronesis* 32.2 (1987), 206–231.

Menn, Stephen. "Avicenna's Metaphysics." In: *Interpreting Avicenna. Critical Essays*. Edited by Peter Adamson. Cambridge: Cambridge University Press, 2013, 143–169.

Menn, Stephen. "Simplicius on the *Theaetetus* (*In Physica* 17,38–18,23 Diels)." In: *Phronesis* 55 (2010), 255–270.

Mesch, Walter. *Reflektierte Gegenwart. Eine Studie über Zeit und Ewigkeit bei Platon, Aristoteles, Plotin und Augustinus*. Philosophische Abhandlungen 86. Frankfurt am Main: Vittorio Klostermann, 2003.

Michot, Yahya. "Avicenna's 'Letter on the Disappearance of the Vain Intelligible Forms After Death.'" In: *Bulletin de philosophie médiévale* 27 (1985), 94–103.

Michot, Yahya. "'L'épître sur la disparition des formes intelligibles vaines après la mort' d'Avicenne. Édition critique, traduction et index." In: *Bulletin de philosophie médiévale* 29 (1987), 152–170.

Miller, Jr., Fred D. "Aristotle on the Reality of Time." In: *Archiv für Geschichte der Philosophie* 56.2 (1974), 132–155.

Miller, Dana R. "Review of *The Order of Nature in Aristotle's Physics: Place and the Elements* by Helen S. Lang." In: *The Review of Metaphysics* 54.1 (2000), 155–157.

Moraux, Paul. *Alexandre d'Aphrodise. Exégète de la noétique d'Aristote*. Bibliothèque de la Faculté de Philosophie et Lettres de l'Université de Liége 99. Liége and Paris: Faculté de Philosophie et Lettres and Librairie E. Droz, 1942.

Moraux, Paul. *Der Aristotelismus bei den Griechen. Von Andronikos bis Alexander von Aphrodisias*. 3 vols. Peripatoi. Philologisch-historische Studien zum Aristotelismus 5–7. Berlin and New York: Walter de Gruyter, 1971–2001.

Moraux, Paul. "Porphyre, commentateur de la *Physique* d'Aristote." In: *Aristotélica. Mélanges offerts à Marcel de Corte*. Edited by André Motte and Christian Rutten. Cahiers de philosophie ancienne 3. Brussels and Liège: Éditions Ousia and Presses Universitaires, 1985, 227–239.

Morison, Benjamin. "Did Theophrastus Reject Aristotle's Account of Place?" In: *Phronesis* 55.1 (2010), 68–103.

Morison, Benjamin. *On Location. Aristotle's Concept of Place*. Oxford Aristotle Studies. Oxford: Clarendon Press, 2002.

Morrison, Donald. "Philoponus and Simplicius on Tekmeriodic Proof." In: *Method and Order in Renaissance Philosophy of Nature. The Aristotle Commentary Tradition*. Edited by Daniel A. Di Liscia, Eckhard Kessler, and Charlotte Methuen. Aldershot and Brookfield: Ashgate, 1997, 1–22.

Mouzala, Melina G. "Aristotle's Method of Understanding the First Principles of Natural Things in the *Physics* I.1." In: *Peitho. Examina Antiqua* 1.3 (2012), 31–50.

Mueller, Ian. "Aristotle's Doctrine of Abstraction in the Commentators." In: *Aristotle Transformed. The Ancient Commentators and Their Influence*. Edited by Richard Sorabji. Ithaca: Cornell University Press, 1990, 463–480.

Müller, Sven. *Naturgemäße Ortsbewegung. Aristoteles' Physik und ihre Rezeption bis Newton*. Philosophische Untersuchungen 16. Tübingen: Mohr Siebeck, 2006.

Nagel, Tilman. "Das Kalifat der Abbasiden." In: *Geschichte der Arabischen Welt*. Edited by Ulrich Haarmann and Heinz Halm. Munich: C. H. Beck, [5]2004, 101–165.

Nikulin, Dmitri. "Physica more geometrico demonstrata. Natural Philosophy in Proclus and Aristotle." In: *Proceedings of the Boston Area Colloquium of Ancient Philosophy* 18 (2003), 183–209.

Nony, Sylvie. "Two Arabic Theories of Impetus." Translated by Peter E. Pormann. In: *Islamic Medical and Scientific Tradition. Critical Concepts in Islamic Studies*. Vol. 3: *The Physical Sciences. Physics, Astronomy, Geodesy*. Edited by Peter E. Pormann. 4 vols. London and New York: Routledge, 2011, 3–32.

O'Brien, Denis. "Plotinus on the Making of Matter, Part I. The Identity of Darkness." In: *The International Journal of the Platonic Tradition* 5.1 (2011), 6–57.

O'Brien, Denis. "Plotinus on the Making of Matter, Part II. 'A Corpse Adorned' (*Enn*. II 4 [12] 5.18)." In: *The International Journal of the Platonic Tradition* 5.2 (2011), 209–261.

O'Brien, Denis. "Plotinus on the Making of Matter, Part III. The Essential Background." In: *The International Journal of the Platonic Tradition* 6.1 (2012), 27–80.

O'Meara, Dominic. *Pythagoras Revived. Mathematics and Philosophy in Late Antiquity*. Clarendon Press, 1989.

O'Neill, William. "Time and Eternity in Proclus." In: *Phronesis* 7.2 (1962), 161–165.

Odzuck, Sebastian. *The Priority of Locomotion in Aristotle's* Physics. Hypomnemata. Untersuchungen zur Antike und zu ihrem Nachleben 196. Göttingen: Vandenhoeck & Ruprecht, 2014.

Opsomer, Jan. "Proclus vs Plotinus on Matter (*De mal. subs*. 30-7)." In: *Phronesis* 46.2 (2001), 154–188.

Opsomer, Jan. "The Integration of Aristotelian Physics in a Neoplatonic Context. Proclus on Movers and Divisibility." In: *Physics and Philosophy of Nature in Greek Neoplatonism*. Proceedings of the European Science Foundation Exploratory Workshop. (Il Ciocco, Castelvecchio Pascoli, 22nd–24th June 2006). Edited by Riccardo Chiaradonna and Franco Trabattoni. Philosophia antiqua. A Series of Studies on Ancient Philosophy 115. Leiden and Boston: Brill, 2009, 189–229.

Opsomer, Jan. "The Natural World." In: *All from One. A Guide to Proclus*. Edited by Pieter d'Hoine and Marije Martijn. Oxford: Oxford University Press, 2017, 139–166.

Owen, Gwilym Ellis Lane. "Aristotle on Time." In: *Motion and Time, Space and Matter. Interrelations in the History of Philosophy and Science*. Edited by Peter K. Machamer and Robert G. Turnbull. Columbus: Ohio State University Press, 1976, 3–27.

Owen, Gwilym Ellis Lane. "Τιθέναι τὰ φαινόμενα." In: *Aristote et les problèmes de méthode*. Communications présentées au Symposium Aristotelicum. (Louvain, 24th Aug.–1st Sept. 1960). Edited by Suzanne Mansion. Aristote. Traductions et études. Louvain and Paris: Publications Universitaires and Béatrice-Nauwelaerts, 1961, 83–103. Reprint in Martha C. Nussbaum, ed. *Logic, Science and Dialectic. Collected Papers in Greek Philosophy*. Ithaca: Cornell University Press, 1986.

Owens, Joseph. "The Universality of the Sensible in the Aristotelian Noetic." In: *Essays in Ancient Philosophy*. Edited by John P. Anton and George L. Kustas. Albany: State University of New York Press, 1971, 462–477.

Pasnau, Robert. "Form and Matter." In: *The Cambridge History of Medieval Philosophy*. Edited by Robert Pasnau and Christina van Dyke. 2 vols. Cambridge: Cambridge University Press, 2010, 635–646.

Pasnau, Robert. *Metaphysical Themes 1274–1671*. Oxford: Clarendon Press, 2011.

Pasnau, Robert and Christina van Dyke, eds. *The Cambridge History of Medieval Philosophy*. 2 vols. Cambridge: Cambridge University Press, 2010.

Périer, Augustin. *Yaḥyā ben ʿAdī. Un philosophe arabe chrétien du Xe siècle*. Paris: J. Gabalda and Paul Geuthner, 1920.

Perkams, Matthias. *Selbstbewusstsein in der Spätantike. Die neuplatonischen Kommentare zu Aristoteles' "De anima."* Quellen und Studien zur Philosophie 85. Berlin and New York: Walter de Gruyter, 2008.

Perkams, Matthias. "Zwei chronologische Anmerkungen zu Ammonios Hermeiou und Johannes Philoponos." In: *Rheinisches Museum für Philologie* 152.3–4 (2009), 385–391.

Pessin, Sarah. "Forms of Hylomorphism." In: *The Routledge Companion to Islamic Philosophy*. Edited by Richard C. Taylor and Luis Xavier López-Farjeat. Routledge Philosophy Companions. London and New York: Routledge, 2016, 197–211.

Peters, Francis E. *Aristoteles Arabus. The Oriental Translations and Commentaries on the Aristotelian* Corpus. Monographs on Mediterranean Antiquity 2. Leiden: E. J. Brill, 1968.

Phillips, John F. "Plotinus on the Generation of Matter." In: *The International Journal of the Platonic Tradition* 3.2 (2009), 103–137.

Pickavé, Martin. "On the Latin Reception of Avicenna's Theory of Individuation." In: *The Arabic, Hebrew and Latin Reception of Avicenna's Metaphysics*. (Villa Vigoni in Loveno di Menaggio, Italy, 2nd–6th July 2008). Edited by Dag Nikolaus Hasse and Amos Bertolacci. Scientia graeco-arabica 7. Berlin and Boston: Walter de Gruyter, 2012, 339–363.

Pietsch, Christian. *Prinzipienfindung bei Aristoteles. Methoden und erkenntnistheoretische Grundlagen*. Beiträge zur Altertumskunde 22. Stuttgart: Teubner, 1992.

Pines, Shlomo. "A New Fragment of Xenocrates and its Implications." In: *Transactions of the American Philosophical Society. New Series* 51.2 (1961), 3–34.

Pines, Shlomo. "A Tenth Century Philosophical Correspondence." In: *Proceedings of the American Academy for Jewish Research* 24 (1955), 103–136.

Pines, Shlomo. "An Arabic Summary of a Lost Work of John Philoponus." In: *Israel Oriental Studies* 2 (1972).

Pines, Shlomo. "Etudes sur Aḥwad al-Zamān Abuʾl-Barakāt al-Baghdādī." In: Pines, Shlomo. *Studies in Abu'l-Barakāt al-Baghdādī. Physics and Metaphysics*. The Collected Works of Shlomo Pines 1. Jerusalem: The Magnes Press, 1979, 1–95. Reprint of "Etudes sur Aḥwad al-Zamān Abuʾl-Barakāt al-Baghdādī." In: *Revue des études juives* 103, 104 (1938, 1939), 3–64, 1–33.

Pines, Shlomo. "Hitherto Unknown Arabic Extracts from Proclus' *Stoicheiôsis Theologikê* and *Stoicheiôsis Physikê*." In: Pines, Shlomo. *Studies in Arabic Versions of Greek Texts and in Medieval Science*. The Collected Works of Shlomo Pines 2. Jerusalem: The Magnes Press, 1986, 287–293.

Pines, Shlomo. "La 'philosophie orientale' d'Avicenne et sa polémique contre les bagdadiens." In: *Archives d'histoire doctrinale et littéraire du Moyen Âge* 27 (1952), 5–37. Reprint in Sarah Stroumsa, ed. *Studies in the History of Arabic Philosophy*. The Collected Works of Shlomo Pines 3. Jerusalem: The Magnes Press, 1996.

Pines, Shlomo. "Les précurseurs musulmans de la théorie de l'impetus." In: *Archeion. Archivio di storia della sciencia* 21.3 (1938), 298–306.

Pines, Shlomo. *Nouvelles etudes sur Aḥwad al-Zamān Abu-l-Barakāt al-Baghdādī*. Memoires de la Société des Études Juives 1. Paris: Librairie Durlacher, 1955. Reprint in *Studies in Abu'l-Barakāt al-Baghdādī. Physics and Metaphysics*. The Collected Works of Shlomo Pines 1. Jerusalem: The Magnes Press, 1979.

Pines, Shlomo. "Omne quod movetur necesse est ab aliquo moveri. A Refutation of Galen by Alexander of Aphrodisias and the Theory of Motion." In: *Isis* 52.1 (1961), 21–54. Reprint in *Studies in Arabic Versions of Greek Texts and in Medieval Science*. The Collected Works of Shlomo Pines 2. Jerusalem: The Magnes Press, 1986.

Pines, Shlomo. *Studies in Arabic Versions of Greek Texts and in Medieval Science*. The Collected Works of Shlomo Pines 2. Jerusalem: The Magnes Press, 1986.

Pines, Shlomo. *Studies in Islamic Atomism*. Edited by Y. Tzvi Langermann. Translated by Michael Schwarz. Jerusalem: The Magnes Press, 1997.

Pines, Shlomo. "The Spiritual Force Permeating the Cosmos According to a Passage in the Treatise *On the Principles of the All* Ascribed to Alexander of Aphrodisias." In: Pines, Shlomo. *Studies in Arabic Versions of Greek Texts and in Medieval Science*. The Collected Works of Shlomo Pines 2. Jerusalem: The Magnes Press, 1986, 252–255.

Pines, Shlomo. "Un précurseur Bagdadien de la théorie de l'impetus." In: *Isis* 44.3 (1953), 247–251.

Pormann, Peter E. *The Oriental Tradition of Paul of Aegina's* Pragmateia. Studies in Ancient Medicine 29. Leiden and Boston: Brill, 2004.

Porro, Pasquale, ed. *The Medieval Concept of Time. The Scholastic Debate and its Reception in Early Modern Philosophy*. Studien und Texte zur Geistesgeschichte des Mittelalters 75. Leiden, Boston, and Cologne: Brill, 2001.

Primavesi, Oliver. "Ein Blick in den Stollen von Skepsis. Vier Kapitel zur frühen Überlieferung des *Corpus Aristotelicum*." In: *Philologus* 151 (2007), 51–77.

al-Qāḍī, Wadād. "*Kitāb Ṣiwān al-ḥikma*. Structure, Composition, Authorship and Sources." In: *Der Islam* 58.1 (1981), 87–124.

Rahman, Fazlur. "Essence and Existence in Ibn Sīnā. The Myth and the Reality." In: *Hamdard Islamicus* 4.1 (1981), 3–14.

Rahman, Fazlur. *Prophecy in Islam. Philosophy and Orthodoxy*. Ethical and Religious Classics of East and West. London: George Allen & Unwin Ltd., 1958.

Rashed, Marwan. "al-Fārābī's Lost Treatise *On Changing Beings* and the Possibility of a Demonstration of the Eternity of the World." In: *Arabic Sciences and Philosophy* 18.1 (2008), 19–58.

Rashed, Marwan. "Alexandre d'Aphrodise et la 'magna quaestio.' Rôle et indépendance des scholies dans la tradition byzantine du corpus aristotélicien." In: *Les études classiques* 63 (1995), 295–351.

Rashed, Marwan. *Essentialisme. Alexandre d'Aphrodise entre logique, physique et cosmologie*. Commentaria in Aristotelem graeca et byzantina. Quellen und Studien 2. Berlin and New York: Walter de Gruyter, 2007.

Rashed, Marwan. "Ibn ʿAdī et Avicenne. Sur les types d'existants." In: *Aristotele e i suoi esegeti neoplatonici. Logica e ontologia nelle interpretazioni greche e arabe*. Atti del convegno internazionale. (Rome, 19th–20th Oct. 2001). Edited by Vincenza Celluprica and Cristina D'Ancona. In collaboration with Riccardo Chiaradonna. Elenchos 40. Naples: Bibliopolis, 2004, 107–171.

Rashed, Marwan. "Natural Philosophy." In: *The Cambridge Companion to Arabic Philosophy*. Edited by Peter Adamson and Richard C. Taylor. Cambridge: Cambridge University Press, 2005, 287–307.

Rashed, Marwan. "Nouveaux fragments antiprocliens de Philopon en version arabe et le problème des origines de la théorie de l''instauration' (*ḥudūth*)." In: *Les études philosophiques* 105.2 (2013), 261–292.

Rashed, Marwan. "Thābit ibn Qurra, la *Physique* d'Aristote et le meilleur des mondes." In: *Thābit ibn Qurra. Science and Philosophy in Ninth-Century Baghdad*. Edited by Roshdi Rashed. Scientia graeco-arabica 4. Berlin and New York: Walter de Gruyter, 2009, 675–714.

Rashed, Marwan. "The Problem of the Composition of the Heavens (529–1610). A New Fragment of Philoponus and its Readers." In: *Philosophy, Science and Exegesis in Greek, Arabic and Latin Commentaries*. Edited by Peter Adamson, Han Baltussen, and Martin W. F. Stone. Vol. 2. 2 vols.

Supplement to the Bulletin of the Institute of Classical Studies 83.1–2. London: Institute of Classical Studies, 2004, 35–58.
Rashed, Roshdi. "Al-Sijzī and Maimonides. A Mathematical and Philosophical Commentary on Proposition II–14 in Apollonius' *Conic Sections*." In: *Maimonides and the Sciences*. Edited by Robert S. Cohen and Hillel Levine. Boston Studies in the Philosophy of Science 211. Dordrecht: Kluwer Academic Publishers, 2000, 159–172.
Rashed, Roshdi. "Le concept de lieu. Ibn al-Haytham, Averroès." In: *La lumière de l'intellect. La pensée scientifique et philosophique d'Averroès dans son temps*. Actes du IVe colloque international de la SIHSPAI (Société Internationale d'Histoire des Sciences et de la Philosophie Arabes et Islamiques). (Córdoba, 9th–12th Dec. 1998). Edited by Ahmad Hasnawi. Ancient and Classical Sciences and Philosophy. With a preface by Roshdi Rashed. Leuven: Peeters, 2011, 3–9.
Rashed, Roshdi. *Les mathématiques infinitésimales du IXe au XIe siécle*. 5 vols. London: al-Furqān Islamic Heritge Foundation, 1996–2006.
Reisman, David C., ed. *Before and After Avicenna*. Proceedings of the First Conference of the Avicenna Study Group. In collaboration with Ahmed H. al-Rahim. Islamic Philosophy, Theology and Science. Texts and Studies 52. Leiden and Boston: E. J. Brill, 2003.
Reisman, David C. "The Life and Times of Avicenna. Patronage and Learning in Medieval Islam." In: *Interpreting Avicenna. Critical Essays*. Edited by Peter Adamson. Cambridge: Cambridge University Press, 2013, 7–27.
Reisman, David C. *The Making of the Avicennan Tradition. The Transmission, Contents, and Structure of Ibn Sīnā's* al-Mubāḥaṯāt *(The Discussions)*. Islamic Philosophy, Theology and Science. Texts and Studies 49. Leiden, Boston, and Cologne: Brill, 2002.
Reisman, David C. "Two Medieval Arabic Treatises on the Nutritive Faculties." In: *Zeitschrift für Geschichte der arabisch-islamischen Wissenschaften* 18 (2008), 287–342.
Rescher, Nicholas. "New Light from Arabic Sources on Galen and the Fourth Figure of the Syllogism." In: *Journal of the History of Philosophy* 3.2 (1965), 27–41.
Rescher, Nicholas. *The Development of Arabic Logic*. University of Pittsburgh Press, 1964.
Richardson, Kara. "Avicenna and Aquinas on Form and Generation." In: *The Arabic, Hebrew and Latin Reception of Avicenna's Metaphysics*. (Villa Vigoni in Loveno di Menaggio, Italy, 2nd–6th July 2008). Edited by Dag Nikolaus Hasse and Amos Bertolacci. Scientia graeco-arabica 7. Berlin and Boston: Walter de Gruyter, 2012, 251–274.
Richardson, Kara. "Avicenna and the Principle of Sufficient Reason." In: *Review of Metaphysics* 67.4 (2014), 743–768.
Richardson, Kara. "Avicenna's Conception of the Efficient Cause." In: *British Journal for the History of Science* 21.2 (2012), 220–239.
Rist, John M. *Plotinus. The Road to Reality*. Cambridge: Cambridge University Press, 1967.
Roark, Tony. *Aristotle on Time. A Study of the* Physics. Cambridge: Cambridge University Press, 2011.
Roark, Tony. "Aristotle's Definition of Time Is not Circular." In: *Ancient Philosophy* 23.2 (2003), 301–318.
Roark, Tony. "Why Aristotle Says There Is no Time without Change." In: *Apeiron. A Journal for Ancient Philosophy and Science* 37.3 (2004), 227–246.
Robinson, Howard M. "Prime Matter in Aristotle." In: *Phronesis* 19.2 (1974), 168–188.
Romano, Francesco. *Porfirio e la fisica aristotelica. In appendice la traduzione dei frammenti e delle testimonianze del* Commentario alla Fisica. Symbolon. Studi e testi di filosofia antica e medievale 3. Catania: Università di Catania, 1985.
Rosenthal, Franz. "aš-Šayḫ al-Yūnānī and the Arabic Plotinus Source." In: *Orientalia* 21 (1952), 461–492.
Rosenthal, Franz. "On the Knowledge of Plato's Philosophy in the Islamic World." In: *Islamic Culture* 14 (1940), 387–422.

Rosenthal, Franz. *The Technique and Approach of Muslim Scholarship*. Analecta Orientalia 24. Rome: Pontificium Institutum Biblicum, 1947.
Rudolph, Enno, ed. *Zeit, Bewegung, Handlung. Studien zur Zeitabhandlung des Aristoteles*. Forschungen und Berichte der evangelischen Studiengemeinschaft 42. Stuttgart: Klett-Cotta, 1988.
Ruffus, Anthony and Jon McGinnis. "Willful Understanding. Avicenna's Philosophy of Action and Theory of the Will." In: *Archiv für Geschichte der Philosophie* 97.2 (2015), 160–195.
Šalaq, ʿAlī. *al-Zamān fī l-fikr al-ʿarabī wa-l-ʿālamī*. Beirut: Dār wa-Maktabat al-Hilāl, 2006.
Saliba, George. "Avicenna's *Shifāʾ (Sufficientia)*. In Defense of Medieval Latin Translators." In: *Journal of the History and Culture of the Middle East* 94.2 (2017), 423–433.
Sambursky, Samuel. *Physics of the Stoics*. London: Routledge & Kegan Paul, 1959.
Sambursky, Samuel. *The Physical World of Late Antiquity*. London: Routledge & Kegan Paul, 1962.
Sattler, Barbara. "A Likely Account of Necessity. Plato's Receptacle as a Physical and Metaphysical Foundation for Space." In: *Journal of the History of Philosophy* 50.2 (2012), 159–195.
Sayılı, Aydın. "Ibn Sīnā and Buridan on the Dynamics of Projectile Motion." In: *İbn Sînâ. Doğumunun bininci yılı armağanı*. Edited by Aydın Sayılı. Türk Tarih Kurumu yayınları. VII. Dizi. Ankara: Türk Tarih Kumuru Basımevi, 1984, 141–160.
Sayılı, Aydın. "Ibn Sīnā and Buridan on the Motion of the Projectile." In: *Annals of the New York Academy of Sciences* 500 (1987), 477–482.
Schreiner, Martin. *Studien über Jeschuʿa Ben Jehuda*. In: *Achtzehnter Bericht über die Lehranstalt für die Wissenschaft des Judentums*. Berlin: Das Curatorium der Lehranstalt für die Wissenschaft des Judentums, 1900.
Schrenk, Lawrence P. "Proclus on Corporeal Space." In: *Archiv für Geschichte der Philosophie* 76 (1994), 151–167.
Schrenk, Lawrence P. "Proclus on Space as Light." In: *Ancient Philosophy* 9.1 (1989), 87–94.
Sedley, David. "Philoponus' Conception of Space." In: *Philoponus and the Rejection of Aristotelian Science*. Edited by Richard Sorabji. London: Duckworth, 1987, 140–153.
Sedley, David. "Two Conceptions of Vacuum." In: *Phronesis* 27.2 (1982), 175–193.
Seeck, Gustav Adolf. "Zeit als Zahl bei Aristoteles." In: *Rheinisches Museum für Philologie* 130 (1987), 107–124.
Shayegan, Yegane. *Avicenna on Time*. PhD thesis. Cambridge: Harvard University, 1986.
Shihadeh, Ayman. "Avicenna's Corporeal Form and Proof of Prime Matter in Twelfth-Century Critical Philosophy. Abū l-Barakāt, al-Masʿūdī and al-Rāzī." In: *Oriens* 42.3–4 (2014), 364–396.
Shihadeh, Ayman. *Doubts on Avicenna. A Study and Edition of Sharaf al-Dīn al-Masʿūdī's Commentary on the* Ishārāt. Islamic Philosophy and Theology. Texts and Studies 95. Leiden and Boston: Brill, 2016.
Silva, José Filipe. *Robert Kilwardby on the Human Soul. Plurality of Forms and Censorship in the Thirteenth Century*. Investigating Medieval Philosophy 3. Leiden and Boston: Brill, 2012.
Sirkel, Riin. "Alexander of Aphrodisias's Account of Universals and its Problems." In: *Journal of the History of Philosophy* 49.3 (2011), 297–314.
Smith, Andrew. "Soul and Time in Plotinus." In: *Ψυχή – Seele – anima*. Festschrift für Karin Alt zum 7. Mai 1998. Edited by Jens Holzhausen. Stuttgart and Leipzig: Teubner, 1998, 335–344.
Smith, Andrew. "The Reception of *On the Cosmos* in Ancient Pagan Philosophy." In: *Cosmic Order and Divine Power*. Edited by Johan C. Thom. Scripta antiquitatis posterioris ad ethicam religionemque pertinentia 23. Tübingen: Mohr Siebeck, 2014, 121–131.
Smith, Andrew. "The Significance of 'Physics' in Porphyry. The Problem of Body and Matter." In: *Neoplatonism and the Philosophy of Nature*. Edited by James Wilberding and Christoph Horn. Oxford: Oxford University Press, 2012, 30–43.
Smith, David Eugene. *The Teaching of Geometry*. Boston: Ginn and Company, 1911.

Solmsen, Friedrich. "Aristotle and Prime Matter. A Reply to Hugh R. King." In: *Journal of the History of Ideas* 19.2 (1958), 243–252.

Solmsen, Friedrich. *Aristotle's System of the Physical World. A Comparison with his Predecessors.* Ithaca: Cornell University Press, 1960.

Sorabji, Richard, ed. *Aristotle Transformed. The Ancient Commentators and Their Influence.* Ithaca: Cornell University Press, 1990.

Sorabji, Richard. "Dating of Philoponus' Commentaries on Aristotle and of his Divergence from his Teacher Ammonius." In: *Aristotle Re-interpreted. New Findings on Seven Hundred Years of the Ancient Commentators.* Edited by Richard Sorabji. London and New York: Bloomsbury, 2016, 367–392.

Sorabji, Richard. "John Philoponus." In: *Philoponus and the Rejection of Aristotelian Science.* Edited by Richard Sorabji. London: Duckworth, 1987, 1–40.

Sorabji, Richard. *Matter, Space, and Motion. Theories in Antiquity and their Sequel.* Ithaca: Cornell University Press, 1988.

Sorabji, Richard. "New Findings on Philoponus." In: *Philoponus and the Rejection of Aristotelian Science.* Edited by Richard Sorabji. Supplement to the Bulletin of the Institute of Classical Studies 103. London: Institute of Classical Studies, ²2010, 1–40.

Sorabji, Richard, ed. *Philoponus and the Rejection of Aristotelian Science.* London: Duckworth, 1987.

Sorabji, Richard, ed. *Philoponus and the Rejection of Aristotelian Science.* Supplement to the Bulletin of the Institute of Classical Studies 103. London: Institute of Classical Studies, ²2010.

Sorabji, Richard. "Simplicius. Prime Matter as Extension." In: *Simplicius. Sa vie, son œvre, sa survie.* Actes du colloque international de Paris. Organisé par le Centre de Recherche sur les Œuvres et la Pensée de Simplicius. (Paris, 28th Sept.–1st Oct. 1985). Edited by Ilsetraut Hadot. Peripatoi. Philologisch-historische Studien zum Aristotelismus 15. Berlin and New York: Walter de Gruyter, 1987, 148–165.

Sorabji, Richard. "The Concept of the Will from Plato to Maximus the Confessor." In: *The Will and Human Action. From Antiquity to the Present Day.* Edited by Thomas Pink and Martin W. F. Stone. London: Routledge, 2003, 6–28.

Sorabji, Richard. *Time, Creation and the Continuum. Theories in Antiquity and the Early Middle Ages.* Chicago: The University of Chicago Press, 1983.

Steel, Carlos. "The Neoplatonic Doctrine of Time and Eternity and its Influence on Medieval Philosophy." In: *The Medieval Concept of Time. The Scholastic Debate and its Reception in Early Modern Philosophy.* Edited by Pasquale Porro. Studien und Texte zur Geistesgeschichte des Mittelalters 75. Leiden, Boston, and Cologne: Brill, 2001, 3–31.

Steel, Carlos. "Why Should We Prefer Plato's Timaeus to Aristotle's Physics? Proclus' Critique of Aristotle's Causal Explanation of the Physical World." In: *Ancient Approaches to Plato's Timaeus.* Edited by Robert W. Sharples and Anne Sheppard. Supplement to the Bulletin of the Institute of Classical Studies 78. London: Institute of Classical Studies, 2003, 175–187.

Steinmetz, Peter. *Die Physik des Theophrastos von Eresos.* Palingenesia. Schriftenreihe für klassische Altertumswissenschaft 1. Bad Homburg v. d. Höhe: Max Gehlen, 1964.

Steinschneider, Moritz. *al-Farabi (Alpharabius). Des arabischen Philosophen Leben und Schriften, mit besonderer Rücksicht auf die Geschichte der griechischen Wissenschaft bei den Arabern.* Saint Petersburg: L'Académie Impériale des sciences, 1869.

Steinschneider, Moritz. *Die arabischen Übersetzungen aus dem Griechischen.* Zwölftes Beiheft zum Centralblatt für Bibliothekswesen. Leipzig: Otto Harrassowitz, 1893.

Stern, Samuel Miklos. "Ibn al-Samḥ." In: *The Journal of the Royal Asiatic Society of Great Britain and Ireland* 1/2 (1956), 31–44.

Stone, Abraham D. "Avicenna." In: *Substantia – Sic et non. Eine Geschichte des Substanzbegriffs von der Antike bis zur Gegenwart in Einzelbeiträgen.* Edited by Holger Gutschmidt, Antonella

Lang-Balestra, and Gianluigi Segalerba. Philosophische Analyse. Philosophical Analysis 27. Heusenstamm: Ontos Verlag, 2008, 133–147.

Stone, Abraham D. "Simplicius and Avicenna on the Essential Corporeity of Material Substance." In: *Aspects of Avicenna*. Edited by Robert Wisnovsky. Princeton: Markus Wiener Publishers, 2001, 73–130.

Street, Tony. "Arabic Logic." In: *Handbook of the History of Logic. Vol. I: Greek, Indian and Arabic Logic*. Edited by Dov M. Gabbay and John Woods. Vol. 1. Amsterdam: Elsevier, 2004, 523–596.

Strobino, Riccardo. "Avicenna's Use of the Arabic Translations of the *Posterior Analytics* and the Ancient Commentary Tradition." In: *Oriens* 40.2 (2012), 355–389.

Stroumsa, Sarah. "From the Earliest Known Judaeo-Arabic Commentary on Genesis." In: *Jerusalem Studies in Arabic and Islam* 27 (2002), 375–395.

Takahashi, Hidemi. "Syriac and Arabic Transmission of *On the Cosmos*." In: *Cosmic Order and Divine Power*. Edited by Johan C. Thom. Scripta antiquitatis posterioris ad ethicam religionemque pertinentia 23. Tübingen: Mohr Siebeck, 2014, 153–167.

Tamer, Georges. *Zeit und Gott. Hellenistische Zeitvorstellungen in der altarabischen Dichtung und im Koran*. Studien zur Geschichte und Kultur des islamischen Orients. Neue Folge 20. Berlin and New York: Walter de Gruyter, 2008.

Tannery, Paul. "Sur un point de la méthode d'Aristote." In: *Archiv für Geschichte der Philosophie* 6.4 (1893), 468–474.

Taylor, Alfred E. *A Commentary on Plato's Timaeus*. Oxford: Clarendon Press, 1928.

Taylor, Richard C. "al-Fārābī and Avicenna. Two Recent Contributions." In: *Middle East Studies Association Bulletin* 39 (2005), 180–182.

Théry, Gabriel. *Autour du décret de 1210*. Vol. 2: Alexandre d'Aphrodisias. Aperçu sur l'influence de sa noétique. Bibliotheque Thomiste 7. Le Saulchoir Kain: Revue des sciences philosophiques et théologiques, 1926.

Thiele, Jan. *Theologie in der jemenitischen Zaydiyya. Die naturphilosophischen Überlegungen des al-Ḥasan ar-Raṣṣāṣ*. Islamic Philosophy and Theology. Texts and Studies 86. Leiden and Boston: Brill, 2013.

Thom, Johan C., ed. *Cosmic Order and Divine Power*. Scripta antiquitatis posterioris ad ethicam religionemque pertinentia 23. Tübingen: Mohr Siebeck, 2014.

Thom, Paul. "The Division of the Categories According to Avicenna." In: *Aristotle and the Arabic Tradition*. Edited by Ahmed Alwishah and Josh Hayes. Cambridge: Cambridge University Press, 2015, 30–49.

Thorp, John. "Aristotle's *Horror Vacui*." In: *Canadian Journal of Philosophy* 20.2 (1990), 149–166.

Tisini, Tayeb. *Die Materieauffassung in der islamisch-arabischen Philosophie des Mittelalters*. Berlin: Akademie Verlag, 1972.

Todd, Robert B. *Alexander of Aphrodisias on Stoic Physics. A Study of the De mixtione with Preliminary Essays, Text, Translation and Commentary*. Philosophia antiqua. A Series of Monographs on Ancient Philosophy 28. Leiden: E. J. Brill, 1976.

Trifogli, Cecilia. "Averroes's Doctrine of Time and its Reception in the Scholastic Debate." In: *The Medieval Concept of Time. The Scholastic Debate and its Reception in Early Modern Philosophy*. Edited by Pasquale Porro. Studien und Texte zur Geistesgeschichte des Mittelalters 75. Leiden, Boston, and Cologne: Brill, 2001, 57–82.

Trifogli, Cecilia. "Change, Time, and Place." In: *The Cambridge History of Medieval Philosophy*. Edited by Robert Pasnau and Christina van Dyke. Vol. 1. 2 vols. Cambridge: Cambridge University Press, 2010, 267–278.

Trifogli, Cecilia. *Oxford Physics in the Thirteenth Century (ca. 1250–1270). Motion, Infinity, Place and Time*. Studien und Texte zur Geistesgeschichte des Mittelalters 72. Leiden, Boston, and Cologne: Brill, 2000.

Troupeau, Gérard. "Un épitomé arabe du 'De contingentia mundi' de Jean Philopon." In: *Mémorial André-Jean Festugière. Antiquité païenne et chrétienne*. Edited by Enzo Lucchesi and Henri Dominique Saffrey. Genève: Patrick Cramer, 1984, 77–88.

Tuominen, Miira. *Apprehension and Argument. Ancient Theories of Starting Points for Knowledge*. Studies in the History of Philosophy of Mind 3. Dordrecht: Springer, 2007.

Tuominen, Miira. "Back to *Posterior Analytics* II 19. Aristotle on the Knowledge of Principles." In: *Apeiron. A Journal for Ancient Philosophy and Science* 43.2–3 (2010): *From Inquiry to Demonstrative Knowledge. New Essays on Aristotle's Posterior Analytics*. Edited by James H. Lesher, 115–144.

Turnbull, Robert G. "'Physics' I. Sense Universals, Principles, Multiplicity, and Motion." In: *Motion and Time, Space and Matter. Interrelations in the History of Philosophy and Science*. Edited by Peter K. Machamer and Robert G. Turnbull. Columbus: Ohio State University Press, 1976, 28–55.

Twetten, David. "Aristotelian Cosmology and Causality in Classical Arabic Philosophy and Its Greek Background." In: *Ideas in Motion in Baghdad and Beyond. Philosophical and Theological Exchanges between Christians and Muslims in the Third/Ninth and Fourth/Tenth Centuries*. Edited by Damien Janos. Leiden and Boston: Brill, 2015, 312–433.

Ullmann, Manfred. *Die Nikomachische Ethik des Aristoteles in arabischer Überlieferung*. 2 vols. Wiesbaden: Harrassowitz Verlag, 2011–2012.

van Ess, Josef. *Theologie und Gesellschaft im 2. und 3. Jahrhundert Hidschra. Eine Geschichte des religiösen Denkens im frühen Islam*. 6 vols. Berlin and New York: Walter de Gruyter, 1991–97.

van Riel, Gerd. "Proclus on Matter and Physical Necessity." In: *Physics and Philosophy of Nature in Greek Neoplatonism*. Proceedings of the European Science Foundation Exploratory Workshop. (Il Ciocco, Castelvecchio Pascoli, 22nd–24th June 2006). Edited by Riccardo Chiaradonna and Franco Trabattoni. Philosophia antiqua. A Series of Studies on Ancient Philosophy 115. Leiden and Boston: Brill, 2009, 231–257.

van Riet, Simone. "Recherches concernant la traduction arabo-latine du Kitāb al-Nafs d'Ibn Sīna. La notion d'idjmāʿ – voluntas." In: *Atti del terzo Congresso di studi arabi e islamici*. (Ravello, 1st–6th Sept. 1966). Naples: Istituto Universitario Orientale, 1967, 641–648.

Verbeke, Gérard. "La nature dans une perspective nouvelle." In: Avicenna. *Liber primus naturalium. Tractatus primus de causis et principiis naturalium*. Edited by Simone van Riet. With an introduction by Gérard Verbeke. Avicenna Latinus. Louvain-la-Neuve and Leiden: Éditions Peeters and E. J. Brill, 1992, 1*–52*.

Verbeke, Gérard. "Notions centrales de la physique d'Avicenne." In: Avicenna. *Liber primus naturalium. Tractatus secundus de motu et de consimilibus*. Edited by Simone van Riet, Jules Janssens, and André Allard. With an introduction by Gérard Verbeke. Avicenna Latinus. Brussels: Académie Royale de Belgique, 2006, 1*–67*.

Verrycken, Koenraad. *God en wereld in de wijsbegeerte van Ioannes Philoponus*. PhD thesis. Université catholique de Louvain, 1985.

Verrycken, Koenraad. "John Philoponus." In: *The Cambridge History of Philosophy in Late Antiquity*. Edited by Lloyd Gerson. Vol. 2. 2 vols. Cambridge: Cambridge University Press, 2010, 733–755.

Verrycken, Koenraad. "The Development of Philoponus' Thought and its Chronology." In: *Aristotle Transformed. The Ancient Commentators and Their Influence*. Edited by Richard Sorabji. Ithaca: Cornell University Press, 1990, 233–274.

von Fritz, Kurt. *Die ἐπαγωγή bei Aristoteles*. Sitzungsberichte der philosophisch-historischen Klasse. Munich: Verlag der Bayerischen Akademie der Wissenschaften, 1964.

von Leyden, Wolfgang. "Time, Number, and Eternity in Plato and Aristotle." In: *The Philosophical Quarterly* 14.54 (1964), 35–52.

von Müller, Iwan. *Ueber Galens Werk vom wissenschaftlichen Beweis*. Aus den Abhandlungen der königlichen bayerischen Akademie der Wissenschaften. Munich: Verlag der königlichen Akademie der Wissenschaften, 1895.

Wakelnig, Elvira. "A New Version of Miskawayh's *Book of Triumph*. An Alternative Recension of *al-Fawz al-aṣghar* or the Lost *Fawz al-akbar*?" In: *Arabic Sciences and Philosophy* 19.1 (2009), 83–119.

Wakelnig, Elvira. "Die Philosophen in der Tradition al-Kindīs. al-ʿĀmirī, al-Isfizārī, Miskawayh, as-Siǧistānī und at-Tawḥīdī." In: *Islamische Philosophie im Mittelalter. Ein Handbuch*. Edited by Heidrun Eichner, Matthias Perkams, and Christian Schäfer. Darmstadt: Wissenschaftliche Buchgesellschaft, 2013, 233–252.

Wakelnig, Elvira. "Proclus in Aristotelian Disguise. Notes on the Arabic transmission of Proclus' *Elements of Theology*." In: *Universalità della ragione. Pluralità delle filosofie nel Medioevo*. Atti del XII Congresso Internazionale di Filosofia Medievale. (16th–22nd Sept. 2007). Edited by Alessandro Musco, Rosanna Gambino, Luciana Pepi, Patrizia Spallino, and Maria Vasallo. Schede Medievali 50. Palermo: Officina di studi medievali, 2012, 165–176.

Wakelnig, Elvira. "The Other Arabic Version of Proclus' *De Aeternitate mundi*. The Surviving First Eight Arguments." In: *Oriens* 40.1 (2012), 51–95.

Walzer, Richard. "Gedanken zur Geschichte der philosophischen Terminologie." In: *Archiv für Geschichte der Philosophie* 50 (1968), 101–114.

Watt, William Montgomery. *The Formative Period of Islamic Thought*. Edinburgh: Edinburgh University Press, 1973. Reprinted as *The Formative Period of Islamic Thought*. Oxford: Oneworld Publications, 2009.

Wedin, Michael V. *Mind and Imagination in Aristotle*. New Haven and London: Yale University Press, 1988.

Weisheipl, James A. "Aristotle's Concept of Nature. Avicenna and Aquinas." In: *Approaches to Nature in the Middle Ages*. Papers of the Tenth Annual Conference of the Center for Medieval & Early Renaissance Studies. Edited by Lawrence D. Roberts. Medieval & Renaissance. Texts & Studies 16. Binghamton: Center for Medieval & Early Renaissance Studies, 1982, 137–160.

Weisheipl, James A. "The Concept of Nature." In: Weisheipl, James A. *Nature and Motion in the Middle Ages*. Edited by William E. Carroll. Studies in Philosophy and the History of Philosophy 11. Washington, D. C.: The Catholic University of America Press, 1985, 1–23. Reprint of "The Concept of Nature." In: *The New Scholasticism* 28.4 (1954), 377–408.

Wieland, Wolfgang. "Aristotle's Physics and the Problem of Inquiry into Principles." In: *Articles on Aristotle*. Edited by Jonathan Barnes, Malcolm Schofield, and Richard Sorabji. Vol. 1: Science. London: Duckworth, 1975, 127–140. Reprint of "Das Problem der Prinzipienforschung und die aristotelische Physik." In: *Kant-Studien* 52 (1961), 206–219.

Wieland, Wolfgang. *Die aristotelische Physik. Untersuchungen über die Grundlegung der Naturwissenschaft und die sprachlichen Bedingungen der Prinzipienforschung bei Aristoteles*. Göttingen: Vandenhoeck & Ruprecht, [3]1992.

Wieland, Wolfgang. "Zur Raumtheorie des Johannes Philoponus." In: *Festschrift für Joseph Klein zum 70. Geburtstag*. Edited by Erich Fries. Göttingen: Vandenhoeck & Ruprecht, 1967, 114–135.

Wilberding, James and Christoph Horn, eds. *Neoplatonism and the Philosophy of Nature*. Oxford: Oxford University Press, 2012.

Wildberg, Christian. *John Philoponus' Criticism of Aristotle's Theory of Aether*. Peripatoi. Philologisch-historische Studien zum Aristotelismus 16. Berlin and New York: Walter de Gruyter, 1988.

Wirmer, David. *Vom Denken der Natur zur Natur des Denkens. Ibn Bāǧǧas Theorie der Potenz als Grundlegung der Psychologie*. Scientia graeco-arabica 13. Berlin, Munich, and Boston: Walter de Gruyter, 2014.

Wisnovsky, Robert, ed. *Aspects of Avicenna*. Princeton: Markus Wiener Publishers, 2001.

Wisnovsky, Robert. *Avicenna on Final Causality*. PhD thesis. Princeton University, 1994.

Wisnovsky, Robert. *Avicenna's Metaphysics in Context.* London: Duckworth, 2003.

Wisnovsky, Robert. "Final and Efficient Causality in Avicenna's Cosmology and Theology." In: *Quaestio. Annuario di storia della metafisica* 2 (2002), 97–123.

Wisnovsky, Robert. "Jowzjāni (Juzjāni), Abu ʿObayd ʿAbd-al-Wāḥed b. Moḥammad." In: *Encyclopædia Iranica.* Edited by Ehsan Yarshater. Vol. 15. London and New York: Routledge & Kegan Paul, 2009, 82–84.

Wisnovsky, Robert. "Towards a History of Avicenna's Distinction between Immanent and Transcendent Causes." In: *Before and After Avicenna.* Proceedings of the First Conference of the Avicenna Study Group. Edited by David C. Reisman. In collaboration with Ahmed H. al-Rahim. Islamic Philosophy, Theology and Science. Texts and Studies 52. Leiden and Boston: E. J. Brill, 2003, 49–68.

Witkam, Jan Just. "Avicenna's Copyists at Work. Codicological Features of the Two Leiden Manuscripts of the *Kitāb al-Shifāʾ*." In: *Oriens* 40.2 (2012), 223–255.

Witkam, Jan Just. *Seven specimens of Arabic Manuscripts. Preserved in the library of the University of Leiden.* Leiden: E. J. Brill, 1978.

Wolff, Michael. *Fallgesetz und Massebegriff. Zwei wissenschaftshistorische Untersuchungen zur Kosmologie des Johannes Philoponus.* Quellen und Studien zur Philosophie 2. Berlin: Walter de Gruyter, 1971.

Wolff, Michael. "Philoponus and the Rise of Preclassical Dynamics." In: *Philoponus and the Rejection of Aristotelian Science.* Edited by Richard Sorabji. London: Duckworth, 1987, 84–120.

Wolfson, Harry A. *The Philosophy of the Kalam.* Structure and Growth of Philosophic Systems from Plato to Spinoza 4. Cambridge and London: Harvard University Press, 1976.

Wolfson, Harry A. "The Problem of the Souls of the Spheres from the Byzantine Commentaries on Aristotle through the Arabs and St. Thomas to Kepler." In: *Dumbarton Oaks Papers* 16 (1962), 65–93.

al-Zarkān, Muḥammad Ṣāliḥ. *Faḫr al-Dīn al-Rāzī wa-ārāʾuhū l-kalāmiyya wa-l-falsafiyya.* Cairo: Dār al-Fikr, 1963.

Zekl, Hans-Günter. *Topos. Die aristotelische Lehre vom Raum.* Paradeigmata 10. Hamburg: Felix Meiner Verlag, 1990.

Zimmermann, Fritz. "al-Farabi und die philosophische Kritik an Galen von Alexander zu Averroes." In: *Akten des VII. Kongresses für Arabistik und Islamwissenschaft.* (Göttingen, 15th–22nd Aug. 1974). Edited by Albert Dietrich. Abhandlungen der Akademie der Wissenschaften in Göttingen. Philologisch-historische Klasse. Dritte Folge 98. Göttingen: Vandenhoeck & Ruprecht, 1976, 401–414.

Zimmermann, Fritz. "Philoponus' Impetus Theory in the Arabic Tradition." In: *Philoponus and the Rejection of Aristotelian Science.* Edited by Richard Sorabji. London: Duckworth, 1987, 121–129.

Zimmermann, Fritz. "Proclus Arabus Rides Again." In: *Arabic Sciences and Philosophy* 4.1 (1994), 9–51.

Zimmermann, Fritz. "The Origins of the So-Called *Theology of Aristotle*." In: *Pseudo-Aristotle in the Middle Ages. The* Theology *and Other Texts.* Edited by Jill Kraye, William F. Ryan, and Charles B. Schmitt. Warburg Institute Surveys and Texts 11. London: The Warburg Institute, 1986, 110–240.

Index

ʿAbbāsids 10, 474, 491n, 510–511
ʿAbd al-Ǧabbār ibn Aḥmad al-Hamadānī see Hamadānī, ʿAbd al-Ǧabbār ibn Aḥmad al-
ʿAbd al-Mutaʿāl, ʿAlāʾ al-Dīn Muḥammad 516
Abraš, Sallām al- 10–16, 39–40
abstraction 50, 64n, 379n, 385, 392, 396, 398, 426
Abū l-Barakāt al-Baġdādī see Baġdādī, Abū l-Barakāt al-
Abū Bišr Mattā ibn Yūnus, see Ibn Yūnus, Abū Bišr Mattā
Abū l-Faraǧ Qudāma ibn Ǧaʿfar al-Kātib al-Baġdādī see Kātib al-Baġdādī, Abū l-Faraǧ Qudāma ibn Ǧaʿfar al-
Abū l-Ḥusayn al-Baṣrī see Baṣrī, Abū l-Ḥusayn al-
accidents 115–117, 118n, 120n, 124, 132–133, 134n, 139, 141n, 142n, 144, 152, 153n, 166n, 168, 170, 177, 179, 189, 198, 209, 352, 367, 372, 374–375, 377, 379, 394–395, 417–418, 424, 430n, 439, 445, 456, 481, 483–484, 510, 512, 514
Active Intellect 50, 170–171, 192–194, 196, 197n
actuality 4, 154, 156–157, 176, 178, 204n, 217, 221n, 250, 419, 522
aether 181n, 200; see also matter, celestial
Aëtius see Ps.-Plutarchus
agent see causes, efficient
air 165, 166n, 170–171, 174, 199, 200, 302–303, 311, 317n, 318, 321, 327–328, 331n, 347–348, 357–359, 363–364, 371, 378, 380, 386, 399, 407–425, 486, 492n
Alexander of Aphrodisias 10, 15–16, 21, 22–25, 27, 29, 32–33, 39, 66, 73n, 88, 92, 102n, 115n, 160, 179–180, 181n, 192n, 203, 217, 222n, 242–245, 253, 261–262, 267, 269–270, 278, 284n, 289, 298, 299n, 307, 310, 315n, 318n, 324, 331n, 334, 336n, 339, 340n, 341n, 369n, 374n, 402–403, 421n, 430n, 432–433, 436, 452n, 453, 455, 457–458, 460, 493n, 495, 498–499, 512, 514, 516, 518, 527, 530
alteration 58, 101, 111, 189, 203n, 204n, 231n, 232, 280, 289, 291, 495, 497; see also quality
ʿĀmirī, Abū l-Ḥasan Muḥammad ibn Yūsuf al- 29n, 267, 269
Ammonius 30n, 103, 139n, 140n, 141n, 160n, 319n, 347n, 440n,
Anaxagoras 328n
animals 54–55, 60, 115n, 134n, 167–168, 171–173, 174n, 195–196, 219, 223–224, 229–233, 241, 245, 249n, 266, 268–269, 271, 285n, 288–289, 290n, 291–298, 300, 301n, 302–303, 305–306, 317, 319, 342n, 526–528
Antiphon 235n
Aristotle 2–23, 25–32, 34–41, 43–46, 48n, 51–63, 64n, 65–70, 73, 75–98, 99n, 102–109, 111n, 112–113, 115–116, 118n, 122, 135–137, 139–141, 143n, 144, 147–148, 150n, 151n, 155, 159–162, 164–165, 175, 178–179, 181, 182n, 200–203, 204n, 205–207, 212n, 213–230, 232n, 233–243, 252–253, 255n, 257, 259, 261–262, 264–280, 284, 285n, 287, 290–302, 304–305, 307–326, 328n, 329–340, 341n, 342–347, 349–351, 353–354, 356–358, 360, 362, 364–382, 384–394, 396–398, 400, 402–404, 405n, 406, 408n, 421–422, 426–427, 429–433, 436n, 437n, 439, 440n, 441n, 443–457, 458n, 459–464, 466, 468, 473n, 478n, 487, 489–502, 503n, 507–517, 521, 525–530
Arnzen, Rüdiger 26–27
Arzhanov, Yury 26–27
Ašʿarī, Abū l-Ḥasan al- 327, 328n, 329n, 332, 346, 501
Ašʿarites 6, 389–390
Asclepius of Tralles 102, 160n
atomism 4n, 21, 106, 135, 189, 362, 386, 388–390, 392, 406, 408, 444n, 490–491
Averroes XV, 6, 35–36, 102, 122–125, 136, 159n, 165, 168, 170, 181–182, 186,

https://doi.org/10.1515/9783110546798-010

216n, 293, 295n, 309n, 336–337, 391, 421n, 429, 447n, 498n

Badawī, ʿAbd al-Raḥmān XV–XVI, 18n, 23–24, 25n, 263, 470n
Baġdād Peripatetics 17, 19n
Baġdādī, Abū l-Barakāt al- 139n, 491n, 503n
Baʿlabakkī, Qusṭā ibn Lūqā al- 15–18, 22n, 23, 33, 39–40, 69, 151n, 226–228, 229n, 255, 257–258, 260, 262–263, 265–266, 271, 315n, 444, 455n
Barmakids 13n
Barnes, Jonathan 79
Basīl 11–12, 14–17, 26, 258n
Baṣrī, Abū l-Ḥusayn al- 17–19, 35
beforeness and afterness 8, 431, 461, 462–479, 481–492, 500, 505–506, 508–515, 523, 530–531
Belo, Catarina 119n, 167, 193–194, 203n, 285n
Bertolacci, Amos 9, 43n, 75n, 79–80, 100n, 102, 171–172, 445, 448n
Bīrūnī, Abū Rayḥān al- 14n, 19n, 28–29, 33, 35, 38, 146, 409–414, 416–417, 422–423, 424n, 456n
Black, Deborah L. 63n, 64n
Bloch, Ernst 121n, 192–193
body 64, 71, 100, 106, 111, 113–115, 118, 119n, 120–134, 136–145, 147–155, 158, 167, 169–170, 172–174, 178, 185, 188–190, 193, 195, 201–202, 205, 211, 216–217, 221–222, 225, 228, 230n, 231–233, 234n, 241, 243, 244n, 249, 256, 260n, 261, 269n, 273–275, 277–279, 282, 284n, 286–289, 297, 301–303, 305–306, 308, 312–320, 322–324, 326, 328–331, 333–338, 342–359, 365–389, 392–407, 410, 415–422, 426, 443n, 459, 503–504, 519, 521, 523, 526–529
– absolute 120n, 121–122, 125, 129, 132–134, 138, 142–143, 153, 165–166, 169, 178–179, 190
– homoeomerous 354
– natural 5, 31, 64, 101, 106, 111, 113–114, 120–121, 127, 133, 138, 153–155, 158, 165, 169, 200–201, 210, 216–217, 225, 228n, 230, 233, 234n, 237, 241–242, 244n, 250, 256, 261, 268, 274–275, 282, 285–287, 289, 300, 305–306, 313, 316, 320, 329n, 335, 376n, 379n, 386, 404–405, 407, 418, 420, 425–426, 525–528
Boethus of Sidon 242, 451–458, 461, 493–494, 498, 505, 512, 530
Bostock, David 58n, 60n, 320, 493,
Buschmann, Elisabeth 119n, 121n, 167, 192–194

causes 5, 7, 31, 39, 46–47, 49–50, 53–55, 59, 64–65, 69n, 75n, 77, 81, 103–104, 116, 157, 159–162, 187, 191, 194, 207–209, 212, 214, 216–217, 219, 221, 222n, 226n, 227, 238n, 244n, 247, 381, 395–396, 405, 407, 410, 413, 416, 420, 422–424, 473, 492, 495–497, 504–511, 513, 516, 520, 523, 530
– Arabic terminology for 162–164
– efficient 100, 156–159, 161–164, 166n, 175–177, 197–198, 201, 212, 216, 219, 221–222, 231–239, 243, 246–247, 249, 251, 261, 271, 276, 292, 298–299, 419–420, 490
– external 64–65, 81, 161–164, 285–286, 296, 301, 305, 405
– final 100, 156–159, 161–164, 175–177, 197, 201, 212, 219, 223, 283, 288–289, 291–292
– formal 161–164, 219
– four 58–59, 63, 100, 155, 159, 161–164, 214, 301
– internal 64–65, 81, 161–164, 290, 301, 305, 403
– material 161–164
celestial spheres and bodies 3n, 60n, 101, 122n, 179–182, 184–186, 188–196, 200, 217n, 223, 237, 249–250, 284n, 285, 288, 289n, 296–298, 300, 306, 324, 326, 333–343, 344n, 349–350, 352, 353n, 365, 378–380, 386, 390n, 391, 397, 399–400, 432, 452–454, 456, 461, 463n, 475, 494, 497, 499–504, 507, 509–514, 519, 521, 529–531
chance and luck 5n, 28, 63, 234, 290
change 58, 64, 71, 82, 95n, 100–101, 111–114, 116, 120, 126, 129n, 130, 145–147, 150, 153–154, 158, 164–165, 166n, 167–168, 170, 177, 180–182, 187, 189–192,

200–212, 215, 225, 228n, 231n, 232n, 234, 235n, 237, 250, 255, 273n, 284, 287–288, 300, 306, 313–315, 317–318, 320, 330–331, 337, 339–343, 345, 356–357, 359–360, 363–365, 367–368, 411–413, 416–418, 422, 424–425, 432, 441n, 443, 454, 476, 495, 512–514, 521, 526–528; see also motion
– accidental 164–165, 166n, 170, 202–203, 417, 424, 483; see also alteration; see also growth (and diminution)
– substantial 56–57, 101, 112, 116n, 118, 150–151, 152n, 157, 164, 165n, 170, 177, 180, 187–189, 193–195, 201–202, 205, 219, 224, 231–233, 242, 268, 288, 314, 337, 342, 345, 495, 520
Charlton, William 44, 61n, 112, 214
clepsydra see phials (and similar devices)
commonality
– numeric vs. generic 155–158, 164–167, 174–180, 182–185, 191–192, 196–199, 201, 211–212, 279, 303n, 306
– of agent 156–158, 175–177, 197, 201, 212
– of end 156–158, 175–177, 197, 201, 212
– of form 154, 165–180, 183–185, 201, 212
– of matter 154, 165, 179–201, 212
– of nature 271, 279, 306
– of privation 211–212
concomitants 58, 75, 108, 127, 131–132, 154, 441, 472n, 496, 507, 510, 512
constituents 54–55, 97, 114, 116–117, 131–132, 140, 149, 153–154, 158, 160–161, 163–164, 174n, 190, 200–201, 207, 209–210, 212, 215–216, 234, 313, 345, 445, 526–527
continuity 4n, 5, 121–122, 124–125, 132–136, 138, 147n, 149–153, 189, 417, 449, 473, 477, 490–491, 504–508, 520, 526, 531
corporeal form 119n, 120n, 121–125, 131–132, 134, 136, 138, 141, 142n, 143–144, 146–150, 152n, 153–154, 165–170, 173–179, 185–186, 190, 395–396, 526–527
corporeality 4, 7, 21, 31, 37, 56, 113–114, 120–123, 125, 127, 129, 131–134, 136–139, 147–149, 153–154, 165, 167–168, 169n, 170n, 174, 176–177, 186, 189–190, 201, 287, 350–353, 425, 525–527; see also body
Damascius 307, 366
Davidson, Herbert A. 194
Democritus 389–390
demonstration 51–53, 58n, 62, 63n, 70, 75–80, 85, 90–92, 94–95, 97–98, 100, 106, 109, 155, 397
density of medium 371n, 405, 417n
desire 230, 234, 241n, 244n, 266, 283, 292–293, 295–297, 494–495
Di Giovanni, Matteo 168
Dimašqī, Abū ʿUṯmān al- 15–16, 18, 23, 33, 39–40
divisibility 121, 123–125, 131n, 132, 134–138, 145–149, 151, 152n, 153–154, 189, 353, 401n, 437, 441, 444–445, 472, 476, 478, 481, 490, 520–521, 523, 526
Dominicus Gundisalvi 185n, 239n, 246n, 254, 256, 384, 424n, 479
Duhem, Pierre 124, 307–308, 366, 426
duration 452–456, 458–460, 478n, 510, 512, 514, 530

earth 178, 199–200, 225, 288, 302–303, 311, 317n, 321, 347, 501
Eleatics 112n
elements, four 59, 101, 140–141, 167, 170, 180, 186, 195–196, 200, 223, 238n, 244n, 249n, 250, 302–304, 311, 314, 347n; see also fire; see also air; see also water; see also earth
emanation 37, 50, 170–171, 193–195, 196n, 197n, 303
end see causes, final
Epicureanism 389
essence 71, 81, 120–122, 125, 131–133, 136, 138, 172–173, 205, 210, 271, 277, 279, 300, 303, 305, 309, 330, 332–333, 344–345, 347, 364, 366, 382, 387, 392, 402–403, 426, 431–433, 462, 472n, 473, 475–477, 482, 485, 488, 492, 496, 500, 507, 512, 517, 523, 529, 531
estimation 296
eternity 29, 31, 36, 57, 117, 140n, 141n, 144, 180, 181n, 182, 193, 197n, 208, 440n, 454, 455n, 456, 458n, 459–460, 478, 488–490, 491n, 497, 499–500, 504, 507, 509–511, 513–514, 516, 526, 530
Euclid 34, 82n, 102–103, 105n, 376n

Eudemus of Rhodes 34, 320, 334, 341n, 378n
experience, methodic 45, 46–51, 62–63, 70, 72, 77, 411–412
experiments 78, 328n, 380, 382, 391–392, 407–410, 414, 415n, 417–418, 420, 422–425
extension, extensionality 120–134, 136–137, 140–142, 143n, 144–145, 147, 151, 153–154, 169n, 174n, 175, 312–314, 315n, 316, 317n, 322–326, 328, 349–354, 355n, 357, 366–368, 371, 373–378, 381–382, 384, 385n, 386–387, 393–397, 401n, 402, 415, 437, 453, 520–522, 526, 529

Falcon, Andrea 56n, 102n, 137n
Fārābī, Abū Naṣr al- 4, 14n, 32, 36–37, 48, 61, 67, 78–79, 80n, 86–88, 90–93, 96, 98, 99n, 104, 155, 160n, 181–182, 186–187, 195–196, 247n, 270, 290n, 310, 328n, 336–338, 340n, 341n, 344, 349, 390–392, 396, 409, 414–419, 421–422, 424–425, 463, 498n
Fazzo, Silvia 21
Fiori, Emiliano 24
fire 47, 52–53, 143n, 181, 200, 225, 241, 282, 290n, 291, 302–303, 311, 321, 378, 412, 424–425
food see nutrition
Forest, Aimé 167
form 1, 4–5, 7, 57, 67, 81, 97, 100, 104, 112–125, 130–133, 134n, 136, 138, 140–141, 142n, 143–180, 182n, 183, 193, 196, 198–206, 209–212, 214–219, 225, 234n, 251n, 255, 256n, 264, 266, 268, 273–274, 278n, 279, 302–304, 312–315, 330–331, 333, 344–345, 361, 363–366, 375, 377–379, 381, 383, 388, 394–396, 398–399, 418, 425, 440, 518–519, 521, 525–527, 529
– multiplicity or plurality of 166–174, 177–178, 184–185, 303n

Galen 16n, 20–23, 28, 151n, 358n, 378n, 379–380, 386, 393, 396, 398, 399n, 400, 436n, 454, 455n, 456, 458, 462–465, 473n, 478n, 507–509
Ġazālī, Abū Ḥāmid al- 14n, 122–123, 124n, 125, 448n, 491n,
Genequand, Charles 24
generation see change, substantial
geometry see mathematics
Gerard of Cremona XV, 23, 36, 59n, 89n, 452
Gerson, Lloyd 103
Giannakis, Elias 9, 15, 18, 23
Gilson, Étienne 166–167
Giver of Forms see Active Intellect
God 5, 11n, 54n, 156–159, 166n, 175, 194–195, 197, 201, 212, 234n, 237, 241n, 249, 254n, 258n, 259, 262, 264, 279, 290n, 327n, 350, 501, 513, 527
Goichon, Amélie-Marie XVI, 119n, 124, 167–169, 194
Grant, Edward 365
growth (and diminution) 58, 60n, 152n, 172, 177, 231–233, 280, 288, 291, 342, 411–412, 417–418, 422, 424, 495; see also quantity
Ǧubbāʾī, Abū Hāšim al- 163n
Ǧubbāʾī, Abū ʿAlī al- 501–502
Ǧurǧānī, ʿAlī ibn Muḥammad al-Sayyid al-Šarīf al- 385n
Gutas, Dimitri 1n, 9, 11n, 14n, 20, 24, 47n, 56n, 148n, 274n, 327n, 409n, 413
Ǧūzǧānī, Abū ʿUbayd al- 38n, 72–73, 74n

Ḥāǧǧī Ḫalīfa 16n, 26
Hamadānī, ʿAbd al-Ǧabbār ibn Aḥmad al- 327, 390
Hārūn al-Rašīd 10, 13n
Hasdai Crescas 122n
Hasnawi, Ahmad 3, 4, 28, 102
Hasse, Dag Nikolaus 1n, 2n, 168n, 294–295, 342n
Hassing, Richard F. 220n, 221n, 230n, 238n, 239n, 255, 306
Hayṯam, Abū ʿAlī Muḥammad ibn al- 35
Hayṯam, al-Ḥasan ibn al-Ḥasan ibn al- 35, 389–390
heavens see celestial spheres and bodies
Hero of Alexandria 408, 409n
Hesiod 312n, 368, 390
Ḥimṣī, ʿAbd al-Masīḥ ibn Nāʿima al- 12–17, 23, 25, 33, 39–40, 258, 260
Hippocrates 260n

Horten, Maximilian 125
Ḥunayn ibn Isḥāq see Ibn Isḥāq, Ḥunayn
Hussey, Edward 313n, 320, 454n, 508n
Hyman, Arthur 119n, 122n, 123–127, 136, 167, 186
hypotheses 31, 72n, 83–94, 96, 98, 100, 103, 105n, 106–108

Iamblichus 103n
Ibn Abī Saʿīd al-Mawṣilī see Mawṣilī, Ibn Abī Saʿīd al-
Ibn ʿAdī, Ibrāhīm 147
Ibn ʿAdī, Yaḥyā 16–18, 21, 22n, 23, 26–27, 35, 40, 66–67, 86, 116n, 142, 147, 179n, 262, 264n, 268, 270, 310, 322n, 334n, 338n, 349–350, 391, 403, 444n, 453–458, 460–461, 462n, 463, 478n, 498, 505, 512–513
Ibn ʿAlī, ʿĪsā 27, 35
Ibn Bāǧǧa, Abū Bakr Muḥammad 6, 35–36, 335–338, 340n, 391
Ibn Basīl, Iṣṭifān 11
Ibn Basīl, Taḏārī 11
Ibn al-Biṭrīq, Yaḥyā XV, 69
Ibn Gabirol, Solomon 168
Ibn al-Ǧarrāḥ, ʿAlī ibn ʿĪsā 27, 35
Ibn al-Ḥakam, Hišām 11n
Ibn al-Ḫammār, al-Ḥasan ibn Suwār 18, 19n, 20, 86, 463, 498n
Ibn Ḥunayn, Isḥāq XV, 17–18, 20, 22n, 23, 37, 39–41, 59n, 67, 69, 84, 164n, 203n, 227–228, 253–254, 263, 264n, 265, 268, 369n, 440n, 444, 445n
Ibn Isḥāq, Ḥunayn XV, 11, 16–17, 21–23, 151n, 452
Ibn Karnīb see Kātib (Ibn Karnīb), Abū Aḥmād ibn Yazīḍ al-
Ibn Manṣūr, Nūḥ 37
Ibn Marwān al-Muqammaṣ, Dāwūd 290n
Ibn Mattawayh, Abū Muḥammad 325n, 327, 328n, 346, 364, 413–414, 415n
Ibn Muḥammad al-Šayḫ al-Mufīd, Abū ʿAbd Allāh Muḥammad 328n, 389n
Ibn al-Murtaḍā, Aḥmad ibn Yaḥyā 163n
Ibn al-Nadīm, Abū l-Faraǧ Muḥammad ibn Isḥāq 9–13, 15–17, 22, 24–28, 34, 260n
Ibn Nāʿima al-Ḥimṣī, ʿAbd al-Masīḥ see Ḥimṣī, ʿAbd al-Masīḥ ibn Nāʿima al-
Ibn al-Qifṭī, ʿAlī ibn Yūsuf 9, 17–18, 26–27, 33–36
Ibn Qurra, Ṯābit 12, 34
Ibn al-Ṣalt, Ibrāhīm 11–13, 16
Ibn al-Samḥ, Abū ʿAlī 17–18, 35, 103–104, 330–331, 349, 394, 432–433, 436, 449, 463
Ibn Suwār ibn al-Ḫammār, al-Ḥasan see Ibn al-Ḫammār, al-Ḥasan ibn Suwār
Ibn al-Ṭayyib, Abū l-Faraǧ 17–18, 27, 33, 35, 270, 463
Ibn Ṭufayl, Abū Bakr Muḥammad 6
Ibn Yūnus, Abū Bišr Mattā XV, 18, 26–28, 35, 84–86, 88, 89n, 181–182, 258n, 268–270, 280, 463
Ibrahim, Bilal 167
Iḫwān al-Ṣafāʾ 14n, 142–143, 168n, 267, 269, 310, 358n, 396–397, 458, 498n
imagination 292, 294–295, 328, 383, 386, 396–400, 426, 449, 519–520, 522–523
impetus 239, 240n, 248n
inclination 4, 31, 209, 230–231, 239–252, 281–283, 284n, 300, 306n, 364n, 417–420, 527–528
induction 46, 48, 51, 53, 62–63, 72
infinity 4n, 5, 67, 106, 205, 315, 369–370, 372, 374, 444n, 475, 503–504, 509–511, 514, 520, 530
inquiry, scientific 4, 43, 45, 51, 54, 59, 60n, 62–64, 70, 72, 75, 77, 79, 112–113, 157, 202, 214, 525,
instruction see teaching and learning
intellect 48–51, 63n, 64n, 65, 68–72, 74, 77–78, 115, 119n, 143n, 156, 170, 173–174, 177n, 192–197, 204, 234, 249, 251, 258–259, 285, 292–293, 296–297, 299, 397, 402, 493–495, 497
interpenetration of extensions or bodies 125n, 345, 357, 373–375, 393–396, 398
al-ʿIrāqī, Muḥammad ʿĀṭif 516–517
Isaac Abravanel 123, 125
Isḥāq ibn Ḥunayn see Ibn Ḥunayn, Isḥāq

Janos, Damien 48n, 182n, 186, 224n, 247n, 258n, 289n
Janssens, Jules 23, 28, 479
Jeck, Udo Reinhold 308–310, 429, 496n, 497n

Kātib (Ibn Karnīb), Abū Aḥmād ibn Yazīḍ al- 34
Kātib al-Baġdādī, Abū l-Farağ Qudāma ibn Ğaʿfar al- 34
Kâtip Çelebi see Ḥāǧǧī Ḫalīfa
Kindī, Abū Yaʿqūb ibn Isḥāq al- 12–13, 14n, 25, 29, 35, 61, 67, 141, 143, 155, 250n, 257–260, 264, 267, 269, 271, 307–308, 310, 368n, 390–391, 396, 447n, 458–459, 498n
Kirmānī, Abū l-Qāsim al- 262, 270
Kraemer, Joel L. 13n, 38n, 454
Kraus, Paul 13n, 21

Lacey, Alan R. 220n, 230n, 255
Lang, Helen S. 222n, 311n, 312n
learning see teaching and learning
Lettinck, Paul 36n, 39, 63, 164n
Leucippus 389–390

Macierowski, Edward M. 220n, 221n, 230n, 238n, 239n, 255, 306
magnitude 5, 8, 11n, 120, 130, 134n, 135–137, 142, 151n, 152, 153n, 169n, 178, 372, 385n, 401n, 416, 431–432, 434n, 435, 437–451, 453, 456, 460–462, 464–465, 468–476, 478, 481, 484, 490–491, 496–497, 500, 502n, 504–505, 508–515, 519–523, 529–531
Maġribī, Abū l-Ḥakam al- 17, 19
Maimonides 36
Marmura, Michael, E. XVI, 16n, 23, 244n, 448n
Marxist interpretations of matter 121n, 192–193
Masīḥī, Abū Sahl al- 9
Masʿūdī, Šaraf al-Dīn al- 152, 153n
mathematics 65n, 82, 100n, 108, 111, 133n, 376n, 378n
matter 1, 4–5, 7, 31, 57–58, 67, 81, 97, 100, 104, 113–119, 120n, 121–124, 130, 131n, 132, 134n, 138–148, 149n, 150–175, 177–203, 205, 209–212, 214–216, 218–219, 223–225, 234n, 254n, 268, 273, 279, 289n, 300n, 303, 305n, 312–315, 330–331, 333, 334n, 344–345, 366, 375–379, 381, 383, 385, 388, 393–401, 417–418, 425, 439, 525–527
– celestial 179–182, 184–201; see also aether
– envolumed 140–143, 153, 375; see also substrate, second
– generation of 182, 184, 192–196
– traditional account of 139–144
– Philoponus' new account of 144–147
– proof for the existence of 148–152
Mawṣilī, Ibn Abī Saʿīd al- 21, 334n, 338n, 349–350, 455n, 457–458, 461
Maʿṣūmī, Abū Saʿīd Aḥmad ibn ʿAlī al- 14n, 412–414, 417, 422, 424n
mayl see inclination
Mayer, Toby 472n, 479n, 488–489, 516, 521
McGinnis, Jon XVI, 3, 119n, 125n, 169–170, 174n, 203n, 246n, 253–254, 261n, 311n, 313n, 339n, 342n, 348n, 358n, 365n, 374n, 384, 392–393, 394n, 401–402, 404n, 405n, 407n, 415n, 429–431, 435, 441n, 443n, 463, 465, 466n, 471–472, 477, 479n, 485n, 488n, 516, 521
McGuire, J. Edward 220n, 221n, 255
measure 127, 129, 134, 138, 399, 442–444, 446n, 447–448, 450–451, 453–461, 465, 470, 478n, 496n, 497, 499, 502–504, 506n, 507, 509, 512–514, 530
Melissus 225
Menn, Stephen 58n, 120n
middle term 47, 50, 77, 95
Miskawayh, Abū ʿAlī Aḥmad 18n, 262, 265–267, 269–270, 280, 458, 460
Moraux, Paul 88, 242n, 339
Morewedge, Parviz 119n
Morison, Benjamin 3n, 315n, 316n, 320, 342
Moses Narboni 123, 125
motion 1, 3–5, 7–8, 21, 23, 28, 31, 36, 40, 56–58, 60, 62n, 67, 94, 100–101, 106, 111–114, 132, 134, 154, 157, 172, 187, 200, 202, 204, 214–217, 219–253, 255, 257–258, 263–265, 267–269, 271–278, 280–289, 290n, 291–293, 296–301, 303–306, 313–314, 316–318, 321, 324–326, 333n, 337–345, 356–368, 371, 381, 391, 404–405, 410–411, 413, 417, 426, 431–444, 445n, 446n, 448–462, 463n, 464–465, 468–482, 484, 486–487, 488n, 490–523, 525, 527–531; see also change

– circular 4, 28, 58, 60, 187, 200, 250, 284–285, 287, 297, 300, 314n, 320, 324, 337, 338n, 339–343, 344n, 391, 405, 452–454, 456, 461, 475, 492, 494, 496–497, 500, 502–504, 509–511, 513–514, 519, 529–530
– definition of 204n, 360–364
– forced 4n, 106, 234n, 236, 239, 247–248, 249n, 301, 405, 416, 418, 503
– form of 361–365, 440, 518–519, 521, 529
– natural 4n, 23, 106, 222, 235, 238n, 239–240, 241n, 244–245, 247–248, 251, 281–286, 303, 311n, 312, 314, 320, 329n, 405, 417, 503
– of the celestial bodies 200, 249, 284–285, 289n, 497
– positional 111n, 280, 282–283, 284n, 314n, 338n, 340–343, 365, 390n, 391, 475n, 529; see also outermost sphere, place and motion of
Muʿtazilites 6, 7, 17, 163n, 310, 325, 327–328, 332–333, 337–338, 344, 362, 364, 386, 389–390, 391n, 392, 406, 409, 413–414, 415n, 417, 422, 427, 501, 528–529

Nāṣer-e Ḫosrow 389n, 498n
nature 1, 4–5, 7, 14n, 19n, 31, 40–41, 47, 58, 63–64, 67, 94, 97, 100–101, 106, 111n, 172, 213–306, 416–422, 424–425, 463
– universal 184n, 271–272, 277–280, 306, 497, 525, 527–528
Nawbaḫtī, Abū Muḥammad al-Ḥaṣan ibn Mūsā al- 341n
Neoplatonism see Platonism and Neoplatonism
Nicolaus of Damascus 293
Nicomachus of Gerasa 143
Nīsābūrī, Abū Rašīd Saʿīd ibn Muḥammad al- 414n, 415n,
now 7, 430, 436n, 448–449, 460, 502, 515–523
Nūḥ ibn Manṣūr see Ibn Manṣūr, Nūḥ
number 143, 442–448, 450–454, 456–465, 467, 472, 477–478, 489–490, 493–499, 502–506, 512–515, 517–518, 529
nutrition 172, 177–178, 232, 386

Olympiodorus 440n
outermost sphere, place and motion of 324, 326, 333–343, 349–350, 353n, 365–366, 390n, 391, 432, 452–454, 456, 461, 475, 497, 499–500, 502–504, 507, 509–514, 519, 529–531

Parmenides 225
particulars 43–44, 54–59, 62, 69–70, 75, 78, 109, 279, 402, 526
Pasnau, Robert 167
perception 44–47, 48n, 49, 51n, 53, 54n, 55, 63n, 68–69, 111n, 219, 292, 294–296, 397, 456
Pessin, Sarah 123
Peters, Francis 9–12, 23n, 260
phials (and similar devices) 328n, 380–382, 391, 407–425, 529
Philo of Alexandria 409n
Philoponus, John 4, 10, 12–19, 23, 27–35, 39–40, 44, 51–59, 60n, 61–63, 65–67, 70, 75, 88, 90–94, 96, 98, 108, 114n, 137n, 139n, 140–148, 153, 155, 160–162, 163n, 180–181, 185, 205–207, 214–215, 218–223, 225–226, 227n, 228n, 229–231, 233–236, 238–246, 251–262, 264–280, 283, 289, 298–299, 304–305, 307–308, 310n, 313n, 314n, 316, 317n, 318n, 319, 321–326, 330–332, 335–339, 342, 344, 347n, 349–351, 353–355, 357, 358n, 364, 366, 368–371, 373n, 374–382, 384–387, 389–401, 405–407, 420, 426–427, 432–433, 436, 440n, 444, 449–451, 460, 493n, 494, 516, 518, 527–530
Pines, Shlomo 16n, 23–24, 66n, 163n, 242n, 244n, 261n, 456n
place 1, 4–5, 7, 20–21, 28, 30n, 31, 35, 40, 57, 106, 111, 190, 232n, 236, 262, 280, 282–283, 303, 306–376, 378, 379n, 380–398, 400n, 408, 410, 415, 417–422, 426–427, 440, 445, 456, 460, 468, 508, 513, 525, 528–529
– natural 189, 233n, 237, 241–244, 247–251, 255, 282–283, 284n, 289, 302–303, 320–321, 329n, 416–418, 420, 425, 528
planets see celestial spheres and bodies

plants 60, 111n, 115, 172–173, 195–196, 223–224, 271, 285n, 288–289, 296–297, 310n, 302–303, 306, 498
Plato 20, 25, 29, 54n, 103, 143, 148, 151n, 160, 175, 180–181, 183, 207, 220–221, 222n, 223, 234, 243n, 271, 273, 278, 298, 331n, 368, 372n, 385n, 429, 454, 455n, 456, 458–460, 478n, 492, 494, 499, 512, 530
Platonic forms 143, 372n
Platonism and Neoplatonism 2n, 8, 25, 34, 53n, 54n, 66, 103, 137, 160–161, 163n, 164, 175, 183–184, 218, 220, 222, 226, 257, 258n, 259–260, 262, 267–271, 273, 275, 277–278, 305, 310n, 325, 331, 364, 427, 440, 450, 455–456, 458n, 460, 462, 478n, 497n, 511–515, 528, 530
Plotinus 25, 30, 141, 143, 147n, 182–183, 197, 218, 220–221, 257–258, 262, 269–270, 429, 450n, 455–456, 459, 478n, 512
Porphyry 11–12, 14, 16, 25–26, 32–34, 102, 111n, 175n, 183, 197, 218, 257, 270–271, 298–299, 455n
posits see hypotheses; see postulates
possibility 126, 146, 200n, 371, 381, 406n, 419, 426, 432–439, 440n, 441, 443–444, 448, 464, 470, 476, 512, 519, 522, 526, 529
postulates 31, 72n, 82n, 83–94, 96, 98, 100, 103, 105n, 106, 108n
potentiality 119n, 126, 136, 149, 152, 154, 177–178, 204, 210, 217, 239n, 243, 248n, 276, 360–361, 363–364, 436
power 4n, 7, 47, 64, 67, 99n, 101, 172–174, 197, 220–221, 224, 230–232, 238, 239n, 249–251, 253–255, 257, 258n, 259–269, 271–280, 282, 285–290, 294–296, 298–300, 302–306, 312n, 329n, 381–382, 391, 396–397, 401, 405, 407, 409, 419, 421, 426, 528
Presocratics 63, 78, 109n, 112, 225
principles XIV, 5, 7, 39, 43, 45, 49–55, 57–60, 63–66, 68, 69n, 70–71, 72n, 74–82, 85, 94–109, 111n, 112–114, 116, 121, 122n, 137–138, 143, 147n, 149n, 150, 153–162, 164–165, 171, 175, 179–181, 193–199, 201–202, 205–212, 214–229, 233–234, 235n, 236–245, 247, 248n, 249–255, 257–258, 261, 263–265, 267–269, 271–280, 282n, 284n, 287, 289–290, 292, 298, 300–301, 305–306, 312n, 313, 352, 363, 365, 374n, 393, 394n, 401, 411n, 425, 494, 499–500, 505, 525–527
– of motion or change 7, 31, 94n, 101, 111n, 114n, 116, 157, 207, 214–216, 219–224, 226n, 227–229, 233–234, 235n, 237–238, 240, 247, 248n, 251, 253, 255, 257–258, 263–265, 267, 271–273, 276–277, 287, 289, 300–301, 305, 363, 494, 525, 527
priority, five sense of 466–469
priority and posteriority 439, 441–443, 448–450, 453–454, 457, 459–462, 464–473, 475, 477–478, 481–488, 491–492, 503–511, 515, 517–519, 530
privation 4, 57, 81, 95n, 104, 112–114, 201–212, 214, 216, 273, 362–363, 375, 527
procession and return 157–158, 184, 194–195
Proclus 28–31, 53n, 54n, 57n, 66, 102–103, 121n, 140n, 141, 144, 146, 160n, 183, 184n, 197, 220, 222n, 223, 257–260, 270, 312, 323n, 362, 440n, 456n, 499
Ps.-Archytas 139n, 455n
Ps.-Plutarchus 69n, 88n, 143n, 151n, 227–228, 229n, 263, 265n, 315n, 444n, 455n, 498n
Pythagoras 103, 143, 390,

quality 140–143, 145, 147, 150, 206, 209, 231, 233n, 250–251, 280, 282–284, 289, 302–303, 322–323, 327, 331n, 337, 339, 342, 352, 372, 375, 377–378, 411–413, 416–418, 422–425
quantity 4n, 5, 97n, 100n, 106, 120, 123, 127, 131–132, 134, 139–144, 146, 152n, 153n, 280, 282–283, 289, 303, 322–323, 337, 339, 350n, 351, 375, 377, 395, 401, 417–418, 420, 424n, 425, 445–446, 447n, 455, 459, 496, 516, 519
Qusṭā ibn Lūqā al-Baʿlabakkī see Baʿlabakkī, Qusṭā ibn Lūqā al-

Rashed, Marwan 22–23, 34, 59, 284n, 340, 341n

Rashed, Roshdi 35
Raṣṣāṣ, al-Ḥasan al- 163n
Rāzī, Abū Bakr Muḥammad ibn Zakariyā᾽ al- 11n, 14n, 259–261, 264, 266, 271, 299, 389–390, 409, 440n, 456n, 458n,
Rāzī, Faḫr al-Dīn al- 226n, 333n, 341n, 407n, 409, 488–490, 503n, 513n
Reisman, David C. 74n
Rescher, Nicholas 16n, 23, 244n
rest 106, 204, 215, 219–220, 223, 226–228, 233, 234n, 238n, 241, 248–250, 252–253, 255, 257–258, 261, 263–265, 267, 271–272, 274–275, 280, 282–283, 285, 300–301, 303, 305, 318, 356–365, 405, 446n, 528–529
Richardson, Kara 168
Ross, William David 44, 56n, 58n, 214, 369n
rotation see motion, circular; see motion, positional

Ṣābi᾽, Abū Rawḥ al- 16, 22n, 23n, 27
Šahrastānī, Muḥammad ibn ʿAbd al-Karīm al- 123, 270–271, 491n
al-Šayḫ al-Mufīd, Abū ʿAbd Allāh Muḥammad ibn Muḥammad see Ibn Muḥammad al-Šayḫ al-Mufīd, Abū ʿAbd Allāh Muḥammad
Scotus, Michael 336
sense perception, sensation see perception
Sergius of Rēš ʿAynā 24
Sharples, Robert W. 24, 452n
Shayegan, Yegane 429–430, 464–465, 471–472, 479n, 511, 516
shellfish 342n
Shihadeh, Ayman 139n, 148n, 152
Siğistānī, Abū Sulaymān al- 18n, 262–267, 269–271, 280, 373n, 459–460, 463, 512
Simplicius 20, 22–23, 31n, 32, 34, 52, 53n, 54n, 56n, 58n, 66, 69, 102, 114n, 137–138, 139n, 141n, 143–144, 147, 178, 181n, 184, 206–207, 209, 215, 217–218, 219n, 221n, 229n, 235–236, 244n, 245, 253, 298, 299, 307, 313n, 314n, 316, 318n, 321, 323–324, 330, 331n, 332, 334, 339–340, 342, 356n, 357, 364, 366, 369n, 373n, 379n, 402–403, 421n, 432, 440n, 462, 493–495
Sīrāfī, Abū Saʿīd al-Ḥasan al- 26
Sorabji, Richard 54n, 180, 221n, 222n, 237, 319, 365, 372–373, 374n, 451n, 493n
soul 50, 56, 60, 74n, 84–85, 98, 99n, 115–116, 118, 119n, 134, 142, 172–174, 177n, 182–183, 195, 200, 216–225, 229–234, 236, 238, 241–246, 247n, 249, 252, 257–259, 265–269, 271, 273, 275–278, 284n, 285, 288–289, 290n, 291, 294–298, 300–306, 309n, 397–398, 429, 448, 454–455, 457, 492–497, 499, 504, 506, 510, 527–528
space 4, 7, 183, 310, 312n, 313n, 315n, 321, 323n, 326, 328, 357, 362, 367–371, 373–382, 384–393, 395–399, 400n, 404, 406–410, 413–415, 420–422, 426, 513, 529
speed 284n, 288, 405, 413, 432–439, 441, 443n, 512, 515, 519, 529
Steinschneider, Moritz 9, 35n, 36
Stoics 66, 141, 147n, 220n, 221n, 257, 267, 269, 278, 390n, 455
Stone, Abraham D. 123, 147n, 149n, 168, 170, 173, 185–186
Strato of Lampsacus 242n, 370n, 382, 409
subject see substrate
substance 105, 111n, 114–121, 125, 127, 129–130, 132, 134, 139, 140–143, 145, 149, 152, 154, 159–160, 165–166, 168, 172–174, 177–179, 181n, 186, 205, 216–217, 220, 223, 252, 257, 259, 264, 269, 277–278, 280, 330, 339, 367–368, 376–377, 380, 393, 397, 401, 430n, 440n, 454, 456, 458–459, 478, 511–512, 514, 526
substrate
– as different from subject 116–118
– second 140–145, 147, 165–166, 170, 178–179
surface 132–134, 137, 149n, 310, 312–315, 317n, 320–328, 330, 332–338, 343–367, 368, 374, 379, 381–384, 388–389, 391–392, 400, 408, 419–422, 425–427, 523, 528–529
syllogism 46–47, 49–50, 52, 58n, 77–78, 80n, 97, 106
Syriac XIII, XV, 10–12, 13n, 15–18, 20–21, 22n, 24, 26–27, 34n, 84, 151n, 163, 261
Syrianus 160n, 452n

Ṭabarī, Abū ʿAmr (or Abū ʿUmar) al- 18, 35,
Ṯābit ibn Qurra see Ibn Qurra, Ṯābit
taǧriba see experience, methodic
Tawḥīdī, ʿAlī Abū Ḥayyān al- 18n, 26, 262, 264–266, 269–271, 368n, 373n, 457n, 458n, 459–460, 498n
teaching and learning 43, 45, 62, 65, 68, 70–75, 77–81, 97–98, 109, 138, 162, 205, 525–526
Themistius 4, 18, 26–28, 31–33, 51, 53, 54n, 56n, 88–94, 96, 98n, 181–182, 229n, 234n, 235–236, 244n, 245, 253, 254n, 255n, 271, 307, 310, 313n, 316n, 317n, 318n, 323n, 324, 331n, 334–337, 338n, 339–340, 343–344, 347n, 349, 358n, 367, 369, 371n, 373–375, 378n, 379–380, 386, 390, 393, 396–397, 399n, 421n, 462, 493–495, 504n, 507–508, 509n, 529
Theophrastus of Eresus 20, 34, 181n, 271, 291, 312, 313n, 323–326, 334, 342n, 349, 355, 366–367, 382
Théry, Gabriel 23
Thomas Aquinas 168
thought experiments 139–140, 376–380, 385–386, 392–393, 396–400, 475–476
three-dimensionality see corporeality; see space; see void
time 1, 3– 5, 7–8, 21–23, 25, 31, 35–37, 40, 57, 106, 281n, 306, 309n, 316, 357, 360–362, 365, 371n, 385n, 403, 429–525, 529–531
– universal 456, 497–500, 509, 513–514, 519
transformation 56, 101, 165, 166n, 167–171, 174, 177–178, 199–200, 486
Ṭūsī, Naṣīr al-Dīn al- 488–489

universals 43–44, 48–51, 53–62, 63n, 64n, 66–72, 75, 77–79, 81, 105, 108–109, 119n, 156, 158, 174–177, 190, 197–199, 402, 526
Usṭāṯ XV, 447

vague particular 63n, 64n
void 4, 7, 36, 141, 240, 309–310, 315n, 324, 327, 328n, 334, 345, 346n, 350, 358n, 367–427, 529
– force of the 380–382, 390n, 391–392, 406–408, 411n, 425, 529

Wagner, Hans 44
Walbridge, John 21
Walzer, Richard 21
Warner, Levinus 17
water 165–166, 170–171, 174, 178–179, 197, 199–200, 233n, 237, 250–251, 278–279, 282, 284, 302–303, 311, 316n, 317–319, 321, 331, 347–348, 353–354, 357–358, 371n, 378, 380–381, 383–384, 386, 399, 407–413, 415–418, 420–421, 423–425, 486, 492n
Weisheipl, James A. 306
Wieland, Wolfgang 79, 214, 378n
Wisnovsky, Robert 4, 120n, 142, 160n, 161n
Wolfson, Harry A. 122–127, 186, 456

Yabrūdī, Abū l-Faraǧ Ǧūrǧīs ibn Ibrāhīm al- 27, 33
Yaḥyā ibn ʿAdī see Ibn ʿAdī, Yaḥyā

Zeno 308–309
Zimmerman, Fritz 21, 245

www.ingramcontent.com/pod-product-compliance
Lightning Source LLC
Chambersburg PA
CBHW080921300426
44115CB00018B/2909